CONTENTS

ON THE COVER: Marshall Faulk. (Photo by Dilip Vishwanat/THE SPORTING NEWS.) Spine photo of Peyton Manning (File photo).

NFL statistics compiled by STATS, Inc., Lincolnwood, Ill.

10 9 8 7 6 5 4 3 2 1

2001 SEASON

NFL directory
Team information
Schedule
College draft
Expansion draft
Playoff plan

NFL DIRECTORY

COMMISSIONER'S OFFICE

Address
280 Park Avenue
New York, NY 10017
Phone
212-450-2000
212-681-7573 (FAX)
Commissioner
Paul Tagliabue
Exec. v.p. for labor rel./chairman NFLMC
Harold Henderson
Executive v.p. & league counsel
Jeff Pash
Exec. v.p. of league and football dev.
Roger Goodell

Executive v.p. of new media/Internet and enterprises
Tom Spock
Chief financial officer
Barbara Kaczynski
Sr. v.p. of broadcasting and gov't affairs
Joe Browne
Senior v.p. of broadcasting & network television
Dennis Lewin
Sr. v.p. of football operations
George Young

COMMUNICATIONS
Vice president of public relations
Greg Aiello
Director of international public affairs
Pete Abitante
Director of community affairs
Beth Colleton
Director of media services
Leslie Hammond
Director of corporate communications
Brian McCarthy

OTHER ORGANIZATIONS

NFL FILMS, INC.

Address
330 Fellowship Road
Mt. Laurel, NJ 08054
Phone
856-778-1600
856-722-6779 (FAX)
President
Steve Sabol

PRO FOOTBALL HALL OF FAME

Address
2121 George Halas Drive, N.W.
Canton, OH 44708
Phone
330-456-8207
330-456-8175 (FAX)
Executive director
John W. Bankert
V.p./communications & exhibits
Joe Horrigan
V.p./operations and marketing
Dave Motts
V.p./merchandising & licensing
Judy Kuntz

NFL PLAYERS ASSOCIATION

Address
2021 L Street, N.W.
Washington, DC 20036
Phone
202-463-2200
202-835-9775 (FAX)
Executive director
Gene Upshaw
Assistant executive director
Doug Allen
Dir. P.R. and NFLPA retired players org.
Frank Woschitz
General counsel
Richard Berthelsen
Director of communications
Carl Francis
Director of player development
Stacey Robinson
Director of research department
Michael Duberstein
Manager/agent/coordinator
Athelia Doggette

NFL ALUMNI ASSOCIATION

Address
3696 N. Federal Highway
Suite 202
Ft. Lauderdale, FL 33308-6263
Phone
954-630-2100
954-630-2535 (FAX)
Executive director/CEO
Frank Krauser
Chairman of the board
Randy Minniear
Vice president/alumni relations
Martin Lerch
V.p./director of communications
Remy Mackowski
Manager of player appearances
Amy Glanzman

ARIZONA CARDINALS
NFC EASTERN DIVISION

2001 SEASON

CLUB DIRECTORY

President
William V. Bidwill
Vice chairman
Thomas J. Guilfoil
Vice president
William V. Bidwill Jr.
Vice president and general counsel
Michael J. Bidwill
Vice president
Nicole Bidwill
Vice president
Larry Wilson
Treasurer and chief financial officer
Charley Schlegel
Vice president/sales and marketing
Ron Minegar
General manager
Bob Ferguson
Assistant to the president
Rod Graves
Pro personnel assistant
Rodd Newhouse
Player personnel administrator
Jay Nienkark
Senior scout
Bo Bolinger
National scouting coordinator
Jerry Hardaway
Scouts
Jim Carmody
Bill DeKraker
Steve Keim
Bob Mazie
Jim Stanley
Head trainer
John Omohundro
Assistant trainers
Jim Shearer
Jeff Herndon
Team physician (orthopedist)
Dr. Russell Chick
Team physician (internist)
Dr. Wayne Kuhl
Equipment manager
Mark Ahlemeier
Assistant equipment manager
Steve Christensen

Head coach
Dave McGinnis

Assistant coaches
Geep Chryst (quarterbacks)
Mike Devlin (asst. off. line/off. QC)
Jeff Fitzgerald (linebackers)
Joe Greene (defensive line)
Pete Hoener (tight ends)
Hank Kuhlmann (special teams)
Stan Kwan (spec. teams asst/def. QC)
Larry Marmie (def. coordinator)
Rich Olson (offensive coordinator)
Kevin Ramsey (defensive backs)
Johnny Roland (running backs)
Bob Rogucki (strength and cond.)
Jerry Sullivan (wide receivers)
George Warhop (offensive line)

Dir. of corp. and broadcasting services
Joe Castor
Director of stadium operations
Steve Walsh
Director of ticketing
Steve Bomar
Director of group sales
Scott Bull
Director of public relations
Paul Jensen
Media coordinator
Greg Gladysiewski
Publications/internet coordinator
Luke Sacks
Video director
Benny Greenberg
Director of player programs
Anthony Edwards

SCHEDULE

Sept.	9— Open date	
Sept.	16— at Washington	1:00
Sept.	23— DENVER	8:35
Sept.	30— ATLANTA	4:05
Oct.	7— at Philadelphia	1:00
Oct.	14— at Chicago	1:00
Oct.	21— KANSAS CITY	4:05
Oct.	28— at Dallas	4:05
Nov.	4— PHILADELPHIA	4:05
Nov.	11— N.Y. GIANTS	4:15
Nov.	18— DETROIT	4:15
Nov.	25— at San Diego	4:05
Dec.	2— at Oakland	4:15
Dec.	9— WASHINGTON	4:05
Dec.	15— at N.Y. Giants (Sat.)	12:30
Dec.	23— DALLAS	4:05
Dec.	30— at Carolina	1:00

All times are Eastern.
All games Sunday unless noted.

DRAFT CHOICES

Leonard Davis, T, Texas (first round/second pick overall).
Kyle Vanden Bosch, DE, Nebraska (2/34).
Michael Stone, DB, Memphis (2/54).
Adrian Wilson, DB, N. Carolina State (3/64).
Bill Gramatica, K, South Florida (4/98).
Marcus Bell, DT, Memphis (4/123).
Mario Fatafehi, DT, Kansas St. (5/133).
Bobby Newcombe, WR, Nebraska (6/166).
Renaldo Hill, DB, Michigan St. (7/202).
Tevita Ofahengaue, TE, BYU (7/246).

2000 REVIEW

RESULTS

Sept. 3—at N.Y. Giants		L	16-21
Sept.10—DALLAS		W	32-31
Sept.17—Open date			
Sept.24—GREEN BAY		L	3-29
Oct. 1—at San Francisco		L	20-27
Oct. 8—CLEVELAND		W	29-21
Oct. 15—PHILADELPHIA		L	14-33
Oct. 22—at Dallas		L	7-48
Oct. 29—NEW ORLEANS		L	10-21
Nov. 5—WASHINGTON		W	16-15
Nov. 12—at Minnesota		L	14-31
Nov. 19—at Philadelphia		L	9-34
Nov. 26—N.Y. GIANTS		L	7-31
Dec. 3—at Cincinnati		L	13-24
Dec. 10—at Jacksonville		L	10-44
Dec. 17—BALTIMORE		L	7-13
Dec. 24—at Washington		L	3-20

RECORDS/RANKINGS

2000 regular-season record: 3-13 (5th in NFC East); 2-6 in division; 2-10 in conference; 3-5 at home; 0-8 on road.
Team record last five years: 29-51 (.363, ranks 26th in league in that span).

2000 team rankings:	No.	NFC	NFL
Total offense	*283.0	12	24
Rushing offense	*79.9	13	27
Passing offense	*203.1	9	17
Scoring offense	210	15	29
Total defense	*358.6	15	30
Rushing defense	*163.1	14	30
Passing defense	*195.5	5	11
Scoring defense	443	14	30
Takeaways	20	T13	T29
Giveaways	44	15	30
Turnover differential	-24	15	30
Sacks	25	T14	T30
Sacks allowed	35	T6	T13

*Yards per game.

TEAM LEADERS

Scoring (kicking): Cary Blanchard, 66 pts. (18/19 PATs, 16/23 FGs).
Scoring (touchdowns): David Boston, 42 pts. (7 receiving).
Passing: Jake Plummer, 2,946 yds. (475 att., 270 comp., 56.8%, 13 TDs, 21 int.).
Rushing: Michael Pittman, 719 yds. (184 att., 3.9 avg., 4 TDs).
Receptions: David Boston, 71 (1,156 yds., 16.3 avg., 7 TDs).
Interceptions: Aeneas Williams, 5 (102 yds., 0 TDs).
Sacks: Simeon Rice, 7.5.
Punting: Scott Player, 44.2 avg. (65 punts, 2,871 yds., 0 blocked).
Punt returns: Mac Cody, 7.2 avg. (31 att., 222 yds., 0 TDs).
Kickoff returns: MarTay Jenkins, 26.7 avg. (82 att., 2,186 yds., 1 TD).

ARIZONA CARDINALS

No.	QUARTERBACKS	Ht./Wt.	Born	NFL Exp.	College	How acq.	'00 Games GP/GS
17	Brown, Dave	6-6/230	2-25-70	10	Duke	FA/98	6/2
14	Greisen, Chris	6-3/227	7-2-76	3	Northwest Missouri State	D7/99	3/0
16	Plummer, Jake	6-2/198	12-19-74	5	Arizona State	D2/97	14/14
	RUNNING BACKS						
26	Jones, Thomas	5-10/211	8-19-78	2	Virginia	D1/00	14/4
34	Makovicka, Joel (FB)	5-11/246	10-6-75	3	Nebraska	D4/99	14/10
39	McKinley, Dennis (FB)	6-2/250	11-3-76	3	Mississippi State	D6c/99	16/0
32	Pittman, Michael	6-0/216	8-14-75	4	Fresno State	D4/98	16/12
	Shields, Paul	6-1/238	1-31-76	2	Arizona	FA/01	*7/0
21	Williams, Clarence	5-9/193	5-16-77	2	Michigan	FA/99	2/0
	RECEIVERS						
89	Boston, David	6-2/211	8-19-78	3	Ohio State	D1a/99	16/16
11	Gilmore, Bryan	6-0/194	7-21-78	1	Midwestern State (Tex.)	FA/00	1/0
80	Hardy, Terry (TE)	6-4/270	5-31-76	4	Southern Mississippi	D5/98	16/15
19	Jenkins, MarTay	6-0/201	2-28-75	3	Nebraska-Omaha	W-Dal./99	16/2
86	Junkin, Trey (TE)	6-2/247	1-23-61	19	Louisiana Tech	W-Oak./96	16/0
	Newcombe, Bobby	5-11/189	8-8-79	R	Nebraska	D6/01	—
	Ofahengaue, Tevita (TE)	6-2/250	7-9-75	R	Brigham Young	D7b/01	—
81	Sanders, Frank	6-2/200	2-17-73	7	Auburn	D2/95	16/16
84	Tant, Jay (TE)	6-3/254	12-4-77	2	Northwestern	D5b/00	5/0
	OFFENSIVE LINEMEN						
65	Clement, Anthony (T)	6-8/351	4-10-76	4	Southwestern Louisiana	D2b/98	16/16
64	Davidds-Garrido, Norberto (T)	6-6/336	10-4-72	6	Southern California	UFA/00	9/2
75	Davis, Leonard (T)	6-6/370	9-5-78	R	Texas	D1/01	—
67	Dishman, Chris (G)	6-3/338	2-27-74	4	Nebraska	D4/97	14/12
60	Gruttadauria, Mike (C)	6-3/286	12-6-72	6	Central Florida	UFA/00	8/8
66	Kendall, Pete (G)	6-5/292	7-9-73	6	Boston College	UFA/00	*16/16
68	Scott, Yusuf (G)	6-3/348	11-30-76	3	Arizona	D5b/99	9/0
70	Shelton, L.J. (T)	6-6/360	3-21-76	3	Eastern Michigan	D1b/99	14/14
50	Starkey, Jason (C)	6-5/270	7-15-77	2	Marshall	FA/00	2/0
	DEFENSIVE LINEMEN						
	Bell, Marcus (T)	6-1/319	6-1-79	R	Memphis	D4b/01	—
95	Burke, Thomas (E)	6-3/275	10-12-76	3	Wisconsin	D3/99	3/0
98	Davis, Russell (T)	6-4/295	3-28-75	3	North Carolina	W-Chi./00	13/9
	Fatafehi, Mario (T)	6-2/307	1-27-79	R	Kansas State	D5/01	—
72	Issa, Jabari (T)	6-5/302	4-18-78	2	Washington	D6/00	10/0
96	Ottis, Brad (E)	6-5/290	8-2-72	7	Wayne State (Neb.)	FA/96	15/11
92	Tanner, Barron (T)	6-3/320	9-14-73	4	Oklahoma	FA/00	4/0
78	Tosi, Mao (E)	6-6/305	12-12-76	2	Idaho	D5a/00	15/10
93	Vanden Bosch, Kyle (E)	6-4/270	11-17-78	R	Nebraska	D2/01	—
90	Wadsworth, Andre (E)	6-4/272	10-19-74	4	Florida State	D1/98	9/8
	LINEBACKERS						
58	Folston, James	6-3/238	8-14-71	8	Northeast Louisiana	FA/99	13/3
59	Fredrickson, Rob	6-4/243	5-13-71	8	Michigan State	UFA/99	13/12
57	McKinnon, Ronald	6-0/255	9-20-73	6	North Alabama	FA/96	16/16
51	Rutledge, Johnny	6-3/243	1-4-77	3	Florida	D2/99	11/3
54	Sanyika, Sekou	6-3/240	3-17-78	2	California	D7/00	16/0
55	Thompson, Raynoch	6-3/222	11-21-77	2	Tennessee	D2/00	11/9
52	Walz, Zack	6-4/229	2-3-76	4	Dartmouth	D6/98	6/5
	DEFENSIVE BACKS						
36	Barrett, David (CB)	5-11/198	12-22-77	2	Arkansas	D4/00	16/0
28	Bennett, Tommy (S)	6-2/212	2-19-73	5	UCLA	FA/96	11/0
25	Chavous, Corey (S)	6-1/202	1-15-76	4	Vanderbilt	D2a/98	16/1
	Hill, Renaldo	5-11/182	11-12-78	R	Michigan State	D7a/01	—
24	Knight, Tom (CB)	6-0/196	12-29-74	5	Iowa	D1/97	16/15
42	Lassiter, Kwamie (S)	6-0/203	12-3-69	7	Kansas	FA/95	16/16
41	Lucas, Justin	5-10/197	7-15-76	3	Abilene Christian	FA/99	16/0
44	Stone, Michael (CB)	5-11/191	2-13-78	R	Memphis	D2b/01	—
40	Tillman, Pat (S)	5-11/199	11-6-76	4	Arizona State	D7b/98	16/16
22	Wilson, Adrian	6-2/213	10-12-79	R	North Carolina State	D3/01	—
	SPECIALISTS						
15	Blanchard, Cary (K)	6-2/222	11-5-68	9	Oklahoma State	UFA/00	16/0
7	Gramatica, Bill (K)	5-10/192	7-10-78	R	South Florida	D4a/01	—
10	Player, Scott (P)	6-1/217	12-17-69	4	Florida State	FA/98	16/0

*Not with Cardinals in 2000.
Other free agent veterans invited to camp: WR Andre Cooper.
Abbreviations: D1—draft pick, first round; SD-2—supplemental draft pick, second round; W—claimed on waivers; T—obtained in trade; PlanB—Plan B free-agent acquisition; FA—free-agent acquisition (other than Plan B); UFA—unconditional free agent acquisition; ED—expansion draft pick.

MISCELLANEOUS TEAM DATA

Stadium (capacity, surface):
Sun Devil Stadium (73,243, grass)
Business address:
P.O. Box 888
Phoenix, AZ 85001-0888
Business phone:
602-379-0101
Ticket information:
602-379-0102
Team colors:
Cardinal red, black and white
Flagship radio station:
KDUS, 1060 AM/KSLX 100.7 FM
Training site:
Northern Arizona University
Flagstaff, Ariz.
520-523-1818

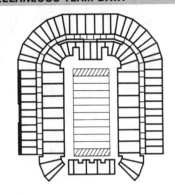

TSN REPORT CARD

Coaching staff	C	The unknown keeps this grade from being higher. Dave McGinnis is entering his first full season as a head coach. Offensive coordinator Rich Olson has never called plays in an entire NFL game. Still, this appears to be an experienced staff with the right mix of veterans and younger assistants.
Quarterbacks	C	Jake Plummer has played poorly the last two seasons, and backup Dave Brown has been average when called upon to play. If Plummer can revert to the player he was in 1998, the Cardinals will be significantly better on offense. If he can't, they won't come within sight of .500.
Running backs	B	Starter Michael Pittman is tough, physical and fast enough to get to the outside. His backup, Thomas Jones, was a disappointment as a rookie, but it's too early to give up on him. Together, they should give the Cardinals a nice change of pace, provided the line can open some holes.
Receivers	A	David Boston appears to be on the verge of stardom, and Rob Moore's rehabilitation from reconstructive knee surgery is ahead of schedule. Frank Sanders could slip from the starting lineup to the No. 3 spot, and MarTay Jenkins should make significant strides this year.
Offensive line	B	If this unit looks as good on the field as it does in the meeting rooms, the Cardinals will have something special. Trouble is, the players haven't done it. Free agent guard Pete Kendall should give the unit some leadership and toughness, while second overall draft pick Leonard Davis will start his career at guard.
Defensive line	D	The Cardinals haven't been able to stop the run the last two years, and it's hard to see how they will do it this year. There is some talent up front, but it's young. This group isn't going to keep offensive coordinators from sleeping the night before games.
Linebackers	C -	Ronald McKinnon on the inside and Rob Fredrickson on the outside are solid players, but nearly everyone else is unproven. Raynoch Thompson and Zack Walz could move into the starting lineup but both have struggled with injuries during their short stints in the league.
Secondary	C -	Cornerback Aeneas Williams is gone, and the Cardinals will be hard-pressed to make up for his loss. Cornerback Tom Knight returns but he doesn't make many big plays. The safeties are solid but this secondary could struggle, especially with no pass rush.
Special teams	B	The kicking battle between rookie Bill Gramatica and 10-year veteran Cary Blanchard will be decided in camp. Punter Scott Player is coming off a Pro Bowl season and MarTay Jenkins is among the league's top kick returners. Rookie Bobby Newcombe will handle punt returns if he makes the team.

ATLANTA FALCONS
NFC WESTERN DIVISION

ATLANTA FALCONS

2001 SEASON

CLUB DIRECTORY

President
Taylor Smith
Executive v.p. of administration
Jim Hay
General manager
Harold Richardson
Vice president of football operations
Ron Hill
Corporate secretary
John O. Knox
Vice president of marketing
Rob Jackson
Vice president of corporate development
Tommy Nobis
Marketing/sales assistants
Mark Fuhrman   Spencer Treadwell
Director of communications
Aaron Salkin
Director of media relations
Frank Kleha
**Executive dir. of the Atlanta Falcons Youth
  Foundation and community relations**
Carol Breeding
Director of community relations
Chris Demos
Director of finance
Greg Beadles
Coordinator of player programs
Billy "White Shoes" Johnson
Director of ticket operations
Jack Ragsdale
Controller
Wallace Norman
Accounting
Carolyn Cathey
Dir. of player personnel/college scouting
Reed Johnson
National scout
Mike Hagen
Scouts
Ken Blair   Melvin Bratton
Billy Campfield   Dick Corrick
Boyd Dowler   Elbert Dubenion
Bill Groman   Bob Harrison
Taylor Morton   Bruce Plummer

**Head coach/
executive v.p.
for football
operations**
Dan Reeves

Assistant coaches
Marvin Bass (asst. to head coach/
  player personnel)
Don Blackmon (def. coordinator)
Greg Brown (secondary)
Jack Burns (quarterbacks)
Rocky Colburn (assistant strength &
  conditioning)
James Daniel (tight ends)
Billy Davis (linebackers)
Joe DeCamillis (special teams)
Thom Kaumeyer (def. quality control)
Pete Mangurian (offensive line)
Al Miller (strength & conditioning)
George Sefcik (off. coord./RBs)
Rennie Simmons (asst. off. line)
Ed West (off. quality control)

Pro personnel assistant
Les Sneed
Admin. assistant/football operations
Kim Mauldin
Head trainer
Ron Medlin
Trainers
Harold King   Tom Reed
Equipment manager
Brian Boigner
Sr. equip. dir./gameday op. coord.
Horace Daniel
Video director
Mike Crews

SCHEDULE

Sept. 9—	at San Francisco	4:15
Sept. 16—	at St. Louis	4:05
Sept. 23—	CAROLINA	1:00
Sept. 30—	at Arizona	4:05
Oct. 7—	CHICAGO	1:00
Oct. 14—	SAN FRANCISCO	1:00
Oct. 21—	at New Orleans	1:00
Oct. 28—	Open date	
Nov. 4—	NEW ENGLAND	1:00
Nov. 11—	DALLAS	1:00
Nov. 18—	at Green Bay	1:00
Nov. 25—	at Carolina	1:00
Dec. 2—	ST. LOUIS	1:00
Dec. 9—	NEW ORLEANS	1:00
Dec. 16—	at Indianapolis	1:00
Dec. 23—	BUFFALO	1:00
Dec. 30—	at Miami	1:00

All times are Eastern.
All games Sunday unless noted.

DRAFT CHOICES

Michael Vick, QB, Virginia Tech (first round/first pick overall).
Alge Crumpler, TE, N. Carolina (2/35).
Robert Garza, C, Texas A&M-Kingsville (4/99).
Matt Stewart, LB, Vanderbilt (4/102).
Vinny Sutherland, WR, Purdue (5/136).
Randy Garner, DE, Arkansas (6/167).
Corey Hall, DB, Appalachian St. (7/215).
Kynan Forney, G, Hawaii (7/219).
Ronald Flemons, DE, Texas A&M (7/226).
Quentin McCord, WR, Kentucky (7/236).

2000 REVIEW

RESULTS

Sept. 3—SAN FRANCISCO	W	36-28
Sept.10—at Denver	L	14-42
Sept.17—at Carolina	W	15-10
Sept.24—ST. LOUIS	L	20-41
Oct. 1—at Philadelphia	L	10-38
Oct. 8—N.Y. GIANTS	L	6-13
Oct. 15—at St. Louis	L	29-45
Oct. 22—NEW ORLEANS	L	19-21
Oct. 29—CAROLINA	W	13-12
Nov. 5—TAMPA BAY	L	14-27
Nov. 12—at Detroit	L	10-13
Nov. 19—at San Francisco	L	6-16
Nov. 26—at Oakland	L	14-41
Dec. 3—SEATTLE	L	10-30
Dec. 10—Open date		
Dec. 17—at New Orleans	L	7-23
Dec. 24—KANSAS CITY	W	29-13

RECORDS/RANKINGS

2000 regular-season record: 4-12 (5th in NFC West); 3-5 in division; 3-9 in conference; 3-5 at home; 1-7 on road.
Team record last five years: 33-47 (.413, ranks 25th in league in that span).

2000 team rankings:	No.	NFC	NFL
Total offense	*249.6	15	30
Rushing offense	*75.9	14	28
Passing offense	*173.8	12	24
Scoring offense	252	13	27
Total defense	*350.4	11	30
Rushing defense	*123.9	13	27
Passing defense	*226.5	11	24
Scoring defense	413	12	26
Takeaways	25	T9	T20
Giveaways	34	11	23
Turnover differential	-9	T10	T23
Sacks	31	T10	T23
Sacks allowed	61	14	30

*Yards per game.

TEAM LEADERS

Scoring (kicking): Morten Andersen, 98 pts. (23/23 PATs, 25/31 FGs).
Scoring (touchdowns): Jamal Anderson, 38 pts. (6 rushing, 1 2-pt. conv.).
Passing: Chris Chandler, 2,236 yds. (331 att., 192 comp., 58.0%, 10 TDs, 12 int.).
Rushing: Jamal Anderson, 1,024 yds. (282 att., 3.6 avg., 6 TDs).
Receptions: Shawn Jefferson, 60 (822 yds., 13.7 avg., 2 TDs).
Interceptions: Ray Buchanan, 6 (114 yds., 0 TDs).
Sacks: Travis Hall, 4.5; Brady Smith, 4.5.
Punting: Dan Stryzinski, 41.0 avg. (84 punts, 3,447 yds., 1 blocked).
Punt returns: Tim Dwight, 9.4 avg. (33 att., 309 yds., 1 TD).
Kickoff returns: Darrick Vaughn, 27.7 avg. (39 att., 1,082 yds., 3 TDs).

ATLANTA FALCONS

No.	QUARTERBACKS	Ht./Wt.	Born	NFL Exp.	College	How acq.	'00 Games GP/GS
12	Chandler, Chris	6-4/226	10-12-65	14	Washington	T-Hou./97	14/13
11	Johnson, Doug	6-2/225	10-27-77	2	Florida	FA/00	4/2
7	Vick, Michael	6-0/214	6-26-80	R	Virginia Tech	D1/01	—
16	Zeier, Eric	6-1/214	9-6-72	7	Georgia	T-TB/01	*3/0
	RUNNING BACKS						
32	Anderson, Jamal	5-11/237	9-30-72	8	Utah	D7/94	16/16
44	Christian, Bob (FB)	5-11/232	11-14-68	9	Northwestern	FA/97	16/14
45	Downs, Gary	6-1/215	6-6-72	8	North Carolina State	FA/97	16/0
36	Jervey, Travis	6-0/222	5-5-72	7	The Citadel	FA/01	*8/0
43	Smith, Maurice	6-0/235	9-7-76	2	North Carolina A & T	FA/01	10/0
20	Thomas, Rodney	5-10/210	3-30-73	7	Texas A&M	FA/01	*16/0
	RECEIVERS						
80	Baker, Eugene	6-0/170	3-18-76	2	Kent	D5/99	1/0
83	Crumpler, Alge (TE)	6-2/264	12-23-77	R	North Carolina	D2/01	—
86	Finneran, Brian	6-5/210	1-31-76	2	Villanova	FA/00	12/0
87	German, Jammi	6-1/191	7-4-74	4	Miami (Fla.)	D3/98	9/0
84	Jefferson, Shawn	5-11/185	2-22-69	11	Central Florida	UFA/00	16/14
89	Kelly, Reggie (TE)	6-3/255	2-27-77	3	Mississippi State	D2/99	16/16
85	Kozlowski, Brian (TE)	6-3/250	10-4-70	8	Connecticut	FA/97	16/3
81	Mathis, Terance	5-10/185	6-7-67	12	New Mexico	UFA/94	16/16
	McCord, Quentin	5-10/195	6-26-78	R	Kentucky	D7d/01	—
49	Neil, Dallas (TE)	6-1/235	9-30-76	2	Montana	FA/00	6/0
82	Philyaw, Mareno	6-2/208	12-19-77	1	Troy (Ala.) State	FA/00	1/0
48	Rackley, Derek (TE)	6-4/250	7-18-77	2	Minnesota	FA/00	16/0
	Sutherland, Vinny	5-8/188	4-22-78	R	Purdue	D5/01	—
	OFFENSIVE LINEMEN						
76	Banks, Chris (G)	6-1/315	4-4-73	4	Kansas	W-Den./00	8/4
71	Claridge, Travis (T)	6-5/300	3-23-78	2	Southern California	D2/00	16/16
68	Collins, Calvin (C)	6-2/310	1-5-74	5	Texas A&M	D6/97	16/16
	Forney, Kynan (G)	6-3/304	9-8-78	R	Hawaii	D7/01	—
	Garza, Robert (C)	6-2/292	3-26-79	R	Texas A&M-Kingsville	D4a/01	—
64	Hallen, Bob (G)	6-4/295	3-9-75	4	Kent	D2/98	16/5
62	McClure, Todd (C)	6-1/288	2-16-77	3	Louisiana State	D7a/99	10/7
61	Redmon, Anthony (G)	6-5/305	4-9-71	8	Auburn	UFA/00	4/4
74	Salaam, Ephraim (T)	6-7/300	6-19-76	4	San Diego State	D7a/98	14/10
67	Shivers, Wes (T)	6-5/298	3-8-77	1	Mississippi State	FA/00	3/0
66	Thompson, Michael (T)	6-4/295	2-11-77	2	Tennessee State	D4/00	2/2
70	Whitfield, Bob (T)	6-5/310	10-18-71	10	Stanford	D1a/92	15/15
	DEFENSIVE LINEMEN						
75	Dronett, Shane (T)	6-6/300	1-12-71	10	Texas	FA/97	3/3
	Flemons, Ronald (E)	6-5/247	10-20-79	R	Texas A&M	D7c/01	—
	Garner, Randy (E)	6-4/273	11-28-77	R	Arkansas	D6/01	—
98	Hall, Travis (T)	6-5/295	8-3-72	7	Brigham Young	D6/95	16/16
95	Jasper, Ed (T)	6-2/293	1-18-73	5	Texas A&M	FA/99	15/15
97	Kerney, Patrick (E)	6-5/273	12-30-76	3	Virginia	D1/99	16/16
91	Smith, Brady (E)	6-5/274	6-5-73	5	Colorado State	UFA/00	15/14
93	Swayda, Shawn (E)	6-5/294	9-4-74	4	Arizona State	FA/98	16/0
99	Wiley, Chuck (E)	6-5/277	3-6-75	4	Louisiana State	W-Car./00	16/0
	LINEBACKERS						
50	Atkins, Corey	6-0/232	11-11-76	2	Southern California	FA/00	12/0
56	Brooking, Keith	6-2/245	10-30-75	4	Georgia Tech	D1/98	5/5
54	Draft, Chris	5-11/232	2-26-76	3	Stanford	W-SF/00	13/8
55	Jordan, Antony	6-3/235	12-19-74	3	Vanderbilt	FA/00	8/0
51	Kelly, Jeff	5-11/242	12-13-75	3	Kansas State	D6a/99	12/6
53	Simoneau, Mark	6-0/234	1-16-77	2	Kansas State	D3/00	14/4
	Stewart, Matt	6-3/232	8-31-79	R	Vanderbilt	D4/01	—
58	Tuggle, Jessie	5-11/230	4-4-65	15	Valdosta (Ga.) State	FA/87	8/7
94	Ulmer, Artie	6-3/247	7-30-73	4	Valdosta (Ga.) State	FA/01	*12/2
	DEFENSIVE BACKS						
33	Ambrose, Ashley (CB)	5-10/185	9-17-70	10	Mississippi Valley State	UFA/00	16/16
23	Bradford, Ronnie (CB)	5-10/198	10-1-70	9	Colorado	UFA/97	16/15
34	Buchanan, Ray (CB)	5-9/186	9-29-71	9	Louisville	FA/97	16/16
25	Carter, Marty (S)	6-1/213	12-17-69	11	Middle Tennessee State	UFA/99	16/16
35	Carty, Johndale (S)	6-0/196	8-27-77	3	Utah State	D4/99	15/0
	Hall, Corey (S)	6-4/190	1-17-79	R	Appalachian State	D7a/01	—
24	Hamilton, Conrad (CB)	5-10/185	11-5-74	4	Eastern New Mexico	FA/01	0/0
47	Hudson, Chris (S)	5-10/199	10-6-71	6	Colorado	UFA/00	0/0
22	McBurrows, Gerald (S)	5-11/208	10-7-73	7	Kansas	UFA/99	16/4
37	Vaughn, Darrick (CB)	5-11/193	10-2-78	2	Southwest Texas State	D7/00	16/0
21	Williams, Elijah (CB)	5-10/180	8-20-75	4	Florida	D6/98	15/3
	SPECIALISTS						
13	Mohr, Chris (P)	6-5/215	5-11-66	12	Alabama	FA/00	*16/0

*Not with Falcons in 2000.
Other free agent veterans invited to camp: DT William Carr, RB Kevin McLeod, DT Ron Moore.

Abbreviations: D1—draft pick, first round; SD-2—supplemental draft pick, second round; W—claimed on waivers; T—obtained in trade; PlanB—Plan B free-agent acquisition; FA—free-agent acquisition (other than Plan B); UFA—unconditional free agent acquisition; ED—expansion draft pick.

ATLANTA FALCONS

MISCELLANEOUS TEAM DATA

Stadium (capacity, surface):
Georgia Dome
(71,228, artificial)
Business address:
4400 Falcon Parkway
Flowery Branch, GA 30542
Business phone:
770-965-3115
Ticket information:
404-223-8444
Team colors:
Black, red, silver and white
Flagship radio station:
WGST, 920 AM
Training site:
4400 Falcon Parkway
Flowery Branch, GA 30542
770-965-3115

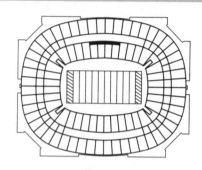

TSN REPORT CARD

Coaching staff — C — The exits of defensive coordinator Rich Brooks and defensive line coach Bill Kollar left the impression that they did not believe Dan Reeves would coach past the 2001 season. Brooks didn't have another job and Kollar made a lateral move. Former linebackers coach Ron Blackmon is in the spotlight as the new defensive coordinator. The change on the offensive line—Art Shell is out and Pete Mangurian is in—was needed.

Quarterbacks — B+ — Chris Chandler still has some touchdown bombs in his right arm. More importantly, he has much knowledge about Reeves' offense. Should Chandler suffer an early season injury, Eric Zeier would be the likely fill-in starter. But by the end of the season expect to see Michael Vick take the first snap. In the meantime, he will have special packages. Vick may make an impact with his legs before he makes a difference with his arm.

Running backs — B — Jamal Anderson should be closer to his 1998 Pro Bowl form now that he has had two years to recover from his 1999 knee surgery. When Vick is in the game, concerns about the quarterback's ability to run east and west may open up some straight-ahead gains for the powerful Anderson. The Falcons made two key pickups, adding veterans Rodney Thomas and special teams standout Travis Jervey, giving the team needed experience behind Anderson. Maurice Smith, quicker and almost as big as Anderson, may play a larger role in his second season.

Receivers — C — One price the Falcons paid by trading up to take Vick in the first round and then picking tight end Alge Crumpler in the second round is they didn't take advantage of the wealth of receivers high in the draft. Instead, two second-day picks—Vinny Sutherland and Quentin McCord—may help replace the traded Tim Dwight as deep threats behind Terance Mathis, 33, and Shawn Jefferson, 32. This may be the last chance for backups Jammi German, Eugene Baker and Brian Finneran. It helps that Crumpler and Reggie Kelly are decent receivers at tight end.

Offensive line — D — A season of juggling only seemed to drag this patchwork outfit down last year. Entering training camp, left tackle Bob Whitfield is the only sure thing for new line coach Pete Mangurian. Ephraim Salaam and Michael Thompson may have a good competition at right tackle, and Travis Claridge will be the man to beat at right guard. Center and left guard are wide open, with Todd McClure and Calvin Collins, respectively, the closest thing to returning starters. If healthy and in good shape, Anthony Redmon could be a factor at one of the guard spots.

Defensive line — C- — If Shane Dronett makes a good return from his season-ending knee injury, there is decent depth at tackle. Travis Hall, Ed Jasper and Dronett are capable starters. Two draft picks—Randy Garner and Ronald Flemons—join the competition at defensive end, where Brady Smith and especially Patrick Kerney did not deliver the expected pass rush as starters. Chuck Wiley helped with his four sacks in a backup role. Expect Smith and Kerney to retain their starting jobs, but improvement will be expected.

Linebackers — B- — Proud warrior Jessie Tuggle returns from a knee injury, confident that at 36 he can still be a productive starter. It is crucial that weakside starter Keith Brooking makes a strong return from a foot injury and fulfills his predicted role as a big-play producer. The big question is on the strongside, where Henri Crockett was not re-signed. Fourth-round pick Matt Stewart, Chris Draft and Mark Simoneau are potential replacements. Draft surprised coaches with his solid fill-in role for Brooking. Simoneau needs to play somewhere but may not be big enough to be a long-term answer at the strongside spot.

Secondary — A- — The Falcons stepped up by keeping Ray Buchanan, who teams with Ashley Ambrose to form one of the top cornerback tandems in the league. The two combined for 10 interceptions last year. It was also important to keep versatile safety Gerald McBurrows, who could push strong safety Marty Carter or free safety Ronnie Bradford. Carter is an established run-stopper who may give way to McBurrows in passing situations.

Special teams — C+ — This is a transition year, with Chris Mohr replacing punter Dan Stryzinski and Jake Arians given the first shot at replacing Morten Andersen. If Andersen does not sign elsewhere, he could still return to Atlanta, but the Falcons saw enough in Arians to keep him on the practice squad last year. Tim Dwight's return skills also will be missed, but Darrick Vaughn set a team record with three kickoff returns for touchdowns. Rookie Vinny Sutherland and free-agent pickup Travis Jervey also can help on returns.

– 10 –

BALTIMORE RAVENS
AFC CENTRAL DIVISION

2001 SEASON

CLUB DIRECTORY

Owner/chief executive officer
Arthur B. Modell
President/chief operating officer
David O. Modell
Vice president of player personnel
Ozzie Newsome
Vice president/public relations
Kevin Byrne
Vice president of administration
Pat Moriarty
Vice president/chief financial officer
Luis Perez
V.p./business dev. and marketing
Dennis Mannion
Sr. dir./corp. & broadcast partnerships
Mark Burdett
Dir. of broadcasting & video production
Larry Rosen
Director of operations and information
Bob Eller
Director of publications
Francine Lubera
Director of ticket operations
Roy Sommerhof
Director of pro personnel
James Harris
Director of college scouting
Phil Savage
Scouting/pro personnel
Eric DeCosta
George Kokinis
Ron Marciniak
Terry McDonough
T.J. McCreight
Art Perkins
Head trainer
Bill Tessendorf
Assistant trainer
Mark Smith

Head coach
Brian Billick

Assistant coaches
Matt Cavanaugh (offensive coordinator)
Jim Colletto (offensive line)
Jack Del Rio (linebackers)
Jeff Friday (strength & conditioning)
Wade Harman (tight ends)
Donnie Henderson (def. backs)
Marvin Lewis (defensive coordinator)
Chip Morton (assistant strength & conditioning)
Mike Nolan (receivers)
Russ Purnell (special teams)
Rex Ryan (defensive line)
Steve Shafer (defensive backs)
Matt Simon (running backs)
Mike Smith (defensive asst.)
Bennie Thompson (assistant special teams)

Team physicians
Dr. Andrew M. Tucker
Dr. Claude T. Moorman III
Dr. Andrew Pollak
Dr. Leigh Ann Curl
Equipment manager
Ed Carroll

SCHEDULE

Sept. 9—	CHICAGO	1:00
Sept. 17—	MINNESOTA (Mon.)	9:00
Sept. 23—	at Cincinnati	1:00
Sept. 30—	at Denver	4:15
Oct. 7—	TENNESSEE	1:00
Oct. 14—	at Green Bay	1:00
Oct. 21—	at Cleveland	12:00
Oct. 28—	JACKSONVILLE	1:00
Nov. 4—	at Pittsburgh	1:00
Nov. 12—	at Tennessee (Mon.)	9:00
Nov. 18—	CLEVELAND	1:00
Nov. 25—	at Jacksonville	1:00
Dec. 2—	INDIANAPOLIS	1:00
Dec. 9—	Open date	
Dec. 16—	PITTSBURGH	8:30
Dec. 23—	CINCINNATI	1:00
Dec. 29—	at Tampa Bay (Sat.)	9:00

All times are Eastern.
All games Sunday unless noted.

DRAFT CHOICES

Todd Heap, TE, Arizona State (first round/31st pick overall).
Gary Baxter, DB, Baylor (2/62).
Casey Rabach, C, Wisconsin (3/92).
Edgerton Hartwell, LB, Western Illinois (4/126).
Chris Barnes, RB, New Mexico State (5/161).
Joe Maese, C, New Mexico (6/194).
Dwayne Missouri, DE, Northwestern (7/231).

2000 REVIEW

RESULTS

Sept. 3—at Pittsburgh	W	16-0
Sept.10—JACKSONVILLE	W	39-36
Sept.17—at Miami	L	6-19
Sept.24—CINCINNATI	W	37-0
Oct. 1—at Cleveland	W	12-0
Oct. 8—at Jacksonville	W	15-10
Oct. 15—at Washington	L	3-10
Oct. 22—TENNESSEE	L	6-14
Oct. 29—PITTSBURGH	L	6-9
Nov. 5—at Cincinnati	W	27-7
Nov. 12—at Tennessee	W	24-23
Nov. 19—DALLAS	W	27-0
Nov. 26—CLEVELAND	W	44-7
Dec. 3—Open date		
Dec. 10—SAN DIEGO	W	24-3
Dec. 17—at Arizona	W	13-7
Dec. 24—N.Y. JETS	W	34-20
Dec. 31—DENVER*	W	21-3
Jan. 7—at Tennessee†	W	27-10
Jan. 14—at Oakland‡	W	16-3
Jan. 28—N.Y. Giants§	W	34-7

*AFC wild-card game.
†AFC divisional playoff game.
‡AFC championship game.
§Super Bowl 35 at Tampa.

RECORDS/RANKINGS

2000 regular-season record: 12-4 (2nd in AFC Central); 8-2 in division; 10-3 in conference; 6-2 at home; 6-2 on road.
Team record last five years: 36-43-1 (.456, ranks 22nd in league in that span).
2000 team rankings:

	No.	AFC	NFL
Total offense	*313.4	9	16
Rushing offense	*137.4	5	5
Passing offense	*175.9	12	22
Scoring offense	333	7	14
Total defense	*247.9	2	2
Rushing defense	*60.6	1	1
Passing defense	*187.3	5	8
Scoring defense	165	1	1
Takeaways	49	1	1
Giveaways	26	T6	T9
Turnover differential	23	1	1
Sacks	35	13	22
Sacks allowed	43	T9	T19

*Yards per game.

TEAM LEADERS

Scoring (kicking): Matt Stover, 135 pts. (30/30 PATs, 35/39 FGs).
Scoring (touchdowns): Jamal Lewis, 38 pts. (6 rushing, 1 2-pt. conv.).
Passing: Tony Banks, 1,578 yds. (274 att., 150 comp., 54.7%, 8 TDs, 8 int.).
Rushing: Jamal Lewis, 1,364 yds. (309 att., 4.4 avg., 6 TDs).
Receptions: Shannon Sharpe, 67 (810 yds., 12.1 avg., 5 TDs).
Interceptions: Duane Starks, 6 (125 yds., 0 TDs).
Sacks: Rob Burnett, 10.5.
Punting: Kyle Richardson, 40.2 avg. (86 punts, 3,457 yds., 0 blocked).
Punt returns: Jermaine Lewis, 16.1 avg. (36 att., 578 yds., 2 TDs).
Kickoff returns: Corey Harris, 23.3 avg. (39 att., 907 yds., 0 TDs).

BALTIMORE RAVENS

No.	QUARTERBACKS	Ht./Wt.	Born	NFL Exp.	College	How acq.	'00 Games GP/GS
	Cunningham, Randall	6-4/213	3-27-63	15	UNLV	UFA/01	*6/3
18	Grbac, Elvis	6-5/240	8-13-70	9	Michigan	FA/01	*15/15
7	Redman, Chris	6-3/223	7-7-77	2	Louisville	D3/00	2/0
	RUNNING BACKS						
30	Ayanbadejo, Obafemi (FB)	6-2/235	3-5-75	4	San Diego State	FA/99	8/4
	Barnes, Chris	6-0/209	7-31-78	R	New Mexico State	D5/01	—
31	Lewis, Jamal	5-11/231	8-28-79	2	Tennessee	D1a/00	16/13
	RECEIVERS						
86	Heap, Todd (TE)	6-5/252	3-16-80	R	Arizona State	D1/01	—
87	Ismail, Qadry	6-0/200	11-8-70	9	Syracuse	FA/99	15/13
83	Johnson, Patrick	5-10/180	8-10-76	4	Oregon	D2/98	13/9
85	Jones, John (TE)	6-4/255	4-4-75	2	Indiana (Pa.)	FA/00	8/0
84	Lewis, Jermaine	5-7/180	10-16-74	6	Maryland	D5/96	15/1
82	Sharpe, Shannon (TE)	6-2/232	6-26-68	12	Savannah (Ga.) State	UFA/00	16/15
80	Stokley, Brandon	5-11/197	6-23-76	3	Southwestern Louisiana	D4a/99	7/1
89	Taylor, Travis	6-1/200	3-30-79	2	Florida	D1b/00	9/8
	OFFENSIVE LINEMEN						
62	Flynn, Mike	6-3/300	6-15-74	4	Maine	FA/97	16/16
	Maese, Joe (C)	6-0/241	12-2-78	R	New Mexico	D7/01	—
64	Mulitalo, Edwin (G)	6-3/340	9-1-74	3	Arizona	D4b/99	16/16
75	Ogden, Jonathan (T)	6-8/340	7-31-74	6	UCLA	D1a/96	15/15
	Rabach, Casey (C)	6-4/301	9-24-77	R	Wisconsin	D3/01	—
72	Searcy, Leon (T)	6-4/320	12-21-69	9	Miami, Fla	FA/00	0/0
70	Swayne, Harry (T)	6-5/300	2-2-65	15	Rutgers	UFA/99	13/13
77	Vickers, Kipp	6-2/300	8-27-69	7	Miami (Fla.)	UFA/00	12/2
78	Williams, Sammy	6-5/318	12-14-74	4	Oklahoma	W-KC/99	1/0
	DEFENSIVE LINEMEN						
95	Adams, Sam (T)	6-3/330	6-13-73	8	Texas A&M	UFA/00	16/16
90	Burnett, Rob (E)	6-4/270	8-27-67	12	Syracuse	D5/90	16/16
91	Dalton, Lional (T)	6-1/309	2-21-75	4	Eastern Michigan	FA/98	16/1
99	McCrary, Michael (E)	6-4/260	7-7-70	9	Wake Forest	UFA/97	16/16
	Missouri, Dwayne (E)	6-5/265	12-23-78	R	Northwestern	D7/01	—
98	Siragusa, Tony (T)	6-3/340	5-14-67	12	Pittsburgh	FA/97	15/15
96	Thomas, Adalius (E)	6-2/270	8-18-77	2	Southern Mississippi	D6a/00	3/0
79	Webster, Larry (T)	6-5/288	1-18-69	10	Maryland	FA/95	5/0
	LINEBACKERS						
58	Boulware, Peter	6-4/255	12-18-74	5	Florida State	D1/97	16/15
	Hartwell, Edgerton	6-1/244	5-27-78	R	Western Illinois	D4/01	—
50	Jackson, Brad	6-0/230	1-11-75	3	Cincinnati	FA/98	10/0
52	Lewis, Ray	6-1/245	5-15-75	6	Miami (Fla.)	D1b/96	16/16
55	Sharper, Jamie	6-3/240	11-23-74	5	Virginia	D2a/97	16/16
	DEFENSIVE BACKS						
28	Baxter, Gary	6-2/204	11-24-78	R	Baylor	D2/01	—
45	Harris, Corey (S)	5-11/200	10-25-69	10	Vanderbilt	FA/98	16/0
25	Love, Clarence (CB)	5-10/181	6-16-76	3	Toledo	FA/99	1/0
21	McAlister, Chris (CB)	6-1/206	6-14-77	3	Arizona	D1/99	16/16
42	Mitchell, Anthony (S)	6-1/211	12-13-74	2	Tuskegee	FA/99	16/0
43	Poindexter, Anthony (S)	6-0/220	7-28-76	3	Virginia	D7/99	10/0
22	Starks, Duane (CB)	5-10/170	5-23-74	4	Miami (Fla.)	D1/98	15/15
38	Trapp, James (CB)	6-0/190	12-28-69	9	Clemson	UFA/99	16/1
26	Woodson, Rod (S)	6-0/205	3-10-65	15	Purdue	FA/98	16/16
	SPECIALISTS						
5	Richardson, Kyle (P)	6-2/210	3-2-73	5	Arkansas State	FA/98	16/0
3	Stover, Matt (K)	5-11/178	1-27-68	12	Louisiana Tech	PlanB/91	16/0

*Not with Ravens in 2000.

Other free agent veterans invited to camp: DT Kelly Gregg.

Abbreviations: D1—draft pick, first round; SD-2—supplemental draft pick, second round; W—claimed on waivers; T—obtained in trade; PlanB—Plan B free-agent acquisition; FA—free-agent acquisition (other than Plan B); UFA—unconditional free agent acquisition; ED—expansion draft pick.

MISCELLANEOUS TEAM DATA

Stadium (capacity, surface):
  PSINet Stadium
  (69,084, grass)
Business address:
  11001 Owings Mills Blvd.
  Owings Mills, MD 21117
Business phone:
  410-654-6200
Ticket information:
  410-261-RAVE
Team colors:
  Purple, black and metallic gold
Flagship radio stations:
  WJFK 1300 AM & WQSR 105.7 FM
Training site:
  Western Maryland College
  Westminster, Md.
  410-654-6200

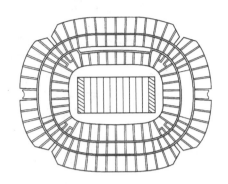

TSN REPORT CARD

Coaching staff	B	Brian Billick is a great organizer, planner and a coach players like to play for. His teams play with emotion, which reflect the character of the coach. Last year he guided the team through a five-game touchdown drought, and the Ravens still won the Super Bowl. But he has yet to provide this franchise with a strong offense, his forte in Minnesota. The Ravens have a capable staff, especially on defense. If the defense plays as well as last season, defensive coordinator Marvin Lewis and linebackers coach Jel Del Rio will probably get hired away by other teams.
Quarterbacks	B	Despite it being his first year in Baltimore, Elvis Grbac should do well in the West Coast offense, a system he had success in at Kansas City. The Ravens have an up-and-coming player in backup Chris Redman, entering his second year.
Running backs	B -	Jamal Lewis proved he was one of the best running backs in the league last season as a rookie, and he should be even better in his second season. But the Ravens don't have a proven backup. Obafemi Ayanbadejo is a solid fullback, but hasn't proved he can play an entire season. He can catch passes out of the backfield, but his blocking ability is suspect.
Receivers	C +	The Ravens will be older, but not necessarily better. This group has some speed, but no one who has proven consistency. Top players to watch are third-year player Brandon Stokley and sophomore Travis Taylor. Tight end Shannon Sharpe could be the go-to receiver again.
Offensive line	C +	The Ravens have a solid tackle tandem in Jonathan Ogden and Leon Searcy, maybe the best in the league, but the middle of the offensive line is shaky. Left guard Edwin Mulitalo is solid as a run blocker, but still needs to improve as a pass protector. Both center Mike Flynn and guard Kipp Vickers are not proven at their respective positions.
Defensive line	A	This group should again anchor the defense. The Ravens have two huge, but athletic tackles up front in Sam Adams and Tony Siragusa. Both ends, Rob Burnett and Michael McCrary, had superb seasons last year. The unit will be dominant again.
Linebackers	A	Ray Lewis is simply the best defensive player in the league, and maybe the best player period. He is joined on the outside by strong side linebacker Peter Boulware, whose shoulder injury won't slow him in 2001. The Ravens also made a bold statement during the offseason by re-signing weakside linebacker Jamie Sharper.
Secondary	B +	Cornerbacks Duane Starks and Chris McAlister elevated their games in the playoffs, and should be able to sustain that level into the 2001 season. The Ravens lost starting strong safety Kim Herring in free agency, but won't miss him much with replacement Corey Harris and veteran Rod Woodson on the weak side.
Special teams	B -	The Ravens have too many young players on these units and it could hurt. Because of salary cap concerns, the team wasn't able to bring back veterans such as O.J. Brigance and Billy Davis. The kicking game, though, should be sound with punter Kyle Richardson and placekicker Matt Stover.

BUFFALO BILLS
AFC EASTERN DIVISION

2001 SEASON

CLUB DIRECTORY

Owner
Ralph C. Wilson Jr.
President/general manager
Tom Donahoe
Vice president/player personnel
Dwight Adams
Vice president, communications
Scott Berchtold
V.p., business dev. & marketing
Russ Brandon
Vice president/operations
Bill Munson
Vice president/administration
Jim Overdorf
Corporate vice president/scout
Linda Bogdan
Consultant
Christy Wilson Hofmann
Treasurer
Jeffrey C. Littmann
Director of administration/ticket sales
Jerry Foran
Controller
Frank Wojnicki
Executive director/marketing
Marc Honan
Director of community affairs
Gretchen Geitter
Director of marketing partnerships
Jeff Fernandez
Director of merchandising
Julie Regan
Director of sales
Pete Guelli
Media relations coordinator
Mark Dalton
Ticket director
June Foran
Video director
Henry Kunttu
Director of stadium operations
George Koch
Director of security
Bill Bambach
Engineering and operations manager
Joe Frandina
Scouts
Brad Forsyth Tom Gibbons
Joe Haering Doug Majeski

Head coach
Gregg Williams

Assistant coaches
Miles Aldridge (linebackers)
Steve Fairchild (running backs)
Fred Graves (wide receivers)
Jerry Gray (defensive coordinator)
Steve Jackson (asst. DBs/third
down specialist)
Rusty Jones (strength and
conditioning coordinator)
Tommy Kaiser (off. assistant/
special teams assistant)
Steve Kragthorpe (quarterbacks)
Chuck Lester (off. asst./admin.
assistant to the head coach)
John Levra (defensive line)
Dan Neal (tight ends)
Danny Smith (special teams
coordinator)
Mike Sheppard (off. coordinator)
Pat Thomas (defensive backs)
Ronnie Vinkarek (offensive line)

Buddy Nix Bob Ryan
Chink Sengel Bobby Williams
Dave G. Smith Dave W. Smith
Head athletic trainer
Bud Carpenter
Assistant athletic trainers
Corey Bennett
Greg McMillen
Equipment manager
Dave Hojnowski
Assistant equipment manager
Woody Ribbeck

SCHEDULE

Sept. 9—	NEW ORLEANS	1:00
Sept. 16—	at Miami	1:00
Sept. 23—	at Indianapolis	1:00
Sept. 30—	PITTSBURGH	1:00
Oct. 7—	N.Y. JETS	4:05
Oct. 14—	Open date	
Oct. 18—	at Jacksonville (Thur.)	8:30
Oct. 28—	at San Diego	4:15
Nov. 4—	INDIANAPOLIS	4:15
Nov. 11—	at New England	1:00
Nov. 18—	SEATTLE	1:00
Nov. 25—	MIAMI	1:00
Dec. 2—	at San Francisco	8:30
Dec. 9—	CAROLINA	1:00
Dec. 16—	NEW ENGLAND	1:00
Dec. 23—	at Atlanta	1:00
Dec. 30—	at N.Y. Jets	1:00

All times are Eastern.
All games Sunday unless noted.

DRAFT CHOICES

Nate Clements, DB, Ohio State (first round/21st pick overall).
Aaron Schobel, DE, Tex. Christian (2/46).
Travis Henry, RB, Tennessee (2/58).
Ron Edwards, DT, Texas A&M (3/76).
Jonas Jennings, T, Georgia (3/95).
Brandon Spoon, LB, N. Carolina (4/110).
Marques Sullivan, T, Illinois (5/144).
Tony Driver, DB, Notre Dame (6/178).
Dan O'Leary, TE, Notre Dame (6/195).
Jimmy Williams, DB, Vanderbilt (6/196).
Reggie Germany, WR, Ohio St. (7/214).
Tyrone Robertson, DT, Hinds C.C. (Miss.) (7/238).

2000 REVIEW

RESULTS

Sept. 3—TENNESSEE	W	16-13
Sept.10—GREEN BAY	W	27-18
Sept.17—at N.Y. Jets	L	14-27
Sept.24—Open date		
Oct. 1—INDIANAPOLIS	L	16-18
Oct. 8—at Miami	L	13-22
Oct. 15—SAN DIEGO (OT)	W	27-24
Oct. 22—at Minnesota	L	27-31
Oct. 29—N.Y. JETS	W	23-20
Nov. 5—at New England (OT)	W	16-13
Nov. 12—CHICAGO	W	20-3
Nov. 19—at Kansas City	W	21-17
Nov. 26—at Tampa Bay	L	17-31
Dec. 3—MIAMI	L	6-33
Dec. 11—at Indianapolis	L	20-44
Dec. 17—NEW ENGLAND	L	10-13
Dec. 23—at Seattle	W	42-23

RECORDS/RANKINGS

2000 regular-season record: 8-8 (4th in AFC East); 2-6 in division; 6-6 in conference; 5-3 at home; 3-5 on road.
Team record last five years: 45-35 (.563, ranks T8th in league in that span).

2000 team rankings:	No.	AFC	NFL
Total offense	*343.6	6	9
Rushing offense	*120.1	8	13
Passing offense	*223.5	6	11
Scoring offense	315	12	20
Total defense	*276.6	3	3
Rushing defense	*97.4	5	6
Passing defense	*179.2	2	4
Scoring defense	350	10	18
Takeaways	29	T9	T16
Giveaways	23	3	4
Turnover differential	6	6	10
Sacks	42	T6	T12
Sacks allowed	59	16	29

*Yards per game.

TEAM LEADERS

Scoring (kicking): Steve Christie, 109 pts. (31/31 PATs, 26/35 FGs).
Scoring (touchdowns): Sammy Morris, 36 pts. (5 rushing, 1 receiving).
Passing: Rob Johnson, 2,125 yds. (306 att., 175 comp., 57.2%, 12 TDs, 7 int.).
Rushing: Shawn Bryson, 591 yds. (161 att., 3.7 avg., 0 TDs).
Receptions: Eric Moulds, 94 (1,326 yds., 14.1 avg., 5 TDs).
Interceptions: Keion Carpenter, 5 (63 yds., 0 TDs).
Sacks: Marcellus Wiley, 10.5.
Punting: Chris Mohr, 38.5 avg. (95 punts, 3,661 yds., 1 blocked).
Punt returns: Chris Watson, 4.9 avg. (33 att., 163 yds., 0 TDs).
Kickoff returns: Chris Watson, 20.3 avg. (44 att., 894 yds., 0 TDs).

BUFFALO BILLS

No.	QUARTERBACKS	Ht./Wt.	Born	NFL Exp.	College	How acq.	'00 Games GP/GS
11	Johnson, Rob	6-4/212	3-18-73	7	Southern California	T-Jax./98	12/11
10	Van Pelt, Alex	6-1/220	5-1-70	7	Pittsburgh	FA/94	1/0
	RUNNING BACKS						
38	Bryson, Shawn	6-1/233	11-30-76	2	Tennessee	D3/99	16/7
37	Centers, Larry	6-0/225	6-1-68	11	Stephen F. Austin State	FA/01	*15/5
25	Henry, Travis	5-9/221	10-29-78	R	Tennessee	D2b/01	—
35	Linton, Jonathan (FB)	6-1/234	11-7-74	4	North Carolina	D5/98	14/2
33	Morris, Sammy	6-0/228	3-23-77	2	Texas Tech	D5/00	12/9
	RECEIVERS						
89	Black, Avion	5-11/181	4-24-77	2	Tennessee State	D4/00	2/0
82	Cavil, Kwame	6-2/203	5-3-79	2	Texas	FA/00	16/0
84	Collins, Bobby (TE)	6-4/248	8-26-76	3	North Alabama	D4b/99	12/2
	Germany, Reggie	6-1/196	3-19-78	R	Ohio State	D7a/01	—
88	Jackson, Sheldon (TE)	6-3/250	7-24-76	3	Nebraska	D7a/99	16/8
86	McDaniel, Jeremy	6-0/197	5-2-76	2	Arizona	FA/99	16/5
80	Moulds, Eric	6-2/204	7-17-73	6	Mississippi State	D1/96	16/16
	O'Leary, Dan (TE)	6-3/260	9-1-77	R	Notre Dame	D6a/01	—
81	Price, Peerless	6-0/190	10-27-76	3	Tennessee	D2/99	16/16
85	Riemersma, Jay (TE)	6-5/254	5-17-73	5	Michigan	D7b/96	12/12
	OFFENSIVE LINEMEN						
79	Brown, Ruben (G)	6-3/304	2-13-72	7	Pittsburgh	D1/95	16/16
65	Carman, Jon (T)	6-7/335	1-14-76	2	Georgia Tech	FA/00	3/0
63	Conaty, Billy (C)	6-2/300	3-8-73	5	Virginia Tech	FA/97	16/0
70	Fina, John (T)	6-5/300	3-11-69	10	Arizona	D1/92	14/14
77	Hicks, Robert (T)	6-7/330	11-17-74	4	Mississippi State	D3/98	14/7
75	Jennings, Jonas (T)	6-3/320	11-21-77	R	Georgia	D3b/01	—
60	Ostroski, Jerry (G)	6-3/327	7-12-70	8	Tulsa	FA/93	16/16
	Sullivan, Marques (T)	6-5/323	2-2-78	R	Illinois	D5/01	—
	DEFENSIVE LINEMEN						
98	Edwards, Ron (T)	6-2/298	7-12-79	R	Texas A&M	D3a/01	—
96	Flowers, Erik (E)	6-4/270	3-1-78	2	Arizona State	D1/00	16/0
90	Hansen, Phil (E)	6-5/273	5-20-68	11	North Dakota State	D2/91	10/9
97	Larsen, Leif (T)	6-4/295	4-3-75	2	Texas-El Paso	D6/00	6/0
91	Price, Shawn (E)	6-4/290	3-28-70	9	Pacific	FA/96	13/6
	Robertson, Tyrone (T)	6-4/287	8-15-79	R	Georgia	D7b/01	—
95	Schobel, Aaron (E)	6-3/261	4-1-77	R	Texas Christian	D2a/01	—
93	Williams, Pat (T)	6-3/310	10-24-72	4	Texas A&M	FA/97	16/3
	LINEBACKERS						
56	Cowart, Sam	6-2/245	2-26-75	4	Florida State	D2/98	12/12
55	Foreman, Jay	6-1/240	2-18-76	3	Nebraska	D5/99	15/4
52	Holecek, John	6-2/242	5-7-72	7	Illinois	D5/95	16/16
99	Jones, Fred	6-2/246	10-18-77	2	Colorado	FA/00	15/0
54	Moore, Corey	5-11/225	3-20-77	2	Virginia Tech	D3/00	9/4
53	Newman, Keith	6-2/245	1-19-77	2	North Carolina	D4a/99	16/16
51	Polk, DaShon	6-2/235	3-13-77	2	Arizona	D7b/00	5/0
	Spoon, Brandon	6-2/244	7-5-78	R	North Carolina	D4/01	—
57	Wright, Kenyatta	6-0/238	2-19-78	2	Oklahoma State	FA/00	16/0
	DEFENSIVE BACKS						
29	Carpenter, Keion (S)	5-11/205	10-31-77	3	Virginia Tech	FA/99	12/12
22	Clements, Nate (CB)	5-11/191	12-12-79	R	Ohio State	D1/01	—
	Driver, Tony (S)	6-1/211	8-4-77	R	Notre Dame	D6/01	—
39	Hill, Raion (S)	6-0/200	9-2-76	2	Louisiana State	FA/99	16/0
24	Hill, Ray (CB)	6-0/192	8-7-75	3	Michigan State	FA/00	8/0
27	Irvin, Ken (CB)	5-11/186	7-11-72	7	Memphis	D4a/95	16/16
20	Jones, Henry (S)	6-0/200	12-29-67	11	Illinois	D1/91	16/16
28	Tillman, Travares (S)	6-1/190	10-8-77	2	Georgia Tech	D2/00	15/4
21	Watson, Chris (CB)	6-1/192	6-30-77	3	Eastern Illinois	T-Den./00	16/4
	Williams, Jimmy (CB)	5-10/184	3-10-79	R	Vanderbilt	D6c/01	—
26	Winfield, Antoine (CB)	5-9/180	6-24-77	3	Ohio State	D1/99	11/11
	SPECIALISTS						
2	Christie, Steve (K)	6-0/190	11-13-67	12	William & Mary	UFA/92	16/0

*Not with Bills in 2000.

Other free agent veterans invited to camp: G Victor Allotey, DB Lance Brown, T Kris Farris, QB Pete Gonzalez, G Corey Holsey.

Abbreviations: D1—draft pick, first round; SD-2—supplemental draft pick, second round; W—claimed on waivers; T—obtained in trade; PlanB—Plan B free-agent acquisition; FA—free-agent acquisition (other than Plan B); UFA—unconditional free agent acquisition; ED—expansion draft pick.

MISCELLANEOUS TEAM DATA

Stadium (capacity, surface):
Ralph Wilson Stadium (73,840, artificial)
Business address:
One Bills Drive
Orchard Park, N.Y. 14127
Business phone:
716-648-1800
Ticket information:
877-BB-TICKS
Team colors:
Royal blue, scarlet and white
Flagship radio station:
WGRF, 96.9 FM (97 ROCK)
Training site:
St. John Fisher College
Rochester, N.Y.
716-648-1800

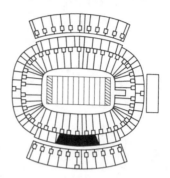

TSN REPORT CARD

Coaching staff	B	It is hard to assign a grade to a staff that hasn't been in game action yet. But Gregg Williams has set the tone with some tough minicamps. His disciplined style has gone over well with the players thus far. Again, it's too early to know for sure, but the players seem to be picking up the new schemes well.
Quarterbacks	B	If he can stay healthy (and that's a big if), Rob Johnson could become one of the league's best passers. All the physical tools are there. Still, he has to prove it on the field. Alex Van Pelt is a solid backup, but is not starting material.
Running backs	C	The search continues for a featured back. The top candidates right now are Shawn Bryson, Sammy Morris and rookie Travis Henry. One of them needs to emerge for the offense to move forward.
Wide receivers	B	Eric Moulds' presence alone is worthy of a good grade, but the play of promising young talents Peerless Price and Jeremy McDaniel give the Bills a chance to have a very explosive passing attack. Moulds is tough to stop one-on-one, but Price and McDaniel are too dangerous for defenses to focus all their attention on one guy.
Offensive line	C	This unit was responsible for allowing most of the team's 59 sacks against last year. The front must get better if the Bills' offense is going to click and for Johnson to stay alive. The starting right side is new, although G Jerry Ostroski is a long-time starter and Robert Hicks was a regular in 1999. Added big T Kris Farris should help. LT John Fina needs to rebound from last year and LG Ruben Brown needs to play up to his Pro Bowl level every Sunday.
Defensive line	C	Without NT Ted Washington and DE Marcellus Wiley, it's hard to imagine this group being as dominant. Someone has to step up and help DT Pat Williams inside. Whether 2000 top draft pick Erik Flowers can fill Wiley's shoes is a key issue this season.
Linebackers	B +	Even with the release of Sam Rogers, this is still one of the best units in the NFL. Inside or outside, LB Sam Cowart is and will continue to be a star. John Holecek is more than capable in the middle and strong side backer Keith Newman is equally adept at stopping the run and rushing the passer.
Secondary	B	If first-rounder Nate Clements is the real deal, the Bills would be set at cornerback. Antoine Winfield is entrenched as a starter, but Ken Irvin will be pushed hard by Clements. SS Henry Jones should have a big year in the new defensive scheme, while Keion Carpenter and Travares Tillman are emerging players at free safety.
Special teams	D	Why the low grade? The Bills had the worst coverage and return units in the league last year. Until there are signs of improvement, the grade stands. Re-signing K Steve Christie was a good move. The team's all-time leading scorer was by far the best thing about this unit, booting four game-deciding field goals.

CAROLINA PANTHERS
NFC WESTERN DIVISION

2001 SEASON

CLUB DIRECTORY

Owner & founder
Jerry Richardson
President of Carolina Panthers
Mark Richardson
Director of football administration
Marty Hurney
Director of player personnel
Jack Bushofsky
President of Carolinas Stadium Corp.
Jon Richardson
Chief financial officer
Dave Olsen
General counsel
Richard Thigpen
Dir. of marketing & sponsorships
Charles Waddell
Director of ticket sales
Phil Youtsey
Director of communications
Charlie Dayton
Director of player relations
Donnie Shell
Director of facilities
Tom Fellows
Director of pro scouting
Mark Koncz
Pro scouts
Hal Hunter   Ted Plumb
Kenny Roberson
Director of college scouting
Tony Softli
College scouts
Hal Athon   Joe Bushofsky
Ryan Cowden   Max McCartney
Jay Mondock   Jeff Morrow
Head groundskeeper
Tom Vaughn
Equipment manager
Jackie Miles

Head coach
George Seifert

Assistant coaches
Paul Boudreau (offensive line)
Don Breaux (tight ends)
Jacob Burney (defensive line)
Chick Harris (running backs)
Carlos Mainord (defensive backs)
John Marshall (assistant head
   coach/defensive coordinator)
Mike McCoy (wide receivers)
Sam Mills (linebackers)
Scott O'Brien (special teams)
Alvin Reynolds (defensive asst.)
Greg Roman (offensive assistant)
Turk Schonert (quarterbacks)
Darrin Simmons (special teams
   assistant/assistant strength &
   conditioning)
Jerry Simmons (strength &
   conditioning)
Richard Williamson (assistant
   head coach/off. coordinator)

Video director
Mark Hobbs
Head trainer
John Kasik
Assistant trainers
Mike Hooper   Dan Ruiz
Orthopedist
Dr. Patt Connor

SCHEDULE

Sept. 9—	at Minnesota	1:00
Sept. 16—	NEW ENGLAND	1:00
Sept. 23—	at Atlanta	1:00
Sept. 30—	GREEN BAY	1:00
Oct. 7—	at San Francisco	8:30
Oct. 14—	NEW ORLEANS	1:00
Oct. 21—	at Washington	1:00
Oct. 28—	N.Y. JETS	1:00
Nov. 4—	at Miami	1:00
Nov. 11—	at St. Louis	1:00
Nov. 18—	SAN FRANCISCO	1:00
Nov. 25—	ATLANTA	1:00
Dec. 2—	at New Orleans	1:00
Dec. 9—	at Buffalo	1:00
Dec. 16—	Open date	
Dec. 23—	ST. LOUIS	1:00
Dec. 30—	ARIZONA	1:00

All times are Eastern.
All games Sunday unless noted.

DRAFT CHOICES

Dan Morgan, LB, Miami, Fla. (first round/11th pick overall).
Kris Jenkins, DT, Maryland (2/44).
Steve Smith, WR, Utah (3/74).
Chris Weinke, QB, Florida State (4/106).
Jarrod Cooper, DB, Kansas State (5/143).
Dee Brown, RB, Syracuse (6/175).
Louis Williams, C, Louisiana State (7/211).
Mike Roberg, TE, Idaho (7/227).

2000 REVIEW

RESULTS

Sept. 3—at Washington	L	17-20
Sept.10—at San Francisco	W	38-22
Sept.17—ATLANTA	L	10-15
Sept.24—Open date		
Oct. 1—DALLAS (OT)	L	13-16
Oct. 8—SEATTLE	W	26-3
Oct. 15—at New Orleans	L	6-24
Oct. 22—SAN FRANCISCO	W	34-16
Oct. 29—at Atlanta	L	12-13
Nov. 5—at St. Louis	W	27-24
Nov. 12—NEW ORLEANS	L	10-20
Nov. 19—at Minnesota	L	17-31
Nov. 27—GREEN BAY	W	31-14
Dec. 3—ST. LOUIS	W	16-3
Dec. 10—at Kansas City	L	14-15
Dec. 17—SAN DIEGO	W	30-22
Dec. 24—at Oakland	L	9-52

RECORDS/RANKINGS

2000 regular-season record: 7-9 (3rd in NFC West); 4-4 in division; 5-7 in conference; 5-3 at home; 2-6 on road.
Team record last five years: 38-42 (.475, ranks T18th in league in that span).
2000 team rankings:

	No.	NFC	NFL
Total offense	*290.9	9	20
Rushing offense	*74.1	15	29
Passing offense	*216.8	6	12
Scoring offense	310	9	21
Total defense	*353.5	12	27
Rushing defense	*121.5	12	26
Passing defense	*232.0	12	26
Scoring defense	310	7	12
Takeaways	38	3	6
Giveaways	35	T12	T24
Turnover differential	3	5	T11
Sacks	27	13	T27
Sacks allowed	69	15	31

*Yards per game.

TEAM LEADERS

Scoring (kicking): Joe Nedney, 98 pts. (20/20 PATs, 26/28 FGs).
Scoring (touchdowns): Muhsin Muhammad, 36 pts. (6 receiving).
Passing: Steve Beuerlein, 3,730 yds. (533 att., 324 comp., 60.8%, 19 TDs, 18 int.).
Rushing: Tim Biakabutuka, 627 yds. (173 att., 3.6 avg., 2 TDs).
Receptions: Muhsin Muhammad, 102 (1,183 yds., 11.6 avg., 6 TDs).
Interceptions: Eric Davis, 5 (14 yds., 0 TDs).
Sacks: Jay Williams, 6.0.
Punting: Ken Walter, 38.4 avg. (64 punts, 2,459 yds., 2 blocked).
Punt returns: Iheanyi Uwaezuoke, 17.3 avg. (10 att., 173 yds., 1 TD).
Kickoff returns: Michael Bates, 22.4 avg. (42 att., 941 yds., 1 TD).

CAROLINA PANTHERS

No.	QUARTERBACKS	Ht./Wt.	Born	NFL Exp.	College	How acq.	'00 Games GP/GS
2	Craig, Dameyune	6-1/200	4-19-74	3	Auburn	FA/98	4/0
8	Lewis, Jeff	6-2/211	4-17-73	5	Northern Arizona	T-Den./99	5/0
9	Lytle, Matt	6-4/225	9-4-75	2	Pittsburgh	FA/00	*2/0
	Weinke, Chris	6-4/238	7-31-72	R	Florida State	D4/01	—
	RUNNING BACKS						
21	Biakabutuka, Tshimanga	6-0/215	1-24-74	6	Michigan	D1/96	12/11
	Brown, Dee	5-10/209	5-12-79	R	Syracuse	D6/01	—
32	Dukes, Chad	6-0/230	12-29-71	1	Pittsburgh	FA/01	*2/0
44	Hetherington, Chris (FB)	6-3/244	11-27-72	6	Yale	FA/99	16/5
45	Hoover, Brad (FB)	6-2/225	11-11-76	2	Western Carolina	FA/00	16/4
22	Murrell, Adrian	5-11/210	10-16-70	7	West Virginia	UFA/01	*15/0
	RECEIVERS						
84	Broughton, Luther (TE)	6-2/248	11-30-74	4	Furman	UFA/01	*15/1
84	Crawford, Casey (TE)	6-6/255	8-1-77	2	Virginia	FA/00	8/0
89	Hankton, Karl	6-2/202	7-24-70	3	Trinity (Ill.)	FA/00	16/0
81	Hayes, Donald	6-4/218	7-13-75	4	Wisconsin	D4/98	15/15
83	Jeffers, Patrick	6-3/218	2-2-73	6	Virginia	FA/99	0/0
86	Mangum, Kris (TE)	6-4/249	8-15-73	4	Mississippi	D7/97	15/7
87	Muhammad, Muhsin	6-2/217	5-5-73	6	Michigan State	D2/96	16/16
	Roberg, Mike (TE)	6-4/263	9-18-77	R	Idaho	D7b/01	—
89	Smith, Steve	5-9/179	5-12-79	R	Utah	D3/01	—
85	Walls, Wesley (TE)	6-5/250	2-26-66	13	Mississippi	UFA/96	8/8
	OFFENSIVE LINEMEN						
65	Donnalley, Kevin (G)	6-5/310	6-10-68	11	North Carolina	UFA/01	*16/16
78	James, Jeno (G)	6-3/292	1-12-77	2	Auburn	D6/00	16/4
60	Mitchell, Jeff (C)	6-4/300	1-29-74	5	Florida	UFA/00	*14/14
63	Nesbit, Jamar (C)	6-4/330	12-17-76	3	South Carolina	FA/99	16/16
75	Steussie, Todd (T)	6-6/308	12-1-70	8	California	FA/01	*16/16
67	Stoltenberg, Bryan (C)	6-1/300	8-25-72	6	Colorado	FA/98	8/1
70	Terry, Chris (T)	6-5/295	8-8-75	3	Georgia	D2a/99	16/16
73	Tuten, Melvin (T)	6-6/305	11-11-71	5	Syracuse	W-Den./00	3/0
	Williams, Louis (C)	6-4/291	4-11-79	R	Louisiana State	D7a/01	—
	DEFENSIVE LINEMEN						
98	Buckner, Brentson (T)	6-2/305	9-30-71	8	Clemson	UFA/01	*16/16
64	Chester, Larry (T)	6-2/310	10-17-75	3	Temple	FA/98	*16/0
94	Gilbert, Sean (T)	6-5/318	4-10-70	9	Pittsburgh	FA/98	15/15
75	Jenkins, Kris (T)	6-4/305	8-3-79	R	Maryland	D2/01	—
71	Lucas, Albert (T)	6-1/294	9-1-78	2	Troy State	FA/00	13/0
98	McKinley, Alvin (T)	6-3/292	6-9-78	2	Mississippi State	D4/00	7/0
90	Morabito, Tim (T)	6-3/296	10-12-73	6	Boston College	W-Cin./97	16/13
97	Peter, Jason (E)	6-4/295	9-13-74	4	Nebraska	D1/98	9/0
93	Rucker, Michael (E)	6-5/258	2-28-75	3	Nebraska	D2b/99	16/1
91	Smith, Chuck (E)	6-2/262	12-21-69	10	Tennessee	UFA/00	2/2
96	Williams, Jay (E)	6-3/280	10-13-71	6	Wake Forest	UFA/00	16/14
	LINEBACKERS						
56	Kyle, Jason	6-3/242	5-12-72	7	Arizona State	UFA/01	*2/0
52	Minor, Kory	6-1/247	12-14-76	2	Notre Dame	FA/99	15/0
55	Morgan, Dan	6-2/233	12-19-78	R	Miami (Fla.)	D1/01	—
53	Navies, Hannibal	6-2/240	7-19-77	3	Colorado	D4/99	13/1
54	Reeves, Jion	6-3/245	2-23-75	3	Purdue	FA/00	*9/0
57	Towns, Lester	6-1/252	8-28-77	2	Washington	D7/00	16/14
95	Wells, Dean	6-3/248	7-20-70	9	Kentucky	UFA/99	16/14
	DEFENSIVE BACKS						
46	Anderson, Rashard	6-2/204	6-14-77	2	Jackson State	D1/00	12/0
	Cooper, Jarrod (S)	6-0/210	3-31-78	R	Kansas State	D5/01	—
33	Evans, Doug (CB)	6-1/190	5-13-70	9	Louisiana Tech	UFA/98	16/16
29	Green, Ray (S)	6-3/187	3-22-77	2	South Carolina	FA/00	16/0
28	Harper, Deveron (CB)	5-11/187	11-15-77	2	Notre Dame	FA/00	16/0
37	Hitchcock, Jimmy (CB)	5-10/187	11-9-70	7	North Carolina	UFA/00	16/2
23	Howard, Reggie (CB)	6-0/190	5-17-77	2	Memphis State	W-NO/00	2/0
30	Minter, Mike (S)	5-10/188	1-15-74	5	Nebraska	D2/97	16/16
39	Richardson, Damien (S)	6-1/210	4-3-76	4	Arizona State	D6/98	16/1
	SPECIALISTS						
5	Sauerbrun, Todd (P)	5-10/204	1-4-73	6	West Virginia	FA/01	*16/0

*Not with Panthers in 2000.

Other free agent veterans invited to camp: P Will Brice, LB O.J. Childress, DT Harry Deligianis, LB Lamont Green, LB Spencer Reid, OL T.J. Washington.

Abbreviations: D1—draft pick, first round; SD-2—supplemental draft pick, second round; W—claimed on waivers; T—obtained in trade; PlanB—Plan B free-agent acquisition; FA—free-agent acquisition (other than Plan B); UFA—unconditional free agent acquisition; ED—expansion draft pick.

Stadium (capacity, surface):
Ericsson Stadium
(73,250, grass)
Business address:
800 S. Mint St.
Charlotte, NC 28202-1502
Business phone:
704-358-7000
Ticket information:
704-358-7800
Team colors:
Blue, black and silver
Flagship radio station:
WRFX-99.7 FM
Training site:
Wofford College
Spartanburg, S.C.
704-358-7000

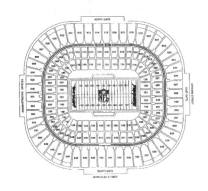

CAROLINA PANTHERS

TSN REPORT CARD

Coaching staff	B	George Seifert is going to have to be more patient than ever as the team rebuilds. It should help that he has stabilized his staff with veterans after going through the disastrous resignation of offensive coordinator Bill Musgrave four games into last season. New coordinator Richard Williamson will have an entire offseason to make adjustments.
Quarterbacks	D -	There is potential and athletic ability here, but none of the quarterbacks on the roster has started an NFL game. There is the possibility one of the quarterbacks could develop into a solid player. But, right now, this might be the weakest collection of quarterbacks in the NFL. Rookie Chris Weinke is the oldest quarterback on the roster.
Running backs	C -	When he's healthy Tshimanga Biakabutuka can be a very productive runner. The problem is he rarely has been healthy. That's why the team tried very hard to upgrade the depth at this position. Rookie Dadrian Brown probably will get a fair amount of carries because the team wants to keep Biakabutuka fresh. Brown also will be used as a receiver out of the backfield. Chris Hetherington will step into the starting fullback spot and needs to show he can be an effective blocker.
Receivers	A	This is the strongest position on the team. Muhsin Muhammad, Patrick Jeffers and Donald Hayes are as good as almost any receiving trio and the Panthers will use plenty of three-receiver sets. All three can stretch the field and make things happen after the catch. Tight end Wesley Walls, who is coming back from a knee injury, is also a top-notch pass catcher and that should help whoever ends up as the quarterback.
Offensive line	C +	The good news is the line can't be any worse than last year's. There has been a near-total overhaul and left tackle Todd Steussie, center Jeff Mitchell and right guard Kevin Donnalley should be upgrades over their predecessors. Right tackle Chris Terry has gotten better each year. The run blocking will be critical because the team wants to run more often.
Defensive line	C -	Last year's grand experiment of putting Reggie White, Eric Swann, Chuck Smith and Sean Gilbert on the same defensive line didn't work. Gilbert remains a solid player in the middle and the team has tried to upgrade at nose tackle. But the real key will be at end where Smith and Jason Peter are recovering from injuries.
Linebackers	C -	This is one of the league's youngest linebacking corps. It's likely rookie Dan Morgan and second-year pro Lester Towns will end up as starters. That's not necessarily a bad thing. Towns is solid in the middle and Morgan could give the team the play-making linebacker it has lacked for several years.
Secondary	C +	This unit lost Eric Davis and Eugene Robinson, but it could be better than a year ago. The emergence of strong safety Mike Minter as a top-notch player helps and Deon Grant should be ready to take over at free safety. Cornerbacks Doug Evans and Jimmy Hitchcock have to avoid giving up big plays.
Special teams	C	The team has lost a Pro Bowl return man (Michael Bates) and veteran punter Ken Walter. Todd Sauerbrun could be an upgrade on Walter, but it's hard to imagine rookie Steve Smith being better than Bates. Kicker John Kasay, who is coming off two knee surgeries, remains a question mark.

CHICAGO BEARS
NFC CENTRAL DIVISION

2001 SEASON

CLUB DIRECTORY

Chairman emeritus
Edward W. McCaskey
Chairman of the board
Michael B. McCaskey
President/chief executive officer
Ted Phillips
Vice president
Timothy E. McCaskey
Secretary
Virginia H. McCaskey
Director/administration
Bill McGrane
Chief marketing officer
Dave Greeley
Director/community relations
John Bostrom
Director of corporate sales
Avery Robbins
Director/public relations
Scott Hagel
Assistant director/public relations
Jim Christman
Director/ticket operations
George McCaskey
Director/pro personnel
Scott Campbell
Assistant director/pro scouting
George Paton
Director/college scouting
Bill Rees
Regional scouts
Marty Barrett   Phil Emery
Pat Roberts   Shemy Schembechler
Jeff Shiver   John Paul Young
Head trainer
Tim Bream
Assistant trainers
Chris Hanks   Bobby Slater
Physical development coordinator
Russ Riederer

Head coach
Dick Jauron

Assistant coaches
Vance Bedford (defensive backs)
Greg Blache (defensive coord.)
Chuck Bullough (quality control
  assistant, defense)
Pete Carmichael Sr. (off. asst.)
Charlie Coiner (quality control
  assistant, offense)
Pat Flaherty (tight ends)
Todd Haley (wide receivers)
Dale Lindsey (linebackers)
Earle Mosley (running backs)
Rex Norris (defensive line)
John Shoop (offensive coord.)
Mike Sweatman (special teams)
Bob Wylie (offensive line)

Asst. physical development coordinator
Steve Little
Equipment manager
Tony Medlin
Assistant equipment managers
Carl Piekarski   Jamal Nelson
Director of video services
Dean Pope
Assistant video director
Dave Hendrickson

SCHEDULE

Sept. 9—	at Baltimore	1:00
Sept. 16—	JACKSONVILLE	4:15
Sept. 23—	MINNESOTA	1:00
Sept. 30—	Open date	
Oct. 7—	at Atlanta	1:00
Oct. 14—	ARIZONA	1:00
Oct. 21—	at Cincinnati	1:00
Oct. 28—	SAN FRANCISCO	1:00
Nov. 4—	CLEVELAND	1:00
Nov. 11—	GREEN BAY	1:00
Nov. 18—	at Tampa Bay	1:00
Nov. 25—	at Minnesota	8:30
Dec. 2—	DETROIT	1:00
Dec. 9—	at Green Bay	1:00
Dec. 16—	TAMPA BAY	1:00
Dec. 23—	at Washington	1:00
Dec. 30—	at Detroit	1:00

All times are Eastern.
All games Sunday unless noted.

DRAFT CHOICES

David Terrell, WR, Michigan (first round/eighth pick overall).
Anthony Thomas, RB, Michigan (2/38).
Mike Gandy, G, Notre Dame (3/68).
Karon Riley, DE, Minnesota (4/103).
Bernard Robertson, C, Tulane (5/138).
John Capel, WR, Florida (7/208).

2000 REVIEW

RESULTS

Sept. 3—at Minnesota	L	27-30
Sept.10—at Tampa Bay	L	0-41
Sept.17—N.Y. GIANTS	L	7-14
Sept.24—DETROIT	L	14-21
Oct. 1—at Green Bay	W	27-24
Oct. 8—NEW ORLEANS	L	10-31
Oct. 15—MINNESOTA	L	16-28
Oct. 22—at Philadelphia	L	9-13
Oct. 29—Open date		
Nov. 5—INDIANAPOLIS	W	27-24
Nov. 12—at Buffalo	L	3-20
Nov. 19—TAMPA BAY	W	13-10
Nov. 26—at N.Y. Jets	L	10-17
Dec. 3—GREEN BAY	L	6-28
Dec. 10—NEW ENGLAND	W	24-17
Dec. 17—at San Francisco	L	0-17
Dec. 24—at Detroit	W	23-20

RECORDS/RANKINGS

2000 regular-season record: 5-11 (5th in NFC Central); 3-5 in division; 3-9 in conference; 3-5 at home; 2-6 on road.
Team record last five years: 26-54 (.325, ranks T28th in league in that span).

2000 team rankings:	No.	NFC	NFL
Total offense	*283.8	11	23
Rushing offense	*108.5	11	21
Passing offense	*175.3	11	23
Scoring offense	216	14	28
Total defense	*327.1	8	16
Rushing defense	*114.2	9	19
Passing defense	*212.9	9	17
Scoring defense	355	9	20
Takeaways	20	T13	T29
Giveaways	29	T6	T15
Turnover differential	-9	T10	T23
Sacks	36	9	21
Sacks allowed	34	T4	T10

*Yards per game.

TEAM LEADERS

Scoring (kicking): Paul Edinger, 84 pts. (21/21 PATs, 21/27 FGs).
Scoring (touchdowns): Marcus Robinson, 30 pts. (5 receiving).
Passing: Cade McNown, 1,646 yds. (280 att., 154 comp., 55.0%, 8 TDs, 9 int.).
Rushing: James Allen, 1,120 yds. (290 att., 3.9 avg., 2 TDs).
Receptions: Marcus Robinson, 55 (738 yds., 13.4 avg., 5 TDs).
Interceptions: Tony Parrish, 3 (81 yds., 1 TD).
Sacks: Brian Urlacher, 8.0.
Punting: Louie Aguiar, 38.8 avg. (52 punts, 2,017 yds., 0 blocked).
Punt returns: Glyn Milburn, 8.6 avg. (35 att., 300 yds., 0 TDs).
Kickoff returns: Glyn Milburn, 23.3 avg. (63 att., 1,468 yds., 0 TDs).

TRAINING CAMP ROSTER

CHICAGO BEARS

No.	QUARTERBACKS	Ht./Wt.	Born	NFL Exp.	College	How acq.	'00 Games GP/GS
9	Matthews, Shane	6-3/196	6-1-70	8	Florida	UFA/99	6/5
8	McNown, Cade	6-1/208	1-12-77	3	UCLA	D1/99	10/9
15	Miller, Jim	6-2/215	2-9-71	8	Michigan State	FA/98	3/2
11	Tolliver, Billy Joe	6-1/217	2-7-66	11	Texas Tech	UFA/01	0/0
	RUNNING BACKS						
20	Allen, James	5-10/215	3-28-75	4	Oklahoma	FA/97	16/15
32	Barnes, Marlon	5-9/215	3-13-76	2	Colorado	FA/00	13/0
45	Dragos, Scott (FB)	6-2/245	10-28-75	2	Boston College	FA/99	9/2
24	Milburn, Glyn	5-8/176	2-19-71	9	Stanford	T-GB/98	16/0
31	Shelton, Daimon (FB)	6-0/254	9-15-72	4	Cal State Sacramento	UFA/01	*16/9
35	Thomas, Anthony	6-1/226	11-11-77	R	Michigan	D2/01	—
	RECEIVERS						
87	Bates, D'Wayne	6-2/215	12-4-75	3	Northwestern	D3b/99	5/0
84	Baxter, Fred (TE)	6-3/265	6-14-71	9	Auburn	FA/01	*9/6
86	Booker, Marty	5-11/215	7-31-76	3	Northeastern Louisiana	D3c/99	15/7
	Capel, John	5-11/170	10-27-78	R	Florida	D7/01	—
81	Engram, Bobby	5-10/185	1-7-73	6	Penn State	D2/96	3/3
89	Lyman, Dustin (TE)	6-4/250	8-5-76	2	Wake Forest	D3b/00	14/7
88	Robinson, Marcus	6-3/215	2-27-75	5	South Carolina	D4b/97	11/11
85	Sinceno, Kaseem (TE)	6-4/255	3-26-76	4	Syracuse	FA/00	11/11
83	Terrell, David	6-3/215	3-13-79	R	Michigan	D1/01	—
80	White, Dez	6-0/219	8-23-79	2	Georgia Tech	D3a/00	15/0
	OFFENSIVE LINEMEN						
78	Brockermeyer, Blake (T)	6-4/300	4-11-73	7	Texas	UFA/99	15/14
75	Gandy, Mike (G)	6-4/313	1-3-79	R	Notre Dame	D3/01	—
74	Herndon, Jimmy (T)	6-8/318	8-30-73	6	Houston	T-Jax./97	10/2
57	Kreutz, Olin (C)	6-2/285	6-9-77	4	Washington	D3/98	7/7
65	Mannelly, Patrick (T)	6-5/270	4-18-75	4	Duke	D6b/98	16/0
	Robertson, Bernard (C)	6-3/297	6-9-79	R	Tulane	D5/01	—
64	Tucker, Rex (G)	6-5/315	12-20-76	3	Texas A&M	D3a/99	6/0
58	Villarrial, Chris (G)	6-4/308	6-9-73	6	Indiana University (Pa.)	D5/96	16/15
71	Williams, James (T)	6-7/331	3-29-68	11	Cheyney (Pa.) State	FA/91	16/16
	DEFENSIVE LINEMEN						
93	Daniels, Phillip (E)	6-5/290	3-4-73	6	Georgia	UFA/00	14/14
64	Newkirk, Robert (T)	6-3/290	3-6-77	2	Michigan State	FA/00	5/0
72	Powell, Carl (T)	6-2/264	1-4-74	2	Louisville	FA/01	*2/0
	Riley, Karon (E)	6-2/251	6-18-80	R	Minnesota	D4/01	—
98	Robinson, Bryan	6-4/300	6-22-74	5	Fresno State	W-St.L./98	16/16
96	Simmons, Clyde (E)	6-5/292	8-4-64	15	Western Carolina	UFA/99	16/2
99	Smeenge, Joel (E)	6-6/265	4-1-68	11	Western Michigan	FA/01	*12/1
94	Traylor, Keith (T)	6-2/304	9-3-69	10	Central Oklahoma	FA/01	*16/16
90	Tuinei, Van (E)	6-4/290	2-16-71	5	Arizona	W-Ind./99	14/2
95	Washington, Ted (T)	6-5/330	4-13-68	11	Louisville	FA/01	*16/16
97	Wells, Mike (T)	6-3/315	1-6-71	9	Iowa	UFA/98	16/14
	LINEBACKERS						
59	Colvin, Rosevelt	6-3/254	9-5-77	3	Purdue	D4b/99	13/8
55	Harris, Sean	6-3/252	2-25-72	7	Arizona	D3/95	15/13
53	Holdman, Warrick	6-1/246	11-22-75	3	Texas A&M	D4a/99	10/10
99	Jones, Greg	6-4/248	5-22-74	5	Colorado	UFA/01	*16/4
92	Minter, Barry	6-2/250	1-28-70	9	Tulsa	T-Dal./93	15/2
91	Samuel, Khari	6-3/240	10-14-76	3	Massachusetts	D5b/99	16/0
54	Urlacher, Brian	6-3/244	5-25-78	R	New Mexico	D1/00	16/14
	DEFENSIVE BACKS						
23	Azumah, Jerry (CB)	5-10/195	9-1-77	3	New Hampshire	D5c/99	14/4
30	Brown, Mike (S)	5-10/202	2-13-78	2	Nebraska	D2/00	16/16
43	Green, Mike (S)	6-0/176	12-6-76	2	Louisiana-Lafayette	D7b/00	7/0
27	Harris, Walt (CB)	5-11/195	8-10-74	6	Mississippi State	D1/96	12/12
47	McElroy, Ray (CB)	5-11/207	7-31-72	6	Eastern Illinois	FA/00	13/0
26	McMillon, Todd (CB)	5-10/183	9-9-73	2	Northern Arizona	FA/00	3/0
21	McQuarters, R.W. (CB)	5-9/198	12-21-76	4	Oklahoma State	T-SF/00	15/2
37	Parrish, Tony (S)	5-10/211	11-23-75	4	Washington	D2/98	16/16
29	Smith, Frankie (S)	5-9/182	10-8-68	9	Baylor	UFA/98	14/0
25	Smith, Thomas (CB)	5-11/190	12-5-70	9	North Carolina	UFA/00	16/16
33	Whigham, Larry (S)	6-2/210	6-23-72	8	Northeast Louisiana	FA/01	*14/4
22	Wooden, Shawn (S)	5-11/205	10-23-73	6	Notre Dame	UFA/00	11/0
	SPECIALISTS						
12	Bartholomew, Brent (P)	6-2/220	10-22-76	3	Ohio State	FA/00	7/0
2	Edinger, Paul (K)	5-10/162	1-17-78	2	Michigan State	D6b/00	16/0
4	Maynard, Brad (P)	6-1/190	2-9-74	5	Ball State	UFA/01	*16/0

*Not with Bears in 2000.

Other free agent veterans invited to camp: TE Shonn Bell, CB Donny Brady, WR Fred Coleman, RB Brian Edwards, FB Conrad Emmerich, DE Alonzo Wallace, WR Gerald Williams.

CHICAGO BEARS

MISCELLANEOUS TEAM DATA

Stadium (capacity, surface):
Soldier Field (66,944, grass)
Business address:
Halas Hall at Conway Park
1000 Football Drive
Lake Forest, IL 60045
Business phone:
847-295-6600
Ticket information:
847-615-2327
Team colors:
Navy blue, orange and white
Flagship radio station:
WBBM, 780 AM
Training site:
University of Wisconsin-Platteville
Platteville, Wis.
608-342-1201

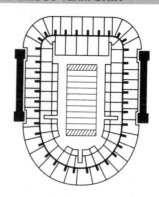

TSN REPORT CARD

Coaching staff	C -	Mistakes last season were costly and the staff needs to regain the players' confidence that they can win even when something doesn't go right.
Quarterbacks	D +	Someone needs to win the job rather than be the only one who didn't lose it. The team believes in Cade McNown and Jim Miller but can they get the job done?
Running backs	B -	James Allen's lack of scoring speed is a problem but he is a solid player. Rookie Anthony Thomas is the workhorse the offense needs.
Receivers	C +	Consistency at quarterback would help but someone other than Marcus Robinson needs to step forward as a threat. Rookie David Terrell looks like the real deal.
Offensive line	B -	Four of five starters begin their third straight season together. Center Olin Kreutz ranks among the NFL's best.
Defensive line	B	Biggest Bears front ever will work against the run but someone needs to at least worry the passer.
Linebackers	A -	Size and speed plus more bulk up front will help let young core of the defense run. Brian Urlacher is already reminding fans of great Bears MLBs of the past.
Secondary	B	Safety tandem very strong with Mike Brown and Tony Parrish, but corners need to win more matchups. A pass rush would be a nice thing to help this group.
Special teams	B -	The kicking game and coverage units are very solid. Return man Glyn Milburn and the blocking were ineffective last year and need to improve to help field position on both sides of the ball.

CINCINNATI BENGALS
AFC CENTRAL DIVISION

2001 SEASON

CLUB DIRECTORY

ADMINISTRATION
President
Mike Brown
Executive vice president
Katie Blackburn
Vice president
John Sawyer
Business development
Troy Blackburn
Business manager
Bill Connelly
Chief financial officer
Bill Scanlon
Controller
Johanna Kappner
Managing director of Paul Brown Stadium
Eric Brown
Director of technology
Jo Ann Ralstin
Director of player relations
Eric Ball

SALES/TICKETING
Director of sales and public affairs
Jeff Berding
Director of corporate sales and marketing
Vince Cicero
Ticket manager
Paul Kelly
Senior corporate sales managers
Tony Kountz, Brian Sells
Corporate sales coordinator
Sara Jackson
Premium seating sales coordinator
Stephanie Mileham
Group sales manager
Kevin Lane
Merchandise manager
Monty Montague
JungleVision producer
Scott Simpson

PUBLIC RELATIONS/INTERNET
Public relations director
Jack Brennan
Assistant public relations director
P.J. Combs
Internet editor/writer
Geoff Hobson

PLAYER PERSONNEL
Senior vice president
Pete Brown

Head coach
Dick LeBeau

Assistant coaches
Paul Alexander (offensive line)
Jim Anderson (running backs)
Ken Anderson (quarterbacks)
Bob Bratkowski (offensive coordinator)
Louie Cioffi (defensive staff assistant)
Kevin Coyle (cornerbacks)
Mark Duffner (def. coord./linebackers)
John Garrett (off. staff assistant)
Rodney Holman (asst. strength & cond.)
Ray Horton (safeties)
Tim Krumrie (defensive line)
Steve Mooshagian (wide receivers)
Al Roberts (special teams)
Frank Verducci (tight ends)
Kim Wood (strength & conditioning)

Vice president
Paul Brown
Director of pro/college personnel
Jim Lippincott
Scouting
Duke Tobin, Frank Smouse

FOOTBALL OPERATIONS
Athletic trainer
Paul Sparling
Assistant athletic trainers
Billy Brooks, Brian Dykhuizen
Equipment manager
Rob Recker
Assistant equipment manager
Jeff Brickner
Video director
Travis Brammer
Assistant video director
Kent Stearman

SCHEDULE

Sept. 9—	NEW ENGLAND	1:00
Sept. 16—	at Tennessee	1:00
Sept. 23—	BALTIMORE	1:00
Sept. 30—	at San Diego	4:15
Oct. 7—	at Pittsburgh	1:00
Oct. 14—	CLEVELAND	1:00
Oct. 21—	CHICAGO	1:00
Oct. 28—	at Detroit	1:00
Nov. 4—	Open date	
Nov. 11—	at Jacksonville	1:00
Nov. 18—	TENNESSEE	1:00
Nov. 25—	at Cleveland	1:00
Dec. 2—	TAMPA BAY	1:00
Dec. 9—	JACKSONVILLE	1:00
Dec. 16—	at N.Y. Jets	1:00
Dec. 23—	at Baltimore	1:00
Dec. 30—	PITTSBURGH	1:00

All times are Eastern.
All games Sunday unless noted.

DRAFT CHOICES

Justin Smith, DE, Missouri (first round/fourth pick overall).
Chad Johnson, WR, Oregon State (2/36).
Sean Brewer, TE, San Jose State (3/66).
Rudi Johnson, RB, Auburn (4/100).
Victor Leyva, G, Arizona State (5/135).
Riall Johnson, LB, Stanford (6/168).
T.J. Houshmandzadeh, WR, Oregon State (7/204).

2000 REVIEW

RESULTS

Date	Opponent	Result	Score
Sept. 3—	Open date		
Sept.10—	CLEVELAND	L	7-24
Sept.17—	at Jacksonville	L	0-13
Sept.24—	at Baltimore	L	0-37
Oct. 1—	MIAMI	L	16-31
Oct. 8—	TENNESSEE	L	14-23
Oct. 15—	at Pittsburgh	L	0-15
Oct. 22—	DENVER	W	31-21
Oct. 29—	CLEVELAND	W	12-3
Nov. 5—	BALTIMORE	L	7-27
Nov. 12—	at Dallas	L	6-23
Nov. 19—	at New England	L	13-16
Nov. 26—	PITTSBURGH	L	28-48
Dec. 3—	ARIZONA	W	24-13
Dec. 10—	at Tennessee	L	3-35
Dec. 17—	JACKSONVILLE	W	17-14
Dec. 24—	at Philadelphia	L	7-16

RECORDS/RANKINGS

2000 regular-season record: 4-12 (5th in AFC Central); 2-8 in division; 3-10 in conference; 3-5 at home; 1-7 on road.
Team record last five years: 26-54 (.325, ranks T28th in league in that span).

2000 team rankings:	No.	AFC	NFL
Total offense	*266.3	15	29
Rushing offense	*144.6	2	2
Passing offense	*121.6	16	31
Scoring offense	185	15	30
Total defense	*342.9	13	22
Rushing defense	*120.3	13	24
Passing defense	*222.6	13	23
Scoring defense	359	12	21
Takeaways	21	16	T27
Giveaways	35	13	T24
Turnover differential	-14	15	T28
Sacks	26	16	29
Sacks allowed	52	13	25

*Yards per game.

TEAM LEADERS

Scoring (kicking): Neil Rackers, 57 pts. (21/21 PATs, 12/21 FGs).
Scoring (touchdowns): Corey Dillon, 42 pts. (7 rushing); Peter Warrick, 42 pts. (2 rushing, 4 receiving, 1 punt return).
Passing: Akili Smith, 1,253 yds. (267 att., 118 comp., 44.2%, 3 TDs, 6 int.).
Rushing: Corey Dillon, 1,435 yds. (315 att., 4.6 avg., 7 TDs).
Receptions: Peter Warrick, 51 (592 yds., 11.6 avg., 4 TDs).
Interceptions: Tom Carter, 2 (40 yds., 0 TDs); Takeo Spikes, 2 (12 yds., 0 TDs).
Sacks: Oliver Gibson, 4.0; Steve Foley, 4.0; Cory Hall, 4.0.
Punting: Daniel Pope, 40.2 avg. (94 punts, 3,775 yds., 0 blocked).
Punt returns: Craig Yeast, 6.6 avg. (34 att., 225 yds., 0 TDs).
Kickoff returns: Tremain Mack, 20.7 avg. (50 att., 1,036 yds., 0 TDs).

2001 SEASON

TRAINING CAMP ROSTER

No.	QUARTERBACKS	Ht./Wt.	Born	NFL Exp.	College	How acq.	'00 Games GP/GS
4	Covington, Scott	6-2/217	1-17-76	3	Miami (Fla.)	D7b/99	0/0
3	Kitna, Jon	6-2/217	9-21-72	5	Central Washington	UFA/01	*15/12
19	Mitchell, Scott	6-6/240	1-2-68	12	Utah	UFA/00	8/5
11	Smith, Akili	6-3/220	8-21-75	3	Oregon	D1/99	12/11
	RUNNING BACKS						
36	Bennett, Brandon	5-11/220	2-3-73	3	South Carolina	FA/98	16/0
28	Dillon, Corey	6-1/225	10-24-75	5	Washington	D2/97	16/16
46	Groce, Clif (FB)	5-11/245	7-30-72	5	Texas A&M	FA/99	8/6
32	Johnson, Rudi	5-10/230	10-1-79	R	Auburn	D4/01	—
29	Keaton, Curtis	5-10/212	10-18-76	2	James Madison	D4/00	6/0
41	Neal, Lorenzo (FB)	5-11/240	12-27-70	9	Fresno State	FA/01	*16/6
30	Williams, Nick (FB)	6-2/267	3-30-77	3	Miami (Fla.)	D5/99	14/4
	RECEIVERS						
89	Battaglia, Marco (TE)	6-3/252	1-25-73	6	Rutgers	D2/96	16/10
	Boyd, LaVell	6-3/215	9-12-76	R	Louisville	FA/00	2/0
	Brewer, Sean (TE)	6-4/255	10-5-77	R	San Jose State	D3/01	—
81	Dugans, Ron	6-2/205	4-27-77	2	Florida State	D3/00	14/5
83	Farmer, Danny	6-3/217	5-21-77	2	UCLA	W-Pit./00	13/2
87	Griffin, Damon	5-9/186	6-14-76	3	Oregon	W-SF/99	8/0
	Houshmandzadeh, T.J.	6-2/205	8-26-77	R	Oregon State	D7/01	—
85	Johnson, Chad	6-1/192	1-9-78	R	Oregon State	D2/01	—
82	McGee, Tony (TE)	6-3/248	4-21-71	9	Michigan	D2/93	14/14
18	Plummer, Chad	6-2/223	11-30-75	2	Cincinnati	FA/00	*3/0
86	Scott, Darnay	6-1/205	7-7-72	8	San Diego State	D2/94	0/0
48	St. Louis, Brad (TE)	6-3/246	8-19-76	2	Southwest Missouri State	D7/00	16/0
80	Warrick, Peter	5-11/195	6-19-77	2	Florida State	D1/00	16/16
84	Yeast, Craig	5-7/165	11-20-76	3	Kentucky	D4/99	15/7
	OFFENSIVE LINEMEN						
71	Anderson, Willie (T)	6-5/340	7-11-75	6	Auburn	D1/96	16/16
74	Braham, Rich (C)	6-4/305	11-6-70	8	West Virginia	UFA/00	9/9
63	Goff, Mike (G)	6-5/316	1-6-76	4	Iowa	D3b/98	16/16
62	Gutierrez, Brock (C)	6-3/304	9-25-73	5	Central Michigan	FA/98	16/7
65	Jackson, John (T)	6-6/297	1-4-65	14	Eastern Kentucky	FA/00	8/5
	Leyva, Victor (G)	6-3/322	12-18-77	R	Arizona State	D5/01	—
72	O'Dwyer, Matt (G)	6-5/308	9-1-72	7	Northwestern	UFA/99	10/10
79	Rehberg, Scott (G)	6-8/330	11-17-73	5	Central Michigan	FA/00	10/6
75	Stephens, Jamain (T)	6-6/335	1-9-74	6	North Carolina A&T	W-Pit./99	5/0
73	Webb, Richmond (T)	6-6/320	1-11-67	12	Texas A&M	UFA/01	*14/14
	DEFENSIVE LINEMEN						
93	Barndt, Tom (T)	6-3/293	3-14-72	6	Pittsburgh	UFA/00	14/5
96	Booker, Vaughn (E)	6-5/300	2-24-68	8	Cincinnati	UFA/00	9/9
	Copeland, John (E)	6-3/280	9-20-70	8	Alabama	D1/93	16/16
99	Gibson, Oliver (T)	6-2/315	3-15-72	7	Notre Dame	UFA/99	16/16
97	Henry, Kevin (E)	6-4/285	10-23-68	9	Mississippi State	FA/01	*15/15
94	Langford, Jevon (E)	6-3/290	2-16-74	6	Oklahoma State	D4/96	11/3
90	Smith, Justin (E)	6-4/270	9-30-79	R	Missouri	D1/01	—
70	Steele, Glen (E)	6-4/295	10-4-74	4	Michigan	D4/98	16/1
91	Williams, Tony (E)	6-1/292	7-9-75	5	Memphis	UFA/01	*14/12
	LINEBACKERS						
98	Curtis, Canute	6-2/257	8-4-74	5	West Virginia	FA/97	15/0
95	Foley, Steve	6-3/260	9-9-75	4	Northeast Louisiana	D3a/98	16/16
	Johnson, Riall	6-3/240	4-20-78	R	Stanford	D6/01	—
57	Ross, Adrian	6-2/250	2-19-75	4	Colorado State	FA/98	13/4
56	Simmons, Brian	6-3/248	6-21-75	4	North Carolina	D1b/98	1/1
59	Spearman, Armegis	6-1/254	4-5-78	2	Mississippi	FA/00	15/11
51	Spikes, Takeo	6-2/243	12-17-76	4	Auburn	D1a/98	16/16
55	Wilson, Reinard	6-2/266	12-17-73	5	Florida State	D1/97	14/0
	DEFENSIVE BACKS						
33	Armour, Jo Juan (S)	5-11/220	7-10-76	3	Miami of Ohio	W-Jax./99	4/0
23	Bean, Robert (CB)	5-11/178	1-6-78	2	Mississippi State	D5/00	12/4
42	Carter, Chris (S)	6-2/209	9-27-74	5	Texas	W-NE/00	16/10
21	Carter, Tom (CB)	6-0/190	9-5-72	9	Notre Dame	W-Chi./99	16/11
26	Hall, Cory (S)	6-0/210	12-5-76	3	Fresno State	D3/99	16/6
27	Hawkins, Artrell (CB)	5-10/190	11-24-75	4	Cincinnati	D2/98	16/6
22	Heath, Rodney (CB)	5-10/175	10-29-74	3	Minnesota	FA/99	13/9
34	Mack, Tremain (S)	6-0/193	11-21-74	5	Miami (Fla.)	D4/97	16/0
20	Roman, Mark (CB)	5-11/188	3-26-77	2	Louisiana State	D2/00	8/2
31	Williams, Darryl (S)	6-0/202	1-8-70	10	Miami (Fla.)	FA/00	16/16
	SPECIALISTS						
8	Cunningham, Richie (K)	5-10/167	8-18-70	4	Southwestern Louisiana	FA/01	*4/0
17	Pope, Daniel (P)	5-10/203	3-28-75	3	Alabama	W-KC/00	16/0
5	Rackers, Neil (K)	6-0/205	8-16-76	2	Illinois	D6/00	16/0

*Not with Bengals in 2000.

Other free agent veterans invited to camp: HB Michael Basnight, T Mike Doughty, TE Jason Gavadza.

Abbreviations: D1—draft pick, first round; SD-2—supplemental draft pick, second round; W—claimed on waivers; T—obtained in trade; PlanB—Plan B free-agent acquisition; FA—free-agent acquisition (other than Plan B); UFA—unconditional free agent acquisition; ED—expansion draft pick.

MISCELLANEOUS TEAM DATA

Stadium (capacity, surface):
Paul Brown Stadium
(65,393, grass)
Business address:
One Paul Brown Stadium
Cincinnati, OH 45202-3492
Business phone:
513-621-3550
Ticket information:
513-621-8383
Team colors:
Black, orange and white
Flagship radio stations:
WCKY 1360 AM; WOFX 92.5 FM
Training site:
Georgetown College
Georgetown, Ky.
502-863-7088

TSN REPORT CARD

Coaching staff	C +	Dick LeBeau's promotion to head coach during the 2000 season was the club's best move in a long time. The players respect him, believe in him, and play hard for him. New coordinators Bob Bratkowski (offense) and Mark Duffner will unveil aggressive, attacking schemes that should enhance the level of play.
Quarterbacks	D	Jon Kitna wouldn't have signed with the Bengals if he were designated as the backup. He was promised a shot at the starting job in an open competition with Akili Smith, and the best man will win the position in the pre-season. An infusion of talented wideouts and a solid running game will help the quarterbacks immensely.
Running backs	B +	Corey Dillon's strength, durability and running power make the ground game go. Last season, he set the NFL's single-game record for rushing yards in a game (278). The Bengals have several players to complement him, but Dillon is the main guy and the complete package. He's worked hard to improve his speed, receiving and blocking skills, and it shows.
Receivers	B	Suddenly, a weakness in 2000 could become a strength in 2001. Darnay Scott's broken left leg has healed and second-rounder Chad Johnson has fine speed. Add lightning quick Peter Warrick to the mix and the receiving corps looks explosive. The tight end position, which disappeared from the offense the past three years, is back. Look for rookie Sean Brewer to beat out incumbent Tony McGee by the end of training camp.
Offensive line	B -	The NFL's No. 2 rushing offense is stronger with the addition of left tackle Richmond Webb, who solidifies the veteran unit. Webb and right tackle Willie Anderson make excellent bookends that will protect the quarterbacks. Center Rich Braham and left guard Matt O'Dwyer are healthy again, and right guard Mike Goff is solid.
Defensive line	C	After getting overpowered in 2000, this unit has been overhauled. A pair of free agents in right tackle Tony Williams and left end Kevin Henry will help tighten up the run defense, and first-round draft pick Justin Smith, who will start at right end, should finally trigger a pass rush that's been missing for years.
Linebackers	A	This is the team's No. 1 area of strength, thanks to middle linebacker Brian Simmons and right linebacker Takeo Spikes. Their ability to pursue the ball with intense speed allows them to cover sideline to sideline and make big plays. This is a pivotal season for left linebacker Steve Foley. He needs to show more pass-rushing skill or he won't be around in 2002.
Secondary	F	Talk about the great unknown, this is it. Second-year cornerbacks Mark Roman and Robert Bean have the kind of speed and ball skills necessary to be starters, but need more experience before they'll be ready to blossom. Cory Hall is the team's top safety and a dangerous blitzer. Another safety needs to step forward.
Special teams	C	Peter Warrick and Tremain Mack are devastating weapons as punt and kickoff returners. But their talent is tempered by the shaky kicking game. Placekicker Neil Rackers, who hit only 7 of 16 field goals outside 29 yards, should benefit from a new grass field at home. Punter Daniel Pope hangs 'em high, but not far.

CLEVELAND BROWNS
AFC CENTRAL DIVISION

2001 SEASON

CLUB DIRECTORY

Owner and chairman
Al Lerner
President and chief executive officer
Carmen Policy
V.p., director of football operations
Dwight Clark
V.p., chief administrative officer
Kofi Bonner
V.p. of finance and treasurer
Doug Jacobs
V.p., director of stadium operations and security
Lew Merletti
V.p., asst. dir. of football operations and general counsel
Lal Heneghan
Director of player personnel
Joe Collins
College personnel coordinator
Phil Neri
Pro personnel coordinator
Keith Kidd
Vice president of operations
Bill Hampton
V.p., marketing and development
Bruce Popko
Director of ticket operations
Mike Jennings
Manager of stadium operations
Diane Downing
Director, Cleveland Browns Foundation
Judge George White
Director of publicity/media relations
Todd Stewart
Director of new media
Dan Arthur
Coordinator of publicity/media relations
Ken Mather
Facilities manager
Greg Hipp

Head coach
Butch Davis

Assistant coaches
Bruce Arians (off. coordinator)
Phil Banko (defensive assistant)
Todd Bowles (defensive assistant)
Keith Butler (linebackers)
Foge Fazio (defensive coordinator)
Pete Garcia (football development)
Pete Hagen (tight ends)
Ray Hamilton (defensive line)
Tim Jorgensen (strength and conditioning)
Todd McNair (running backs)
Chuck Pagano (defensive backs)
Rob Phillips (assistant strength and conditioning)
Terry Robiske (wide receivers)
Jerry Rosburg (special teams)
Carl Smith (quarterbacks)
Larry Zierlein (offensive line)

Head athletic trainer
Mike Colello
Equipment manager
Bobby Monica
Video director
Pat Dolan
Head groundskeeper
Chris Powell

SCHEDULE

Sept. 9—	SEATTLE	12:00
Sept. 16—	at Pittsburgh	8:30
Sept. 23—	DETROIT	12:00
Sept. 30—	at Jacksonville	4:15
Oct. 7—	SAN DIEGO	12:00
Oct. 14—	at Cincinnati	1:00
Oct. 21—	BALTIMORE	12:00
Oct. 28—	Open date	
Nov. 4—	at Chicago	1:00
Nov. 11—	PITTSBURGH	12:00
Nov. 18—	at Baltimore	1:00
Nov. 25—	CINCINNATI	1:00
Dec. 2—	TENNESSEE	1:00
Dec. 9—	at New England	1:00
Dec. 16—	JACKSONVILLE	1:00
Dec. 23—	at Green Bay	1:00
Dec. 30—	at Tennessee	1:00

All times are Eastern.
All games Sunday unless noted.

DRAFT CHOICES

Gerard Warren, DT, Florida (first round/third pick overall).
Quincy Morgan, WR, Kansas State (2/33).
James Jackson, RB, Miami, Fla. (3/65).
Anthony Henry, DB, South Florida (4/97).
Jeremiah Pharms, LB, Washington (5/134).
Michael Jameson, DB, Texas A&M (6/165).
Paul Zukauskas, G, Boston College (7/203).
Andre King, WR, Miami, Fla. (7/245).

2000 REVIEW

RESULTS

Sept. 3—JACKSONVILLE	L	7-27
Sept.10—at Cincinnati	W	24-7
Sept.17—PITTSBURGH	W	23-20
Sept.24—at Oakland	L	10-36
Oct. 1—BALTIMORE	L	0-12
Oct. 8—at Arizona	L	21-29
Oct. 15—at Denver	L	10-44
Oct. 22—at Pittsburgh	L	0-22
Oct. 29—at Cincinnati	L	3-12
Nov. 5—N.Y. GIANTS	L	3-24
Nov. 12—NEW ENGLAND	W	19-11
Nov. 19—at Tennessee	L	10-24
Nov. 26—at Baltimore	L	7-44
Dec. 3—at Jacksonville	L	0-48
Dec. 10—PHILADELPHIA	L	24-35
Dec. 17—TENNESSEE	L	0-24
Dec. 24—Open date		

RECORDS/RANKINGS

2000 regular-season record: 3-13 (6th in AFC Central); 2-8 in division; 3-10 in conference; 2-6 at home; 1-7 on road.
Team record last five years: 5-27 (.156, ranks 31st in league in that span).

2000 team rankings:	No.	AFC	NFL
Total offense	*220.6	16	31
Rushing offense	*67.8	15	30
Passing offense	*152.8	15	30
Scoring offense	161	16	31
Total defense	*352.7	15	26
Rushing defense	*156.6	16	29
Passing defense	*196.1	7	12
Scoring defense	419	15	27
Takeaways	25	12	T20
Giveaways	28	9	T13
Turnover differential	-3	11	19
Sacks	42	T6	T12
Sacks allowed	40	8	18

*Yards per game.

TEAM LEADERS

Scoring (kicking): Phil Dawson, 59 pts. (17/17 PATs, 14/17 FGs).
Scoring (touchdowns): Travis Prentice, 48 pts. (7 rushing, 1 receiving).
Passing: Tim Couch, 1,483 yds. (215 att., 137 comp., 63.7%, 7 TDs, 9 int.).
Rushing: Travis Prentice, 512 yds. (173 att., 3.0 avg., 7 TDs).
Receptions: Kevin Johnson, 57 (669 yds., 11.7 avg., 0 TDs).
Interceptions: Corey Fuller, 3 (0 yds., 0 TDs).
Sacks: Keith McKenzie, 8.0.
Punting: Chris Gardocki, 45.5 avg. (108 punts, 4,919 yds., 0 blocked).
Punt returns: Dennis Northcutt, 10.7 avg. (27 att., 289 yds., 0 TDs).
Kickoff returns: Jamel White, 21.7 avg. (43 att., 935 yds., 0 TDs).

CLEVELAND BROWNS

No.	QUARTERBACKS	Ht./Wt.	Born	NFL Exp.	College	How acq.	'00 Games GP/GS
2	Couch, Tim	6-4/227	7-31-77	3	Kentucky	D1/99	7/7
11	Detmer, Ty	6-0/194	10-30-67	10	Brigham Young	T-SF/99	0/0
10	Holcomb, Kelly	6-2/212	7-9-73	5	Middle Tennessee State	FA/01	0/0
16	Thompson, Kevin	6-5/236	7-27-77	2	Penn State	FA/00	1/0
13	Wynn, Spergon	6-3/226	8-10-78	2	Southwest Texas State	D6a/00	7/1
	RUNNING BACKS						
34	Floyd, Chris (FB)	6-2/235	6-23-75	4	Michigan	FA/00	13/0
29	Jackson, James	5-10/209	8-4-76	R	Miami (Fla.)	D3/01	—
41	Prentice, Travis	5-11/221	12-8-76	2	Miami of Ohio	D3a/00	16/11
23	Rhett, Errict	5-11/211	12-11-70	8	Florida	UFA/00	5/4
44	Sellers, Mike (FB)	6-3/260	7-21-75	4	None	FA/01	*15/7
30	White, Jamel	5-9/208	2-11-77	2	South Dakota	FA/00	13/0
	RECEIVERS						
89	Brown, Bobby	6-2/197	3-26-77	2	Notre Dame	FA/00	6/0
83	Campbell, Mark (TE)	6-6/253	12-6-75	3	Michigan	FA/99	16/10
84	Chiaverini, Darrin	6-2/210	10-12-77	3	Colorado	D5/99	10/2
88	Dawson, JaJuan	6-1/197	11-5-77	2	Tulane	D3b/00	2/2
82	Dudley, Rickey (TE)	6-6/255	7-15-72	6	Ohio State	UFA/01	*16/16
81	Jackson, Lenzie	6-0/184	6-17-77	3	Arizona State	FA/00	5/0
85	Johnson, Kevin	5-11/195	7-15-76	3	Syracuse	D2a/99	16/16
	King, Andre	6-0/200	11-26-73	R	Miami (Fla.)	D7b/01	—
5	Morgan, Quincy	6-1/209	9-23-77	R	Kansas State	D2/01	—
86	Northcutt, Dennis	5-10/175	12-22-77	2	Arizona	D2/00	15/8
87	Santiago, O.J. (TE)	6-7/264	4-4-74	5	Kent	W-Dal./00	*11/0
80	Shea, Aaron (TE)	6-3/244	12-5-76	2	Michigan	D4b/00	15/8
	OFFENSIVE LINEMEN						
63	Bedell, Brad	6-4/299	2-12-77	2	Colorado	D6b/00	12/0
65	Bundren, Jim (C)	6-3/303	10-6-74	3	Clemson	ED/99 (NYJ)	11/9
69	Chanoine, Roger (T)	6-4/295	8-11-76	2	Temple	FA/99	7/0
	Johnson, Tré (G)	6-2/326	8-30-71	7	Temple	FA/01	*4/4
79	Lamontagne, Noel	6-4/301	3-9-77	2	Virginia	FA/00	2/0
61	Lindsay, Everett	6-4/302	9-18-70	8	Mississippi	FA/00	16/16
60	O'Hara, Shaun (C)	6-3/287	6-23-77	2	Rutgers	FA/00	8/4
72	Oben, Roman (T)	6-4/305	10-9-72	6	Louisville	UFA/00	16/16
71	Pyne, Jim	6-2/297	11-23-71	8	Virginia Tech	ED/99 (Det.)	2/2
77	Verba, Ross	6-4/308	10-31-73	5	Iowa	UFA/01	*16/16
64	Wohlabaugh, Dave (C)	6-3/292	4-13-72	7	Syracuse	UFA/99	12/12
75	Zahursky, Steve (G)	6-6/305	9-2-76	3	Kent	FA/99	16/16
	Zukauskas, Paul (G)	6-6/318	7-12-79	R	Boston College	D7a/01	—
	DEFENSIVE LINEMEN						
94	Alexander, Derrick (E)	6-4/286	11-13-73	7	Florida State	UFA/99	0/0
92	Brown, Courtney (E)	6-4/266	2-14-78	2	Penn State	D1/00	16/16
93	Colinet, Stalin (T)	6-6/288	7-19-74	5	Boston College	T-Min./99	16/16
73	Holland, Darius (T)	6-5/330	11-10-73	7	Colorado	UFA/99	16/1
97	Kuehl, Ryan (T)	6-5/290	1-18-72	5	Virginia	FA/99	16/0
90	McKenzie, Keith	6-3/273	10-17-73	6	Ball State	UFA/00	16/16
98	Miller, Arnold (E)	6-3/239	1-3-75	3	Louisiana State	FA/99	12/0
78	Rogers, Tyrone (E)	6-5/236	10-11-76	2	Alabama State	FA/99	16/0
99	Roye, Orpheus	6-4/288	1-21-74	6	Florida State	UFA/00	16/16
94	Smith, Mark (T)	6-4/294	8-28-74	5	Auburn	UFA/01	*14/7
91	Spriggs, Marcus (T)	6-4/314	7-26-76	3	Troy (Ala.) State	D6a/99	8/0
70	Warren, Gerald (T)	6-4/322	7-25-78	R	Florida	D1/01	—
	LINEBACKERS						
53	Abdullah, Rahim	6-5/251	3-22-76	3	Clemson	D2b/99	13/4
52	Boyer, Brant	6-1/230	6-27-71	8	Arizona	FA/01	*12/5
54	Burnett, Chester	5-10/230	4-15-75	2	Arizona	FA/99	7/0
51	Jones, Lenoy	6-1/235	9-25-74	6	Texas Christian	ED/99 (Ten.)	8/1
95	Miller, Jamir	6-5/266	11-19-73	8	UCLA	UFA/99	16/16
55	Moore, Marty	6-1/245	3-19-71	8	Kentucky	UFA/00	16/9
	Pharms, Jeremiah	6-0/251	6-24-78	R	Washington	D5/01	—
58	Rainer, Wali	6-2/245	4-19-77	3	Virginia	D4/99	16/16
57	Rudd, Dwayne	6-2/237	2-3-76	5	Alabama	UFA/01	*14/13
50	Saleh, Tarek	6-0/240	11-7-74	5	Wisconsin	ED/99 (Car.)	16/0
	DEFENSIVE BACKS						
28	Barnes, Rashidi	5-11/205	6-26-78	2	Colorado	D7c/00	14/0
27	Chapman, Lamar	6-0/186	11-6-76	2	Kansas State	D5b/00	7/0
43	Ellsworth, Percy	6-2/225	10-19-74	6	Virginia	UFA/00	16/6
22	Franz, Todd (CB)	6-0/194	4-12-76	1	Tulsa	FA/00	7/0
24	Fuller, Corey	5-10/205	5-1-71	7	Florida State	UFA/99	15/15
	Henry, Anthony (CB)	6-0/205	3-29-79	R	South Florida	D4/01	—
31	Jackson, Raymond	5-10/189	2-17-73	6	Colorado State	FA/00	9/1
	Jameson, Michael	5-11/187	7-14-79	R	Texas A&M	D6/01	—

No.	DEFENSIVE BACKS	Ht./Wt.	Born	NFL Exp.	College	How acq.	'00 Games GP/GS
20	Little, Earl	6-0/198	3-10-73	4	Miami (Fla.)	W-NO/99	16/0
26	Malbrough, Anthony	5-10/185	12-9-76	2	Texas Tech	D5a/00	9/1
33	McCutcheon, Daylon (CB)	5-10/180	12-9-76	3	Southern California	D3a/99	15/15
25	Sanders, Lewis	6-0/200	6-22-78	2	Maryland	D4a/00	11/2
21	Smith, Marquis	6-2/213	1-13-75	3	California	D3b/99	16/16
	SPECIALISTS						
4	Dawson, Phil (K)	5-11/190	1-23-75	3	Texas	FA/99	16/0
17	Gardocki, Chris (P)	6-1/200	2-7-70	11	Clemson	UFA/99	16/0

*Not with Browns in 2000.

Other free agent veterans invited to camp: QB Jeff Brohm, TE Rod Monroe, WR Joseph Natasi.

Abbreviations: D1—draft pick, first round; SD-2—supplemental draft pick, second round; W—claimed on waivers; T—obtained in trade; PlanB—Plan B free-agent acquisition; FA—free-agent acquisition (other than Plan B); UFA—unconditional free agent acquisition; ED—expansion draft pick.

MISCELLANEOUS TEAM DATA

Stadium (capacity, surface):
Cleveland Browns Stadium
(73,200, grass)
Business address:
76 Lou Groza Boulevard
Berea, Ohio 44017
Business phone:
440-891-5000
Ticket information:
440-891-5050
Team colors:
Brown, orange and white
Flagship radio stations:
WMJI, 105.7 FM
Training site:
76 Lou Groza Boulevard
Berea, Ohio
440-891-5000

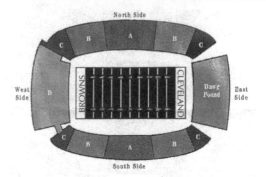

TSN REPORT CARD

Coaching staff — B +
Having Butch Davis on board makes all the difference in the world on this team. He's a proven winner who is used to resurrecting downtrodden programs. And the Browns are in that boat right now. In addition, he has capable coordinators in Foge Fazio (defense) and Bruce Arians (offense) and a receivers coach in Terry Robiskie who has something to prove after being part of the Washington Redskins purge.

Quarterbacks — B
This is the season when Tim Couch must stay healthy for all 16 games, and if he can, he should have a big, big season. This pitch-and-catch passing scheme he now gets to operate is similar to what he used at Kentucky when he set all kinds of school and SEC records.

Running backs — D -
There is no healthy, proven go-to back on the roster right now. All have important shortcomings. Maybe the Browns will find a diamond in the rough, but more probably, they'll have to use James Jackson on first and second down, Jamel White on third down and Travis Prentice as a backup.

Receivers — C +
If Quincy Morgan can be more consistent, he'll give the Browns the big, athletic, strong wide receiver to go over the middle and make the tough catch. JaJuan Dawson will be a big key, too. Kevin Johnson must adapt to this new offense, which may not be easy.

Offensive line — C -
Getting Ross Verba in free agency helped immensely. He'll fill a big hole at right tackle. Center Dave Wohlabaugh and left guard Jim Pyne are returning from injuries. Left tackle Roman Oben is decent, but there are still plenty of questions at right guard.

Defensive line — A
This is undoubtedly the strongest position on the team. The Browns are solid two-deep across the line. Drafting Gerard Warren was the key, of course. With him at right tackle and Courtney Brown at right end, the Browns have potentially their best end/tackle tandem ever.

Linebackers — C
Once again, the Browns helped themselves a great deal in free agency by getting weak-sider Dwayne Rudd. His quickness fits this defense like a glove. Middle man Wali Rainer will be more productive now that he won't be getting blocked so much.

Secondary — D +
The Browns are decent at cornerback, but they have all kinds of problems at safety, where there has been absolutely no production for two straight years. Free safety Percy Ellsworth was a huge disappointment last year. He must improve for the secondary to improve.

Special teams — C -
Punter Chris Gardocki is outstanding, and place kicker Phil Dawson has been pretty productive in the limited opportunities he's been given. But the Browns must do much, much better in their return game and in coverage. Those units have been horrible.

DALLAS COWBOYS
NFC EASTERN DIVISION

2001 SEASON

CLUB DIRECTORY

President/general manager
Jerry Jones
Vice presidents
Charlotte Anderson
George Hays
Jerry Jones Jr.
Stephen Jones
Treasurer
Robert Nunez
Director of public relations
Rich Dalrymple
Assistant director of public relations
Brett Daniels
Ticket manager
Carol Padgett
Director of college and pro scouting
Larry Lacewell
Scouts
Tom Ciskowski
Jim Garrett
Tommy Hart
Jim Hess
Walter Juliff
Henry Sroka
Walt Yowarsky
Head athletic trainer
Jim Maurer
Assistant athletic trainers
Britt Brown
Greg Gaither
Physicians
Dan Cooper
Andrew Dossett
Robert Fowler
J.R. Zamorano

Head coach
Dave Campo

Assistant coaches
Joe Avezzano (special teams/
  tight ends)
Bill Bates (def. nickel package/
  assistant special teams)
Wes Chandler (wide receivers)
George Edwards (linebackers)
Steve Hoffman (kickers/quality
  control)
Hudson Houck (offensive line)
Jim Jeffcoat (defensive ends)
Joe Juraszek (strength & cond.)
Andre Patterson (def. tackles)
Clancy Pendergrast (secondary)
Jack Reilly (off. coordinator)
Clarence Shelmon (running backs)
Glenn Smith (offensive assistant)
Wade Wilson (quarterbacks)
Mike Zimmer (def. coordinator)

Equipment/practice fields manager
Mike McCord
Video director
Robert Blackwell
Director of operations
Bruce Mays

SCHEDULE

Sept. 9—	TAMPA BAY	1:00
Sept. 16—	at Detroit	1:00
Sept. 23—	SAN DIEGO	1:00
Sept. 30—	at Philadelphia	8:30
Oct. 7—	Open date	
Oct. 15—	WASHINGTON (Mon.)	9:00
Oct. 21—	at Oakland	4:15
Oct. 28—	ARIZONA	4:05
Nov. 4—	at N.Y. Giants	1:00
Nov. 11—	at Atlanta	1:00
Nov. 18—	PHILADELPHIA	1:00
Nov. 22—	DENVER (Thanks.)	4:05
Dec. 2—	at Washington	4:15
Dec. 9—	N.Y. GIANTS	1:00
Dec. 16—	at Seattle	4:15
Dec. 23—	at Arizona	4:05
Dec. 30—	SAN FRANCISCO	1:00

All times are Eastern.
All games Sunday unless noted.

DRAFT CHOICES

Quincy Carter, QB, Georgia (second round/53rd pick overall).
Tony Dixon, DB, Alabama (2/56).
Willie Blade, DT, Mississippi St. (3/93).
Markus Steele, LB, USC (4/122).
Matt Lehr, C, Virginia Tech (5/137).
Daleroy Stewart, DT, Southern Mississippi (6/171).
Colston Weatherington, DE, Central Missouri (7/207).
John Nix, DT, Southern Mississippi (7/240).
Char-ron Dorsey, T, Florida State (7/242).

2000 REVIEW

RESULTS

Sept. 3—PHILADELPHIA	L	14-41
Sept.10—at Arizona	L	31 -32
Sept.18—at Washington	W	27-21
Sept.24—SAN FRANCISCO	L	24-41
Oct. 1—at Carolina (OT)	W	16-13
Oct. 8—Open date		
Oct. 15—at N.Y. Giants	L	14-19
Oct. 22—ARIZONA	W	48-7
Oct. 29—JACKSONVILLE (OT)	L	17-23
Nov. 5—at Philadelphia (OT)	L	13-16
Nov. 12—CINCINNATI	W	23-6
Nov. 19—at Baltimore	L	0-27
Nov. 23—MINNESOTA	L	15-27
Dec. 3—at Tampa Bay	L	7-27
Dec. 10—WASHINGTON	W	32-13
Dec. 17—N.Y. GIANTS	L	13 -17
Dec. 25—at Tennessee	L	0-31

RECORDS/RANKINGS

2000 regular-season record: 5-11 (4th in NFC East); 3-5 in division; 4-8 in conference; 3-5 at home; 2-6 on road.
Team record last five years: 39-41 (.488, ranks T15th in league in that span).

2000 team rankings:	No.	NFC	NFL
Total offense	*279.7	13	25
Rushing offense	*122.1	5	12
Passing offense	*157.6	15	28
Scoring offense	294	11	23
Total defense	*333.1	9	19
Rushing defense	*164.8	15	31
Passing defense	*168.3	2	3
Scoring defense	361	10	22
Takeaways	25	T9	T20
Giveaways	39	14	28
Turnover differential	-14	14	T28
Sacks	25	T14	T30
Sacks allowed	35	T6	T13

*Yards per game.

TEAM LEADERS

Scoring (kicking): Tim Seder, 102 pts. (27/27 PATs, 25/33 FGs).
Scoring (touchdowns): Emmitt Smith, 54 pts. (9 rushing).
Passing: Troy Aikman, 1,632 yds. (262 att., 156 comp., 59.5%, 7 TDs, 14 int.).
Rushing: Emmitt Smith, 1,203 yds. (294 att., 4.1 avg., 9 TDs).
Receptions: James McKnight, 52 (926 yds., 17.8 avg., 2 TDs).
Interceptions: Phillippi Sparks, 5 (59 yds., 0 TDs).
Sacks: Ebenezer Ekuban, 6.5.
Punting: Micah Knorr, 42.8 avg. (58 punts, 2,481 yds., 0 blocked).
Punt returns: Wane McGarity, 11.8 avg. (30 att., 353 yds., 2 TDs).
Kickoff returns: Jason Tucker, 21.5 avg. (51 att., 1,099 yds., 0 TDs).

2001 SEASON
TRAINING CAMP ROSTER

No.	QUARTERBACKS	Ht./Wt.	Born	NFL Exp.	College	How acq.	'00 Games GP/GS
3	Banks, Tony	6-4/225	4-5-73	6	Michigan State	FA/01	*11/8
17	Carter, Quincy	6-2/225	10-13-77	R	Georgia	D2a/01	—
5	Stoerner, Clint	6-2/210	12-29-77	2	Arkansas	FA/00	1/0
2	Wright, Anthony	6-1/195	2-14-76	3	South Carolina	FA/00	4/2
	RUNNING BACKS						
42	Hambrick, Troy	6-1/235	11-6-76	2	Savannah State	FA/00	3/0
22	Smith, Emmitt	5-9/209	5-15-69	12	Florida	D1/90	16/16
44	Thomas, Robert (FB)	6-1/252	12-1-74	4	Henderson State (Ark.)	FA/98	16/15
32	Wiley, Michael	5-11/189	1-5-78	2	Ohio State	D5/00	10/0
	RECEIVERS						
85	Brazzell, Chris	6-2/193	5-22-76	3	Angelo State (Texas)	W-NYJ/99	9/0
15	Dunn, Damon	5-9/182	3-15-76	2	Stanford	FA/01	*4/0
84	Galloway, Joey	5-11/188	11-20-71	7	Ohio State	T-Sea./00	1/1
88	Harris, Jackie (TE)	6-4/250	1-4-68	12	Northeast Louisiana	UFA/00	16/7
16	Hodge, Damon	6-1/192	2-16-77	2	Alabama State	FA/00	8/0
81	Ismail, Rocket	5-11/190	11-18-69	9	Notre Dame	UFA/99	9/9
89	LaFleur, David (TE)	6-7/272	1-29-74	5	Louisiana State	D1/97	15/10
83	McGarity, Wane	5-8/197	9-30-76	3	Texas	D4a/99	14/0
87	Tucker, Jason	6-1/182	6-24-76	3	Texas Christian	FA/99	16/7
46	Whalen, James (TE)	6-2/228	12-11-77	2	Kentucky	FA/00	3/0
18	Yamini, Bashir	6-3/190	9-10-77	1	Iowa	FA/01	*6/0
	OFFENSIVE LINEMEN						
76	Adams, Flozell (T)	6-7/335	5-18-75	4	Michigan State	D2/98	16/16
73	Allen, Larry (G)	6-3/326	11-27-71	8	Sonoma State (Calif.)	D2/94	16/16
	Dorsey, Char-Ron (T)	6-7/367	11-5-77	R	Florida State	D7c/01	—
66	Fricke, Ben (G)	6-0/295	11-3-75	3	Houston	FA/99	9/5
71	Jackson, Al (G)	6-3/306	5-18-77	2	Louisiana State	FA/00	3/0
	Lehr, Matt (C)	6-2/292	4-25-79	R	Virginia Tech	D5/01	—
62	Page, Craig (C)	6-3/303	1-17-76	2	Georgia Tech	FA/00	2/0
77	Page, Solomon (G)	6-4/321	2-27-76	3	West Virginia	D2/99	16/16
53	Stepnoski, Mark (C)	6-2/265	1-20-67	13	Pittsburgh	UFA/99	11/11
79	Williams, Erik (T)	6-6/311	9-7-68	10	Central State (Ohio)	D3c/91	16/16
	DEFENSIVE LINEMEN						
99	Blade, Willie (T)	6-3/319	2-7-79	R	Mississippi State	D3/01	—
96	Ekuban, Ebenezer (E)	6-3/265	5-29-76	3	North Carolina	D1/99	12/2
98	Ellis, Greg (E)	6-6/286	8-14-75	4	North Carolina	D1/98	16/16
97	Fields, Aaron (E)	6-4/243	1-9-76	2	Troy State	FA/00	3/0
95	Hennings, Chad (T)	6-6/291	10-20-65	9	Air Force	D11/88	8/8
94	Myers, Michael	6-2/288	1-20-76	4	Alabama	D4/98	13/7
	Nix, John (T)	6-2/278	11-24-76	R	Southern Mississippi	D7b/01	—
75	Noble, Brandon (T)	6-2/285	4-10-74	3	Penn State	FA/99	16/9
90	Scarlett, Noel (T)	6-3/320	1-21-74	1	Langston University (Okla.)	FA/00	1/0
64	Stewart, Daleroy (T)	6-4/309	11-1-78	R	Southern Mississippi	D7/01	—
91	Underwood, Dimitrius	6-6/276	3-29-77	2	Michigan State	FA/00	15/0
67	Weatherington, Colston (E)	6-5/274	10-29-77	R	Central Missouri State	D7a/01	—
92	White, Chris (E)	6-3/285	9-28-76	2	Southern	FA./00	*5/0
93	Zellner, Peppi (E)	6-5/257	3-14-75	3	Fort Valley (Ga.) State	D4b/99	12/0
	LINEBACKERS						
58	Bowden, Joe	5-11/235	2-25-70	10	Oklahoma	UFA/00	16/0
52	Coakley, Dexter	5-10/228	10-20-72	5	Appalachian State	D3a/97	16/16
56	Grant, Orantes	6-0/225	3-18-78	2	Georgia	D7/00	13/0
54	Hambrick, Darren	6-2/227	8-30-75	4	South Carolina	D5a/98	16/16
59	Nguyen, Dat	5-11/231	9-25-75	3	Texas A&M	D3/99	10/5
51	Steele, Markus	6-3/240	7-24-79	R	Southern California	D4/01	—
	DEFENSIVE BACKS						
24	Dixon, Tony (S)	6-1/213	6-18-79	R	Alabama	D2b/01	—
27	Edwards, Mario (CB)	6-0/191	12-1-75	2	Florida State	D6/00	11/1
23	Goodrich, Dwayne (CB)	5-11/198	5-29-78	2	Tennessee	D2/00	5/0
38	Hawthorne, Duane (CB)	5-10/175	8-26-76	3	Northern Illinois	FA/99	14/0
41	Larrimore, Kareem (CB)	5-11/190	4-21-76	2	West Texas A&M	D4/00	15/4
43	Reese, Izell (S)	6-2/190	5-7-74	4	Alabama-Birmingham	D6/98	16/7
20	Sparks, Phillippi (CB)	5-11/195	4-15-69	10	Arizona State	UFA/00	16/12
31	Teague, George (S)	6-1/196	2-18-71	9	Alabama	UFA/00	9/9
28	Woodson, Darren (S)	6-1/219	4-25-69	10	Arizona State	D2b/92	11/11
	SPECIALISTS						
4	Knorr, Micah (P)	6-2/193	1-9-75	2	Utah State	FA/00	14/0
6	Seder, Tim (K)	5-9/180	9-17-74	2	Ashland University	FA/00	15/0

*Not with Cowboys in 2000.

Other free agent veterans invited to camp: RB John Avery, TE Ryan Collins, TE Chris Fontenot, G Kelvin Garmon, CB Jermaine Jones, TE Mike Lucky, DE Ben Williams.

Abbreviations: D1—draft pick, first round; SD-2—supplemental draft pick, second round; W—claimed on waivers; T—obtained in trade; PlanB—Plan B free-agent acquisition; FA—free-agent acquisition (other than Plan B); UFA—unconditional free agent acquisition; ED—expansion draft pick.

MISCELLANEOUS TEAM DATA

Stadium (capacity, surface):
Texas Stadium
(65,675, artificial)
Business address:
One Cowboys Parkway
Irving, TX 75063
Business phone:
972-556-9900
Ticket information:
972-785-5000
Team colors:
Blue, metallic silver blue and white
Flagship radio station:
KVIL, 103.7 FM
Training site:
Midwestern State Univ. (July 20-Aug. 10)
Wichita Falls, Tex.
972-556-9900
Oxnard, Calif. (Aug. 11-24)
972-556-9900

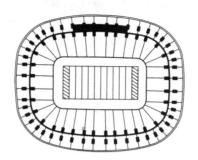

TSN REPORT CARD

Coaching staff	C -	Offensive coordinator Jack Reilly and defensive coordinator Mike Zimmer will start the season on the hot seat. Each must do a substantially better job of delegating responsibility and getting the most out of their assistants. This is a young team and a good coaching job could get Dallas an extra 2-3 wins.
Quarterbacks	D	Tony Banks is an average NFL quarterback who looks terrific some weeks and terrible other weeks. He's not proven he can be a consistent performer. His backups—Anthony Wright and second-round pick Quincy Carter—are very unproven.
Running backs	B	Emmitt Smith remains productive and needs a little more than 1,500 yards to become the NFL's all-time leading rusher. Fullback Robert Thomas is a solid player, but the Cowboys can't afford for either one to have an injury because there's no proven depth behind them.
Receivers	C +	The key is whether Joey Galloway and Raghib Ismail can recover from knee injuries last season and return to their high standards. Dallas still needs a third-down possession receiver, who can beat single coverage because Galloway and Ismail will be doubled. Second-year receiver Damon Hodge can be a factor, if given a chance.
Offensive line	B	The only question is at right guard, where Al Jackson holds a slight edge over Kelvin Garmon and rookie Matt Lehr. Left tackle Flozell Adams is an unrestricted free agent after the season, which means he should be motivated to have the best season of his career.
Defensive line	D	Dallas hasn't improved its personnel enough to suggest it can substantially improve the run defense, which finished 31st in the NFL last season. Their best hope is that Dimitrius Underwood can sustain the talent he flashed on various occasions last season and defensive ends Greg Ellis and Ebenezer Ekuban can each record 10 sacks.
Linebackers	C -	The Cowboys have a group of undersized linebackers that rely on the defensive tackles to keep them from getting run over by offensive linemen. Dexter Coakley is a speed player who will play all three positions at various times this season. But the key will be whether Dat Nguyen can play the run strong and withstand the rigors of a 16-game season.
Secondary	D	None of the four cornerbacks on the Cowboys' roster is proven, which means it could be a long season. Kareem Larrimore probably has the most talent, but hasn't figured out how to consistently work hard to get better. Dwayne Goodrich still hasn't showed why he was the club's second-round pick last season, but his attitude is a lot better this season. Mario Edwards and Duane Hawthorne are the starters, but there's no guarantee how long they keep their jobs.
Special teams	B	Micah Knorr is a terrific punter and Tim Seder was solid last year. Each should be better this season because they're more concerned with improving their technique than making the team. John Avery could give the Cowboys a chance to make big plays on special teams.

DENVER BRONCOS
AFC WESTERN DIVISION

2001 SEASON

CLUB DIRECTORY

President/chief executive officer
Pat Bowlen
General manager
Neal Dahlen
Vice president of business operations
Joe Ellis
Chief financial officer
Allen Fears
Dir. of ticket operations/business dev.
Rick Nichols
General manager of stadium
Mac Freeman
Senior director of media relations
Jim Saccomano
Director of operations
Bill Harpole
Director of pro personnel
Rick Smith
Director of college scouting
Ted Sundquist
Director of special services
Fred Fleming
Director of player relations
Billy Thompson
Scouts
Bob Beers
Scott DiStefano
Jim Goodman
Cornell Green
Dan Rambo
Dale Strahm
Head trainer
Steve Antonopulos
Assistant trainers
Jim Keller
Corey Oshikoya
Physician
Richard Hawkins
Equipment manager
Doug West

Head coach
Mike Shanahan

Assistant coaches
Frank Bush (special teams)
Larry Coyer (linebackers)
Rick Dennison (offensive line)
Karl Dorrell (wide receivers)
George Dyer (defensive line)
David Gibbs (safeties)
Gary Kubiak (offensive coordinator/
quarterbacks)
Anthony Lynn (special teams asst.)
Pat McPherson (off. assistant)
Ron Milus (defensive backs)
Brian Pariani (tight ends)
Ray Rhodes (def. coordinator)
Greg Saporta (assistant strength
& conditioning)
Cedric Smith (assistant strength
& conditioning)
John Teerlinck (pass rush
specialist)
Bobby Turner (running backs)
Rich Tuten (strength & cond.)
Steve Watson (defensive assistant)
Zaven Yaralian (head coach's asst.)

Director/video operations
Kent Erickson

SCHEDULE

Sept. 10—	N.Y. GIANTS (Mon.)	9:00
Sept. 16—	at Indianapolis	1:00
Sept. 23—	at Arizona	8:35
Sept. 30—	BALTIMORE	4:15
Oct. 7—	KANSAS CITY	4:05
Oct. 14—	at Seattle	4:15
Oct. 21—	at San Diego	4:05
Oct. 28—	NEW ENGLAND	4:15
Nov. 5—	at Oakland (Mon.)	9:00
Nov. 11—	SAN DIEGO	4:05
Nov. 18—	WASHINGTON	4:15
Nov. 22—	at Dallas (Thanks.)	4:05
Dec. 2—	at Miami	1:00
Dec. 9—	SEATTLE	8:30
Dec. 16—	at Kansas City	1:00
Dec. 23—	Open date	
Dec. 30—	OAKLAND	4:15

All times are Eastern.
All games Sunday unless noted.

DRAFT CHOICES

Willie Middlebrooks, DB, Minnesota
(first round/24th pick overall).
Paul Toviessi, DE, Marshall (2/51).
Reggie Hayward, DE, Iowa State (3/87).
Ben Hamilton, C, Minnesota (4/113).
Nick Harris, P, California (4/120).
Kevin Kasper, WR, Iowa (6/190).

2000 REVIEW

RESULTS

Sept. 4—at St. Louis	L	36-41
Sept.10—ATLANTA	W	42-14
Sept.17—at Oakland	W	33-24
Sept.24—KANSAS CITY	L	22-23
Oct. 1—NEW ENGLAND	L	19-28
Oct. 8—at San Diego	W	21-7
Oct. 15—CLEVELAND	W	44-10
Oct. 22—at Cincinnati	L	21-31
Oct. 29—Open date		
Nov. 5—at N.Y. Jets	W	30-23
Nov. 13—OAKLAND	W	27-24
Nov. 19—SAN DIEGO	W	38-37
Nov. 26—at Seattle	W	38-31
Dec. 3—at New Orleans	W	38-23
Dec. 10—SEATTLE	W	31-24
Dec. 17—at Kansas City	L	7-20
Dec. 23—SAN FRANCISCO	W	38-9
Dec. 31—at Baltimore*	L	3-21

*AFC wild-card game.

RECORDS/RANKINGS

2000 regular-season record: 11-5 (2nd
in AFC West); 6-2 in division; 8-4 in conference; 6-2 at home; 5-3 on road.
Team record last five years: 56-24 (.700),
ranks 1st in league in that span).

2000 team rankings:	No.	AFC	NFL
Total offense	*409.6	1	2
Rushing offense	*144.4	3	3
Passing offense	*265.2	2	3
Scoring offense	485	1	2
Total defense	*346.5	14	24
Rushing defense	*99.9	6	7
Passing defense	*246.6	16	31
Scoring defense	369	13	23
Takeaways	44	2	2
Giveaways	25	T4	T7
Turnover differential	19	2	2
Sacks	44	4	T9
Sacks allowed	30	6	8

*Yards per game.

TEAM LEADERS

Scoring (kicking): Jason Elam, 103 pts.
(49/49 PATs, 18/24 FGs).
Scoring (touchdowns): Mike Anderson,
92 pts. (15 rushing, 1 2-pt. conv.).
Passing: Brian Griese, 2,688 yds. (336
att., 216 comp., 64.3%, 19 TDs, 4 int.).
Rushing: Mike Anderson, 1,487 yds. (297
att., 5.0 avg., 15 TDs).
Receptions: Rod Smith, 100 (1,602 yds.,
16.0 avg., 8 TDs).
Interceptions: Terrell Buckley, 6 (110
yds., 1 TD).
Sacks: Trevor Pryce, 12.0.
Punting: Tom Rouen, 40.2 avg. (61 punts,
2,455 yds., 1 blocked).
Punt returns: Deltha O'Neal, 10.4 avg. (34
att., 354 yds., 0 TDs).
Kickoff returns: Deltha O'Neal, 24.0 avg.
(46 att., 1,102 yds., 1 TD).

DENVER BRONCOS

No.	QUARTERBACKS	Ht./Wt.	Born	NFL Exp.	College	How acq.	'00 Games GP/GS
	Beuerlein, Steve	6-3/220	3-7-65	15	Notre Dame	FA/01	*16/16
12	Frerotte, Gus	6-3/225	7-31-71	8	Tulsa	UFA/00	10/6
14	Griese, Brian	6-3/215	3-18-75	4	Michigan	D3/98	10/10
17	Jackson, Jarious	6-0/228	5-3-77	2	Notre Dame	D7a/00	2/0
	RUNNING BACKS						
38	Anderson, Mike	6-0/230	9-21-73	2	Utah	D6/00	16/12
37	Carter, Tony (FB)	6-0/235	8-23-72	8	Minnesota	UFA/01	*16/6
21	Coleman, KaRon	5-7/198	5-22-78	2	Stephen F. Austin State	FA/00	9/0
30	Davis, Terrell	5-11/210	10-28-72	7	Georgia	D6b/95	5/4
22	Gary, Olandis	5-11/218	5-18-75	3	Georgia	D4/99	1/0
29	Griffith, Howard (FB)	6-0/240	11-17-67	9	Illinois	UFA/97	14/14
	Mitchell, Basil	5-10/200	9-7-75	2	Texas Christian	FA/01	*1/0
42	Smith, Detron (FB)	5-10/230	2-25-74	6	Texas A&M	D3a/96	16/0
	RECEIVERS						
89	Carswell, Dwayne (TE)	6-3/260	1-18-72	8	Liberty (Va.)	FA/94	16/16
88	Clark, Desmond (TE)	6-3/255	4-20-77	3	Wake Forest	D6a/99	16/2
84	Cole, Chris	6-0/195	11-12-77	2	Texas A&M	D3/00	8/0
82	Hape, Patrick (TE)	6-4/262	6-6-74	5	Alabama	UFA/01	*16/2
	Kasper, Kevin	6-0/193	12-23-77	R	Iowa	D6/01	—
11	Kennison, Eddie	6-1/190	1-20-73	6	Louisiana State	UFA/01	*16/10
87	McCaffrey, Ed	6-5/215	8-17-68	11	Stanford	UFA/95	16/16
83	McGriff, Travis	5-8/185	6-24-76	3	Florida	D3b/99	15/0
82	Miller, Billy (TE)	6-3/230	4-24-77	3	Southern California	D7a/99	12/0
81	Montgomery, Scottie	6-1/195	5-26-78	2	Duke	FA/00	4/0
80	Smith, Rod	6-0/200	5-15-70	7	Missouri Southern	FA/94	16/16
	OFFENSIVE LINEMEN						
76	Brooks, Ethan (T)	6-6/297	4-27-72	5	Williams (Conn.)	UFA/01	*14/3
65	Carlisle, Cooper (G)	6-5/295	8-11-77	2	Florida	D4b/00	14/0
67	Fordham, Todd (T)	6-5/308	10-9-73	5	Florida State	UFA/01	*16/8
64	Friedman, Lennie (G)	6-3/285	10-13-76	3	Duke	D2b/99	16/8
	Hamilton, Ben (C)	6-4/283	8-18-77	R	Minnesota	D4a/01	—
60	Jones, K.C (C)	6-1/275	3-28-74	5	Miami (Fla.)	FA/97	16/0
78	Lepsis, Matt (T)	6-4/290	1-13-74	5	Colorado	FA/97	16/16
66	Nalen, Tom (C)	6-3/286	5-13-71	8	Boston College	D7c/94	16/16
62	Neil, Dan (G)	6-2/285	10-21-73	5	Texas	D3/97	16/16
72	Neujahr, Quentin (C)	6-4/302	1-30-71	7	Kansas State	FA/01	*16/2
63	Ostrowski, Phil (G)	6-4/291	9-23-75	4	Penn State	FA/01	*13/0
70	Teague, Trey (T)	6-5/292	12-27-74	4	Tennessee	D7a/98	2/0
	DEFENSIVE LINEMEN						
92	Archambeau, Lester (E)	6-5/275	6-27-67	12	Stanford	UFA/00	3/0
96	Hasselbach, Harald (E)	6-6/285	9-22-67	8	Washington	FA/94	16/1
69	Hayward, Reggie (E)	6-5/255	3-14-79	R	Iowa State	D3/01	—
78	Lett, Leon (T)	6-6/290	10-12-68	11	Emporia (Kan.) State	UFA/01	*9/7
91	McGlockton, Chester (T)	6-4/334	9-16-69	10	Clemson	FA/01	*15/15
95	Pittman, Kavika (E)	6-6/273	10-9-74	6	McNeese State	UFA/00	15/15
93	Pryce, Trevor (T)	6-5/295	8-3-75	5	Clemson	D1/97	16/16
99	Reagor, Montae (E)	6-2/280	6-29-77	3	Texas Tech	D2a/99	13/0
98	Tanuvasa, Maa (T)	6-2/270	11-6-70	8	Hawaii	FA/95	16/16
68	Toviessi, Paul (E)	6-6/260	2-26-78	R	Marshall	D2/01	—
97	Washington, Keith (E)	6-4/275	12-18-72	7	UNLV	FA/01	*16/0
	LINEBACKERS						
59	Crockett, Henri	6-2/238	10-28-74	5	Florida State	UFA/01	*15/12
52	Gold, Ian	6-0/223	8-23-78	2	Michigan	D2a/00	16/0
51	Mobley, John	6-1/236	10-10-73	6	Kutztown (Pa.) University	D1/96	15/14
53	Romanowski, Bill	6-4/245	4-2-66	14	Boston College	UFA/96	16/16
56	Wilson, Al	6-0/240	6-21-77	3	Tennessee	D1/99	15/14
58	Woodall, Lee	6-1/230	10-31-69	8	West Chester (Pa.) University	FA/01	*16/16
	DEFENSIVE BACKS						
26	Brown, Eric (S)	6-0/210	3-20-75	4	Mississippi State	D2/98	16/16
48	Coghill, George (S)	6-0/210	3-30-70	5	Wake Forest	FA/97	16/0
32	Jenkins, Billy (S)	5-10/205	7-8-74	4	Howard	T-St.L./00	16/16
28	Kennedy, Kenoy (S)	6-1/215	11-15-77	2	Arkansas	D2b/00	13/0
20	Lewis, Darryll (CB)	5-9/188	12-16-68	11	Arizona	FA/01	*15/7
23	Middlebrooks, Willie (CB)	6-1/200	2-12-79	R	Minnesota	D1/01	—
24	O'Neal, Deltha (CB)	5-10/196	1-30-77	2	California	D1/00	16/0
	Poole, Tyrone	5-8/188	2-3-72	6	Fort Valley (Ga.) State	T-Car./98	*15/12
31	Pounds, Darryl (CB)	5-10/189	7-21-72	7	Nicholls State	UFA/00	9/0
33	Spencer, Jimmy (CB)	5-9/180	3-29-69	10	Florida	FA/00	16/6
35	Suttle, Jason (CB)	5-10/182	12-2-74	2	Wisconsin	FA/00	5/0
25	Walker, Denard (CB)	6-1/190	8-9-73	5	Louisiana State	UFA/01	*15/14
	SPECIALISTS						
1	Elam, Jason (K)	5-11/200	3-8-70	9	Hawaii	D3b/93	13/0
	Harris, Nick (P)	6-2/221	7-28-76	R	California	D4b/01	—
2	Lindsey, Steve (K)	6-1/185	11-25-74	3	Mississippi	FA/00	16/0
16	Rouen, Tom (P)	6-3/225	6-9-68	9	Colorado	FA/93	16/0

*Not with Broncos in 2000.

Other free agent veterans invited to camp: DE Bert Berry, CB DeAuntae Brown, DT Jerry Johnson, LB Antonio London, QB Ronnie McAda, LB Ricardo McDonald, WR Muneer Moore, T Chris Ruhman, CB Cordell Taylor, WR Ryan Thelwell.

Abbreviations: D1—draft pick, first round; SD-2—supplemental draft pick, second round; W—claimed on waivers; T—obtained in trade; PlanB—Plan B free-agent acquisition; FA—free-agent acquisition (other than Plan B); UFA—unconditional free agent acquisition; ED—expansion draft pick.

MISCELLANEOUS TEAM DATA

Stadium (capacity, surface):
Invesco Field at Mile High
(76,125, grass)
Business address:
13655 Broncos Parkway
Englewood, CO 80112
Business phone:
303-649-9000
Ticket information:
To be announced
Team colors:
Orange, navy blue and white
Flagship radio station:
KOA, 850 AM
Training site:
University of Northern Colorado
Greeley, Colo.
303-623-5212

TSN REPORT CARD

Coaching staff	B +	Mike Shanahan remains one of the game's premier offensive minds. He and offensive coordinator Gary Kubiak put together game plans that leave other teams reeling. But the loss of offensive line coach Alex Gibbs is huge (he will work as a part-time "consultant" in 2001), and new defensive coordinator Ray Rhodes will be on the hot seat as he attempts to beef up the Broncos' weak link.
Quarterbacks	A -	Brian Griese shut up his critics with a sizzling performance in 2000. He was one of the league's smartest, most efficient quarterbacks and his 102.9 passer rating proved it. Now he must prove he can carry his team an entire season on his fragile right shoulder. In Gus Frerotte, the Broncos have a reliable backup.
Running backs	A	With three quality backs to choose from, the Broncos running game is in good hands. If Mike Anderson or Olandis Gary is the primary back, The running game will be better than good. If Terrell Davis returns anywhere close to his old form, the running game will be great again.
Wide receivers	B +	In Rod Smith and Ed McCaffrey, Denver may have the NFL's best one-two punch. Each of them are coming off of 100-reception seasons. Moreover, they block like demons. The big question is who will be receiver No. 3. It's an ongoing question the Broncos haven't answered during Shanahan's tenure.
Offensive line	B	Three key figures, coach Alex Gibbs, left tackle Tony Jones and left guard Mark Schlereth are gone for good. How Denver's line adjusts to the shock is one of the key questions of its season. Lennie Friedman should be able to fill Schlereth's shoes, but the talented Matt Lepsis must prove he can fill the big hole at left tackle.
Defensive line	C +	The Broncos are betting that castoffs Leon Lett and Chester McGlockton still have some games in them. The hope is that they will free up Pro Bowl left tackle Trevor Pryce to do his thing. What the Broncos really need is a dominate, pass-rushing defensive end. They still don't have one, unless Lett makes a quantum leap when he moves outside.
Linebackers	A -	A strong, athletic unit with few questions. The biggest is Bill Romanowski's age, but the additions of Lee Woodall and Henri Crockett gives the Broncos excellent depth. Expect John Mobley to have a big year now that he's a full season removed from knee surgery. The player of the future is Ian Gold, the second-year man out of Michigan.
Secondary	C -	The weakest link last season and the biggest question mark this season is the secondary. The acquisition of Denard Walker was a good start, but the other cornerback spot remains vulnerable—for this season at least. Denver's safeties have to be more than big hitters, they have to be sure tacklers.
Special teams	B +	Punter Nick Harris, a fourth-round draft choice, gives the Broncos a chance to pin teams against the goal line. After last season's back injury, Jason Elam should regain his place as an elite place-kicker. And if Deltha O'Neal ever cuts loose and follows his instincts, the return game will blossom.

DETROIT LIONS
NFC CENTRAL DIVISION

2001 SEASON

CLUB DIRECTORY

Chairman and owner
William Clay Ford
Vice chairman
William Clay Ford, Jr.
President and CEO
Matt Millen
Senior vice president
Bill Keenist
Senior vice president
Kevin Warren
Asst. to president/finance & special projects
Kent Newhart
V.p. of stadium dev. and salary cap
Tom Lewand
Executive director of player personnel
Bill Tobin
V.p. of corporate sales & sponsorships
Steve Harms
V.p. of finance and chief financial officer
Tom Lesnau
V.p. of ticket sales/operations
Jennifer Manzo
Secretary
David Hempstead
Dir. of football administration/staff counsel
Martin Mayhew
Sr. director of community affairs
Tim Pendell
Director of media relations
Matt Barnhart
Director of pro personnel
Sheldon White
Director of college scouting
Scott McEwen
Pro and college scouts
Russ Bollinger   Chad Henry
Lance Newmark   Charlie Sanders
Dave Uyrus
Hessley Hempstead (BLESTO)
Head athletic trainer
Al Bellamy
Physicians
Kyle Anderson   Keith Burch
David Collon

Head coach
Marty
Mornhinweg

Assistant coaches
Jason Arapoff (strength and
   conditioning)
Malcolm Blacken (assistant strength
   and conditioning)
Maurice Carthon (running backs)
Don Clemons (defensive
   assistant/quality control)
Charles Haley (asst. defensive
   line/pass rush specialist)
Kevin Higgins (quarterbacks)
Larry Kirksey (wide receivers)
Sean Kugler (tight ends)
Carl Mauck (offensive line)
Mike McHugh (offensive
   assistant/quality control)
Glenn Pires (linebackers)
Chuck Priefer (special teams)
Richard Selcer (defensive backs)
Vince Tobin (defensive coordinator)
Bill Young (defensive line)

Equipment manager
Mark Glenn
Video director
Steve Hermans
Groundskeeper
Charlie Coffin
Director of security
Allen Hughes
Director of broadcasting & new media
Bryan Bender
Director of ticket operations
Mark Graham

SCHEDULE

Sept. 9—	at Green Bay	1:00
Sept. 16—	DALLAS	1:00
Sept. 23—	at Cleveland	12:00
Sept. 30—	Open date	
Oct. 8—	ST. LOUIS (Mon.)	9:00
Oct. 14—	at Minnesota	1:00
Oct. 21—	TENNESSEE	1:00
Oct. 28—	CINCINNATI	1:00
Nov. 4—	at San Francisco	4:05
Nov. 11—	TAMPA BAY	1:00
Nov. 18—	at Arizona	4:15
Nov. 22—	GREEN BAY (Thanks.)	12:30
Dec. 2—	at Chicago	1:00
Dec. 9—	at Tampa Bay	1:00
Dec. 16—	MINNESOTA	1:00
Dec. 23—	at Pittsburgh	1:00
Dec. 30—	CHICAGO	1:00

All times are Eastern.
All games Sunday unless noted.

DRAFT CHOICES

Jeff Backus, T, Michigan (first round/
18th pick overall).
Dominic Raiola, C, Nebraska (2/50).
Shaun Rogers, DT, Texas (2/61).
Scotty Anderson, WR, Grambling
(5/148).
Mike McMahon, QB, Rutgers (5/149).
Jason Glenn, LB, Texas A&M (6/173).

2000 REVIEW

RESULTS

Sept. 3—	at New Orleans	W	14-10
Sept.10—	WASHINGTON	W	15-10
Sept.17—	TAMPA BAY	L	10-31
Sept.24—	at Chicago	W	21-14
Oct. 1—	MINNESOTA	L	24-31
Oct. 8—	GREEN BAY	W	31-24
Oct. 15—	Open date		
Oct. 19—	at Tampa Bay	W	28-14
Oct. 29—	at Indianapolis	L	18-30
Nov. 5—	MIAMI	L	8-23
Nov. 12—	ATLANTA	W	13-10
Nov. 19—	at N.Y. Giants	W	31-21
Nov. 23—	NEW ENGLAND	W	34-9
Nov. 30—	at Minnesota	L	17-24
Dec. 10—	at Green Bay	L	13-26
Dec. 17—	at N.Y. Jets	W	10-7
Dec. 24—	CHICAGO	L	20-23

RECORDS/RANKINGS

2000 regular-season record: 9-7 (3rd in
NFC Central); 3-5 in division; 7-5 in conference; 4-4 at home; 5-3 on road.
Team record last five years: 36-44 (.450,
ranks 23rd in league in that span).

2000 team rankings:	No.	NFC	NFL
Total offense	*276.4	14	27
Rushing offense	*109.2	10	20
Passing offense	*167.2	13	25
Scoring offense	307	10	22
Total defense	*314.6	6	14
Rushing defense	*113.9	8	18
Passing defense	*200.6	7	15
Scoring defense	307	6	11
Takeaways	42	1	3
Giveaways	31	8	20
Turnover differential	11	2	7
Sacks	28	12	26
Sacks allowed	53	13	T26

*Yards per game.

TEAM LEADERS

Scoring (kicking): Jason Hanson, 101
pts. (29/29 PATs, 24/30 FGs).
Scoring (touchdowns): James Stewart,
72 pts. (10 rushing, 1 receiving, 3 2-pt.
conv.).
Passing: Charlie Batch, 2,489 yds. (412
att., 221 comp., 53.6%, 13 TDs, 15 int.).
Rushing: James Stewart, 1,184 yds. (339
att., 3.5 avg., 10 TDs).
Receptions: Johnnie Morton, 61 (788
yds., 12.9 avg., 3 TDs).
Interceptions: Kurt Schulz, 7 (53 yds., 0
TDs).
Sacks: Robert Porcher, 8.0.
Punting: John Jett, 43.5 avg. (93 punts,
4,044 yds., 2 blocked).
Punt returns: Desmond Howard, 14.7
avg. (31 att., 457 yds., 1 TD).
Kickoff returns: Desmond Howard, 24.6
avg. (57 att., 1,401 yds., 0 TDs).

DETROIT LIONS

No.	QUARTERBACKS	Ht./Wt.	Born	NFL Exp.	College	How acq.	'00 Games GP/GS
10	Batch, Charlie	6-2/220	12-5-74	4	Eastern Michigan	D2b/98	15/15
9	Harbaugh, Jim	6-3/215	12-23-63	15	Michigan	UFA/01	*7/5
	McMahon, Mike	6-2/213	2-8-79	R	Rutgers	D5b/01	—
	RUNNING BACKS						
21	Droughns, Reuben	5-11/207	8-21-78	2	Oregon	D3/00	0/0
33	Irvin, Sedrick	5-11/226	3-30-78	3	Michigan State	D4/99	6/0
31	Lee, Amp	5-11/200	10-1-71	10	Florida State	FA/01	*3/0
26	Olivo, Brock (FB)	6-0/232	6-24-76	4	Missouri	FA/98	13/0
30	Schlesinger, Cory (FB)	6-0/246	6-23-72	7	Nebraska	D6b/95	16/8
34	Stewart, James	6-1/226	12-27-71	7	Tennessee	UFA/00	16/16
25	Warren, Lamont	5-11/202	1-4-73	7	Colorado	FA/01	0/0
	RECEIVERS						
	Anderson, Scotty	6-2/184	11-24-79	R	Grambling State	D5a/01	—
89	Banta, Bradford (TE)	6-6/255	12-14-70	8	Southern California	UFA/01	*16/0
82	Crowell, Germane	6-3/216	9-13-76	4	Virginia	D2a/98	9/7
17	Foster, Larry	5-10/196	11-7-76	2	Louisiana State	FA/00	10/0
80	Howard, Desmond	5-10/185	5-15-70	10	Michigan	FA/99	15/0
48	Mitchell, Pete (TE)	6-2/248	10-9-71	7	Boston College	UFA/01	*14/5
84	Moore, Herman	6-4/224	10-20-69	11	Virginia	D1/91	15/11
87	Morton, Johnnie	6-0/190	10-7-71	8	Southern California	D1/94	16/16
86	Sloan, David (TE)	6-6/260	6-8-72	7	New Mexico	D3/95	15/10
	OFFENSIVE LINEMEN						
74	Atkins, James (T)	6-6/306	1-28-70	7	Southwestern Louisiana	UFA/00	2/1
76	Backus, Jeff (T)	6-5/308	9-21-77	R	Michigan	D1/01	—
79	Beverly, Eric (C)	6-3/294	3-28-74	4	Miami of Ohio	FA/97	16/7
65	Blaise, Kerlin (G)	6-5/323	12-25-74	4	Miami (Fla.)	FA/98	12/0
71	Gibson, Aaron (T)	6-4/380	9-27-77	3	Wisconsin	D1b/99	10/10
75	Joyce, Matt (G)	6-7/305	3-30-72	7	Richmond	FA/01	*13/13
73	McDougle, Stockar (T)	6-6/350	1-11-77	2	Oklahoma	D1/00	8/8
51	Raiola, Dominic (C)	6-1/303	12-30-78	R	Nebraska	D2a/01	—
	Roberts, Ray (T)	6-6/320	6-3-69	9	Virginia	FA/96	10/10
66	Stai, Brenden (G)	6-4/312	3-30-72	7	Nebraska	FA/00	*16/16
	DEFENSIVE LINEMEN						
95	DeVries, Jared (E)	6-4/280	6-11-76	3	Iowa	D3/99	15/1
94	Elliss, Luther (T)	6-5/305	3-22-73	7	Utah	D1/95	16/16
96	Hall, James (E)	6-2/271	2-4-77	2	Michigan	FA/00	5/0
98	Jones, James (T)	6-2/295	2-6-69	11	Northern Iowa	UFA/99	16/16
67	Kirschke, Travis (E)	6-3/287	9-6-74	5	UCLA	FA/97	13/0
91	Porcher, Robert (E)	6-3/282	7-30-69	10	South Carolina State	D1/92	16/16
92	Rogers, Shaun (T)	6-4/331	3-12-79	R	Texas	D2b/01	—
97	Scroggins, Tracy (E)	6-3/273	9-11-69	10	Tulsa	D2a/92	16/15
	LINEBACKERS						
55	Aldridge, Allen	6-1/254	5-30-72	8	Houston	UFA/98	16/14
57	Boyd, Stephen	6-0/242	8-22-72	7	Boston College	D5a/95	15/15
50	Claiborne, Chris	6-3/255	7-26-78	3	Southern California	D1a/99	16/14
	Glenn, Jason	6-0/231	8-20-79	R	Texas A&M	D6/01	—
54	Green, Barrett	6-0/217	10-29-77	2	West Virginia	D2/00	9/0
52	Kowalkowski, Scott	6-2/220	8-23-68	11	Notre Dame	FA/94	16/2
58	Kriewaldt, Clint	6-1/236	3-17-76	3	Wisconsin-Stevens Point	D6/99	13/1
	DEFENSIVE BACKS						
	Bailey, Robert	5-10/182	9-3-68	10	Miami (Fla.)	FA/01	*16/0
39	Campbell, Lamar (CB)	5-11/183	8-29-76	4	Wisconsin	FA/98	16/2
23	Fair, Terry (CB)	5-9/184	7-20-76	4	Tennessee	D1/98	15/15
24	Lyght, Todd (CB)	6-0/190	2-9-69	11	Notre Dame	UFA/01	*14/12
28	Rice, Ron (S)	6-1/217	11-9-72	7	Eastern Michigan	FA/95	14/14
45	Schulz, Kurt (S)	6-1/208	12-12-68	10	Eastern Washington	UFA/00	11/11
29	Supernaw, Kywin (S)	6-1/207	6-2-75	4	Indiana	FA/98	13/3
32	Westbrook, Bryant (CB)	6-0/198	12-19-74	5	Texas	D1/97	13/13
35	Wyrick, Jimmy (CB)	5-9/179	12-31-76	2	Minnesota	FA/00	6/0
	SPECIALISTS						
4	Hanson, Jason (K)	5-11/182	6-17-70	10	Washington State	D2b/92	16/0
19	Jett, John (P)	6-0/197	11-11-68	9	East Carolina	UFA/97	16/0

*Not with Lions in 2000.
Other free agent veterans invited to camp: QB Cory Sauter.
Abbreviations: D1—draft pick, first round; SD-2—supplemental draft pick, second round; W—claimed on waivers; T—obtained in trade; PlanB—Plan B free-agent acquisition; FA—free-agent acquisition (other than Plan B); UFA—unconditional free agent acquisition; ED—expansion draft pick.

MISCELLANEOUS TEAM DATA

Stadium (capacity, surface):
Pontiac Silverdome
(80,311, artificial)
Business address:
1200 Featherstone Road
Pontiac, MI 48342
Business phone:
248-335-4131
Ticket information:
248-335-4151
Team colors:
Honolulu blue and silver
Flagship radio station:
WXYT, 1270 AM
Training site:
Saginaw Valley State University
Saginaw, Mich.
248-972-3700

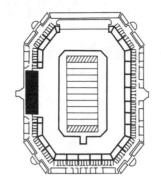

TSN REPORT CARD

Coaching staff	B	It's hard to judge at this point because everybody is new, but they have a definite plan of action and everything is geared toward that attitude and philosophy. Marty Mornhinweg is his own offensive coordinator so there should be a lot of creativity in the play-calling.
Quarterbacks	C -	After three years of being the starter, Charlie Batch is still unknown. Injuries have hampered his progress during each season, especially in 2000, and his development has been stunted. He has the tools to be very effective in a West Coast offense, but he hasn't shown he can do it yet.
Running backs	C	James Stewart is an effective running back, but he'll have to show more skills as a receiver in the West Coast offense. He was pulled for a third-down back last season, but the new system uses nickel plays in all situations. Fullback Cory Schlesinger must improve his receiving skills.
Receivers	B -	Germane Crowell and Johnnie Morton are consistent and can make big plays, but didn't get many opportunities last season. This offense places a premium on running after the catch and they both do that well. There will be a glaring lack of experienced backup help if Herman Moore doesn't return—unless Jerry Rice is signed.
Offensive line	D	Yes, there's a significant upgrade in young talent, but four of the five projected starters haven't played a full NFL season yet. Also, right tackle Aaron Gibson has been sidelined for all or part of the last two years with shoulder problems. These guys should be better, but it'll take time.
Defensive line	D	That grade reflects their production last season, not their talent, which would be considerably higher. Defensive end Robert Porcher sets the tone for this group and if his mind is right, this unit could be dominating. First, though, Detroit must find a complete player for the right side.
Linebackers	C -	A solid group against the run, but they don't have a lot of speed and can be vulnerable against the pass. Stephen Boyd is dependable in the middle while weak side backer Chris Claiborne has to be more consistent. He's still young, though, and could develop into a force.
Secondary	B	Bryant Westbrook is expected to return 100 percent from Achilles tendon surgery and, with the addition of free agent Todd Lyght, the Lions are in excellent shape. The situation at safety is also very good but, as the Lions proved last year, their production falls off considerably when they can't stay healthy.
Special teams	A	They'll give up a big play from time to time, but over the course of the season all of these units play at a consistently high level. Kicker Jason Hanson is in the midst of his prime while return specialist Desmond Howard has proved that he still has a lot of high-octane in his tank.

GREEN BAY PACKERS
NFC CENTRAL DIVISION

GREEN BAY PACKERS

2001 SEASON

CLUB DIRECTORY

President/chief executive officer
Robert E. Harlan
Executive assistant to the president
Phil Pionek
Senior v.p. of administration
John Jones
Vice president/general counsel
Lance Lopes
Vice president of football operations
Mark Hatley
Corporate security officer
Jerry Parins
Director of administrative affairs
Mark Schiefelbein
Executive director/public relations
Lee Remmel
Associate director/public relations
Jeff Blumb
Asst. director of p.r./travel coordinator
Aaron Popkey
Director/marketing
Jeff Cieply
Exe. dir. of player programs & comm. affairs
Edgar Bennett
Director of community relations
Jeanne McKenna
Director of family programs
Sherry Schuldes
Ticket director
Mark Wagner
Vice president of personnel
Ken Herock
Dir. of player finance/football ops.
Andrew Brandt
Dir. of football admin./asst. to the g.m.
Bruce Warwick
Pro personnel director
Reggie McKenzie
Pro personnel assistant
Vince Workman
Scouting coordinator
Danny Mock
Assistant director of college scouting
Shaun Herock
Scouts
John 'Red' Cochran, Lee Gissendaner, Brian Gutekunst, Alonzo Highsmith, Marc Lillibridge, Lenny McGill, Sam Seale
Video director
Bob Eckberg

General manager/ head coach
Mike Sherman

Assistant coaches
Larry Beightol (offensive line)
Darrell Bevell (offensive assistant/ quality control)
Sylvester Croom (running backs)
Ed Donatell (defensive coordinator)
Stan Drayton (off. quality control/ special teams assistant)
Jethro Franklin (defensive line)
Jeff Jagodzinski (tight ends)
Mark Lovat (strength and conditioning assistant)
Brad Miller (def. asst./quality control)
Frank Novak (special teams)
Bo Pelini (linebackers)
Tom Rossley (offensive coordinator)
Barry Rubin (strength & conditioning)
Pat Ruel (assistant offensive line)
Ray Sherman (wide receivers)
Bob Slowik (defensive backs)
Lionel Washington (defensive backs assistant)

Equipment manager
Gordon 'Red' Batty
Assistant equipment manager
Tom Bakken   Brian Nehring
Head trainer
Pepper Burruss
Assistant trainers
Bryan Engel   Kurt Fielding
Building supervisor
Ted Eisenreich
Fields supervisor
Allen Johnson

SCHEDULE

Sept. 9—	DETROIT	1:00
Sept. 16—	at N.Y. Giants	1:00
Sept. 24—	WASHINGTON (Mon.)	9:00
Sept. 30—	at Carolina	1:00
Oct. 7—	at Tampa Bay	4:15
Oct. 14—	BALTIMORE	1:00
Oct. 21—	at Minnesota	4:15
Oct. 28—	Open date	
Nov. 4—	TAMPA BAY	1:00
Nov. 11—	at Chicago	1:00
Nov. 18—	ATLANTA	1:00
Nov. 22—	at Detroit (Thanks.)	12:30
Dec. 3—	at Jacksonville (Mon.)	9:00
Dec. 9—	CHICAGO	1:00
Dec. 16—	at Tennessee	4:15
Dec. 23—	CLEVELAND	1:00
Dec. 30—	MINNESOTA	1:00

All times are Eastern.
All games Sunday unless noted.

DRAFT CHOICES

Jamal Reynolds, DE, Florida State (first round/10th pick overall).
Robert Ferguson, WR, Texas A&M (2/41).
Bhawoh Jue, DB, Penn State (3/71).
Torrance Marshall, LB, Oklahoma (3/72).
Bill Ferrario, G, Wisconsin (4/105).
David Martin, TE, Tennessee (6/198).

2000 REVIEW

RESULTS

Sept. 3—N.Y. JETS	L	16-20
Sept.10—at Buffalo	L	18-27
Sept.17—PHILADELPHIA	W	6-3
Sept.24—at Arizona	W	29-3
Oct. 1—CHICAGO	L	24-27
Oct. 8—at Detroit	L	24-31
Oct. 15—SAN FRANCISCO	W	31-28
Oct. 22—Open date		
Oct. 29—at Miami	L	20-28
Nov. 6—MINNESOTA (OT)	W	26-20
Nov. 12—at Tampa Bay	L	15-20
Nov. 19—INDIANAPOLIS	W	26-24
Nov. 27—at Carolina	L	14-31
Dec. 3—at Chicago	W	28-6
Dec. 10—DETROIT	W	26-13
Dec. 17—at Minnesota	W	33-28
Dec. 24—TAMPA BAY (OT)	W	17-14

RECORDS/RANKINGS

2000 regular-season record: 9-7 (3rd in NFC Central); 5-3 in division; 8-4 in conference; 6-2 at home; 3-5 on road.
Team record last five years: 54-26 (.675, ranks T2nd in league in that span).
2000 team rankings:

	No.	NFC	NFL
Total offense	*332.6	7	15
Rushing offense	*102.7	12	23
Passing offense	*229.9	4	8
Scoring offense	353	6	11
Total defense	*316.8	7	15
Rushing defense	*101.1	2	8
Passing defense	*215.7	10	19
Scoring defense	323	8	14
Takeaways	28	8	19
Giveaways	33	T9	T21
Turnover differential	-5	9	T20
Sacks	38	T7	T19
Sacks allowed	34	T4	T10

*Yards per game.

TEAM LEADERS

Scoring (kicking): Ryan Longwell, 131 pts. (32/32 PATs, 33/38 FGs).
Scoring (touchdowns): Ahman Green, 78 pts. (10 rushing, 3 receiving).
Passing: Brett Favre, 3,812 yds. (580 att., 338 comp., 58.3%, 20 TDs, 16 int.).
Rushing: Ahman Green, 1,175 yds. (263 att., 4.5 avg., 10 TDs).
Receptions: Bill Schroeder, 65 (999 yds., 15.4 avg., 4 TDs).
Interceptions: Darren Sharper, 9 (109 yds., 0 TDs).
Sacks: John Thierry, 6.5.
Punting: Josh Bidwell, 38.5 avg. (78 punts, 3,003 yds., 0 blocked).
Punt returns: Allen Rossum, 8.6 avg. (29 att., 248 yds., 0 TDs).
Kickoff returns: Allen Rossum, 25.8 avg. (50 att., 1,288 yds., 1 TD).

GREEN BAY PACKERS

No.	QUARTERBACKS	Ht./Wt.	Born	NFL Exp.	College	How acq.	'00 Games GP/GS
4	Favre, Brett	6-2/225	10-10-69	11	Southern Mississippi	T-Atl./92	16/16
18	Pederson, Doug	6-3/220	1-31-68	9	Northeast Louisiana	FA/01	*11/8
	RUNNING BACKS						
29	Goodman, Herbert	5-11/203	8-31-77	2	Graceland College (Iowa)	FA/00	5/0
30	Green, Ahman	6-0/217	2-16-77	4	Nebraska	T-Sea./00	16/11
33	Henderson, William (FB)	6-1/253	2-19-71	7	North Carolina	D3b/95	16/6
25	Levens, Dorsey	6-1/230	5-21-70	8	Georgia Tech	D5b/94	5/5
22	Parker, De'Mond	5-10/185	12-24-76	3	Oklahoma	D5a/99	8/0
44	Snider, Matt (FB)	6-2/240	1-26-76	3	Richmond	W-Car./99	16/0
	RECEIVERS						
85	Bradford, Corey	6-1/197	12-8-75	4	Jackson State	D5/98	2/2
81	Davis, Tyrone (TE)	6-4/260	6-30-72	6	Virginia	T-NYJ/97	14/9
80	Driver, Donald	6-0/177	2-2-75	3	Alcorn State	D7b/99	16/2
89	Ferguson, Robert	6-1/209	12-17-79	R	Texas A&M	D2/01	—
88	Franks, Bubba (TE)	6-6/260	1-6-78	2	Miami (Fla.)	D1/00	16/13
86	Freeman, Antonio	6-1/198	5-27-72	7	Virginia Tech	D3d/95	15/15
82	Lee, Charles	6-2/202	11-19-77	2	Central Florida	D7c/00	15/1
	Martin, David	6-3/214	3-13-79	R	Tennessee	D6/01	—
84	Schroeder, Bill	6-3/205	1-9-71	6	Wisconsin-La Crosse	FA/96	16/16
	OFFENSIVE LINEMEN						
76	Clifton, Chad (T)	6-5/325	6-26-76	2	Tennessee	D2/00	13/10
61	Curry, Scott (T)	6-5/300	12-25-75	3	Montana	D6b/99	0/0
60	Davis, Rob (C)	6-3/286	12-10-68	6	Shippensburg (Pa.)	FA/97	16/0
72	Dotson, Earl (T)	6-4/317	12-17-70	9	Texas A&I	D3/93	2/2
	Flanigan, Jim (T)	6-2/288	8-27-71	7	Notre Dame	FA/01	*16/14
63	Ferrario, Bill (G)	6-2/313	9-22-78	R	Wisconsin	D4/01	—
58	Flanagan, Mike (C)	6-5/297	11-10-73	6	UCLA	D3a/96	16/2
69	Mercier, Richard (G)	6-3/300	5-13-75	2	Miami (Fla.)	W-Den./00	0/0
62	Rivera, Marco (G)	6-4/310	4-26-72	6	Penn State	D6/96	16/16
79	Stokes, Barry (T)	6-4/310	12-20-73	4	Eastern Michigan	FA/00	8/0
65	Tauscher, Mark (T)	6-3/313	6-17-77	2	Wisconsin	D7a/00	16/14
68	Wahle, Mike (G)	6-6/310	3-29-77	4	Navy	SD-2/98	16/6
52	Winters, Frank (C)	6-3/305	1-23-64	15	Western Illinois	UFA/92	14/14
	DEFENSIVE LINEMEN						
96	Bowens, David (E)	6-2/261	7-3-77	3	Western Illinois	T-Den./00	14/0
93	Brown, Gilbert (T)	6-2/339	2-22-71	8	Kansas	W-Min./93	0/0
71	Dotson, Santana (T)	6-5/285	12-19-69	10	Baylor	UFA/96	12/11
94	Gbaja-Biamila, Kabeer (E)	6-4/245	9-24-77	2	San Diego State	D5a/00	7/0
90	Holliday, Vonnie (E)	6-5/290	12-11-75	4	North Carolina	D1/98	12/9
97	Hunt, Cletidus (T)	6-4/299	1-2-76	3	Kentucky State	D3b/99	16/11
98	Lyon, Billy (E)	6-5/295	12-10-73	4	Marshall	FA/97	11/1
67	Maryland, Russell (T)	6-1/308	3-22-69	11	Miami (Fla.)	FA/00	16/16
99	Reynolds, Jamal (E)	6-3/266	2-20-79	R	Florida State	D1/01	—
91	Thierry, John (E)	6-4/262	9-4-71	8	Alcorn State	UFA/00	16/16
95	Warren, Steve (T)	6-1/298	1-22-78	2	Nebraska	D3/00	13/0
	LINEBACKERS						
59	Diggs, Na'il	6-4/234	7-8-78	2	Ohio State	D4a/00	13/12
57	Gizzi, Chris	6-0/235	3-8-75	2	Air Force	W-Den./00	11/0
55	Harris, Bernardo	6-2/246	10-15-71	7	North Carolina	FA/95	16/16
51	Marshall, Torrance	6-2/245	6-12-77	R	Oklahoma	D3b/01	—
56	McCaslin, Eugene	6-1/226	7-12-77	1	Florida	D7d/00	1/0
56	Morton, Mike	6-4/235	3-28-72	6	North Carolina	UFA/00	16/0
54	Wayne, Nate	6-0/230	1-12-75	4	Mississippi	T-Den./00	16/13
50	Williams, K.D.	6-0/235	4-21-73	3	Henderson State (Ark.)	T-NO/00	16/3
	DEFENSIVE BACKS						
31	Akins, Chris (S)	5-11/195	11-29-76	3	Arkansas-Pine Bluff	W-Dal./00	10/0
21	Berry, Gary (S)	5-11/199	10-24-77	2	Ohio State	D4c/00	4/0
36	Butler, LeRoy (S)	6-0/203	7-19-68	12	Florida State	D2/90	16/16
25	Darden, Tony (CB)	5-11/193	8-11-75	3	Texas Tech	W-SD/01	*16/3
24	Edwards, Antuan (CB)	6-1/205	5-26-77	3	Clemson	D1/99	12/3
21	Jue, Bhawoh (CB)	6-0/197	5-24-79	R	Penn State	D3a/01	—
27	McBride, Tod (S)	6-1/207	1-26-76	3	UCLA	W-Sea./99	15/6
43	McGarrahan, Scott (S)	6-1/198	2-12-74	4	New Mexico	D6a/98	16/0
34	McKenzie, Mike (CB)	6-0/190	4-26-76	3	Memphis	D3a/99	10/8
20	Rossum, Allen (CB)	5-8/178	10-22-75	4	Notre Dame	T-Phi./00	16/0
42	Sharper, Darren (S)	6-2/205	11-3-75	5	William & Mary	D2/97	16/16
37	Williams, Tyrone (CB)	5-11/193	5-31-73	6	Nebraska	D3b/96	16/16
	SPECIALISTS						
9	Bidwell, Josh (P)	6-3/225	3-13-76	2	Oregon	D4b/99	16/0
8	Longwell, Ryan (K)	6-0/198	8-16-74	5	California	W-SF/97	16/0

*Not with Packers in 2000.

Other free agent veterans invited to camp: QB Henry Burris, LB Vernon Crawford, CB Gana Joseph, WR Anthony Lucas, RB Rondell Mealey, G Glen Rountree, C Tom Schau, CB Hurley Tarver.

Abbreviations: D1—draft pick, first round; SD-2—supplemental draft pick, second round; W—claimed on waivers; T—obtained in trade; PlanB—Plan B free-agent acquisition; FA—free-agent acquisition (other than Plan B); UFA—unconditional free agent acquisition; ED—expansion draft pick.

MISCELLANEOUS TEAM DATA

Stadium (capacity, surface):
Lambeau Field
(60,890, grass)
Business address:
P.O. Box 10628
Green Bay, WI 54307-0628
Business phone:
920-496-5700
Ticket information:
920-496-5719
Team colors:
Dark green, gold and white
Flagship radio station:
WTMJ, 620 AM
Training site:
St. Norbert College
West De Pere, Wis.
920-496-5700

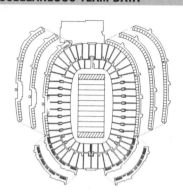

TSN REPORT CARD

Coaching staff	B	This will be a critical year for Mike Sherman and his staff. Sherman will be balancing duties as general manager and head coach and there will be times when his assistants will have to take on a bigger burden. Sherman did a great job last year of keeping together a team decimated by injury. But this year the expectations are a lot higher and he must prove he can take a team to a higher level. His offensive know-how will be put to the test after a year in which the team didn't score consistently until the end of the season. Opposing coaches have had an off-season to study defensive coordinator Ed Donatell's system and so his challenge will be to stay a step ahead.
Quarterbacks	B +	As long as he has weapons around him, Brett Favre is going to make things happen. He might not be as elusive as he once was, but he is showing more maturity and is not trying to do it all by himself as much. The backup position isn't settled after Matt Hasselbeck was traded to Seattle and could be a problem area if it is not upgraded before training camp.
Running backs	B +	The days of having more than one option are back. Ahman Green is a 1,000-yard rusher and should continue to improve. Dorsey Levens is good enough to start, but his career is still in limbo because of knee problems. Together, the two would be a perfect complement of speed and power. The return of Rondell Mealey from a knee injury should provide insurance if Levens can't play. The fullback position is solid with William Henderson and Matt Snider.
Receivers	C -	This is a totally unproven group. Antonio Freeman is at a crossroads in his career and must get his act together or face being phased out. Corey Bradford is being counted on for big things, but he has not been able to stay healthy. Bill Schroeder is the incumbent starter at split end but has been rather ordinary. Much will be expected of rookie Robert Ferguson, who has the size and strength to be effective over the middle. There's no sign tight end Bubba Franks is ready to break out yet.
Offensive line	B	This could be the best group the club has had in more than a decade. But a couple of things have to be settled. First, right tackle Earl Dotson has to show his back is healthy enough for him to start. Then, a decision has to be made whether to move Mark Tauscher from right tackle to left guard. Having Dotson and Tauscher together in the lineup would be ideal. Mike Flanagan is penciled in to replace Frank Winters at center and should add more athletic ability. Left tackle Chad Clifton will have to avoid a letdown after having a terrific rookie season.
Defensive line	C -	Much will be expected from rookie end Jamal Reynolds, but there's only so much a single speed rusher can add. It will be imperative that end Vonnie Holliday take a big step forward and become an effective pass rusher. The inside positions are a problem with Santana Dotson and Steve Warren recovering from injury and Russell Maryland increasing in age. Cletidus Hunt could be a big contributor inside if he doesn't have to rotate from end to tackle. This group set the tone for the defense last year with its hustle, but it didn't provide much pass rush.
Linebackers	C	The coaches think strongside linebacker Na'il Diggs is headed for stardom. They will increase his role so that he does more than just shadow the tight end. Nate Wayne takes over on the weakside full-time and will have to be more assignment-sure. He is active but can be overrun at the line of scrimmage. Bernardo Harris has been consistent in the middle, but will get some pressure from rookie Torrance Marshall, a tremendous athlete who needs a lot of work on the scheme.
Secondary	B +	A lot will depend on whether safety Darren Sharper has the same kind of year. He was dominant last year as a blitzer, run-stuffer and deep coverage man. He's the one guy in the division who can give Randy Moss a run for his money. The cornerback position is solid if Mike McKenzie can stay healthy. There is depth at the corner position but not at safety. The club can't afford an injury at the latter. Overall, this group should be able to hold up if the coaches decide to blitz a lot again.
Special teams	B -	Kicker Ryan Longwell makes this group. He is consistent and effective in poor weather. The same can't be said for punter Josh Bidwell, who struggled in his first year. He will be under pressure to be more consistent and will receive competition from rookie Kevin Stemke. The return game is in good hands with Allen Rossum and the coverage units should get a boost with the addition of rookie linebacker Marshall.

INDIANAPOLIS COLTS
AFC EASTERN DIVISION

CLUB DIRECTORY

Owner and CEO
James Irsay
President
Bill Polian
Senior executive v.p.-administration
Pete Ward
Senior vice president
Bob Terpening
General counsel
Daniel Luther
Vice president of finance
Kurt Humphrey
Vice president of ticket operations
Larry Hall
Controller
Herm Stonitsch
Vice president of public relations
Craig Kelley
Assistant director of public relations
Ryan Robinson
Sponsorship accounting manager
Brad Beery
Director of football operations
Dom Anile
Director of pro player personnel
Clyde Powers
Director of college scouting
Mike Butler
Director of pro scouting
Chris Polian
Director of player development
Steve Champlin
College scouts
David Caldwell
Tom Gamble
Bo Guarani
Byron Lusby
Paul Roell
Tom Telesco
Todd Vasvari

Head coach
Jim Mora

Assistant coaches
George Catavolos (asst. head
coach/defensive secondary)
Vic Fangio (def. coordinator)
Todd Grantham (defensive line)
Richard Howell (asst. strength
& conditioning)
Gene Huey (running backs)
John Hufnagel (quarterbacks)
Tony Marciano (tight ends)
Tom Moore (off. coordinator)
Howard Mudd (offensive line)
Mike Murphy (linebackers)
Jay Norvell (receivers)
John Pagano (def. assistant)
Kevin Spencer (special teams)
Jon Torine (strength &
conditioning)

Equipment manager
Jon Scott
Video director
Marty Heckscher
Head trainer
Hunter Smith
Assistant equipment manager
Mike Mays
Assistant trainers
Dave Hammer
Dave Walston

SCHEDULE

Sept. 9—	at N.Y. Jets	1:00
Sept. 16—	DENVER	1:00
Sept. 23—	BUFFALO	1:00
Sept. 30—	at New England	1:00
Oct. 7—	Open date	
Oct. 14—	OAKLAND	8:30
Oct. 21—	NEW ENGLAND	1:00
Oct. 28—	at Kansas City	1:00
Nov. 4—	at Buffalo	4:15
Nov. 11—	MIAMI	1:00
Nov. 18—	at New Orleans	1:00
Nov. 25—	SAN FRANCISCO	1:00
Dec. 2—	at Baltimore	1:00
Dec. 10—	at Miami	9:00
Dec. 16—	ATLANTA	1:00
Dec. 23—	N.Y. JETS	8:30
Dec. 30—	at St. Louis	1:00

All times are Eastern.
All games Sunday unless noted.

DRAFT CHOICES

Reggie Wayne, WR, Miami, Fla. (first round/30th pick overall).
Idrees Bashir, DB, Memphis (2/37).
Cory Bird, DB, Virginia Tech (3/91).
Ryan Diem, G, Northern Illinois (4/118).
Raymond Walls, DB, Southern Mississippi (5/152).
Jason Doering, DB, Wisconsin (6/193).
Rick DeMulling, G, Idaho (7/220).

2000 REVIEW

RESULTS

Sept. 3—at Kansas City	W	27-14
Sept.10—OAKLAND	L	31-38
Sept.17—Open date		
Sept.25—JACKSONVILLE	W	43-14
Oct. 1—at Buffalo	W	18-16
Oct. 8—at New England	L	16-24
Oct. 15—at Seattle	W	37-24
Oct. 22—NEW ENGLAND	W	30-23
Oct. 29—DETROIT	W	30-18
Nov. 5—at Chicago	L	24-27
Nov. 12—N.Y. JETS	W	23-15
Nov. 19—at Green Bay	L	24-26
Nov. 26—MIAMI	L	14-17
Dec. 3—at N.Y. Jets	L	17-27
Dec. 11—BUFFALO	W	44-20
Dec. 17—at Miami	W	20-13
Dec. 24—MINNESOTA	W	31-10
Dec. 30—at Miami (OT)*	L	17-23

*AFC wild-card game.

RECORDS/RANKINGS

2000 regular-season record: 10-6 (2nd in AFC East); 5-3 in division; 8-4 in conference; 6-2 at home; 4-4 on road.
Team record last five years: 38-42 (.475, ranks T18th in league in that span).

2000 team rankings:

	No.	AFC	NFL
Total offense	*383.8	2	3
Rushing offense	*116.2	10	16
Passing offense	*267.6	1	2
Scoring offense	429	3	4
Total defense	*334.8	12	21
Rushing defense	*120.9	14	25
Passing defense	*213.9	7	15
Scoring defense	326	7	15
Takeaways	22	T14	T25
Giveaways	29	T10	T15
Turnover differential	-7	13	22
Sacks	42	T6	T12
Sacks allowed	20	T1	T1

*Yards per game.

TEAM LEADERS

Scoring (kicking): Mike Vanderjagt, 121 pts. (46/46 PATs, 25/27 FGs).
Scoring (touchdowns): Edgerrin James, 110 pts. (13 rushing, 5 receiving, 1 2-pt. conv.).
Passing: Peyton Manning, 4,413 yds. (571 att., 357 comp., 62.5%, 33 TDs, 15 int.).
Rushing: Edgerrin James, 1,709 yds. (387 att., 4.4 avg., 13 TDs).
Receptions: Marvin Harrison, 102 (1,413 yds., 13.9 avg., 14 TDs).
Interceptions: Jeff Burris, 4 (38 yds., 1 TD).
Sacks: Chad Bratzke, 7.5.
Punting: Hunter Smith, 44.7 avg. (65 punts, 2,906 yds., 0 blocked).
Punt returns: Terrence Wilkins, 8.3 avg. (29 att., 240 yds., 0 TDs).
Kickoff returns: Jerome Pathon, 22.4 avg. (26 att., 583 yds., 0 TDs).

TRAINING CAMP ROSTER

INDIANAPOLIS COLTS

No.	QUARTERBACKS	Ht./Wt.	Born	NFL Exp.	College	How acq.	'00 Games GP/GS
12	Hobert, Billy Joe	6-3/230	1-8-71	7	Washington	UFA/00	0/0
18	Manning, Peyton	6-5/225	3-24-76	4	Tennessee	D1/98	16/16
	RUNNING BACKS						
33	al-Jabbar, Abdul-Karim	5-10/205	6-28-74	4	UCLA	UFA/00	1/0
36	Finn, Jim	6-0/235	12-9-76	2	Pennsylvania	FA/00	16/1
30	Gordon, Lennox	6-0/201	4-9-78	3	New Mexico	FA/99	9/0
32	James, Edgerrin	6-0/214	8-1-78	3	Miami (Fla.)	D1/99	16/16
43	McDougal, Kevin	5-11/203	5-18-77	2	Colorado State	FA/00	6/0
	RECEIVERS						
85	Dilger, Ken (TE)	6-5/253	2-2-71	7	Illinois	D2/95	16/16
84	Green, E.G.	5-11/188	6-28-75	4	Florida State	D3/98	7/0
88	Harrison, Marvin	6-0/178	8-25-72	6	Syracuse	D1/96	16/16
83	Keur, Josh (TE)	6-4/270	9-4-76	2	Michigan State	FA/99	1/0
86	Pathon, Jerome	6-0/182	12-16-75	4	Washington	D2/98	16/10
81	Pollard, Marcus (TE)	6-4/252	2-8-72	7	Bradley	FA/95	16/14
48	Snow, Justin (TE)	6-3/234	12-21-76	2	Baylor	FA/00	16/0
87	Wayne, Reggie	6-0/197	11-17-78	R	Miami (Fla.)	D1/01	—
80	Wilkins, Terrence	5-8/178	7-29-75	3	Virginia	FA/99	14/7
	OFFENSIVE LINEMEN						
54	Armour, Phillip (C)	6-3/318	12-9-76	1	North Texas State	FA/99	3/0
	DeMulling, Rick (G)	6-4/313	7-21-77	R	Idaho	D7/01	—
71	Diem, Ryan (G)	6-6/332	7-1-79	R	Northern Illinois	D4/01	—
78	Glenn, Tarik (T)	6-5/332	5-25-76	5	California	D1/97	16/16
74	Jackson, Waverly (G)	6-2/315	12-19-72	4	Virginia Tech	FA/98	16/0
76	McKinney, Steve (G)	6-4/295	10-15-75	4	Texas A&M	D4/98	16/16
73	Meadows, Adam (T)	6-5/295	1-25-74	5	Georgia	D2/97	16/16
50	Moore, Larry (G)	6-2/296	6-1-75	4	Brigham Young	FA/98	16/16
63	Saturday, Jeff (C)	6-2/293	6-8-75	3	North Carolina	FA/99	16/16
	DEFENSIVE LINEMEN						
93	Barnes, Lionel (E)	6-4/274	4-19-76	3	Northeast Louisiana	W-St.L./00	2/0
92	Bratzke, Chad (E)	6-5/272	9-15-71	8	Eastern Kentucky	UFA/99	16/16
79	Holsey, Bernard	6-2/286	12-10-73	6	Duke	UFA/00	16/13
62	Johnson, Ellis (T)	6-2/288	10-30-73	7	Florida	D1/95	13/13
95	King, Shawn (E)	6-3/275	6-24-72	6	Northeast Louisiana	UFA/99	0/0
65	Miller, Brandon (T)	6-0/299	11-27-75	2	Georgia	FA/00	1/0
91	Nwokorie, Chukie (E)	6-3/280	7-10-75	3	Purdue	FA/99	1/0
97	Peter, Christian (T)	6-3/292	10-5-72	5	Nebraska	UFA/01	*16/15
99	Scioli, Brad (E)	6-3/274	9-6-76	3	Penn State	D5/99	16/2
90	Thomas, Mark (E)	6-5/265	5-6-69	10	North Carolina State	W-Chi./98	14/1
96	Williams, Josh (T)	6-3/284	8-9-76	2	Michigan	D4/00	14/7
	LINEBACKERS						
54	Glover, Phil	5-11/241	12-17-75	2	Utah	FA/00	9/0
94	Morris, Rob	6-2/238	1-18-75	2	Brigham Young	D1/00	7/0
52	Peterson, Mike	6-1/232	6-17-76	3	Florida	D2/99	16/16
98	Sword, Sam	6-1/245	12-9-74	3	Michigan	FA/00	3/0
55	Thomas, Ratcliff	6-0/240	1-2-74	4	Maryland	FA/98	12/0
53	Washington, Marcus	6-3/255	10-17-77	2	Auburn	D2/00	16/0
	DEFENSIVE BACKS						
47	Austin, Billy	5-10/195	3-8-75	2	New Mexico	FA/98	16/0
	Bashir, Idrees	6-2/206	12-7-78	R	Memphis	D2/01	—
41	Bird, Cory	5-10/216	8-10-78	R	Virginia Tech	D3/01	—
26	Blevins, Tony	6-0/165	1-29-75	3	Kansas	W-SF/98	16/1
20	Burris, Jeff	6-0/190	6-7-72	8	Notre Dame	UFA/98	16/16
37	Cota, Chad	6-0/196	8-8-71	7	Oregon	UFA/99	16/16
	Doering, Jason	6-0/200	4-22-78	R	Wisconsin	D6/01	—
27	Macklin, David	5-9/193	7-14-78	2	Penn State	D3/00	16/2
21	Muhammad, Mustafah	5-9/180	10-19-73	3	Fresno State	FA/99	13/3
	Walls, Raymond (CB)	5-10/175	7-24-79	R	Southern Mississippi	D5/01	—
	SPECIALISTS						
7	Kight, Danny (K)	6-1/214	8-18-71	3	Augusta (Ga.) State	FA/99	16/0
17	Smith, Hunter (P)	6-2/212	8-9-77	3	Notre Dame	D7a/99	16/0
13	Vanderjagt, Mike (K)	6-5/210	3-24-70	4	West Virginia	FA/98	16/0

*Not with Colts in 2000.

Other free agent veterans invited to camp: DB Rodregis Brooks, DB Clifton Crosby, WR Drew Haddad, DT Rob Renes.

Abbreviations: D1—draft pick, first round; SD-2—supplemental draft pick, second round; W—claimed on waivers; T—obtained in trade; PlanB—Plan B free-agent acquisition; FA—free-agent acquisition (other than Plan B); UFA—unconditional free agent acquisition; ED—expansion draft pick.

MISCELLANEOUS TEAM DATA

Stadium (capacity, surface):
RCA Dome (56,500, artificial)
Business address:
P.O. Box 535000
Indianapolis, IN 46253
Business phone:
317-297-2658
Ticket information:
317-297-7000
Team colors:
Royal blue and white
Flagship radio stations:
WNDE, 1260 AM
WFBQ, 94.5 FM
Training site:
Rose Hulman Technical Institute
Terre Haute, Ind.
317-297-2658

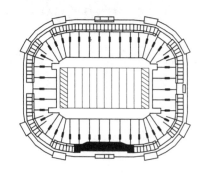

TSN REPORT CARD

Coaching staff:	B	Coach Jim Mora needs to break his 0-for-6 playoff drought, but the man on the spot is defensive coordinator Vic Fangio. His group must elevate its play even though Fangio will rely on several new faces, many of them rookies.
Quarterbacks:	A -	Peyton Manning is as good as it gets, and there is every reason to believe he's going to get better. And what better time for the kid from New Orleans to lead his team to the Super Bowl? It will be played in the Big Easy next January.
Running backs:	A -	The last player to lead the league in rushing for three consecutive seasons was Dallas' Emmitt Smith (1991-93). Anyone want to bet against another Florida native, Edgerrin James, being the next? The guy with dreadlocks, gold teeth and a perpetual motor shows no sign of slowing down.
Receivers:	B +	Marvin Harrison has totaled 220 catches, 3,076 yards and 26 TDs the past two years. Imagine the numbers he'll tack up if first-round draft pick Reggie Wayne can help eliminate the double-teaming tactics of defenses. Few teams have a better tight-end duo than the Colts' Ken Dilger and Marcus Pollard.
Offensive line:	B +	It's hard to imagine how an offense can be so explosive and send three skill players to the Pro Bowl, yet no one from the trenches gets recognized. The tackle tandem of Tarik Glenn and Adam Meadows is a solid one.
Defensive line:	C	Whether the front four can be an effective unit largely rests with the contributions of left tackle Christian Peter, an offseason pickup from the Giants, and left end Shawn King, who returns after missing the 2000 season.
Linebackers:	C -	So much youth, so many questions. The corps should be OK, if middle linebacker Rob Morris is fully recovered from a ruptured quadriceps tendon in his right knee and if strongside linebacker Marcus Washington can replace Cornelius Bennett. There is no question that weakside linebacker Mike Peterson is the real deal.
Secondary:	C -	Another area where uncertainty abounds. left cornerback Jeff Burris and strong safety Chad Cota return, but either Mustafah Muhammad or David Macklin must emerge at right cornerback and second-round draft pick Idrees Bashir must step in at free safety. The majority of the backups lack pro experience.
Special teams:	B	Mike Vanderjagt is the most accurate kicker in NFL history (89.3 percent), his 49-yard miss in overtime in the playoffs at Miami notwithstanding. P Hunter Smith is a solid complement. However, the return and coverage teams need to be upgraded.

JACKSONVILLE JAGUARS
AFC CENTRAL DIVISION

2001 SEASON

CLUB DIRECTORY

Chairman & CEO
Wayne Weaver
Senior vice president/football operations
Michael Huyghue
Senior v.p./marketing
Dan Connell
Vice president/chief financial officer
Bill Prescott
V.p., administration/general counsel
Paul Vance
Exec. dir of comm. & broadcasting
Dan Edwards
Director of player personnel
Rick Reiprish
Director of pro scouting
Fran Foley
Director of college scouting
Gene Smith
Director of finance
Kim Dodson
Director of football operations
Skip Richardson
Director of information technology
Bruce Swindell
Director of corporate sponsorship
Macky Weaver
Director of special events
Bo Reed
Director of ticket sales
Steve Swetoha
Director of ticket operations
Tim Bishko
Head athletic trainer
Mike Ryan
Video director
Mike Perkins
Equipment manager
Drew Hampton

Head coach
Tom Coughlin

Assistant coaches
John Bonamego (assistant
  special teams)
Perry Fewell (secondary)
Greg Finnegan (asst. strength &
  conditioning)
Frank Gansz (special teams
  coordinator)
Paul Haynes (def. quality control)
Fred Hoaglin (tight ends)
Jerald Ingram (running backs)
Mike Maser (offensive line)
Garrick McGee (off. qual. control)
John McNulty (wide receivers)
Gary Moeller (def. coordinator)
Jerry Palmieri (strength &
  conditioning)
John Pease (assistant head
  coach/defensive line)
Bob Petrino (off. coordinator)
Lucious Selmon (outside line-
  backers)
Steve Szabo (inside linebackers)

SCHEDULE

Sept. 9—	PITTSBURGH	1:00
Sept. 16—	at Chicago	4:15
Sept. 23—	TENNESSEE	1:00
Sept. 30—	CLEVELAND	4:15
Oct. 7—	at Seattle	4:05
Oct. 14—	Open date	
Oct. 18—	BUFFALO (Thur.)	8:30
Oct. 28—	at Baltimore	1:00
Nov. 4—	at Tennessee	2:00
Nov. 11—	CINCINNATI	1:00
Nov. 18—	at Pittsburgh	4:05
Nov. 25—	BALTIMORE	1:00
Dec. 3—	GREEN BAY (Mon.)	9:00
Dec. 9—	at Cincinnati	1:00
Dec. 16—	at Cleveland	1:00
Dec. 23—	at Minnesota	4:15
Dec. 30—	KANSAS CITY	1:00

All times are Eastern.
All games Sunday unless noted.

DRAFT CHOICES

Marcus Stroud, DT, Georgia (first round/
13th pick overall).
Maurice Williams, T, Michigan (2/43).
Eric Westmoreland, LB, Tennessee
(3/73).
James Boyd, DB, Penn State (3/94).
David Leaverton, P, Tennessee (5/142).
Chad Ward, G, Washington (6/170).
Anthony Denman, LB, Notre Dame
(7/213).
Marlon McCree, DB, Kentucky (7/233).
Richmond Flowers, WR, UT Chattanooga
(7/235).
Randy Chevrier, DT, McGill (7/241).

2000 REVIEW

RESULTS

Sept. 3—at Cleveland	W	27-7	
Sept.10—at Baltimore	L	36-39	
Sept.17—CINCINNATI	W	13-0	
Sept.25—at Indianapolis	L	14-43	
Oct. 1—PITTSBURGH	L	13-24	
Oct. 8—BALTIMORE	L	10-15	
Oct. 16—at Tennessee	L	13-27	
Oct. 22—WASHINGTON	L	16-35	
Oct. 29—at Dallas (OT)	W	23-17	
Nov. 5—Open date			
Nov. 12—SEATTLE	L	21-28	
Nov. 19—at Pittsburgh	W	34-24	
Nov. 26—TENNESSEE	W	16-13	
Dec. 3—CLEVELAND	W	48-0	
Dec. 10—ARIZONA	W	44-10	
Dec. 17—at Cincinnati	L	14-17	
Dec. 23—at N.Y. Giants	L	25-28	

RECORDS/RANKINGS

2000 regular-season record: 7-9 (4th in
AFC Central); 5-5 in division; 5-7 in conference; 4-4 at home; 3-5 on road.
Team record last five years: 52-28 (.650),
ranks 4th in league in that span).

2000 team rankings:

	No.	AFC	NFL
Total offense	*355.6	4	7
Rushing offense	*127.0	7	10
Passing offense	*228.6	5	9
Scoring offense	367	4	8
Total defense	*302.8	7	12
Rushing defense	*105.3	7	11
Passing defense	*197.5	8	14
Scoring defense	327	8	16
Takeaways	30	T7	T14
Giveaways	29	T10	T15
Turnover differential	1	8	15
Sacks	40	T9	T15
Sacks allowed	54	15	28

*Yards per game.

TEAM LEADERS

Scoring (kicking): Mike Hollis, 105 pts.
(33/33 PATs, 24/26 FGs).
Scoring (touchdowns): Fred Taylor, 84
pts. (12 rushing, 2 receiving).
Passing: Mark Brunell, 3,640 yds. (512
att., 311 comp., 60.7%, 20 TDs, 14 int.).
Rushing: Fred Taylor, 1,399 yds. (292 att.,
4.8 avg., 12 TDs).
Receptions: Jimmy Smith, 91 (1,213
yds., 13.3 avg., 8 TDs).
Interceptions: Rayna Stewart, 2 (37 yds.,
0 TDs); Donovin Darius, 2 (26 yds., 0
TDs); Mike Logan, 2 (14 yds., 0 TDs).
Sacks: Tony Brackens, 7.5.
Punting: Bryan Barker, 42.0 avg. (76
punts, 3,194 yds., 0 blocked).
Punt returns: Reggie Barlow, 6.9 avg. (29
att., 200 yds., 0 TDs).
Kickoff returns: Shyrone Stith, 23.8 avg.
(33 att., 785 yds., 0 TDs).

JACKSONVILLE JAGUARS

No.	QUARTERBACKS	Ht./Wt.	Born	NFL Exp.	College	How acq.	'00 Games GP/GS
8	Brunell, Mark	6-1/217	9-17-70	9	Washington	T-GB/95	16/16
10	Martin, Jamie	6-2/208	2-8-70	7	Weber State	UFA/00	5/0
12	Quinn, Jonathon	6-6/239	2-27-75	4	Middle Tennessee State	D3/98	1/0
	RUNNING BACKS						
34	Mack, Stacey (FB)	6-1/237	6-26-75	3	Temple	FA/99	6/2
33	Stith, Shyrone	5-7/206	4-2-78	2	Virginia Tech	D7c/00	14/0
28	Taylor, Fred	6-1/200	1-27-76	4	Florida	D1a/98	13/13
	RECEIVERS						
80	Brady, Kyle (TE)	6-6/277	1-14-72	7	Penn State	FA/99	16/15
	Dawkins, Sean	6-4/218	2-3-71	9	California	FA/01	*16/16
	Flowers, Richmond	5-11/192	5-4-78	R	UT-Chattanooga	D7b/01	—
88	Jones, Damon (TE)	6-5/266	9-18-74	4	Southern Illinois	D5/97	1/0
87	McCardell, Keenan	6-1/190	1-6-70	10	UNLV	UFA/96	16/16
83	Neufeld, Ryan (TE)	6-4/240	11-22-75	3	UCLA	FA/00	3/0
89	Smith, Emanuel	6-1/210	2-3-76	1	Arkansas	D6/00	1/0
82	Smith, Jimmy	6-1/204	2-9-69	9	Jackson State	FA/95	15/14
81	Soward, R. Jay	5-11/178	1-16-78	2	Southern California	D1/00	13/2
86	Whitted, Alvis	6-0/182	9-4-74	4	North Carolina State	D7a/98	16/3
	OFFENSIVE LINEMEN						
69	Baniewicz, Mark (T)	6-6/304	3-24-77	2	Syracuse	D7e/00	0/0
71	Boselli, Tony (T)	6-7/318	4-17-72	7	Southern California	D1a/95	16/16
64	Koch, Aaron (G)	6-3/300	2-1-78	2	Oregon State	FA/00	8/0
76	Ledford, Dwayne (G)	6-3/295	11-2-76	1	East Carolina	FA/00	*1/0
63	Meester, Brad (G)	6-3/300	3-23-77	2	Northern Iowa	D2/00	16/16
79	Nelson, Reggie (T)	6-3/321	6-23-76	2	McNeese State	FA/00	1/0
73	Smith, Jeff (C)	6-3/316	5-25-73	6	Tennessee	FA/00	14/12
66	Wade, John (C)	6-5/300	1-25-75	4	Marshall	D5/98	2/2
	Ward, Chad (G)	6-4/339	1-12-77	R	Washington	D6/01	—
77	Wiegert, Zach (T)	6-5/310	8-16-72	7	Nebraska	FA/99	8/8
74	Williams, Maurice (T)	6-5/307	1-26-79	R	Michigan	D2/01	—
	DEFENSIVE LINEMEN						
90	Brackens, Tony (E)	6-4/271	12-26-74	6	Texas	D2a/96	16/16
	Chevrier, Randy (T)	6-2/293	6-6-76	R	McGill (Quebec)	D7d/01	—
92	Meier, Rob (E)	6-5/270	8-29-77	2	Washington State	D7b/00	16/0
91	Payne, Seth (T)	6-4/290	2-12-75	5	Cornell	D4/97	16/14
94	Smith, Larry (T)	6-5/284	12-4-74	3	Florida State	D2/99	14/4
95	Spicer, Paul (E)	6-4/271	8-18-75	2	Saginaw Valley State (Mich.)	FA/00	3/0
99	Stroud, Marcus (T)	6-6/317	6-25-78	R	Georgia	D1/01	—
96	Walker, Gary (T)	6-2/301	2-28-73	7	Auburn	UFA/99	15/14
97	Wynn, Renaldo (E)	6-3/288	9-3-74	5	Notre Dame	D1/97	14/14
	LINEBACKERS						
55	Clark, Danny	6-2/240	5-9-77	2	Illinois	D7d/00	16/0
	Denman, Anthony	6-1/237	10-30-79	R	Notre Dame	D7a/01	—
51	Hardy, Kevin	6-4/248	7-24-73	6	Illinois	D1/96	16/16
58	Marts, Lonnie	6-2/250	11-10-68	12	Tulane	FA/99	7/3
56	Nickerson, Hardy	6-2/235	9-1-65	15	California	UFA/00	6/6
54	Pelshak, Troy	6-2/242	3-6-77	3	North Carolina A&T	FA/00	4/0
53	Slaughter, T.J.	6-0/239	2-20-77	2	Southern Mississippi	D3/00	16/7
59	Thomas, Edward	6-0/235	9-27-74	1	Georgia Southern	FA/00	8/0
52	Westmoreland, Eric	5-11/236	3-11-77	R	Tennessee	D3a/01	—
	DEFENSIVE BACKS						
21	Beasley, Aaron (CB)	6-0/195	7-7-73	6	West Virginia	D3/96	14/14
42	Boyd, James (S)	5-11/208	10-17-77	R	Penn State	D3b/01	—
25	Bryant, Fernando (CB)	5-10/176	3-26-77	3	Alabama	D1/99	14/14
29	Craft, Jason (CB)	5-10/178	2-13-76	3	Colorado State	D5/99	16/3
27	Criss, Shad (CB)	5-11/184	1-11-76	2	Missouri	FA/00	3/0
20	Darius, Donovin (S)	6-1/216	8-12-75	4	Syracuse	D1b/98	16/16
37	Lake, Carnell (S)	6-1/213	7-15-67	13	UCLA	UFA/99	0/0
	McCree, Marlon (S)	5-10/187	3-17-77	R	Kentucky	D7b/01	—
24	Miller, Craig (S)	5-11/199	10-4-77	1	Utah State	FA/00	4/2
45	Olson, Erik (S)	6-1/210	1-4-77	2	Colorado State	D7a/00	14/0
41	Thomas, Kiwaukee (CB)	5-11/182	6-19-77	2	Georgia Southern	D5/00	16/3
	SPECIALISTS						
1	Hollis, Mike (K)	5-7/174	5-22-72	7	Idaho	FA/95	12/0
	Leaverton, David (P)	6-3/211	4-1-78	R	Tennessee	D5/01	—
5	Tarle, Jim (K)	6-0/221	12-27-72	2	Arkansas State	FA/00	6/0

*Not with Jaguars in 2000.

Other free agent veterans invited to camp: S Kerry Cooks, TE Lawrence Hart, LB Richard Hogans.

Abbreviations: D1—draft pick, first round; SD-2—supplemental draft pick, second round; W—claimed on waivers; T—obtained in trade; PlanB—Plan B free-agent acquisition; FA—free-agent acquisition (other than Plan B); UFA—unconditional free agent acquisition; ED—expansion draft pick.

MISCELLANEOUS TEAM DATA

Stadium (capacity, surface):
ALLTEL Stadium (73,000, grass)
Business address:
One ALLTEL Stadium Place
Jacksonville, FL 32202
Business phone:
904-633-6000
Ticket information:
904-633-2000
Team colors:
Teal, black and gold
Flagship radio station:
WOKV, 690 AM
Training site:
ALLTEL Stadium
Jacksonville, Fla.
904-633-6000

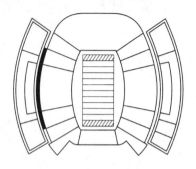

TSN REPORT CARD

Coaching staff	B -	Tom Coughlin is sometimes too conservative, but he did one of his better coaching jobs last season, when the Jaguars started 3-7 but recovered to win four consecutive games and push for a .500 record. A pressing question: What will happen to the defense with Gary Moeller replacing Dom Capers as coordinator?
Quarterbacks	B +	Mark Brunell will turn 31 this season, and although he's not the scrambler he once was, he has turned into a reliable pocket passer. He still needs to prove he can come up big late in big games, but he's still one of the best in the NFL.
Running backs	A	The key to this grade is health. If Fred Taylor isn't hurt, he's one of the best two or three backs in the NFL. He rushed for 1,399 yards in 13 games last season, including a streak of nine consecutive 100-yard games.
Receivers	B +	Again, the key is health. Jimmy Smith underwent two abdominal surgeries in the offseason, and if he's not 100 percent, the offense is in real trouble. If he is fully healthy, the Jaguars have one of the best trios— Smith, Keenan McCardell and tight end Kyle Brady—in the NFL.
Offensive line	B -	Left tackle Tony Boselli is still one of the best in the NFL, but the Jaguars need rookie Maurice Williams to emerge as the starter at right tackle. Zach Wiegert can start at the spot, but the team needs Williams to develop to give them the depth needed for a playoff run.
Defensive line	C +	The grade here could go up in a hurry if defensive tackle Marcus Stroud fulfills his first-round potential. He's a run-stuffer who can occupy blockers, which could free up end Tony Brackens and tackle Gary Walker to return to their '99 pass-rushing form.
Linebackers	C -	Middle linebacker Hardy Nickerson will be 36 next season and outside linebacker Kevin Hardy slipped from his 1999 Pro Bowl form last season. With middle linebacker T. J. Slaughter probably moving to the weak side, the linebacking corps appears too mish-mash.
Secondary	C +	Potentially, this group could be a strength. If safety Carnell Lake can return to his pre-injury form of 1998, he's one of the best safeties in the NFL. Fernando Bryant and Aaron Beasley were hurt last season by a pass rush that never matched its effectiveness of 1999.
Special teams	C +	Punter Bryan Barker wasn't re-signed as a free agent, which hurts the team because he was the only punter in team history and the only holder kicker Mike Hollis ever has had. R. Jay Soward was drafted in the first round in 2000 to be an impact punt returner, but he never developed into that role last season.

KANSAS CITY CHIEFS
AFC WESTERN DIVISION

2001 SEASON

CLUB DIRECTORY

Founder
Lamar Hunt
Chairman of the board
Jack Steadman
President/g.m./chief executive officer
Carl Peterson
Executive vice president/assistant g.m.
Dennis Thum
Senior vice president
Dennis Watley
Secretary/legal
Jim Seigfried
Treasurer and director/finance
Dale Young
Vice president/sales and marketing
Wallace Bennett
Director/operations
Steve Schneider
Director/development
Ken Blume
Director/corporate sponsorship sales
Anita Bailey
Director/sales
Gary Spani
Director/public relations
Bob Moore
Associate director/public relations
Peter Moris
V.p. of football ops. and player personnel
Lynn Stiles
Director of pro personnel
Bill Kuharich
Director of college scouting
Chuck Cook
Scouts
Scott Campbell   Jeff Ireland
Quintin Smith
Trainer
Dave Kendall
Assistant trainer
Bud Epps

Head coach
Dick
Vermeil

Assistant coaches
Irv Eatman (asst. offensive line)
Frank Gansz Jr. (special teams)
Peter Giunta (defensive backs)
Carl Hairston (defensive lines)
Jeff Hurd (strength and
  conditioning)
Charlie Joiner (wide receivers)
Bob Karmelowicz (defensive line)
Billy Long (asst. strength and
  conditioning)
Greg Robinson (def. coordinator)
Keith Rowen (tight ends)
Al Saunders (asst. head coach/
  offensive coordinator)
James Saxon (running backs)
Terry Shea (quarterbacks)
Mike Solari (offensive line)
Jason Verduzco (offensive asst./
  quality control)
Joe Vitt (linebackers)
Darvin Wallis (defensive asst./
  quality control)

Physicians
Cris Barnthouse   Joseph Brewer
Jon Browne   Mike Monaco
Equipment manager
Mike Davidson

SCHEDULE

Sept. 9—	OAKLAND	1:00
Sept. 16—	at Seattle	4:15
Sept. 23—	N.Y. GIANTS	1:00
Sept. 30—	at Washington	1:00
Oct. 7—	at Denver	4:05
Oct. 14—	PITTSBURGH	1:00
Oct. 21—	at Arizona	4:05
Oct. 28—	INDIANAPOLIS	1:00
Nov. 4—	at San Diego	4:15
Nov. 11—	at N.Y. Jets	1:00
Nov. 18—	Open date	
Nov. 25—	SEATTLE	1:00
Nov. 29—	PHILADELPHIA (Thur.)	8:30
Dec. 9—	at Oakland	4:15
Dec. 16—	DENVER	1:00
Dec. 23—	SAN DIEGO	1:00
Dec. 30—	at Jacksonville	1:00

All times are Eastern.
All games Sunday unless noted.

DRAFT CHOICES

Eric Downing, DT, Syracuse (third round/
75th pick overall).
Marvin Minnis, WR, Florida State (3/77).
Monty Beisel, DE, Kansas State (4/107).
George Layne, RB, Texas Christian
(4/108).
Billy Baber, TE, Virginia (5/141).
Derrick Blaylock, RB, Stephen F. Austin
State (5/150).
Alex Sulfsted, T, Miami of Ohio (6/176).
Shaunard Harts, DB, Boise State (7/212).
Terdell Sands, DT, UT Chattanooga
(7/243).

2000 REVIEW

RESULTS

Sept. 3—INDIANAPOLIS	L	14-27
Sept.10—at Tennessee (OT)	L	14-17
Sept.17—SAN DIEGO	W	42-10
Sept.24—at Denver	W	23-22
Oct. 2—SEATTLE	W	24-17
Oct. 8—Open date		
Oct. 15—OAKLAND	L	17-20
Oct. 22—ST. LOUIS	W	54-34
Oct. 29—at Seattle	W	24-19
Nov. 5—at Oakland	L	31-49
Nov. 12—at San Francisco	L	7-21
Nov. 19—BUFFALO	L	17-21
Nov. 26—at San Diego	L	16-17
Dec. 4—at New England	L	24 -30
Dec. 10—CAROLINA	W	15-14
Dec. 17—DENVER	W	20-7
Dec. 24—at Atlanta	L	13-29

RECORDS/RANKINGS

2000 regular-season record: 7-9 (3rd in
AFC West); 5-3 in division; 5-7 in conference; 5-3 at home; 2-6 on road.
Team record last five years: 45-35 (.563,
ranks T8th in league in that span).
2000 team rankings:

	No.	AFC	NFL
Total offense	*350.9	5	8
Rushing offense	*91.6	13	25
Passing offense	*259.3	3	5
Scoring offense	355	5	9
Total defense	*330.0	10	18
Rushing defense	*113.1	10	17
Passing defense	*216.9	10	20
Scoring defense	354	11	19
Takeaways	29	T9	T16
Giveaways	26	T6	T9
Turnover differential	3	7	T11
Sacks	51	2	T4
Sacks allowed	34	7	T10

*Yards per game.

TEAM LEADERS

Scoring (kicking): Todd Peterson, 70 pts.
(25/25 PATs, 15/20 FGs).
Scoring (touchdowns): Derrick Alexander,
60 pts. (10 receiving).
Passing: Elvis Grbac, 4,169 yds. (547 att.,
326 comp., 59.6%, 28 TDs, 14 int.).
Rushing: Tony Richardson, 697 yds. (147
att., 4.7 avg., 3 TDs).
Receptions: Derrick Alexander, 78 (1,391
yds., 17.8 avg., 10 TDs).
Interceptions: James Hasty, 4 (53 yds., 0
TDs).
Sacks: Eric Hicks, 14.0.
Punting: Todd Sauerbrun, 44.6 avg. (82
punts, 3,656 yds., 0 blocked).
Punt returns: Kevin Lockett, 8.0 avg. (26
att., 208 yds., 0 TDs).
Kickoff returns: Mike Cloud, 21.6 avg. (36
att., 779 yds., 0 TDs).

KANSAS CITY CHIEFS

No.	QUARTERBACKS	Ht./Wt.	Born	NFL Exp.	College	How acq.	'00 Games GP/GS
6	Brister, Bubby	6-3/215	8-15-62	15	Northeast Louisiana	UFA/01	*2/0
10	Green, Trent	6-3/215	7-9-70	8	Indiana	T-St.L./01	*8/5
	RUNNING BACKS						
	Blaylock, Derrick	5-9/188	8-23-79	R	Stephen F. Austin State	D5b/01	
34	Cloud, Mike	5-10/205	7-1-75	3	Boston College	D2/99	16/4
31	Holmes, Priest	5-9/205	10-7-73	5	Texas	UFA/01	*16/2
38	Layne, George (FB)	5-11/243	10-9-78	R	Texas Christian	D4b/01	—
22	Moreau, Frank	6-0/223	9-9-76	2	Louisville	D4/00	11/0
49	Richardson, Tony (FB)	6-1/233	12-17-71	7	Auburn	FA/95	16/16
43	Williams, Jermaine	6-0/235	8-14-73	3	Houston	FA/01	*7/0
	RECEIVERS						
82	Alexander, Derrick	6-2/200	11-6-71	8	Michigan	UFA/98	16/16
	Baber, Billy (TE)	6-3/248	1-17-79	R	Virginia	D5a/01	
89	Dunn, Jason (TE)	6-4/260	11-15-73	5	Eastern Kentucky	FA/00	14/2
83	Gammon, Kendall (TE)	6-4/258	10-23-68	10	Pittsburg (Kan.) State	UFA/00	16/0
88	Gonzalez, Tony (TE)	6-4/249	2-27-76	5	California	D1/97	16/16
20	Hall, Dante	5-8/193	9-1-78	2	Texas A&M	D5a/00	5/0
81	Horne, Tony	5-9/173	3-21-76	4	Clemson	FA/01	*11/0
13	Minnis, Marvin	6-1/171	2-6-77	R	Florida State	D3/01	—
84	Morris, Sylvester	6-3/206	10-6-77	2	Jackson State	D1/00	15/14
80	Parker, Larry	6-1/205	7-14-76	3	Southern California	D4/99	16/0
85	Ricks, Mikhael	6-5/237	11-14-74	4	Stephen F. Austin State	FA/00	4/1
87	Thomas, Chris	6-2/190	7-16-71	5	Cal Poly-SLO	UFA/01	*16/0
	OFFENSIVE LINEMEN						
72	Alford, Darnell (T)	6-4/328	6-11-77	2	Boston College	D6/00	1/0
69	Blackshear, Jeff (G)	6-6/316	3-29-69	8	Northeast Louisiana	FA/00	16/15
66	Riley, Victor (T)	6-5/328	11-4-74	4	Auburn	D1/98	16/16
68	Shields, Will (G)	6-3/311	9-15-71	9	Nebraska	D3/93	16/16
70	Spears, Marcus (G)	6-4/312	9-28-71	8	Northwestern State (La.)	FA/97	13/0
	Sulfsted, Alex (T)	6-5/310	12-21-77	R	Miami (Ohio)	D6/01	
76	Tait, John (T)	6-6/305	1-26-75	3	Brigham Young	D1/99	15/15
54	Waters, Brian (C)	6-3/293	2-18-73	2	North Texas	FA/00	6/0
62	Wiegmann, Casey (C)	6-3/285	7-20-75	5	Iowa	UFA/01	*16/10
60	Willis, Donald (G)	6-3/330	7-15-73	4	North Carolina A&T	FA/00	16/2
	DEFENSIVE LINEMEN						
71	Beisel, Monty (E)	6-3/270	8-20-78	R	Kansas State	D4a/01	—
93	Browning, John (T)	6-4/289	9-30-73	6	West Virginia	D3/96	16/16
99	Clemons, Duane (E)	6-5/277	5-23-74	6	California	UFA/00	12/12
	Downing, Eric (T)	6-4/294	9-16-78	R	Syracuse	D3a/01	
98	Hicks, Eric (E)	6-6/286	6-17-76	4	Maryland	FA/98	13/11
90	Martin, Steve (T)	6-4/312	5-31-74	6	Missouri	UFA/00	16/0
75	McCleary, Norris (T)	6-4/305	5-10-77	1	East Carolina	FA/00	3/0
97	Owens, Rich (E)	6-6/275	5-22-72	7	Lehigh	UFA/01	*12/3
95	Ransom, Derrick (T)	6-3/310	9-13-76	4	Cincinnati	D6/98	10/0
	Sands, Terdell (T)	6-6/280	10-31-79	R	Tennessee-Chattanooga	D7b/01	—
92	Williams, Dan (T)	6-4/288	12-15-69	8	Toledo	FA/97	12/10
96	Williams, Tyrone (E)	6-4/292	10-22-72	4	Wyoming	FA/00	13/0
	LINEBACKERS						
35	Atkins, Larry	6-3/225	7-21-75	3	UCLA	D3b/99	15/0
56	Bush, Lew	6-2/247	12-2-69	7	Washington State	FA/00	16/8
59	Edwards, Donnie	6-2/227	4-6-73	6	UCLA	D4/96	16/16
55	George, Ron	6-2/247	3-20-70	8	Stanford	FA/98	16/0
57	Maslowski, Mike	6-1/251	7-11-74	3	Wisconsin-La Crosse	FA/99	16/5
52	O'Neal, Andre	6-1/235	12-12-75	2	Marshall	FA/00	10/0
53	Patton, Marvcus	6-2/237	5-1-67	12	UCLA	UFA/99	16/15
55	Stills, Gary	6-2/235	7-11-74	3	West Virginia	D3a/99	12/0
	DEFENSIVE BACKS						
26	Allen, Taje (CB)	5-11/185	11-6-73	5	Texas	UFA/01	*11/1
24	Bartee, William (CB)	6-1/196	6-25-77	2	Oklahoma	D2/00	16/3
39	Crockett, Ray (CB)	5-10/184	1-5-67	13	Baylor	FA/01	*13/11
41	Dennis, Pat (CB)	6-0/207	6-3-78	2	Louisiana-Monroe	D5b/00	16/13
23	Gray, Carlton (CB)	6-0/202	6-26-71	9	UCLA	FA/99	4/1
	Harts, Shaunard (S)	6-0/200	8-4-78	R	Boise State	D7a/01	—
38	McCullough, George (CB)	5-10/187	2-18-75	3	Baylor	FA/01	*11/0
27	Walker, Bracey (S)	6-0/206	6-11-70	8	North Carolina	FA/98	15/0
44	Warfield, Eric (CB)	6-0/198	3-3-76	4	Nebraska	D7a/98	13/3
25	Wesley, Greg (S)	6-2/208	3-19-76	2	Arkansas-Pine Bluff	D3/00	16/16
21	Woods, Jerome (S)	6-2/207	3-17-73	6	Memphis	D1/96	16/16
	SPECIALISTS						
2	Peterson, Todd (K)	5-10/177	2-4-70	7	Georgia	FA/00	11/0
4	Stryzinski, Dan (P)	6-2/200	5-15-65	12	Indiana	UFA/01	*16/0

*Not with Chiefs in 2000.

Other free agent veterans invited to camp: QB Todd Collins, G Robert Hunt, LB Richard Jordan, LB Kazadi Muandianvita, G Brad Kubik, TE Mark Thomas, DE Jabbar Threats, LB Casey Tisdale.

Abbreviations: D1—draft pick, first round; SD-2—supplemental draft pick, second round; W—claimed on waivers; T—obtained in trade; PlanB—Plan B free-agent acquisition; FA—free-agent acquisition (other than Plan B); UFA—unconditional free agent acquisition; ED—expansion draft pick.

MISCELLANEOUS TEAM DATA

Stadium (capacity, surface):
Arrowhead Stadium
(79,451, grass)
Business address:
One Arrowhead Drive
Kansas City, MO 64129
Business phone:
816-920-9300
Ticket information:
816-920-9400
Team colors:
Red, gold and white
Flagship radio station:
KYYS, 99.7 FM
Training site:
U. of Wisconsin-River Falls
River Falls, Wis.
715-425-4580

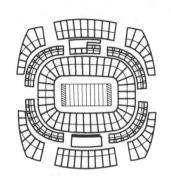

KANSAS CITY CHIEFS

TSN REPORT CARD

Coaching staff	B	Dick Vermeil may have had a couple of rocky seasons in St. Louis, but he eventually got the job done. That has inspired hopes of a similar turnaround in Kansas City. Vermeil assembled a quality staff, led by veterans Al Saunders (offensive coordinator) and Greg Robinson (defensive coordinator).
Quarterbacks	C +	Trent Green did a nice job in Washington in 1998, but that was his last regular gig as a starter. He filled in nicely for Kurt Warner last season, but there are concerns about his surgically repaired knee. The backups are Todd Collins, who hasn't taken a regular-season snap in three years, and 38-year-old journeyman Bubby Brister.
Running backs	B -	Much depends on free agent addition Priest Holmes and fifth-round draft pick Derrick Blaylock. The Chiefs are counting on them to bring speed and quickness to an offense that demands those qualities from its backs. Tony Richardson is a complete player at fullback.
Receivers	B +	Tony Gonzalez is the best receiving tight end in the game. Wide receiver Derrick Alexander should excel in the new offensive system. If Sylvester Morris develops into a consistent player and Tony Horne becomes a dangerous downfield weapon, the Chiefs will have one of the league's best receiving groups.
Offensive line	B	The Chiefs lost two longtime starters in Tim Grunhard and Dave Szott but appear to have made the transition without losing much of a beat. The addition of center Casey Wiegmann and guard Marcus Spears makes the line less physical but more athletic and mobile.
Defensive line	B -	If healthy, the line is capable of big things. But three of the front four starters lost part of last season to injury and those ailments were lingering for end Duane Clemons and tackle Dan Williams. Left end Eric Hicks is healthy and may be headed for a Pro Bowl season.
Linebackers	B -	Weak-side linebacker Donnie Edwards is one of the league's most versatile linebackers and may be more effective as the Chiefs allow him to put more pressure on the quarterback. Marvcus Patton is steady in the middle, but the Chiefs need more from Lew Bush on the strong side.
Secondary	C +	The Chiefs are hoping to get a solid season or two from free-agent addition Ray Crockett at one corner. They have nobody proven on the other side, though Eric Warfield has the potential. Strong safety Greg Wesley and free safety Jerome Woods make a nice combination.
Special teams	C	The Chiefs are counting on several new elements to improve what was a woeful product in 2000. Punter Dan Stryzinski and kickoff returner Tony Horne should make a difference. The Chiefs still had issues to settle on field goals, kickoffs and punt returns.

MIAMI DOLPHINS
AFC EASTERN DIVISION

2001 SEASON

CLUB DIRECTORY

Owner/chairman of the board
H. Wayne Huizenga
President/chief operating officer
Eddie J. Jones
Sr. vice president/business operations
Bryan Wiedmeier
Sr. vice president/finance and admin.
Jill R. Strafaci
Sr. vice president/sales and marketing
Bill Galante
Vice president/player personnel
Rick Spielman
Director of pro personnel
Tom Heckert Jr.
Director of college scouting
Ron Labadie
College scouting coordinator
Adam Engroff
Vice president/media relations
Harvey Greene
Director of media relations
Neal Gulkis
Vice president/sales and marketing
Jim Ross
Director of publications & Internet
Scott Stone
Sr. dir./community & alumni relations
Fudge Browne
Scouts
Tom Braatz, Mike Cartwright, John
Crea, Chris Grier, Anthony Hunt,
Johnathon Stigall, Nate Sullivan
Head trainer
Kevin O'Neill
Trainers
Troy Maurer
Ben Westby

Head coach
Dave Wannstedt

Assistant coaches
Keith Armstrong (special teams)
Jim Bates (defensive coordinator)
Doug Blevins (kicking)
Clarence Brooks (defensive line)
Joel Collier (running backs)
Robert Ford (wide receivers)
Chan Gailey (off. coordinator)
John Gamble (strength &
conditioning)
Judd Garrett (offensive assistant)
Pat Jones (tight ends)
Bill Lewis (defensive nickel package)
Robert Nunn (def. assistant)
Mel Phillips (secondary)
Brad Roll (assistant strength and
conditioning)
Bob Sanders (linebackers)
Mike Shula (quarterbacks)
Tony Wise (offensive line)

Physicians
George Caldwell
Daniel Kanell
Equipment manager
Tony Egues
Video director
Dave Hack

SCHEDULE

Sept.	9— at Tennessee	8:30
Sept.	16— BUFFALO	1:00
Sept.	23— OAKLAND	1:00
Sept.	30— at St. Louis	1:00
Oct.	7— NEW ENGLAND	1:00
Oct.	14— at N.Y. Jets	4:15
Oct.	21— Open date	
Oct.	28— at Seattle	4:15
Nov.	4— CAROLINA	1:00
Nov.	11— at Indianapolis	1:00
Nov.	18— N.Y. JETS	1:00
Nov.	25— at Buffalo	1:00
Dec.	2— DENVER	1:00
Dec.	10— INDIANAPOLIS	9:00
Dec.	16— at San Francisco	4:05
Dec.	22— at New England (Sat.)	12:30
Dec.	30— ATLANTA	1:00

All times are Eastern.
All games Sunday unless noted.

DRAFT CHOICES

Jamar Fletcher, DB, Wisconsin (first round/26th pick overall).
Chris Chambers, WR, Wisconsin (2/52).
Travis Minor, RB, Florida State (3/85).
Morlon Greenwood, LB, Syracuse (3/88).
Shawn Draper, T, Alabama (5/156).
Brandon Winey, T, Louisiana State (6/164).
Josh Heupel, QB, Oklahoma (6/177).
Otis Leverette, DE, Alabama-Birmingham (6/187).
Rick Crowell, LB, Colorado St. (6/188).

2000 REVIEW

RESULTS

Sept. 3—SEATTLE	W	23-0
Sept.10—at Minnesota	L	7-13
Sept.17—BALTIMORE	W	19-6
Sept.24—NEW ENGLAND	W	10-3
Oct. 1—at Cincinnati	W	31-16
Oct. 8—BUFFALO	W	22-13
Oct. 15—Open date		
Oct. 23—at N.Y. Jets (OT)	L	37-40
Oct. 29—GREEN BAY	W	28-20
Nov. 5—at Detroit	W	23-8
Nov. 12—at San Diego	W	17-7
Nov. 19—N.Y. JETS	L	3-20
Nov. 26—at Indianapolis	W	17-14
Dec. 3—at Buffalo	W	33-6
Dec. 10—TAMPA BAY	L	13-16
Dec. 17—INDIANAPOLIS	L	13-20
Dec. 24—at New England	W	27-24
Dec. 30—INDIANAPOLIS (OT)*	W	23-17
Jan. 6—at Oakland†	L	0-27

*AFC wild-card game.
†AFC divisional playoff game.

RECORDS/RANKINGS

2000 regular-season record: 11-5 (1st in AFC East); 5-3 in division; 9-3 in conference; 5-3 at home; 6-2 on road.
Team record last five years: 47-33 (.588, ranks T6th in league in that span).
2000 team rankings:

	No.	AFC	NFL
Total offense	*278.8	13	26
Rushing offense	*118.4	9	14
Passing offense	*160.4	13	27
Scoring offense	323	8	16
Total defense	*289.8	4	6
Rushing defense	*108.5	9	14
Passing defense	*181.3	3	5
Scoring defense	226	3	3
Takeaways	41	3	T4
Giveaways	26	T6	T9
Turnover differential	15	4	5
Sacks	48	3	7
Sacks allowed	28	T4	T5

*Yards per game.

TEAM LEADERS

Scoring (kicking): Olindo Mare, 117 pts. (33/34 PATs, 28/31 FGs).
Scoring (touchdowns): Lamar Smith, 96 pts. (14 rushing, 2 receiving).
Passing: Jay Fiedler, 2,402 yds. (357 att., 204 comp., 57.1%, 14 TDs, 14 int.).
Rushing: Lamar Smith, 1,139 yds. (309 att., 3.7 avg., 14 TDs).
Receptions: Oronde Gadsden, 56 (786 yds., 14.0 avg., 6 TDs).
Interceptions: Brian Walker, 7 (80 yds., 0 TDs).
Sacks: Trace Armstrong, 16.5.
Punting: Matt Turk, 42.1 avg. (92 punts, 3,870 yds., 0 blocked).
Punt returns: Jeff Ogden, 17.0 avg. (19 att., 323 yds., 1 TD).
Kickoff returns: Autry Denson, 24.8 avg. (20 att., 495 yds., 0 TDs).

MIAMI DOLPHINS

No.	QUARTERBACKS	Ht./Wt.	Born	NFL Exp.	College	How acq.	'00 Games GP/GS
9	Fiedler, Jay	6-2/225	12-29-71	6	Dartmouth	UFA/00	15/15
	Heupel, Josh	6-1/216	3-22-78	R	Oklahoma	D6a/01	—
6	Lucas, Ray	6-3/215	8-6-72	4	Rutgers	FA/01	*7/0
4	Quinn, Mike	6-4/215	4-15-74	5	Stephen F. Austin State	FA/00	1/0
	RUNNING BACKS						
28	Denson, Autry	5-10/193	12-8-76	3	Notre Dame	FA/99	11/0
33	Dyer, Deon (FB)	6-0/255	10-2-77	2	North Carolina	D4/00	16/1
32	Johnson, J.J.	6-1/230	4-20-74	3	Mississippi State	D2a/99	13/1
44	Konrad, Rob (FB)	6-3/255	11-12-76	3	Syracuse	D2b/99	15/14
34	Minor, Travis	5-10/194	6-30-79	R	Florida State	D3a/01	—
26	Smith, Lamar	5-11/229	11-29-70	8	Houston	FA/00	15/15
	RECEIVERS						
84	Chambers, Chris	5-11/212	8-12-77	R	Wisconsin	D2/01	—
86	Gadsden, Oronde	6-2/215	8-20-71	4	Winston-Salem	FA/98	16/16
83	Goodwin, Hunter (TE)	6-5/270	10-10-72	6	Texas A&M	FA/99	16/16
48	Heffner-Liddiard, Brody (TE)	6-4/234	6-12-77	2	Colorado	FA/00	5/0
85	Mayes, Alonzo (TE)	6-4/265	6-4-75	4	Oklahoma State	T-Chi./00	*5/3
81	McDuffie, O.J.	5-10/195	12-2-69	9	Penn State	D1/93	9/1
80	McKnight, James	6-1/200	6-17-72	9	Liberty (Va.)	UFA/01	*16/15
88	Ogden, Jeff	6-0/190	2-22-75	4	Eastern Washington	T-Dal./00	16/0
89	Perry, Ed (TE)	6-4/270	9-1-74	5	James Madison	D6d/97	9/0
85	Thomas, Lamar	6-1/170	2-12-70	8	Miami, Fla	FA/96	0/0
87	Ward, Dedric	5-9/185	9-29-74	5	Northern Iowa	UFA/01	*16/16
82	Weaver, Jed (TE)	6-4/246	8-11-76	3	Oregon	W-Phi./00	16/0
	OFFENSIVE LINEMEN						
62	Andersen, Jason (C)	6-6/315	9-3-75	4	Brigham Young	FA/00	*7/0
63	Dixon, Mark (G)	6-4/300	11-26-70	4	Virginia	FA/98	15/15
	Draper, Shawn (T)	6-3/294	7-5-79	R	Alabama	D5/01	—
66	Irwin, Heath (G)	6-4/300	6-27-73	6	Colorado	UFA/00	13/0
75	Perry, Todd (G)	6-5/308	11-28-70	9	Kentucky	UFA/01	*16/16
61	Ruddy, Tim (C)	6-3/305	4-27-72	8	Notre Dame	D2b/94	16/16
74	Smith, Brent (T)	6-5/315	11-21-73	5	Mississippi State	D3d/97	16/2
76	Spriggs, Marcus (T)	6-3/315	5-17-74	5	Houston	UFA/01	*16/11
71	Wade, Todd (T)	6-8/325	10-30-76	2	Mississippi	D2/00	16/16
	Winey, Brandon (T)	6-7/294	1-27-78	R	Louisiana State	D6a/01	—
	DEFENSIVE LINEMEN						
95	Bowens, Tim (T)	6-4/320	2-7-73	8	Mississippi	D1/94	15/15
91	Bromell, Lorenzo (E)	6-6/275	9-23-75	4	Clemson	D4/98	8/0
92	Gardener, Daryl (T)	6-6/315	2-25-73	6	Baylor	D1/96	10/10
97	Grant, Ernest (T)	6-5/310	5-17-76	2	Arkansas-Pine Bluff	D6/00	2/0
94	Haley, Jermaine (T)	6-4/305	2-13-73	2		D7a/99	15/4
	Leverette, Otis (E)	6-6/285	5-31-78	R	Alabama-Birmingham	D6c/01	—
79	Mixon, Kenny (E)	6-4/285	5-31-75	4	Louisiana State	D2b/98	16/16
99	Taylor, Jason (E)	6-6/260	9-1-74	5	Akron	D3a/97	16/16
	LINEBACKERS						
	Crowell, Rick	6-2/238	5-21-77	R	Colorado State	D6c/01	—
58	Galyon, Scott	6-2/245	3-23-74	6	Tennessee	UFA/00	6/1
52	Greenwood, Morlon	6-0/239	7-17-78	R	Syracuse	D3b/01	—
51	Hendricks, Tommy	6-2/231	10-23-78	· 2	Michigan	FA/00	8/0
59	Rodgers, Derrick	6-1/230	10-14-71	5	Arizona State	D3b/97	16/14
56	Russell, Twan	6-1/228	4-25-74	5	Miami, Fla	FA/00	16/2
54	Thomas, Zach	5-11/235	9-1-73	6	Texas Tech	D5c/96	11/11
	DEFENSIVE BACKS						
21	Cousin, Terry (CB)	5-9/182	4-11-75	5	South Carolina	UFA/01	*15/0
24	Fletcher, Jamar (CB)	5-9/177	8-28-79	R	Wisconsin	D1/01	—
27	Freeman, Arturo (S)	6-0/195	10-27-76	2	South Carolina	D5/00	8/0
42	Gamble, Trent (S)	5-9/195	7-24-77	2	Wyoming	FA/00	16/0
20	Kelly, Ben (CB)	5-9/185	9-15-78	2	Colorado	D3/00	2/0
29	Madison, Sam (CB)	5-11/185	4-23-74	5	Louisville	D2/97	16/16
22	Porter, Daryl (CB)	5-9/190	1-16-74	4	Boston College	FA/01	*16/0
23	Surtain, Patrick (CB)	5-11/192	6-19-76	4	Southern Mississippi	D2a/98	16/16
45	Walker, Brian (S)	6-1/205	5-31-72	6	Washington State	UFA/00	16/16
38	Williams, Kevin (S)	6-0/190	8-4-75	4	Oklahoma State	FA/00	11/7
	SPECIALISTS						
10	Mare, Olindo (K)	5-10/195	6-6-73	5	Syracuse	FA/97	16/0
1	Turk, Matt (P)	6-5/250	6-16-68	7	Wisconsin-Whitewater	T-Was./00	16/0

*Not with Dolphins in 2000.

Other free agent veterans invited to camp: WR Brian Alford, WR Ronnie Anderson, G Anthony Cesario, P Chris Hanson, LB Nate Hemsley, LB Tyrus McCloud, T Dan Palmer.

Abbreviations: D1—draft pick, first round; SD-2—supplemental draft pick, second round; W—claimed on waivers; T—obtained in trade; PlanB—Plan B free-agent acquisition; FA—free-agent acquisition (other than Plan B); UFA—unconditional free agent acquisition; ED—expansion draft pick.

MISCELLANEOUS TEAM DATA

Stadium (capacity, surface):
Pro Player Stadium
(75,192, grass)
Business address:
7500 S.W. 30th St.
Davie, FL 33314
Business phone:
954-452-7000
Ticket information:
305-620-2578
Team colors:
Aqua, coral, blue and white
Flagship radio station:
WQAM, 560 AM
Training site:
Nova Southeastern University
Davie, Fla.
954-452-7000

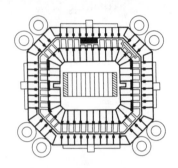

TSN REPORT CARD

Coaching staff	B +	Dave Wannstedt has to prove he can do it in back-to-back years, but he has a very good staff, led by strong coordinators in Chan Gailey and Jim Bates. He lets them coach, and he trusts them, which a lot of head coaches don't do all the time. His motivation skills have been a hit.
Quarterbacks	C +	Forget the Jay Fiedler you saw at the end of last season and look at the one in the middle of the year. He was making enough plays to win and not making bad plays that cost the team wins. If he continues to improve, the Dolphins should be fine. If not, that's why they got Ray Lucas.
Running backs	C	Lamar Smith is still an enigma, and if he can't do it again there's even more questions behind him. J.J. Johnson needs to improve, and the Dolphins need Autry Denson or Travis Minor to develop into a good third-down back. At fullback, they are set with an improving Rob Konrad and second-year man Deon Dyer.
Receivers	B	They have upgraded themselves from a year ago with James McKnight, Dedric Ward and Chris Chambers. This group was missing breakaway speed last year, but they have it with those three. Oronde Gadsden is a tough, sure-handed receiver who can make plays. This group gets a lot better if O.J. McDuffie can contribute.
Offensive line	B	A surprise last year, the success of the team hinges on this group. They got into a rhythm last year, but they have two new starters this year. If Brent Smith can handle the left tackle spot and if Todd Perry provides solid play, then they shouldn't miss a beat.
Defensive line	B +	The Dolphins will miss Trace Armstrong but more for his presence than sacks. Lorenzo Bromell and Kenny Mixon can approach those numbers, and Jason Taylor is a difference maker. On the inside, few are better than Daryl Gardener and Tim Bowens. The key here is depth.
Linebackers	B	Zach Thomas is one of the best middle linebackers in the game, and he should become the team's leader. Don't be fooled by Derrick Rodgers' numbers; he is asked to be steady not spectacular. They need a strong-side backer to step up and depth is a concern.
Secondary	A	Name two corners on the same team better than Sam Madison and Patrick Surtain. You can't. They are the best tandem in the league because of their style of play. Rookie Jamar Fletcher is cut from the same clothe, and there's enough depth. Brian Walker is poised for a big year and Arturo Freeman has all the tools at free safety.
Special teams	B	Olindo Mare is the game's highest-paid kicker for a reason, and when going good Matt Turk is among the best punters. The coverage units are above average, but you''d like to see more from the return teams. New special teams coach Keith Armstrong is under some pressure.

MINNESOTA VIKINGS
NFC CENTRAL DIVISION

2001 SEASON

CLUB DIRECTORY

Owner
Red McCombs
President
Gary Woods
Head coach & v.p. of football operations
Dennis Green
Executive v.p. of business operations
Mike Kelly
Vice president of player personnel
Frank Gilliam
National scout
Jerry Reichow
Director of pro personnel
Richard Solomon
V.p. of football administration
Rob Brzezinski
Player personnel coordinator
Scott Studwell
Vice president of finance
Steve Poppen
Vice president of sales & marketing
Steve LaCroixl
Director of public relations
Bob Hagan
Director of ticket sales
Phil Huebner
Director of operations
Breck Spinner
Equipment manager
Dennis Ryan
Coordinator of medical services
Fred Zamberletti
Head athletic trainer
Chuck Barta

Head coach
Dennis Green

Assistant coaches
Charlie Baggett (wide receivers)
Brian Baker (defensive line)
Dean Dalton (quality control)
Carl Hargrave (running backs)
Chuck Knox Jr. (outside LBs)
Daryl Lawrence (asst. strength & conditioning)
Sherman Lewis (off. coordinator)
Willie Shaw (defensive backs/assistant head coach)
Richard Solomon (defensive backs/asst. head coach)
Emmitt Thomas (defensive coordinator)
John Tice (tight ends)
Mike Tice (off. line/asst. head coach)
Trent Walters (defensive asst.)
Steve Wetzel (strength & conditioning)
Alex Wood (quarterbacks)
Gary Zauner (special teams)

SCHEDULE

Sept. 9—	CAROLINA	1:00
Sept. 17—	at Baltimore (Mon.)	9:00
Sept. 23—	at Chicago	1:00
Sept. 30—	TAMPA BAY	1:00
Oct. 7—	at New Orleans	1:00
Oct. 14—	DETROIT	1:00
Oct. 21—	GREEN BAY	4:15
Oct. 28—	at Tampa Bay	1:00
Nov. 4—	Open date	
Nov. 11—	at Philadelphia	4:15
Nov. 19—	N.Y. GIANTS (Mon.)	9:00
Nov. 25—	CHICAGO	8:30
Dec. 2—	at Pittsburgh	1:00
Dec. 9—	TENNESSEE	1:00
Dec. 16—	at Detroit	1:00
Dec. 23—	JACKSONVILLE	4:15
Dec. 30—	at Green Bay	1:00

All times are Eastern.
All games Sunday unless noted.

DRAFT CHOICES

Michael Bennett, RB, Wisconsin (first round/27th pick overall).
Willie Howard, DE, Stanford (2/57).
Eric Kelly, DB, Kentucky (3/69).
Shawn Worthen, DT, Texas Christian (4/130).
Cedric James, WR, Texas Christian (4/131).
Patrick Chukwurah, LB, Wyoming (5/157).
Carey Scott, DB, Kentucky State (6/189).
Brian Crawford, T, Western Oregon (7/225).

2000 REVIEW

RESULTS

Sept. 3—CHICAGO	W	30-27
Sept.10—MIAMI	W	13-7
Sept.17—at New England	W	21-13
Sept.24—Open date		
Oct. 1—at Detroit	W	31-24
Oct. 9—TAMPA BAY	W	30-23
Oct. 15—at Chicago	W	28-16
Oct. 22—BUFFALO	W	31-27
Oct. 29—at Tampa Bay	L	13-41
Nov. 6—at Green Bay (OT)	L	20-26
Nov. 12—ARIZONA	W	31-14
Nov. 19—CAROLINA	W	31-17
Nov. 23—at Dallas	W	27-15
Nov. 30—DETROIT	W	24-17
Dec. 10—at St. Louis	L	29-40
Dec. 17—GREEN BAY	L	28-33
Dec. 24—at Indianapolis	L	10-31
Jan. 6—NEW ORLEANS*	W	34-16
Jan. 14—at N.Y. Giants†	L	0-41

*NFC divisional playoff game.
†NFC championship game.

RECORDS/RANKINGS

2000 regular-season record: 11-5 (1st in NFC Central); 5-3 in division; 8-4 in conference; 7-1 at home; 4-4 on road.
Team record last five years: 54-26 (.675, ranks T2nd in league in that span).

2000 team rankings:

	No.	NFC	NFL
Total offense	*372.6	3	5
Rushing offense	*133.1	1	6
Passing offense	*239.5	3	7
Scoring offense	397	2	5
Total defense	*356.3	13	28
Rushing defense	*111.8	6	15
Passing defense	*244.6	14	28
Scoring defense	371	11	24
Takeaways	18	15	31
Giveaways	28	5	T13
Turnover differential	-10	T12	T26
Sacks	31	T10	T23
Sacks allowed	35	T6	T13

*Yards per game.

TEAM LEADERS

Scoring (kicking): Gary Anderson, 111 pts. (45/45 PATs, 22/23 FGs).
Scoring (touchdowns): Randy Moss, 92 pts. (15 receiving, 1 2-pt. conv.).
Passing: Daunte Culpepper, 3,937 yds. (474 att., 297 comp., 62.7%, 33 TDs, 16 int.).
Rushing: Robert Smith, 1,521 yds. (295 att., 5.2 avg., 7 TDs).
Receptions: Randy Moss, 77 (1,437 yds., 18.7 avg., 15 TDs).
Interceptions: Kailee Wong, 2 (28 yds., 0 TDs); Robert Tate, 2 (12 yds., 0 TDs).
Sacks: John Randle, 8.0.
Punting: Mitch Berger, 44.7 avg. (62 punts, 2,773 yds., 0 blocked).
Punt returns: Troy Walters, 14.5 avg. (15 att., 217 yds., 0 TDs).
Kickoff returns: Troy Walters, 23.1 avg. (30 att., 692 yds., 0 TDs).

MINNESOTA VIKINGS

No.	QUARTERBACKS	Ht./Wt.	Born	NFL Exp.	College	How acq.	'00 Games GP/GS
	Bouman, Todd	6-2/229	8-1-72	4	St. Cloud State	FA/97	0/0
11	Culpepper, Daunte	6-4/260	1-28-77	3	Central Florida	D1a/99	16/16
	RUNNING BACKS						
23	Bennett, Michael	5-9/211	8-13-78	R	Wisconsin	D1/01	—
34	Chapman, Doug	5-10/213	8-22-77	2	Marshall	D3/00	0/0
40	Kleinsasser, Jim (FB)	6-3/274	1-31-77	3	North Dakota	D2/99	14/8
33	Morrow, Harold (FB)	5-11/232	2-24-73	6	Auburn	W-Dal./96	16/0
21	Williams, Moe	6-1/210	7-26-74	6	Kentucky	D3/96	16/0
	RECEIVERS						
80	Carter, Cris	6-3/208	11-25-65	15	Ohio State	W-Phi./90	16/16
48	Cercone, Matt (TE)	6-5/252	11-30-75	1	Arizona State	FA/99	2/0
87	Chamberlain, Byron (TE)	6-1/264	10-17-71	6	Wayne State (Neb.)	UFA/01	*15/0
89	Davis, John (TE)	6-4/271	5-14-73	5	Emporia (Kan.) State	UFA/00	15/9
83	Jacquet, Nate	6-0/185	9-2-75	4	San Diego State	FA/00	12/0
13	James, Cedric	6-1/199	3-19-76	R	Texas Christian	D4b/01	—
85	Jordan, Andrew (TE)	6-6/263	6-21-72	7	Western Carolina	FA/99	16/4
84	Moss, Randy	6-4/204	2-13-77	4	Marshall	D1/98	16/16
86	Reed, Jake	6-3/213	9-28-67	11	Grambling State	FA/01	*7/6
82	Walters, Troy	5-7/173	12-15-76	2	Stanford	D5/00	12/0
	OFFENSIVE LINEMEN						
74	Badger, Brad (T)	6-4/319	1-11-75	5	Stanford	FA/00	16/0
78	Birk, Matt (C)	6-4/308	7-23-76	4	Harvard	D6/98	16/16
	Crawford, Brian (T)	6-8/315	8-27-77	R	Western Oregon	D7/01	—
71	Dixon, David (G)	6-5/359	1-5-69	8	Arizona State	FA/94	16/16
76	Liwienski, Chris (G)	6-5/321	8-2-75	3	Indiana	FA/99	14/1
77	Stringer, Korey (T)	6-4/335	5-8-74	7	Ohio State	D1b/95	16/16
60	Withrow, Cory (C)	6-2/281	4-5-75	2	Washington State	FA/99	12/0
	DEFENSIVE LINEMEN						
96	Boireau, Michael (E)	6-4/274	7-24-78	2	Miami (Fla.)	D2b/00	0/0
99	Hovan, Chris (T)	6-2/294	5-12-78	2	Boston College	D1/00	16/13
91	Howard, Willie (E)	6-3/298	12-26-77	R	Stanford	D2/01	—
51	Johnstone, Lance (E)	6-4/253	6-11-73	6	Temple	FA/01	*14/9
98	Robbins, Fred (T)	6-4/312	3-25-77	2	Wake Forest	D2a/00	8/0
97	Sawyer, Talance (E)	6-2/270	6-14-76	3	UNLV	D6a/99	16/16
92	Smith, Fernando (E)	6-6/284	8-2-71	8	Jackson State	UFA/00	3/0
95	Worthen, Shawn (T)	6-0/316	9-12-78	4	Texas Christian	D4a/01	—
	LINEBACKERS						
	Chukwurah, Patrick	6-2/238	3-1-79	R	Wyoming	D5/01	—
55	Hall, Lemanski	6-0/235	11-24-70	7	Alabama	UFA/00	15/1
58	McDaniel, Ed	5-11/234	2-23-69	10	Clemson	D5/92	16/15
56	Nelson, Jim	6-1/234	4-16-75	3	Penn State	W-GB/00	16/0
90	Northern, Gabe	6-3/241	6-8-74	6	Louisiana State	FA/00	9/2
57	Palmer, Mitch	6-4/257	9-2-73	4	Colorado State	FA/00	16/0
59	Sauer, Craig	6-1/241	12-13-72	6	Minnesota	UFA/00	9/0
54	Wilson, Antonio	6-2/247	12-29-77	2	Texas A&M-Commerce	D4a/00	1/0
52	Wong, Kailee	6-2/250	5-23-76	4	Stanford	D2/98	16/16
	DEFENSIVE BACKS						
30	Banks, Antonio (CB)	5-10/195	3-12-73	3	Virginia Tech	D4/97	14/0
22	Carter, Tyrone (S)	5-8/190	3-31-76	2	Minnesota	D4b/00	15/7
24	Griffith, Robert (S)	5-11/198	11-30-70	8	San Diego State	FA/94	16/16
25	Kelly, Eric (CB)	5-10/197	1-15-77	R	Kentucky	D3/01	—
31	Morgan, Don (S)	5-11/202	9-18-75	1	Nevada-Reno	FA/99	2/0
41	Scott, Carey (CB)	6-0/180	8-11-78	R	Kentucky State	D6/01	—
29	Serwanga, Wasswa (CB)	5-11/203	7-23-76	3	UCLA	FA/00	7/2
28	Tate, Robert (CB)	5-10/193	10-19-73	5	Cincinnati	D6/97	16/16
42	Thomas, Orlando (S)	6-1/225	10-21-72	7	Southwestern Louisiana	D2a/95	9/9
20	Wright, Kenny (CB)	6-1/205	9-14-77	3	Northwestern (La.) State	D4a/99	16/7
	SPECIALISTS						
1	Anderson, Gary (K)	5-11/170	7-16-59	20	Syracuse	UFA/98	16/0
17	Berger, Mitch (P)	6-4/228	6-24-72	6	Colorado	FA/96	16/0

*Not with Vikings in 2000.

Other free agent veterans invited to camp: OL Jay Humphrey, WR Joey Kent, DB Carl Kidd, OL Mike Malano.

Abbreviations: D1—draft pick, first round; SD-2—supplemental draft pick, second round; W—claimed on waivers; T—obtained in trade; PlanB—Plan B free-agent acquisition; FA—free-agent acquisition (other than Plan B); UFA—unconditional free agent acquisition; ED—expansion draft pick.

MISCELLANEOUS TEAM DATA

Stadium (capacity, surface):
Metrodome (64,121, artificial)
Business address:
9520 Viking Drive
Eden Prairie, MN 55344
Business phone:
952-828-6500
Ticket information:
612-333-8828
Team colors:
Purple, gold and white
Flagship radio station:
KFAN, 1130 AM
Training site:
Minnesota State University-Mankato
Mankato, Minn.
952-828-6500

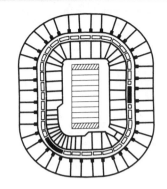

MINNESOTA VIKINGS

TSN REPORT CARD

Coaching staff	A	Dennis Green is simply one of the best coaches in the NFL. He's a great football mind who gets the most out of his team. By now, we've learned not to count him out. Offensive coordinator Sherman Lewis and defensive coordinator Emmitt Thomas are also both good, dedicated teachers. The addition of defensive backs coach Willie Shaw should be a serious upgrade. Offensive line coach Mike Tice is a future head coach.
Quarterback	B +	By this time next year, Daunte Culpepper should be grade A material. This superstar in-the-making is still learning. And that's the scary part. In his first season as a starter, Culpepper was brilliant and parlayed it into a Pro Bowl start. At 6-foot-4, 255 pounds, he can run and throw. Simply a dominant presence.
Running back	C +	Michael Bennett was an excellent draft pick and he should be a very fine player. However, with just one season of college experience the excitement has to be tempered. But the Vikings expect him to be the same type of home-run threat that his retired predecessor Robert Smith was. Fullback Jim Kleinsasser is a fine blocker.
Receivers	A	Cris Carter doesn't age and Randy Moss keeps getting better. Thus, this continues to be the premier wide receiving tandem in the league. Carter says this will be his final season, so you know he'll try to make it a great one. Moss is simply the most exciting player in football. New tight end Byron Chamberlain will get an opportunity to catch a lot of passes.
Offensive line	B -	Like last year, this unit will have new starters. Brad Badger replaces Todd Steussie at left tackle and Chris Liwienski replaces Corbin Lacina at left guard. However, the rest of the line is very stable and very good. Center Matt Birk and right tackle Korey Stringer are Pro Bowl performers and right guard David Dixon is steady.
Defensive line	C -	This is the most intriguing position on the team. Right now, it's not very strong, but it could be decent. New right end Lance Johnstone is a potential 10-plus sack artist and second-round pick Willie Howard could vie to start at either left end or at under tackle. Tackle Chris Hovan was solid as a rookie last year.
Linebackers	C -	Their best linebacker last year, Dwayne Rudd, departed to Cleveland through free agency. Special teamer Craig Sauer will replace him. Outside linebacker Ed McDaniel is aging. Middle linebacker Kailee Wong has talent but he's still learning. There are more questions than answers.
Secondary	F	This is by far the weakest position on the team and by far the weakest secondary in the league. It cost the Vikings several games last year and was humiliated in the NFC championship game in New York. New coach Willie Shaw, a former defensive coordinator in the NFL, has his hands full.
Special teams	B	This is a very aggressive and talented group. The Vikings are one of proudest special teams in the league. Kicker Gary Anderson is ageless and punter Mitch Berger is very solid. However, returner Troy Walters is nothing special.

NEW ENGLAND PATRIOTS
AFC EASTERN DIVISION

2001 SEASON

CLUB DIRECTORY

Chairman and owner
Robert K. Kraft
Vice chairman
Jonathan A. Kraft
Senior v.p. & chief operating officer
Andy Wasynczuk
Assistant director of player personnel
Scott Pioli
Vice president, finance
James Hausmann
Vice president of marketing
Lou Imbriano
V.p., player dev. and com. relations
Donald Lowery
Director of college scouting
Larry Cook
Director of operations
Nick Carparelli
Director of media relations
Stacey James
Controller
Jim Nolan
Director of ticket operations
John Traverse
Corporate sales executive
Jon Levy
General manager of Foxboro Stadium
Dan Murphy
Building services manager
Bernie Reinhart
Head trainer
Ron O'Neil
Equipment manager
Don Brocher

Head coach
Bill Belichick

Assistant coaches
Romeo Crennel (def. coordinator)
Jeff Davidson (asst. off. line)
Ivan Fears (wide receivers)
Eric Mangini (defensive backs)
Randy Melvin (defensive line)
Markus Paul (assistant strength and conditioning)
Dick Rehbein (quarterbacks)
Rob Ryan (linebackers)
Dante Scarnecchia (assistant head coach/offensive line)
Brad Seely (special teams)
Charlie Weis (off. coordinator/ running backs)
Mike Woicik (strength and conditioning)

SCHEDULE

Sept.	9— at Cincinnati	1:00
Sept.	16— at Carolina	1:00
Sept.	23— N.Y. JETS	4:05
Sept.	30— INDIANAPOLIS	1:00
Oct.	7— at Miami	1:00
Oct.	14— SAN DIEGO	1:00
Oct.	21— at Indianapolis	1:00
Oct.	28— at Denver	4:15
Nov.	4— at Atlanta	1:00
Nov.	11— BUFFALO	1:00
Nov.	18— ST. LOUIS	8:30
Nov.	25— NEW ORLEANS	4:05
Dec.	2— at N.Y. Jets	1:00
Dec.	9— CLEVELAND	1:00
Dec.	16— at Buffalo	1:00
Dec.	22— MIAMI (Sat.)	12:30
Dec.	30— Open date	

All times are Eastern.
All games Sunday unless noted.

DRAFT CHOICES

Richard Seymour, DT, Georgia (first round/sixth pick overall).
Matt Light, G, Purdue (2/48).
Brock Williams, DB, Notre Dame (3/86).
Kenyatta Jones, G, South Florida (4/96).
Jabari Holloway, TE, Notre Dame (4/119).
Hakim Akbar, DB, Washington (5/163).
Arther Love, TE, S.C. State (6/180).
Leonard Myers, DB, Miami, Fla. (6/200).
Owen Pochman, K, BYU (7/216).
T.J. Turner, LB, Michigan State (7/239).

2000 REVIEW

RESULTS

Sept. 3—TAMPA BAY	L	16-21
Sept.11—at N.Y. Jets	L	19-20
Sept.17—MINNESOTA	L	13-21
Sept.24—at Miami	L	3-10
Oct. 1—at Denver	W	28-19
Oct. 8—INDIANAPOLIS	W	24-16
Oct. 15—N.Y. JETS	L	17-34
Oct. 22—at Indianapolis	L	23-30
Oct. 29—Open date		
Nov. 5—BUFFALO (OT)	L	13-16
Nov. 12—at Cleveland	L	11-19
Nov. 19—CINCINNATI	W	16-13
Nov. 23—at Detroit	L	9-34
Dec. 4—KANSAS CITY	W	30-24
Dec. 10—at Chicago	L	17-24
Dec. 17—at Buffalo	W	13-10
Dec. 24—MIAMI	L	24-27

RECORDS/RANKINGS

2000 regular-season record: 5-11 (5th in AFC East); 2-6 in division; 5-7 in conference; 3-5 at home; 2-6 on road.
Team record last five years: 43-37 (.538), ranks T12th in league in that span).

2000 team rankings:	No.	AFC	NFL
Total offense	*285.7	12	22
Rushing offense	*86.9	14	26
Passing offense	*198.8	10	19
Scoring offense	276	13	25
Total defense	*334.6	11	20
Rushing defense	*114.4	11	T20
Passing defense	*220.1	11	21
Scoring defense	338	9	17
Takeaways	23	13	24
Giveaways	25	T4	T7
Turnover differential	-2	10	18
Sacks	29	14	25
Sacks allowed	48	12	24

*Yards per game.

TEAM LEADERS

Scoring (kicking): Adam Vinatieri, 106 pts. (25/25 PATs, 27/33 FGs).
Scoring (touchdowns): Terry Glenn, 36 pts. (6 receiving).
Passing: Drew Bledsoe, 3,291 yds. (531 att., 312 comp., 58.8%, 17 TDs, 13 int.).
Rushing: Kevin Faulk, 570 yds. (164 att., 3.5 avg., 4 TDs).
Receptions: Terry Glenn, 79 (963 yds., 12.2 avg., 6 TDs).
Interceptions: Ty Law, 2 (32 yds., 0 TDs); Tebucky Jones, 2 (20 yds., 0 TDs); Lawyer Milloy, 2 (2 yds., 0 TDs).
Sacks: Willie McGinest, 6.0; Greg Spires, 6.0.
Punting: Lee Johnson, 42.7 avg. (89 punts, 3,798 yds., 1 blocked).
Punt returns: Troy Brown, 12.9 avg. (39 att., 504 yds., 1 TD).
Kickoff returns: Kevin Faulk, 21.5 avg. (38 att., 816 yds., 0 TDs).

NEW ENGLAND PATRIOTS

No.	QUARTERBACKS	Ht./Wt.	Born	NFL Exp.	College	How acq.	'00 Games GP/GS
7	Bishop, Michael	6-2/217	5-15-76	3	Kansas State	D7a/99	8/0
11	Bledsoe, Drew	6-5/240	2-14-72	9	Washington State	D1/93	16/16
12	Brady, Tom	6-4/210	8-3-77	2	Michigan	D6b/00	1/0
19	Huard, Damon	6-3/215	7-9-73	5	Washington	FA/01	*16/1
	RUNNING BACKS						
44	Edwards, Marc (FB)	6-0/240	11-17-74	5	Notre Dame	UFA/01	*16/8
47	Edwards, Robert	5-11/220	10-2-74	3	Georgia	D1a/98	0/0
33	Faulk, Kevin	5-8/200	6-15-76	3	Louisiana State	D2/99	16/9
35	Pass, Patrick	5-10/215	12-31-77	2	Georgia	D7b/00	5/2
46	Paulk, Jeff (FB)	6-0/240	4-26-76	3	Arizona State	FA/00	1/0
21	Redmond, J.R.	5-11/210	9-28-77	2	Arizona State	D3/00	12/5
	RECEIVERS						
80	Brown, Troy	5-10/190	7-2-71	9	Marshall	D8/93	16/15
84	Davis, Shockmain	6-0/205	8-20-77	2	Angelo State	FA/00	12/1
86	Eitzmann, Chris (TE)	6-5/255	4-1-77	2	Harvard	FA/00	5/1
17	Emanuel, Bert	5-10/185	10-26-70	8	Rice	UFA/01	*11/0
88	Glenn, Terry	5-11/195	7-23-74	6	Ohio State	D1/96	16/16
49	Holloway, Jabari (TE)	6-3/255	12-18-78	R	Notre Dame	D4b/01	—
82	Jackson, Curtis	5-10/190	9-22-73	2	Texas	FA/00	5/2
	Johnson, Charles	6-0/200	1-3-72	8	Colorado	FA/01	*16/16
	Love, Arther (TE)	6-4/252	9-18-77	R	South Carolina State	D6/01	—
	McWilliams, Johnny	6-4/271	12-14-72	4	Southern California	UFA/01	*15/7
15	Patten, David	5-10/195	8-19-74	5	Western Carolina	UFA/01	*14/11
66	Paxton, Lonie (TE)	6-2/260	3-13-78	2	Sacramento State	FA/00	16/0
83	Rutledge, Rod (TE)	6-5/270	8-12-75	4	Alabama	D2b/98	16/11
81	Simmons, Tony	6-1/210	12-8-74	4	Wisconsin	D2a/98	12/2
	Small, Torrance	6-3/209	9-4-70	10	Alcorn State	FA/01	*14/14
85	Wiggins, Jermaine (TE)	6-2/255	1-18-75	2	Georgia	W-NYJ/00	15/2
	OFFENSIVE LINEMEN						
63	Andruzzi, Joe (G)	6-3/315	8-23-75	5	Southern Connecticut State	FA/00	11/11
64	Compton, Mike	6-6/300	9-18-70	9	West Virginia	UFA/01	*16/16
60	Jones, Kenyatta	6-3/315	1-18-79	R	South Florida	D4/01	—
70	Klemm, Adrian (T)	6-3/310	5-21-77	2	Hawaii	D2/00	5/4
71	Light, Matt (T)	6-4/305	6-23-78	R	Purdue	D2/01	—
74	Panos, Joe (G)	6-3/300	1-24-71	7	Wisconsin	FA/01	*13/0
77	Robinson-Randall, Greg (T)	6-5/315	6-23-78	2	Michigan State	D4/00	12/4
67	Ruegamer, Grey (G)	6-5/310	6-1-76	2	Arizona State	FA/00	6/0
63	Scott, Lance (C)	6-3/295	2-15-72	6	Utah	FA/00	0/0
76	Williams, Grant (T)	6-7/325	5-10-74	6	Louisiana Tech	UFA/00	15/8
65	Woody, Damien (C)	6-3/315	11-3-77	3	Boston College	D1a/99	16/16
	DEFENSIVE LINEMEN						
97	Grimes, Reggie (E)	6-4/290	11-7-76	2	Alabama	FA/00	8/0
91	Hamilton, Bobby (E)	6-5/280	1-7-71	7	Southern Mississippi	UFA/00	16/16
60	Johnson, Garrett (T)	6-3/295	12-31-75	2	Illinois	FA/99	8/2
	Leroy, Emarlos (T)	6-1/304	7-31-75	3	Georgia	W-Jax./01	*9/1
55	McGinest, Willie (E)	6-5/270	12-11-71	8	Southern California	D1/94	14/14
99	Mitchell, Brandon (E)	6-3/285	6-19-75	5	Texas A&M	D2/97	11/9
92	Nugent, David (E)	6-4/300	10-27-77	2	Purdue	D6c/00	6/0
98	Pleasant, Anthony (E)	6-5/280	1-27-68	12	Tennessee State	UFA/01	*16/16
93	Seymour, Richard (T)	6-6/300	10-6-79	R	Georgia	D1/01	—
94	Spires, Greg (E)	6-1/265	8-12-74	4	Florida State	D3b/98	16/2
	LINEBACKERS						
54	Bruschi, Tedy	6-1/245	6-9-73	6	Arizona	D3/96	16/16
58	Chatham, Matt	6-4/240	6-28-77	2	South Dakota	W-St.L./00	6/0
90	Dalton, Antico	6-1/240	12-31-75	1	Hampton University	FA/00	3/0
50	Holmberg, Rob	6-3/240	5-6-71	8	Penn State	FA/00	16/5
53	Izzo, Larry	5-10/228	9-26-74	5	Rice	UFA/01	*16/0
52	Johnson, Ted	6-4/255	12-4-72	7	Colorado	D2/95	13/11
59	Katzenmoyer, Andy	6-3/255	12-2-77	3	Ohio State	D1b/99	8/3
96	Tuitele, Maugaula	6-2/255	5-26-78	1	Colorado State	FA/00	1/0
	Turner, T.J.	6-2/252	10-1-78	R	Michigan State	D7b/01	—
51	Vrabel, Mike	6-4/250	8-14-75	5	Ohio State	UFA/01	*15/0
	DEFENSIVE BACKS						
	Akbar, Hakim (S)	6-0/211	8-11-80	R	Washington	D5/01	—
41	George, Tony (S)	5-11/205	8-10-75	3	Florida	D3/99	15/0
23	Harris, Antwan (CB)	5-9/190	5-29-77	2	Virginia	D6a/00	14/0
34	Jones, Tebucky (S)	6-2/220	10-6-74	4	Syracuse	D1b/98	15/9
24	Law, Ty (CB)	5-11/200	2-10-74	7	Michigan	D1/95	15/15
36	Milloy, Lawyer (S)	6-0/210	11-14-73	6	Washington	D2/96	16/16
	Myers, Leonard (CB)	6-0/201	12-18-78	R	Miami (Fla.)	D6/01	—
31	Serwanga, Kato (CB)	6-0/198	7-23-76	3	California	FA/98	15/0
22	Shaw, Terrance (CB)	5-11/190	11-11-73	7	Stephen F. Austin State	FA/00	*11/3
45	Smith, Otis (CB)	5-11/195	10-22-65	12	Missouri	FA/00	16/14
26	Stevens, Matt (S)	6-0/206	6-15-73	5	Appalachian State	W-Was./00	16/4
27	Williams, Brock (CB)	5-10/185	8-12-79	R	Notre Dame	D3/01	—

NEW ENGLAND PATRIOTS

SPECIALISTS

10	Johnson, Lee (P).........................	6-2/200	11-27-61	17	Brigham Young	FA/99	16/0
	Pochman, Owen (K).....................	5-11/179	8-2-77	R	Brigham Young	D7a/01	—
4	Vinatieri, Adam (K).......................	6-0/200	12-28-72	6	South Dakota State	FA/96	16/0

*Not with Patriots in 2000.
Other free agent veterans invited to camp: FB Larry Bowie, P Brad Costello, DB Sean Morey, DT Chuck Osborne.
Abbreviations: D1—draft pick, first round; SD-2—supplemental draft pick, second round; W—claimed on waivers; T—obtained in trade; PlanB—Plan B free-agent acquisition; FA—free-agent acquisition (other than Plan B); UFA—unconditional free agent acquisition; ED—expansion draft pick.

MISCELLANEOUS TEAM DATA

Stadium (capacity, surface):
Foxboro Stadium
(60,292, grass)
Business address:
60 Washington St.
Foxboro, MA 02035
Business phone:
508-543-8200
Ticket information:
508-543-1776
Team colors:
Silver, red, white and blue
Flagship radio station:
WBCN, 104.1 FM
Training site:
Bryant College
Smithfield, R.I.
508-543-8200

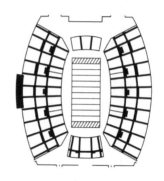

TSN REPORT CARD

Coaching staff	C	When you win five games, you should get a D or an F, but Bill Belichick deserves a break because he was handed bad players. He won't be able to use that excuse much longer, though. Belichick has now had one winning season in his six years as an NFL head coach.
Quarterback	B	Given the large number of bad quarterbacks in the league right now, the Patriots should consider themselves lucky. This isn't to say Drew Bledsoe is an elite quarterback, however. He can help himself by continuing to improve his footwork and mobility.
Running backs	D	Maybe J.R. Redmond will be able to carry the ball 20-25 times a game. Maybe Kevin Faulk will learn to hold on to the ball. Maybe Patrick Pass will be another late-round steal from Georgia. Maybe Robert Edwards will complete his miracle comeback. Then again, maybe not.
Recievers	C +	Talk about top-heavy. The Pats have Terry Glenn and Troy Brown and a whole bunch of question marks. The biggest need is a deep threat to take heat off of Glenn and allow Brown to return to the slot. The Pats could also use more size—not to mention a tight end.
Offensive line	F	There is nowhere to go but up for this unit. The additions of Mike Compton and Joe Panos should help at guard while there is enough youth to have a spirited competition at tackle. Whether that translates into fewer hits on Bledsoe remains to be seen. At least Damien Woods is a good center.
Defensive line	C	Chad Eaton was huge in Belichick's scheme. Now he's gone and there's no viable replacement. Top pick Richard Seymour will make an immediate impact, but because of Eaton's departure, the unit will merely tread water. Veterans Bobby Hamilton, Anthony Pleasant and Brandon Mitchell are serviceable.
Linebackers	C	Too many injuries and not enough young talent. Veterans Larry Izzo, Mike Vrabel and Rob Holmberg weren't good enough to start anywhere else, but they may get the chance in New England. If Ted Johnson can stay on the field everything changes.
Secondary	C -	The individual talent is there; the cohesion is not. It's up to Belichick to make this unit better. Lawyer Milloy is the best player on the team and Ty Law has all the talent in the world. The coach should be able to find a few more pieces and make it all work.
Special teams	B -	Watching Brown return punts game-in, game-out is a delight. The coverage teams should be much improved with the additions of Izzo and Vrabel. The kicking game could be in flux in the near future as both punter Lee Johnson and kicker Adam Vinatieri will face competition in 2001.

NEW ORLEANS SAINTS
NFC WESTERN DIVISION

2001 SEASON

CLUB DIRECTORY

Owner
Tom Benson

FOOTBALL OPERATIONS
General manager of football operations
Randy Mueller
Director of football administration
Mickey Loomis
Assistant g.m of football operations
Charles Bailey
Director of player personnel
Rick Mueller
College scouting coordinator
Rick Thompson
Scouting supervisor
Pat Mondock
Pro scouts
Mike Baugh   Bill Quinter
Area scouts
Cornell Gowdy, Tim Heffelfinger, James
Jefferson, Mark Sadowski
Combine scout
Andy Weidl
Player personnel assistant
Grant Neill
Football operations assistants
John "Chip" Beake, T.D. Cox, Barrett Wiley
Dir. of player dev. and community relations
Ricky Porter
Equipment manager
Dan Simmons
Assistant equipment manager
Glennon "Silky" Powell
Equipment assistant
Nolan Castex
Head athletic trainer
Scottie B. Patton
Assistant athletic trainer
Kevin Mangum
Assistant athletic trainer
Aaron Miller
Video director
Joe Malota
Assistant video director
Jeff Jacobs
Director of media & public relations
Greg Bensel
Media & public relations managers
Paul Corliss, Justin Macione, Chris Pika
New media manager
Ricky Zeller

Head coach
Jim Haslett

Assistant coaches
Hubbard Alexander (wide receivers)
Dave Atkins (running backs)
Joe Baker (secondary/special teams
  assistant)
Frank Cignetti Jr. (quarterbacks)
Sam Clancy (defensive line)
Al Everest (special teams)
Rock Gullickson (strength & cond.)
Jack Henry (offensive line)
Jim Hostler (offensive assistant)
Mike McCarthy (off. coordinator)
Evan Marcus (asst. strength &
  conditioning)
Winston Moss (linebackers)
Bob Palcic (tight ends)
Rick Venturi (asst. head coach/
  secondary)
Mike Woodford (defensive assistant)
Ron Zook (defensive coordinator)

Director of photography
Michael C. Hebert

ADMINISTRATION
Director of administration
Arnold D Fielkow
Chief financial officer
Dennis Lauscha
Dir. of marketing & business development
Wayne Hodes
Dir. of regional sales & marketing
Mike Feder
Director of operations & team logistics
James Nagaoka
Director of ticket sales
Mike Stanfield

SCHEDULE

Sept. 9—	at Buffalo	1:00
Sept. 16—	SAN FRANCISCO	1:00
Sept. 23—	Open date	
Sept. 30—	at N.Y. Giants	1:00
Oct. 7—	MINNESOTA	1:00
Oct. 14—	at Carolina	1:00
Oct. 21—	ATLANTA	1:00
Oct. 28—	at St. Louis	1:00
Nov. 4—	N.Y. JETS	8:30
Nov. 11—	at San Francisco	4:15
Nov. 18—	INDIANAPOLIS	1:00
Nov. 25—	at New England	4:05
Dec. 2—	CAROLINA	1:00
Dec. 9—	at Atlanta	1:00
Dec. 17—	ST. LOUIS (Mon.)	9:00
Dec. 23—	at Tampa Bay	1:00
Dec. 30—	WASHINGTON	8:30

All times are Eastern.
All games Sunday unless noted.

DRAFT CHOICES

Deuce McAllister, RB, Mississippi (first round/23rd pick overall).
Sedrick Hodge, LB, North Carolina (3/70).
Kenny Smith, DT, Alabama (3/81).
Moran Norris, RB, Kansas (4/115).
Onome Ojo, WR, UC Davis (5/153).
Mitch White, T, Oregon State (6/185).
Ennis Davis, DT, Southern California (7/221).

2000 REVIEW

RESULTS

Sept. 3—DETROIT	L	10-14
Sept.10—at San Diego	W	28-27
Sept.17—at Seattle	L	10-20
Sept.24—PHILADELPHIA	L	7-21
Oct. 1—Open date		
Oct. 8—at Chicago	W	31-10
Oct. 15—CAROLINA	W	24-6
Oct. 22—at Atlanta	W	21-19
Oct. 29—at Arizona	W	21-10
Nov. 5—SAN FRANCISCO	W	31-15
Nov. 12—at Carolina	W	20-10
Nov. 19—OAKLAND	L	22-31
Nov. 26—at St. Louis	W	31-24
Dec. 3—DENVER	L	23-38
Dec. 10—at San Francisco	W	31-27
Dec. 17—ATLANTA	W	23-7
Dec. 24—ST. LOUIS	L	21-26
Dec. 30—ST. LOUIS*	W	31-28
Jan. 6—at Minnesota†	L	16-34

*NFC wild-card game.
†NFC divisional playoff game.

RECORDS/RANKINGS

2000 regular-season record: 10-6 (1st in NFC West); 7-1 in division; 9-3 in conference; 3-5 at home; 7-1 on road.
Team record last five years: 28-52 (.350, ranks 27th in league in that span).

2000 team rankings:

	No.	NFC	NFL
Total offense	*337.3	T4	T10
Rushing offense	*129.3	2	8
Passing offense	*208.1	8	14
Scoring offense	354	5	10
Total defense	*296.4	3	8
Rushing defense	*104.5	4	10
Passing defense	*191.9	4	10
Scoring defense	305	5	10
Takeaways	35	4	T8
Giveaways	26	4	T9
Turnover differential	9	3	8
Sacks	66	1	1
Sacks allowed	39	10	17

*Yards per game.

TEAM LEADERS

Scoring (kicking): Doug Brien, 106 pts. (37/37 PATs, 23/29 FGs).
Scoring (touchdowns): Ricky Williams, 54 pts. (8 rushing, 1 receiving).
Passing: Jeff Blake, 2,025 yds. (302 att., 184 comp., 60.9%, 13 TDs, 9 int.).
Rushing: Ricky Williams, 1,000 yds. (248 att., 4.0 avg., 8 TDs).
Receptions: Joe Horn, 94 (1,340 yds., 14.3 avg., 8 TDs).
Interceptions: Sammy Knight, 5 (68 yds., 2 TDs).
Sacks: La'Roi Glover, 17.0.
Punting: Toby Gowin, 41.1 avg. (74 punts, 3,043 yds., 0 blocked).
Punt returns: Chad Morton, 9.3 avg. (30 att., 278 yds., 0 TDs).
Kickoff returns: Chad Morton, 23.4 avg. (44 att., 1,029 yds., 0 TDs).

NEW ORLEANS SAINTS

No.	QUARTERBACKS	Ht./Wt.	Born	NFL Exp.	College	How acq.	'00 Games GP/GS
18	Blake, Jeff	6-0/210	12-4-70	10	East Carolina	UFA/00	11/11
2	Brooks, Aaron	6-4/205	3-24-76	3	Virginia	T-GB/00	8/5
	RUNNING BACKS						
47	Houser, Kevin (FB)	6-2/250	8-23-77	2	Ohio State	D7/00	16/0
26	McAfee, Fred	5-10/198	6-20-68	11	Mississippi College	UFA/00	12/0
	McAllister, Deuce	6-1/222	12-27-78	R	Mississippi	D1/01	—
44	Milne, Brian (FB)	6-3/254	1-7-73	6	Penn State	UFA/00	16/2
32	Moore, Jerald	5-9/230	11-20-74	5	Oklahoma	W-Oak./00	11/1
30	Morton, Chad	5-8/186	4-4-77	2	Southern California	D5c/00	16/3
	Norris, Moran	6-1/244	6-16-78	R	Kansas	D4/01	—
41	Smith, Terrelle (FB)	6-0/246	3-12-78	2	Arizona State	D4/00	14/9
34	Williams, Ricky	5-10/236	5-21-77	3	Texas	D1/99	10/10
	RECEIVERS						
85	Cleeland, Cam (TE)	6-4/272	4-15-75	3	Washington	D2/98	0/0
83	Connell, Albert	6-0/179	5-13-74	5	Texas A&M	UFA/01	*16/13
81	Hall, Lamont (TE)	6-4/260	11-16-74	3	Clemson	T-GB/00	16/5
87	Horn, Joe	6-1/206	1-16-72	6	None	UFA/00	16/16
88	Jackson, Willie	6-1/212	8-16-71	8	Florida	UFA/00	15/7
	Ojo, Onome	6-6/265	8-11-78	R	UC Davis	D5/01	—
83	Poole, Keith	6-0/193	6-18-74	5	Arizona State	D4b/97	15/4
89	Stachelski, Dave (TE)	6-3/250	3-1-77	2	Boise State	FA/00	4/0
84	Wheatley, Austin (TE)	6-5/254	11-16-77	2	Iowa	D5b/00	4/0
16	Wilson, Robert	5-11/176	6-23-74	3	Florida A&M	FA/00	15/0
	OFFENSIVE LINEMEN						
69	Ackerman, Tom (G)	6-3/296	9-6-72	6	Eastern Washington	D5b/96	15/0
62	Fontenot, Jerry (C)	6-3/300	11-21-66	13	Texas A&M	UFA/97	16/16
65	Naeole, Chris (G)	6-3/313	12-25-74	5	Colorado	D1/97	16/16
70	Price, Marcus (T)	6-6/321	3-3-72	4	Louisiana State	FA/00	7/0
77	Roaf, Willie (T)	6-5/312	4-18-70	9	Louisiana Tech	D1/93	16/16
78	Terrell, Daryl (T)	6-5/296	1-25-75	3	Southern Mississippi	FA/98	16/0
68	Turley, Kyle (T)	6-5/300	9-24-75	4	San Diego State	D1/98	16/16
63	Williams, Wally (G)	6-2/321	2-19-71	9	Florida A&M	UFA/99	16/16
	DEFENSIVE LINEMEN						
92	Chase, Martin (T)	6-2/310	12-19-74	4	Oklahoma	W-Bal./00	9/0
	Davis, Ennis (T)	6-4/303	12-2-77	R	Southern California	D7/01	—
95	Douglas, Marques (E)	6-2/270	3-5-77	1	Howard	W-Bal./00	1/0
97	Glover, La'Roi (T)	6-2/285	7-4-74	6	San Diego State	W-Oak./97	16/16
99	Hand, Norman (T)	6-3/310	9-4-72	7	Mississippi	UFA/00	15/15
93	Howard, Darren (E)	6-3/281	11-19-76	2	Kansas State	D2/00	16/16
94	Johnson, Joe (E)	6-4/270	7-11-72	8	Louisville	D1/94	16/15
	Smith, Kenny (T)	6-3/289	9-8-77	R	Alabama	D3b/01	—
98	Whitehead, Willie (E)	6-3/285	1-26-73	3	Auburn	FA/99	16/2
	LINEBACKERS						
51	Clarke, Phil	6-0/241	1-9-77	3	Pittsburgh	FA/99	14/4
56	Clemons, Charlie	6-2/250	7-4-72	4	Georgia	FA/00	0/0
	Hodge, Sedrick	6-3/235	9-13-78	R	North Carolina	D3a/01	—
53	Jones, Donta	6-2/235	8-27-72	7	Nebraska	FA/00	12/0
59	Mitchell, Keith	6-2/245	7-24-74	5	Texas A&M	FA/97	16/14
59	Smith, Darrin	6-1/230	4-15-70	9	Miam, Fla	FA/00	16/11
50	Terry, Corey	6-3/246	3-6-76	3	Tennessee	FA/00	7/0
50	Ward, Phillip	6-3/230	11-11-74	1	UCLA	FA/00	2/0
	DEFENSIVE BACKS						
	Bellamy, Jay (S)	5-11/199	7-8-72	8	Rutgers	UFA/01	*16/16
37	Gleason, Steve	5-11/215	3-19-77	1	Washington State	FA/00	3/0
26	Harris, Corey (CB)	5-10/191	11-28-76	1	North Alabama	FA/99	3/1
36	Hawthorne, Michael (CB)	6-3/196	1-26-77	2	Purdue	D6b/00	11/1
21	Israel, Steve (CB)	5-11/194	3-16-69	9	Pittsburgh	UFA/00	0/0
27	Kelly, Rob (S)	6-0/199	6-21-74	5	Ohio State	D2a/97	12/0
29	Knight, Sammy (S)	6-0/205	9-10-75	5	Southern California	FA/97	16/16
23	Mathis, Kevin (CB)	5-9/181	4-29-74	5	East Texas State	T-Dal./00	16/16
28	Oldham, Chris	5-9/200	10-26-68	11	Oregon	UFA/00	13/1
39	Perry, Darren (S)	5-11/200	12-29-68	9	Penn State	FA/00	16/16
22	Thomas, Fred (CB)	5-9/172	9-11-73	6	Tennessee-Martin	UFA/00	11/0
24	Weary, Fred (CB)	5-10/181	4-12-74	4	Florida	D4a/98	12/12
	SPECIALISTS						
4	Gowin, Toby (P)	5-10/167	3-30-75	5	North Texas	FA/00	16/0
5	Hall, Jeff (K)	5-11/190	7-30-76	2	Tennessee	FA/01	*3/0

*Not with Saints in 2000.

Other free agent veterans invited to camp: QB Jake Delhomme, RB Derrick Harris, FB Jason Nevadomsky, T Tutan Reyes, DT Richard Seals.

Abbreviations: D1—draft pick, first round; SD-2—supplemental draft pick, second round; W—claimed on waivers; T—obtained in trade; PlanB—Plan B free-agent acquisition; FA—free-agent acquisition (other than Plan B); UFA—unconditional free agent acquisition; ED—expansion draft pick.

MISCELLANEOUS TEAM DATA

Stadium (capacity, surface):
Louisiana Superdome
(65,900, artificial)
Business address:
5800 Airline Drive
Metairie, LA 70003
Business phone:
504-733-0255
Ticket information:
504-731-1700
Team colors:
Old gold, black and white
Flagship radio station:
WWL-870 AM
Training site:
Nicholls State University
Thibodaux, La.
504-448-4282

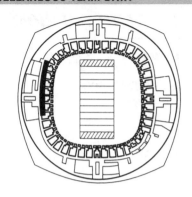

TSN REPORT CARD

Coaching staff	A	The Saints are a reflection of the aggressive, hard-working, intense group Jim Haslett assembled. He was that way as a player, and he's brought it with him to the coaching ranks. Coordinators Mike McCarthy and Ron Zook should be in line for head coaching jobs soon.
Quarterbacks	B +	The Saints and Broncos are the only teams with two returning quarterbacks with passer efficiency ratings above 80. Aaron Brooks and Jeff Blake are mobile and own strong arms. Both are capable of leading the team to the playoffs but neither has shown enough consistency to be dominant.
Running backs	A	Some teams go decades without a feature back (See: Miami). The Saints have two of them. Ricky Williams and Deuce McAllister are a potent one-two punch. Williams wears defenses down with his interior blasts. McAllister is a home-run threat on every down. Durability is question mark for each. Fullback is a concern because of Terrelle Smith's lingering back injury.
Receivers	B	This should be a much improved position thanks to the addition of deep threat Albert Connell and the healthy return of tight end Cam Cleeland. Both could have big seasons if defenses concentrate too much on go-to receiver Joe Horn. Willie Jackson is one of the league's most dependable slot receivers.
Offensive line	A	It's hard to find a weakness in this starting five. Willie Roaf and Kyle Turley are one of the league's most athletic tackle tandems. Wally Williams and Chris Naeole are solid at guard. And Jerry Fontenot is the leader under center. This group is smart, dependable and tough. It has few equals.
Defensive line	A	The starting quartet is as good as they come. Ends Joe Johnson and Darren Howard play the run as well as put heat on the passer. Norman Hand is a run stuffer supreme at tackle. La'Roi Glover is the quiet leader of the group. His relentless sets the tone for the group.
Linebackers	B	Haslett said he has seen few threesomes more athletic than Charlie Clemons, Darrin Smith and Keith Mitchell. It's a big year for Clemons, in his first season as a first-year starter in the middle. The group needs to produce more big plays. Depth is a concern with unproved rookie Sedrick Hodge the primary backup at both outside spots.
Secondary	B -	No Champ Baileys or Charles Woodsons here but the Saints have five solid corners that can get the job done. If Fred Weary and/or Steve Israel return to 100 percent this group could be excellent. Safeties Sammy Knight and Jay Bellamy are solid in coverage and run support.
Special teams	D	Coverage units need an upgrade after costing the team at least one and maybe two games a year ago. Kicking is a major question, with three unproven legs battling for the starting job. Return men Chad Morton and McAllister have great potential. Punter Toby Gowin is steady but not spectacular.

NEW YORK GIANTS
NFC EASTERN DIVISION

2001 SEASON

CLUB DIRECTORY

President/co-CEO
Wellington T. Mara
Chairman/co-CEO
Preston Robert Tisch
Exec. v.p./general counsel
John K. Mara
Vice president/general manager
Ernie Accorsi
Treasurer
Jonathan Tisch
Assistant general manager
Rick Donohue
Controller
Christine Procops
Director/player personnel
Marv Sunderland
Director of administration
Jim Phelan
Vice president, marketing
Rusty Hawley
Director/promotion
Francis X. Mara
Ticket manager
John Gorman
Director/pro personnel
Dave Gettleman
Assistant director/pro personnel
Jerry Reese
Director/research and development
Raymond J. Walsh Jr.
Director/college scouting
Jerry Shay
Vice president of communications
Pat Hanlon
Director of corporate sponsorships
Bill Smith
Head trainer
Ronnie Barnes
Assistant trainers
Byron Hansen   Steve Kennelly
Director of player development
Greg Gabriel

Head coach
Jim Fassel

Assistant coaches
Dave Brazil (def. quality control)
John Dunn (strength & cond.)
John Fox (defensive coordinator)
Johnnie Lynn (defensive backs)
Denny Marcin (defensive line)
Jim McNally (offensive line)
Tom Olivadotti (linebackers)
Sean Payton (off. coordinator)
Mike Pope (tight ends)
Jay Robertson (off. quality control)
Jimmy Robinson (wide receivers)
Craig Stoddard (assistant strength
    & conditioning)
Eric Studesville (running backs)
Fred von Appen (special teams)

Scouts
Rosey Brown   Jeremiah Davis
Donnie Etheridge   Ryan Jones
Steve Verderosa
Team physician
Russell Warren
Locker room/equipment manager
Ed Wagner Jr.
Assistant equipment managers
Ed Skiba   Joe Skiba
Tim Slaman
Video director
John Mancuso

SCHEDULE

Sept. 10—	at Denver (Mon.)	9:00
Sept. 16—	GREEN BAY	1:00
Sept. 23—	at Kansas City	1:00
Sept. 30—	NEW ORLEANS	1:00
Oct. 7—	WASHINGTON	1:00
Oct. 14—	at St. Louis	1:00
Oct. 22—	PHILADELPHIA (Mon.)	9:00
Oct. 28—	at Washington	8:30
Nov. 4—	DALLAS	1:00
Nov. 11—	at Arizona	4:15
Nov. 19—	at Minnesota (Mon.)	9:00
Nov. 25—	OAKLAND	4:15
Dec. 2—	Open date	
Dec. 9—	at Dallas	1:00
Dec. 15—	ARIZONA (Sat.)	12:30
Dec. 23—	SEATTLE	1:00
Dec. 30—	at Philadelphia	1:05

All times are Eastern.
All games Sunday unless noted.

DRAFT CHOICES

Will Allen, DB, Syracuse (first round/
22nd pick overall).
William Peterson, DB, Western Illinois
(3/78).
Cedric Scott, DE, Southern Mississippi
(4/114).
Jesse Palmer, QB, Florida (4/125).
John Markham, K, Vanderbilt (5/160).
Jonathan Carter, WR, Troy State (5/162).
Ross Kolodziej, DT, Wisconsin (7/230).

2000 REVIEW

RESULTS

Sept. 3—ARIZONA	W	21-16
Sept. 10—at Philadelphia	W	33-18
Sept. 17—at Chicago	W	14-7
Sept. 24—WASHINGTON	L	6-16
Oct. 1—at Tennessee	L	14-28
Oct. 8—at Atlanta	W	13-6
Oct. 15—DALLAS	W	19-14
Oct. 22—Open date		
Oct. 29—PHILADELPHIA	W	24-7
Nov. 5—at Cleveland	W	24-3
Nov. 12—ST. LOUIS	L	24-38
Nov. 19—DETROIT	L	21-31
Nov. 26—at Arizona	W	31-7
Dec. 3—at Washington	W	9-7
Dec. 10—PITTSBURGH	W	30-10
Dec. 17—at Dallas	W	17-13
Dec. 23—JACKSONVILLE	W	28-25
Jan. 7—PHILADELPHIA*	W	20-10
Jan. 14—MINNESOTA†	W	41-0
Jan. 28—Baltimore‡	L	7-34

*NFC divisional playoff game.
†NFC championship game.
‡Super Bowl 35 at Tampa.

RECORDS/RANKINGS

2000 regular-season record: 12-4 (1st in
NFC East); 7-1 in division; 9-3 in conference; 5-3 at home; 7-1 on road.
Team record last five years: 43-36-1
(.544, ranks 11th in league in that span).
2000 team rankings:

	No.	NFC	NFL
Total offense	*336.0	6	13
Rushing offense	*125.6	4	11
Passing offense	*210.4	7	13
Scoring offense	328	8	15
Total defense	*284.1	2	5
Rushing defense	*72.3	1	2
Passing defense	*211.9	8	16
Scoring defense	246	2	5
Takeaways	31	T6	T12
Giveaways	24	T2	T5
Turnover differential	7	4	9
Sacks	44	6	T9
Sacks allowed	28	2	T5

*Yards per game.

TEAM LEADERS

Scoring (kicking): Brad Daluiso, 85 pts.
(34/34 PATs, 17/23 FGs).
Scoring (touchdowns): Tiki Barber, 54
pts. (8 rushing, 1 receiving).
Passing: Kerry Collins, 3,610 yds. (529
att., 311 comp., 58.8%, 22 TDs, 13 int.).
Rushing: Tiki Barber, 1,006 yds. (213 att.,
4.7 avg., 8 TDs).
Receptions: Amani Toomer, 78 (1,094
yds., 14.0 avg., 7 TDs).
Interceptions: Emmanuel McDaniel, 6 (30
yds., 0 TDs).
Sacks: Keith Hamilton, 10.0.
Punting: Brad Maynard, 40.6 avg. (79
punts, 3,210 yds., 1 blocked).
Punt returns: Tiki Barber, 8.5 avg. (39 att.,
332 yds., 0 TDs).
Kickoff returns: Ron Dixon, 21.2 avg. (31
att., 658 yds., 0 TDs).

NEW YORK GIANTS

No.	QUARTERBACKS	Ht./Wt.	Born	NFL Exp.	College	How acq.	'00 Games GP/GS
5	Collins, Kerry	6-5/245	12-30-72	7	Penn State	UFA/99	16/16
17	Garrett, Jason	6-2/200	3-28-66	9	Princeton	UFA/00	2/0
12	Palmer, Jesse	6-2/219	10-5-79	R	Florida	D4b/01	—
	RUNNING BACKS						
21	Barber, Tiki	5-10/200	4-7-75	5	Virginia	D2/97	16/12
44	Bennett, Sean	6-1/230	11-9-75	3	Northwestern	D4/99	0/0
34	Comella, Greg (FB)	6-1/248	7-29-75	4	Stanford	FA/98	16/12
27	Dayne, Ron	5-10/253	3-14-78	2	Wisconsin	D1/00	16/4
33	Montgomery, Joe	5-10/230	6-8-76	3	Ohio State	D2/99	3/0
29	Washington, Damon	5-11/193	2-20-77	2	Colorado State	FA/00	3/0
	RECEIVERS						
89	Campbell, Dan (TE)	6-5/260	4-13-76	3	Texas A&M	D3/99	16/5
	Carter, Jonathan	6-0/182	3-20-79	R	Troy State	D5/01	—
87	Cross, Howard (TE)	6-5/270	8-8-67	13	Alabama	D6/89	16/11
82	Davis, Thabiti	6-2/205	3-24-75	2	Wake Forest	FA/00	13/0
86	Dixon, Ron	6-0/190	5-28-76	2	Lambuth University	D3/00	12/0
88	Hilliard, Ike	5-11/195	4-5-76	5	Florida	D1/97	14/14
84	Jurevicius, Joe	6-5/230	12-23-74	4	Penn State	D2/98	14/3
81	Toomer, Amani	6-3/208	9-8-74	6	Michigan	D2/96	16/14
	OFFENSIVE LINEMEN						
76	Brown, Lomas (T)	6-4/280	3-30-63	17	Florida	FA/00	16/16
62	Parker, Glenn (G)	6-5/312	4-22-66	12	Arizona	UFA/00	13/13
77	Petitgout, Luke (T)	6-6/310	6-16-76	3	Notre Dame	D1/99	16/16
78	Rosenthal, Mike (G)	6-7/315	6-10-77	3	Notre Dame	D5/99	8/2
65	Stone, Ron (G)	6-5/320	7-20-71	9	Boston College	FA/96	15/15
66	Whittle, Jason (G)	6-4/305	3-7-75	3	Southwest Missouri State	FA/98	16/2
52	Zeigler, Dusty (C)	6-5/303	9-27-73	6	Notre Dame	UFA/00	16/16
74	Ziemann, Chris (T)	6-7/315	9-20-76	2	Michigan	FA/00	8/0
	DEFENSIVE LINEMEN						
97	Griffin, Cornelius (T)	6-3/300	12-3-76	2	Alabama	D2/00	15/0
93	Hale, Ryan (T)	6-4/300	7-10-75	3	Arkansas	D7a/99	16/0
75	Hamilton, Keith (T)	6-6/295	5-25-71	10	Pittsburgh	D4/92	16/16
90	Holmes, Kenny (E)	6-4/270	10-24-73	6	Miami (Fla.)	UFA/01	*14/13
79	Parker, Jeremiah (E)	6-5/250	11-15-77	2	California	D7/00	4/0
96	Scott, Cedric (E)	6-5/274	10-19-77	R	Southern Mississippi	D4a/01	—
92	Strahan, Michael (E)	6-5/275	11-21-71	9	Texas Southern	D2/93	16/16
	LINEBACKERS						
98	Armstead, Jessie	6-1/240	10-26-70	9	Miami (Fla.)	D8/93	16/16
58	Barrow, Mike	6-2/240	4-19-70	9	Miami (Fla.)	FA/00	15/15
57	Golden, Jack	6-1/240	1-28-77	2	Oklahoma State	FA/00	16/0
59	Lewis, Kevin	6-1/230	10-6-78	2	Duke	FA/00	7/0
53	Short, Brandon	6-3/255	7-11-77	2	Penn State	D4/00	11/0
	DEFENSIVE BACKS						
25	Allen, Will (CB)	5-10/192	8-5-78	R	Syracuse	D1/01	—
22	Brown, Ralph (CB)	5-10/185	9-9-78	2	Nebraska	D5/00	2/0
20	Garnes, Sam (S)	6-3/225	7-12-74	5	Cincinnati	D5/97	15/15
26	McDaniel, Emmanuel (CB)	5-9/180	7-27-72	6	East Carolina	W-Mia./99	16/3
24	Peterson, Will (CB)	6-0/197	6-15-79	R	Western Illinois	D3/01	—
31	Sehorn, Jason (CB)	6-2/215	4-15-71	8	Southern California	D2b/94	14/14
26	Stoutmire, Omar (S)	5-11/198	7-9-74	4	Fresno State	FA/00	16/0
41	Thomas, Dave (CB)	6-3/218	8-25-68	9	Tennessee	UFA/00	16/16
35	Weathers, Andre (CB)	6-0/190	8-6-76	3	Michigan	D6b/99	1/0
36	Williams, Shaun (S)	6-2/215	10-10-76	4	UCLA	D1/98	16/16
	SPECIALISTS						
19	Holmes, Jaret (K)	6-0/203	3-3-76	3	Auburn	FA/00	4/0
	Markham, John (K)	6-1/212	4-27-79	R	Vanderbilt	D5b/01	—

*Not with Giants in 2000.

Other free agent veterans invited to camp: LB Dhani Jones, FB Mike Kacmarynski, P Rodney Williams.

Abbreviations: D1—draft pick, first round; SD-2—supplemental draft pick, second round; W—claimed on waivers; T—obtained in trade; PlanB—Plan B free-agent acquisition; FA—free-agent acquisition (other than Plan B); UFA—unconditional free agent acquisition; ED—expansion draft pick.

NEW YORK GIANTS

Stadium (capacity, surface):
Giants Stadium
(79,593, grass)
Business address:
East Rutherford, NJ 07073
Business phone:
201-935-8111
Ticket information:
201-935-8222
Team colors:
Blue, white and red
Flagship radio station:
WFAN, 660 AM; WNEW, 102.7 FM
Training site:
University at Albany
Albany, N.Y.

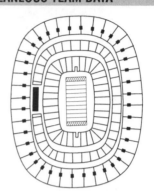

TSN REPORT CARD

Coaching staff	A -	Jim Fassel earned a place in Giants lore with his playoff guarantee last year, which solidified his status in the locker room. The team lucked out when defensive coordinator John Fox did not get the head job in Buffalo. Fox and Sean Payton form one of the league's best coordinator duos.
Quarterbacks	B	Kerry Collins' five TD passes against the Vikings in the NFC championship game vindicated the team's faith in him. Now he must bounce back from the four interceptions in the Super Bowl. Jason Garrett is a heady backup, but can't be counted on for the long haul if Collins goes down. Jesse Palmer is an intriguing new No. 3.
Running backs	B+	Tiki Barber was team MVP in 2000; repeating that feat after getting a big new contract will be tough. Ideally, Ron Dayne will help keep Barber fresh, but he must bounce back after a dreary finish to his rookie year. Joe Montgomery offers quality depth; Greg Comella is a solid fullback.
Receivers	B	Amani Toomer has had his ups and downs, but he is establishing himself as an elite wide receiver. Ike Hilliard is a nice complement, but he has been banged up. Joe Jurevicius has not emerged as hoped as a third receiver; maybe Ron Dixon will. Warhorse Howard Cross heads a shaky tight end corps.
Offensive line	B	If everyone stays reasonably healthy, the line should again be strong. But that could be a longshot given the mileage on the left side of the line with Lomas Brown and Glenn Parker. The depth all along the line is a huge question mark, with a number of young, unproven players vying for jobs.
Defensive line	A	The addition of free agent Kenny Holmes and the ascension of second-year man Cornelius Griffin make this potentially one of the best front fours in the NFL. Tackle Keith Hamilton had a brilliant all-around season in 2000 and three-time Pro Bowler Michael Strahan finished with a flourish.
Linebackers	B	Jessie Armstead is a four-time Pro Bowler on the weak side and Mike Barrow finished strongly in the middle after a lackluster start in 2000. But there are uncertainties on the strong side, where unproven Brandon Short is expected to take over, and on the bench, where the depth is almost non-existent.
Secondary	B	Jason Sehorn is back to hold the fort at right corner, but the other side is in flux, with veteran Dave Thomas and rookies Will Allen and William Peterson jockeying for position. Safeties Shaun Williams and Sam Garnes both are in their primes and form a big, hard-hitting one-two punch.
Special teams	C	Coach Larry Mac Duff has been replaced by veteran Fred Von Appen, and there is much work to do. Ron Dixon became the first player ever to return two kickoffs for touchdowns in the playoffs, but there will be a new kicker and punter to break in for the first time in years.

NEW YORK JETS
AFC EASTERN DIVISION

2001 SEASON

CLUB DIRECTORY

Owner and CEO
Robert Wood Johnson IV
President
Jay Cross
General manager
Terry Bradway
Director of player personnel
Dick Haley
**Director of player development/
player contract negotiations**
Mike Tannenbaum
Director of player development
Kevin Winston
Director of security
Steve Yarnell
Treasurer & chief financial officer
Mike Gerstle
Exec. director of business operations
Bob Parente
Director of public relations
Frank Ramos
Director of operations
Mike Kensil
Sr. manager of pro player development
JoJo Wooden
Scout of other pro football leagues
Brian Gaine
Talent scouts
Trent Baalke, Ron Brockington, Joey
Clinkscales, Jim Cochran, Michael Davis,
Sid Hall, Jessie Kaye, Bob Schmitz, Gary
Smith
Jets development
Thad Sheely
Director of team travel
Kevin Coyle
College scouting coordinator
John Griffin
Assistant director of public relations
Douglas Miller
Public relations assistants
Sharon Czark   Jared Winley
Community relations manager
Kimberlee Fields
Coordinator of special projects
Ken Ilchuk

Head coach
Herman
Edwards

Assistant coaches
Bill Bradley (defensive backs)
Rubin Carter (defensive line)
Ted Cottrell (asst. head coach/
defensive coordinator)
Paul Hackett (off. coordinator)
Bishop Harris (running backs)
Mike Henning (off. asst./QC)
Lou Hernandez (assistant strength &
conditioning)
John Lott (strength & conditioning)
David Merritt (defensive assistant)
Bill Muir (offensive line)
Phil Pettey (tight ends)
Eric Price (off. asst./QC)
Mose Rison (wide receivers)
Bob Sutton (linebackers)
Mike Westhoff (special teams)

Controller
Mike Minarczyk
Sr. dir. of marketing & business dev.
Marc Riccio
Director of ticket operations
John Buschhorn
Head athletic trainer
David Price
Assistant athletic trainer
John Melody
Equipment manager
Clay Hampton
Assistant equipment director
Gus Granneman
Video director
John Seiter

SCHEDULE

Sept. 9—	INDIANAPOLIS	1:00
Sept. 16—	at Oakland	4:15
Sept. 23—	at New England	4:05
Sept. 30—	Open date	
Oct. 1—	SAN FRANCISCO (Mon.)	9:00
Oct. 7—	at Buffalo	4:05
Oct. 14—	MIAMI	4:15
Oct. 21—	ST. LOUIS	1:00
Oct. 28—	at Carolina	1:00
Nov. 4—	at New Orleans	8:30
Nov. 11—	KANSAS CITY	1:00
Nov. 18—	at Miami	1:00
Dec. 2—	NEW ENGLAND	1:00
Dec. 9—	at Pittsburgh	4:15
Dec. 16—	CINCINNATI	1:00
Dec. 23—	at Indianapolis	8:30
Dec. 30—	BUFFALO	1:00

All times are Eastern.
All games Sunday unless noted.

DRAFT CHOICES

Santana Moss, WR, Miami, Fla. (first round/16th pick overall).
LaMont Jordan, RB, Maryland (2/49).
Kareem McKenzie, T, Penn State (3/79).
Jamie Henderson, DB, Georgia (4/101).
James Reed, DT, Iowa State (7/206).
Siitupe Peko, C, Michigan State (7/217).

2000 REVIEW

RESULTS

Sept. 3—at Green Bay	W	20-16
Sept.11—NEW ENGLAND	W	20-19
Sept.17—BUFFALO	W	27-14
Sept.24—at Tampa Bay	W	21-17
Oct. 1—Open date		
Oct. 8—PITTSBURGH	L	3-20
Oct. 15—at New England	W	34-17
Oct. 23—MIAMI (OT)	W	40-37
Oct. 29—at Buffalo	L	20-23
Nov. 5—DENVER	L	23-30
Nov. 12—at Indianapolis	L	15-23
Nov. 19—at Miami	W	20-3
Nov. 26—CHICAGO	W	17-10
Dec. 3—INDIANAPOLIS	W	27-17
Dec. 10—at Oakland	L	7-31
Dec. 17—DETROIT	L	7-10
Dec. 24—at Baltimore	L	20-34

RECORDS/RANKINGS

2000 regular-season record: 9-7 (3rd in AFC East); 6-2 in division; 6-6 in conference; 5-3 at home; 4-4 on road.
Team record last five years: 39-41 (.488, ranks T15th in league in that span).

2000 team rankings:

	No.	AFC	NFL
Total offense	*337.2	7	12
Rushing offense	*91.9	12	24
Passing offense	*245.3	4	6
Scoring offense	321	T9	T17
Total defense	*301.3	6	T10
Rushing defense	*118.0	12	23
Passing defense	*183.3	4	6
Scoring defense	321	6	13
Takeaways	35	T5	T8
Giveaways	40	15	29
Turnover differential	-5	12	T20
Sacks	40	T9	T15
Sacks allowed	20	T1	T1

*Yards per game.

TEAM LEADERS

Scoring (kicking): John Hall, 93 pts. (30/30 PATs, 21/32 FGs).
Scoring (touchdowns): Curtis Martin, 66 pts. (9 rushing, 2 receiving).
Passing: Vinny Testaverde, 3,732 yds. (590 att., 328 comp., 55.6%, 21 TDs, 25 int.).
Rushing: Curtis Martin, 1,204 yds. (316 att., 3.8 avg., 9 TDs).
Receptions: Wayne Chrebet, 69 (937 yds., 13.6 avg., 8 TDs).
Interceptions: Victor Green, 6 (144 yds., 1 TD).
Sacks: Mo Lewis, 10.0.
Punting: Tom Tupa, 44.7 avg. (83 punts, 3,714 yds., 0 blocked).
Punt returns: Dedric Ward, 7.9 avg. (27 att., 214 yds., 0 TDs).
Kickoff returns: Kevin Williams, 26.2 avg. (21 att., 551 yds., 1 TD).

NEW YORK JETS

No.	QUARTERBACKS	Ht./Wt.	Born	NFL Exp.	College	How acq.	'00 Games GP/GS
10	Pennington, Chad	6-3/225	6-26-76	2	Marshall	D1c/00	1/0
16	Testaverde, Vinny	6-5/235	11-13-63	15	Miami (Fla.)	FA/98	16/16
	RUNNING BACKS						
20	Anderson, Richie (FB)	6-2/230	9-13-71	9	Penn State	D6/93	16/10
34	Jordan, LaMont	5-10/230	11-11-78	R	Maryland	D2/01	—
28	Martin, Curtis	5-11/210	5-1-73	7	Pittsburgh	FA/98	16/16
37	Moreland, Jake (FB)	6-3/255	1-18-77	2	Western Michigan	FA/00	7/1
33	Sowell, Jerald (FB)	6-0/245	1-21-74	5	Tulane	W-GB/97	16/0
	RECEIVERS						
88	Becht, Anthony (TE)	6-5/267	8-8-77	2	West Virginia	D1d/00	14/10
80	Chrebet, Wayne	5-10/188	8-14-73	7	Hofstra	FA/95	16/16
87	Coles, Laveranues	5-11/190	12-29-77	2	Florida State	D3/00	13/3
89	Hatchette, Matthew	6-3/193	5-1-74	6	Langston University (Okla.)	UFA/01	*14/4
86	Hayes, Windrell	5-11/198	12-14-76	2	Southern California	D5/00	8/1
82	Johnson, Malcolm	6-5/215	8-27-77	2	Notre Dame	FA/00	5/0
83	Moss, Santana	5-10/185	6-1-79	R	Miami (Fla.)	D1/01	—
	OFFENSIVE LINEMEN						
76	Elliott, Jumbo (T)	6-7/308	4-1-65	14	Michigan	UFA/96	10/0
69	Fabini, Jason (T)	6-7/312	8-25-74	4	Cincinnati	D4/98	16/16
71	Jenkins, Kerry (G)	6-5/305	9-6-73	4	Troy (Ala.) State	FA/97	16/16
79	Loverne, David (G)	6-3/299	5-22-76	3	San Jose State	D3/99	16/0
63	Machado, J.P. (C)	6-4/300	1-6-76	3	Illinois	D6b/99	16/0
68	Mawae, Kevin (C)	6-4/305	1-23-71	8	Louisiana State	UFA/98	16/16
67	McKenzie, Kareem (T)	6-6/327	5-24-79	R	Penn State	D3/01	—
	Peko, Tupe (C)	6-4/300	8-19-78	R	Michigan State	D7b/01	—
77	Thomas, Randy (G)	6-4/301	1-19-76	3	Mississippi State	D2/99	16/16
74	Young, Ryan (T)	6-5/320	6-28-76	3	Kansas State	D7a/99	16/16
	DEFENSIVE LINEMEN						
98	Burton, Shane (E)	6-6/305	1-18-74	6	Tennessee	UFA/00	16/16
92	Ellis, Shaun (E)	6-5/280	6-24-77	2	Tennessee	D1a/00	16/3
72	Ferguson, Jason (T)	6-3/305	11-28-74	5	Georgia	D7b/97	15/11
95	Lyle, Rick (E)	6-5/290	2-26-71	7	Missouri	UFA/97	14/14
99	Ogbogu, Eric (E)	6-4/285	7-18-75	4	Maryland	D6a/98	0/0
	Reed, James (T)	6-0/285	2-3-77	R	Iowa State	D7a/01	—
91	Wiltz, Jason (T)	6-4/300	11-23-76	3	Nebraska	D4/99	15/1
	LINEBACKERS						
44	Abraham, John	6-4/250	5-6-78	2	South Carolina	D1b/00	6/0
52	Colman, Doug	6-2/250	6-4-73	6	Nebraska	FA/01	*5/0
51	Darling, James	6-0/250	12-29-74	5	Washington State	UFA/01	*16/0
58	Farrior, James	6-2/244	1-6-75	5	Virginia	D1/97	16/6
55	Jones, Marvin	6-2/250	6-28-72	9	Florida State	D1/93	16/16
53	Ledyard, Courtney	6-2/250	3-9-77	2	Michigan State	FA/99	4/0
57	Lewis, Mo.	6-3/258	10-21-69	11	Georgia	D3/91	16/16
	DEFENSIVE BACKS						
42	Coleman, Marcus (CB)	6-2/210	5-24-74	6	Texas Tech	D5/96	16/16
25	Ferguson, Nick (CB)	5-11/201	11-27-73	2	Georgia Tech	FA/00	7/0
47	Frost, Scott (S)	6-3/219	1-4-75	4	Nebraska	D3a/98	16/1
31	Glenn, Aaron (CB)	5-9/185	7-16-72	8	Texas A&M	D1/94	16/16
21	Green, Victor (S)	5-11/210	12-8-69	9	Akron	FA/93	16/16
30	Hayes, Chris (S)	6-0/206	5-7-72	5	Washington State	T-GB/96	16/8
23	Henderson, Jamie (CB)	6-2/202	1-1-79	R	Georgia	D4/01	—
24	Mickens, Ray (CB)	5-8/184	1-4-73	6	Texas A&M	D3/96	16/0
38	Moreland, Earthwind (CB)	5-11/185	6-13-77	2	Georgia Southern	FA/00	1/0
22	Robinson, Damien (S)	6-2/214	12-22-73	5	Iowa	UFA/01	*16/16
27	Scott, Tony (CB)	5-10/193	10-3-76	2	North Carolina State	D6/00	16/0
	SPECIALISTS						
9	Hall, John (K)	6-3/228	3-17-74	5	Wisconsin	FA/97	15/0
7	Tupa, Tom (P)	6-4/225	2-6-66	13	Ohio State	UFA/99	16/0

*Not with Jets in 2000.

Other free agent veterans invited to camp: TE James Dearth, WR-KR Desmond Kitchings, WR Shannon Myers, TE Scott Slutzker, LB J.J. Syvrud.

Abbreviations: D1—draft pick, first round; SD-2—supplemental draft pick, second round; W—claimed on waivers; T—obtained in trade; PlanB—Plan B free-agent acquisition; FA—free-agent acquisition (other than Plan B); UFA—unconditional free agent acquisition; ED—expansion draft pick.

MISCELLANEOUS TEAM DATA

Stadium (capacity, surface):
Giants Stadium
(79,466, grass)
Business address:
1000 Fulton Avenue
Hempstead, NY 11550
Business phone:
516-560-8100
Ticket information:
516-560-8200
Team colors:
Green and white
Flagship radio station:
MSG Radio, 770 AM & 1880 AM
Training site:
Hofstra University
Hempstead, N.Y.
516-560-8288

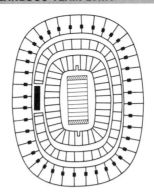

TSN REPORT CARD

Coaching staff	B	Rookie head coach Herman Edwards should thrive in the areas of motivation and communication, but he's largely an unknown. He's never worked as a coordinator, let alone a head coach. He did hire an experienced trio of coordinators, and that will relieve some of the pressure.
Quarterback	C +	Is there any magic left in Vinny Testaverde's 37-year-old right arm? The Jets better hope so because their season could be riding on it. If he can't do any better than last year—see a league-leading 25 interceptions—it will be time to ring in the Chad Pennington era.
Running back	A -	Curtis Martin remains one of the top five backs in the AFC. He has a lot of mileage on his odometer, but he shows no signs of letting up. He and Pro Bowl FB Richie Anderson might be the best pass-catching tandem around. Rookie LaMont Jordan provides fresh legs.
Receivers	B -	Keyshawn who? The Jets upgraded by adding size (6-2 Matthew Hatchette) and speed (No. 1 pick Santana Moss). They will join old reliable, Wayne Chrebet. TE Anthony Becht could be a factor in the new West Coast passing attack, but he's a liability as a blocker.
Offensive line	B	The starting unit, together for two seasons, should be ready to peak. Pro Bowl C Kevin Mawae is the best of the bunch, with RG Randy Thomas a close second. The entire group must do a better job in the running game, which was non-existent during last year's homestretch.
Defensive line	B -	Shaun Ellis, Jason Ferguson and former LB John Abraham form a potentially formidable trio, but who's the fourth starter? It probably will be Shane Burton. Depth also is a major concern. Ellis and Abraham should combine for at least 20 sacks.
Linebacker	B +	There's not much to worry about with Marvin Jones in the middle and Mo Lewis on the strongside. The weakside is just that - the weak side, where former No. 1 pick James Farrior will be pushed by former Eagle James Darling. Bryan Cox' leadership will be missed.
Secondary	B	The Jets stabilized a perennial weak spot, signing former Bucs FS Damien Robinson. He and SS Victor Green form one of the most physical safety tandems in the league. The cornerback positions are set, with Marcus Coleman and Aaron Glenn. Nickel back Ray Mickens will have to fight for his job.
Special teams	C +	This unit should be improved, especially with the dynamic Moss returning punts, but there are concerns about PK John Hall's head and P Tom Tupa's groin. Hall is coming back from a late-season benching and Tupa is rebounding from offseason surgery.

OAKLAND RAIDERS
AFC WESTERN DIVISION

OAKLAND RAIDERS

2001 SEASON

CLUB DIRECTORY

Owner
Al Davis
Chief executive
Amy Trask
Executive assistant
Al LoCasale
General counsel
Jeff Birren
Senior assistant
Bruce Allen
Personnel
Chet Franklin   Mike Lombardi
Legal affairs
Roxanne Kosarzycki
Finance
Marc Badain   Ron LaVelle
Derek Person
Finance/technology
Tom Blanda
Special projects
Jim Otto
Senior administrator
Morris Bradshaw
Senior executive
John Herrera
Business affairs
Scott Fink   Wendy Reicher
Dawn Roberts
Public relations director
Mike Taylor
Public relations
Craig Long
Broadcast and multimedia
Billy Zagger
Ticket operations
Peter Eiges
Head trainer
H. Rod Martin
Assistant trainers
Mark Mayer
Scott Touchet
Equipment manager
Bob Romanski
Video director
Dave Nash

Head coach
Jon Gruden

Assistant coaches
Fred Biletnikoff (wide receivers)
Chuck Bresnahan (def. coord.)
Willie Brown (squad development)
Bill Callahan (offensive
  coordinator/offensive line)
Bob Casullo (special teams)
Jim Erkenbeck (tight ends)
Garrett Giemont (strength &
  conditioning)
Aaron Kromer (offensive assistant)
Ron Lynn (defensive backs)
Don Martin (quality control-def.)
John Morton (offensive assistant)
Fred Pagac (linebackers)
Skip Peete (running backs)
David Shaw (quarterbacks)
Marc Trestman (sr. asst. coach)
Mike Waufle (defensive line)

Video operations
Jim Otten
Computer operations
John Otten
Information technology
Moses Cathey
Computer support
El Aranas
Internet services
Jerry Knaak
Player development/community relations
Terry Burton

SCHEDULE

Sept. 9—	at Kansas City	1:00
Sept. 16—	N.Y. JETS	4:15
Sept. 23—	at Miami	1:00
Sept. 30—	SEATTLE	4:15
Oct. 7—	Open date	
Oct. 14—	at Indianapolis	8:30
Oct. 21—	DALLAS	4:15
Oct. 28—	at Philadelphia	4:15
Nov. 5—	DENVER (Mon.)	9:00
Nov. 11—	at Seattle	8:30
Nov. 18—	SAN DIEGO	4:05
Nov. 25—	at N.Y. Giants	4:15
Dec. 2—	ARIZONA	4:15
Dec. 9—	KANSAS CITY	4:15
Dec. 15—	at San Diego (Sat.)	4:00
Dec. 22—	TENNESSEE (Sat.)	9:00
Dec. 30—	at Denver	4:15

All times are Eastern.
All games Sunday unless noted.

DRAFT CHOICES

Derrick Gibson, DB, Florida State (first round/28th pick overall).
Marques Tuiasosopo, QB, Washington (2/59).
DeLawrence Grant, DE, Oregon State (3/89).
Raymond Perryman, DB, Northern Arizona (5/158).
Chris Cooper, DT, Nebraska-Omaha (6/184).
Derek Combs, RB, Ohio State (7/228).
Ken-Yon Rambo, WR, Ohio St. (7/229).

2000 REVIEW

RESULTS

Sept. 3—SAN DIEGO	W	9-6	
Sept.10—at Indianapolis	W	38-31	
Sept.17—DENVER	L	24-33	
Sept.24—CLEVELAND	W	36-10	
Oct. 1—Open date			
Oct. 8—at San Francisco (OT)	W	34-28	
Oct. 15—at Kansas City	W	20-17	
Oct. 22—SEATTLE	W	31-3	
Oct. 29—at San Diego	W	15-13	
Nov. 5—KANSAS CITY	W	49-31	
Nov. 13—at Denver	L	24-27	
Nov. 19—at New Orleans	W	31-22	
Nov. 26—ATLANTA	W	41-14	
Dec. 3—at Pittsburgh	L	20-21	
Dec. 10—N.Y. JETS	W	31-7	
Dec. 16—at Seattle	L	24-27	
Dec. 24—CAROLINA	W	52-9	
Jan. 6—MIAMI*	W	27-0	
Jan. 14—BALTIMORE†	L	3-16	

*AFC divisional playoff game.
†AFC championship game.

RECORDS/RANKINGS

2000 regular-season record: 12-4 (1st in AFC West); 5-3 in division; 8-4 in conference; 7-1 at home; 5-3 on road.
Team record last five years: 39-41 (.488, ranks T15th in league in that span).

2000 team rankings:	No.	AFC	NFL
Total offense	*361.0	3	6
Rushing offense	*154.4	1	1
Passing offense	*206.6	7	15
Scoring offense	479	2	3
Total defense	*328.1	9	17
Rushing defense	*96.9	4	5
Passing defense	*231.1	14	25
Scoring defense	299	5	9
Takeaways	37	4	7
Giveaways	20	1	2
Turnover differential	17	3	T3
Sacks	43	5	11
Sacks allowed	28	T4	T5

*Yards per game.

TEAM LEADERS

Scoring (kicking): Sebastian Janikowski, 112 pts. (46/46 PATs, 22/32 FGs).
Scoring (touchdowns): Tim Brown, 66 pts. (11 receiving).
Passing: Rich Gannon, 3,430 yds. (473 att., 284 comp., 60.0%, 28 TDs, 11 int.).
Rushing: Tyrone Wheatley, 1,046 yds. (232 att., 4.5 avg., 9 TDs).
Receptions: Tim Brown, 76 (1,128 yds., 14.8 avg., 11 TDs).
Interceptions: Eric Allen, 6 (145 yds., 3 TDs); William Thomas, 6 (68 yds., 1 TD).
Sacks: Grady Jackson, 8.0.
Punting: Shane Lechler, 45.9 avg. (65 punts, 2,984 yds., 1 blocked).
Punt returns: Darrien Gordon, 8.9 avg. (29 att., 258 yds., 0 TDs).
Kickoff returns: David Dunn, 24.4 avg. (44 att., 1,073 yds., 1 TD).

OAKLAND RAIDERS

No.	QUARTERBACKS	Ht./Wt.	Born	NFL Exp.	College	How acq.	'00 Games GP/GS
12	Gannon, Rich	6-3/210	12-20-65	14	Delaware	UFA/99	16/16
14	Hoying, Bobby	6-3/220	9-20-72	6	Ohio State	T-Phi./99	4/0
16	Peete, Rodney	6-0/225	3-16-66	13	Southern California	FA/00	0/0
	Tuiasosopo, Marques	6-1/219	3-22-79	R	Washington	D2/01	—
	RUNNING BACKS						
	Combs, Derek	5-11/197	2-28-79	R	Ohio State	D7a/01	—
32	Crockett, Zack	6-2/240	12-2-72	6	Florida State	UFA/99	16/4
25	Garner, Charlie	5-9/187	2-13-72	8	Tennessee	UFA/01	*16/15
24	Howard, Chris	5-10/226	5-5-75	3	Michigan	FA/01	*2/1
28	Jordan, Randy	5-11/215	6-6-70	8	North Carolina	UFA/98	16/0
42	Kirby, Terry	6-1/213	1-20-70	8	Virginia	UFA/99	2/0
40	Ritchie, Jon	6-1/250	9-4-74	4	Stanford	D3/98	13/12
47	Wheatley, Tyrone	6-0/235	1-19-72	7	Michigan	FA/99	14/13
	RECEIVERS						
84	Barlow, Reggie	6-0/186	1-22-73	6	Alabama State	FA/01	*16/0
86	Bjornson, Eric (TE)	6-4/236	12-15-71	7	Washington	FA/01	*8/6
87	Brigham, Jeremy (TE)	6-6/255	3-22-75	4	Washington	D5a/98	15/3
81	Brown, Tim	6-0/195	7-22-66	14	Notre Dame	D1/88	16/16
88	Dunn, David	6-3/210	6-10-72	7	Fresno State	FA/00	15/0
48	Fulcher, Mondriel (TE)	6-3/250	10-15-76	2	Miami (Fla.)	D7a/00	10/0
82	Jett, James	5-10/170	12-28-70	9	West Virginia	FA/93	16/13
21	Metcalf, Eric	5-10/188	1-23-68	11	Texas	UFA/00	0/0
1	Porter, Jerry	6-2/225	7-14-78	2	West Virginia	D2/00	12/0
	Rambo, Ken-Yon	6-0/191	10-4-78	R	Ohio State	D7b/01	—
89	Rison, Andre	6-1/199	3-18-67	13	Michigan State	FA/00	16/0
86	Van Dyke, Alex	6-0/205	7-24-74	6	Nevada	FA/01	*4/0
86	Williams, Roland (TE)	6-5/269	4-27-75	3	Syracuse	T-St.L./01	*16/11
	OFFENSIVE LINEMEN						
73	Ashmore, Darryl (G)	6-7/310	11-1-69	10	Northwestern	FA/98	16/0
79	Collins, Mo (T)	6-4/325	9-22-76	4	Florida	D1b/98	16/16
72	Kennedy, Lincoln (T)	6-6/335	2-12-71	9	Washington	T-Atl./96	16/16
73	Middleton, Frank (G)	6-3/334	10-25-74	5	Arizona	UFA/01	*16/16
63	Robbins, Barret (C)	6-3/320	8-26-73	7	Texas Christian	D2/95	16/16
65	Sims, Barry (G)	6-5/295	12-1-74	3	Utah	FA/99	16/8
74	Stinchcomb, Matt (T)	6-6/310	6-3-77	2	Georgia	D1/99	13/9
62	Treu, Adam (C)	6-5/300	6-24-74	5	Nebraska	D3/97	16/0
76	Wisniewski, Steve (G)	6-4/305	4-7-67	13	Penn State	D2/89	16/16
	DEFENSIVE LINEMEN						
93	Armstrong, Trace (E)	6-4/270	10-5-65	13	Florida	UFA/01	*16/0
94	Bryant, Tony (E)	6-6/275	9-3-76	3	Florida State	D2/99	16/16
57	Coleman, Roderick (E)	6-2/265	8-16-76	3	East Carolina	D5b/99	13/1
	Cooper, Chris (T)	6-6/270	12-27-77	R	Nebraska-Omaha	D6/01	—
	Grant, DeLawrence (E)	6-2/267	11-18-79	R	Oregon State	D3/01	—
90	Jackson, Grady (T)	6-2/325	1-21-73	5	Knoxville (Tenn.) College	D6b/97	16/15
96	Russell, Darrell (T)	6-5/325	5-27-76	5	Southern California	D1/97	16/16
99	Taves, Josh (E)	6-7/280	5-13-72	2	Northeastern	FA/00	16/0
91	Upshaw, Regan (E)	6-4/260	8-12-75	6	California	UFA/00	16/7
	LINEBACKERS						
58	Alexander, Elijah	6-2/235	8-2-70	9	Kansas State	FA/00	16/16
50	Barton, Eric	6-2/245	9-29-77	3	Maryland	D5a/99	4/0
54	Biekert, Greg	6-2/255	3-14-69	9	Colorado	D7/93	16/16
55	Brooks, Bobby	6-2/240	3-3-76	2	Fresno State	FA/99	16/0
91	Phillips, Ryan	6-4/252	2-7-74	5	Idaho	UFA/01	*16/15
53	Smith, Travian	6-4/240	8-26-75	3	Oklahoma	D5b/98	16/0
51	Taylor, Ryan	6-2/230	12-11-76	2	Auburn	FA/01	*4/0
51	Thomas, William	6-2/223	8-13-68	11	Texas A&M	FA/00	16/16
	DEFENSIVE BACKS						
21	Allen, Eric	5-10/185	11-22-65	14	Arizona State	T-NO/98	16/15
27	Branch, Calvin (S)	5-11/195	5-8-74	5	Colorado State	D6/97	16/0
33	Dorsett, Anthony (S)	5-11/200	9-14-73	6	Pittsburgh	UFA/00	16/16
	Gibson, Derrick (S)	6-1/211	3-22-79	R	Florida State	D1/01	—
37	Harris, Johnnie (S)	6-2/210	8-21-72	2	Mississippi State	FA/99	15/2
20	James, Tory (CB)	6-2/185	5-18-73	6	Louisiana State	UFA/00	16/1
39	Jennings, Brandon (S)	6-0/195	7-15-78	2	Texas A&M	FA/00	2/0
41	Johnson, Eric (S)	6-0/210	6-30-76	2	Nebraska	FA/00	16/0
25	McDonald, Ramos (CB)	5-11/194	4-30-76	4	New Mexico	FA/01	*3/0
	Perryman, Raymond	6-0/200	11-27-78	R	Northern Arizona	D5/01	—
49	Pope, Marquez	5-11/193	10-29-70	10	Fresno State	FA/00	15/14
24	Woodson, Charles	6-1/205	10-7-76	4	Michigan	D1a/98	16/16
	SPECIALISTS						
11	Janikowski, Sebastian (K)	6-1/255	3-2-78	2	Florida State	D1/00	14/0
9	Lechler, Shane (P)	6-2/230	8-7-76	2	Texas A&M	D5/00	16/0

*Not with Raiders in 2000.

Other free agent veterans invited to camp: DB Clifton Black, G Lamont Burns, TE Pete Chryplewicz, DE Emil Ekiyor, WR Yatil Green, DE Jon Harris, DE Junior Ioane, WR Andy McCullough, WR Terry Mickens, T Toby Myles, T Nathan Parks, RB Corey Walker.

Abbreviations: D1—draft pick, first round; SD-2—supplemental draft pick, second round; W—claimed on waivers; T—obtained in trade; PlanB—Plan B free-agent acquisition; FA—free-agent acquisition (other than Plan B); UFA—unconditional free agent acquisition; ED—expansion draft pick.

MISCELLANEOUS TEAM DATA

Stadium (capacity, surface):
Network Associates Coliseum
(63,142, grass)
Business address:
1220 Harbor Bay Parkway
Alameda, CA 94502
Business phone:
510-864-5000
Ticket information:
800-949-2626
Team colors:
Silver and black
Flagship radio station:
The Ticket, 1050 AM
Training site:
Napa, Calif.
510-864-5000

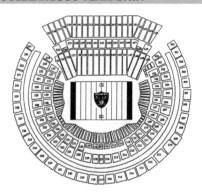

TSN REPORT CARD

Coaching staff	A -	Coach Jon Gruden gets the most out of his players and knows how to push all the right buttons. Defensive coordinator Chuck Bresnahan made a seamless transition from assistant coach and implements solid game plans. Bob Casullo transformed special teams from a perennial weakness into an integral part of the Raiders success.
Quarterbacks	B	Rich Gannon improvises as well as any quarterback, and he always seems to find a way to win. He is an accurate passer who doesn't throw many interceptions or get sacked often. In addition, he is durable, dependable and a leader on and off the field. Bobby Hoying is a bit rusty, but he's a capable backup.
Running backs	A	The Raiders led the league in rushing in 2000. They should be even more potent this season with the addition of Charlie Garner to complement leading rusher Tyrone Wheatley. Garner isn't as fast as the retired Napoleon Kaufman, but he is a better fit for Gruden's offense because of his superb pass-catching ability.
Receivers	C -	Tim Brown remains the go-to guy, but he lacks a suitable complement unless Andre Rison re-signs or someone such as James Jett, Jerry Porter, Reggie Barlow or Ken-yon Rambo emerges. They also lack a reliable deep threat. Roland Williams and Eric Bjornson should combine for more production than the Raiders received from departed tight end Rickey Dudley.
Offensive line	A	A unit that spearheaded the league's top rushing attack and allowed only 28 sacks is back intact and healthy. Left guard Steve Wisniewski and center Barret Robbins are among the best at their respective positions. Backups Frank Middleton, Matt Stinchcomb and Darryl Ashmore give the Raiders tremendous depth and flexibility.
Defensive line	B +	End Trace Armstrong replaces departed fixture Lance Johnstone on a line that got better and better as the season wore on in 2000. Tackle Grady Jackson has the potential to be one of the top linemen in the game. Tackle Darrell Russell and ends Tony Bryant and Regan Upshaw also are key parts of a seven- and eight-man rotation.
Linebackers	C	Middle linebacker Greg Biekert is fresh from another solid, if not spectacular, season. He remains the heart of the defense. William Thomas is very effective on the weak side. Elijah Alexander is solid on the strong-side. The backups are inexperienced and unknown commodities.
Secondary	B -	Cornerbacks Charles Woodson and Eric Allen played as well as any tandem in the league last season. Safeties Anthony Dorsett and Marquez Pope and nickel backs Tory James likely will be more effective this season in their second year with Oakland. This unit can become the strength of the team if the safeties cut down on missed tackles and assignments and rookie Derrick Gibson develops into a starter right away.
Special teams	B +	Punter Shane Lechler looks like the second coming of Ray Guy. David Dunn continually gives the Raiders good field position on kickoff returns. Kick coverage is dependable and solid. Kicker Sebastian Janikowski possesses perhaps the strongest leg around, but he needs to improve his field goal accuracy and depth on kickoffs.

PHILADELPHIA EAGLES
NFC EASTERN DIVISION

2001 SEASON

CLUB DIRECTORY

President/chief executive officer
Jeffrey Lurie
Executive v.p./chief operating officer
Joe Banner
Director of football operations
Tom Modrak
Senior v.p./business operations
Len Komoroski
Senior v.p./chief financial officer
Don Smolenski
Executive dir. of Eagles Youth Partnership
Sarah Helfman
Vice president, corporate sales
Dave Rowan
Vice president of sales
Jason Gonella
Director of pro scouting
Mike McCartney
Director of college scouting
Marc Ross
Dir. of public and community relations
Ron Howard
Coordinator of football media relations
Derek Boyko
Football media relations assistants
Rich Burg   Bob Lange
Dir. of player and community relations
Harold Carmichael
Ticket manager
Leo Carlin
Director of merchandising
Steve Strawbridge
Travel coordinator
Tracey Bucher
Director of security
Anthony Buchanico
Director of penthouse operations
Christiana Noyalas
Director of broadcasting
Rob Alberino

Head coach & exec. v.p. for football operations
Andy Reid

Assistant coaches
Tommy Brasher (defensive line)
Juan Castillo (offensive line)
Brad Childress (quarterbacks)
Dave Culley (wide receivers)
Rod Dowhower (off. coordinator)
Leslie Frazier (defensive backs)
John Harbaugh (special teams)
Jim Johnson (def. coordinator)
Sean McDermott (def. assistant/ quality control)
Tom Melvin (offensive assistant/ quality control)
Ron Rivera (linebackers)
Pat Shurmur (tight ends/ assistant offensive line)
Steve Spagnuolo (def. backs)
Dave Toub (special teams quality control)
Ted Williams (running backs)
Mike Wolf (strength & cond.)

Head athletic trainer
Rick Burkholder
Assistant athletic trainers
Chris Peduzzi   Eric Sugarman
Video director
Mike Dougherty
Equipment manager
John Hatfield

SCHEDULE

Sept. 9—	ST. LOUIS	4:15
Sept. 16—	at Tampa Bay	1:00
Sept. 23—	at Seattle	4:15
Sept. 30—	DALLAS	8:30
Oct. 7—	ARIZONA	1:00
Oct. 14—	Open date	
Oct. 22—	at N.Y. Giants (Mon.)	9:00
Oct. 28—	OAKLAND	4:15
Nov. 4—	at Arizona	4:05
Nov. 11—	MINNESOTA	4:15
Nov. 18—	at Dallas	1:00
Nov. 25—	WASHINGTON	1:00
Nov. 29—	at Kansas City (Thur.)	8:30
Dec. 9—	SAN DIEGO	1:00
Dec. 16—	at Washington	1:00
Dec. 22—	at San Francisco (Sat.)	4:00
Dec. 30—	N.Y. GIANTS	1:05

All times are Eastern.
All games Sunday unless noted.

DRAFT CHOICES

Freddie Mitchell, WR, UCLA (first round/ 25th pick overall).
Quinton Caver, LB, Arkansas (2/55).
Derrick Burgess, DE, Mississippi (3/63).
Correll Buckhalter, RB, Nebraska (4/121).
Tony Stewart, TE, Penn State (5/147).
A.J. Feeley, QB, Oregon (5/155).

2000 REVIEW

RESULTS

Sept. 3—at Dallas	W	41-14
Sept.10—N.Y. GIANTS	L	18-33
Sept.17—at Green Bay	L	3-6
Sept.24—at New Orleans	W	21-7
Oct. 1—ATLANTA	W	38-10
Oct. 8—WASHINGTON	L	14-17
Oct. 15—at Arizona	W	33-14
Oct. 22—CHICAGO	W	13-9
Oct. 29—at N.Y. Giants	L	7-24
Nov. 5—DALLAS (OT)	W	16-13
Nov. 12—at Pittsburgh (OT)	W	26-23
Nov. 19—ARIZONA	W	34-9
Nov. 26—at Washington	W	23-20
Dec. 3—TENNESSEE	L	13-15
Dec. 10—at Cleveland	W	35-24
Dec. 17—Open date		
Dec. 24—CINCINNATI	W	16-7
Dec. 31—TAMPA BAY*	W	21-3
Jan. 7—at N.Y. Giants†	L	10-20

*NFC wild-card game.
†NFC divisional playoff game.

RECORDS/RANKINGS

2000 regular-season record: 11-5 (2nd in NFC East); 5-3 in division; 8-4 in conference; 5-3 at home; 6-2 on road.
Team record last five years: 35-44-1 (.444, ranks 24th in league in that span).

2000 team rankings:

	No.	NFC	NFL
Total offense	*312.9	8	17
Rushing offense	*117.6	6	15
Passing offense	*195.3	10	20
Scoring offense	351	7	12
Total defense	*301.3	5	T10
Rushing defense	*114.4	10	T20
Passing defense	*186.9	3	7
Scoring defense	245	1	4
Takeaways	31	T6	T12
Giveaways	29	T6	T15
Turnover differential	2	T6	T13
Sacks	50	4	6
Sacks allowed	45	12	22

*Yards per game.

TEAM LEADERS

Scoring (kicking): David Akers, 121 pts. (34/36 PATs, 29/33 FGs).
Scoring (touchdowns): Charles Johnson, 42 pts. (7 receiving).
Passing: Donovan McNabb, 3,365 yds. (569 att., 330 comp., 58.0%, 21 TDs, 13 int.).
Rushing: Donovan McNabb, 629 yds. (86 att., 7.3 avg., 6 TDs).
Receptions: Chad Lewis, 69 (735 yds., 10.7 avg., 3 TDs).
Interceptions: Troy Vincent, 5 (34 yds., 0 TDs).
Sacks: Hugh Douglas, 15.0.
Punting: Sean Landeta, 42.3 avg. (86 punts, 3,635 yds., 0 blocked).
Punt returns: Brian Mitchell, 10.5 avg. (32 att., 335 yds., 1 TD).
Kickoff returns: Brian Mitchell, 23.9 avg. (47 att., 1,124 yds., 1 TD).

PHILADELPHIA EAGLES

No.	QUARTERBACKS	Ht./Wt.	Born	NFL Exp.	College	How acq.	'00 Games GP/GS
10	Detmer, Koy	6-1/195	7-5-73	5	Colorado	D7a/97	16/0
	Feeley, A.J.	6-4/220	5-16-77	R	Oregon	D5/01	—
5	McNabb, Donovan	6-2/226	11-25-76	3	Syracuse	D1/99	16/16
	RUNNING BACKS						
24	Autry, Darnell	5-10/210	6-19-76	3	Northwestern	FA/98	11/7
28	Buckhalter, Correll	6-0/222	10-6-78	R	Nebraska	D4/01	—
38	Martin, Cecil (FB)	6-0/235	7-8-75	3	Wisconsin	D6a/99	16/9
30	Mitchell, Brian	5-10/221	8-18-68	12	Southwestern Louisiana	FA/00	16/1
36	Pritchett, Stanley	6-1/240	12-22-73	6	South Carolina	UFA/00	16/2
22	Staley, Duce	5-11/220	2-27-75	5	South Carolina	D3/97	5/5
	RECEIVERS						
88	Bartrum, Mike (TE)	6-4/245	6-23-70	8	Marshall	FA/00	16/0
85	Brown, Na	6-0/196	2-22-77	3	North Carolina	D4c/99	14/2
82	Douglas, Dameane	6-0/195	3-15-76	3	California	W-Oak./99	6/0
89	Lewis, Chad (TE)	6-6/252	10-5-71	4	Brigham Young	W-St.L./99	16/16
84	Mitchell, Freddie	5-11/184	11-28-78	R	UCLA	D1/01	—
87	Pinkston, Todd	6-2/170	4-23-77	2	Southern Mississippi	D2a/00	16/1
86	Scott, Gari	6-0/191	6-2-78	2	Michigan State	D4/00	0/0
48	Stewart, Tony (TE)	6-5/255	8-9-79	R	Penn State	D5a/01	—
	Thomason, Jeff (TE)	6-5/255	12-30-69	8	Oregon	T-GB/00	16/5
80	Thrash, James	6-0/200	4-28-75	5	Missouri Southern	UFA/01	*16/9
	OFFENSIVE LINEMEN						
74	Brzezinski, Doug (G)	6-4/305	3-11-76	3	Boston College	D3/99	16/0
71	Mayberry, Jermane (G)	6-4/325	8-29-73	6	Texas A&M-Kingsville	D1/96	16/16
65	Miller, Bubba (C)	6-1/305	1-24-73	6	Tennessee	FA/96	16/16
69	Runyan, Jon (T)	6-7/330	11-27-73	6	Michigan	UFA/00	16/16
67	Schau, Ryan (T)	6-6/300	12-30-75	3	Illinois	FA/99	10/0
72	Thomas, Tra (T)	6-7/349	11-20-74	4	Florida State	D1/98	16/16
76	Welbourn, John (T)	6-5/318	3-30-76	3	California	D4a/99	16/16
66	Williams, Bobbie (G)	6-3/320	9-25-76	2	Arkansas	D2b/00	0/0
	DEFENSIVE LINEMEN						
77	Burgess, Derrick (E)	6-2/266	8-12-78	R	Mississippi	D3/01	—
93	Davis, Pernell (T)	6-2/320	5-19-76	3	Alabama-Birmingham	D7b/99	0/0
96	Grasmanis, Paul (T)	6-2/298	8-2-74	6	Notre Dame	UFA/00	16/0
91	Hamiter, Uhuru (E)	6-4/280	3-14-73	4	Delaware State	FA/00	7/0
79	Jefferson, Greg (E)	6-3/280	8-31-71	7	Central Florida	D3a/95	0/0
62	Johnson, Dwight (E)	6-4/285	1-30-77	2	Baylor	FA/00	4/0
94	Kalu, Ndukwe (E)	6-3/265	8-3-75	5	Rice	UFA/00	*15/0
90	Simon, Corey (T)	6-2/293	3-2-77	2	Florida State	D1/00	16/16
78	Thomas, Hollis (T)	6-0/306	1-10-74	6	Northern Illinois	FA/96	16/16
97	Walker, Darwin (T)	6-3/294	6-15-77	2	Tennessee	W-Ari./00	*1/0
98	Whiting, Brandon (T)	6-3/285	7-30-76	4	California	D4a/98	16/11
	LINEBACKERS						
56	Caldwell, Mike	6-2/237	8-31-71	9	Middle Tennessee State	FA/98	16/3
55	Caver, Quinton	6-4/230	8-22-78	R	Arkansas	D2/01	—
53	Douglas, Hugh	6-2/280	8-23-71	7	Central State (Ohio)	T-NYJ/98	16/15
51	Emmons, Carlos	6-5/250	9-3-73	6	Arkansas State	UFA/00	16/13
52	Gardner, Barry	6-0/248	12-13-76	3	Northwestern	D2/99	16/13
58	Reese, Ike	6-2/222	10-16-73	4	Michigan State	D5/98	16/0
54	Trotter, Jeremiah	6-1/261	1-20-77	4	Stephen F. Austin State	D3a/98	16/16
	DEFENSIVE BACKS						
32	Bostic, Jason (S)	5-9/181	6-30-76	2	Georgia Tech	FA/99	16/0
42	Cook, Rashard (S)	5-11/197	4-18-77	3	Southern California	W-Chi./99	14/0
20	Dawkins, Brian (S)	5-11/200	10-13-73	6	Clemson	D2b/96	13/13
31	Harris, Al (CB)	6-1/185	12-7-74	4	Texas A&M-Kingsville	W-TB/98	16/4
24	Montgomery, Monty (CB)	5-11/197	12-8-73	5	Houston	UFA/01	*15/9
43	Moore, Damon (S)	5-11/215	9-15-76	3	Ohio State	D4b/99	16/16
21	Taylor, Bobby (CB)	6-3/216	12-28-73	7	Notre Dame	D2a/95	16/15
23	Vincent, Troy (CB)	6-1/200	6-8-71	10	Wisconsin	FA/96	16/16
	SPECIALISTS						
2	Akers, David (K)	5-10/200	12-9-74	3	Louisville	FA/99	16/0
7	Landeta, Sean (P)	6-0/215	1-6-62	17	Towson State	UFA/99	16/0

*Not with Eagles in 2000.

Other free agent veterans invited to camp: DE John Frank, RB Thomas Hamner, WR Kenny Mitchell, C-G John Romero, T Joe Wong.

Abbreviations: D1—draft pick, first round; SD-2—supplemental draft pick, second round; W—claimed on waivers; T—obtained in trade; PlanB—Plan B free-agent acquisition; FA—free-agent acquisition (other than Plan B); UFA—unconditional free agent acquisition; ED—expansion draft pick.

MISCELLANEOUS TEAM DATA

Stadium (capacity, surface):
Veterans Stadium
(65,352, artificial)
Business address:
NovaCare Complex
One NovaCare Way
Philadelphia, PA 19145
Business phone:
215-463-2500
Ticket information:
215-463-5500
Team colors:
Midnight green, silver and white
Flagship radio station:
WYSP, 94.1 FM
Training site:
Lehigh University
Bethlehem, Pa.
610-758-6868

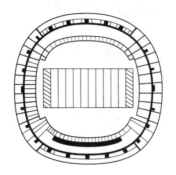

TSN REPORT CARD

Coaching staff	B	Andy Reid did a good job in turning the team around from 5-11 to 11-5 last season, and is second to none when it comes to organization and detail. His game-day decisions raise some eyebrows, and he may be taking on a little too much as he becomes the team's personnel man as well.
Quarterbacks	B	Donovan McNabb was a one-man show for the Eagles last season, and may have to be again this year. In his third year McNabb is the unquestioned leader of the team, and will have to have another MVP-type season for the team to progress. Koy Detmer is a better No. 2 than most people think.
Running backs	C -	If Duce Staley is 100 percent healthy this grade rises dramatically. The problem is the team won't know for sure about Staley until the start of the season. The backups are either unproven, or proven to be inadequate.
Receivers	D +	This group will improve as the year goes on, but to start it's a mess. Only James Thrash has any experience, and he has all of one year with Washington. Todd Pinkston still does not look ready. And Freddie Mitchell is a rookie trying to learn the West Coast offense.
Offensive line	C +	Tra Thomas and Jon Runyan make the Eagles solid at tackles, and guards Jermane Mayberry and John Welbourn are good pass blockers. Center Bubba Miller is a good leader for the line. The problems come in the running game where the line has been inconsistent.
Defensive line	B +	Hugh Douglas is coming off his first All-Pro season and should have another double-digit sack season. His play against the run was better, but still not great. Corey Simon and Hollis Thomas are a good set of tackles, and Brandon Whiting is smart and solid on the left end. N.D. Kalu gives the team a nickel pass rusher.
Linebackers	B	Jeremiah Trotter is an All-Pro in the middle, and should be for a long time. Strongside linebacker Carlos Emmons is solid over the tight end, both against the run and in coverage. The weakside spot is open, and rookie Quinton Caver could take it.
Secondary	A	Troy Vincent might be the best cornerback in the NFC. He's a complete player, excellent in run support and coverage. Bobby Taylor is strong on the other side and rarely makes mistakes. Brian Dawkins is also one of the top free safeties in the game. The question is at strong safety where Damon Moore, a good run supporter, has to become more complete.
Special teams	B	Kicker David Akers showed tremendous accuracy and coolness under pressure last year. He has to avoid a second-year jinx. Punter Sean Landeta, who turned 39 years old in January, shows no signs of age. He had one of his best seasons last year. Returnman Brian Mitchell wore down a little bit last year, but came back to play well in the playoffs.

PITTSBURGH STEELERS
AFC CENTRAL DIVISION

2001 SEASON

CLUB DIRECTORY

President
Daniel M. Rooney
Vice president/general counsel
Arthur J. Rooney II
Administration advisor
Charles H. Noll
Director of business
Mark Hart
Chief negotiator and travel coordinator
Omar Kahn
Accounts coordinator
Jim Ellenberger
Office ticket coordinator
Geraldine Glenn
Director of football operations
Kevin Colbert
Player relations
Anthony Griggs
Communications coordinator
Ron Wahl
Public relations/media manager
Dave Lockett
Pro scouting personnel
Doug Whaley
College scouting coordinator
Bill Baker
College scouts
Mark Gorscak
Phil Kreidler
Doug Kretz
Bob Lane
Bruce McNorton
Dan Rooney
Director of marketing
Tony Quatrini
Trainers
John Norwig
Ryan Grove

Head coach
Bill Cowher

Assistant coaches
Mike Archer (linebackers)
Tom Clements (quarterbacks)
Russ Grimm (offensive line)
Jay Hayes (special teams)
Dick Hoak (running backs)
Kenny Jackson (wide receivers)
Tim Lewis (defensive coordinator)
John Mitchell (defensive line)
Mike Mularkey (off. coordinator)
Willy Robinson (defensive backs)
Ken Whisenhunt (tight ends)

Physicians
James P. Bradley
Joseph Maroon
Anthony P. Yates
Equipment manager
Rodgers Freyvogel
Field manager
Rich Baker
Video coordinator
Bob McCartney
Video assistant
Andy Lizanich
Photographer
Mike Fabus

SCHEDULE

Sept. 9—	at Jacksonville	1:00
Sept. 16—	CLEVELAND	8:30
Sept. 23—	Open date	
Sept. 30—	at Buffalo	1:00
Oct. 7—	CINCINNATI	1:00
Oct. 14—	at Kansas City	1:00
Oct. 21—	at Tampa Bay	1:00
Oct. 29—	TENNESSEE (Mon.)	9:00
Nov. 4—	BALTIMORE	1:00
Nov. 11—	at Cleveland	12:00
Nov. 18—	JACKSONVILLE	4:05
Nov. 25—	at Tennessee	1:00
Dec. 2—	MINNESOTA	1:00
Dec. 9—	N.Y. JETS	4:15
Dec. 16—	at Baltimore	8:30
Dec. 23—	DETROIT	1:00
Dec. 30—	at Cincinnati	1:00

All times are Eastern.
All games Sunday unless noted.

DRAFT CHOICES

Casey Hampton, DT, Texas (first round/19th pick overall).
Kendrell Bell, LB, Georgia (2/39).
Mathias Nkwenti, T, Temple (4/111).
Chukky Okobi, C, Purdue (5/146).
Rodney Bailey, DE, Ohio State (6/181).
Roger Knight, LB, Wisconsin (6/182).
Chris Taylor, WR, Texas A&M (7/218).

2000 REVIEW

RESULTS

Sept. 3—	BALTIMORE	L	0-16
Sept.10—	Open date		
Sept.17—	at Cleveland	L	20-23
Sept.24—	TENNESSEE	L	20-23
Oct. 1—	at Jacksonville	W	24-13
Oct. 8—	at N.Y. Jets	W	20-3
Oct. 15—	CINCINNATI	W	15-0
Oct. 22—	CLEVELAND	W	22-0
Oct. 29—	at Baltimore	W	9-6
Nov. 5—	at Tennessee	L	7-9
Nov. 12—	PHILADELPHIA (OT)	L	23-26
Nov. 19—	JACKSONVILLE	L	24-34
Nov. 26—	at Cincinnati	W	48-28
Dec. 3—	OAKLAND	W	21-20
Dec. 10—	at N.Y. Giants	L	10-30
Dec. 16—	WASHINGTON	W	24-3
Dec. 24—	at San Diego	W	34-21

RECORDS/RANKINGS

2000 regular-season record: 9-7 (3rd in AFC Central); 5-5 in division; 8-5 in conference; 4-4 at home; 5-3 on road.
Team record last five years: 43-37 (.538, ranks T12th in league in that span).
2000 team rankings:

	No.	AFC	NFL
Total offense	*297.9	10	18
Rushing offense	*140.5	4	4
Passing offense	*157.4	14	29
Scoring offense	321	T9	T17
Total defense	*294.6	5	7
Rushing defense	*105.8	8	12
Passing defense	*188.8	6	9
Scoring defense	255	4	6
Takeaways	35	T5	T8
Giveaways	21	2	3
Turnover differential	14	5	6
Sacks	39	T11	T17
Sacks allowed	43	T9	T19

*Yards per game.

TEAM LEADERS

Scoring (kicking): Kris Brown, 107 pts. (32/33 PATs, 25/30 FGs).
Scoring (touchdowns): Jerome Bettis, 48 pts. (8 rushing).
Passing: Kordell Stewart, 1,860 yds. (289 att., 151 comp., 52.2%, 11 TDs, 8 int.).
Rushing: Jerome Bettis, 1,341 yds. (355 att., 3.8 avg., 8 TDs).
Receptions: Hines Ward, 48 (672 yds., 14.0 avg., 4 TDs); Bobby Shaw, 40 (672 yds., 16.8 avg., 4 TDs).
Interceptions: Dewayne Washington, 5 (59 yds., 0 TDs); Chad Scott, 5 (49 yds., 0 TDs).
Sacks: Jason Gildon, 13.5.
Punting: Josh Miller, 43.8 avg. (90 punts, 3,944 yds., 1 blocked).
Punt returns: Hank Poteat, 13.0 avg. (36 att., 467 yds., 1 TD).
Kickoff returns: Hank Poteat, 19.4 avg. (24 att., 465 yds., 0 TDs).

TRAINING CAMP ROSTER

PITTSBURGH STEELERS

No.	QUARTERBACKS	Ht./Wt.	Born	NFL Exp.	College	How acq.	'00 Games GP/GS
11	Graham, Kent	6-5/245	11-1-68	10	Ohio State	UFA/00	12/5
17	Martin, Tee	6-1/221	7-25-78	2	Tennessee	D5b/00	2/0
10	Stewart, Kordell	6-1/211	10-16-72	7	Colorado	D2/95	16/11
	RUNNING BACKS						
36	Bettis, Jerome	5-11/250	2-16-72	9	Notre Dame	T-St.L./96	16/16
45	Fuamatu-Ma'afala, Chris	5-11/252	3-4-77	4	Utah	D6a/98	7/1
33	Huntley, Richard	5-11/225	9-18-72	5	Winston-Salem (N.C.) State	FA/98	13/0
35	Kreider, Dan (FB)	5-11/242	3-11-77	2	New Hampshire	FA/00	10/7
	Rivers, Ron	5-8/205	11-13-71	5	Fresno State	UFA/01	*6/0
38	Witman, Jon (FB)	6-1/240	6-1-72	6	Penn State	D3b/96	6/5
21	Zereoue, Amos	5-8/202	10-8-76	3	West Virginia	D3c/99	12/0
	RECEIVERS						
89	Blackwell, Will	6-0/190	7-9-75	5	San Diego State	D2/97	5/0
87	Bruener, Mark (TE)	6-4/261	9-16-72	7	Washington	D1/95	16/16
80	Burress, Plaxico	6-5/229	8-12-77	2	Michigan State	D1/00	12/9
48	Cushing, Matt (TE)	6-3/258	7-2-75	3	Illinois	FA/98	7/1
81	Edwards, Troy	5-9/192	4-7-77	3	Louisiana Tech	D1/99	14/1
85	Geason, Corey (TE)	6-3/255	8-12-75	2	Tulane	FA/99	9/3
82	Shaw, Bobby	6-0/186	4-23-75	4	California	FA/98	16/0
	Taylor, Chris	5-10/176	4-25-79	R	Texas A&M	D7/01	—
84	Tuman, Jerame (TE)	6-3/250	3-24-76	3	Michigan	D5a/99	16/1
86	Ward, Hines	6-0/197	3-8-76	4	Georgia	D3b/98	16/15
	OFFENSIVE LINEMEN						
62	Duffy, Roger (G)	6-3/299	7-16-67	12	Penn State	UFA/98	13/7
66	Faneca, Alan (G)	6-4/315	12-7-76	4	Louisiana State	D1/98	16/16
72	Gandy, Wayne (T)	6-5/310	2-10-71	8	Auburn	UFA/99	16/16
64	Hartings, Jeff (G)	6-3/295	9-7-72	7	Penn State	UFA/01	*16/16
61	Myslinski, Tom (G)	6-3/293	12-7-68	9	Tennessee	UFA/00	6/0
78	Nkwenti, Mathias (T)	6-3/300	5-11-78	R	Temple	D4/01	—
	Okobi, Chukky (C)	6-2/310	10-18-78	R	Purdue	D5/01	—
54	Schneck, Mike (C)	6-0/242	8-4-77	3	Wisconsin	FA/99	16/0
77	Smith, Marvel (T)	6-5/320	8-6-78	2	Arizona State	D2/00	12/9
71	Tharpe, Larry (T)	6-4/305	11-19-70	9	Tennessee State	UFA/00	12/5
65	Tylski, Rich (G)	6-5/308	2-27-71	6	Utah State	UFA/00	16/16
	DEFENSIVE LINEMEN						
	Bailey, Rodney (E)	6-3/270	10-7-79	R	Ohio State	D6a/01	—
96	Clancy, Kendrick (T)	6-1/280	9-17-78	2	Mississippi	D3a/00	9/0
73	Combs, Chris (E)	6-4/284	12-15-76	2	Duke	D6a/00	6/0
53	Haggans, Clark (E)	6-3/250	1-10-77	2	Colorado State	D5a/00	2/0
98	Hampton, Casey (T)	6-1/321	9-3-77	R	Texas	D1/01	—
91	Smith, Aaron (E)	6-5/281	4-9-76	3	Northern Colorado	D4/99	16/15
74	Sullivan, Chris	6-4/285	3-14-73	6	Boston College	UFA/00	15/2
67	von Oelhoffen, Kimo	6-4/305	1-30-71	8	Boise State	UFA/00	16/16
	LINEBACKERS						
97	Bell, Kendrell	6-1/236	7-17-80	R	Georgia	D2/01	—
57	Fiala, John	6-2/235	11-25-73	4	Washington	FA/98	16/0
92	Gildon, Jason	6-3/255	7-31-72	8	Oklahoma State	D3a/94	16/16
50	Holmes, Earl	6-2/250	4-28-73	6	Florida A&M	D4a/96	16/16
51	Jones, Mike	6-1/240	4-15-69	11	Missouri	UFA/01	*16/16
	Knight, Roger	6-2/234	10-11-78	R	Wisconsin	D6b/01	—
55	Porter, Joey	6-2/240	3-22-77	3	Colorado State	D3a/99	16/16
	DEFENSIVE BACKS						
27	Alexander, Brent (S)	5-11/196	7-10-71	8	Tennessee State	FA/00	16/16
28	Battles, Ainsley (S)	5-10/190	11-6-77	2	Vanderbilt	FA/00	16/1
40	Bell, Myron (S)	5-11/203	9-15-71	R	Michigan State	FA/00	1/0
24	Codie, Nakia	6-2/208	1-20-76	2	Baylor	FA/00	6/0
41	Flowers, Lee (S)	6-0/211	1-14-73	7	Georgia Tech	D5a/95	14/14
31	Logan, Mike	6-0/209	9-15-74	5	West Virginia	UFA/01	*15/11
22	Poteat, Hank (CB)	5-10/190	8-30-77	2	Pittsburgh	D3b/00	15/0
30	Scott, Chad	6-1/192	9-6-74	5	Maryland	D1/97	16/16
47	Shields, Scott (S)	6-4/228	3-29-76	3	Weber State	D2/99	10/1
23	Simmons, Jason (CB)	5-8/186	3-30-76	4	Arizona State	D5/98	15/0
26	Townsend, Deshea (CB)	5-10/175	9-8-75	4	Alabama	D4a/98	16/0
20	Washington, Dewayne (CB)	6-0/193	12-27-72	8	North Carolina State	UFA/98	16/16
43	Williams, Payton	5-7/170	11-19-78	1	Fresno State	FA/00	*7/0
	SPECIALISTS						
3	Brown, Kris (K)	5-10/204	12-23-76	3	Nebraska	D7c/99	16/0
4	Miller, Josh (P)	6-3/219	7-14-70	6	Arizona	FA/96	16/0

*Not with Steelers in 2000.

Other free agent veterans invited to camp: WR Kamil Loud, G Oliver Ross.

Abbreviations: D1—draft pick, first round; SD-2—supplemental draft pick, second round; W—claimed on waivers; T—obtained in trade; PlanB—Plan B free-agent acquisition; FA—free-agent acquisition (other than Plan B); UFA—unconditional free agent acquisition; ED—expansion draft pick.

PITTSBURGH STEELERS

Stadium (capacity, surface):
To be announced
(65,000, grass)
Business address:
3400 South Water St.
Pittsburgh, PA 15203-2349
Business phone:
412-432-7800
Ticket information:
412-323-1200
Team colors:
Black and gold
Flagship radio station:
WDVE, 102.7 FM
Training site:
St. Vincent College
Latrobe, Pa.
412-539-8515

Stadium diagram not available
at press time.

TSN REPORT CARD

Coaching staff	B	The team made several changes offensively, promoting Mike Mularkey from tight ends coach to offensive coordinator and bringing in a quarterbacks coach, Tom Clements, for Kordell Stewart. Both moves will improve the offensive cohesion for Bill Cowher's team.
Quarterbacks	C +	Kordell Stewart has to prove that last year, when he won seven of the 11 games he started, was no fluke. But the team has to be careful to promote Tee Martin to No. 2 too quickly. The Steelers need an experienced man behind Stewart.
Running backs	B	Re-signing Jerome Bettis was a key because of his dependability, durability and production. There has been a return to emphasizing the running game, and Bettis does that very well.
Receivers	C -	Until Plaxico Burress and Troy Edwards prove they were worth No. 1 picks, this will be an unsettled position. Hines Ward has made it difficult for the coaches to take him out of the lineup because he is their most dependable and productive receiver. But Burress has to step up and be a star.
Offensive line	B	This unit made the biggest improvement in 2000, particularly because of the play of LT Wayne Gandy and the development of No. 2 pick, RT Marvel Smith. Adding Jeff Hartings to replace an ailing Dermontti Dawson will be a plus because the team played only 16 games the past two seasons with Dawson.
Defensive line	D	Despite drafting NT Casey Hampton with the top pick, the team still does not have a defensive lineman who can generate pressure on the passer, an area the team wanted to address in the offseason. Moving Kimo von Oelhoffen to end is not the answer. Hampton has to step in and start right away or the team will have to keep von Oelhoffen at the nose. That will leave a hole at defensive end.
Linebackers	C +	This used to be the strongest area on the team. Now it is one of the most puzzling. The team wanted to improve its speed inside, which is why they signed free agent Mike Jones to replace aging Levon Kirkland. But, with no pass rush from the defensive line, that will mean added pressure on OLB Jason Gildon and Joey Porter to get to the quarterback.
Secondary	B	A pretty solid group with tough, aggressive corners. Dewayne Washington has been a great free-agent pickup, but the team needs to add a little speed over the middle. That's why the Steelers signed FS Mike Logan from the Jaguars.
Special teams	B	The team has a pair of young, strong-legged kickers with P Josh Miller and K Kris Brown. And Hank Poteat looks as though he could become one of the league's dangerous punt returners. But the team needs to improve its kick coverage and kick returns. They had to re-sign Will Blackwell, a non-productive wide receiver, because he's been the only consistent kick returner.

ST. LOUIS RAMS
NFC WESTERN DIVISION

2001 SEASON

CLUB DIRECTORY

Chairman
Georgia Frontiere
Vice chairman
Stan Kroenke
President
John Shaw
President/football operations
Jay Zygmunt
General manager
Charley Armey
Sr. v.p./administration, gen. counsel
Bob Wallace
Director of college scouting
Lawrence McCutcheon
Director of pro scouting
Mike Ackerley
Treasurer
Jeff Brewer
Vice president/finance
Adrian Barr-Bracy
Director of operations
John Oswald
Vice president/marketing and sales
Phil Thomas
Vice president of ticket operations
Michael T. Naughton
Director of public relations
Rick Smith
Assistant director of public relations
Duane Lewis
Scouts
Dick Daniels   Ryan Grigson
Tom Marino   Kevin McCabe
David Razzano   Pete Russell
Harley Sewell
Head trainer
Jim Anderson
Assistant trainers
Ron DuBuque
Dake Walden
Physicians
Dr. Bernard Garfinkel Dr. James Loomis
Dr. George Paletta   Dr. Rick Wright

Head coach
Mike Martz

Assistant coaches
Bobby April (special teams)
Chris Clausen (strength and
   conditioning)
Henry Ellard (off. assistant)
Mike Haluchak (linebackers)
Jim Hanifan (offensive line)
Bobby Jackson (associate head
   coach/offensive coordinator/
   running backs)
Bill Kollar (defensive line)
Dana LeDuc (strength and
   conditioning)
John Matsko (assistant head
   coach/offensive line)
Ron Meeks (secondary)
Wilbert Montgomery (tight ends)
Ray Ogas (player programs)
John Ramsdell (quarterbacks)
Matt Sheldon (def. assistant)
Lovie Smith (def. coordinator)
Ken Zampese (wide receivers)

Equipment manager
Todd Hewitt
Assistant equipment manager
Jim Lake
Video director
Larry Clerico
Assistant video director
Bob Whitener

SCHEDULE

Sept. 9—	at Philadelphia	4:15
Sept. 16—	ATLANTA	4:05
Sept. 23—	at San Francisco	4:15
Sept. 30—	MIAMI	1:00
Oct. 8—	at Detroit (Mon.)	9:00
Oct. 14—	N.Y. GIANTS	1:00
Oct. 21—	at N.Y. Jets	1:00
Oct. 28—	NEW ORLEANS	1:00
Nov. 4—	Open date	
Nov. 11—	CAROLINA	1:00
Nov. 18—	at New England	8:30
Nov. 26—	TAMPA BAY (Mon.)	9:00
Dec. 2—	at Atlanta	1:00
Dec. 9—	SAN FRANCISCO	1:00
Dec. 17—	at New Orleans (Mon.)	9:00
Dec. 23—	at Carolina	1:00
Dec. 30—	INDIANAPOLIS	1:00

All times are Eastern.
All games Sunday unless noted.

DRAFT CHOICES

Damione Lewis, DT, Miami, Fla. (first
round/12th pick overall).
Adam Archuleta, DB, Arizona St. (1/20).
Ryan Pickett, DT, Ohio State (1/29).
Tommy Polley, LB, Florida State (2/42).
Brian Allen, LB, Florida State (3/83).
Milton Wynn, WR, Washington State
(4/116).
Brandon Manumaleuna, TE, Arizona
(4/129).
Jeremetrius Butler, DB, Kansas State
(5/145).
Francis St. Paul, WR, Northern Arizona
(6/197).

2000 REVIEW

RESULTS

Sept. 4—DENVER	W	41-36
Sept.10—at Seattle	W	37-34
Sept.17—SAN FRANCISCO	W	41-13
Sept.24—at Atlanta	W	41-20
Oct. 1—SAN DIEGO	W	57-31
Oct. 8—Open date		
Oct. 15—ATLANTA	W	45-29
Oct. 22—at Kansas City	L	34-54
Oct. 29—at San Francisco	W	34-24
Nov. 5—CAROLINA	L	24-27
Nov. 12—at N.Y. Giants	W	38-24
Nov. 20—WASHINGTON	L	20 -33
Nov. 26—NEW ORLEANS	L	24-31
Dec. 3—at Carolina	L	3-16
Dec. 10—MINNESOTA	W	40-29
Dec. 18—at Tampa Bay	L	35-38
Dec. 24—at New Orleans	W	26-21
Dec. 30—at New Orleans*	L	28-31

*NFC wild-card game.

RECORDS/RANKINGS

2000 regular-season record: 10-6 (1st in
NFC West); 5-3 in division; 7-5 in conference; 5-3 at home; 5-3 on road.
Team record last five years: 38-42 (.475,
ranks T18th in league in that span).
2000 team rankings:

	No.	NFC	NFL
Total offense	*442.2	1	1
Rushing offense	*115.2	7	17
Passing offense	*327.0	1	1
Scoring offense	540	1	1
Total defense	*343.4	10	23
Rushing defense	*106.1	5	13
Passing defense	*237.3	13	27
Scoring defense	471	15	31
Takeaways	25	T9	T20
Giveaways	35	T12	T24
Turnover differential	-10	T12	T26
Sacks	51	3	T4
Sacks allowed	44	11	21

*Yards per game.

TEAM LEADERS

Scoring (kicking): Jeff Wilkins, 89 pts.
(38/38 PATs, 17/17 FGs).
Scoring (touchdowns): Marshall Faulk,
160 pts. (18 rushing, 8 receiving, 2 2-pt.
conv.).
Passing: Kurt Warner, 3,429 yds. (347
att., 235 comp., 67.7%, 21 TDs, 18 int.).
Rushing: Marshall Faulk, 1,359 yds. (253
att., 5.4 avg., 18 TDs).
Receptions: Torry Holt, 82 (1,635 yds.,
19.9 avg., 6 TDs).
Interceptions: Dexter McCleon, 8 (28
yds., 0 TDs).
Sacks: Grant Wistrom, 11.0.
Punting: John Baker, 40.4 avg. (43 punts,
1,736 yds., 1 blocked).
Punt returns: Az-Zahir Hakim, 15.3 avg.
(32 att., 489 yds., 1 TD).
Kickoff returns: Tony Horne, 24.2 avg.
(57 att., 1,379 yds., 1 TD).

ST. LOUIS RAMS

No.	QUARTERBACKS	Ht./Wt.	Born	NFL Exp.	College	How acq.	'00 Games GP/GS
9	Germaine, Joe	6-0/220	8-11-75	3	Ohio State	D4/99	0/0
16	Justin, Paul	6-4/211	5-19-68	6	Arizona State	FA/00	0/0
13	Warner, Kurt	6-2/220	6-22-71	4	Northern Iowa	FA/98	11/11
	RUNNING BACKS						
24	Canidate, Trung	5-11/205	3-3-77	2	Arizona	D1/00	3/0
28	Faulk, Marshall	5-10/211	2-26-73	8	San Diego State	T-Ind./99	14/14
42	Hodgins, James	6-1/270	4-30-77	3	San Jose State	FA/99	15/2
25	Holcombe, Robert	5-11/225	12-11-75	4	Illinois	D2/98	14/9
44	Walendy, Craig	6-2/228	7-11-77	2	UCLA	FA/01	*12/0
33	Watson, Justin	6-0/220	1-7-75	3	San Diego State	FA/99	14/2
	RECEIVERS						
83	Blevins, Darrius	6-2/215	4-21-76	1	Memphis State	FA/99	5/0
80	Bruce, Isaac	6-0/188	11-10-72	8	Memphis State	D2/94	16/16
84	Conwell, Ernie (TE)	6-2/265	8-17-72	6	Washington	D2b/96	16/1
81	Hakim, Az-Zahir	5-10/182	6-3-77	4	San Diego State	D4a/98	16/4
88	Holt, Torry	6-0/190	6-5-76	3	North Carolina State	D1/99	16/15
	Manumaleuna, Brandon (TE)	6-2/288	1-4-80	R	Arizona	D4b/01	—
87	Proehl, Ricky	6-0/190	3-7-68	12	Wake Forest	UFA/98	12/4
45	Robinson, Jeff (TE)	6-4/275	2-20-70	9	Idaho	UFA/97	16/2
	St. Paul, Francis	5-9/175	3-25-79	R	Northern Arizona	D6/01	—
	OFFENSIVE LINEMEN						
64	Garcia, Frank (C)	6-2/302	1-28-72	7	Washington	FA/01	*16/16
72	Kline, Andrew (G)	6-2/303	10-5-76	1	San Diego State	D7/00	0/0
67	McCollum, Andy (G)	6-4/295	6-2-70	8	Toledo	UFA/99	16/16
71	Noa, Kaulana (T)	6-3/307	12-29-76	2	Hawaii	D4/00	0/0
61	Nutten, Tom (G)	6-5/304	6-8-71	5	Western Michigan	FA/98	16/16
76	Pace, Orlando (T)	6-7/325	11-4-75	5	Ohio State	D1/97	16/16
73	Spikes, Cameron (G)	6-2/323	11-6-76	3	Texas A&M	D5/99	9/0
70	St. Clair, John (T)	6-4/315	7-15-77	2	Virginia	D3/00	0/0
68	Swanson, Pete (G)	6-5/315	3-26-74	3	Stanford	FA/00	3/0
62	Timmerman, Adam (G)	6-4/300	8-14-71	7	South Dakota State	UFA/99	16/15
50	Tucker, Ryan (T)	6-5/305	6-12-75	5	Texas Christian	D4/97	16/16
	DEFENSIVE LINEMEN						
99	Agnew, Ray (T)	6-3/285	12-9-67	11	North Carolina State	UFA/98	15/15
94	Hyder, Gaylon (T)	6-5/317	10-18-74	3	Texas Christian	FA/99	5/1
97	Jackson, Tyoka	6-2/280	11-22-71	7	Penn State	FA/01	*16/1
95	Jones, Cedric (E)	6-4/290	4-30-74	5	Oklahoma	FA/01	*16/16
92	Lewis, Damione (T)	6-2/301	3-1-78	R	Miami (Fla.)	D1a/01	—
57	Little, Leonard (E)	6-3/257	10-19-74	4	Tennessee	D3/98	14/0
77	Moran, Sean (E)	6-3/280	6-5-73	6	Colorado State	UFA/00	15/3
79	Pickett, Ryan (T)	6-2/310	10-8-79	R	Ohio State	D1c/01	—
98	Wistrom, Grant (E)	6-4/272	7-3-76	4	Nebraska	D1/98	16/16
66	Young, Brian (E)	6-2/290	7-8-77	2	Texas-El Paso	D5/00	11/0
90	Zgonina, Jeff (T)	6-2/300	5-24-70	9	Purdue	UFA/99	16/11
	LINEBACKERS						
51	Allen, Brian	6-1/238	4-1-78	R	Florida State	D3/01	—
	Collins, Todd	6-2/248	5-27-70	9	Carson-Newman (Tenn.)	UFA/99	14/11
58	Davis, Don	6-1/234	12-17-72	4	Kansas	UFA/01	*16/0
55	Fields, Mark	6-2/244	11-9-72	6	Washington State	FA/01	*16/14
59	Fletcher, London	5-10/241	5-19-75	4	John Carroll	FA/98	16/15
53	Miller, Keith	6-1/238	7-9-76	2	California	FA/00	16/0
52	Polley, Tommy	6-3/240	1-11-78	R	Florida State	D2a/01	—
	DEFENSIVE BACKS						
31	Archuleta, Adam (S)	6-0/215	11-27-77	R	Arizona State	D1b/01	—
32	Bly, Dre' (CB)	5-9/185	5-22-77	3	North Carolina	D2/99	16/3
39	Bowen, Matt (S)	6-1/208	11-12-76	2	Iowa	D6/00	16/2
23	Bush, Devin (S)	6-0/210	7-3-73	7	Florida State	UFA/99	13/12
37	Butler, Jerametrius (CB)	5-10/181	11-28-78	R	Kansas State	D5/01	—
38	Coady, Rich (S)	6-0/203	1-26-76	3	Texas A&M	D3/99	12/2
20	Herring, Kim (S)	6-0/200	9-10-75	5	Penn State	UFA/01	*16/16
21	McCleon, Dexter (CB)	5-10/195	10-9-73	5	Clemson	D2/97	16/16
22	Shepherd, Jacoby (CB)	6-1/195	8-31-79	2	Oklahoma State	D2/00	15/1
35	Williams, Aeneas (CB)	5-11/200	1-29-68	11	Southern	T-Ari./01	*16/16
	SPECIALISTS						
4	Baker, John (P)	6-3/223	4-22-77	2	North Texas State	T-Ind./00	15/0
14	Wilkins, Jeff (K)	6-2/205	4-19-72	8	Youngstown State	FA/97	11/0

*Not with Rams in 2000.

Other free agent veterans invited to camp: CB Darwin Brown, DE Jonathan Brown, QB Marc Bulger, TE Giles Cole, CB Buddy Crutchfield, WR Sherrod Gideon, OL Jeff Marriott, CB Damien Wheeler, DE Mark Word.

Abbreviations: D1—draft pick, first round; SD-2—supplemental draft pick, second round; W—claimed on waivers; T—obtained in trade; PlanB—Plan B free-agent acquisition; FA—free-agent acquisition (other than Plan B); UFA—unconditional free agent acquisition; ED—expansion draft pick.

MISCELLANEOUS TEAM DATA

Stadium (capacity, surface):
To be announced (66,000, artificial)
Business address:
1 Rams Way
St. Louis, MO 63045
Business phone:
314-982-7267
Ticket information:
314-425-8830
Team colors:
Rams millennium blue, Rams century
gold
Flagship radio station:
KLOU, 103.3 FM; KATZ, 1600 AM
Training site:
Western Illinois University
Macomb, Ill.
309-298-4400

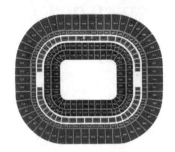

TSN REPORT CARD

Coaching staff	B	Mike Martz made some rookie mistakes last season, but seems determined to learn from them. During the offseason, he added two of the best assistants in the business in Bill Kollar (defensive line) and Bobby April (special teams). Lovie Smith must prove himself as a defensive coordinator, but overall this will be a better-coached team in 2001.
Quarterbacks	B	Before suffering a broken pinky finger that sidelined him for five games in the middle of the season, Kurt Warner proved he was no one-year wonder in guiding the Rams to a 6-0 start. He has toughness, a quick release, and has mastered this offense, but he must cut down on his interception total. The Trent Green trade makes Joe Germaine the backup, and he's thrown only 16 NFL passes.
Running backs	A	Marshall Faulk may be the best all-purpose back in NFL history. Robert Holcombe, a high second-round pick in '98, and Trung Canidate, a low first-rounder in 2000, are quality backups. But Canidate must prove he can stay healthy after a disastrous rookie year. At fullback, James Hodgins has emerged as a punishing lead blocker, although he's very limited offensively.
Receivers	A	This remains the best wide receiver corps in the league. Isaac Bruce, Torry Holt, and Az-Zahir Hakim all can stretch defenses and are elusive in the open field. Ricky Proehl seems to get better with age in his role as a possession receiver who can move the chains. You can slow these guys down, but no one has shut them down in two years.
Offensive line	B	There are Pro Bowlers at left tackle (Orlando Pace) and right guard (Adam Timmerman). LG Tom Nutten is one of the most underrated guards in the league. RT Ryan Tucker was a pleasant surprise in his first year as a starter, and C Andy McCollum performed better than expected in his first year as a Rams starter. As a unit, they're undersized, intelligent, quick and tenacious.
Defensive line	C	This unit is the biggest question mark on the team. Leonard Little, at about 260 pounds, replaces the 300-pound Kevin Carter as the starter at left end. Rookie Damione Lewis and steady journeyman Jeff Zgonina figure to be the starters at tackle. That leaves right end Grant Wistrom as the only returning starter from a year ago. This unit will have a lot to prove.
Linebackers	C -	Middle linebacker London Fletcher is the only returning starter. With only 11 career tackles, former Tampa Bay Buc Don Davis starts at strongside linebacker, with former New Orleans Saint Mark Fields starting at weakside. Two rookies from Florida State, Tommy Polley and Brian Allen, will provide depth. This group can run, but how quickly can it gel?
Secondary	B -	A work in progress, like the rest of the defense. Right corner Dexter McCleon is the only returning starter. But former Cardinal Aeneas Williams adds leadership—and skill—at left corner. Free safety Kim Herring, the former Raven, has the look of a rising star—if he can stay healthy. Rookie Adam Archuleta must make the switch from college linebacker to NFL strong safety.
Special teams	B	The mere addition of April as special teams coach should lead to better play. Hakim must improve his ball security as a punt returner. Canidate is the leading contender for the kickoff return job, replacing Tony Horne. But rookies Milton Wynn and Francis St. Paul will get a look there as well. K Jeff Wilkins is solid; P John Baker must improve.

SAN DIEGO CHARGERS
AFC WESTERN DIVISION

2001 SEASON

CLUB DIRECTORY

Chairman of the board
Alex G. Spanos
President/vice chairman
Dean A. Spanos
Executive vice president
Michael A. Spanos
General manager
John Butler
Vice president/finance
Jeremiah T. Murphy
Chief financial & administrative officer
Jeanne Bonk
Assistant general manager
A.J. Smith
Coordinator/football operations
Ed McGuire
Director of player personnel
Buddy Nix
Business manager
John Hinek
Director/ticket operations
Mike Dougherty
Director/public relations
Bill Johnston
Director/sales and marketing
John Shean
Director/security
Dick Lewis
Trainer
James Collins
Equipment manager
Bob Wick

Head coach
Mike Riley

Assistant coaches
Mark Banker (defensive
assistant/secondary)
Joe Bugel (offensive line)
Paul Chryst (tight ends)
Craig Dickenson (off. assistant)
John Hastings (strength &
conditioning)
Mike Johnson (quarterbacks)
Andrew McClave (def. assistant)
Wayne Nunnely (defensive line)
Joe Pascale (defensive coordinator)
Rod Perry (defensive backs)
Bruce Read (special teams)
Mike Sanford (wide receivers)
Mike Schleelein (assistant
strength & conditioning)
Norv Turner (off. coordinator)
Jim Vechiarella (linebackers)
Ollie Wilson (running backs)

Director/video operations
Brian Duddy

SCHEDULE

Sept. 9—	WASHINGTON	4:15
Sept. 16—	Open date	
Sept. 23—	at Dallas	1:00
Sept. 30—	CINCINNATI	4:15
Oct. 7—	at Cleveland	12:00
Oct. 14—	at New England	1:00
Oct. 21—	DENVER	4:05
Oct. 28—	BUFFALO	4:15
Nov. 4—	KANSAS CITY	4:15
Nov. 11—	at Denver	4:05
Nov. 18—	at Oakland	4:05
Nov. 25—	ARIZONA	4:05
Dec. 2—	at Seattle	4:05
Dec. 9—	at Philadelphia	1:00
Dec. 15—	OAKLAND (Sat.)	4:00
Dec. 23—	at Kansas City	1:00
Dec. 30—	SEATTLE	4:15

All times are Eastern.
All games Sunday unless noted.

DRAFT CHOICES

LaDainian Tomlinson, RB, Texas
Christian (first round/fifth pick overall).
Drew Brees, QB, Purdue (2/32).
Tay Cody, DB, Florida State (3/67).
Carlos Polk, LB, Nebraska (4/112).
Elliot Silvers, T, Washington (5/132).
Zeke Moreno, LB, Southern California
(5/139).
Brandon Gorin, T, Purdue (7/201).
Robert Carswell, DB, Clemson (7/244).

2000 REVIEW

RESULTS

Sept. 3—at Oakland	L	6-9
Sept.10—NEW ORLEANS	L	27-28
Sept.17—at Kansas City	L	10-42
Sept.24—SEATTLE	L	12-20
Oct. 1—at St. Louis	L	31-57
Oct. 8—DENVER	L	7-21
Oct. 15—at Buffalo (OT)	L	24-27
Oct. 22—Open date		
Oct. 29—OAKLAND	L	13-15
Nov. 5—at Seattle	L	15-17
Nov. 12—MIAMI	L	7-17
Nov. 19—at Denver	L	37-38
Nov. 26—KANSAS CITY	W	17-16
Dec. 3—SAN FRANCISCO	L	17-45
Dec. 10—at Baltimore	L	3-24
Dec. 17—at Carolina	L	22-30
Dec. 24—PITTSBURGH	L	21-34

RECORDS/RANKINGS

2000 regular-season record: 1-15 (5th in
AFC West); 1-7 in division; 1-11 in conference; 1-7 at home; 0-8 on road.
Team record last five years: 26-54 (.325,
ranks T28th in league in that span).

2000 team rankings:

	No.	AFC	NFL
Total offense	*268.8	14	28
Rushing offense	*66.4	16	31
Passing offense	*202.4	9	18
Scoring offense	269	14	26
Total defense	*309.9	8	13
Rushing defense	*88.9	3	4
Passing defense	*221.1	12	22
Scoring defense	440	16	29
Takeaways	22	T14	T25
Giveaways	50	16	31
Turnover differential	-28	16	31
Sacks	39	T11	T17
Sacks allowed	53	14	T26

*Yards per game.

TEAM LEADERS

Scoring (kicking): John Carney, 81 pts.
(27/27 PATs, 18/25 FGs).
Scoring (touchdowns): Curtis Conway, 30
pts. (5 receiving); Freddie Jones, 30 pts.
(5 receiving).
Passing: Ryan Leaf, 1,883 yds. (322 att.,
161 comp., 50.0%, 11 TDs, 18 int.).
Rushing: Terrell Fletcher, 384 yds. (116
att., 3.3 avg., 3 TDs).
Receptions: Jeff Graham, 55 (907 yds.,
16.5 avg., 4 TDs).
Interceptions: Rodney Harrison, 6 (97
yds., 1 TD).
Sacks: John Parrella, 7.0.
Punting: Darren Bennett, 46.2 avg. (92
punts, 4,248 yds., 0 blocked).
Punt returns: Nate Jacquet, 7.0 avg. (30
att., 211 yds., 0 TDs).
Kickoff returns: Ronney Jenkins, 22.9
avg. (67 att., 1,531 yds., 1 TD).

SAN DIEGO CHARGERS

No.	QUARTERBACKS	Ht./Wt.	Born	NFL Exp.	College	How acq.	'00 Games GP/GS
9	Brees, Drew	6-0/221	1-15-79	R	Purdue	D2/01	—
7	Flutie, Doug	5-10/178	10-23-62	8	Boston College	FA/00	*11/5
	RUNNING BACKS						
35	Fazande, Jermaine	6-2/255	1-14-75	3	Oklahoma	D2/99	13/7
41	Fletcher, Terrell	5-8/196	9-14-73	7	Wisconsin	D2b/95	16/6
28	Jenkins, Ronney	5-11/188	5-25-77	2	Northern Arizona	FA/00	16/0
44	McCrary, Fred (FB)	6-0/235	9-19-72	5	Mississippi State	FA/99	15/12
21	Tomlinson, LaDainian	5-10/221	6-23-79	R	Texas Christian	D1/01	—
	RECEIVERS						
80	Conway, Curtis	6-1/196	3-13-71	9	Southern California	UFA/00	14/14
84	Davis, Reggie (TE)	6-3/233	9-3-76	3	Washington	FA/99	10/0
85	Dwight, Tim	5-9/180	7-13-75	4	Iowa	T-Atl./01	*14/1
82	Gaylor, Trevor	6-3/195	11-3-77	2	Miami of Ohio	D4a/00	14/2
81	Graham, Jeff	6-2/206	2-14-69	11	Ohio State	FA/99	14/13
83	Heiden, Steve (TE)	6-5/270	9-21-76	3	South Dakota State	D3/99	15/3
88	Jones, Freddie (TE)	6-5/270	9-16-74	5	North Carolina	D2/97	16/16
87	Jones, Reggie	6-0/195	5-8-71	2	Louisiana State	FA/00	11/2
	OFFENSIVE LINEMEN						
50	Binn, David (C)	6-3/245	2-6-72	8	California	FA/94	16/0
69	Ellis, Ed (T)	6-7/325	10-13-75	5	Buffalo	UFA/01	*12/0
67	Fortin, Roman (C)	6-5/297	2-26-67	12	San Diego State	FA/98	16/16
	Gorin, Brandon (T)	6-6/304	7-17-78	R	Purdue	D7a/01	—
71	Graham, DeMingo (G)	6-3/310	9-10-73	3	Hofstra	FA/98	14/1
64	Jacox, Kendyl (C)	6-2/330	6-10-75	4	Kansas State	FA/98	16/3
77	McIntosh, Damion (T)	6-4/325	3-25-77	2	Kansas State	D3/00	3/0
70	Parker, Vaughn (T)	6-3/300	6-5-71	8	UCLA	D2b/94	16/16
74	Roundtree, Raleigh (G)	6-4/295	8-31-75	5	South Carolina State	D4/97	16/15
68	Silvers, Elliot (T)	6-7/321	2-19-78	R	Washington	D5a/01	—
63	Thomas, Jason (C)	6-3/300	6-10-77	1	Hampton	D7/00	0/0
	DEFENSIVE LINEMEN						
96	Carson, Leonardo (T)	6-2/285	2-11-77	2	Auburn	D4b/00	4/0
90	Dingle, Adrian (E)	6-3/272	6-25-77	3	Clemson	D5a/99	14/1
95	Fontenot, Al (E)	6-4/287	9-17-70	9	Baylor	FA/99	15/15
99	Johnson, Raylee (E)	6-3/272	6-1-70	9	Arkansas	D4a/93	0/0
98	Mohring, Michael (T)	6-5/295	3-22-74	5	Pittsburgh	FA/97	7/0
97	Parrella, John (T)	6-3/300	11-22-69	9	Nebraska	FA/94	16/16
91	Pringley, Mike (E)	6-4/277	5-22-76	3	North Carolina	FA/00	2/0
75	Wiley, Marcellus (E)	6-4/275	11-30-74	5	Columbia	UFA/01	*16/15
76	Williams, Jamal (T)	6-3/305	4-28-76	4	Oklahoma State	SD-2/98	16/16
	LINEBACKERS						
51	Dixon, Gerald	6-3/250	6-20-69	9	South Carolina	UFA/98	16/16
53	Humphrey, Deon	6-3/240	5-7-76	2	Florida State	FA/00	10/0
57	Moreno, Zeke	6-2/246	10-10-78	R	Southern California	D5b/01	—
52	Polk, Carlos	6-2/250	2-22-77	R	Nebraska	D4/01	—
	Rogers, Sam	6-3/245	5-30-70	7	Colorado	FA/01	*11/11
56	Ruff, Orlando	6-3/247	9-28-76	3	Furman	FA/99	16/14
55	Seau, Junior	6-3/250	1-19-69	12	Southern California	D1/90	16/16
94	Taylor, Shannon	6-3/247	2-16-75	2	Virginia	D6a/00	11/0
	DEFENSIVE BACKS						
42	Beckett, Rogers (S)	6-3/205	1-31-77	2	Marshall	D2/00	16/3
24	Brown, Fakhir (CB)	5-11/192	9-21-77	3	Grambling State	FA/99	9/8
	Carswell, Robert (S)	5-11/215	10-26-78	R	Clemson	D7b/01	—
27	Cody, Tay (CB)	5-9/180	10-6-77	R	Florida State	D3/01	—
25	Denton, Tim	5-11/182	2-2-73	3	Sam Houston State	FA/00	5/0
37	Harrison, Rodney (S)	6-1/207	12-15-72	8	Western Illinois	D5b/94	16/16
29	Hatcher, Armon (S)	6-0/212	7-15-76	2	Oregon State	FA/00	4/0
47	McNeil, Ryan (CB)	6-2/192	10-4-70	9	Miami (Fla.)	FA/01	*16/16
25	Molden, Alex (CB)	5-10/190	8-4-73	6	Oregon	UFA/01	*15/6
31	Perry, Jason (S)	6-0/200	8-1-76	3	North Carolina State	D4/99	1/0
25	Rusk, Reggie (S)	5-10/190	12-19-72	4	Kentucky	FA/98	7/0
	SPECIALISTS						
2	Bennett, Darren (P)	6-5/235	1-9-65	7	None	FA/94	16/0
5	Richey, Wade (K)	6-3/205	5-19-76	4	Louisiana State	FA/01	*16/0

*Not with Chargers in 2000.

Other free agent veterans invited to camp: QB Dave Dickenson, WR Rodney Williams.

Abbreviations: D1—draft pick, first round; SD-2—supplemental draft pick, second round; W—claimed on waivers; T—obtained in trade; PlanB—Plan B free-agent acquisition; FA—free-agent acquisition (other than Plan B); UFA—unconditional free agent acquisition; ED—expansion draft pick.

MISCELLANEOUS TEAM DATA

Stadium (capacity, surface):
Qualcomm Stadium
(71,000, grass)
Business address:
P.O. Box 609609
San Diego, CA 92160-9609
Business phone:
858-874-4500
Ticket information:
619-280-2121
Team colors:
Navy blue, white and gold
Flagship radio station:
KFMB, 760 AM/STAR 100.7 FM
Training site:
UC San Diego
La Jolla, Calif.
858-455-1976

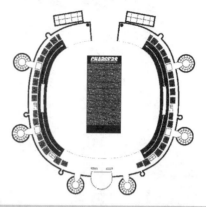

TSN REPORT CARD

Coaching staff	C	Head coach Mike Riley, one of the truly good people in sports, was able to survive a 1-15 record primarily because smart people knew it wasn't all his fault. He did make mistakes on game day, some of them seemingly out of desperation. With new offensive coordinator Norv Turner calling plays now, Riley can concentrate on game management.
Quarterbacks	B -	Ryan Leaf and Jim Harbaugh, last year's primary starters, are gone. In steps 38-year-old Doug Flutie, who may be short, but has a habit of winning games. He's a football player. Rookie Drew Brees, the most productive passer in college football at Purdue in 2000, can watch, learn, and probably play some. A great improvement.
Running backs	B -	The plodding, literally three-yards-and-a-cloud-of-dust running game appears to be gone. Rookie running back LaDanian Tomlinson, last year's collegiate rushing champ at TCU, will start right away ahead of incumbent Jermaine Fazande, who had an unproductive year. Terrell Fletcher is a fine third-down back who can blitz block with the best.
Receivers	C -	Speed has been added, now that wideout Tim Dwight is on board following the trade with Atlanta that gave the Falcons Michael Vick. Wideout Jeff Graham is a smart, terrific pro, but speedy Curtis Conway must stay healthy to make things go. Tight end Freddie Jones is one of the best there is, capable of dominating a secondary.
Offensive line	F +	Right tackle Vaughn Parker, the best lineman, is being moved to left tackle, which he doesn't prefer. Parker and center Roman Fortin are the only two returning starters. Newcomer Ed Ellis, on his third team in three years, is set to start at right tackle. He has one career start. Inexperienced Kendyl Jacox, who has promise, will be the right guard. The left guard is Raleigh Roundtree, who did not start the final game last year due to subpar play.
Defensive line	A -	Much improved. Rush end Marcellus Wiley has been brought in from Buffalo, where he had 10.5 sacks last year, to start on the left side. Left end Raylee Johnson, who missed all of last year with a knee injury—he had 10.5 sacks in 1999—is back. There will be a pass rush. Tackles John Parrella and Jamal Williams are terrific run-stoppers.
Linebackers	B	Perennial Pro Bowler Junior Seau and Gerald Dixon will start on the outside but Orlando Ruff could receive stiff competition from Carlos Polk, a powerful run-stopper out of Nebraska, in the middle. The addition of Polk and another rookie, Zeke Moreno out of USC, should give this group depth, which it didn't have last year.
Secondary	C +	A major problem last year at corner. DeRon Jenkins, a high-priced bust, is gone and free agents Ryan McNeil and Alex Molden have been brought in to man the corner spots. Strong safety Rodney Harrison should have made the Pro Bowl last year and second-year pro Rogers Beckett will start at free safety. He has a lot of upside. Depth has been added at corner.
Special teams	C -	The big news is that placekicker and all-time team scoring leader John Carney is gone. In from the 49ers is Wade Richey, who has a bigger leg than Carney—who lacked depth on kickoffs—and he frequently kicks off into the end zone. Darren Bennett is a Pro Bowl punter. The speedy Dwight will handle punts and kickoffs, along with Ronney Jenkins. More dangerous. Last season's horrible coverage teams, however, must improve.

SAN FRANCISCO 49ERS
NFC WESTERN DIVISION

2001 SEASON

CLUB DIRECTORY

Owner
Denise DeBartolo-York
Owner's representative
John York
V.p./general manager
Terry Donahue
V.p./consultant
Bill Walsh
V.p./director of football administration
John McVay
Chief operating officer
Les Schmidt
V,p. of business development
David Goldman
Pro personnel director
Bill McPherson
Controller
Debye Whelchel
Senior director of communications
Rodney Knox
Director of public relations
Kirk Reynolds
Public relations assistants
Cindy Jensen
Kristin Johnson
Darla Maeda
Chad Steele
Scouts
Jim Abrams   John Brunner
Todd Brunner   Brian Gardner
Jim Gruden   Oscar Lofton
Head trainer
Lindsy McLean
Assistant trainers
Todd Lazenby
Jeff Tanaka
Physicians
Michael Dillingham, M.D.
James Klint, M.D.

Head coach
Steve Mariucci

Assistant coaches
Jerry Attaway (physical
   development coordinator)
Tom Batta (tight ends)
Chris Beake (defensive assistant)
Dwaine Board (defensive line)
Bruce DeHaven (special teams)
Terrell Jones (strength
   development coordinator)
Greg Knapp (off. coordinator)
Brett Maxie (defensive assistant/
   secondary)
Jim Mora (defensive coordinator)
Patrick Morris (offensive line)
Greg Olson (quarterbacks)
Dan Quinn (def. quality control)
Tom Rathman (running backs)
Richard Smith (linebackers)
George Stewart (wide receivers)
Andy Sugarman (off. assistant)
Jason Tarver (off. quality control)

Stadium operations director
Murlan "Mo" Fowell
Equipment manager
Kevin "Tique" Lartigue
Equipment assistants
Nick Pettit
Steve Urbaniak

SCHEDULE

Sept. 9—	ATLANTA	4:15
Sept. 16—	at New Orleans	1:00
Sept. 23—	ST. LOUIS	4:15
Sept. 30—	Open date	
Oct. 1—	at N.Y. Jets (Mon.)	9:00
Oct. 7—	CAROLINA	8:30
Oct. 14—	at Atlanta	1:00
Oct. 28—	at Chicago	1:00
Nov. 4—	DETROIT	4:05
Nov. 11—	NEW ORLEANS	4:15
Nov. 18—	at Carolina	1:00
Nov. 25—	at Indianapolis	1:00
Dec. 2—	BUFFALO	8:30
Dec. 9—	at St. Louis	1:00
Dec. 16—	MIAMI	4:05
Dec. 22—	PHILADELPHIA (Sat.)	4:00
Dec. 30—	at Dallas	1:00

All times are Eastern.
All games Sunday unless noted.

DRAFT CHOICES

Andre Carter, DE, California (first round/
seventh pick overall).
Jamie Winborn, LB, Vanderbilt (2/47).
Kevan Barlow, RB, Pittsburgh (3/80).
Cedrick Wilson, WR, Tennessee (6/169).
Rashad Holman, DB, Louisville (6/179).
Menson Holloway, DE, Texas-El Paso
(6/191).
Alex Lincoln, LB, Auburn (7/209).
Eric Johnson, TE, Yale (7/224).

2000 REVIEW

RESULTS

Sept. 3	—at Atlanta	L	28-36
Sept.10	—CAROLINA	L	22-38
Sept.17	—at St. Louis	L	24-41
Sept.24	—at Dallas	W	41-24
Oct. 1	—ARIZONA	W	27-20
Oct. 8	—OAKLAND (OT)	L	28-34
Oct. 15	—at Green Bay	L	28-31
Oct. 22	—at Carolina	L	16-34
Oct. 29	—ST. LOUIS	L	24-34
Nov. 5	—at New Orleans	L	15-31
Nov. 12	—KANSAS CITY	W	21-7
Nov. 19	—ATLANTA	W	16-6
Nov. 26	—Open date		
Dec. 3	—at San Diego	W	45-17
Dec. 10	—NEW ORLEANS	L	27-31
Dec. 17	—CHICAGO	W	17-0
Dec. 23	—at Denver	L	9-38

RECORDS/RANKINGS

2000 regular-season record: 6-10 (4th in
NFC West); 1-7 in division; 4-8 in conference; 4-4 at home; 2-6 on road.
Team record last five years: 47-33 (.588,
ranks T6th in league in that span).

2000 team rankings:	No.	NFC	NFL
Total offense	*377.5	2	4
Rushing offense	*112.6	8	18
Passing offense	*264.9	2	4
Scoring offense	388	T3	T6
Total defense	*356.8	14	29
Rushing defense	*112.1	7	16
Passing defense	*244.7	15	29
Scoring defense	422	13	28
Takeaways	21	12	T27
Giveaways	19	1	1
Turnover differential	2	T6	T13
Sacks	38	T7	T19
Sacks allowed	25	1	3
*Yards per game.			

TEAM LEADERS

Scoring (kicking): Wade Richey, 88 pts.
(43/45 PATs, 15/22 FGs).
Scoring (touchdowns): Terrell Owens, 80
pts. (13 receiving, 1 2-pt. conv.).
Passing: Jeff Garcia, 4,278 yds. (561 att.,
355 comp., 63.3%, 31 TDs, 10 int.).
Rushing: Charlie Garner, 1,142 yds. (258
att., 4.4 avg., 7 TDs).
Receptions: Terrell Owens, 97 (1,451
yds., 15.0 avg., 13 TDs).
Interceptions: Zack Bronson, 3 (75 yds.,
0 TDs); Delmonico Montgomery, 3 (68
yds., 1 TD).
Sacks: Bryant Young, 9.5.
Punting: Chad Stanley, 39.5 avg. (69
punts, 2,727 yds., 1 blocked).
Punt returns: Kevin Williams, 8.5 avg. (26
att., 220 yds., 0 TDs).
Kickoff returns: Kevin Williams, 17.9 avg.
(30 att., 536 yds., 0 TDs).

SAN FRANCISCO 49ERS

No.	QUARTERBACKS	Ht./Wt.	Born	NFL Exp.	College	How acq.	'00 Games GP/GS
5	Garcia, Jeff	6-1/195	2-24-70	3	San Jose State	FA/99	16/16
3	Mirer, Rick	6-3/212	3-19-70	8	Notre Dame	FA/00	1/0
13	Rattay, Tim	6-0/215	3-15-77	2	Louisiana Tech	D7a/00	1/0
	RUNNING BACKS						
32	Barlow, Kevan	6-1/238	1-7-79	R	Pittsburgh	D3/01	—
40	Beasley, Fred (FB)	6-0/235	9-18-74	4	Auburn	D6/98	15/15
20	Hearst, Garrison	5-11/215	1-4-71	9	Georgia	FA/97	0/0
22	Jackson, Terry	6-0/232	1-10-76	3	Florida	D5a/99	15/1
43	Lewis, Jonas	5-9/210	12-27-76	2	San Diego State	FA/00	10/0
27	Smith, Paul	5-11/234	1-31-78	2	Texas-El Paso	D5a/00	10/0
	RECEIVERS						
85	Clark, Greg (TE)	6-4/251	4-7-72	5	Stanford	D3/97	15/15
86	Jennings, Brian (TE)	6-5/245	10-14-76	2	Arizona State	D7/00	16/0
	Johnson, Eric (TE)	6-3/230	8-15-79	R	Yale	D7b/01	—
81	Owens, Terrell	6-3/217	12-7-73	6	Tennessee-Chattanooga	D3/96	14/13
80	Rice, Jerry	6-2/196	10-13-62	17	Mississippi Valley State	D1//85	16/16
83	Stokes, J.J.	6-4/217	10-6-72	7	UCLA	D1//95	16/3
89	Streets, Tai	6-1/193	4-20-77	3	Michigan	D6/99	15/1
88	Swift, Justin (TE)	6-3/265	8-14-75	2	Kansas State	FA/00	16/1
14	Wilson, Cedrick	5-9/179	12-17-78	R	Tennessee	D6a/01	—
	OFFENSIVE LINEMEN						
65	Brown, Ray (G)	6-5/318	12-12-62	15	Arkansas State	FA//96	16/16
67	Dalman, Chris (C)	6-3/297	3-15-70	9	Stanford	D6//93	0/0
63	Deese, Derrick (T)	6-3/289	5-17-70	10	Southern California	FA/92	13/13
79	Dercher, Dan (T)	6-5/293	6-2-76	2	Kansas	FA/99	2/0
74	Fiore, Dave (T)	6-4/290	8-10-74	6	Hofstra	FA/97	15/15
78	Gragg, Scott (T)	6-8/325	2-28-72	7	Montana	D2/95	16/16
66	Hopson, Tyrone (G)	6-2/305	5-28-76	3	Eastern Kentucky	D5b/99	3/1
60	Lynch, Ben (C)	6-4/295	11-18-72	3	California	FA/99	9/0
62	Newberry, Jeremy (G)	6-5/315	3-23-76	4	California	D2/98	16/16
77	Willig, Matt (T)	6-8/317	1-21-69	10	Southern California	UFA/00	16/3
	DEFENSIVE LINEMEN						
90	Bryant, Junior (T)	6-4/278	1-16-71	6	Notre Dame	FA/93	3/3
96	Carter, Andre (E)	6-4/265	5-12-79	R	California	D1/01	—
95	Engelberger, John (E)	6-4/260	10-18-76	2	Virginia Tech	D2a/00	16/13
95	Hobgood-Chittick, Nate (T)	6-3/290	11-30-74	3	North Carolina	W-St.L./00	10/0
	Holloway, Menson (E)	6-2/270	7-12-78	R	Texas-El Paso	D6b/01	—
71	Killings, Cedric (T)	6-2/290	12-14-77	2	Carson-Newman (Tenn.)	FA/00	14/1
92	McGrew, Reggie (T)	6-1/301	12-16-76	3	Florida	D1/99	10/0
99	Milem, John (E)	6-7/290	6-9-75	2	Lenoir-Rhyne College (N.C.)	D5b/00	16/0
91	Okeafor, Chike (E)	6-4/248	3-27-76	3	Purdue	D3/99	15/0
94	Stubblefield, Dana (T)	6-2/315	11-14-70	9	Kansas	FA/01	*15/14
97	Young, Bryant (T)	6-3/291	1-27-72	8	Notre Dame	D1//94	15/15
	LINEBACKERS						
	Lincoln, Alex	6-0/237	11-17-77	R	Auburn	D7a/01	—
98	Peterson, Julian	6-3/235	7-28-78	2	Michigan State	D1a/00	13/7
50	Smith, Derek	6-2/239	1-18-75	5	Arizona State	UFA/01	*16/14
53	Ulbrich, Jeff	6-0/249	2-17-77	2	Hawaii	D3b/00	4/0
55	Winborn, Jamie	6-0/242	5-14-79	R	Vanderbilt	D2/01	—
	DEFENSIVE BACKS						
31	Bronson, Zack (S)	6-1/195	1-28-74	4	McNeese State	FA/97	9/7
38	Heard, Ronnie (S)	6-2/215	10-5-76	2	Mississippi	FA/00	13/3
28	Keith, John (S)	6-0/207	2-4-77	2	Furman	D4/00	6/3
21	Parker, Anthony (CB)	6-1/200	12-4-75	3	Weber State	D4a/99	16/0
29	Plummer, Ahmed (CB)	5-11/191	3-26-76	2	Ohio State	D1b/00	16/14
23	Prioleau, Pierson (CB)	5-10/191	8-6-77	3	Virginia Tech	D4b/99	14/6
30	Schulters, Lance (S)	6-2/195	5-27-75	4	Hofstra	D4/98	12/12
36	Webster, Jason (CB)	5-9/180	9-8-77	2	Texas A&M	D2b/00	16/10
	SPECIALISTS						
4	Stanley, Chad (P)	6-3/205	1-29-76	3	Stephen F. Austin State	FA/99	16/0

*Not with 49ers in 2000.

Other free agent veterans invited to camp: QB Giovanni Carmazzi, CB Dee Moronkola.

Abbreviations: D1—draft pick, first round; SD-2—supplemental draft pick, second round; W—claimed on waivers; T—obtained in trade; PlanB—Plan B free-agent acquisition; FA—free-agent acquisition (other than Plan B); UFA—unconditional free agent acquisition; ED—expansion draft pick.

Stadium (capacity, surface):
 3Com Park at Candlestick Point
 (70,270, grass)
Business address:
 4949 Centennial Blvd.
 Santa Clara, CA 95054-1229
Business phone:
 408-562-4949
Ticket information:
 415-656-4900
Team colors:
 Forty Niners gold and cardinal
Flagship radio station:
 KGO, 810 AM
Training site:
 University of Pacific
 Stockton, Calif.
 209-932-4949

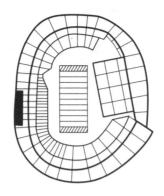

SAN FRANCISCO 49ERS

TSN REPORT CARD

Coaching staff — B + — Equal doses of optimism, enthusiasm and patience make this a perfect staff for the rebuilding project at hand. The 49ers still have some of the best West Coast offense minds in the game as they proved last year with the NFL's fourth-ranked offense.

Quarterbacks — B - — Jeff Garcia's emergence can't be written off as a fluke since coaches spoke of the promise he showed throughout the spring and the summer. He is a comfortable fit in the 49ers' offense. But he won't take defenses by surprise anymore, and he has lost some firepower without Charlie Garner and Jerry Rice.

Running backs — C - — A Garrison Hearst return from an ankle injury that has kept him sidelined for two years would be a triumphant story, but he likely won't be able to carry a heavy load. No other tailback is proven. And teams rarely flourish with a committee approach at tailback. The 49ers need someone to emerge, but they will benefit from having experienced fullback Fred Beasley.

Receivers — B — If Tai Streets returns healthy from a broken leg, he could more than make up for the loss of Jerry Rice. Along with Terrell Owens and J.J. Stokes, the 49ers could have an impressive trio. It all starts with Owens, who is arguably the most complete receiver in the game today. Stokes, a disappointment the past two seasons, needs a career resurgence.

Offensive line — B + — The veterans are another year older, but both Derrick Deese and Ray Brown played some of their best football last year. Why should things be different, especially since all five starters (and top backup Matt Willig) return intact after a stellar year?

Defensive line — B - — The 49ers added an inexperienced end and a struggling tackle in the offseason, and they've never been more excited about their defense's prospects. Why? Because the tackle, Dana Stubblefield, once starred in San Francisco, and the rookie end, Andre Carter, is their most highly-touted draft pick in recent memory. Bryant Young remains the defense's anchor.

Linebackers — C - — The 49ers figure to see both the negatives of inexperience and the positives of athleticism as they replace veterans Ken Norton Jr. and Winfred Tubbs with younger athletes. But the scariest proposition here is their lack of depth. Julian Peterson should have a breakout season.

Defensive backs — C — Three rookie starters from last year are all a year older, but it's still a pretty inexperienced unit. If safeties Lance Schulters and John Keith can return strong from season-ending injuries, the 49ers will be more stable. And everyone should benefit from a stronger pass rush.

Special teams — C - — A lot will hinge on whether the 49ers can adequately replace kicker Wade Richey. They figure to be in a lot of tight games and will need a sturdy leg. Plus, Richey excelled at deep kickoffs. The coverage and return units should both be stocked with young athletes. Punter Chad Stanley is mediocre.

SEATTLE SEAHAWKS
AFC WESTERN DIVISION

2001 SEASON

CLUB DIRECTORY

Owner
Paul Allen
Vice chairman
Bert Kolde
President
Bob Whitsitt
Senior vice president
Mike Reinfeldt
Vice president/football operations
Ted Thompson
V.p./ticket sales & services
Duane McLean
V.p./communications
Gary Wright
Public relations director
Dave Pearson
Community outreach director
Sandy Gregory
Player relations director
Nesby Glasgow
Assistant to the general manager
Gary Reynolds
Admin. assistant/football operations
Bill Nayes
Director of player personnel
John Schneider
College scouting director
Scott McCloughan
Pro scouting director
Will Lewis
Scouts
Bucky Brooks   Derrick Jensen
Matt Malaspina   Mike Murphy
John Peterson   Eric Stokes
Head trainer
Paul Federici
Assistant trainers
James Oglesby Jr.
Sam Ramsden
Ken Smith

Executive v.p. of football ops. /g.m. and head coach
Mike Holmgren

Assistant coaches
Larry Brooks (defensive line)
Jerry Colquitt (off. qual. control)
Nolan Cromwell (wide receivers)
Ken Flajole (defensive backs)
Gil Haskell (off. coordinator)
Johnny Holland (linebackers)
Kent Johnston (strength and
   conditioning)
Jim Lind (tight ends)
Clayton Lopez (defensive quality
   control and defensive backs)
Tom Lovat (asst. head coach/
   offensive line)
Mark Michaels (assistant special
   teams)
Stump Mitchell (running backs)
Pete Rodriguez (special teams)
Steve Sidwell (def. coordinator)
Rod Springer (assistant strength
   and conditioning)
Jim Zorn (quarterbacks)

Equipment manager
Erik Kennedy
Assistant equipment managers
Jeff Bower
Brad Melland
Video director
Thom Fermstad

SCHEDULE

Sept.	9— at Cleveland	12:00
Sept.	16— KANSAS CITY	4:15
Sept.	23— PHILADELPHIA	4:15
Sept.	30— at Oakland	4:15
Oct.	7— JACKSONVILLE	4:05
Oct.	14— DENVER	4:15
Oct.	21— Open date	
Oct.	28— MIAMI	4:15
Nov.	4— at Washington	4:15
Nov.	11— OAKLAND	8:30
Nov.	18— at Buffalo	1:00
Nov.	25— at Kansas City	1:00
Dec.	2— SAN DIEGO	4:05
Dec.	9— at Denver	8:30
Dec.	16— DALLAS	4:15
Dec.	23— at N.Y. Giants	1:00
Dec.	30— at San Diego	4:15

All times are Eastern.
All games Sunday unless noted.

DRAFT CHOICES

Koren Robinson, WR, North Carolina State (first round/ninth pick overall).
Steve Hutchinson, G, Michigan (1/17).
Ken Lucas, DB, Mississippi (2/40).
Heath Evans, RB, Auburn (3/82).
Orlando Huff, LB, Fresno State (4/104).
Curtis Fuller, DB, TCU (4/127).
Floyd Womack, T, Miss. State (4/128).
Alex Bannister, WR, E. Kentucky (5/140).
Josh Booty, QB, Louisiana State (6/172).
Harold Blackmon, DB, Northwestern (7/210).
Dennis Norman, T, Princeton (7/222).
Kris Kocurek, DT, Texas Tech (7/237).

2000 REVIEW

RESULTS

Sept. 3—at Miami	L	0-23
Sept.10—ST. LOUIS	L	34-37
Sept.17—NEW ORLEANS	W	20-10
Sept.24—at San Diego	W	20-12
Oct. 2—at Kansas City	L	17 -24
Oct. 8—at Carolina	L	3-26
Oct. 15—INDIANAPOLIS	L	24-37
Oct. 22—at Oakland	L	3-31
Oct. 29—KANSAS CITY	L	19-24
Nov. 5—SAN DIEGO	W	17-15
Nov. 12—at Jacksonville	W	28-21
Nov. 19—Open date		
Nov. 26—DENVER	L	31-38
Dec. 3—at Atlanta	W	30-10
Dec. 10—at Denver	L	24-31
Dec. 16—OAKLAND	W	27-24
Dec. 23—BUFFALO	L	23-42

RECORDS/RANKINGS

2000 regular-season record: 6-10 (4th in AFC West); 3-5 in division; 4-8 in conference; 3-5 at home; 3-5 on road.
Team record last five years: 38-42 (.475, ranks T18th in league in that span).
2000 team rankings:

	No.	AFC	NFL
Total offense	*292.5	11	19
Rushing offense	*107.5	11	22
Passing offense	*185.0	11	21
Scoring offense	320	11	19
Total defense	*399.4	16	31
Rushing defense	*153.4	15	28
Passing defense	*246.1	15	30
Scoring defense	405	14	25
Takeaways	29	T9	T16
Giveaways	38	14	27
Turnover differential	-9	14	T23
Sacks	27	15	T27
Sacks allowed	46	11	23

*Yards per game.

TEAM LEADERS

Scoring (kicking): Rian Lindell, 70 pts. (25/25 PATs, 15/17 FGs).
Scoring (touchdowns): Ricky Watters, 54 pts. (7 rushing, 2 receiving).
Passing: Jon Kitna, 2,658 yds. (418 att., 259 comp., 62.0%, 18 TDs, 19 int.).
Rushing: Ricky Watters, 1,242 yds. (278 att., 4.5 avg., 7 TDs).
Receptions: Sean Dawkins, 63 (731 yds., 11.6 avg., 5 TDs).
Interceptions: Jay Bellamy, 4 (132 yds., 1 TD); Willie Williams, 4 (74 yds., 1 TD).
Sacks: Chad Brown, 6.0; Lamar King, 6.0.
Punting: Jeff Feagles, 40.0 avg. (74 punts, 2,960 yds., 1 blocked).
Punt returns: Charlie Rogers, 14.0 avg. (26 att., 363 yds., 0 TDs).
Kickoff returns: Charlie Rogers, 24.7 avg. (66 att., 1,629 yds., 1 TD).

TRAINING CAMP ROSTER

SEATTLE SEAHAWKS

No.	QUARTERBACKS	Ht./Wt.	Born	NFL Exp.	College	How acq.	'00 Games GP/GS
2	Booty, Josh	6-2/221	4-29-75	R	Louisiana State	D6/01	—
5	Brown, Travis	6-3/218	7-17-77	2	Northern Arizona	FA/00	1/0
8	Hasselbeck, Matt	6-4/220	9-25-75	3	Boston College	T-GB/01	*16/0
11	Huard, Brock	6-4/228	4-15-76	3	Washington	D3a/99	5/4
	RUNNING BACKS						
37	Alexander, Shaun	5-11/218	8-30-77	2	Alabama	D1a/00	16/1
34	Brown, Reggie (FB)	6-0/244	6-26-73	6	Fresno State	D3b/96	12/1
44	Evans, Heath (FB)	6-0/246	12-30-78	R	Auburn	D3/01	—
38	Strong, Mack (FB)	6-0/235	9-11-71	8	Georgia	FA/93	16/13
32	Watters, Ricky	6-1/217	4-7-69	11	Notre Dame	UFA/98	16/16
	RECEIVERS						
83	Bailey, Karsten	5-10/201	4-26-77	3	Auburn	D3b/99	9/0
18	Bannister, Alex	6-5/201	4-23-79	R	Eastern Kentucky	D5/01	—
19	Bownes, Fabien	5-11/192	2-29-72	4	Western Illinois	W-Chi./99	16/0
52	Darche, Jean-Philippe (TE)	6-0/242	2-28-75	2	McGill (Montreal)	FA/00	16/0
86	Fauria, Christian (TE)	6-4/245	9-22-71	7	Colorado	D2/95	15/10
85	Hill, James (TE)	6-4/246	10-25-74	2	Abilene Christian	FA/00	10/0
82	Jackson, Darrell	6-0/197	12-6-78	2	Florida	D3/00	16/9
89	Mili, Itula (TE)	6-4/265	4-20-73	5	Brigham Young	D6/97	16/6
81	Robinson, Koren	6-1/211	3-19-80	R	North Carolina State	D1a/01	—
88	Williams, James	5-10/180	3-6-78	2	Marshall	D6a/00	10/0
	OFFENSIVE LINEMEN						
63	Beede, Frank (G)	6-4/296	5-1-73	6	Panhandle State (Okla.)	FA/96	7/0
62	Gray, Chris (G)	6-4/305	6-19-70	9	Auburn	UFA/98	16/16
76	Hutchinson, Steve (G)	6-5/306	11-1-77	R	Michigan	D1b/01	—
71	Jones, Walter (T)	6-5/300	1-19-74	5	Florida State	D1b/97	16/16
75	McIntosh, Chris (T)	6-6/315	2-20-77	2	Wisconsin	D1b/00	14/10
	Norman, Dennis (T)	6-4/280	1-26-80	R	Princeton	D7b/01	—
79	Overhauser, Chad (T)	6-4/316	6-17-75	4	UCLA	T-Chi./00	0/0
61	Tobeck, Robbie (C)	6-4/298	3-6-70	8	Washington State	UFA/00	4/0
69	Wedderburn, Floyd (T)	6-5/333	5-5-76	3	Penn State	D5a/99	16/16
74	Weiner, Todd (T)	6-4/300	9-16-75	4	Kansas State	D2/98	16/6
77	Womack, Floyd (T)	6-4/345	11-15-78	R	Mississippi State	D4c/01	—
	DEFENSIVE LINEMEN						
78	Cochran, Antonio (T)	6-4/297	6-21-76	3	Georgia	D4/99	15/0
90	Eaton, Chad (T)	6-5/300	4-6-72	6	Washington State	UFA/01	*14/13
95	Hilliard, John (E)	6-2/285	4-16-76	2	Mississippi State	D6c/00	5/0
92	King, Lamar (E)	6-3/294	8-10-75	3	Saginaw Valley State (Mich.)	D1/99	14/14
	Kocurek, Kris (T)	6-5/293	11-15-78	R	Texas Tech	D7c/01	—
91	LaBounty, Matt (T)	6-4/275	1-3-69	9	Oregon	T-GB/96	12/2
93	Randle, John (T)	6-1/287	12-12-67	12	Texas A&I	FA/01	*16/16
70	Sinclair, Michael (E)	6-4/275	1-31-68	11	Eastern New Mexico	D6/91	16/16
73	Staat, Jeremy (E)	6-5/300	10-10-76	4	Arizona State	FA/01	*7/0
	LINEBACKERS						
55	Bell, Marcus	6-1/237	7-19-77	2	Arizona	D4a/00	16/0
94	Brown, Chad	6-2/240	7-12-70	9	Colorado	UFA/97	16/16
57	Huff, Orlando	6-2/245	8-14-78	R	Fresno State	D4a/01	—
58	Kacyvenski, Isaiah	6-1/250	10-3-77	2	Harvard	D4b/00	16/0
99	Kirkland, Levon	6-1/270	2-17-69	10	Clemson	FA/01	*16/16
51	Simmons, Anthony	6-0/230	6-20-76	4	Clemson	D1/98	16/16
59	Terry, Tim	6-2/239	7-26-74	3	Temple	FA/00	6/0
	DEFENSIVE BACKS						
	Blackmon, Harold (CB)	5-11/210	5-20-78	R	Northwestern	D7a/01	—
23	Charlton, Ike (S)	5-11/205	10-6-77	2	Virginia Tech	D2/00	16/0
29	Fuller, Curtis (S)	5-10/186	7-25-78	R	Texas Christian	D4b/01	—
33	Kelly, Maurice (S)	6-2/205	10-9-72	2	East Tennessee State	FA/00	16/0
26	Lucas, Ken (CB)	6-0/200	1-23-79	R	Mississippi	D2/01	—
22	Miranda, Paul (CB)	5-10/182	5-2-76	3	Central Florida	FA/00	3/0
31	Robertson, Marcus (S)	5-11/205	10-2-69	11	Iowa State	FA/01	*15/15
24	Springs, Shawn (CB)	6-0/195	3-11-75	5	Ohio State	D1a/97	16/16
25	Tongue, Reggie (S)	6-0/206	4-11-73	6	Oregon State	UFA/00	16/6
27	Williams, Willie (CB)	5-9/180	12-26-70	8	Western Carolina	UFA/97	16/15
	SPECIALISTS						
10	Feagles, Jeff (P)	6-1/207	3-7-66	14	Miami (Fla.)	UFA/98	16/0
9	Lindell, Rian (K)	6-3/241	1-20-77	2	Washington State	FA/00	12/0
20	Rogers, Charlie (KR)	5-9/179	6-19-76	3	Georgia Tech	D5b/99	15/0

*Not with Seahawks in 2000.

Other free agent veterans invited to camp: G Chris Brymer, TE Rufus French, RB Jay Graham, T Eric King, CB Chris Rogers, S Tawambi Settles, CB Fred Vinson, DT Tim Watson, DT Cedric Woodard.

Abbreviations: D1—draft pick, first round; SD-2—supplemental draft pick, second round; W—claimed on waivers; T—obtained in trade; PlanB—Plan B free-agent acquisition; FA—free-agent acquisition (other than Plan B); UFA—unconditional free agent acquisition; ED—expansion draft pick.

MISCELLANEOUS TEAM DATA

Stadium (capacity, surface):
Husky Stadium (72,500, artificial)
Business address:
11220 N.E. 53rd Street
Kirkland, WA 98033
Business phone:
425-827-9777
Ticket information:
800-635-4295
Team colors:
Blue, green and silver
Flagship radio station:
KIRO, 710 AM
Training site:
Eastern Washington University
Cheney, Wash.
206-827-9777

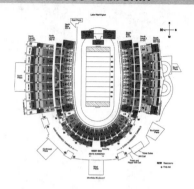

TSN REPORT CARD

Coaching staff	B -	Mike Holmgren has one of the best offensive minds in the game. Steve Sidwell has one of the most innovative defensive minds in the game. But together they produced never-mind results last year, when the Seahawks were hamstrung by problems that have been laid on personnel. If this team is going to improve, it must start at the top.
Quarterbacks	C	Newcomer Matt Hasselbeck leads a group that is greener even than the rain-drenched spring grass in Seattle. How emerald are they? Hasselbeck has thrown 29 regular-season passes. At 26, baseball-playing rookie Josh Booty is the oldest quarterback on the roster. But Holmgren is counting on Hasselbeck to be as good in November and December as he was in August preseason games while in Green Bay.
Running backs	B +	How good was the rejuvenated Ricky Watters last year? Good enough to keep first-round draft choice Shaun Alexander on the sideline. Alexander is good enough to replace Watters, but it hasn't happened yet. They give the Seahawks a productive 1-2 punch.
Receivers	C	The Seahawks' catchers are almost as inexperienced as their passers. But what they lack in actual NFL production they make up for with potential. First-round draft choice Koren Robinson brings the run-after-the-catch element that has been missing since Joey Galloway's departure, and his presence should only make Darrell Jackson, the league's best rookie receiver last year, that much better.
Offensive line	B	A unit that only improved as the season progressed last year only got better with the addition of G Steve Hutchinson in the first round of the draft. He joins Walter Jones, Robbie Tobeck, Floyd Wedderburn and Chris McIntosh to give the Seahawks a young, talented line that is the best in franchise history—and also one that averages 315 pounds.
Defensive line	C +	How can a unit add DTs John Randle and Chad Eaton in free agency and be only average? Because last year this group was a combined failure—with a capital F. If Randle's high-rev motor has anything left and Eaton's energy can be channeled in the right direction, they have the potential to be much better than average.
Linebackers	A -	This unit lacks depth, but you'd have to search for a long time, and probably in vain, to find a better starting trio than Chad Brown, Levon Kirkland and Anthony Simmons. Whatever Kirkland has left at age 32 will be better than what the Seahawks had in the middle last year, and his presence will only help make Brown and Simmons better.
Secondary	C -	CB Shawn Springs should find himself surrounded by three new starters this season—FS Marcus Robertson, who was signed in free agency; SS Reggie Tongue, who was a disappointment and eventually benched after being signed in free agency last year; and a cornerback to be named. This mix-and-match unit must be a better mix than what the Seahawks had a year ago.
Special teams	A	5-1-5. A new area code? No, the Seahawks' special teams ranking the past three seasons, and an indication that this is an area where the Seahawks continue to excel. They are set to challenge for another Top 5 finish with reliable K Rian Lindell, relentless return man Charlie Rogers and some of the best coverage units to ever run down a football field.

TAMPA BAY BUCCANEERS
NFC CENTRAL DIVISION

2001 SEASON

CLUB DIRECTORY

Owner
Malcolm Glazer
Executive vice president
Bryan Glazer
Executive vice president
Joel Glazer
Executive vice president
Edward Glazer
General manager
Rich McKay
Chief financial officer
Tom Alas
Director of player personnel
Jerry Angelo
Director of college scouting
Tim Ruskell
Director of football administration
John Idzik
Executive director of the Glazer Foundation
Veronica (Roni) Costello
Director of communications
Reggie Roberts
Director of marketing
George Woods
Director of special events
Maury Wilks
Director of community relations
Stephanie Waller
Dir. of ticketing and luxury suite relations
Mike Newquist
Director of player development
Cedric Saunders
Coordinator of pro personnel
Mark Dominik
Pro scout
Lloyd Richards Jr.
College scouts
Mike Ackerley, Joe DiMarzo Jr., Frank
Dorazio, Dennis Hickey, Ruston Webster,
Mike Yowarsky
Communications manager
Jeff Kamis
Communications coordinator
Zack Bolno

Head coach
Tony Dungy

Assistant coaches
Mark Asanovich (strength &
conditioning)
Joe Barry (linebackers)
Jim Caldwell (quarterbacks)
Clyde Christensen (off. coordinator)
Les Ebert (asst. strength & condit.)
Chris Foerster (offensive line)
Monte Kiffin (def. coordinator)
Joe Marciano (special teams)
Rod Marinelli (defensive line)
Tony Nathan (running backs)
Kevin O'Dea (offensive assistant)
Ricky Thomas (tight ends)
Mike Tomlin (defensive backs)
Alan Williams (defensive assistant)
Charlie Williams (wide receivers)

Internet manager
Scott Smith
Trainer
Todd Toriscelli
Assistant trainer
Jim Whalen
Video director
Dave Levy
Assistant video director
Pat Brazil
Equipment manager
Darin Kerns
Assistant equipment manager
Mark Meschede

SCHEDULE

Sept. 9—	at Dallas	1:00
Sept. 16—	PHILADELPHIA	1:00
Sept. 23—	Open date	
Sept. 30—	at Minnesota	1:00
Oct. 7—	GREEN BAY	4:15
Oct. 14—	at Tennessee	1:00
Oct. 21—	PITTSBURGH	1:00
Oct. 28—	MINNESOTA	1:00
Nov. 4—	at Green Bay	1:00
Nov. 11—	at Detroit	1:00
Nov. 18—	CHICAGO	1:00
Nov. 26—	at St. Louis (Mon.)	9:00
Dec. 2—	at Cincinnati	1:00
Dec. 9—	DETROIT	1:00
Dec. 16—	at Chicago	1:00
Dec. 23—	NEW ORLEANS	1:00
Dec. 29—	BALTIMORE (Sat.)	9:00

All times are Eastern.
All games Sunday unless noted.

DRAFT CHOICES

Kenyatta Walker, T, Florida (first round/
14th pick overall).
Dwight Smith, DB, Akron (3/84).
John Howell, DB, Colorado St. (4/117).
Russ Hochstein, G, Nebraska (5/151).
Jameel Cook, RB, Illinois (6/174).
Ellis Wyms, DE, Mississippi St. (6/183).
Dauntae' Finger, TE, North Carolina
(7/205).
Than Merrill, DB, Yale (7/223).
Joe Tafoya, DE, Arizona (7/234).

2000 REVIEW

RESULTS

Sept. 3	at New England	W	21-16
Sept.10	CHICAGO	W	41-0
Sept.17	at Detroit	W	31-10
Sept.24	N.Y. JETS	L	17-21
Oct. 1	at Washington	L	17-20
Oct. 9	at Minnesota	L	23-30
Oct. 15	Open date		
Oct. 19	DETROIT	L	14-28
Oct. 29	MINNESOTA	W	41-13
Nov. 5	at Atlanta	W	27-14
Nov. 12	GREEN BAY	W	20-15
Nov. 19	at Chicago	L	10-13
Nov. 26	BUFFALO	W	31-17
Dec. 3	DALLAS	W	27-7
Dec. 10	at Miami	W	16-13
Dec. 18	ST. LOUIS	W	38-35
Dec. 24	at Green Bay (OT)	L	14-17
Dec. 31	at Philadelphia*	L	3-21
*NFC wild-card game.			

RECORDS/RANKINGS

2000 regular-season record: 10-6 (2nd
in NFC Central); 4-4 in division; 7-5 in
conference; 6-2 at home; 4-4 on road.
Team record last five years: 45-35 (.563,
ranks T8th in league in that span).

2000 team rankings:	No.	NFC	NFL
Total offense	*290.6	10	21
Rushing offense	*129.1	3	9
Passing offense	*161.4	14	26
Scoring offense	388	T3	T6
Total defense	*300.0	4	9
Rushing defense	*103.0	3	9
Passing defense	*197.0	6	13
Scoring defense	269	T3	T7
Takeaways	41	2	T4
Giveaways	24	T2	T5
Turnover differential	17	1	T3
Sacks	55	2	T2
Sacks allowed	38	9	16
*Yards per game.			

TEAM LEADERS

Scoring (kicking): Martin Gramatica, 126
pts. (42/42 PATs, 28/34 FGs).
Scoring (touchdowns): Warrick Dunn, 54
pts. (8 rushing, 1 receiving).
Passing: Shaun King, 2,769 yds. (428
att., 233 comp., 54.4%, 18 TDs, 13 int.).
Rushing: Warrick Dunn, 1,133 yds. (248
att., 4.6 avg., 8 TDs).
Receptions: Keyshawn Johnson, 71 (874
yds., 12.3 avg., 8 TDs).
Interceptions: Donnie Abraham, 7 (82
yds., 0 TDs).
Sacks: Warren Sapp, 16.5.
Punting: Mark Royals, 41.8 avg. (85
punts, 3,551 yds., 0 blocked).
Punt returns: Karl Williams, 9.2 avg. (31
att., 286 yds., 1 TD).
Kickoff returns: Aaron Stecker, 22.9 avg.
(29 att., 663 yds., 0 TDs).

TAMPA BAY BUCCANEERS

No.	QUARTERBACKS	Ht./Wt.	Born	NFL Exp.	College	How acq.	'00 Games GP/GS
1	Hamilton, Joe	5-10/190	3-13-77	2	Georgia Tech	D7/00	1/0
14	Johnson, Brad	6-5/224	9-13-68	10	Florida State	UFA/01	*12/11
10	King, Shaun	6-0/225	5-29-77	3	Tulane	D2/99	16/16
16	Leaf, Ryan	6-5/235	5-15-76	4	Washington State	W-SD/01	*11/9
	RUNNING BACKS						
27	Abdullah, Rabih	6-1/227	4-27-75	4	Lehigh	FA/98	12/0
40	Alstott, Mike (FB)	6-1/248	12-21-73	6	Purdue	D2/96	13/13
	Cook, Jameel (FB)	5-10/227	2-8-79	R	Illinois	D6a/01	—
28	Dunn, Warrick	5-8/180	1-5-75	5	Florida State	D1a/97	16/14
48	Kirby, Charles (FB)	6-1/249	11-27-74	3	Virginia	FA/00	6/2
22	Stecker, Aaron	5-10/205	11-13-75	2	Western Illinois	FA/00	10/0
	RECEIVERS						
85	Anthony, Reidel	5-11/180	10-20-76	5	Florida	D1b/97	16/1
	Finger, Dauntaé (TE)	6-3/255	4-5-77	R	North Carolina	D7a/01	—
81	Green, Jacquez	5-9/168	1-15-76	4	Florida	D2a/98	16/16
19	Johnson, Keyshawn	6-4/212	7-22-72	6	Southern California	T-NYJ/00	16/16
83	Moore, Dave (TE)	6-2/258	11-11-69	9	Pittsburgh	FA/92	16/16
87	Murphy, Frank	6-0/206	2-11-77	1	Kansas State	FA/00	1/0
86	Williams, Karl	5-10/177	4-10-71	6	Texas A&M-Kingsville	FA/96	13/0
80	Yoder, Todd (TE)	6-4/234	3-18-78	2	Vanderbilt	FA/00	9/0
	OFFENSIVE LINEMEN						
62	Christy, Jeff (C)	6-2/285	2-3-69	9	Pittsburgh	UFA/00	16/16
60	Coleman, Cosey (G)	6-4/322	10-27-78	2	Tennessee	D2/00	8/0
79	Hegamin, George (T)	6-7/331	2-14-73	8	North Carolina State	FA/99	16/1
65	Hochstein, Russ (G)	6-3/288	10-7-77	R	Nebraska	D5/01	—
64	McDaniel, Randall (G)	6-3/287	12-19-64	14	Arizona State	FA/00	16/16
69	Pierson, Pete (T)	6-5/315	2-4-71	7	Washington	D5/94	15/15
67	Walker, Kenyatta (T)	6-5/302	2-1-79	R	Florida	D1/01	—
75	Washington, Todd (C)	6-3/324	7-19-76	4	Virginia Tech	D4/98	10/0
71	Wunsch, Jerry (T)	6-6/339	1-21-74	5	Wisconsin	D2/97	16/16
	DEFENSIVE LINEMEN						
98	Cannida, James (T)	6-2/291	1-3-75	4	Nevada-Reno	D6a/98	16/0
78	Jones, Marcus (E)	6-6/278	8-15-73	6	North Carolina	D1b/96	16/16
92	McFarland, Anthony (T)	6-0/300	12-18-77	3	Louisiana State	D1/99	16/16
95	McLaughlin, John (E)	6-4/247	11-13-75	3	California	D5/99	6/0
97	Rice, Simeon (E)	6-5/268	2-24-74	6	Illinois	UFA/01	*15/11
99	Sapp, Warren (T)	6-2/303	12-19-72	7	Miami (Fla.)	D1a/95	16/15
	Tafoya, Joe (E)	6-4/258	9-6-77	R	Arizona	D7b/01	—
94	White, Steve (E)	6-2/271	10-25-73	6	Tennessee	FA/96	15/0
	Wyms, Ellis (E)	6-3/279	4-12-79	R	Mississippi State	D6b/01	—
	LINEBACKERS						
55	Brooks, Derrick	6-0/235	4-18-73	7	Florida State	D1b/95	16/16
59	Duncan, Jamie	6-0/242	7-20-75	4	Vanderbilt	D3/98	15/15
50	Gooch, Jeff	5-11/225	10-31-74	6	Austin Peay State	FA/01	16/0
53	Quarles, Shelton	6-1/230	9-11-71	5	Vanderbilt	FA/97	14/13
51	Singleton, Alshermond	6-2/228	8-7-75	5	Temple	D4/97	13/1
52	Webster, Nate	5-11/225	11-29-77	2	Miami (Fla.)	D3/00	16/0
	DEFENSIVE BACKS						
21	Abraham, Donnie (CB)	5-10/192	10-8-73	6	East Tennessee State	D3/96	16/16
20	Barber, Ronde (CB)	5-10/184	4-7-75	5	Virginia	D3b/97	16/16
46	Gibson, David (S)	6-1/210	11-5-77	2	Southern California	D6/00	9/0
38	Howell, John (S)	5-11/196	4-28-78	R	Colorado State	D4/01	—
34	Jackson, Dexter (S)	6-0/196	7-28-77	3	Florida State	D4/99	13/0
25	Kelly, Brian (CB)	5-11/193	1-14-76	4	Southern California	D2b/98	16/3
47	Lynch, John (S)	6-2/220	9-25-71	9	Stanford	D3/93	16/16
	Merril, Than (CB)	6-1/225	12-17-77	R	Yale	D7b/01	—
26	Smith, Dwight (CB)	5-10/201	8-13-78	R	Akron	D3/01	—
33	Vance, Eric (S)	6-2/218	7-14-75	4	Vanderbilt	FA/00	14/0
	SPECIALISTS						
7	Gramatica, Martin (K)	5-8/170	11-27-75	3	Kansas State	D3/99	16/0
3	Royals, Mark (P)	6-5/215	6-22-65	13	Appalachian State	FA/99	16/0

*Not with Buccaneers in 2000.

Other free agent veterans invited to camp: G Wilbert Brown, DT Chartric Darby, CB Anthony Midget, TE Randy Palmer, TE Damian Vaughn, LB Jude Waddy, DE Ron Warner.

Abbreviations: D1—draft pick, first round; SD-2—supplemental draft pick, second round; W—claimed on waivers; T—obtained in trade; PlanB—Plan B free-agent acquisition; FA—free-agent acquisition (other than Plan B); UFA—unconditional free agent acquisition; ED—expansion draft pick.

Stadium (capacity, surface):
Raymond James Stadium (65,699, grass)
Business address:
One Buccaneer Place
Tampa, FL 33607
Business phone:
813-870-2700
Ticket information:
813-879-2827
Team colors:
Buccaneer red, pewter, black and orange
Flagship radio station:
WQYK, 99.5 FM
Training site:
University of Tampa
Tampa, Fla.
813-253-6215

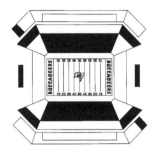

TAMPA BAY BUCCANEERS

TSN REPORT CARD

Coaching staff	B	Players love playing for Tony Dungy. He always treats his players like professionals and has an easy-going style that works well with today's athletes. Defensive coordinator Monte Kiffin is among the best in the league, but there are new faces almost everywhere else. Clyde Christensen is an unproven offensive coordinator and Dungy can only hope that rookie linebackers coach Joe Carroll and secondary coach Mike Tomlin can get the same results as their predecessors. New quarterbacks coach Jim Caldwell has a wealth of experience at the college level but has never dealt with the egos at the NFL level.
Quarterbacks	A	Brad Johnson is the most accurate passer in the league today. He's not going to blow a team up with bombs but pick them apart spraying bullets all over the field. He's smart and experienced but tends to miss a few games each year due to injury. Ryan Leaf is as talented a player as there is anywhere. If he can mature and accept the backup role he'll be a solid addition. Shaun King has led this team to the playoffs two years in a row. He's neither a polished athlete or a polished quarterback, but he finds a way to get the job done.
Running backs	A -	Warrick Dunn and Mike Alstott form the best one-two running back punch in the league. Although there are some questions about Dunn, both have proved durable and both can hurt you either as ball carriers or pass catchers. The duo's downside is that Alstott doesn't block very well and he puts the ball on the ground too much. That's one reason his role will be altered this year, with Dunn getting the majority of the carries and Alstott working more as a pass catcher.
Receivers	A -	Keyshawn Johnson is easily one of the game's top all-around receivers. He creates matchup problems with his size, makes big plays and blocks better than some tight ends. Jacquez Green is a perfect complement to Johnson. He is a true deep threat who can stretch the field and create room underneath. Reidel Anthony has a lot of the same skills as Green and can be devastating on third down. TE Dave Moore is underrated. He has an uncanny ability to get open in the red zone and has good hands. He's a solid blocker as well. The unit has plenty of depth with veteran Karl Williams and rookie Frank Murphy in reserve.
Offensive line	C +	Kenyatta Walker is a rookie but he should provide the team with an upgrade at left tackle, where journeymen Pete Pierson and George Hegamin platooned a year ago. Perennial Pro Bowler Randall McDaniel is nearing the end of a Hall of Fame career but he still gets the job done without incident at left guard. Center Jeff Christy is one of the most athletic players at his position and RG Cosey Coleman is a fine complement. Both allow the Bucs to run outside more because of their athleticism. Jerry Wunsch is a mauler but the team wins with him. He's improving thanks to experience and now has Hegamin behind him.
Defensive line	A	The best defensive front in the league only got better with the addition of RE Simeon Rice. This group alone could set an NFL record for sacks this year. Warren Sapp leads the way, and he creates so many problems inside that the ends are often left on an island that they can easily get off of. NT Anthony McFarland is improving and could approach the 10-sack mark this year. Marcus Jones moves from right end to left end this year, but he's more natural on that side so a slip in performance is not expected.
Linebackers	B +	Outside of Derrick Brooks, you won't recognize a lot of the names here. You will make note of their work, though. Through speed and athleticism, this group gets the job done as well as any in the league. All the players here are smart, speedy and instinctual. All are great pursuit players, which is what the Bucs want them to do. Jamie Duncan starts in the middle but he'll yield time to second-year pro Nate Webster. Shelton Quarles is the starter at strongside backer, but Al Singleton works a platoon there.
Secondary	B +	This unit plays such a big part in the team's blitz package that they often look like linebackers. SS John Lynch certainly plays his spot that way. He's solid against the run and is one of the hardest hitters on the team. He used to be considered the best blitzer in the unit but Ronde Barber proved last year (6.5 sacks) that his timing and effectiveness in that role may be even better. As his Pro Bowl election proves, Donnie Abraham is one of the best cover corners in the game. The team believes it upgraded itself at free safety with the promotion to starter of Dexter Jackson, who replaces Damien Robinson.
Special teams	C	K Martin Gramatica hits on about 83 percent of his kicks and is capable of hitting anything between 50 and 60 yards with the same degree of accuracy. He tends to be a little short on kickoffs but solid coverage units usually eliminate the concern associated with that. P Mark Royals can drop the ball anywhere you need it and is a dependable holder on kicks for Gramatica. Karl Williams is a solid punt returner but the team has yet to find an impact kick returner and it sometimes struggles in punt coverage.

TENNESSEE TITANS
AFC CENTRAL DIVISION

2001 SEASON

CLUB DIRECTORY

Owner
K.S. "Bud" Adams Jr.
President/chief operating officer
Jeff Diamond
Executive v.p./general manager
Floyd Reese
Executive assistant to owner
Thomas S. Smith
Vice president/legal counsel
Steve Underwood
Vice president/finance
Jackie Curley
Exec. v.p./broadcasting and marketing
Don MacLachlan
Director of player personnel
Rich Snead
Director/sales operations
Stuart Spears
Dir. of media relations and services
Robbie Bohren
Vice president for community affairs
Bob Hyde
Director/ticket operations
Marty Collins
Director/security
Steve Berk
Director/player programs
Al Smith
Asst. dir. of media rel. and services
William Bryant
Head trainer
Brad Brown
Scouts
Ray Biggs   C.O. Brocato
Dub Fesperman
Equipment manager
Paul Noska

Head coach
Jeff Fisher

Assistant coaches
Chuck Cecil (defensive assistant)
Gunther Cunningham (asst. head
  coach/linebackers)
Mike Heimerdinger (offensive
  coordinator)
George Henshaw (asst. head
  coach/offense)
Craig Johnson (off. assistant)
Alan Lowry (special teams)
Mike Munchak (offensive line)
Jim Schwartz (def. coordinator)
Sherman Smith (running backs)
Steve Walters (wide receivers)
Jim Washburn (defensive line)
Steve Watterson (strength &
  rehabilitation)
Everett Withers (defensive backs)

Videotape coordinator
Anthony Pastrana
Team physicians
Burton Elrod
Craig Rutland
John Williams

SCHEDULE

Sept. 9—	MIAMI	8:30
Sept. 16—	CINCINNATI	1:00
Sept. 23—	at Jacksonville	1:00
Sept. 30—	Open date	
Oct. 7—	at Baltimore	1:00
Oct. 14—	TAMPA BAY	1:00
Oct. 21—	at Detroit	1:00
Oct. 29—	at Pittsburgh (Mon.)	9:00
Nov. 4—	JACKSONVILLE	2:00
Nov. 12—	BALTIMORE (Mon.)	9:00
Nov. 18—	at Cincinnati	1:00
Nov. 25—	PITTSBURGH	1:00
Dec. 2—	at Cleveland	1:00
Dec. 9—	at Minnesota	1:00
Dec. 16—	GREEN BAY	4:15
Dec. 22—	at Oakland (Sat.)	9:00
Dec. 30—	CLEVELAND	1:00

All times are Eastern.
All games Sunday unless noted.

DRAFT CHOICES

Andre Dyson, DB, Utah (second round/
60th pick overall).
Shad Meier, TE, Kansas State (3/90).
Justin McCareins, WR, Northern Illinois
(4/124).
Eddie Berlin, WR, Northern Iowa (5/159).
Dan Alexander, RB, Nebraska (6/192).
Adam Haayer, T, Minnesota (6/199).
Keith Adams, LB, Clemson (7/232).

2000 REVIEW

RESULTS

Sept. 3—at Buffalo	L	13-16
Sept.10—KANSAS CITY (OT)	W	17-14
Sept.17—Open date		
Sept.24—at Pittsburgh	W	23-20
Oct. 1—N.Y. GIANTS	W	28-14
Oct. 8—at Cincinnati	W	23-14
Oct. 16—JACKSONVILLE	W	27-13
Oct. 22—at Baltimore	W	14-6
Oct. 30—at Washington	W	27-21
Nov. 5—PITTSBURGH	W	9-7
Nov. 12—BALTIMORE	L	23-24
Nov. 19—CLEVELAND	W	24-10
Nov. 26—at Jacksonville	L	13-16
Dec. 3—at Philadelphia	W	15-13
Dec. 10—CINCINNATI	W	35-3
Dec. 17—at Cleveland	W	24-0
Dec. 25—DALLAS	W	31-0
Jan. 7—BALTIMORE*	L	10-27

*AFC divisional playoff game.

RECORDS/RANKINGS

2000 regular-season record: 13-3 (1st in
AFC Central); 8-2 in division; 9-3 in conference; 7-1 at home; 6-2 on road.
Team record last five years: 50-30 (.625,
ranks 5th in league in that span).

2000 team rankings:

	No.	AFC	NFL
Total offense	*334.4	8	14
Rushing offense	*130.3	6	7
Passing offense	*204.1	8	16
Scoring offense	346	6	13
Total defense	*238.3	1	1
Rushing defense	*86.9	2	3
Passing defense	*151.4	1	1
Scoring defense	191	2	2
Takeaways	30	T7	T14
Giveaways	30	12	19
Turnover differential	0	9	T16
Sacks	55	1	T2
Sacks allowed	27	3	4

*Yards per game.

TEAM LEADERS

Scoring (kicking): Al Del Greco, 118 pts.
(37/38 PATs, 27/33 FGs).
Scoring (touchdowns): Eddie George, 96
pts. (14 rushing, 2 receiving).
Passing: Steve McNair, 2,847 yds. (396
att., 248 comp., 62.6%, 15 TDs, 13 int.).
Rushing: Eddie George, 1,509 yds. (403
att., 3.7 avg., 14 TDs).
Receptions: Derrick Mason, 63 (895 yds.,
14.2 avg., 5 TDs).
Interceptions: Samari Rolle, 7 (140 yds.,
1 TD).
Sacks: Jevon Kearse, 11.5.
Punting: Craig Hentrich, 40.8 avg. (76
punts, 3,101 yds., 0 blocked).
Punt returns: Derrick Mason, 13.0 avg.
(51 att., 662 yds., 1 TD).
Kickoff returns: Derrick Mason, 27.0 avg.
(42 att., 1,132 yds., 0 TDs).

TENNESSEE TITANS

No.	QUARTERBACKS	Ht./Wt.	Born	NFL Exp.	College	How acq.	'00 Games GP/GS
9	McNair, Steve	6-2/225	2-14-73	7	Alcorn State	D1/95	16/15
14	O'Donnell, Neil	6-3/228	7-3-66	12	Maryland	UFA/99	7/1
	Volek, Billy	6-2/210	4-28-76	2	Fresno State	FA/00	1/0
	RUNNING BACKS						
	Alexander, Dan	6-0/244	3-17-78	R	Nebraska	D6/01	
27	George, Eddie	6-3/240	9-24-73	6	Ohio State	D1/96	16/16
22	Green, Mike	6-0/249	9-2-76	2	Houston	D7a/00	1/0
	RECEIVERS						
	Berlin, Eddie	5-11/186	1-14-78	R	Northern Iowa	D5/01	—
	Coleman, Chris	6-0/202	5-8-77	2	North Carolina State	FA/00	13/0
87	Dyson, Kevin	6-1/201	6-23-75	4	Utah	D1/98	2/2
	Jackson, Chris	6-2/204	2-26-75	R	Washington State	FA/00	1/0
88	Kinney, Erron (TE)	6-5/272	7-28-77	2	Florida	D3a/00	16/9
	Leach, Mike (TE)	6-4/238	10-18-76	2	William and Mary	FA/00	15/0
85	Mason, Derrick	5-10/188	1-17-74	5	Michigan State	D4a/97	16/10
	McCareins, Justin	6-2/200	12-11-78	R	Northern Illinois	D4/01	—
	Meier, Shad (TE)	6-4/250	6-7-78	R	Kansas State	D3/01	—
81	Sanders, Chris	6-1/188	5-8-72	7	Ohio State	D3a/95	16/14
89	Wycheck, Frank (TE)	6-3/250	10-14-71	9	Maryland	W-Was./95	16/16
	OFFENSIVE LINEMEN						
	Haayer, Adam (T)	6-6/297	2-22-77	R	Minnesota	D6b/01	—
72	Hopkins, Brad (T)	6-3/305	9-5-70	9	Illinois	D1/93	15/15
60	Long, Kevin (C)	6-5/295	5-2-75	4	Florida State	D7b/98	16/16
76	Mathews, Jason (T)	6-5/304	2-9-71	8	Texas A&M	FA/98	16/1
74	Matthews, Bruce (G)	6-5/305	8-8-61	19	Southern California	D1/83	16/16
71	Miller, Fred (T)	6-7/315	2-6-73	6	Baylor	UFA/00	16/16
75	Olson, Benji (G)	6-3/315	6-5-75	4	Washington	D5/98	16/16
69	Piller, Zach (G)	6-5/330	5-2-76	3	Florida	D3/99	16/0
	DEFENSIVE LINEMEN						
	Carter, Kevin (E)	6-5/280	9-21-73	7	Florida	T-St.L./01	*16/13
	Embray, Keith (E)	6-4/265	11-29-74	2	Utah	FA/00	14/0
91	Evans, Josh (T)	6-2/288	9-6-72	6	Alabama-Birmingham	FA/95	0/0
97	Fisk, Jason (T)	6-3/295	9-4-72	7	Stanford	UFA/99	15/15
92	Ford, Henry (T)	6-3/295	10-30-71	8	Arkansas	D1/94	14/3
90	Kearse, Jevon (E)	6-4/265	9-3-76	3	Florida	D1/99	16/16
95	Salave'a, Joe (T)	6-3/290	3-23-75	4	Arizona	D4/98	15/1
98	Smith, Robaire (E)	6-4/271	11-15-77	2	Michigan State	D6/00	7/0
78	Thornton, John (T)	6-2/295	10-2-76	3	West Virginia	D2/99	16/16
	LINEBACKERS						
	Adams, Keith	5-11/223	11-22-79	R	Clemson	D7/01	—
53	Bulluck, Keith	6-3/232	4-4-77	2	Syracuse	D1/00	16/1
57	Chamberlin, Frank	6-1/250	1-2-78	2	Boston College	D5b/00	12/0
51	Favors, Greg	6-1/244	9-30-74	4	Mississippi State	W-KC/99	16/15
56	Godfrey, Randall	6-2/245	4-6-73	6	Georgia	UFA/00	16/16
55	Robinson, Eddie	6-1/243	4-13-70	10	Alabama State	FA/98	16/16
59	Sirmon, Peter	6-2/246	2-18-77	2	Oregon	D4b/00	5/0
	DEFENSIVE BACKS						
23	Bishop, Blaine (S)	5-9/203	7-24-70	9	Ball State	D8/93	16/16
	Dyson, Andre (CB)	5-10/177	5-25-79	R	Utah	D2/01	—
28	Morris, Aric (S)	5-10/208	7-22-77	2	Michigan State	D5a/00	15/0
32	Myers, Bobby (S)	6-1/189	10-11-76	2	Wisconsin	D4a/00	16/1
35	Phenix, Perry (S)	5-11/208	11-14-74	4	Southern Mississippi	FA/00	16/0
21	Rolle, Samari (CB)	6-0/175	8-10-76	4	Florida State	D2/98	15/15
37	Sidney, Dainon (CB)	6-0/188	5-30-75	4	Alabama-Birmingham	D3/98	11/2
	SPECIALISTS						
15	Hentrich, Craig (P)	6-3/205	5-18-71	8	Notre Dame	UFA/98	16/0
6	Nedney, Joe (K)	6-5/220	3-22-73	6	San Jose State	UFA/01	*15/0

*Not with Titans in 2000.

Other free agent veterans invited to camp: G Gennaro DiNapoli, DE Byron Frisch, CB Donald Mitchell.

Abbreviations: D1—draft pick, first round; SD-2—supplemental draft pick, second round; W—claimed on waivers; T—obtained in trade; PlanB—Plan B free-agent acquisition; FA—free-agent acquisition (other than Plan B); UFA—unconditional free agent acquisition; ED—expansion draft pick.

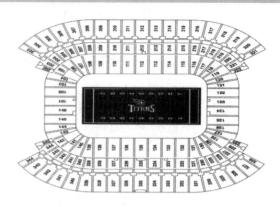

MISCELLANEOUS TEAM DATA

Stadium (capacity, surface):
Adelphia Coliseum
(68,498, grass)
Business address:
460 Great Circle Road
Nashville, TN 37228
Business phone:
615-565-4000
Ticket information:
615-341-SNAP
Team colors:
Navy, red, Titan blue and white
Flagship radio station:
WGFX, 104.5 FM
Training site:
460 Great Circle Road
Nashville, TN 37228
615-565-4000

TSN REPORT CARD

Coaching staff	B +	Head coach Jeff Fisher suffered some staff losses on defense—So Jim Schwartz will now get his first crack at being a defensive coordinator, with former Chiefs coach Gunther Cunningham taking over Schwartz's spot with the linebackers. Overall, it's a well-prepared group that should have a team than can compete with the league's best.
Quarterbacks	B	Steve McNair battled a severe shoulder infection earlier in the year and will have to show he can come back to full speed by the time training camp opens. Neil O'Donnell is a proven veteran at the backup spot, giving the team as good a 1-2 as there is in the league. But until McNair throws full speed against a defense, the jury is out.
Running backs	B +	Eddie George is the man, having been to four consecutive Pro Bowls and pushed the Titans into the league's elite. But there isn't much—if any—proven depth. Rookie Dan Alexander will get a chance to show what he's got in the preseason.
Receivers	C	After diving into the draft and grabbing two wide receivers and later signing six undrafted rookie free agents, it's clear the Titans simply wanted more bodies at this position. Derrick Mason had his break-through season last year and Kevin Dyson is scheduled to be back from knee surgery. Tight end Frank Wycheck, who has led the team in receptions in each of the last four seasons, and Mason are the front-line options. But there's not enough proven depth.
Offensive line	A -	The only real question here, with all five starters returning, is where 19-year veteran Bruce Matthews will play. It will either be left guard or center but no matter which one, the Titans will still pound the ball in the run game.
Defensive line	A	Suddenly this is the deepest position on the team. The addition of Kevin Carter at left defensive end will move Jevon Kearse to the right side and will also give Kearse more room to work. They are deep and powerful at tackle with Jason Fisk and John Thornton heading a group that includes Josh Evans, who was suspended for all of the 2000 season for violating the league's substance abuse program.
Linebackers	A	Randall Godfrey should have been a Pro Bowler last season; he gives the Titans an every-down player in the middle. Eddie Robinson, heading into his 10th season, will be at one outside spot while Keith Bulluck and Greg Favors will fight for the other. There is plenty of depth, so those who don't start will be the foundation of the special teams.
Secondary	B	There are some question marks here given the departure of Denard Walker in free agency and the release of Marcus Robertson. Walker's spot is open to full-scale competition while second-year safety Bobby Myers will play in Robertson's old spot at free safety. But with Samari Rolle at the other corner and Blaine Bishop at the other safety spot, the team will find a combination that works.
Special teams	A	Newcomer Joe Nedney has a big leg and will get plenty of chances with the close-to-the-vest Titans to see if he has what it takes with the game on the line. Craig Hentrich is a dominant punter and Derrick Mason was the Pro Bowl returner last season. The coverage teams are well-stocked and the Titans cover kicks with an attitude.

WASHINGTON REDSKINS
NFC EASTERN DIVISION

2001 SEASON

CLUB DIRECTORY

Chairman and chief executive officer
Daniel M. Snyder
President
Steve Baldacci
House counsel
Bob Gordon
Assistant general manager
Bobby Mitchell
Vice president of finance
Jeff Ochs
Senior vice president of operations
Michael Dillow
Contract negotiator
Mark Levin
Director of player programs
John Jefferson
Director of college scouting
To be announced
Scouts
To be announced
Director of public relations
Michelle Tessier
Publications/Internet director
Terence J. (Casey) Husband
Community relations manager
Catherine Augustyn
Director of leadership council
Alex Hahn
Director of administration
Russ Ball
Video director
Rob Porteus
Assistant video director
Mike Bracken
Ticket manager
Jeff Ritter
Head trainer
Bubba Tyer

Head coach
Marty
Schottenheimer

Assistant coaches
Bill Arnsparger (def. assistant)
Pete Carmichael Jr. (offensive
   assistant/quality control)
Jerry Holmes (secondary)
Hue Jackson (running backs)
Richard Mann (wide receivers)
Greg Manusky (linebackers)
Kirk Olivadotti (def. assistant/
   quality control)
Joe Pendry (offensive line)
Jimmy Raye (off. coordinator)
Dave Redding (strength and
   conditioning)
Matt Schiotz (assistant strength
   and conditioning)
Brian Schottenheimer (QBs)
Kurt Schottenheimer (def. coord.)
Tony Sparano (tight ends)
Mike Stock (special teams)
Mike Trgovac (defensive line)

Assistant trainers
Eric Steward
Ryan Vermillion
Equipment manager
Brad Berlin
Asst. equipment manager
Andy Beutel

SCHEDULE

Sept. 9—	at San Diego	4:15
Sept. 16—	ARIZONA	1:00
Sept. 24—	at Green Bay (Mon.)	9:00
Sept. 30—	KANSAS CITY	1:00
Oct. 7—	at N.Y. Giants	1:00
Oct. 15—	at Dallas (Mon.)	9:00
Oct. 21—	CAROLINA	1:00
Oct. 28—	N.Y GIANTS	8:30
Nov. 4—	SEATTLE	4:15
Nov. 11—	Open date	
Nov. 18—	at Denver	4:15
Nov. 25—	at Philadelphia	1:00
Dec. 2—	DALLAS	4:15
Dec. 9—	at Arizona	4:05
Dec. 16—	PHILADELPHIA	1:00
Dec. 23—	CHICAGO	1:00
Dec. 30—	at New Orleans	8:30

All times are Eastern.
All games Sunday unless noted.

DRAFT CHOICES

Rod Gardner, WR, Clemson (first round/
15th pick overall).
Fred Smoot, DB, Mississippi State
(2/45).
Sage Rosenfels, QB, Iowa State (4/109).
Darnerien McCants, WR, Delaware State
(5/154).
Mario Monds, DT, Cincinnati (6/186).

2000 REVIEW

RESULTS

Sept. 3—CAROLINA	W	20-17
Sept.10—at Detroit	L	10-15
Sept.18—DALLAS	L	21-27
Sept.24—at N.Y. Giants	W	16-6
Oct. 1—TAMPA BAY	W	20-17
Oct. 8—at Philadelphia	W	17-14
Oct. 15—BALTIMORE	W	10-3
Oct. 22—at Jacksonville	W	35-16
Oct. 30—TENNESSEE	L	21-27
Nov. 5—at Arizona	L	15-16
Nov. 12—Open date		
Nov. 20—at St. Louis	W	33-20
Nov. 26—PHILADELPHIA	L	20-23
Dec. 3—N.Y. GIANTS	L	7-9
Dec. 10—at Dallas	L	13-32
Dec. 16—at Pittsburgh	L	3-24
Dec. 24—ARIZONA	W	20-3

RECORDS/RANKINGS

2000 regular-season record: 8-8 (3rd in
NFC East); 3-5 in division; 6-6 in conference; 4-4 at home; 4-4 on road.
Team record last five years: 41-38-1
(.519, ranks 14th in league in that span).

2000 team rankings:	No.	NFC	NFL
Total offense	*337.3	T4	T10
Rushing offense	*109.3	9	19
Passing offense	*228.0	5	10
Scoring offense	281	12	24
Total defense	*279.6	1	4
Rushing defense	*115.8	11	22
Passing defense	*163.8	1	2
Scoring defense	269	T3	T7
Takeaways	33	5	11
Giveaways	33	T9	T21
Turnover differential	0	8	T16
Sacks	45	5	8
Sacks allowed	32	3	9

*Yards per game.

TEAM LEADERS

Scoring (kicking): Eddie Murray, 31 pts.
(7/8 PATs, 8/12 FGs).
Scoring (touchdowns): Stephen Davis, 66
pts. (11 rushing).
Passing: Brad Johnson, 2,505 yds. (365
att., 228 comp., 62.5%, 11 TDs, 15 int.).
Rushing: Stephen Davis, 1,318 yds. (332
att., 4.0 avg., 11 TDs).
Receptions: Albert Connell, 39 (762 yds.,
19.5 avg., 3 TDs).
Interceptions: Champ Bailey, 5 (48 yds., 0
TDs).
Sacks: Marco Coleman, 12.0.
Punting: Tommy Barnhardt, 40.0 avg. (79
punts, 3,160 yds., 0 blocked).
Punt returns: Deion Sanders, 7.4 avg. (25
att., 185 yds., 0 TDs).
Kickoff returns: James Thrash, 22.2 avg.
(45 att., 1,000 yds., 0 TDs).

2001 SEASON

TRAINING CAMP ROSTER

No.	QUARTERBACKS	Ht./Wt.	Born	NFL Exp.	College	How acq.	'00 Games GP/GS
3	George, Jeff	6-4/215	12-8-67	11	Illinois	UFA/00	7/5
8	Husak, Todd	6-3/216	7-6-78	2	Stanford	D6/00	1/0
18	Rosenfels, Sage	6-4/221	3-6-78	R	Iowa State	D4/01	—
	RUNNING BACKS						
32	Bennett, Donnell (FB)	6-0/245	9-14-72	8	Miami (Fla.)	UFA/01	*7/2
48	Davis, Stephen	6-0/234	3-1-74	6	Auburn	D4/96	15/15
47	Johnson, Bryan (FB)	6-1/234	1-18-78	1	Boise State	FA/00	1/0
	RECEIVERS						
80	Alexander, Stephen (TE)	6-4/246	11-7-75	4	Oklahoma	D2/98	16/16
89	Flemister, Zeron (TE)	6-4/249	9-8-76	2	Iowa	FA/00	5/0
87	Gardner, Rod	6-2/216	10-26-77	R	Clemson	D1/01	—
81	Lockett, Kevin	6-0/187	9-8-74	5	Kansas State	UFA/01	*16/2
	McCants, Darnerien	6-4/210	8-1-77	R	Delaware State	D5/01	—
86	Rasby, Walter (TE)	6-3/251	9-7-72	8	Wake Forest	UFA/01	*16/8
13	Thompson, Derrius	6-2/215	7-5-77	3	Baylor	FA/99	4/0
82	Westbrook, Michael	6-3/220	7-7-72	6	Colorado	D1/95	2/2
	OFFENSIVE LINEMEN						
77	Albright, Ethan	6-5/268	5-1-71	8	North Carolina	FA/01	*16/0
66	Campbell, Matt (G)	6-4/300	7-14-72	7	South Carolina	UFA/01	*14/14
51	Fischer, Mark (C)	6-3/303	7-29-74	4	Purdue	D5/98	16/16
65	Fletcher, Derrick (T)	6-6/348	9-9-75	3	Baylor	FA/00	3/2
76	Jansen, Jon (T)	6-6/302	1-28-76	3	Michigan	D2/99	16/16
66	Moore, Michael (G)	6-3/320	11-1-76	1	Troy (Ala.) State	D4/00	5/1
52	Raymer, Cory (C)	6-2/289	3-3-73	6	Wisconsin	D2/95	0/0
60	Samuels, Chris (T)	6-5/325	7-28-77	2	Alabama	D1b/00	16/16
	DEFENSIVE LINEMEN						
99	Coleman, Marco (E)	6-3/267	12-18-69	10	Georgia Tech	UFA/99	16/16
75	Ham, Derrick (E)	6-4/257	3-23-75	1	Miami (Fla.)	FA/99	1/0
90	Lang, Kenard (E)	6-4/277	1-31-75	5	Miami (Fla.)	D1/97	16/0
78	Smith, Bruce (E)	6-4/279	6-18-63	17	Virginia Tech	FA/00	16/16
95	Wilkinson, Dan (T)	6-5/313	3-13-73	8	Ohio State	T-Cin./98	16/16
	LINEBACKERS						
56	Arrington, LaVar	6-3/250	6-20-78	2	Penn State	D1a/00	16/11
59	Barber, Shawn	6-2/224	1-14-75	4	Richmond	D4/98	14/14
53	Mason, Eddie	6-0/236	1-9-72	5	North Carolina	FA/99	16/2
55	Mitchell, Kevin	6-1/254	1-1-71	7	Syracuse	UFA/00	16/0
	DEFENSIVE BACKS						
24	Bailey, Champ (CB)	6-1/184	6-22-78	3	Georgia	D1/99	16/16
27	Carrier, Mark (S)	6-1/190	4-28-68	12	Southern California	UFA/00	15/15
28	Green, Darrell (CB)	5-8/184	2-15-60	19	Texas A&I	D1/83	13/2
25	Greer, Donovan	5-9/178	9-11-74	5	Texas A&M	UFA/01	*13/1
41	Harrison, Lloyd (CB)	5-10/190	6-21-77	2	North Carolina State	D3/00	2/0
21	Sanders, Deion (CB)	6-1/198	8-9-67	13	Florida State	FA/00	16/15
29	Shade, Sam (S)	6-1/201	6-14-73	7	Alabama	UFA/99	16/14
23	Smoot, Fred (CB)	5-11/179	4-17-79	R	Mississippi State	D2/01	—
34	Symonette, Josh (S)	5-10/180	5-8-78	1	Tennessee Tech	FA/00	3/0
31	Terrell, David (CB)	6-1/188	7-8-75	2	Texas-El Paso	FA/99	16/0
	SPECIALISTS						
4	Barker, Bryan (P)	6-2/199	6-28-64	12	Santa Clara	UFA/01	*16/0
3	Bentley, Scott (K)	6-0/203	4-10-74	3	Florida State	FA/00	7/0
5	Conway, Brett (K)	6-2/192	3-8-75	5	Penn State	UFA/01	*4/0

*Not with Redskins in 2000.
Other free agent veterans invited to camp: DT Delbert Cowsette.
Abbreviations: D1—draft pick, first round; SD-2—supplemental draft pick, second round; W—claimed on waivers; T—obtained in trade; PlanB—Plan B free-agent acquisition; FA—free-agent acquisition (other than Plan B); UFA—unconditional free agent acquisition; ED—expansion draft pick.

MISCELLANEOUS TEAM DATA

Stadium (capacity, surface):
FedEx Field (85,407, grass)
Business address:
21300 Redskins Park Drive
Ashburn, Va. 20147
Business phone:
703-478-8900
Ticket information:
301-276-6050
Team colors:
Burgundy and gold
Flagship radio station:
WJFK, 106.7 FM
Training site:
Dickinson College
Carlisle, Pa.
703-478-8900

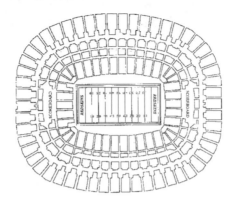

TSN REPORT CARD

Coaching staff	B	There is plenty of experience, and Marty Schottenheimer, entering his 16th season as an NFL head coach, commands respect. His attention to detail and the staff's ability to understand what Schottenheimer wants should be assets. There is no doubt that Schottenheimer is in charge and has final say on all personnel matters. That lets the players know to whom they are responsible.
Quarterbacks	C	Jeff George still has the physical tools to get the job done. His arm is strong, his release quick, his passes very catchable. But until he proves otherwise, his attitude will be the major question mark. Depth is a problem. Behind George are young, unproven players. Todd Husak one day will be an effective NFL quarterback, but it isn't clear he'll get a chance to show that in Washington.
Running backs	B -	A healthy, well-conditioned Stephen Davis is among the best backs in the league and is capable of leading the league in rushing. Things drop off dramatically without Davis, though, after the Redskins decided to part ways with Skip Hicks. Bryan Johnson should provide some pop in the backfield and some enthusiasm on the field.
Receivers	C	So much depends on the recovery of Michael Westbrook from major knee surgery, although rookie Rod Gardner could assume Westbrook's role, in time. Kevin Lockett is a good addition and rookie Darnerien McCants has the potential to be a playmaker. Stephen Alexander is due for a big year at tight end.
Offensive line	B -	Finding a better pair of young tackles anywhere in the league would be difficult. Jon Jansen and Chris Samuels can be standouts at their jobs for a decade. The questions are in the middle where Cory Raymer is coming back from a knee injury and the guards—Mookie Moore, Derrick Fletcher and Mark Fischer—are unproven and untested.
Defensive line	C	The question is how much age is catching up with Bruce Smith and Marco Coleman on the ends. Dan Wilkinson is solid in the middle, but his motor needs to be turned up a few revolutions. Kenard Lang might not have the size to endure a season at tackle. Depth is a problem.
Linebackers	B	With a year's experience and with the hoopla of last year behind him, LaVar Arrington should be able to settle in and start making the big plays that are expected of him. Shawn Barber is a dynamic playmaker on the outside, and Kevin Mitchell should be solid in the middle.
Secondary	C	A youthful cadre of cornerbacks has been assembled quickly, which is good considering that Deion Sanders might not be back and Darrell Green finally is showing his age. Mark Carrier and Sam Shade will be pushed for playing time by David Terrell and Josh Symonette.
Special teams	C -	Brett Conway and Bryan Barker were solid free-agent signings and will upgrade what was a dreadful kicking game in 2000. Winston October could bring some needed electricity to the return game. There are enough young players and good coaches to make the cover units effective. There is much to prove and make up for from last year, and until that is done, these are suspect units.

SCHEDULE

PRESEASON
(All times Eastern)

HALL OF FAME WEEKEND

FRIDAY, AUGUST 3

Pittsburgh at Atlanta	7:30

SATURDAY, AUGUST 4

Cincinnati at Chicago	8:00
Dallas at Oakland	9:00

MONDAY, AUGUST 6

Miami vs. St. Louis at Canton, Ohio	8:00

WEEK 1

FRIDAY, AUGUST 10

Carolina at Jacksonville	7:30
Cincinnati at Detroit	7:30
N.Y. Giants at New England	8:00

SATURDAY, AUGUST 11

Atlanta at N.Y. Jets	8:00
Chicago at Tennessee	8:00
Green Bay at Cleveland	8:00
Minnesota vs. New Orleans at San Antonio, Tex.	8:00
Seattle at Indianapolis	8:00
Denver at Dallas	9:00
San Francisco at San Diego	10:30
Oakland at Arizona	11:00

SUNDAY, AUGUST 12

St. Louis at Buffalo	7:30
Washington at Kansas City	8:30

MONDAY, AUGUST 13

Baltimore at Philadelphia	7:30
Miami at Tampa Bay	8:00
Open date: Pittsburgh	

WEEK 2

THURSDAY, AUGUST 16

Jacksonville at N.Y. Giants	8:00
Pittsburgh at Minnesota	8:00

FRIDAY, AUGUST 17

Atlanta at Washington	8:00
Tennessee at St. Louis	8:00

SATURDAY, AUGUST 18

San Diego at Miami	7:00
New England at Carolina	7:30
Philadelphia at Buffalo	7:30
Baltimore at N.Y. Jets	8:00
Dallas at New Orleans	8:00
Detroit at Indianapolis	8:00
Tampa Bay at Cleveland	8:00
Chicago at Kansas City	8:30
Arizona at Seattle	9:30

SUNDAY, AUGUST 19

Oakland at San Francisco	7:00

MONDAY, AUGUST 20

Denver at Green Bay	8:00
Open date: Cincinnati	

WEEK 3

THURSDAY, AUGUST 23

Carolina at Baltimore	7:30
Kansas City at Jacksonville	7:30
Philadelphia at Tennessee	8:00

FRIDAY, AUGUST 24

Cleveland at Washington	8:00
Indianapolis at Minnesota	8:00

SATURDAY, AUGUST 25

Detroit at Pittsburgh	1:00
Buffalo at Cincinnati	7:30
New England at Tampa Bay	7:30
Arizona at Chicago	8:00
Miami at Green Bay	8:00
N.Y. Jets at N.Y. Giants	8:00
New Orleans at Denver	9:00
Seattle at San Francisco	9:00
St. Louis at San Diego	10:00

MONDAY, AUGUST 27

Oakland vs. Dallas at Mexico City	8:00
Open date: Atlanta	

WEEK 4

THURSDAY, AUGUST 30

Buffalo at Pittsburgh	7:30
Indianapolis at Cincinnati	7:30
N.Y. Jets at Philadelphia	7:30
Tennessee at Detroit	7:30
Washington at New England	8:00
Jacksonville at Dallas	8:30

FRIDAY, AUGUST 31

N.Y. Giants at Baltimore	12:00
Minnesota at Miami	7:00
Tampa Bay at Atlanta	7:30
Cleveland at Carolina	8:00
Kansas City at St. Louis	8:00
Green Bay at Oakland	9:00
San Francisco at Denver	9:00
San Diego at Arizona	10:00

SATURDAY, SEPTEMBER 1

New Orleans at Seattle	4:00
Open date: Chicago	

REGULAR SEASON
(All times Eastern)

WEEK 1

SUNDAY, SEPTEMBER 9

Atlanta at San Francisco	4:15
Carolina at Minnesota	1:00
Chicago at Baltimore	1:00
Detroit at Green Bay	1:00
Indianapolis at N.Y. Jets	1:00
New England at Cincinnati	1:00
New Orleans at Buffalo	1:00
Oakland at Kansas City	1:00
Pittsburgh at Jacksonville	1:00
St. Louis at Philadelphia	4:15
Seattle at Cleveland	12:00
Tampa Bay at Dallas	1:00

Washington at San Diego 4:15
Miami at Tennessee 8:30

MONDAY, SEPTEMBER 10

N.Y. Giants at Denver.. 9:00
  Open date: Arizona

WEEK 2

SUNDAY, SEPTEMBER 16

Arizona at Washington.. 1:00
Atlanta at St. Louis 4:05
Buffalo at Miami 1:00
Cincinnati at Tennessee 1:00
Dallas at Detroit... 1:00
Denver at Indianapolis 1:00
Green Bay at N.Y. Giants... 1:00
Jacksonville at Chicago 4:15
Kansas City at Seattle 4:15
New England at Carolina.. 1:00
N.Y. Jets at Oakland... 4:15
Philadelphia at Tampa Bay... 1:00
San Francisco at New Orleans 1:00
Cleveland at Pittsburgh.. 8:30

MONDAY, SEPTEMBER 17

Minnesota at Baltimore.. 9:00
  Open date: San Diego

WEEK 3

SUNDAY, SEPTEMBER 23

Baltimore at Cincinnati.. 1:00
Buffalo at Indianapolis 1:00
Carolina at Atlanta 1:00
Detroit at Cleveland 12:00
Minnesota at Chicago 1:00
N.Y. Giants at Kansas City 1:00
N.Y. Jets at New England... 4:05
Oakland at Miami... 1:00
Philadelphia at Seattle 4:15
St. Louis at San Francisco 4:15
San Diego at Dallas 1:00
Tennessee at Jacksonville.. 1:00
Denver at Arizona 8:35

MONDAY, SEPTEMBER 24

Washington at Green Bay 9:00
  Open date: New Orleans, Pittsburgh, Tampa Bay

WEEK 4

SUNDAY, SEPTEMBER 30

Atlanta at Arizona.. 4:05
Baltimore at Denver... 4:15
Cincinnati at San Diego 4:15
Cleveland at Jacksonville... 4:15
Green Bay at Carolina 1:00
Indianapolis at New England 1:00
Kansas City at Washington 1:00
Miami at St. Louis 1:00
New Orleans at N.Y. Giants.. 1:00
Pittsburgh at Buffalo.. 1:00
Seattle at Oakland 4:15
Tampa Bay at Minnesota.. 1:00
Dallas at Philadelphia.. 8:30

MONDAY, OCTOBER 1

San Francisco at N.Y. Jets 9:00
  Open date: Chicago, Detroit, Tennessee

WEEK 5

SUNDAY, OCTOBER 7

Arizona at Philadelphia 1:00
Chicago at Atlanta.. 1:00

Cincinnati at Pittsburgh 1:00
Green Bay at Tampa Bay 4:15
Jacksonville at Seattle 4:05
Kansas City at Denver.. 4:05
Minnesota at New Orleans.. 1:00
New England at Miami.. 1:00
N.Y. Jets at Buffalo 4:05
San Diego at Cleveland.. 12:00
Tennessee at Baltimore.. 1:00
Washington at N.Y. Giants 1:00
Carolina at San Francisco 8:30

MONDAY, OCTOBER 8

St. Louis at Detroit 9:00
  Open date: Dallas, Indianapolis, Oakland

WEEK 6

SUNDAY, OCTOBER 14

Arizona at Chicago... 1:00
Baltimore at Green Bay 1:00
Cleveland at Cincinnati.. 1:00
Denver at Seattle 4:15
Detroit at Minnesota 1:00
Miami at N.Y. Jets.. 4:15
New Orleans at Carolina 1:00
N.Y. Giants at St. Louis.. 1:00
Pittsburgh at Kansas City 1:00
San Diego at New England 1:00
San Francisco at Atlanta 1:00
Tampa Bay at Tennessee 1:00
Oakland at Indianapolis 8:30

MONDAY, OCTOBER 15

Washington at Dallas.. 9:00
  Open date: Buffalo, Jacksonville, Philadelphia

WEEK 7

THURSDAY, OCTOBER 18

Buffalo at Jacksonville.. 8:30

SUNDAY, OCTOBER 21

Atlanta at New Orleans 1:00
Baltimore at Cleveland... 12:00
Carolina at Washington 1:00
Chicago at Cincinnati... 1:00
Dallas at Oakland 4:15
Denver at San Diego 4:05
Green Bay at Minnesota... 4:15
Kansas City at Arizona... 4:05
New England at Indianapolis 1:00
Pittsburgh at Tampa Bay.. 1:00
St. Louis at N.Y. Jets... 1:00
Tennessee at Detroit.. 1:00

MONDAY, OCTOBER 22

Philadelphia at N.Y. Giants... 9:00
  Open date: Miami, San Francisco, Seattle

WEEK 8

SUNDAY, OCTOBER 28

Arizona at Dallas.. 4:05
Buffalo at San Diego 4:15
Cincinnati at Detroit... 1:00
Indianapolis at Kansas City.. 1:00
Jacksonville at Baltimore 1:00
Miami at Seattle 4:15
Minnesota at Tampa Bay.. 1:00
New England at Denver 4:15
New Orleans at St. Louis 1:00
N.Y. Jets at Carolina.. 1:00
Oakland at Philadelphia 4:15
San Francisco at Chicago 1:00
N.Y. Giants at Washington 8:30

MONDAY, OCTOBER 29

Tennessee at Pittsburgh	9:00

Open date: Atlanta, Cleveland, Green Bay

WEEK 9

SUNDAY, NOVEMBER 4

Baltimore at Pittsburgh	1:00
Carolina at Miami	1:00
Cleveland at Chicago	1:00
Dallas at N.Y. Giants	1:00
Detroit at San Francisco	4:05
Indianapolis at Buffalo	4:15
Jacksonville at Tennessee	2:00
Kansas City at San Diego	4:15
New England at Atlanta	1:00
Philadelphia at Arizona	4:05
Seattle at Washington	4:15
Tampa Bay at Green Bay	1:00
N.Y. Jets at New Orleans	8:30

MONDAY, NOVEMBER 5

Denver at Oakland	9:00

Open date: Cincinnati, Minnesota, St. Louis

WEEK 10

SUNDAY, NOVEMBER 11

Buffalo at New England	1:00
Carolina at St. Louis	1:00
Cincinnati at Jacksonville	1:00
Dallas at Atlanta	1:00
Green Bay at Chicago	1:00
Kansas City at N.Y. Jets	1:00
Miami at Indianapolis	1:00
Minnesota at Philadelphia	4:15
New Orleans at San Francisco	4:15
N.Y. Giants at Arizona	4:15
Pittsburgh at Cleveland	12:00
San Diego at Denver	4:05
Tampa Bay at Detroit	1:00
Oakland at Seattle	8:30

MONDAY, NOVEMBER 12

Baltimore at Tennessee	9:00

Open date: Washington

WEEK 11

SUNDAY, NOVEMBER 18

Atlanta at Green Bay	1:00
Chicago at Tampa Bay	1:00
Cleveland at Baltimore	1:00
Detroit at Arizona	4:15
Indianapolis at New Orleans	1:00
Jacksonville at Pittsburgh	4:05
N.Y. Jets at Miami	1:00
Philadelphia at Dallas	1:00
San Diego at Oakland	4:05
San Francisco at Carolina	1:00
Seattle at Buffalo	1:00
Tennessee at Cincinnati	1:00
Washington at Denver	4:15
St. Louis at New England	8:30

MONDAY, NOVEMBER 19

N.Y. Giants at Minnesota	9:00

Open date: Kansas City

WEEK 12

THURSDAY, NOVEMBER 22

Green Bay at Detroit	12:30
Denver at Dallas	4:05

SUNDAY, NOVEMBER 25

Arizona at San Diego	4:05
Atlanta at Carolina	1:00
Baltimore at Jacksonville	1:00
Cincinnati at Cleveland	1:00
Miami at Buffalo	1:00
New Orleans at New England	4:05
Oakland at N.Y. Giants	4:15
Pittsburgh at Tennessee	1:00
San Francisco at Indianapolis	1:00
Seattle at Kansas City	1:00
Washington at Philadelphia	1:00
Chicago at Minnesota	8:30

MONDAY, NOVEMBER 26

Tampa Bay at St. Louis	9:00

Open date: N.Y. Jets

WEEK 13

THURSDAY, NOVEMBER 29

Philadelphia at Kansas City	8:30

SUNDAY, DECEMBER 2

Arizona at Oakland	4:15
Carolina at New Orleans	1:00
Dallas at Washington	4:15
Denver at Miami	1:00
Detroit at Chicago	1:00
Indianapolis at Baltimore	1:00
Minnesota at Pittsburgh	1:00
New England at N.Y. Jets	1:00
St. Louis at Atlanta	1:00
San Diego at Seattle	4:05
Tampa Bay at Cincinnati	1:00
Tennessee at Cleveland	1:00
Buffalo at San Francisco	8:30

MONDAY, DECEMBER 3

Green Bay at Jacksonville	9:00

Open date: N.Y. Giants

WEEK 14

SUNDAY, DECEMBER 9

Carolina at Buffalo	1:00
Chicago at Green Bay	1:00
Cleveland at New England	1:00
Detroit at Tampa Bay	1:00
Jacksonville at Cincinnati	1:00
Kansas City at Oakland	4:15
New Orleans at Atlanta	1:00
N.Y. Giants at Dallas	1:00
N.Y. Jets at Pittsburgh	4:15
San Diego at Philadelphia	1:00
San Francisco at St. Louis	1:00
Tennessee at Minnesota	1:00
Washington at Arizona	4:05
Seattle at Denver	8:30

SUNDAY, DECEMBER 10

Indianapolis at Miami	9:00

Open date: Baltimore

WEEK 15

SATURDAY, DECEMBER 15

Arizona at N.Y. Giants	12:30
Oakland at San Diego	4:00

SUNDAY, DECEMBER 16

Atlanta at Indianapolis	1:00
Cincinnati at N.Y. Jets	1:00
Dallas at Seattle	4:15
Denver at Kansas City	1:00
Green Bay at Tennessee	4:15
Jacksonville at Cleveland	1:00

Miami at San Francisco	4:05
Minnesota at Detroit	1:00
New England at Buffalo	1:00
Philadelphia at Washington	1:00
Tampa Bay at Chicago	1:00
Pittsburgh at Baltimore	8:30

St. Louis at New Orleans	9:00
Open date: Carolina	

WEEK 16

SATURDAY, DECEMBER 22

Miami at New England	12:30
Philadelphia at San Francisco	4:00
Tennessee at Oakland	9:00

SUNDAY, DECEMBER 23

Buffalo at Atlanta	1:00
Chicago at Washington	1:00
Cincinnati at Baltimore	1:00
Cleveland at Green Bay	1:00
Dallas at Arizona	4:05
Detroit at Pittsburgh	1:00
Jacksonville at Minnesota	4:15
New Orleans at Tampa Bay	1:00

St. Louis at Carolina	1:00
San Diego at Kansas City	1:00
Seattle at N.Y. Giants	1:00
N.Y. Jets at Indianapolis	8:30
Open date: Denver	

WEEK 17

SATURDAY, DECEMBER 29

Baltimore at Tampa Bay	9:00

SUNDAY, DECEMBER 30

Arizona at Carolina	1:00
Atlanta at Miami	1:00
Buffalo at N.Y. Jets	1:00
Chicago at Detroit	1:00
Cleveland at Tennessee	1:00
Indianapolis at St. Louis	1:00
Kansas City at Jacksonville	1:00
Minnesota at Green Bay	1:00
N.Y. Giants at Philadelphia	1:05
Oakland at Denver	4:15
Pittsburgh at Cincinnati	1:00
San Francisco at Dallas	1:00
Seattle at San Diego	4:15
Washington at New Orleans	8:30
Open date: New England	

2001 SEASON *Schedule*

NATIONALLY TELEVISED GAMES

(All times Eastern)

PRESEASON

Mon.	Aug.	6—	Miami vs. St. Louis at Canton, Ohio (8:00, ABC)
Sat.	Aug.	11—	Minnesota vs. New Orleans at San Antonio, Tex. (8:00, ESPN)
Mon.	Aug.	13—	Miami at Tampa Bay (8:00, ESPN)
Thur.	Aug.	16—	Jacksonville at N.Y. Giants (8:00, ESPN)
Fri.	Aug.	17—	Tennessee at St. Louis (8:00, FOX)
Sat.	Aug.	18—	Baltimore at N.Y. Jets (8:00, CBS)
Mon.	Aug.	20—	Denver at Green Bay (8:00, ABC)
Thur.	Aug.	23—	Philadelphia at Tennessee (8:00, CBS)
Fri.	Aug.	24—	Indianapolis at Minnesota (8:00, FOX)
Mon.	Aug.	27—	Oakland vs. Dallas at Mexico City (8:00, ABC)
Fri.	Aug.	31—	Kansas City at St. Louis (8:00, ESPN)

REGULAR SEASON

Sun.	Sept.	9—	St. Louis at Philadelphia (4:15, FOX)
			Miami at Tennessee (8:30, ESPN)
Mon.	Sept.	10—	N.Y. Giants at Denver (9:00, ABC)
Sun.	Sept.	16—	N.Y. Jets at Oakland (4:15, CBS)
			Cleveland at Pittsburgh (8:30, ESPN)
Mon.	Sept.	17—	Minnesota at Baltimore (9:00, ABC)
Sun.	Sept.	23—	St. Louis at San Francisco (4:15, FOX)
			Denver at Arizona (8:35, ESPN)
Mon.	Sept.	24—	Washington at Green Bay (9:00, ABC)
Sun.	Sept.	30—	Baltimore at Denver (4:15, CBS)
			Dallas at Philadelphia (8:30, ESPN)
Mon.	Oct.	1—	San Francisco at N.Y. Jets (9:00, ABC)
Sun.	Oct.	7—	Green Bay at Tampa Bay (4:15, FOX)
			Carolina at San Francisco (8:30, ESPN)
Mon.	Oct.	8—	St. Louis at Detroit (9:00, ABC)
Sun.	Oct.	14—	Miami at N.Y. Jets (4:15, CBS)
			Oakland at Indianapolis (8:30, ESPN)
Mon.	Oct.	15—	Washington at Dallas (9:00, ABC)
Thur.	Oct.	18—	Buffalo at Jacksonville (8:30, ESPN)
Sun.	Oct.	21—	Green Bay at Minnesota (4:15, FOX)
Mon.	Oct.	22—	Philadelphia at N.Y. Giants (9:00, ABC)
Sun.	Oct.	28—	Oakland at Philadelphia (4:15, CBS)
			N.Y. Giants at Washington (8:30, ESPN)
Mon.	Oct.	29—	Tennessee at Pittsburgh (9:00, ABC)
Sun.	Nov.	4—	Seattle at Washington (4:15, CBS)
			N.Y. Jets at New Orleans (8:30, ESPN)
Mon.	Nov.	5—	Denver at Oakland (9:00, ABC)
Sun.	Nov.	11—	Minnesota at Philadelphia (4:15, FOX)
			Oakland at Seattle (8:30, ESPN)
Mon.	Nov.	12—	Baltimore at Tennessee (9:00, ABC)
Sun.	Nov.	18—	Washington at Denver (4:15, FOX)
			St. Louis at New England (8:30, ESPN)
Mon.	Nov.	19—	N.Y. Giants at Minnesota (9:00, ABC)
Thur.	Nov.	22—	Green Bay at Detroit (12:30, FOX)
			Denver at Dallas (4:05, CBS)
Sun.	Nov.	25—	Oakland at N.Y. Giants (4:15, CBS)
			Chicago at Minnesota (8:30, ESPN)
Mon.	Nov.	26—	Tampa Bay at St. Louis (9:00, ABC)
Thur.	Nov.	29—	Philadelphia at Kansas City (8:30, ESPN)
Sun.	Dec.	2—	Dallas at Washington (4:15, FOX)
			Buffalo at San Francisco (8:30, ESPN)
Mon.	Dec.	3—	Green Bay at Jacksonville (9:00, ABC)
Sun.	Dec.	9—	Kansas City at Oakland (4:15, CBS)
			Seattle at Denver (8:30, ESPN)
Sun.	Dec.	10—	Indianapolis at Miami (9:00, ABC)
Sat.	Dec.	15—	Arizona at N.Y. Giants (12:30, FOX)
			Oakland at San Diego (4:00, CBS)
Sun.	Dec.	16—	Green Bay at Tennessee (4:15, FOX)
			Pittsburgh at Baltimore (8:30, ESPN)
Mon.	Dec.	17—	St. Louis at New Orleans (9:00, ABC)
Sat.	Dec.	22—	Miami at New England (12:30, CBS)
			Philadelphia at San Francisco (4:00, FOX)
			Tennessee at Oakland (9:00, ABC)
Sun.	Dec.	23—	Jacksonville at Minnesota (4:15, CBS)
			N.Y. Jets at Indianapolis (8:30, ESPN)
Sat.	Dec.	29—	Baltimore at Tampa Bay (9:00, ABC)
Sun.	Dec.	30—	Oakland at Denver (4:15, CBS)
			Washington at New Orleans (8:30, ESPN)

POSTSEASON

Sat.	Jan.	5—	AFC, NFC wild-card playoffs (ABC)
Sun.	Jan.	6—	AFC, NFC wild-card playoffs (CBS, FOX)
Sat.	Jan.	12—	AFC, NFC divisional playoffs (CBS, FOX)
Sun.	Jan.	13—	AFC, NFC divisional playoffs (CBS, FOX)
Sun.	Jan.	20—	AFC, NFC championship games (CBS, FOX)
Sun.	Jan.	27—	Super Bowl at Louisiana Superdome, New Orleans (FOX)
Sun.	Feb.	3—	Pro Bowl at Honolulu (ABC)

INTERCONFERENCE GAMES

(All times Eastern)

Sun.	Sept. 9—	Chicago at Baltimore	1:00
		New Orleans at Buffalo	1:00
		Washington at San Diego	4:15
Mon.	Sept. 10—	N.Y. Giants at Denver	9:00
Sun.	Sept. 16—	Jacksonville at Chicago	4:15
		New England at Carolina	1:00
Mon.	Sept. 17—	Minnesota at Baltimore	9:00
Sun.	Sept. 23—	Detroit at Cleveland	12:00
		N.Y. Giants at Kansas City	1:00
		Philadelphia at Seattle	4:15
		San Diego at Dallas	1:00
		Denver at Arizona	8:35
Sun.	Sept. 30—	Kansas City at Washington	1:00
		Miami at St. Louis	1:00
Mon.	Oct. 1—	San Francisco at N.Y. Jets	9:00
Sun.	Oct. 14—	Baltimore at Green Bay	1:00
		Tampa Bay at Tennessee	1:00
Sun.	Oct. 21—	Chicago at Cincinnati	1:00
		Dallas at Oakland	4:15
		Kansas City at Arizona	4:05
		Pittsburgh at Tampa Bay	1:00
		St. Louis at N.Y. Jets	1:00
		Tennessee at Detroit	1:00
Sun.	Oct. 28—	Cincinnati at Detroit	1:00
		N.Y. Jets at Carolina	1:00
		Oakland at Philadelphia	4:15
Sun.	Nov. 4—	Carolina at Miami	1:00
		Cleveland at Chicago	1:00
		New England at Atlanta	1:00
		Seattle at Washington	4:15

		N.Y. Jets at New Orleans	8:30
Sun.	Nov. 18—	Indianapolis at New Orleans	1:00
		Washington at Denver	4:15
		St. Louis at New England	8:30
Thur.	Nov. 22—	Denver at Dallas	4:05
Sun.	Nov. 25—	Arizona at San Diego	4:05
		New Orleans at New England	4:05
		Oakland at N.Y. Giants	4:15
		San Francisco at Indianapolis	1:00
Thur.	Nov. 29—	Philadelphia at Kansas City	8:30
Sun.	Dec. 2—	Arizona at Oakland	4:15
		Minnesota at Pittsburgh	1:00
		Tampa Bay at Cincinnati	1:00
		Buffalo at San Francisco	8:30
Mon.	Dec. 3—	Green Bay at Jacksonville	9:00
Sun.	Dec. 9—	Carolina at Buffalo	1:00
		San Diego at Philadelphia	1:00
		Tennessee at Minnesota	1:00
Sun.	Dec. 16—	Atlanta at Indianapolis	1:00
		Dallas at Seattle	4:15
		Green Bay at Tennessee	4:15
		Miami at San Francisco	4:05
Sun.	Dec. 23—	Buffalo at Atlanta	1:00
		Cleveland at Green Bay	1:00
		Detroit at Pittsburgh	1:00
		Jacksonville at Minnesota	4:15
		Seattle at N.Y. Giants	1:00
Sat.	Dec. 29—	Baltimore at Tampa Bay	9:00
Sun.	Dec. 30—	Atlanta at Miami	1:00
		Indianapolis at St. Louis	1:00

2001 STRENGTH OF SCHEDULE

(Teams are ranked from most difficult to easiest schedules, based on 2001 opponents' combined 2000 records)

	Team	Opp. Wins	Opp. Losses	Opp. Pct.		Team	Opp. Wins	Opp. Losses	Opp. Pct.
1.	Minnesota (5)	147	109	.574		Cincinnati (T15)	127	129	.496
2.	Tampa Bay (9)	142	114	.555		New Orleans (26)	127	129	.496
3.	Indianapolis (3)	138	118	.539	20.	New England (T6)	126	130	.492
4.	Green Bay (10)	136	120	.531	21.	Cleveland (14)	125	131	.488
5.	Miami (2)	133	123	.520		Chicago (T11)	125	131	.488
	N.Y. Jets (4)	133	123	.520	23.	Carolina (21)	124	132	.484
7.	Tennessee (24)	132	124	.516		Oakland (T28)	124	132	.484
	Pittsburgh (T15)	132	124	.516	25.	Detroit (T11)	123	133	.480
9.	St. Louis (30)	131	125	.512	26.	Atlanta (T22)	122	134	.477
10.	San Francisco (25)	130	126	.508	27.	Buffalo (1)	120	136	.469
	N.Y. Giants (20)	130	126	.508	28.	San Diego (19)	119	137	.465
12.	Kansas City (8)	129	127	.504		Philadelphia (31)	119	137	.465
13.	Jacksonville (T22)	128	128	.500	30.	Washington (T11)	118	138	.461
	Baltimore (18)	128	128	.500		Denver (27)	118	138	.461
	Arizona (T28)	128	128	.500		NOTE: Number in parentheses is 2000 rank.			
16.	Dallas (T15)	127	129	.496					
	Seattle (T6)	127	129	.496					

COLLEGE DRAFT

FIRST ROUND

Team	Player selected	Pos.	College	Draft pick origination
1. Atlanta	Michael Vick	QB	Virginia Tech	From San Diego
2. Arizona	Leonard Davis	T	Texas	
3. Cleveland	Gerard Warren	DT	Florida	
4. Cincinnati	Justin Smith	DE	Missouri	
5. San Diego	LaDainian Tomlinson	RB	Texas Christian	From Atlanta
6. New England	Richard Seymour	DT	Georgia	
7. San Francisco	Andre Carter	DE	California	From Dallas through Seattle
8. Chicago	David Terrell	WR	Michigan	
9. Seattle	Koren Robinson	WR	North Carolina State	From San Francisco
10. Green Bay	Jamal Reynolds	DE	Florida State	From Seattle
11. Carolina	Dan Morgan	LB	Miami, Fla.	
12. St. Louis	Damione Lewis	DT	Miami, Fla.	From Kansas City
13. Jacksonville	Marcus Stroud	DT	Georgia	
14. Tampa Bay	Kenyatta Walker	T	Florida	From Buffalo
15. Washington	Rod Gardner	WR	Clemson	
16. N.Y. Jets	Santana Moss	WR	Miami, Fla.	From Pittsburgh
17. Seattle	Steve Hutchinson	G	Michigan	From Green Bay
18. Detroit	Jeff Backus	T	Michigan	
19. Pittsburgh	Casey Hampton	DT	Texas	From N.Y. Jets
20. St. Louis	Adam Archuleta	DB	Arizona State	
21. Buffalo	Nate Clements	DB	Ohio State	From Tampa Bay
22. N.Y. Giants	Will Allen	DB	Syracuse	From Indianapolis
23. New Orleans	Deuce McAllister	RB	Mississippi	
24. Denver	Willie Middlebrooks	DB	Minnesota	
25. Philadelphia	Freddie Mitchell	WR	UCLA	
26. Miami	Jamar Fletcher	DB	Wisconsin	
27. Minnesota	Michael Bennett	RB	Wisconsin	
28. Oakland	Derrick Gibson	DB	Florida State	
29. St. Louis	Ryan Pickett	DT	Ohio State	From Tennessee
30. Indianapolis	Reggie Wayne	WR	Miami, Fla.	From N.Y. Giants
31. Baltimore	Todd Heap	TE	Arizona State	

SECOND ROUND

Team	Player selected	Pos.	College	Draft pick origination
32. San Diego	Drew Brees	QB	Purdue	
33. Cleveland	Quincy Morgan	WR	Kansas State	
34. Arizona	Kyle Vanden Bosch	DE	Nebraska	
35. Atlanta	Alge Crumpler	TE	North Carolina	
36. Cincinnati	Chad Johnson	WR	Oregon State	
37. Indianapolis	Idrees Bashir	DB	Memphis	From Dallas
38. Chicago	Anthony Thomas	RB	Michigan	
39. Pittsburgh	Kendrell Bell	LB	Georgia	From New England
40. Seattle	Ken Lucas	DB	Mississippi	
41. Green Bay	Robert Ferguson	WR	Texas A&M	From San Francisco
42. St. Louis	Tommy Polley	LB	Florida State	From Kansas City
43. Jacksonville	Maurice Williams	T	Michigan	
44. Carolina	Kris Jenkins	DT	Maryland	
45. Washington	Fred Smoot	DB	Mississippi State	
46. Buffalo	Aaron Schobel	DE	Texas Christian	
47. San Francisco	Jamie Winborn	LB	Vanderbilt	From Green Bay
48. New England	Matt Light	G	Purdue	From Detroit
49. N.Y. Jets	LaMont Jordan	RB	Maryland	
50. Detroit	Dominic Raiola	C	Nebraska	From Pittsburgh through New England
51. Denver	Paul Toviessi	DE	Marshall	From Tampa Bay through Buffalo
52. Miami	Chris Chambers	WR	Wisconsin	From Indianapolis through Dallas
53. Dallas	Quincy Carter	QB	Georgia	From New Orleans
54. Arizona	Michael Stone	DB	Memphis	From St. Louis
55. Philadelphia	Quinton Caver	LB	Arkansas	
56. Dallas	Tony Dixon	DB	Alabama	From Miami
57. Minnesota	Willie Howard	DE	Stanford	
58. Buffalo	Travis Henry	RB	Tennessee	From Denver
59. Oakland	Marques Tuiasosopo	QB	Washington	
60. Tennessee	Andre Dyson	DB	Utah	
61. Detroit	Shaun Rogers	DT	Texas	From N.Y. Giants
62. Baltimore	Gary Baxter	DB	Baylor	

THIRD ROUND

	Team	Player selected	Pos.	College	Draft pick origination
63.	Philadelphia	Derrick Burgess	DE	Mississippi	From San Diego
64.	Arizona	Adrian Wilson	DB	North Carolina State	
65.	Cleveland	James Jackson	RB	Miami, Fla.	
66.	Cincinnati	Sean Brewer	TE	San Jose State	
67.	San Diego	Tay Cody	DB	Florida State	From Atlanta
68.	Chicago	Mike Gandy	G	Notre Dame	
69.	Minnesota	Eric Kelly	DB	Kentucky	From New England
70.	New Orleans	Sedrick Hodge	LB	North Carolina	From Dallas
71.	Green Bay	Bhawoh Jue	DB	Penn State	From San Francisco
72.	Green Bay	Torrance Marshall	LB	Oklahoma	From Seattle
73.	Jacksonville	Eric Westmoreland	LB	Tennessee	
74.	Carolina	Steve Smith	WR	Utah	
75.	Kansas City	Eric Downing	DT	Syracuse	
76.	Buffalo	Ron Edwards	DT	Texas A&M	
77.	Kansas City	Marvin Minnis	WR	Florida State	From Washington
78.	N.Y. Giants	William Peterson	DB	Western Illinois	From Detroit
79.	N.Y. Jets	Kareem McKenzie	T	Penn State	
	Pittsburgh forfeited its pick for 1998 salary cap violations				
80.	San Francisco	Kevan Barlow	RB	Pittsburgh	From Green Bay
81.	New Orleans	Kenny Smith	DT	Alabama	From Indianapolis through Dallas
82.	Seattle	Heath Evans	RB	Auburn	From New Orleans through G.B. and S.F.
83.	St. Louis	Brian Allen	LB	Florida State	
84.	Tampa Bay	Dwight Smith	DB	Akron	
85.	Miami	Travis Minor	RB	Florida State	
86.	New England	Brock Williams	DB	Notre Dame	From Minnesota
87.	Denver	Reggie Hayward	DE	Iowa State	
88.	Miami	Morlon Greenwood	LB	Syracuse	From Philadelphia
89.	Oakland	DeLawrence Grant	DE	Oregon State	
90.	Tennessee	Shad Meier	TE	Kansas State	
91.	Indianapolis	Cory Bird	DB	Virginia Tech	From N.Y. Giants
92.	Baltimore	Casey Rabach	C	Wisconsin	
93.	Dallas*	Willie Blade	DT	Mississippi State	
94.	Jacksonville*	James Boyd	DB	Penn State	
95.	Buffalo*	Jonas Jennings	T	Georgia	

FOURTH ROUND

	Team	Player selected	Pos.	College	Draft pick origination
96.	New England	Kenyatta Jones	G	South Florida	From San Diego
97.	Cleveland	Anthony Henry	DB	South Florida	
98.	Arizona	Bill Gramatica	K	South Florida	
99.	Atlanta	Robert Garza	C	Texas A&M-Kingsville	
100.	Cincinnati	Rudi Johnson	RB	Auburn	
101.	N.Y. Jets	Jamie Henderson	DB	Georgia	From New England
102.	Atlanta	Matt Stewart	LB	Vanderbilt	From Dallas
103.	Chicago	Karon Riley	DE	Minnesota	
104.	Seattle	Orlando Huff	LB	Fresno State	
105.	Green Bay	Bill Ferrario	G	Wisconsin	From San Francisco
106.	Carolina	Chris Weinke	QB	Florida State	
107.	Kansas City	Monty Beisel	DE	Kansas State	
108.	Kansas City	George Layne	RB	Texas Christian	From Jacksonville
109.	Washington	Sage Rosenfels	QB	Iowa State	
110.	Buffalo	Brandon Spoon	LB	North Carolina	From Buffalo through Denver
111.	Pittsburgh	Mathias Nkwenti	T	Temple	From N.Y. Jets
112.	San Diego	Carlos Polk	LB	Nebraska	From Pittsburgh through New England
113.	Denver	Ben Hamilton	C	Minnesota	From Green Bay
114.	N.Y. Giants	Cedric Scott	DE	Southern Mississippi	From Detroit
115.	New Orleans	Moran Norris	RB	Kansas	
116.	St. Louis	Milton Wynn	WR	Washington State	
117.	Tampa Bay	John Howell	DB	Colorado State	
118.	Indianapolis	Ryan Diem	G	Northern Illinois	
119.	New England	Jabari Holloway	TE	Notre Dame	From Minnesota
120.	Denver	Nick Harris	P	California	
121.	Philadelphia	Correll Buckhalter	RB	Nebraska	
122.	Dallas	Markus Steele	LB	Southern California	From Miami
123.	Arizona	Marcus Bell	DT	Memphis	From Oakland through St. Louis
124.	Tennessee	Justin McCareins	WR	Northern Illinois	
125.	N.Y. Giants	Jesse Palmer	QB	Florida	
126.	Baltimore	Edgerton Hartwell	LB	Western Illinois	
127.	Seattle*	Curtis Fuller	DB	Texas Christian	
128.	Seattle*	Floyd Womack	T	Mississippi State	

Team	Player selected	Pos.	College	Draft pick origination
129. St. Louis*	Brandon Manumaleuna	TE	Arizona	
130. Minnesota*	Shawn Worthen	DT	Texas Christian	
131. Minnesota*	Cedric James	WR	Texas Christian	

FIFTH ROUND

Team	Player selected	Pos.	College	Draft pick origination
132. San Diego	Elliot Silvers	T	Washington	
133. Arizona	Mario Fatafehi	DT	Kansas State	
134. Cleveland	Jeremiah Pharms	LB	Washington	
135. Cincinnati	Victor Leyva	G	Arizona State	
136. Atlanta	Vinny Sutherland	WR	Purdue	
137. Dallas	Matt Lehr	C	Virginia Tech	
138. Chicago	Bernard Robertson	C	Tulane	
139. San Diego	Zeke Moreno	LB	Southern California	From New England

San Francisco forfeited its pick for 1997 salary cap violations

Team	Player selected	Pos.	College	Draft pick origination
140. Seattle	Alex Bannister	WR	Eastern Kentucky	
141. Kansas City	Billy Baber	TE	Virginia	
142. Jacksonville	David Leaverton	P	Tennessee	
143. Carolina	Jarrod Cooper	DB	Kansas State	
144. Buffalo	Marques Sullivan	T	Illinois	
145. St. Louis	Jeremetrius Butler	DB	Kansas State	From Washington
146. Pittsburgh	Chukky Okobi	C	Purdue	
147. Philadelphia	Tony Stewart	TE	Penn State	From Green Bay
148. Detroit	Scotty Anderson	WR	Grambling	
149. Detroit	Mike McMahon	QB	Rutgers	From N.Y. Jets through New England
150. Kansas City	Derrick Blaylock	RB	Stephen F. Austin State	From St. Louis
151. Tampa Bay	Russ Hochstein	G	Nebraska	
152. Indianapolis	Raymond Walls	DB	Southern Mississippi	
153. New Orleans	Onome Ojo	WR	UC Davis	
154. Washington	Darnerien McCants	WR	Delaware State	From Denver through St. Louis
155. Philadelphia	A.J. Feeley	QB	Oregon	
156. Miami	Shawn Draper	T	Alabama	
157. Minnesota	Patrick Chukwurah	LB	Wyoming	
158. Oakland	Raymond Perryman	DB	Northern Arizona	
159. Tennessee	Eddie Berlin	WR	Northern Iowa	
160. N.Y. Giants	John Markham	K	Vanderbilt	
161. Baltimore	Chris Barnes	RB	New Mexico State	
162. N.Y. Giants*	Jonathan Carter	WR	Troy State	
163. New England*	Hakim Akbar	DB	Washington	

SIXTH ROUND

Team	Player selected	Pos.	College	Draft pick origination
164. Miami	Brandon Winey	T	Louisiana State	From San Diego
165. Cleveland	Michael Jameson	DB	Texas A&M	
166. Arizona	Bobby Newcombe	WR	Nebraska	
167. Atlanta	Randy Garner	DE	Arkansas	
168. Cincinnati	Riall Johnson	LB	Stanford	
169. San Francisco	Cedrick Wilson	WR	Tennessee	From Chicago
170. Jacksonville	Chad Ward	G	Washington	From New England
171. Dallas	Daleroy Stewart	DT	Southern Mississippi	
172. Seattle	Josh Booty	QB	Louisiana State	
173. Detroit	Jason Glenn	LB	Texas A&M	From San Francisco through New England
174. Tampa Bay	Jameel Cook	RB	Illinois	From Jacksonville
175. Carolina	Dee Brown	RB	Syracuse	
176. Kansas City	Alex Sulfsted	T	Miami of Ohio	
177. Miami	Josh Heupel	QB	Oklahoma	From Washington
178. Buffalo	Tony Driver	DB	Notre Dame	
179. San Francisco	Rashad Holman	DB	Louisville	From Green Bay
180. New England	Arther Love	TE	South Carolina State	From Detroit
181. Pittsburgh	Rodney Bailey	DE	Ohio State	From N.Y. Jets
182. Pittsburgh	Roger Knight	LB	Wisconsin	
183. Tampa Bay	Ellis Wyms	DE	Mississippi State	
184. Oakland	Chris Cooper	DT	Nebraska-Omaha	From Indianapolis
185. New Orleans	Mitch White	T	Oregon State	
186. Washington	Mario Monds	DT	Cincinnati	From St. Louis
187. Miami	Otis Leverette	DE	Alabama-Birmingham	From Philadelphia
188. Miami	Rick Crowell	LB	Colorado State	
189. Minnesota	Carey Scott	DB	Kentucky State	
190. Denver	Kevin Kasper	WR	Iowa	
191. San Francisco	Menson Holloway	DE	Texas-El Paso	From Oakland through Seattle
192. Tennessee	Dan Alexander	RB	Nebraska	

Team	Player selected	Pos.	College	Draft pick origination
193. Indianapolis	Jason Doering	DB	Wisconsin	From N.Y. Giants
194. Baltimore	Joe Maese	C	New Mexico	
195. Buffalo*	Dan O'Leary	TE	Notre Dame	
196. Buffalo*	Jimmy Williams	DB	Vanderbilt	
197. St. Louis*	Francis St. Paul	WR	Northern Arizona	
198. Green Bay*	David Martin	TE	Tennessee	
199. Tennessee*	Adam Haayer	T	Minnesota	
200. New England*	Leonard Myers	DB	Miami, Fla.	

SEVENTH ROUND

Team	Player selected	Pos.	College	Draft pick origination
201. San Diego	Brandon Gorin	T	Purdue	
202. Arizona	Renaldo Hill	DB	Michigan State	
203. Cleveland	Paul Zukauskas	G	Boston College	
204. Cincinnati	T.J. Houshmandzadeh	WR	Oregon State	
205. Tampa Bay	Dauntae' Finger	TE	North Carolina	From Atlanta
206. N.Y. Jets	James Reed	DT	Iowa State	From New England
207. Dallas	Colston Weatherington	DE	Central Missouri	
208. Chicago	John Capel	WR	Florida	
209. San Francisco	Alex Lincoln	LB	Auburn	
210. Seattle	Harold Blackmon	DB	Northwestern	
211. Carolina	Louis Williams	C	Louisiana State	
212. Kansas City	Shaunard Harts	DB	Boise State	
213. Jacksonville	Anthony Denman	LB	Notre Dame	
214. Buffalo	Reggie Germany	WR	Ohio State	
215. Atlanta	Corey Hall	DB	Appalachian State	From Washington through Denver
216. New England	Owen Pochman	K	Brigham Young	From Detroit
217. N.Y. Jets	Siitupe Peko	C	Michigan State	
218. Pittsburgh	Chris Taylor	WR	Texas A&M	
219. Atlanta	Kynan Forney	G	Hawaii	From Green Bay through Denver
220. Indianapolis	Rick DeMulling	G	Idaho	
221. New Orleans	Ennis Davis	DT	Southern California	
222. Seattle	Dennis Norman	T	Princeton	From St. Louis through Green Bay and S.F.
223. Tampa Bay	Than Merrill	DB	Yale	
224. San Francisco	Eric Johnson	TE	Yale	From Miami through Washington
225. Minnesota	Brian Crawford	T	Western Oregon	
226. Atlanta	Ronald Flemons	DE	Texas A&M	From Denver
227. Carolina	Mike Roberg	TE	Idaho	From Philadelphia
228. Oakland	Derek Combs	RB	Ohio State	
229. Oakland	Ken-Yon Rambo	WR	Ohio State	From Tennessee
230. N.Y. Giants	Ross Kolodziej	DT	Wisconsin	
231. Baltimore	Dwayne Missouri	DE	Northwestern	
232. Tennessee*	Keith Adams	LB	Clemson	
233. Jacksonville*	Marlon McCree	DB	Kentucky	
234. Tampa Bay*	Joe Tafoya	DE	Arizona	
235. Jacksonville*	Richmond Flowers	WR	UT Chattanooga	
236. Atlanta*	Quentin McCord	WR	Kentucky	
237. Seattle*	Kris Kocurek	DT	Texas Tech	
238. Buffalo*	Tyrone Robertson	DT	Hinds C.C. (Miss.)	
239. New England*	T.J. Turner	LB	Michigan State	
240. Dallas*	John Nix	DT	Southern Mississippi	
241. Jacksonville*	Randy Chevrier	DT	McGill	
242. Dallas*	Char-ron Dorsey	T	Florida State	
243. Kansas City*	Terdell Sands	DT	UT Chattanooga	
244. San Diego*	Robert Carswell	DB	Clemson	
245. Cleveland*	Andre King	WR	Miami, Fla.	
246. Arizona*	Tevita Ofahengaue	TE	Brigham Young	

*Compensatory selection.

PLAYOFF PLAN

TIEBREAKING PROCEDURES

DIVISION TIES

TWO CLUBS

1. Head-to-head (best won-lost-tied percentage in games between the clubs).
2. Best won-lost-tied percentage in games played within the division.
3. Best won-lost-tied percentage in games played within the conference.
4. Best won-lost-tied percentage in common games, if applicable.
5. Best net points in division games.
6. Best net points in all games.
7. Strength of schedule.
8. Best net touchdowns in all games.
9. Coin toss.

THREE OR MORE CLUBS

(Note: If two clubs remain tied after other clubs are eliminated during any step, tie-breaker reverts to step 1 of two-club format.)
1. Head-to-head (best won-lost-tied percentage in games among the clubs).
2. Best won-lost-tied percentage in games played within the division.
3. Best won-lost-tied percentage in games played within the conference.
4. Best won-lost-tied percentage in common games.
5. Best net points in division games.
6. Best net points in all games.
7. Strength of schedule.
8. Best net touchdowns in all games.
9. Coin toss.

WILD-CARD TIES

If necessary to break ties to determine the three wild-card clubs from each conference, the following steps will be taken:
1. If all the tied clubs are from the same division, apply division tie-breaker.
2. If the tied clubs are from different divisions, apply the steps listed below.
3. When the first wild-card team has been identified, the procedure is repeated to name the second wild card (i.e., eliminate all but the highest-ranked club in each division prior to proceeding to step 2), and repeated a third time, if necessary, to identify the third wild card. In situations where three or more teams from the same division are involved in the procedure, the original seeding of the teams remains the same for subsequent applications of the tie-breaker if the top-ranked team in that division qualifies for a wild-card berth.

TWO CLUBS

1. Head-to-head, if applicable.
2. Best won-lost-tied percentage in games played within the conference.
3. Best won-lost-tied percentage in common games, minimum of four.
4. Best average net points in conference games.
5. Best net points in all games.
6. Strength of schedule.
7. Best net touchdowns in all games.
8. Coin toss.

THREE OR MORE CLUBS

(Note: If two clubs remain tied after other clubs are eliminated, tie-breaker reverts to step 1 of two-club format.)
1. Apply division tie-breaker to eliminate all but highest-ranked club in each division prior to proceeding to step 1. The original seeding within a division upon application of the division tie-breaker remains the same for all subsequent applications of the procedure that are necessary to identify the three wild-card participants.
2. Head-to-head sweep (applicable only if one club has defeated each of the others or one club has lost to each of the others).
3. Best won-lost-tied percentage in games played within the conference.
4. Best won-lost-tied percentage in common games, minimum of four.
5. Best average net points in conference games.
6. Best net points in all games.
7. Strength of schedule.
8. Best net touchdowns in all games.
9. Coin toss.

2000 REVIEW

Year in review
Final standings
Weeks 1 through 17
Wild-card games
Divisional playoffs
Conference championships
Super Bowl 35
Pro Bowl
Player participation
Attendance
Trades

YEAR IN REVIEW

After the 10th concussion of his career, Troy Aikman was waived by the Cowboys and then retired. (Photo by Bob Leverone/The Sporting News)

Like the previous season, the 2000 NFL season will be a year remembered for significant change, change on the field and off the field.

In 2000, we were reminded that defense does win championships. We watched a Super Bowl in which the marquee players were rebounding from the very depths of personal problems. We saw a championship coach have second thoughts and make a return to the league. We saw yet another concussion end the career of a future Hall of Fame quarterback, and we saw the last of a future Hall of Fame receiver in 49er colors.

And long after the season had ended, we saw perhaps the most significant change, a future of realigned divisions.

IN DEFENSE OF DEFENSE

If the Baltimore Ravens' defense in 2000 wasn't the best in NFL history - and some will argue that it was - it certainly is among the best of all-time. The numbers say this: The Ravens allowed 10.3 points per game.

They gave up just 970 rushing yards for the season, an average of just 2.7 yards per rushing attempt. They did not allow any opposing rusher to gain 100 yards in a single game.

More numbers: The Ravens' defense had 49 takeaways and 35 sacks, and they set the NFL record for fewest points allowed, just 165, in a 16-game season.

It culminated in a dominating Super Bowl performance, a 34-7 victory over the New York Giants. The Ravens' allowed New York just 66 rushing yards in that game, 86 passing yards. But for a kickoff return in the third quarter, the Ravens were well on their way to shutting out the NFC champs.

"Our defense has been doing this all year long," said Ray Lewis, the Ravens' middle linebacker, the leader of this defensive pack and the MVP of the Super Bowl. "We didn't do anything different (in the Super Bowl). We didn't change anything. We just came out and showed that we are the best defense."

Lewis' personal saga embodied that change. A year ago, in January of 2000, Lewis stood accused and charged with murder in an incident at the Super Bowl in Atlanta. A year later, he stood at the pinnacle of football success, with an MVP and Super Bowl championships trophy.

Too, Kerry Collins, who quarterbacked the Giants into the Super Bowl, spent a nomadic couple of seasons, playing in Carolina and New Orleans before earning a shot in New York. Given that opportunity, Collins helped engineer a surprising 14-5 season, a dominating performance against the Vikings in the NFC Championship Game and a Super Bowl appearance.

A NEW CHIEF

A year ago, with a championship trophy in his own hands, Dick Vermeil stepped aside as coach of the St. Louis Rams, handing over the reins to Mike Martz.

But Vermeil's teary departure from the league barely lasted a season, when he conceded and accepted an offer from the Kansas City Chiefs to return to the league once again.

Vermeil's return ushered in a war of words between the Rams and Chiefs, who battled over compensation for Vermeil's signing. It also ushered in a significant change for the Chiefs on the field, with Elvis Grbac out as the Chiefs' quarterback and Trent Green, who had been relegated to backup with Kurt Warner's rise in St. Louis, in.

HARD-HEADED DECISIONS

Having suffered yet another concussion, having missed five games during the season, Cowboys quarterback Troy Aikman ended his career in the offseason.

The Cowboys had waived Aikman in March, and while Aikman considered his options to continue playing, he announced his retirement in March. Aikman finished his 12-year career with three Super Bowl trophies.

Another legend, Jerry Rice, played out his final season as a San Francisco 49er. Rice was expected to be released by San Francisco for salary cap reasons. A number of teams had expressed interest in signing him for the 2001 season.

REALIGNMENT

In their offseason meetings, the NFL announced a significant realignment plan. With the addition of the Houston Texans in 2002, the realignment, which was approved unanimously, creates eight four-team divisions.

Jerry Rice may have caught his last pass with the 49ers, but it likely will not be the last pass of his career. (Photo by John Cordes for The Sporting News)

NFC East	AFC East
Dallas	Buffalo
New York Giants	Miami
Philadelphia	New England
Washington	New York Jets

NFC South	AFC South
Atlanta	Houston
Carolina	Indianapolis
New Orleans	Jacksonville
Tampa Bay	Tennessee

NFC North	AFC North
Chicago	Baltimore
Detroit	Cincinnati
Green Bay	Cleveland
Minnesota	Pittsburgh

NFC West	AFC West
Arizona	Denver
St. Louis	Kansas City
San Francisco	Oakland
Seattle	San Diego

The most significant shifts affect the Seahawks and the Cardinals. Seattle moves from the AFC to the NFC; the Cardinals shift from the NFC East to the NFC West.

A FINAL FAREWELL

After 30 years and 255 Steelers games, Three Rivers Stadium closed its doors after the Steelers' season. The record books will always show a 181-74 Steelers home mark, the final game on December 16, 2000 against the Washington Redskins.

The record books cannot show the enduring memories of Three Rivers. The Immaculate Reception ... the Terrible Towels ... and the Steel Curtain.

Brian Griese had big shoes to fill in Denver, but the Broncos' decision paid off. (Photo by Dilip Vishwanat/The Sporting News.)

By CHRIS BAHR, DAVE DARLING, MIKE KIL-DUFF, CARL MORITZ, DAVE SLOAN and SEAN STEWART of The Sporting News

Reprinted from the January 1, 2000 issue of The Sporting News

AFC East

Best surprise: Lamar Smith, RB, Dolphins. He wasn't slated as even the No. 2 guy going into training camp, but he emerged as the starter and had a career year.

Biggest bust: Antowain Smith, RB, Bills. Take away his season-finale 147-yard, three-TD performance against the Seahawks, and he had 207 yards and one TD.

Best Band-Aid: Marcellus Wiley, DE, Bills. With the departure of Bruce Smith, he had some huge shoes to fill. The fourth-year pro delivered by more than doubling his career high for sacks with a team-leading 10.5.

Most painful injury: Rob Johnson, QB, Bills. Doug Flutie played well, but Johnson's injury-filled season did nothing but further Buffalo's silly QB controversy.

Play to remember: Jets RB Curtis Martin, not even gripping the laces of the football, hitting Wayne "Flashlight" Chrebet in the back of the Tampa Bay end zone with 52 seconds left for a 21-17 win in Week 4.

Play to forget: Ravens' Chris McAlister's 98-yard TD return off a horrible pass by Jets QB Vinny Testaverde on Sunday. Basically, it killed the Jets' season.

Change for the better: Four years after Jimmy Johnson first cried "run the ball!" in Miami, the Dolphins finally did. But for Dave Wannstedt, not Johnson.

Change for the worse: Although no one may admit it, the Jets, especially Testaverde, missed Keyshawn.

Free-agent flop: The Patriots signed Antonio Langham, hoping he would team with Ty Law to form a solid cover tandem. Instead, Langham got beat repeatedly, had just one interception and dropped a key pick in the end zone that could have preserved a Week 2 win over the Jets.

About to cash in: Eric Moulds, WR, Bills. He has become one of the elite receivers in the league (94 receptions, 1,326 yards, five TDs this season). The Bills, obviously, would like to keep him, but it's unclear whether they are willing to pay the price.

One thing we were wrong about: We told you after the games in Week 14 that the Colts, 7-6 after three straight defeats, were done for the season and one of the league's biggest disappointments of 2000. Oops. Yeah, but we sure nailed this one: After starting 5-1 we told you the Jets would fall apart in the second half and finish out of the playoffs. Voila.

AFC Central

Best surprise: Sam Adams, DT, Ravens. They said he was an underachiever, but Adams anchored the middle of the line on the league's stingiest defense.

Biggest bust (tie): Plaxico Burress, WR, Steelers, R. Jay Soward, WR, Jaguars. It's hard to say which rookie did less this season. Burress (the No. 8 pick in the draft) failed to score a touchdown; Soward (No. 29) failed to catch even 15 passes. Neither could hold a starting job.

Best Band-Aid: Derrick Mason, WR/KR, Titans. He did it all this season: stepping in as a starting WR when Kevin Dyson got hurt and continuing as one of the league's top return men. His Pro Bowl invitation was well deserved.

Most painful injury: Tim Couch, QB, Browns. The Browns weren't going to the playoffs anyway, but their offense absolutely collapsed after Couch hurt his thumb in Week 7; it averaged 7.3 ppg without its No. 1 QB.

Play to remember: Tony Banks hitting Shannon Sharpe with a 29-yard TD pass in the final minute in Week 2, giving the Ravens their first win ever over the Jaguars.

Play to forget: Cleveland G Jim Pyne injuring his knee while celebrating a Couch TD pass in Week 2. The Browns' best lineman missed the rest of the year.

Change for the better: When Ravens coach Brian Billick stopped trying to make his offense what it isn't (a passing threat) and settled for what it can be (a devastating running attack with RB Jamal Lewis).

Change for the worse: Troy Edwards caught 61 passes playing split end for the Steelers in 1999. To make room for Burress, the team moved him to flanker. Edwards caught 17 passes and didn't score all season.

Free-agent flop: Hardy Nickerson, LB, Jaguars. The Jags handed him a fat four-year contract last February in hopes that he had something left at 35. He played in just six games because of injuries and was ineffective.

About to cash in: Corey Dillon, RB, Bengals. He is about to find out what a career-best, 1,435-yard season and an NFL-record 278-yard game is really worth.

One thing we were wrong about: That the Steelers would finish with their worst record since 1969 (1-13). Yeah, but we sure nailed this one: That the Bengals wouldn't win a game as long as Akili Smith remained their starting quarterback.

AFC West

Best surprise: Brian Griese, QB, Broncos. They actually considered bringing in Steve Young. Instead, they were stuck with Griese, who missed most of seven games but finished as the league's top-rated passer.

Biggest bust: Steve Sidwell, coordinator, Seahawks. He was hired to improved last year's No. 23 defense, but the unit was worse, finishing No. 31 in the league.

Best Band-Aid: Mike Anderson, RB, Broncos. Terrell Who? Olandis Why-do-we-care?

Most painful injury: Dave Szott, LG, Chiefs. He tore his biceps muscle on the third play of 2000, and the K.C. running game never recovered. He is expected to retire.

Play to remember: Anderson's 80-yard TD run late in the Broncos' 38-31 win in Seattle. Part of an impressive run of games by Anderson and the Denver offensive line.

Play to forget: Forget is a good word here. Uh, Elvis, did you forget how much time was left in the game? It's the only explanation for Grbac throwing short of the end zone to TE Tony Gonzalez in the middle of the field with no timeouts in the waning seconds against the Patriots.

Daunte Culpepper was behind the Vikings' success all season ... until the NFC Championship Game against the Giants. (Photo by John Dunn for The Sporting News.)

Change for the better: The Raiders' fortunes turned along with the new year. They closed out the 1999 season with a 41-38 OT win over the Chiefs on January 2. They never lost the momentum and finished this season by winning their first division title since 1990.

Change for the worse: The Chiefs going to the air. It was mostly because the running game went AWOL.

Free-agent flop: DeRon Jenkins, CB, Chargers. The Chargers paid big bucks to lure him from Baltimore. He didn't do much to help San Diego's defense, and the Ravens didn't seem to miss him.

About to cash in: They're not as sexy as the so-called skill position players, but Seattle G Pete Kendall and Kansas City G Will Shields showed up when their teams didn't. Some teams will reward them for their effort.

One thing we were wrong about: We said the Chargers' first win would come Week 9 against Oakland, then tried again in Week 12 vs. the Broncos. We gave up on them one week too early, or 12 weeks too late. Yeah, but we sure nailed this one: We said the Chargers would be the last team to win a game. We just didn't know it would be their only win.

Keyshawn Johnson made his mark in Tampa Bay, just not as he wanted to against his ex-teammates. (Photo by Mark Bolton for The Sporting News.)

NFC East

Best surprise: Donovan McNabb, QB, Eagles. He led his team to the playoffs without a quality wide receiver and no running game for more than half of the season.

Biggest bust: The Redskins proved that money can't buy a Super Bowl. Washington imploded because of injuries, poor play and Danny boy.

Best Band-Aid: David Boston, WR, Cardinals. He had a strong season despite having to fill the void left by Rob Moore's injury, his team's bad offensive line and an ineffective quarterback.

Most painful injury: Joey Galloway, WR, Cowboys. The way he went out—with a torn knee ligament suffered late in a blowout loss in Week 1, when he should have been out of the game—was just plain stupid.

Play to remember: McNabb's 21-yard scamper for a touchdown against the Redskins in Week 13. He outran one Redskin, schooled another and carried a third the final 3 yards into the end zone.

Play to forget: In Week 16, Steelers RB Richard Huntley bounced off a tackle by Washington's Mark Carrier and ran over Champ Bailey to score on a 30-yard run, sealing the Redskins' non-playoff fate.

Change for the better: One of the Cardinals'

few bright spots was KR MarTay Jenkins, who helped the team finish near the top of the league in at least one department (kickoff return yardage) this season.

Change for the worse: Dallas drafted CBs Dwayne Goodrich and Kareem Larrimore to help fill the void left by Deion Sanders. They were woefully overmatched.

Free-agent flop: Sanders, Redskins. At 33, his days as the NFL's best cover corner are over.

About to cash in: Jeremiah Trotter, MLB, Eagles. The team already cut a deal with TE Chad Lewis, who also was a first-time Pro Bowl selection. Trotter, a restricted free agent, moves to the top of the club's list.

One thing we were wrong about: That Dallas QB Troy Aikman would bounce back from a poor game against Carolina with a good game against the Giants in Week 7. He threw five INTs in a 19-14 Giants victory. Yeah, but we sure nailed this one: The Giants would beat the Eagles in Week 9 to improve to 4-1 in the NFC East. New York obliged, 24-7.

NFC Central

Best surprise: Daunte Culpepper, QB, Vikings. No one (not even Denny Green) could have expected someone who hadn't thrown an NFL pass to have such an impact.

Biggest bust: Curtis Enis, RB, Bears. Injuries and inconsistency have plagued him his entire career, but this year was his—and his team's—biggest nightmare.

Best Band-Aid: Ahman Green, RB, Packers. His breakthrough season (1,175 yards rushing) has made the oft-injured Dorsey Levens expendable.

Most painful injury: The Bears—and QB Cade McNown—never recovered after No. 1 receiver Bobby Engram was lost for the season in Week 3.

Play to remember: Warrick Dunn's pitch to Shaun King in Week 16 against the Rams. That electrifying play (and the ensuing late-hit penalty) saved Tampa Bay's season and nearly killed St. Louis'.

Play to forget: That bruising Thanksgiving day hit laid on Lions QB Charlie Batch by Patriots SS Lawyer Milloy. Batch's ribs never healed, and the Lions' offense never was the same.

Change for the better: C Matt Birk and LG Corbin Lacina stepped in for Pro Bowl linemen Jeff Christy and Randall McDaniel in Minnesota, and the Vikings' offensive line never missed a beat.

Change for the worse: The Mark Chmura saga haunted the Packers all season. It completely changed their draft strategy, and the tight end position went from being a strength to a liability with the inexperienced Bubba Franks and the inconsistent Tyrone Davis.

Free-agent flop: Bryce Paup, DE, Vikings. Minnesota planned to use him mainly at end on passing downs, but Paup had little impact because of a broken leg.

About to cash in: Darren Sharper, FS, Packers. He had a breakout season (nine INTs, a trip to the Pro Bowl), but his price tag probably is out of Green Bay's range now.

One thing we were wrong about: The Lions will win the Super Bowl. 'Nuff said. Yeah, but we sure nailed this one: Check out this Week 4 prediction from our preview issue: "Keyshawn Johnson gets reacquainted with his old teammates when the Jets visit Tampa Bay. Johnson fumbles away a reception late in the game." Not bad, huh?

NFC West

Best surprise: Jeff Garcia, QB, 49ers. At the start of the year, he was regarded as nothing more than a stopgap at the position. By the end of the year, he was voted to the Pro Bowl and considered a franchise cornerstone.

Biggest bust (tie): Kevin Carter, DE, Todd Lyght, CB, Rams. Unhappy over contract issues, they seemed unprepared for the season. Both were slow and sluggish and shells of what they were as Pro Bowl players in 1999.

Best Band-Aid: Aaron Brooks, QB, Saints. After Jeff Blake was hurt, Brooks sustained the Saints' march to the NFC West title. He may not let go of the job.

Most painful injury: Patrick Jeffers, WR, Panthers. His season-ending knee injury in an exhibition game took the steam out of Carolina's big-play passing game.

Play to remember: With a 10-6, fourth-quarter lead over Carolina in Week 7, the Saints pulled a fake punt on a fourth-and-1 from their 35. Up back Fred McAfee took the snap and raced 40 yards, setting up a game-icing TD. That typified the Saints' aggressive, unpredictable style.

Play to forget: In a microcosm of the Rams' awful defensive season, Carter could not get Bucs RB Warrick Dunn to the ground in the Monday game in Week 16. Dunn lateraled to Shaun King, who set up the winning TD.

Change for the better: The 49ers loaded up on defense in the draft and had five rookies starting on that unit by the end of the year. The future of the D—and team - is bright.

Change for the worse: Atlanta let a couple of offensive line starters leave, and a mediocre line

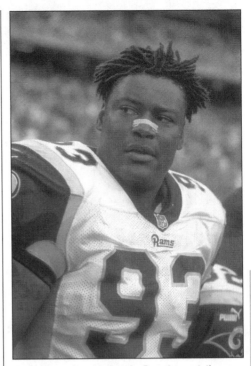

Kevin Carter played below the Rams' expectations, leading to an offseason trade to Tennessee. (Photo by Peter Newcomb for The Sporting News.)

became worse. Chris Chandler was pummeled, and the season fell apart.

Free-agent flop: Chuck Smith, DE, Panthers. The Panthers blew it by signing an older guy with a chronic knee problem. He was supposed to be the pass-rushing cornerstone but played in only two games.

About to cash in: Mike Minter, SS, Panthers. As Carolina's best defensive player, he will be hotly pursued in free agency. He's a big hitter and playmaker.

One thing we were wrong about: That the Saints would fail to make the playoffs after Williams and Blake went out. But did anyone know Brooks would be so poised? Yeah, but we sure nailed this one: We said the Rams would win last Sunday because Bud Carson's defensive strategy would contain Brooks. It did.

FINAL STANDINGS

AMERICAN FOOTBALL CONFERENCE

EASTERN DIVISION

	W	L	T	Pct.	Pts.	Opp.	Home	Away	Vs. AFC	Vs. NFC	Vs.AFC East
Miami*	11	5	0	.688	323	226	5-3	6-2	9-3	2-2	5-3
Indianapolis†	10	6	0	.625	429	326	6-2	4-4	8-4	2-2	5-3
N.Y. Jets	9	7	0	.563	321	321	5-3	4-4	6-6	3-1	6-2
Buffalo	8	8	0	.500	315	350	5-3	3-5	6-6	2-2	2-6
New England	5	11	0	.313	276	338	3-5	2-6	5-7	0-4	2-6

CENTRAL DIVISION

	W	L	T	Pct.	Pts.	Opp.	Home	Away	Vs. AFC	Vs. NFC	Vs.AFC Central
Tennessee*	13	3	0	.813	346	191	7-1	6-2	9-3	4-0	8-2
Baltimore†	12	4	0	.750	333	165	6-2	6-2	10-3	2-1	8-2
Pittsburgh	9	7	0	.563	321	255	4-4	5-3	8-5	1-2	5-5
Jacksonville	7	9	0	.438	367	327	4-4	3-5	5-7	2-2	5-5
Cincinnati	4	12	0	.250	185	359	3-5	1-7	3-10	1-2	2-8
Cleveland	3	13	0	.188	161	419	2-6	1-7	3-10	0-3	2-8

WESTERN DIVISION

	W	L	T	Pct.	Pts.	Opp.	Home	Away	Vs. AFC	Vs. NFC	Vs.AFC West
Oakland*	12	4	0	.750	479	299	7-1	5-3	8-4	4-0	5-3
Denver†	11	5	0	.688	485	369	6-2	5-3	8-4	3-1	6-2
Kansas City	7	9	0	.438	355	354	5-3	2-6	5-7	2-2	5-3
Seattle	6	10	0	.375	320	405	3-5	3-5	4-8	2-2	3-5
San Diego	1	15	0	.063	269	440	1-7	0-8	1-11	0-4	1-7

*Division champion. †Wild-card team.

NATIONAL FOOTBALL CONFERENCE

EASTERN DIVISION

	W	L	T	Pct.	Pts.	Opp.	Home	Away	Vs. AFC	Vs. NFC	Vs.NFC East
N.Y. Giants*	12	4	0	.750	328	246	5-3	7-1	3-1	9-3	7-1
Philadelphia†	11	5	0	.688	351	245	5-3	6-2	3-1	8-4	5-3
Washington	8	8	0	.500	281	269	4-4	4-4	2-2	6-6	3-5
Dallas	5	11	0	.313	294	361	3-5	2-6	1-3	4-8	3-5
Arizona	3	13	0	.188	210	443	3-5	0-8	1-3	2-10	2-6

CENTRAL DIVISION

	W	L	T	Pct.	Pts.	Opp.	Home	Away	Vs. AFC	Vs. NFC	Vs.NFC Central
Minnesota*	11	5	0	.688	397	371	7-1	4-4	3-1	8-4	5-3
Tampa Bay†	10	6	0	.625	388	269	6-2	4-4	3-1	7-5	4-4
Green Bay	9	7	0	.563	353	323	6-2	3-5	1-3	8-4	5-3
Detroit	9	7	0	.563	307	307	4-4	5-3	2-2	7-5	3-5
Chicago	5	11	0	.313	216	355	3-5	2-6	2-2	3-9	3-5

WESTERN DIVISION

	W	L	T	Pct.	Pts.	Opp.	Home	Away	Vs. AFC	Vs. NFC	Vs.NFC West
New Orleans*	10	6	0	.625	354	305	3-5	7-1	1-3	9-3	7-1
St. Louis†	10	6	0	.625	540	471	5-3	5-3	3-1	7-5	5-3
Carolina	7	9	0	.438	310	310	5-3	2-6	2-2	5-7	4-4
San Francisco	6	10	0	.375	388	422	4-4	2-6	2-2	4-8	1-7
Atlanta	4	12	0	.250	252	413	3-5	1-7	1-3	3-9	3-5

*Division champion. †Wild-card team.

AFC PLAYOFFS

AFC wild card: Miami 23, Indianapolis 17 (OT)
Baltimore 21, Denver 3
AFC semifinals: Oakland 27, Miami 0
Baltimore 24, Tennessee 10
AFC championship: Baltimore 16, Oakland 3

NFC PLAYOFFS

NFC wild card: New Orleans 31, St. Louis 28
Philadelphia 21, Tampa Bay 3
NFC semifinals: Minnesota 34, New Orleans 16
N.Y. Giants 20, Philadelphia 10
NFC championship: N.Y. Giants 41, Minnesota 0

SUPER BOWL

Baltimore 34, N.Y. Giants 7

WEEK 1

AFC EAST

	W	L	T	Pct.
Buffalo	1	0	0	1.000
Indianapolis	1	0	0	1.000
Miami	1	0	0	1.000
N.Y. Jets	1	0	0	1.000
New England	0	1	0	.000

AFC CENTRAL

	W	L	T	Pct.
Baltimore	1	0	0	1.000
Jacksonville	1	0	0	1.000
Cincinnati	0	0	0	.000
Cleveland	0	1	0	.000
Pittsburgh	0	1	0	.000
Tennessee	0	1	0	.000

AFC WEST

	W	L	T	Pct.
Oakland	1	0	0	1.000
Denver	0	1	0	.000
Kansas City	0	1	0	.000
San Diego	0	1	0	.000
Seattle	0	1	0	.000

NFC EAST

	W	L	T	Pct.
N.Y. Giants	1	0	0	1.000
Philadelphia	1	0	0	1.000
Washington	1	0	0	1.000
Arizona	0	1	0	.000
Dallas	0	1	0	.000

NFC CENTRAL

	W	L	T	Pct.
Detroit	1	0	0	1.000
Minnesota	1	0	0	1.000
Tampa Bay	1	0	0	1.000
Chicago	0	1	0	.000
Green Bay	0	1	0	.000

NFC WEST

	W	L	T	Pct.
Atlanta	1	0	0	1.000
St. Louis	1	0	0	1.000
Carolina	0	1	0	.000
New Orleans	0	1	0	.000
San Francisco	0	1	0	.000

TOP PERFORMANCES

100-YARD RUSHING GAMES

Player, Team & Opponent	Att.	Yds.	TD
Duce Staley, Phi. at Dal.	26	201	1
Lamar Smith, Mia. vs. Sea.	27	145	1
Tiki Barber, NYG vs. Ari.	13	144	2
Stephen Davis, Wash. vs. Car.	23	133	1
Edgerrin James, Ind. at K.C.	28	124	1
Priest Holmes, Balt. at Pit.	27	119	0
Curtis Martin, NYJ at G.B.	30	110	1
Robert Smith, Min. vs. Chi.	14	109	0

300-YARD PASSING GAMES

Player, Team & Opponent	Att.	Comp.	Yds.	TD	Int.
Kurt Warner, St.L. vs. Den.	35	25	441	3	3
Jake Plummer, Ari. at NYG	49	28	318	2	3
Brian Griese, Den. at St.L.	29	19	307	2	0
Mark Brunell, Jack. at Cle.	34	24	301	1	0

100-YARD RECEIVING GAMES

Player, Team & Opponent	Rec.	Yds.	TD
Shawn Jefferson, Atl. vs. S.F.	7	148	1
David Boston, Ari. at NYG	9	128	2
Az-Zahir Hakim, St.L. vs. Den.	5	116	1
Marvin Harrison, Ind. at K.C.	9	115	0
Ed McCaffrey, Den. at St.L.	7	115	0
Keenan McCardell, Jack. at Cle.	9	115	0
Dedric Ward, NYJ at G.B.	5	104	0
Torry Holt, St.L. vs. Den.	6	103	0
Qadry Ismail, Balt. at Pit.	7	102	1
Marshall Faulk, St.L. vs. Den.	4	100	1

RESULTS

SUNDAY, SEPTEMBER 3

ATLANTA 36, San Francisco 28
Baltimore 16, PITTSBURGH 0
BUFFALO 16, Tennessee 13
Detroit 14, NEW ORLEANS 10
Indianapolis 27, KANSAS CITY 14
Jacksonville 27, CLEVELAND 7
MIAMI 23, Seattle 0
MINNESOTA 30, Chicago 27
N.Y. GIANTS 21, Arizona 16
N.Y. Jets 20, GREEN BAY 16
OAKLAND 9, San Diego 6
Philadelphia 41, DALLAS 14
Tampa Bay 21, NEW ENGLAND 16
WASHINGTON 20, Carolina 17

MONDAY, SEPTEMBER 4

ST. LOUIS 41, Denver 36
  Open date: Cincinnati

2000 REVIEW Week 1

BILLS 16, TITANS 13

Sunday, September 3

Tennessee	0	6	0	7—13
Buffalo	0	7	3	6—16

Second Quarter
Buf.—P. Price 15 pass from Johnson (Christie kick), 2:31.
Ten.—FG, Del Greco 38, 10:43.
Ten.—FG, Del Greco 27, 14:49.

Third Quarter
Buf.—FG, Christie 42, 11:00.

Fourth Quarter
Buf.—FG, Christie 41, 0:41.
Ten.—E. George 2 run (Del Greco kick), 6:16.
Buf.—FG, Christie 33, 14:29.
  Attendance—72,492.

	Tennessee	Buffalo
First downs	9	17
Rushes-yards	20-53	35-129
Passing	119	137
Punt returns	6-60	5-10
Kickoff returns	5-182	3-35
Interception returns	0-0	1-8
Comp.-att.-int.	17-31-1	13-26-0
Sacked-yards lost	4-33	5-37
Punts	9-38	9-42
Fumbles-lost	1-0	0-0
Penalties-yards	12-112	6-91
Time of possession	26:49	33:11

INDIVIDUAL STATISTICS

RUSHING—Tennessee, E. George 17-37, McNair 2-15, Thomas 1-1. Buffalo, A. Smith 17-42, Bryson 10-16, Johnson 6-60, Morris 2-11.

PASSING—Tennessee, McNair 17-31-1-152. Buffalo, Johnson 9-18-0-107, Van Pelt 4-8-0-67.

RECEIVING—Tennessee, E. George 6-44, Wycheck 4-51, Roan 3-12, Pickens 2-23, Sanders 1-18, Thigpen 1-4. Buffalo, P. Price 4-42, McDaniel 3-40, Moulds 2-46, Riemersma 2-9, Bryson 1-23, Morris 1-14.

MISSED FIELD GOAL ATTEMPTS—Tennessee, Hentrich 60. Buffalo, Christie 51.

INTERCEPTIONS—Buffalo, Carpenter 1-8.

KICKOFF RETURNS—Tennessee, Mason 5-182. Buffalo, Watson 3-35.

PUNT RETURNS—Tennessee, Mason 6-60. Buffalo, Watson 5-10.

SACKS—Tennessee, Favors 2, Fisk 1, Holmes 1, Killens 1. Buffalo, Newman 2, P. Williams 1, Hansen 1.

JETS 20, PACKERS 16

Sunday, September 3

N.Y. Jets	7	3	0	10—20
Green Bay	7	3	3	3—16

First Quarter
G.B.—T. Davis 4 pass from Favre (Longwell kick), 5:27.
NYJ—Martin 2 run (Hall kick), 13:11.

Second Quarter
G.B.—FG, Longwell 45, 9:00.
NYJ—FG, Hall 23, 14:38.

Third Quarter
G.B.—FG, Longwell 42, 12:17.

Fourth Quarter
NYJ—FG, Hall 39, 6:08.
G.B.—FG, Longwell 42, 8:22.
NYJ—Martin 3 pass from Testaverde (Hall kick), 11:32.
  Attendance—59,870.

	N.Y. Jets	Green Bay
First downs	24	13
Rushes-yards	34-118	16-62
Passing	261	149
Punt returns	1-0	1-43
Kickoff returns	5-92	5-116
Interception returns	1-0	1-29
Comp.-att.-int.	23-44-1	14-34-1
Sacked-yards lost	0-0	1-3
Punts	3-48	4-36
Fumbles-lost	0-0	3-1
Penalties-yards	10-75	10-81
Time of possession	37:50	22:15

INDIVIDUAL STATISTICS

RUSHING—New York, Martin 30-110, Testaverde 3-9, Parmalee 1-(minus 1). Green Bay, Green 12-41, Favre 2-13, Mitchell 2-8.

PASSING—New York, Testaverde 23-44-1-261. Green Bay, Favre 14-34-1-152.

RECEIVING—New York, Martin 6-34, Ward 5-104, Chrebet 5-47, R. Anderson 3-41, Brisby 2-25, Parmalee 2-10. Green Bay, Freeman 3-59, Schroeder 3-38, Green 3-21, T. Davis 2-15, Lee 1-11, Franks 1-4, Henderson 1-4.

MISSED FIELD GOAL ATTEMPTS—New York, Hall 52, 48.

INTERCEPTIONS—New York, V. Green 1-0. Green Bay, Sharper 1-29.

KICKOFF RETURNS—New York, Glenn 3-51, Coles 2-41. Green Bay, Rossum 3-77, Mitchell 1-26, Morton 1-13.

PUNT RETURNS—New York, Ward 1-0. Green Bay, Rossum 1-43.

SACKS—New York, Ellis 1.

EAGLES 41, COWBOYS 14

Sunday, September 3

Philadelphia	14	10	3	14—41
Dallas	0	6	0	8—14

First Quarter
Phi.—Thomason 1 pass from McNabb (Akers kick), 4:01.
Phi.—Staley 1 run (Akers kick), 14:58.

Second Quarter
Phi.—Trotter 27 interception return (Akers kick), 1:20.
Phi.—FG, Akers 33, 8:37.
Dal.—FG, Seder 34, 12:07.
Dal.—FG, Seder 38, 15:00.

Third Quarter
Phi.—FG, Akers 37, 8:30.

Fourth Quarter
Phi.—McNabb 3 run (Akers kick), 0:04.
Phi.—Mitchell 6 run (Akers kick), 2:38.
Dal.—Galloway 4 pass from Cunningham (Ismail pass from Cunningham), 8:15.
  Attendance—62,872.

	Philadelphia	Dallas
First downs	27	10
Rushes-yards	46-306	13-67
Passing	119	100
Punt returns	3-20	1-2
Kickoff returns	1-29	5-118
Interception returns	2-35	3-38
Comp.-att.-int.	16-29-3	13-31-2
Sacked-yards lost	1-11	5-35
Punts	2-44	7-45
Fumbles-lost	0-0	0-0
Penalties-yards	4-25	9-93
Time of possession	39:30	20:30

INDIVIDUAL STATISTICS

RUSHING—Philadelphia, Staley 26-201, Mitchell 8-39, Pritchett 6-29, McNabb 5-29, C. Johnson 1-8. Dallas, E. Smith 7-29, Warren 3-0, Ismail 2-33, Cunningham 1-5.

PASSING—Philadelphia, McNabb 16-28-2-130, Detmer 0-1-1-0. Dallas, Cunningham 13-26-1-135, Aikman 0-5-1-0.

RECEIVING—Philadelphia, Staley 4-61, Pinkston 3-29, Broughton 2-12, Van Dyke 1-8, Lewis 1-6, Mitchell 1-5, C. Johnson 1-5, C. Martin 1-2, Small 1-1, Thomason 1-1. Dallas, Galloway 4-62, Ismail 3-36, Harris 2-3, McGarity 1-10, Wiley 1-10, McKnight 1-9, Warren 1-5.

MISSED FIELD GOAL ATTEMPTS—None.

INTERCEPTIONS—Philadelphia, Trotter 1-27, Emmons 1-8. Dallas, Nguyen 1-24, Reese 1-14, Sparks 1-0.

KICKOFF RETURNS—Philadelphia, Mitchell 1-29. Dallas, Tucker 5-118.

PUNT RETURNS—Philadelphia, Mitchell 3-20. Dallas, Galloway 1-2.

SACKS—Philadelphia, H. Douglas 1.5, Mamula 1, Simon 1, Emmons 1, Darling 0.5. Dallas, Spellman 1.

GIANTS 21, CARDINALS 16

Sunday, September 3

Arizona	0	0	3	13—16
N.Y. Giants	7	7	0	7—21

First Quarter
NYG—Barber 10 run (Daluiso kick), 15:00.

Second Quarter
NYG—Barber 78 run (Daluiso kick), 5:29.

Third Quarter
Ariz.—FG, Blanchard 32, 15:00.

Fourth Quarter
NYG—Dayne 7 run (Daluiso kick), 7:32.
Ariz.—Boston 9 pass from Plummer (Blanchard kick), 13:05.
Ariz.—Boston 25 pass from Plummer (pass failed), 14:28.
Attendance—77,434.

	Arizona	N.Y. Giants
First downs	19	20
Rushes-yards	20-43	41-223
Passing	312	172
Punt returns	2-17	3-18
Kickoff returns	4-133	2-27
Interception returns	1-11	3-42
Comp.-att.-int.	28-49-3	17-25-1
Sacked-yards lost	1-6	0-0
Punts	5-42	6-43
Fumbles-lost	2-1	3-1
Penalties-yards	1-5	9-68
Time of possession	28:30	31:30

INDIVIDUAL STATISTICS
RUSHING—Arizona, Jones 12-16, Plummer 4-18, Pittman 4-9. New York, Dayne 23-78, Barber 13-144, Collins 5-1.
PASSING—Arizona, Plummer 28-49-3-318. New York, Collins 17-25-1-172.
RECEIVING—Arizona, Boston 9-128, Pittman 6-71, Sanders 5-78, Jones 4-18, Makovicka 2-2, Jenkins 1-13, Cody 1-8. New York, Comella 5-42, Toomer 4-35, Hilliard 3-62, Barber 3-25, Campbell 1-10, Dayne 1-(minus 2).
MISSED FIELD GOAL ATTEMPTS—None.
INTERCEPTIONS—Arizona, Lassiter 1-11. New York, McDaniel 2-2, S. Williams 1-40.
KICKOFF RETURNS—Arizona, Jenkins 4-92. New York, Dixon 2-27.
PUNT RETURNS—Arizona, Cody 1-16, Jenkins 1-1. New York, Barber 3-18.
SACKS—New York, Barrow 1.

RAVENS 16, STEELERS 0

Sunday, September 3

Baltimore	10	3	3	0—16
Pittsburgh	0	0	0	0— 0

First Quarter
Bal.—FG, Stover 23, 8:10.
Bal.—Ismail 53 pass from Banks (Stover kick), 11:02.

Second Quarter
Bal.—FG, Stover 26, 15:00.

Third Quarter
Bal.—FG, Stover 33, 3:29.
Attendance—55,049.

	Baltimore	Pittsburgh
First downs	18	12
Rushes-yards	36-140	18-30
Passing	196	193
Punt returns	5-50	0-0
Kickoff returns	1-38	2-48
Interception returns	0-0	0-0
Comp.-att.-int.	18-32-0	17-39-0
Sacked-yards lost	1-3	1-6
Punts	7-40	6-51
Fumbles-lost	0-0	3-1
Penalties-yards	6-42	2-15
Time of possession	35:07	24:53

INDIVIDUAL STATISTICS
RUSHING—Baltimore, Holmes 27-119, Ja. Lewis 5-16, Banks 2-5, Ayanbadejo 2-0. Pittsburgh, Bettis 9-8, Huntley 7-31, Stewart 1-0, Edwards 1-(minus 9).

PASSING—Baltimore, Banks 18-32-0-199. Pittsburgh, Graham 17-38-0-199, Stewart 0-1-0-0.
RECEIVING—Baltimore, Ismail 7-102, Taylor 4-50, Holmes 4-32, Ayanbadejo 2-10, Coates 1-5. Pittsburgh, Burress 4-77, Shaw 4-49, Bruener 2-27, Ward 2-20, Huntley 2-12, Edwards 2-7, Bettis 1-7.
MISSED FIELD GOAL ATTEMPTS—Pittsburgh, K. Brown 45.
INTERCEPTIONS—None.
KICKOFF RETURNS—Baltimore, Ismail 1-38. Pittsburgh, Poteat 1-25, Ward 1-23.
PUNT RETURNS—Baltimore, J. Lewis 5-50.
SACKS—Baltimore, Burnett 1. Pittsburgh, Vrabel 1.

RAIDERS 9, CHARGERS 6

Sunday, September 3

San Diego	0	0	0	6—6
Oakland	0	0	2	7—9

Third Quarter
Oak.—Chancey tackled in end zone by Russell for a safety, 7:37.

Fourth Quarter
S.D.—Chancey 3 run (pass failed), 5:19.
Oak.—Rison 10 pass from Gannon (Janikowski kick), 12:23.
Attendance—56,373.

	San Diego	Oakland
First downs	17	13
Rushes-yards	28-76	25-67
Passing	179	166
Punt returns	2-7	3-12
Kickoff returns	1-26	3-65
Interception returns	0-0	3-41
Comp.-att.-int.	19-42-3	20-35-0
Sacked-yards lost	2-18	4-10
Punts	7-49	10-42
Fumbles-lost	2-1	2-0
Penalties-yards	4-35	8-60
Time of possession	28:30	31:30

INDIVIDUAL STATISTICS
RUSHING—San Diego, Chancey 23-74, Fletcher 3-8, Leaf 2-(minus 6). Oakland, Wheatley 13-47, Gannon 6-17, Kaufman 4-0, Brown 1-3, Crockett 1-0.
PASSING—San Diego, Leaf 17-39-3-180, Moreno 2-3-0-17. Oakland, Gannon 20-35-0-176.
RECEIVING—San Diego, Conway 5-50, F. Jones 5-43, J. Graham 4-62, Fletcher 1-12, McCrary 1-10, Davis 1-8, Chancey 1-6, Ricks 1-6. Oakland, Rison 5-49, Brown 5-39, Wheatley 3-25, Ritchie 2-30, Brigham 1-13, Jett 1-12, Porter 1-6, Dudley 1-5, Jordan 1-(minus 3).
MISSED FIELD GOAL ATTEMPTS—Oakland, Janikowski 41.
INTERCEPTIONS—Oakland, Pope 1-25, Woodson 1-13, W. Thomas 1-3.
KICKOFF RETURNS—San Diego, R. Jenkins 1-26. Oakland, Kaufman 2-48, Gordon 1-17.
PUNT RETURNS—San Diego, J. Graham 2-7. Oakland, Gordon 3-12.
SACKS—San Diego, Harrison 1, Seau 1, Dixon 1, Dingle 1. Oakland, Taves 1, Johnstone 1.

REDSKINS 20, PANTHERS 17

Sunday, September 3

Carolina	10	0	0	7—17
Washington	7	0	3	10—20

First Quarter
Was.—Davis 2 run (Conway kick), 7:09.
Car.—Bates 92 kickoff return (Cunningham kick), 7:24.
Car.—FG, Cunningham 29, 13:29.

Third Quarter
Was.—FG, Conway 24, 6:51.

Fourth Quarter
Was.—B. Johnson 1 run (Conway kick), 2:46.
Was.—FG, Conway 21, 10:01.
Car.—Walls 20 pass from Beuerlein (Cunningham kick), 13:08.
Attendance—80,257.

	Carolina	Washington
First downs	12	23
Rushes-yards	20-112	31-162
Passing	124	234
Punt returns	0-0	3-15
Kickoff returns	5-189	3-53

	Carolina	Washington
Interception returns	0-0	0-0
Comp.-att.-int.	17-26-0	25-36-0
Sacked-yards lost	6-59	0-0
Punts	5-43	4-40
Fumbles-lost	1-1	0-0
Penalties-yards	9-65	7-64
Time of possession	26:46	33:14

INDIVIDUAL STATISTICS

RUSHING—Carolina, Biakabutuka 15-88, Beuerlein 2-10, Hetherington 2-7, Hoover 1-7. Washington, Davis 23-133, Centers 4-26, B. Johnson 2-0, Thrash 1-4, Murrell 1-(minus 1).

PASSING—Carolina, Beuerlein 17-26-0-183. Washington, B. Johnson 25-36-0-234.

RECEIVING—Carolina, Muhammad 6-48, Hayes 4-71, Walls 3-28, Biakabutuka 2-20, Mangum 1-12, Floyd 1-4. Washington, Centers 7-56, Westbrook 5-53, Davis 4-37, Thrash 3-22, Connell 2-27, Alexander 2-9, Fryar 1-22, Flemister 1-8.

MISSED FIELD GOAL ATTEMPTS—Carolina, Cunningham 27.

INTERCEPTIONS—None.

KICKOFF RETURNS—Carolina, Bates 4-164, Burks 1-25. Washington, Thrash 3-53.

PUNT RETURNS—Washington, Sanders 3-15.

SACKS—Washington, Coleman 2, B. Smith 2, Kev. Mitchell 1, D. Smith 1.

COLTS 27, CHIEFS 14

Sunday, September 3

Indianapolis	0	7	7	13—27
Kansas City	0	7	7	0—14

Second Quarter
Ind.—James 1 run (Vanderjagt kick), 0:45.
K.C.—Richardson 11 pass from Grbac (Stoyanovich kick), 9:37.

Third Quarter
Ind.—James 27 pass from Manning (Vanderjagt kick), 6:37.
K.C.—Alexander 21 pass from Grbac (Stoyanovich kick), 10:35.

Fourth Quarter
Ind.—FG, Vanderjagt 23, 1:23.
Ind.—Burris 27 interception return (Vanderjagt kick), 2:22.
Ind.—FG, Vanderjagt 40, 10:59.
Attendance—78,357.

	Indianapolis	Kansas City
First downs	20	17
Rushes-yards	32-119	24-74
Passing	267	206
Punt returns	4-80	2-18
Kickoff returns	2-33	5-111
Interception returns	1-27	1-3
Comp.-att.-int.	22-32-1	16-37-1
Sacked-yards lost	1-6	1-6
Punts	4-57	8-47
Fumbles-lost	1-1	0-0
Penalties-yards	7-78	6-50
Time of possession	33:13	26:47

INDIVIDUAL STATISTICS

RUSHING—Indianapolis, James 28-124, Manning 3-(minus 3), al-Jabbar 1-(minus 2). Kansas City, Richardson 13-58, Bennett 6-(minus 4), Moreau 3-15, Cloud 2-5.

PASSING—Indianapolis, Manning 22-32-1-273. Kansas City, Grbac 16-37-1-212.

RECEIVING—Indianapolis, Harrison 9-115, James 6-40, Pathon 3-55, Green 2-35, Dilger 2-28. Kansas City, Alexander 5-50, Morris 3-58, Gonzalez 2-34, Lockett 2-29, Richardson 2-24, Bennett 2-17.

MISSED FIELD GOAL ATTEMPTS—None.

INTERCEPTIONS— Indianapolis, Burris 1-27. Kansas City, Edwards 1-3.

KICKOFF RETURNS—Indianapolis, P. Williams 2-33. Kansas City, Cloud 5-111.

PUNT RETURNS—Indianapolis, P. Williams 4-80. Kansas City, L. Parker 2-18.

SACKS—Indianapolis, Chester 1. Kansas City, Hicks 1.

DOLPHINS 23, SEAHAWKS 0

Sunday, September 3

Seattle	0	0	0	0— 0
Miami	10	13	0	0—23

First Quarter
Mia.—L. Smith 4 run (Mare kick), 7:17.
Mia.—FG, Mare 48, 13:38.

Second Quarter
Mia.—FG, Mare 25, 1:06.
Mia.—FG, Mare 30, 4:09.
Mia.—Gadsden 16 pass from Fiedler (Mare kick), 14:17.
Attendance—72,949.

	Seattle	Miami
First downs	8	16
Rushes-yards	19-71	41-181
Passing	72	127
Punt returns	4-52	5-24
Kickoff returns	6-108	1-26
Interception returns	0-0	4-50
Comp.-att.-int.	10-24-4	15-24-0
Sacked-yards lost	4-12	2-7
Punts	6-42	7-40
Fumbles-lost	3-2	1-1
Penalties-yards	2-10	6-36
Time of possession	21:40	38:20

INDIVIDUAL STATISTICS

RUSHING—Seattle, Watters 11-59, Alexander 2-5, Kitna 2-5, R. Brown 2-3, Huard 1-4, J. Williams 1-(minus 5). Miami, L. Smith 27-145, Konrad 2-19, Fiedler 3-9, T. Thomas 3-9, Emanuel 1-(minus 1).

PASSING—Seattle, Kitna 6-13-4-54, Huard 4-11-0-30. Miami, Fiedler 15-24-0-134.

RECEIVING—Seattle, Watters 3-32, Jackson 2-15, R. Brown 2-9, Mili 1-10, J. Williams 1-9, Mayes 1-9. Miami, Shepherd 3-30, T. Thomas 3-22, Gadsden 2-21, Martin 2-19, Konrad 2-6, Emanuel 1-16, L. Smith 1-12, Goodwin 1-8.

MISSED FIELD GOAL ATTEMPTS—Seattle, Heppner 52.

INTERCEPTIONS—Miami, Madison 2-38, Surtain 1-12, Marion 1-0.

KICKOFF RETURNS—Seattle, Rogers 6-108. Miami, Marion 1-26.

PUNT RETURNS—Seattle, Rogers 4-52. Miami, Kelly 3-13, Shepherd 2-11.

SACKS—Seattle, King 1, Simmons 1. Miami, Armstrong 2.5, Z. Thomas 0.5, Gardener 0.5, Taylor 0.5.

LIONS 14, SAINTS 10

Sunday, September 3

Detroit	0	6	8	0—14
New Orleans	7	0	0	3—10

First Quarter
N.O.—Knight 37 interception return (Brien kick), 5:22.

Second Quarter
Det.—FG, Hanson 24, 9:25.
Det.—FG, Hanson 30, 13:07.

Third Quarter
Det.—Howard 95 punt return (J. Stewart run), 12:54.

Fourth Quarter
N.O.—FG, Brien 48, 1:03.
Attendance—64,900.

	Detroit	New Orleans
First downs	10	13
Rushes-yards	32-98	25-106
Passing	89	146
Punt returns	4-119	6-36
Kickoff returns	3-50	4-105
Interception returns	1-6	1-37
Comp.-att.-int.	13-25-1	18-34-1
Sacked-yards lost	2-11	5-23
Punts	7-42	7-49
Fumbles-lost	2-1	5-2
Penalties-yards	8-74	12-89
Time of possession	30:49	29:11

INDIVIDUAL STATISTICS

RUSHING—Detroit, J. Stewart 25-78, Case 3-17, Irvin 3-3, Jett 1-0. New Orleans, R. Williams 20-84, Blake 5-22.

PASSING—Detroit, Case 13-25-1-100. New Orleans, Blake 18-34-1-169.

RECEIVING—Detroit, Morton 4-52, Sloan 2-10, Crowell 2-5, Irvin 1-10, Stablein 1-11, Schlesinger 1-6, J. Stewart 1-1, Rasby 1-1. New Orleans, Horn 5-58, R. Williams 4-29, Reed 3-46, Poole 3-14, Jackson 2-19, Morton 1-3.

MISSED FIELD GOAL ATTEMPTS—New Orleans, Brien 52.

INTERCEPTIONS—Detroit, Schulz 1-6. New Orleans, Knight 1-37.

KICKOFF RETURNS—Detroit, Howard 3-50. New Orleans, Morton 4-105.

PUNT RETURNS—Detroit, Howard 4-119. New Orleans, Morton 6-36.

SACKS—Detroit, Scroggins 2, Elliss 1, Aldridge 1, Pritchett 1. New Orleans, L. Glover 1, Oldham 1.

VIKINGS 30, BEARS 27

Sunday, September 3

Chicago	7	6	7	7—27
Minnesota	6	3	7	14—30

First Quarter
Min.—FG, Anderson 35, 4:44.
Chi.—Allred 18 pass from McNown (Edinger kick),11:02.
Min.—FG, Anderson 38, 13:44.

Second Quarter
Chi.—FG, Edinger 29, 9:41.
Min.—FG, Anderson 45, 13:09.
Chi.—FG, Edinger 49, 14:44.

Third Quarter
Chi.—M. Robinson 48 pass from McNown (Edinger kick), 4:50.
Min.—Culpepper 1 run (Anderson kick), 9:36.

Fourth Quarter
Min.—Culpepper 7 run (Anderson kick), 4:01.
Min.—Culpepper 4 run (Anderson kick), 10:25.
Chi.—McNown 8 run (Edinger kick), 13:43.
Attendance—64,104.

	Chicago	Minnesota
First downs	23	17
Rushes-yards	25-153	30-186
Passing	272	188
Punt returns	1-12	0-0
Kickoff returns	7-175	5-124
Interception returns	1-2	0-0
Comp.-att.-int.	27-41-0	13-23-1
Sacked-yards lost	2-18	1-2
Punts	4-31	2-39
Fumbles-lost	2-1	2-0
Penalties-yards	5-45	4-20
Time of possession	32:34	26:59

INDIVIDUAL STATISTICS
RUSHING—Chicago, McNown 10-87, Allen 9-60, Enis 4-11, Engram 1-1, Booker 1-(minus 6). Minnesota, Smith 14-109, Culpepper 13-73, Kleinsasser 2-5, M. Williams 1-(minus 1).

PASSING—Chicago, McNown 27-41-0-290. Minnesota, Culpepper 13-23-1-190.

RECEIVING—Chicago, Engram 8-61, M. Robinson 7-86, Booker 6-59, Allred 2-36, Kennison 2-16, Allen 1-17, Enis 1-15. Minnesota, Moss 4-89, Kleinsasser 2-32, J. Davis 2-31, C. Carter 2-26, Smith 2-3, Jordan 1-9.

MISSED FIELD GOAL ATTEMPTS—None.

INTERCEPTIONS—Chicago, Azumah 1-2.

KICKOFF RETURNS—Chicago, Milburn 7-175. Minnesota, T. Carter 5-124.

PUNT RETURNS—Chicago, Milburn 1-12.

SACKS—Chicago, Daniels 1. Minnesota, E. McDaniel 1, Burrough 1.

JAGUARS 27, BROWNS 7

Sunday, September 3

Jacksonville	0	10	10	7—27
Cleveland	0	7	0	0— 7

Second Quarter
Jac.—J. Smith 2 pass from Brunell (Hollis kick), 3:17.
Cle.—J. Dawson 13 pass from Couch (P. Dawson kick), 11:27.
Jac.—FG, Hollis 50, 14:30.

Third Quarter
Jac.—Mack 3 run (Hollis kick), 7:21.
Jac.—FG, Hollis 25, 13:40.

Fourth Quarter
Jac.—Howard 9 run (Hollis kick), 10:32.
Attendance—72,418.

	Jacksonville	Cleveland
First downs	28	9
Rushes-yards	40-119	16-96
Passing	279	153
Punt returns	3-17	0-0
Kickoff returns	1-24	5-89
Interception returns	0-0	0-0
Comp.-att.-int.	24-34-0	19-27-0
Sacked-yards lost	4-22	1-7
Punts	3-39	5-51
Fumbles-lost	1-0	1-1
Penalties-yards	1-5	3-25
Time of possession	36:17	22:50

INDIVIDUAL STATISTICS
RUSHING—Jacksonville, Mack 23-74, Howard 13-45, Martin 3-(minus 5), Brunell 1-5. Cleveland, Rhett 14-64, Couch 2-32.

PASSING—Jacksonville, Brunell 24-34-0-301. Cleveland, Couch 19-27-0-160.

RECEIVING—Jacksonville, McCardell 9-115, J. Smith 6-52, Brady 5-85, Howard 1-13, Jones 1-12, Shelton 1-12, Whitted 1-12. Cleveland, J. Dawson 6-83, Rhett 5-13, Johnson 3-32, Patten 2-9, Shea 1-24, Northcutt 1-0, Edwards 1-(minus 1).

MISSED FIELD GOAL ATTEMPTS—None.

INTERCEPTIONS—None.

KICKOFF RETURNS—Jacksonville, Barlow 1-24. Cleveland, White 3-51, Patten 2-38.

PUNT RETURNS—Jacksonville, Barlow 3-17.

SACKS—Jacksonville, Brackens 1. Cleveland, Roye 1, K. McKenzie 1, L. Jones 1, A. Miller 1.

FALCONS 36, 49ERS 28

Sunday, September 3

San Francisco	7	7	7	7—28
Atlanta	6	16	14	0—36

First Quarter
S.F.—Beasley 4 pass from Garcia (Richey kick), 4:35.
Atl.—FG, Andersen 43, 7:00.
Atl.—FG, Andersen 44, 13:13.

Second Quarter
Atl.—FG, Andersen 24, 5:19.
Atl.—FG, Andersen 44, 9:22.
Atl.—Mathis 44 pass from Chandler (Andersen kick), 12:48.
S.F.—Beasley 1 run (Richey kick), 13:53.
Atl.—FG, Andersen 48, 15:00.

Third Quarter
Atl.—Jefferson 48 pass from Chandler (Andersen kick), 0:54.
S.F.—Beasley 4 pass from Garcia (Richey kick), 5:50.
Atl.—Ambrose 36 interception return (Andersen kick), 8:35.

Fourth Quarter
S.F.—Owens 6 pass from Garcia (Richey kick), 12:10.
Attendance—54,626.

	San Francisco	Atlanta
First downs	23	22
Rushes-yards	24-92	32-95
Passing	247	264
Punt returns	1-0	2-21
Kickoff returns	5-85	5-145
Interception returns	0-0	1-36
Comp.-att.-int.	23-36-1	16-31-0
Sacked-yards lost	1-6	0-0
Punts	5-39	2-48
Fumbles-lost	3-0	2-1
Penalties-yards	7-42	4-51
Time of possession	27:28	31:39

INDIVIDUAL STATISTICS
RUSHING—San Francisco, Garner 15-62, Beasley 5-10, Garcia 2-22, Jackson 1-0, Rice 1-(minus 2). Atlanta, Anderson 24-77, Chandler 4-12, Christian 3-5, Jefferson 1-1.

PASSING—San Francisco, Garcia 23-36-1-253. Atlanta, Chandler 16-31-0-264.

RECEIVING—San Francisco, Owens 7-72, Rice 5-59, Clark 4-27, Garner 3-45, Beasley 3-25, Stokes 1-25. Atlanta, Jefferson 7-148, Mathis 3-72, R. Kelly 2-10, Anderson 1-20, Christian 1-12, Kozlowski 1-6, Chandler 1-(minus 4).

MISSED FIELD GOAL ATTEMPTS—None.

INTERCEPTIONS—Atlanta, Ambrose 1-36.

KICKOFF RETURNS—San Francisco, K. Williams 3-48, Stokes 1-19, Jervey 1-18. Atlanta, Dwight 3-74, Vaughn 1-57, Kozlowski 1-14.

PUNT RETURNS—San Francisco, K. Williams 1-0. Atlanta, Dwight 2-21.

SACKS—Atlanta, Crockett 1.

BUCCANEERS 21, PATRIOTS 16

Sunday, September 3

Tampa Bay	0	14	7	0—21
New England	3	7	0	6—16

First Quarter
N.E.—FG, Vinatieri 30, 2:41.

Second Quarter
T.B.—Alstott 5 run (Gramatica kick), 4:19.
N.E.—Brown 66 punt return (Vinatieri kick), 7:35.
T.B.—Anthony 8 pass from King (Gramatica kick), 14:29.

Third Quarter
T.B.—Alstott 3 run (Gramatica kick), 11:51.

Fourth Quarter
N.E.—Glenn 39 pass from Bledsoe (run failed), 11:59.
Attendance—60,292.

	Tampa Bay	New England
First downs	17	14
Rushes-yards	38-140	21-88
Passing	156	190
Punt returns	3-13	4-118
Kickoff returns	3-88	3-85
Interception returns	0-0	0-0
Comp.-att.-int.	12-24-0	26-39-0
Sacked-yards lost	1-11	6-26
Punts	10-40	9-41
Fumbles-lost	2-1	2-1
Penalties-yards	4-25	5-33
Time of possession	31:35	28:25

INDIVIDUAL STATISTICS

RUSHING—Tampa Bay, Dunn 16-56, Alstott 16-54, King 4-21, Green 1-6, K. Johnson 1-3. New England, Faulk 10-21, Bledsoe 8-30, Brown 2-33, T. Carter 1-4.

PASSING—Tampa Bay, King 12-24-0-167. New England, Bledsoe 26-39-0-216.

RECEIVING—Tampa Bay, K. Johnson 4-64, Green 2-67, Anthony 1-8, Williams 1-8, Alstott 1-6, Moore 1-6, Dunn 1-5, Abdullah 1-3. New England, Faulk 11-62, Brown 7-70, Glenn 4-56, Bjornson 2-15, Simmons 1-9, Rutledge 1-4.

MISSED FIELD GOAL ATTEMPTS—New England, Vinatieri 55.

INTERCEPTIONS—None.

KICKOFF RETURNS—Tampa Bay, Williams 3-88. New England, Faulk 3-85.

PUNT RETURNS—Tampa Bay, Williams 3-13. New England, Brown 4-118.

SACKS—Tampa Bay, Sapp 1.5, Jones 1.5, Quarles 1, Barber 1, White 1. New England, McGinest 1.

RAMS 41, BRONCOS 36

Monday, September 4

Denver	7	10	10	9—36
St. Louis	7	14	14	6—41

First Quarter
Den.—Griese 8 run (Elam kick), 4:57.
St.L.—Hakim 86 punt return (Wilkins kick), 12:55.

Second Quarter
Den.—FG, Elam 32, 1:18.
St.L.—Faulk 5 run (Wilkins kick), 6:07.
Den.—R. Smith 25 pass from Griese (Elam kick), 11:10.
St.L.—Proehl 7 pass from Warner (Wilkins kick), 14:22.

Third Quarter
Den.—FG, Elam 38, 5:41.
St.L.—Faulk 72 pass from Warner (Wilkins kick), 6:51.
St.L.—Hakim 80 pass from Warner (Wilkins kick), 10:58.
Den.—Clark 7 pass from Griese (Elam kick), 14:09.

Fourth Quarter
Den.—FG, Elam 36, 7:28.
Den.—Buckley 32 interception return (run failed), 8:25.
St.L.—Holcombe 1 run (pass failed), 12:02.
Attendance—65,956.

	Denver	St. Louis
First downs	25	23
Rushes-yards	28-150	18-80
Passing	274	433
Punt returns	0-0	1-86
Kickoff returns	5-98	8-145
Interception returns	3-33	0-0
Comp.-att.-int.	19-29-0	25-35-3
Sacked-yards lost	4-33	2-8
Punts	2-45	1-34
Fumbles-lost	1-0	0-0
Penalties-yards	5-27	5-56
Time of possession	32:13	27:47

INDIVIDUAL STATISTICS

RUSHING—Denver, Gary 13-80, Davis 9-34, Griese 4-28, R. Smith 1-8, Griffith 1-0. St. Louis, Faulk 14-78, Warner 3-1, Holcombe 1-1.

PASSING—Denver, Griese 19-29-0-307. St. Louis, Warner 25-35-3-441.

RECEIVING—Denver, McCaffrey 7-115, R. Smith 3-88, Gary 3-10, Carswell 2-27, Griffith 2-22, Chamberlain 1-38, Clark 1-7. St. Louis, Holt 6-103, Hakim 5-116, Faulk 4-100, Bruce 4-60, Proehl 3-40, Holcombe 2-19, Robinson 1-3.

MISSED FIELD GOAL ATTEMPTS—None.

INTERCEPTIONS—Denver, Wilson 2-1, Buckley 1-32.

KICKOFF RETURNS—Denver, O'Neal 5-98. St. Louis, Horne 8-145.

PUNT RETURNS—St. Louis, Hakim 1-86.

SACKS—Denver, Romanowski 1, Pittman 1. St. Louis, Fletcher 2, Carter 1, Farr 1.

STANDINGS

AFC EAST

	W	L	T	Pct.
Buffalo	2	0	0	1.000
N.Y. Jets	2	0	0	1.000
Indianapolis	1	1	0	.500
Miami	1	1	0	.500
New England	0	2	0	.000

AFC CENTRAL

	W	L	T	Pct.
Baltimore	2	0	0	1.000
Cleveland	1	1	0	.500
Jacksonville	1	1	0	.500
Tennessee	1	1	0	.500
Cincinnati	0	1	0	.000
Pittsburgh	0	1	0	.000

AFC WEST

	W	L	T	Pct.
Oakland	2	0	0	1.000
Denver	1	1	0	.500
Kansas City	0	2	0	.000
San Diego	0	2	0	.000
Seattle	0	2	0	.000

NFC EAST

	W	L	T	Pct.
N.Y. Giants	2	0	0	1.000
Arizona	1	1	0	.500
Philadelphia	1	1	0	.500
Washington	1	1	0	.500
Dallas	0	2	0	.000

NFC CENTRAL

	W	L	T	Pct.
Detroit	2	0	0	1.000
Minnesota	2	0	0	1.000
Tampa Bay	2	0	0	1.000
Chicago	0	2	0	.000
Green Bay	0	2	0	.000

NFC WEST

	W	L	T	Pct.
St. Louis	2	0	0	1.000
Atlanta	1	1	0	.500
Carolina	1	1	0	.500
New Orleans	1	1	0	.500
San Francisco	0	2	0	.000

TOP PERFORMANCES

100-YARD RUSHING GAMES

Player, Team & Opponent	Att.	Yds.	TD
Mike Anderson, Den. vs. Atl.	31	131	2

300-YARD PASSING GAMES

Player, Team & Opponent	Att.	Comp.	Yds.	TD	Int.
Mark Brunell, Jack. at Balt.	50	28	386	3	2
Kurt Warner, St.L. at Sea.	47	35	386	1	1
Peyton Manning, Ind. vs. Oak.	48	33	367	3	2
Steve Beuerlein, Car. at S.F.	32	24	364	3	1
Daunte Culpepper, Min. vs. Mia.	37	23	355	1	1

100-YARD RECEIVING GAMES

Player, Team & Opponent	Rec.	Yds.	TD
Jimmy Smith, Jack. at Balt.	15	291	3
Cris Carter, Min. vs. Mia.	9	168	0
Marvin Harrison, Ind. vs. Oak.	10	141	1
Tony Martin, Mia. at Min.	6	120	0
Rod Smith, Den. vs. Atl.	7	117	2
Joe Horn, N.O. at S.D.	12	116	2
Donald Hayes, Car. at S.F.	6	115	1
Muhsin Muhammad, Car. at S.F.	8	108	1
Kevin Dyson, Ten. vs. K.C.*	6	104	1
Jacquez Green, T.B. vs. Chi.	5	104	1
Eric Moulds, Buf. vs. G.B.	7	103	0
David Boston, Ari. vs. Dal.	6	102	0
Torry Holt, St.L. at Sea.	6	101	0
Dedric Ward, NYJ vs. N.E.	4	100	0

*Overtime game.

RESULTS

SUNDAY, SEPTEMBER 10

ARIZONA 32, Dallas 31
BALTIMORE 39, Jacksonville 36
BUFFALO 27, Green Bay 18
Carolina 38, San Francisco 22
Cleveland 24, CINCINNATI 7
DENVER 42, Atlanta 14
DETROIT 15, Washington 10
MINNESOTA 13, Miami 7
New Orleans 28, SAN DIEGO 27
N.Y. Giants 33, PHILADELPHIA 18
Oakland 38, INDIANAPOLIS 31
St. Louis 37, SEATTLE 34
TAMPA BAY 41, Chicago 0
TENNESSEE 17, Kansas City 14 (OT)

MONDAY, SEPTEMBER 11

N.Y. JETS 20, New England 19
 Open date: Pittsburgh

2000 REVIEW Week 2

CARDINALS 32, COWBOYS 31

Sunday, September 10

Dallas	7	14	3	7—31
Arizona	3	10	10	9—32

First Quarter
Ariz.—FG, Blanchard 19, 5:58.
Dal.—McGarity 64 punt return (Seder kick), 10:26.

Second Quarter
Ariz.—Pittman 1 run (Blanchard kick), 2:55.
Dal.—McKnight 47 pass from Cunningham (Seder kick), 5:56.
Dal.—Harris 1 pass from Cunningham (Seder kick), 14:34.
Ariz.—FG, Blanchard 54, 15:00.

Third Quarter
Dal.—FG, Seder 44, 6:44.
Ariz.—Sanders 4 pass from Plummer (Blanchard kick), 12:26.
Ariz.—FG, Blanchard 35, 14:48.

Fourth Quarter
Dal.—Wiley 15 pass from Cunningham (Seder kick), 6:07.
Ariz.—FG, Blanchard 51, 9:43.
Ariz.—Sanders 17 pass from Plummer (run failed), 13:06.
Attendance—66,009.

	Dallas	Arizona
First downs	17	21
Rushes-yards	22-90	33-98
Passing	240	224
Punt returns	2-65	1-7
Kickoff returns	6-97	5-129
Interception returns	0-0	0-0
Comp.-att.-int.	24-34-0	18-24-0
Sacked-yards lost	1-3	2-19
Punts	2-57	2-47
Fumbles-lost	2-2	4-1
Penalties-yards	5-102	2-15
Time of possession	28:40	31:20

INDIVIDUAL STATISTICS
RUSHING—Dallas, E. Smith 16-59, Cunningham 5-34, Ismail 1-(minus 3). Arizona, Jones 23-70, Pittman 9-28, Plummer 1-0.
PASSING—Dallas, Cunningham 24-34-0-243. Arizona, Plummer 18-24-0-243.
RECEIVING—Dallas, Harris 7-56, McKnight 5-86, Ismail 5-69, Wiley 3-23, Thomas 2-8, LaFleur 1-2, E. Smith 1-(minus 1). Arizona, Boston 6-102, Sanders 4-56, Jones 2-30, Hardy 2-19, Pittman 2-12, Cody 1-19, Gedney 1-5.
MISSED FIELD GOAL ATTEMPTS—None.
INTERCEPTIONS—None.
KICKOFF RETURNS—Dallas, Tucker 6-97. Arizona, Jenkins 4-111, Cody 1-18.
PUNT RETURNS—Dallas, McGarity 2-65. Arizona, Cody 1-7.
SACKS—Dallas, Zellner 1, Ekuban 0.5, Lett 0.5. Arizona, Rice 1.

SAINTS 28, CHARGERS 27

Sunday, September 10

New Orleans	7	6	6	9—28
San Diego	3	21	0	3—27

First Quarter
S.D.—FG, Carney 42, 8:21.
N.O.—Horn 6 pass from Blake (Brien kick), 13:00.

Second Quarter
S.D.—Chancey 3 run (Carney kick), 0:40.
S.D.—Conway 20 pass from Leaf (Carney kick), 7:56.
N.O.—FG, Brien 20, 13:06.
S.D.—R. Jenkins 93 kickoff return (Carney kick), 13:23.
N.O.—FG, Brien 20, 15:00.

Third Quarter
N.O.—R. Williams 13 pass from Blake (pass failed), 12:06.

Fourth Quarter
N.O.—FG, Brien 31, 0:08.
S.D.—FG, Carney 49, 9:52.
N.O.—Horn 8 pass from Blake (pass failed), 14:13.
Attendance—51,300.

	New Orleans	San Diego
First downs	28	15
Rushes-yards	31-64	20-72
Passing	259	116
Punt returns	4-93	2-32
Kickoff returns	6-138	6-221
Interception returns	2-51	2-21
Comp.-att.-int.	33-46-2	13-26-2
Sacked-yards lost	0-0	5-21
Punts	3-39	4-44
Fumbles-lost	2-1	2-0
Penalties-yards	7-37	7-85
Time of possession	36:06	23:54

INDIVIDUAL STATISTICS
RUSHING—New Orleans, R. Williams 24-50, Blake 6-13, Morton 1-1. San Diego, Chancey 15-59, Bynum 3-9, Conway 1-9, Leaf 1-(minus 5).
PASSING—New Orleans, Blake 33-46-2-259. San Diego, Leaf 12-24-2-134, Chancey 0-1-0-0, Moreno 1-1-0-3.
RECEIVING—New Orleans, Horn 12-116, Reed 5-51, R. Williams 4-27, A. Glover 4-23, T. Smith 3-14, Morton 3-11, Jackson 2-17. San Diego, Gaylor 4-21, J. Graham 3-46, Conway 3-31, F. Jones 1-19, McCrary 1-19, R. Jenkins 1-1.
MISSED FIELD GOAL ATTEMPTS—None.
INTERCEPTIONS—New Orleans, Weary 1-27, Molden 1-24. San Diego, Ruff 1-18, Lewis 1-3.
KICKOFF RETURNS—New Orleans, Morton 6-138. San Diego, R. Jenkins 6-221.
PUNT RETURNS—New Orleans, Morton 4-93. San Diego, Jacquet 2-32.
SACKS—New Orleans, Howard 2, L. Glover 2, Weary 1.

RAIDERS 38, COLTS 31

Sunday, September 10

Oakland	0	7	24	7—38
Indianapolis	14	10	0	7—31

First Quarter
Ind.—Pollard 13 pass from Manning (Vanderjagt kick), 4:43.
Ind.—James 6 run (Vanderjagt kick), 10:03.

Second Quarter
Ind.—James 10 pass from Manning (Vanderjagt kick), 3:32.
Oak.—Gannon 3 run (Janikowski kick), 12:09.
Ind.—FG, Vanderjagt 31, 14:57.

Third Quarter
Oak.—Gannon 7 run (Janikowski kick), 4:04.
Oak.—FG, Janikowski 24, 7:30.
Oak.—Gannon 6 run (Janikowski kick), 11:02.
Oak.—Wheatley 6 run (Janikowski kick), 14:19.

Fourth Quarter
Oak.—Wheatley 1 run (Janikowski kick), 9:21.
Ind.—Harrison 50 pass from Manning (Vanderjagt kick), 10:53.
Attendance—56,769.

	Oakland	Indianapolis
First downs	21	28
Rushes-yards	38-152	20-111
Passing	207	351
Punt returns	2-36	3-28
Kickoff returns	4-77	4-80
Interception returns	2-25	0-0
Comp.-att.-int.	15-22-0	33-48-2
Sacked-yards lost	0-0	2-16
Punts	3-53	2-58
Fumbles-lost	1-0	1-1
Penalties-yards	5-35	7-41
Time of possession	30:59	28:55

INDIVIDUAL STATISTICS
RUSHING—Oakland, Wheatley 20-49, Gannon 10-37, Kaufman 8-66. Indianapolis, James 18-91, Manning 2-20.
PASSING—Oakland, Gannon 15-22-0-207. Indianapolis, Manning 33-48-2-367.
RECEIVING—Oakland, Brown 4-68, Dudley 3-35, Rison 2-47, Wheatley 2-26, Brigham 2-10, Ritchie 1-13, Jett 1-8. Indianapolis, Harrison 10-141, Dilger 8-96, James 6-36, Pathon 5-61, Pollard 2-17, Green 2-16.
MISSED FIELD GOAL ATTEMPTS—Oakland, Janikowski 50. Indianapolis, Vanderjagt 47.

INTERCEPTIONS—Oakland, James 2-25.
KICKOFF RETURNS—Oakland, Kaufman 4-77. Indianapolis, Muhammad 2-45, P. Williams 2-35.
PUNT RETURNS—Oakland, Dunn 2-36. Indianapolis, P. Williams 3-28.
SACKS—Oakland, Johnstone 1, Russell 1.

BRONCOS 42, FALCONS 14

Sunday, September 10

Atlanta	0	7	7	0—14
Denver	13	21	8	0—42

First Quarter
Den.—Anderson 2 run (Elam kick), 6:35.
Den.—FG, Elam 29, 7:46.
Den.—FG, Elam 51, 13:18.

Second Quarter
Den.—Griffith 6 pass from Griese (Elam kick), 2:46.
Den.—Anderson 20 run (Elam kick), 6:33.
Den.—R. Smith 11 pass from Griese (Elam kick), 14:04.
Atl.—Vaughn 100 kickoff return (Andersen kick), 14:17.

Third Quarter
Den.—R. Smith 37 pass from Griese (Anderson run), 4:07.
Atl.—Dwight 35 pass from Chandler (Andersen kick), 11:56.
Attendance—75,466.

	Atlanta	Denver
First downs	12	29
Rushes-yards	13-47	39-152
Passing	139	255
Punt returns	3-50	3-33
Kickoff returns	8-257	2-38
Interception returns	0-0	0-0
Comp.-att.-int.	12-29-0	20-33-0
Sacked-yards lost	6-32	2-13
Punts	7-39	5-43
Fumbles-lost	5-3	0-0
Penalties-yards	10-71	7-54
Time of possession	22:57	37:03

INDIVIDUAL STATISTICS
RUSHING—Atlanta, Anderson 7-38, Rivers 3-4, Dwight 2-5, Chandler 1-0. Denver, Anderson 31-131, Coleman 7-21, Griese 1-0.
PASSING—Atlanta, Chandler 9-22-0-128, Johnson 3-7-0-43. Denver, Griese 20-33-0-268.
RECEIVING—Atlanta, Christian 3-16, Dwight 2-60, Mathis 2-42, Jefferson 2-37, Finneran 1-10, Kozlowski 1-6, Anderson 1-0. Denver, R. Smith 7-117, Carswell 5-54, Brooks 2-46, Clark 2-17, Griffith 2-11, Anderson 1-18, McCaffrey 1-5.
MISSED FIELD GOAL ATTEMPTS—None.
INTERCEPTIONS—None.
KICKOFF RETURNS—Atlanta, Dwight 6-149, Vaughn 1-100, Kozlowski 1-8. Denver, O'Neal 1-21, Cole 1-17.
PUNT RETURNS—Atlanta, Dwight 3-50. Denver, O'Neal 3-33.
SACKS—Atlanta, Brooking 1, Hall 1. Denver, Pryce 2, Tanuvasa 1, E. Brown 1, Hasselbach 1, Reagor 1.

TITANS 17, CHIEFS 14

Sunday, September 10

Kansas City	0	7	0	7	0—14
Tennessee	0	7	0	7	3—17

Second Quarter
Ten.—Dyson 30 pass from Wycheck (Del Greco kick), 13:18.
K.C.—Edwards 42 interception return (Stoyanovich kick), 14:48.

Fourth Quarter
K.C.—Alexander 16 pass from Grbac (Stoyanovich kick), 0:05.
Ten.—Thigpen 8 pass from O'Donnell (Del Greco kick), 14:10.

Overtime
Ten.—FG, Del Greco 36, 2:58.
Attendance—68,203.

	Kansas City	Tennessee
First downs	14	23
Rushes-yards	33-62	29-121
Passing	127	232
Punt returns	0-0	3-37
Kickoff returns	3-63	3-92

	Kansas City	Tennessee
Interception returns	2-80	0-0
Comp.-att.-int.	13-21-0	23-36-2
Sacked-yards lost	3-17	4-23
Punts	7-39	4-40
Fumbles-lost	2-0	1-1
Penalties-yards	10-72	7-70
Time of possession	29:53	33:05

INDIVIDUAL STATISTICS
RUSHING—Kansas City, Richardson 14-28, Cloud 7-10, Moreau 7-4, Grbac 3-19, Anders 2-1. Tennessee, E. George 21-80, McNair 7-42, O'Donnell 1-(minus 1).
PASSING—Kansas City, Grbac 13-21-0-144. Tennessee, McNair 11-18-2-93, O'Donnell 11-17-0-132, Wycheck 1-1-0-30.
RECEIVING—Kansas City, Alexander 5-54, Morris 3-44, Lockett 2-28, Gonzalez 2-16, Richardson 1-2. Tennessee, Dyson 6-104, Wycheck 6-50, Pickens 3-43, Thigpen 3-24, E. George 3-17, Kinney 2-17.
MISSED FIELD GOAL ATTEMPTS—Kansas City, Stoyanovich 36.
INTERCEPTIONS—Kansas City, Edwards 1-42, Hasty 1-38.
KICKOFF RETURNS—Kansas City, L. Parker 3-63. Tennessee, Mason 3-92.
PUNT RETURNS—Tennessee, Mason 3-37.
SACKS—Kansas City, Clemons 2, D. Williams 1, Hicks 1. Tennessee, Thornton 1, Holmes 1, Kearse 1.

RAMS 37, SEAHAWKS 34

Sunday, September 10

St. Louis	3	10	7	17—37	
Seattle	3	7	10	14—34	

First Quarter
Sea.—FG, Heppner 19, 9:00.
St.L.—FG, Wilkins 48, 14:28.

Second Quarter
Sea.—Bellamy 84 interception return (Heppner kick), 8:02.
St.L.—FG, Wilkins 48, 11:49.
St.L.—Holcombe 1 run (Wilkins kick), 14:43.

Third Quarter
Sea.—Watters 3 run (Heppner kick), 5:04.
St.L.—Faulk 1 run (Wilkins kick), 10:19.
Sea.—FG, Heppner 43, 14:40.

Fourth Quarter
St.L.—R. Williams 4 pass from Warner (Wilkins kick), 3:28.
Sea.—Watters 1 run (Heppner kick), 7:20.
St.L.—Bush 15 fumble return (Wilkins kick), 9:48.
Sea.—Jackson 34 pass from Kitna (Heppner kick), 12:55.
St.L.—FG, Wilkins 27, 14:37.
Attendance—64,869.

	St. Louis	Seattle
First downs	28	24
Rushes-yards	22-97	24-101
Passing	379	239
Punt returns	0-0	1-13
Kickoff returns	6-134	7-192
Interception returns	2-9	1-84
Comp.-att.-int.	35-47-1	20-31-2
Sacked-yards lost	1-7	3-6
Punts	2-35	2-38
Fumbles-lost	2-0	1-1
Penalties-yards	4-16	1-10
Time of possession	33:33	26:27

INDIVIDUAL STATISTICS
RUSHING—St. Louis, Faulk 15-68, Holcombe 4-17, Warner 2-11, Canidate 1-1. Seattle, Watters 16-59, Kitna 3-24, Alexander 3-18, Strong 1-1, Jackson 1-(minus 1).
PASSING—St. Louis, Warner 35-47-1-386. Seattle, Kitna 20-31-2-245.
RECEIVING—St. Louis, Faulk 9-85, Holt 6-101, Bruce 6-97, Hakim 6-41, Proehl 4-44, Robinson 1-8, Holcombe 1-4, R. Williams 1-4, Conwell 1-2. Seattle, Dawkins 6-70, Watters 5-44, Mili 3-52, Jackson 2-42, Mayes 2-20, Strong 2-17.
MISSED FIELD GOAL ATTEMPTS—None.
INTERCEPTIONS—St. Louis, Lyle 1-9, Lyght 1-0. Seattle, Bellamy 1-84.
KICKOFF RETURNS—St. Louis, Horne 6-134. Seattle, Rogers 7-192.
PUNT RETURNS—Seattle, Rogers 1-13.
SACKS—St. Louis, Collins 1, M. Jones 1, Agnew 1. Seattle, C. Brown 0.5, Sinclair 0.5.

PANTHERS 38, 49ERS 22

Sunday, September 10

Carolina	14	14	10	0—38
San Francisco	0	0	7	15—22

First Quarter
Car.—Floyd 1 run (Cunningham kick), 5:34.
Car.—Hayes 24 pass from Beuerlein (Cunningham kick), 10:20.

Second Quarter
Car.—Muhammad 3 pass from Beuerlein (Cunningham kick), 6:45.
Car.—Biakabutuka 1 run (Cunningham kick), 12:44.

Third Quarter
S.F.—Jackson 1 run (Richey kick), 4:20.
Car.—Walls 9 pass from Beuerlein (Cunningham kick), 8:33.
Car.—FG, Cunningham 24, 10:34.

Fourth Quarter
S.F.—Stokes 17 pass from Mirer (Richey kick), 3:34.
S.F.—Beasley 2 run (Owens pass from Mirer), 13:16.
Attendance—66,879.

	Carolina	San Francisco
First downs	27	21
Rushes-yards	34-98	21-95
Passing	352	296
Punt returns	1-20	1-16
Kickoff returns	1-10	6-84
Interception returns	1-3	1-31
Comp.-att.-int.	24-32-1	22-40-1
Sacked-yards lost	2-12	2-11
Punts	3-31	4-44
Fumbles-lost	1-0	1-1
Penalties-yards	6-50	9-67
Time of possession	36:07	23:53

INDIVIDUAL STATISTICS
RUSHING—Carolina, Biakabutuka 22-75, Lewis 4-11, Hoover 3-6, Hetherington 2-5, Floyd 2-2, Beuerlein 1-(minus 1). San Francisco, Garner 11-73, Beasley 4-2, Garcia 3-14, Mirer 2-5, Jackson 1-1.
PASSING—Carolina, Beuerlein 24-32-1-364. San Francisco, Garcia 12-20-1-181, Mirer 10-20-0-126.
RECEIVING—Carolina, Muhammad 8-108, Hayes 6-115, Walls 5-99, Floyd 3-21, Biakabutuka 1-16, Bates 1-5. San Francisco, Stokes 5-98, Owens 5-97, Garner 4-22, Beasley 3-56, Rice 3-22, Clark 2-12.
MISSED FIELD GOAL ATTEMPTS—None.
INTERCEPTIONS—Carolina, Davis 1-3. San Francisco, Peterson 1-31.
KICKOFF RETURNS—Carolina, Hetherington 1-10. San Francisco, K. Williams 6-84.
PUNT RETURNS—Carolina, Davis 1-20. San Francisco, K. Williams 1-16.
SACKS—Carolina, McKinley 1, Rucker 0.5, White 0.5. San Francisco, Keith 1, Peterson 1.

LIONS 15, REDSKINS 10

Sunday, September 10

Washington	0	7	3	0—10
Detroit	3	3	3	6—15

First Quarter
Det.—FG, Hanson 49, 6:06.

Second Quarter
Det.—FG, Hanson 20, 1:47.
Was.—Alexander 5 pass from B. Johnson (Conway kick), 10:30.

Third Quarter
Det.—FG, Hanson 54, 8:25.
Was.—FG, Conway 26, 12:56.

Fourth Quarter
Det.—FG, Hanson 37, 3:24.
Det.—FG, Hanson 35, 8:36.
Attendance—74,159.

	Washington	Detroit
First downs	20	15
Rushes-yards	23-104	24-62
Passing	229	182
Punt returns	1-4	1-6
Kickoff returns	4-132	2-61
Interception returns	2-0	4-84
Comp.-att.-int.	23-35-4	16-31-2

	Washington	Detroit
Sacked-yards lost	1-16	2-12
Punts	3-36	2-44
Fumbles-lost	1-0	0-0
Penalties-yards	6-55	7-50
Time of possession	30:55	29:05

INDIVIDUAL STATISTICS
RUSHING—Washington, Davis 17-59, B. Johnson 5-44, Murrell 1-1. Detroit, J. Stewart 21-65, Batch 2-(minus 3), Irvin 1-0.
PASSING—Washington, B. Johnson 23-35-4-245. Detroit, Batch 16-31-2-194.
RECEIVING—Washington, Centers 4-53, Westbrook 4-50, Murrell 4-26, Fryar 3-35, Davis 3-28, Alexander 3-19, Connell 2-34. Detroit, Crowell 6-51, Morton 5-88, Moore 2-27, Irvin 2-25, Sloan 1-3.
MISSED FIELD GOAL ATTEMPTS—None.
INTERCEPTIONS—Washington, Bailey 2-0. Detroit, Pritchett 1-78, Schulz 1-6, Westbrook 1-0, Fair 1-0.
KICKOFF RETURNS—Washington, Thrash 4-132. Detroit, Howard 2-61.
PUNT RETURNS—Washington, Sanders 1-4. Detroit, Howard 1-6.
SACKS—Washington, Coleman 1, Wilkinson 1. Detroit, Aldridge 1.

VIKINGS 13, DOLPHINS 7

Sunday, September 10

Miami	0	0	0	7— 7
Minnesota	3	0	0	10—13

First Quarter
Min.—FG, Anderson 28, 12:14.

Fourth Quarter
Min.—FG, Anderson 49, 3:30.
Min.—Moss 15 pass from Culpepper (Anderson kick), 13:04.
Mia.—T. Thomas 2 pass from Fiedler (Mare kick), 13:58.
Attendance—64,112.

	Miami	Minnesota
First downs	10	24
Rushes-yards	16-49	28-125
Passing	160	340
Punt returns	2-14	4-16
Kickoff returns	4-88	2-40
Interception returns	3-15	1-0
Comp.-att.-int.	12-31-1	23-37-3
Sacked-yards lost	3-15	3-15
Punts	9-44	4-45
Fumbles-lost	0-0	3-1
Penalties-yards	7-40	7-60
Time of possession	22:41	37:19

INDIVIDUAL STATISTICS
RUSHING—Miami, L. Smith 11-27, Fiedler 4-22, Emanuel 1-0. Minnesota, Smith 18-72, Culpepper 8-37, Moss 1-9, Kleinsasser 1-7.
PASSING—Miami, Fiedler 12-31-1-175. Minnesota, Culpepper 23-37-3-355.
RECEIVING—Miami, Martin 6-120, Gadsden 2-24, L. Smith 1-12, Weaver 1-12, Emanuel 1-5, T. Thomas 1-2. Minnesota, C. Carter 9-168, Moss 6-87, Jordan 3-27, J. Davis 2-42, Walsh 1-20, Smith 1-11, Kleinsasser 1-0.
MISSED FIELD GOAL ATTEMPTS—None.
INTERCEPTIONS—Miami, Marion 1-14, Walker 1-1, Bowens 1-0. Minnesota, Thibodeaux 1-0.
KICKOFF RETURNS—Miami, Marion 3-82, Goodwin 1-6. Minnesota, T. Carter 1-25, Thomas 1-15.
PUNT RETURNS—Miami, Shepherd 2-14. Minnesota, D. Palmer 4-16.
SACKS—Miami, Mixon 1, Armstrong 1, Bowens 1. Minnesota, E. McDaniel 1, Griffith 1, Wong 1.

GIANTS 33, EAGLES 18

Sunday, September 10

N.Y. Giants	3	17	7	6—33
Philadelphia	0	3	9	6—18

First Quarter
NYG—FG, Daluiso 32, 10:55.

Second Quarter
NYG—FG, Daluiso 36, 3:17.
Phi.—FG, Akers 33, 9:38.
NYG—Toomer 25 pass from Collins (Daluiso kick), 14:00.
NYG—Barber 31 run (Daluiso kick), 14:46.

Third Quarter

Phi.—FG, Akers 29, 5:51.
NYG—Hilliard 30 pass from Collins (Daluiso kick), 10:59.
Phi.—McNabb 15 run (kick blocked), 14:04.

Fourth Quarter

NYG—FG, Daluiso 44, 6:20.
NYG—FG, Daluiso 23, 11:01.
Phi.—Lewis 7 pass from McNabb (pass failed), 13:38.
Attendance—65,530.

	N.Y. Giants	Philadelphia
First downs	24	13
Rushes-yards	39-167	12-56
Passing	220	181
Punt returns	3-34	0-0
Kickoff returns	4-117	6-121
Interception returns	0-0	0-0
Comp.-att.-int.	21-29-0	19-33-0
Sacked-yards lost	1-0	3-33
Punts	2-35	4-51
Fumbles-lost	1-0	0-0
Penalties-yards	4-35	5-40
Time of possession	38:44	21:16

INDIVIDUAL STATISTICS

RUSHING—New York, Dayne 21-50, Barber 11-96, Collins 5-2, Comella 2-19. Philadelphia, Staley 7-11, McNabb 5-45.

PASSING—New York, Collins 21-29-0-220. Philadelphia, McNabb 19-33-0-214.

RECEIVING—New York, Hilliard 8-84, Toomer 7-80, Barber 3-29, Comella 2-12, Dixon 1-15. Philadelphia, Staley 7-58, C. Johnson 5-48, Lewis 4-67, Pinkston 1-23, D. Douglas 1-9, Miller 1-9.

MISSED FIELD GOAL ATTEMPTS—None.

INTERCEPTIONS—None.

KICKOFF RETURNS—New York, Dixon 4-117. Philadelphia, Mitchell 5-106, Pritchett 1-15.

PUNT RETURNS—New York, Barber 3-34.

SACKS—New York, Armstead 1, Phillips 1, Monty 1. Philadelphia, H. Douglas 1.

BUCCANEERS 41, BEARS 0

Sunday, September 10

Chicago	0	0	0	0— 0
Tampa Bay	0	20	14	7—41

Second Quarter

T.B.—FG, Gramatica 23, 4:32.
T.B.—FG, Gramatica 47, 12:14.
T.B.—King 3 run (Gramatica kick), 13:06.
T.B.—Barber 24 fumble return (Gramatica kick), 13:43.

Third Quarter

T.B.—K. Johnson 13 pass from King (Gramatica kick), 6:33.
T.B.—Green 58 pass from King (Gramatica kick), 7:27.

Fourth Quarter

T.B.—Alstott 20 run (Gramatica kick), 4:44.
Attendance—65,569.

	Chicago	Tampa Bay
First downs	9	21
Rushes-yards	22-116	36-156
Passing	49	171
Punt returns	3-23	4-17
Kickoff returns	7-166	1-31
Interception returns	0-0	2-19
Comp.-att.-int.	15-29-2	13-24-0
Sacked-yards lost	5-47	2-15
Punts	7-38	5-44
Fumbles-lost	3-2	0-0
Penalties-yards	9-64	3-20
Time of possession	26:24	33:36

INDIVIDUAL STATISTICS

RUSHING—Chicago, Enis 11-20, Allen 6-47, McNown 5-49. Tampa Bay, Alstott 15-71, Dunn 14-53, Stecker 5-26, King 2-6.

PASSING—Chicago, McNown 15-29-2-96. Tampa Bay, King 10-21-0-167, Zeier 3-3-0-19.

RECEIVING—Chicago, Engram 4-10, Allen 3-14, M. Robinson 2-25, Brooks 2-19, White 2-15, Mayes 1-8, Kennison 1-5. Tampa Bay, Green 5-104, K. Johnson 2-32, Dunn 2-5, Williams 1-27, Hape 1-13, Alstott 1-4, Yoder 1-1.

MISSED FIELD GOAL ATTEMPTS—Chicago, Edinger 42.

INTERCEPTIONS—Tampa Bay, Abraham 2-19.

KICKOFF RETURNS—Chicago, Milburn 7-166. Tampa Bay, Stecker 1-31.

PUNT RETURNS—Chicago, Milburn 3-23. Tampa Bay, Williams 4-17.

SACKS—Chicago, Daniels 1, F. Smith 1. Tampa Bay, Barber 2.5, T. Jackson 1, Sapp 1, Jones 0.5.

BROWNS 24, BENGALS 7

Sunday, September 10

Cleveland	7	7	3	7—24
Cincinnati	0	7	0	0— 7

First Quarter

Cle.—Prentice 16 run (P. Dawson kick), 11:17.

Second Quarter

Cin.—Dugans 4 pass from Smith (Rackers kick), 0:27.
Cle.—Campbell 5 pass from Couch (P. Dawson kick), 3:40.

Third Quarter

Cle.—FG, P. Dawson 30, 8:31.

Fourth Quarter

Cle.—Edwards 5 pass from Couch (P. Dawson kick), 3:13.
Attendance—64,006.

	Cleveland	Cincinnati
First downs	17	17
Rushes-yards	33-105	19-111
Passing	249	207
Punt returns	2-5	7-35
Kickoff returns	2-42	5-124
Interception returns	2-7	1-5
Comp.-att.-int.	19-31-1	15-43-2
Sacked-yards lost	1-10	7-43
Punts	7-48	6-41
Fumbles-lost	1-0	3-1
Penalties-yards	6-60	7-65
Time of possession	34:03	25:57

INDIVIDUAL STATISTICS

RUSHING—Cleveland, Rhett 20-53, Prentice 8-46, Couch 4-7, Northcutt 1-(minus 1). Cincinnati, Dillon 12-41, Smith 2-26, Bennett 2-5, Pope 1-22, N. Williams 1-9, Warrick 1-8.

PASSING—Cleveland, Couch 19-31-1-259. Cincinnati, Smith 15-43-2-250.

RECEIVING—Cleveland, Johnson 5-59, Patten 3-95, J. Dawson 3-14, Rhett 2-11, Shea 1-30, Chiaverini 1-18, Northcutt 1-12, Prentice 1-10, Campbell 1-5, Edwards 1-5. Cincinnati, Warrick 3-80, Groce 3-12, Dillon 2-46, Yeast 2-38, Bennett 2-30, Dugans 2-10, McGee 1-34.

MISSED FIELD GOAL ATTEMPTS—Cincinnati, Rackers 42.

INTERCEPTIONS—Cleveland, Little 1-7, Sanders 1-0. Cincinnati, Spikes 1-5.

KICKOFF RETURNS—Cleveland, Patten 1-22, White 1-20. Cincinnati, Mack 4-124, N. Williams 1-0.

PUNT RETURNS—Cleveland, Northcutt 2-5. Cincinnati, Yeast 7-35.

SACKS—Cleveland, K. McKenzie 3, J. Miller 2, Colinet 1, M. Thompson 1. Cincinnati, Simmons 1.

BILLS 27, PACKERS 18

Sunday, September 10

Green Bay	0	0	10	8—18
Buffalo	0	10	10	7—27

Second Quarter

Buf.—McDaniel 6 pass from Johnson (Christie kick), 14:16.
Buf.—FG, Christie 45, 15:00.

Third Quarter

Buf.—Riemersma 6 pass from Johnson (Christie kick), 3:02.
G.B.—Freeman 7 pass from Favre (Longwell kick), 7:07.
Buf.—FG, Christie 20, 10:18.
G.B.—FG, Longwell 24, 14:20.

Fourth Quarter

Buf.—Riemersma 14 pass from Johnson (Christie kick), 3:15.
G.B.—Freeman 18 pass from Favre (T. Davis pass from Favre), 14:25.
Attendance—72,722.

	Green Bay	Buffalo
First downs	14	20
Rushes-yards	16-40	34-89
Passing	234	220

	Green Bay	Buffalo
Punt returns	1-5	3-3
Kickoff returns	4-94	4-83
Interception returns	1-3	0-0
Comp.-att.-int.	25-35-0	18-26-1
Sacked-yards lost	4-35	5-39
Punts	7-43	7-37
Fumbles-lost	4-3	0-0
Penalties-yards	2-12	5-33
Time of possession	26:37	33:23

INDIVIDUAL STATISTICS

RUSHING—Green Bay, Green 11-46, Favre 3-(minus 2), Freeman 1-2, Goodman 1-(minus 6). Buffalo, Bryson 12-31, A. Smith 12-17, Johnson 7-31, Morris 2-6, Moulds 1-4.

PASSING—Green Bay, Favre 25-35-0-269. Buffalo, Johnson 18-26-1-259.

RECEIVING—Green Bay, Freeman 7-80, Green 4-18, Henderson 3-31, Lee 3-30, Driver 2-58, T. Davis 2-24, Schroeder 2-16, Franks 2-12. Buffalo, Moulds 7-103, Riemersma 4-70, McDaniel 3-38, P. Price 3-36, Jackson 1-12.

MISSED FIELD GOAL ATTEMPTS—None.

INTERCEPTIONS—Green Bay, Holliday 1-3.

KICKOFF RETURNS—Green Bay, Rossum 4-94. Buffalo, Watson 2-62, Linton 1-17, H. Jones 1-4.

PUNT RETURNS—Green Bay, Rossum 1-5. Buffalo, Watson 3-3.

SACKS—Green Bay, Sharper 1, Wayne 1, Thierry 1, Butler 1, B. Harris 1. Buffalo, Hansen 1, Wiley 1, Washington 1, P. Williams 1.

RAVENS 39, JAGUARS 36

Sunday, September 10

Jacksonville	17	6	3	10	36
Baltimore	0	7	15	17	39

First Quarter

Jac.—FG, Hollis 36, 3:45.
Jac.—J. Smith 45 pass from Brunell (Hollis kick), 7:11.
Jac.—J. Smith 43 pass from Brunell (Hollis kick), 12:28.

Second Quarter

Bal.—Taylor 14 pass from Banks (Stover kick), 0:12.
Jac.—FG, Hollis 45, 11:24.
Jac.—FG, Hollis 48, 14:16.

Third Quarter

Bal.—Taylor 23 pass from Banks (Coates pass from Banks), 1:29.
Jac.—FG, Hollis 34, 8:13.
Bal.—Ayanbadejo 5 pass from Banks (Stover kick), 13:58.

Fourth Quarter

Bal.—Je. Lewis 12 pass from Banks (Stover kick), 5:00.
Bal.—FG, Stover 44, 8:00.
Jac.—FG, Hollis 48, 11:07.
Jac.—J. Smith 40 pass from Brunell (Hollis kick), 13:15.
Bal.—Sharpe 29 pass from Banks (Stover kick), 14:19.
Attendance—68,843.

	Jacksonville	Baltimore
First downs	22	17
Rushes-yards	21-46	18-89
Passing	375	242
Punt returns	5-25	0-0
Kickoff returns	5-118	9-173
Interception returns	2-37	2-32
Comp.-att.-int.	28-50-2	23-40-2
Sacked-yards lost	4-11	3-20
Punts	3-38	7-41
Fumbles-lost	4-2	1-0
Penalties-yards	10-60	8-65
Time of possession	31:23	28:37

INDIVIDUAL STATISTICS

RUSHING—Jacksonville, Mack 11-36, Howard 8-7, Brunell 2-3. Baltimore, Holmes 10-54, Ja. Lewis 5-7, Banks 2-5, J. Lewis 1-23.

PASSING—Jacksonville, Brunell 28-50-2-386. Baltimore, Banks 23-40-2-262.

RECEIVING—Jacksonville, J. Smith 15-291, McCardell 7-61, Howard 2-13, Brady 2-12, Soward 2-9. Baltimore, Ayanbadejo 7-53, Taylor 4-80, Holmes 4-18, Sharpe 3-50, J. Lewis 3-27, B. Davis 2-34.

MISSED FIELD GOAL ATTEMPTS—None.

INTERCEPTIONS—Jacksonville, R. Stewart 2-37. Baltimore, Herring 1-30, Harris 1-2.

KICKOFF RETURNS—Jacksonville, Barlow 3-58, Stith 2-60. Baltimore, Harris 7-153, Ismail 1-13, Holmes 1-7.

PUNT RETURNS—Jacksonville, Barlow 5-25.

SACKS—Jacksonville, Brackens 1, Smeenge 1, Wynn 1. Baltimore, Boulware 2, Burnett 1, Trapp 1.

JETS 20, PATRIOTS 19

Monday, September 11

New England	3	9	0	7	19
N.Y. Jets	7	0	0	13	20

First Quarter

N.E.—FG, Vinatieri 32, 5:09.
NYJ—Baxter 4 pass from Testaverde (Hall kick), 11:12.

Second Quarter

N.E.—FG, Vinatieri 35, 2:37.
N.E.—FG, Vinatieri 30, 3:47.
N.E.—FG, Vinatieri 33, 12:15.

Fourth Quarter

N.E.—Bjornson 6 pass from Bledsoe (Vinatieri kick), 5:04.
NYJ—Chrebet 2 pass from Testaverde (Hall kick), 8:35.
NYJ—Chrebet 28 pass from Testaverde (run failed), 13:05.
Attendance—77,687.

	New England	N.Y. Jets
First downs	21	18
Rushes-yards	34-100	17-59
Passing	193	271
Punt returns	4-93	2-5
Kickoff returns	3-75	6-108
Interception returns	1-24	0-0
Comp.-att.-int.	25-43-0	16-37-1
Sacked-yards lost	6-36	2-10
Punts	4-39	6-50
Fumbles-lost	0-0	2-0
Penalties-yards	3-8	6-69
Time of possession	38:00	22:00

INDIVIDUAL STATISTICS

RUSHING—New England, Faulk 21-82, Redmond 5-2, Bledsoe 3-10, T. Carter 2-7, Bishop 1-2, Floyd 1-(minus 1), Glenn 1-(minus 2). New York, Martin 11-47, Testaverde 3-0, R. Anderson 2-10, W. Hayes 1-2.

PASSING—New England, Bledsoe 25-43-0-229. New York, Testaverde 16-37-1-281.

RECEIVING—New England, Glenn 6-81, Bjornson 6-39, Brown 4-27, Faulk 4-23, T. Carter 2-11, Calloway 1-22, Floyd 1-21, Simmons 1-5. New York, R. Anderson 6-88, Ward 4-100, Chrebet 4-71, Brisby 1-18, Baxter 1-4.

MISSED FIELD GOAL ATTEMPTS—New England, Vinatieri 29.

INTERCEPTIONS—New England, Langham 1-24.

KICKOFF RETURNS—New England, Faulk 3-75. New York, Williams 3-73, Dunn 2-35, Becht 1-0.

PUNT RETURNS—New England, Brown 4-93. New York, Ward 1-5, Dunn 1-0.

SACKS—New England, Thomas 1.5, Hamilton 0.5. New York, Abraham 1.5, Ellis 1.5, Lewis 1, Farrior 1, Wiltz 1.

WEEK 3

AFC EAST

	W	L	T	Pct.
N.Y. Jets	3	0	0	1.000
Buffalo	2	1	0	.667
Miami	2	1	0	.667
Indianapolis	1	1	0	.500
New England	0	3	0	.000

AFC CENTRAL

	W	L	T	Pct.
Baltimore	2	1	0	.667
Cleveland	2	1	0	.667
Jacksonville	2	1	0	.667
Tennessee	1	1	0	.500
Cincinnati	0	2	0	.000
Pittsburgh	0	2	0	.000

AFC WEST

	W	L	T	Pct.
Denver	2	1	0	.667
Oakland	2	1	0	.667
Kansas City	1	2	0	.333
Seattle	1	2	0	.333
San Diego	0	3	0	.000

NFC EAST

	W	L	T	Pct.
N.Y. Giants	3	0	0	1.000
Arizona	1	1	0	.500
Dallas	1	2	0	.333
Philadelphia	1	2	0	.333
Washington	1	2	0	.333

NFC CENTRAL

	W	L	T	Pct.
Minnesota	3	0	0	1.000
Tampa Bay	3	0	0	1.000
Detroit	2	1	0	.667
Green Bay	1	2	0	.333
Chicago	0	3	0	.000

NFC WEST

	W	L	T	Pct.
St. Louis	3	0	0	1.000
Atlanta	2	1	0	.667
Carolina	1	2	0	.333
New Orleans	1	2	0	.333
San Francisco	0	3	0	.000

TOP PERFORMANCES

100-YARD RUSHING GAMES

Player, Team & Opponent	Att.	Yds.	TD
Mike Anderson, Den. at Oak.	32	187	0
Marshall Faulk, St.L. vs. S.F.	25	134	3
Jerome Bettis, Pit. at Cle.	24	133	1
Ricky Williams, N.O. at Sea.	23	107	0
Ricky Watters, Sea. vs. N.O.	22	105	1

300-YARD PASSING GAMES

Player, Team & Opponent	Att.	Comp.	Yds.	TD	Int.
Kurt Warner, St.L. vs. S.F.	34	23	394	2	2
Tim Couch, Cle. vs. Pit.	31	23	316	2	0

100-YARD RECEIVING GAMES

Player, Team & Opponent	Rec.	Yds.	TD
Isaac Bruce, St.L. vs. S.F.	8	188	1
Sylvester Morris, K.C. vs. S.D.	6	112	3
Keenan McCardell, Jack. vs. Cin.	10	108	1
Terrell Owens, S.F. at St.L.	6	108	1

RESULTS

SUNDAY, SEPTEMBER 17

Atlanta 15, CAROLINA 10
CLEVELAND 23, Pittsburgh 20
Denver 33, OAKLAND 24
GREEN BAY 6, Philadelphia 3
JACKSONVILLE 13, Cincinnati 0
KANSAS CITY 42, San Diego 10
MIAMI 19, Baltimore 6
Minnesota 21, NEW ENGLAND 13
N.Y. Giants 14, CHICAGO 7
N.Y. JETS 27, Buffalo 14
ST. LOUIS 41, San Francisco 24
SEATTLE 20, New Orleans 10
Tampa Bay 31, DETROIT 10

MONDAY, SEPTEMBER 18

Dallas 27, WASHINGTON 21
Open date: Arizona, Indianapolis, Tennessee

2000 REVIEW *Week 3*

- 129 -

DOLPHINS 19, RAVENS 6

Sunday, September 17

Baltimore	0	0	3	3— 6
Miami	3	3	7	6—19

First Quarter
Mia.—FG, Mare 42, 10:05.

Second Quarter
Mia.—FG, Mare 41, 2:23.

Third Quarter
Mia.—L. Smith 7 run (Mare kick), 3:13.
Bal.—FG, Stover 27, 11:47.

Fourth Quarter
Mia.—L. Smith 8 pass from Fiedler (kick failed), 1:45.
Bal.—FG, Stover 33, 5:25.
Attendance—73,464.

	Baltimore	Miami
First downs	18	15
Rushes-yards	18-118	34-106
Passing	144	152
Punt returns	0-0	3-59
Kickoff returns	5-96	2-42
Interception returns	1-3	1-43
Comp.-att.-int.	19-31-1	11-16-1
Sacked-yards lost	6-45	1-8
Punts	4-41	3-48
Fumbles-lost	3-0	0-0
Penalties-yards	4-20	6-38
Time of possession	28:49	31:11

INDIVIDUAL STATISTICS
RUSHING—Baltimore, Ja. Lewis 9-76, Holmes 6-25, Banks 2-11, Ayanbadejo 1-6. Miami, L. Smith 22-63, Johnson 5-10, Fiedler 4-8, T. Thomas 3-25.
PASSING—Baltimore, Banks 19-31-1-189. Miami, Fiedler 11-16-1-160.
RECEIVING—Baltimore, Sharpe 5-56, Ayanbadejo 4-49, Johnson 2-23, Ja. Lewis 2-22, Holmes 2-18, Coates 2-11, Taylor 2-10. Miami, L. Smith 3-47, T. Thomas 3-31, Shepherd 3-30, Weaver 1-41, Gadsden 1-11.
MISSED FIELD GOAL ATTEMPTS—Baltimore, Stover 30.
INTERCEPTIONS—Baltimore, Trapp 1-3. Miami, Surtain 1-43.
KICKOFF RETURNS—Baltimore, Harris 4-79, Washington 1-17. Miami, Marion 2-42.
PUNT RETURNS—Miami, Shepherd 2-28, Ogden 1-31.
SACKS—Baltimore, McCrary 1. Miami, Taylor 2.5, Walker 1, Armstrong 1, Haley 1, Mixon 0.5.

JAGUARS 13, BENGALS 0

Sunday, September 17

Cincinnati	0	0	0	0— 0
Jacksonville	10	0	0	3—13

First Quarter
Jac.—McCardell 21 pass from Brunell (Lindsey kick), 7:46.
Jac.—FG, Lindsey 30, 9:23.

Fourth Quarter
Jac.—FG, Lindsey 19, 13:15.
Attendance—45,653.

	Cincinnati	Jacksonville
First downs	14	15
Rushes-yards	23-71	29-84
Passing	159	157
Punt returns	6-54	3-40
Kickoff returns	4-82	1-22
Interception returns	1-1	2-49
Comp.-att.-int.	18-41-2	20-32-1
Sacked-yards lost	5-24	4-19
Punts	7-42	7-42
Fumbles-lost	3-2	0-0
Penalties-yards	6-44	7-76
Time of possession	28:31	31:29

INDIVIDUAL STATISTICS
RUSHING—Cincinnati, Dillon 17-32, Smith 5-34, Groce 1-5. Jacksonville, Mack 20-35, Brunell 5-25, Dukes 2-2, Soward 1-20, Shelton 1-2.

PASSING—Cincinnati, Smith 18-41-2-183. Jacksonville, Brunell 20-32-1-176.
RECEIVING—Cincinnati, Warrick 5-75, Dillon 4-34, Yeast 3-31, McGee 3-23, Dugans 2-18, Groce 1-2. Jacksonville, McCardell 10-108, J. Smith 6-41, Brady 4-27.
MISSED FIELD GOAL ATTEMPTS—Cincinnati, Rackers 44, 47. Jacksonville, Lindsey 33.
INTERCEPTIONS—Cincinnati, Foley 1-1. Jacksonville, Beasley 1-39, Nickerson 1-10.
KICKOFF RETURNS—Cincinnati, Mack 4-82. Jacksonville, Barlow 1-22.
PUNT RETURNS—Cincinnati, Yeast 6-54. Jacksonville, Barlow 3-40.
SACKS—Cincinnati, Gibson 2, Spikes 1, Hall 1. Jacksonville, Walker 2, Nickerson 1, Brackens 1, Smeenge 1.

SEAHAWKS 20, SAINTS 10

Sunday, September 17

New Orleans	7	3	0	0—10
Seattle	7	0	3	10—20

First Quarter
Sea.—Watters 7 run (Heppner kick), 6:25.
N.O.—Poole 49 pass from Blake (Brien kick), 14:03.

Second Quarter
N.O.—FG, Brien 23, 12:23.

Third Quarter
Sea.—FG, Heppner 31, 6:59.

Fourth Quarter
Sea.—Mili 1 pass from Kitna (Heppner kick), 5:37.
Sea.—FG, Heppner 45, 11:13.
Attendance—59,513.

	New Orleans	Seattle
First downs	13	22
Rushes-yards	26-116	31-126
Passing	147	169
Punt returns	1-6	4-21
Kickoff returns	5-125	3-76
Interception returns	1-0	0-0
Comp.-att.-int.	14-24-0	22-29-1
Sacked-yards lost	2-12	4-24
Punts	5-41	3-41
Fumbles-lost	1-0	0-0
Penalties-yards	4-40	4-32
Time of possession	25:13	34:47

INDIVIDUAL STATISTICS
RUSHING—New Orleans, R. Williams 23-107, Blake 2-10, Morton 1-(minus 1). Seattle, Watters 22-105, Alexander 5-19, Kitna 4-2.
PASSING—New Orleans, Blake 14-24-0-159. Seattle, Kitna 22-29-1-193.
RECEIVING—New Orleans, Horn 7-68, R. Williams 5-35, Poole 1-49, Morton 1-7. Seattle, Jackson 5-59, Mili 4-22, Strong 3-33, Watters 3-19, Alexander 2-21, Fauria 2-16, Dawkins 1-8, J. Williams 1-8, Bailey 1-7.
MISSED FIELD GOAL ATTEMPTS—Seattle, Heppner 37.
INTERCEPTIONS—New Orleans, Molden 1-0.
KICKOFF RETURNS—New Orleans, Morton 5-125. Seattle, J. Williams 3-76.
PUNT RETURNS—New Orleans, Morton 1-6. Seattle, Canty 4-21.
SACKS—New Orleans, Johnson 2, Clarke 1, Howard 1. Seattle, Bellamy 1, King 1.

FALCONS 15, PANTHERS 10

Sunday, September 17

Atlanta	3	7	0	5—15
Carolina	0	10	0	0—10

First Quarter
Atl.—FG, Andersen 31, 5:56.

Second Quarter
Atl.—Anderson 26 run (Andersen kick), 4:03.
Car.—FG, Cunningham 33, 10:38.
Car.—Muhammad 9 pass from Beuerlein (Cunningham kick), 14:45.

Fourth Quarter
Atl.—FG, Andersen 27, 10:50.
Atl.—Evans returned Anderson fumble to own end zone, play ruled a safety, 12:48.
Attendance—73,025.

	Atlanta	Carolina
First downs	10	17
Rushes-yards	30-108	16-59
Passing	154	225
Punt returns	2-0	2-5
Kickoff returns	4-77	3-87
Interception returns	2-75	0-0
Comp.-att.-int.	21-27-0	21-38-2
Sacked-yards lost	2-20	4-16
Punts	6-43	5-29
Fumbles-lost	3-2	3-2
Penalties-yards	7-57	4-28
Time of possession	33:14	26:46

INDIVIDUAL STATISTICS

RUSHING—Atlanta, Anderson 22-97, Chandler 6-4, Christian 2-7. Carolina, Biakabutuka 12-45, Beuerlein 4-14.

PASSING—Atlanta, Chandler 21-27-0-174. Carolina, Beuerlein 21-37-2-241, Walter 0-1-0-0.

RECEIVING—Atlanta, Christian 6-26, Jefferson 5-77, Mathis 5-42, Finneran 3-17, Anderson 2-12. Carolina, Biakabutuka 5-62, Muhammad 5-34, Hayes 4-69, Walls 3-45, Mangum 2-16, Floyd 1-9, Byrd 1-6.

MISSED FIELD GOAL ATTEMPTS—Atlanta, Andersen 50, 47. Carolina, Cunningham 25.

INTERCEPTIONS—Atlanta, Buchanan 1-38, Ambrose 1-37.

KICKOFF RETURNS—Atlanta, Vaughn 3-66, Oliver 1-11. Carolina, Bates 2-57, Byrd 1-30.

PUNT RETURNS—Atlanta, Oliver 2-0. Carolina, Bates 1-5, Hitchcock 1-0.

SACKS—Atlanta, Wiley 2, Dronett 1, Hall 1. Carolina, Peter 1, White 1.

CHIEFS 42, CHARGERS 10

Sunday, September 17

San Diego	10	0	0	0—10
Kansas City	0	14	14	14—42

First Quarter
S.D.—Dumas 56 interception return (Carney kick), 4:38.
S.D.—FG, Carney 54, 13:41.

Second Quarter
K.C.—Morris 36 pass from Grbac (Stoyanovich kick), 4:48.
K.C.—Richardson 1 pass from Grbac (Stoyanovich kick), 14:13.

Third Quarter
K.C.—Morris 9 pass from Grbac (Stoyanovich kick), 7:34.
K.C.—Drayton 2 pass from Grbac (Stoyanovich kick), 10:22.

Fourth Quarter
K.C.—Morris 20 pass from Grbac (Stoyanovich kick), 2:34.
K.C.—Moreau 1 run (Stoyanovich kick), 13:03.
Attendance—77,604.

	San Diego	Kansas City
First downs	10	25
Rushes-yards	14-49	34-117
Passing	138	232
Punt returns	4-31	5-50
Kickoff returns	7-172	3-69
Interception returns	1-56	1-33
Comp.-att.-int.	17-35-1	20-33-1
Sacked-yards lost	6-31	2-3
Punts	6-57	5-50
Fumbles-lost	1-1	2-0
Penalties-yards	8-66	6-30
Time of possession	24:51	35:09

INDIVIDUAL STATISTICS

RUSHING—San Diego, Moreno 4-20, Bynum 4-17, Chancey 4-8, Fletcher 2-4. Kansas City, Moreau 18-58, Cloud 8-21, Richardson 6-40, Grbac 2-(minus 2).

PASSING—San Diego, Moreno 11-22-0-107, Leaf 6-13-1-62. Kansas City, Grbac 20-33-1-235.

RECEIVING—San Diego, Fletcher 7-66, F. Jones 4-45, Conway 2-18, Bynum 2-13, McCrary 1-19, Gaylor 1-8. Kansas City, Morris 6-112, Alexander 4-48, Gonzalez 2-43, Richardson 4-22, L. Parker 1-8, Drayton 1-2.

MISSED FIELD GOAL ATTEMPTS—San Diego, Carney 51.

INTERCEPTIONS—San Diego, Dumas 1-56. Kansas City, Bush 1-33.

KICKOFF RETURNS—San Diego, R. Jenkins 6-156, Bynum 1-16. Kansas City, L. Parker 2-44, Lockett 1-25.

PUNT RETURNS—San Diego, Jacquet 4-31. Kansas City, L. Parker 3-32, Lockett 2-18.

SACKS—San Diego, Beckett 1, Parrella 0.5, N. Smith 0.5. Kansas City, Hicks 2, D. Williams 2, Browning 1, McGlockton 1.

BROWNS 23, STEELERS 20

Sunday, September 17

Pittsburgh	0	10	10	0—20
Cleveland	14	0	3	6—23

First Quarter
Cle.—Shea 2 pass from Couch (P. Dawson kick), 4:26.
Cle.—Edwards 21 pass from Couch (P. Dawson kick), 11:25.

Second Quarter
Pit.—Huntley 4 run (K. Brown kick), 1:26.
Pit.—FG, K. Brown 41, 13:16.

Third Quarter
Pit.—FG, K. Brown 31, 2:21.
Cle.—FG, P. Dawson 23, 4:48.
Pit.—Bettis 10 run (K. Brown kick), 9:13.

Fourth Quarter
Cle.—FG, P. Dawson 28, 4:11.
Cle.—FG, P. Dawson 19, 12:15.
Attendance—73,018.

	Pittsburgh	Cleveland
First downs	19	14
Rushes-yards	30-159	23-61
Passing	187	316
Punt returns	4-60	1-5
Kickoff returns	5-138	5-145
Interception returns	0-0	1-0
Comp.-att.-int.	15-30-1	23-31-0
Sacked-yards lost	3-15	0-0
Punts	4-39	4-49
Fumbles-lost	1-0	1-1
Penalties-yards	4-35	4-26
Time of possession	31:12	28:48

INDIVIDUAL STATISTICS

RUSHING—Pittsburgh, Bettis 23-122, Huntley 3-6, Fuamatu-Ma'afala 2-22, Graham 1-7, Witman 1-2. Cleveland, Rhett 18-55, Prentice 4-3, Couch 1-3.

PASSING—Pittsburgh, Graham 14-28-0-193, Bettis 0-1-1-0, Stewart 1-1-0-9. Cleveland, Couch 23-31-0-316.

RECEIVING—Pittsburgh, Ward 5-85, Shaw 3-66, Witman 2-17, Fuamatu-Ma'afala 2-8, Bettis 1-11, Burress 1-10, Bruener 1-5. Cleveland, Chiavarini 5-26, Johnson 4-97, Shea 4-43, Patten 3-81, Northcutt 2-27, Rhett 2-11, Prentice 2-10, Edwards 1-21.

MISSED FIELD GOAL ATTEMPTS—None.

INTERCEPTIONS—Cleveland, Fuller 1-0.

KICKOFF RETURNS—Pittsburgh, Poteat 4-81, Ward 1-57. Cleveland, Patten 3-114, L. Jackson 2-31.

PUNT RETURNS—Pittsburgh, Poteat 2-43, Shaw 2-17. Cleveland, Northcutt 1-5.

SACKS—Cleveland, C. Brown 3.

BUCCANEERS 31, LIONS 10

Sunday, September 17

Tampa Bay	14	7	3	7—31
Detroit	3	7	0	0—10

First Quarter
Det.—FG, Hanson 38, 2:18.
T.B.—King 6 run (Gramatica kick), 9:12.
T.B.—Alstott 4 run (Gramatica kick), 14:24.

Second Quarter
T.B.—R. McDaniel 2 pass from King (Gramatica kick), 12:44.
Det.—Crowell 50 pass from Batch (Hanson kick), 15:00.

Third Quarter
T.B.—FG, Gramatica 24, 9:31.

Fourth Quarter
T.B.—Dunn 1 run (Gramatica kick), 9:21.
Attendance—76,928.

	Tampa Bay	Detroit
First downs	22	13
Rushes-yards	39-120	10-17
Passing	211	226
Punt returns	2-42	1-17
Kickoff returns	1-15	6-218
Interception returns	2-49	0-0
Comp.-att.-int.	18-30-0	26-36-2

	Tampa Bay	Detroit
Sacked-yards lost	0-0	7-51
Punts	4-39	5-29
Fumbles-lost	0-0	2-1
Penalties-yards	5-45	10-51
Time of possession	36:04	23:56

INDIVIDUAL STATISTICS

RUSHING—Tampa Bay, Alstott 21-68, Dunn 10-34, King 4-17, Stecker 3-2, Zeier 1-(minus 1). Detroit, J. Stewart 8-13, Batch 2-4.

PASSING—Tampa Bay, King 18-30-0-211. Detroit, Batch 26-36-2-277.

RECEIVING—Tampa Bay, K. Johnson 8-84, Green 3-56, Dunn 3-49, Anthony 2-17, Alstott 1-3, R. McDaniel 1-2. Detroit, Crowell 6-93, Moore 5-41, Sloan 4-53, J. Stewart 4-22, Morton 3-37, Olivo 1-14, Pupunu 1-6, Schlesinger 1-6, Stablein 1-5.

MISSED FIELD GOAL ATTEMPTS—Tampa Bay, Gramatica 38. Detroit, Hanson 34.

INTERCEPTIONS—Tampa Bay, Lynch 1-36, Abraham 1-13.

KICKOFF RETURNS—Tampa Bay, Stecker 1-15. Detroit, Howard 6-218.

PUNT RETURNS—Tampa Bay, Williams 2-42. Detroit, Howard 1-17.

SACKS—Tampa Bay, Sapp 3, McFarland 2.5, Jones 1, Ahanotu 0.5.

VIKINGS 21, PATRIOTS 13

Sunday, September 17

Minnesota	7	14	0	0—21
New England	7	0	0	6—13

First Quarter
Min.—Smith 4 run (Anderson kick), 8:54.
N.E.—Faulk 2 run (Vinatieri kick), 10:45.

Second Quarter
Min.—McWilliams 1 pass from Culpepper (Anderson kick), 5:07.
Min.—Hatchette 39 pass from Culpepper (Anderson kick), 9:42.

Fourth Quarter
N.E.—Glenn 8 pass from Bledsoe (run failed), 3:49.
Attendance—60,292.

	Minnesota	New England
First downs	23	18
Rushes-yards	43-154	18-103
Passing	161	164
Punt returns	2-8	4-35
Kickoff returns	2-51	3-88
Interception returns	1-0	1-0
Comp.-att.-int.	19-28-1	21-35-1
Sacked-yards lost	4-16	3-26
Punts	5-41	4-38
Fumbles-lost	2-1	0-0
Penalties-yards	5-61	9-64
Time of possession	39:08	20:52

INDIVIDUAL STATISTICS

RUSHING—Minnesota, Smith 29-91, Culpepper 12-59, Kleinsasser 2-4. New England, Faulk 13-80, Bledsoe 3-21, T. Carter 1-1, Pass 1-1.

PASSING—Minnesota, Culpepper 19-28-1-177. New England, Bledsoe 21-35-1-190.

RECEIVING—Minnesota, C. Carter 7-67, McWilliams 3-16, Hatchette 2-46, Moss 2-20, Smith 2-12, Walsh 1-8, J. Davis 1-5, Kleinsasser 1-3. New England, Glenn 8-69, Brown 7-62, Faulk 3-31, Bjornson 2-13, Calloway 1-15.

MISSED FIELD GOAL ATTEMPTS—New England, Vinatieri 44.

INTERCEPTIONS—Minnesota, Dishman 1-0. New England, Milloy 1-0.

KICKOFF RETURNS—Minnesota, M. Williams 1-27, T. Carter 1-24. New England, Faulk 2-56, S. Davis 1-32.

PUNT RETURNS—Minnesota, Walsh 1-11, D. Palmer 1-(minus 3). New England, Faulk 3-22, Brown 1-13.

SACKS—Minnesota, Paup 1, Hovan 1, Thomas 1. New England, Spires 1.5, Bruschi 1, Slade 1, Thomas 0.5.

BRONCOS 33, RAIDERS 24

Sunday, September 17

Denver	17	7	3	6—33
Oakland	7	17	0	0—24

First Quarter
Den.—McCaffrey 10 pass from Griese (Nedney kick), 6:15.
Den.—Pryce 28 fumble return (Nedney kick), 6:34.
Den.—FG, Nedney 24, 8:36.
Oak.—Brown 11 pass from Gannon (Janikowski kick), 12:24.

Second Quarter
Den.—Griffith 1 pass from Griese (Nedney kick), 0:33.
Oak.—FG, Janikowski 19, 4:35.
Oak.—Brown 9 pass from Gannon (Janikowski kick), 5:37.
Oak.—Jordan 3 blocked punt return (Janikowski kick), 7:12.

Third Quarter
Den.—FG, Nedney 32, 11:07.

Fourth Quarter
Den.—FG, Nedney 22, 1:53.
Den.—FG, Nedney 21, 10:12.
Attendance—62,078.

	Denver	Oakland
First downs	25	16
Rushes-yards	38-182	19-123
Passing	205	140
Punt returns	1-8	0-0
Kickoff returns	5-97	7-161
Interception returns	2-14	0-0
Comp.-att.-int.	21-31-0	13-21-2
Sacked-yards lost	2-8	4-19
Punts	1-0	2-47
Fumbles-lost	1-1	2-2
Penalties-yards	3-30	5-51
Time of possession	37:06	22:54

INDIVIDUAL STATISTICS

RUSHING—Denver, Anderson 32-187, Griese 5-(minus 5), Griffith 1-0. Oakland, Wheatley 12-27, Kaufman 5-86, Gannon 2-10.

PASSING—Denver, Griese 21-31-0-213. Oakland, Gannon 13-21-2-159.

RECEIVING—Denver, McCaffrey 7-92, R. Smith 7-63, Clark 2-22, Griffith 2-17, Carswell 2-17, Anderson 1-2. Oakland, Brown 7-92, Wheatley 2-15, Brigham 1-19, Dudley 1-13, Kaufman 1-12, Jordan 1-8.

MISSED FIELD GOAL ATTEMPTS—Oakland, Janikowski 49.

INTERCEPTIONS—Denver, Mobley 1-9, Buckley 1-5.

KICKOFF RETURNS—Denver, Cole 3-84, B. Miller 1-13, Carswell 1-0. Oakland, Dunn 4-88, Kaufman 3-73.

PUNT RETURNS—Denver, O'Neal 1-8.

SACKS—Denver, Pittman 2, Wilson 1.5, Romanowski 0.5. Oakland, Jackson 2.

GIANTS 14, BEARS 7

Sunday, September 17

N.Y. Giants	7	0	7	0—14
Chicago	0	7	0	0— 7

First Quarter
NYG—Dixon 34 pass from Collins (Daluiso kick), 4:22.

Second Quarter
Chi.—Kennison 2 pass from McNown (Edinger kick), 14:46.

Third Quarter
NYG—Barber 3 run (Daluiso kick), 9:34.
Attendance—66,944.

	N.Y. Giants	Chicago
First downs	23	12
Rushes-yards	41-172	16-48
Passing	235	174
Punt returns	3-26	2-20
Kickoff returns	1-9	3-68
Interception returns	0-0	0-0
Comp.-att.-int.	24-33-0	23-36-0
Sacked-yards lost	2-14	4-28
Punts	4-41	7-43
Fumbles-lost	1-1	2-1
Penalties-yards	2-15	2-30
Time of possession	38:11	21:49

INDIVIDUAL STATISTICS

RUSHING—New York, Dayne 19-69, Barber 17-86, Collins 3-1, Dixon 1-12, Comella 1-4. Chicago, Allen 10-31, Enis 5-13, McNown 1-4.

PASSING—New York, Collins 24-33-0-249. Chicago, McNown 23-36-0-202.

RECEIVING—New York, Barber 6-58, Toomer 5-24, Hilliard 4-54, Comella 4-31, Mitchell 2-17, Dixon 1-34, Cross 1-18, Campbell 1-13. Chicago, M. Robinson 9-84, Engram 4-38, Enis 3-26, Brooks 3-26, Allred 1-18, Allen 1-8, Kennison 1-2, White 1-0.

MISSED FIELD GOAL ATTEMPTS—New York, Daluiso 34, 41, 31. Chicago, Edinger 49.

INTERCEPTIONS—None.

KICKOFF RETURNS—New York, Comella 1-9. Chicago, Milburn 3-68.

PUNT RETURNS—New York, Barber 3-26. Chicago, Milburn 2-20.

SACKS—New York, Armstead 1, Barrow 1, Strahan 1, K. Hamilton 1. Chicago, Urlacher 1, Wilson 1.

JETS 27, BILLS 14

Sunday, September 17

Buffalo	7	7	0	0—14
N.Y. Jets	7	14	3	3—27

First Quarter

Buf.—Moulds 3 pass from Johnson (Christie kick), 8:50.

NYJ—Williams 97 kickoff return (Hall kick), 9:09.

Second Quarter

NYJ—Martin 5 run (Hall kick), 7:19.

Buf.—McDaniel 74 pass from Johnson (Christie kick), 13:53.

NYJ—Coleman 45 pass from Testaverde (Hall kick), 15:00.

Third Quarter

NYJ—FG, Hall 51, 7:45.

Fourth Quarter

NYJ—FG, Hall 27, 13:04.

Attendance—77,884.

	Buffalo	N.Y. Jets
First downs	16	15
Rushes-yards	23-80	36-91
Passing	274	188
Punt returns	3-22	3-27
Kickoff returns	5-94	2-117
Interception returns	1-2	1-1
Comp.-att.-int.	21-36-1	16-32-1
Sacked-yards lost	2-17	0-0
Punts	6-40	6-46
Fumbles-lost	3-3	0-0
Penalties-yards	7-66	3-10
Time of possession	26:49	33:11

INDIVIDUAL STATISTICS

RUSHING—Buffalo, Bryson 12-40, A. Smith 5-13, Johnson 3-18, Morris 3-9. New York, Martin 29-84, R. Anderson 3-3, Ward 2-10, Testaverde 1-(minus 1), Lucas 1-(minus 5).

PASSING—Buffalo, Johnson 21-36-1-291. New York, Testaverde 16-32-1-188.

RECEIVING—Buffalo, Moulds 8-78, Riemersma 3-48, Collins 3-33, Morris 3-11, McDaniel 2-93, P. Price 1-20, Jackson 1-8. New York, Martin 4-44, Chrebet 4-36, R. Anderson 4-29, Coleman 1-45, Brisby 1-17, Ward 1-14, Wiggins 1-3.

MISSED FIELD GOAL ATTEMPTS—Buffalo, Christie 43. New York, Hall 33.

INTERCEPTIONS—Buffalo, Cowart 1-2. New York, Frost 1-1.

KICKOFF RETURNS—Buffalo, Watson 4-77, Morris 1-17. New York, Williams 2-117.

PUNT RETURNS—Buffalo, Watson 3-22. New York, Ward 3-27.

SACKS—New York, Phifer 1, Cox 0.5, Abraham 0.5.

RAMS 41, 49ERS 24

Sunday, September 17

San Francisco	7	10	0	7—24
St. Louis	3	14	7	17—41

First Quarter

S.F.—Beasley 29 pass from Garcia (Richey kick), 0:31.

St.L.—FG, Wilkins 47, 4:00.

Second Quarter

S.F.—FG, Richey 21, 4:15.

St.L.—Horne 18 pass from Warner (Wilkins kick), 9:51.

S.F.—Garner 20 pass from Garcia (Richey kick), 12:46.

St.L.—Bruce 78 pass from Warner (Wilkins kick), 13:07.

Third Quarter

St.L.—Faulk 1 run (Wilkins kick), 6:32.

Fourth Quarter

St.L.—FG, Wilkins 25, 0:03.

S.F.—Owens 12 pass from Garcia (Richey kick), 2:58.

St.L.—Faulk 4 run (Wilkins kick), 7:21.

St.L.—Faulk 1 run (Wilkins kick), 13:18.

Attendance—65,945.

	San Francisco	St. Louis
First downs	16	32
Rushes-yards	21-111	28-140
Passing	290	389
Punt returns	2-19	3-7
Kickoff returns	4-86	4-76
Interception returns	2-11	2-22
Comp.-att.-int.	21-34-2	23-34-2
Sacked-yards lost	0-0	1-5
Punts	6-40	3-51
Fumbles-lost	0-0	2-0
Penalties-yards	7-53	3-25
Time of possession	26:53	33:07

INDIVIDUAL STATISTICS

RUSHING—San Francisco, Garner 15-87, Beasley 3-10, Garcia 2-12, Jackson 1-2. St. Louis, Faulk 25-134, Hakim 1-4, Holcombe 1-3, Warner 1-(minus 1).

PASSING—San Francisco, Garcia 21-34-2-290. St. Louis, Warner 23-34-2-394.

RECEIVING—San Francisco, Owens 6-108, Garner 5-40, Beasley 4-47, Rice 3-44, Clark 2-13, Streets 1-38. St. Louis, Bruce 8-188, Faulk 7-65, Holt 4-94, Hakim 2-18, Horne 1-18, R. Williams 1-11.

MISSED FIELD GOAL ATTEMPTS—None.

INTERCEPTIONS—San Francisco, Tubbs 1-11, Keith 1-0. St. Louis, Bly 1-22, McCleon 1-0.

KICKOFF RETURNS—San Francisco, Jervey 3-73, Milem 1-13. St. Louis, Horne 3-59, Fletcher 1-17.

PUNT RETURNS—San Francisco, K. Williams 2-19. St. Louis, Hakim 3-7.

SACKS—San Francisco, Engelberger 1.

PACKERS 6, EAGLES 3

Sunday, September 17

Philadelphia	0	3	0	0—3
Green Bay	0	0	3	3—6

Second Quarter

Phi.—FG, Akers 43, 13:00.

Third Quarter

G.B.—FG, Longwell 37, 8:52.

Fourth Quarter

G.B.—FG, Longwell 38, 14:57.

Attendance—59,869.

	Philadelphia	Green Bay
First downs	12	19
Rushes-yards	22-85	29-79
Passing	86	157
Punt returns	4-30	5-45
Kickoff returns	2-47	2-46
Interception returns	3-20	1-7
Comp.-att.-int.	15-31-1	18-33-3
Sacked-yards lost	5-32	5-32
Punts	9-46	5-45
Fumbles-lost	1-0	1-1
Penalties-yards	12-115	5-31
Time of possession	27:40	32:20

INDIVIDUAL STATISTICS

RUSHING—Philadelphia, Staley 17-60, McNabb 3-20, Mitchell 2-5. Green Bay, Levens 24-74, Green 3-3, Favre 2-2.

PASSING—Philadelphia, McNabb 15-31-1-118. Green Bay, Favre 18-33-3-189.

RECEIVING—Philadelphia, Staley 8-62, C. Johnson 3-20, C. Martin 2-17, Broughton 1-10, Pritchett 1-9. Green Bay, T. Davis 5-41, Freeman 3-35, Franks 3-13, Driver 2-50, Levens 2-15, Schroeder 1-18, Green 1-16, Henderson 1-1.

MISSED FIELD GOAL ATTEMPTS—Green Bay, Longwell 40.

INTERCEPTIONS—Philadelphia, Moore 1-20, Dawkins 1-0, Vincent 1-0. Green Bay, Sharper 1-7.

KICKOFF RETURNS—Philadelphia, Mitchell 2-47. Green Bay, Rossum 1-24, Berry 1-22.

PUNT RETURNS—Philadelphia, Mitchell 4-30. Green Bay, Rossum 5-45.

SACKS—Philadelphia, H. Douglas 2.5, H. Thomas 1, Grasmanis 1, Mamula 0.5. Green Bay, S. Dotson 1.5, B. Harris 1, Bowens 1, Thierry 1, McGarrahan 0.5.

COWBOYS 27, REDSKINS 21

Monday, September 18

Dallas	7	7	3	10—27
Washington	7	0	7	7—21

First Quarter
Was.—Davis 7 run (Husted kick), 6:47.
Dal.—Warren 76 pass from Cunningham (Seder kick), 12:28.

Second Quarter
Dal.—E. Smith 3 run (Seder kick), 4:15.

Third Quarter
Dal.—FG, Seder 32, 5:19.
Was.—Davis 1 run (Husted kick), 10:23.

Fourth Quarter
Dal.—Harris 16 pass from Cunningham (Seder kick), 5:41.
Was.—Sellers 7 pass from B. Johnson (Husted kick), 9:26.
Dal.—FG, Seder 38, 13:14.
Attendance—84,431.

	Dallas	Washington
First downs	15	24
Rushes-yards	31-153	29-107
Passing	179	227
Punt returns	4-12	3-54

	Dallas	Washington
Kickoff returns	4-89	5-111
Interception returns	1-46	1-0
Comp.-att.-int.	10-23-1	30-49-1
Sacked-yards lost	1-6	3-14
Punts	5-46	7-40
Fumbles-lost	2-1	3-1
Penalties-yards	4-20	6-82
Time of possession	24:54	35:06

INDIVIDUAL STATISTICS

RUSHING—Dallas, E. Smith 24-83, Cunningham 3-32, Ismail 2-30, Warren 2-8. Washington, Davis 25-91, B. Johnson 2-2, Centers 1-11, Murrell 1-3.

PASSING—Dallas, Cunningham 10-23-1-185. Washington, B. Johnson 30-49-1-241.

RECEIVING—Dallas, Warren 3-86, Ismail 3-65, Harris 2-28, McKnight 1-6, E. Smith 1-0. Washington, Murrell 8-48, Fryar 6-47, Davis 5-54, Thrash 3-21, Centers 3-20, Connell 2-20, Alexander 1-15, Reed 1-9, Sellers 1-7.

MISSED FIELD GOAL ATTEMPTS—None.

INTERCEPTIONS—Dallas, Reese 1-46. Washington, Shade 1-0.

KICKOFF RETURNS—Dallas, Wiley 4-89. Washington, Thrash 5-111.

PUNT RETURNS—Dallas, Tucker 3-12, McGarity 1-0. Washington, Sanders 3-0.

SACKS—Dallas, Lett 1, Ekuban 1, Ellis 1. Washington, Coleman 1.

WEEK 4

STANDINGS

AFC EAST

	W	L	T	Pct.
N.Y. Jets	4	0	0	1.000
Miami	3	1	0	.750
Buffalo	2	1	0	.667
Indianapolis	2	1	0	.667
New England	0	4	0	.000

AFC CENTRAL

	W	L	T	Pct.
Baltimore	3	1	0	.750
Tennessee	2	1	0	.667
Cleveland	2	2	0	.500
Jacksonville	2	2	0	.500
Cincinnati	0	3	0	.000
Pittsburgh	0	3	0	.000

AFC WEST

	W	L	T	Pct.
Oakland	3	1	0	.750
Denver	2	2	0	.500
Kansas City	2	2	0	.500
Seattle	2	2	0	.500
San Diego	0	4	0	.000

NFC EAST

	W	L	T	Pct.
N.Y. Giants	3	1	0	.750
Philadelphia	2	2	0	.500
Washington	2	2	0	.500
Arizona	1	2	0	.333
Dallas	1	3	0	.250

NFC CENTRAL

	W	L	T	Pct.
Minnesota	3	0	0	1.000
Detroit	3	1	0	.750
Tampa Bay	3	1	0	.750
Green Bay	2	2	0	.500
Chicago	0	4	0	.000

NFC WEST

	W	L	T	Pct.
St. Louis	4	0	0	1.000
Atlanta	2	2	0	.500
Carolina	1	2	0	.333
New Orleans	1	3	0	.250
San Francisco	1	3	0	.250

TOP PERFORMANCES

100-YARD RUSHING GAMES

Player, Team & Opponent	Att.	Yds.	TD
Charlie Garner, S.F. at Dal.	36	201	1
Jamal Lewis, Balt. vs. Cin.	25	116	1
Ricky Williams, N.O. vs. Phi.	20	103	0

300-YARD PASSING GAMES

Player, Team & Opponent	Att.	Comp.	Yds.	TD	Int.
Peyton Manning, Ind. vs. Jack.	36	23	440	4	0
Kurt Warner, St.L. at Atl.	19	12	336	4	1

100-YARD RECEIVING GAMES

Player, Team & Opponent	Rec.	Yds.	TD
Torry Holt, St.L. at Atl.	3	189	2
Terrence Wilkins, Ind. vs. Jack.	9	148	1
Rod Smith, Den. vs. K.C.	8	134	0
Jimmy Smith, Jack. at Ind.	9	132	2
James McKnight, Dal. vs. S.F.	6	129	0
Tony Gonzalez, K.C. at Den.	10	127	1
Albert Connell, Wash. at NYG	4	122	0
Carl Pickens, Ten. at Pit.	2	105	0
Marvin Harrison, Ind. vs. Jack.	2	103	1

RESULTS

SUNDAY, SEPTEMBER 24

BALTIMORE 37, Cincinnati 0
Detroit 21, CHICAGO 14
Green Bay 29, ARIZONA 3
Kansas City 23, DENVER 22
MIAMI 10, New England 3
N.Y. Jets 21, TAMPA BAY 17
OAKLAND 36, Cleveland 10
Philadelphia 21, NEW ORLEANS 7
St. Louis 41, ATLANTA 20
San Francisco 41, DALLAS 24
Seattle 20, SAN DIEGO 12
Tennessee 23, PITTSBURGH 20
Washington 16, N.Y. GIANTS 6

MONDAY, SEPTEMBER 25

INDIANAPOLIS 43, Jacksonville 14
Open date: Buffalo, Carolina, Minnesota

RAVENS 37, BENGALS 0

Sunday, September 24

Cincinnati	0	0	0	0— 0
Baltimore	10	14	3	10—37

First Quarter
Bal.—FG, Stover 30, 6:22.
Bal.—Taylor 8 pass from Banks (Stover kick), 14:10.

Second Quarter
Bal.—Ja. Lewis 11 run (Stover kick), 0:04.
Bal.—Sharpe 1 pass from Banks (Stover kick), 11:55.

Third Quarter
Bal.—FG, Stover 37, 11:57.

Fourth Quarter
Bal.—Ayanbadejo 1 run (Stover kick), 8:21.
Bal.—FG, Stover 19, 13:03.
Attendance—68,481.

	Cincinnati	Baltimore
First downs	7	27
Rushes-yards	16-4	38-176
Passing	90	215
Punt returns	1-9	2-37
Kickoff returns	8-147	1-26
Interception returns	0-0	2-2
Comp.-att.-int.	15-24-2	22-39-0
Sacked-yards lost	4-15	0-0
Punts	4-37	1-33
Fumbles-lost	2-2	1-1
Penalties-yards	8-53	10-90
Time of possession	21:16	38:44

INDIVIDUAL STATISTICS
RUSHING—Cincinnati, Dillon 12-9, Bennett 2-(minus 7), S. Mitchell 1-3, Groce 1-(minus 1). Baltimore, Ja. Lewis 25-116, Holmes 8-51, Ayanbadejo 4-9, Redman 1-0.
PASSING—Cincinnati, S. Mitchell 14-23-2-97, Smith 1-1-0-8. Baltimore, Banks 20-36-0-196, Redman 2-3-0-19.
RECEIVING—Cincinnati, Groce 4-24, Dillon 3-22, Warrick 3-15, Dugans 2-19, N. Williams 2-18, Farmer 1-7. Baltimore, Sharpe 5-40, Holmes 4-48, Taylor 4-32, Ayanbadejo 3-22, J. Lewis 2-33, Ja. Lewis 2-25, Ismail 2-15.
MISSED FIELD GOAL ATTEMPTS—None.
INTERCEPTIONS—Baltimore, Woodson 1-2, Starks 1-0.
KICKOFF RETURNS—Cincinnati, Griffin 5-85, Mack 2-40, Heath 1-22. Baltimore, Harris 1-26.
PUNT RETURNS—Cincinnati, Griffin 1-9. Baltimore, J. Lewis 2-37.
SACKS—Baltimore, Burnett 2, Brown 1, Boulware 1.

EAGLES 21, SAINTS 7

Sunday, September 24

Philadelphia	0	14	7	0—21
New Orleans	7	0	0	0— 7

First Quarter
N.O.—Blake 10 run (Brien kick), 7:16.

Second Quarter
Phi.—Lewis 16 pass from McNabb (Akers kick), 1:45.
Phi.—C. Johnson 21 pass from McNabb (Akers kick), 2:05.

Third Quarter
Phi.—Mitchell 72 punt return (Akers kick), 10:58.
Attendance—64,900.

	Philadelphia	New Orleans
First downs	14	17
Rushes-yards	25-67	24-141
Passing	201	146
Punt returns	2-72	3-9
Kickoff returns	2-53	4-68
Interception returns	2-17	0-0
Comp.-att.-int.	20-32-0	19-39-2
Sacked-yards lost	3-21	5-22
Punts	7-42	7-39
Fumbles-lost	3-2	2-2
Penalties-yards	10-64	5-40
Time of possession	29:21	30:39

INDIVIDUAL STATISTICS
RUSHING—Philadelphia, Staley 18-44, McNabb 7-23. New Orleans, R. Williams 20-103, Blake 4-38.
PASSING—Philadelphia, McNabb 20-32-0-222. New Orleans, Blake 19-39-2-168.
RECEIVING—Philadelphia, Small 5-74, Lewis 5-43, C. Johnson 3-48, Staley 3-16, Broughton 2-22, Pinkston 1-11, Brown 1-8. New Orleans, R. Williams 7-52, Reed 5-67, Horn 4-34, T. Smith 2-7, Jackson 1-8.
MISSED FIELD GOAL ATTEMPTS—None.
INTERCEPTIONS—Philadelphia, Vincent 2-17.
KICKOFF RETURNS—Philadelphia, Mitchell 2-53. New Orleans, Morton 4-68.
PUNT RETURNS—Philadelphia, Mitchell 1-72, Jas. Bostic 1-0. New Orleans, Morton 3-9.
SACKS—Philadelphia, H. Douglas 1.5, Simon 1.5, H. Thomas 1, Grasmanis 1. New Orleans, Kei. Mitchell 1, Whitehead 1, Howard 1.

RAMS 41, FALCONS 20

Sunday, September 24

St. Louis	3	14	10	14—41
Atlanta	7	6	0	7—20

First Quarter
Atl.—Anderson 3 run (Andersen kick), 4:08.
St.L.—FG, Wilkins 30, 8:27.

Second Quarter
St.L.—Bruce 14 pass from Warner (Wilkins kick), 1:46.
Atl.—FG, Andersen 37, 12:23.
St.L.—Holt 80 pass from Warner (Wilkins kick), 12:46.
Atl.—FG, Andersen 45, 15:00.

Third Quarter
St.L.—Lyle 94 fumble return (Wilkins kick), 3:02.
St.L.—FG, Wilkins 30, 5:27.

Fourth Quarter
St.L.—Holt 85 pass from Warner (Wilkins kick), 3:05.
Atl.—R. Kelly 37 pass from Chandler (Andersen kick), 5:24.
St.L.—Bruce 66 pass from Warner (Wilkins kick), 5:45.
Attendance—58,761.

	St. Louis	Atlanta
First downs	14	18
Rushes-yards	25-74	21-68
Passing	321	218
Punt returns	3-(-1)	0-0
Kickoff returns	2-58	4-90
Interception returns	2-11	1-8
Comp.-att.-int.	12-19-1	22-38-2
Sacked-yards lost	3-15	8-46
Punts	3-43	5-41
Fumbles-lost	2-1	3-2
Penalties-yards	10-90	5-42
Time of possession	27:16	32:44

INDIVIDUAL STATISTICS
RUSHING—St. Louis, Faulk 20-78, Watson 2-2, Warner 2-(minus 3), Horne 1-(minus 3). Atlanta, Anderson 15-41, Rivers 5-23, Christian 1-4.
PASSING—St. Louis, Warner 12-19-1-336. Atlanta, Chandler 21-35-2-255, Kanell 1-3-0-9.
RECEIVING—St. Louis, Holt 3-189, Bruce 3-92, Faulk 3-18, Hakim 1-20, Holcombe 1-10, Robinson 1-7. Atlanta, Mathis 8-82, Jefferson 5-51, R. Kelly 4-83, Christian 2-20, Anderson 1-12, Finneran 1-8, Kozlowski 1-8.
MISSED FIELD GOAL ATTEMPTS—None.
INTERCEPTIONS—St. Louis, Bly 1-8, McCleon 1-3. Atlanta, Kerney 1-8.
KICKOFF RETURNS—St. Louis, Horne 2-58. Atlanta, Vaughn 4-90.
PUNT RETURNS—St. Louis, Hakim 2-(minus 1), McCleon 1-0.
SACKS—St. Louis, Wistrom 3, Styles 1, Bly 1, Zgonina 1, Carter 1, Hobgood-Chittick 1. Atlanta, Crockett 1, Hall 1, Kerney 1.

LIONS 21, BEARS 14

Sunday, September 24

Detroit	7	7	0	7—21
Chicago	0	0	14	0—14

First Quarter
Det.—Morton 13 pass from Batch (Hanson kick), 8:30.

– 136 –

Second Quarter

Det.—Crowell 36 pass from Batch (Hanson kick), 14:42.

Third Quarter

Chi.—M. Robinson 55 pass from McNown (Edinger kick), 6:20.
Chi.—McNown 14 run (Edinger kick), 11:47.

Fourth Quarter

Det.—J. Stewart 1 run (Hanson kick), 5:24.
Attendance—66,944.

	Detroit	Chicago
First downs	15	16
Rushes-yards	29-80	31-147
Passing	194	254
Punt returns	1-22	4-30
Kickoff returns	3-47	4-63
Interception returns	3-8	1-0
Comp.-att.-int.	20-37-1	21-35-3
Sacked-yards lost	3-13	1-7
Punts	10-41	6-27
Fumbles-lost	1-0	6-2
Penalties-yards	6-39	9-78
Time of possession	31:38	28:22

INDIVIDUAL STATISTICS

RUSHING—Detroit, J. Stewart 23-71, Batch 4-2, Bates 2-7. Chicago, Allen 19-87, McNown 10-52, Enis 1-5, Barnes 1-3.

PASSING—Detroit, Batch 20-37-1-207. Chicago, McNown 21-35-3-261.

RECEIVING—Detroit, Morton 5-55, J. Stewart 5-25, Sloan 3-23, Crowell 2-65, Moore 2-21, Irvin 2-14, Howard 1-4. Chicago, M. Robinson 5-97, Booker 5-56, Kennison 5-35, Mayes 2-25, Brooks 2-15, Allred 1-25, Allen 1-8.

MISSED FIELD GOAL ATTEMPTS—Detroit, Hanson 32.

INTERCEPTIONS—Detroit, Schulz 3-8. Chicago, Urlacher 1-0.

KICKOFF RETURNS—Detroit, Howard 3-47. Chicago, Milburn 3-63, Tucker 1-0.

PUNT RETURNS—Detroit, Howard 1-22. Chicago, Milburn 4-30.

SACKS—Detroit, Scroggins 1. Chicago, Urlacher 1, Daniels 1, Flanigan 1.

49ERS 41, COWBOYS 24

Sunday, September 24

San Francisco	3	14	10	14—41
Dallas	0	10	0	14—24

First Quarter

S.F.—FG, Richey 38, 13:44.

Second Quarter

Dal.—FG, Seder 40, 3:55.
S.F.—Garner 1 run (Richey kick), 7:58.
S.F.—Owens 3 pass from Garcia (Richey kick), 12:11.
Dal.—E. Smith 1 run (Seder kick), 13:18.

Third Quarter

S.F.—Rice 68 pass from Garcia (Richey kick), 1:46.
S.F.—FG, Richey 47, 4:17.

Fourth Quarter

S.F.—Rice 5 pass from Garcia (Richey kick), 0:45.
Dal.—Harris 11 pass from Aikman (Seder kick), 3:52.
S.F.—Owens 1 pass from Garcia (Richey kick), 10:55.
Dal.—Harris 16 pass from Stoerner (Seder kick), 11:37.
Attendance—64,127.

	San Francisco	Dallas
First downs	27	18
Rushes-yards	47-261	14-76
Passing	178	222
Punt returns	1-15	0-0
Kickoff returns	4-69	6-127
Interception returns	1-2	0-0
Comp.-att.-int.	16-27-0	19-32-1
Sacked-yards lost	0-0	3-28
Punts	1-52	3-45
Fumbles-lost	0-0	2-2
Penalties-yards	8-94	5-62
Time of possession	37:13	22:47

INDIVIDUAL STATISTICS

RUSHING—San Francisco, Garner 36-201, Garcia 6-43, Beasley 4-11, Lewis 1-6. Dallas, E. Smith 11-31, Coakley 1-26, Warren 1-18, Wiley 1-1.

PASSING—San Francisco, Garcia 16-26-0-178, Rice 0-1-0-0. Dallas, Aikman 15-26-1-197, Stoerner 4-6-0-53.

RECEIVING—San Francisco, Owens 5-51, Rice 4-73, Garner 3-34, Clark 2-13, Streets 1-6, Beasley 1-1. Dallas, McKnight 6-129, Harris 3-32, Thomas 3-28, Ismail 2-38, Warren 2-14, Tucker 2-1, Wiley 1-8.

MISSED FIELD GOAL ATTEMPTS—None.

INTERCEPTIONS—San Francisco, Peterson 1-2.

KICKOFF RETURNS—San Francisco, K. Williams 4-69. Dallas, Wiley 3-64, Tucker 2-55, Noble 1-8.

PUNT RETURNS—San Francisco, K. Williams 1-15.

SACKS—San Francisco, Killings 1, Buckner 1, Engelberger 1.

TITANS 23, STEELERS 20

Sunday, September 24

Tennessee	10	0	3	10—23
Pittsburgh	3	3	0	14—20

First Quarter

Ten.—E. George 20 run (Del Greco kick), 3:36.
Pit.—FG, K. Brown 32, 8:10.
Ten.—FG, Del Greco 24, 13:30.

Second Quarter

Pit.—FG, K. Brown 32, 4:49.

Third Quarter

Ten.—FG, Del Greco 40, 8:48.

Fourth Quarter

Pit.—Stewart 1 run (K. Brown kick), 0:02.
Ten.—FG, Del Greco 40, 2:18.
Pit.—Bettis 5 run (K. Brown kick), 7:10.
Ten.—Kinney 18 pass from McNair (Del Greco kick), 13:35.
Attendance—51,769.

	Tennessee	Pittsburgh
First downs	15	20
Rushes-yards	31-85	25-115
Passing	287	249
Punt returns	5-70	0-0
Kickoff returns	5-117	6-146
Interception returns	0-0	3-36
Comp.-att.-int.	16-30-3	19-37-0
Sacked-yards lost	1-5	3-11
Punts	4-42	7-48
Fumbles-lost	1-0	1-1
Penalties-yards	3-25	5-35
Time of possession	30:32	29:28

INDIVIDUAL STATISTICS

RUSHING—Tennessee, E. George 27-74, McNair 2-8, O'Donnell 2-3. Pittsburgh, Bettis 19-77, Fuamatu-Ma'afala 4-21, Stewart 2-17.

PASSING—Tennessee, O'Donnell 13-27-3-237, McNair 3-3-0-55. Pittsburgh, Graham 18-33-0-254, Stewart 1-4-0-6.

RECEIVING—Tennessee, Mason 5-71, Sanders 4-54, Pickens 2-105, Kinney 2-35, Wycheck 1-24, E. George 1-2, Neal 1-1. Pittsburgh, Ward 5-59, Edwards 3-50, Fuamatu-Ma'afala 3-36, Bettis 3-20, Shaw 2-38, Geason 1-36, Burress 1-17, Bruener 1-4.

MISSED FIELD GOAL ATTEMPTS—Pittsburgh, K. Brown 50.

INTERCEPTIONS—Pittsburgh, Scott 2-38, Washington 1-(minus 2).

KICKOFF RETURNS—Tennessee, Mason 4-102, Neal 1-15. Pittsburgh, Edwards 3-77, Ward 3-69.

PUNT RETURNS—Tennessee, Mason 5-70.

SACKS—Tennessee, Salave'a 2, Embray 1. Pittsburgh, Gildon 1.

DOLPHINS 10, PATRIOTS 3

Sunday, September 24

New England	0	3	0	0— 3
Miami	0	10	0	0—10

Second Quarter

N.E.—FG, Vinatieri 40, 0:17.
Mia.—Emanuel 53 pass from Fiedler (Mare kick), 3:30.
Mia.—FG, Mare 43, 14:53.
Attendance—73,344.

	New England	Miami
First downs	12	12
Rushes-yards	29-56	33-99
Passing	150	143
Punt returns	3-25	4-50
Kickoff returns	2-27	1-25
Interception returns	2-48	1-3

	New England	Miami
Comp.-att.-int.	16-33-1	12-24-2
Sacked-yards lost	2-11	1-10
Punts	6-47	6-44
Fumbles-lost	2-1	1-1
Penalties-yards	3-30	5-40
Time of possession	29:58	30:02

INDIVIDUAL STATISTICS

RUSHING—New England, Faulk 21-46, Shaw 3-2, T. Carter 2-8, Bledsoe 2-5, Brown 1-(minus 5). Miami, L. Smith 20-42, Fiedler 8-21, T. Thomas 4-37, Emanuel 1-(minus 1).

PASSING—New England, Bledsoe 16-33-1-161. Miami, Fiedler 12-24-2-153.

RECEIVING—New England, Glenn 5-65, Brown 4-38, Bjornson 2-15, Shaw 2-11, Calloway 1-17, Simmons 1-9, Faulk 1-6. Miami, Gadsden 4-60, Shepherd 3-23, Emanuel 2-58, Konrad 2-11, T. Thomas 1-1.

MISSED FIELD GOAL ATTEMPTS—New England, Vinatieri 53.

INTERCEPTIONS—New England, Law 1-32, Thomas 1-16. Miami, Jeffries 1-3.

KICKOFF RETURNS—New England, Faulk 1-14, S. Davis 1-13. Miami, Marion 1-25.

PUNT RETURNS—New England, Brown 3-25. Miami, Shepherd 2-32, Kelly 2-18.

SACKS—New England, T. Johnson 0.5, Slade 0.5. Miami, Armstrong 2.

CHIEFS 23, BRONCOS 22

Sunday, September 24

Kansas City	7	0	7	9—23
Denver	3	9	10	0—22

First Quarter
K.C.—Richardson 1 run (Stoyanovich kick), 5:50.
Den.—FG, Nedney 22, 12:58.

Second Quarter
Den.—FG, Nedney 20, 6:07.
Den.—Crockett 26 interception return (pass failed), 8:20.

Third Quarter
Den.—Anderson 16 run (Nedney kick), 3:34.
K.C.—Gonzalez 15 pass from Grbac (Stoyanovich kick), 7:37.
Den.—FG, Nedney 43, 11:04.

Fourth Quarter
K.C.—FG, Stoyanovich 42, 6:41.
K.C.—Alexander 22 pass from Grbac (pass failed), 12:39.
Attendance—74,596.

	Kansas City	Denver
First downs	21	21
Rushes-yards	27-49	30-145
Passing	245	197
Punt returns	0-0	3-37
Kickoff returns	5-108	5-122
Interception returns	1-15	2-26
Comp.-att.-int.	21-33-2	18-31-1
Sacked-yards lost	1-5	1-11
Punts	4-50	2-47
Fumbles-lost	1-1	2-2
Penalties-yards	8-48	6-71
Time of possession	30:19	29:41

INDIVIDUAL STATISTICS

RUSHING—Kansas City, Richardson 14-35, Moreau 6-8, Cloud 4-5, Grbac 3-1. Denver, Anderson 22-85, Davis 6-41, Frerotte 2-19.

PASSING—Kansas City, Grbac 21-33-2-250. Denver, Frerotte 18-31-1-208.

RECEIVING—Kansas City, Gonzalez 10-127, Alexander 3-35, Richardson 2-35, Lockett 2-16, Morris 2-13, Cloud 1-13, Drayton 1-11. Denver, R. Smith 8-134, Carswell 3-27, Anderson 3-19, McCaffrey 2-20, Griffith 2-8.

MISSED FIELD GOAL ATTEMPTS—Denver, Nedney 50.

INTERCEPTIONS—Kansas City, Patton 1-15. Denver, Crockett 2-26.

KICKOFF RETURNS—Kansas City, Hall 5-108. Denver, Cole 5-122.

PUNT RETURNS—Denver, O'Neal 3-37.

SACKS—Kansas City, Wesley 1. Denver, Pittman 1.

RAIDERS 36, BROWNS 10

Sunday, September 24

Cleveland	7	0	3	0—10
Oakland	7	21	0	8—36

First Quarter
Cle.—Chiaverini 15 pass from Couch (P. Dawson kick), 4:43.
Oak.—Wheatley 2 run (Janikowski kick), 7:39.

Second Quarter
Oak.—Wheatley 2 run (Janikowski kick), 1:33.
Oak.—Crockett 2 run (Janikowski kick), 13:43.
Oak.—W. Thomas 46 interception return (Janikowski kick), 14:18.

Third Quarter
Cle.—FG, P. Dawson 29, 12:11.

Fourth Quarter
Oak.—FG, Janikowski 37, 1:46.
Oak.—FG, Janikowski 31, 9:09.
Oak.—Couch intentionally grounded ball in end zone for a safety, 9:26.
Attendance—45,702.

	Cleveland	Oakland
First downs	14	18
Rushes-yards	21-89	36-113
Passing	141	179
Punt returns	4-40	3-13
Kickoff returns	5-65	1-14
Interception returns	0-0	2-58
Comp.-att.-int.	18-34-2	14-25-0
Sacked-yards lost	3-15	1-0
Punts	5-45	6-47
Fumbles-lost	1-0	0-0
Penalties-yards	8-46	5-40
Time of possession	27:03	32:57

INDIVIDUAL STATISTICS

RUSHING—Cleveland, Rhett 15-85, Couch 3-3, Prentice 3-1. Oakland, Wheatley 21-63, Kaufman 7-37, Jordan 4-6, Hoying 2-(minus 3), Gannon 1-8, Crockett 1-2.

PASSING—Cleveland, Couch 16-29-2-141, Wynn 2-5-0-15. Oakland, Gannon 14-23-0-179, Hoying 0-2-0-0.

RECEIVING—Cleveland, Prentice 5-45, Johnson 3-19, Chiaverini 2-24, Rhett 2-22, Campbell 2-16, Shea 2-7, Edwards 1-15, Northcutt 1-8. Oakland, Brown 3-54, Rison 3-54, Dudley 3-44, Ritchie 3-13, Kaufman 1-13, Jordan 1-1.

MISSED FIELD GOAL ATTEMPTS—Cleveland, P. Dawson 42.

INTERCEPTIONS—Oakland, W. Thomas 2-58.

KICKOFF RETURNS—Cleveland, Patten 4-53, Campbell 1-12. Oakland, Dunn 1-14.

PUNT RETURNS—Cleveland, Northcutt 4-40. Oakland, Gordon 3-13.

SACKS—Cleveland, Holland 1. Oakland, Jackson 1, Bryant 1, Coleman 1.

SEAHAWKS 20, CHARGERS 12

Sunday, September 24

Seattle	10	3	7	0—20
San Diego	6	6	0	0—12

First Quarter
Sea.—FG, Heppner 25, 4:55.
S.D.—FG, Carney 41, 11:23.
S.D.—FG, Carney 28, 13:56.
Sea.—Jackson 68 pass from Kitna (Heppner kick), 14:55.

Second Quarter
S.D.—FG, Carney 24, 11:04.
Sea.—FG, Heppner 26, 14:24.
S.D.—FG, Carney 45, 15:00.

Third Quarter
Sea.—W. Williams 69 interception return (Heppner kick), 8:10.
Attendance—47,233.

	Seattle	San Diego
First downs	15	15
Rushes-yards	25-108	24-91
Passing	161	212
Punt returns	5-44	3-9
Kickoff returns	4-95	5-100
Interception returns	2-69	0-0
Comp.-att.-int.	11-21-0	24-40-2
Sacked-yards lost	5-35	2-8
Punts	5-45	6-45
Fumbles-lost	2-2	3-0
Penalties-yards	5-45	9-71
Time of possession	26:44	33:16

INDIVIDUAL STATISTICS

RUSHING—Seattle, Watters 16-67, Kitna 6-22, Alexander 3-19. San Diego, Fazande 11-36, Fletcher 5-40, McCrary 5-9, Leaf 2-3, Harbaugh 1-3.

PASSING—Seattle, Kitna 11-21-0-196. San Diego, Leaf 16-26-1-153, Harbaugh 8-14-1-67.

RECEIVING—Seattle, Mili 3-45, Dawkins 3-37, Jackson 1-68, Watters 1-14, Fauria 1-13, Bailey 1-10, Strong 1-9. San Diego, F. Jones 8-82, Conway 4-45, Ricks 2-29, R. Jones 2-15, Heiden 2-9, Fazande 2-6, Fletcher 2-3, Jacquet 1-25, McCrary 1-6.

MISSED FIELD GOAL ATTEMPTS—Seattle, Heppner 34.

INTERCEPTIONS—Seattle, W. Williams 1-69, Springs 1-0.

KICKOFF RETURNS—Seattle, Rogers 4-95. San Diego, R. Jenkins 3-49, Bynum 2-51.

PUNT RETURNS—Seattle, Rogers 5-44. San Diego, Jacquet 3-9.

SACKS—Seattle, Simmons 1, Sinclair 1. San Diego, Parrella 2, Harrison 1, Rusk 1, Dingle 1.

PACKERS 29, CARDINALS 3

Sunday, September 24

Green Bay	7	10	6	6—29
Arizona	0	3	0	0— 3

First Quarter
G.B.—Green 19 run (Longwell kick), 10:24.

Second Quarter
G.B.—Schroeder 55 pass from Favre (Longwell kick), 0:55.
Ariz.—FG, Blanchard 31, 6:12.
G.B.—FG, Longwell 38, 12:54.

Third Quarter
G.B.—FG, Longwell 47, 6:13.
G.B.—FG, Longwell 48, 14:11.

Fourth Quarter
G.B.—FG, Longwell 37, 5:27.
G.B.—FG, Longwell 22, 6:07.
Attendance—71,801.

	Green Bay	Arizona
First downs	23	12
Rushes-yards	36-176	13-28
Passing	279	181
Punt returns	3-19	1-11
Kickoff returns	2-39	7-182
Interception returns	4-24	0-0
Comp.-att.-int.	18-32-0	21-43-4
Sacked-yards lost	1-9	1-8
Punts	2-41	6-48
Fumbles-lost	1-1	0-0
Penalties-yards	6-53	5-45
Time of possession	36:28	23:32

INDIVIDUAL STATISTICS

RUSHING—Green Bay, Levens 17-42, Green 12-93, Favre 4-38, Goodman 2-4, Hasselbeck 1-(minus 1). Arizona, Jones 10-24, Pittman 3-4.

PASSING—Green Bay, Favre 17-31-0-277, Hasselbeck 1-1-0-11. Arizona, Plummer 21-43-4-189.

RECEIVING—Green Bay, Schroeder 4-94, Franks 3-34, Driver 3-27, Green 2-49, T. Davis 2-22, Freeman 1-20, Levens 1-19, Henderson 1-12, Lee 1-11. Arizona, Sanders 7-60, Pittman 4-43, Cody 3-44, Boston 3-23, Jones 2-3, Hardy 1-11, Jenkins 1-5.

MISSED FIELD GOAL ATTEMPTS—None.

INTERCEPTIONS—Green Bay, Sharper 2-0, T. Williams 1-21, Butler 1-3.

KICKOFF RETURNS—Green Bay, Rossum 2-39. Arizona, Jenkins 7-177.

PUNT RETURNS—Green Bay, Rossum 3-19. Arizona, Cody 1-11.

SACKS—Green Bay, Bowens 1. Arizona, Smith 1.

JETS 21, BUCCANEERS 17

Sunday, September 24

N.Y. Jets	3	3	0	15—21
Tampa Bay	3	7	7	0—17

First Quarter
T.B.—FG, Gramatica 22, 7:32.
NYJ—FG, Hall 41, 12:49.

Second Quarter
T.B.—Moore 3 pass from King (Gramatica kick), 3:07.
NYJ—FG, Hall 27, 13:45.

Third Quarter
T.B.—Barber 37 interception return (Gramatica kick), 11:13.

Fourth Quarter
NYJ—Martin 6 pass from Testaverde (Coles pass from Testaverde), 13:06.
NYJ—Chrebet 18 pass from Martin (Hall kick), 14:08.
Attendance—65,619.

	N.Y. Jets	Tampa Bay
First downs	16	12
Rushes-yards	24-98	32-119
Passing	198	120
Punt returns	5-46	4-40
Kickoff returns	3-93	2-56
Interception returns	2-17	3-48
Comp.-att.-int.	24-44-3	7-19-2
Sacked-yards lost	1-6	2-15
Punts	7-50	7-50
Fumbles-lost	1-0	2-2
Penalties-yards	4-25	8-75
Time of possession	31:29	28:31

INDIVIDUAL STATISTICS

RUSHING—New York, Martin 18-90, Testaverde 5-(minus 1), Lucas 1-9. Tampa Bay, Alstott 16-60, Dunn 13-53, King 2-8, Stecker 1-(minus 2).

PASSING—New York, Testaverde 22-42-3-181, Martin 1-1-0-18, Lucas 1-1-0-5. Tampa Bay, King 7-19-2-135.

RECEIVING—New York, R. Anderson 7-42, Martin 7-27, Ward 3-44, Coles 2-34, Chrebet 2-32, Becht 2-20, Baxter 1-5. Tampa Bay, Moore 2-10, Green 1-75, Alstott 1-21, Anthony 1-18, Dunn 1-10, K. Johnson 1-1.

MISSED FIELD GOAL ATTEMPTS—None.

INTERCEPTIONS—New York, V. Green 1-17, Glenn 1-0. Tampa Bay, Barber 1-37, Duncan 1-10, Robinson 1-1.

KICKOFF RETURNS—New York, Williams 3-93. Tampa Bay, Stecker 2-56.

PUNT RETURNS—New York, Ward 5-46. Tampa Bay, Williams 4-40.

SACKS—New York, Abraham 1, Lewis 1. Tampa Bay, Ahanotu 1.

REDSKINS 16, GIANTS 6

Sunday, September 24

Washington	0	10	6	0—16
N.Y. Giants	0	0	0	6— 6

Second Quarter
Was.—Fryar 23 pass from B. Johnson (Husted kick), 2:27.
Was.—FG, Husted 25, 8:33.

Third Quarter
Was.—Reed 21 pass from B. Johnson (kick failed), 1:54.

Fourth Quarter
NYG—Hilliard 7 pass from Collins (run failed), 12:35.
Attendance—78,216.

	Washington	N.Y. Giants
First downs	17	21
Rushes-yards	39-110	22-93
Passing	284	168
Punt returns	3-15	1-6
Kickoff returns	1-0	4-64
Interception returns	1-32	0-0
Comp.-att.-int.	14-20-0	21-44-1
Sacked-yards lost	1-5	4-42
Punts	5-35	8-42
Fumbles-lost	1-0	0-0
Penalties-yards	4-25	6-59
Time of possession	31:22	28:38

INDIVIDUAL STATISTICS

RUSHING—Washington, Davis 30-89, Murrell 5-22, B. Johnson 3-(minus 3), Sellers 1-2. New York, Barber 16-65, Dayne 5-23, Toomer 1-5.

PASSING—Washington, B. Johnson 14-20-0-289. New York, Collins 21-44-1-210.

RECEIVING—Washington, Connell 4-122, Reed 4-37, Fryar 2-32, Alexander 2-28, Thrash 1-46, Sellers 1-24. New York, Hilliard 7-85, Barber 6-41, Toomer 3-31, Comella 2-11, Mitchell 1-18, Dixon 1-14, Jurevicius 1-10.

MISSED FIELD GOAL ATTEMPTS—Washington, Husted 30.

INTERCEPTIONS—Washington, Sanders 1-32.

KICKOFF RETURNS—Washington, Murrell 1-0. New York, Dixon 4-64.

PUNT RETURNS—Washington, Sanders 3-15. New York, Barber 1-6.

SACKS—Washington, Barber 1, B. Smith 1, Lang 1, Coleman 1. New York, K. Hamilton 1.

COLTS 43, JAGUARS 14

Monday, September 25

Jacksonville	0	14	0	0—14
Indianapolis	7	14	5	17—43

First Quarter
Ind.—Harrison 76 pass from Manning (Vanderjagt kick), 4:01.

Second Quarter
Jac.—J. Smith 9 pass from Brunell (Lindsey kick), 7:24.
Ind.—Wilkins 27 pass from Manning (Vanderjagt kick), 9:51.
Ind.—Pathon 16 pass from Manning (Vanderjagt kick), 13:32.
Jac.—J. Smith 26 pass from Brunell (Lindsey kick), 14:49.

Third Quarter
Ind.—FG, Vanderjagt 41, 9:28.
Ind.—Safety, Brunell sacked in end zone by Bratzke, 13:50.

Fourth Quarter
Ind.—FG, Vanderjagt 22, 3:29.
Ind.—Dilger 4 pass from Manning (Vanderjagt kick), 6:18.
Ind.—James 14 run (Vanderjagt kick), 9:05.
Attendance—56,816.

	Jacksonville	Indianapolis
First downs	18	21
Rushes-yards	24-97	28-93
Passing	189	440
Punt returns	2-21	4-20
Kickoff returns	7-136	3-90
Interception returns	0-0	2-8
Comp.-att.-int.	21-36-2	23-36-0
Sacked-yards lost	5-40	0-0
Punts	9-43	5-47
Fumbles-lost	1-0	1-1
Penalties-yards	4-40	11-90
Time of possession	27:38	32:22

INDIVIDUAL STATISTICS

RUSHING—Jacksonville, Taylor 14-57, Brunell 6-35, Johnson 2-4, Shelton 1-1, Soward 1-0. Indianapolis, James 22-89, Manning 6-4.

PASSING—Jacksonville, Brunell 21-36-2-229. Indianapolis, Manning 23-36-0-440.

RECEIVING—Jacksonville, J. Smith 9-132, McCardell 4-48, Johnson 3-9, Soward 2-20, Brady 2-12, Whitted 1-8. Indianapolis, Wilkins 9-148, Dilger 5-38, Pathon 3-67, Harrison 2-103, James 2-65, Pollard 2-19.

MISSED FIELD GOAL ATTEMPTS—None.

INTERCEPTIONS—Indianapolis, Peterson 1-5, Cota 1-3.

KICKOFF RETURNS—Jacksonville, Mack 4-86, Barlow 3-50. Indianapolis, P. Williams 2-42, Pathon 1-48.

PUNT RETURNS—Jacksonville, Soward 2-21. Indianapolis, Wilkins 4-20.

SACKS—Indianapolis, E. Johnson 2, Bratzke 2, Belser 1.

WEEK 5

STANDINGS

AFC EAST

	W	L	T	Pct.
N.Y. Jets	4	0	0	1.000
Miami	4	1	0	.800
Indianapolis	3	1	0	.750
Buffalo	2	2	0	.500
New England	1	4	0	.200

AFC CENTRAL

	W	L	T	Pct.
Baltimore	4	1	0	.800
Tennessee	3	1	0	.750
Cleveland	2	3	0	.400
Jacksonville	2	3	0	.400
Pittsburgh	1	3	0	.250
Cincinnati	0	4	0	.000

AFC WEST

	W	L	T	Pct.
Oakland	3	1	0	.750
Kansas City	3	2	0	.600
Denver	2	3	0	.400
Seattle	2	3	0	.400
San Diego	0	5	0	.000

NFC EAST

	W	L	T	Pct.
N.Y. Giants	3	2	0	.600
Philadelphia	3	2	0	.600
Washington	3	2	0	.600
Dallas	2	3	0	.400
Arizona	1	3	0	.250

NFC CENTRAL

	W	L	T	Pct.
Minnesota	4	0	0	1.000
Detroit	3	2	0	.600
Tampa Bay	3	2	0	.600
Green Bay	2	3	0	.400
Chicago	1	4	0	.200

NFC WEST

	W	L	T	Pct.
St. Louis	5	0	0	1.000
Atlanta	2	3	0	.400
San Francisco	2	3	0	.400
Carolina	1	3	0	.250
New Orleans	1	3	0	.250

TOP PERFORMANCES

100-YARD RUSHING GAMES

Player, Team & Opponent	Att.	Yds.	TD
Stephen Davis, Wash. vs. T.B.*	28	141	1
Robert Smith, Min. at Det.	16	134	1
Emmitt Smith, Dal. at Car.*	24	132	1
Eddie George, Ten. vs. NYG	35	125	1
James Stewart, Det. vs. Min.	20	123	0
Corey Dillon, Cin. vs. Mia.	22	110	0
Brian Mitchell, Phi. vs. Atl.	2	105	1
Justin Watson, St.L. vs. S.D.	14	102	1

300-YARD PASSING GAMES

Player, Team & Opponent	Att.	Comp.	Yds.	TD	Int.
Kurt Warner, St.L. vs. S.D.	30	24	390	4	0
Brian Griese, Den. vs. N.E.	50	31	361	1	1
Jim Harbaugh, S.D. at St.L.	40	27	348	2	1
Brett Favre, G.B. vs. Chi.	48	31	333	3	1
Donovan McNabb, Phi. vs. Atl.	44	30	311	2	1

100-YARD RECEIVING GAMES

Player, Team & Opponent	Rec.	Yds.	TD
Randy Moss, Min. at Det.	7	168	3
Isaac Bruce, St.L. vs. S.D.	9	167	2
Rod Smith, Den. vs. N.E.	13	160	0
Derrick Alexander, K.C. vs. Sea.	5	153	1
Keenan McCardell, Jack. vs. Pit.	11	137	1
Marcus Robinson, Chi. at G.B.	2	126	2
Torrance Small, Phi. vs. Atl.	4	122	1
Marshall Faulk, St.L. vs. S.D.	6	116	2
David Patten, Cle. vs. Balt.	7	113	0
Eric Moulds, Buf. vs. Ind.	9	112	1
Troy Brown, N.E. at Den.	5	108	2
Bill Schroeder, G.B. vs. Chi.	8	108	2
Jeff Graham, S.D. at St.L.	7	107	0
Az-Zahir Hakim, St.L. vs. S.D.	5	104	0
Derrick Mason, Ten. vs. NYG	6	103	1

*Overtime game.

RESULTS

SUNDAY, OCTOBER 1

Baltimore 12, CLEVELAND 0
Chicago 27, GREEN BAY 24
Dallas 16, CAROLINA 13 (OT)
Indianapolis 18, BUFFALO 16
Miami 31, CINCINNATI 16
Minnesota 31, DETROIT 24
New England 28, DENVER 19
PHILADELPHIA 38, Atlanta 10
Pittsburgh 24, JACKSONVILLE 13
ST. LOUIS 57, San Diego 31
SAN FRANCISCO 27, Arizona 20
WASHINGTON 20, Tampa Bay 17

MONDAY, OCTOBER 2

KANSAS CITY 24, Seattle 17
Open date: New Orleans, N.Y. Jets, Oakland

2000 REVIEW Week 5

RAVENS 12, BROWNS 0

Sunday, October 1

Baltimore	3	6	3	0—12
Cleveland	0	0	0	0— 0

First Quarter
Bal.—FG, Stover 45, 8:03.

Second Quarter
Bal.—FG, Stover 30, 3:35.
Bal.—FG, Stover 44, 5:48.

Third Quarter
Bal.—FG, Stover 22, 10:04.
Attendance—73,018.

	Baltimore	Cleveland
First downs	22	11
Rushes-yards	37-188	13-23
Passing	160	207
Punt returns	4-74	2-16
Kickoff returns	0-0	5-116
Interception returns	3-5	1-0
Comp.-att.-int.	18-34-1	21-36-3
Sacked-yards lost	1-9	0-0
Punts	3-43	4-51
Fumbles-lost	0-0	3-1
Penalties-yards	6-62	8-60
Time of possession	36:44	23:16

INDIVIDUAL STATISTICS
RUSHING—Baltimore, Holmes 20-82, Ja. Lewis 13-86, Ayanbadejo 2-8, Taylor 1-12, Banks 1-0. Cleveland, Prentice 7-13, Rhett 4-1, Edwards 2-9.
PASSING—Baltimore, Banks 18-34-1-169. Cleveland, Couch 20-35-3-203, Pederson 1-1-0-4.
RECEIVING—Baltimore, Sharpe 6-83, Taylor 5-39, Ayanbadejo 2-14, Ismail 2-14, Holmes 2-12, Ja. Lewis 1-7. Cleveland, Patten 7-113, Northcutt 4-43, Prentice 4-15, Rhett 3-21, Johnson 2-11, Edwards 1-4.
MISSED FIELD GOAL ATTEMPTS—Baltimore, Stover 51.
INTERCEPTIONS—Baltimore, Starks 1-4, R. Lewis 1-1, Woodson 1-0. Cleveland, Fuller 1-0.
KICKOFF RETURNS—Cleveland, Patten 3-61, L. Jackson 2-55.
PUNT RETURNS—Baltimore, J. Lewis 3-69, Starks 1-5. Cleveland, Northcutt 2-16.
SACKS—Cleveland, Colinet 1.

COWBOYS 16, PANTHERS 13

Sunday, October 1

Dallas	0	10	3	0	3—16
Carolina	0	10	0	3	0—13

Second Quarter
Car.—Biakabutuka 1 run (Cunningham kick), 2:14.
Dal.—K. Walter tackled in the end zone by I. Reese for a safety, 7:47.
Dal.—E. Smith 8 run (Harris pass from Aikman), 12:26.
Car.—FG, Cunningham 39, 14:58.
Dal.—FG, Seder 27, 10:47.

Third Quarter

Fourth Quarter
Car.—FG, Cunningham 23, 2:25.

Overtime
Dal.—FG, Seder 24, 3:52.
Attendance—73,310.

	Dallas	Carolina
First downs	20	13
Rushes-yards	38-173	29-119
Passing	118	153
Punt returns	1-(-3)	2-16
Kickoff returns	5-73	3-67
Interception returns	0-0	2-14
Comp.-att.-int.	15-23-2	17-29-0
Sacked-yards lost	2-13	1-8
Punts	4-44	3-40
Fumbles-lost	0-0	5-2
Penalties-yards	4-45	5-55
Time of possession	36:03	27:49

INDIVIDUAL STATISTICS
RUSHING—Dallas, E. Smith 24-132, Warren 8-27, Thomas 3-12, Aikman 2-2, Ismail 1-0. Carolina, Biakabutuka 20-86, Beuerlein 4-22, Floyd 2-1, Hoover 1-6, Muhammad 1-4, Walter 1-0.
PASSING—Dallas, Aikman 15-23-2-131. Carolina, Beuerlein 17-29-0-161.
RECEIVING—Dallas, McKnight 3-37, Ismail 3-25, Harris 3-20, E. Smith 3-17, Warren 2-28, Tucker 1-4. Carolina, Biakabutuka 6-48, Muhammad 5-52, Hayes 3-21, Walls 2-26, Floyd 1-14.
MISSED FIELD GOAL ATTEMPTS—Dallas, Seder 45.
INTERCEPTIONS—Carolina, Wells 1-14, Davis 1-0.
KICKOFF RETURNS—Dallas, Tucker 4-60, Santiago 1-13. Carolina, Bates 3-67.
PUNT RETURNS—Dallas, Tucker 1-(minus 3). Carolina, Bates 2-16.
SACKS—Dallas, Zellner 1. Carolina, Swann 1, White 1.

COLTS 18, BILLS 16

Sunday, October 1

Indianapolis	0	7	0	11—18
Buffalo	3	6	0	7—16

First Quarter
Buf.—FG, Christie 19, 7:41.

Second Quarter
Buf.—FG, Christie 30, 0:48.
Buf.—FG, Christie 27, 6:06.
Ind.—Harrison 14 pass from Manning (Vanderjagt kick), 10:51.

Fourth Quarter
Ind.—Wilkins 10 pass from Manning (James run), 0:50.
Buf.—Moulds 40 pass from Johnson (Christie kick), 13:52.
Ind.—FG, Vanderjagt 45, 15:00.
Attendance—72,617.

	Indianapolis	Buffalo
First downs	14	21
Rushes-yards	24-81	33-170
Passing	184	215
Punt returns	1-14	2-23
Kickoff returns	5-54	2-39
Interception returns	0-0	1-8
Comp.-att.-int.	16-27-1	21-32-0
Sacked-yards lost	1-3	4-31
Punts	5-47	5-39
Fumbles-lost	0-0	1-0
Penalties-yards	3-20	8-60
Time of possession	24:01	35:59

INDIVIDUAL STATISTICS
RUSHING—Indianapolis, James 19-60, Manning 5-21. Buffalo, Linton 13-58, Bryson 11-43, Johnson 5-41, Morris 4-28.
PASSING—Indianapolis, Manning 16-27-1-187. Buffalo, Johnson 21-32-0-246.
RECEIVING—Indianapolis, James 4-43, Harrison 3-45, Pathon 3-28, Pollard 3-25, Dilger 2-36, Wilkins 1-10. Buffalo, Moulds 9-112, Morris 4-44, McDaniel 3-73, P. Price 1-14, Collins 1-5, Linton 1-3, Bryson 1-1, Johnson 1-(minus 6).
MISSED FIELD GOAL ATTEMPTS—None.
INTERCEPTIONS—Buffalo, Winfield 1-8.
KICKOFF RETURNS—Indianapolis, Pathon 4-54, Macklin 1-0. Buffalo, Watson 2-39.
PUNT RETURNS—Indianapolis, Wilkins 1-14. Buffalo, Watson 2-23.
SACKS—Indianapolis, Bratzke 1, Hollier 1, Washington 1, Bennett 1. Buffalo, Newman 1.

VIKINGS 31, LIONS 24

Sunday, October 1

Minnesota	7	3	7	14—31
Detroit	7	3	0	14—24

First Quarter
Det.—Crowell 9 pass from Batch (Hanson kick), 3:55.
Min.—Moss 61 pass from Culpepper (Anderson kick), 6:14.

Second Quarter
Det.—FG, Hanson 21, 10:52.
Min.—FG, Anderson 20, 14:57.

Third Quarter
Min.—Moss 17 pass from Culpepper (Anderson kick), 14:46.
Fourth Quarter
Det.—Batch 5 run (Hanson kick), 2:51.
Min.—Moss 50 pass from Culpepper (Anderson kick), 6:12.
Min.—Smith 65 run (Anderson kick), 8:37.
Det.—Bates 1 run (Hanson kick), 14:57.
Attendance—76,438.

	Minnesota	Detroit
First downs	19	27
Rushes-yards	29-178	25-129
Passing	261	226
Punt returns	3-27	4-32
Kickoff returns	4-82	6-107
Interception returns	1-0	0-0
Comp.-att.-int.	17-29-0	25-44-1
Sacked-yards lost	2-8	2-13
Punts	6-44	5-43
Fumbles-lost	0-0	0-0
Penalties-yards	10-72	9-55
Time of possession	28:42	31:18

INDIVIDUAL STATISTICS
RUSHING—Minnesota, Smith 16-134, Culpepper 7-29, M. Williams 4-12, Kleinsasser 1-4, Moss 1-(minus 1). Detroit, J. Stewart 20-123, Bates 4-1, Batch 1-5.

PASSING—Minnesota, Culpepper 17-29-0-269. Detroit, Batch 25-44-1-239.

RECEIVING—Minnesota, Moss 7-168, J. Davis 4-34, C. Carter 3-30, Smith 2-19, Walsh 1-18. Detroit, Crowell 8-85, Morton 6-50, Bates 3-37, J. Stewart 2-16, Moore 2-15, Schlesinger 2-12, Olivo 1-19, Sloan 1-12.

MISSED FIELD GOAL ATTEMPTS—Detroit, Hanson 43.

INTERCEPTIONS—Minnesota, Thomas 1-0.

KICKOFF RETURNS—Minnesota, T. Carter 4-82. Detroit, Howard 4-82, Olivo 2-25.

PUNT RETURNS—Minnesota, Walters 3-27. Detroit, Howard 4-32.

SACKS—Minnesota, T. Williams 1, Sawyer 1. Detroit, Porcher 1, Elliss 1.

RAMS 57, CHARGERS 31
Sunday, October 1

San Diego	3	7	7	14—31
St. Louis	17	13	17	10—57

First Quarter
St.L.—FG, Wilkins 51, 2:32.
St.L.—Bruce 9 pass from Warner (Wilkins kick), 8:22.
St.L.—Faulk 13 pass from Warner (Wilkins kick), 9:16.
S.D.—FG, Carney 37, 14:20.
Second Quarter
St.L.—FG, Wilkins 21, 3:01.
S.D.—Fazande 2 run (Carney kick), 8:25.
St.L.—Holt 7 pass from Warner (Wilkins kick), 12:19.
St.L.—FG, Wilkins 31, 15:00.
Third Quarter
S.D.—McCrary 3 pass from Harbaugh (Carney kick), 3:00.
St.L.—Bruce 12 pass from Warner (Wilkins kick), 4:03.
St.L.—FG, Wilkins 33, 6:45.
St.L.—Faulk 48 pass from Green (Wilkins kick), 11:00.
Fourth Quarter
St.L.—FG, Wilkins 20, 3:24.
S.D.—Fletcher 6 run (Carney kick), 7:18.
St.L.—Watson 14 run (Wilkins kick), 11:41.
S.D.—Gaylor 62 pass from Harbaugh (Carney kick), 13:08.
Attendance—66,010.

	San Diego	St. Louis
First downs	23	29
Rushes-yards	15-48	26-163
Passing	333	451
Punt returns	0-0	3-64
Kickoff returns	9-209	5-108
Interception returns	0-0	1-0
Comp.-att.-int.	27-40-1	27-34-0
Sacked-yards lost	3-15	2-14
Punts	3-165	0-0
Fumbles-lost	1-1	0-0
Penalties-yards	3-15	4-36
Time of possession	29:35	30:25

INDIVIDUAL STATISTICS
RUSHING—San Diego, Fazande 8-19, Fletcher 4-23, R. Jenkins 2-6, Harbaugh 1-0. St. Louis, Watson 14-102, Faulk 7-55, Green 3-(minus 3), Warner 1-6, Hodgins 1-3.

PASSING—San Diego, Harbaugh 27-40-1-348. St. Louis, Warner 24-30-0-390, Green 3-4-0-75.

RECEIVING—San Diego, J. Graham 7-107, F. Jones 7-50, R. Jones 5-67, Fletcher 4-38, McCrary 3-24, Gaylor 1-62. St. Louis, Bruce 9-167, Faulk 6-116, Hakim 5-104, R. Williams 3-36, Holt 3-34, Holcombe 1-8.

MISSED FIELD GOAL ATTEMPTS—San Diego, Carney 49.

INTERCEPTIONS—St. Louis, Shepherd 1-0.

KICKOFF RETURNS—San Diego, R. Jenkins 8-187, Bynum 1-22. St. Louis, Horne 5-108.

PUNT RETURNS—St. Louis, Hakim 2-32, Horne 1-16.

SACKS—San Diego, Harrison 1, Dixon 1. St. Louis, Carter 1, Wistrom 1, Agnew 1.

STEELERS 24, JAGUARS 13
Sunday, October 1

Pittsburgh	7	10	7	0—24
Jacksonville	3	3	0	7—13

First Quarter
Jac.—FG, Lindsey 19, 5:03.
Pit.—Fuamatu-Ma'afala 5 run (K. Brown kick), 14:19.
Second Quarter
Pit.—FG, K. Brown 19, 8:08.
Pit.—Bettis 1 run (K. Brown kick), 11:47.
Jac.—FG, Lindsey 48, 14:29.
Third Quarter
Pit.—Bettis 3 run (K. Brown kick), 10:33.
Fourth Quarter
Jac.—McCardell 11 pass from Martin (Lindsey kick), 14:51.
Attendance—64,351.

	Pittsburgh	Jacksonville
First downs	22	17
Rushes-yards	44-209	16-26
Passing	123	180
Punt returns	3-51	1-9
Kickoff returns	3-73	3-91
Interception returns	1-0	1-0
Comp.-att.-int.	10-16-1	23-45-1
Sacked-yards lost	2-9	7-45
Punts	3-34	4-50
Fumbles-lost	2-2	1-1
Penalties-yards	7-55	10-75
Time of possession	35:10	24:50

INDIVIDUAL STATISTICS
RUSHING—Pittsburgh, Bettis 28-97, Stewart 9-61, Fuamatu-Ma'afala 7-51. Jacksonville, Taylor 15-24, Brunell 1-2.

PASSING—Pittsburgh, Stewart 10-16-1-132. Jacksonville, Brunell 15-32-1-137, Martin 8-13-0-88.

RECEIVING—Pittsburgh, Burress 3-40, Fuamatu-Ma'afala 2-39, Ward 2-23, Edwards 1-20, Bruener 1-5, Witman 1-5. Jacksonville, McCardell 11-137, Taylor 4-14, Brady 3-37, J. Smith 2-20, Johnson 2-15, Soward 1-2.

MISSED FIELD GOAL ATTEMPTS—None.

INTERCEPTIONS—Pittsburgh, Flowers 1-0. Jacksonville, Bryant 1-0.

KICKOFF RETURNS—Pittsburgh, Edwards 2-42, Poteat 1-31. Jacksonville, Stith 3-91.

PUNT RETURNS—Pittsburgh, Edwards 2-44, Poteat 1-7. Jacksonville, Soward 1-9.

SACKS—Pittsburgh, Gildon 2, A. Smith 2, Townsend 1, Porter 1, Team 1. Jacksonville, Beasley 2.

TITANS 28, GIANTS 14
Sunday, October 1

N.Y. Giants	0	0	7	7—14
Tennessee	7	14	0	7—28

First Quarter
Ten.—Wycheck 14 pass from McNair (Del Greco kick), 6:25.
Second Quarter
Ten.—E. George 7 run (Del Greco kick), 6:12.
Ten.—Mason 29 pass from McNair (Del Greco kick), 12:06.
Third Quarter
NYG—Hilliard 14 pass from Collins (Holmes kick), 9:35.

Fourth Quarter
Ten.—Wycheck 3 pass from McNair (Del Greco kick), 2:34.
NYG—Campbell 1 pass from Collins (Holmes kick), 7:56.
Attendance—68,341.

	N.Y. Giants	Tennessee
First downs	14	28
Rushes-yards	12-24	43-152
Passing	191	284
Punt returns	2-18	2-10
Kickoff returns	5-135	1-27
Interception returns	0-0	3-64
Comp.-att.-int.	17-36-3	24-35-0
Sacked-yards lost	1-6	2-9
Punts	5-55	4-41
Fumbles-lost	2-1	1-1
Penalties-yards	7-48	6-64
Time of possession	17:14	42:46

INDIVIDUAL STATISTICS
RUSHING—New York, Barber 5-2, Collins 3-19, Dayne 3-(minus 1), Comella 1-4. Tennessee, E. George 35-125, McNair 4-21, Thomas 4-6.

PASSING—New York, Collins 17-36-3-197. Tennessee, McNair 24-35-0-293.

RECEIVING—New York, Toomer 5-81, Barber 5-49, Hilliard 4-59, Jurevicius 1-6, Campbell 1-1, Mitchell 1-1. Tennessee, Mason 6-103, Kinney 5-60, Wycheck 5-42, E. George 4-52, Sanders 2-14, Pickens 1-15, Thomas 1-7.

MISSED FIELD GOAL ATTEMPTS—Tennessee, Del Greco 46.

INTERCEPTIONS—Tennessee, Rolle 1-41, Sidney 1-19, Walker 1-4.

KICKOFF RETURNS—New York, Dixon 5-135. Tennessee, Mason 1-27.

PUNT RETURNS—New York, Barber 2-18. Tennessee, Mason 2-10.

SACKS—New York, K. Hamilton 1, Strahan 1. Tennessee, Holmes 1.

REDSKINS 20, BUCCANEERS 17
Sunday, October 1

Tampa Bay	7	0	0	10	0—17
Washington	0	7	3	7	3—20

First Quarter
T.B.—Alstott 2 run (Gramatica kick), 13:22.

Second Quarter
Was.—Davis 50 run (Husted kick), 11:46.

Third Quarter
Was.—FG, Husted 28, 7:09.

Fourth Quarter
Was.—Centers 8 pass from B. Johnson (Husted kick), 11:03.
T.B.—Anthony 46 pass from King (Gramatica kick), 13:00.
T.B.—FG, Gramatica 42, 15:00.

Overtime
Was.—FG, Husted 20, 4:09.
Attendance—83,532.

	Tampa Bay	Washington
First downs	16	14
Rushes-yards	28-72	32-145
Passing	183	185
Punt returns	5-13	7-86
Kickoff returns	4-101	2-64
Interception returns	0-0	1-0
Comp.-att.-int.	19-38-1	20-32-0
Sacked-yards lost	4-19	3-22
Punts	9-46	10-44
Fumbles-lost	3-1	3-1
Penalties-yards	4-40	8-48
Time of possession	31:32	32:37

INDIVIDUAL STATISTICS
RUSHING—Tampa Bay, Alstott 15-46, Dunn 10-3, King 3-23. Washington, Davis 28-141, B. Johnson 2-2, Centers 1-2, Murrell 1-0.

PASSING—Tampa Bay, King 19-38-1-202. Washington, B. Johnson 20-32-0-207.

RECEIVING—Tampa Bay, K. Johnson 6-42, Moore 4-47, Dunn 4-36, Hape 2-12, Anthony 1-46, Alstott 1-12, Green 1-7. Washington, Centers 8-53, Fryar 4-61, Alexander 3-28, Connell 1-47, Murrell 1-6, Davis 1-5, Thrash 1-4, Sellers 1-3.

MISSED FIELD GOAL ATTEMPTS—Tampa Bay, Gramatica 40. Washington, Husted 35.

INTERCEPTIONS—Washington, Green 1-0.

KICKOFF RETURNS—Tampa Bay, Stecker 4-101. Washington, Thrash 2-64.
PUNT RETURNS—Tampa Bay, Williams 3-12, Green 2-1. Washington, Sanders 7-86.
SACKS—Tampa Bay, Jones 1, McFarland 1, Sapp 1. Washington, Coleman 3, Arrington 1.

PATRIOTS 28, BRONCOS 19
Sunday, October 1

New England	14	7	7	0—28
Denver	0	3	8	8—19

First Quarter
N.E.—Brown 11 pass from Bledsoe (Vinatieri kick), 3:12.
N.E.—Brown 44 pass from Bledsoe (Vinatieri kick), 7:01.

Second Quarter
Den.—FG, Nedney 20, 4:27.
N.E.—Redmond 12 pass from Bledsoe (Vinatieri kick), 14:35.

Third Quarter
Den.—L. Johnson stepped out of bounds in the end zone for a safety, 9:46.
Den.—O'Neal 87 kickoff return (run failed), 10:04.
N.E.—Glenn 9 pass from Bledsoe (Vinatieri kick), 14:17.

Fourth Quarter
Den.—McGriff 43 pass from Griese (McCaffrey pass from Griese), 13:04.
Attendance—75,684.

	New England	Denver
First downs	19	26
Rushes-yards	27-54	21-79
Passing	260	326
Punt returns	3-22	2-18
Kickoff returns	3-73	4-153
Interception returns	1-0	1-9
Comp.-att.-int.	18-27-1	31-50-1
Sacked-yards lost	3-11	4-35
Punts	6-45	5-49
Fumbles-lost	0-0	2-1
Penalties-yards	5-17	7-50
Time of possession	27:12	32:48

INDIVIDUAL STATISTICS
RUSHING—New England, Faulk 9-40, Redmond 6-15, Bledsoe 4-(minus 2), Shaw 3-3, Bishop 2-1, Floyd 1-0, T. Carter 1-(minus 1), L. Johnson 1-(minus 1). Denver, Davis 9-24, Griese 6-29, Anderson 6-26.

PASSING—New England, Bledsoe 18-27-1-271. Denver, Griese 31-50-1-361.

RECEIVING—New England, Brown 6-124, Glenn 5-60, Bjornson 2-20, Redmond 2-17, Faulk 1-26, Calloway 1-13, Simmons 1-11. Denver, R. Smith 13-160, McCaffrey 9-91, Carswell 3-21, Chamberlain 2-35, McGriff 1-43, Anderson 1-6, Clark 1-4, Griffith 1-1.

MISSED FIELD GOAL ATTEMPTS—Denver, Nedney 43.

INTERCEPTIONS—New England, Jones 1-0. Denver, Buckley 1-9.

KICKOFF RETURNS—New England, Faulk 3-73. Denver, O'Neal 2-112, Cole 2-41.

PUNT RETURNS—New England, Brown 3-22. Denver, O'Neal 2-18.

SACKS—New England, Slade 1, McGinest 1, Serwanga 1, Spires 1. Denver, Pryce 1.5, Traylor 1, Wilson 0.5.

DOLPHINS 31, BENGALS 16
Sunday, October 1

Miami	0	10	14	7—31
Cincinnati	10	3	0	3—16

First Quarter
Cin.—Warrick 9 pass from Smith (Rackers kick), 6:55.
Cin.—FG, Rackers 23, 14:14.

Second Quarter
Cin.—FG, Rackers 38, 1:47.
Mia.—FG, Mare 40, 14:04.
Mia.—Taylor 29 fumble return (Mare kick), 15:00.

Third Quarter
Mia.—L. Smith 18 run (Mare kick), 7:45.
Mia.—Gadsden 7 pass from Fiedler (Mare kick), 10:21.

Fourth Quarter
Mia.—Gadsden 21 pass from Fiedler (Mare kick), 2:34.
Cin.—FG, Rackers 34, 7:34.
Attendance—61,535.

	Miami	Cincinnati
First downs	18	24
Rushes-yards	29-159	35-191
Passing	143	159
Punt returns	0-0	1-1
Kickoff returns	4-78	4-70
Interception returns	0-0	1-7
Comp.-att.-int.	14-21-1	20-38-0
Sacked-yards lost	2-12	3-19
Punts	3-60	4-31
Fumbles-lost	1-1	1-1
Penalties-yards	8-61	10-123
Time of possession	26:20	33:40

INDIVIDUAL STATISTICS

RUSHING—Miami, L. Smith 12-66, Denson 8-32, Johnson 5-16, Fiedler 4-45. Cincinnati, Dillon 22-110, Bennett 7-35, Smith 5-43, Warrick 1-3.

PASSING—Miami, Fiedler 14-21-1-155. Cincinnati, Smith 20-38-0-178.

RECEIVING—Miami, Gadsden 6-73, Shepherd 3-39, L. Smith 2-17, Ogden 1-12, Emanuel 1-9, Denson 1-5. Cincinnati, McGee 6-74, Bennett 5-28, Warrick 4-45, Battaglia 2-19, Yeast 1-5, Dillon 1-4, Groce 1-3.

MISSED FIELD GOAL ATTEMPTS—None.

INTERCEPTIONS—Cincinnati, Spikes 1-7.

KICKOFF RETURNS—Miami, Marion 3-63, Weaver 1-15. Cincinnati, Mack 4-70.

PUNT RETURNS—Cincinnati, Yeast 1-1.

SACKS—Miami, Bowens 2, Taylor 1. Cincinnati, Copeland 1, Gibson 1.

BEARS 27, PACKERS 24

Sunday, October 1

Chicago	10	7	7	3—27
Green Bay	0	3	7	14—24

First Quarter

Chi.—McNown 1 run (Edinger kick), 2:42.
Chi.—FG, Edinger 19, 10:22.

Second Quarter

Chi.—M. Robinson 68 pass from McNown (Edinger kick), 5:53.
G.B.—FG, Longwell 42, 10:12.

Third Quarter

Chi.—M. Robinson 58 pass from McNown (Edinger kick), 9:25.
G.B.—Freeman 14 pass from Favre (Longwell kick), 12:24.

Fourth Quarter

G.B.—Schroeder 17 pass from Favre (Longwell kick), 6:16.
Chi.—FG, Edinger 47, 11:45.
G.B.—Schroeder 17 pass from Favre (Longwell kick), 13:02.
Attendance—59,869.

	Chicago	Green Bay
First downs	13	22
Rushes-yards	36-178	14-44
Passing	192	320
Punt returns	0-0	2-10
Kickoff returns	2-65	6-148
Interception returns	1-36	0-0
Comp.-att.-int.	11-20-0	31-48-1
Sacked-yards lost	5-11	2-13
Punts	8-39	6-41
Fumbles-lost	2-0	2-2
Penalties-yards	8-65	4-35
Time of possession	31:50	28:10

INDIVIDUAL STATISTICS

RUSHING—Chicago, Allen 24-72, McNown 10-51, Kennison 1-52, Enis 1-3. Green Bay, Levens 11-24, Green 3-20.

PASSING—Chicago, McNown 11-20-0-203. Green Bay, Favre 31-48-1-333.

RECEIVING—Chicago, Allred 4-28, M. Robinson 2-126, Booker 2-15, Kennison 1-21, Mayes 1-7, Enis 1-6. Green Bay, Schroeder 8-108, Franks 5-54, Levens 5-41, Green 5-41, Driver 3-43, Freeman 3-32, Henderson 2-14.

MISSED FIELD GOAL ATTEMPTS—Chicago, Edinger 42.

INTERCEPTIONS—Chicago, Parrish 1-36.

KICKOFF RETURNS—Chicago, Milburn 2-65. Green Bay, Rossum 5-136, Bowens 1-12.

PUNT RETURNS—Green Bay, Rossum 2-10.

SACKS—Chicago, Urlacher 1, Daniels 1. Green Bay, Hunt 2, S. Dotson 1, Thierry 1, B. Williams 0.5, K. Williams 0.5.

EAGLES 38, FALCONS 10

Sunday, October 1

Atlanta	0	0	7	3—10
Philadelphia	3	3	11	21—38

First Quarter

Phi.—FG, Akers 39, 4:25.

Second Quarter

Phi.—FG, Akers 38, 14:51.

Third Quarter

Phi.—Small 70 pass from McNabb (Small pass from McNabb), 3:36.
Atl.—Dwight 70 punt return (Andersen kick), 10:09.
Phi.—FG, Akers 19, 15:00.

Fourth Quarter

Phi.—C. Johnson 11 pass from McNabb (Akers kick), 6:21.
Atl.—FG, Andersen 48, 8:18.
Phi.—Mitchell 89 kickoff return (Akers kick), 8:34.
Phi.—Mitchell 85 run (Akers kick), 13:08.
Attendance—65,424.

	Atlanta	Philadelphia
First downs	13	22
Rushes-yards	22-61	22-191
Passing	139	311
Punt returns	3-85	2-15
Kickoff returns	7-141	3-176
Interception returns	2-12	1-9
Comp.-att.-int.	15-35-1	30-45-2
Sacked-yards lost	2-17	0-0
Punts	8-37	3-46
Fumbles-lost	0-0	1-1
Penalties-yards	2-10	9-110
Time of possession	28:08	31:52

INDIVIDUAL STATISTICS

RUSHING—Atlanta, Anderson 19-47, M. Smith 2-13, Chandler 1-1. Philadelphia, Staley 11-28, McNabb 7-57, Mitchell 2-105, C. Johnson 1-1, C. Martin 1-0.

PASSING—Atlanta, Chandler 14-34-1-151, Kanell 1-1-0-5. Philadelphia, McNabb 30-44-1-311, Small 0-1-1-0.

RECEIVING—Atlanta, Jefferson 4-43, Mathis 4-33, Dwight 3-55, Christian 3-20, M. Smith 1-5. Philadelphia, Lewis 7-52, C. Johnson 6-47, Small 4-122, Mitchell 3-35, Staley 3-4, C. Martin 2-22, Broughton 2-8, Pinkston 1-11, Thomason 1-6, Brown 1-4.

MISSED FIELD GOAL ATTEMPTS—None.

INTERCEPTIONS—Atlanta, Bradford 1-12, Buchanan 1-0. Philadelphia, H. Douglas 1-9.

KICKOFF RETURNS—Atlanta, Dwight 5-102, Kozlowski 1-21, Vaughn 1-18. Philadelphia, Mitchell 2-135, D. Douglas 1-41.

PUNT RETURNS—Atlanta, Dwight 3-85. Philadelphia, Mitchell 2-15.

SACKS—Philadelphia, Mamula 1, Simon 1.

49ERS 27, CARDINALS 20

Sunday, October 1

Arizona	0	10	0	10—20
San Francisco	7	10	7	3—27

First Quarter

S.F.—Rice 5 pass from Garcia (Richey kick), 12:32.

Second Quarter

Ariz.—FG, Blanchard 32, 2:53.
S.F.—FG, Richey 33, 13:07.
S.F.—Garner 1 run (Richey kick), 14:11.
Ariz.—Boston 56 pass from Plummer (Blanchard kick), 14:42.

Third Quarter

S.F.—Garner 1 run (Richey kick), 8:47.

Fourth Quarter

S.F.—FG, Richey 29, 2:42.
Ariz.—FG, Blanchard 27, 8:15.
Ariz.—Jones 4 run (Blanchard kick), 12:45.
Attendance—66,985.

	Arizona	San Francisco
First downs	16	18
Rushes-yards	24-126	32-130
Passing	239	215
Punt returns	5-32	1-3
Kickoff returns	5-114	4-49

	Arizona	San Francisco
Interception returns	0-0	0-0
Comp.-att.-int.	24-41-0	22-33-0
Sacked-yards lost	0-0	1-5
Punts	4-44	6-38
Fumbles-lost	4-2	1-1
Penalties-yards	4-40	6-40
Time of possession.................................	27:50	32:10

INDIVIDUAL STATISTICS

RUSHING—Arizona, Pittman 11-72, Jones 10-36, Plummer 3-18. San Francisco, Garner 21-77, Garcia 6-36, Beasley 5-17.

PASSING—Arizona, Plummer 24-41-0-239. San Francisco, Garcia 22-33-0-220.

RECEIVING—Arizona, Pittman 6-72, Boston 5-87, Jones 4-15, Cody 3-30, Hardy 3-14, Sanders 2-10, Jenkins 1-11. San Francisco, Rice 7-66, Stokes 4-62, Streets 4-47, Beasley 3-8, Clark 2-24, Garner 2-13.

MISSED FIELD GOAL ATTEMPTS—Arizona, Blanchard 51.

INTERCEPTIONS—None.

KICKOFF RETURNS—Arizona, Jenkins 5-114. San Francisco, K. Williams 2-31, Jervey 1-18, Plummer 1-0.

PUNT RETURNS—Arizona, Cody 5-32. San Francisco, K. Williams 1-3.

SACKS—Arizona, Maddox 0.5, Davis 0.5.

CHIEFS 24, SEAHAWKS 17

Monday, October 2

Seattle	7	7	3	0—17
Kansas City........................	0	7	7	10—24

First Quarter
Sea.—Mili 1 pass from Kitna (Lindell kick), 13:26.

Second Quarter
K.C.—Gonzalez 15 pass from Grbac (Stoyanovich kick), 8:01.
Sea.—Alexander 7 run (Lindell kick), 14:12.

Third Quarter
Sea.—FG, Lindell 27, 8:36.
K.C.—Alexander 17 pass from Grbac (Stoyanovich kick), 12:45.

Fourth Quarter
K.C.—FG, Stoyanovich 27, 3:18.
K.C.—Cloud 15 run (Stoyanovich kick), 10:34.
  Attendance—82,893.

	Seattle	Kansas City
First downs	20	18
Rushes-yards..	34-186	26-136
Passing	103	242
Punt returns..	3-46	2-27
Kickoff returns	4-82	4-101
Interception returns	0-0	1-0
Comp.-att.-int.	17-28-1	16-27-0
Sacked-yards lost	5-37	2-14
Punts	6-39	6-43
Fumbles-Lost..	4-1	0-0
Penalties-yards	7-45	12-77
Time of possession.................................	34:52	25:08

INDIVIDUAL STATISTICS

RUSHING—Seattle, Watters 16-97, Alexander 11-74, Kitna 7-15. Kansas City, Richardson 11-53, Anders 7-45, Cloud 6-36, Grbac 2-2.

PASSING—Seattle, Kitna 17-28-1-140. Kansas City, Grbac 16-27-0-256.

RECEIVING—Seattle, Jackson 4-51, Fauria 4-25, Dawkins 3-24, Mayes 2-20, Alexander 2-13, Strong 1-6, Mili 1-1. Kansas City, Alexander 5-153, Morris 3-40, Gonzalez 3-34, Drayton 1-11, Lockett 1-8, Richardson 1-6, Cloud 1-3, Anders 1-1.

MISSED FIELD GOAL ATTEMPTS—Kansas City, Stoyanovich 37.

INTERCEPTIONS—Kansas City, Woods 1-0.

KICKOFF RETURNS—Seattle, Rogers 4-82. Kansas City, Hall 3-81, Cloud 1-20.

PUNT RETURNS—Seattle, Rogers 2-21, Joseph 1-25. Kansas City, Hall 2-27.

SACKS—Seattle, Koonce 1, King 1. Kansas City, Hicks 3, D. Williams 1, McGlockton 1.

WEEK 6

STANDINGS

AFC EAST

	W	L	T	Pct.
Miami	5	1	0	.833
N.Y. Jets	4	1	0	.800
Indianapolis	3	2	0	.600
Buffalo	2	3	0	.400
New England	2	4	0	.333

AFC CENTRAL

	W	L	T	Pct.
Baltimore	5	1	0	.833
Tennessee	4	1	0	.800
Pittsburgh	2	3	0	.400
Cleveland	2	4	0	.333
Jacksonville	2	4	0	.333
Cincinnati	0	5	0	.000

AFC WEST

	W	L	T	Pct.
Oakland	4	1	0	.800
Kansas City	3	2	0	.600
Denver	3	3	0	.500
Seattle	2	4	0	.333
San Diego	0	6	0	.000

NFC EAST

	W	L	T	Pct.
N.Y. Giants	4	2	0	.667
Washington	4	2	0	.667
Philadelphia	3	3	0	.500
Arizona	2	3	0	.400
Dallas	2	3	0	.400

NFC CENTRAL

	W	L	T	Pct.
Minnesota	5	0	0	1.000
Detroit	4	2	0	.667
Tampa Bay	3	3	0	.500
Green Bay	2	4	0	.333
Chicago	1	5	0	.167

NFC WEST

	W	L	T	Pct.
St. Louis	5	0	0	1.000
Carolina	2	3	0	.400
New Orleans	2	3	0	.400
Atlanta	2	4	0	.333
San Francisco	2	4	0	.333

TOP PERFORMANCES

100-YARD RUSHING GAMES

Player, Team & Opponent	Att.	Yds.	TD
Eddie George, Ten. at Cin.	36	181	1
Ricky Williams, N.O. at Chi.	30	128	1
Charlie Garner, S.F. vs. Oak.*	24	109	0
Jerome Bettis, Pit. at NYJ	25	107	1
Michael Pittman, Ari. vs. Cle.	16	107	0
Tim Biakabutuka, Car. vs. Sea.	23	103	0

300-YARD PASSING GAMES

Player, Team & Opponent	Att.	Comp.	Yds.	TD	Int.
Jeff Garcia, S.F. vs. Oak.*	41	28	336	4	0
Peyton Manning, Ind. at N.E.	54	31	334	1	3
Steve Beuerlein, Car. vs. Sea.	39	27	332	2	1
Rich Gannon, Oak. at S.F.*	43	21	310	2	1

100-YARD RECEIVING GAMES

Player, Team & Opponent	Rec.	Yds.	TD
Terrell Owens, S.F. vs. Oak.*	12	176	2
Tim Brown, Oak. at S.F.*	7	172	2
Marvin Harrison, Ind. at N.E.	13	159	1
Jacquez Green, T.B. at Min.	11	131	0
Randy Moss, Min. vs. T.B.	5	118	1
Wesley Walls, Car. vs. Sea.	7	102	0
Reggie Jones, S.D. vs. Den.	7	101	0

*Overtime game.

RESULTS

SUNDAY, OCTOBER 8

ARIZONA 29, Cleveland 21
Baltimore 15, JACKSONVILLE 10
CAROLINA 26, Seattle 3
Denver 21, SAN DIEGO 7
DETROIT 31, Green Bay 24
MIAMI 22, Buffalo 13
NEW ENGLAND 24, Indianapolis 16
New Orleans 31, CHICAGO 10
N.Y. Giants 13, ATLANTA 6
Oakland 34, SAN FRANCISCO 28 (OT)
Pittsburgh 20, N.Y. JETS 3
Tennessee 23, CINCINNATI 14
Washington 17, PHILADELPHIA 14

MONDAY, OCTOBER 9

MINNESOTA 30, Tampa Bay 23
  Open date: Dallas, Kansas City, St. Louis

TITANS 23, BENGALS 14

Sunday, October 8

Tennessee	3	7	10	3—23
Cincinnati	0	14	0	0—14

First Quarter
Ten.—FG, Del Greco 22, 7:35.

Second Quarter
Cin.—Dillon 80 run (Rackers kick), 1:12.
Ten.—Mason 19 pass from McNair (Del Greco kick), 8:15.
Cin.—D. Williams 36 interception return (Rackers kick), 12:12.

Third Quarter
Ten.—E. George 5 run (Del Greco kick), 6:12.
Ten.—FG, Del Greco 41, 11:32.

Fourth Quarter
Ten.—FG, Del Greco 34, 12:54.
Attendance—63,406.

	Tennessee	Cincinnati
First downs	21	7
Rushes-yards	44-203	20-129
Passing	214	84
Punt returns	5-53	1-6
Kickoff returns	3-77	5-87
Interception returns	0-0	1-36
Comp.-att.-int.	19-31-1	10-23-0
Sacked-yards Lost	2-16	1-1
Punts	5-39	7-37
Fumbles-Lost	1-1	3-2
Penalties-yards	6-50	2-10
Time of possession	41:22	18:38

INDIVIDUAL STATISTICS
RUSHING—Tennessee, E. George 36-181, McNair 5-17, Thomas 3-5. Cincinnati, Dillon 15-95, Smith 3-33, Bennett 1-1, Groce 1-0.
PASSING—Tennessee, McNair 19-31-1-230. Cincinnati, Smith 10-23-0-85.
RECEIVING—Tennessee, Wycheck 7-68, Mason 6-65, E. George 3-33, Sanders 2-56, Kinney 1-8. Cincinnati, Dugans 3-25, Bennett 1-17, Battaglia 1-15, Warrick 1-10, Dillon 1-7, Farmer 1-5, McGee 1-4, Groce 1-2.
MISSED FIELD GOAL ATTEMPTS—Tennessee, Del Greco 33. Cincinnati, Rackers 35, 46.
INTERCEPTIONS—Cincinnati, D. Williams 1-36.
KICKOFF RETURNS—Tennessee, Mason 3-77. Cincinnati, Yeast 3-39, Mack 1-36, N. Williams 1-12.
PUNT RETURNS—Tennessee, Mason 5-53. Cincinnati, Yeast 1-6.
SACKS—Tennessee, Holmes 1. Cincinnati, Foley 1, Steele 1.

STEELERS 20, JETS 3

Sunday, October 8

Pittsburgh	3	7	0	10—20
N.Y. Jets	0	3	0	0— 3

First Quarter
Pit.—FG, K. Brown 43, 15:00.

Second Quarter
Pit.—Bettis 12 run (K. Brown kick), 13:20.
NYJ—FG, Hall 40, 15:00.

Fourth Quarter
Pit.—Shaw 10 pass from Stewart (K. Brown kick), 3:27.
Pit.—FG, K. Brown 29, 11:59.
Attendance—78,441.

	Pittsburgh	N.Y. Jets
First downs	21	12
Rushes-yards	41-193	21-112
Passing	137	94
Punt returns	3-25	1-6
Kickoff returns	1-21	4-110
Interception returns	2-40	0-0
Comp.-att.-int.	17-26-0	13-26-2
Sacked-yards Lost	1-3	1-5
Punts	5-33	4-46
Fumbles-Lost	0-0	2-2
Penalties-yards	8-57	6-45
Time of possession	37:43	22:17

INDIVIDUAL STATISTICS
RUSHING—Pittsburgh, Bettis 25-107, Fuamatu-Ma'afala 7-35, Stewart 6-33, Witman 2-3, Edwards 1-15. New York, Martin 15-59, Lucas 3-31, Ward 1-12, Coles 1-7, R. Anderson 1-3.
PASSING—Pittsburgh, Stewart 17-26-0-140. New York, Lucas 13-25-2-99, Testaverde 0-1-0-0.
RECEIVING—Pittsburgh, Edwards 4-27, Burress 3-26, Fuamatu-Ma'afala 2-23, Shaw 2-20, Ward 2-18, Witman 2-11, Geason 1-8, Bruener 1-7. New York, Chrebet 4-32, Martin 3-16, Becht 2-19, Ward 2-15, Coles 1-18, R. Anderson 1-(minus 1).
MISSED FIELD GOAL ATTEMPTS—New York, Hall 29.
INTERCEPTIONS—Pittsburgh, Washington 1-31, Alexander 1-9.
KICKOFF RETURNS—Pittsburgh, Edwards 1-21. New York, Stone 2-63, Williams 2-47.
PUNT RETURNS—Pittsburgh, Poteat 3-25. New York, Ward 1-6.
SACKS—Pittsburgh, Porter 1. New York, Phifer 1.

SAINTS 31, BEARS 10

Sunday, October 8

New Orleans	0	17	7	7—31
Chicago	7	0	0	3—10

First Quarter
Chi.—Brown 35 interception return (Edinger kick), 4:19.

Second Quarter
N.O.—Horn 4 pass from Blake (Brien kick), 1:34.
N.O.—Horn 47 pass from Blake (Brien kick), 8:12.
N.O.—FG, Brien 44, 13:08.

Third Quarter
N.O.—R. Williams 2 run (Brien kick), 12:39.

Fourth Quarter
Chi.—FG, Edinger 38, 1:37.
N.O.—A. Glover 29 pass from Blake (Brien kick), 7:09.
Attendance—66,944.

	New Orleans	Chicago
First downs	24	13
Rushes-yards	49-186	15-72
Passing	217	173
Punt returns	3-25	3-33
Kickoff returns	3-69	6-169
Interception returns	3-15	1-35
Comp.-att.-int.	18-25-1	18-37-3
Sacked-yards Lost	2-15	5-29
Punts	6-35	5-38
Fumbles-Lost	0-0	0-0
Penalties-yards	10-149	5-45
Time of possession	38:28	21:32

INDIVIDUAL STATISTICS
RUSHING—New Orleans, R. Williams 30-128, Blake 12-66, Brooks 3-(minus 2), Morton 3-(minus 3), Horn 1-(minus 3). Chicago, Allen 10-24, McNown 5-48.
PASSING—New Orleans, Blake 18-25-1-232. Chicago, McNown 18-37-3-202.
RECEIVING—New Orleans, Horn 4-78, R. Williams 4-57, Poole 4-30, T. Smith 3-18, A. Glover 1-29, Jackson 1-14, Reed 1-6. Chicago, Kennison 8-89, Booker 3-44, Brooks 2-33, Bates 2-18, Sinceno 2-16, Allred 1-2.
MISSED FIELD GOAL ATTEMPTS—Chicago, Edinger 30.
INTERCEPTIONS—New Orleans, D. Smith 1-15, Knight 1-0, Oldham 1-0. Chicago, Brown 1-35.
KICKOFF RETURNS—New Orleans, Morton 3-69. Chicago, Milburn 6-169.
PUNT RETURNS—New Orleans, Morton 3-25. Chicago, Milburn 3-33.
SACKS—New Orleans, L. Glover 3, Kei. Mitchell 1, Howard 1. Chicago, Urlacher 1, B. Robinson 1.

LIONS 31, PACKERS 24

Sunday, October 8

Green Bay	0	6	11	7—24
Detroit	10	14	7	0—31

First Quarter
Det.—FG, Hanson 30, 3:37.
Det.—Morton 42 pass from Batch (Hanson kick), 5:35.

Second Quarter
G.B.—FG, Longwell 44, 0:10.
Det.—J. Stewart 13 pass from Batch (Hanson kick), 4:57.
Det.—Campbell 42 interception return (Hanson kick), 13:27.
G.B.—FG, Longwell 51, 14:51.

Third Quarter
G.B.—FG, Longwell 31, 7:41.
Det.—Moore 30 pass from Batch (Hanson kick), 10:21.
G.B.—Freeman 5 pass from Favre (Driver pass from Favre), 13:41.

Fourth Quarter
G.B.—Henderson 7 pass from Favre (Longwell kick), 7:45.
Attendance—77,549.

	Green Bay	Detroit
First downs	19	11
Rushes-yards	22-69	24-74
Passing	270	179
Punt returns	5-41	2-9
Kickoff returns	5-148	6-115
Interception returns	1-22	3-61
Comp.-att.-int.	27-43-3	13-26-1
Sacked-yards Lost	4-23	3-20
Punts	4-33	7-46
Fumbles-Lost	5-2	0-0
Penalties-yards	4-29	6-50
Time of possession	34:36	25:24

INDIVIDUAL STATISTICS
RUSHING—Green Bay, Green 22-69. Detroit, J. Stewart 20-56, Batch 2-6, Crowell 1-12, Bates 1-0.
PASSING—Green Bay, Favre 27-43-3-293. Detroit, Batch 13-26-1-199.
RECEIVING—Green Bay, Green 8-76, Freeman 6-98, Henderson 5-28, Franks 3-18, Lee 2-46, Driver 2-27, Goodman 1-0. Detroit, J. Stewart 5-67, Morton 3-73, Crowell 3-21, Moore 1-30, Schlesinger 1-8.
MISSED FIELD GOAL ATTEMPTS—None.
INTERCEPTIONS—Green Bay, Butler 1-22. Detroit, Campbell 1-42, Schulz 1-19, Fair 1-0.
KICKOFF RETURNS—Green Bay, Goodman 4-129, Rossum 1-19. Detroit, Howard 6-115.
PUNT RETURNS—Green Bay, Lee 4-50, Rossum 1-(minus 9). Detroit, Howard 2-9.
SACKS—Green Bay, S. Dotson 1, Hunt 1, Bowens 1. Detroit, Scroggins 1.5, Elliss 1, Porcher 1, Pritchett 0.5.

CARDINALS 29, BROWNS 21

Sunday, October 8

Cleveland	7	7	0	7—21
Arizona	0	16	10	3—29

First Quarter
Cle.—Prentice 1 run (P. Dawson kick), 13:09.

Second Quarter
Cle.—Prentice 1 run (P. Dawson kick), 0:34.
Ariz.—Jones 10 run (Blanchard kick), 3:00.
Ariz.—Sanders 53 pass from Plummer (run failed), 5:52.
Ariz.—FG, Blanchard 36, 13:47.

Third Quarter
Ariz.—FG, Blanchard 47, 6:05.
Ariz.—Sanders 5 pass from Plummer (Blanchard kick), 13:05.

Fourth Quarter
Cle.—Prentice 6 run (P. Dawson kick), 2:17.
Ariz.—FG, Blanchard 28, 12:00.
Attendance—44,296.

	Cleveland	Arizona
First downs	12	20
Rushes-yards	31-104	31-146
Passing	136	169
Punt returns	3-27	5-26
Kickoff returns	6-125	3-93
Interception returns	0-0	0-0
Comp.-att.-int.	16-22-0	17-30-0
Sacked-yards lost	1-2	1-2
Punts	7-42	3-48
Fumbles-lost	0-0	3-2
Penalties-yards	8-86	3-20
Time of possession	28:57	31:03

INDIVIDUAL STATISTICS
RUSHING—Cleveland, Prentice 28-97, White 2-6, Couch 1-1. Arizona, Pittman 16-107, Plummer 7-(minus 1), Jones 6-9, Boston 1-24, Makovicka 1-7.
PASSING—Cleveland, Couch 16-22-0-138. Arizona, Plummer 17-30-0-171.
RECEIVING—Cleveland, Northcutt 3-67, Patten 3-27, Shea 3-12, Prentice 3-7, Edwards 2-17, Campbell 1-4, Johnson 1-4. Arizona, Boston 5-63, Sanders 4-76, Pittman 2-10, Jenkins 2-8, Gedney 2-7, Hardy 1-5, Makovicka 1-2.
MISSED FIELD GOAL ATTEMPTS—Cleveland, P. Dawson 42.
INTERCEPTIONS—None.
KICKOFF RETURNS—Cleveland, Patten 3-64, White 2-53, Saleh 1-8. Arizona, Jenkins 3-93.
PUNT RETURNS—Cleveland, Northcutt 3-27. Arizona, Cody 5-26.
SACKS—Cleveland, L. Jones 1. Arizona, Ottis 1.

DOLPHINS 22, BILLS 13

Sunday, October 8

Buffalo	3	0	0	10—13
Miami	3	10	2	7—22

First Quarter
Mia.—FG, Mare 30, 6:21.
Buf.—FG, Christie 45, 13:10.

Second Quarter
Mia.—FG, Mare 33, 8:34.
Mia.—Shepherd 20 pass from Fiedler (Mare kick), 13:09.

Third Quarter
Mia.—J. Linton tackled in end zone by J. Haley for a safety, 4:22.

Fourth Quarter
Buf.—FG, Christie 23, 2:59.
Buf.—Morris 3 run (Christie kick), 6:26.
Mia.—Madison 20 fumble return (Mare kick), 10:15.
Attendance—73,901.

	Buffalo	Miami
First downs	15	15
Rushes-yards	21-76	37-120
Passing	178	134
Punt returns	1-0	3-31
Kickoff returns	5-76	4-72
Interception returns	1-0	1-19
Comp.-att.-int.	14-32-1	14-24-1
Sacked-yards Lost	6-44	1-8
Punts	6-43	7-38
Fumbles-Lost	4-1	0-0
Penalties-yards	3-40	5-64
Time of possession	25:38	34:22

INDIVIDUAL STATISTICS
RUSHING—Buffalo, Linton 7-11, Morris 5-17, Bryson 5-4, Johnson 4-44. Miami, L. Smith 24-62, T. Thomas 7-24, Fiedler 5-29, Denson 1-5.
PASSING—Buffalo, Johnson 11-26-0-178, Flutie 3-6-1-44. Miami, Fiedler 14-24-1-142.
RECEIVING—Buffalo, Moulds 4-51, McDaniel 3-48, P. Price 2-61, Morris 2-6, Bryson 1-32, Collins 1-23, Linton 1-1. Miami, Gadsden 3-33, T. Thomas 3-26, Shepherd 2-21, L. Smith 2-9, Emanuel 1-35, Martin 1-11, Goodwin 1-4, Denson 1-3.
MISSED FIELD GOAL ATTEMPTS—None.
INTERCEPTIONS—Buffalo, Irvin 1-0. Miami, Wilson 1-19.
KICKOFF RETURNS—Buffalo, Watson 3-41, Foreman 1-19, Bryson 1-16. Miami, Marion 2-35, Denson 1-23, Shepherd 1-14.
PUNT RETURNS—Buffalo, Watson 1-0. Miami, Shepherd 2-21, Ogden 1-10.
SACKS—Buffalo, Newman 1. Miami, Armstrong 3.5, Mixon 1, Taylor 1, Owens 0.5.

REDSKINS 17, EAGLES 14

Sunday, October 8

Washington	7	0	0	10—17
Philadelphia	0	7	0	7—14

First Quarter
Was.—Davis 12 run (Husted kick), 4:14.

Second Quarter
Phi.—C. Johnson 30 pass from McNabb (Akers kick), 13:31.

Fourth Quarter
Phi.—Brown 8 pass from McNabb (Akers kick), 0:03.
Was.—Hicks 3 run (Husted kick), 4:45.
Was.—FG, Husted 24, 14:58.
   Attendance—65,491.

	Washington	Philadelphia
First downs	23	16
Rushes-yards	31-141	18-79
Passing	266	196
Punt returns	5-47	2-28
Kickoff returns	3-66	3-59
Interception returns	2-48	1-4
Comp.-att.-int.	25-36-1	18-35-2
Sacked-yards Lost	3-23	2-11
Punts	6-37	7-45
Fumbles-Lost	1-1	3-2
Penalties-yards	12-80	5-48
Time of possession	36:27	23:33

INDIVIDUAL STATISTICS

RUSHING—Washington, Davis 23-84, Thrash 2-41, Murrell 2-14, Centers 2-0, Hicks 1-3, B. Johnson 1-(minus 1). Philadelphia, Autry 7-15, McNabb 5-43, Mitchell 3-8, C. Martin 2-10, Pritchett 1-3.

PASSING—Washington, B. Johnson 25-36-1-289. Philadelphia, McNabb 17-34-2-186, Mitchell 1-1-0-21.

RECEIVING—Washington, Connell 6-83, Centers 5-46, Thrash 5-45, Alexander 3-48, Davis 3-37, Sellers 1-12, Fryar 1-9, Reed 1-9. Philadelphia, Lewis 5-77, C. Johnson 4-52, C. Martin 3-17, Small 2-44, Broughton 1-10, Brown 1-8, Autry 1-4, Mitchell 1-(minus 5).

MISSED FIELD GOAL ATTEMPTS—Washington, Husted 33, 42.

INTERCEPTIONS—Washington, Green 1-33, Shade 1-15. Philadelphia, Moore 1-4.

KICKOFF RETURNS—Washington, Thrash 3-43. Philadelphia, Mitchell 2-50, D. Douglas 1-9.

PUNT RETURNS—Washington, Sanders 5-47. Philadelphia, Mitchell 2-28.

SACKS—Washington, Coleman 1, Wilkinson 1. Philadelphia, H. Douglas 2, Simon 1.

BRONCOS 21, CHARGERS 7

Sunday, October 8

Denver	7	0	7	7—21
San Diego	0	7	0	0— 7

First Quarter
Den.—McCaffrey 2 pass from Griese (Elam kick), 6:03.

Second Quarter
S.D.—F. Jones 26 pass from Harbaugh (Carney kick), 14:08.

Third Quarter
Den.—McCaffrey 5 pass from Griese (Elam kick), 8:44.

Fourth Quarter
Den.—Carswell 14 pass from Griese (Elam kick), 13:35.
   Attendance—56,079.

	Denver	San Diego
First downs	18	17
Rushes-yards	30-96	20-65
Passing	208	212
Punt returns	3-72	3-10
Kickoff returns	2-50	4-65
Interception returns	3-81	0-0
Comp.-att.-int.	27-40-0	18-43-3
Sacked-yards lost	2-27	4-25
Punts	9-36	8-47
Fumbles-lost	0-0	1-0
Penalties-yards	9-113	6-57
Time of possession	34:26	25:34

INDIVIDUAL STATISTICS

RUSHING—Denver, Coleman 14-37, Anderson 13-52, Harris 2-0, Griese 1-7. San Diego, Fazande 14-61, Harbaugh 2-3, R. Jenkins 2-1, Fletcher 2-0.

PASSING—Denver, Griese 27-40-0-235. San Diego, Harbaugh 18-43-3-237.

RECEIVING—Denver, McCaffrey 10-71, Chamberlain 6-55, R. Smith 3-52, Carswell 3-29, Harris 2-19, Coleman 1-5, Griffith 1-3, Anderson 1-1. San Diego, R. Jones 7-101, F. Jones 5-72, J. Graham 2-41, Fazande 2-15, Fletcher 2-7.

MISSED FIELD GOAL ATTEMPTS—San Diego, Carney 34.

INTERCEPTIONS—Denver, Buckley 2-64, Jenkins 1-17.

KICKOFF RETURNS—Denver, O'Neal 2-50. San Diego, R. Jenkins 2-40, Bynum 1-17, Jacox 1-8.

PUNT RETURNS—Denver, O'Neal 3-72. San Diego, Jacquet 3-10.

SACKS—Denver, Pryce 3, Tanuvasa 1. San Diego, Dixon 1, Dingle 1.

PATRIOTS 24, COLTS 16

Sunday, October 8

Indianapolis	0	10	3	3—16
New England	3	7	0	14—24

First Quarter
N.E.—FG, Vinatieri 21, 4:59.

Second Quarter
Ind.—Harrison 17 pass from Manning (Vanderjagt kick), 6:36.
Ind.—FG, Vanderjagt 33, 14:50.
N.E.—Simmons 44 pass from Bishop (Vinatieri kick), 15:00.

Third Quarter
Ind.—FG, Vanderjagt 33, 10:19.

Fourth Quarter
N.E.—Bjornson 2 pass from Bledsoe (Vinatieri kick), 0:04.
N.E.—Glenn 4 pass from Bledsoe (Vinatieri kick), 7:34.
Ind.—FG, Vanderjagt 34, 14:24.
   Attendance—60,292.

	Indianapolis	New England
First downs	27	19
Rushes-yards	26-84	28-124
Passing	324	177
Punt returns	2-6	1-15
Kickoff returns	3-62	4-83
Interception returns	0-0	3-31
Comp.-att.-int.	31-54-3	17-25-0
Sacked-yards lost	2-10	4-27
Punts	3-42	6-44
Fumbles-lost	1-0	0-0
Penalties-yards	5-52	7-34
Time of possession	33:10	26:50

INDIVIDUAL STATISTICS

RUSHING—Indianapolis, James 24-75, Manning 1-7, Wilkins 1-2. New England, Redmond 14-45, Faulk 12-64, Bledsoe 2-15.

PASSING—Indianapolis, Manning 31-54-3-334. New England, Bledsoe 15-23-0-142, Bishop 1-1-0-44, L. Johnson 1-1-0-18.

RECEIVING—Indianapolis, Harrison 13-159, Wilkins 6-78, Pathon 6-42, James 3-34, Dilger 2-17, Pollard 1-4. New England, Glenn 5-51, Faulk 4-25, Bjornson 3-22, Simmons 1-44, Calloway 1-20, Brown 1-10, T. Carter 1-4.

MISSED FIELD GOAL ATTEMPTS—None.

INTERCEPTIONS—New England, Jones 1-20, Harris 1-11, Law 1-0.

KICKOFF RETURNS—Indianapolis, P. Williams 2-45, Pathon 1-17. New England, Faulk 3-44, Simmons 1-39.

PUNT RETURNS—Indianapolis, Wilkins 2-6. New England, Brown 1-15.

SACKS—Indianapolis, Holsey 1, Washington 1, Burris 0.5, E. Johnson 0.5, Bennett 0.5, J. Williams 0.5. New England, Spires 2.

GIANTS 13, FALCONS 6

Sunday, October 8

N.Y. Giants	10	3	0	0—13
Atlanta	0	3	3	0— 6

First Quarter
NYG—Dayne 2 run (Holmes kick), 4:53.
NYG—FG, Holmes 34, 14:52.

Second Quarter
Atl.—FG, Andersen 42, 9:35.
NYG—FG, Holmes 27, 15:00.

Third Quarter
Atl.—FG, Andersen 28, 5:38.
   Attendance—50,947.

	N.Y. Giants	Atlanta
First downs	14	17
Rushes-yards	33-104	14-13
Passing	151	225
Punt returns	1-6	3-(-2)
Kickoff returns	3-44	3-70
Interception returns	2-30	2-24
Comp.-att.-int.	14-25-2	23-48-2

	N.Y. Giants	Atlanta
Sacked-yards lost	0-0	4-30
Punts	7-35	5-37
Fumbles-lost	0-0	1-1
Penalties-yards	8-71	2-13
Time of possession	29:45	30:15

INDIVIDUAL STATISTICS

RUSHING—New York, Barber 14-50, Dayne 12-31, Collins 4-5, Comella 2-1, Hilliard 1-17. Atlanta, Anderson 12-12, Dwight 2-1.

PASSING—New York, Collins 14-25-2-151. Atlanta, Kanell 15-36-1-166, Chandler 8-12-1-89.

RECEIVING—New York, Barber 5-50, Comella 4-43, Hilliard 2-25, Toomer 1-17, Dixon 1-9, Jurevicius 1-7. Atlanta, Jefferson 5-72, Christian 5-42, R. Kelly 4-49, Kozlowski 3-44, Mathis 3-25, Anderson 1-12, German 1-10, Dwight 1-1.

MISSED FIELD GOAL ATTEMPTS—Atlanta, Andersen 45.

INTERCEPTIONS—New York, Sehorn 1-32, Armstead 1-(minus 2). Atlanta, Ambrose 1-24, Bradford 1-0.

KICKOFF RETURNS—New York, Dixon 3-44. Atlanta, Dwight 2-50, Vaughn 1-20.

PUNT RETURNS—New York, Barber 1-6. Atlanta, Dwight 2-(minus 2), Oliver 1-0.

SACKS—New York, Monty 1, Strahan 1, Griffin 1, K. Hamilton 1.

PANTHERS 26, SEAHAWKS 3

Sunday, October 8

Seattle	0	0	3	0—	3
Carolina	7	13	3	3—	26

First Quarter
Car.—Hayes 43 pass from Beuerlein (Nedney kick), 10:10.

Second Quarter
Car.—Floyd 5 pass from Beuerlein (Nedney kick), 3:24.
Car.—FG, Nedney 44, 12:55.
Car.—FG, Nedney 42, 15:00.

Third Quarter
Car.—FG, Nedney 22, 10:55.
Sea.—FG, Lindell 42, 14:06.

Fourth Quarter
Car.—FG, Nedney 29, 6:56.
Attendance—72,192.

	Seattle	Carolina
First downs	10	26
Rushes-yards	11-63	33-125
Passing	146	322
Punt returns	0-0	6-24
Kickoff returns	6-129	2-33
Interception returns	1-0	0-0
Comp.-att.-int.	19-34-0	27-39-1
Sacked-yards lost	3-26	2-10
Punts	7-41	2-36
Fumbles-lost	1-0	2-0
Penalties-yards	12-80	5-30
Time of possession	20:20	39:40

INDIVIDUAL STATISTICS

RUSHING—Seattle, Watters 10-63, Alexander 1-0. Carolina, Biakabutuka 23-103, Floyd 4-10, Hoover 4-10, Beuerlein 1-3, Lewis 1-(minus 1).

PASSING—Seattle, Huard 19-34-0-172. Carolina, Beuerlein 27-39-1-332.

RECEIVING—Seattle, Jackson 6-45, Dawkins 5-61, Fauria 3-24, J. Williams 2-31, Mili 1-12, Strong 1-3, Watters 1-(minus 4). Carolina, Walls 7-102, Byrd 6-49, Hayes 5-93, Biakabutuka 4-38, Floyd 3-24, Mangum 1-18, Muhammad 1-8.

MISSED FIELD GOAL ATTEMPTS—Carolina, Nedney 34.

INTERCEPTIONS—Seattle, C. Brown 1-0.

KICKOFF RETURNS—Seattle, Rogers 6-129. Carolina, Bates 2-33.

PUNT RETURNS—Carolina, Bates 4-14, Byrd 1-10, Green 1-0.

SACKS—Seattle, C. Brown 1.5, Koonce 0.5. Carolina, J. Williams 2, Navies 1.

RAIDERS 34, 49ERS 28

Sunday, October 8

Oakland	3	3	15	7	6—34
San Francisco	0	14	0	14	0—28

First Quarter
Oak.—FG, Janikowski 23, 2:16.

Second Quarter
Oak.—FG, Janikowski 35, 3:19.
S.F.—Owens 4 pass from Garcia (Richey kick), 8:39.
S.F.—Rice 5 pass from Garcia (Richey kick), 14:41.

Third Quarter
Oak.—Wheatley 1 run (Gannon run), 5:04.
Oak.—Brown 30 pass from Gannon (Janikowski kick), 10:10.

Fourth Quarter
Oak.—Gannon 13 run (Janikowski kick), 0:12.
S.F.—Owens 31 pass from Garcia (Richey kick), 5:09.
S.F.—Garner 9 pass from Garcia (Richey kick), 6:22.

Overtime
Oak.—Brown 31 pass from Gannon, 10:15.
Attendance—68,344.

	Oakland	San Francisco
First downs	31	28
Rushes-yards	33-164	34-136
Passing	307	336
Punt returns	1-12	0-0
Kickoff returns	4-90	4-83
Interception returns	0-0	1-13
Comp.-att.-int.	21-43-1	28-41-0
Sacked-yards lost	1-3	0-0
Punts	4-44	5-24
Fumbles-lost	1-1	2-2
Penalties-yards	10-74	13-124
Time of possession	35:29	34:43

INDIVIDUAL STATISTICS

RUSHING—Oakland, Wheatley 15-50, Gannon 12-85, Kaufman 6-29. San Francisco, Garner 24-109, Garcia 4-16, Beasley 3-1, Stokes 1-6, Owens 1-4, Jervey 1-0.

PASSING—Oakland, Gannon 21-43-1-310. San Francisco, Garcia 28-41-0-336.

RECEIVING—Oakland, Brown 7-172, Rison 5-83, Jett 3-26, Wheatley 3-16, Crockett 2-1, Kaufman 1-12. San Francisco, Owens 12-176, Rice 5-46, Garner 5-28, Clark 2-19, Beasley 2-15, Streets 1-36, Jackson 1-16.

MISSED FIELD GOAL ATTEMPTS—Oakland, Janikowski 41, 35. San Francisco, Richey 29.

INTERCEPTIONS—San Francisco, Prioleau 1-13.

KICKOFF RETURNS—Oakland, Dunn 3-66, Branch 1-24. San Francisco, K. Williams 2-51, Jervey 2-32.

PUNT RETURNS—Oakland, Gordon 1-12.

SACKS—San Francisco, Tubbs 1.

RAVENS 15, JAGUARS 10

Sunday, October 8

Baltimore	3	3	3	6—15
Jacksonville	3	0	0	7—10

First Quarter
Jac.—FG, Lindsey 49, 6:56.
Bal.—FG, Stover 47, 13:37.

Second Quarter
Bal.—FG, Stover 32, 14:39.

Third Quarter
Bal.—FG, Stover 43, 2:23.

Fourth Quarter
Bal.—FG, Stover 21, 1:22.
Bal.—FG, Stover 24, 5:16.
Jac.—Taylor 1 run (Lindsey kick), 10:56.
Attendance—65,194.

	Baltimore	Jacksonville
First downs	10	22
Rushes-yards	24-55	27-95
Passing	138	253
Punt returns	2-24	6-38
Kickoff returns	2-62	5-68
Interception returns	3-87	0-0
Comp.-att.-int.	17-39-0	29-43-3
Sacked-yards lost	2-16	3-7
Punts	9-42	5-38
Fumbles-lost	1-1	8-3
Penalties-yards	6-30	6-35
Time of possession	28:12	31:48

INDIVIDUAL STATISTICS

RUSHING—Baltimore, Ja. Lewis 16-43, Banks 3-6, Ayanbadejo 2-8, Holmes 2-(minus 6), J. Lewis 1-4. Jacksonville, Taylor 17-54, Brunell 8-32, Johnson 1-7, Martin 1-2.

PASSING—Baltimore, Banks 17-39-0-154. Jacksonville, Brunell 18-28-2-167, Martin 11-15-1-93.

RECEIVING—Baltimore, Ismail 9-85, Ayanbadejo 4-17, J. Lewis 2-19, Sharpe 1-26, Taylor 1-7. Jacksonville, J. Smith 8-95, McCardell 8-63, Taylor 7-45, Brady 5-45, Shelton 1-12.

MISSED FIELD GOAL ATTEMPTS—Jacksonville, Lindsey 31.

INTERCEPTIONS—Baltimore, Herring 2-69, Woodson 1-18.

KICKOFF RETURNS—Baltimore, Harris 2-62. Jacksonville, Stith 2-50, Mack 2-18, Fordham 1-0.

PUNT RETURNS—Baltimore, J. Lewis 2-24. Jacksonville, Soward 6-38.

SACKS—Baltimore, Boulware 1.5, Adams 1, R. Lewis 0.5. Jacksonville, Beasley 2.

VIKINGS 30, BUCCANEERS 23

Monday, October 9

Tampa Bay	7	3	6	7—23
Minnesota	7	10	3	10—30

First Quarter
Min.—Culpepper 27 run (Anderson kick), 0:24.
T.B.—King 11 run (Gramatica kick), 10:59.

Second Quarter
Min.—FG, Anderson 37, 2:46.
Min.—J. Davis 26 pass from Culpepper (Anderson kick), 3:49.
T.B.—FG, Gramatica 23, 13:54.

Third Quarter
Min.—FG, Anderson 42, 3:48.
T.B.—FG, Gramatica 33, 6:49.
T.B.—FG, Gramatica 35, 14:16.

Fourth Quarter
T.B.—Abraham 53 blocked FG return (Gramatica kick), 2:47.
Min.—Moss 42 pass from Culpepper (Anderson kick), 6:18.
Min.—FG, Anderson 19, 14:01.
Attendance—64,162.

	Tampa Bay	Minnesota
First downs	22	17
Rushes-yards	20-63	30-115
Passing	283	207
Punt returns	2-24	1-3
Kickoff returns	7-160	6-134
Interception returns	1-0	0-0
Comp.-att.-int.	26-41-0	15-19-1
Sacked-yards lost	2-12	6-24
Punts	1-53	2-52
Fumbles-lost	3-3	3-1
Penalties-yards	7-58	4-44
Time of possession	29:26	30:34

INDIVIDUAL STATISTICS

RUSHING—Tampa Bay, Dunn 10-32, Alstott 6-10, King 3-22, Green 1-(minus 1). Minnesota, Smith 22-81, Culpepper 7-35, M. Williams 1-(minus 1).

PASSING—Tampa Bay, King 26-40-0-295, Alstott 0-1-0-0. Minnesota, Culpepper 15-19-1-231.

RECEIVING—Tampa Bay, Green 11-131, K. Johnson 5-71, Dunn 4-47, Alstott 2-24, Moore 2-12, Anthony 1-7, Hape 1-3. Minnesota, Moss 5-118, C. Carter 3-43, Smith 3-19, J. Davis 2-41, Hatchette 1-5, Walters 1-5.

MISSED FIELD GOAL ATTEMPTS—Tampa Bay, Gramatica 53. Minnesota, Anderson 51.

INTERCEPTIONS—Tampa Bay, Robinson 1-0.

KICKOFF RETURNS—Tampa Bay, Stecker 7-160. Minnesota, T. Carter 6-134.

PUNT RETURNS—Tampa Bay, Hastings 2-24. Minnesota, Walters 1-3.

SACKS—Tampa Bay, Jones 2, McFarland 1, Barber 1, Sapp 1, Ahanotu 1. Minnesota, Sawyer 1, Randle 1.

STANDINGS

AFC EAST

	W	L	T	Pct.
Miami	5	1	0	.833
N.Y. Jets	5	1	0	.833
Indianapolis	4	2	0	.667
Buffalo	3	3	0	.500
New England	2	5	0	.286

AFC CENTRAL

	W	L	T	Pct.
Tennessee	5	1	0	.833
Baltimore	5	2	0	.714
Pittsburgh	3	3	0	.500
Jacksonville	2	4	0	.333
Cleveland	2	5	0	.286
Cincinnati	0	6	0	.000

AFC WEST

	W	L	T	Pct.
Oakland	5	1	0	.833
Denver	4	3	0	.571
Kansas City	3	3	0	.500
Seattle	2	5	0	.286
San Diego	0	7	0	.000

NFC EAST

	W	L	T	Pct.
N.Y. Giants	5	2	0	.714
Washington	5	2	0	.714
Philadelphia	4	3	0	.571
Arizona	2	4	0	.333
Dallas	2	4	0	.333

NFC CENTRAL

	W	L	T	Pct.
Minnesota	6	0	0	1.000
Detroit	4	2	0	.667
Tampa Bay	3	3	0	.500
Green Bay	3	4	0	.429
Chicago	1	6	0	.143

NFC WEST

	W	L	T	Pct.
St. Louis	6	0	0	1.000
New Orleans	3	3	0	.500
Carolina	2	4	0	.333
Atlanta	2	5	0	.286
San Francisco	2	5	0	.286

TOP PERFORMANCES

100-YARD RUSHING GAMES

Player, Team & Opponent	Att.	Yds.	TD
Edgerrin James, Ind. at Sea.	38	219	3
Marshall Faulk, St.L. vs. Atl.	25	208	1
Robert Smith, Min. at Chi.	23	170	1
Eddie George, Ten. vs. Jack.	29	167	1
Ricky Williams, N.O. vs. Car.	38	144	2
Curtis Martin, NYJ at N.E.	34	143	3
Fred Taylor, Jack. at Ten.	20	112	0
Ron Dayne, NYG vs. Dal.	21	108	1
Mike Anderson, Den. vs. Cle.	20	103	1
Jerome Bettis, Pit. vs. Cin.	29	101	0

300-YARD PASSING GAMES

Player, Team & Opponent	Att.	Comp.	Yds.	TD	Int.
Jeff Garcia, S.F. at G.B.	42	27	336	4	0
Brian Griese, Den. vs. Cle.	34	19	336	3	0
Rob Johnson, Buf. vs. S.D.*	47	29	321	1	1
Kurt Warner, St.L. vs. Atl.	40	24	313	3	1

100-YARD RECEIVING GAMES

Player, Team & Opponent	Rec.	Yds.	TD
Eric Moulds, Buf. vs. S.D.*	11	170	0
Curtis Conway, S.D. at Buf.*	7	143	1
Marvin Harrison, Ind. at Sea.	7	134	0
Ed McCaffrey, Den. vs. Cle.	5	129	0
David Boston, Ari. vs. Phi.	6	123	1
Sean Dawkins, Sea. vs. Ind.	6	118	0
Antonio Freeman, G.B. vs. S.F.	6	116	1
Jeff Graham, S.D. at Buf.*	9	113	1
Cris Carter, Min. at Chi.	7	111	1
Rod Smith, Den. vs. Cle.	5	111	3
Tony Gonzalez, K.C. vs. Oak.	7	100	1

*Overtime game.

RESULTS

SUNDAY, OCTOBER 15

BUFFALO 27, San Diego 24 (OT)
DENVER 44, Cleveland 10
GREEN BAY 31, San Francisco 28
Indianapolis 37, SEATTLE 24
Minnesota 28, CHICAGO 16
NEW ORLEANS 24, Carolina 6
N.Y. GIANTS 19, Dallas 14
N.Y. Jets 34, NEW ENGLAND 17
Oakland 20, KANSAS CITY 17
Philadelphia 33, ARIZONA 14
PITTSBURGH 15, Cincinnati 0
ST. LOUIS 45, Atlanta 29
WASHINGTON 10, Baltimore 3

MONDAY, OCTOBER 16

TENNESSEE 27, Jacksonville 13
Open date: Detroit, Miami, Tampa Bay

2000 REVIEW Week 7

JETS 34, PATRIOTS 17

Sunday, October 15

N.Y. Jets	14	10	7	3—34
New England	3	7	0	7—17

First Quarter

NYJ—Martin 2 run (Hall kick), 6:31.
NYJ—V. Green 21 interception return (Hall kick), 7:26.
N.E.—FG, Vinatieri 23, 11:29.

Second Quarter

N.E.—Faulk 9 run (Vinatieri kick), 4:16.
NYJ—Martin 4 run (Hall kick), 12:49.
NYJ—FG, Hall 38, 14:55.

Third Quarter

NYJ—Martin 2 run (Hall kick), 10:47.

Fourth Quarter

N.E.—Bledsoe 13 run (Vinatieri kick), 5:22.
NYJ—FG, Hall 27, 11:04.
Attendance—60,292.

	N.Y. Jets	New England
First downs	20	16
Rushes-yards	43-164	14-51
Passing	130	198
Punt returns	3-17	3-35
Kickoff returns	4-76	6-129
Interception returns	4-80	0-0
Comp.-att.-int.	15-23-0	18-41-4
Sacked-yards lost	3-9	7-46
Punts	6-42	5-36
Fumbles-lost	1-1	2-2
Penalties-yards	5-68	4-30
Time of possession	37:54	22:06

INDIVIDUAL STATISTICS

RUSHING—New York, Martin 34-143, R. Anderson 3-10, Testaverde 3-3, Chrebet 2-5, Lewis 1-3. New England, Faulk 9-26, Bledsoe 2-16, T. Carter 2-7, Redmond 1-2.

PASSING—New York, Testaverde 15-23-0-139. New England, Bledsoe 16-35-3-208, Bishop 2-6-1-36.

RECEIVING—New York, Coles 6-53, R. Anderson 4-34, Chrebet 2-22, Martin 2-18, Ward 1-12. New England, Brown 5-73, Faulk 5-27, Simmons 3-76, Glenn 2-45, Bjornson 2-17, T. Carter 1-6.

MISSED FIELD GOAL ATTEMPTS—New York, Hall 46.

INTERCEPTIONS—New York, V. Green 2-57, Lewis 1-23, Glenn 1-0.

KICKOFF RETURNS—New York, Williams 3-66, Stone 1-10. New England, Faulk 5-105, Simmons 1-24.

PUNT RETURNS—New York, Ward 3-17. New England, Brown 3-35.

SACKS—New York, Abraham 2, Lewis 1, Lyle 1, Ellis 1, Ferguson 1, Cox 0.5, Burton 0.5. New England, Thomas 1, McGinest 1, Slade 1.

RAIDERS 20, CHIEFS 17

Sunday, October 15

Oakland	7	0	3	10—20
Kansas City	0	17	0	0—17

First Quarter

Oak.—Kaufman 4 pass from Gannon (Janikowski kick), 9:51.

Second Quarter

K.C.—FG, Peterson 27, 8:22.
K.C.—Gonzalez 14 pass from Grbac (Peterson kick), 12:11.
K.C.—Richardson 15 pass from Grbac (Peterson kick), 14:48.

Third Quarter

Oak.—FG, Janikowski 47, 4:44.

Fourth Quarter

Oak.—Wheatley 7 pass from Gannon (Janikowski kick), 5:35.
Oak.—FG, Janikowski 43, 14:35.
Attendance—79,025.

	Oakland	Kansas City
First downs	23	20
Rushes-yards	33-161	19-58
Passing	230	288
Punt returns	1-17	1-11
Kickoff returns	4-106	4-108
Interception returns	0-0	0-0
Comp.-att.-int.	28-33-0	23-40-0
Sacked-yards lost	2-14	1-0
Punts	3-51	4-51
Fumbles-lost	1-1	1-1
Penalties-yards	8-69	6-40
Time of possession	34:01	25:59

INDIVIDUAL STATISTICS

RUSHING—Oakland, Wheatley 15-76, Kaufman 10-47, Gannon 8-38. Kansas City, Moreau 7-18, Richardson 5-25, Anders 4-8, Cloud 3-7.

PASSING—Oakland, Gannon 28-33-0-244. Kansas City, Grbac 23-40-0-288.

RECEIVING—Oakland, Ritchie 7-48, Brown 5-89, Wheatley 4-37, Kaufman 3-9, Brigham 2-19, Jett 2-15, Rison 2-15, Jordan 2-4, Woodson 1-8. Kansas City, Gonzalez 7-100, Alexander 5-78, Richardson 5-31, Morris 4-64, Lockett 1-13, Drayton 1-2.

MISSED FIELD GOAL ATTEMPTS—Oakland, Janikowski 47, 59. Kansas City, Peterson 44.

INTERCEPTIONS—None.

KICKOFF RETURNS—Oakland, Dunn 4-106. Kansas City, Hall 3-84, Cloud 1-24.

PUNT RETURNS—Oakland, Gordon 1-17. Kansas City, Hall 1-11.

SACKS—Oakland, Team 1. Kansas City, Browning 1, Bartee 1.

STEELERS 15, BENGALS 0

Sunday, October 15

Cincinnati	0	0	0	0— 0
Pittsburgh	7	3	3	2—15

First Quarter

Pit.—Ward 77 pass from Graham (K. Brown kick), 1:07.

Second Quarter

Pit.—FG, K. Brown 36, 14:56.

Third Quarter

Pit.—FG, K. Brown 28, 12:41.

Fourth Quarter

Pit.—S. Mitchell sacked in end zone by J. Porter for a safety, 8:28.
Attendance—54,328.

	Cincinnati	Pittsburgh
First downs	12	13
Rushes-yards	26-120	32-103
Passing	111	171
Punt returns	6-40	6-78
Kickoff returns	3-49	2-35
Interception returns	0-0	2-45
Comp.-att.-int.	14-36-2	13-33-0
Sacked-yards lost	4-25	1-2
Punts	10-44	12-44
Fumbles-lost	1-1	0-0
Penalties-yards	6-46	8-65
Time of possession	28:39	31:21

INDIVIDUAL STATISTICS

RUSHING—Cincinnati, Dillon 15-36, Smith 3-24, Keaton 3-12, Warrick 2-48, Bennett 2-5, Rackers 1-(minus 5). Pittsburgh, Bettis 29-101, Graham 2-4, Huntley 1-(minus 2).

PASSING—Cincinnati, Smith 10-20-0-97, S. Mitchell 4-16-2-39. Pittsburgh, Graham 13-33-0-173.

RECEIVING—Cincinnati, Warrick 4-21, McGee 3-23, Dugans 2-29, Yeast 1-22, Griffin 1-16, Battaglia 1-14, Dillon 1-9, Groce 1-2. Pittsburgh, Burress 4-33, Shaw 3-36, Ward 2-91, Fuamatu-Ma'afala 2-1, Edwards 1-7, Bruener 1-5.

MISSED FIELD GOAL ATTEMPTS—None.

INTERCEPTIONS—Pittsburgh, Washington 1-30, Alexander 1-15.

KICKOFF RETURNS—Cincinnati, Mack 2-42, Bush 1-7. Pittsburgh, Edwards 2-35.

PUNT RETURNS—Cincinnati, Yeast 5-30, Warrick 1-10. Pittsburgh, Poteat 6-78.

SACKS—Cincinnati, Wilson 1. Pittsburgh, Porter 3, Gildon 1.

EAGLES 33, CARDINALS 14

Sunday, October 15

Philadelphia	7	10	7	9—33
Arizona	0	0	7	7—14

First Quarter
Phi.—Pritchett 1 run (Akers kick), 9:31.

Second Quarter
Phi.—FG, Akers 31, 3:28.
Phi.—McNabb 3 run (Akers kick), 14:35.

Third Quarter
Phi.—Lewis 9 pass from McNabb (Akers kick), 5:44.
Ariz.—Boston 70 pass from Plummer (Blanchard kick), 10:27.

Fourth Quarter
Ariz.—Pittman 10 pass from Plummer (Blanchard kick), 4:13.
Phi.—Autry 1 run (kick failed), 9:32.
Phi.—FG, Akers 29, 12:16.
Attendance—38,293.

	Philadelphia	Arizona
First downs	28	17
Rushes-yards	38-172	14-93
Passing	219	207
Punt returns	2-0	2-8
Kickoff returns	3-76	7-168
Interception returns	2-43	0-0
Comp.-att.-int.	24-35-0	18-30-2
Sacked-yards lost	3-7	1-6
Punts	3-47	3-46
Fumbles-lost	0-0	1-1
Penalties-yards	10-95	9-65
Time of possession	39:34	20:26

INDIVIDUAL STATISTICS
RUSHING—Philadelphia, Autry 20-64, McNabb 7-35, Pritchett 6-29, Mitchell 3-16, Akers 1-15, C. Martin 1-13. Arizona, Pittman 8-37, Jones 3-35, Plummer 2-43, Boston 1-(minus 22).

PASSING—Philadelphia, McNabb 24-34-0-226, Mitchell 0-1-0-0. Arizona, Plummer 18-30-2-213.

RECEIVING—Philadelphia, Lewis 7-62, Small 5-44, C. Johnson 4-68, Autry 3-28, C. Martin 3-5, Pritchett 1-11, Brown 1-8. Arizona, Boston 6-123, Pittman 4-27, Gedney 2-13, Cody 1-18, Sanders 1-13, Jenkins 1-7, Hardy 1-5, Makovicka 1-4, Jones 1-3.

MISSED FIELD GOAL ATTEMPTS—None.

INTERCEPTIONS—Philadelphia, Taylor 1-25, Vincent 1-17.

KICKOFF RETURNS—Philadelphia, Mitchell 3-76. Arizona, Jenkins 7-168.

PUNT RETURNS—Philadelphia, Mitchell 2-0. Arizona, Cody 2-8.

SACKS—Philadelphia, H. Douglas 1. Arizona, Folston 2, Rice 1.

PACKERS 31, 49ERS 28

Sunday, October 15

San Francisco	0	7	7	14—28
Green Bay	7	7	7	10—31

First Quarter
G.B.—Freeman 67 pass from Favre (Longwell kick), 12:43.

Second Quarter
S.F.—Garner 39 pass from Garcia (Richey kick), 9:33.
G.B.—Green 2 run (Longwell kick), 14:09.

Third Quarter
G.B.—Levens 1 run (Longwell kick), 6:09.
S.F.—Stokes 23 pass from Garcia (Richey kick), 12:50.

Fourth Quarter
S.F.—Owens 16 pass from Garcia (Richey kick), 3:24.
G.B.—Green 1 run (Longwell kick), 6:59.
S.F.—Owens 37 pass from Garcia (Richey kick), 9:30.
G.B.—FG, Longwell 35, 14:06.
Attendance—59,870.

	San Francisco	Green Bay
First downs	23	22
Rushes-yards	19-95	31-132
Passing	319	246
Punt returns	2-7	0-0
Kickoff returns	5-97	5-129
Interception returns	0-0	0-0
Comp.-att.-int.	27-42-0	20-27-0
Sacked-yards lost	2-17	2-20
Punts	5-34	5-38
Fumbles-lost	1-0	0-0
Penalties-yards	4-53	9-65
Time of possession	27:36	32:24

INDIVIDUAL STATISTICS
RUSHING—San Francisco, Garner 14-84, Garcia 4-6, Beasley 1-5. Green Bay, Levens 17-57, Green 11-40, Favre 3-35.

PASSING—San Francisco, Garcia 27-42-0-336. Green Bay, Favre 20-27-0-266.

RECEIVING—San Francisco, Owens 8-93, Rice 6-77, Garner 5-92, Streets 3-25, Beasley 3-14, Stokes 2-35. Green Bay, Freeman 6-116, Levens 4-42, Franks 4-40, Green 2-25, Schroeder 2-23, Driver 1-10, Henderson 1-10.

MISSED FIELD GOAL ATTEMPTS—None.

INTERCEPTIONS—None.

KICKOFF RETURNS—San Francisco, Smith 3-67, K. Williams 2-30. Green Bay, Rossum 5-129.

PUNT RETURNS—San Francisco, K. Williams 2-7.

SACKS—San Francisco, B. Young 1, Buckner 0.5, Posey 0.5. Green Bay, Hunt 1, Thierry 0.5, Gbaja-Biamila 0.5.

BILLS 27, CHARGERS 24

Sunday, October 15

San Diego	3	7	14	0	0—24
Buffalo	0	14	0	10	3—27

First Quarter
S.D.—FG, Carney 36, 14:47.

Second Quarter
Buf.—Morris 32 run (Christie kick), 0:55.
Buf.—Ostroski recovered fumble in end zone (Christie kick), 4:07.
S.D.—Conway 60 pass from Harbaugh (Carney kick), 5:45.

Third Quarter
S.D.—Fazande 2 run (Carney kick), 4:30.
S.D.—J. Graham 52 pass from Harbaugh (Carney kick), 6:51.

Fourth Quarter
Buf.—Bryson 11 pass from Johnson (Christie kick), 1:12.
Buf.—FG, Christie 29, 14:53.

Overtime
Buf.—FG, Christie 46, 8:26.
Attendance—72,351.

	San Diego	Buffalo
First downs	15	25
Rushes-yards	27-52	28-95
Passing	251	329
Punt returns	6-51	1-0
Kickoff returns	5-49	5-101
Interception returns	1-0	2-2
Comp.-att.-int.	21-34-2	31-50-1
Sacked-yards lost	4-36	4-22
Punts	7-42	10-43
Fumbles-lost	4-2	3-1
Penalties-yards	12-88	10-103
Time of possession	32:54	35:32

INDIVIDUAL STATISTICS
RUSHING—San Diego, Fazande 19-51, Harbaugh 5-1, Fletcher 2-0, Moreno 1-0. Buffalo, Bryson 9-22, Morris 8-60, Linton 8-10, Johnson 3-3.

PASSING—San Diego, Harbaugh 21-33-2-287, Moreno 0-1-0-0. Buffalo, Johnson 29-47-1-321, Flutie 2-3-0-30.

RECEIVING—San Diego, J. Graham 9-113, Conway 7-143, R. Jones 2-20, Fazande 2-7, Fletcher 1-4. Buffalo, Moulds 11-170, P. Price 6-75, Bryson 6-47, McDaniel 4-44, Morris 3-4, Collins 1-11.

MISSED FIELD GOAL ATTEMPTS—None.

INTERCEPTIONS—San Diego, Harrison 1-0. Buffalo, Cowart 1-2, H. Jones 1-0.

KICKOFF RETURNS—San Diego, Bynum 2-28, R. Jenkins 2-21, D. Graham 1-0. Buffalo, Watson 5-101.

PUNT RETURNS—San Diego, Jacquet 6-51. Buffalo, Watson 1-0.

SACKS—San Diego, Harrison 1, Dixon 1, Parrella 1, Fontenot 1. Buffalo, Wiley 2, Cowart 1, Flowers 1.

SAINTS 24, PANTHERS 6

Sunday, October 15

Carolina	0	6	0	0— 6
New Orleans	0	10	0	14—24

Second Quarter
N.O.—R. Williams 2 run (Brien kick), 0:47.
Car.—FG, Nedney 52, 10:42.
N.O.—FG, Brien 29, 14:47.
Car.—FG, Nedney 46, 15:00.

Fourth Quarter

N.O.—R. Williams 1 run (Brien kick), 9:44.

N.O.—Horn 29 pass from Blake (Brien kick), 11:50.

 Attendance—50,015.

	Carolina	New Orleans
First downs	8	21
Rushes-yards	12-10	47-215
Passing	131	182
Punt returns	1-12	4-27
Kickoff returns	5-95	2-40
Interception returns	0-0	1-0
Comp.-att.-int.	15-31-1	12-24-0
Sacked-yards lost	8-41	1-13
Punts	9-33	5-37
Fumbles-lost	1-1	4-3
Penalties-yards	7-45	8-59
Time of possession	24:02	35:58

INDIVIDUAL STATISTICS

RUSHING—Carolina, Biakabutuka 10-5, Floyd 1-3, Beuerlein 1-2. New Orleans, R. Williams 38-144, T. Smith 4-22, Blake 4-9, McAfee 1-40.

PASSING—Carolina, Beuerlein 15-28-1-172, Lewis 0-3-0-0. New Orleans, Blake 11-23-0-161, R. Williams 1-1-0-34.

RECEIVING—Carolina, Hayes 5-67, Walls 4-53, Muhammad 2-27, Floyd 2-12, Kinchen 1-7, Biakabutuka 1-6. New Orleans, Horn 5-97, R. Williams 3-35, A. Glover 2-29, Poole 1-34, Morton 1-0.

MISSED FIELD GOAL ATTEMPTS—New Orleans, Brien 51.

INTERCEPTIONS—New Orleans, Mathis 1-0.

KICKOFF RETURNS—Carolina, Bates 4-94, Green 1-1. New Orleans, Morton 2-40.

PUNT RETURNS—Carolina, Uwaezuoke 1-12. New Orleans, Morton 4-27.

SACKS—Carolina, J. Williams 1. New Orleans, L. Glover 3, Kei. Mitchell 2, Howard 2, Johnson 1.

RAMS 45, FALCONS 29

Sunday, October 15

Atlanta	14	7	0	8—29
St. Louis	7	22	8	8—45

First Quarter

Atl.—Vaughn 96 kickoff return (Andersen kick), 0:16.

St.L.—Horne 103 kickoff return (Wilkins kick), 0:36.

Atl.—Mathis 16 pass from Chandler (Andersen kick), 4:46.

Second Quarter

St.L.—Horne 3 pass from Warner (Fletcher pass from Lyle), 0:05.

St.L.—Watson 2 run (run failed), 11:44.

Atl.—Anderson 4 run (Andersen kick), 13:04.

St.L.—Hakim 30 pass from Warner (Faulk run), 14:57.

Third Quarter

St.L.—Holcombe 12 pass from Warner (Faulk run), 8:03.

Fourth Quarter

Atl.—Dwight 16 pass from Chandler (Anderson run), 10:33.

St.L.—Faulk 3 run (R. Williams pass from Warner), 13:51.

 Attendance—66,019.

	Atlanta	St. Louis
First downs	21	29
Rushes-yards	16-61	31-227
Passing	198	302
Punt returns	1-(-1)	1-1
Kickoff returns	7-178	5-163
Interception returns	1-3	1-0
Comp.-att.-int.	18-30-1	24-40-1
Sacked-yards lost	3-22	3-11
Punts	5-43	3-35
Fumbles-lost	0-0	0-0
Penalties-yards	8-40	11-96
Time of possession	25:16	34:44

INDIVIDUAL STATISTICS

RUSHING—Atlanta, Anderson 14-64, M. Smith 2-(minus 3). St. Louis, Faulk 25-208, Holcombe 3-12, Watson 2-6, Warner 1-1.

PASSING—Atlanta, Chandler 18-30-1-220. St. Louis, Warner 24-40-1-313.

RECEIVING—Atlanta, Anderson 4-67, Dwight 3-35, Mathis 3-32, Christian 3-29, Finneran 2-25, Jefferson 2-17, R. Kelly 1-15. St. Louis, Faulk 7-78, Hakim 7-73, Bruce 3-88, Holt 3-51, Horne 2-8, Holcombe 1-12, Watson 1-3.

MISSED FIELD GOAL ATTEMPTS—None.

INTERCEPTIONS—Atlanta, Buchanan 1-3. St. Louis, McCleon 1-0.

KICKOFF RETURNS—Atlanta, Dwight 3-56, Kozlowski 2-7, Vaughn 1-96, E. Williams 1-19. St. Louis, Horne 5-163.

PUNT RETURNS—Atlanta, Oliver 1-(minus 1). St. Louis, Hakim 1-1.

SACKS—Atlanta, McBurrows 1, Simoneau 1, Hall 1. St. Louis, M. Jones 1, Wistrom 1, Moran 1.

GIANTS 19, COWBOYS 14

Sunday, October 15

Dallas	0	0	14	0—14
N.Y. Giants	0	7	6	6—19

Second Quarter

NYG—Mitchell 1 pass from Collins (Daluiso kick), 8:18.

Third Quarter

NYG—FG, Daluiso 24, 3:51.

Dal.—Thomas 1 pass from Aikman (Seder kick), 4:58.

NYG—FG, Daluiso 20, 8:47.

Dal.—E. Smith 3 run (Seder kick), 13:41.

Fourth Quarter

NYG—Dayne 3 run (run failed), 5:00.

 Attendance—78,189.

	Dallas	N.Y. Giants
First downs	23	17
Rushes-yards	27-76	33-203
Passing	193	108
Punt returns	3-22	3-47
Kickoff returns	5-205	2-41
Interception returns	0-0	5-19
Comp.-att.-int.	22-42-5	14-25-0
Sacked-yards lost	2-18	2-11
Punts	3-43	7-40
Fumbles-lost	0-0	0-0
Penalties-yards	9-81	9-72
Time of possession	30:42	29:18

INDIVIDUAL STATISTICS

RUSHING—Dallas, E. Smith 19-61, Warren 5-4, Aikman 2-7, Thomas 1-4. New York, Dayne 21-108, Barber 9-73, Collins 3-22.

PASSING—Dallas, Aikman 22-42-5-211. New York, Collins 14-25-0-119.

RECEIVING—Dallas, Warren 6-62, Thomas 5-24, Hodge 3-52, Tucker 2-26, Ismail 2-14, E. Smith 2-10, LaFleur 1-19, Harris 1-4. New York, Jurevicius 4-25, Hilliard 3-42, Comella 2-19, Toomer 2-17, Barber 2-15, Mitchell 1-1.

MISSED FIELD GOAL ATTEMPTS—None.

INTERCEPTIONS—New York, S. Williams 1-12, Barrow 1-7, Thomas 1-0, Sehorn 1-0, Stephens 1-0.

KICKOFF RETURNS—Dallas, Tucker 5-205. New York, Dixon 2-41.

PUNT RETURNS—Dallas, McGarity 3-22. New York, Barber 3-47.

SACKS—Dallas, Lett 1, Hambrick 1. New York, Jones 1, McDaniel 1.

COLTS 37, SEAHAWKS 24

Sunday, October 15

Indianapolis	7	13	14	3—37
Seattle	0	17	0	7—24

First Quarter

Ind.—James 26 run (Vanderjagt kick), 3:55.

Second Quarter

Ind.—FG, Vanderjagt 23, 0:48.

Sea.—Jackson 8 pass from Huard (Lindell kick), 4:57.

Ind.—James 3 run (Vanderjagt kick), 8:06.

Sea.—Mili 7 pass from Huard (Lindell kick), 13:04.

Ind.—FG, Vanderjagt 38, 14:37.

Sea.—FG, Lindell 51, 15:00.

Third Quarter

Ind.—Dilger 17 pass from Manning (Vanderjagt kick), 6:27.

Ind.—James 2 run (Vanderjagt kick), 14:48.

Fourth Quarter

Ind.—FG, Vanderjagt 40, 4:20.

Sea.—Bailey 6 pass from Huard (Lindell kick), 9:48.

 Attendance—63,593.

	Indianapolis	Seattle
First downs	28	21
Rushes-yards	39-219	16-65
Passing	280	252

	Indianapolis	Seattle
Punt returns	1-5	1-17
Kickoff returns	4-64	8-268
Interception returns	1-0	0-0
Comp.-att.-int.	20-30-0	24-32-1
Sacked-yards lost	1-1	6-31
Punts	1-45	3-35
Fumbles-lost	2-2	2-2
Penalties-yards	3-25	5-39
Time of possession	36:09	23:51

INDIVIDUAL STATISTICS

RUSHING—Indianapolis, James 38-219, Manning 1-0. Seattle, Watters 8-24, Alexander 5-20, Huard 3-21.

PASSING—Indianapolis, Manning 20-30-0-281. Seattle, Huard 19-26-1-226, Kitna 5-6-0-57.

RECEIVING—Indianapolis, Harrison 7-134, Dilger 6-93, Wilkins 5-32, Pathon 1-13, James 1-9. Seattle, Dawkins 6-118, Jackson 6-66, Mili 4-21, Watters 3-31, J. Williams 2-31, Bailey 2-11, Strong 1-5.

MISSED FIELD GOAL ATTEMPTS—Seattle, Lindell 21.

INTERCEPTIONS—Indianapolis, Cota 1-0.

KICKOFF RETURNS—Indianapolis, P. Williams 2-37, Pathon 1-27, Peterson 1-0. Seattle, Rogers 6-198, Bownes 1-44, Strong 1-26.

PUNT RETURNS—Indianapolis, Wilkins 1-5. Seattle, Rogers 1-17.

SACKS—Indianapolis, J. Williams 1.5, Bennett 1, Burris 1, E. Johnson 1, Washington 1, Bratzke 0.5. Seattle, C. Brown 0.5, Sinclair 0.5.

BRONCOS 44, BROWNS 10

Sunday, October 15

Cleveland	3	0	7	0—10
Denver	3	17	14	10—44

First Quarter
Den.—FG, Elam 22, 1:39.
Cle.—FG, P. Dawson 45, 13:42.

Second Quarter
Den.—R. Smith 22 pass from Griese (Elam kick), 6:13.
Den.—R. Smith 17 pass from Griese (Elam kick), 10:31.
Den.—FG, Elam 45, 14:49.

Third Quarter
Cle.—Prentice 3 pass from Couch (P. Dawson kick), 4:06.
Den.—Anderson 26 run (Elam kick), 5:45.
Den.—R. Smith 32 pass from Griese (Elam kick), 10:12.

Fourth Quarter
Den.—Jenkins 36 interception return (Elam kick), 1:38.
Den.—FG, Elam 46, 6:05.
Attendance—75,811.

	Cleveland	Denver
First downs	12	24
Rushes-yards	9-38	31-146
Passing	240	353
Punt returns	1-22	3-31
Kickoff returns	9-179	3-114
Interception returns	0-0	3-49
Comp.-att.-int.	26-45-3	22-40-0
Sacked-yards lost	5-47	0-0
Punts	8-46	4-40
Fumbles-lost	0-0	3-0
Penalties-yards	9-116	2-14
Time of possession	28:09	31:51

INDIVIDUAL STATISTICS

RUSHING—Cleveland, Prentice 6-27, Wynn 2-12, Couch 1-(minus 1). Denver, Anderson 20-103, Harris 8-22, Griese 1-14, R. Smith 1-8, Frerotte 1-(minus 1).

PASSING—Cleveland, Couch 24-40-3-266, Wynn 2-5-0-21. Denver, Griese 19-34-0-336, Frerotte 3-6-0-17.

RECEIVING—Cleveland, Johnson 8-60, Shea 6-76, Northcutt 5-80, Patten 4-54, Prentice 3-17. Denver, McCaffrey 5-129, R. Smith 5-111, Carswell 5-30, Clark 4-46, Anderson 2-28, Chamberlain 1-9.

MISSED FIELD GOAL ATTEMPTS—Denver, Elam 45.

INTERCEPTIONS—Denver, Jenkins 2-44, Crockett 1-5.

KICKOFF RETURNS—Cleveland, White 4-88, Patten 2-44, L. Jackson 2-36, Saleh 1-11. Denver, O'Neal 3-114.

PUNT RETURNS—Cleveland, Northcutt 1-22. Denver, O'Neal 2-20, Buckley 1-11.

SACKS—Denver, Pryce 2, Pittman 2, Wilson 1.

REDSKINS 10, RAVENS 3

Sunday, October 15

Baltimore	0	3	0	0— 3
Washington	0	3	0	7—10

Second Quarter
Was.—FG, Heppner 37, 7:15.
Bal.—FG, Stover 51, 11:46.

Fourth Quarter
Was.—Davis 33 run (Heppner kick), 0:42.
Attendance—83,252.

	Baltimore	Washington
First downs	15	15
Rushes-yards	25-91	29-101
Passing	108	145
Punt returns	2-14	2-23
Kickoff returns	2-67	2-60
Interception returns	1-6	1-0
Comp.-att.-int.	16-27-1	18-27-1
Sacked-yards lost	3-27	1-13
Punts	7-40	4-42
Fumbles-lost	0-0	1-1
Penalties-yards	7-41	6-51
Time of possession	31:04	28:56

INDIVIDUAL STATISTICS

RUSHING—Baltimore, Ja. Lewis 16-34, Holmes 4-25, Banks 2-18, J. Lewis 1-11, Ayanbadejo 1-4, Taylor 1-(minus 1). Washington, Davis 21-91, B. Johnson 4-(minus 4), Hicks 3-7, Thrash 1-7.

PASSING—Baltimore, Banks 16-27-1-135. Washington, B. Johnson 18-27-1-158.

RECEIVING—Baltimore, Sharpe 4-50, J. Lewis 3-24, Ja. Lewis 3-4, Ismail 2-38, Taylor 2-10, Coates 1-6, Ayanbadejo 1-3. Washington, Thrash 6-62, Centers 6-51, Alexander 4-35, Davis 1-5, Hicks 1-5.

MISSED FIELD GOAL ATTEMPTS—None.

INTERCEPTIONS—Baltimore, Starks 1-6. Washington, Kev. Mitchell 1-0.

KICKOFF RETURNS—Baltimore, Harris 2-67. Washington, Thrash 2-60.

PUNT RETURNS—Baltimore, J. Lewis 2-14. Washington, Thrash 2-23.

SACKS—Baltimore, Burnett 1. Washington, Barber 1, Lang 1, Stubblefield 0.5, Wilkinson 0.5.

VIKINGS 28, BEARS 16

Sunday, October 15

Minnesota	0	14	7	7—28
Chicago	6	3	0	7—16

First Quarter
Chi.—White 25 pass from McNown (run failed), 11:14.

Second Quarter
Chi.—FG, Edinger 22, 6:02.
Min.—Smith 72 run (Anderson kick), 6:25.
Min.—C. Carter 24 pass from Culpepper (Anderson kick), 9:34.

Third Quarter
Min.—Hatchette 24 pass from Culpepper (Anderson kick), 4:59.

Fourth Quarter
Chi.—Allen 6 run (Edinger kick), 0:04.
Min.—Moss 7 pass from Culpepper (Anderson kick), 5:34.
Attendance—66,944.

	Minnesota	Chicago
First downs	17	17
Rushes-yards	29-191	26-98
Passing	177	196
Punt returns	2-32	3-29
Kickoff returns	4-91	5-92
Interception returns	0-0	0-0
Comp.-att.-int.	15-26-0	19-33-0
Sacked-yards lost	3-21	2-14
Punts	5-41	7-35
Fumbles-lost	2-1	1-0
Penalties-yards	7-73	8-53
Time of possession	27:25	32:35

INDIVIDUAL STATISTICS

RUSHING—Minnesota, Smith 23-170, Culpepper 4-15, M. Williams 2-6. Chicago, Allen 22-71, McNown 4-27.

PASSING—Minnesota, Culpepper 15-26-0-198. Chicago, McNown 19-33-0-210.

RECEIVING—Minnesota, C. Carter 7-111, Moss 4-29, Hatchette 1-24, Walsh 1-18, McWilliams 1-9, Smith 1-7. Chicago, M. Robinson 7-88, Sinceno 4-32, Brooks 3-25, Booker 2-32, White 1-25, Allen 1-4, Kennison 1-4.

MISSED FIELD GOAL ATTEMPTS—None.

INTERCEPTIONS—None.

KICKOFF RETURNS—Minnesota, M. Williams 3-56, Walters 1-35. Chicago, Milburn 5-92.

PUNT RETURNS—Minnesota, Walters 2-32. Chicago, Milburn 2-15, W. Harris 1-14.

SACKS—Minnesota, Burrough 1, Randle 1. Chicago, Urlacher 2, Wells 1.

TITANS 27, JAGUARS 13

Monday, October 16

Jacksonville	3	0	0	10	13
Tennessee	7	10	7	3	27

First Quarter

Jac.—FG, Hollis 23, 7:23.

Ten.—Wycheck 4 pass from McNair (Del Greco kick), 10:49.

Second Quarter

Ten.—Mason 22 pass from McNair (Del Greco kick), 2:19.

Ten.—FG, Del Greco 26, 8:16.

Third Quarter

Ten.—E. George 19 run (Del Greco kick), 6:12.

Fourth Quarter

Jac.—FG, Hollis 45, 1:41.

Ten.—FG, Del Greco 28, 11:23.

Jac.—Johnson 2 run (Hollis kick), 14:07.

Attendance—68,498.

	Jacksonville	Tennessee
First downs	13	18
Rushes-yards	26-143	38-173
Passing	161	234
Punt returns	2-25	3-32
Kickoff returns	6-150	3-128
Interception returns	0-0	0-0
Comp.-att.-int.	18-27-0	13-21-0
Sacked-yards lost	5-35	0-0
Punts	5-45	3-49
Fumbles-lost	2-2	1-1
Penalties-yards	5-40	10-89
Time of possession	26:53	33:07

INDIVIDUAL STATISTICS

RUSHING—Jacksonville, Taylor 20-112, Brunell 3-18, Johnson 2-9, Stith 1-4. Tennessee, E. George 30-165, McNair 5-4, Thomas 3-4.

PASSING—Jacksonville, Brunell 18-27-0-196. Tennessee, McNair 13-21-0-234.

RECEIVING—Jacksonville, McCardell 5-64, Soward 3-18, Whitted 3-12, Johnson 2-55, Taylor 2-27, Brady 2-11, J. Smith 1-9. Tennessee, Wycheck 5-47, E. George 3-42, Thigpen 2-54, Mason 2-37, Sanders 1-54.

MISSED FIELD GOAL ATTEMPTS—Tennessee, Del Greco 44.

INTERCEPTIONS—None.

KICKOFF RETURNS—Jacksonville, Stith 4-107, Barlow 2-43. Tennessee, Mason 2-101, Coleman 1-27.

PUNT RETURNS—Jacksonville, Soward 2-25. Tennessee, Mason 2-23, Thigpen 1-9.

SACKS—Tennessee, Smith 1.5, Robinson 1, Embray 1, Thornton 1, Kearse 0.5.

WEEK 8

STANDINGS

AFC EAST

	W	L	T	Pct.
N.Y. Jets	6	1	0	.857
Indianapolis	5	2	0	.714
Miami	5	2	0	.714
Buffalo	3	4	0	.429
New England	2	6	0	.250

AFC CENTRAL

	W	L	T	Pct.
Tennessee	6	1	0	.857
Baltimore	5	3	0	.625
Pittsburgh	4	3	0	.571
Cleveland	2	6	0	.250
Jacksonville	2	6	0	.250
Cincinnati	1	6	0	.143

AFC WEST

	W	L	T	Pct.
Oakland	6	1	0	.857
Kansas City	4	3	0	.571
Denver	4	4	0	.500
Seattle	2	6	0	.250
San Diego	0	7	0	.000

NFC EAST

	W	L	T	Pct.
Washington	6	2	0	.750
N.Y. Giants	5	2	0	.714
Philadelphia	5	3	0	.625
Dallas	3	4	0	.429
Arizona	2	5	0	.286

NFC CENTRAL

	W	L	T	Pct.
Minnesota	7	0	0	1.000
Detroit	5	2	0	.714
Green Bay	3	4	0	.429
Tampa Bay	3	4	0	.429
Chicago	1	7	0	.125

NFC WEST

	W	L	T	Pct.
St. Louis	6	1	0	.857
New Orleans	4	3	0	.571
Carolina	3	4	0	.429
Atlanta	2	6	0	.250
San Francisco	2	6	0	.250

TOP PERFORMANCES

100-YARD RUSHING GAMES

Player, Team & Opponent	Att.	Yds.	TD
Corey Dillon, Cin. vs. Den.	22	278	2
Tyrone Wheatley, Oak. vs. Sea.	15	156	1
Ricky Williams, N.O. at Atl.	29	156	3
Lamar Smith, Mia. at NYJ*	23	155	2
Edgerrin James, Ind. vs. N.E.	20	124	1
Fred Taylor, Jack. vs. Wash.	22	124	0
James Stewart, Det. at T.B.	29	116	3
Stephen Davis, Wash. at Jack.	24	114	2
Emmitt Smith, Dal. vs. Ari.	24	112	1
Jerome Bettis, Pit. vs. Cle.	33	105	1
Kimble Anders, K.C. vs. St.L.	13	102	2

300-YARD PASSING GAMES

Player, Team & Opponent	Att.	Comp.	Yds.	TD	Int.
Vinny Testaverde, NYJ vs. Mia.*	59	36	378	5	3
Brian Griese, Den. at Cin.	45	30	365	2	1
Steve Beuerlein, Car. vs. S.F.	44	28	309	3	0
Jeff Garcia, S.F. at Car.	39	25	307	2	1

100-YARD RECEIVING GAMES

Player, Team & Opponent	Rec.	Yds.	TD
Albert Connell, Wash. at Jack.	7	211	3
Marvin Harrison, Ind. vs. N.E.	5	156	2
Ed McCaffrey, Den. at Cin.	10	136	0
Eric Moulds, Buf. at Min.	12	135	1
Isaac Bruce, St.L. at K.C.	8	129	2
Muhsin Muhammad, Car. vs. S.F.	9	127	0
Oronde Gadsden, Mia. at NYJ*	7	119	0
Derrick Alexander, K.C. vs. St.L.	5	117	1
Tony Gonzalez, K.C. vs. St.L.	5	117	1
Charlie Garner, S.F. at Car.	7	112	0
Kyle Brady, Jack. vs. Wash.	8	111	0
Randy Moss, Min. vs. Buf.	5	110	1
Rod Smith, Den. at Cin.	7	110	1
Richie Anderson, NYJ vs. Mia.*	12	109	0
Cris Carter, Min. vs. Buf.	7	107	2
Wayne Chrebet, NYJ vs. Mia.*	6	104	2
Shannon Sharpe, Balt. vs. Ten.	8	104	0

*Overtime game.

RESULTS

THURSDAY, OCTOBER 19
Detroit 28, TAMPA BAY 14
SUNDAY, OCTOBER 22
CAROLINA 34, San Francisco 16
CINCINNATI 31, Denver 21
DALLAS 48, Arizona 7
INDIANAPOLIS 30, New England 23
KANSAS CITY 54, St. Louis 34
MINNESOTA 31, Buffalo 27
New Orleans 21, ATLANTA 19
OAKLAND 31, Seattle 3
PHILADELPHIA 13, Chicago 9
PITTSBURGH 22, Cleveland 0
Tennessee 14, BALTIMORE 6
Washington 35, JACKSONVILLE 16
MONDAY, OCTOBER 23
N.Y. JETS 40, Miami 37 (OT)
    Open date: Green Bay, N.Y. Giants, San Diego

LIONS 28, BUCCANEERS 14

Thursday, October 19

Detroit	0	11	3	14—28
Tampa Bay	6	5	0	3—14

First Quarter
T.B.—FG, Gramatica 27, 6:31.
T.B.—FG, Gramatica 43, 10:00.

Second Quarter
T.B.—R. Rice tackled in end zone following blocked punt for a safety, 3:13.
Det.—FG, Hanson 32, 7:15.
T.B.—FG, Gramatica 50, 9:36.
Det.—J. Stewart 4 run (J. Stewart run), 14:22.

Third Quarter
Det.—FG, Hanson 47, 3:31.

Fourth Quarter
T.B.—FG, Gramatica 55, 1:50.
Det.—J. Stewart 4 run (Hanson kick), 10:32.
Det.—J. Stewart 1 run (Hanson kick), 13:07.
Attendance—65,557.

	Detroit	Tampa Bay
First downs	21	12
Rushes-yards	37-170	19-109
Passing	107	149
Punt returns	1-6	3-26
Kickoff returns	4-107	6-123
Interception returns	3-17	0-0
Comp.-att.-int.	13-31-0	17-34-3
Sacked-yards lost	7-37	0-0
Punts	6-37	3-45
Fumbles-lost	0-0	1-1
Penalties-yards	7-55	7-54
Time of possession	36:35	23:25

INDIVIDUAL STATISTICS
RUSHING—Detroit, J. Stewart 29-116, Bates 3-24, Batch 3-16, Foster 1-15, Morton 1-(minus 1). Tampa Bay, Dunn 8-46, Alstott 6-30, King 5-33.
PASSING—Detroit, Batch 13-31-0-144. Tampa Bay, King 17-34-3-149.
RECEIVING—Detroit, Morton 5-84, J. Stewart 2-8, Bates 1-11, Moore 1-9, Rasby 1-9, Schlesinger 1-8, Sloan 1-8, Stablein 1-7. Tampa Bay, K. Johnson 6-79, Green 3-27, Dunn 3-19, Moore 3-18, Alstott 2-6.
MISSED FIELD GOAL ATTEMPTS—Detroit, Hanson 40.
INTERCEPTIONS—Detroit, Westbrook 2-16, Claiborne 1-1.
KICKOFF RETURNS—Detroit, Howard 4-107. Tampa Bay, Stecker 5-112, Green 1-11.
PUNT RETURNS—Detroit, Howard 1-6. Tampa Bay, Hastings 3-26.
SACKS—Tampa Bay, Jones 4, Sapp 2, McFarland 1.

COWBOYS 48, CARDINALS 7

Sunday, October 22

Arizona	0	0	0	7— 7
Dallas	14	13	14	7—48

First Quarter
Dal.—E. Smith 1 run (Seder kick), 11:34.
Dal.—McGarity 59 punt return (Seder kick), 13:59.

Second Quarter
Dal.—Warren 32 run (Seder kick), 4:08.
Dal.—FG, Seder 32, 13:30.
Dal.—FG, Seder 23, 15:00.

Third Quarter
Dal.—Ismail 24 pass from Aikman (Seder kick), 8:10.
Dal.—Warren 10 run (Seder kick), 10:57.

Fourth Quarter
Dal.—Thomas 2 pass from Aikman (Seder kick), 2:39.
Ariz.—Pittman 1 run (Blanchard kick), 9:31.
Attendance—62,981.

	Arizona	Dallas
First downs	15	23
Rushes-yards	24-109	40-200
Passing	167	147
Punt returns	1-4	4-68
Kickoff returns	6-164	1-8
Interception returns	0-0	3-43
Comp.-att.-int.	20-31-3	9-15-0
Sacked-yards lost	1-13	1-7
Punts	5-43	3-42
Fumbles-lost	1-0	0-0
Penalties-yards	11-59	5-30
Time of possession	29:15	30:45

INDIVIDUAL STATISTICS
RUSHING—Arizona, Jones 11-50, Pittman 9-21, Plummer 3-36, Makovicka 1-2. Dallas, E. Smith 24-112, Warren 10-64, Thomas 3-14, Cunningham 2-(minus 1), Ismail 1-11.
PASSING—Arizona, Plummer 20-31-3-180. Dallas, Aikman 9-15-0-154.
RECEIVING—Arizona, Pittman 7-24, Boston 3-50, Cody 2-24, Jones 2-15, Sanders 2-14, Gedney 1-24, Jenkins 1-20, Makovicka 1-5, Hardy 1-4. Dallas, McKnight 3-75, Ismail 2-46, Thomas 2-9, Harris 1-13, Warren 1-11.
MISSED FIELD GOAL ATTEMPTS—None.
INTERCEPTIONS—Dallas, Sparks 1-43, C. Williams 1-0, Woodson 1-0.
KICKOFF RETURNS—Arizona, Jenkins 6-164. Dallas, LaFleur 1-8.
PUNT RETURNS—Arizona, Cody 1-4. Dallas, McGarity 4-68.
SACKS—Arizona, McKinnon 1. Dallas, Underwood 1.

PANTHERS 34, 49ERS 16

Sunday, October 22

San Francisco	0	13	3	0—16
Carolina	7	17	7	3—34

First Quarter
Car.—Byrd 3 pass from Beuerlein (Nedney kick), 7:33.

Second Quarter
S.F.—Owens 32 pass from Garcia (kick failed), 0:08.
Car.—Biakabutuka 2 pass from Beuerlein (Nedney kick), 6:09.
Car.—Minter 30 interception return (Nedney kick), 6:28.
S.F.—Rice 16 pass from Garcia (Richey kick), 9:19.
Car.—FG, Nedney 30, 13:56.

Third Quarter
Car.—Biakabutuka 8 pass from Beuerlein (Nedney kick), 2:44.
S.F.—FG, Richey 38, 9:41.

Fourth Quarter
Car.—FG, Nedney 38, 6:29.
Attendance—73,169.

	San Francisco	Carolina
First downs	20	26
Rushes-yards	18-128	25-98
Passing	283	292
Punt returns	0-0	1-13
Kickoff returns	5-77	1-19
Interception returns	0-0	1-30
Comp.-att.-int.	25-39-1	28-44-0
Sacked-yards lost	3-24	3-17
Punts	1-37	2-42
Fumbles-lost	3-1	0-0
Penalties-yards	13-82	6-63
Time of possession	26:23	33:37

INDIVIDUAL STATISTICS
RUSHING—San Francisco, Garner 10-87, Beasley 3-7, Smith 2-20, Garcia 2-12, Owens 1-2. Carolina, Biakabutuka 19-85, Beuerlein 2-3, Floyd 2-2, Hetherington 1-4, Hoover 1-4.
PASSING—San Francisco, Garcia 25-39-1-307. Carolina, Beuerlein 28-44-0-309.
RECEIVING—San Francisco, Garner 7-112, Owens 6-96, Beasley 4-32, Rice 3-35, Clark 2-14, Swift 1-8, Streets 1-6, Stokes 1-4. Carolina, Muhammad 9-127, Hayes 6-90, Biakabutuka 6-42, Walls 3-22, Byrd 2-24, Floyd 1-2, Mangum 1-2.
MISSED FIELD GOAL ATTEMPTS—None.
INTERCEPTIONS—Carolina, Minter 1-30.
KICKOFF RETURNS—San Francisco, Smith 5-77. Carolina, Byrd 1-19.
PUNT RETURNS—Carolina, Uwaezuoke 1-13.
SACKS—San Francisco, Ulmer 1, Killings 1, Pleasant 1. Carolina, Rucker 1, White 1, Peter 1.

2000 REVIEW *Week 8*

VIKINGS 31, BILLS 27

Sunday, October 22

Buffalo	0	10	7	10—27
Minnesota	3	3	7	18—31

First Quarter
Min.—FG, Anderson 38, 12:33.

Second Quarter
Buf.—Moulds 25 pass from Flutie (Christie kick), 1:22.
Buf.—FG, Christie 25, 14:06.
Min.—FG, Anderson 20, 15:00.

Third Quarter
Min.—C. Carter 6 pass from Culpepper (Anderson kick), 5:43.
Buf.—Morris 1 run (Christie kick), 13:47.

Fourth Quarter
Buf.—Morris 18 pass from Flutie (Christie kick), 0:41.
Min.—C. Carter 11 pass from Culpepper (M. Williams pass from Culpepper), 5:26.
Buf.—FG, Christie 48, 8:21.
Min.—Moss 39 pass from Culpepper (Anderson kick), 11:18.
Min.—FG, Anderson 21, 13:56.
Attendance—64,116.

	Buffalo	Minnesota
First downs	21	17
Rushes-yards	28-120	22-97
Passing	286	251
Punt returns	2-23	2-41
Kickoff returns	3-73	6-106
Interception returns	1-10	0-0
Comp.-att.-int.	28-43-0	17-29-1
Sacked-yards lost	1-8	0-0
Punts	4-40	4-42
Fumbles-lost	2-1	1-0
Penalties-yards	11-72	9-55
Time of possession	35:38	24:22

INDIVIDUAL STATISTICS
RUSHING—Buffalo, Morris 14-31, Bryson 11-72, Linton 2-9, Flutie 1-8. Minnesota, Smith 16-68, Culpepper 6-29.
PASSING—Buffalo, Flutie 28-43-0-294. Minnesota, Culpepper 17-29-1-251.
RECEIVING—Buffalo, Moulds 12-135, McDaniel 5-39, Morris 4-39, P. Price 3-42, Cavil 2-22, Bryson 2-17. Minnesota, C. Carter 7-107, Moss 5-110, McWilliams 3-12, Hatchette 1-13, Smith 1-9.
MISSED FIELD GOAL ATTEMPTS—None.
INTERCEPTIONS—Buffalo, Rogers 1-10.
KICKOFF RETURNS—Buffalo, Watson 3-73. Minnesota, Walters 3-39, M. Williams 2-50, Morrow 1-17.
PUNT RETURNS—Buffalo, Watson 2-23. Minnesota, Walters 2-41.
SACKS—Minnesota, Wong 1.

TITANS 14, RAVENS 6

Sunday, October 22

Tennessee	0	7	7	0—14
Baltimore	3	3	0	0— 6

First Quarter
Bal.—FG, Stover 21, 9:56.

Second Quarter
Bal.—FG, Stover 38, 4:16.
Ten.—Thomas 9 pass from McNair (Del Greco kick), 14:16.

Third Quarter
Ten.—Godfrey 24 interception return (Del Greco kick), 1:38.
Attendance—69,200.

	Tennessee	Baltimore
First downs	7	24
Rushes-yards	26-90	29-113
Passing	101	255
Punt returns	2-37	3-11
Kickoff returns	3-57	3-75
Interception returns	4-27	1-19
Comp.-att.-int.	11-21-1	25-46-4
Sacked-yards lost	0-0	5-35
Punts	7-46	5-37
Fumbles-lost	2-1	7-0
Penalties-yards	4-20	8-52
Time of possession	23:59	36:01

INDIVIDUAL STATISTICS
RUSHING—Tennessee, Thomas 18-53, McNair 7-33, E. George 1-4. Baltimore, Ja. Lewis 17-58, Holmes 6-30, Banks 4-13, Dilfer 2-12.
PASSING—Tennessee, McNair 11-21-1-101. Baltimore, Banks 17-32-3-229, Dilfer 7-13-1-58, J. Lewis 1-1-0-3.
RECEIVING—Tennessee, Sanders 3-60, Thomas 3-13, Mason 2-17, Wycheck 2-5, Thigpen 1-6. Baltimore, Sharpe 8-104, Ismail 4-76, Taylor 3-25, J. Lewis 3-18, Holmes 3-5, Ja. Lewis 2-36, Coates 1-22, Johnson 1-4.
MISSED FIELD GOAL ATTEMPTS—None.
INTERCEPTIONS—Tennessee, Godfrey 2-25, Booker 1-2, Sidney 1-0. Baltimore, Herring 1-19.
KICKOFF RETURNS—Tennessee, Mason 3-57. Baltimore, Harris 3-75.
PUNT RETURNS—Tennessee, Mason 2-37. Baltimore, J. Lewis 3-11.
SACKS—Tennessee, Holmes 2, Bishop 1, Fisk 1, Kearse 1.

EAGLES 13, BEARS 9

Sunday, October 22

Chicago	0	0	0	9— 9
Philadelphia	3	7	3	0—13

First Quarter
Phi.—FG, Akers 51, 14:57.

Second Quarter
Phi.—Thomason 3 pass from McNabb (Akers kick), 14:14.

Third Quarter
Phi.—FG, Akers 29, 8:25.

Fourth Quarter
Chi.—FG, Edinger 25, 2:24.
Chi.—FG, Edinger 33, 10:21.
Chi.—FG, Edinger 40, 10:50.
Attendance—65,553.

	Chicago	Philadelphia
First downs	14	17
Rushes-yards	25-114	27-97
Passing	160	201
Punt returns	3-0	3-19
Kickoff returns	4-82	1-8
Interception returns	1-7	1-30
Comp.-att.-int.	20-43-1	22-35-1
Sacked-yards lost	3-17	1-6
Punts	7-42	7-41
Fumbles-lost	1-0	2-1
Penalties-yards	7-50	4-35
Time of possession	29:02	30:58

INDIVIDUAL STATISTICS
RUSHING—Chicago, Allen 21-87, Miller 2-2, Kennison 1-23, McNown 1-2. Philadelphia, Autry 14-37, McNabb 5-25, Pritchett 4-21, Mitchell 2-2, Detmer 1-8, C. Martin 1-4.
PASSING—Chicago, Miller 14-34-1-128, McNown 6-9-0-49. Philadelphia, McNabb 22-35-1-207.
RECEIVING—Chicago, Kennison 5-62, Brooks 5-29, M. Robinson 4-55, Booker 3-13, Allen 2-9, Sinceno 1-9. Philadelphia, C. Johnson 6-57, Autry 5-70, C. Martin 3-27, Small 2-25, Lewis 2-12, Thomason 2-10, Pritchett 1-3, Mitchell 1-3.
MISSED FIELD GOAL ATTEMPTS—None.
INTERCEPTIONS—Chicago, Parrish 1-7. Philadelphia, Dawkins 1-30.
KICKOFF RETURNS—Chicago, Milburn 4-82. Philadelphia, Mitchell 1-8.
PUNT RETURNS—Chicago, Milburn 3-0. Philadelphia, Mitchell 3-19.
SACKS—Chicago, Urlacher 1. Philadelphia, H. Douglas 1.5, H. Thomas 1, Grasmanis 0.5.

BENGALS 31, BRONCOS 21

Sunday, October 22

Denver	7	7	0	7—21
Cincinnati	0	10	7	14—31

First Quarter
Den.—D. Smith 1 pass from Griese (Elam kick), 6:47.

Second Quarter
Cin.—FG, Rackers 24, 2:19.
Den.—Anderson 3 run (Elam kick), 9:20.
Cin.—Warrick 77 run (Rackers kick), 9:47.

Third Quarter
Cin.—Bennett 19 run (Rackers kick), 6:07.

Fourth Quarter

Cin.—Dillon 65 run (Rackers kick), 10:02.
Den.—R. Smith 28 pass from Griese (Elam kick), 11:17.
Cin.—Dillon 41 run (Rackers kick), 13:11.
    Attendance—61,603.

	Denver	Cincinnati
First downs	32	15
Rushes-yards	32-142	37-407
Passing	358	14
Punt returns	2-10	0-0
Kickoff returns	5-116	4-85
Interception returns	0-0	1-6
Comp.-att.-int.	30-45-1	2-14-0
Sacked-yards lost	2-7	2-20
Punts	2-35	5-47
Fumbles-lost	3-2	1-1
Penalties-yards	6-38	9-69
Time of possession	37:33	22:27

INDIVIDUAL STATISTICS

RUSHING—Denver, Anderson 19-92, Coleman 10-34, Griese 3-16. Cincinnati, Dillon 22-278, Bennett 7-19, Warrick 3-90, Smith 3-12, S. Mitchell 2-8.

PASSING—Denver, Griese 30-45-1-365. Cincinnati, Smith 2-9-0-34, S. Mitchell 0-5-0-0.

RECEIVING—Denver, McCaffrey 10-136, R. Smith 7-110, Clark 6-44, Carswell 4-68, Anderson 2-6, D. Smith 1-1. Cincinnati, McGee 1-25, Warrick 1-9.

MISSED FIELD GOAL ATTEMPTS—Denver, Elam 48, 48.

INTERCEPTIONS—Cincinnati, C. Carter 1-6.

KICKOFF RETURNS—Denver, O'Neal 4-102, D. Smith 1-14. Cincinnati, Mack 3-71, Keaton 1-14.

PUNT RETURNS—Denver, O'Neal 2-10.

SACKS—Denver, Wilson 1, Reagor 1. Cincinnati, Foley 1, Curtis 1.

CHIEFS 54, RAMS 34

Sunday, October 22

St. Louis	0	14	14	6—34
Kansas City	20	7	13	14—54

First Quarter

K.C.—Moreau 2 run (Peterson kick), 1:56.
K.C.—FG, Peterson 34, 5:51.
K.C.—FG, Peterson 20, 10:27.
K.C.—Cloud 6 blocked punt return (Peterson kick), 12:04.

Second Quarter

St.L.—Faulk 1 run (Stoyanovich kick), 5:17.
K.C.—Gonzalez 9 pass from Grbac (Peterson kick), 8:11.
St.L.—Holt 18 pass from Warner (Stoyanovich kick), 9:45.

Third Quarter

K.C.—Alexander 30 pass from Grbac (Peterson kick), 1:30.
St.L.—R. Williams 31 pass from Green (Stoyanovich kick), 6:10.
K.C.—Anders 6 run (pass failed), 13:34.
St.L.—Bruce 22 pass from Green (Stoyanovich kick), 14:42.

Fourth Quarter

K.C.—Anders 4 run (Peterson kick), 4:09.
K.C.—Drayton 8 pass from Moon (Peterson kick), 9:33.
St.L.—Bruce 4 pass from Green (pass failed), 12:07.
    Attendance—79,142.

	St. Louis	Kansas City
First downs	24	21
Rushes-yards	20-66	22-106
Passing	362	362
Punt returns	1-7	2-(-2)
Kickoff returns	8-267	6-95
Interception returns	0-0	3-38
Comp.-att.-int.	30-46-3	22-34-0
Sacked-yards lost	4-28	2-13
Punts	5-33	4-39
Fumbles-lost	2-1	1-0
Penalties-yards	8-87	6-50
Time of possession	34:49	25:11

INDIVIDUAL STATISTICS

RUSHING—St. Louis, Faulk 17-67, Holcombe 1-1, Warner 1-0, Green 1-(minus 2). Kansas City, Anders 13-102, Moreau 4-6, Grbac 3-(minus 4), Richardson 2-2.

PASSING—St. Louis, Warner 15-25-2-185, Green 15-21-1-205. Kansas City, Grbac 18-30-0-266, Moon 3-3-0-78, Morris 1-1-0-31.

RECEIVING—St. Louis, Bruce 8-129, Faulk 6-32, Holt 5-93, Hakim 4-54, R. Williams 2-34, Watson 2-21, Proehl 2-20, Holcombe 1-7. Kansas City, Alexander 5-117, Gonzalez 5-117, Morris 5-64, Lockett 3-49, Drayton 2-12, Richardson 1-16, Anders 1-0.

MISSED FIELD GOAL ATTEMPTS—Kansas City, Peterson 42.

INTERCEPTIONS—Kansas City, Wesley 1-28, Hasty 1-10, Browning 1-0.

KICKOFF RETURNS—St. Louis, Horne 8-267. Kansas City, Cloud 3-60, Hall 2-24, Spears 1-11.

PUNT RETURNS—St. Louis, Hakim 1-7. Kansas City, Hall 2-(minus 2).

SACKS—St. Louis, Little 2. Kansas City, Browning 1, Woods 1, Dennis 1, D. Williams 1.

SAINTS 21, FALCONS 19

Sunday, October 22

New Orleans	7	0	7	7—21
Atlanta	3	10	0	6—19

First Quarter

Atl.—FG, Andersen 50, 3:40.
N.O.—R. Williams 12 run (Brien kick), 10:40.

Second Quarter

Atl.—FG, Andersen 44, 9:28.
Atl.—Dwight 52 pass from Chandler (Andersen kick), 13:38.

Third Quarter

N.O.—R. Williams 26 run (Brien kick), 9:15.

Fourth Quarter

N.O.—R. Williams 1 run (Brien kick), 10:50.
Atl.—Mathis 33 pass from Chandler (pass failed), 12:02.
    Attendance—56,508.

	New Orleans	Atlanta
First downs	25	13
Rushes-yards	37-200	17-75
Passing	202	203
Punt returns	1-13	0-0
Kickoff returns	4-78	4-95
Interception returns	0-0	1-13
Comp.-att.-int.	19-31-1	15-20-0
Sacked-yards lost	2-7	6-37
Punts	3-40	4-44
Fumbles-lost	0-0	0-0
Penalties-yards	6-45	7-48
Time of possession	33:52	25:58

INDIVIDUAL STATISTICS

RUSHING—New Orleans, R. Williams 29-156, Blake 5-30, T. Smith 3-14. Atlanta, Anderson 17-75.

PASSING—New Orleans, Blake 19-31-1-209. Atlanta, Chandler 15-20-0-240.

RECEIVING—New Orleans, Horn 4-54, R. Williams 4-37, Poole 4-35, Jackson 3-47, Hall 2-20, T. Smith 2-16. Atlanta, Dwight 3-85, Mathis 3-55, Christian 3-24, Jefferson 2-37, R. Kelly 2-22, Anderson 1-15, Kozlowski 1-2.

MISSED FIELD GOAL ATTEMPTS—Atlanta, Andersen 33.

INTERCEPTIONS—Atlanta, Bradford 1-13.

KICKOFF RETURNS—New Orleans, Morton 4-78. Atlanta, Vaughn 2-67, Oliver 1-24, Carter 1-4.

PUNT RETURNS—New Orleans, Morton 1-13.

SACKS—New Orleans, Fields 2, L. Glover 2, Kei. Mitchell 1, Hand 1. Atlanta, Simoneau 1, Swayda 1.

COLTS 30, PATRIOTS 23

Sunday, October 22

New England	7	6	10	0—23
Indianapolis	7	0	7	16—30

First Quarter

N.E.—Redmond 19 pass from Bledsoe (Vinatieri kick), 8:43.
Ind.—Harrison 51 pass from Manning (Vanderjagt kick), 12:22.

Second Quarter

N.E.—FG, Vinatieri 27, 4:34.
N.E.—FG, Vinatieri 26, 14:57.

Third Quarter

N.E.—FG, Vinatieri 28, 8:09.
Ind.—Harrison 78 pass from Manning (Vanderjagt kick), 8:27.
N.E.—Bledsoe 1 run (Vinatieri kick), 12:33.

Fourth Quarter
Ind.—James 1 pass from Manning (Vanderjagt kick), 8:44.
Ind.—James 3 run (pass failed), 12:51.
Ind.—FG, Vanderjagt 36, 14:42.
Attendance—56,828.

	New England	Indianapolis
First downs	24	20
Rushes-yards	42-155	21-130
Passing	231	268
Punt returns	0-0	2-28
Kickoff returns	3-55	6-140
Interception returns	0-0	0-0
Comp.-att.-int.	23-34-0	16-20-0
Sacked-yards lost	0-0	0-0
Punts	2-51	2-35
Fumbles-lost	3-1	1-1
Penalties-yards	6-48	8-106
Time of possession	39:01	20:59

INDIVIDUAL STATISTICS
RUSHING—New England, Redmond 22-97, Faulk 12-41, Bledsoe 3-4, Bishop 3-3, T. Carter 2-10. Indianapolis, James 20-124, Wilkins 1-6.
PASSING—New England, Bledsoe 23-34-0-231. Indianapolis, Manning 16-20-0-268.
RECEIVING—New England, Brown 6-78, Redmond 5-35, Glenn 3-36, Faulk 3-27, Rutledge 3-24, Simmons 2-20, Bjornson 1-11. Indianapolis, Harrison 5-156, Wilkins 4-33, Pollard 2-33, Pathon 2-26, James 2-5, Dilger 1-15.
MISSED FIELD GOAL ATTEMPTS—None.
INTERCEPTIONS—None.
KICKOFF RETURNS—New England, Faulk 3-55. Indianapolis, Pathon 4-94, P. Williams 2-46.
PUNT RETURNS—Indianapolis, Wilkins 2-28.
SACKS—None.

REDSKINS 35, JAGUARS 16

Sunday, October 22

Washington	7	14	7	7—35
Jacksonville	3	13	0	0—16

First Quarter
Was.—Davis 1 run (Heppner kick), 5:20.
Jac.—FG, Hollis 23, 11:38.

Second Quarter
Jac.—Soward 33 pass from Brunell (Hollis kick), 2:46.
Was.—Connell 11 pass from B. Johnson (Heppner kick), 5:07.
Was.—Connell 49 pass from B. Johnson (Heppner kick), 9:21.
Jac.—FG, Hollis 33, 12:45.
Jac.—FG, Hollis 51, 14:29.

Third Quarter
Was.—Connell 77 pass from B. Johnson (Heppner kick), 4:38.

Fourth Quarter
Was.—Davis 16 run (Heppner kick), 10:28.
Attendance—69,061.

	Washington	Jacksonville
First downs	18	21
Rushes-yards	30-130	26-146
Passing	269	239
Punt returns	2-32	3-15
Kickoff returns	3-54	6-132
Interception returns	2-21	1-0
Comp.-att.-int.	16-24-1	21-42-2
Sacked-yards lost	0-0	6-32
Punts	6-45	5-48
Fumbles-lost	1-1	3-2
Penalties-yards	6-59	5-42
Time of possession	27:42	32:18

INDIVIDUAL STATISTICS
RUSHING—Washington, Davis 24-114, Hicks 3-2, Thrash 2-13, Centers 1-1. Jacksonville, Taylor 22-124, Brunell 2-12, Soward 1-8, Stith 1-2.
PASSING—Washington, B. Johnson 16-24-1-269. Jacksonville, Brunell 21-42-2-271.
RECEIVING—Washington, Connell 7-211, Centers 3-17, Alexander 3-17, Thrash 2-16, Hicks 1-8. Jacksonville, Brady 8-111, Taylor 4-33, McCardell 3-51, Soward 2-40, J. Smith 2-17, Whitted 1-11, Shelton 1-8.
MISSED FIELD GOAL ATTEMPTS—None.

INTERCEPTIONS—Washington, Sanders 1-21, Stevens 1-0. Jacksonville, Logan 1-0.
KICKOFF RETURNS—Washington, Murrell 3-54. Jacksonville, Stith 4-85, Barlow 1-27, Whitted 1-20.
PUNT RETURNS—Washington, Thrash 2-32. Jacksonville, Soward 2-9, Barlow 1-6.
SACKS—Washington, Mason 2, Shade 1, B. Smith 1, Wilkinson 1, Kalu 1.

RAIDERS 31, SEAHAWKS 3

Sunday, October 22

Seattle	3	0	0	0— 3
Oakland	7	14	0	10—31

First Quarter
Sea.—FG, Lindell 44, 4:13.
Oak.—Brown 16 pass from Gannon (Janikowski kick), 11:55.

Second Quarter
Oak.—Brown 9 pass from Gannon (Janikowski kick), 3:09.
Oak.—Wheatley 80 run (Janikowski kick), 7:24.

Fourth Quarter
Oak.—FG, Janikowski 32, 1:27.
Oak.—Jett 23 pass from Gannon (Janikowski kick), 6:32.
Attendance—57,490.

	Seattle	Oakland
First downs	17	17
Rushes-yards	32-137	27-206
Passing	146	174
Punt returns	3-45	1-0
Kickoff returns	4-87	1-15
Interception returns	1-0	1-0
Comp.-att.-int.	15-30-1	15-22-1
Sacked-yards lost	2-3	1-2
Punts	5-45	5-50
Fumbles-lost	3-2	1-0
Penalties-yards	10-68	10-90
Time of possession	29:40	30:20

INDIVIDUAL STATISTICS
RUSHING—Seattle, Watters 17-95, Alexander 9-29, Kitna 5-9, Huard 1-4. Oakland, Wheatley 15-156, Kaufman 6-34, Gannon 3-14, Jordan 3-2.
PASSING—Seattle, Kitna 11-18-0-85, Huard 4-12-1-64. Oakland, Gannon 15-22-1-176.
RECEIVING—Seattle, Mili 5-33, Jackson 4-26, Watters 2-56, Dawkins 2-28, Fauria 1-6, Strong 1-0. Oakland, Jordan 2-35, Rison 2-28, Brown 2-25, Dudley 2-21, Wheatley 2-18, Brigham 2-16, Jett 1-23, Kaufman 1-11, Ritchie 1-(minus 1).
MISSED FIELD GOAL ATTEMPTS—Seattle, Lindell 43.
INTERCEPTIONS—Seattle, W. Williams 1-0. Oakland, Allen 1-0.
KICKOFF RETURNS—Seattle, Rogers 3-63, Bownes 1-24. Oakland, Dunn 1-15.
PUNT RETURNS—Seattle, Rogers 3-45. Oakland, Gordon 1-0.
SACKS—Seattle, C. Brown 1. Oakland, Bryant 1, Upshaw 1.

STEELERS 22, BROWNS 0

Sunday, October 22

Cleveland	0	0	0	0— 0
Pittsburgh	3	10	3	6—22

First Quarter
Pit.—FG, K. Brown 44, 13:10.

Second Quarter
Pit.—Bettis 1 run (K. Brown kick), 7:19.
Pit.—FG, K. Brown 20, 13:06.

Third Quarter
Pit.—FG, K. Brown 31, 7:17.

Fourth Quarter
Pit.—FG, K. Brown 26, 3:00.
Pit.—FG, K. Brown 33, 13:26.
Attendance—57,659.

	Cleveland	Pittsburgh
First downs	5	17
Rushes-yards	19-49	45-143
Passing	55	105
Punt returns	1-7	5-83
Kickoff returns	7-164	1-10
Interception returns	0-0	3-11

	Cleveland	Pittsburgh
Comp.-att.-int.	10-23-3	10-25-0
Sacked-yards lost	1-8	3-15
Punts	8-48	5-45
Fumbles-lost	0-0	1-0
Penalties-yards	8-77	5-47
Time of possession	20:25	39:35

INDIVIDUAL STATISTICS

RUSHING—Cleveland, Prentice 14-48, Pederson 2-4, White 2-0, Northcutt 1-(minus 3). Pittsburgh, Bettis 33-105, Stewart 6-15, Huntley 4-5, Fuamatu-Ma'afala 1-20, Edwards 1-(minus 2).

PASSING—Cleveland, Pederson 9-20-3-61, Wynn 1-3-0-2. Pittsburgh, Stewart 7-13-0-74, Graham 3-12-0-46.

RECEIVING—Cleveland, Prentice 3-8, Northcutt 2-22, Johnson 2-5, Shea 1-21, L. Jackson 1-5, Campbell 1-2. Pittsburgh, Shaw 3-60, Burress 2-25, Edwards 2-15, Hawkins 1-16, Ward 1-5, Huntley 1-(minus 1).

MISSED FIELD GOAL ATTEMPTS—Cleveland, P. Dawson 42.

INTERCEPTIONS—Pittsburgh, Alexander 1-7, Scott 1-3, Kirkland 1-1.

KICKOFF RETURNS—Cleveland, White 4-118, L. Jackson 3-46. Pittsburgh, Edwards 1-10.

PUNT RETURNS—Cleveland, Northcutt 1-7. Pittsburgh, Poteat 4-74, Hawkins 1-9.

SACKS—Cleveland, C. Brown 1, J. Miller 1, McCutcheon 1. Pittsburgh, Gildon 1.

JETS 40, DOLPHINS 37

Monday, October 23

Miami	17	6	7	7	0	—37
N.Y. Jets	0	7	0	30	3	—40

First Quarter
Mia.—FG, Mare 28, 7:38.
Mia.—Shepherd 42 pass from Fiedler (Mare kick), 9:57.
Mia.—L. Smith 68 run (Mare kick), 11:51.

Second Quarter
Mia.—FG, Mare 42, 2:03.
NYJ—Chrebet 10 pass from Testaverde (Hall kick), 14:07.
Mia.—FG, Mare 44, 14:58.

Third Quarter
Mia.—L. Smith 3 run (Mare kick), 14:48.

Fourth Quarter
NYJ—Coles 30 pass from Testaverde (pass failed), 1:11.
NYJ—Wiggins 1 pass from Testaverde (Hall kick), 5:09.
NYJ—FG, Hall 34, 9:17.
NYJ—Chrebet 24 pass from Testaverde (Hall kick), 11:05.
Mia.—Shepherd 46 pass from Fiedler (Mare kick), 11:27.
NYJ—Elliott 3 pass from Testaverde (Hall kick), 14:18.

Overtime
NYJ—FG, Hall 40, 6:47.
Attendance—78,389.

	Miami	N.Y. Jets
First downs	20	31
Rushes-yards	38-198	22-79
Passing	235	376
Punt returns	2-35	3-25
Kickoff returns	7-193	8-139
Interception returns	3-12	3-7
Comp.-att.-int.	16-35-3	36-59-3
Sacked-yards lost	2-15	1-2
Punts	8-40	6-42
Fumbles-lost	0-0	1-1
Penalties-yards	13-95	3-30
Time of possession	36:11	30:36

INDIVIDUAL STATISTICS

RUSHING—Miami, L. Smith 23-155, Konrad 5-11, Fiedler 4-24, T. Thomas 4-2, Johnson 2-6. New York, Martin 14-65, R. Anderson 6-3, Testaverde 1-7, Stone 1-4.

PASSING—Miami, Fiedler 16-35-3-250. New York, Testaverde 36-59-3-378.

RECEIVING—Miami, Gadsden 7-119, Shepherd 3-94, Goodwin 2-13, L. Smith 2-9, T. Thomas 1-8, Konrad 1-7. New York, R. Anderson 12-109, Martin 8-72, Chrebet 6-104, Coles 4-55, Ward 3-40, Elliott 1-3, Wiggins 1-1, Sowell 1-(minus 6).

MISSED FIELD GOAL ATTEMPTS—Miami, Mare 36.

INTERCEPTIONS—Miami, Walker 1-12, Surtain 1-0, Madison 1-0. New York, Coleman 3-7.

KICKOFF RETURNS—Miami, Marion 7-193. New York, Williams 6-113, Stone 1-19, Coles 1-7.

PUNT RETURNS—Miami, Shepherd 2-35. New York, Ward 3-25.

SACKS—Miami, Taylor 1. New York, Cox 1, Ellis 1.

WEEK 9

AFC EAST

	W	L	T	Pct.
Indianapolis	6	2	0	.750
Miami	6	2	0	.750
N.Y. Jets	6	2	0	.750
Buffalo	4	4	0	.500
New England	2	6	0	.250

AFC CENTRAL

	W	L	T	Pct.
Tennessee	7	1	0	.875
Pittsburgh	5	3	0	.625
Baltimore	5	4	0	.556
Jacksonville	3	6	0	.333
Cincinnati	2	6	0	.250
Cleveland	2	7	0	.222

AFC WEST

	W	L	T	Pct.
Oakland	7	1	0	.875
Kansas City	5	3	0	.625
Denver	4	4	0	.500
Seattle	2	7	0	.222
San Diego	0	8	0	.000

NFC EAST

	W	L	T	Pct.
N.Y. Giants	6	2	0	.750
Washington	6	3	0	.667
Philadelphia	5	4	0	.556
Dallas	3	5	0	.375
Arizona	2	6	0	.250

NFC CENTRAL

	W	L	T	Pct.
Minnesota	7	1	0	.875
Detroit	5	3	0	.625
Tampa Bay	4	4	0	.500
Green Bay	3	5	0	.375
Chicago	1	7	0	.125

NFC WEST

	W	L	T	Pct.
St. Louis	7	1	0	.875
New Orleans	5	3	0	.625
Carolina	3	5	0	.375
Atlanta	3	6	0	.333
San Francisco	2	7	0	.222

TOP PERFORMANCES

100-YARD RUSHING GAMES

Player, Team & Opponent	Att.	Yds.	TD
Edgerrin James, Ind. vs. Det.	31	139	1
Corey Dillon, Cin. at Cle.	27	137	1
Fred Taylor, Jack. at Dal.*	31	107	0
Emmitt Smith, Dal. vs. Jack.*	24	102	0

300-YARD PASSING GAMES

Player, Team & Opponent	Att.	Comp.	Yds.	TD	Int.
Elvis Grbac, K.C. at Sea.	35	22	342	3	3
Daunte Culpepper, Min. at T.B.	53	29	313	1	2
Trent Green, St.L. at S.F.	39	22	310	2	1

100-YARD RECEIVING GAMES

Player, Team & Opponent	Rec.	Yds.	TD
Kyle Brady, Jack. at Dal.*	10	138	1
Derrick Alexander, K.C. at Sea.	4	137	2
Eric Moulds, Buf. vs. NYJ	6	137	0
Laveranues Coles, NYJ at Buf.	5	131	0
Isaac Bruce, St.L. at S.F.	8	129	0
Keyshawn Johnson, T.B. vs. Min.	6	121	1
Cris Carter, Min. at T.B.	7	115	0
Terrell Owens, S.F. vs. St.L.	8	115	2
James McKnight, Dal. vs. Jack.*	6	113	0
Freddie Jones, S.D. vs. Oak.	10	111	2
Marvin Harrison, Ind. vs. Det.	9	109	1
Amani Toomer, NYG vs. Phi.	9	108	1
Kevin Johnson, Cle. vs. Cin.	6	102	0
Tony Gonzalez, K.C. at Sea.	8	101	0

*Overtime game.

RESULTS

SUNDAY, OCTOBER 29

ATLANTA 13, Carolina 12
BUFFALO 23, N.Y. Jets 20
CINCINNATI 12, Cleveland 3
INDIANAPOLIS 30, Detroit 18
Jacksonville 23, DALLAS 17 (OT)
Kansas City 24, SEATTLE 19
MIAMI 28, Green Bay 20
New Orleans 21, ARIZONA 10
N.Y. GIANTS 24, Philadelphia 7
Oakland 15, SAN DIEGO 13
Pittsburgh 9, BALTIMORE 6
St. Louis 34, SAN FRANCISCO 24
TAMPA BAY 41, Minnesota 13

MONDAY, OCTOBER 30

Tennessee 27, WASHINGTON 21
Open date: Chicago, Denver, New England

2000 REVIEW Week 9

STEELERS 9, RAVENS 6

Sunday, October 29

Pittsburgh	0	0	9	0—9
Baltimore	0	6	0	0—6

Second Quarter
Bal.—FG, Stover 51, 3:40.
Bal.—FG, Stover 49, 13:08.

Third Quarter
Pit.—Ward 45 pass from Stewart (kick failed), 5:09.
Pit.—FG, K. Brown 24, 9:07.
Attendance—69,405.

	Pittsburgh	Baltimore
First downs	14	14
Rushes-yards	34-120	28-135
Passing	111	139
Punt returns	0-0	2-27
Kickoff returns	3-63	3-55
Interception returns	1-0	0-0
Comp.-att.-int.	9-18-0	11-24-1
Sacked-yards lost	5-22	3-13
Punts	7-40	4-32
Fumbles-lost	2-1	2-2
Penalties-yards	3-20	4-20
Time of possession	31:58	28:02

INDIVIDUAL STATISTICS

RUSHING—Pittsburgh, Bettis 18-65, Stewart 9-31, Huntley 7-24. Baltimore, Ja. Lewis 19-93, Holmes 5-19, Dilfer 3-23, Taylor 1-0.

PASSING—Pittsburgh, Stewart 9-18-0-133. Baltimore, Dilfer 11-24-1-152.

RECEIVING—Pittsburgh, Ward 2-55, Shaw 2-30, Burress 2-16, Kreider 1-14, Bruener 1-11, Huntley 1-7. Baltimore, Ja. Lewis 3-53, Ismail 3-41, Sharpe 3-35, Taylor 2-23.

MISSED FIELD GOAL ATTEMPTS—None.

INTERCEPTIONS—Pittsburgh, Washington 1-0.

KICKOFF RETURNS—Pittsburgh, Poteat 3-63. Baltimore, Harris 3-55.

PUNT RETURNS—Baltimore, J. Lewis 2-27.

SACKS—Pittsburgh, Porter 2, A. Smith 1. Baltimore, R. Lewis 1, Burnett 1, McCrary 1, Herring 1, Adams 1.

BENGALS 12, BROWNS 3

Sunday, October 29

Cincinnati	0	7	3	2—12
Cleveland	0	0	3	0— 3

Second Quarter
Cin.—Dillon 1 run (Rackers kick), 2:46.

Third Quarter
Cin.—FG, Rackers 39, 5:07.
Cle.—FG, P. Dawson 18, 13:04.

Fourth Quarter
Cin.—Holding penalty on Cleveland enforced in the end zone for a safety, 6:34.
Attendance—73,118.

	Cincinnati	Cleveland
First downs	18	10
Rushes-yards	51-179	20-54
Passing	61	128
Punt returns	3-21	3-47
Kickoff returns	3-68	3-69
Interception returns	1-30	1-5
Comp.-att.-int.	7-20-1	13-32-1
Sacked-yards lost	4-23	2-19
Punts	8-40	8-42
Fumbles-lost	2-0	0-0
Penalties-yards	6-84	9-71
Time of possession	36:42	23:18

INDIVIDUAL STATISTICS

RUSHING—Cincinnati, Dillon 27-137, Bennett 17-39, Smith 5-(minus 1), Keaton 1-3, Warrick 1-1. Cleveland, Prentice 16-40, Pederson 2-10, White 2-4.

PASSING—Cincinnati, Smith 7-20-1-84. Cleveland, Pederson 6-16-0-65, Wynn 7-16-1-82.

RECEIVING—Cincinnati, Warrick 3-25, Bennett 1-21, Yeast 1-19, McGee 1-13, Battaglia 1-6. Cleveland, Johnson 6-102, Northcutt 4-23, Edwards 1-12, Patten 1-7, Shea 1-3.

MISSED FIELD GOAL ATTEMPTS—None.

INTERCEPTIONS—Cincinnati, T. Carter 1-30. Cleveland, Rainer 1-5.

KICKOFF RETURNS—Cincinnati, Yeast 1-29, Keaton 1-22, Mack 1-17. Cleveland, White 2-57, Saleh 1-12.

PUNT RETURNS—Cincinnati, Yeast 3-21. Cleveland, Northcutt 3-47.

SACKS—Cincinnati, C. Carter 1, Hall 1. Cleveland, Rainer 1, C. Brown 1, Moore 1, Team 1.

FALCONS 13, PANTHERS 12

Sunday, October 29

Carolina	3	3	3	3—12
Atlanta	3	0	0	10—13

First Quarter
Car.—FG, Nedney 35, 7:58.
Atl.—FG, Andersen 35, 14:06.

Second Quarter
Car.—FG, Nedney 48, 5:17.

Third Quarter
Car.—FG, Nedney 25, 11:31.

Fourth Quarter
Car.—FG, Nedney 24, 2:20.
Atl.—Anderson 2 run (Andersen kick), 9:56.
Atl.—FG, Andersen 31, 12:07.
Attendance—46,178.

	Carolina	Atlanta
First downs	16	16
Rushes-yards	20-30	27-97
Passing	179	184
Punt returns	2-11	3-23
Kickoff returns	2-29	4-71
Interception returns	2-8	3-55
Comp.-att.-int.	21-41-3	19-29-2
Sacked-yards lost	4-23	1-7
Punts	3-52	3-40
Fumbles-lost	1-1	2-1
Penalties-yards	9-58	8-98
Time of possession	28:23	31:37

INDIVIDUAL STATISTICS

RUSHING—Carolina, Biakabutuka 14-23, Floyd 3-6, Beuerlein 3-1. Atlanta, Anderson 25-90, Chandler 2-7.

PASSING—Carolina, Beuerlein 21-41-3-202. Atlanta, Chandler 19-29-2-191.

RECEIVING—Carolina, Biakabutuka 4-51, Walls 4-47, Hayes 4-41, Byrd 3-26, Floyd 3-20, Mangum 2-10, Muhammad 1-7. Atlanta, Mathis 7-89, Anderson 5-15, Dwight 3-37, R. Kelly 2-29, Christian 2-21.

MISSED FIELD GOAL ATTEMPTS—Atlanta, Andersen 46, 42.

INTERCEPTIONS—Carolina, Minter 1-8, Gilbert 1-0. Atlanta, Buchanan 2-13, Ambrose 1-42.

KICKOFF RETURNS—Carolina, Bates 1-16, Byrd 1-13. Atlanta, Vaughn 4-71.

PUNT RETURNS—Carolina, Uwaezuoke 2-11. Atlanta, Dwight 3-23.

SACKS—Carolina, Navies 1. Atlanta, Jasper 1, Hall 1, Wiley 1, B. Smith 1.

BUCCANEERS 41, VIKINGS 13

Sunday, October 29

Minnesota	3	10	0	0—13
Tampa Bay	14	17	3	7—41

First Quarter
T.B.—K. Johnson 9 pass from King (Gramatica kick), 4:27.
Min.—FG, Anderson 30, 8:25.
T.B.—Dunn 23 pass from King (Gramatica kick), 11:20.

Second Quarter
Min.—Moss 7 pass from Culpepper (Anderson kick), 3:03.
T.B.—Moore 20 pass from King (Gramatica kick), 5:14.
T.B.—Brooks 34 interception return (Gramatica kick), 7:02.
T.B.—FG, Gramatica 47, 11:22.
Min.—FG, Anderson 37, 14:40.

Third Quarter

T.B.—FG, Gramatica 26, 8:35.

Fourth Quarter

T.B.—Anthony 16 pass from King (Gramatica kick), 9:55.

Attendance—65,589.

	Minnesota	Tampa Bay
First downs	25	23
Rushes-yards	17-99	25-152
Passing	302	261
Punt returns	0-0	0-0
Kickoff returns	7-149	3-63
Interception returns	0-0	2-39
Comp.-att.-int.	29-53-2	16-23-0
Sacked-yards lost	2-11	1-6
Punts	1-49	0-0
Fumbles-lost	1-1	0-0
Penalties-yards	6-46	4-34
Time of possession	32:13	27:47

INDIVIDUAL STATISTICS

RUSHING—Minnesota, Smith 12-61, Culpepper 4-35, Kleinsasser 1-3. Tampa Bay, Dunn 11-89, Alstott 10-56, King 2-4, Stecker 1-4, Zeier 1-(minus 1).

PASSING—Minnesota, Culpepper 29-53-2-313. Tampa Bay, King 16-23-0-267.

RECEIVING—Minnesota, C. Carter 7-115, Moss 7-65, Smith 7-53, Hatchette 4-42, Kleinsasser 2-22, J. Davis 1-11, M. Williams 1-5. Tampa Bay, K. Johnson 6-121, Green 3-45, Anthony 3-36, Moore 2-27, Dunn 1-23, Stecker 1-15.

MISSED FIELD GOAL ATTEMPTS—None.

INTERCEPTIONS—Tampa Bay, Brooks 1-34, Abraham 1-5.

KICKOFF RETURNS—Minnesota, Walters 6-128, M. Williams 1-21. Tampa Bay, Stecker 3-63.

PUNT RETURNS—None.

SACKS—Minnesota, Robbins 1. Tampa Bay, Barber 1, Sapp 1.

DOLPHINS 28, PACKERS 20

Sunday, October 29

Green Bay	10	7	0	3—20
Miami	0	7	21	0—28

First Quarter

G.B.—FG, Longwell 51, 5:50.

G.B.—Levens 1 run (Longwell kick), 13:58.

Second Quarter

G.B.—Levens 7 run (Longwell kick), 3:07.

Mia.—Fiedler 1 run (Mare kick), 13:45.

Third Quarter

Mia.—Gadsden 15 pass from Fiedler (Mare kick), 4:11.

Mia.—L. Smith 4 run (Mare kick), 8:57.

Mia.—Ogden 81 punt return (Mare kick), 11:51.

Fourth Quarter

G.B.—FG, Longwell 48, 4:10.

Attendance—73,740.

	Green Bay	Miami
First downs	21	17
Rushes-yards	24-133	30-140
Passing	186	156
Punt returns	2-13	2-88
Kickoff returns	5-116	4-86
Interception returns	0-0	1-24
Comp.-att.-int.	21-34-1	16-25-0
Sacked-yards lost	2-8	1-2
Punts	5-35	6-39
Fumbles-lost	2-1	2-1
Penalties-yards	7-59	7-104
Time of possession	31:41	28:19

INDIVIDUAL STATISTICS

RUSHING—Green Bay, Green 15-94, Levens 8-27, Henderson 1-12. Miami, L. Smith 20-71, Fiedler 5-6, T. Thomas 3-10, Izzo 1-39, Shepherd 1-14.

PASSING—Green Bay, Favre 21-34-1-194. Miami, Fiedler 16-25-0-158.

RECEIVING—Green Bay, Schroeder 4-48, Levens 4-29, Franks 3-42, Green 3-19, T. Davis 3-19, Henderson 2-27, Freeman 2-10. Miami, Gadsden 5-70, Shepherd 3-60, McDuffie 3-17, T. Thomas 2-11, L. Smith 2-1, Konrad 1-(minus 1).

MISSED FIELD GOAL ATTEMPTS—Green Bay, Longwell 53.

INTERCEPTIONS—Miami, Marion 1-24.

KICKOFF RETURNS—Green Bay, Rossum 4-94, Henderson 1-22. Miami, Marion 3-47, Denson 1-39.

PUNT RETURNS—Green Bay, Rossum 2-13. Miami, Ogden 1-81, Shepherd 1-7.

SACKS—Green Bay, Holliday 1. Miami, Taylor 1, Armstrong 1.

COLTS 30, LIONS 18

Sunday, October 29

Detroit	0	0	11	7—18
Indianapolis	7	16	0	7—30

First Quarter

Ind.—Pollard 31 pass from Manning (Vanderjagt kick), 12:24.

Second Quarter

Ind.—Harrison 3 pass from Manning (Vanderjagt kick), 8:34.

Ind.—C. Batch sacked in end zone for a safety, 12:05.

Ind.—Dilger 12 pass from Manning (Vanderjagt kick), 14:18.

Third Quarter

Det.—Bates 9 run (J. Stewart run), 5:55.

Det.—FG, Hanson 21, 12:54.

Fourth Quarter

Det.—Moore 5 pass from Batch (Hanson kick), 12:28.

Ind.—James 24 run (Vanderjagt kick), 13:18.

Attendance—56,971.

	Detroit	Indianapolis
First downs	18	24
Rushes-yards	23-154	31-139
Passing	174	281
Punt returns	4-94	3-26
Kickoff returns	5-136	3-65
Interception returns	2-16	2-1
Comp.-att.-int.	18-39-2	22-33-2
Sacked-yards lost	3-16	1-7
Punts	7-50	6-51
Fumbles-lost	2-2	3-3
Penalties-yards	9-57	3-20
Time of possession	25:46	34:14

INDIVIDUAL STATISTICS

RUSHING—Detroit, J. Stewart 16-63, Batch 4-62, Bates 3-29. Indianapolis, James 31-139.

PASSING—Detroit, Batch 18-39-2-190. Indianapolis, Manning 22-33-2-288.

RECEIVING—Detroit, Foster 4-24, Sloan 4-20, J. Stewart 3-66, Moore 2-31, Bates 2-20, Olivo 1-17, Morton 1-7, Stablein 1-5. Indianapolis, Harrison 9-109, Dilger 5-52, Pollard 3-74, Wilkins 2-27, James 2-37, Finn 1-2.

MISSED FIELD GOAL ATTEMPTS—Detroit, Hanson 29.

INTERCEPTIONS—Detroit, Westbrook 1-9, Rice 1-7. Indianapolis, Poole 1-1, Macklin 1-0.

KICKOFF RETURNS—Detroit, Howard 5-136. Indianapolis, Wilkins 2-45, Pathon 1-20.

PUNT RETURNS—Detroit, Howard 4-94. Indianapolis, Wilkins 3-26.

SACKS—Detroit, Jones 1. Indianapolis, Belser 1, Bratzke 1, J. Williams 1.

BILLS 23, JETS 20

Sunday, October 29

N.Y. Jets	7	0	10	3—20
Buffalo	7	10	0	6—23

First Quarter

Buf.—Morris 1 run (Christie kick), 9:59.

NYJ—Baxter 12 pass from Testaverde (Hall kick), 14:01.

Second Quarter

Buf.—FG, Christie 20, 9:44.

Buf.—H. Jones 45 interception return (Christie kick), 10:11.

Third Quarter

NYJ—FG, Hall 40, 8:41.

NYJ—Chrebet 10 pass from Testaverde (Hall kick), 13:56.

Fourth Quarter

Buf.—FG, Christie 29, 8:46.

NYJ—FG, Hall 36, 12:40.

Buf.—FG, Christie 34, 15:00.

Attendance—72,861.

	N.Y. Jets	Buffalo
First downs	19	18
Rushes-yards	20-51	29-86
Passing	286	252
Punt returns	2-20	2-22
Kickoff returns	5-122	5-107
Interception returns	0-0	2-67
Comp.-att.-int.	28-38-2	18-35-0
Sacked-yards lost	1-7	1-1
Punts	2-43	3-49
Fumbles-lost	2-2	0-0
Penalties-yards	2-20	5-45
Time of possession	29:37	30:23

INDIVIDUAL STATISTICS

RUSHING—New York, Martin 18-46, R. Anderson 2-5. Buffalo, Morris 19-54, Bryson 6-17, Flutie 4-15.

PASSING—New York, Testaverde 28-38-2-293. Buffalo, Flutie 18-35-0-253.

RECEIVING—New York, Chrebet 6-69, Martin 6-31, R. Anderson 6-24, Coles 5-131, Ward 3-25, Baxter 2-13. Buffalo, Moulds 6-137, Morris 5-39, McDaniel 3-44, Bryson 2-3, P. Price 1-17, Riemersma 1-13.

MISSED FIELD GOAL ATTEMPTS—Buffalo, Christie 44.

INTERCEPTIONS—Buffalo, H. Jones 1-45, Carpenter 1-22.

KICKOFF RETURNS—New York, Stone 3-80, Williams 2-42. Buffalo, Watson 4-92, Bryson 1-15.

PUNT RETURNS—New York, Ward 2-20. Buffalo, Watson 2-22.

SACKS—New York, Cox 1. Buffalo, Rogers 1.

JAGUARS 23, COWBOYS 17

Sunday, October 29

Jacksonville	0	17	0	0	6—23
Dallas	7	0	3	7	0—17

First Quarter
Dal.—Harris 13 pass from Aikman (Seder kick), 7:19.

Second Quarter
Jac.—FG, Hollis 42, 5:27.
Jac.—Brady 3 pass from Brunell (Hollis kick), 13:40.
Jac.—Whitted 3 pass from Brunell (Hollis kick), 14:51.

Third Quarter
Dal.—FG, Seder 19, 7:59.

Fourth Quarter
Dal.—Cunningham 1 run (Seder kick), 13:53.

Overtime
Jac.—Whitted 37 pass from Brunell, 3:44.
Attendance—63,554.

	Jacksonville	Dallas
First downs	18	22
Rushes-yards	38-161	32-118
Passing	231	207
Punt returns	0-0	2-23
Kickoff returns	3-74	3-68
Interception returns	1-21	0-0
Comp.-att.-int.	20-24-0	17-25-1
Sacked-yards lost	0-0	2-13
Punts	5-44	3-41
Fumbles-lost	0-0	3-2
Penalties-yards	8-50	7-54
Time of possession	33:36	30:08

INDIVIDUAL STATISTICS

RUSHING—Jacksonville, Taylor 31-107, Brunell 5-41, Stith 1-12, Johnson 1-1. Dallas, E. Smith 24-102, Cunningham 3-(minus 3), Warren 2-9, Thomas 2-8, Ismail 1-2.

PASSING—Jacksonville, Brunell 20-24-0-231. Dallas, Cunningham 13-20-1-177, Aikman 4-5-0-43.

RECEIVING—Jacksonville, Brady 10-138, Whitted 3-55, McCardell 3-19, Taylor 2-9, Johnson 1-11, Soward 1-(minus 1). Dallas, McKnight 6-113, Ismail 5-57, Harris 3-34, Thomas 2-11, LaFleur 1-5.

MISSED FIELD GOAL ATTEMPTS—Jacksonville, Hollis 49.

INTERCEPTIONS—Jacksonville, Darius 1-21.

KICKOFF RETURNS—Jacksonville, Stith 3-74. Dallas, Tucker 3-68.

PUNT RETURNS—Dallas, McGarity 2-23.

SACKS—Jacksonville, Spicer 1, Beasley 1.

CHIEFS 24, SEAHAWKS 19

Sunday, October 29

Kansas City	7	14	0	3—24
Seattle	3	7	0	9—19

First Quarter
Sea.—FG, Lindell 50, 12:37.
K.C.—Alexander 59 pass from Grbac (Peterson kick), 14:07.

Second Quarter
Sea.—Fauria 2 pass from Kitna (Lindell kick), 6:30.
K.C.—Alexander 50 pass from Grbac (Peterson kick), 9:06.
K.C.—Lockett 34 pass from Grbac (Peterson kick), 12:40.

Fourth Quarter
Sea.—FG, Lindell 24, 0:03.
Sea.—Watters 14 pass from Kitna (pass failed), 9:07.
K.C.—FG, Peterson 37, 14:18.
Attendance—62,141.

	Kansas City	Seattle
First downs	17	22
Rushes-yards	26-76	25-143
Passing	334	208
Punt returns	1-1	3-65
Kickoff returns	4-61	4-99
Interception returns	3-0	3-39
Comp.-att.-int.	22-35-3	26-42-3
Sacked-yards lost	1-8	3-16
Punts	6-42	5-40
Fumbles-lost	1-0	1-1
Penalties-yards	7-53	10-99
Time of possession	30:40	29:20

INDIVIDUAL STATISTICS

RUSHING—Kansas City, Anders 19-54, Richardson 4-18, Moreau 3-4. Seattle, Watters 21-90, Alexander 4-53.

PASSING—Kansas City, Grbac 22-35-3-342. Seattle, Kitna 26-42-3-224.

RECEIVING—Kansas City, Gonzalez 8-101, Alexander 4-137, Lockett 4-77, Anders 4-17, Richardson 2-10. Seattle, Dawkins 7-64, Fauria 5-50, Watters 5-38, Mayes 3-29, Jackson 2-17, Strong 2-7, Mili 1-12, Alexander 1-7.

MISSED FIELD GOAL ATTEMPTS—None.

INTERCEPTIONS—Kansas City, Dennis 1-0, Hasty 1-0, Wesley 1-0. Seattle, Bellamy 2-32, Simmons 1-7.

KICKOFF RETURNS—Kansas City, Hall 4-61. Seattle, Rogers 4-99.

PUNT RETURNS—Kansas City, Hall 1-1. Seattle, Rogers 3-65.

SACKS—Kansas City, Woods 1, Edwards 1, D. Williams 1. Seattle, Kennedy 1.

RAMS 34, 49ERS 24

Sunday, October 29

St. Louis	7	7	10	10—34
San Francisco	7	10	7	0—24

First Quarter
S.F.—Garner 4 run (Richey kick), 1:35.
St.L.—Faulk 1 run (Stoyanovich kick), 11:01.

Second Quarter
S.F.—FG, Richey 44, 1:59.
St.L.—Faulk 1 run (Stoyanovich kick), 12:06.
S.F.—Owens 53 pass from Garcia (Richey kick), 13:16.

Third Quarter
St.L.—FG, Stoyanovich 48, 2:10.
S.F.—Owens 17 pass from Garcia (Richey kick), 6:50.
St.L.—Faulk 19 pass from Green (Stoyanovich kick), 11:22.

Fourth Quarter
St.L.—Faulk 16 pass from Green (Stoyanovich kick), 4:39.
St.L.—FG, Stoyanovich 46, 11:15.
Attendance—68,109.

	St. Louis	San Francisco
First downs	22	15
Rushes-yards	30-149	18-92
Passing	298	233
Punt returns	3-91	3-23
Kickoff returns	4-90	6-153
Interception returns	0-0	1-8
Comp.-att.-int.	22-39-1	26-44-0
Sacked-yards lost	2-12	2-10

	St. Louis	San Francisco
Punts	5-42	6-44
Fumbles-lost	1-0	2-0
Penalties-yards	11-90	8-80
Time of possession	33:58	26:02

INDIVIDUAL STATISTICS

RUSHING—St. Louis, Faulk 19-83, Green 5-6, Watson 4-43, Conwell 1-17, Holcombe 1-0. San Francisco, Garner 10-28, Garcia 4-51, Beasley 3-11, Smith 1-2.

PASSING—St. Louis, Green 22-39-1-310. San Francisco, Garcia 26-44-0-243.

RECEIVING—St. Louis, Bruce 8-129, Faulk 6-61, Holt 5-64, Hakim 2-18, Proehl 1-27, Holcombe 0-11. San Francisco, Owens 8-115, Rice 6-53, Garner 6-30, Clark 3-17, Beasley 2-14, Stokes 1-14.

MISSED FIELD GOAL ATTEMPTS—San Francisco, Richey 53, 49.

INTERCEPTIONS—San Francisco, Webster 1-8.

KICKOFF RETURNS—St. Louis, Horne 4-90. San Francisco, K. Williams 3-53, Jervey 1-68, Smith 1-23, Jackson 1-9.

PUNT RETURNS—St. Louis, Hakim 3-91. San Francisco, K. Williams 3-23.

SACKS—St. Louis, Wistrom 1.5, Carter 0.5. San Francisco, Engelberger 1, Buckner 1.

GIANTS 24, EAGLES 7

Sunday, October 29

Philadelphia	0	0	0	7— 7
N.Y. Giants	7	7	0	10—24

First Quarter
NYG—Dayne 1 run (Daluiso kick), 8:56.

Second Quarter
NYG—Toomer 27 pass from Collins (Daluiso kick), 13:29.

Fourth Quarter
NYG—FG, Daluiso 31, 1:54.
NYG—Montgomery 4 run (Daluiso kick), 9:04.
Phi.—C. Johnson 25 pass from McNabb (Akers kick), 9:48.
Attendance—78,087.

	Philadelphia	N.Y. Giants
First downs	8	25
Rushes-yards	11-72	44-152
Passing	120	232
Punt returns	3-57	5-2
Kickoff returns	5-94	2-25
Interception returns	0-0	1-1
Comp.-att.-int.	10-31-1	22-37-0
Sacked-yards lost	4-9	3-21
Punts	9-37	6-46
Fumbles-lost	0-0	5-0
Penalties-yards	8-74	5-35
Time of possession	16:19	43:41

INDIVIDUAL STATISTICS

RUSHING—Philadelphia, Pritchett 6-17, McNabb 3-42, C. Johnson 1-15, Mitchell 1-(minus 2). New York, Dayne 25-93, Barber 14-52, Collins 4-3, Montgomery 1-4.

PASSING—Philadelphia, McNabb 10-31-1-129. New York, Collins 22-37-0-253.

RECEIVING—Philadelphia, Pritchett 3-25, Lewis 1-26, C. Johnson 1-25, Lee 1-20, Brown 1-13, Mitchell 1-12, Small 1-7, C. Martin 1-1. New York, Toomer 9-108, Hilliard 5-39, Barber 4-71, Mitchell 2-13, Dayne 1-12, Comella 1-10.

MISSED FIELD GOAL ATTEMPTS—Philadelphia, Akers 48.

INTERCEPTIONS—New York, McDaniel 1-1.

KICKOFF RETURNS—Philadelphia, Mitchell 4-76, Whiting 1-18. New York, Dixon 1-22, Jurevicius 1-3.

PUNT RETURNS—Philadelphia, Mitchell 3-57. New York, Barber 4-2, West 1-0.

SACKS—Philadelphia, Vincent 1, Simon 1, H. Douglas 1. New York, Barrow 1.5, Peter 1, Armstead 0.5, Griffin 0.5, Jones 0.5.

SAINTS 21, CARDINALS 10

Sunday, October 29

New Orleans	7	0	7	7—21
Arizona	7	3	0	0—10

First Quarter
N.O.—Hall 1 pass from Blake (Brien kick), 12:29.
Ariz.—Hardy 3 pass from Plummer (Blanchard kick), 14:48.

Second Quarter
Ariz.—FG, Blanchard 34, 9:37.

Third Quarter
N.O.—Kei. Mitchell 40 interception return (Brien kick), 9:53.

Fourth Quarter
N.O.—R. Williams 1 run (Brien kick), 4:28.
Attendance—35,286.

	New Orleans	Arizona
First downs	17	24
Rushes-yards	29-89	27-125
Passing	158	269
Punt returns	2-12	2-9
Kickoff returns	3-57	4-97
Interception returns	2-40	1-0
Comp.-att.-int.	16-26-1	26-47-2
Sacked-yards lost	2-9	3-20
Punts	5-47	2-46
Fumbles-lost	0-0	2-2
Penalties-yards	5-55	4-27
Time of possession	26:41	33:19

INDIVIDUAL STATISTICS

RUSHING—New Orleans, R. Williams 21-54, Blake 6-16, Horn 1-16, T. Smith 1-3. Arizona, Pittman 20-86, Jones 6-26, Plummer 1-13.

PASSING—New Orleans, Blake 16-26-1-167. Arizona, Plummer 26-47-2-289.

RECEIVING—New Orleans, R. Williams 9-92, Jackson 2-19, Horn 2-10, A. Glover 1-24, Morton 1-21, Hall 1-1. Arizona, Hardy 7-45, Boston 5-49, Pittman 3-40, Jones 3-19, Sanders 2-54, Cody 2-24, Jenkins 1-31, Mitchell 1-18, Makovicka 1-5, Tant 1-4.

MISSED FIELD GOAL ATTEMPTS—New Orleans, Brien 45. Arizona, Blanchard 42, 30.

INTERCEPTIONS—New Orleans, Kei. Mitchell 1-40, Knight 1-0. Arizona, Chavous 1-0.

KICKOFF RETURNS—New Orleans, Morton 3-57. Arizona, Jenkins 4-97.

PUNT RETURNS—New Orleans, Morton 2-12. Arizona, Cody 2-9.

SACKS—New Orleans, L. Glover 2, Johnson 1. Arizona, Tillman 1, McKinnon 1.

RAIDERS 15, CHARGERS 13

Sunday, October 29

Oakland	9	3	0	3—15
San Diego	0	0	7	6—13

First Quarter
Oak.—FG, Janikowski 40, 5:23.
Oak.—FG, Janikowski 40, 10:26.
Oak.—FG, Janikowski 54, 14:46.

Second Quarter
Oak.—FG, Janikowski 29, 8:05.

Third Quarter
S.D.—F. Jones 8 pass from Harbaugh (Carney kick), 6:09.

Fourth Quarter
S.D.—F. Jones 21 pass from Harbaugh (pass failed), 9:02.
Oak.—FG, Janikowski 24, 14:47.
Attendance—66,659.

	Oakland	San Diego
First downs	19	18
Rushes-yards	28-83	20-29
Passing	145	195
Punt returns	4-35	2-18
Kickoff returns	3-75	5-118
Interception returns	1-0	1-0
Comp.-att.-int.	16-35-1	25-35-1
Sacked-yards lost	1-11	3-27
Punts	3-47	5-47
Fumbles-lost	0-0	2-1
Penalties-yards	8-50	11-88
Time of possession	31:44	28:16

INDIVIDUAL STATISTICS

RUSHING—Oakland, Wheatley 12-21, Gannon 7-27, Kaufman 6-27, Crockett 3-8. San Diego, Fletcher 9-23, Fazande 5-9, R. Jenkins 3-(minus 3), McCrary 2-(minus 1), Harbaugh 1-1.

PASSING—Oakland, Gannon 16-35-1-156. San Diego, Harbaugh 25-35-1-222.

RECEIVING—Oakland, Rison 5-67, Brown 3-29, Wheatley 3-12, Brigham 1-15, Kaufman 1-11, Dunn 1-10, Dudley 1-6, Ritchie 1-6. San Diego, F. Jones 10-111, Fletcher 5-30, R. Jones 4-35, J. Graham 4-30, Conway 2-16.

MISSED FIELD GOAL ATTEMPTS—Oakland, Janikowski 42. San Diego, Carney 40.

INTERCEPTIONS—Oakland, Pope 1-0. San Diego, Seau 1-0.

KICKOFF RETURNS—Oakland, Dunn 3-75. San Diego, R. Jenkins 4-100, Bynum 1-18.

PUNT RETURNS—Oakland, Gordon 4-35. San Diego, R. Jones 2-18.

SACKS—Oakland, W. Thomas 1, Bryant 1, Upshaw 1. San Diego, Mickell 1.

TITANS 27, REDSKINS 21

Monday, October 30

Tennessee	0	20	0	7	27
Washington	7	0	7	7	21

First Quarter
Was.—Sellers 5 pass from B. Johnson (Heppner kick), 10:02.

Second Quarter
Ten.—FG, Del Greco 46, 1:53.
Ten.—Mason 69 punt return (Del Greco kick), 3:48.
Ten.—FG, Del Greco 21, 14:02.
Ten.—Rolle 81 interception return (Del Greco kick), 15:00.

Third Quarter
Was.—Davis 1 run (Heppner kick), 14:03.

Fourth Quarter
Ten.—Wycheck 18 pass from McNair (Del Greco kick), 4:48.
Was.—Centers 3 pass from B. Johnson (Heppner kick), 8:18.
Attendance—83,472.

	Tennessee	Washington
First downs	13	21
Rushes-yards	27-96	24-90
Passing	93	176
Punt returns	1-69	0-0
Kickoff returns	4-96	5-117
Interception returns	3-81	0-0
Comp.-att.-int.	14-18-0	21-40-3
Sacked-yards lost	1-3	3-26
Punts	5-35	3-37
Fumbles-lost	0-0	0-0
Penalties-yards	10-56	7-62
Time of possession	29:19	30:41

INDIVIDUAL STATISTICS

RUSHING—Tennessee, E. George 22-71, McNair 3-16, Thomas 2-9. Washington, Davis 21-62, B. Johnson 1-13, Barnhardt 1-11, Centers 1-4.

PASSING—Tennessee, McNair 14-18-0-96. Washington, B. Johnson 21-40-3-202.

RECEIVING—Tennessee, E. George 5-42, Wycheck 5-28, Mason 2-12, Sanders 1-12, Thomas 1-2. Washington, Centers 6-39, Alexander 4-38, Fryar 3-55, Thrash 3-20, Connell 2-33, Reed 1-10, Sellers 1-5, Davis 1-2.

MISSED FIELD GOAL ATTEMPTS—None.

INTERCEPTIONS—Tennessee, Rolle 2-81, Sidney 1-0.

KICKOFF RETURNS—Tennessee, Mason 3-80, Thornton 1-16. Washington, Thrash 5-117.

PUNT RETURNS—Tennessee, Mason 1-69.

SACKS—Tennessee, Robinson 1, Smith 1, Thornton 1. Washington, Arrington 1.

WEEK 10

STANDINGS

AFC EAST

	W	L	T	Pct.
Miami	7	2	0	.778
Indianapolis	6	3	0	.667
N.Y. Jets	6	3	0	.667
Buffalo	5	4	0	.556
New England	2	7	0	.222

AFC CENTRAL

	W	L	T	Pct.
Tennessee	8	1	0	.889
Baltimore	6	4	0	.600
Pittsburgh	5	4	0	.556
Jacksonville	3	6	0	.333
Cincinnati	2	7	0	.222
Cleveland	2	8	0	.222

AFC WEST

	W	L	T	Pct.
Oakland	8	1	0	.889
Denver	5	4	0	.556
Kansas City	5	4	0	.556
Seattle	3	7	0	.300
San Diego	0	9	0	.000

NFC EAST

	W	L	T	Pct.
N.Y. Giants	7	2	0	.778
Philadelphia	6	4	0	.600
Washington	6	4	0	.600
Arizona	3	6	0	.333
Dallas	3	6	0	.333

NFC CENTRAL

	W	L	T	Pct.
Minnesota	7	2	0	.778
Detroit	5	4	0	.556
Tampa Bay	5	4	0	.556
Green Bay	4	5	0	.444
Chicago	2	7	0	.222

NFC WEST

	W	L	T	Pct.
St. Louis	7	2	0	.778
New Orleans	6	3	0	.667
Carolina	4	5	0	.444
Atlanta	3	7	0	.300
San Francisco	2	8	0	.200

TOP PERFORMANCES

100-YARD RUSHING GAMES

Player, Team & Opponent	Att.	Yds.	TD
Emmitt Smith, Dal. at Phi.*	26	134	1
Lamar Smith, Mia. at Det.	24	125	2
Stephen Davis, Wash. at Ari.	30	124	1
Robert Smith, Min. at G.B.*	24	122	0
Terrell Davis, Den. at NYJ	33	115	1
Tyrone Wheatley, Oak. vs. K.C.	20	112	1
Jamal Lewis, Balt. at Cin.	22	109	0

300-YARD PASSING GAMES

Player, Team & Opponent	Att.	Comp.	Yds.	TD	Int.
Elvis Grbac, K.C. at Oak.	53	39	504	2	2
Trent Green, St.L. vs. Car.	42	29	431	2	0
Brian Griese, Den. at NYJ	35	22	327	2	1
Peyton Manning, Ind. at Chi.	39	26	302	2	1

100-YARD RECEIVING GAMES

Player, Team & Opponent	Rec.	Yds.	TD
Joe Horn, N.O. vs. S.F.	10	180	1
Az-Zahir Hakim, St.L. vs. Car.	8	147	1
Derrick Alexander, K.C. at Oak.	9	139	2
Tony Gonzalez, K.C. at Oak.	9	134	0
Rod Smith, Den. at NYJ	5	134	0
Torry Holt, St.L. vs. Car.	4	130	0
Randy Moss, Min. at G.B.*	6	130	0
Antonio Freeman, G.B. vs. Min.*	5	118	1
Sylvester Morris, K.C. at Oak.	6	102	0
James Thrash, Wash. at Ari.	6	102	0
Amani Toomer, NYG at Cle.	6	100	2

*Overtime game.

RESULTS

SUNDAY, NOVEMBER 5

ARIZONA 16, Washington 15
Baltimore 27, CINCINNATI 7
Buffalo 16, NEW ENGLAND 13 (OT)
Carolina 27, ST. LOUIS 24
CHICAGO 27, Indianapolis 24
Denver 30, N.Y. JETS 23
Miami 23, DETROIT 8
NEW ORLEANS 31, San Francisco 15
N.Y. Giants 24, CLEVELAND 3
OAKLAND 49, Kansas City 31
PHILADELPHIA 16, Dallas 13 (OT)
SEATTLE 17, San Diego 15
TENNESSEE 9, Pittsburgh 7
Tampa Bay 27, ATLANTA 14

MONDAY, NOVEMBER 6

GREEN BAY 26, Minnesota 20 (OT)
  Open date: Jacksonville

BEARS 27, COLTS 24

Sunday, November 5

Indianapolis	0	0	8	16—24
Chicago	10	10	7	0—27

First Quarter
Chi.—Enis 11 run (Edinger kick), 9:39.
Chi.—FG, Edinger 41, 14:58.

Second Quarter
Chi.—M. Robinson 34 pass from Miller (Edinger kick), 10:48.
Chi.—FG, Edinger 37, 15:00.

Third Quarter
Chi.—W. Harris 35 interception return (Edinger kick), 1:18.
Ind.—James 1 run (Pollard pass from Manning), 9:00.

Fourth Quarter
Ind.—FG, Vanderjagt 19, 4:27.
Ind.—James 21 pass from Manning (run failed), 8:21.
Ind.—Pathon 19 pass from Manning (Vanderjagt), 13:24.
Attendance—66,944.

	Indianapolis	Chicago
First downs	20	20
Rushes-yards	20-90	35-143
Passing	281	227
Punt returns	0-0	2-18
Kickoff returns	5-104	3-61
Interception returns	0-0	1-35
Comp.-att.-int.	26-39-1	25-36-0
Sacked-yards lost	2-21	0-0
Punts	4-39	3-37
Fumbles-lost	1-1	0-0
Penalties-yards	7-81	8-58
Time of possession	24:37	35:23

INDIVIDUAL STATISTICS
RUSHING—Indianapolis, James 17-68, Manning 3-22. Chicago, Allen 16-85, Enis 9-25, Barnes 5-23, Miller 4-1, M. Robinson 1-9.
PASSING—Indianapolis, Manning 26-39-1-302. Chicago, Miller 24-35-0-214, Aguiar 1-1-0-13.
RECEIVING—Indianapolis, Harrison 6-42, Dilger 5-66, Green 5-45, James 4-49, Pathon 3-58, Pollard 3-42. Chicago, M. Robinson 8-90, Allen 5-37, Kennison 5-37, Sinceno 2-21, Brooks 2-16, Wells 1-13, Booker 1-11, White 1-2.
MISSED FIELD GOAL ATTEMPTS—None.
INTERCEPTIONS—Chicago, W. Harris 1-35.
KICKOFF RETURNS—Indianapolis, Pathon 4-87, Wilkins 1-17. Chicago, Milburn 2-50, Enis 1-11.
PUNT RETURNS—Chicago, Milburn 2-18.
SACKS—Chicago, Colvin 1, Daniels 1.

RAVENS 27, BENGALS 7

Sunday, November 5

Baltimore	3	21	0	3—27
Cincinnati	0	0	7	0— 7

First Quarter
Bal.—FG, Stover 38, 12:32.

Second Quarter
Bal.—Stokley 14 pass from Dilfer (Stover kick), 0:53.
Bal.—Sharpe 18 pass from Dilfer (Stover kick), 8:35.
Bal.—Sharpe 19 pass from Dilfer (Stover kick), 12:56.

Third Quarter
Cin.—Warrick 4 run (Rackers kick), 8:47.

Fourth Quarter
Bal.—FG, Stover 32, 6:02.
Attendance—54,759.

	Baltimore	Cincinnati
First downs	19	11
Rushes-yards	31-142	27-44
Passing	236	130
Punt returns	2-28	3-43
Kickoff returns	1-26	6-144
Interception returns	0-0	0-0

	Baltimore	Cincinnati
Comp.-att.-int.	23-34-0	15-27-0
Sacked-yards lost	1-8	2-7
Punts	6-41	8-43
Fumbles-lost	0-0	2-1
Penalties-yards	6-50	6-40
Time of possession	33:13	26:47

INDIVIDUAL STATISTICS
RUSHING—Baltimore, Ja. Lewis 22-109, Dilfer 5-6, Holmes 3-8, Johnson 1-19. Cincinnati, Dillon 16-23, Smith 5-8, Keaton 2-9, Bennett 2-7, Warrick 2-(minus 3).
PASSING—Baltimore, Dilfer 23-34-0-244. Cincinnati, Smith 15-27-0-137.
RECEIVING—Baltimore, Sharpe 7-66, Ismail 4-42, J. Lewis 4-25, Ja. Lewis 3-70, Johnson 2-24, Stokley 1-14, Gash 1-3, Holmes 1-0. Cincinnati, Bennett 4-19, Yeast 3-26, McGee 2-41, Warrick 2-22, Battaglia 2-11, Dillon 1-9, Dugans 1-9.
MISSED FIELD GOAL ATTEMPTS—None.
INTERCEPTIONS—None.
KICKOFF RETURNS—Baltimore, Harris 1-26. Cincinnati, Mack 4-107, Keaton 2-37.
PUNT RETURNS—Baltimore, J. Lewis 2-28. Cincinnati, Yeast 3-43.
SACKS—Baltimore, McCrary 1, Boulware 1. Cincinnati, Hall 1.

DOLPHINS 23, LIONS 8

Sunday, November 5

Miami	14	3	6	0—23
Detroit	0	0	0	8— 8

First Quarter
Mia.—L. Smith 46 run (Mare kick), 0:21.
Mia.—L. Smith 8 run (Mare kick), 6:29.

Second Quarter
Mia.—FG, Mare 40, 4:08.

Third Quarter
Mia.—FG, Mare 38, 2:25.
Mia.—FG, Mare 41, 14:08.

Fourth Quarter
Det.—J. Stewart 3 run (Morton pass from Case), 3:59.
Attendance—77,813.

	Miami	Detroit
First downs	15	14
Rushes-yards	37-189	22-99
Passing	104	154
Punt returns	3-45	2-15
Kickoff returns	1-56	5-118
Interception returns	1-15	0-0
Comp.-att.-int.	13-18-0	15-27-1
Sacked-yards lost	1-8	4-15
Punts	5-41	6-39
Fumbles-lost	1-0	2-2
Penalties-yards	7-62	5-40
Time of possession	33:45	26:15

INDIVIDUAL STATISTICS
RUSHING—Miami, L. Smith 24-125, Fiedler 8-42, Konrad 3-9, T. Thomas 1-12, Shepherd 1-1. Detroit, J. Stewart 18-71, Batch 2-6, Foster 1-16, Morton 1-6.
PASSING—Miami, Fiedler 13-18-0-112. Detroit, Batch 8-16-0-95, Case 7-11-1-74.
RECEIVING—Miami, Gadsden 4-41, L. Smith 4-17, Konrad 2-10, Weaver 1-33, Shepherd 1-7, T. Thomas 1-4. Detroit, Moore 4-45, Sloan 3-64, Foster 2-30, J. Stewart 2-11, Bates 2-8, Morton 1-8, Schlesinger 1-3.
MISSED FIELD GOAL ATTEMPTS—None.
INTERCEPTIONS—Miami, Denson 1-15.
KICKOFF RETURNS—Miami, Denson 1-56. Detroit, Fair 5-118.
PUNT RETURNS—Miami, Ogden 3-45. Detroit, Fair 2-15.
SACKS—Miami, Taylor 2, Gardener 1.5, Armstrong 0.5. Detroit, Jones 1.

TITANS 9, STEELERS 7

Sunday, November 5

Pittsburgh	0	0	0	7—7
Tennessee	0	3	0	6—9

Second Quarter
Ten.—FG, Del Greco 21, 14:08.
Fourth Quarter
Ten.—FG, Del Greco 31, 2:11.
Pit.—Bruener 30 pass from Stewart (K. Brown kick), 6:33.
Ten.—FG, Del Greco 29, 14:56.
Attendance—68,498.

	Pittsburgh	Tennessee
First downs	10	21
Rushes-yards	20-74	40-148
Passing	93	216
Punt returns	2-1	4-24
Kickoff returns	4-44	2-31
Interception returns	1-0	1-2
Comp.-att.-int.	7-22-1	20-31-1
Sacked-yards lost	2-19	1-11
Punts	6-46	5-41
Fumbles-lost	4-2	1-0
Penalties-yards	4-25	14-115
Time of possession	20:30	39:30

INDIVIDUAL STATISTICS

RUSHING—Pittsburgh, Bettis 13-42, Stewart 6-31, Huntley 1-1. Tennessee, E. George 34-98, McNair 5-50, Thomas 1-0.

PASSING—Pittsburgh, Stewart 7-22-1-112. Tennessee, McNair 20-31-1-227.

RECEIVING—Pittsburgh, Bruener 1-30, Burress 1-25, Geason 1-22, Bettis 1-12, Kreider 1-8, Shaw 1-8, Ward 1-7. Tennessee, Mason 8-92, Wycheck 3-40, Sanders 4-70, Kinney 1-19, Thomas 1-5, E. George 1-3.

MISSED FIELD GOAL ATTEMPTS—Tennessee, Del Greco 24.

INTERCEPTIONS—Pittsburgh, Porter 1-0. Tennessee, Rolle 1-2.

KICKOFF RETURNS—Pittsburgh, Edwards 2-40, Poteat 1-23, Tuman 1-(minus 1). Tennessee, Mason 2-31.

PUNT RETURNS—Pittsburgh, Hawkins 1-1, Poteat 1-0. Tennessee, Mason 4-24.

SACKS—Pittsburgh, Gildon 1. Tennessee, Favors 1, Godfrey 0.5, Robinson 0.5.

BILLS 16, PATRIOTS 13

Sunday, November 5

Buffalo	3	7	0	3	3—16
New England	0	3	0	10	0—13

First Quarter
Buf.—FG, Christie 19, 13:41.
Second Quarter
Buf.—Riemersma 9 pass from Flutie (Christie kick), 4:50.
N.E.—FG, Vinatieri 48, 14:40.
Fourth Quarter
N.E.—Redmond 1 run (Vinatieri kick), 6:00.
N.E.—FG, Vinatieri 43, 12:57.
Buf.—FG, Christie 48, 14:56.
Overtime
Buf.—FG, Christie 32, 4:32.
Attendance—60,292.

	Buffalo	New England
First downs	20	14
Rushes-yards	31-141	34-89
Passing	174	100
Punt returns	3-14	5-64
Kickoff returns	4-22	5-79
Interception returns	2-1	0-0
Comp.-att.-int.	18-37-0	14-27-2
Sacked-yards lost	1-5	3-16
Punts	8-36	8-42
Fumbles-lost	2-1	1-0
Penalties-yards	7-73	8-103
Time of possession	31:54	32:38

INDIVIDUAL STATISTICS

RUSHING—Buffalo, Bryson 13-60, Morris 10-45, Flutie 5-23, A. Smith 3-13. New England, Redmond 24-68, T. Carter 6-19, Faulk 2-2, Bledsoe 1-5, Brown 1-(minus 1).

PASSING—Buffalo, Flutie 18-37-0-179. New England, Friesz 11-21-1-66, Bledsoe 3-5-1-50, Bishop 0-1-0-0.

RECEIVING—Buffalo, Riemersma 6-49, Morris 4-41, Moulds 4-29, P. Price 3-36, McDaniel 1-24. New England, Redmond 5-19, Brown 3-49, Glenn 3-25, Simmons 1-22, T. Carter 1-6, Faulk 1-(minus 5).

MISSED FIELD GOAL ATTEMPTS—None.

INTERCEPTIONS—Buffalo, Irvin 1-1, Holecek 1-0.

KICKOFF RETURNS—Buffalo, Watson 1-22, Cavil 1-1, A. Smith 1-0, Bryson 1-(minus 1). New England, Simmons 2-19, Faulk 1-28, Redmond 1-25, Bruschi 1-7.

PUNT RETURNS—Buffalo, Watson 3-14. New England, Brown 5-64.

SACKS—Buffalo, Cowart 1, Wiley 1, Rogers 1. New England, Thomas 1.

GIANTS 24, BROWNS 3

Sunday, November 5

N.Y. Giants	0	10	7	7—24	
Cleveland	3	0	0	0— 3	

First Quarter
Cle.—FG, P. Dawson 19, 13:15.
Second Quarter
NYG—FG, Daluiso 39, 3:41.
NYG—Hilliard 28 pass from Collins (Daluiso kick), 13:05.
Third Quarter
NYG—Toomer 17 pass from Collins (Daluiso kick), 9:41.
Fourth Quarter
NYG—Toomer 32 pass from Collins (Daluiso kick), 2:22.
Attendance—72,718.

	N.Y. Giants	Cleveland
First downs	24	12
Rushes-yards	43-155	16-41
Passing	215	152
Punt returns	3-30	1-12
Kickoff returns	2-41	5-91
Interception returns	1-6	0-0
Comp.-att.-int.	19-31-0	17-29-1
Sacked-yards lost	3-42	4-24
Punts	3-45	6-49
Fumbles-lost	2-1	0-0
Penalties-yards	3-28	4-55
Time of possession	36:40	23:20

INDIVIDUAL STATISTICS

RUSHING—New York, Dayne 19-64, Barber 15-53, Collins 4-1, Comella 3-16, Toomer 1-27, Hilliard 1-(minus 6). Cleveland, Prentice 11-15, White 3-12, Pederson 2-14.

PASSING—New York, Collins 19-31-0-257. Cleveland, Pederson 17-29-1-176.

RECEIVING—New York, Toomer 6-100, Comella 5-58, Hilliard 3-60, Barber 2-15, Davis 1-13, Jurevicius 1-10, Campbell 1-1. Cleveland, Johnson 5-76, Shea 4-27, Northcutt 3-34, White 2-27, Prentice 2-3, Edwards 1-9.

MISSED FIELD GOAL ATTEMPTS—None.

INTERCEPTIONS—New York, McDaniel 1-6.

KICKOFF RETURNS—New York, Levingston 2-41. Cleveland, White 4-73, Burnett 1-18.

PUNT RETURNS—New York, Barber 3-30. Cleveland, Northcutt 1-12.

SACKS—New York, Strahan 2, Griffin 1, K. Hamilton 1. Cleveland, Rainer 1, J. Miller 1, K. McKenzie 1.

EAGLES 16, COWBOYS 13

Sunday, November 5

Dallas	0	7	3	3	0—13
Philadelphia	0	0	0	13	3—16

Second Quarter
Dal.—E. Smith 7 run (Seder kick), 10:18.
Third Quarter
Dal.—FG, Seder 48, 13:02.
Fourth Quarter
Phi.—FG, Akers 34, 2:00.
Phi.—Autry 23 pass from McNabb (Akers kick), 7:22.
Dal.—FG, Seder 27, 13:09.
Phi.—FG, Akers 34, 14:49.
Overtime
Phi.—FG, Akers 32, 7:55.
Attendance—65,636.

	Dallas	Philadelphia
First downs	16	23
Rushes-yards	46-204	31-129
Passing	91	228
Punt returns	3-37	1-2

	Dallas	Philadelphia
Kickoff returns	2-70	3-71
Interception returns	2-13	1-0
Comp.-att.-int.	14-22-1	23-42-2
Sacked-yards lost	3-18	0-0
Punts	5-36	6-44
Fumbles-lost	3-1	1-0
Penalties-yards	12-97	7-91
Time of possession	34:50	33:05

INDIVIDUAL STATISTICS

RUSHING—Dallas, E. Smith 26-134, Warren 10-48, Cunningham 9-22, Thomas 1-0. Philadelphia, Autry 19-65, McNabb 5-58, Pritchett 3-8, C. Martin 2-2, Lee 1-2, C. Johnson 1-(minus 6).

PASSING—Dallas, Cunningham 14-22-1-109. Philadelphia, McNabb 23-41-2-228, Mitchell 0-1-0-0.

RECEIVING—Dallas, McGarity 3-19, Warren 3-14, Thomas 3-14, McKnight 2-41, Harris 2-6, E. Smith 1-15. Philadelphia, C. Martin 6-40, Pritchett 5-40, Autry 3-57, C. Johnson 3-34, Lewis 3-23, Mitchell 2-19, Small 1-15.

MISSED FIELD GOAL ATTEMPTS—Philadelphia, Akers 40.

INTERCEPTIONS—Dallas, Woodson 1-12, Wortham 1-1. Philadelphia, Dawkins 1-0.

KICKOFF RETURNS—Dallas, Tucker 2-70. Philadelphia, Mitchell 3-71.

PUNT RETURNS—Dallas, McGarity 3-37. Philadelphia, Mitchell 1-2.

SACKS—Philadelphia, Whiting 2, H. Douglas 1.

BRONCOS 30, JETS 23

Sunday, November 5

Denver	10	10	3	7—30
N.Y. Jets	0	10	10	3—23

First Quarter
Den.—McCaffrey 1 pass from Griese (Elam kick), 10:42.
Den.—FG, Elam 31, 13:36.

Second Quarter
Den.—Davis 4 run (Elam kick), 9:27.
NYJ—Martin 1 run (Hall kick), 11:55.
Den.—FG, Elam 41, 13:47.
NYJ—FG, Hall 45, 14:51.

Third Quarter
NYJ—Becht 1 pass from Testaverde (Hall kick), 4:56.
NYJ—FG, Hall 26, 9:36.
Den.—FG, Elam 23, 15:00.

Fourth Quarter
Den.—McCaffrey 47 pass from Griese (Elam kick), 6:00.
NYJ—FG, Hall 28, 10:15.
Attendance—78,305.

	Denver	N.Y. Jets
First downs	23	22
Rushes-yards	39-130	17-88
Passing	317	293
Punt returns	1-15	1-0
Kickoff returns	4-73	7-124
Interception returns	2-0	1-0
Comp.-att.-int.	22-35-1	21-42-2
Sacked-yards lost	1-10	0-0
Punts	3-30	2-61
Fumbles-lost	0-0	1-1
Penalties-yards	6-57	2-10
Time of possession	36:47	23:13

INDIVIDUAL STATISTICS

RUSHING—Denver, Davis 33-115, Griese 5-12, Anderson 1-3. New York, Martin 14-71, R. Anderson 1-9, Coles 1-8, Testaverde 1-0.

PASSING—Denver, Griese 22-35-1-327. New York, Testaverde 21-42-2-293.

RECEIVING—Denver, McCaffrey 6-96, R. Smith 5-134, Carswell 4-31, Clark 2-28, Davis 2-4, Chamberlain 1-21, McGriff 1-8, Brooks 1-5. New York, Martin 6-68, Chrebet 5-82, Ward 4-61, Becht 3-41, R. Anderson 2-10, Coles 1-31.

MISSED FIELD GOAL ATTEMPTS—None.

INTERCEPTIONS—Denver, E. Brown 1-0, Kennedy 1-0. New York, Farrior 1-0.

KICKOFF RETURNS—Denver, O'Neal 4-73. New York, Stone 5-97, Baxter 1-15, Wiggins 1-12.

PUNT RETURNS—Denver, O'Neal 1-15. New York, Ward 1-0.

SACKS—New York, Lewis 1.

BUCCANEERS 27, FALCONS 14

Sunday, November 5

Tampa Bay	7	7	3	10—27
Atlanta	0	0	7	7—14

First Quarter
T.B.—Moore 1 pass from King (Gramatica kick), 7:32.

Second Quarter
T.B.—K. Johnson 5 pass from King (Gramatica kick), 10:01.

Third Quarter
Atl.—Mathis 19 pass from Kanell (Andersen kick), 7:55.
T.B.—FG, Gramatica 51, 14:15.

Fourth Quarter
T.B.—K. Johnson 29 pass from King (Gramatica kick), 7:01.
T.B.—FG, Gramatica 34, 10:33.
Atl.—Mathis 16 pass from Kanell (Andersen kick), 14:57.
Attendance—70,097.

	Tampa Bay	Atlanta
First downs	15	22
Rushes-yards	36-126	15-59
Passing	141	224
Punt returns	1-12	4-33
Kickoff returns	2-32	5-59
Interception returns	4-44	1-60
Comp.-att.-int.	12-26-1	30-50-4
Sacked-yards lost	2-5	4-23
Punts	4-48	5-35
Fumbles-lost	1-1	0-0
Penalties-yards	4-43	5-25
Time of possession	30:15	29:45

INDIVIDUAL STATISTICS

RUSHING—Tampa Bay, Dunn 18-77, Alstott 10-20, King 3-19, Green 2-11, Stecker 2-1, Hamilton 1-(minus 2). Atlanta, Anderson 15-59.

PASSING—Tampa Bay, King 11-25-1-110, Royals 1-1-0-36. Atlanta, Kanell 26-43-2-218, Chandler 4-7-2-29.

RECEIVING—Tampa Bay, K. Johnson 3-47, Green 2-44, Moore 2-11, Dunn 2-(minus 1), Robinson 1-36, Hape 1-5, Alstott 1-4. Atlanta, Anderson 9-48, Mathis 6-65, Jefferson 6-55, Christian 4-24, Dwight 3-41, R. Kelly 2-14.

MISSED FIELD GOAL ATTEMPTS—None.

INTERCEPTIONS—Tampa Bay, Abraham 2-45, Robinson 1-0, Duncan 1-(minus 1). Atlanta, Buchanan 1-60.

KICKOFF RETURNS—Tampa Bay, Stecker 2-32. Atlanta, Dwight 3-39, Kozlowski 1-12, Vaughn 1-8.

PUNT RETURNS—Tampa Bay, Williams 1-12. Atlanta, Dwight 4-33.

SACKS—Tampa Bay, Cannida 1.5, McFarland 1, White 1, Lynch 0.5. Atlanta, Wiley 1, Draft 1.

SAINTS 31, 49ERS 15

Sunday, November 5

San Francisco	0	0	7	8—15
New Orleans	7	21	3	0—31

First Quarter
N.O.—A. Glover 1 pass from Blake (Brien kick), 8:31.

Second Quarter
N.O.—Jackson 4 pass from Blake (Brien kick), 1:19.
N.O.—Horn 43 pass from Blake (Brien kick), 10:26.
N.O.—R. Williams 1 run (Brien kick), 14:51.

Third Quarter
N.O.—FG, Brien 44, 2:59.
S.F.—Garner 1 run (Richey kick), 7:08.

Fourth Quarter
S.F.—Jackson 11 pass from Garcia (Jackson run), 14:13.
Attendance—64,900.

	San Francisco	New Orleans
First downs	19	25
Rushes-yards	20-84	39-124
Passing	262	236
Punt returns	1-1	1-6
Kickoff returns	5-131	1-16
Interception returns	0-0	2-0
Comp.-att.-int.	22-36-2	20-26-0
Sacked-yards lost	0-0	4-39

	San Francisco	New Orleans
Punts	3-39	3-46
Fumbles-lost	1-0	0-0
Penalties-yards	14-97	10-54
Time of possession	23:10	36:50

INDIVIDUAL STATISTICS

RUSHING—San Francisco, Garner 13-49, Garcia 4-24, Beasley 2-11, Jackson 1-0. New Orleans, R. Williams 27-81, Blake 6-23, T. Smith 2-6, Brooks 2-(minus 2), Horn 1-13, Morton 1-3.

PASSING—San Francisco, Garcia 22-36-2-262. New Orleans, Blake 20-26-0-275.

RECEIVING—San Francisco, Owens 6-97, Clark 4-53, Stokes 4-51, Rice 3-28, Jackson 3-20, Streets 1-7, Garner 1-6. New Orleans, Horn 9-167, Jackson 4-34, A. Glover 3-37, R. Williams 2-17, Morton 1-14, Hall 1-6.

MISSED FIELD GOAL ATTEMPTS—San Francisco, Richey 34.

INTERCEPTIONS—New Orleans, Knight 1-0, Weary 1-0.

KICKOFF RETURNS—San Francisco, Streets 4-98, K. Williams 1-33. New Orleans, Morton 1-16.

PUNT RETURNS—San Francisco, K. Williams 1-1. New Orleans, Morton 1-6.

SACKS—San Francisco, Peterson 2, B. Young 2.

CARDINALS 16, REDSKINS 15

Sunday, November 5

Washington	3	9	3	0—15
Arizona	10	0	6	0—16

First Quarter
Ariz.—Williams 104 fumble return (Blanchard kick), 4:22.
Ariz.—FG, Blanchard 30, 7:32.
Was.—FG, Heppner 35, 11:42.

Second Quarter
Was.—Davis 1 run (run failed), 6:17.
Was.—FG, Heppner 28, 13:08.

Third Quarter
Ariz.—Pittman 7 run (run failed), 1:16.
Was.—FG, Heppner 29, 10:17.
Attendance—52,244.

	Washington	Arizona
First downs	27	11
Rushes-yards	37-164	24-45
Passing	267	133
Punts	0-0	3-46
Kickoff returns	4-84	5-183
Interception returns	1-32	2-26
Comp.-att.-int.	20-39-2	12-19-1
Sacked-yards lost	1-9	1-13
Punt returns	2-0	0-0
Fumbles-lost	1-1	2-1
Penalties-yards	8-59	8-65
Time of possession	37:26	22:34

INDIVIDUAL STATISTICS

RUSHING—Washington, Davis 30-124, Hicks 6-25, Thrash 1-15. Arizona, Pittman 15-30, Jones 4-16, Plummer 4-0, Makovicka 1-(minus 1).

PASSING—Washington, George 20-39-2-276. Arizona, Plummer 12-19-1-146.

RECEIVING—Washington, Thrash 6-102, Alexander 5-3, Centers 4-33, Davis 2-62, Fryar 2-15, Connell 1-11. Arizona, Boston 3-57, Pittman 3-28, Mitchell 2-9, Jenkins 1-34, Sanders 1-9, Jones 1-5, Hardy 1-4.

MISSED FIELD GOAL ATTEMPTS—Washington, Heppner 51, 33. Arizona, Blanchard 56.

INTERCEPTIONS—Washington, Sanders 1-32. Arizona, Williams 1-26, Walz 1-0.

KICKOFF RETURNS—Washington, Thrash 4-84. Arizona, Jenkins 5-183.

PUNT RETURNS—Washington, Sanders 1-0, Thrash 1-0.

SACKS—Washington, Lang 1. Arizona, Issa 1.

SEAHAWKS 17, CHARGERS 15

Sunday, November 5

San Diego	0	3	9	3—15
Seattle	0	14	0	3—17

Second Quarter
Sea.—Dawkins 10 pass from Kitna (Lindell kick), 2:03.
Sea.—Fauria 10 pass from Kitna (Lindell kick), 6:26.
S.D.—FG, Carney 19, 15:00.

Third Quarter
S.D.—FG, Carney 41, 5:49.
S.D.—Conway 10 pass from Harbaugh (run failed), 10:48.

Fourth Quarter
S.D.—FG, Carney 28, 9:24.
Sea.—FG, Lindell 48, 15:00.
Attendance—59,884.

	San Diego	Seattle
First downs	22	9
Rushes-yards	33-116	25-50
Passing	282	78
Punt returns	3-2	0-0
Kickoff returns	3-32	4-128
Interception returns	1-3	1-8
Comp.-att.-int.	26-37-1	11-19-1
Sacked-yards lost	1-1	1-7
Punts	2-28	6-34
Fumbles-lost	3-2	0-0
Penalties-yards	9-53	5-34
Time of possession	39:51	20:09

INDIVIDUAL STATISTICS

RUSHING—San Diego, Fazande 22-74, Harbaugh 6-16, Fletcher 4-13, Conway 1-13. Seattle, Watters 21-55, Alexander 4-(minus 5).

PASSING—San Diego, Harbaugh 22-32-1-236, Moreno 4-5-0-47. Seattle, Kitna 11-19-1-85.

RECEIVING—San Diego, F. Jones 5-86, J. Graham 5-67, Fletcher 5-40, Fazande 5-37, Conway 3-30, McCrary 2-12, R. Jones 1-11. Seattle, Watters 4-20, Dawkins 3-26, Jackson 2-27, Fauria 1-10, Mayes 1-2.

MISSED FIELD GOAL ATTEMPTS—San Diego, Carney 51.

INTERCEPTIONS—San Diego, Harrison 1-0. Seattle, Simmons 1-8.

KICKOFF RETURNS—San Diego, R. Jenkins 3-32. Seattle, Rogers 3-94, Joseph 1-34.

PUNT RETURNS—San Diego, Dumas 1-1, Jacquet 1-1, R. Jones 1-0.

SACKS—San Diego, Seau 1. Seattle, Bellamy 1.

RAIDERS 49, CHIEFS 31

Sunday, November 5

Kansas City	0	10	7	14—31
Oakland	14	14	7	14—49

First Quarter
Oak.—Rison 10 pass from Gannon (Lechler kick), 5:23.
Oak.—Crockett 1 run (Lechler kick), 13:57.

Second Quarter
K.C.—Richardson 1 run (Peterson kick), 1:13.
Oak.—Rison 6 pass from Gannon (Lechler kick), 7:20.
Oak.—Wheatley 1 run (Lechler kick), 11:39.
K.C.—FG, Peterson 28, 14:33.

Third Quarter
Oak.—Dudley 20 pass from Gannon (Lechler kick), 10:11.
K.C.—Alexander 9 pass from Grbac (Peterson kick), 13:53.

Fourth Quarter
K.C.—Alexander 48 pass from Grbac (Peterson kick), 6:41.
Oak.—Dudley 2 pass from Gannon (Lechler kick), 11:07.
K.C.—Grbac 3 run (Peterson kick), 13:13.
Oak.—Jordan 43 run (Lechler kick), 13:23.
Attendance—62,428.

	Kansas City	Oakland
First downs	31	31
Rushes-yards	9-39	42-231
Passing	474	242
Punt returns	0-0	3-38
Kickoff returns	7-148	5-137
Interception returns	0-0	2-47
Comp.-att.-int.	39-53-2	20-31-0
Sacked-yards lost	4-30	3-44
Punts	3-56	3-44
Fumbles-lost	1-1	0-0
Penalties-yards	9-80	9-81
Time of possession	21:31	38:29

INDIVIDUAL STATISTICS

RUSHING—Kansas City, Richardson 3-18, Bennett 3-(minus 2), Anders 2-20, Grbac 1-3. Oakland, Wheatley 20-112, Kaufman 11-32, Gannon 5-33, Jordan 3-46, Crockett 2-1, Brown 1-7.

PASSING—Kansas City, Grbac 39-53-2-504. Oakland, Gannon 20-31-0-242.

RECEIVING—Kansas City, Alexander 9-139, Gonzalez 9-134, Lockett 7-57, Richardson 7-51, Morris 6-102, Drayton 1-21. Oakland, Brown 5-74, Dudley 4-56, Jordan 3-37, Ritchie 3-25, Crockett 2-28, Rison 2-16, Jett 1-6.

MISSED FIELD GOAL ATTEMPTS—Oakland, Lechler 33.

INTERCEPTIONS—Oakland, Taves 1-24, Woodson 1-23.

KICKOFF RETURNS—Kansas City, L. Parker 5-90, Cloud 2-58. Oakland, Dunn 4-113, Branch 1-24.

PUNT RETURNS—Oakland, Gordon 3-38.

SACKS—Oakland, Coleman 2, Russell 1.5, Bryant 0.5.

PANTHERS 27, RAMS 24

Sunday, November 5

Carolina	6	7	3	11	27
St. Louis	7	3	14	0	24

First Quarter

Car.—FG, Nedney 35, 4:01.
St.L.—Hakim 14 pass from Green (Stoyanovich kick), 10:35.
Car.—FG, Nedney 45, 14:49.

Second Quarter

St.L.—FG, Stoyanovich 28, 4:22.
Car.—Crawford 16 pass from Beuerlein (Nedney kick), 9:05.

Third Quarter

Car.—FG, Nedney 24, 5:07.
St.L.—Bruce 4 pass from Green (Stoyanovich kick), 9:41.
St.L.—Watson 3 run (Stoyanovich kick), 12:34.

Fourth Quarter

Car.—Hayes 13 pass from Beuerlein (Beuerlein run), 4:17.
Car.—FG, Nedney 46, 14:20.
Attendance—66,048.

	Carolina	St. Louis
First downs	18	20
Rushes-yards	24-90	16-31
Passing	178	395
Punt returns	1-9	1-14
Kickoff returns	4-89	6-110
Interception returns	0-0	1-0
Comp.-att.-int.	15-25-1	29-42-0
Sacked-yards lost	5-36	5-36
Punts	2-44	2-31
Fumbles-lost	1-1	3-2
Penalties-yards	5-40	7-52
Time of possession	28:35	31:25

INDIVIDUAL STATISTICS

RUSHING—Carolina, Biakabutuka 19-77, Beuerlein 3-4, Floyd 2-9. St. Louis, Watson 12-12, Green 2-12, Hakim 2-7.

PASSING—Carolina, Beuerlein 15-25-1-214. St. Louis, Green 29-42-0-431.

RECEIVING—Carolina, Muhammad 6-83, Hayes 3-62, Byrd 2-23, Crawford 1-16, Hankton 1-14, Floyd 1-10, Biakabutuka 1-6. St. Louis, Hakim 8-147, Bruce 7-69, Holt 4-130, Watson 4-27, Proehl 3-38, Conwell 2-18, Hodgins 1-2.

MISSED FIELD GOAL ATTEMPTS—St. Louis, Stoyanovich 50, 37.

INTERCEPTIONS—St. Louis, McCleon 1-0.

KICKOFF RETURNS—Carolina, Bates 3-64, Byrd 1-25. St. Louis, Horne 6-110.

PUNT RETURNS—Carolina, Uwaezuoke 1-9. St. Louis, Hakim 1-14.

SACKS—Carolina, White 2, Morabito 1, J. Williams 1, Gilbert 1. St. Louis, Wistrom 1, McCleon 1, Agnew 1, Little 1, Moran 1.

PACKERS 26, VIKINGS 20

Monday, November 6

Minnesota	3	10	7	0	0	20
Green Bay	0	10	10	0	6	26

First Quarter

Min.—FG, Anderson 30, 6:35.

Second Quarter

G.B.—FG, Longwell 24, 0:07.
Min.—C. Carter 12 pass from Culpepper (Anderson kick), 4:57.
G.B.—Green 5 pass from Favre (Longwell kick), 8:09.
Min.—FG, Anderson 48, 15:00.

Third Quarter

G.B.—FG, Longwell 31, 6:12.
Min.—Smith 45 pass from Culpepper (Anderson kick), 11:00.
G.B.—Green 2 run (Longwell kick), 11:28.

Overtime

G.B.—Freeman 43 pass from Favre, 3:39.
Attendance—59,854.

	Minnesota	Green Bay
First downs	22	19
Rushes-yards	33-157	26-81
Passing	250	217
Punt returns	3-15	1-3
Kickoff returns	5-103	4-129
Interception returns	0-0	4-48
Comp.-att.-int.	17-35-4	17-36-0
Sacked-yards lost	3-26	2-18
Punts	4-42	8-35
Fumbles-lost	1-1	0-0
Penalties-yards	11-129	8-63
Time of possession	35:53	27:46

INDIVIDUAL STATISTICS

RUSHING—Minnesota, Smith 24-122, Culpepper 4-20, Kleinsasser 2-9, M. Williams 2-9, Moss 1-(minus 3). Green Bay, Green 23-68, Schroeder 1-12, Favre 1-2, Parker 1-(minus 1).

PASSING—Minnesota, Culpepper 17-34-3-276, Berger 0-1-1-0. Green Bay, Favre 17-36-0-235.

RECEIVING—Minnesota, Moss 6-130, C. Carter 5-59, Smith 2-67, Walsh 2-11, Hatchette 1-5, Jordan 1-4. Green Bay, Freeman 5-118, Green 5-34, Schroeder 4-63, Henderson 3-20.

MISSED FIELD GOAL ATTEMPTS—None.

INTERCEPTIONS—Green Bay, Sharper 2-22, M. McKenzie 1-26, T. Williams 1-0.

KICKOFF RETURNS—Minnesota, D. Palmer 4-82, M. Williams 1-21. Green Bay, Rossum 4-129.

PUNT RETURNS—Minnesota, D. Palmer 3-15. Green Bay, Rossum 1-3.

SACKS—Minnesota, Randle 1, Sawyer 1. Green Bay, Holliday 1, Bowens 1, S. Dotson 0.5, Maryland 0.5.

WEEK 11

STANDINGS

AFC EAST
	W	L	T	Pct.
Miami	8	2	0	.800
Indianapolis	7	3	0	.700
Buffalo	6	4	0	.600
N.Y. Jets	6	4	0	.600
New England	2	8	0	.200

AFC CENTRAL
	W	L	T	Pct.
Tennessee	8	2	0	.800
Baltimore	7	4	0	.636
Pittsburgh	5	5	0	.500
Jacksonville	3	7	0	.300
Cleveland	3	8	0	.273
Cincinnati	2	8	0	.200

AFC WEST
	W	L	T	Pct.
Oakland	8	2	0	.800
Denver	6	4	0	.600
Kansas City	5	5	0	.500
Seattle	4	7	0	.364
San Diego	0	10	0	.000

NFC EAST
	W	L	T	Pct.
N.Y. Giants	7	3	0	.700
Philadelphia	7	4	0	.636
Washington	6	4	0	.600
Dallas	4	6	0	.400
Arizona	3	7	0	.300

NFC CENTRAL
	W	L	T	Pct.
Minnesota	8	2	0	.800
Detroit	6	4	0	.600
Tampa Bay	6	4	0	.600
Green Bay	4	6	0	.400
Chicago	2	8	0	.200

NFC WEST
	W	L	T	Pct.
St. Louis	8	2	0	.800
New Orleans	7	3	0	.700
Carolina	4	6	0	.400
Atlanta	3	8	0	.273
San Francisco	3	8	0	.273

TOP PERFORMANCES

100-YARD RUSHING GAMES
Player, Team & Opponent	Att.	Yds.	TD
Jerome Bettis, Pit. vs. Phi.*	30	134	1
Edgerrin James, Ind. vs. NYJ	31	131	1
Jamal Anderson, Atl. at Det.	25	119	1
Robert Smith, Min. vs. Ari.	20	117	0
Fred Taylor, Jack. vs. Sea.	21	103	1
Charlie Garner, S.F. vs. K.C.	25	102	1

300-YARD PASSING GAMES
Player, Team & Opponent	Att.	Comp.	Yds.	TD	Int.
Rich Gannon, Oak. at Den.	53	30	382	1	2
Mark Brunell, Jack. vs. Sea.	33	24	340	1	0
Troy Aikman, Dal. vs. Cin.	37	24	308	1	0
Daunte Culpepper, Min. vs. Ari.	32	25	302	3	1

100-YARD RECEIVING GAMES
Player, Team & Opponent	Rec.	Yds.	TD
James McKnight, Dal. vs. Cin.	8	164	1
Keenan McCardell, Jack. vs. Sea.	6	156	1
Wayne Chrebet, NYJ at Ind.	8	140	0
Tim Brown, Oak. at Den.	10	122	1
Cris Carter, Min. vs. Ari.	11	119	1
Andre Rison, Oak. at Den.	6	117	0
Jimmy Smith, Jack. vs. Sea.	10	117	0
Ike Hilliard, NYG vs. St.L.	5	110	2
Randy Moss, Min. vs. Ari.	7	104	1

*Overtime game.

RESULTS

SUNDAY, NOVEMBER 12

Baltimore 24, TENNESSEE 23
BUFFALO 20, Chicago 3
CLEVELAND 19, New England 11
DALLAS 23, Cincinnati 6
DETROIT 13, Atlanta 10
INDIANAPOLIS 23, N.Y. Jets 15
Miami 17, SAN DIEGO 7
MINNESOTA 31, Arizona 14
New Orleans 20, CAROLINA 10
Philadelphia 26, PITTSBURGH 23 (OT)
St. Louis 38, N.Y. GIANTS 24
SAN FRANCISCO 21, Kansas City 7
Seattle 28, JACKSONVILLE 21
TAMPA BAY 20, Green Bay 15

MONDAY, NOVEMBER 13

DENVER 27, Oakland 24
Open date: Washington

LIONS 13, FALCONS 10

Sunday, November 12

Atlanta	0	7	3	0—10
Detroit	7	0	0	6—13

First Quarter
Det.—J. Stewart 1 run (Hanson kick), 4:30.

Second Quarter
Atl.—Anderson 14 run (Andersen kick), 8:24.

Third Quarter
Atl.—FG, Andersen 42, 4:36.

Fourth Quarter
Det.—FG, Hanson 18, 9:46.
Det.—FG, Hanson 44, 13:17.
Attendance—74,309.

	Atlanta	Detroit
First downs	17	12
Rushes-yards	29-114	33-107
Passing	104	115
Punt returns	8-34	3-13
Kickoff returns	4-85	2-49
Interception returns	1-1	2-12
Comp.-att.-int.	14-34-2	12-27-1
Sacked-yards lost	3-22	2-13
Punts	10-44	10-49
Fumbles-lost	3-0	0-0
Penalties-yards	10-82	9-70
Time of possession	30:32	29:28

INDIVIDUAL STATISTICS

RUSHING—Atlanta, Anderson 25-119, Christian 2-0, Kanell 1-0, Mathis 1-(minus 5). Detroit, J. Stewart 25-71, Bates 4-5, Batch 3-4, Morton 1-27.

PASSING—Atlanta, Kanell 14-34-2-126. Detroit, Batch 12-27-1-128.

RECEIVING—Atlanta, Anderson 5-36, Mathis 4-43, Jefferson 3-20, Dwight 2-27. Detroit, Moore 5-76, Pupunu 2-26, J. Stewart 2-(minus 6), Rasby 1-17, Morton 1-10, Foster 1-5.

MISSED FIELD GOAL ATTEMPTS—None.

INTERCEPTIONS—Atlanta, E. Williams 1-1. Detroit, C. Brown 1-12, Westbrook 1-0.

KICKOFF RETURNS—Atlanta, Dwight 4-85. Detroit, Howard 2-49.

PUNT RETURNS—Atlanta, Dwight 8-34. Detroit, Howard 3-13.

SACKS—Atlanta, Carter 1, B. Smith 1. Detroit, Porcher 2, Jones 1.

RAVENS 24, TITANS 23

Sunday, November 12

Baltimore	7	10	0	7—24
Tennessee	0	14	0	9—23

First Quarter
Bal.—Ismail 46 pass from Dilfer (Stover kick), 5:02.

Second Quarter
Bal.—Ja. Lewis 2 run (Stover kick), 2:34.
Ten.—Mason 10 pass from McNair (Del Greco kick), 6:50.
Bal.—FG, Stover 45, 13:56.
Ten.—Neal 4 pass from McNair (Del Greco kick), 14:57.

Fourth Quarter
Ten.—FG, Del Greco 23, 6:37.
Ten.—Phenix 87 interception return (kick failed), 12:30.
Bal.—Johnson 2 pass from Dilfer (Stover kick), 14:35.
Attendance—68,490.

	Baltimore	Tennessee
First downs	19	17
Rushes-yards	29-103	16-62
Passing	258	224
Punt returns	2-34	3-14
Kickoff returns	5-107	5-163
Interception returns	0-0	1-87
Comp.-att.-int.	23-36-1	21-34-0
Sacked-yards lost	5-23	1-4
Punts	6-38	5-49
Fumbles-lost	5-0	3-2
Penalties-yards	8-72	8-64
Time of possession	34:14	25:46

INDIVIDUAL STATISTICS

RUSHING—Baltimore, Ja. Lewis 23-99, Ayanbadejo 3-2, Holmes 3-2. Tennessee, E. George 12-28, McNair 4-34.

PASSING—Baltimore, Dilfer 23-36-1-281. Tennessee, McNair 21-34-0-228.

RECEIVING—Baltimore, Sharpe 8-92, Ismail 3-65, Johnson 3-24, Holmes 2-15, J. Lewis 2-15, Gash 2-12, Coates 1-28, Ja. Lewis 1-15, Stokley 1-15. Tennessee, Mason 5-63, Wycheck 5-56, E. George 5-36, Sanders 3-55, Kinney 2-14, Neal 1-4.

MISSED FIELD GOAL ATTEMPTS—Tennessee, Del Greco 43.

INTERCEPTIONS—Tennessee, Phenix 1-87.

KICKOFF RETURNS—Baltimore, Harris 4-107, Brown 1-0. Tennessee, Mason 4-136, Coleman 1-27.

PUNT RETURNS—Baltimore, J. Lewis 2-34. Tennessee, Mason 3-14.

SACKS—Baltimore, Burnett 1. Tennessee, Kearse 3, Thornton 1, Embray 1.

SAINTS 20, PANTHERS 10

Sunday, November 12

New Orleans	0	7	7	6—20
Carolina	0	3	0	7—10

Second Quarter
N.O.—Horn 43 pass from Blake (Brien kick), 5:41.
Car.—FG, Nedney 38, 8:50.

Third Quarter
N.O.—Kei. Mitchell 90 fumble return (Brien kick), 11:27.

Fourth Quarter
N.O.—FG, Brien 40, 0:38.
Car.—Muhammad 13 pass from Beuerlein (Nedney kick), 6:16.
N.O.—FG, Brien 42, 11:37.
Attendance—72,981.

	New Orleans	Carolina
First downs	16	21
Rushes-yards	31-157	17-53
Passing	165	258
Punt returns	1-11	0-0
Kickoff returns	2-59	5-115
Interception returns	2-46	1-0
Comp.-att.-int.	14-23-1	24-42-2
Sacked-yards lost	2-14	8-37
Punts	2-35	3-41
Fumbles-lost	4-1	4-3
Penalties-yards	8-99	3-22
Time of possession	28:37	31:23

INDIVIDUAL STATISTICS

RUSHING—New Orleans, R. Williams 16-93, Morton 6-33, Blake 6-20, T. Smith 2-9, Moore 1-2. Carolina, Biakabutuka 13-22, Beuerlein 4-31.

PASSING—New Orleans, Blake 14-23-1-179. Carolina, Beuerlein 24-42-2-295.

RECEIVING—New Orleans, Horn 5-89, Jackson 3-30, R. Williams 2-28, T. Smith 2-10, Poole 1-18, Morton 1-4. Carolina, Hayes 7-78, Muhammad 5-99, Byrd 4-47, Biakabutuka 3-40, Hetherington 2-12, Hankton 1-14, Uwaezuoke 1-7, Floyd 1-(minus 2).

MISSED FIELD GOAL ATTEMPTS—New Orleans, Brien 33.

INTERCEPTIONS—New Orleans, D. Howard 1-46, Perry 1-0. Carolina, Davis 1-0.

KICKOFF RETURNS—New Orleans, Morton 2-59. Carolina, Bates 4-97, Byrd 1-18.

PUNT RETURNS—New Orleans, Morton 1-11.

SACKS—New Orleans, Johnson 3, Hand 1, Kei. Mitchell 1, Knight 1, L. Glover 1, Whitehead 1. Carolina, Minter 1, Gilbert 1.

VIKINGS 31, CARDINALS 14

Sunday, November 12

Arizona	7	0	0	7—14
Minnesota	7	3	7	14—31

First Quarter
Min.—Smith 33 pass from Culpepper (Anderson kick), 8:18.
Ariz.—Pittman 1 run (Blanchard kick), 14:47.

Second Quarter
Min.—FG, Anderson 33, 15:00.

Third Quarter
Min.—Moss 4 pass from Culpepper (Anderson kick), 4:45.

Fourth Quarter
Min.—Culpepper 3 run (Anderson kick), 4:49.
Min.—C. Carter 12 pass from Culpepper (Anderson kick), 11:15.
Ariz.—Jenkins 98 kickoff return (Blanchard kick), 11:30.
    Attendance—64,223.

	Arizona	Minnesota
First downs	14	29
Rushes-yards	17-62	33-158
Passing	187	302
Punt returns	0-0	2-5
Kickoff returns	4-173	2-38
Interception returns	1-13	0-0
Comp.-att.-int.	19-28-0	26-34-1
Sacked-yards lost	3-32	1-4
Punts	4-43	1-39
Fumbles-lost	3-2	1-1
Penalties-yards	8-65	4-35
Time of possession	25:52	34:08

INDIVIDUAL STATISTICS
RUSHING—Arizona, Pittman 12-50, Jones 3-3, Plummer 2-9. Minnesota, Smith 20-117, Culpepper 5-26, M. Williams 5-14, Brister 2- (minus 3), Kleinsasser 1-4.

PASSING—Arizona, Plummer 19-28-0-219. Minnesota, Culpepper 25-32-1-302, Brister 1-2-0-4.

RECEIVING—Arizona, Pittman 8-63, Sanders 5-82, Boston 2-34, Jones 2-17, Gedney 1-13, Hardy 1-10. Minnesota, C. Carter 11-119, Moss 7-104, Smith 4-52, M. Williams 1-12, Hatchette 1-8, J. Davis 1-7, Jordan 1-4.

MISSED FIELD GOAL ATTEMPTS—None.

INTERCEPTIONS—Arizona, Williams 1-13.

KICKOFF RETURNS—Arizona, Jenkins 4-173. Minnesota, D. Palmer 2-38.

PUNT RETURNS—Minnesota, D. Palmer 2-5.

SACKS—Arizona, Rice 1. Minnesota, Rudd 1, T. Williams 1, Sawyer 0.5, Randle 0.5.

EAGLES 26, STEELERS 23
Sunday, November 12

Philadelphia	3	7	3	10	3—26
Pittsburgh	0	6	7	10	0—23

First Quarter
Phi.—FG, Akers 26, 12:56.

Second Quarter
Phi.—Thomason 2 pass from McNabb (Akers kick), 3:13.
Pit.—FG, K. Brown 38, 12:01.
Pit.—FG, K. Brown 52, 14:38.

Third Quarter
Phi.—FG, Akers 45, 2:07.
Pit.—Bettis 7 run (K. Brown kick), 11:41.

Fourth Quarter
Pit.—Porter 32 fumble return (K. Brown kick), 2:04.
Pit.—FG, K. Brown 40, 11:18.
Phi.—Mitchell 13 pass from McNabb (Akers kick), 12:31.
Phi.—FG, Akers 42, 15:00.

Overtime
Phi.—FG, Akers 42, 4:16.
    Attendance—56,702.

	Philadelphia	Pittsburgh
First downs	21	21
Rushes-yards	22-88	37-182
Passing	202	140
Punt returns	3-36	4-5
Kickoff returns	7-144	4-73
Interception returns	1-38	0-0
Comp.-att.-int.	26-55-0	14-31-1
Sacked-yards lost	3-11	3-19
Punts	7-41	7-42
Fumbles-lost	1-1	0-0
Penalties-yards	9-61	13-141
Time of possession	31:10	33:06

INDIVIDUAL STATISTICS
RUSHING—Philadelphia, Pritchett 7-49, Autry 7-7, McNabb 5-27, Mitchell 2-4, Small 1-1. Pittsburgh, Bettis 30-134, Huntley 4-31, Stewart 3-17.

PASSING—Philadelphia, McNabb 26-55-0-213. Pittsburgh, Stewart 14-31-1-159.

RECEIVING—Philadelphia, Pritchett 6-30, Lewis 5-41, C. Johnson 4-18, Small 3-42, Autry 3-31, C. Martin 2-35, Mitchell 2-14, Thomason 1-2. Pittsburgh, Hawkins 4-71, Edwards 2-25, Ward 2-22, Bettis 2-4, Shaw 1-25, Huntley 1-5, Burress 1-4, Cushing 1-3.

MISSED FIELD GOAL ATTEMPTS—Philadelphia, Akers 38.

INTERCEPTIONS—Philadelphia, Taylor 1-38.

KICKOFF RETURNS—Philadelphia, Mitchell 6-134, Thomason 1-10. Pittsburgh, Poteat 2-39, Edwards 2-34.

PUNT RETURNS—Philadelphia, Mitchell 3-36. Pittsburgh, Poteat 3-5, Hawkins 1-0.

SACKS—Philadelphia, Gardner 1, Mamula 1, Simon 0.5, Whiting 0.5. Pittsburgh, Gildon 1, A. Smith 1, von Oelhoffen 1.

BILLS 20, BEARS 3
Sunday, November 12

Chicago	0	3	0	0— 3
Buffalo	0	6	7	7—20

Second Quarter
Buf.—FG, Christie 27, 1:24.
Chi.—FG, Edinger 24, 10:04.
Buf.—FG, Christie 42, 13:59.

Third Quarter
Buf.—Flutie 1 run (Christie kick), 8:03.

Fourth Quarter
Buf.—Porter 23 fumble return (Christie kick), 12:20.
    Attendance—72,420.

	Chicago	Buffalo
First downs	12	14
Rushes-yards	21-99	35-105
Passing	135	194
Punt returns	2-11	5-34
Kickoff returns	5-67	2-51
Interception returns	1-0	3-31
Comp.-att.-int.	20-37-3	18-29-1
Sacked-yards lost	2-11	1-6
Punts	7-40	5-39
Fumbles-lost	1-1	2-0
Penalties-yards	3-20	3-15
Time of possession	24:44	35:16

INDIVIDUAL STATISTICS
RUSHING—Chicago, Allen 16-87, Enis 3-5, Matthews 1-5, Miller 1-2. Buffalo, A. Smith 13-29, Morris 10-30, Flutie 6-6, Bryson 5-21, Johnson 1-19.

PASSING—Chicago, Matthews 11-24-3-106, Miller 9-13-0-40. Buffalo, Flutie 16-26-1-171, Johnson 2-3-0-29.

RECEIVING—Chicago, Kennison 6-55, M. Robinson 5-37, Booker 4-17, Sinceno 2-12, Allen 1-12, Brooks 1-9, Dragos 1-4. Buffalo, Moulds 5-91, Morris 4-32, Bryson 4-11, P. Price 2-26, McDaniel 1-24, A. Smith 1-9, Riemersma 1-7.

MISSED FIELD GOAL ATTEMPTS—Buffalo, Christie 39.

INTERCEPTIONS—Chicago, W. Harris 1-0. Buffalo, Carpenter 2-31, Porter 1-0.

KICKOFF RETURNS—Chicago, Milburn 3-36, Enis 1-19, Sinceno 1-12. Buffalo, Watson 2-51.

PUNT RETURNS—Chicago, Milburn 2-11. Buffalo, Watson 5-34.

SACKS—Chicago, Flanigan 1. Buffalo, Rogers 1, Cowart 1.

COWBOYS 23, BENGALS 6
Sunday, November 12

Cincinnati	0	6	0	0— 6
Dallas	0	7	13	3—23

Second Quarter
Cin.—FG, Rackers 22, 4:05.
Dal.—McKnight 35 pass from Aikman (Seder kick), 6:20.
Cin.—FG, Rackers 37, 10:46.

Third Quarter
Dal.—FG, Seder 43, 5:14.
Dal.—Seder 1 run (Seder kick), 8:38.
Dal.—FG, Seder 35, 13:04.

Fourth Quarter
Dal.—FG, Seder 42, 6:11.
    Attendance—62,170.

	Cincinnati	Dallas
First downs	15	22
Rushes-yards	32-139	32-97
Passing	56	308
Punt returns	0-0	2-11
Kickoff returns	6-118	3-51
Interception returns	0-0	1-7
Comp.-att.-int.	10-25-1	24-37-0
Sacked-yards lost	3-12	0-0
Punts	3-36.7	0-0
Fumbles-lost	2-1	2-1
Penalties-yards	7-94	13-100
Time of possession	24:35	35:25

INDIVIDUAL STATISTICS

RUSHING—Cincinnati, Dillon 20-94, Smith 5-25, Bennett 5-24, Pope 1-0, Warrick 1-(minus 4). Dallas, E. Smith 17-16, Warren 9-59, McGarity 2-15, Thomas 2-7, Seder 1-1, Aikman 1-(minus 1).

PASSING—Cincinnati, Smith 10-25-1-68. Dallas, Aikman 24-37-0-308.

RECEIVING—Cincinnati, Warrick 4-36, McGee 2-14, Yeast 2-8, Battaglia 1-7, N. Williams 1-3. Dallas, McKnight 8-164, McGarity 4-51, Warren 4-23, Harris 3-15, Thomas 2-9, E. Smith 1-19, Tucker 1-14, LaFleur 1-13.

MISSED FIELD GOAL ATTEMPTS—Dallas, Seder 39, 44, 51.

INTERCEPTIONS—Dallas, Nguyen 1-7.

KICKOFF RETURNS—Cincinnati, Mack 5-102, Yeast 1-16. Dallas, Tucker 2-42, Larrimore 1-9.

PUNT RETURNS—Dallas, McGarity 2-11.

SACKS—Dallas, Ellis 1, Noble 1, Ekuban 1.

BROWNS 19, PATRIOTS 11

Sunday, November 12

New England	3	0	0	8—11
Cleveland	3	10	3	3—19

First Quarter
Cle.—FG, P. Dawson 39, 10:24.
N.E.—FG, Vinatieri 38, 13:54.

Second Quarter
Cle.—Shea 9 pass from Pederson (P. Dawson kick), 10:51.
Cle.—FG, P. Dawson 43, 14:30.

Third Quarter
Cle.—FG, P. Dawson 35, 14:40.

Fourth Quarter
Cle.—FG, P. Dawson 35, 2:36.
N.E.—Rutledge 2 pass from Bledsoe (Faulk run), 9:12.
Attendance—72,618.

	New England	Cleveland
First downs	18	18
Rushes-yards	22-102	35-139
Passing	184	133
Punt returns	3-51	4-47
Kickoff returns	6-115	2-38
Interception returns	0-0	1-0
Comp.-att.-int.	21-35-1	20-37-0
Sacked-yards lost	4-28	1-5
Punts	5-44	6-42
Fumbles-lost	3-3	0-0
Penalties-yards	5-40	4-25
Time of possession	25:36	34:24

INDIVIDUAL STATISTICS

RUSHING—New England, Redmond 10-60, Faulk 5-26, Bledsoe 3-6, T. Carter 3-5, Shaw 1-5. Cleveland, Prentice 19-84, White 12-37, Pederson 4-18.

PASSING—New England, Bledsoe 21-35-1-212. Cleveland, Pederson 20-37-0-138.

RECEIVING—New England, Faulk 8-96, Glenn 6-65, Rutledge 3-20, Simmons 2-21, Brown 2-10. Cleveland, Northcutt 4-32, Edwards 4-27, Prentice 4-19, Johnson 3-23, White 3-22, Shea 1-9, Dunn 1-6.

MISSED FIELD GOAL ATTEMPTS—None.

INTERCEPTIONS—Cleveland, Holland 1-0.

KICKOFF RETURNS—New England, Faulk 5-109, Brown 1-6. Cleveland, White 2-38.

PUNT RETURNS—New England, Brown 3-51. Cleveland, Northcutt 4-47.

SACKS—New England, Slade 0.5, Spires 0.5. Cleveland, K. McKenzie 1.5, Colinet 1.5, J. Miller 0.5, L. Jones 0.5.

BUCCANEERS 20, PACKERS 15

Sunday, November 12

Green Bay	0	3	6	6—15
Tampa Bay	0	14	0	6—20

Second Quarter
T.B.—K. Johnson 5 pass from King (Gramatica kick), 2:29.
G.B.—FG, Longwell 52, 3:42.
T.B.—Anthony 19 pass from King (Gramatica kick), 13:07.

Third Quarter
G.B.—FG, Longwell 42, 6:22.
G.B.—FG, Longwell 45, 9:31.

Fourth Quarter
G.B.—Franks 27 pass from Hasselbeck (pass failed), 0:59.
T.B.—FG, Gramatica 54, 4:48.
T.B.—FG, Gramatica 51, 8:10.
Attendance—65,621.

	Green Bay	Tampa Bay
First downs	16	14
Rushes-yards	19-97	30-108
Passing	205	164
Punt returns	2-41	2-16
Kickoff returns	2-41	5-106
Interception returns	1-4	0-0
Comp.-att.-int.	23-43-0	16-27-1
Sacked-yards lost	1-5	0-0
Punts	5-39	6-39
Fumbles-lost	1-1	0-0
Penalties-yards	4-35	6-37
Time of possession	27:57	32:03

INDIVIDUAL STATISTICS

RUSHING—Green Bay, Green 16-65, Parker 2-16, Rossum 1-16. Tampa Bay, Dunn 14-55, Alstott 9-38, King 6-13, K. Johnson 1-2.

PASSING—Green Bay, Favre 14-25-0-117, Hasselbeck 9-18-0-93. Tampa Bay, King 16-27-1-164.

RECEIVING—Green Bay, Green 7-35, Schroeder 4-54, Freeman 4-36, Franks 3-45, Driver 2-13, Lee 1-16, Parker 1-6, Wetnight 1-5. Tampa Bay, K. Johnson 5-51, Moore 3-57, Green 3-16, Dunn 2-13, Alstott 2-8, Anthony 1-19.

MISSED FIELD GOAL ATTEMPTS—Green Bay, Longwell 53.

INTERCEPTIONS—Green Bay, Edwards 1-4.

KICKOFF RETURNS—Green Bay, Rossum 2-41. Tampa Bay, Williams 4-87, Anthony 1-19.

PUNT RETURNS—Green Bay, Rossum 2-41. Tampa Bay, Williams 2-16.

SACKS—Tampa Bay, Sapp 1.

SEAHAWKS 28, JAGUARS 21

Sunday, November 12

Seattle	0	14	7	7—28
Jacksonville	7	14	0	0—21

First Quarter
Jac.—Brunell 2 run (Hollis kick), 12:47.

Second Quarter
Sea.—Watters 1 run (Lindell kick), 3:36.
Jac.—Taylor 10 run (Hollis kick), 12:00.
Jac.—McCardell 67 pass from Brunell (Hollis kick), 13:44.
Sea.—Dawkins 15 pass from Kitna (Lindell kick), 14:47.

Third Quarter
Sea.—Mayes 8 pass from Kitna (Lindell kick), 10:43.

Fourth Quarter
Sea.—Watters 4 pass from Kitna (Lindell kick), 12:59.
Attendance—68,063.

	Seattle	Jacksonville
First downs	22	24
Rushes-yards	32-96	26-122
Passing	230	315
Punt returns	1-43	2-14
Kickoff returns	4-66	5-93
Interception returns	0-0	0-0
Comp.-att.-int.	22-33-0	24-33-0
Sacked-yards lost	1-1	5-25
Punts	6-45	4-43
Fumbles-lost	3-0	2-1
Penalties-yards	5-40	7-55
Time of possession	29:12	30:48

INDIVIDUAL STATISTICS

RUSHING—Seattle, Watters 24-80, Kitna 5-3, Alexander 3-13. Jacksonville, Taylor 21-103, Brunell 4-15, Johnson 1-4.

PASSING—Seattle, Kitna 22-33-0-231. Jacksonville, Brunell 24-33-0-340.

RECEIVING—Seattle, Dawkins 6-92, Watters 5-46, Mayes 4-39, Fauria 3-25, Strong 2-9, Jackson 1-12, Mili 1-8. Jacksonville, J. Smith 10-117, McCardell 6-156, Taylor 5-34, Brady 2-30, Johnson 1-3.

MISSED FIELD GOAL ATTEMPTS—None.

INTERCEPTIONS—None.

KICKOFF RETURNS—Seattle, Rogers 2-36, Bownes 1-15, Joseph 1-15. Jacksonville, Soward 4-93, Leroy 1-0.

PUNT RETURNS—Seattle, Rogers 1-43. Jacksonville, Barlow 2-14.

SACKS—Seattle, C. Brown 2, King 1, Sinclair 1, Cochran 0.5, LaBounty 0.5. Jacksonville, Brackens 1.

RAMS 38, GIANTS 24

Sunday, November 12

St. Louis	14	14	10	0—38
N.Y. Giants	0	7	10	7—24

First Quarter
St.L.—R. Williams 1 pass from Green (Wilkins kick), 4:27.
St.L.—Holt 5 pass from Green (Hall kick), 13:05.

Second Quarter
NYG—Barber 13 pass from Collins (Daluiso kick), 2:18.
St.L.—Proehl 8 pass from Green (Hall kick), 9:17.
St.L.—Green 18 run (Hall kick), 12:19.

Third Quarter
NYG—Hilliard 46 pass from Collins (Daluiso kick), 1:02.
NYG—FG, Daluiso 20, 3:26.
St.L.—FG, Hall 50, 7:40.
St.L.—Bruce 34 pass from Green (Hall kick), 12:36.

Fourth Quarter
NYG—Hilliard 34 pass from Collins (Daluiso kick), 6:34.
Attendance—78,174.

	St. Louis	N.Y. Giants
First downs	28	14
Rushes-yards	28-141	19-135
Passing	256	213
Punt returns	3-92	2-16
Kickoff returns	4-106	7-173
Interception returns	2-14	1-10
Comp.-att.-int.	27-45-1	17-34-2
Sacked-yards lost	2-16	3-27
Punts	6-40	6-51
Fumbles-lost	0-0	4-1
Penalties-yards	2-10	7-49
Time of possession	36:40	23:20

INDIVIDUAL STATISTICS

RUSHING—St. Louis, Watson 17-62, Green 6-54, Canidate 2-5, Horne 1-9, Holt 1-7, Lyle 1-4. New York, Dayne 9-66, Barber 9-61, Hilliard 1-8.

PASSING—St. Louis, Green 27-45-1-272. New York, Collins 17-34-2-240.

RECEIVING—St. Louis, Holt 8-86, Proehl 6-53, Bruce 4-75, Watson 3-5, Hakim 2-39, Horne 1-6, Canidate 1-4, Hodgins 1-3, R. Williams 1-1. New York, Hilliard 5-110, Barber 4-32, Mitchell 3-33, Jurevicius 2-31, Comella 2-14, Toomer 1-20.

MISSED FIELD GOAL ATTEMPTS—St. Louis, Hall 47.

INTERCEPTIONS—St. Louis, Fletcher 1-12, McCleon 1-2. New York, Phillips 1-10.

KICKOFF RETURNS—St. Louis, Horne 4-106. New York, Levingston 4-92, Stoutmire 2-41, Stephens 1-40.

PUNT RETURNS—St. Louis, Hakim 3-92. New York, Barber 1-16, Comella 1-0.

SACKS—St. Louis, McCleon 1, Little 1, Wistrom 0.5, Agnew 0.5. New York, Strahan 1.5, K. Hamilton 0.5.

COLTS 23, JETS 15

Sunday, November 12

N.Y. Jets	0	0	7	8—15
Indianapolis	7	10	3	3—23

First Quarter
Ind.—Harrison 6 pass from Manning (Vanderjagt kick), 6:35.

Ind.—James 2 run (Vanderjagt kick), 0:43.
Ind.—FG, Vanderjagt 26, 14:55.

Third Quarter
Ind.—FG, Vanderjagt 38, 11:00.
NYJ—Ward 16 pass from Testaverde (Hall kick), 14:55.

Fourth Quarter
Ind.—FG, Vanderjagt 35, 4:03.
NYJ—Martin 9 run (Coleman pass from Testaverde), 9:49.
Attendance—56,657.

	N.Y. Jets	Indianapolis
First downs	22	25
Rushes-yards	22-96	38-148
Passing	271	210
Punt returns	2-15	1-6
Kickoff returns	6-128	2-43
Interception returns	0-0	2-12
Comp.-att.-int.	20-38-2	21-35-0
Sacked-yards lost	0-0	0-0
Punts	2-50	3-43
Fumbles-lost	0-0	1-1
Penalties-yards	6-65	4-64
Time of possession	26:01	33:59

INDIVIDUAL STATISTICS

RUSHING—New York, Martin 21-93, R. Anderson 1-3. Indianapolis, James 31-131, Manning 4-2, Smith 1-11, Pathon 1-1, Finn 1-1.

PASSING—New York, Testaverde 20-38-2-271. Indianapolis, Manning 21-35-0-210.

RECEIVING—New York, Chrebet 8-140, R. Anderson 4-19, Ward 3-54, Martin 3-26, Coles 2-32. Indianapolis, James 5-24, Harrison 4-34, Pollard 3-65, Pathon 3-42, Green 3-24, Dilger 2-11, Wilkins 1-10.

MISSED FIELD GOAL ATTEMPTS—New York, Hall 47, 51.

INTERCEPTIONS—Indianapolis, Burris 1-11, Washington 1-1.

KICKOFF RETURNS—New York, Coles 5-103, Stone 1-25. Indianapolis, Wilkins 1-22, Pathon 1-21.

PUNT RETURNS—New York, Ward 2-15. Indianapolis, Wilkins 1-6.

SACKS—None.

49ERS 21, CHIEFS 7

Sunday, November 12

Kansas City	0	0	0	7— 7
San Francisco	0	21	0	0—21

Second Quarter
S.F.—Garner 1 run (Richey kick), 0:44.
S.F.—Garcia 2 run (Richey kick), 8:16.
S.F.—Garcia 1 run (Richey kick), 14:37.

Fourth Quarter
K.C.—Bennett 1 run (Peterson kick), 8:33.
Attendance—68,002.

	Kansas City	San Francisco
First downs	20	25
Rushes-yards	15-50	37-149
Passing	240	240
Punt returns	2-13	2-15
Kickoff returns	4-92	2-36
Interception returns	0-0	1-23
Comp.-att.-int.	22-40-1	20-25-0
Sacked-yards lost	3-31	1-4
Punts	4-43	5-33
Fumbles-lost	1-0	0-0
Penalties-yards	7-50	6-53
Time of possession	23:50	36:10

INDIVIDUAL STATISTICS

RUSHING—Kansas City, Bennett 6-16, Richardson 4-19, Anders 3-21, Grbac 1-1, L. Parker 1-(minus 7). San Francisco, Garner 25-102, Garcia 8-37, Smith 2-7, Jackson 1-3, Streets 1-0.

PASSING—Kansas City, Grbac 22-40-1-271. San Francisco, Garcia 20-25-0-244.

RECEIVING—Kansas City, Richardson 8-81, Gonzalez 4-46, Morris 3-49, Anders 3-26, Alexander 2-48, Drayton 1-11, Lockett 1-10. San Francisco, Garner 5-39, Clark 4-41, Rice 4-31, Stokes 3-66, Smith 2-55, Streets 1-6, Owens 1-6.

MISSED FIELD GOAL ATTEMPTS—Kansas City, Peterson 34. San Francisco, Richey 43.

INTERCEPTIONS—San Francisco, Bronson 1-23.

KICKOFF RETURNS—Kansas City, Cloud 3-68, L. Parker 1-24. San Francisco, K. Williams 2-36.

PUNT RETURNS—Kansas City, Lockett 2-13. San Francisco, K. Williams 2-15.

SACKS—Kansas City, Browning 1. San Francisco, B. Young 2, Buckner 1.

DOLPHINS 17, CHARGERS 7

Sunday, November 12

Miami	7	7	3	0—17
San Diego	0	0	0	7— 7

First Quarter
Mia.—L. Smith 2 run (Mare kick), 1:41.

Second Quarter
Mia.—L. Smith 6 run (Mare kick), 0:44.

Third Quarter
Mia.—FG, Mare 35, 8:31.

Fourth Quarter
S.D.—McCrary 8 pass from Leaf (Carney kick), 0:05.
Attendance—56,896.

	Miami	San Diego
First downs	15	18
Rushes-yards	41-84	16-82
Passing	160	156
Punt returns	2-20	2-8
Kickoff returns	2-50	4-106
Interception returns	4-60	0-0
Comp.-att.-int.	13-20-0	20-47-4
Sacked-yards lost	0-0	3-22
Punts	7-41	6-48
Fumbles-lost	0-0	3-0
Penalties-yards	8-60	8-88
Time of possession	32:46	27:14

INDIVIDUAL STATISTICS

RUSHING—Miami, L. Smith 27-69, Denson 5-5, T. Thomas 3-17, Fiedler 3-8, Shepherd 2-(minus 12), McDuffie 1-(minus 3). San Diego, Fletcher 10-52, Fazande 3-8, Leaf 2-20, R. Jenkins 1-2.

PASSING—Miami, Fiedler 13-20-0-160. San Diego, Leaf 9-21-1-92, Moreno 9-21-2-67, Harbaugh 2-5-1-19.

RECEIVING—Miami, McDuffie 3-36, L. Smith 3-12, Shepherd 2-19, Martin 2-15, Gadsden 1-61, T. Thomas 1-12, Konrad 1-5. San Diego, Fletcher 4-40, F. Jones 4-39, Gaylor 3-53, Conway 2-18, J. Graham 2-10, McCrary 2-8, Fazande 2-6, R. Jones 1-4.

MISSED FIELD GOAL ATTEMPTS—San Diego, Carney 43.

INTERCEPTIONS—Miami, Walker 2-38, Madison 1-22, Surtain 1-0.

KICKOFF RETURNS—Miami, Denson 2-50. San Diego, R. Jenkins 4-106.

PUNT RETURNS—Miami, Ogden 1-20, Shepherd 1-0. San Diego, R. Jones 1-8, J. Graham 1-0.

SACKS—Miami, Wilson 1, Taylor 1, Armstrong 1.

BRONCOS 27, RAIDERS 24

Monday, November 13

Oakland	3	7	0	14—24
Denver	7	0	10	10—27

First Quarter
Den.—Davis 5 run (Elam kick), 3:28.
Oak.—FG, Conway 19, 12:54.

Second Quarter
Oak.—Crockett 1 run (Conway kick), 12:05.

Third Quarter
Den.—FG, Elam 23, 7:35.
Den.—Gold 12 blocked punt return (Elam kick), 9:40.

Fourth Quarter
Den.—Chamberlain 11 pass from Griese (Elam kick), 1:57.
Oak.—Crockett 1 run (Conway kick), 8:30.
Oak.—Brown 22 pass from Gannon (Conway kick), 13:54.
Den.—FG, Elam 41, 15:00.
Attendance—75,951.

	Oakland	Denver
First downs	25	18
Rushes-yards	18-38	23-71
Passing	373	258
Punt returns	3-24	2-20
Kickoff returns	5-122	5-94
Interception returns	1-1	2-(-3)
Comp.-att.-int.	30-53-2	26-39-1
Sacked-yards lost	4-9	1-8
Punts	4-37	6-44
Fumbles-lost	2-1	2-1
Penalties-yards	9-54	5-45
Time of possession	30:08	29:52

INDIVIDUAL STATISTICS

RUSHING—Oakland, Kaufman 7-8, Crockett 5-16, Gannon 3-16, Jordan 1-3, Brown 1-2, Dudley 1-(minus 7). Denver, Davis 21-68, Griese 2-3.

PASSING—Oakland, Gannon 30-53-2-382. Denver, Griese 25-37-1-262, Frerotte 1-2-0-4.

RECEIVING—Oakland, Brown 10-122, Rison 6-117, Jordan 5-47, Kaufman 3-27, Ritchie 3-11, Dudley 2-44, Dunn 1-14. Denver, McCaffrey 7-58, R. Smith 6-76, Chamberlain 5-58, Carswell 5-50, Clark 2-17, Griffith 1-7.

MISSED FIELD GOAL ATTEMPTS—None.

INTERCEPTIONS—Oakland, W. Thomas 1-1. Denver, Crockett 1-0, Romanowski 1-(minus 3).

KICKOFF RETURNS—Oakland, Dunn 5-122. Denver, O'Neal 4-82, Chamberlain 1-12.

PUNT RETURNS—Oakland, Gordon 3-24. Denver, O'Neal 2-20.

SACKS—Oakland, Allen 1. Denver, Spencer 1, Pryce 1, Tanuvasa 1, Gold 1.

STANDINGS

AFC EAST

	W	L	T	Pct.
Miami	8	3	0	.727
Buffalo	7	4	0	.636
Indianapolis	7	4	0	.636
N.Y. Jets	7	4	0	.636
New England	3	8	0	.273

AFC CENTRAL

	W	L	T	Pct.
Tennessee	9	2	0	.818
Baltimore	8	4	0	.667
Pittsburgh	5	6	0	.455
Jacksonville	4	7	0	.364
Cleveland	3	9	0	.250
Cincinnati	2	9	0	.182

AFC WEST

	W	L	T	Pct.
Oakland	9	2	0	.818
Denver	7	4	0	.636
Kansas City	5	6	0	.455
Seattle	4	7	0	.364
San Diego	0	11	0	.000

NFC EAST

	W	L	T	Pct.
Philadelphia	8	4	0	.667
N.Y. Giants	7	4	0	.636
Washington	7	4	0	.636
Dallas	4	7	0	.364
Arizona	3	8	0	.273

NFC CENTRAL

	W	L	T	Pct.
Minnesota	9	2	0	.818
Detroit	7	4	0	.636
Tampa Bay	6	5	0	.545
Green Bay	5	6	0	.455
Chicago	3	8	0	.273

NFC WEST

	W	L	T	Pct.
St. Louis	8	3	0	.727
New Orleans	7	4	0	.636
Carolina	4	7	0	.364
San Francisco	4	8	0	.333
Atlanta	3	9	0	.250

TOP PERFORMANCES

100-YARD RUSHING GAMES

Player, Team & Opponent	Att.	Yds.	TD
Fred Taylor, Jack. at Pit.	30	234	3
Jamal Lewis, Balt. vs. Dal.	28	187	0
Ahman Green, G.B. vs. Ind.	24	153	0
Eddie George, Ten. vs. Cle.	36	134	3
Robert Smith, Min. vs. Car.	23	103	1

300-YARD PASSING GAMES

Player, Team & Opponent	Att.	Comp.	Yds.	TD	Int.
Gus Frerotte, Den. vs. S.D.	58	36	462	5	4
Trent Green, St.L. vs. Wash.	38	23	366	2	1
Daunte Culpepper, Min. vs. Car.	29	22	357	3	0
Kerry Collins, NYG vs. Det.	51	29	350	2	1
Elvis Grbac, K.C. vs. Buf.	48	28	341	2	1
Ryan Leaf, S.D. at Den.	27	13	311	3	1
Brett Favre, G.B. vs. Ind.	36	23	301	2	1

100-YARD RECEIVING GAMES

Player, Team & Opponent	Rec.	Yds.	TD
Rod Smith, Den. vs. S.D.	11	187	1
Bill Schroeder, G.B. vs. Ind.	8	155	0
Ed McCaffrey, Den. vs. S.D.	10	148	2
Derrick Alexander, K.C. vs. Buf.	7	146	0
Jeff Graham, S.D. at Den.	4	144	2
Cris Carter, Min. vs. Car.	8	138	1
Terry Glenn, N.E. vs. Cin.	11	129	0
Torry Holt, St.L. vs. Wash.	4	125	0
Curtis Conway, S.D. at Den.	4	118	1
Troy Brown, N.E. vs. Cin.	8	110	0
Amani Toomer, NYG vs. Det.	8	108	0
Randy Moss, Min. vs. Car.	5	106	1
Shannon Sharpe, Balt. vs. Dal.	5	101	1

RESULTS

SUNDAY, NOVEMBER 19

BALTIMORE 27, Dallas 0
Buffalo 21, KANSAS CITY 17
CHICAGO 13, Tampa Bay 10
DENVER 38, San Diego 37
Detroit 31, N.Y. GIANTS 21
GREEN BAY 26, Indianapolis 24
Jacksonville 34, PITTSBURGH 24
MINNESOTA 31, Carolina 17
NEW ENGLAND 16, Cincinnati 13
N.Y. Jets 20, MIAMI 3
Oakland 31, NEW ORLEANS 22
PHILADELPHIA 34, Arizona 9
SAN FRANCISCO 16, Atlanta 6
TENNESSEE 24, Cleveland 10

MONDAY, NOVEMBER 20

Washington 33, ST. LOUIS 20
Open date: Seattle

BEARS 13, BUCCANEERS 10

Sunday, November 19

Tampa Bay	0	3	7	0—10
Chicago	3	7	0	3—13

First Quarter
Chi.—FG, Edinger 34, 9:02.

Second Quarter
T.B.—FG, Gramatica 33, 0:05.
Chi.—Parrish 38 interception return (Edinger kick), 14:12.

Third Quarter
T.B.—King 9 run (Gramatica kick), 5:37.

Fourth Quarter
Chi.—FG, Edinger 48, 4:58.
Attendance—66,944.

	Tampa Bay	Chicago
First downs	14	15
Rushes-yards	33-165	28-83
Passing	60	160
Punt returns	1-6	0-0
Kickoff returns	4-93	3-80
Interception returns	1-0	2-57
Comp.-att.-int.	12-19-2	20-34-1
Sacked-yards lost	4-31	1-5
Punts	5-33	5-33
Fumbles-lost	1-1	0-0
Penalties-yards	1-8	4-25
Time of possession	29:52	30:08

INDIVIDUAL STATISTICS
RUSHING—Tampa Bay, Dunn 17-75, King 11-72, Abdullah 2-18, Alstott 2-3, Green 1-(minus 3). Chicago, Allen 20-67, Matthews 4-5, Barnes 3-11, Enis 1-0.
PASSING—Tampa Bay, King 12-19-2-91. Chicago, Matthews 20-34-1-165.
RECEIVING—Tampa Bay, Green 3-30, Moore 2-25, K. Johnson 2-13, Dunn 2-1, Anthony 1-11, Hape 1-6, Alstott 1-5. Chicago, M. Robinson 5-53, Kennison 4-54, Allen 4-15, Brooks 3-16, Enis 2-11, Sinceno 1-9, Booker 1-7.
MISSED FIELD GOAL ATTEMPTS—Chicago, Edinger 38.
INTERCEPTIONS—Tampa Bay, Robinson 1-0. Chicago, Parrish 1-38, Urlacher 1-19.
KICKOFF RETURNS—Tampa Bay, Stecker 4-93. Chicago, Milburn 3-80.
PUNT RETURNS—Tampa Bay, Williams 1-6.
SACKS—Tampa Bay, Jones 1. Chicago, Parrish 1, B. Robinson 1, Daniels 1, F. Smith 1.

TITANS 24, BROWNS 10

Sunday, November 19

Cleveland	0	0	10	0—10
Tennessee	0	0	14	10—24

Third Quarter
Cle.—Ellsworth 33 interception return (P. Dawson kick), 1:36.
Ten.—E. George 4 run (Del Greco kick), 4:09.
Cle.—FG, P. Dawson 38, 9:43.
Ten.—E. George 1 run (Del Greco kick), 14:47.

Fourth Quarter
Ten.—FG, Del Greco 22, 4:11.
Ten.—E. George 1 run (Del Greco kick), 12:35.
Attendance—68,498.

	Cleveland	Tennessee
First downs	5	23
Rushes-yards	18-45	47-182
Passing	80	210
Punt returns	0-0	6-117
Kickoff returns	5-106	3-47
Interception returns	3-33	1-17
Comp.-att.-int.	13-20-1	17-25-3
Sacked-yards lost	4-23	3-12
Punts	8-46	1-52
Fumbles-lost	0-0	4-4
Penalties-yards	7-61	5-45
Time of possession	21:41	38:19

INDIVIDUAL STATISTICS
RUSHING—Cleveland, White 8-27, Prentice 7-14, Pederson 2-1, Wynn 1-3. Tennessee, E. George 36-134, McNair 8-51, Thomas 2-(minus 1), Neal 1-(minus 2).
PASSING—Cleveland, Pederson 13-20-1-103. Tennessee, McNair 17-25-3-222.
RECEIVING—Cleveland, White 3-30, Northcutt 3-30, Campbell 2-11, Johnson 2-9, Shea 1-9, Edwards 1-8, Prentice 1-6. Tennessee, Mason 6-89, Wycheck 4-73, Sanders 3-29, E. George 2-15, Kinney 1-10, Neal 1-6.
MISSED FIELD GOAL ATTEMPTS—None.
INTERCEPTIONS—Cleveland, Ellsworth 1-33, J. Miller 1-0, Chapman 1-0. Tennessee, Rolle 1-17.
KICKOFF RETURNS—Cleveland, White 4-84, Patten 1-22. Tennessee, Leach 2-32, Mason 1-15.
PUNT RETURNS—Tennessee, Mason 6-117.
SACKS—Cleveland, K. McKenzie 1, Rogers 1, McCutcheon 1. Tennessee, Robinson 1, Kearse 1, Holmes 1, Killens 1.

RAVENS 27, COWBOYS 0

Sunday, November 19

Dallas	0	0	0	0—0
Baltimore	10	7	0	10—27

First Quarter
Bal.—Ismail 40 pass from Dilfer (Stover kick), 3:35.
Bal.—FG, Stover 25, 9:58.

Second Quarter
Bal.—Sharpe 59 pass from Dilfer (Stover kick), 12:53.

Fourth Quarter
Bal.—FG, Stover 19, 7:18.
Bal.—Holmes 5 run (Stover kick), 11:08.
Attendance—69,416.

	Dallas	Baltimore
First downs	9	22
Rushes-yards	14-55	44-250
Passing	137	229
Punt returns	0-0	3-24
Kickoff returns	6-105	1-15
Interception returns	2-16	3-42
Comp.-att.-int.	19-33-3	18-24-2
Sacked-yards lost	1-1	2-13
Punts	7-37	3-38
Fumbles-lost	1-0	0-0
Penalties-yards	3-15	6-55
Time of possession	21:38	38:22

INDIVIDUAL STATISTICS
RUSHING—Dallas, E. Smith 11-48, Aikman 2-0, Warren 1-7. Baltimore, Ja. Lewis 28-187, Holmes 13-64, Banks 2-(minus 3), Dilfer 1-2.
PASSING—Dallas, Aikman 19-33-3-138. Baltimore, Dilfer 18-24-2-242.
RECEIVING—Dallas, McGarity 6-40, McKnight 4-50, Warren 4-19, Thomas 3-12, Tucker 1-11, Harris 1-6. Baltimore, Sharpe 5-101, Holmes 4-34, Ja. Lewis 4-20, Ismail 3-51, Stokley 1-32, Coates 1-4.
MISSED FIELD GOAL ATTEMPTS—Dallas, Seder 46. Baltimore, Stover 47.
INTERCEPTIONS—Dallas, Sparks 2-16. Baltimore, Harris 1-42, R. Lewis 1-0, Woodson 1-0.
KICKOFF RETURNS—Dallas, Tucker 6-105. Baltimore, Harris 1-15.
PUNT RETURNS—Baltimore, J. Lewis 3-24.
SACKS—Dallas, Spellman 1, Underwood 1. Baltimore, McCrary 1.

RAIDERS 31, SAINTS 22

Sunday, November 19

Oakland	3	14	0	14—31
New Orleans	0	7	6	9—22

First Quarter
Oak.—FG, Janikowski 49, 10:26.

Second Quarter
Oak.—Rison 34 pass from Gannon (Janikowski kick), 3:22.
Oak.—Crockett 6 run (Janikowski kick), 8:45.
N.O.—Jackson 53 pass from Brooks (Brien kick), 11:07.

Third Quarter
N.O.—FG, Brien 42, 6:06.
N.O.—FG, Brien 40, 11:51.

Fourth Quarter

Oak.—Brown 21 pass from Gannon (Janikowski kick), 2:55.
N.O.—FG, Brien 33, 7:19.
Oak.—Crockett 6 run (Janikowski kick), 13:05.
N.O.—Jackson 9 pass from Brooks (pass failed), 13:51.
Attendance—64,900.

	Oakland	New Orleans
First downs	19	19
Rushes-yards	36-159	30-133
Passing	134	200
Punt returns	4-36	4-51
Kickoff returns	5-122	5-159
Interception returns	1-0	0-0
Comp.-att.-int.	14-21-0	16-27-1
Sacked-yards lost	5-34	3-26
Punts	4-55	4-41
Fumbles-lost	1-1	1-0
Penalties-yards	5-32	12-93
Time of possession	32:23	27:37

INDIVIDUAL STATISTICS

RUSHING—Oakland, Crockett 17-44, Kaufman 9-49, Gannon 7-55, Jordan 3-11. New Orleans, Moore 13-42, Brooks 7-5, Morton 5-45, T. Smith 4-42, Horn 1-(minus 1).

PASSING—Oakland, Gannon 14-21-0-168. New Orleans, Brooks 14-22-1-187, Blake 2-5-0-39.

RECEIVING—Oakland, Brown 4-69, Dudley 2-17, Jordan 2-11, Crockett 2-4, Rison 1-34, Kaufman 1-25, Jett 1-6, Ritchie 1-2. New Orleans, Morton 6-62, Jackson 4-85, Horn 3-33, Poole 2-33, A. Glover 1-13.

MISSED FIELD GOAL ATTEMPTS—None.

INTERCEPTIONS—Oakland, Woodson 1-0.

KICKOFF RETURNS—Oakland, Dunn 5-122. New Orleans, Morton 4-145, McAfee 1-14.

PUNT RETURNS—Oakland, Gordon 4-36. New Orleans, Morton 4-40.

SACKS—Oakland, Jackson 2, Johnstone 1. New Orleans, Johnson 2, Kei. Mitchell 1, D. Howard 1, Weary 1.

PATRIOTS 16, BENGALS 13

Sunday, November 19

Cincinnati	0	10	3	0—13
New England	7	3	0	6—16

First Quarter

N.E.—T. Carter 1 run (Vinatieri kick), 13:03.

Second Quarter

Cin.—Warrick 13 pass from S. Mitchell (Rackers kick), 9:00.
N.E.—FG, Vinatieri 38, 13:01.
Cin.—FG, Rackers 28, 15:00.

Third Quarter

Cin.—FG, Rackers 45, 8:18.

Fourth Quarter

N.E.—FG, Vinatieri 21, 0:03.
N.E.—FG, Vinatieri 22, 14:57.
Attendance—60,292.

	Cincinnati	New England
First downs	25	17
Rushes-yards	37-137	22-39
Passing	228	252
Punt returns	2-10	2-11
Kickoff returns	5-83	3-61
Interception returns	1-0	1-2
Comp.-att.-int.	20-38-1	22-36-1
Sacked-yards lost	1-8	1-6
Punts	5-43	6-44
Fumbles-lost	2-1	2-0
Penalties-yards	8-75	9-69
Time of possession	32:28	27:32

INDIVIDUAL STATISTICS

RUSHING—Cincinnati, Dillon 28-79, Bennett 7-32, Yeast 1-15, S. Mitchell 1-11. New England, Pass 12-39, Bledsoe 5-(minus 4), T. Carter 4-0, Faulk 1-4.

PASSING—Cincinnati, S. Mitchell 20-38-1-236. New England, Bledsoe 22-36-1-258.

RECEIVING—Cincinnati, Warrick 7-79, Yeast 4-57, Farmer 3-36, McGee 2-26, Dillon 2-18, N. Williams 1-17, Battaglia 1-3. New England, Glenn 11-129, Brown 8-110, Pass 2-16, Rutledge 1-3.

MISSED FIELD GOAL ATTEMPTS—Cincinnati, Rackers 30.

INTERCEPTIONS—Cincinnati, Bean 1-0. New England, Milloy 1-2.

KICKOFF RETURNS—Cincinnati, Mack 3-57, Keaton 1-16, Yeast 1-10. New England, Faulk 3-61.

PUNT RETURNS—Cincinnati, Yeast 2-10. New England, Brown 2-11.

SACKS—Cincinnati, Gibson 0.5, Spearman 0.5. New England, Spires 1.

VIKINGS 31, PANTHERS 17

Sunday, November 19

Carolina	7	7	0	3—17
Minnesota	14	10	7	0—31

First Quarter

Car.—Beuerlein 1 run (Nedney kick), 6:51.
Min.—Moss 36 pass from Culpepper (Anderson kick), 9:19.
Min.—Smith 53 pass from Culpepper (Anderson kick), 14:31.

Second Quarter

Min.—Smith 3 run (Anderson kick), 4:25.
Car.—Hetherington 1 run (Nedney kick), 14:40.
Min.—FG, Anderson 43, 15:00.

Third Quarter

Min.—C. Carter 15 pass from Culpepper (Anderson kick), 12:58.

Fourth Quarter

Car.—FG, Nedney 28, 10:33.
Attendance—64,208.

	Carolina	Minnesota
First downs	23	19
Rushes-yards	26-78	26-117
Passing	252	329
Punt returns	1-27	0-0
Kickoff returns	4-67	2-25
Interception returns	0-0	2-37
Comp.-att.-int.	26-44-2	22-29-0
Sacked-yards lost	5-20	1-28
Punts	4-36	4-44
Fumbles-lost	1-1	4-2
Penalties-yards	5-30	8-53
Time of possession	33:09	26:51

INDIVIDUAL STATISTICS

RUSHING—Carolina, Hoover 18-59, Hetherington 3-6, Bates 2-12, Beuerlein 2-2, Craig 1-(minus 1). Minnesota, Smith 23-103, M. Williams 2-14, Culpepper 1-0.

PASSING—Carolina, Beuerlein 26-44-2-272. Minnesota, Culpepper 22-29-0-357.

RECEIVING—Carolina, Muhammad 6-76, Hetherington 6-59, Mangum 4-47, Byrd 3-32, Hayes 3-24, Uwaezuoke 2-18, Hoover 2-16. Minnesota, C. Carter 8-138, Moss 5-106, Smith 3-70, J. Davis 3-28, Hatchette 1-7, Walsh 1-6, Morrow 1-2.

MISSED FIELD GOAL ATTEMPTS—None.

INTERCEPTIONS—Minnesota, Wong 1-14, Tate 1-0.

KICKOFF RETURNS—Carolina, Bates 3-55, Byrd 1-12. Minnesota, Walters 1-19, Walsh 1-6.

PUNT RETURNS—Carolina, Uwaezuoke 1-27.

SACKS—Carolina, Rucker 1. Minnesota, Randle 2, Sawyer 2, T. Williams 1.

BILLS 21, CHIEFS 17

Sunday, November 19

Buffalo	7	0	0	14—21
Kansas City	0	3	7	7—17

First Quarter

Buf.—Moulds 9 pass from Johnson (Christie kick), 5:01.

Second Quarter

K.C.—FG, Peterson 19, 9:48.

Third Quarter

K.C.—Gonzalez 13 pass from Grbac (Peterson kick), 5:53.

Fourth Quarter

Buf.—Riemersma 18 pass from Johnson (Christie kick), 1:25.
K.C.—Gonzalez 9 pass from Grbac (Peterson kick), 7:05.
Buf.—Johnson 12 run (Christie kick), 12:02.
Attendance—78,457.

	Buffalo	Kansas City
First downs	21	24
Rushes-yards	27-74	19-103
Passing	225	275

	Buffalo	Kansas City
Punt returns	2-15	6-42
Kickoff returns	3-56	4-82
Interception returns	1-2	0-0
Comp.-att.-int.	22-37-0	28-48-1
Sacked-yards lost	3-15	5-66
Punts	7-40	4-47
Fumbles-lost	0-0	2-1
Penalties-yards	6-45	7-57
Time of possession	31:20	28:40

INDIVIDUAL STATISTICS

RUSHING—Buffalo, A. Smith 12-21, Bryson 10-12, Johnson 5-41. Kansas City, Richardson 8-44, Bennett 5-9, Anders 4-41, Alexander 1-8, Grbac 1-1.

PASSING—Buffalo, Johnson 21-36-0-196, Mohr 1-1-0-44. Kansas City, Grbac 28-48-1-341.

RECEIVING—Buffalo, Moulds 8-67, P. Price 4-45, Riemersma 4-41, McDaniel 3-39, Bryson 2-4, Porter 1-44. Kansas City, Gonzalez 9-76, Alexander 7-146, Richardson 4-30, L. Parker 2-33, Lockett 2-21, Anders 2-10, Morris 1-19, Dunn 1-6.

MISSED FIELD GOAL ATTEMPTS—Kansas City, Peterson 35.

INTERCEPTIONS—Buffalo, Carpenter 1-2.

KICKOFF RETURNS—Buffalo, Watson 2-43, Bryson 1-13. Kansas City, Cloud 3-65, L. Parker 1-17.

PUNT RETURNS—Buffalo, Watson 2-15. Kansas City, Lockett 6-42.

SACKS—Buffalo, Wiley 2, Rogers 2, Newman 1. Kansas City, Clemons 1, D. Williams 1, T. Williams 1.

EAGLES 34, CARDINALS 9

Sunday, November 19

Arizona	3	0	0	6— 9
Philadelphia	0	10	7	17—34

First Quarter

Ariz.—FG, Blanchard 42, 6:58.

Second Quarter

Phi.—FG, Akers 38, 6:08.

Phi.—Thomason 1 pass from McNabb (Akers kick), 14:41.

Third Quarter

Phi.—McNabb 7 run (Akers kick), 8:32.

Fourth Quarter

Phi.—FG, Akers 46, 5:58.

Phi.—Caldwell 26 interception return (Akers kick), 7:20.

Ariz.—Boston 44 pass from Da. Brown (pass failed), 10:17.

Phi.—Autry 1 run (Akers kick), 13:03.

Attendance—65,356.

	Arizona	Philadelphia
First downs	12	21
Rushes-yards	17-54	31-134
Passing	156	204
Punt returns	2-33	2-15
Kickoff returns	7-153	2-39
Interception returns	1-8	1-26
Comp.-att.-int.	19-28-1	25-34-1
Sacked-yards lost	8-35	3-13
Punts	7-40	3-33
Fumbles-lost	0-0	2-1
Penalties-yards	9-114	5-35
Time of possession	25:09	34:49

INDIVIDUAL STATISTICS

RUSHING—Arizona, Pittman 13-49, Plummer 2-11, Jones 1-(minus 2), Jenkins 1-(minus 4). Philadelphia, Autry 16-59, Pritchett 7-29, McNabb 5-29, C. Martin 3-17.

PASSING—Arizona, Plummer 8-15-0-51, Da. Brown 11-13-1-140. Philadelphia, McNabb 25-34-1-217.

RECEIVING—Arizona, Boston 6-94, Pittman 6-29, Jones 3-38, Sanders 2-19, Jenkins 1-8, Hardy 1-3. Philadelphia, Lewis 5-52, Autry 5-31, Pritchett 4-47, Broughton 3-36, Thomason 2-12, Mitchell 2-6, Brown 1-18, Small 1-12, McNabb 1-2, C. Martin 1-1.

MISSED FIELD GOAL ATTEMPTS—None.

INTERCEPTIONS—Arizona, Fredrickson 1-8. Philadelphia, Caldwell 1-26.

KICKOFF RETURNS—Arizona, Jenkins 6-144, McKinnon 1-9. Philadelphia, Broughton 2-39, Mitchell 1-19.

PUNT RETURNS—Arizona, Cody 2-33. Philadelphia, Mitchell 2-15.

SACKS—Arizona, Rice 3. Philadelphia, Trotter 2, Dawkins 2, Simon 1.5, Grasmanis 1, Mamula 1, Whiting 0.5.

PACKERS 26, COLTS 24

Sunday, November 19

Indianapolis	0	0	3	21—24
Green Bay	5	14	0	7—26

First Quarter

G.B.—P. Manning tackled in end zone by R. Maryland for a safety, 2:45.

G.B.—FG, Longwell 42, 12:27.

Second Quarter

G.B.—T. Davis 1 pass from Favre (Longwell kick), 5:15.

G.B.—Freeman 17 pass from Favre (Longwell kick), 11:01.

Third Quarter

Ind.—FG, Vanderjagt 38, 6:40.

Fourth Quarter

Ind.—Green 34 pass from Manning (Vanderjagt kick), 4:25.

Ind.—Finn 5 pass from Manning (Vanderjagt kick), 10:28.

G.B.—Rossum 92 kickoff return (Longwell kick), 10:44.

Ind.—Pathon 11 pass from Manning (Vanderjagt kick), 12:21.

Attendance—59,869.

	Indianapolis	Green Bay
First downs	25	25
Rushes-yards	17-71	28-145
Passing	267	287
Punt returns	1-0	1-5
Kickoff returns	5-104	6-179
Interception returns	1-(-1)	1-0
Comp.-att.-int.	25-44-1	23-37-1
Sacked-yards lost	4-27	2-14
Punts	4-40	4-35
Fumbles-lost	2-1	0-0
Penalties-yards	5-69	7-46
Time of possession	25:51	34:09

INDIVIDUAL STATISTICS

RUSHING—Indianapolis, James 17-71. Green Bay, Green 24-153, Parker 3-(minus 5), Favre 1-(minus 3).

PASSING—Indianapolis, Manning 25-44-1-294. Green Bay, Favre 23-36-1-301, Green 0-1-0-0.

RECEIVING—Indianapolis, James 7-66, Green 6-81, Dilger 4-39, Pathon 3-45, Wilkins 2-30, Harrison 2-28, Finn 1-5. Green Bay, Schroeder 8-155, Green 4-27, Freeman 3-37, Henderson 3-22, Franks 2-34, Driver 1-24, Parker 1-1, T. Davis 1-1.

MISSED FIELD GOAL ATTEMPTS—Green Bay, Longwell 28.

INTERCEPTIONS—Indianapolis, E. Johnson 1-(minus 1). Green Bay, McBride 1-0.

KICKOFF RETURNS—Indianapolis, Wilkins 4-79, Pathon 1-25. Green Bay, Rossum 4-173, Henderson 1-6, Wetnight 1-0.

PUNT RETURNS—Indianapolis, Muhammad 1-0. Green Bay, Rossum 1-5.

SACKS—Indianapolis, E. Johnson 1, Whittington 1. Green Bay, S. Dotson 2, Thierry 1, Maryland 1.

LIONS 31, GIANTS 21

Sunday, November 19

Detroit	0	21	7	3—31
N.Y. Giants	0	0	14	7—21

Second Quarter

Det.—Rasby 5 pass from Batch (Hanson kick), 0:48.

Det.—J. Stewart 1 run (Hanson kick), 5:38.

Det.—Moore 7 pass from Batch (Hanson kick), 14:35.

Third Quarter

Det.—Morton 32 pass from Batch (Hanson kick), 3:26.

NYG—Collins 4 run (Daluiso kick), 7:46.

NYG—Campbell 2 pass from Collins (Daluiso kick), 14:38.

Fourth Quarter

Det.—FG, Hanson 19, 7:22.

NYG—Jurevicius 13 pass from Collins (Daluiso kick), 13:13.

Attendance—77,897.

	Detroit	N.Y. Giants
First downs	22	25
Rushes-yards	35-95	15-53
Passing	219	320
Punt returns	2-80	3-37
Kickoff returns	4-65	6-101
Interception returns	1-14	1-0
Comp.-att.-int.	20-32-1	29-51-1

	Detroit	N.Y. Giants
Sacked-yards lost	1-6	4-30
Punts	5-40	5-34
Fumbles-lost	2-1	3-3
Penalties-yards	6-55	10-103
Time of possession	33:53	26:07

INDIVIDUAL STATISTICS

RUSHING—Detroit, J. Stewart 22-52, Bates 8-20, Batch 4-30, Morton 1-(minus 7). New York, Barber 8-30, Dayne 4-5, Collins 3-18.

PASSING—Detroit, Batch 20-32-1-225. New York, Collins 29-51-1-350.

RECEIVING—Detroit, Morton 6-78, Moore 4-38, Sloan 2-39, Rasby 2-17, J. Stewart 2-16, Schlesinger 1-13, Bates 1-11, Foster 1-7, Stablein 1-6. New York, Toomer 8-108, Barber 8-99, Mitchell 5-70, Jurevicius 2-23, Comella 2-5, Davis 1-27, Hilliard 1-19, Campbell 1-2, Cross 1-(minus 3).

MISSED FIELD GOAL ATTEMPTS—Detroit, Hanson 44.

INTERCEPTIONS—Detroit, Schulz 1-14. New York, S. Williams 1-0.

KICKOFF RETURNS—Detroit, Howard 3-65, Olivo 1-0. New York, Stoutmire 3-52, Stephens 2-29, Levingston 1-20.

PUNT RETURNS—Detroit, Howard 2-80. New York, Barber 3-37.

SACKS—Detroit, Porcher 3, Hall 1. New York, Garnes 1.

JAGUARS 34, STEELERS 24

Sunday, November 19

Jacksonville	0	17	17	0—34
Pittsburgh	7	3	0	14—24

First Quarter

Pit.—Ward 32 pass from Stewart (K. Brown kick), 10:50.

Second Quarter

Jac.—Taylor 25 run (Hollis kick), 5:44.
Pit.—FG, K. Brown 40, 9:11.
Jac.—Taylor 16 pass from Brunell (Hollis kick), 13:40.
Jac.—FG, Hollis 36, 14:56.

Third Quarter

Jac.—FG, Hollis 33, 6:11.
Jac.—Taylor 2 run (Hollis kick), 6:56.
Jac.—Taylor 26 run (Hollis kick), 11:33.

Fourth Quarter

Pit.—Stewart 2 run (pass failed), 0:05.
Pit.—Stewart 45 run (Huntley run), 7:18.
Attendance—50,925.

	Jacksonville	Pittsburgh
First downs	20	15
Rushes-yards	36-240	24-147
Passing	177	159
Punt returns	2-7	4-28
Kickoff returns	5-114	6-115
Interception returns	2-5	1-8
Comp.-att.-int.	17-31-1	13-27-2
Sacked-yards lost	3-13	5-29
Punts	5-43	4-46
Fumbles-lost	1-1	3-3
Penalties-yards	8-55	4-30
Time of possession	34:20	25:40

INDIVIDUAL STATISTICS

RUSHING—Jacksonville, Taylor 30-234, Stith 3-5, Brunell 3-1. Pittsburgh, Bettis 12-57, Stewart 6-59, Huntley 6-31.

PASSING—Jacksonville, Brunell 17-31-1-190. Pittsburgh, Stewart 13-27-2-188.

RECEIVING—Jacksonville, J. Smith 6-85, Brady 5-62, McCardell 3-29, Taylor 3-14. Pittsburgh, Shaw 5-81, Ward 3-60, Cushing 2-9, Huntley 1-18, Hawkins 1-12, Bruener 1-8.

MISSED FIELD GOAL ATTEMPTS—Pittsburgh, K. Brown 42.

INTERCEPTIONS—Jacksonville, Darius 1-5, Hardy 1-0. Pittsburgh, Scott 1-8.

KICKOFF RETURNS—Jacksonville, Stith 5-114. Pittsburgh, Ward 2-47, Edwards 2-39, Poteat 2-29.

PUNT RETURNS—Jacksonville, Barlow 2-7. Pittsburgh, Poteat 4-28.

SACKS—Jacksonville, Logan 1, Boyer 1, Smeenge 1, Wynn 1, Walker 1. Pittsburgh, Porter 1, Flowers 1, Gildon 1.

JETS 20, DOLPHINS 3

Sunday, November 19

N.Y. Jets	3	3	0	14—20
Miami	0	3	0	0— 3

First Quarter

NYJ—FG, Hall 39, 13:58.

Second Quarter

Mia.—FG, Mare 47, 13:52.
NYJ—FG, Hall 33, 15:00.

Fourth Quarter

NYJ—Parmalee 18 run (Hall kick), 8:08.
NYJ—Parmalee 7 run (Hall kick), 11:48.
Attendance—74,320.

	N.Y. Jets	Miami
First downs	18	10
Rushes-yards	32-133	22-83
Passing	95	117
Punt returns	0-0	4-30
Kickoff returns	2-40	4-89
Interception returns	3-1	2-0
Comp.-att.-int.	13-28-2	16-29-3
Sacked-yards lost	2-7	3-11
Punts	6-49	6-36
Fumbles-lost	1-0	1-1
Penalties-yards	4-29	11-99
Time of possession	31:58	28:02

INDIVIDUAL STATISTICS

RUSHING—New York, Parmalee 14-57, Martin 14-54, Testaverde 2-14, Stone 1-9, R. Anderson 1-(minus 1). Miami, Johnson 10-50, Denson 6-21, L. Smith 6-12.

PASSING—New York, Testaverde 13-28-2-102. Miami, Huard 16-29-3-128.

RECEIVING—New York, R. Anderson 5-53, Chrebet 2-22, Becht 2-8, Ward 1-12, Parmalee 1-8, Sowell 1-0, Martin 1-(minus 1). Miami, Johnson 4-24, Denson 3-14, Gadsden 2-42, Shepherd 2-15, Konrad 2-6, McDuffie 1-18, Weaver 1-6, L. Smith 1-3.

MISSED FIELD GOAL ATTEMPTS—None.

INTERCEPTIONS—New York, Ellis 1-1, C. Hayes 1-0, Scott 1-0. Miami, Walker 1-0, Shaw 1-0.

KICKOFF RETURNS—New York, Coles 2-40. Miami, Denson 4-89.

PUNT RETURNS—Miami, Ogden 3-14, Shepherd 1-16.

SACKS—New York, Lewis 1, Ellis 1. Miami, Walker 1, Armstrong 1.

49ERS 16, FALCONS 6

Sunday, November 19

Atlanta	0	3	3	0— 6
San Francisco	3	3	7	3—16

First Quarter

S.F.—FG, Richey 32, 3:43.

Second Quarter

Atl.—FG, Andersen 21, 3:25.
S.F.—FG, Richey 30, 11:07.

Third Quarter

S.F.—Webster 70 interception return (Richey kick), 5:03.
Atl.—FG, Andersen 51, 10:47.

Fourth Quarter

S.F.—FG, Richey 26, 4:06.
Attendance—67,447.

	Atlanta	San Francisco
First downs	11	17
Rushes-yards	20-93	32-127
Passing	118	210
Punt returns	2-26	0-0
Kickoff returns	5-89	3-48
Interception returns	0-0	1-70
Comp.-att.-int.	16-33-1	16-31-0
Sacked-yards lost	4-36	0-0
Punts	5-44	4-39
Fumbles-lost	1-0	1-1
Penalties-yards	6-40	9-85
Time of possession	27:35	32:25

INDIVIDUAL STATISTICS

RUSHING—Atlanta, Anderson 17-76, M. Smith 2-15, Dwight 1-2. San Francisco, Garner 18-59, Garcia 9-50, Beasley 3-9, Smith 2-9.

PASSING—Atlanta, Chandler 16-33-1-154. San Francisco, Garcia 16-31-0-210.

RECEIVING—Atlanta, Jefferson 6-60, Anderson 3-17, Dwight 2-29, Christian 2-19, R. Kelly 2-11, Kozlowski 1-18. San Francisco, Garner 6-76, Streets 4-73, Rice 4-31, Stokes 1-27, Clark 1-3.

MISSED FIELD GOAL ATTEMPTS—None.

INTERCEPTIONS—San Francisco, Webster 1-70.

KICKOFF RETURNS—Atlanta, Vaughn 5-89. San Francisco, K. Williams 1-18, Streets 1-16, Lewis 1-14.

PUNT RETURNS—Atlanta, Dwight 2-26.

SACKS—San Francisco, B. Young 2, Buckner 1, Okeafor 1.

BRONCOS 38, CHARGERS 37

Sunday, November 19

San Diego	3	21	10	3—37
Denver	0	10	7	21—38

First Quarter
S.D.—FG, Carney 41, 10:19.

Second Quarter
Den.—McCaffrey 1 pass from Frerotte (Elam kick), 0:13.
S.D.—Conway 68 pass from Leaf (Carney kick), 1:54.
S.D.—J. Graham 45 pass from Leaf (Carney kick), 11:45.
S.D.—Turner 75 interception return (Carney kick), 13:35.
Den.—FG, Elam 26, 14:36.

Third Quarter
S.D.—FG, Carney 31, 3:35.
Den.—Carswell 5 pass from Frerotte (Elam kick), 9:52.
S.D.—J. Graham 83 pass from Leaf (Carney kick), 14:52.

Fourth Quarter
Den.—R. Smith 26 pass from Frerotte (Elam kick), 2:00.
S.D.—FG, Carney 33, 7:47.
Den.—Clark 10 pass from Frerotte (Elam kick), 10:01.
Den.—McCaffrey 5 pass from Frerotte (Elam kick), 13:27.
Attendance—75,218.

	San Diego	Denver
First downs	14	34
Rushes-yards	27-86	22-93
Passing	299	443
Punt returns	1-10	2-24
Kickoff returns	6-127	7-173
Interception returns	4-96	1-3
Comp.-att.-int.	13-27-1	36-58-4
Sacked-yards lost	3-12	3-19
Punts	3-44	2-38
Fumbles-lost	5-2	1-1
Penalties-yards	9-62	7-63
Time of possession	26:34	33:26

INDIVIDUAL STATISTICS

RUSHING—San Diego, Fazande 14-49, Leaf 7-19, Fletcher 6-18. Denver, Anderson 19-97, Frerotte 3-(minus 4).

PASSING—San Diego, Leaf 13-27-1-311. Denver, Frerotte 36-58-4-462.

RECEIVING—San Diego, J. Graham 4-144, Conway 4-118, F. Jones 3-35, Heiden 1-10, Fletcher 1-4. Denver, R. Smith 11-187, McCaffrey 10-148, Anderson 6-41, Chamberlain 3-36, Carswell 3-27, Clark 2-15, Griffith 1-8.

MISSED FIELD GOAL ATTEMPTS—Denver, Elam 42.

INTERCEPTIONS—San Diego, Turner 1-75, D. Jenkins 1-16, Beckett 1-7, F. Brown 1-(minus 2). Denver, Romanowski 1-3.

KICKOFF RETURNS—San Diego, R. Jenkins 5-109, Bynum 1-18. Denver, O'Neal 6-157, D. Smith 1-16.

PUNT RETURNS—San Diego, Jacquet 1-10. Denver, O'Neal 1-25, Buckley 1-(minus 1).

SACKS—San Diego, J. Williams 1, Fontenot 1, Lewis 1. Denver, Wilson 1, Pryce 1, Romanowski 1.

REDSKINS 33, RAMS 20

Monday, November 20

Washington	3	10	12	8—33
St. Louis	10	3	7	0—20

First Quarter
St.L.—FG, Hall 30, 4:39.
St.L.—Faulk 19 pass from Green (Hall kick), 5:25.
Was.—FG, Murray 37, 14:17.

Second Quarter
St.L.—FG, Hall 43, 8:15.
Was.—Thrash 19 pass from George (Murray kick), 13:10.
Was.—FG, Murray 47, 15:00.

Third Quarter
Was.—Centers 3 pass from George (kick failed), 5:41.
St.L.—Proehl 15 pass from Green (Hall kick), 9:47.
Was.—Fryar 34 pass from George (pass failed), 14:35.

Fourth Quarter
Was.—FG, Murray 41, 3:17.
Was.—FG, Murray 39, 4:22.
Was.—T.Green sacked in end zone by B.Smith for a safety, 11:16.
Attendance—66,087.

	Washington	St. Louis
First downs	21	18
Rushes-yards	32-138	14-50
Passing	262	344
Punt returns	2-34	2-7
Kickoff returns	6-105	6-139
Interception returns	1-48	1-23
Comp.-att.-int.	24-34-1	23-38-1
Sacked-yards lost	2-7	6-22
Punts	4-38	2-54
Fumbles-lost	1-0	2-2
Penalties-yards	9-67	8-52
Time of possession	32:37	27:23

INDIVIDUAL STATISTICS

RUSHING—Washington, Davis 19-85, Hicks 6-19, George 3-12, Thrash 2-12, Centers 2-10. St. Louis, Faulk 9-33, Holcombe 3-11, Green 1-3, Hakim 1-3.

PASSING—Washington, George 24-34-1-269. St. Louis, Green 23-38-1-366.

RECEIVING—Washington, Connell 5-96, Thrash 5-51, Fryar 3-58, Davis 3-21, Centers 3-11, Alexander 2-21, Sellers 2-13, Hicks 1-(minus 2). St. Louis, Faulk 9-88, Bruce 5-91, Holt 4-125, Proehl 2-37, Hakim 2-13, Conwell 1-12.

MISSED FIELD GOAL ATTEMPTS—None.

INTERCEPTIONS—Washington, Bailey 1-48. St. Louis, McCleon 1-23.

KICKOFF RETURNS—Washington, Thrash 4-90, Arrington 1-16, Sanders 1-(minus 1). St. Louis, Horne 6-139.

PUNT RETURNS—Washington, Thrash 2-34. St. Louis, Hakim 2-7.

SACKS—Washington, B. Smith 3, Arrington 2, Coleman 0.5, Stubblefield 0.5. St. Louis, Carter 2.

WEEK 13

STANDINGS

AFC EAST
	W	L	T	Pct.
Miami	9	3	0	.750
N.Y. Jets	8	4	0	.667
Buffalo	7	5	0	.583
Indianapolis	7	5	0	.583
New England	3	9	0	.250

AFC CENTRAL
	W	L	T	Pct.
Tennessee	9	3	0	.750
Baltimore	9	4	0	.692
Pittsburgh	6	6	0	.500
Jacksonville	5	7	0	.417
Cleveland	3	10	0	.231
Cincinnati	2	10	0	.167

AFC WEST
	W	L	T	Pct.
Oakland	10	2	0	.833
Denver	8	4	0	.667
Kansas City	5	7	0	.417
Seattle	4	8	0	.333
San Diego	1	11	0	.083

NFC EAST
	W	L	T	Pct.
Philadelphia	9	4	0	.692
N.Y. Giants	8	4	0	.667
Washington	7	5	0	.583
Dallas	4	8	0	.333
Arizona	3	9	0	.250

NFC CENTRAL
	W	L	T	Pct.
Minnesota	10	2	0	.833
Detroit	8	4	0	.667
Tampa Bay	7	5	0	.583
Green Bay	5	7	0	.417
Chicago	3	9	0	.250

NFC WEST
	W	L	T	Pct.
New Orleans	8	4	0	.667
St. Louis	8	4	0	.667
Carolina	5	7	0	.417
San Francisco	4	8	0	.333
Atlanta	3	10	0	.231

TOP PERFORMANCES

100-YARD RUSHING GAMES
Player, Team & Opponent	Att.	Yds.	TD
Mike Anderson, Den. at Sea.	30	195	2
Jamal Lewis, Balt. vs. Cle.	30	170	2
Robert Smith, Min. at Dal.	21	148	1
Corey Dillon, Cin. vs. Pit.	23	128	2
Donovan McNabb, Phi. at Wash.	11	125	1
James Allen, Chi. at NYJ	25	122	0
Edgerrin James, Ind. vs. Mia.	26	118	0
Brad Hoover, Car. vs. G.B.	24	117	1
Warrick Dunn, T.B. vs. Buf.	20	106	2
Fred Taylor, Jack. vs. Ten.	24	104	0
Emmitt Smith, Dal. vs. Min.	12	100	0

300-YARD PASSING GAMES
None

100-YARD RECEIVING GAMES
Player, Team & Opponent	Rec.	Yds.	TD
Randy Moss, Min. at Dal.	7	144	2
Muhsin Muhammad, Car. vs. G.B.	11	131	2
Ricky Watters, Sea. vs. Den.	9	126	0
James Thrash, Wash. vs. Phi.	5	121	1
Eddie George, Ten. at Jack.	7	109	0
Shawn Jefferson, Atl. at Oak.	7	109	0
Eric Moulds, Buf. at T.B.	8	102	1

RESULTS

THURSDAY, NOVEMBER 23
DETROIT 34, New England 9
Minnesota 27, DALLAS 15

SUNDAY, NOVEMBER 26
BALTIMORE 44, Cleveland 7
Denver 38, SEATTLE 31
JACKSONVILLE 16, Tennessee 13
Miami 17, INDIANAPOLIS 14
New Orleans 31, ST. LOUIS 24
N.Y. Giants 31, ARIZONA 7
N.Y. JETS 17, Chicago 10
OAKLAND 41, Atlanta 14
Philadelphia 23, WASHINGTON 20
Pittsburgh 48, CINCINNATI 28
SAN DIEGO 17, Kansas City 16
TAMPA BAY 31, Buffalo 17

MONDAY, NOVEMBER 27
CAROLINA 31, Green Bay 14
Open date: San Francisco

LIONS 34, PATRIOTS 9

Thursday, November 23

New England	6	0	3	0—	9
Detroit	3	3	7	21—	34

First Quarter
Det.—FG, Hanson 31, 1:43.
N.E.—FG, Vinatieri 24, 9:19.
N.E.—FG, Vinatieri 47, 13:37.

Second Quarter
Det.—FG, Hanson 36, 2:12.

Third Quarter
N.E.—FG, Vinatieri 43, 6:09.
Det.—Sloan 1 pass from Batch (Hanson kick), 11:15.

Fourth Quarter
Det.—J. Stewart 1 run (Hanson kick), 3:42.
Det.—Batch 10 run (Hanson kick), 6:05.
Det.—Westbrook 101 interception return (Hanson kick), 10:47.
Attendance—77,923.

	New England	Detroit
First downs	15	17
Rushes-yards	20-66	28-110
Passing	149	189
Punt returns	1-2	2-22
Kickoff returns	6-111	4-136
Interception returns	0-0	2-113
Comp.-att.-int.	18-35-2	17-25-0
Sacked-yards lost	2-5	2-15
Punts	5-50	2-48
Fumbles-lost	0-0	4-1
Penalties-yards	9-81	10-99
Time of possession	30:27	29:33

INDIVIDUAL STATISTICS
RUSHING—New England, Redmond 11-30, Bledsoe 4-27, Pass 3-9, T. Carter 2-0. Detroit, J. Stewart 18-51, Irvin 4-45, Batch 4-17, Case 2-(minus 3).
PASSING—New England, Bledsoe 17-32-2-148, Brady 1-3-0-6. Detroit, Batch 16-24-0-194, Case 1-1-0-10.
RECEIVING—New England, Glenn 5-76, Brown 4-27, Rutledge 4-25, S. Davis 2-12, T. Carter 1-15, Redmond 1-5, Pass 1-(minus 6). Detroit, Morton 4-46, Moore 4-42, Sloan 3-66, Rasby 2-14, Stablein 2-14, Irvin 1-18, Schlesinger 1-4.
MISSED FIELD GOAL ATTEMPTS—None.
INTERCEPTIONS—Detroit, Westbrook 1-101, M. Walker 1-12.
KICKOFF RETURNS—New England, Faulk 6-111. Detroit, Howard 4-136.
PUNT RETURNS—New England, Faulk 1-2. Detroit, Howard 2-22.
SACKS—New England, Eaton 1, Serwanga 1. Detroit, Scroggins 1, Boyd 0.5, C. Brown 0.5.

VIKINGS 27, COWBOYS 15

Thursday, November 23

Minnesota	0	10	17	0—	27
Dallas	3	6	0	6—	15

First Quarter
Dal.—FG, Seder 37, 4:59.

Second Quarter
Dal.—FG, Seder 43, 2:33.
Min.—FG, Anderson 49, 6:50.
Min.—Smith 15 run (Anderson kick), 13:08.
Dal.—FG, Seder 36, 15:00.

Third Quarter
Min.—Moss 7 pass from Culpepper (Anderson kick), 2:35.
Min.—FG, Anderson 29, 8:49.
Min.—Moss 36 pass from Culpepper (Anderson kick), 14:42.

Fourth Quarter
Dal.—LaFleur 6 pass from Aikman (run failed), 12:28.
Attendance—63,878.

	Minnesota	Dallas
First downs	18	22
Rushes-yards	27-168	24-128
Passing	192	276

	Minnesota	Dallas
Punt returns	1-10	2-20
Kickoff returns	3-54	6-104
Interception returns	1-25	0-0
Comp.-att.-int.	15-22-0	30-43-1
Sacked-yards lost	2-13	0-0
Punts	4-45	3-36
Fumbles-lost	1-0	1-1
Penalties-yards	4-21	5-45
Time of possession	28:09	31:51

INDIVIDUAL STATISTICS
RUSHING—Minnesota, Smith 21-148, M. Williams 4-12, Culpepper 2-8. Dallas, E. Smith 12-100, Warren 8-10, Aikman 2-3, McGarity 1-11, Tucker 1-4.
PASSING—Minnesota, Culpepper 15-22-0-205. Dallas, Aikman 30-43-1-276.
RECEIVING—Minnesota, Moss 7-144, McWilliams 2-26, C. Carter 2-22, Hatchette 2-16, Walsh 1-3, Smith 1-(minus 6). Dallas, Tucker 6-57, LaFleur 6-45, McGarity 5-54, Warren 5-40, McKnight 3-41, Harris 2-21, E. Smith 1-8, Wiley 1-8, Brazzell 1-2.
MISSED FIELD GOAL ATTEMPTS—Dallas, Seder 26.
INTERCEPTIONS—Minnesota, Griffith 1-25.
KICKOFF RETURNS—Minnesota, Walters 1-35, M. Williams 1-16, Walsh 1-3. Dallas, Tucker 5-91, LaFleur 1-13.
PUNT RETURNS—Minnesota, Walters 1-10. Dallas, McGarity 2-20.
SACKS—Dallas, Ekuban 1, Underwood 1.

RAVENS 44, BROWNS 7

Sunday, November 26

Cleveland	7	0	0	0—	7
Baltimore	7	24	6	7—	44

First Quarter
Cle.—Prentice 4 run (P. Dawson kick), 4:30.
Bal.—Ja. Lewis 1 run (Stover kick), 10:54.

Second Quarter
Bal.—Gash 2 pass from Dilfer (Stover kick), 1:20.
Bal.—Johnson 46 pass from Dilfer (Stover kick), 3:21.
Bal.—FG, Stover 39, 10:25.
Bal.—Ja. Lewis 36 run (Stover kick), 12:05.

Third Quarter
Bal.—FG, Stover 26, 3:08.
Bal.—FG, Stover 38, 9:59.

Fourth Quarter
Bal.—Holmes 3 run (Stover kick), 9:37.
Attendance—68,361.

	Cleveland	Baltimore
First downs	5	25
Rushes-yards	17-28	51-247
Passing	84	214
Punt returns	2-30	9-126
Kickoff returns	6-125	2-38
Interception returns	1-3	1-14
Comp.-att.-int.	13-25-1	14-26-1
Sacked-yards lost	6-54	0-0
Punts	10-49	4-47
Fumbles-lost	2-2	2-1
Penalties-yards	3-11	3-25
Time of possession	21:28	38:32

INDIVIDUAL STATISTICS
RUSHING—Cleveland, Prentice 11-13, White 4-12, Pederson 2-3. Baltimore, Ja. Lewis 30-170, Holmes 17-64, Dilfer 2-10, Johnson 1-2, Gash 1-1.
PASSING—Cleveland, Pederson 8-16-1-108, Wynn 5-9-0-30. Baltimore, Dilfer 12-23-1-169, Banks 2-3-0-45.
RECEIVING—Cleveland, Johnson 4-85, Patten 4-23, Campbell 2-25, Edwards 1-4, Prentice 1-3, White 1-(minus 2). Baltimore, Stokley 4-68, Ismail 3-39, Johnson 2-54, Sharpe 2-17, Gash 2-8, B. Davis 1-28.
MISSED FIELD GOAL ATTEMPTS—None.
INTERCEPTIONS—Cleveland, Moore 1-3. Baltimore, McAlister 1-14.
KICKOFF RETURNS—Cleveland, White 6-125. Baltimore, Harris 2-38.
PUNT RETURNS—Cleveland, Northcutt 2-30. Baltimore, Starks 5-71, J. Lewis 4-55.
SACKS—Baltimore, R. Lewis 2, Boulware 1, Brown 1, McCrary 1, Trapp 1.

BUCCANEERS 31, BILLS 17

Sunday, November 26

Buffalo	0	7	0	10—17
Tampa Bay	3	7	0	21—31

First Quarter
T.B.—FG, Gramatica 45, 2:43.

Second Quarter
Buf.—Linton 4 pass from Johnson (Christie kick), 5:18.
T.B.—King 2 run (Gramatica kick), 11:26.

Fourth Quarter
T.B.—Dunn 6 run (Gramatica kick), 3:22.
Buf.—Moulds 19 pass from Johnson (Christie kick), 6:04.
T.B.—Williams 73 punt return (Gramatica kick), 9:26.
Buf.—FG, Christie 28, 12:33.
T.B.—Dunn 39 run (Gramatica kick), 12:52.
Attendance—65,546.

	Buffalo	Tampa Bay
First downs	25	13
Rushes-yards	27-139	25-114
Passing	294	66
Punt returns	4-(-3)	3-95
Kickoff returns	6-124	3-104
Interception returns	0-0	0-0
Comp.-att.-int.	28-49-0	10-18-0
Sacked-yards lost	6-25	7-40
Punts	7-36	7-43
Fumbles-lost	2-2	0-0
Penalties-yards	8-70	7-71
Time of possession	36:17	23:43

INDIVIDUAL STATISTICS
RUSHING—Buffalo, A. Smith 11-30, Bryson 8-32, Johnson 4-19, Flutie 2-11, P. Price 1-27, Moulds 1-20. Tampa Bay, Dunn 20-106, King 5-8.
PASSING—Buffalo, Johnson 24-39-0-262, Flutie 4-10-0-57. Tampa Bay, King 10-18-0-106.
RECEIVING—Buffalo, Moulds 8-102, P. Price 6-44, Riemersma 5-82, McDaniel 3-43, Jackson 2-15, Bryson 1-17, A. Smith 1-7, Cavil 1-5, Linton 1-4. Tampa Bay, Green 4-51, Moore 3-17, K. Johnson 2-15, Dunn 1-23.
MISSED FIELD GOAL ATTEMPTS—Buffalo, Christie 42.
INTERCEPTIONS—None.
KICKOFF RETURNS—Buffalo, Watson 5-108, Bryson 1-16. Tampa Bay, Anthony 2-69, Williams 1-35.
PUNT RETURNS—Buffalo, Watson 4-(minus 3). Tampa Bay, Williams 3-95.
SACKS—Buffalo, Cowart 2.5, Wiley 2, Washington 1.5, Moore 1. Tampa Bay, Sapp 2, Brooks 1, Jones 1, Quarles 1, T. Jackson 1.

EAGLES 23, REDSKINS 20

Sunday, November 26

Philadelphia	7	3	7	6—23
Washington	7	7	3	3—20

First Quarter
Was.—Thrash 36 pass from George (Murray kick), 2:38.
Phi.—Thomason 3 pass from McNabb (Akers kick), 6:44.

Second Quarter
Phi.—FG, Akers 27, 6:47.
Was.—Alexander 19 pass from George (Murray kick), 11:52.

Third Quarter
Phi.—McNabb 21 run (Akers kick), 5:57.
Was.—FG, Murray 26, 12:44.

Fourth Quarter
Phi.—FG, Akers 33, 3:17.
Was.—FG, Murray 20, 9:18.
Phi.—FG, Akers 30, 12:00.
Attendance—83,284.

	Philadelphia	Washington
First downs	14	20
Rushes-yards	26-171	19-44
Passing	118	282
Punt returns	1-6	2-1
Kickoff returns	4-85	6-117
Interception returns	0-0	1-0
Comp.-att.-int.	19-31-1	25-43-0

	Philadelphia	Washington
Sacked-yards lost	4-19	1-6
Punts	4-39	4-41
Fumbles-lost	2-1	3-2
Penalties-yards	11-98	6-46
Time of possession	29:13	30:47

INDIVIDUAL STATISTICS
RUSHING—Philadelphia, McNabb 11-125, Autry 9-25, Pritchett 5-18, C. Martin 1-3. Washington, Hicks 10-22, Murrell 7-14, George 2-8.
PASSING—Philadelphia, McNabb 19-30-1-137, Mitchell 0-1-0-0. Washington, George 25-43-0-288.
RECEIVING—Philadelphia, Lewis 6-53, C. Johnson 3-17, Autry 2-24, Thomason 2-7, Small 1-18, Brown 1-9, Broughton 1-6, Pinkston 1-6, C. Martin 1-0, Pritchett 1-(minus 3). Washington, Centers 7-33, Thrash 5-121, Fryar 4-50, Alexander 4-39, Murrell 3-13, Hicks 2-32.
MISSED FIELD GOAL ATTEMPTS—Washington, Murray 44.
INTERCEPTIONS—Washington, Bailey 1-0.
KICKOFF RETURNS—Philadelphia, Mitchell 4-85. Washington, Thrash 6-117.
PUNT RETURNS—Philadelphia, Mitchell 1-6. Washington, Thrash 2-1.
SACKS—Philadelphia, Mamula 1. Washington, B. Smith 1, Jones 1, Stubblefield 1, Coleman 1.

STEELERS 48, BENGALS 28

Sunday, November 26

Pittsburgh	14	10	21	3—48
Cincinnati	7	7	7	7—28

First Quarter
Pit.—Ward 34 pass from Stewart (K. Brown kick), 2:54.
Cin.—Bennett 37 run (Rackers kick), 4:56.
Pit.—Stewart 1 run (K. Brown kick), 11:17.

Second Quarter
Cin.—Dillon 20 run (Rackers kick), 1:04.
Pit.—Bruener 11 pass from Stewart (K. Brown kick), 6:00.
Pit.—FG, K. Brown 44, 14:44.

Third Quarter
Cin.—Dillon 4 run (Rackers kick), 5:14.
Pit.—Shaw 45 pass from Stewart (K. Brown kick), 8:44.
Pit.—Bettis 7 run (K. Brown kick), 13:29.
Pit.—Gildon 22 fumble return (K. Brown kick), 15:00.

Fourth Quarter
Cin.—Warrick 5 pass from Smith (Rackers kick), 12:10.
Pit.—FG, K. Brown 28, 13:11.
Attendance—63,925.

	Pittsburgh	Cincinnati
First downs	21	23
Rushes-yards	38-185	41-209
Passing	187	100
Punt returns	2-5	3-0
Kickoff returns	3-44	8-96
Interception returns	0-0	0-0
Comp.-att.-int.	12-22-0	10-20-0
Sacked-yards lost	4-22	4-29
Punts	4-41	4-36
Fumbles-lost	0-0	8-3
Penalties-yards	4-35	3-15
Time of possession	30:49	29:11

INDIVIDUAL STATISTICS
RUSHING—Pittsburgh, Bettis 23-93, Stewart 6-31, Zereoue 3-5, Ward 2-38, Huntley 2-20, Graham 2-(minus 2). Cincinnati, Dillon 23-128, Smith 6-15, Bennett 5-55, N. Williams 5-16, Warrick 2-(minus 5).
PASSING—Pittsburgh, Stewart 11-20-0-182, Graham 1-2-0-27. Cincinnati, Smith 10-20-0-129.
RECEIVING—Pittsburgh, Ward 4-70, Shaw 2-66, Bruener 2-25, Edwards 1-27, Hawkins 1-17, Cushing 1-5, Bettis 1-(minus 1). Cincinnati, Farmer 3-59, Warrick 3-25, Yeast 2-37, Bennett 2-8.
MISSED FIELD GOAL ATTEMPTS—None.
INTERCEPTIONS—None.
KICKOFF RETURNS—Pittsburgh, Blackwell 1-25, Poteat 1-19, Kreider 1-0. Cincinnati, Mack 5-73, Bush 2-11, Yeast 1-12.
PUNT RETURNS—Pittsburgh, Hawkins 1-5, Poteat 1-0. Cincinnati, Yeast 2-0, Warrick 1-0.
SACKS—Pittsburgh, Gildon 2, Porter 1, Townsend 1. Cincinnati, Ross 1, Curtis 1, Foley 1, Hall 1.

SAINTS 31, RAMS 24

Sunday, November 26

New Orleans	7	14	3	7—31
St. Louis	7	3	7	7—24

First Quarter
St.L.—Holcombe 1 run (Hall kick), 12:17.
N.O.—Milne 4 pass from Brooks (Brien kick), 14:52.

Second Quarter
N.O.—Moore 3 run (Brien kick), 4:32.
N.O.—Brooks 2 run (Brien kick), 13:05.
St.L.—FG, Hall 28, 15:00.

Third Quarter
N.O.—FG, Brien 30, 5:33.
St.L.—Hakim 35 pass from Green (Hall kick), 8:10.

Fourth Quarter
St.L.—Proehl 19 pass from Green (Hall kick), 3:54.
N.O.—Brooks 1 run (Brien kick), 11:10.
Attendance—66,064.

	New Orleans	St. Louis
First downs	23	21
Rushes-yards	44-147	10-28
Passing	185	251
Punt returns	0-0	4-80
Kickoff returns	4-104	5-104
Interception returns	1-0	2-17
Comp.-att.-int.	17-29-2	20-41-1
Sacked-yards lost	1-5	6-38
Punts	4-38	3-35
Fumbles-lost	0-0	5-3
Penalties-yards	17-116	14-132
Time of possession	39:26	20:34

INDIVIDUAL STATISTICS
RUSHING—New Orleans, Moore 18-61, Morton 12-35, Brooks 7-34, T. Smith 5-20, McAfee 1-(minus 3). St. Louis, Faulk 8-27, Holcombe 1-1, Green 1-0.
PASSING—New Orleans, Brooks 17-29-2-190. St. Louis, Green 20-41-1-289.
RECEIVING—New Orleans, Horn 7-77, Jackson 4-64, Morton 2-12, Poole 1-18, Wilson 1-9, A. Glover 1-6, Milne 1-4. St. Louis, Holt 6-89, Bruce 4-59, Hakim 4-54, Proehl 3-66, Faulk 2-16, R. Williams 1-5.
MISSED FIELD GOAL ATTEMPTS—New Orleans, Brien 44.
INTERCEPTIONS—New Orleans, Oldham 1-0. St. Louis, Fletcher 2-17.
KICKOFF RETURNS—New Orleans, Morton 4-104. St. Louis, Bly 5-104.
PUNT RETURNS—St. Louis, Hakim 4-80.
SACKS—New Orleans, L. Glover 3, D. Howard 1, D. Smith 1, Johnson 1. St. Louis, Fletcher 0.5, Wistrom 0.5.

JAGUARS 16, TITANS 13

Sunday, November 26

Tennessee	7	3	0	3—13
Jacksonville	10	0	3	3—16

First Quarter
Jac.—FG, Hollis 27, 4:10.
Ten.—E. George 7 run (Del Greco kick), 9:41.
Jac.—Taylor 10 pass from Brunell (Hollis kick), 12:53.

Second Quarter
Ten.—FG, Del Greco 30, 7:25.

Third Quarter
Jac.—FG, Hollis 20, 6:22.

Fourth Quarter
Ten.—FG, Del Greco 38, 0:05.
Jac.—FG, Hollis 38, 15:00.
Attendance—65,454.

	Tennessee	Jacksonville
First downs	17	16
Rushes-yards	31-117	28-111
Passing	217	223
Punt returns	2-46	3-13
Kickoff returns	4-61	4-84
Interception returns	2-(-1)	0-0
Comp.-att.-int.	13-24-0	15-25-2
Sacked-yards lost	2-11	3-14
Punts	5-38	3-54
Fumbles-lost	1-0	0-0
Penalties-yards	4-40	4-25
Time of possession	30:41	29:19

INDIVIDUAL STATISTICS
RUSHING—Tennessee, E. George 24-69, McNair 5-46, Thomas 2-2. Jacksonville, Taylor 24-104, Brunell 3-1, Johnson 1-6.
PASSING—Tennessee, McNair 13-24-0-228. Jacksonville, Brunell 15-25-2-237.
RECEIVING—Tennessee, E. George 7-109, Mason 2-33, Wycheck 2-18, Thigpen 1-37, Sanders 1-31. Jacksonville, Taylor 4-22, McCardell 3-53, J. Smith 3-45, Brady 3-28, Soward 1-45, Johnson 1-44.
MISSED FIELD GOAL ATTEMPTS—Tennessee, Del Greco 28.
INTERCEPTIONS—Tennessee, Rolle 2-(minus 1).
KICKOFF RETURNS—Tennessee, Mason 4-61. Jacksonville, Stith 4-84.
PUNT RETURNS—Tennessee, Mason 2-46. Jacksonville, Barlow 3-13.
SACKS—Tennessee, Bishop 1, Godfrey 1, Ford 1. Jacksonville, Brackens 1, Hardy 0.5, L. Smith 0.5.

JETS 17, BEARS 10

Sunday, November 26

Chicago	0	0	3	7—10
N.Y. Jets	7	10	0	0—17

First Quarter
NYJ—Becht 2 pass from Testaverde (Hall kick), 10:28.

Second Quarter
NYJ—FG, Hall 20, 4:20.
NYJ—R. Anderson 15 pass from Testaverde (Hall kick), 14:28.

Third Quarter
Chi.—FG, Edinger 39, 13:08.

Fourth Quarter
Chi.—Booker 6 pass from Matthews (Edinger kick), 9:46.
Attendance—77,354.

	Chicago	N.Y. Jets
First downs	13	17
Rushes-yards	30-135	32-59
Passing	98	218
Punt returns	3-45	1-2
Kickoff returns	3-90	3-82
Interception returns	1-21	0-0
Comp.-att.-int.	13-32-0	21-35-1
Sacked-yards lost	0-0	0-0
Punts	5-35	7-40
Fumbles-lost	4-3	0-0
Penalties-yards	5-29	4-35
Time of possession	24:59	35:01

INDIVIDUAL STATISTICS
RUSHING—Chicago, Allen 25-122, Barnes 3-11, Enis 1-2, Matthews 1-0. New York, Martin 17-29, Parmalee 10-26, R. Anderson 2-5, Testaverde 2-(minus 2), Ward 1-1.
PASSING—Chicago, Matthews 13-32-0-98. New York, Testaverde 20-34-1-215, Lucas 1-1-0-3.
RECEIVING—Chicago, Booker 5-45, Allen 3-23, Brooks 2-19, Barnes 1-7, Kennison 1-7, M. Robinson 1-(minus 3). New York, Ward 6-93, R. Anderson 6-69, Parmalee 6-48, Chrebet 1-8, Becht 1-2, Martin 1-(minus 2).
MISSED FIELD GOAL ATTEMPTS—New York, Hall 46.
INTERCEPTIONS—Chicago, Wells 1-21.
KICKOFF RETURNS—Chicago, Milburn 3-90. New York, Stone 3-82.
PUNT RETURNS—Chicago, Milburn 3-45. New York, Ward 1-2.
SACKS—None.

CHARGERS 17, CHIEFS 16

Sunday, November 26

Kansas City	3	3	10	0—16
San Diego	7	7	0	3—17

First Quarter
K.C.—FG, Peterson 39, 8:26.
S.D.—F. Jones 20 pass from Leaf (Carney kick), 10:37.

Second Quarter
S.D.—F. Jones 7 pass from Leaf (Carney kick), 1:48.
K.C.—FG, Peterson 34, 10:28.

Third Quarter

K.C.—Patton 24 interception return (Peterson kick), 1:02.

K.C.—FG, Peterson 30, 13:09.

Fourth Quarter

S.D.—FG, Carney 52, 12:46.

Attendance—47,228.

	Kansas City	San Diego
First downs	10	14
Rushes-yards	31-77	22-52
Passing	84	149
Punt returns	6-65	6-50
Kickoff returns	3-48	5-122
Interception returns	2-29	1-2
Comp.-att.-int.	12-31-1	17-30-2
Sacked-yards lost	5-46	6-28
Punts	10-43	8-49
Fumbles-lost	1-0	3-3
Penalties-yards	11-90	5-43
Time of possession	31:03	28:57

INDIVIDUAL STATISTICS

RUSHING—Kansas City, Anders 16-20, Richardson 9-52, Bennett 4-3, Moon 2-2. San Diego, Fletcher 14-40, Fazande 4-13, Leaf 4-(minus 1).

PASSING—Kansas City, Moon 12-31-1-130. San Diego, Leaf 17-30-2-177.

RECEIVING—Kansas City, Alexander 4-67, Richardson 3-27, Anders 2-18, Morris 2-18. San Diego, F. Jones 4-47, Fletcher 4-15, J. Graham 3-48, Conway 2-32, McCrary 2-19, Fazande 2-16.

MISSED FIELD GOAL ATTEMPTS—None.

INTERCEPTIONS—Kansas City, Patton 1-24, Hasty 1-5. San Diego, Seau 1-2.

KICKOFF RETURNS—Kansas City, Cloud 3-48. San Diego, R. Jenkins 5-122.

PUNT RETURNS—Kansas City, Lockett 6-65. San Diego, Jacquet 6-50.

SACKS—Kansas City, Hicks 2, Maslowski 1, Clemons 1, Hasty 1, D. Williams 1. San Diego, Harrison 2, Dumas 1, Parrella 1, Mickell 1.

BRONCOS 38, SEAHAWKS 31

Sunday, November 26

Denver	0	10	7	21—38
Seattle	0	14	10	7—31

Second Quarter

Sea.—Sinclair 63 fumble return (Lindell kick), 3:21.

Den.—FG, Elam 35, 8:27.

Sea.—Watters 1 run (Lindell kick), 12:06.

Den.—Clark 43 pass from Frerotte (Elam kick), 13:24.

Third Quarter

Den.—Anderson 15 run (Elam kick), 8:03.

Sea.—C. Brown 10 fumble return (Lindell kick), 12:48.

Sea.—FG, Lindell 42, 14:33.

Fourth Quarter

Den.—R. Smith 50 run (Elam kick), 2:23.

Den.—Spencer 21 interception return (Elam kick), 9:06.

Sea.—Dawkins 8 pass from Kitna (Lindell kick), 10:58.

Den.—Anderson 80 run (Elam kick), 11:26.

Attendance—68,661.

	Denver	Seattle
First downs	25	17
Rushes-yards	41-301	21-85
Passing	237	269
Punt returns	3-4	2-17
Kickoff returns	6-109	7-140
Interception returns	2-30	2-8
Comp.-att.-int.	15-31-2	23-48-2
Sacked-yards lost	1-7	1-5
Punts	4-36	6-38
Fumbles-lost	4-3	2-1
Penalties-yards	5-53	5-43
Time of possession	34:25	25:35

INDIVIDUAL STATISTICS

RUSHING—Denver, Anderson 30-195, Frerotte 6-23, R. Smith 3-78, Griffith 1-3, Coleman 1-2. Seattle, Watters 16-77, Alexander 3-1, Strong 1-4, Kitna 1-3.

PASSING—Denver, Frerotte 15-31-2-244. Seattle, Kitna 20-42-2-226, Huard 3-6-0-48.

RECEIVING—Denver, R. Smith 4-82, Clark 3-73, Carswell 3-42, McCaffrey 3-33, Anderson 2-14. Seattle, Watters 9-126, Dawkins 7-54, Fauria 3-16, Mayes 2-49, Jackson 1-19, Strong 1-10.

MISSED FIELD GOAL ATTEMPTS—None.

INTERCEPTIONS—Denver, Spencer 1-21, E. Brown 1-9. Seattle, Springs 1-8, W. Williams 1-0.

KICKOFF RETURNS—Denver, O'Neal 5-97, D. Smith 1-12. Seattle, Rogers 7-140.

PUNT RETURNS—Denver, O'Neal 3-4. Seattle, Rogers 2-17.

SACKS—Denver, Mobley 1. Seattle, Simmons 1.

DOLPHINS 17, COLTS 14

Sunday, November 26

Miami	0	3	7	7—17
Indianapolis	7	0	0	7—14

First Quarter

Ind.—Harrison 27 pass from Manning (Vanderjagt kick), 5:14.

Second Quarter

Mia.—FG, Mare 28, 14:57.

Third Quarter

Mia.—Johnson 3 run (Mare kick), 7:31.

Fourth Quarter

Ind.—Harrison 8 pass from Manning (Vanderjagt kick), 0:46.

Mia.—Gadsden 17 pass from Huard (Mare kick), 13:50.

Attendance—56,935.

	Miami	Indianapolis
First downs	17	19
Rushes-yards	24-82	31-144
Passing	171	209
Punt returns	2-37	5-71
Kickoff returns	2-65	2-16
Interception returns	1-19	0-0
Comp.-att.-int.	22-33-0	16-34-1
Sacked-yards lost	2-12	0-0
Punts	7-50	6-47
Fumbles-lost	1-0	0-0
Penalties-yards	4-30	10-78
Time of possession	29:05	30:55

INDIVIDUAL STATISTICS

RUSHING—Miami, Johnson 21-60, Denson 3-22. Indianapolis, James 26-118, Manning 5-26.

PASSING—Miami, Huard 22-33-0-183. Indianapolis, Manning 16-34-1-209.

RECEIVING—Miami, Shepherd 7-41, Denson 6-63, Johnson 5-29, Gadsden 2-30, Martin 1-11, Emanuel 1-9. Indianapolis, James 5-37, Harrison 4-74, Wilkins 2-34, Pollard 2-30, Pathon 2-19, Dilger 1-15.

MISSED FIELD GOAL ATTEMPTS—Indianapolis, Vanderjagt 59.

INTERCEPTIONS—Miami, Marion 1-19.

KICKOFF RETURNS—Miami, Ogden 1-39, Denson 1-26. Indianapolis, Wilkins 1-16, Dilger 1-0.

PUNT RETURNS—Miami, Ogden 2-37. Indianapolis, Wilkins 4-67, Muhammad 1-4.

SACKS—Indianapolis, M. Thomas 1, E. Johnson 1.

RAIDERS 41, FALCONS 14

Sunday, November 26

Atlanta	7	0	0	7—14
Oakland	3	21	14	3—41

First Quarter

Atl.—Anderson 5 run (Andersen kick), 3:29.

Oak.—FG, Janikowski 24, 10:17.

Second Quarter

Oak.—Wheatley 1 run (Janikowski kick), 2:38.

Oak.—Brown 28 pass from Gannon (Janikowski kick), 6:53.

Oak.—Crockett 8 run (Janikowski kick), 13:51.

Third Quarter

Oak.—Dunn 88 kickoff return (Janikowski kick), 0:19.

Oak.—Jett 84 pass from Gannon (Janikowski kick), 6:10.

Fourth Quarter

Atl.—Kozlowski 4 pass from Johnson (Andersen kick), 0:30.

Oak.—FG, Janikowski 35, 3:35.

Attendance—55,175.

2000 REVIEW Week 13

	Atlanta	Oakland
First downs	15	24
Rushes-yards	13-31	38-270
Passing	150	222
Punt returns	1-0	3-3
Kickoff returns	8-180	3-136
Interception returns	0-0	1-15
Comp.-att.-int.	18-29-1	15-22-0
Sacked-yards lost	6-32	2-9
Punts	8-39	3-38
Fumbles-lost	2-1	3-1
Penalties-yards	10-55	12-108
Time of possession	24:53	35:07

INDIVIDUAL STATISTICS

RUSHING—Atlanta, Anderson 12-26, Chandler 1-5. Oakland, Wheatley 12-85, Crockett 10-48, Jordan 7-33, Kaufman 5-40, Gannon 4-64.

PASSING—Atlanta, Johnson 11-17-0-85, Chandler 7-12-1-97. Oakland, Gannon 15-22-0-231.

RECEIVING—Atlanta, Jefferson 7-109, R. Kelly 3-23, Anderson 2-21, Christian 2-17, Dwight 2-(minus 1), Mathis 1-9. Oakland, Brown 6-95, Jordan 2-14, Jett 1-84, Dudley 1-11, Wheatley 1-7, Kaufman 1-7, Brigham 1-6, Ritchie 1-4, Dunn 1-3.

MISSED FIELD GOAL ATTEMPTS—None.

INTERCEPTIONS—Oakland, Allen 1-15.

KICKOFF RETURNS—Atlanta, Vaughn 7-165, E. Williams 1-15. Oakland, Dunn 3-136.

PUNT RETURNS—Atlanta, Dwight 1-0. Oakland, Gordon 3-3.

SACKS—Atlanta, B. Smith 1.5, Crockett 0.5. Oakland, Biekert 1, Dorsett 1, Jackson 1, Bryant 1, Taves 1, Upshaw 1.

GIANTS 31, CARDINALS 7

Sunday, November 26

N.Y. Giants	7	7	7	10	—31
Arizona	0	0	7	0	— 7

First Quarter
NYG—Campbell 5 pass from Collins (Daluiso kick), 5:28.

Second Quarter
NYG—Dayne 1 run (Daluiso kick), 4:45.

Third Quarter
NYG—Barber 23 run (Daluiso kick), 8:36.
Ariz.—Pittman 36 pass from Da. Brown (Blanchard kick), 12:59.

Fourth Quarter
NYG—Toomer 19 run (Daluiso kick), 4:54.
NYG—FG, Daluiso 25, 8:11.
Attendance—42,094.

	N.Y. Giants	Arizona
First downs	25	14
Rushes-yards	40-146	16-88
Passing	225	179
Punt returns	2-2	1-9
Kickoff returns	2-36	6-158
Interception returns	1-4	0-0
Comp.-att.-int.	20-30-0	20-39-1
Sacked-yards lost	1-7	6-32
Punts	4-41	5-44
Fumbles-lost	2-1	3-3
Penalties-yards	4-45	12-99
Time of possession	34:43	25:17

INDIVIDUAL STATISTICS

RUSHING—New York, Dayne 24-85, Barber 12-32, Toomer 2-31, Garrett 2-(minus 2). Arizona, Pittman 13-77, Jones 2-11, Da. Brown 1-0.

PASSING—New York, Collins 20-30-0-232. Arizona, Da. Brown 18-36-1-192, Greisen 2-3-0-19.

RECEIVING—New York, Jurevicius 6-70, Toomer 4-58, Barber 4-52, Mitchell 3-28, Dixon 1-13, Cross 1-6, Campbell 1-5. Arizona, Pittman 10-96, Sanders 3-44, Hardy 2-13, Boston 1-32, Jenkins 1-13, Gedney 1-6, Jones 1-4, Cody 1-3.

MISSED FIELD GOAL ATTEMPTS—None.

INTERCEPTIONS—New York, Stephens 1-4.

KICKOFF RETURNS—New York, Dixon 2-36. Arizona, Jenkins 6-158.

PUNT RETURNS—New York, Barber 2-2. Arizona, Cody 1-9.

SACKS—New York, K. Hamilton 3, Griffin 2, Phillips 1. Arizona, McKinnon 1.

PANTHERS 31, PACKERS 14

Monday, November 27

Green Bay	0	14	0	0	—14
Carolina	14	3	7	7	—31

First Quarter
Car.—Hetherington 3 pass from Beuerlein (Nedney kick), 4:39.
Car.—Muhammad 12 pass from Beuerlein (Nedney kick), 7:57.

Second Quarter
G.B.—Green 26 run (Longwell kick), 3:03.
G.B.—Driver 32 pass from Favre (Longwell kick), 12:58.
Car.—FG, Nedney 26, 13:59.

Third Quarter
Car.—Muhammad 3 pass from Beuerlein (Nedney kick), 1:55.

Fourth Quarter
Car.—Hoover 1 run (Nedney kick), 5:46.
Attendance—73,295.

	Green Bay	Carolina
First downs	20	24
Rushes-yards	14-87	31-133
Passing	239	223
Punt returns	4-25	1-8
Kickoff returns	5-88	3-61
Interception returns	1-46	3-36
Comp.-att.-int.	31-51-3	22-37-1
Sacked-yards lost	3-28	2-20
Punts	5-37	5-38
Fumbles-lost	3-2	2-1
Penalties-yards	6-55	2-25
Time of possession	28:03	31:57

INDIVIDUAL STATISTICS

RUSHING—Green Bay, Green 12-61, Parker 2-26. Carolina, Hoover 24-117, Beuerlein 4-6, Craig 1-5, Bates 1-4, Hetherington 1-1.

PASSING—Green Bay, Favre 31-51-3-267. Carolina, Beuerlein 22-37-1-243.

RECEIVING—Green Bay, Green 9-56, Schroeder 6-70, Freeman 4-43, Parker 4-18, Lee 2-20, Henderson 2-16, Franks 2-11, Driver 1-32, T. Davis 1-1. Carolina, Muhammad 11-131, Hoover 3-41, Hetherington 2-12, Hankton 2-10, Bates 2-7, Mangum 1-31, Crawford 1-11.

MISSED FIELD GOAL ATTEMPTS—None.

INTERCEPTIONS—Green Bay, T. Williams 1-46. Carolina, Hitchcock 1-28, Davis 1-8, Navies 1-0.

KICKOFF RETURNS—Green Bay, Rossum 5-88. Carolina, Bates 3-61.

PUNT RETURNS—Green Bay, Rossum 2-23, Lee 1-2, M. McKenzie 1-0. Carolina, Uwaezuoke 1-8.

SACKS—Green Bay, Wayne 1, Butler 1. Carolina, J. Williams 2, Gilbert 1.

STANDINGS

AFC EAST

	W	L	T	Pct.
Miami	10	3	0	.769
N.Y. Jets	9	4	0	.692
Buffalo	7	6	0	.538
Indianapolis	7	6	0	.538
New England	4	9	0	.308

AFC CENTRAL

	W	L	T	Pct.
Tennessee	10	3	0	.769
Baltimore	9	4	0	.692
Pittsburgh	7	6	0	.538
Jacksonville	6	7	0	.462
Cincinnati	3	10	0	.231
Cleveland	3	11	0	.214

AFC WEST

	W	L	T	Pct.
Oakland	10	3	0	.769
Denver	9	4	0	.692
Kansas City	5	8	0	.385
Seattle	5	8	0	.385
San Diego	1	12	0	.077

NFC EAST

	W	L	T	Pct.
N.Y. Giants	9	4	0	.692
Philadelphia	9	5	0	.643
Washington	7	6	0	.538
Dallas	4	9	0	.308
Arizona	3	10	0	.231

NFC CENTRAL

	W	L	T	Pct.
Minnesota	11	2	0	.846
Detroit	8	5	0	.615
Tampa Bay	8	5	0	.615
Green Bay	6	7	0	.462
Chicago	3	10	0	.231

NFC WEST

	W	L	T	Pct.
New Orleans	8	5	0	.615
St. Louis	8	5	0	.615
Carolina	6	7	0	.462
San Francisco	5	8	0	.385
Atlanta	3	11	0	.214

TOP PERFORMANCES

100-YARD RUSHING GAMES

Player, Team & Opponent	Att.	Yds.	TD
Mike Anderson, Den. at N.O.	37	251	4
Corey Dillon, Cin. vs. Ari.	35	216	1
Warrick Dunn, T.B. vs. Dal.	22	210	2
Curtis Martin, NYJ vs. Ind.	30	203	1
Fred Taylor, Jack. vs. Cle.	30	181	3
Jerome Bettis, Pit. vs. Oak.	24	128	0
Robert Smith, Min. vs. Det.	17	115	2
Eddie George, Ten. at Phi.	32	101	0
Lamar Smith, Mia. at Buf.	28	100	0

300-YARD PASSING GAMES

Player, Team & Opponent	Att.	Comp.	Yds.	TD	Int.
Aaron Brooks, N.O. vs. Den.	48	30	441	2	2
Elvis Grbac, K.C. at N.E.	46	25	350	3	1
Peyton Manning, Ind. at NYJ	51	27	339	2	2
Jeff Garcia, S.F. at S.D.	32	18	323	2	0

100-YARD RECEIVING GAMES

Player, Team & Opponent	Rec.	Yds.	TD
David Boston, Ari. at Cin.	9	184	2
Joe Horn, N.O. vs. Den.	10	170	0
Tony Gonzalez, K.C. at N.E.	11	147	1
Robert Wilson, N.O. vs. Den.	8	122	0
Troy Brown, N.E. vs. K.C.	12	119	1
Bill Schroeder, G.B. at Chi.	6	119	0
Derrick Alexander, K.C. at N.E.	5	116	1
Terrence Wilkins, Ind. at NYJ	7	109	1
Larry Foster, Det. at Min.	8	106	1
Jimmy Smith, Jack. vs. Cle.	6	104	0

RESULTS

THURSDAY, NOVEMBER 30
MINNESOTA 24, Detroit 17
SUNDAY, DECEMBER 3

CAROLINA 16, St. Louis 3
CINCINNATI 24, Arizona 13
Denver 38, NEW ORLEANS 23
Green Bay 28, CHICAGO 6
JACKSONVILLE 48, Cleveland 0
Miami 33, BUFFALO 6
N.Y. Giants 9, WASHINGTON 7
N.Y. JETS 27, Indianapolis 17
PITTSBURGH 21, Oakland 20
San Francisco 45, SAN DIEGO 17
Seattle 30, ATLANTA 10
TAMPA BAY 27, Dallas 7
Tennessee 15, PHILADELPHIA 13
MONDAY, DECEMBER 4
NEW ENGLAND 30, Kansas City 24
Open date: Baltimore

2000 REVIEW Week 14

GAME SUMMARIES

VIKINGS 24, LIONS 17

Thursday, November 30

Detroit	0	3	0	14—17
Minnesota	7	10	0	7—24

First Quarter
Min.—Smith 1 run (Anderson kick), 7:21.

Second Quarter
Min.—C. Carter 4 pass from Culpepper (Anderson kick), 0:04.
Det.—FG, Hanson 52, 13:48.
Min.—FG, Anderson 40, 14:56.

Fourth Quarter
Det.—J. Stewart 3 run (Hanson kick), 1:01.
Min.—Smith 43 run (Anderson kick), 11:56.
Det.—Foster 40 pass from Case (Hanson kick), 14:47.
Attendance—64,214.

	Detroit	Minnesota
First downs	20	19
Rushes-yards	25-139	25-145
Passing	213	160
Punt returns	1-4	3-78
Kickoff returns	4-46	1-22
Interception returns	2-4	1-14
Comp.-att.-int.	25-36-1	19-32-2
Sacked-yards lost	5-33	0-0
Punts	6-44	5-49
Fumbles-lost	1-1	0-0
Penalties-yards	5-35	6-59
Time of possession	34:54	25:06

INDIVIDUAL STATISTICS
RUSHING—Detroit, J. Stewart 15-67, Case 6-62, Batch 1-3, Bates 1-3, Schlesinger 1-3, Irvin 1-1. Minnesota, Smith 17-115, Culpepper 6-25, Kleinsasser 1-4, M. Williams 1-1.
PASSING—Detroit, Case 23-33-1-230, Batch 2-3-0-16. Minnesota, Culpepper 19-32-2-160.
RECEIVING—Detroit, Foster 8-106, Morton 4-53, Moore 3-21, Irvin 2-19, Sloan 2-17, Bates 2-5, Howard 1-10, Rasby 1-6, Stablein 1-5, Schlesinger 1-3. Minnesota, C. Carter 7-45, McWilliams 3-28, Moss 3-26, Walsh 2-21, M. Williams 2-14, Smith 1-13, Hatchette 1-13.
MISSED FIELD GOAL ATTEMPTS—None.
INTERCEPTIONS—Detroit, Aldridge 1-4, C. Brown 1-0. Minnesota, Wong 1-14.
KICKOFF RETURNS—Detroit, Howard 2-35, Schlesinger 1-11, Beverly 1-0. Minnesota, Walters 1-22.
PUNT RETURNS—Detroit, Howard 1-4. Minnesota, Walters 3-78.
SACKS—Minnesota, Randle 2, Hovan 1, Sawyer 1, Paup 1.

SEAHAWKS 30, FALCONS 10

Sunday, December 3

Seattle	17	7	6	0—30
Atlanta	0	3	0	7—10

First Quarter
Sea.—Jackson 6 pass from Kitna (Lindell kick), 3:42.
Sea.—Koonce 27 interception return (Lindell kick), 4:03.
Sea.—FG, Lindell 46, 12:14.

Second Quarter
Atl.—FG, Andersen 36, 11:47.
Sea.—Watters 1 run (Lindell kick), 13:22.

Third Quarter
Sea.—FG, Lindell 45, 3:18.
Sea.—FG, Lindell 29, 10:41.

Fourth Quarter
Atl.—R. Kelly 19 pass from Johnson (Andersen kick), 1:12.
Attendance—44,680.

	Seattle	Atlanta
First downs	17	20
Rushes-yards	25-83	24-97
Passing	252	204
Punt returns	0-0	0-0
Kickoff returns	2-39	7-129
Interception returns	2-41	0-0

	Seattle	Atlanta
Comp.-att.-int.	25-34-0	17-33-2
Sacked-yards lost	0-0	4-29
Punts	2-40	3-36
Fumbles-lost	0-0	2-2
Penalties-yards	5-35	4-25
Time of possession	30:25	29:35

INDIVIDUAL STATISTICS
RUSHING—Seattle, Watters 21-79, Alexander 3-5, Kitna 1-(minus 1). Atlanta, Anderson 12-43, M. Smith 9-42, Johnson 2-9, Christian 1-3.
PASSING—Seattle, Kitna 25-34-0-252. Atlanta, Johnson 17-33-2-233.
RECEIVING—Seattle, Watters 7-58, Jackson 5-98, Mayes 5-36, Strong 3-20, J. Williams 2-20, Dawkins 2-11, Fauria 1-9. Atlanta, R. Kelly 4-44, Jefferson 3-59, Mathis 3-41, Christian 3-16, Dwight 2-37, Kozlowski 2-36.
MISSED FIELD GOAL ATTEMPTS—None.
INTERCEPTIONS—Seattle, Koonce 1-27, Kennedy 1-14.
KICKOFF RETURNS—Seattle, Rogers 2-39. Atlanta, Vaughn 5-94, Dwight 1-20, Kozlowski 1-15.
PUNT RETURNS—None.
SACKS—Seattle, King 2, Simmons 1, W. Williams 1.

BENGALS 24, CARDINALS 13

Sunday, December 3

Arizona	0	0	7	6—13
Cincinnati	7	7	7	3—24

First Quarter
Cin.—McGee 2 pass from S. Mitchell (Rackers kick), 4:14.

Second Quarter
Cin.—Dillon 1 run (Rackers kick), 14:14.

Third Quarter
Cin.—Bennett 7 run (Rackers kick), 3:26.
Ariz.—Boston 38 pass from Plummer (Blanchard kick), 10:52.

Fourth Quarter
Ariz.—Boston 15 pass from Plummer (kick failed), 1:15.
Cin.—FG, Rackers 32, 13:58.
Attendance—50,289.

	Arizona	Cincinnati
First downs	15	27
Rushes-yards	19-72	54-292
Passing	268	106
Punt returns	4-19	1-10
Kickoff returns	5-114	3-38
Interception returns	1-7	1-10
Comp.-att.-int.	22-44-1	11-23-1
Sacked-yards lost	1-10	1-3
Punts	3-39	4-33
Fumbles-lost	1-1	1-0
Penalties-yards	6-39	5-47
Time of possession	24:12	35:48

INDIVIDUAL STATISTICS
RUSHING—Arizona, Pittman 19-72. Cincinnati, Dillon 35-216, Bennett 17-62, N. Williams 1-8, S. Mitchell 1-6.
PASSING—Arizona, Plummer 22-44-1-278. Cincinnati, S. Mitchell 11-23-1-109.
RECEIVING—Arizona, Boston 9-184, Pittman 6-31, Sanders 3-21, Jenkins 2-35, C. Williams 1-5, Gedney 1-2. Cincinnati, Warrick 3-42, McGee 3-23, Yeast 2-15, N. Williams 1-15, Bennett 1-8, Battaglia 1-6.
MISSED FIELD GOAL ATTEMPTS—Arizona, Blanchard 31. Cincinnati, Rackers 36, 45.
INTERCEPTIONS—Arizona, A. Williams 1-7. Cincinnati, T. Carter 1-10.
KICKOFF RETURNS—Arizona, Jenkins 4-97, Bennett 1-17. Cincinnati, Mack 2-26, Griffin 1-12.
PUNT RETURNS—Arizona, Cody 4-19. Cincinnati, Yeast 1-10.
SACKS—Arizona, Fredrickson 1. Cincinnati, Steele 1.

STEELERS 21, RAIDERS 20

Sunday, December 3

Oakland	0	17	0	3—20
Pittsburgh	7	0	7	7—21

– 196 –

First Quarter
Pit.—Shaw 19 pass from Stewart (K. Brown kick), 4:47.

Second Quarter
Oak.—FG, Janikowski 40, 0:49.
Oak.—Allen 27 interception return (Janikowski kick), 1:06.
Oak.—Jordan 21 pass from Gannon (Janikowski kick), 13:54.

Third Quarter
Pit.—Bruener 6 pass from Stewart (K. Brown kick), 9:10.

Fourth Quarter
Pit.—Stewart 17 run (K. Brown kick), 0:12.
Oak.—FG, Janikowski 42, 3:22.
Attendance—55,811.

	Oakland	Pittsburgh
First downs	20	19
Rushes-yards	28-117	32-199
Passing	273	112
Punt returns	2-32	2-23
Kickoff returns	4-80	5-90
Interception returns	1-27	0-0
Comp.-att.-int.	21-40-0	15-26-1
Sacked-yards lost	0-0	5-31
Punts	4-43	7-43
Fumbles-lost	2-2	2-0
Penalties-yards	3-31	3-15
Time of possession	28:07	31:53

INDIVIDUAL STATISTICS
RUSHING—Oakland, Wheatley 16-60, Gannon 6-39, Kaufman 5-16, Crockett 1-2. Pittsburgh, Bettis 24-128, Stewart 3-33, Kreider 2-24, Huntley 2-11, Ward 1-3.
PASSING—Oakland, Gannon 21-40-0-273. Pittsburgh, Stewart 14-23-0-136, Graham 1-3-1-7.
RECEIVING—Oakland, Brown 7-99, Jett 3-42, Rison 3-35, Ritchie 3-22, Dudley 2-39, Jordan 2-30, Dunn 1-6. Pittsburgh, Ward 4-36, Shaw 3-34, Hawkins 3-29, Huntley 2-20, Bruener 2-11, Bettis 1-13.
MISSED FIELD GOAL ATTEMPTS—Oakland, Janikowski 44.
INTERCEPTIONS—Oakland, Allen 1-27.
KICKOFF RETURNS—Oakland, Dunn 4-80. Pittsburgh, Poteat 3-54, Blackwell 2-36.
PUNT RETURNS—Oakland, Gordon 2-32. Pittsburgh, Poteat 2-23.
SACKS—Oakland, Upshaw 2, Biekert 1, Jackson 1, Coleman 1.

BRONCOS 38, SAINTS 23

Sunday, December 3

Denver	7	21	3	7—38
New Orleans	7	6	3	7—23

First Quarter
Den.—Anderson 13 run (Elam kick), 11:37.
N.O.—A. Glover 19 pass from Brooks (Brien kick), 14:25.

Second Quarter
Den.—Anderson 5 run (Elam kick), 5:15.
N.O.—FG, Brien 30, 8:16.
Den.—Carswell 43 pass from Frerotte (Elam kick), 9:06.
Den.—Anderson 7 run (Elam kick), 12:31.
N.O.—FG, Brien 19, 15:00.

Third Quarter
Den.—FG, Elam 22, 4:56.
N.O.—FG, Brien 42, 10:01.

Fourth Quarter
Den.—Anderson 2 run (Elam kick), 6:41.
N.O.—Jackson 28 pass from Brooks (Brien kick), 14:15.
Attendance—64,900.

	Denver	New Orleans
First downs	24	19
Rushes-yards	49-283	9-21
Passing	200	425
Punt returns	3-29	0-0
Kickoff returns	3-69	7-140
Interception returns	2-2	0-0
Comp.-att.-int.	11-16-0	30-48-2
Sacked-yards lost	1-1	3-16
Punts	4-36	3-46
Fumbles-lost	1-0	2-1
Penalties-yards	4-21	6-45
Time of possession	35:03	24:57

INDIVIDUAL STATISTICS
RUSHING—Denver, Anderson 37-251, Coleman 8-31, Griffith 2-1, Frerotte 2-0. New Orleans, Brooks 3-13, Morton 3-5, Moore 1-6, Allen 1-0, T. Smith 1-(minus 3).
PASSING—Denver, Frerotte 11-16-0-201. New Orleans, Brooks 30-48-2-441.
RECEIVING—Denver, Carswell 3-62, McCaffrey 3-56, R. Smith 2-25, Clark 1-44, Griffith 1-9, Anderson 1-5. New Orleans, Horn 10-170, Wilson 8-122, Morton 7-29, A. Glover 2-58, Jackson 2-46, Turley 1-16.
MISSED FIELD GOAL ATTEMPTS—New Orleans, Brien 43.
INTERCEPTIONS—Denver, Spencer 1-2, E. Brown 1-0.
KICKOFF RETURNS—Denver, O'Neal 2-52, D. Smith 1-17. New Orleans, Mathis 5-115, Morton 2-25.
PUNT RETURNS—Denver, O'Neal 3-29.
SACKS—Denver, Pryce 2, Gold 1. New Orleans, D. Howard 1.

PANTHERS 16, RAMS 3

Sunday, December 3

St. Louis	3	0	0	0—3
Carolina	0	0	7	9—16

First Quarter
St.L.—FG, Wilkins 38, 5:01.

Third Quarter
Car.—Hitchcock 88 interception return (Nedney kick), 9:41.

Fourth Quarter
Car.—FG, Nedney 20, 4:42.
Car.—FG, Nedney 23, 10:47.
Car.—FG, Nedney 37, 13:03.
Attendance—73,358.

	St. Louis	Carolina
First downs	15	20
Rushes-yards	16-99	33-68
Passing	179	169
Punt returns	1-0	0-0
Kickoff returns	4-59	2-43
Interception returns	2-25	4-91
Comp.-att.-int.	18-36-4	20-30-2
Sacked-yards lost	2-10	7-26
Punts	1-34	4-31
Fumbles-lost	4-3	0-0
Penalties-yards	9-72	1-10
Time of possession	22:05	37:55

INDIVIDUAL STATISTICS
RUSHING—St. Louis, Faulk 15-94, Hakim 1-5. Carolina, Hoover 22-63, Beuerlein 6-4, Hetherington 3-4, Bates 2-(minus 3).
PASSING—St. Louis, Warner 18-36-4-189. Carolina, Beuerlein 20-30-2-195.
RECEIVING—St. Louis, Bruce 6-74, Faulk 5-34, Hakim 3-28, Holt 2-18, Holcombe 1-19, Proehl 1-16. Carolina, Muhammad 10-95, Hoover 3-7, Hayes 2-23, Bates 1-23, Uwaezuoke 1-21, Mangum 1-13, Crawford 1-9, Craig 1-4.
MISSED FIELD GOAL ATTEMPTS—None.
INTERCEPTIONS—St. Louis, Lyght 1-21, Fletcher 1-4. Carolina, Hitchcock 2-88, Davis 1-3, Evans 1-0.
KICKOFF RETURNS—St. Louis, Bly 4-59. Carolina, Bates 2-43.
PUNT RETURNS—St. Louis, Hakim 1-0.
SACKS—St. Louis, Carter 3, Fletcher 1, Zgonina 1, Wistrom 1, Agnew 1. Carolina, Minter 1, Gilbert 1.

GIANTS 9, REDSKINS 7

Sunday, December 3

N.Y. Giants	0	6	3	0—9
Washington	0	0	0	7—7

Second Quarter
NYG—FG, Daluiso 46, 11:28.
NYG—FG, Daluiso 27, 14:56.

Third Quarter
NYG—FG, Daluiso 28, 8:42.

Fourth Quarter
Was.—Fryar 5 pass from George (Murray kick), 10:12.
Attendance—83,485.

	N.Y. Giants	Washington
First downs	13	15
Rushes-yards	36-141	13-29

	N.Y. Giants	Washington
Passing	164	261
Punt returns	2-25	1-16
Kickoff returns	2-46	4-62
Interception returns	2-21	1-6
Comp.-att.-int.	18-29-1	24-47-2
Sacked-yards lost	0-0	2-8
Punts	5-34	7-39
Fumbles-lost	2-2	1-0
Penalties-yards	3-20	4-35
Time of possession	33:18	26:42

INDIVIDUAL STATISTICS

RUSHING—New York, Dayne 18-57, Barber 14-82, Collins 3-1, Comella 1-1. Washington, Davis 12-29, B. Johnson 1-0.

PASSING—New York, Collins 18-29-1-164. Washington, B. Johnson 14-29-2-126, George 10-18-0-143.

RECEIVING—New York, Jurevicius 6-83, Barber 4-26, Toomer 3-26, Mitchell 2-10, Campbell 1-11, Dixon 1-7, Dayne 1-1. Washington, Connell 5-55, Centers 5-33, Thrash 4-73, Fryar 4-55, Davis 4-21, Alexander 2-32.

MISSED FIELD GOAL ATTEMPTS—Washington, Murray 39, 49.

INTERCEPTIONS—New York, McDaniel 1-17, Garnes 1-4. Washington, Sanders 1-6.

KICKOFF RETURNS—New York, Barber 1-28, Dixon 1-18. Washington, Murrell 2-45, Hicks 1-17, Sellers 1-0.

PUNT RETURNS—New York, Barber 2-25. Washington, Thrash 1-16.

SACKS—New York, Barrow 1, Griffin 1.

DOLPHINS 33, BILLS 6

Sunday, December 3

Miami	7	17	6	3—	33
Buffalo	0	0	0	6—	6

First Quarter
Mia.—L. Smith 6 pass from Fiedler (Mare kick), 4:22.

Second Quarter
Mia.—Gadsden 6 pass from Fiedler (Mare kick), 8:45.
Mia.—FG, Mare 32, 11:55.
Mia.—Shepherd 14 pass from Fiedler (Mare kick), 14:10.

Third Quarter
Mia.—FG, Mare 31, 5:17.
Mia.—FG, Mare 20, 12:38.

Fourth Quarter
Buf.—A. Smith 1 run (run failed), 0:03.
Mia.—FG, Mare 26, 8:31.
Attendance—73,002.

	Miami	Buffalo
First downs	15	14
Rushes-yards	37-133	26-160
Passing	200	36
Punt returns	1-7	1-5
Kickoff returns	2-32	8-144
Interception returns	3-49	0-0
Comp.-att.-int.	13-21-0	8-27-3
Sacked-yards lost	2-14	6-39
Punts	4-40	5-29
Fumbles-lost	1-1	2-0
Penalties-yards	10-86	4-30
Time of possession	33:49	26:11

INDIVIDUAL STATISTICS

RUSHING—Miami, L. Smith 28-100, Johnson 6-23, Denson 2-10, Fiedler 1-0. Buffalo, Bryson 12-88, A. Smith 10-39, Johnson 3-16, Flutie 1-17.

PASSING—Miami, Fiedler 13-21-0-214. Buffalo, Johnson 6-18-2-44, Flutie 2-9-1-31.

RECEIVING—Miami, L. Smith 4-23, Shepherd 3-67, Gadsden 3-43, Martin 1-39, McDuffie 1-24, Konrad 1-18. Buffalo, Moulds 2-31, McDaniel 2-27, Bryson 2-(minus 4), P. Price 1-11, Riemersma 1-10.

MISSED FIELD GOAL ATTEMPTS—Buffalo, Christie 47.

INTERCEPTIONS—Miami, Walker 1-29, Madison 1-20, Surtain 1-0. Buffalo, none.

KICKOFF RETURNS—Miami, Denson 2-32. Buffalo, Black 5-97, Watson 3-47.

PUNT RETURNS—Miami, Ogden 1-7. Buffalo, P. Price 1-5.

SACKS—Miami, Taylor 3, Armstrong 2, Bromell 1. Buffalo, Wiley 1.5, P. Williams 0.5.

49ERS 45, CHARGERS 17

Sunday, December 3

San Francisco	0	17	10	18—	45
San Diego	7	3	0	7—	17

First Quarter
S.D.—Fletcher 7 run (Carney kick), 9:17.

Second Quarter
S.F.—FG, Richey 22, 2:29.
S.F.—Beasley 1 run (Richey kick), 8:56.
S.F.—Rice 1 pass from Garcia (Richey kick), 13:50.
S.D.—FG, Carney 34, 14:54.

Third Quarter
S.F.—FG, Richey 28, 8:29.
S.F.—Garner 4 run (Richey kick), 12:04.

Fourth Quarter
S.D.—Conway 17 pass from Leaf (Carney kick), 2:13.
S.F.—FG, Richey 38, 5:37.
S.F.—Rice 12 pass from Garcia (Stokes pass from Garcia), 6:16.
S.F.—Montgomery 46 interception return (Richey kick), 13:21.
Attendance—57,255.

	San Francisco	San Diego
First downs	19	18
Rushes-yards	28-73	13-49
Passing	312	254
Punt returns	3-34	2-7
Kickoff returns	4-92	9-179
Interception returns	4-115	0-0
Comp.-att.-int.	19-33-0	24-47-4
Sacked-yards lost	2-7	2-12
Punts	4-40	6-42
Fumbles-lost	0-0	1-1
Penalties-yards	8-60	8-68
Time of possession	33:48	26:12

INDIVIDUAL STATISTICS

RUSHING—San Francisco, Garner 13-28, Beasley 5-16, Smith 5-11, Garcia 3-19, Rattay 2-(minus 1). San Diego, Fletcher 12-47, Leaf 1-2.

PASSING—San Francisco, Garcia 18-32-0-323, Rattay 1-1-0-(minus 4). San Diego, Leaf 24-47-4-266.

RECEIVING—San Francisco, Owens 4-93, Garner 4-14, Stokes 3-74, Clark 3-62, Rice 3-41, Streets 1-39, Beasley 1-(minus 4). San Diego, Conway 7-88, F. Jones 7-69, J. Graham 4-67, Gaylor 3-29, Fletcher 2-13, McCrary 1-0.

MISSED FIELD GOAL ATTEMPTS—None.

INTERCEPTIONS—San Francisco, Montgomery 2-63, Bronson 2-52.

KICKOFF RETURNS—San Francisco, Streets 1-36, K. Williams 1-22, Okeafor 1-17, Lewis 1-17. San Diego, R. Jenkins 8-164, Bynum 1-15.

PUNT RETURNS—San Francisco, K. Williams 3-34. San Diego, Jacquet 2-7.

SACKS—San Francisco, Tubbs 1, Montgomery 0.5, Schulters 0.5. San Diego, Seau 1, Dixon 1.

BUCCANEERS 27, COWBOYS 7

Sunday, December 3

Dallas	0	0	7	0—	7
Tampa Bay	17	3	0	7—	27

First Quarter
T.B.—FG, Gramatica 28, 1:12.
T.B.—Dunn 70 run (Gramatica kick), 4:21.
T.B.—Kelly 9 interception return (Gramatica kick), 11:53.

Second Quarter
T.B.—FG, Gramatica 25, 4:23.

Third Quarter
Dal.—E. Smith 4 run (Seder kick), 9:02.

Fourth Quarter
T.B.—Dunn 4 run (Gramatica kick), 7:06.
Attendance—65,621.

	Dallas	Tampa Bay
First downs	19	17
Rushes-yards	28-113	36-250
Passing	153	51
Punt returns	3-7	3-14
Kickoff returns	5-73	2-24
Interception returns	0-0	1-9

	Dallas	Tampa Bay
Comp.-att.-int.	17-33-1	9-15-0
Sacked-yards lost	2-15	2-14
Punts	5-42	5-40
Fumbles-lost	4-3	1-1
Penalties-yards	7-58	6-35
Time of possession	30:17	29:43

INDIVIDUAL STATISTICS

RUSHING—Dallas, E. Smith 20-80, Wiley 6-32, Thomas 1-3, McGarity 1-(minus 2). Tampa Bay, Dunn 22-210, Abdullah 10-38, King 4-2.

PASSING—Dallas, Aikman 16-30-1-158, Wright 1-3-0-10. Tampa Bay, King 9-15-0-65.

RECEIVING—Dallas, McKnight 4-42, McGarity 3-44, Wiley 3-13, Harris 2-11, Tucker 1-15, LaFleur 1-14, E. Smith 1-11, Brazzell 1-10, Hodge 1-8. Tampa Bay, K. Johnson 4-28, Green 2-15, Dunn 2-11, Abdullah 1-11.

MISSED FIELD GOAL ATTEMPTS—Dallas, Seder 34.

INTERCEPTIONS—Tampa Bay, Kelly 1-9.

KICKOFF RETURNS—Dallas, Tucker 4-51, Wiley 1-22. Tampa Bay, Murphy 2-24.

PUNT RETURNS—Dallas, McGarity 3-7. Tampa Bay, Williams 2-14, Yoder 1-0.

SACKS—Dallas, Spellman 1, Underwood 1. Tampa Bay, Ahanotu 1, Jones 1.

PACKERS 28, BEARS 6

Sunday, December 3

Green Bay	0	14	7	7—28
Chicago	0	3	0	3— 6

Second Quarter
G.B.—Green 2 run (Longwell kick), 0:04.
Chi.—FG, Edinger 32, 6:13.
G.B.—Freeman 5 pass from Favre (Longwell kick), 10:37.

Third Quarter
G.B.—Green 8 run (Longwell kick), 8:57.

Fourth Quarter
G.B.—T. Williams 38 interception return (Longwell kick), 1:00.
Chi.—FG, Edinger 46, 5:55.
Attendance—66,944.

	Green Bay	Chicago
First downs	17	17
Rushes-yards	28-81	23-104
Passing	223	226
Punt returns	0-0	1-7
Kickoff returns	2-39	5-103
Interception returns	2-42	0-0
Comp.-att.-int.	19-31-0	22-44-2
Sacked-yards lost	1-2	1-7
Punts	7-34	6-38
Fumbles-lost	0-0	0-0
Penalties-yards	5-42	5-41
Time of possession	30:13	29:47

INDIVIDUAL STATISTICS

RUSHING—Green Bay, Green 20-69, Parker 3-8, Hasselbeck 3-(minus 3), Henderson 1-4, Freeman 1-3. Chicago, Allen 17-80, Matthews 3-23, Milburn 1-6, Bates 1-(minus 2), Kennison 1-(minus 3).

PASSING—Green Bay, Favre 19-31-0-225. Chicago, Matthews 22-43-2-233, Hartsell 0-1-0-0.

RECEIVING—Green Bay, Schroeder 6-119, Freeman 4-51, Henderson 4-10, Green 3-16, Franks 1-20, Wetnight 1-9. Chicago, Allen 11-93, Sinceno 4-47, Kennison 3-22, White 2-20, Booker 1-41, Enis 1-10.

MISSED FIELD GOAL ATTEMPTS—None.

INTERCEPTIONS—Green Bay, T. Williams 1-38, Sharper 1-4.

KICKOFF RETURNS—Green Bay, Rossum 2-39. Chicago, Milburn 5-103.

PUNT RETURNS—Chicago, Milburn 1-7.

SACKS—Green Bay, Lyon 1. Chicago, Culpepper 1.

JAGUARS 48, BROWNS 0

Sunday, December 3

Cleveland	0	0	0	0— 0
Jacksonville	3	17	21	7—48

First Quarter
Jac.—FG, Hollis 40, 4:16.

Second Quarter
Jac.—Taylor 3 run (Hollis kick), 0:04.
Jac.—FG, Hollis 24, 11:51.
Jac.—McCardell 14 pass from Brunell (Hollis kick), 14:32.

Third Quarter
Jac.—Taylor 2 run (Hollis kick), 7:15.
Jac.—Brunell 8 run (Hollis kick), 7:40.
Jac.—Taylor 1 run (Hollis kick), 13:27.

Fourth Quarter
Jac.—Stith 3 run (Hollis kick), 9:33.
Attendance—51,262.

	Cleveland	Jacksonville
First downs	2	28
Rushes-yards	18-62	47-244
Passing	-9	205
Punt returns	3-18	7-70
Kickoff returns	9-127	1-25
Interception returns	0-0	0-0
Comp.-att.-int.	7-18-0	16-33-0
Sacked-yards lost	6-42	2-13
Punts	12-43	5-39
Fumbles-lost	2-1	0-0
Penalties-yards	9-85	9-59
Time of possession	22:49	37:11

INDIVIDUAL STATISTICS

RUSHING—Cleveland, Prentice 10-33, White 7-29, K. Thompson 1-0. Jacksonville, Taylor 30-181, Stith 11-27, Johnson 2-24, Brunell 2-14, Quinn 2-(minus 2).

PASSING—Cleveland, Wynn 5-16-0-17, K. Thompson 1-1-0-8, Pederson 1-1-0-8. Jacksonville, Brunell 15-31-0-165, Martin 1-2-0-53.

RECEIVING—Cleveland, White 2-11, Prentice 2-6, Johnson 1-8, Patten 1-8, Northcutt 1-0. Jacksonville, J. Smith 6-104, McCardell 4-46, Brady 3-41, Soward 2-21, Taylor 1-6.

MISSED FIELD GOAL ATTEMPTS—None.

INTERCEPTIONS—None.

KICKOFF RETURNS—Cleveland, Patten 3-51, White 3-50, Campbell 2-18, Little 1-8. Jacksonville, Stith 1-25.

PUNT RETURNS—Cleveland, Northcutt 2-18, Barnes 1-0. Jacksonville, Barlow 6-64, Soward 1-6.

SACKS—Cleveland, M. Smith 1, Abdullah 1. Jacksonville, Hardy 1, Darius 1, Meier 1, Brackens 1, Smeenge 1, Walker 1.

TITANS 15, EAGLES 13

Sunday, December 3

Tennessee	0	6	3	6—15
Philadelphia	3	3	0	7—13

First Quarter
Phi.—FG, Akers 23, 4:12.

Second Quarter
Ten.—FG, Del Greco 26, 4:14.
Ten.—FG, Del Greco 42, 13:30.
Phi.—FG, Akers 40, 14:42.

Third Quarter
Ten.—FG, Del Greco 22, 6:37.

Fourth Quarter
Ten.—FG, Del Greco 44, 9:37.
Phi.—McNabb 2 run (Akers kick), 11:49.
Ten.—FG, Del Greco 50, 15:00.
Attendance—65,639.

	Tennessee	Philadelphia
First downs	24	14
Rushes-yards	36-118	17-56
Passing	213	206
Punt returns	3-28	2-6
Kickoff returns	3-56	5-89
Interception returns	0-0	0-0
Comp.-att.-int.	24-39-0	18-31-0
Sacked-yards lost	2-11	5-33
Punts	5-37	8-41
Fumbles-lost	1-1	1-0
Penalties-yards	1-5	6-34
Time of possession	38:42	21:18

INDIVIDUAL STATISTICS

RUSHING—Tennessee, E. George 32-101, McNair 4-17. Philadelphia, McNabb 7-39, Autry 6-14, Pritchett 3-0, Mitchell 1-3.

PASSING—Tennessee, McNair 23-37-0-210, O'Donnell 1-2-0-14. Philadelphia, McNabb 18-31-0-239.

RECEIVING—Tennessee, Mason 7-93, Wycheck 7-59, E. George 4-24, Sanders 3-22, Neal 2-4, Thigpen 1-22. Philadelphia, Small 5-55, Lewis 4-55, C. Johnson 4-41, Autry 2-30, Pinkston 1-45, C. Martin 1-8, Brown 1-5.

MISSED FIELD GOAL ATTEMPTS—None.

INTERCEPTIONS—None.

KICKOFF RETURNS—Tennessee, Mason 3-56. Philadelphia, Mitchell 5-89.

PUNT RETURNS—Tennessee, Mason 3-28. Philadelphia, Mitchell 2-6.

SACKS—Tennessee, Holmes 2, Kearse 1, Favors 1, Salave'a 1. Philadelphia, H. Douglas 1, Team 1.

JETS 27, COLTS 17

Sunday, December 3

Indianapolis	0	0	10	7—17
N.Y. Jets	14	6	0	7—27

First Quarter
NYJ—Chrebet 11 pass from Testaverde (Hall kick), 6:13.
NYJ—Ward 13 pass from Testaverde (Hall kick), 10:25.

Second Quarter
NYJ—FG, Hall 45, 4:35.
NYJ—FG, Hall 21, 15:00.

Third Quarter
Ind.—FG, Vanderjagt 32, 2:38.
Ind.—Harrison 17 pass from Manning (Vanderjagt kick), 13:59.

Fourth Quarter
Ind.—Wilkins 43 pass from Manning (Vanderjagt kick), 5:10.
NYJ—Martin 2 run (Hall kick), 11:43.
Attendance—78,138.

	Indianapolis	N.Y. Jets
First downs	21	26
Rushes-yards	12-49	39-211
Passing	326	280
Punt returns	1-9	1-18
Kickoff returns	5-119	4-62
Interception returns	1-35	2-63
Comp.-att.-int.	27-51-2	26-41-1
Sacked-yards lost	3-13	2-15
Punts	5-37	5-30
Fumbles-lost	2-1	0-0
Penalties-yards	2-20	4-54
Time of possession	18:35	41:25

INDIVIDUAL STATISTICS

RUSHING—Indianapolis, James 11-49, Manning 1-0. New York, Martin 30-203, R. Anderson 4-9, Parmalee 2-5, Testaverde 1-3, Sowell 1-1, Stone 1-(minus 10).

PASSING—Indianapolis, Manning 27-51-2-339. New York, Testaverde 26-41-1-295.

RECEIVING—Indianapolis, Harrison 8-90, Wilkins 7-109, Pathon 6-73, James 3-31, Pollard 2-26, Dilger 1-10. New York, Chrebet 8-77, R. Anderson 5-75, W. Hayes 4-84, Martin 4-9, Ward 3-31, Becht 2-19.

MISSED FIELD GOAL ATTEMPTS—New York, Hall 49.

INTERCEPTIONS—Indianapolis, Macklin 1-35. New York, V. Green 1-43, N. Ferguson 1-20.

KICKOFF RETURNS—Indianapolis, Pathon 4-95, Wilkins 1-24. New York, Stone 3-62, Scott 1-0.

PUNT RETURNS—Indianapolis, Wilkins 1-9. New York, Ward 1-18.

SACKS—Indianapolis, Belser 1, M. Thomas 1. New York, Cox 2, Lewis 1.

PATRIOTS 30, CHIEFS 24

Monday, December 4

Kansas City	3	7	0	14—24
New England	10	10	7	3—30

First Quarter
N.E.—FG, Vinatieri 48, 2:42.
K.C.—FG, Peterson 42, 6:33.
N.E.—Faulk 1 run (Vinatieri kick), 13:31.

Second Quarter
K.C.—Alexander 81 pass from Grbac (Peterson kick), 6:21.
N.E.—Brown 17 pass from Bledsoe (Vinatieri kick), 13:00.
N.E.—FG, Vinatieri 53, 15:00.

Third Quarter
N.E.—Wiggins 1 pass from Bledsoe (Vinatieri kick), 7:51.

Fourth Quarter
K.C.—Gonzalez 4 pass from Grbac (Peterson kick), 1:17.
N.E.—FG, Vinatieri 27, 7:37.
K.C.—Lockett 19 pass from Grbac (Peterson kick), 11:02.
Attendance—60,292.

	Kansas City	New England
First downs	18	24
Rushes-yards	19-68	31-105
Passing	350	263
Punt returns	3-32	2-34
Kickoff returns	6-157	5-133
Interception returns	0-0	1-56
Comp.-att.-int.	25-46-1	33-48-0
Sacked-yards lost	0-0	3-19
Punts	6-38	6-39
Fumbles-lost	2-2	1-1
Penalties-yards	7-40	5-65
Time of possession	23:18	36:42

INDIVIDUAL STATISTICS

RUSHING—Kansas City, Richardson 6-30, Anders 6-19, Grbac 4-17, Bennett 3-2. New England, Faulk 22-52, Bledsoe 3-5, Glenn 2-37, Pass 2-9, Shaw 2-2.

PASSING—Kansas City, Grbac 25-46-1-350. New England, Bledsoe 33-48-0-282.

RECEIVING—Kansas City, Gonzalez 11-147, Alexander 5-116, Richardson 3-32, Morris 3-17, Lockett 2-34, Anders 1-4. New England, Brown 12-119, Wiggins 5-41, Faulk 5-32, Rutledge 3-27, Jackson 2-17, Glenn 2-15, T. Carter 2-10, Simmons 1-14, Pass 1-7.

MISSED FIELD GOAL ATTEMPTS—New England, Vinatieri 37.

INTERCEPTIONS—New England, Smith 1-56.

KICKOFF RETURNS—Kansas City, Cloud 6-157. New England, Jackson 4-117, T. Carter 1-16.

PUNT RETURNS—Kansas City, Lockett 3-32. New England, Faulk 2-34.

SACKS—Kansas City, Patton 1, McGlockton 1, Hicks 1.

WEEK 15

STANDINGS

AFC EAST

	W	L	T	Pct.
Miami	10	4	0	.714
N.Y. Jets	9	5	0	.643
Indianapolis	8	6	0	.571
Buffalo	7	7	0	.500
New England	4	10	0	.286

AFC CENTRAL

	W	L	T	Pct.
Tennessee	11	3	0	.786
Baltimore	10	4	0	.714
Jacksonville	7	7	0	.500
Pittsburgh	7	7	0	.500
Cincinnati	3	11	0	.214
Cleveland	3	12	0	.200

AFC WEST

	W	L	T	Pct.
Oakland	11	3	0	.786
Denver	10	4	0	.714
Kansas City	6	8	0	.429
Seattle	5	9	0	.357
San Diego	1	13	0	.071

NFC EAST

	W	L	T	Pct.
N.Y. Giants	10	4	0	.714
Philadelphia	10	5	0	.667
Washington	7	7	0	.500
Dallas	5	9	0	.357
Arizona	3	11	0	.214

NFC CENTRAL

	W	L	T	Pct.
Minnesota	11	3	0	.786
Tampa Bay	9	5	0	.643
Detroit	8	6	0	.571
Green Bay	7	7	0	.500
Chicago	4	10	0	.286

NFC WEST

	W	L	T	Pct.
New Orleans	9	5	0	.643
St. Louis	9	5	0	.643
Carolina	6	8	0	.429
San Francisco	5	9	0	.357
Atlanta	3	11	0	.214

TOP PERFORMANCES

100-YARD RUSHING GAMES

Player, Team & Opponent	Att.	Yds.	TD
Emmitt Smith, Dal. vs. Wash.	23	150	1
Fred Taylor, Jack. vs. Ari.	23	137	2
Marshall Faulk, St.L. vs. Min.	25	135	4
Mike Anderson, Den. vs. Sea.	29	131	2
Ahman Green, G.B. vs. Det.	27	118	1
Edgerrin James, Ind. vs. Buf.	27	111	3
Aaron Brooks, N.O. at S.F.	11	108	0

300-YARD PASSING GAMES

Player, Team & Opponent	Att.	Comp.	Yds.	TD	Int.
Donovan McNabb, Phi. at Cle.	36	23	390	4	0
Kurt Warner, St.L. vs. Min.	32	27	346	0	0
Kerry Collins, NYG vs. Pit.	35	24	333	2	0
Elvis Grbac, K.C. vs. Car.	44	31	315	1	2
Doug Pederson, Cle. vs. Phi.	40	29	309	1	2
Jeff Garcia, S.F. vs. N.O.	38	25	305	2	2

100-YARD RECEIVING GAMES

Player, Team & Opponent	Rec.	Yds.	TD
Torry Holt, St.L. vs. Min.	9	172	0
Jimmy Smith, Jack. vs. Ari.	8	147	1
Amani Toomer, NYG vs. Pit.	9	136	1
Terrell Owens, S.F. vs. N.O.	6	129	1
Ed McCaffrey, Den. vs. Sea.	8	112	1
Joe Horn, N.O. at S.F.	5	105	0
Richie Anderson, NYJ at Oak.	8	103	0
David Patten, Cle. vs. Phi.	7	103	1
Muhsin Muhammad, Car. at K.C.	8	102	0
Eddie Kennison, Chi. vs. N.E.	8	100	1
Chad Lewis, Phi. at Cle.	5	100	0

RESULTS

SUNDAY, DECEMBER 10
BALTIMORE 24, San Diego 3
CHICAGO 24, New England 17
DALLAS 32, Washington 13
DENVER 31, Seattle 24
GREEN BAY 26, Detroit 13
JACKSONVILLE 44, Arizona 10
KANSAS CITY 15, Carolina 14
New Orleans 31, SAN FRANCISCO 27
N.Y. GIANTS 30, Pittsburgh 10
OAKLAND 31, N.Y. Jets 7
Philadelphia 35, CLEVELAND 24
ST. LOUIS 40, Minnesota 29
Tampa Bay 16, MIAMI 13
TENNESSEE 35, Cincinnati 3

MONDAY, DECEMBER 11
INDIANAPOLIS 44, Buffalo 20
  Open date: Atlanta

BEARS 24, PATRIOTS 17

Sunday, December 10

New England	0	10	0	7—17
Chicago	3	7	7	7—24

First Quarter
Chi.—FG, Edinger 24, 8:54.

Second Quarter
N.E.—Glenn 12 pass from Bledsoe (Vinatieri kick), 1:50.
N.E.—FG, Vinatieri 40, 9:29.
Chi.—Kennison 9 pass from Matthews (Edinger kick), 14:50.

Third Quarter
Chi.—Allen 16 run (Edinger kick), 4:08.

Fourth Quarter
Chi.—Allen 6 pass from Matthews (Edinger kick), 0:04.
N.E.—Brown 7 pass from Bledsoe (Vinatieri kick), 4:07.
Attendance—66,944.

	New England	Chicago
First downs	15	21
Rushes-yards	13-38	39-102
Passing	207	237
Punt returns	3-14	4-37
Kickoff returns	5-64	4-100
Interception returns	0-0	0-0
Comp.-att.-int.	25-46-0	22-27-0
Sacked-yards lost	2-18	1-2
Punts	6-43	5-35
Fumbles-lost	1-0	1-1
Penalties-yards	7-60	3-35
Time of possession	22:50	37:10

INDIVIDUAL STATISTICS
RUSHING—New England, Redmond 6-18, R. Harris 3-14, Bledsoe 3-6, Faulk 1-0. Chicago, Allen 37-97, Barnes 1-3, Matthews 1-2.
PASSING—New England, Bledsoe 25-46-0-225. Chicago, Matthews 22-27-0-239.
RECEIVING—New England, Glenn 5-63, Brown 5-46, Wiggins 4-39, Redmond 4-22, Jackson 3-27, Faulk 2-27, R. Harris 2-1. Chicago, Kennison 8-100, Sinceno 3-36, Allen 3-27, Booker 2-24, Dragos 2-14, Bates 1-16, Brooks 1-9, Milburn 1-8, White 1-5.
MISSED FIELD GOAL ATTEMPTS—Chicago, Edinger 47.
INTERCEPTIONS—None.
KICKOFF RETURNS—New England, Jackson 3-55, Brown 1-9, Hamilton 1-0. Chicago, Milburn 4-100.
PUNT RETURNS—New England, Brown 3-14. Chicago, Milburn 4-37.
SACKS—New England, Hamilton 1. Chicago, Colvin 1, Simmons 0.5, B. Robinson 0.5.

EAGLES 35, BROWNS 24

Sunday, December 10

Philadelphia	7	14	14	0—35
Cleveland	0	14	0	10—24

First Quarter
Phi.—Autry 3 run (Akers kick), 11:58.

Second Quarter
Cle.—Patten 9 pass from Pederson (P. Dawson kick), 0:40.
Cle.—Prentice 1 run (P. Dawson kick), 4:47.
Phi.—Small 24 pass from McNabb (Akers kick), 6:54.
Phi.—Small 8 pass from McNabb (Akers kick), 13:56.

Third Quarter
Phi.—C. Johnson 11 pass from McNabb (Akers kick), 2:47.
Phi.—C. Johnson 38 pass from McNabb (Akers kick), 10:57.

Fourth Quarter
Cle.—FG, P. Dawson 29, 3:38.
Cle.—Prentice 1 run (P. Dawson kick), 6:06.
Attendance—72,318.

	Philadelphia	Cleveland
First downs	23	25
Rushes-yards	15-41	30-101
Passing	350	317
Punt returns	1-15	1-13
Kickoff returns	5-126	6-140
Interception returns	3-33	0-0
Comp.-att.-int.	23-36-0	30-43-3
Sacked-yards lost	5-40	3-15
Punts	4-39	3-39
Fumbles-lost	2-2	6-1
Penalties-yards	4-21	6-55
Time of possession	25:43	34:17

INDIVIDUAL STATISTICS
RUSHING—Philadelphia, Autry 10-28, McNabb 3-12, Pritchett 2-1. Cleveland, Prentice 17-46, Northcutt 7-37, White 3-15, Pederson 3-3.
PASSING—Philadelphia, McNabb 23-36-0-390. Cleveland, Pederson 29-40-2-309, Johnson 1-3-1-23.
RECEIVING—Philadelphia, Small 7-92, Lewis 5-100, C. Johnson 5-93, Pinkston 2-56, C. Martin 2-30, Pritchett 1-11, Thomason 1-8. Cleveland, Patten 7-103, Johnson 6-76, Northcutt 5-44, Prentice 4-29, Shea 3-33, Campbell 3-17, Saleh 1-22, B. Brown 1-8.
MISSED FIELD GOAL ATTEMPTS—None.
INTERCEPTIONS—Philadelphia, Dawkins 1-32, Taylor 1-1, Vincent 1-0.
KICKOFF RETURNS—Philadelphia, Mitchell 5-126. Cleveland, White 6-140.
PUNT RETURNS—Philadelphia, Mitchell 1-15. Cleveland, Northcutt 1-13.
SACKS—Philadelphia, Trotter 1, H. Douglas 1, Simon 1. Cleveland, Spriggs 2, McCutcheon 1, J. Miller 1, K. McKenzie 1.

JAGUARS 44, CARDINALS 10

Sunday, December 10

Arizona	0	3	0	7—10
Jacksonville	10	17	10	7—44

First Quarter
Jac.—FG, Hollis 36, 5:49.
Jac.—Taylor 1 run (Hollis kick), 7:45.

Second Quarter
Jac.—Brady 8 pass from Brunell (Hollis kick), 2:11.
Jac.—Taylor 4 run (Hollis kick), 8:29.
Ariz.—FG, Blanchard 32, 13:52.
Jac.—FG, Hollis 50, 14:56.

Third Quarter
Jac.—FG, Hollis 40, 5:56.
Jac.—McCardell 25 pass from Brunell (Hollis kick), 9:27.

Fourth Quarter
Jac.—J. Smith 65 pass from Martin (Hollis kick), 0:33.
Ariz.—Sanders 26 pass from Greisen (Blanchard kick), 5:15.
Attendance—53,472.

	Arizona	Jacksonville
First downs	11	25
Rushes-yards	19-40	45-214
Passing	149	255
Punt returns	1-11	4-33
Kickoff returns	9-213	2-36
Interception returns	0-0	1-12
Comp.-att.-int.	15-26-1	15-21-0
Sacked-yards lost	4-32	0-0
Punts	5-48	1-55
Fumbles-lost	0-0	0-0
Penalties-yards	4-53	2-15
Time of possession	25:04	34:56

INDIVIDUAL STATISTICS
RUSHING—Arizona, Pittman 11-(minus 1), Jones 7-40, Greisen 1-1. Jacksonville, Taylor 23-137, Johnson 13-39, Martin 3-(minus 3), Brunell 2-30, J. Williams 2-8, Stith 2-3.
PASSING—Arizona, Da. Brown 11-19-1-135, Greisen 4-7-0-46. Jacksonville, Brunell 13-18-0-182, Martin 2-3-0-73.
RECEIVING—Arizona, Sanders 4-90, Boston 2-25, Pittman 2-17, Hardy 2-12, Jenkins 2-12, Cody 1-11, McKinley 1-9, Gedney 1-5. Jacksonville, J. Smith 8-147, McCardell 3-65, Brady 2-21, Taylor 1-14, Johnson 1-8.
MISSED FIELD GOAL ATTEMPTS—Arizona, Blanchard 47.
INTERCEPTIONS—Jacksonville, Boyer 1-12.
KICKOFF RETURNS—Arizona, Jenkins 8-193, McKinley 1-20. Jacksonville, Stith 2-36.
PUNT RETURNS—Arizona, Cody 1-11. Jacksonville, McCardell 3-25, Barlow 1-8.
SACKS—Jacksonville, Boyer 2, Walker 1, Brackens 1.

GIANTS 30, STEELERS 10

Sunday, December 10

Pittsburgh..........................	0	3	0	7—10
N.Y. Giants	3	10	7	10—30

First Quarter
NYG—FG, Daluiso 38, 2:06.

Second Quarter
NYG—FG, Daluiso 40, 0:13.
NYG—Barber 3 run (Daluiso kick), 6:33.
Pit.—FG, K. Brown 32, 14:25.

Third Quarter
NYG—Hilliard 9 pass from Collins (Daluiso kick), 9:36.

Fourth Quarter
NYG—FG, Daluiso 21, 1:33.
NYG—Toomer 2 pass from Collins (Daluiso kick), 12:26.
Pit.—Shaw 5 pass from Stewart (K. Brown kick), 13:56.
Attendance—78,164.

	Pittsburgh	N.Y. Giants
First downs	17	20
Rushes-yards	20-47	26-68
Passing	217	326
Punt returns	0-0	3-27
Kickoff returns	7-132	2-58
Interception returns	0-0	1-0
Comp.-att.-int.	20-34-1	24-35-0
Sacked-yards lost	2-7	1-7
Punts	3-45	1-25
Fumbles-lost	0-0	0-0
Penalties-yards	5-42	6-91
Time of possession	27:46	32:14

INDIVIDUAL STATISTICS
RUSHING—Pittsburgh, Bettis 17-39, Stewart 3-8. New York, Barber 12-22, Dayne 11-20, Garrett 2-(minus 2), Toomer 1-28.
PASSING—Pittsburgh, Stewart 20-34-1-224. New York, Collins 24-35-0-333.
RECEIVING—Pittsburgh, Shaw 6-88, Ward 6-64, Blackwell 2-23, Kreider 2-10, Hawkins 2-7, Edwards 1-25, Bettis 1-7. New York, Toomer 9-136, Barber 6-75, Hilliard 5-90, Mitchell 2-25, Jurevicius 1-6, Comella 1-1.
MISSED FIELD GOAL ATTEMPTS—Pittsburgh, K. Brown 36, 44.
INTERCEPTIONS—New York, Stephens 1-0.
KICKOFF RETURNS—Pittsburgh, Poteat 5-88, Blackwell 2-44. New York, Stoutmire 1-47, Comella 1-11.
PUNT RETURNS—New York, Barber 3-27.
SACKS—Pittsburgh, Battles 1. New York, Jones 1, Armstead 1.

TITANS 35, BENGALS 3

Sunday, December 10

Cincinnati	0	3	0	0— 3
Tennessee........................	14	7	7	7—35

First Quarter
Ten.—Thigpen 56 pass from McNair (Del Greco kick), 6:15.
Ten.—E. George 5 run (Del Greco kick), 12:12.

Second Quarter
Cin.—FG, Rackers 45, 1:03.
Ten.—E. George 7 pass from McNair (Del Greco kick), 6:03.

Third Quarter
Ten.—E. George 3 pass from McNair (Del Greco kick), 6:07.

Fourth Quarter
Ten.—Neal 1 pass from O'Donnell (Del Greco kick), 6:37.
Attendance—68,498.

	Cincinnati	Tennessee
First downs	9	21
Rushes-yards	25-60	36-112
Passing	111	331
Punt returns	3-15	3-23
Kickoff returns	6-120	2-58
Interception returns	0-0	0-0
Comp.-att.-int.	12-26-0	23-33-0
Sacked-yards lost	4-20	2-14
Punts	9-45	5-42
Fumbles-lost	0-0	4-1
Penalties-yards	4-34	7-39
Time of possession	25:12	34:48

INDIVIDUAL STATISTICS
RUSHING—Cincinnati, Dillon 18-42, Bennett 4-(minus 3), S. Mitchell 2-14, N. Williams 1-7. Tennessee, E. George 24-81, Thomas 5-23, McNair 3-10, O'Donnell 3-(minus 3), Mason 1-1.
PASSING—Cincinnati, S. Mitchell 12-26-0-131. Tennessee, McNair 16-26-0-229, O'Donnell 6-6-0-93, Wycheck 1-1-0-23.
RECEIVING—Cincinnati, Warrick 2-32, Bennett 2-18, Dillon 2-8, Yeast 1-27, Battaglia 1-15, Griffin 1-9, McGee 1-9, Bush 1-8, Farmer 1-5. Tennessee, Mason 5-92, Wycheck 5-41, E. George 4-20, Thigpen 2-89, Pickens 2-56, Sanders 2-38, Kinney 1-9, Neal 1-1, Thomas 1-(minus 1).
MISSED FIELD GOAL ATTEMPTS—None.
INTERCEPTIONS—None.
KICKOFF RETURNS—Cincinnati, Mack 5-103, Griffin 1-17. Tennessee, Mason 2-58.
PUNT RETURNS—Cincinnati, Yeast 3-15. Tennessee, Mason 2-23, Coleman 1-0.
SACKS—Cincinnati, Wilson 2. Tennessee, Favors 2, Ford 1, Kearse 1.

RAMS 40, VIKINGS 29

Sunday, December 10

Minnesota..........................	0	7	14	8—29
St. Louis...........................	14	6	13	7—40

First Quarter
St.L.—Faulk 1 run (Wilkins kick), 6:04.
St.L.—Faulk 1 run (Wilkins kick), 10:06.

Second Quarter
St.L.—FG, Wilkins 26, 1:12.
Min.—McWilliams 22 pass from Culpepper (Anderson kick), 7:46.
St.L.—FG, Wilkins 19, 13:49.

Third Quarter
Min.—Culpepper 8 run (Anderson kick), 3:40.
St.L.—Faulk 5 run (pass failed), 6:41.
St.L.—Faulk 1 run (Wilkins kick), 10:24.
Min.—C. Carter 2 pass from Culpepper (Anderson kick), 14:28.

Fourth Quarter
St.L.—Watson 6 run (Wilkins kick), 6:50.
Min.—Moss 32 pass from Culpepper (Moss pass from Culpepper), 12:33.
Attendance—66,273.

	Minnesota	St. Louis
First downs	23	32
Rushes-yards	19-104	34-162
Passing	208	346
Punt returns	0-0	4-61
Kickoff returns	5-127	3-38
Interception returns	0-0	0-0
Comp.-att.-int.	21-33-0	27-32-0
Sacked-yards lost	4-13	0-0
Punts	5-50	1-38
Fumbles-lost	1-0	0-0
Penalties-yards	7-60	7-43
Time of possession	25:36	34:24

INDIVIDUAL STATISTICS
RUSHING—Minnesota, Smith 15-67, Culpepper 4-37. St. Louis, Faulk 25-135, Warner 5-1, Holcombe 2-14, Conwell 1-6, Watson 1-6.
PASSING—Minnesota, Culpepper 21-33-0-221. St. Louis, Warner 27-32-0-346.
RECEIVING—Minnesota, C. Carter 7-66, McWilliams 5-53, Moss 4-63, Smith 2-0, Kleinsasser 1-15, Walsh 1-13, Hatchette 1-11. St. Louis, Holt 9-172, Bruce 7-74, Faulk 6-43, Robinson 2-34, Proehl 2-18, Hakim 1-5.
MISSED FIELD GOAL ATTEMPTS—None.
INTERCEPTIONS—None.
KICKOFF RETURNS—Minnesota, Walters 5-127. St. Louis, Blevins 2-36, Proehl 1-2.
PUNT RETURNS—St. Louis, Hakim 4-61.
SACKS—St. Louis, Fletcher 2, Wistrom 1, Little 1.

COWBOYS 32, REDSKINS 13

Sunday, December 10

Washington	0	7	0	6—13
Dallas...............................	6	6	10	10—32

First Quarter
Dal.—FG, Seder 33, 3:36.
Dal.—FG, Seder 19, 8:35.

Second Quarter

Was.—Davis 1 run (Murray kick), 7:03.
Dal.—McGarity 22 run (pass failed), 9:18.

Third Quarter

Dal.—E. Smith 2 run (Seder kick), 3:38.
Dal.—FG, Seder 20, 11:44.

Fourth Quarter

Dal.—Tucker 17 run (Seder kick), 7:28.
Was.—Fryar 32 pass from George (pass failed), 10:58.
Dal.—FG, Seder 43, 13:05.
 Attendance—63,467.

	Washington	Dallas
First downs	17	19
Rushes-yards	22-79	43-242
Passing	191	72
Punt returns	1-11	5-79
Kickoff returns	8-143	2-48
Interception returns	0-0	1-0
Comp.-att.-int.	19-33-1	5-8-0
Sacked-yards lost	5-44	3-17
Punts	6-42	3-45
Fumbles-lost	2-1	1-0
Penalties-yards	11-121	6-35
Time of possession	29:00	31:00

INDIVIDUAL STATISTICS

RUSHING—Washington, Davis 16-57, Centers 3-14, George 2-4, Murrell 1-4. Dallas, E. Smith 23-150, Wiley 11-38, Wright 5-1, Tucker 2-29, McGarity 1-22, Aikman 1-2.

PASSING—Washington, George 19-33-1-235. Dallas, Wright 3-5-0-73, Aikman 2-3-0-16.

RECEIVING—Washington, Thrash 5-62, Centers 5-54, Fryar 3-56, Reed 2-24, Alexander 2-8, Bailey 1-24, Davis 1-7. Dallas, McKnight 2-58, Harris 2-20, LaFleur 1-11.

MISSED FIELD GOAL ATTEMPTS—Dallas, Seder 47.

INTERCEPTIONS—Dallas, McNeil 1-0.

KICKOFF RETURNS—Washington, Murrell 4-67, Thrash 3-65, Sellers 1-11. Dallas, Tucker 2-48.

PUNT RETURNS—Washington, Sanders 1-11. Dallas, McGarity 5-79.

SACKS—Washington, Coleman 1, Wilkinson 1, N. Harrison 1. Dallas, Ekuban 2, Spellman 2, Ellis 1.

CHIEFS 15, PANTHERS 14

Sunday, December 10

Carolina	0	7	7	0—14
Kansas City	0	3	3	9—15

Second Quarter

Car.—Hetherington 1 run (Nedney kick), 11:00.
K.C.—FG, Peterson 35, 13:27.

Third Quarter

Car.—Mangum 15 pass from Beuerlein (Nedney kick), 5:28.
K.C.—FG, Peterson 24, 11:14.

Fourth Quarter

K.C.—Gonzalez 6 pass from Grbac (pass failed), 2:29.
K.C.—FG, Peterson 33, 11:17.
 Attendance—77,481.

	Carolina	Kansas City
First downs	21	26
Rushes-yards	16-23	26-138
Passing	234	315
Punt returns	0-0	2-20
Kickoff returns	5-81	3-58
Interception returns	2-17	1-0
Comp.-att.-int.	23-31-1	31-44-2
Sacked-yards lost	6-18	0-0
Punts	5-42	0-0
Fumbles-lost	0-0	2-2
Penalties-yards	5-47	5-35
Time of possession	27:54	32:06

INDIVIDUAL STATISTICS

RUSHING—Carolina, Hoover 10-13, Hetherington 5-8, Beuerlein 1-2. Kansas City, Richardson 17-89, Grbac 5-20, Moreau 3-3, Alexander 1-26.

PASSING—Carolina, Beuerlein 23-31-1-252. Kansas City, Grbac 31-44-2-315.

RECEIVING—Carolina, Muhammad 8-102, Hayes 5-77, Hoover 4-27, Mangum 3-32, Crawford 1-11, Bates 1-3, Craig 1-0. Kansas City, Gonzalez 10-96, Richardson 8-56, Alexander 6-81, Morris 4-38, Lockett 2-24, Dunn 1-20.

MISSED FIELD GOAL ATTEMPTS—Carolina, Nedney 48.

INTERCEPTIONS—Carolina, Evans 1-17, Robinson 1-0. Kansas City, Woods 1-0.

KICKOFF RETURNS—Carolina, Bates 3-46, Byrd 2-35. Kansas City, Cloud 2-40, L. Parker 1-18.

PUNT RETURNS—Kansas City, Lockett 2-20.

SACKS—Kansas City, Clemons 2, Hicks 2, McGlockton 1, Browning 1.

RAVENS 24, CHARGERS 3

Sunday, December 10

San Diego	0	3	0	0— 3
Baltimore	3	7	14	0—24

First Quarter

Bal.—FG, Stover 32, 11:25.

Second Quarter

Bal.—Ismail 28 pass from Dilfer (Stover kick), 10:44.
S.D.—FG, Carney 47, 14:12.

Third Quarter

Bal.—Ja. Lewis 1 run (Stover kick), 4:13.
Bal.—Stokley 22 pass from Dilfer (Stover kick), 10:09.
 Attendance—68,805.

	San Diego	Baltimore
First downs	9	19
Rushes-yards	26-64	40-110
Passing	64	166
Punt returns	3-10	2-52
Kickoff returns	5-96	2-50
Interception returns	2-19	1-9
Comp.-att.-int.	9-23-1	16-24-2
Sacked-yards lost	2-14	3-21
Punts	4-45	3-40
Fumbles-lost	5-4	2-1
Penalties-yards	4-20	3-15
Time of possession	22:24	37:36

INDIVIDUAL STATISTICS

RUSHING—San Diego, Fletcher 16-44, Fazande 7-17, Leaf 3-3. Baltimore, Ja. Lewis 29-91, Holmes 7-16, Dilfer 3-2, Gash 1-1.

PASSING—San Diego, Leaf 9-23-1-78. Baltimore, Dilfer 16-24-2-187.

RECEIVING—San Diego, Conway 3-32, Fletcher 2-5, Fazande 1-17, F. Jones 1-11, McCrary 1-7, Heiden 1-6. Baltimore, Ismail 6-80, Stokley 4-55, Ja. Lewis 3-39, Holmes 2-6, Sharpe 1-7.

MISSED FIELD GOAL ATTEMPTS—None.

INTERCEPTIONS—San Diego, Harrison 2-19. Baltimore, McAlister 1-9.

KICKOFF RETURNS—San Diego, R. Jenkins 4-82, Bynum 1-14. Baltimore, Harris 2-50.

PUNT RETURNS—San Diego, Jacquet 2-10, D. Jenkins 1-0. Baltimore, J. Lewis 2-32.

SACKS—San Diego, Fontenot 1, Parrella 1, Mickell 1. Baltimore, McCrary 1, Brown 1.

BRONCOS 31, SEAHAWKS 24

Sunday, December 10

Seattle	3	0	7	14—24
Denver	7	7	10	7—31

First Quarter

Sea.—FG, Lindell 23, 5:55.
Den.—McCaffrey 5 pass from Frerotte (Elam kick), 9:52.

Second Quarter

Den.—Spencer 79 interception return (Elam kick), 3:14.

Third Quarter

Den.—Anderson 1 run (Elam kick), 7:09.
Den.—FG, Elam 38, 8:44.
Sea.—Dawkins 4 pass from Kitna (Lindell kick), 14:02.

Fourth Quarter

Sea.—Jackson 9 pass from Kitna (Lindell kick), 5:39.
Den.—Anderson 6 run (Elam kick), 9:03.
Sea.—Dawkins 22 pass from Kitna (Lindell kick), 12:32.
 Attendance—75,218.

	Seattle	Denver
First downs	22	20
Rushes-yards	26-107	36-131
Passing	298	182
Punt returns	0-0	3-20
Kickoff returns	4-80	4-66
Interception returns	1-16	3-99
Comp.-att.-int.	26-41-3	14-25-1
Sacked-yards lost	0-0	1-19
Punts	4-37	4-44
Fumbles-lost	3-1	3-0
Penalties-yards	4-38	2-15
Time of possession	31:28	28:32

INDIVIDUAL STATISTICS

RUSHING—Seattle, Watters 16-57, Kitna 7-27, Alexander 1-16, Strong 1-4, R. Brown 1-3. Denver, Anderson 29-131, Frerotte 3-0, Coleman 2-6, R. Smith 1-5, Rouen 1-(minus 11).

PASSING—Seattle, Kitna 26-41-3-298. Denver, Frerotte 14-25-1-201.

RECEIVING—Seattle, Dawkins 6-85, Watters 6-49, Jackson 5-76, Mayes 5-27, Mili 2-51, Fauria 1-9, Strong 1-1. Denver, McCaffrey 8-112, R. Smith 5-82, B. Miller 1-7.

MISSED FIELD GOAL ATTEMPTS—None.

INTERCEPTIONS—Seattle, Bellamy 1-16. Denver, Spencer 1-79, Wilson 1-20, Jenkins 1-0.

KICKOFF RETURNS—Seattle, Rogers 3-58, Joseph 1-22. Denver, O'Neal 3-52, D. Smith 1-14.

PUNT RETURNS—Denver, O'Neal 3-20.

SACKS—Seattle, Sinclair 1.

SAINTS 31, 49ERS 27

Sunday, December 10

New Orleans	3	0	11	17—31
San Francisco	7	7	0	13—27

First Quarter

S.F.—Garcia 8 run (Richey kick), 4:36.
N.O.—FG, Brien 40, 7:53.

Second Quarter

S.F.—Garcia 1 run (Richey kick), 14:48.

Third Quarter

N.O.—FG, Brien 41, 6:41.
N.O.—A. Glover 15 pass from Brooks (Allen run), 13:01.

Fourth Quarter

S.F.—Clark 4 pass from Garcia (Richey kick), 2:02.
N.O.—FG, Brien 28, 6:10.
S.F.—Owens 69 pass from Garcia (run failed), 6:33.
N.O.—Jackson 22 pass from Brooks (Brien kick), 9:14.
N.O.—Allen 1 run (Brien kick), 14:14.
Attendance—67,892.

	New Orleans	San Francisco
First downs	21	21
Rushes-yards	38-216	21-110
Passing	172	288
Punt returns	3-30	2-30
Kickoff returns	5-125	6-105
Interception returns	2-3	0-0
Comp.-att.-int.	12-29-0	25-38-2
Sacked-yards lost	5-31	2-17
Punts	5-41	5-44
Fumbles-lost	1-0	1-1
Penalties-yards	1-5	2-15
Time of possession	32:46	27:14

INDIVIDUAL STATISTICS

RUSHING—New Orleans, Allen 18-80, Brooks 11-108, T. Smith 6-18, Morton 2-11, Horn 1-(minus 1). San Francisco, Garner 11-50, Garcia 5-42, Beasley 3-19, Smith 2-(minus 1).

PASSING—New Orleans, Brooks 12-29-0-203. San Francisco, Garcia 25-38-2-305.

RECEIVING—New Orleans, Horn 5-105, A. Glover 3-33, Morton 2-21, Jackson 1-22, Poole 1-22. San Francisco, Owens 6-129, Rice 6-62, Garner 4-49, Clark 4-24, Beasley 3-15, Stokes 1-22, Streets 1-4.

MISSED FIELD GOAL ATTEMPTS—None.

INTERCEPTIONS—New Orleans, Perry 2-3.

KICKOFF RETURNS—New Orleans, Mathis 3-72, McAfee 2-53. San Francisco, K. Williams 2-42, Lewis 2-33, Streets 2-30.

PUNT RETURNS—New Orleans, Canty 2-25, Mathis 1-5. San Francisco, K. Williams 2-30.

SACKS—New Orleans, D. Smith 1, D. Howard 1. San Francisco, B. Young 2.5, Buckner 1, Killings 1, Okeafor 0.5.

BUCCANEERS 16, DOLPHINS 13

Sunday, December 10

Tampa Bay	0	10	0	6—16
Miami	3	0	10	0—13

First Quarter

Mia.—FG, Mare 35, 11:49.

Second Quarter

T.B.—Duncan 31 interception return (Gramatica kick), 0:59.
T.B.—FG, Gramatica 38, 15:00.

Third Quarter

Mia.—FG, Mare 23, 6:35.
Mia.—L. Smith 1 run (Mare kick), 11:42.

Fourth Quarter

T.B.—FG, Gramatica 30, 4:24.
T.B.—FG, Gramatica 46, 6:48.
Attendance—74,307.

	Tampa Bay	Miami
First downs	14	17
Rushes-yards	38-100	27-84
Passing	121	170
Punt returns	3-10	2-9
Kickoff returns	3-48	4-90
Interception returns	4-36	1-0
Comp.-att.-int.	11-15-1	13-28-4
Sacked-yards lost	4-26	1-5
Punts	6-37	4-44
Fumbles-lost	1-0	1-1
Penalties-yards	7-63	6-46
Time of possession	31:50	28:10

INDIVIDUAL STATISTICS

RUSHING—Tampa Bay, Dunn 28-59, King 6-27, Abdullah 4-14. Miami, L. Smith 23-79, Denson 2-3, Fiedler 2-2.

PASSING—Tampa Bay, King 11-15-1-147. Miami, Fiedler 13-28-4-175.

RECEIVING—Tampa Bay, Dunn 6-84, K. Johnson 4-41, Moore 1-22. Miami, Martin 5-67, Gadsden 4-75, Konrad 2-21, L. Smith 1-8, McDuffie 1-4.

MISSED FIELD GOAL ATTEMPTS—Tampa Bay, Gramatica 34.

INTERCEPTIONS—Tampa Bay, Duncan 1-31, Quarles 1-5, Robinson 1-0, Abraham 1-0. Miami, Walker 1-0.

KICKOFF RETURNS—Tampa Bay, Williams 2-32, Abdullah 1-16. Miami, Denson 3-64, Johnson 1-26.

PUNT RETURNS—Tampa Bay, Williams 3-10. Miami, Ogden 2-9.

SACKS—Tampa Bay, Cannida 1. Miami, Z. Thomas 1, Surtain 1, Armstrong 1, Gardener 0.5, Taylor 0.5.

PACKERS 26, LIONS 13

Sunday, December 10

Detroit	0	0	3	10—13
Green Bay	6	0	3	17—26

First Quarter

G.B.—FG, Longwell 22, 4:01.
G.B.—FG, Longwell 27, 11:24.

Third Quarter

Det.—FG, Hanson 26, 7:30.
G.B.—FG, Longwell 26, 14:17.

Fourth Quarter

G.B.—FG, Longwell 45, 3:11.
Det.—J. Stewart 1 run (Hanson kick), 7:56.
G.B.—Green 3 pass from Favre (Longwell kick), 10:35.
Det.—FG, Hanson 36, 12:43.
G.B.—Green 39 run (Longwell kick), 13:06.
Attendance—59,854.

	Detroit	Green Bay
First downs	15	16
Rushes-yards	31-103	32-128
Passing	190	202
Punt returns	2-8	3-23
Kickoff returns	7-153	3-102
Interception returns	1-5	3-43

	Detroit	Green Bay
Comp.-att.-int.	17-33-3	15-36-1
Sacked-yards lost	0-0	2-6
Punts	4-45	3-39
Fumbles-lost	2-2	3-1
Penalties-yards	3-30	2-11
Time of possession	28:46	31:14

INDIVIDUAL STATISTICS

RUSHING—Detroit, J. Stewart 22-66, Batch 8-35, Bates 1-2. Green Bay, Green 27-118, Favre 2-7, Hasselbeck 2-(minus 3), Parker 1-6.

PASSING—Detroit, Batch 17-33-3-190. Green Bay, Favre 15-36-1-208.

RECEIVING—Detroit, Morton 5-56, Crowell 3-86, Bates 3-5, Rasby 2-14, J. Stewart 2-12, Moore 1-14, Foster 1-3. Green Bay, Freeman 5-80, Green 4-17, Schroeder 2-64, T. Davis 2-13, Franks 1-25, Driver 1-9.

MISSED FIELD GOAL ATTEMPTS—Green Bay, Longwell 45.

INTERCEPTIONS—Detroit, D. Walker 1-5. Green Bay, McBride 1-43, Sharper 1-0, Edwards 1-0.

KICKOFF RETURNS—Detroit, Howard 5-108, Fair 1-31, Schlesinger 1-14. Green Bay, Rossum 3-102.

PUNT RETURNS—Detroit, Howard 2-8. Green Bay, Rossum 3-23.

SACKS—Detroit, Porcher 1, Claiborne 0.5, Kirschke 0.5.

RAIDERS 31, JETS 7

Sunday, December 10

N.Y. Jets	0	0	0	7—	7
Oakland	0	21	0	10—	31

Second Quarter

Oak.—Allen 50 interception return (Janikowski kick), 2:29.
Oak.—Rison 7 pass from Gannon (Janikowski kick), 8:59.
Oak.—Wheatley 1 run (Janikowski kick), 13:51.

Fourth Quarter

Oak.—Brown 4 pass from Gannon (Janikowski kick), 0:44.
Oak.—FG, Janikowski 32, 13:10.
NYJ—Chrebet 5 pass from Pennington (Hall kick), 14:36.
Attendance—62,632.

	N.Y. Jets	Oakland
First downs	14	17
Rushes-yards	20-10	38-180
Passing	290	150
Punt returns	3-11	5-48
Kickoff returns	6-111	1-23
Interception returns	1-34	4-72
Comp.-att.-int.	22-44-4	11-23-1
Sacked-yards lost	5-25	2-11
Punts	8-42	7-44
Fumbles-lost	0-0	1-0
Penalties-yards	6-27	7-60
Time of possession	28:19	31:41

INDIVIDUAL STATISTICS

RUSHING—New York, Martin 17-11, Lucas 1-7, Pennington 1-0, Chrebet 1-(minus 8). Oakland, Wheatley 18-88, Jordan 8-37, Gannon 7-28, Kaufman 4-28, Crockett 1-(minus 1).

PASSING—New York, Testaverde 14-25-2-149, Lucas 6-14-2-99, Pennington 2-5-0-67. Oakland, Gannon 11-23-1-161.

RECEIVING—New York, R. Anderson 8-103, Martin 5-51, Chrebet 3-44, Ward 3-24, Sowell 1-62, Coles 1-16, Becht 1-15. Oakland, Brown 3-31, Jett 2-77, Rison 2-15, Dudley 2-12, Jordan 1-23, Brigham 1-3.

MISSED FIELD GOAL ATTEMPTS—None.

INTERCEPTIONS—New York, Glenn 1-34. Oakland, Allen 2-66, W. Thomas 2-6.

KICKOFF RETURNS—New York, L. Johnson 3-57, Stone 3-54. Oakland, Dunn 1-23.

PUNT RETURNS—New York, L. Johnson 3-11. Oakland, Dunn 5-48.

SACKS—New York, Frost 1, Cox 0.5, Ellis 0.5. Oakland, Coleman 2, Alexander 1, Taves 1, Jackson 0.5, Russell 0.5.

COLTS 44, BILLS 20

Monday, December 11

Buffalo	3	3	6	8—20
Indianapolis	3	6	14	21—44

First Quarter

Buf.—FG, Christie 29, 8:05.
Ind.—FG, Vanderjagt 37, 12:32.

Second Quarter

Ind.—FG, Vanderjagt 23, 2:43.
Buf.—FG, Christie 46, 8:28.
Ind.—FG, Vanderjagt 39, 15:00.

Third Quarter

Ind.—James 1 run (Vanderjagt kick), 4:08.
Ind.—Holsey 48 fumble return (Vanderjagt kick), 11:02.
Buf.—Morris 1 run (run failed), 14:25.

Fourth Quarter

Ind.—James 1 run (Vanderjagt kick), 4:45.
Ind.—Muhammad 40 interception return (Vanderjagt kick), 5:09.
Buf.—P. Price 29 pass from Flutie (Bryson run), 8:36.
Ind.—James 13 run (Vanderjagt kick), 10:49.
Attendance—56,671.

	Buffalo	Indianapolis
First downs	16	20
Rushes-yards	22-66	32-121
Passing	228	116
Punt returns	1-12	4-39
Kickoff returns	6-140	4-80
Interception returns	0-0	2-40
Comp.-att.-int.	18-34-2	13-24-0
Sacked-yards lost	9-42	2-16
Punts	6-34	5-44
Fumbles-lost	1-1	2-0
Penalties-yards	10-106	7-67
Time of possession	31:52	28:08

INDIVIDUAL STATISTICS

RUSHING—Buffalo, Bryson 15-45, Morris 5-7, Johnson 2-14. Indianapolis, James 27-111, Gordon 2-12, Manning 2-(minus 2), Wilkins 1-0.

PASSING—Buffalo, Johnson 12-22-2-188, Flutie 6-12-0-82. Indianapolis, Manning 13-24-0-132.

RECEIVING—Buffalo, Bryson 6-75, P. Price 4-93, Morris 4-27, Moulds 2-47, McDaniel 2-28. Indianapolis, Pathon 3-31, James 3-21, Wilkins 2-37, Harrison 2-27, Pollard 1-9, Dilger 1-7, Finn 1-0.

MISSED FIELD GOAL ATTEMPTS—None.

INTERCEPTIONS—Indianapolis, Muhammad 1-40, Burris 1-0.

KICKOFF RETURNS—Buffalo, Watson 3-77, Bryson 3-63. Indianapolis, Pathon 3-70, Holsey 1-10.

PUNT RETURNS—Buffalo, P. Price 1-12. Indianapolis, Wilkins 4-39.

SACKS—Buffalo, Newman 1, S. Price 1. Indianapolis, Scioli 2, Bennett 2, Burris 1, Belser 1, Bratzke 1, Chester 1, M. Thomas 1.

STANDINGS

AFC EAST

	W	L	T	Pct.
Miami	10	5	0	.667
Indianapolis	9	6	0	.600
N.Y. Jets	9	6	0	.600
Buffalo	7	8	0	.467
New England	5	10	0	.333

AFC CENTRAL

	W	L	T	Pct.
Tennessee	12	3	0	.800
Baltimore	11	4	0	.733
Pittsburgh	8	7	0	.533
Jacksonville	7	8	0	.467
Cincinnati	4	11	0	.267
Cleveland	3	13	0	.188

AFC WEST

	W	L	T	Pct.
Oakland	11	4	0	.733
Denver	10	5	0	.667
Kansas City	7	8	0	.467
Seattle	6	9	0	.400
San Diego	1	14	0	.067

NFC EAST

	W	L	T	Pct.
N.Y. Giants	11	4	0	.733
Philadelphia	10	5	0	.667
Washington	7	8	0	.467
Dallas	5	10	0	.333
Arizona	3	12	0	.200

NFC CENTRAL

	W	L	T	Pct.
Minnesota	11	4	0	.733
Tampa Bay	10	5	0	.667
Detroit	9	6	0	.600
Green Bay	8	7	0	.533
Chicago	4	11	0	.267

NFC WEST

	W	L	T	Pct.
New Orleans	10	5	0	.667
St. Louis	9	6	0	.600
Carolina	7	8	0	.467
San Francisco	6	9	0	.400
Atlanta	3	12	0	.200

TOP PERFORMANCES

100-YARD RUSHING GAMES

Player, Team & Opponent	Att.	Yds.	TD
Eddie George, Ten. at Cle.	34	176	3
Ricky Watters, Sea. vs. Oak.	26	168	0
James Stewart, Det. at NYJ	37	164	0
Ahman Green, G.B. at Min.	25	161	0
Tony Richardson, K.C. vs. Den.	23	156	1
Tyrone Wheatley, Oak. at Sea.	26	146	0
Warrick Dunn, T.B. vs. St.L.	22	145	3
Jamal Lewis, Balt. at Ari.	29	126	1
Edgerrin James, Ind. at Mia.	32	112	0
Fred Taylor, Jack. at Cin.	32	110	1
Jerome Bettis, Pit. vs. Wash.	25	104	0

300-YARD PASSING GAMES

Player, Team & Opponent	Att.	Comp.	Yds.	TD	Int.
Jeff Garcia, S.F. vs. Chi.	44	36	402	2	0
Daunte Culpepper, Min. vs. G.B.	38	23	335	3	1
Kurt Warner, St.L. at T.B.	32	20	316	2	3

100-YARD RECEIVING GAMES

Player, Team & Opponent	Rec.	Yds.	TD
Terrell Owens, S.F. vs. Chi.	20	283	1
Torry Holt, St.L. at T.B.	9	165	1
Randy Moss, Min. vs. G.B.	4	136	1
Joe Horn, N.O. vs. Atl.	7	116	0
Keyshawn Johnson, T.B. vs. St.L.	7	116	2
Danny Farmer, Cin. vs. Jack.	5	102	0
Rod Smith, Den. at K.C.	6	101	0

RESULTS

SATURDAY, DECEMBER 16

PITTSBURGH 24, Washington 3
SEATTLE 27, Oakland 24

SUNDAY, DECEMBER 17

Baltimore 13, ARIZONA 7
CAROLINA 30, San Diego 22
CINCINNATI 17, Jacksonville 14
Detroit 10, N.Y. JETS 7
Green Bay 33, MINNESOTA 28
Indianapolis 20, MIAMI 13
KANSAS CITY 20, Denver 7
New England 13, BUFFALO 10
NEW ORLEANS 23, Atlanta 7
N.Y. Giants 17, DALLAS 13
SAN FRANCISCO 17, Chicago 0
Tennessee 24, CLEVELAND 0

MONDAY, DECEMBER 18

TAMPA BAY 38, St. Louis 35
Open date: Philadelphia

2000 REVIEW *Week 16*

STEELERS 24, REDSKINS 3

Saturday, December 16

Washington	3	0	0	0— 3
Pittsburgh	0	17	0	7—24

First Quarter
Was.—FG, Murray 32, 11:58.

Second Quarter
Pit.—FG, K. Brown 28, 5:04.
Pit.—Poteat 53 punt return (K. Brown kick), 11:25.
Pit.—Huntley 3 run (K. Brown kick), 14:32.

Fourth Quarter
Pit.—Huntley 30 run (K. Brown kick), 4:18.
  Attendance—58,183.

	Washington	Pittsburgh
First downs	14	21
Rushes-yards	21-64	45-190
Passing	207	174
Punt returns	1-7	2-56
Kickoff returns	5-102	2-36
Interception returns	0-0	2-0
Comp.-att.-int.	18-32-2	11-21-0
Sacked-yards lost	3-24	1-1
Punts	5-41	5-43
Fumbles-lost	3-3	4-1
Penalties-yards	7-70	6-40
Time of possession	24:53	35:07

INDIVIDUAL STATISTICS
RUSHING—Washington, Davis 16-39, Centers 4-35, Thrash 1-(minus 10). Pittsburgh, Bettis 25-104, Stewart 8-9, Huntley 7-56, Zereoue 3-9, Ward 1-12, Miller 1-0.
PASSING—Washington, George 15-27-2-178, B. Johnson 3-5-0-53. Pittsburgh, Stewart 11-21-0-175.
RECEIVING—Washington, Centers 7-67, Alexander 4-85, Fryar 2-28, Davis 2-12, Connell 1-17, Reed 1-14, Thrash 1-8. Pittsburgh, Shaw 3-71, Ward 3-31, Hawkins 2-15, Bettis 1-25, Bruener 1-21, Edwards 1-12.
MISSED FIELD GOAL ATTEMPTS—None.
INTERCEPTIONS—Pittsburgh, Washington 1-0, Scott 1-0.
KICKOFF RETURNS—Washington, Thrash 3-54, Murrell 2-48. Pittsburgh, Blackwell 2-36.
PUNT RETURNS—Washington, Sanders 1-7. Pittsburgh, Poteat 2-56.
SACKS—Washington, Stubblefield 1. Pittsburgh, Gildon 1.5, Porter 1, Alexander 0.5.

SEAHAWKS 27, RAIDERS 24

Saturday, December 16

Oakland	7	3	7	7—24
Seattle	10	3	0	14—27

First Quarter
Sea.—Strong 13 pass from Kitna (Lindell kick), 3:17.
Oak.—Rison 14 pass from Gannon (Janikowski kick), 7:48.
Sea.—FG, Lindell 40, 14:02.

Second Quarter
Oak.—FG, Janikowski 25, 8:56.
Sea.—FG, Lindell 52, 15:00.

Third Quarter
Oak.—Jordan 6 run (Janikowski kick), 8:02.

Fourth Quarter
Oak.—Jordan 7 run (Janikowski kick), 3:12.
Sea.—Alexander 4 run (pass failed), 9:44.
Sea.—M.Pope tackled in end zone by J.Williams for a safety, 12:36.
Sea.—Jackson 9 pass from Kitna (run failed), 14:32.
  Attendance—68,681.

	Oakland	Seattle
First downs	15	18
Rushes-yards	42-227	31-173
Passing	134	153
Punt returns	1-15	2-17
Kickoff returns	3-64	6-144
Interception returns	1-0	3-35

	Oakland	Seattle
Comp.-att.-int.	5-17-3	19-32-1
Sacked-yards lost	1-2	3-24
Punts	4-46	6-32
Fumbles-lost	1-0	5-1
Penalties-yards	7-45	5-55
Time of possession	31:06	28:54

INDIVIDUAL STATISTICS
RUSHING—Oakland, Wheatley 26-146, Jordan 11-55, Gannon 5-26. Seattle, Watters 26-168, Kitna 3-1, Alexander 2-4.
PASSING—Oakland, Gannon 5-17-3-136. Seattle, Kitna 19-30-1-177, T. Brown 0-1-0-0, Feagles 0-1-0-0.
RECEIVING—Oakland, Brown 2-52, Jordan 1-55, Dudley 1-15, Rison 1-14. Seattle, Jackson 4-52, Watters 4-37, Dawkins 4-30, Strong 3-19, Mili 1-21, Mayes 1-10, Fauria 1-8.
MISSED FIELD GOAL ATTEMPTS—Oakland, Janikowski 50.
INTERCEPTIONS—Oakland, Woodson 1-0. Seattle, Bell 1-30, W. Williams 1-5, Kacyvenski 1-0.
KICKOFF RETURNS—Oakland, Dunn 3-64. Seattle, Rogers 5-125, R. Brown 1-19.
PUNT RETURNS—Oakland, Dunn 1-15. Seattle, Rogers 2-17.
SACKS—Oakland, Pope 1, Upshaw 1, Bryant 1. Seattle, Sinclair 1.

PACKERS 33, VIKINGS 28

Sunday, December 17

Green Bay	10	10	3	10—33
Minnesota	7	7	7	7—28

First Quarter
G.B.—FG, Longwell 34, 7:22.
G.B.—Freeman 18 pass from Favre (Longwell kick), 12:56.
Min.—Moss 78 pass from Culpepper (Anderson kick), 13:24.

Second Quarter
G.B.—Green 6 pass from Favre (Longwell kick), 3:09.
G.B.—FG, Longwell 35, 12:19.
Min.—Culpepper 3 run (Anderson kick), 14:40.

Third Quarter
G.B.—FG, Longwell 43, 6:21.
Min.—McWilliams 22 pass from Culpepper (Anderson kick), 11:02.

Fourth Quarter
G.B.—Schroeder 3 pass from Favre (Longwell kick), 0:04.
G.B.—FG, Longwell 36, 8:09.
Min.—C. Carter 5 pass from Culpepper (Anderson kick), 12:22.
  Attendance—64,183.

	Green Bay	Minnesota
First downs	28	19
Rushes-yards	30-159	17-68
Passing	275	332
Punt returns	2-13	0-0
Kickoff returns	3-59	8-177
Interception returns	1-47	0-0
Comp.-att.-int.	26-38-0	23-38-1
Sacked-yards lost	2-15	1-3
Punts	1-53	3-49
Fumbles-lost	2-0	2-1
Penalties-yards	3-25	8-67
Time of possession	35:41	24:19

INDIVIDUAL STATISTICS
RUSHING—Green Bay, Green 25-161, Favre 4-(minus 2), Parker 1-0. Minnesota, Smith 10-26, Culpepper 7-42.
PASSING—Green Bay, Favre 26-38-0-290. Minnesota, Culpepper 23-38-1-335.
RECEIVING—Green Bay, Schroeder 8-78, Freeman 6-97, Henderson 5-27, Green 4-31, T. Davis 1-41, Parker 1-10, Driver 1-6. Minnesota, C. Carter 7-91, Moss 4-136, Walsh 3-44, McWilliams 3-32, Smith 3-16, Kleinsasser 1-15, J. Davis 1-3, D. Palmer 1-(minus 2).
MISSED FIELD GOAL ATTEMPTS—None.
INTERCEPTIONS—Green Bay, Sharper 1-47.
KICKOFF RETURNS—Green Bay, Rossum 2-43, Henderson 1-16. Minnesota, Walters 8-177.
PUNT RETURNS—Green Bay, Rossum 2-13.
SACKS—Green Bay, Holliday 1. Minnesota, E. McDaniel 1, T. Williams 1.

BENGALS 17, JAGUARS 14

Sunday, December 17

Jacksonville	0	7	7	0—14
Cincinnati	0	0	7	10—17

Second Quarter
Jac.—J. Smith 3 pass from Brunell (Hollis kick), 14:33.

Third Quarter
Cin.—Warrick 82 punt return (Rackers kick), 4:03.
Jac.—Taylor 5 run (Hollis kick), 10:03.

Fourth Quarter
Cin.—S. Mitchell 12 run (Rackers kick), 13:45.
Cin.—FG, Rackers 27, 15:00.
Attendance—50,469.

	Jacksonville	Cincinnati
First downs	17	15
Rushes-yards	34-114	27-106
Passing	162	157
Punt returns	2-6	3-87
Kickoff returns	3-59	2-26
Interception returns	1-14	0-0
Comp.-att.-int.	19-28-0	10-22-1
Sacked-yards lost	1-8	4-14
Punts	8-29	5-36
Fumbles-lost	3-1	3-3
Penalties-yards	6-47	6-40
Time of possession	37:15	22:45

INDIVIDUAL STATISTICS
RUSHING—Jacksonville, Taylor 32-110, Brunell 1-2, Stith 1-2. Cincinnati, Dillon 17-76, Bennett 7-14, Warrick 2-4, S. Mitchell 1-12.
PASSING—Jacksonville, Brunell 19-28-0-170. Cincinnati, S. Mitchell 10-22-1-171.
RECEIVING—Jacksonville, J. Smith 9-58, McCardell 4-61, Brady 4-38, Taylor 2-13. Cincinnati, Farmer 5-102, Warrick 3-38, N. Williams 2-31.
MISSED FIELD GOAL ATTEMPTS—Jacksonville, Hollis 28.
INTERCEPTIONS—Jacksonville, Logan 1-14.
KICKOFF RETURNS—Jacksonville, Stith 3-59. Cincinnati, Griffin 1-15, Mack 1-11.
PUNT RETURNS—Jacksonville, Barlow 2-6. Cincinnati, Warrick 3-87.
SACKS—Jacksonville, Payne 1.5, Brackens 1.5, Smeenge 1. Cincinnati, Spikes 1.

CHIEFS 20, BRONCOS 7

Sunday, December 17

Denver	0	7	0	0— 7
Kansas City	3	0	7	10—20

First Quarter
K.C.—FG, Peterson 40, 7:31.

Second Quarter
Den.—Suttle recovered fumble in end zone (Elam kick), 3:34.

Third Quarter
K.C.—Moreau 2 run (Peterson kick), 5:37.

Fourth Quarter
K.C.—Richardson 28 run (Peterson kick), 7:46.
K.C.—FG, Peterson 27, 14:27.
Attendance—78,406.

	Denver	Kansas City
First downs	11	24
Rushes-yards	14-66	41-264
Passing	225	160
Punt returns	3-24	4-8
Kickoff returns	5-92	2-43
Interception returns	0-0	0-0
Comp.-att.-int.	22-35-0	14-28-0
Sacked-yards lost	2-9	0-0
Punts	7-42	6-44
Fumbles-lost	1-1	4-2
Penalties-yards	7-51	6-51
Time of possession	25:26	34:34

INDIVIDUAL STATISTICS
RUSHING—Denver, Anderson 12-62, Frerotte 2-4. Kansas City, Richardson 23-156, Moreau 14-59, Grbac 3-38, Alexander 1-11.
PASSING—Denver, Frerotte 22-34-0-234, Jackson 0-1-0-0. Kansas City, Grbac 14-28-0-160.

RECEIVING—Denver, McCaffrey 8-84, R. Smith 6-101, Anderson 3-29, Chamberlain 2-16, Carswell 2-2, Griffith 1-2. Kansas City, Alexander 5-79, Gonzalez 4-46, Richardson 3-13, Morris 2-22.
MISSED FIELD GOAL ATTEMPTS—Denver, Elam 37.
INTERCEPTIONS—None.
KICKOFF RETURNS—Denver, O'Neal 4-79, Chamberlain 1-13. Kansas City, Cloud 2-43.
PUNT RETURNS—Denver, O'Neal 3-24. Kansas City, Lockett 4-8.
SACKS—Kansas City, Hicks 2.

SAINTS 23, FALCONS 7

Sunday, December 17

Atlanta	0	0	7	0— 7
New Orleans	0	13	7	3—23

Second Quarter
N.O.—FG, Brien 20, 0:44.
N.O.—Knight 31 interception return (Brien kick), 2:30.
N.O.—FG, Brien 46, 15:00.

Third Quarter
Atl.—Vaughn 88 kickoff return (Andersen kick), 0:17.
N.O.—Allen 2 run (Brien kick), 5:15.

Fourth Quarter
N.O.—FG, Brien 47, 10:06.
Attendance—64,900.

	Atlanta	New Orleans
First downs	9	19
Rushes-yards	21-64	30-92
Passing	99	281
Punt returns	2-16	5-5
Kickoff returns	5-175	2-46
Interception returns	0-0	2-31
Comp.-att.-int.	9-20-2	24-35-0
Sacked-yards lost	5-27	1-4
Punts	7-40	5-44
Fumbles-lost	1-1	1-1
Penalties-yards	5-33	7-50
Time of possession	25:26	34:34

INDIVIDUAL STATISTICS
RUSHING—Atlanta, Anderson 18-53, Chandler 2-9, Johnson 1-2. New Orleans, Allen 21-82, Brooks 5-7, Gowin 1-5, Morton 1-4, Milne 1-0, Horn 1-(minus 6).
PASSING—Atlanta, Chandler 4-10-1-81, Johnson 5-10-1-45. New Orleans, Brooks 24-35-0-285.
RECEIVING—Atlanta, Anderson 3-79, Kozlowski 2-15, Christian 2-8, Mathis 1-15, R. Kelly 1-9. New Orleans, Horn 7-116, Jackson 4-47, Poole 3-40, A. Glover 3-29, Morton 3-24, Milne 2-9, Wilson 1-13, Allen 1-7.
MISSED FIELD GOAL ATTEMPTS—None.
INTERCEPTIONS—New Orleans, Knight 1-31, Molden 1-0.
KICKOFF RETURNS—Atlanta, Dwight 3-58, Vaughn 2-117. New Orleans, McAfee 2-46.
PUNT RETURNS—Atlanta, Dwight 2-16. New Orleans, Canty 5-5.
SACKS—Atlanta, Jasper 1. New Orleans, Johnson 2, Knight 1, Whitehead 1, Fields 0.5, D. Howard 0.5.

TITANS 24, BROWNS 0

Sunday, December 17

Tennessee	10	7	0	7—24
Cleveland	0	0	0	0— 0

First Quarter
Ten.—FG, Del Greco 33, 4:49.
Ten.—E. George 1 run (Del Greco kick), 9:17.

Second Quarter
Ten.—E. George 2 run (Del Greco kick), 3:11.

Fourth Quarter
Ten.—E. George 35 run (Del Greco kick), 2:09.
Attendance—72,318.

	Tennessee	Cleveland
First downs	19	6
Rushes-yards	47-212	17-50
Passing	93	63
Punt returns	3-24	1-5
Kickoff returns	1-35	5-89
Interception returns	0-0	1-0

	Tennessee	Cleveland
Comp.-att.-int.	12-20-1	13-30-0
Sacked-yards lost	2-12	2-12
Punts	4-37	7-40
Fumbles-lost	1-0	4-2
Penalties-yards	3-25	7-66
Time of possession	38:53	21:07

INDIVIDUAL STATISTICS

RUSHING—Tennessee, E. George 34-176, Thomas 11-27, McNair 2-9. Cleveland, Prentice 12-32, White 4-3, Pederson 1-15.

PASSING—Tennessee, McNair 10-18-1-79, O'Donnell 2-2-0-26. Cleveland, Pederson 13-30-0-75.

RECEIVING—Tennessee, Wycheck 3-9, Thigpen 2-27, Sanders 2-13, Neal 2-8, Mason 1-33, Kinney 1-15, E. George 1-0. Cleveland, Patten 3-26, Prentice 2-13, White 2-12, Shea 2-8, Johnson 2-3, Edwards 1-7, B. Brown 1-6.

MISSED FIELD GOAL ATTEMPTS—None.

INTERCEPTIONS—Cleveland, Fuller 1-0.

KICKOFF RETURNS—Tennessee, Mason 1-35. Cleveland, White 2-38, Edwards 1-24, Saleh 1-15, Little 1-12.

PUNT RETURNS—Tennessee, Mason 3-24. Cleveland, Chapman 1-5.

SACKS—Tennessee, Kearse 1, Salave'a 1. Cleveland, Abdullah 1, Rogers 1.

49ERS 17, BEARS 0

Sunday, December 17

Chicago	0	0	0	0—0
San Francisco	7	3	7	0—17

First Quarter
S.F.—Clark 1 pass from Garcia (Richey kick), 6:01.

Second Quarter
S.F.—FG, Richey 28, 14:57.

Third Quarter
S.F.—Owens 27 pass from Garcia (Richey kick), 7:45.
Attendance—68,306.

	Chicago	San Francisco
First downs	8	26
Rushes-yards	18-39	27-78
Passing	65	378
Punt returns	4-39	6-36
Kickoff returns	3-44	1-19
Interception returns	0-0	1-5
Comp.-att.-int.	9-29-1	36-44-0
Sacked-yards lost	2-8	5-24
Punts	9-44	6-45
Fumbles-lost	0-0	4-1
Penalties-yards	4-30	9-80
Time of possession	20:52	39:08

INDIVIDUAL STATISTICS

RUSHING—Chicago, Allen 16-31, Booker 1-5, McNown 1-3. San Francisco, Garner 14-43, Garcia 7-16, Beasley 3-9, Smith 2-5, Owens 1-5.

PASSING—Chicago, McNown 9-29-1-73. San Francisco, Garcia 36-44-0-402.

RECEIVING—Chicago, Booker 5-47, Kennison 1-10, Bates 1-8, Lyman 1-4, Sinceno 1-4. San Francisco, Owens 20-283, Rice 7-76, Garner 4-18, Clark 3-20, Stokes 1-3, Beasley 1-2.

MISSED FIELD GOAL ATTEMPTS—San Francisco, Richey 33.

INTERCEPTIONS—San Francisco, Montgomery 1-5.

KICKOFF RETURNS—Chicago, Milburn 2-42, Tuinei 1-2. San Francisco, Lewis 1-19.

PUNT RETURNS—Chicago, Milburn 4-39. San Francisco, K. Williams 6-36.

SACKS—Chicago, S. Harris 1, Urlacher 1, Colvin 1, Parrish 1, Tuinei 1. San Francisco, Peterson 1, Heard 1.

PANTHERS 30, CHARGERS 22

Sunday, December 17

San Diego	2	14	6	0—22
Carolina	7	0	13	10—30

First Quarter
Car.—Muhammad 11 pass from Beuerlein (Nedney kick), 5:35.
S.D.—Beuerlein sacked in end zone by A. Fontenot for a safety, 13:28.

Second Quarter
S.D.—Fletcher 25 pass from Leaf (Carney kick), 2:15.
S.D.—Dixon 36 interception return (Carney kick), 7:42.

Third Quarter
Car.—Byrd 34 pass from Beuerlein (Nedney kick), 2:14.
S.D.—Heiden 4 pass from Leaf (run failed), 7:02.
Car.—Uwaezuoke 64 punt return (pass failed), 13:08.

Fourth Quarter
Car.—FG, Nedney 18, 1:20.
Car.—Evans 54 blocked FG return (Nedney kick), 5:27.
Attendance—72,159.

	San Diego	Carolina
First downs	19	13
Rushes-yards	34-100	15-11
Passing	258	158
Punt returns	1-3	3-93
Kickoff returns	4-68	4-76
Interception returns	1-36	1-0
Comp.-att.-int.	23-43-1	18-40-1
Sacked-yards lost	1-1	3-22
Punts	9-38	8-39
Fumbles-lost	3-1	1-0
Penalties-yards	10-95	7-45
Time of possession	35:08	24:52

INDIVIDUAL STATISTICS

RUSHING—San Diego, Fletcher 16-47, Fazande 12-31, Leaf 5-13, Conway 1-9. Carolina, Beuerlein 4-5, Hoover 4-3, Biakabutuka 3-(minus 11), Hetherington 2-1, Muhammad 1-8, Lewis 1-5.

PASSING—San Diego, Leaf 23-43-1-259. Carolina, Beuerlein 12-27-0-139, Lewis 6-13-1-41.

RECEIVING—San Diego, Fletcher 7-66, Conway 5-63, F. Jones 4-43, J. Graham 3-59, McCrary 2-15, Gaylor 1-9, Heiden 1-4. Carolina, Muhammad 9-72, Hayes 3-29, Hetherington 3-21, Mangum 2-24, Byrd 1-34.

MISSED FIELD GOAL ATTEMPTS—San Diego, Carney 37.

INTERCEPTIONS—San Diego, Dixon 1-36. Carolina, Woodall 1-0.

KICKOFF RETURNS—San Diego, Bynum 2-43, R. Jenkins 1-14, R. Jones 1-11. Carolina, Bates 3-65, Hetherington 1-11.

PUNT RETURNS—San Diego, R. Jones 1-3. Carolina, Uwaezuoke 3-93.

SACKS—San Diego, Mickell 2, Fontenot 1. Carolina, Morabito 1.

RAVENS 13, CARDINALS 7

Sunday, December 17

Baltimore	3	0	10	0—13
Arizona	0	0	7	0— 7

First Quarter
Bal.—FG, Stover 42, 7:48.

Third Quarter
Ariz.—Sanders 27 pass from Plummer (Blanchard kick), 5:19.
Bal.—Ja. Lewis 1 run (Stover kick), 8:42.
Bal.—FG, Stover 42, 14:39.
Attendance—37,452.

	Baltimore	Arizona
First downs	14	18
Rushes-yards	37-177	23-51
Passing	37	258
Punt returns	3-59	3-31
Kickoff returns	2-47	4-88
Interception returns	2-75	1-3
Comp.-att.-int.	12-22-1	23-43-2
Sacked-yards lost	4-33	2-8
Punts	7-39	4-45
Fumbles-lost	3-1	3-2
Penalties-yards	6-64	3-15
Time of possession	31:57	28:03

INDIVIDUAL STATISTICS

RUSHING—Baltimore, Ja. Lewis 29-126, Holmes 4-28, Dilfer 3-17, Stokley 1-6. Arizona, Jones 14-39, Pittman 5-6, Plummer 4-6.

PASSING—Baltimore, Dilfer 12-22-1-70. Arizona, Plummer 23-43-2-266.

RECEIVING—Baltimore, Sharpe 4-37, Ja. Lewis 3-5, Johnson 2-27, Coates 2-8, Holmes 1-(minus 7). Arizona, Jones 7-41, Boston 5-93, Sanders 5-76, Cody 2-31, Hardy 2-18, McKinley 1-4, Pittman 1-3.

MISSED FIELD GOAL ATTEMPTS—Arizona, Blanchard 46.

INTERCEPTIONS—Baltimore, Sharper 1-45, Starks 1-30. Arizona, Tillman 1-3.

KICKOFF RETURNS—Baltimore, Harris 2-47. Arizona, Jenkins 4-88.

PUNT RETURNS—Baltimore, Starks 3-59. Arizona, Cody 3-31.

SACKS—Baltimore, Burnett 2. Arizona, Smith 2, Knight 1, Wadsworth 1.

LIONS 10, JETS 7

Sunday, December 17

Detroit	0	0	3	7—10
N.Y. Jets	7	0	0	0— 7

First Quarter
NYJ—Martin 1 run (Hall kick), 9:11.

Third Quarter
Det.—FG, Hanson 35, 8:19.

Fourth Quarter
Det.—Hartings recovered fumble in end zone (Hanson kick), 9:17.
Attendance—77,513.

	Detroit	N.Y. Jets
First downs	16	12
Rushes-yards	44-210	18-51
Passing	78	189
Punt returns	1-15	4-37
Kickoff returns	3-66	2-30
Interception returns	1-0	1-27
Comp.-att.-int.	8-18-1	21-36-1
Sacked-yards lost	5-32	1-5
Punts	7-42	7-41
Fumbles-lost	1-0	2-1
Penalties-yards	4-25	7-45
Time of possession	34:18	25:42

INDIVIDUAL STATISTICS
RUSHING—Detroit, J. Stewart 37-164, Batch 4-12, Bates 3-34. New York, Martin 16-52, Testaverde 1-0, Sowell 1-(minus 1).
PASSING—Detroit, Batch 8-18-1-110. New York, Testaverde 21-36-1-194.
RECEIVING—Detroit, Morton 2-31, Sloan 2-31, Crowell 2-5, J. Stewart 1-32, Schlesinger 1-11. New York, Martin 5-57, R. Anderson 5-22, Ward 4-25, Chrebet 3-43, Sowell 2-20, W. Hayes 1-22, Becht 1-5.
MISSED FIELD GOAL ATTEMPTS—New York, Hall 47, 35.
INTERCEPTIONS—Detroit, Boyd 1-0. New York, V. Green 1-27.
KICKOFF RETURNS—Detroit, Howard 3-66. New York, Stone 1-21, Sowell 1-9.
PUNT RETURNS—Detroit, Howard 1-15. New York, Ward 3-33, L. Johnson 1-4.
SACKS—Detroit, Aldridge 1. New York, Ellis 2, Phifer 2, Lewis 1.

PATRIOTS 13, BILLS 10

Sunday, December 17

New England	3	0	0	7	3—13
Buffalo	0	3	0	7	0—10

First Quarter
N.E.—FG, Vinatieri 22, 15:00.

Second Quarter
Buf.—FG, Christie 25, 8:41.

Fourth Quarter
Buf.—Jackson 1 pass from Flutie (Christie kick), 3:29.
N.E.—Faulk 13 run (Vinatieri kick), 10:15.

Overtime
N.E.—FG, Vinatieri 24, 14:41.
Attendance—47,230.

	New England	Buffalo
First downs	19	19
Rushes-yards	48-189	40-178
Passing	142	169
Punt returns	5-33	3-10
Kickoff returns	3-85	3-33
Interception returns	0-0	0-0
Comp.-att.-int.	13-26-0	16-28-0
Sacked-yards lost	1-14	4-28
Punts	7-42	7-29
Fumbles-lost	5-0	4-1
Penalties-yards	9-75	6-54
Time of possession	39:38	35:03

INDIVIDUAL STATISTICS
RUSHING—New England, Redmond 20-66, Faulk 14-52, T. Carter 9-34, Brown 2-23, Bledsoe 2-14, L. Johnson 1-0. Buffalo, Bryson 19-82, Morris 11-43, Flutie 9-50, A. Smith 1-3.
PASSING—New England, Bledsoe 13-26-0-156. Buffalo, Flutie 15-25-0-193, Johnson 1-3-0-4.

RECEIVING—New England, Glenn 6-70, Wiggins 3-42, Brown 2-15, T. Carter 1-21, Faulk 1-8. Buffalo, P. Price 3-68, McDaniel 3-38, Bryson 3-34, Morris 3-11, Moulds 2-26, Riemersma 1-19, Jackson 1-1.
MISSED FIELD GOAL ATTEMPTS—New England, Vinatieri 27. Buffalo, Christie 23, 30.
INTERCEPTIONS—None.
KICKOFF RETURNS—New England, Jackson 3-85. Buffalo, Watson 2-26, Linton 1-7.
PUNT RETURNS—New England, Brown 5-33. Buffalo, P. Price 3-10.
SACKS—New England, Eaton 2, McGinest 2. Buffalo, Wiley 1.

COLTS 20, DOLPHINS 13

Sunday, December 17

Indianapolis	7	10	3	0—20
Miami	0	3	7	3—13

First Quarter
Ind.—Pollard 50 pass from Manning (Vanderjagt kick), 4:49.

Second Quarter
Ind.—Manning 4 run (Vanderjagt kick), 2:38.
Mia.—FG, Mare 25, 13:06.
Ind.—FG, Vanderjagt 48, 15:00.

Third Quarter
Ind.—FG, Vanderjagt 31, 8:19.
Mia.—L. Smith 8 run (Mare kick), 12:17.

Fourth Quarter
Mia.—FG, Mare 31, 11:35.
Attendance—73,884.

	Indianapolis	Miami
First downs	20	14
Rushes-yards	35-132	26-140
Passing	195	132
Punt returns	3-7	2-2
Kickoff returns	3-44	3-63
Interception returns	1-0	0-0
Comp.-att.-int.	21-28-0	12-26-1
Sacked-yards lost	1-11	4-18
Punts	6-37	5-40
Fumbles-lost	2-2	2-2
Penalties-yards	4-35	8-45
Time of possession	33:50	26:10

INDIVIDUAL STATISTICS
RUSHING—Indianapolis, James 32-112, Manning 3-20. Miami, L. Smith 22-97, Denson 2-11, Fiedler 1-29, Johnson 1-3.
PASSING—Indianapolis, Manning 21-28-0-206. Miami, Fiedler 12-25-1-150, L. Smith 0-1-0-0.
RECEIVING—Indianapolis, Harrison 6-47, Pollard 5-74, James 5-31, Pathon 3-39, Dilger 2-15. Miami, Martin 4-67, Gadsden 3-40, L. Smith 3-10, Weaver 1-24, Denson 1-9.
MISSED FIELD GOAL ATTEMPTS—None.
INTERCEPTIONS—Indianapolis, Burris 1-0.
KICKOFF RETURNS—Indianapolis, Wilkins 3-44. Miami, Denson 2-39, Williams 1-24.
PUNT RETURNS—Indianapolis, Wilkins 3-7. Miami, Ogden 2-2.
SACKS—Indianapolis, M. Thomas 2, J. Williams 0.5, Bratzke 0.5, Team 1. Miami, Taylor 1.

GIANTS 17, COWBOYS 13

Sunday, December 17

N.Y. Giants	0	0	7	10—17
Dallas	7	6	0	0—13

First Quarter
Dal.—E. Smith 1 run (Seder kick), 10:40.

Second Quarter
Dal.—FG, Seder 47, 2:23.
Dal.—FG, Seder 43, 12:44.

Third Quarter
NYG—Toomer 33 pass from Collins (Daluiso kick), 12:31.

Fourth Quarter
NYG—Barber 13 run (Daluiso kick), 6:45.
NYG—FG, Daluiso 44, 13:11.
Attendance—61,311.

	N.Y. Giants	Dallas
First downs	12	15
Rushes-yards	31-99	30-75
Passing	126	70
Punt returns	2-35	1-5
Kickoff returns	4-91	4-80
Interception returns	1-4	1-0
Comp.-att.-int.	12-26-1	13-25-1
Sacked-yards lost	1-14	5-49
Punts	6-32	5-43
Fumbles-lost	1-0	2-2
Penalties-yards	7-79	7-75
Time of possession	28:36	31:24

INDIVIDUAL STATISTICS

RUSHING—New York, Barber 20-80, Dayne 8-19, Collins 2-(minus 1), Dixon 1-1. Dallas, E. Smith 24-46, Wright 4-26, Thomas 1-3, Wiley 1-0.

PASSING—New York, Collins 12-26-1-140. Dallas, Wright 13-25-1-119.

RECEIVING—New York, Barber 4-47, Toomer 3-58, Mitchell 2-12, Cross 1-9, Comella 1-7, Hilliard 1-7. Dallas, Wiley 4-14, Harris 3-28, McKnight 2-45, McGarity 2-17, Tucker 1-13, Thomas 1-2.

MISSED FIELD GOAL ATTEMPTS—New York, Daluiso 45, 40.

INTERCEPTIONS—New York, McDaniel 1-4. Dallas, Sparks 1-0.

KICKOFF RETURNS—New York, Dixon 4-91. Dallas, Tucker 4-80.

PUNT RETURNS—New York, Barber 2-35. Dallas, McGarity 1-5.

SACKS—New York, Strahan 2.5, K. Hamilton 1.5, Armstead 1. Dallas, Ekuban 1.

BUCCANEERS 38, RAMS 35

Monday, December 18

St. Louis	7	7	7	14—35
Tampa Bay	10	14	7	7—38

First Quarter
T.B.—FG, Gramatica 35, 1:52.
St.L.—Faulk 2 run (Wilkins kick), 8:35.
T.B.—Dunn 2 run (Gramatica kick), 14:20.

Second Quarter
St.L.—Faulk 16 run (Wilkins kick), 4:00.
T.B.—K. Johnson 8 pass from King (Gramatica kick), 10:58.
T.B.—K. Johnson 17 pass from King (Gramatica kick), 14:00.

Third Quarter
St.L.—Faulk 27 pass from Warner (Wilkins kick), 14:40.
T.B.—Dunn 52 run (Gramatica kick), 15:00.

Fourth Quarter
St.L.—Faulk 9 run (Wilkins kick), 4:07.
St.L.—Holt 72 pass from Warner (Wilkins kick), 9:42.
T.B.—Dunn 1 run (Gramatica kick), 14:12.
Attendance—65,653.

	St. Louis	Tampa Bay
First downs	19	27
Rushes-yards	23-90	32-205
Passing	298	241
Punt returns	1-8	1-6
Kickoff returns	6-108	6-146
Interception returns	2-0	3-11
Comp.-att.-int.	20-32-3	18-38-2
Sacked-yards lost	2-18	2-15
Punts	3-37	2-37
Fumbles-lost	0-0	0-0
Penalties-yards	2-20	5-40
Time of possession	28:31	31:29

INDIVIDUAL STATISTICS

RUSHING—St. Louis, Faulk 22-79, Bruce 1-11. Tampa Bay, Dunn 22-145, King 7-58, Alstott 3-2.

PASSING—St. Louis, Warner 20-32-3-316. Tampa Bay, King 18-38-2-256.

RECEIVING—St. Louis, Holt 9-165, Faulk 4-53, Bruce 3-36, Proehl 2-50, R. Williams 1-8, Hakim 1-4. Tampa Bay, K. Johnson 7-116, Dunn 5-53, Green 4-55, Anthony 1-22, Moore 1-10.

MISSED FIELD GOAL ATTEMPTS—None.

INTERCEPTIONS—St. Louis, McCleon 2-0. Tampa Bay, Barber 1-9, Lynch 1-2, Robinson 1-0.

KICKOFF RETURNS—St. Louis, Blevins 4-73, Faulk 1-18, Moran 1-17. Tampa Bay, Williams 6-146.

PUNT RETURNS—St. Louis, Hakim 1-8. Tampa Bay, Williams 1-6.

SACKS—St. Louis, Bush 1, Carter 1. Tampa Bay, Sapp 2.

WEEK 17

STANDINGS

AFC EAST

	W	L	T	Pct.
Miami	11	5	0	.688
Indianapolis	10	6	0	.625
N.Y. Jets	9	7	0	.562
Buffalo	8	8	0	.500
New England	5	11	0	.312

AFC CENTRAL

	W	L	T	Pct.
Tennessee	13	3	0	.813
Baltimore	12	4	0	.750
Pittsburgh	9	7	0	.562
Jacksonville	7	9	0	.438
Cincinnati	4	12	0	.250
Cleveland	3	13	0	.188

AFC WEST

	W	L	T	Pct.
Oakland	12	4	0	.750
Denver	11	5	0	.688
Kansas City	7	9	0	.438
Seattle	6	10	0	.375
San Diego	1	15	0	.062

NFC EAST

	W	L	T	Pct.
N.Y. Giants	12	4	0	.750
Philadelphia	11	5	0	.688
Washington	8	8	0	.500
Dallas	5	11	0	.313
Arizona	3	13	0	.188

NFC CENTRAL

	W	L	T	Pct.
Minnesota	11	5	0	.688
Tampa Bay	10	6	0	.625
Detroit	9	7	0	.562
Green Bay	9	7	0	.562
Chicago	5	11	0	.313

NFC WEST

	W	L	T	Pct.
New Orleans	10	6	0	.625
St. Louis	10	6	0	.625
Carolina	7	9	0	.438
San Francisco	6	10	0	.375
Atlanta	4	12	0	.250

TOP PERFORMANCES

100-YARD RUSHING GAMES

Player, Team & Opponent	Att.	Yds.	TD
Marshall Faulk, St.L. at N.O.	32	220	2
Antowain Smith, Buf. at Sea.	17	147	3
Edgerrin James, Ind. vs. Min.	26	128	0
Stephen Davis, Wash. vs. Ari.	27	120	0
Jamal Anderson, Atl. vs. K.C.	28	107	0

300-YARD PASSING GAMES

Player, Team & Opponent	Att.	Comp.	Yds.	TD	Int.
Vinny Testaverde, NYJ at Balt.	69	36	481	2	3
Doug Flutie, Buf. at Sea.	25	20	366	3	0
Kerry Collins, NYG vs. Jack.	39	22	321	2	1
Drew Bledsoe, N.E. vs. Mia.	34	18	312	2	2

100-YARD RECEIVING GAMES

Player, Team & Opponent	Rec.	Yds.	TD
Amani Toomer, NYG vs. Jack.	8	193	1
Dedric Ward, NYJ at Balt.	8	147	1
Richie Anderson, NYJ at Balt.	11	139	1
Peerless Price, Buf. at Sea.	8	132	1
Keenan McCardell, Jack. at NYG	11	131	0
Torry Holt, St.L. at N.O.	5	121	0
Muhsin Muhammad, Car. at Oak.	10	114	0
Jeff Graham, S.D. vs. Pit.	5	113	1
Marvin Harrison, Ind. vs. Min.	12	109	3
Troy Brown, N.E. vs. Mia.	8	102	0
Eric Moulds, Buf. at Sea.	4	101	0

RESULTS

SATURDAY, DECEMBER 23

Buffalo 42, SEATTLE 23
DENVER 38, San Francisco 9
N.Y. GIANTS 28, Jacksonville 25

SUNDAY, DECEMBER 24

ATLANTA 29, Kansas City 13
BALTIMORE 34, N.Y. Jets 20
Chicago 23, DETROIT 20
GREEN BAY 17, Tampa Bay 14 (OT)
INDIANAPOLIS 31, Minnesota 10
Miami 27, NEW ENGLAND 24
OAKLAND 52, Carolina 9
PHILADELPHIA 16, Cincinnati 7
Pittsburgh 34, SAN DIEGO 21
St. Louis 26, NEW ORLEANS 21
WASHINGTON 20, Arizona 3

MONDAY, DECEMBER 25

TENNESSEE 31, Dallas 0
Open date: Cleveland

BRONCOS 38, 49ERS 9

Saturday, December 23

San Francisco	0	0	0	9—	9
Denver	0	17	21	0—	38

Second Quarter
Den.—FG, Elam 20, 4:03.
Den.—Coleman 24 run (Elam kick), 7:27.
Den.—Anderson 1 run (Elam kick), 14:18.

Third Quarter
Den.—McCaffrey 25 pass from Frerotte (Elam kick), 4:27.
Den.—Frerotte 13 run (Elam kick), 6:09.
Den.—Anderson 1 run (Elam kick), 14:45.

Fourth Quarter
S.F.—FG, Richey 44, 5:56.
S.F.—Stokes 8 pass from Garcia (kick failed), 14:21.
Attendance—76,098.

	San Francisco	Denver
First downs	16	28
Rushes-yards	15-46	42-159
Passing	146	203
Punt returns	1-21	2-15
Kickoff returns	4-85	1-13
Interception returns	0-0	1-0
Comp.-att.-int.	18-40-1	20-31-0
Sacked-yards lost	6-42	4-16
Punts	4-42	2-39
Fumbles-lost	2-1	2-1
Penalties-yards	11-110	8-90
Time of possession	23:53	36:07

INDIVIDUAL STATISTICS

RUSHING—San Francisco, Garner 8-3, Beasley 3-9, Smith 2-19, Garcia 2-15. Denver, Anderson 26-85, Coleman 12-52, Frerotte 3-23, Jackson 1-(minus 1).

PASSING—San Francisco, Garcia 18-40-1-188. Denver, Frerotte 18-29-0-205, Griese 2-2-0-14.

RECEIVING—San Francisco, Rice 6-61, Garner 4-29, Stokes 3-43, Owens 3-35, Jackson 1-12, Beasley 1-8. Denver, R. Smith 8-80, McCaffrey 5-71, Griffith 2-13, Carswell 2-8, De. Clark 1-22, Chamberlain 1-15, Montgomery 1-10.

MISSED FIELD GOAL ATTEMPTS—San Francisco, Richey 48. Denver, Elam 41.

INTERCEPTIONS—Denver, Buckley 1-0.

KICKOFF RETURNS—San Francisco, Lewis 4-85. Denver, O'Neal 1-13.

PUNT RETURNS—San Francisco, K. Williams 1-21. Denver, O'Neal 2-15.

SACKS—San Francisco, Buckner 1.5, Pleasant 1, Heard 1, Okeafor 0.5. Denver, Romanowski 1, Mobley 1, Crockett 1, Hasselbach 1, Pittman 1, Pryce 1.

GIANTS 28, JAGUARS 25

Saturday, December 23

Jacksonville	0	7	3	15—	25
N.Y. Giants	7	0	0	21—	28

First Quarter
NYG—Barber 3 run (Daluiso kick), 14:15.

Second Quarter
Jac.—Taylor 44 run (Hollis kick), 1:37.

Third Quarter
Jac.—FG, Hollis 36, 1:41.

Fourth Quarter
NYG—Hilliard 5 pass from Collins (Daluiso kick), 3:49.
NYG—Toomer 54 pass from Collins (Daluiso kick), 11:55.
Jac.—Brady 5 pass from Brunell (Brady pass from Brunell), 13:04.
NYG—Sehorn 38 kickoff return (Daluiso kick), 13:09.
Jac.—Whitted 12 pass from Brunell (Hollis kick), 14:41.
Attendance—77,924.

	Jacksonville	N.Y. Giants
First downs	14	19
Rushes-yards	18-70	31-80
Passing	257	293
Punt returns	1-0	2-9
Kickoff returns	5-97	4-96
Interception returns	1-7	1-12
Comp.-att.-int.	23-41-1	22-39-1
Sacked-yards lost	2-5	3-28
Punts	7-42	5-30
Fumbles-lost	1-1	0-0
Penalties-yards	3-25	1-10
Time of possession	25:39	34:21

INDIVIDUAL STATISTICS

RUSHING—Jacksonville, Taylor 13-52, Johnson 5-18. New York, Barber 24-78, Dayne 6-3, Collins 1-(minus 1).

PASSING—Jacksonville, Brunell 23-41-1-262. New York, Collins 22-39-1-321.

RECEIVING—Jacksonville, McCardell 11-131, Whitted 4-39, Brady 4-31, Barlow 1-28, Shelton 1-16, Taylor 1-9, Johnson 1-8. New York, Toomer 8-193, Hilliard 4-51, Barber 4-35, Comella 4-22, Mitchell 1-17, Campbell 1-3.

MISSED FIELD GOAL ATTEMPTS—New York, Daluiso 39.

INTERCEPTIONS—Jacksonville, Brackens 1-7. New York, Phillips 1-12.

KICKOFF RETURNS—Jacksonville, Whitted 3-47, J. Williams 2-50. New York, Dixon 3-58, Sehorn 1-38.

PUNT RETURNS—Jacksonville, Barlow 1-0. New York, Barber 2-9.

SACKS—Jacksonville, Hardy 1, Smeenge 1, Wynn 1. New York, Jones 1, Griffin 0.5, K. Hamilton 0.5.

BILLS 42, SEAHAWKS 23

Saturday, December 23

Buffalo	21	7	7	7—	42
Seattle	7	7	3	6—	23

First Quarter
Buf.—Bryson 11 pass from Flutie (Christie kick), 4:40.
Buf.—P. Price 18 pass from Flutie (Christie kick), 11:37.
Sea.—Rogers 81 kickoff return (Lindell kick), 11:52.
Buf.—A. Smith 9 run (Christie kick), 13:31.

Second Quarter
Sea.—Kitna 1 run (Lindell kick), 5:20.
Buf.—Riemersma 6 pass from Flutie (Christie kick), 13:51.

Third Quarter
Sea.—FG, Lindell 38, 8:14.
Buf.—A. Smith 2 run (Christie kick), 14:34.

Fourth Quarter
Sea.—Watters 6 run (pass failed), 5:31.
Buf.—A. Smith 4 run (Christie kick), 8:17.
Attendance—61,025.

	Buffalo	Seattle
First downs	27	17
Rushes-yards	37-213	26-126
Passing	366	186
Punt returns	0-0	1-4
Kickoff returns	5-84	7-199
Interception returns	1-0	0-0
Comp.-att.-int.	20-25-0	18-29-1
Sacked-yards lost	0-0	5-9
Punts	1-34	3-38
Fumbles-lost	2-2	5-3
Penalties-yards	2-10	4-45
Time of possession	32:56	27:04

INDIVIDUAL STATISTICS

RUSHING—Buffalo, A. Smith 17-147, Flutie 8-31, Linton 8-24, Bryson 3-6, P. Price 1-5. Seattle, Watters 17-67, Alexander 5-42, Kitna 4-17.

PASSING—Buffalo, Flutie 20-25-0-366. Seattle, Kitna 18-29-1-195.

RECEIVING—Buffalo, P. Price 8-132, Moulds 4-101, Riemersma 3-24, McDaniel 2-55, Cavil 1-39, Bryson 1-11, A. Smith 1-4. Seattle, Watters 5-47, Jackson 3-40, Mayes 3-23, Bailey 2-34, Fauria 2-26, Dawkins 2-23, Strong 1-2.

MISSED FIELD GOAL ATTEMPTS—Buffalo, Christie 26.

INTERCEPTIONS—Buffalo, Flowers 1-0.

KICKOFF RETURNS—Buffalo, Black 4-68, Linton 1-16. Seattle, Rogers 4-171, Mili 1-19, Fauria 1-9, R. Brown 1-0.

PUNT RETURNS—Seattle, Rogers 1-4.

SACKS—Buffalo, Newman 2, F. Jones 1, Flowers 1, Larsen 1.

RAMS 26, SAINTS 21

Sunday, December 24

St. Louis	7	3	9	7—26
New Orleans	0	7	0	14—21

First Quarter
St.L.—Faulk 13 pass from Warner (Wilkins kick), 5:45.

Second Quarter
N.O.—D. Smith 41 interception return (Brien kick), 4:31.
St.L.—FG, Wilkins 19, 13:42.

Third Quarter
St.L.—FG, Wilkins 39, 3:19.
St.L.—Faulk 9 run (run failed), 12:15.

Fourth Quarter
N.O.—Jackson 28 pass from Brooks (Brien kick), 5:39.
St.L.—Faulk 1 run (Wilkins kick), 11:33.
N.O.—Horn 22 pass from Brooks (Brien kick), 12:36.
Attendance—64,900.

	St. Louis	New Orleans
First downs	26	12
Rushes-yards	42-246	15-73
Passing	228	196
Punt returns	3-4	2-15
Kickoff returns	4-66	5-144
Interception returns	1-14	1-41
Comp.-att.-int.	18-27-1	16-31-1
Sacked-yards lost	3-20	2-12
Punts	4-42	7-39
Fumbles-lost	0-0	3-0
Penalties-yards	6-65	7-48
Time of possession	37:42	22:18

INDIVIDUAL STATISTICS
RUSHING—St. Louis, Faulk 32-220, Holcombe 4-10, Watson 2-16, Warner 2-1, Holt 1-0, Green 1-(minus 1). New Orleans, Allen 6-17, Moore 4-45, Brooks 3-7, Morton 1-3, Milne 1-1.

PASSING—St. Louis, Warner 12-17-1-133, Green 6-10-0-115. New Orleans, Brooks 16-31-1-208.

RECEIVING—St. Louis, Faulk 7-41, Holt 5-121, Bruce 2-43, Proehl 2-32, Conwell 1-8, R. Williams 1-3. New Orleans, Horn 5-60, Jackson 4-71, Reed 2-36, Milne 2-20, Wilson 1-10, Hall 1-6, Morton 1-5.

MISSED FIELD GOAL ATTEMPTS—None.

INTERCEPTIONS—St. Louis, Bly 1-14. New Orleans, D. Smith 1-41.

KICKOFF RETURNS—St. Louis, Blevins 3-64, Hakim 1-2. New Orleans, McAfee 5-138.

PUNT RETURNS—St. Louis, Hakim 3-4. New Orleans, Canty 2-15.

SACKS—St. Louis, Lyght 1, Carter 1. New Orleans, Hand 1, L. Glover 1, Whitehead 1.

RAVENS 34, JETS 20

Sunday, December 24

N.Y. Jets	14	0	3	3—20
Baltimore	0	20	7	7—34

First Quarter
NYJ—Ward 37 pass from Testaverde (Conway kick), 2:24.
NYJ—R. Anderson 35 pass from Testaverde (Conway kick), 6:11.

Second Quarter
Bal.—Ismail 7 pass from Dilfer (Stover kick), 2:53.
Bal.—FG, Stover 42, 4:47.
Bal.—C. Martin tackled in end zone by M. McCrary for a safety, 8:39.
Bal.—McAlister 98 interception return (Ja. Lewis run), 14:53.

Third Quarter
NYJ—FG, Conway 40, 4:02.
Bal.—Je. Lewis 54 punt return (Stover kick), 8:41.

Fourth Quarter
NYJ—FG, Conway 19, 3:01.
Bal.—Je. Lewis 89 punt return (Stover kick), 9:58.
Attendance—69,184.

	N.Y. Jets	Baltimore
First downs	22	5
Rushes-yards	21-51	26-64
Passing	473	78
Punt returns	6-47	4-173
Kickoff returns	6-118	6-130
Interception returns	2-(-1)	3-183

	N.Y. Jets	Baltimore
Comp.-att.-int.	36-69-3	11-25-2
Sacked-yards lost	1-8	4-21
Punts	6-50	10-42
Fumbles-lost	4-3	0-0
Penalties-yards	4-19	5-32
Time of possession	32:14	27:46

INDIVIDUAL STATISTICS
RUSHING—New York, Martin 18-47, Testaverde 2-0, R. Anderson 1-4. Baltimore, Ja. Lewis 22-52, Holmes 2-7, Dilfer 1-3, Banks 1-2.

PASSING—New York, Testaverde 36-69-3-481. Baltimore, Dilfer 11-25-2-99.

RECEIVING—New York, R. Anderson 11-139, Ward 8-147, Martin 8-55, Chrebet 5-97, Becht 2-15, W. Hayes 1-20, Sowell 1-8. Baltimore, Sharpe 5-46, Holmes 3-40, Gash 1-7, Ismail 1-7, Dilfer 1-(minus 1).

MISSED FIELD GOAL ATTEMPTS—Baltimore, Stover 45.

INTERCEPTIONS—New York, Glenn 1-0, Coleman 1-(minus 1). Baltimore, Starks 2-85, McAlister 1-98.

KICKOFF RETURNS—New York, L. Johnson 3-60, Stone 2-42, Coles 1-16. Baltimore, Harris 5-107, J. Lewis 1-23.

PUNT RETURNS—New York, L. Johnson 6-47. Baltimore, J. Lewis 4-173.

SACKS—New York, Lewis 2, M. Jones 1, Burton 1. Baltimore, Burnett 1.

EAGLES 16, BENGALS 7

Sunday, December 24

Cincinnati	0	0	0	7— 7
Philadelphia	10	3	0	3—16

First Quarter
Phi.—FG, Akers 32, 9:52.
Phi.—C. Johnson 39 pass from McNabb (Akers kick), 11:03.

Second Quarter
Phi.—FG, Akers 45, 13:54.

Fourth Quarter
Cin.—Warrick 17 pass from S. Mitchell (Rackers kick), 11:48.
Phi.—FG, Akers 33, 13:12.
Attendance—64,902.

	Cincinnati	Philadelphia
First downs	15	22
Rushes-yards	26-102	35-138
Passing	169	183
Punt returns	2-26	1-14
Kickoff returns	5-86	2-22
Interception returns	1-12	1-0
Comp.-att.-int.	18-34-1	23-40-1
Sacked-yards lost	2-14	2-15
Punts	5-37	3-43
Fumbles-lost	3-2	3-3
Penalties-yards	6-39	4-34
Time of possession	22:50	37:10

INDIVIDUAL STATISTICS
RUSHING—Cincinnati, Dillon 16-39, Bennett 5-36, N. Williams 2-14, S. Mitchell 2-7, Warrick 1-6. Philadelphia, Warren 15-42, Pritchett 8-21, Autry 4-20, McNabb 4-20, C. Martin 2-28, Mitchell 1-7, C. Johnson 1-0.

PASSING—Cincinnati, S. Mitchell 18-34-1-183. Philadelphia, McNabb 23-40-1-198.

RECEIVING—Cincinnati, Farmer 5-54, Warrick 3-38, Bush 2-31, Yeast 2-16, Dugans 2-15, Battaglia 2-9, Bennett 1-19, Dillon 1-1. Philadelphia, Lewis 9-66, C. Johnson 4-69, C. Martin 3-14, Pritchett 2-20, Small 2-18, Brown 1-7, McNabb 1-3, Warren 1-1.

MISSED FIELD GOAL ATTEMPTS—Cincinnati, Rackers 31. Philadelphia, Akers 41.

INTERCEPTIONS—Cincinnati, Hall 1-12. Philadelphia, Emmons 1-0.

KICKOFF RETURNS—Cincinnati, Mack 4-75, Keaton 1-11. Philadelphia, Mitchell 1-20, Dawkins 1-2.

PUNT RETURNS—Cincinnati, Warrick 2-26. Philadelphia, Mitchell 1-14.

SACKS—Cincinnati, Spearman 1, Foley 1. Philadelphia, H. Thomas 1, Whiting 1.

FALCONS 29, CHIEFS 13

Sunday, December 24

Kansas City	7	0	0	6—13
Atlanta	7	6	6	10—29

First Quarter
Atl.—Jefferson 17 pass from Chandler (Andersen kick), 8:12.
K.C.—Gonzalez 21 pass from Grbac (Peterson kick), 14:41.

Second Quarter
Atl.—FG, Andersen 24, 8:22.
Atl.—FG, Andersen 48, 12:20.

Third Quarter
Atl.—FG, Andersen 42, 10:19.
Atl.—FG, Andersen 23, 14:46.

Fourth Quarter
Atl.—Kozlowski 6 pass from Chandler (Andersen kick), 8:04.
Atl.—FG, Andersen 36, 13:04.
K.C.—Moreau 1 run (pass failed), 14:50.
    Attendance—41,017.

	Kansas City	Atlanta
First downs	15	20
Rushes-yards	12-49	36-131
Passing	210	157
Punt returns	1-10	3-63
Kickoff returns	7-122	3-49
Interception returns	0-0	0-0
Comp.-att.-int.	18-32-0	20-29-0
Sacked-yards lost	4-20	3-6
Punts	5-46	2-44
Fumbles-lost	2-1	1-0
Penalties-yards	5-25	4-30
Time of possession	18:42	41:18

INDIVIDUAL STATISTICS
RUSHING—Kansas City, Richardson 8-30, Grbac 2-15, Moreau 2-4. Atlanta, Anderson 28-107, Chandler 4-22, M. Smith 4-2.

PASSING—Kansas City, Grbac 18-32-0-230. Atlanta, Chandler 20-29-0-163.

RECEIVING—Kansas City, Gonzalez 5-86, Lockett 4-51, Alexander 4-43, Richardson 4-32, Morris 1-18. Atlanta, Mathis 4-34, R. Kelly 4-31, Anderson 4-28, Jefferson 3-37, Christian 3-21, Kozlowski 2-12.

MISSED FIELD GOAL ATTEMPTS—Kansas City, Peterson 43.

INTERCEPTIONS—None.

KICKOFF RETURNS—Kansas City, Cloud 5-85, L. Parker 1-23, Anders 1-14. Atlanta, Dwight 2-47, Finneran 1-2.

PUNT RETURNS—Kansas City, Lockett 1-10. Atlanta, Dwight 3-23.

SACKS—Kansas City, Clemons 1, Browning 1, T. Williams 1. Atlanta, B. Smith 2, Carter 1, Hall 1.

REDSKINS 20, CARDINALS 3
Sunday, December 24

Arizona	0	3	0	0—	3
Washington	14	6	0	0—	20

First Quarter
Was.—Bailey 7 run (Murray kick), 4:04.
Was.—Fryar 7 pass from B. Johnson (Murray kick), 8:21.

Second Quarter
Was.—FG, Murray 41, 0:04.
Was.—FG, Bentley 50, 5:45.
Ariz.—FG, Blanchard 37, 13:54.
    Attendance—65,711.

	Arizona	Washington
First downs	14	18
Rushes-yards	21-104	34-140
Passing	141	175
Punt returns	2-6	1-11
Kickoff returns	5-134	2-31
Interception returns	2-83	3-32
Comp.-att.-int.	14-32-3	20-33-2
Sacked-yards lost	1-3	2-15
Punts	4-41	5-38
Fumbles-lost	3-2	0-0
Penalties-yards	7-50	8-85
Time of possession	23:07	36:53

INDIVIDUAL STATISTICS
RUSHING—Arizona, Pittman 16-72, Plummer 4-30, Boston 1-2. Washington, Davis 27-120, Fryar 2-16, Bailey 1-7, B. Johnson 1-5, Centers 1-0, Husak 1-(minus 1), Murrell 1-(minus 7).

PASSING—Arizona, Plummer 14-31-3-144, Da. Brown 0-1-0-0. Washington, B. Johnson 18-31-2-192, Husak 2-2-0-(minus 2).

RECEIVING—Arizona, Sanders 4-47, Pittman 3-13, Mitchell 2-53, Jenkins 2-22, Hardy 2-(minus 3), Boston 1-12. Washington, Centers 7-34, Alexander 3-35, Fryar 3-25, Davis 3-22, Bailey 2-54, Sellers 1-14, Connell 1-6.

MISSED FIELD GOAL ATTEMPTS—Washington, Murray 43.

INTERCEPTIONS—Arizona, A. Williams 2-56. Washington, Carrier 1-30, Green 1-2, Bailey 1-0.

KICKOFF RETURNS—Arizona, Jenkins 5-134. Washington, Sellers 1-21, Thrash 1-10.

PUNT RETURNS—Arizona, Cody 2-6. Washington, Bailey 1-11.

SACKS—Arizona, McKinnon 1, Rice 1. Washington, B. Smith 1.

BEARS 23, LIONS 20
Sunday, December 24

Chicago	0	6	7	10—23	
Detroit	10	0	0	10—20	

First Quarter
Det.—FG, Hanson 41, 7:51.
Det.—Sloan 9 pass from Batch (Hanson kick), 8:08.

Second Quarter
Chi.—FG, Edinger 37, 1:11.
Chi.—FG, Edinger 50, 10:23.

Third Quarter
Chi.—Booker 27 pass from McNown (Edinger kick), 13:13.

Fourth Quarter
Det.—Case 13 run (Hanson kick), 3:46.
Chi.—McQuarters 61 interception return (Edinger kick), 8:29.
Det.—FG, Hanson 26, 13:04.
Chi.—FG, Edinger 54, 14:58.
    Attendance—71,957.

	Chicago	Detroit
First downs	15	18
Rushes-yards	26-105	26-100
Passing	181	140
Punt returns	1-10	2-10
Kickoff returns	4-87	5-126
Interception returns	1-61	0-0
Comp.-att.-int.	19-29-0	19-36-1
Sacked-yards lost	1-2	5-30
Punts	5-38	6-42
Fumbles-lost	3-2	1-1
Penalties-yards	5-28	2-20
Time of possession	28:56	31:04

INDIVIDUAL STATISTICS
RUSHING—Chicago, Allen 22-72, Barnes 2-30, McNown 2-3. Detroit, J. Stewart 20-57, Case 5-41, Bates 1-2.

PASSING—Chicago, Matthews 14-18-0-123, McNown 5-11-0-60. Detroit, Case 12-21-1-89, Batch 7-15-0-81.

RECEIVING—Chicago, Booker 7-79, Kennison 3-30, Allen 3-24, Sinceno 3-20, White 2-20, Dragos 1-10. Detroit, Morton 6-60, Sloan 4-33, Moore 4-24, Crowell 2-19, J. Stewart 1-17, Bates 1-12, Schlesinger 1-5.

MISSED FIELD GOAL ATTEMPTS—None.

INTERCEPTIONS—Chicago, McQuarters 1-61.

KICKOFF RETURNS—Chicago, Milburn 4-87. Detroit, Howard 5-126.

PUNT RETURNS—Chicago, Milburn 1-10. Detroit, Howard 2-10.

SACKS—Chicago, B. Robinson 2, Urlacher 1, S. Harris 1, T. Smith 1. Detroit, Scroggins 1.

DOLPHINS 27, PATRIOTS 24
Sunday, December 24

Miami	3	14	0	10—27	
New England	7	14	3	0—24	

First Quarter
Mia.—FG, Mare 47, 5:04.
N.E.—T. Carter 1 run (Vinatieri kick), 10:55.

Second Quarter
N.E.—Faulk 52 pass from Bledsoe (Vinatieri kick), 6:44.
Mia.—Goodwin 9 pass from Fiedler (Mare kick), 11:20.
Mia.—L. Smith 1 run (Mare kick), 12:47.
N.E.—Glenn 16 pass from Bledsoe (Vinatieri kick), 14:57.

Third Quarter
N.E.—FG, Vinatieri 33, 8:43.

Fourth Quarter

Mia.—L. Smith 1 run (Mare kick), 10:51.
Mia.—FG, Mare 49, 14:51.
  Attendance—60,292.

	Miami	New England
First downs	25	18
Rushes-yards	24-47	21-37
Passing	263	311
Punt returns	2-67	2-10
Kickoff returns	5-78	4-72
Interception returns	2-2	0-0
Comp.-att.-int.	31-46-0	18-35-2
Sacked-yards lost	2-8	1-1
Punts	5-38	5-34
Fumbles-lost	0-0	1-1
Penalties-yards	5-25	5-58
Time of possession	35:39	24:21

INDIVIDUAL STATISTICS

RUSHING—Miami, L. Smith 20-26, Fiedler 2-22, Denson 2-(minus 1). New England, Faulk 12-34, Redmond 6-3, T. Carter 2-(minus 4), Glenn 1-4.

PASSING—Miami, Fiedler 30-45-0-264, Huard 1-1-0-7. New England, Bledsoe 18-34-2-312, Bishop 0-1-0-0.

RECEIVING—Miami, Gadsden 7-43, Weaver 5-63, McDuffie 5-44, Martin 4-44, L. Smith 2-21, Dyer 2-14, Denson 2-11, Goodwin 2-11, Ogden 1-12, Johnson 1-8. New England, Brown 8-102, Wiggins 4-81, Faulk 2-80, Glenn 2-41, Redmond 2-8.

MISSED FIELD GOAL ATTEMPTS—Miami, Mare 47, 28.

INTERCEPTIONS—Miami, Taylor 1-2, Z. Thomas 1-0.

KICKOFF RETURNS—Miami, Williams 2-40, Denson 2-38, Goodwin 1-0. New England, Jackson 3-66, Bruschi 1-6.

PUNT RETURNS—Miami, Ogden 2-67. New England, Brown 2-10.

SACKS—Miami, Bromell 1. New England, McGinest 1, A. Harris 1.

COLTS 31, VIKINGS 10

Sunday, December 24

Minnesota	7	3	0	0—10
Indianapolis	7	14	7	3—31

First Quarter

Ind.—Harrison 4 pass from Manning (Vanderjagt kick), 7:28.
Min.—Moss 42 pass from Culpepper (Anderson kick), 11:53.

Second Quarter

Ind.—James 52 pass from Manning (Vanderjagt kick), 5:48.
Min.—FG, Anderson 31, 9:56.
Ind.—Harrison 15 pass from Manning (Vanderjagt kick), 13:41.

Third Quarter

Ind.—Harrison 18 pass from Manning (Vanderjagt kick), 7:13.

Fourth Quarter

Ind.—FG, Vanderjagt 28, 5:06.
  Attendance—56,672.

	Minnesota	Indianapolis
First downs	11	25
Rushes-yards	21-67	29-128
Passing	169	283
Punt returns	3-26	3-13
Kickoff returns	5-133	3-57
Interception returns	1-12	1-3
Comp.-att.-int.	16-28-1	25-36-1
Sacked-yards lost	1-6	0-0
Punts	7-46	4-48
Fumbles-lost	2-0	1-0
Penalties-yards	6-53	3-20
Time of possession	26:01	33:59

INDIVIDUAL STATISTICS

RUSHING—Minnesota, R. Smith 15-37, Brister 3-23, Kleinsasser 1-3, Walters 1-3, M. Williams 1-1. Indianapolis, James 26-128, Gordon 2-1, Manning 1-(minus 1).

PASSING—Minnesota, Brister 9-18-1-78, Culpepper 7-10-0-97. Indianapolis, Manning 25-36-1-283.

RECEIVING—Minnesota, C. Carter 4-67, Walsh 4-29, Jordan 2-19, Kleinsasser 2-11, McWilliams 2-4, Moss 1-42, R. Smith 1-3. Indianapolis, Harrison 12-109, James 5-79, Pathon 4-47, Wilkins 2-21, Pollard 1-21, Finn 1-6.

MISSED FIELD GOAL ATTEMPTS—None.

INTERCEPTIONS—Minnesota, Tate 1-12. Indianapolis, Peterson 1-3.

KICKOFF RETURNS—Minnesota, Walters 4-110, M. Williams 1-23. Indianapolis, Wilkins 2-32, Pathon 1-25.

PUNT RETURNS—Minnesota, Walters 3-26. Indianapolis, Wilkins 3-13.

SACKS—Indianapolis, Belser 1.

PACKERS 17, BUCCANEERS 14

Sunday, December 24

Tampa Bay	0	0	3	11	0—14
Green Bay	7	0	7	0	3—17

First Quarter

G.B.—Green 3 run (Longwell kick), 9:05.

Third Quarter

G.B.—Green 2 run (Longwell kick), 4:59.
T.B.—FG, Gramatica 38, 12:57.

Fourth Quarter

T.B.—K. Johnson 18 pass from King (King run), 5:58.
T.B.—FG, Gramatica 43, 7:10.

Overtime

G.B.—FG, Longwell 22, 6:31.
  Attendance—59,692.

	Tampa Bay	Green Bay
First downs	16	21
Rushes-yards	23-67	38-135
Passing	205	184
Punt returns	2-3	3-14
Kickoff returns	3-65	5-97
Interception returns	2-20	0-0
Comp.-att.-int.	21-42-0	20-42-2
Sacked-yards lost	5-32	1-12
Punts	11-40	8-42
Fumbles-lost	1-0	3-2
Penalties-yards	4-54	6-43
Time of possession	28:36	37:55

INDIVIDUAL STATISTICS

RUSHING—Tampa Bay, Dunn 15-40, King 6-20, Alstott 2-7. Green Bay, Green 27-74, Parker 5-35, Favre 4-23, Driver 1-4, Schroeder 1-(minus 1).

PASSING—Tampa Bay, King 21-42-0-237. Green Bay, Favre 20-42-2-196.

RECEIVING—Tampa Bay, K. Johnson 6-69, Dunn 5-44, Green 4-50, Anthony 3-48, Moore 3-26. Green Bay, Green 9-78, Schroeder 3-51, Driver 2-23, Parker 2-15, Henderson 2-12, Franks 1-11, Wetnight 1-6.

MISSED FIELD GOAL ATTEMPTS—Tampa Bay, Gramatica 40.

INTERCEPTIONS—Tampa Bay, Duncan 1-15, Lynch 1-5.

KICKOFF RETURNS—Tampa Bay, Williams 3-65. Green Bay, Rossum 3-61, Henderson 2-36.

PUNT RETURNS—Tampa Bay, Williams 2-3. Green Bay, Rossum 3-14.

SACKS—Tampa Bay, Sapp 1. Green Bay, Holliday 2, Thierry 2, Gbaja-Biamila 1.

RAIDERS 52, PANTHERS 9

Sunday, December 24

Carolina	3	6	0	0— 9
Oakland	7	17	14	14—52

First Quarter

Oak.—Brigham 4 pass from Gannon (Janikowski kick), 6:47.
Car.—FG, Nedney 46, 8:14.

Second Quarter

Oak.—FG, Janikowski 42, 0:04.
Car.—FG, Nedney 21, 4:53.
Oak.—Dudley 1 pass from Gannon (Janikowski kick), 11:52.
Oak.—Brown 9 pass from Gannon (Janikowski kick), 14:41.
Car.—FG, Nedney 51, 15:00.

Third Quarter

Oak.—Dudley 21 pass from Gannon (Janikowski kick), 2:47.
Oak.—Allen 37 interception return (Janikowski kick), 3:44.

Fourth Quarter

Oak.—Brigham 2 pass from Gannon (Janikowski kick), 2:54.
Oak.—Gordon 74 fumble return (Janikowski kick), 15:00.
  Attendance—60,637.

	Carolina	Oakland
First downs	19	28
Rushes-yards	12-79	39-179
Passing	218	230
Punt returns	0-0	1-36
Kickoff returns	6-99	3-49
Interception returns	0-0	1-37
Comp.-att.-int.	22-37-1	26-32-0
Sacked-yards lost	2-17	0-0
Punts	3-30	1-38
Fumbles-lost	3-3	0-0
Penalties-yards	5-70	7-60
Time of possession	21:36	38:24

INDIVIDUAL STATISTICS

RUSHING—Carolina, Hetherington 4-29, Biakabutuka 3-29, Lewis 2-21, Beuerlein 2-(minus 2), Hoover 1-2. Oakland, Wheatley 17-66, Kirby 11-51, Jordan 6-20, Gannon 3-32, Crockett 2-10.

PASSING—Carolina, Beuerlein 12-21-1-156, Lewis 10-16-0-79. Oakland, Gannon 26-32-0-230.

RECEIVING—Carolina, Muhammad 10-114, Hayes 6-66, Hoover 3-21, Hetherington 1-12, Biakabutuka 1-12, Mangum 1-10. Oakland, Jett 4-57, Jordan 4-37, Dudley 4-32, Crockett 4-29, Kirby 3-19, Brown 3-18, Rison 2-32, Brigham 2-6.

MISSED FIELD GOAL ATTEMPTS—None.

INTERCEPTIONS—Oakland, Allen 1-37.

KICKOFF RETURNS—Carolina, Bates 5-79, Byrd 1-20. Oakland, Dunn 3-49.

PUNT RETURNS—Oakland, Gordon 1-36.

SACKS—Oakland, Jackson 1.5, Johnstone 0.5.

STEELERS 34, CHARGERS 21

Sunday, December 24

Pittsburgh	7	17	0	10—34
San Diego	14	0	7	0—21

First Quarter
S.D.—J. Graham 71 pass from Leaf (Carney kick), 1:58.
Pit.—Blackwell 98 kickoff return (K. Brown kick), 2:19.
S.D.—Harrison 63 interception return (Carney kick), 4:40.

Second Quarter
Pit.—Hawkins 5 pass from Stewart (K. Brown kick), 6:17.
Pit.—FG, K. Brown 32, 12:46.
Pit.—Stewart 19 run (K. Brown kick), 14:05.

Third Quarter
S.D.—Fletcher 1 run (Carney kick), 10:15.

Fourth Quarter
Pit.—Stewart 1 run (K. Brown kick), 2:09.
Pit.—FG, K. Brown 28, 10:53.
Attendance—50,809.

	Pittsburgh	San Diego
First downs	21	6
Rushes-yards	41-131	12-31
Passing	185	140
Punt returns	5-84	4-24
Kickoff returns	4-153	5-102
Interception returns	1-14	2-78
Comp.-att.-int.	16-33-2	15-29-1
Sacked-yards lost	2-5	6-31
Punts	6-46	8-51
Fumbles-lost	1-0	1-1
Penalties-yards	1-10	8-82
Time of possession	39:21	20:39

INDIVIDUAL STATISTICS

RUSHING—Pittsburgh, Bettis 26-51, Stewart 10-81, Graham 3-(minus 2), Huntley 2-1. San Diego, Fletcher 11-25, Leaf 1-6.

PASSING—Pittsburgh, Stewart 16-32-2-190, Bettis 0-1-0-0. San Diego, Leaf 15-29-1-171.

RECEIVING—Pittsburgh, Hawkins 5-71, Ward 4-36, Bruener 2-33, Huntley 2-30, Bettis 2-10, Kreider 1-10. San Diego, J. Graham 5-113, Conway 4-28, F. Jones 3-14, Fletcher 1-11, Heiden 1-3, McCrary 1-2.

MISSED FIELD GOAL ATTEMPTS—None.

INTERCEPTIONS—Pittsburgh, Codie 1-14. San Diego, Harrison 2-78.

KICKOFF RETURNS—Pittsburgh, Blackwell 3-140, Poteat 1-13. San Diego, R. Jenkins 5-102.

PUNT RETURNS—Pittsburgh, Poteat 5-84. San Diego, R. Jones 4-24.

SACKS—Pittsburgh, Gildon 2, Porter 1.5, Townsend 1.5, Alexander 1. San Diego, Parrella 1, Mickell 1.

TITANS 31, COWBOYS 0

Monday, December 25

Dallas	0	0	0	0— 0
Tennessee	7	0	24	0—31

First Quarter
Ten.—Mason 17 pass from McNair (Del Greco kick), 6:08.

Third Quarter
Ten.—George 11 run (Del Greco kick), 0:53.
Ten.—Ford 30 fumble return (Del Greco kick), 3:03.
Ten.—Bulluck 8 interception return (Del Greco kick), 9:29.
Ten.—FG, Del Greco 21, 14:06.
Attendance—68,498.

	Dallas	Tennessee
First downs	6	23
Rushes-yards	29-86	35-159
Passing	9	215
Punt returns	2-16	3-27
Kickoff returns	6-140	1-(-57)
Interception returns	2-4	2-8
Comp.-att.-int.	5-20-2	20-33-2
Sacked-yards lost	3-26	1-1
Punts	10-40	5-37
Fumbles-lost	8-3	2-2
Penalties-yards	7-51	7-51
Time of possession	25:26	34:34

INDIVIDUAL STATISTICS

RUSHING—Dallas, Hambrick 6-28, E. Smith 12-20, Wiley 5-17, Wright 3-9, Tucker 1-9, McGarity 1-3, Thomas 1-0. Tennessee, George 19-83, Thomas 9-46, McNair 4-31, O'Donnell 1-(minus 3).

PASSING—Dallas, Wright 5-20-2-35. Tennessee, McNair 17-23-2-188, O'Donnell 3-10-0-28.

RECEIVING—Dallas, McKnight 2-30, Harris 2-9, Wiley 1-(minus 4). Tennessee, Mason 6-95, Wycheck 5-45, Thigpen 2-26, George 1-14, Kinney 3-10, Sanders 1-10, Thomas 1-9, Neal 1-7.

MISSED FIELD GOAL ATTEMPTS—None.

INTERCEPTIONS—Dallas, McNeil 1-2, Wortham 1-2. Tennessee, Walker 1-0, Bulluck 1-8.

KICKOFF RETURNS—Dallas, Wiley 5-128, Goodrich 1-12. Tennessee, Myers 1-(-57).

PUNT RETURNS—Dallas, McGarity 2-16. Tennessee, Mason 2-27, Walker 1-0.

SACKS—Dallas, Ellis 1. Tennessee, Godfrey 2, Kearse 1.

WILD-CARD GAMES

By DENNIS DILLON

Reprinted from the January 8, 2001 issue of The Sporting News

Extra Points: Observations on the wild-card playoffs

If I'm a Vegas oddsmaker, I list the over/under for the Ravens-Titans game at $5^{1}/_{2}$ points. If I'm a bettor, I take the under. The teams' defenses are simply superb. ...

You could make a lot of arguments why Jim Haslett should be the coach of the year, but here's the most convincing one: His Saints dominated the Rams with an entire unit of backup skill players. No Ricky Williams. No Jeff Blake. No Joe Horn (after the third play of last Saturday's game). New Orleans ran up a 31-7 lead with QB Aaron Brooks, RB Terry Allen and journeyman WR Willie (three touchdowns) Jackson propelling the offense. ...

Even those Dolphins fans who forked over money to buy tickets to the game against the Colts that was blacked out locally missed RB Lamar Smith's final carry. Smith rushed 40 times (an NFL postseason record) for 209 yards, including a 17-yard TD run in overtime that lifted the Dolphins to victory. In the locker room after the game, a giddy coach Dave Wannstedt handed Smith a game ball, then jumped on Smith's back. ...

The Broncos hoisted a white flag when they brought in third-string QB Jarious Jackson with 4:31

GAME SUMMARIES

DOLPHINS 23, COLTS 17

Saturday, December 30

Indianapolis	3	11	0	3	0—17
Miami	0	0	7	10	6—23

First Quarter
Ind.—FG, Vanderjagt 32, 7:11.

Second Quarter
Ind.—FG, Vanderjagt 26, 5:27.
Ind.—Pathon 17 pass from Manning (Dilger pass from Manning), 7:13.

Third Quarter
Mia.—L. Smith 2 run (Mare kick), 6:51.

Fourth Quarter
Mia.—FG, Mare 38, 4:37.
Ind.—FG, Vanderjagt 50, 10:05.
Mia.—Weaver 9 pass from Fiedler (Mare kick), 14:26.

Overtime
Mia.—L. Smith 17 run, 11:26.
Attendance—73,193.

	Indianapolis	Miami
First downs	14	26
Rushes-yards	23-99	48-258
Passing	194	176
Punt returns	1-0	3-30
Kickoff returns	2-35	4-90
Interception returns	3-27	0-0
Comp.-att.-int.	17-32-0	19-34-3
Sacked-yards lost	0-0	2-9
Punts	4-43	3-46
Fumbles-lost	0-0	0-0
Penalties-yards	1-10	7-55
Time of possession	27:46	43:40

INDIVIDUAL STATISTICS
RUSHING—Indianapolis, James 21-107, Manning 1-(minus 2), Smith 1-(minus 6). Miami, L. Smith 40-209, Fiedler 7-43, Martin 1-6.
PASSING—Indianapolis, Manning 17-32-0-194. Miami, Fiedler 19-34-3-185.
RECEIVING—Indianapolis, Pathon 5-69, Harrison 5-63, James 3-33, Dilger 3-16, Pollard 1-13. Miami, McDuffie 4-57, Gadsden 4-38, L. Smith 3-18, Martin 2-21, Johnson 2-18, Denson 2-18, Weaver 1-9, Ogden 1-6.
MISSED FIELD GOAL ATTEMPTS—Indianapolis, Vanderjagt 49. Miami, Mare 38.
INTERCEPTIONS—Indianapolis, Cota 2-23, Bratzke 1-4.
KICKOFF RETURNS—Indianapolis, Wilkins 2-35. Miami, Williams 3-59, Denson 1-31.
PUNT RETURNS—Indianapolis, Wilkins 1-0. Miami, Ogden 3-30.
SACKS—Indianapolis, E. Johnson 1, Belser 0.5, Whittington 0.5.

RAVENS 21, BRONCOS 3

Sunday, December 31

Denver	0	3	0	0—	3
Baltimore	0	14	7	0—	21

Second Quarter
Bal.—Ja. Lewis 1 run (Stover kick), 3:17.
Den.—FG, Elam 31, 10:29.
Bal.—Sharpe 58 pass from Dilfer (Stover kick), 10:54.

Third Quarter
Bal.—Ja. Lewis 27 run (Stover kick), 11:41.
Attendance—69,638.

	Denver	Baltimore
First downs	9	13
Rushes-yards	18-42	38-122
Passing	135	118
Punt returns	4-13	4-26
Kickoff returns	3-43	2-23
Interception returns	0-0	1-4
Comp.-att.-int.	18-38-1	9-15-0
Sacked-yards lost	5-43	2-12
Punts	9-38	10-38
Fumbles-lost	0-0	1-0
Penalties-yards	6-33	4-30
Time of possession	27:37	32:23

INDIVIDUAL STATISTICS
RUSHING—Denver, Anderson 15-40, R. Smith 2-3, Frerotte 1-(minus 1). Baltimore, Ja. Lewis 30-110, Holmes 5-6, J. Lewis 1-5, Dilfer 1-2, Banks 1-(minus 1).
PASSING—Denver, Frerotte 13-28-1-124, Jackson 5-10-0-54. Baltimore, Dilfer 9-14-0-130, Banks 0-1-0-0.
RECEIVING—Denver, McCaffrey 8-75, R. Smith 3-58, Anderson 2-10, Carswell 2-8, Griffith 1-16, McGriff 1-6, De. Clark 1-5. Baltimore, Ismail 4-35, Sharpe 3-73, Ja. Lewis 1-15, Gash 1-7.
MISSED FIELD GOAL ATTEMPTS—None.
INTERCEPTIONS—Baltimore, R. Lewis 1-4.
KICKOFF RETURNS—Denver, D. Smith 1-15, Chamberlain 1-15, O'Neal 1-13. Baltimore, Harris 1-15, Coates 1-8.
PUNT RETURNS—Denver, O'Neal 3-13, D. Smith 1-0. Baltimore, J. Lewis 4-26.
SACKS—Denver, Jenkins 1, Tanuvasa 1. Baltimore, McCrary 3, Boulware 1, Burnett 1.

2000 REVIEW *Wild-card games*

left in their loss to the Ravens, but it looked like they had given up long before then. Yes, the Ravens had the best rushing defense in the NFL this season (60.6 yards per game), but the Broncos barely tried to test it with 1,500-yard rusher Mike Anderson. ...

It's both unjust and myopic to lay blame for the Rams' loss to New Orleans at the feet of PR Az-Zahir Hakim, whose muffed punt at the 8-yard line with 1:43 to play put the kibosh on the defending Super Bowl champs' season. Those faultfinders are forgetting the three interceptions and one lost fumble by QB Kurt Warner. And the ridiculous holding penalty on TE Roland Williams that wiped out a 51-yard run by Marshall Faulk when the game was tied, 7-7. And another underwhelming performance by the St. Louis defense. Fact is, the Rams looked like they were suffering from a collective concussion before they mounted their frenetic comeback attempt after the Saints took a 31-7 lead with 11:57 left in the game. ...

The Buccaneers' defensive line is arguably the best in the NFL, but the Eagles' O-line steamrollered Warren Sapp and Co. It didn't help that the Bucs were missing 13-sack man Marcus Jones (foot injury). ...

Two hundred fifty-eight rushing yards by a Miami team? In a playoff game? Daniel, Michael, Joseph, Alexandra and Niki Lin Marino, these are not your father's Dolphins. ...

Something tells me defense will be a high priority on both the Colts' and Rams' draft shopping lists. ...

The Saints' most valuable offensive players are Willie Roaf, Wally Williams, Jerry Fontenot, Chris Naeole and Kyle Turley. It's because of the play of those five linemen that the Saints have been able to overcome the losses of their offensive skill players. ...

Here's a sobering thought for those half-naked Eagles fans who were yelling, "We want New York!" near the end of the Eagles' victory over the Bucs. Under coach Jim Fassel, the Giants are 8-0 vs. Philadelphia.

GAME SUMMARIES

SAINTS 31, RAMS 28

Saturday, December 30

St. Louis	7	0	0	21—28
New Orleans	0	10	7	14—31

First Quarter
St.L.—Bruce 17 pass from Warner (Wilkins kick), 9:02.
Second Quarter
N.O.—Wilson 12 pass from Brooks (Brien kick), 0:04.
N.O.—FG, Brien 33, 13:30.
Third Quarter
N.O.—Jackson 10 pass from Brooks (Brien kick), 6:20.
Fourth Quarter
N.O.—Jackson 49 pass from Brooks (Brien kick), 1:38.
N.O.—Jackson 16 pass from Brooks (Brien kick), 3:03.
St.L.—Proehl 17 pass from Warner (run failed), 5:24.
St.L.—Faulk 25 pass from Warner (Wilkins kick), 11:08.
St.L.—Warner 5 run (Faulk pass from Warner), 12:24.
Attendance—64,900.

	St. Louis	New Orleans
First downs	17	17
Rushes-yards	16-34	32-50
Passing	350	251
Punt returns	3-59	3-32
Kickoff returns	5-69	5-83
Interception returns	1-6	3-64
Comp.-att.-int.	24-40-3	16-29-1
Sacked-yards lost	2-15	2-15
Punts	5-43	6-41
Fumbles-lost	3-2	4-1
Penalties-yards	9-60	5-40
Time of possession	28:29	31:31

INDIVIDUAL STATISTICS
RUSHING—St. Louis, Faulk 14-24, Warner 1-5, Watson 1-5. New Orleans, Allen 16-21, Brooks 10-26, Moore 3-1, Morton 2-5, Jackson 1-(minus 3).

PASSING—St. Louis, Warner 24-40-3-365. New Orleans, Brooks 16-29-1-266.

RECEIVING—St. Louis, Bruce 7-127, Faulk 7-99, Proehl 3-46, R. Williams 3-25, Hakim 2-42, Holt 2-26. New Orleans, Jackson 6-142, Wilson 3-41, Reed 3-27, Morton 2-34, A. Glover 1-16, Allen 1-6.

MISSED FIELD GOAL ATTEMPTS—None.

INTERCEPTIONS—St. Louis, Bush 1-6. New Orleans, Knight 2-56, Oldham 1-8.

KICKOFF RETURNS—St. Louis, Horne 5-69. New Orleans, McAfee 3-81, D. Smith 1-2, Mathis 1-0.

PUNT RETURNS—St. Louis, Hakim 3-59. New Orleans, Morton 3-32.

SACKS—St. Louis, Wistrom 1, Little 1. New Orleans, Kei. Mitchell 1, Whitehead 1.

EAGLES 21, BUCCANEERS 3

Sunday, December 31

Tampa Bay	0	3	0	0— 3
Philadelphia	0	14	0	7—21

Second Quarter
T.B.—FG, Gramatica 29, 4:44.
Phi.—McNabb 5 run (Akers kick), 11:39.
Phi.—Brown 5 pass from McNabb (Akers kick), 14:48.
Fourth Quarter
Phi.—Thomason 2 pass from McNabb (Akers kick), 0:47.
Attendance—65,813.

	Tampa Bay	Philadelphia
First downs	11	20
Rushes-yards	19-50	33-126
Passing	149	151
Punt returns	2-12	3-38
Kickoff returns	3-42	2-48
Interception returns	1-0	0-0
Comp.-att.-int.	17-31-0	24-33-1
Sacked-yards lost	4-22	2-10
Punts	6-41	5-37
Fumbles-lost	2-1	1-0
Penalties-yards	7-62	2-20
Time of possession	25:07	34:53

INDIVIDUAL STATISTICS
RUSHING—Tampa Bay, Dunn 8-1, Alstott 7-42, King 4-7. Philadelphia, Warren 22-85, McNabb 8-32, Mitchell 3-9.

PASSING—Tampa Bay, King 17-31-0-171. Philadelphia, McNabb 24-33-1-161.

RECEIVING—Tampa Bay, K. Johnson 6-106, Dunn 5-28, Alstott 2-14, Moore 2-12, Anthony 1-6, Hape 1-5. Philadelphia, C. Johnson 5-47, Mitchell 5-37, Small 3-30, Lewis 3-24, C. Martin 2-8, Pritchett 2-(minus 1), Brown 1-5, Pinkston 1-5, Warren 1-4, Thomason 1-2.

MISSED FIELD GOAL ATTEMPTS—Philadelphia, Akers 36.

INTERCEPTIONS—Tampa Bay, Abraham 1-0.

KICKOFF RETURNS—Tampa Bay, Green 1-21, Williams 1-14, Anthony 1-7. Philadelphia, Mitchell 1-24, D. Douglas 1-24.

PUNT RETURNS—Tampa Bay, Williams 2-12. Philadelphia, Mitchell 3-38.

SACKS—Tampa Bay, White 1, Singleton 0.5, Webster 0.5. Philadelphia, H. Douglas 2, Caldwell 1, H. Thomas 1.

DIVISIONAL PLAYOFFS

By DENNIS DILLON

Reprinted from the January 15, 2001 issue of The Sporting News

Extra Points: Observations on the divisional playoffs

Ray Lewis, you have shown me something. And I think you're going to show a lot more before these playoffs are over. The Ravens' middle linebacker simply is the best player still on the field, and that's why Baltimore will buck the postseason venue trend—home teams have won seven of the eight games—and beat the Raiders in Oakland in the AFC championship game. Lewis was a dominant force in the Ravens' 24-10 victory over the Titans, scoring a

TKO in his one-on-one battle with Tennessee RB Eddie George. In two games in the playoffs, Lewis has 13 solo tackles, six assists, two interceptions, three passes defensed and one touchdown. ...

The Raiders had the No. 1 rushing offense during the regular season; the Ravens had the No. 1 rushing defense. Get ready for a turf war. ...

The Giants' two best players in their ninth straight win over the Eagles were a pair of linemen. OT Lomas Brown, getting occasional help from TE Howard Cross or a chip-blocking running back, reduced DE Hugh Douglas to a non-factor. Douglas' name didn't even appear on the Eagles' defensive stats sheet. Giants DE Michael Strahan (three tackles, one assist, two sacks, one forced fumble) dominated Jon Runyan, overwhelming the Eagles' right offensive tackle on several plays. ...

GAME SUMMARIES

RAIDERS 27, DOLPHINS 0

Saturday, January 6

Miami	0	0	0	0— 0
Oakland	10	10	7	0—27

First Quarter
Oak.—James 90 interception return (Janikowski kick), 3:24.
Oak.—FG, Janikowski 36, 10:08.

Second Quarter
Oak.—FG, Janikowski 33, 6:24.
Oak.—Jett 6 pass from Gannon (Janikowski kick), 13:07.

Third Quarter
Oak.—Wheatley 2 run (Janikowski kick), 9:04.
Attendance—61,998.

	Miami	Oakland
First downs	10	20
Rushes-yards	17-40	45-140
Passing	164	127
Punt returns	4-76	2-26
Kickoff returns	5-116	1-28
Interception returns	0-0	3-98
Comp.-att.-int.	18-37-3	12-18-0
Sacked-yards lost	2-12	3-16
Punts	6-34	5-47
Fumbles-lost	1-1	1-1
Penalties-yards	8-55	6-40
Time of possession	22:36	37:24

INDIVIDUAL STATISTICS

RUSHING—Miami, L. Smith 8-4, Johnson 3-12, Denson 3-12, Fiedler 3-12. Oakland, Wheatley 19-56, Kirby 11-37, Gannon 5-31, Jordan 5-15, Hoying 2-(minus 2), Kaufman 1-4, Crockett 1-3, Jett 1-(minus 4).

PASSING—Miami, Fiedler 18-37-3-176. Oakland, Gannon 12-18-0-143.

RECEIVING—Miami, Denson 6-42, Shepherd 4-20, McDuffie 3-43, Martin 2-27, Gadsden 1-33, Johnson 1-7, L. Smith 1-4. Oakland, Kirby 2-35, Rison 2-28, Brown 2-27, Jordan 2-14, Jett 2-13, Brigham 1-17, Crockett 1-9.

MISSED FIELD GOAL ATTEMPTS—Oakland, Janikowski 58.

INTERCEPTIONS—Oakland, James 2-98, Allen 1-0.

KICKOFF RETURNS—Miami, Denson 5-116. Oakland, Dunn 1-28.

PUNT RETURNS—Miami, Ogden 3-66, McDuffie 1-10. Oakland, Gordon 2-26.

SACKS—Miami, Jones 1, Bromell 1, Armstrong 1. Oakland, Bryant 1, Coleman 1.

RAVENS 24, TITANS 10

Sunday, January 7

Baltimore	0	7	3	14—24
Tennessee	7	0	3	0—10

First Quarter
Ten.—E. George 2 run (Del Greco kick), 7:17.

Second Quarter
Bal.—Ja. Lewis 1 run (Stover kick), 5:14.

Third Quarter
Ten.—FG, Del Greco 21, 6:46.
Bal.—FG, Stover 38, 11:55.

Fourth Quarter
Bal.—A. Mitchell 90 blocked FG return (Stover kick), 2:48.
Bal.—R. Lewis 50 interception return (Stover kick), 8:19.
Attendance—68,527.

	Baltimore	Tennessee
First downs	6	23
Rushes-yards	23-49	33-126
Passing	85	191
Punt returns	1-4	2-5
Kickoff returns	3-69	4-55
Interception returns	1-50	0-0
Comp.-att.-int.	5-17-0	25-47-1
Sacked-yards lost	3-32	1-4
Punts	8-28	5-38
Fumbles-lost	0-0	0-0
Penalties-yards	7-50	6-55
Time of possession	19:31	40:29

INDIVIDUAL STATISTICS

RUSHING—Baltimore, Ja. Lewis 17-47, Dilfer 4-1, J. Lewis 1-1, Gash 1-0. Tennessee, E. George 27-91, McNair 5-31, Thomas 1-4.

PASSING—Baltimore, Dilfer 5-16-0-117, Banks 0-1-0-0. Tennessee, McNair 24-46-1-176, O'Donnell 1-1-0-19.

RECEIVING—Baltimore, Ismail 3-53, Sharpe 1-56, Stokley 1-8. Tennessee, E. George 8-52, Mason 7-88, Wycheck 5-31, Thigpen 3-25, Kinney 1-9, McNair 1-(minus 10).

MISSED FIELD GOAL ATTEMPTS—Tennessee, Del Greco 45, 31, 37.

INTERCEPTIONS—Baltimore, R. Lewis 1-50.

KICKOFF RETURNS—Baltimore, J. Lewis 2-49, Harris 1-20. Tennessee, Mason 4-55.

PUNT RETURNS—Baltimore, J. Lewis 1-4. Tennessee, Mason 2-5.

SACKS—Baltimore, Adams 1. Tennessee, Godfrey 1, Fisk 1, Ford 1.

2000 REVIEW Divisional playoffs

Show of hands: How many of you predicted that Trent Dilfer and Kerry Collins would be two of the four quarterbacks in the conference championship games? I said, raise your hands if ... Oh. ...

If I'm Giants defensive coordinator John Fox, here's how I try to defend Vikings WR Randy Moss: sign every member of the U.S. Olympic 4x100-meter relay team; make each of them a defensive back; stack them 5 yards apart in a single-file formation on whatever side Moss lines up; and have all of them mirror every move by Moss. ...

One thing the Ravens might work on this week is punt protection. It's hard to believe they survived two blocked punts (both right up the gut) in a game of field position against the Titans. ...

If you were asked to predict which Raiders cornerback would excel in the game against the Dolphins, your first answer would have been Charles Woodson. Your second would have been Eric Allen. But it was Tory James who had a career day. ...

The Titans couldn't have run a more effective opening offensive series against Baltimore—11 plays (five for first downs) for 68 yards in 7:17, capped off by George's 2-yard TD run. After that, Tennessee scored only three more points. Logical explanation: a great job of adjusting by Ravens defensive coordinator Marvin Lewis. ...

If you love offense, you probably were disappointed by Sunday's two games (Ravens-Titans, Giants-Eagles). Of the seven combined touchdowns, two were scored on defense and two on special teams. And the Eagles' only TD was set up by a blocked punt. ...

At least Haslett won't have to answer any more questions about whether Ricky Williams will play. ...

Are there any Raiders fans who don't paint their faces; wear masks, eye patches or spikes; carry medieval-style maces; or have skulls growing out of their shoulders? ...

In their last three divisional playoff games, the Dolphins have been outscored by a combined 127-10 by the Broncos, Jaguars and Raiders.

GAME SUMMARIES

VIKINGS 34, SAINTS 16

Saturday, January 6

New Orleans	3	0	7	6—16
Minnesota	10	7	10	7—34

First Quarter
Min.—Moss 53 pass from Culpepper (Anderson kick), 3:03.
N.O.—FG, Brien 33, 7:14.
Min.—FG, Anderson 24, 13:24.

Second Quarter
Min.—C. Carter 17 pass from Culpepper (Anderson kick), 13:31.

Third Quarter
Min.—Moss 68 pass from Culpepper (Anderson kick), 1:27.
N.O.—Stachelski 2 pass from Brooks (Brien kick), 5:27.
Min.—FG, Anderson 44, 10:29.

Fourth Quarter
Min.—R. Smith 2 run (Anderson kick), 4:14.
N.O.—Jackson 48 pass from Brooks (pass failed), 12:41.
Attendance—63,881.

	New Orleans	Minnesota
First downs	19	18
Rushes-yards	17-69	32-127
Passing	286	302
Punt returns	3-33	3-25
Kickoff returns	7-139	4-72
Interception returns	0-0	2-2
Comp.-att.-int.	30-48-2	17-31-0
Sacked-yards lost	2-9	0-0
Punts	5-39	5-45
Fumbles-lost	0-0	1-0
Penalties-yards	7-40	5-60
Time of possession	27:49	32:11

INDIVIDUAL STATISTICS
RUSHING—New Orleans, R. Williams 6-14, Brooks 5-29, Morton 5-25, Allen 1-1. Minnesota, R. Smith 25-74, Culpepper 4-51, Morrow 3-2.

PASSING—New Orleans, Brooks 30-48-2-295. Minnesota, Culpepper 17-31-0-302.

RECEIVING—New Orleans, Morton 13-106, Jackson 9-125, Reed 2-29, Poole 2-12, Wilson 1-14, A. Glover 1-5, R. Williams 1-2, Stachelski 1-2. Minnesota, C. Carter 8-120, Moss 2-121, R. Smith 2-25, Kleinsasser 2-18, Walters 1-7, Jordan 1-6, McWilliams 1-5.

MISSED FIELD GOAL ATTEMPTS—None.

INTERCEPTIONS—Minnesota, Wong 1-1, Tate 1-1.

KICKOFF RETURNS—New Orleans, McAfee 7-139. Minnesota, Walters 3-68, Hatchette 1-4.

PUNT RETURNS—New Orleans, Morton 3-33. Minnesota, Walters 3-25.

SACKS—Minnesota, Burrough 1, Randle 1.

GIANTS 20, EAGLES 10

Sunday, January 7

Philadelphia	0	3	0	7—10
N.Y. Giants	7	10	0	3—20

First Quarter
NYG—Dixon 97 kickoff return (Daluiso kick), 0:17.

Second Quarter
NYG—FG, Daluiso 37, 0:05.
NYG—Sehorn 32 interception return (Daluiso kick), 13:20.
Phi.—FG, Akers 28, 14:34.

Fourth Quarter
NYG—FG, Daluiso 25, 6:19.
Phi.—Small 10 pass from McNabb (Akers kick), 13:04.
Attendance—78,765.

	Philadelphia	N.Y. Giants
First downs	11	15
Rushes-yards	14-46	43-112
Passing	140	125
Punt returns	1-2	6-36
Kickoff returns	5-125	3-119
Interception returns	0-0	1-32
Comp.-att.-int.	20-41-1	12-19-0
Sacked-yards lost	6-41	1-0
Punts	8-42	7-32
Fumbles-lost	3-2	3-3
Penalties-yards	6-50	4-18
Time of possession	23:51	36:09

INDIVIDUAL STATISTICS
RUSHING—Philadelphia, Warren 6-11, McNabb 5-17, Mitchell 3-18. New York, Dayne 17-53, Barber 15-35, Collins 8-17, Toomer 1-6, Comella 1-2, Hilliard 1-(minus 1).

PASSING—Philadelphia, McNabb 20-41-1-181. New York, Collins 12-19-0-125.

RECEIVING—Philadelphia, C. Johnson 5-53, Small 4-39, Mitchell 3-27, Lewis 3-27, Warren 2-14, Broughton 1-13, Brown 1-4, C. Martin 1-4. New York, Hilliard 3-35, Barber 3-13, Mitchell 2-47, Toomer 2-23, Dayne 1-4, Comella 1-3.

MISSED FIELD GOAL ATTEMPTS—Philadelphia, Akers 30.

INTERCEPTIONS—New York, Sehorn 1-32.

KICKOFF RETURNS—Philadelphia, Mitchell 5-125. New York, Dixon 2-119, Hilliard 1-0.

PUNT RETURNS—Philadelphia, Mitchell 1-2. New York, Toomer 5-34, Hilliard 1-2.

SACKS—Philadelphia, Trotter 1. New York, Strahan 2, Griffin 1.5, Hale 1, Armstead 0.5, McDaniel 0.5, K. Hamilton 0.5.

CONFERENCE CHAMPIONSHIPS

By DENNIS DILLON

Reprinted from the January 22, 2001 issue of The Sporting News

Extra Points: Observations on the conference championships

First, let us correct a mistake that was in our NFL preview issue. We meant to predict that the Giants and Ravens would play in Super Bowl 35. The Sporting News sincerely regrets the error. ...

There hasn't been a defense as impressive as Baltimore's since Buddy Ryan's '85 Bears outfit. To come into Oakland and hold the NFL's No. 1 rushing offense (154.4 yards per game in the regular season) to 24 yards on the ground and three points was an extraordinary achievement for the Ravens. They were particularly impressive in two goal-line situations during the second half of the AFC championship game. They held the Raiders to a field goal the first time and no points the second time. ...

The Giants' offense sure disposed of that frumpy tag against Minnesota. Offensive coordinator Sean Payton went into the game in an aerial-attack mode against the league's 28th-ranked pass defense, and it worked. Giants QB Kerry Collins looked like Y.A. Tittle passing against a Minnesota secondary that looked a) out of position, b) confused, or c) both all day. ...

It wasn't necessary for Ravens DT Tony Siragusa to collapse his 350-something pounds on Rich Gannon after the Raiders' quarterback threw a pass in the second quarter. That move would fit nicely in a WWF script. Although no penalty was called, it was not much different than driving a quarterback into the ground. Gannon injured his left shoulder on the play

GAME SUMMARIES

RAVENS 16, RAIDERS 3

Sunday, January 14

Baltimore	0	10	3	3—16
Oakland	0	0	3	0— 3

Second Quarter
Bal.—Sharpe 96 pass from Dilfer (Stover kick), 3:52.
Bal.—FG, Stover 31, 6:41.

Third Quarter
Oak.—FG, Janikowski 24, 4:53.
Bal.—FG, Stover 28, 9:52.

Fourth Quarter
Bal.—FG, Stover 21, 7:32.
Attendance—62,784.

	Baltimore	Oakland
First downs	12	12
Rushes-yards	46-110	17-24
Passing	172	167
Punt returns	3-58	2-9
Kickoff returns	2-45	4-72
Interception returns	4-59	1-2
Comp.-att.-int.	9-18-1	19-37-4
Sacked-yards lost	2-18	4-20
Punts	7-41	7-45
Fumbles-lost	2-1	2-1
Penalties-yards	10-95	5-36
Time of possession	34:38	25:22

INDIVIDUAL STATISTICS
RUSHING—Baltimore, Ja. Lewis 29-79, Holmes 9-31, Dilfer 7-4, Ismail 1-(minus 4). Oakland, Wheatley 12-7, Hoying 3-13, Gannon 1-2, Jordan 1-2.

PASSING—Baltimore, Dilfer 9-18-1-190. Oakland, Gannon 11-21-2-80, Hoying 8-16-2-107.

RECEIVING—Baltimore, Stokley 3-31, Ja. Lewis 3-21, Sharpe 1-96, Coates 1-24, Ismail 1-18. Oakland, Brown 5-48, Jett 3-16, Kirby 2-41, Brigham 2-22, Crockett 2-9, Porter 1-19, Rison 1-16, Dudley 1-7, Ritchie 1-5, Wheatley 1-4.

MISSED FIELD GOAL ATTEMPTS—Baltimore, Stover 36.

INTERCEPTIONS—Baltimore, Starks 2-44, Sharper 1-15, Bailey 1-0. Oakland, Jo. Harris 1-2.

KICKOFF RETURNS—Baltimore, J. Lewis 1-29, Harris 1-16. Oakland, Dunn 4-72.

PUNT RETURNS—Baltimore, J. Lewis 3-58. Oakland, Gordon 2-9.

SACKS—Baltimore, Sharper 2, Boulware 1, McCrary 1. Oakland, Russell 1, W. Thomas 1.

GIANTS 41, VIKINGS 0

Sunday, January 14

Minnesota	0	0	0	0— 0
N.Y. Giants	14	20	7	0—41

First Quarter
NYG—Hilliard 46 pass from Collins (Daluiso kick), 1:57.
NYG—Comella 18 pass from Collins (Daluiso kick), 2:13.

Second Quarter
NYG—FG, Daluiso 21, 0:04.
NYG—Jurevicius 8 pass from Collins (Daluiso kick), 4:36.
NYG—FG, Daluiso 22, 9:38.
NYG—Hilliard 7 pass from Collins (Daluiso kick), 14:48.

Third Quarter
NYG—Toomer 7 pass from Collins (Daluiso kick), 2:54.
Attendance—79,310.

	Minnesota	N.Y. Giants
First downs	9	31
Rushes-yards	9-54	41-138
Passing	60	380
Punt returns	0-0	2-2
Kickoff returns	8-128	1-16
Interception returns	2-5	3-13
Comp.-att.-int.	13-28-3	29-40-2
Sacked-yards lost	4-18	1-5
Punts	6-35	1-30
Fumbles-lost	2-2	1-0
Penalties-yards	5-61	4-36
Time of possession	17:38	42:22

INDIVIDUAL STATISTICS
RUSHING—Minnesota, R. Smith 7-44, Culpepper 2-10. New York, Montgomery 16-43, Barber 12-69, Dayne 10-29, Garrett 3-(minus 3).

PASSING—Minnesota, Culpepper 13-28-3-78. New York, Collins 28-39-2-381, Garrett 1-1-0-4.

RECEIVING—Minnesota, C. Carter 3-24, Walsh 3-23, Moss 2-18, R. Smith 2-(minus 2), McWilliams 1-9, Jordan 1-4, Hatchette 1-2. New York, Hilliard 10-155, Toomer 6-88, Comella 4-36, Barber 4-21, Dixon 2-62, Jurevicius 2-15, Dayne 1-8.

MISSED FIELD GOAL ATTEMPTS—New York, Daluiso 43.

INTERCEPTIONS—Minnesota, Tate 1-4, Morgan 1-1. New York, Garnes 1-13, McDaniel 1-0, Sehorn 1-0.

KICKOFF RETURNS—Minnesota, Walters 6-113, M. Williams 2-15. New York, Washington 1-16.

PUNT RETURNS—New York, Hilliard 2-2.

SACKS—Minnesota, Paup 1. New York, Armstead 1, Barrow 1, Strahan 1, S. Williams 1.

and wasn't the same for the rest of the game. ...

If Giants LB Pete Monty ever starts and plays a complete game, will it be known as a full Monty? ...

Before the NFC championship game, Fox TV reported that Giants CBs Jason Sehorn and Dave Thomas planned to focus more on playing and watching the ball when they defended Vikings WR Randy Moss. In retrospect, it looked like a pretty good plan. Other cornerbacks might want to note that strategy. ...

Moss still looks uncomfortable on routes where he has to cut across the middle. Did you notice how he pulled up on one play when he saw S Omar Stoutmire moving into position for a possible kill shot? When Moss hesitated, QB Daunte Culpepper's pass sailed harmlessly away. ...

Dumbest Move I: Raiders CB Charles Woodson shoving Ravens WR Qadry Ismail to the ground after the play midway through the fourth quarter. It allowed the Ravens to bleed a couple more minutes off the clock before kicking a field goal for a 16-3 lead. Dumbest Move II: James Trapp of the Ravens slamming into Darrien Gordon as the Raiders' return man was signaling for a fair catch on a punt with 16 seconds remaining. ...

Giants DE Michael Strahan has turned in back-to-back dominating performances against RTs Jon Runyan (Eagles) and Korey Stringer (Vikings). Harry Swayne, beware. ...

Look for Ravens defensive coordinator Marvin Lewis to get a head-coaching position soon. He won't be approachable until after the Super Bowl, but if I'm running the Bills, Browns or Jets—the three teams with head-coaching vacancies—I wait it out. Let's see if any of those teams are smart enough to have patience. ...

Don't look now, Tampa, but Trent Dilfer is coming back to town—as a Super Bowl quarterback. ...

This Super Bowl shapes up as a battle of defenses and field position. Look for Ravens P Kyle Richardson to be a key contributor. Richardson was the league leader in placing punts inside the 20 for the second season in a row, and produced four in the AFC championship game. ...

Brace yourselves, Kerry Collins and Ray Lewis. Given the horde of reporters who will be in Tampa during the week before the Super Bowl, you're sure to get an onslaught of questions about life off the field. ...

The Ravens still have allowed fewer points (181) in 19 games this season than the 1986 Bears gave up when Chicago set the record (187) for a 16-game schedule.

SUPER BOWL 35

By PAUL ATTNER

Reprinted from the February 5, 2001 issue of The Sporting News

Showstoppers

They have the self-proclaimed best defense in NFL history, and whether that is true or not, it certainly was inspired enough for the Ravens to capture Super Bowl 35 in a most powerful fashion. And until this league changes, this is the way it will be. We will have Super Bowls that will be dominated by defensive teams like the Ravens even when they feature bland quarterbacks like Trent Dilfer guiding offenses that play not to lose.

And the result will be, as we found last Sunday, a championship game limited in excitement, uneven in its quality of play and vulnerable to setting such yawn-generating records as total punts by both teams. You walk away from Baltimore's 34-7 victory over the Giants truly impressed with the Ravens' amazing defensive quickness, continuity and determination—and their ability to back up cockiness with results. You know this is a defense for the ages, but neither team was good enough offensively to produce a game for the ages, and that's the rub.

As long as defenses rule the league, Super Bowls will never be memorable. But don't fret. This defensive bullying, both in this championship game and the league in general this season, will not be a lasting trend. Indeed, it is just a glitch on the NFL pizzazz meter that may fizzle within another year or two. So if you hated this fall, if you were turned off by this Super Bowl, be patient. There is every sign that the stars will return to correct alignment, and offense once again will be restored to its proper place as the lead dog that pulls the league's popularity.

And when we talk "stars" here, let's be specific. We are talking quarterbacks, and the fact the NFL is going through a transition period at the position is the very reason we found ourselves watching a championship game in 2001 featuring Dilfer and Kerry Collins. These were two of the least glamorous players to be starting quarterbacks in a Super Bowl, a pairing unmatched in the history of this QB-driven game. But they are an accurate reflection of the state of the league.

And of Super Bowl 35. Pro football's title game never can be described as unglamorous; the pure nature of the beast, with its array of activities, parties, celebrities, expensive tickets and layers of attention, automatically qualifies it as a special event even if the Bengals are participating. But it's not quite the same as having Brett Favre dueling John Elway (Super Bowl 32) or Troy Aikman taking on Jim Kelly (Super Bowls 27 and 28). So the buildup to this Super Bowl suffered. The major story during the days preceding this game was of Ray Lewis'

Jamal Lewis and the Ravens offense ran roughshod over a Giants defense coming off a 41-0 rout of the Vikings in the NFC championship game. (Photo by Bob Leverone/The Sporting News.)

unrepentant stance regarding the events surrounding a double murder in Atlanta the night of Super Bowl 34 last January. But not much was expected from a matchup between these two flawed teams, even if the Ravens were trying to make a case for their place in history.

And this is what happens when you match a Kerry Collins against a defense as magnificent as the Ravens. You get four interceptions, tying a Super Bowl record, you get an embarrassing 86 net passing yards and 152 total yards—the third lowest in Super Bowl history. You get a quarterback so confused and unsure of himself that by the second half, virtually every pass seemed destined to be picked off. You needed a quarterback who had to be nearly perfect, who had to connect when the rare opportunities popped open, who could stand up against a relentless rush. And Collins did not come close to meeting any of these musts.

Nor, for that matter, did the other quarterbacks who faced the Ravens in the playoffs. This is the splendor of this Baltimore defense: In four postseason games, it gave up just one touchdown and three field goals. The only Giants score came on a 97-yard

Duane Starks scored Baltimore's second touchdown on a 49-yard interception return to increase the Ravens' lead to 17-0. (Photo by Robert Seale/The Sporting News.)

kickoff return by Ron Dixon. Two weeks ago, the Giants beat the Vikings, 41-0, for the NFC title. On this night, they crossed into Ravens territory twice, never in the second half. And when they got to the Baltimore 29 late in the second quarter, Collins promptly made a terrible throw that was intercepted. Lewis was the game's MVP, but it just as well could have gone to the entire defense.

"Our defense has been doing this all year long," Lewis said. "We didn't do anything different. We didn't change anything. We just came out and showed that we are the best defense."

Of course, no one in Baltimore is complaining about the game's outcome. Art Modell, in his 40th year of NFL ownership, is celebrating his first Super Bowl victory—and his second NFL title—and the city is toasting an unexpected championship in the fifth year since the franchise's arrival. Give coach Brian Billick much of the credit; in only his second season with the team, he backed off almost all of his prevailing offensive instincts, stopped trying to win with the pass and tailored his offense to make sure it did not get in the way of his defense.

Billick knows full well what is going on in this league. "There's no dominant quarterback play," he said after the Super Bowl. "And I think that plays to the strengths of defenses. The athletes are so good now on defense that you need dominant quarterback play to keep the upper hand."

Simply put, the state of the league is this: The level of quality at quarterback is just not very good. Gone are the pillars from the historical class of 1983. Dan Marino, Kelly and Elway are all retired; possibly all three will wind up in the Hall of Fame. Steve Young, another Canton-bound talent, also has stopped playing. And although Aikman may contin-

ue to play, his struggles with concussions and back problems have limited his effectiveness the past two seasons and dropped him from the elite level. Drew Bledsoe came close to moving into this level, but now he too has fallen back.

Look around. You want to know why we had the Ravens and Giants in Super Bowl 35? Then identify the glamour quarterbacks still left in the NFL. Favre remains one, for sure, even if the Packers haven't been in the playoffs for two years. Peyton Manning has been productive enough in his three seasons to be included. And Kurt Warner certainly is close; if he's not yet a member, then he would qualify with one more year like his previous two. Mark Brunell is no stiff, and Steve McNair has been solid, but are they as good as Favre, Manning and Warner? No way. It's a short list of greatness.

Think about it. Among the starting quarterbacks in the playoffs were Jay Fiedler, Aaron Brooks, Donovan McNabb, Daunte Culpepper, Shaun King, Gus Frerotte and Rich Gannon. The first five were in their first year as full-time starters; Frerotte is a journeyman backup, and Gannon finally had a magnificent season after laboring for 11 years in the league. Compare the state of NFL quarterbacking now to even five years ago. That's when you had Favre, Young, Elway, Marino, Aikman and Bledsoe. At least one of those six played in Super Bowls 27 through 33, and the MVP of Super Bowl 34 was Warner.

Packers general manager Ron Wolf—who is among the most astute judges of quarterback talent in the NFL (he drafted Brunell, Brooks and Ty Detmer, traded for Favre and signed Warner as a free agent)—sees a league in quarterback flux. "Overall, you'd have to say the quarterback level is in transition," he says. "When you are a defense, it is easier to defend against younger quarterbacks. But I look at this as a natural change in the maturation of the league. Every position is going to have dips, and it just so happens that quarterback is the position in question right now."

Seahawks coach Mike Holmgren, who won a Super Bowl at Green Bay with Favre, is in the market for a new starting quarterback. But until he can build up his offense, he sees his team and the rest of the league following the same blueprint as the Ravens. "Until we have more maturity around the league at quarterback, to win games you are going to have to think defense, whether it is through free agency or the draft," he says. "That is how I can see getting our team competitive faster. I am not taking anything away from the quarterbacks in this Super Bowl, but clearly defensive teams dominated these playoffs, and you have to be smart enough to learn from that."

That formula is what drove the NFL this season and promises to do so for another year or two. If your favorite team has a defense that is very good to overwhelming and a veteran quarterback experienced enough to avoid damaging mistakes, you've got a chance, in this transition period, to advance to a Super Bowl. The Giants and Ravens showed that.

"I think it is more difficult to build a good offen-

Although strong safety Kim Herring missed on an interception here, he did have one of the Ravens' four picks of Giants quarterback Kerry Collins. (Photo by Albert Dickson/The Sporting News.)

sive team than a good defensive team," says Holmgren. "That is the nature of the beast."

Holmgren contends that a great athlete with raw skills can play effectively much sooner on defense than on offense.

"Now the burden is on us so-called offensive coaches to build this thing back up and get the playing field level again," he says.

Indeed, it becomes a matter of waiting—waiting for the quarterback class of 1999 (McNabb, Culpepper, Brooks, Tim Couch, King, Akili Smith, Cade McNown)—to grow into quality players and give these Super Bowls an offensive transfusion. The Jets also have hopes for the Class of 2000's Chad Pennington, and Michael Vick is arriving next season from Virginia Tech. McNair still has plenty of room to improve as a passer, and this season could serve as a springboard for Collins, who was the fifth player chosen in the 1995 draft. The 49ers continue to be surprised by the growth of Jeff Garcia; perhaps he is talented enough to escalate that franchise's return to glory.

"When these young guys grow up, it will be an offensive league again," says Saints general manager Randy Mueller, who acquired Brooks (the Packers' fourth-round pick in the 1999 draft) from Wolf in the offseason. "These are guys with great potential, that's for sure. These guys (from the Class of '99) are similar; they can beat you with their feet and their passing from the pocket. You've never seen guys like this, 6-4 and they can run, too.

"It is all cyclical. Two years ago, you wondered where the young quarterbacks would show up. Now there are several who could be really special. It is still the key position. You have to have one to win, and it is the hardest position to defense. They can control the game if they are good."

Unfortunately, quarterback brilliance doesn't happen overnight. As good as Manning is, he still is developing his short passing touch and has yet to lead the Colts to a conference championship game, much less a Super Bowl. But he's close to being dominant, and, based on this season, Culpepper and McNabb may not be far behind. Imagine the advantage their teams have, considering how many other franchises are quarterback-poor. Imagine what the league will be like if four or five quarterbacks blossom within the next three or four years.

"Right now, having a strong defense really pays dividends," says Ozzie Newsome, the Ravens' vice president of player personnel who constructed Baltimore's Super Bowl club. "It's not like they are facing really strong offenses every week anymore. You play against these young quarterbacks, and they can give you fits with their mobility, but they also make mistakes. They haven't seen a lot yet as far as coverages and complex schemes, and it takes awhile. So if your defense can confuse them, it gives you a huge advantage."

But Bill Walsh, the 49ers' general manager and Hall of Fame coach, thinks offenses could shorten their period as the league's punching bag if coaches

Collins' miserable night included four interceptions, 86 net passing yards and a 7.1 passer rating. (Photo by Bob Leverone/The Sporting News.)

would rethink their game-planning. He sees too little attention being paid to the protection of quarterbacks, leaving them far too susceptible to blitzes, mistakes and turnovers.

"They are too much in love with empty backfield alignments, where they have four or five receivers into patterns and no fullbacks and tight ends kept in for blocking," says Walsh. "That is playing into the hands of defenses. It is too easy to get to a quarterback, to hit him or force quick passes. If you have a young quarterback, he just has little chance. Or he learns to rely too much on running. Defenses like Baltimore see these protection weaknesses, and they have so much speed, they just simply run their players upfield and overwhelm quarterbacks. To have any chance, you've got to protect these players and give them time to perfect their passing skills. That is the only way they will become effective quarterbacks over time."

Owners obviously have noticed this defensive swing, too. Now defensive-oriented coaches are the hot head-coaching prospects. Dave McGinnis (Cardinals), Dick LeBeau (Bengals), Herm Edwards (Jets), Dom Capers (expansion Texans) and Marty Schottenheimer (Redskins) have been hired as head coaches since the start of the 2000 season, and all have defensive backgrounds. And Marvin Lewis,

the Ravens' brilliant defensive coordinator, is expected to be hired in Buffalo or Cleveland.

Still, teams understand how quickly they could move to the top of the league if they could field a quality quarterback and link him with a defense, say, that ranks in the top 12. That's why Denver's Mike Shanahan, who is very high on the oft-injured Brian Griese, took a major step toward improving his inconsistent defense with the hiring of Ray Rhodes as coordinator. And why Dilfer, despite his 11-1 record as a starter with the Ravens and the team's current 11-game winning streak, probably won't return as No. 1 next season.

The Ravens know they could make a run at becoming a long-term powerhouse if they could strengthen the quarterback position even a little. They are willing to allow two members of their defense, linebacker Jamie Sharper and safety Kim Herring, to leave as free agents, so they will have enough cap room to sign a veteran quarterback, most likely Brad Johnson.

With Johnson, who made the Pro Bowl two years ago as playoff quarterback with the Redskins before losing his starting spot to Jeff George, Billick would be able to open up his offense and expand its passing scheme. The Ravens would have the potential to generate more points, taking pressure off the defense and turning Baltimore into a much more dangerous and versatile team. That would make the Ravens odds-on favorites to win Super Bowl 36. Billick and Johnson, who worked together for many years when Billick was the Vikings' offensive coordinator, are extremely comfortable together. Few franchises in the league are equipped to neutralize the potential that would be generated by Johnson's addition to the Ravens.

That has to be a scary possibility to the rest of the NFL, considering how the current Ravens manhandled the Giants. New York, despite its late-season surge, never seemed more than an overachieving team incapable of winning a Super Bowl. Still, Baltimore eventually even wore out the Giants' very good defense, which obviously was disheartened by the inability of the team's offense to make any headway against the Ravens. New York wound up surrendering 102 yards to running back Jamal Lewis, an unsightly amount against the league's No. 2-rated rushing defense.

Indeed, a sharper Baltimore quarterback easily could have turned the Super Bowl into an early rout. The Ravens decided their receivers could beat the man coverage of the Giants' cornerbacks. And when New York blitzed, the Baltimore offensive line protected Dilfer well enough to allow him to go long, but he misfired frequently. On one occasion, wide receiver Patrick Johnson was wide open, by 10 yards, after cornerback Jason Sehorn fell, but Dilfer's pass sailed out of bounds. But Dilfer did complete one particularly nifty throw, a down-the-seam toss to receiver Brandon Stokley for a 38-yard, first-quarter touchdown when the Giants chose to double-team tight end Shannon Sharpe and leave Stokley alone against Sehorn.

When Matt Stover added a 47-yard field goal in the second quarter following a 44-yard completion to Qadry Ismail, the Ravens' defense declared the game over. "Give us 10 points and we'll win," Marvin and Ray Lewis told some offensive players before kickoff.

They were prophetic. The Giants' lone spark came on Dixon's kickoff return that cut the Ravens' lead to 17-7—cornerback Duane Starks had just returned a Collins pass 49 yards for a touchdown—but even that celebration was short-lived when Jermaine Lewis took the ensuing kickoff back 84 yards for a 24-7 advantage. Ultimately, the Ravens, who were No. 1 in the league in takeaway-giveaway differential, created five turnovers while turning it over not once.

"I sucked," said Collins about his 15-for-39, 112-yard, four-interception stinker. He admitted he was confused and bewildered at times by a Ravens defense that pounded him and forced him to hurry his throws. He found out that this defense plays even faster and hits even harder than it appears on tape, which is something every opponent learns when first exposed to the Ravens' whirlwind.

This defense was good enough in October to push the Ravens to two wins amid a five-game streak in which the offense didn't score a touchdown. It was difficult then to believe this was a potential Super Bowl champion. But that was before any of us realized that in this NFL, it is only appropriate that a defensive team should be in possession of the Lombardi Trophy.

Senior writer Paul Attner covers the NFL for The Sporting News.

RAVENS 34, GIANTS 7

Sunday, January 14

Baltimore	7	3	14	10—34
N.Y. Giants	0	0	7	0— 7

First Quarter
Bal.—Stokley 38 pass from Dilfer (Stover kick), 8:10.

Second Quarter
Bal.—FG, Stover 47, 13:19.

Third Quarter
Bal.—Starks 49 interception return (Stover kick), 11:11.
NYG—Dixon 97 kickoff return (Daluiso kick), 11:29.
Bal.—Je. Lewis 84 kickoff return (Stover kick), 11:47.

Fourth Quarter
Bal.—Ja. Lewis 3 run (Stover kick), 6:15.
Bal.—FG, Stover 34, 9:33.
Attendance—71,921.

	Baltimore	N.Y. Giants
First downs	13	11
Rushes-yards	33-111	16-66
Passing	133	86
Punt returns	3-34	5-46
Kickoff returns	2-111	7-171
Interception returns	4-59	0-0
Comp.-att.-int.	12-26-0	15-39-4
Sacked-yards lost	3-20	4-26
Punts	10-43	11-38
Fumbles-lost	2-0	2-1
Penalties-yards	9-70	6-27
Time of possession	34:06	25:54

INDIVIDUAL STATISTICS

RUSHING—Baltimore, Ja. Lewis 27-102, Holmes 4-8, Je. Lewis 1-1, Dilfer 1-0. New York, Barber 11-49, Collins 3-12, Montgomery 2-5.

PASSING—Baltimore, Dilfer 12-25-0-153, Banks 0-1-0-0. New York, Collins 15-39-4-112.

RECEIVING—Baltimore, Stokley 3-52, Coates 3-30, Ismail 1-44, Johnson 1-8, Je. Lewis 1-6, Sharpe 1-5, Holmes 1-4, Ja. Lewis 1-4. New York, Barber 6-26, Hilliard 3-30, Toomer 2-24, Dixon 1-16, Cross 1-7, Mitchell 1-7, Comella 1-2.

MISSED FIELD GOAL ATTEMPTS—Baltimore, Stover 41.

INTERCEPTIONS—Baltimore, Starks 1-49, McAlister 1-4, Sharper 1-4, Herring 1-2.

KICKOFF RETURNS—Baltimore, Je. Lewis 2-111. New York, Dixon 6-154, Washington 1-17.

PUNT RETURNS—Baltimore, Je. Lewis 3-34. New York, Hilliard 3-33, Barber 2-13.

SACKS—Baltimore, McCrary 2, Washington 1, Burnett 1. New York, Strahan 1.5, Griffin 1.5.

2000 REVIEW *Super Bowl 35*

PRO BOWL

NFC SQUAD

OFFENSE

WR— Isaac Bruce, St. Louis*
Cris Carter, Minnesota*
Torry Holt, St. Louis
Joe Horn, New Orleans
Randy Moss, Minnesota
Terrell Owens, San Francisco
TE— Chad Lewis, Philadelphia*
Stephen Alexander, Washington
T— Orlando Pace, St. Louis*
William Roaf, New Orleans*
Korey Stringer, Minnesota
G— Larry Allen, Dallas*
Randall McDaniel, Tampa Bay*
Ron Stone, N.Y. Giants
C— Jeff Christy, Tampa Bay*
Matt Birk, Minnesota
QB— Daunte Culpepper, Minnesota*
Jeff Garcia, San Francisco
Donovan McNabb, Philadelphia
Kurt Warner, St. Louis
RB— Marshall Faulk, St. Louis*
Stephen Davis, Washington
Warrick Dunn, Tampa Bay
Charlie Garner, San Francisco
Robert Smith, Minnesota
FB— Mike Alstott, Tampa Bay*
NOTE: WR Bruce replaced due to injury by Holt; WR Moss
replaced due to injury by Horn; QB Warner replaced due
to injury by McNabb; RB Faulk replaced due to injury by
Davis; RB Smith replaced due to injury by Dunn.

DEFENSE

DE— Hugh Douglas, Philadelphia*
Joe Johnson, New Orleans*
Marco Coleman, Washington
DT— La'Roi Glover, New Orleans*
Warren Sapp, Tampa Bay*
Luther Elliss, Detroit
OLB— Jessie Armstead, N.Y. Giants*
Derrick Brooks, Tampa Bay*
Mark Fields, New Orleans†
Keith Mitchell, New Orleans
ILB— Stephen Boyd, Detroit*
Jeremiah Trotter, Philadelphia
Brian Urlacher, Chicago
CB— Champ Bailey, Washington*
Troy Vincent, Philadelphia*
Donnie Abraham, Tampa Bay
SS— John Lynch, Tampa Bay*
Robert Griffith, Minnesota
FS— Darren Sharper, Green Bay*
NOTE: ILB Boyd replaced due to injury by Urlacher.

SPECIALISTS

P— Scott Player, Arizona
K— Martin Gramatica, Tampa Bay
KR— Desmond Howard, Detroit
ST— Michael Bates, Carolina

AFC SQUAD

OFFENSE

WR— Marvin Harrison, Indianapolis*
Eric Moulds, Buffalo*
Jimmy Smith, Jacksonville
Rod Smith, Denver
TE— Tony Gonzalez, Kansas City*
Frank Wycheck, Tennessee
T— Jonathan Ogden, Baltimore*
Tony Boselli, Jacksonville*
Brad Hopkins, Tennessee
Lincoln Kennedy, Oakland
G— Ruben Brown, Buffalo*
Bruce Matthews, Tennessee*
Will Shields, Kansas City
Steve Wisniewski, Oakland
C— Kevin Mawae, N.Y. Jets*
Tom Nalen, Denver
Tim Ruddy, Miami
QB— Rich Gannon, Oakland*
Elvis Grbac, Kansas City
Brian Griese, Denver
Peyton Manning, Indianapolis
Steve McNair, Tennessee
RB— Edgerrin James, Indianapolis*
Corey Dillon, Cincinnati
Eddie George, Tennessee
FB— Richie Anderson, N.Y. Jets*
NOTE: T Boselli replaced due to injury by Kennedy; G Matthews
replaced due to injury by Shields; C Nalen replaced due
to injury by Ruddy; QB Griese replaced due to injury by
McNair, who was replaced due to injury by Grbac.

DEFENSE

DE— Trace Armstrong, Miami*
Jason Taylor, Miami
Jevon Kearse, Tennessee
DT— Sam Adams, Baltimore*
Trevor Pryce, Denver*
Ted Washington, Buffalo
OLB— Mo Lewis, N.Y. Jets*
Junior Seau, San Diego*
Jason Gildon, Pittsburgh
ILB— Ray Lewis, Baltimore*
Sam Cowart, Buffalo
Zach Thomas, Miami†
CB— Sam Madison, Miami*
Samari Rolle, Tennessee*
Charles Woodson, Oakland
SS— Blaine Bishop, Tennessee*
FS— Rod Woodson, Baltimore*
Brock Marion, Miami

SPECIALISTS

P— Darren Bennett, San Diego
K— Matt Stover, Baltimore
KR— Derrick Mason, Tennessee
ST— Larry Izzo, Miami
*Elected starter.
†Selected as need player

AFC 38, NFC 17

Sunday, February 4

NFC	0	3	14	0—17
AFC	14	10	7	7—38

First Quarter
AFC—Gonzalez 8 pass from Gannon (Stover kick), 5:22.
AFC—Harrison 16 pass from Gannon (Stover kick), 10:52.

Second Quarter
AFC—FG Stover 29, 1:19.
NFC—FG Gramatica 48, 5:43.
AFC—Smith 2 pass from Manning (Stover kick), 14:06.

Third Quarter
NFC—Owens 17 pass from McNabb (Gramatica kick), 1:21.
AFC—Harrison 24 pass from Manning (Stover kick), 3:50.
NFC—Holt 20 pass from Culpepper (Gramatica kick), 11:38.

Fourth Quarter
AFC—James 20 run (Stover kick), 3:41.
Attendance—50,128.

	NFC	AFC
First downs	20	29
Rushes-yards	9-36	23-83
Passing	297	348
Punt returns	1-11	2-33
Kickoff returns	7-187	3-70
Interception returns	1-0	3-17
Comp.-att.-int.	28-56-3	32-42-1
Sacked-yards lost	0-0	4-21
Punts	3-49	3-39
Fumbles-lost	1-1	1-0
Penalties-yards	1-17	7-55
Time of possession	25:42	34:18

INDIVIDUAL STATISTICS

RUSHING—NFC, Culpepper 2-16, Dunn 2-13, Alstott 2-7, Garner 2-3, Garcia 1-(minus 3). AFC, George 8-31, James 4-26, Dillon 5-16, Grbac 3-7, Anderson 2-4, Manning 1-(minus 1).

PASSING—NFC, Culpepper 9-21-1-81, Garcia 15-28-1-144, McNabb 4-7-1-72. AFC, Gannon 12-14-0-160, Manning 16-22-0-150, Grbac 4-6-1-59.

RECEIVING—NFC, Holt 7-103, Dunn 7-69, Owens 5-50, Carter 5-41, Alexander 1-16, C. Lewis 1-11, Alstott 1-4, Garner 1-3. AFC, Harrison 8-84, Gonzalez 6-108, Moulds 6-65, Wycheck 3-23, Dillon 2-36, J. Smith 2-12, Anderson 2-8, James 1-15, R. Smith 1-12, Mason 1-6.

MISSED FIELD GOAL ATTEMPTS—None.

INTERCEPTIONS—NFC, Bailey 1-0. AFC, M. Lewis 1-16, Rolle 1-1, Marion 1-0.

2000 REVIEW Pro Bowl

COMPLETE LIST

Player, Team	GP	GS
Abdullah, Rabih, Tampa Bay	12	0
Abdullah, Rahim, Cleveland	13	4
Abraham, Donnie, Tampa Bay	16	16
Abraham, John, N.Y. Jets	6	0
Ackerman, Tom, New Orleans	15	0
Adams, Flozell, Dallas	16	16
Adams, Sam, Baltimore	16	16
Agnew, Ray, St. Louis	15	15
Aguiar, Louie, Chicago	9	0
Ahanotu, Chidi, Tampa Bay	16	16
Aikman, Troy, Dallas	11	11
Akers, David, Philadelphia	16	0
Akins, Chris, Dal.-G.B.	10	0
Albright, Ethan, Buffalo	16	0
Aldridge, Allen, Detroit	16	14
Alexander, Brent, Pittsburgh	16	16
Alexander, Derrick S., K.C.	16	16
Alexander, Elijah, Oakland	16	16
Alexander, Shaun, Seattle	16	1
Alexander, Stephen, Was.	16	16
Alford, Darnell, Kansas City	1	0
al-Jabbar, Karim Abdul, Ind.	1	0
Allen, Eric, Oakland	16	15
Allen, James, Chicago	16	15
Allen, Larry, Dallas	16	16
Allen, Taje, St. Louis	11	1
Allen, Terry, New Orleans	4	3
Allred, John, Chicago	5	3
Alstott, Mike, Tampa Bay	13	13
Ambrose, Ashley, Atlanta	16	16
Anders, Kimble, Kansas City	15	7
Andersen, Jason, New England	7	0
Andersen, Morten, Atlanta	16	0
Anderson, Gary, Minnesota	16	0
Anderson, Jamal, Atlanta	16	16
Anderson, Mike, Denver	16	12
Anderson, Rashard, Carolina	12	0
Anderson, Richie, N.Y. Jets	16	10
Anderson, Willie, Cincinnati	16	16
Andruzzi, Joe, New England	11	11
Anthony, Reidel, Tampa Bay	16	1
Archambeau, Lester, Denver	3	0
Armour, JoJuan, Cincinnati	4	0
Armour, Phil, Indianapolis	3	0
Armstead, Jessie, N.Y. Giants	16	16
Armstrong, Bruce, N.E.	16	16
Armstrong, Trace, Miami	16	0
Arrington, LaVar, Washington	16	11
Ashmore, Darryl, Oakland	16	0
Atkins, Corey, Atlanta	12	0
Atkins, James, Detroit	2	1
Atkins, Larry, Kansas City	15	0
Austin, Billy, Indianapolis	16	0
Autry, Darnell, Philadelphia	11	7
Ayanbadejo, Obafemi, Baltimore	8	4
Azumah, Jerry, Chicago	14	4
Badger, Brad, Minnesota	16	0
Bailey, Champ, Washington	16	16
Bailey, Karsten, Seattle	9	0
Bailey, Robert, Baltimore	16	0
Baker, Eugene, Atlanta	1	0
Baker, John, St. Louis	15	0
Banks, Antonio, Minnesota	14	0
Banks, Chris, Atlanta	8	4
Banks, Tony, Baltimore	11	8
Bankston, Michael, Cincinnati	16	14

Player, Team	GP	GS
Banta, Brad, N.Y. Jets	16	0
Barber, Ronde, Tampa Bay	16	16
Barber, Shawn, Washington	14	14
Barber, Tiki, N.Y. Giants	16	12
Barker, Bryan, Jacksonville	16	0
Barker, Roy, Minnesota	4	0
Barlow, Reggie, Jacksonville	16	0
Barndt, Tom, Cincinnati	14	5
Barnes, Lionel, St.L.-Ind.	2	0
Barnes, Marlon, Chicago	13	0
Barnes, Rashidi, Cleveland	14	0
Barnhardt, Tommy, Washington	16	0
Barrett, David, Arizona	16	0
Barrow, Micheal, N.Y. Giants	15	15
Bartee, William, Kansas City	16	3
Bartholomew, Brent, Chicago	7	0
Barton, Eric, Oakland	4	0
Bartrum, Mike, Philadelphia	16	0
Batch, Charlie, Detroit	15	15
Bates, D'Wayne, Chicago	5	0
Bates, Mario, Detroit	13	0
Bates, Michael, Carolina	16	0
Battaglia, Marco, Cincinnati	16	10
Battles, Ainsley, Pittsburgh	16	1
Baxter, Fred, N.Y. Jets	9	6
Bean, Robert, Cincinnati	12	4
Beasley, Aaron, Jacksonville	14	14
Beasley, Fred, San Francisco	15	15
Becht, Anthony, N.Y. Jets	14	10
Beckett, Rogers, San Diego	16	3
Bedell, Brad, Cleveland	12	0
Beede, Frank, Seattle	7	0
Bell, Marcus, Seattle	16	0
Bell, Myron, Pittsburgh	1	0
Bellamy, Jay, Seattle	16	16
Belser, Jason, Indianapolis	16	16
Bennett, Brandon, Cincinnati	16	0
Bennett, Cornelius, Indianapolis	16	15
Bennett, Darren, San Diego	16	0
Bennett, Donnell, Kansas City	7	2
Bennett, Tommy, Arizona	11	0
Bentley, Scott, Den.-Was.	7	0
Bercich, Pete, Minnesota	2	0
Berger, Mitch, Minnesota	16	0
Berry, Gary, Green Bay	4	0
Bettis, Jerome, Pittsburgh	16	16
Beuerlein, Steve, Carolina	16	16
Beverly, Eric, Detroit	16	7
Biakabutuka, Tim, Carolina	12	11
Bidwell, Josh, Green Bay	16	0
Biekert, Greg, Oakland	16	16
Binn, David, San Diego	16	0
Birk, Matt, Minnesota	16	16
Bishop, Blaine, Tennessee	16	16
Bishop, Michael, New England	8	0
Bjornson, Eric, New England	8	6
Black, Avion, Buffalo	2	0
Blackshear, Jeff, Kansas City	16	15
Blackwell, Will, Pittsburgh	5	0
Blaise, Kerlin, Detroit	12	0
Blake, Jeff, New Orleans	11	11
Blanchard, Cary, Arizona	16	0
Bledsoe, Drew, New England	16	16
Blevins, Darrius, St. Louis	5	0
Blevins, Tony, Indianapolis	16	1
Bly, Dre', St. Louis	16	3

Player, Team	GP	GS
Bobo, Orlando, Baltimore	7	0
Bock, John, Miami	6	1
Booker, Marty, Chicago	15	7
Booker, Michael, Tennessee	15	1
Booker, Vaughn, Cincinnati	9	9
Boose, Dorian, N.Y. Jets	10	0
Bordano, Chris, Atlanta	2	0
Boselli, Tony, Jacksonville	16	16
Bostic, Jason, Philadelphia	16	0
Boston, David, Arizona	16	16
Boulware, Peter, Baltimore	16	15
Bowden, Joe, Dallas	16	0
Bowen, Matt, St. Louis	16	2
Bowens, David, Green Bay	14	0
Bowens, Tim, Miami	15	15
Bownes, Fabien, Seattle	16	0
Boyd, LaVell, Cincinnati	2	0
Boyd, Stephen, Detroit	15	15
Boyer, Brant, Jacksonville	12	5
Brackens, Tony, Jacksonville	16	16
Bradford, Corey, Green Bay	2	2
Bradford, Ronnie, Atlanta	16	15
Brady, Kyle, Jacksonville	16	15
Brady, Tom, New England	1	0
Braham, Rich, Cincinnati	9	9
Branch, Calvin, Oakland	16	0
Bratzke, Chad, Indianapolis	16	16
Brazzell, Chris, Dallas	9	0
Brien, Doug, New Orleans	16	0
Brigance, O.J., Baltimore	16	0
Brigham, Jeremy, Oakland	15	3
Brisby, Vincent, N.Y. Jets	3	1
Brister, Bubby, Minnesota	2	0
Brockermeyer, Blake, Chicago	15	14
Bromell, Lorenzo, Miami	8	0
Bronson, Zack, San Francisco	9	7
Brooking, Keith, Atlanta	5	5
Brooks, Aaron, New Orleans	8	5
Brooks, Barrett, Detroit	15	4
Brooks, Bobby, Oakland	16	0
Brooks, Derrick, Tampa Bay	16	16
Brooks, Ethan, Arizona	14	3
Brooks, Macey, Chicago	16	3
Brooks, Robert, Denver	4	0
Broughton, Luther, Philadelphia	15	1
Brown, Bobby, Cleveland	6	0
Brown, Chad, Seattle	16	16
Brown, Cornell, Baltimore	16	1
Brown, Corwin, Detroit	14	4
Brown, Courtney, Cleveland	16	16
Brown, Dave, Arizona	6	2
Brown, Eric, Denver	16	16
Brown, Fakhir, San Diego	9	8
Brown, J.B., Detroit	3	0
Brown, James, Cleveland	7	5
Brown, Kris, Pittsburgh	16	0
Brown, Lomas, N.Y. Giants	16	16
Brown, Mike, Chicago	16	16
Brown, Na, Philadelphia	14	2
Brown, Ralph, N.Y. Giants	2	0
Brown, Ray, San Francisco	16	16
Brown, Reggie, Seattle	12	1
Brown, Ruben, Buffalo	16	16
Brown, Tim, Oakland	16	16
Brown, Travis, Seattle	1	0
Brown, Troy, New England	16	15

Player, Team	GP	GS
Browning, John, Kansas City	16	16
Bruce, Isaac, St. Louis	16	16
Bruener, Mark, Pittsburgh	16	16
Brunell, Mark, Jacksonville	16	16
Bruschi, Tedy, New England	16	16
Bryant, Fernando, Jacksonville	14	14
Bryant, Junior, San Francisco	3	3
Bryant, Tony, Oakland	16	16
Bryson, Shawn, Buffalo	16	7
Brzezinski, Doug, Philadelphia	16	0
Buchanan, Ray, Atlanta	16	16
Buckley, Terrell, Denver	16	16
Buckner, Brentson, S.F.	16	16
Bulluck, Keith, Tennessee	16	1
Bundren, Jim, Cleveland	11	9
Burke, Tom, Arizona	2	0
Burks, Dialleo, Carolina	1	0
Burnett, Chester, Cleveland	7	0
Burnett, Rob, Baltimore	16	16
Burns, Keith, Denver	13	0
Burress, Plaxico, Pittsburgh	12	9
Burris, Jeff, Indianapolis	16	16
Burrough, John, Minnesota	14	6
Burton, Shane, N.Y. Jets	16	16
Bush, Devin, St. Louis	13	12
Bush, Lewis, Kansas City	16	8
Bush, Steve, Cincinnati	16	0
Butler, LeRoy, Green Bay	16	16
Bynum, Kenny, San Diego	14	0
Byrd, Isaac, Carolina	15	4
Cadrez, Glenn, Denver	16	3
Caldwell, Mike, Philadelphia	16	3
Calloway, Chris, New England	7	2
Campbell, Dan, N.Y. Giants	16	5
Campbell, Lamar, Detroit	16	2
Campbell, Mark, Cleveland	16	10
Campbell, Matt, Carolina	14	14
Canidate, Trung, St. Louis	3	0
Cannida, James, Tampa Bay	16	0
Cantrell, Barry, Dallas	2	0
Canty, Chris, Sea.-N.O.	15	1
Carlisle, Cooper, Denver	14	0
Carman, Jon, Buffalo	3	0
Carney, John, San Diego	16	0
Carpenter, Keion, Buffalo	12	12
Carrier, Mark, Washington	15	15
Carson, Leonardo, San Diego	4	0
Carswell, Dwayne, Denver	16	16
Carter, Chris, Cincinnati	16	10
Carter, Cris, Minnesota	16	16
Carter, Kevin, St. Louis	16	13
Carter, Marty, Atlanta	16	13
Carter, Tom, Cincinnati	16	11
Carter, Tony, New England	16	6
Carter, Tyrone, Minnesota	15	7
Carty, Johndale, Atlanta	15	0
Case, Stoney, Detroit	5	1
Cavil, Kwame, Buffalo	16	0
Centers, Larry, Washington	15	5
Cercone, Matt, Minnesota	2	0
Chamberlain, Byron, Denver	15	0
Chamberlin, Frank, Tennessee	12	0
Chancey, Robert, San Diego	4	3
Chandler, Chris, Atlanta	14	13
Chanoine, Roger, Cleveland	7	0
Chapman, Lamar, Cleveland	7	0
Charlton, Ike, Seattle	16	0
Chase, Martin, New Orleans	9	0
Chatham, Matt, New England	6	0
Chavous, Corey, Arizona	16	1
Cherry, Je'Rod, Philadelphia	13	0
Chester, Larry, Indianapolis	16	0
Chiaverini, Darrin, Cleveland	10	2
Chrebet, Wayne, N.Y. Jets	16	16
Christian, Bob, Atlanta	16	14
Christie, Steve, Buffalo	16	0
Christy, Jeff, Tampa Bay	16	16
Claiborne, Chris, Detroit	16	14
Clancy, Kendrick, Pittsburgh	9	0
Claridge, Travis, Atlanta	16	16
Clark, Danny, Jacksonville	16	0
Clark, Desmond, Denver	16	2
Clark, Greg, San Francisco	15	15
Clarke, Phil, New Orleans	14	4
Clement, Anthony, Arizona	16	16
Clemons, Duane, Kansas City	12	12
Clifton, Chad, Green Bay	13	10
Cloud, Mike, Kansas City	16	4
Coady, Rich, St. Louis	12	2
Coakley, Dexter, Dallas	16	16
Coates, Ben, Baltimore	16	9
Cochran, Antonio, Seattle	15	0
Codie, Nakia, Pittsburgh	6	0
Cody, Mac, Arizona	15	1
Coghill, George, Denver	16	0
Cole, Chris, Denver	8	0
Coleman, Ben, San Diego	16	16
Coleman, Chris, Tennessee	13	0
Coleman, Cosey, Tampa Bay	8	0
Coleman, KaRon, Denver	9	0
Coleman, Marco, Washington	16	16
Coleman, Marcus, N.Y. Jets	16	16
Coleman, Roderick, Oakland	13	1
Coles, Laveranues, N.Y. Jets	13	3
Colinet, Stalin, Cleveland	16	16
Collins, Bobby, Buffalo	12	2
Collins, Calvin, Atlanta	16	16
Collins, Kerry, N.Y. Giants	16	16
Collins, Mo, Oakland	16	16
Collins, Todd F., St. Louis	14	11
Colman, Doug, Cleveland	5	0
Colvin, Rosevelt, Chicago	13	8
Combs, Chris, Pittsburgh	6	0
Comella, Greg, N.Y. Giants	16	12
Compton, Mike, Detroit	16	16
Conaty, Bill, Buffalo	16	0
Connell, Albert, Washington	16	13
Conway, Brett, Was.-Oak.-NYJ	4	0
Conway, Curtis, San Diego	14	14
Conwell, Ernie, St. Louis	16	1
Cook, Rashard, Philadelphia	14	0
Copeland, John, Cincinnati	16	16
Cota, Chad, Indianapolis	16	16
Couch, Tim, Cleveland	7	7
Cousin, Terry, Atlanta	15	0
Cowart, Sam, Buffalo	12	12
Cox, Bryan, N.Y. Jets	15	14
Craft, Jason, Jacksonville	16	3
Craig, Dameyune, Carolina	4	0
Crawford, Casey, Carolina	8	0
Criss, Shadwick, Jacksonville	3	0
Crockett, Henri, Atlanta	15	12
Crockett, Ray, Denver	13	11
Crockett, Zack, Oakland	16	4
Cross, Howard, N.Y. Giants	16	11
Crowell, Germane, Detroit	9	7
Culpepper, Brad, Chicago	12	1
Culpepper, Daunte, Minnesota	16	16
Cunningham, Randall, Dallas	6	3
Cunningham, Richie, Carolina	4	0
Curtis, Canute, Cincinnati	15	0
Cushing, Matt, Pittsburgh	7	1
Dalton, Antico, New England	3	0
Dalton, Lional, Baltimore	16	1
Daluiso, Brad, N.Y. Giants	14	0
Daniels, Phillip, Chicago	14	14
Darche, Jean-Philippe, Seattle	16	0
Darden, Tony, San Diego	16	3
Darius, Donovin, Jacksonville	16	16
Darling, James, Philadelphia	16	0
Davidds-Garrido, Norberto, Ari.	9	2
Davis, Anthony, Baltimore	14	0
Davis, Billy, Baltimore	16	1
Davis, Don, Tampa Bay	16	0
Davis, Eric, Carolina	16	16
Davis, John, Minnesota	15	9
Davis, Reggie, San Diego	10	0
Davis, Rob, Green Bay	16	0
Davis, Russell, Arizona	13	9
Davis, Shockmain, New England	12	1
Davis, Stephen, Washington	15	15
Davis, Terrell, Denver	5	4
Davis, Thabiti, N.Y. Giants	13	0
Davis, Tyrone, Green Bay	14	9
Dawkins, Brian, Philadelphia	13	13
Dawkins, Sean, Seattle	16	16
Dawson, Dermontti, Pittsburgh	9	9
Dawson, JaJuan, Cleveland	2	2
Dawson, Phil, Cleveland	16	0
Dayne, Ron, N.Y. Giants	16	4
Deese, Derrick, San Francisco	13	13
Del Greco, Al, Tennessee	16	0
DeLong, Greg, Jacksonville	4	1
Dennis, Pat, Kansas City	16	13
Denson, Autry, Miami	11	0
Denton, Tim, San Diego	5	0
Dercher, Dan, San Francisco	2	0
Derney, Patrick, Atlanta	16	16
Detmer, Koy, Philadelphia	16	0
DeVries, Jared, Detroit	15	1
Dexter, James, Carolina	9	2
Diaz, Jorge, Dallas	9	0
Diggs, Na'il, Green Bay	13	12
Dilfer, Trent, Baltimore	11	8
Dilger, Ken, Indianapolis	16	16
Dillon, Corey, Cincinnati	16	16
Dingle, Adrian, San Diego	14	1
Dishman, Chris, Arizona	14	12
Dishman, Cris, Minnesota	11	9
Dixon, David, Minnesota	16	16
Dixon, Gerald, San Diego	16	16
Dixon, Mark, Miami	15	15
Dixon, Ron, N.Y. Giants	12	0
Donnalley, Kevin, Miami	16	16
Dorsett, Anthony, Oakland	16	16
Dotson, Earl, Green Bay	2	2
Dotson, Santana, Green Bay	12	11
Douglas, Dameane, Philadelphia	6	0
Douglas, Hugh, Philadelphia	16	16
Douglas, Marques, New Orleans	1	0
Downs, Gary, Atlanta	16	0
Draft, Chris, Atlanta	13	8
Dragos, Scott, Chicago	9	2
Drakeford, Tyronne, Washington	9	1
Drayton, Troy, Kansas City	16	1
Driver, Donald, Green Bay	16	2
Dronett, Shane, Atlanta	3	3
Dudley, Rickey, Oakland	16	16
Duffy, Roger, Pittsburgh	13	7
Dugans, Ron, Cincinnati	14	5
Dukes, Chad, Was.-Jac.	2	0
Dumas, Mike, San Diego	12	12
Duncan, Jamie, Tampa Bay	15	15
Dunn, Damon, NYJ-Cle.	4	0
Dunn, David, Oakland	15	0
Dunn, Jason, Kansas City	14	2

Player, Team	GP	GS
Dunn, Warrick, Tampa Bay	16	14
Dwight, Tim, Atlanta	14	1
Dyer, Deon, Miami	16	1
Dyson, Kevin, Tennessee	2	2
Eaton, Chad, New England	14	13
Edinger, Paul, Chicago	16	0
Edwards, Antuan, Green Bay	12	3
Edwards, Donnie, Kansas City	16	16
Edwards, Marc, Cleveland	16	8
Edwards, Mario, Dallas	11	1
Edwards, Troy, Pittsburgh	14	1
Eitzmann, Chris, New England	5	1
Ekuban, Ebenezer, Dallas	12	2
Elam, Jason, Denver	13	0
Elliott, Jumbo, N.Y. Jets	10	0
Ellis, Ed, Washington	12	0
Ellis, Greg, Dallas	16	16
Ellis, Shaun, N.Y. Jets	16	3
Elliss, Luther, Detroit	16	16
Ellsworth, Percy, Cleveland	16	16
Emanuel, Bert, Miami	11	0
Embray, Keith, Tennessee	14	0
Emmons, Carlos, Philadelphia	16	13
Engelberger, John, S.F.	16	13
Engler, Derek, N.Y. Giants	8	0
Engram, Bobby, Chicago	3	3
Enis, Curtis, Chicago	12	5
Evans, Chuck, Baltimore	1	0
Evans, Doug, Carolina	16	16
Everitt, Steve, St. Louis	4	1
Fabini, Jason, N.Y. Jets	16	16
Fair, Terry, Detroit	15	15
Faneca, Alan, Pittsburgh	16	16
Farmer, Danny, Cincinnati	13	2
Farr, D'Marco, St. Louis	10	5
Farrior, James, N.Y. Jets	16	6
Faulk, Kevin, New England	16	9
Faulk, Marshall, St. Louis	14	14
Fauria, Christian, Seattle	15	10
Favors, Greg, Tennessee	16	15
Favre, Brett, Green Bay	16	16
Fazande, Jermaine, San Diego	13	7
Feagles, Jeff, Seattle	16	0
Ferguson, Jason, N.Y. Jets	15	11
Ferguson, Nick, N.Y. Jets	7	0
Fiala, John, Pittsburgh	16	0
Fiedler, Jay, Miami	15	15
Fields, Aaron, Dallas	3	0
Fields, Mark, New Orleans	16	14
Fina, John, Buffalo	14	14
Finn, Jim, Indianapolis	16	1
Finneran, Brian, Atlanta	12	0
Fiore, Dave, San Francisco	15	15
Fischer, Mark, Washington	16	16
Fisk, Jason, Tennessee	15	15
Flanagan, Mike, Green Bay	16	2
Flanigan, Jim, Chicago	16	14
Flemister, Zeron, Washington	5	0
Fletcher, Derrick, N.E.-Was.	3	2
Fletcher, London, St. Louis	16	15
Fletcher, Terrell, San Diego	16	6
Flowers, Erik, Buffalo	16	0
Flowers, Lethon, Pittsburgh	14	14
Floyd, Chris, N.E.-Cle.	13	0
Floyd, William, Carolina	10	8
Flutie, Doug, Buffalo	11	5
Flynn, Mike, Baltimore	16	16
Folau, Spencer, Baltimore	11	4
Foley, Steve, Cincinnati	16	16
Folston, James, Arizona	13	3
Fontenot, Albert, San Diego	15	15
Fontenot, Jerry, New Orleans	16	16
Ford, Henry, Tennessee	14	3
Fordham, Todd, Jacksonville	16	8
Foreman, Jay, Buffalo	15	4
Fortin, Roman, San Diego	16	16
Foster, Larry, Detroit	10	0
Franks, Bubba, Green Bay	16	13
Franz, Todd, N.O.-Cle.	7	0
Fredrickson, Rob, Arizona	13	12
Freeman, Antonio, Green Bay	15	15
Freeman, Arturo, Miami	8	0
Frerotte, Gus, Denver	10	6
Fricke, Ben, Dallas	9	5
Friedman, Lennie, Denver	16	8
Friesz, John, New England	1	0
Frost, Scott, N.Y. Jets	16	1
Fryar, Irving, Washington	14	5
Fuamatu-Ma'afala, Chris, Pit.	7	1
Fulcher, Mondriel, Oakland	10	0
Fuller, Corey, Cleveland	15	15
Gadsden, Oronde, Miami	16	16
Galloway, Joey, Dallas	1	1
Galyon, Scott, Miami	6	1
Gamble, Trent, Miami	16	0
Gammon, Kendall, Kansas City	16	0
Gandy, Wayne, Pittsburgh	16	16
Gannon, Rich, Oakland	16	16
Garcia, Frank, Carolina	16	16
Garcia, Jeff, San Francisco	16	16
Gardener, Daryl, Miami	10	10
Gardner, Barry, Philadelphia	16	13
Gardocki, Chris, Cleveland	16	0
Garner, Charlie, San Francisco	16	15
Garnes, Sam, N.Y. Giants	15	15
Garrett, Jason, N.Y. Giants	2	0
Gary, Olandis, Denver	1	0
Gash, Sam, Baltimore	15	4
Gaylor, Trevor, San Diego	14	2
Gbaja-Biamila, Kabeer, G.B.	7	0
Geason, Corey, Pittsburgh	9	3
Gedney, Chris, Arizona	13	3
George, Eddie, Tennessee	16	16
George, Jeff, Washington	7	5
George, Ron, Kansas City	16	0
George, Tony, New England	15	0
German, Jammi, Atlanta	9	0
Gibson, Aaron, Detroit	10	10
Gibson, David, Tampa Bay	9	0
Gibson, Oliver, Cincinnati	16	16
Gilbert, Sean, Carolina	15	15
Gildon, Jason, Pittsburgh	16	16
Gilmore, Bryan, Arizona	1	0
Givens, Reggie, Washington	9	0
Gizzi, Chris, Green Bay	11	0
Gleason, Steve, New Orleans	3	0
Glenn, Aaron, N.Y. Jets	16	16
Glenn, Tarik, Indianapolis	16	16
Glenn, Terry, New England	16	16
Glover, Andrew, New Orleans	16	14
Glover, La'Roi, New Orleans	16	16
Glover, Phil, Indianapolis	9	0
Godfrey, Randall, Tennessee	16	16
Goff, Mike, Cincinnati	16	16
Gogan, Kevin, San Diego	14	14
Gold, Ian, Denver	16	0
Golden, Jack, N.Y. Giants	16	0
Gonzalez, Tony, Kansas City	16	16
Gooch, Jeff, Tampa Bay	16	0
Goodman, Herbert, Green Bay	5	0
Goodrich, Dwayne, Dallas	5	0
Goodwin, Hunter, Miami	16	16
Gordon, Darrien, Oakland	13	0
Gordon, Dwayne, N.Y. Jets	15	1
Gordon, Lennox, Indianapolis	9	0
Gowin, Toby, New Orleans	16	0
Gragg, Scott, San Francisco	16	16
Graham, DeMingo, San Diego	14	1
Graham, Jeff, San Diego	14	13
Graham, Kent, Pittsburgh	12	5
Gramatica, Martin, Tampa Bay	16	0
Grant, Ernest, Miami	2	0
Grant, Orantes, Dallas	13	0
Granville, Billy, Cincinnati	14	0
Grasmanis, Paul, Philadelphia	16	0
Gray, Carlton, Kansas City	4	1
Gray, Chris, Seattle	16	16
Grbac, Elvis, Kansas City	15	15
Green, Ahman, Green Bay	16	11
Green, Barrett, Detroit	9	0
Green, Darrell, Washington	13	2
Green, E.G., Indianapolis	7	0
Green, Jacquez, Tampa Bay	16	16
Green, Michael, Chicago	7	0
Green, Mike, Tennessee	1	0
Green, Ray, Carolina	16	0
Green, Trent, St. Louis	8	5
Green, Victor, N.Y. Jets	16	16
Greer, Donovan, Buffalo	13	1
Greisen, Chris, Arizona	3	0
Griese, Brian, Denver	10	10
Griffin, Cornelius, N.Y. Giants	15	0
Griffin, Damon, Cincinnati	8	0
Griffith, Howard, Denver	14	14
Griffith, Rich, Jacksonville	16	1
Griffith, Robert, Minnesota	16	16
Grimes, Reggie, New England	8	0
Groce, Clif, Cincinnati	8	6
Grunhard, Tim, Kansas City	15	15
Gruttadauria, Mike, Arizona	8	8
Gutierrez, Brock, Cincinnati	16	7
Haggans, Clark, Pittsburgh	2	0
Hakim, Az-Zahir, St. Louis	16	4
Hale, Ryan, N.Y. Giants	16	0
Haley, Jermaine, Miami	15	4
Hall, Cory, Cincinnati	16	6
Hall, Dante, Kansas City	5	0
Hall, James, Detroit	5	0
Hall, Jeff, St. Louis	3	0
Hall, John, N.Y. Jets	15	0
Hall, Lamont, New Orleans	16	5
Hall, Lemanski, Minnesota	15	1
Hall, Travis, Atlanta	16	16
Hallen, Bob, Atlanta	16	5
Hallock, Ty, Chicago	2	0
Ham, Derrick, Washington	1	0
Hambrick, Darren, Dallas	16	16
Hambrick, Troy, Dallas	3	0
Hamilton, Bobby, New England	16	16
Hamilton, Joe, Tampa Bay	1	0
Hamilton, Keith, N.Y. Giants	16	16
Hamilton, Michael, Mia.-Cle.	4	0
Hamiter, Uhuru, Philadelphia	7	0
Hand, Norman, New Orleans	15	15
Hankton, Karl, Carolina	16	0
Hansen, Phil, Buffalo	10	9
Hanson, Jason, Detroit	16	0
Hape, Patrick, Tampa Bay	16	2
Harbaugh, Jim, San Diego	7	5
Hardy, Kevin, Jacksonville	16	16
Hardy, Terry, Arizona	16	15
Harper, Deveron, Carolina	16	0
Harris, Al, Philadelphia	16	4
Harris, Antwan, New England	14	0
Harris, Bernardo, Green Bay	16	16
Harris, Corey, New Orleans	3	1

Player, Team	GP	GS	Player, Team	GP	GS	Player, Team	GP	GS
Harris, Corey L., Baltimore	16	0	Hopson, Tyrone, San Francisco	3	1	Johnson, Dwight, Philadelphia	4	0
Harris, Jackie, Dallas	16	7	Horn, Joe, New Orleans	16	16	Johnson, Ellis, Indianapolis	13	13
Harris, Johnnie, Oakland	15	2	Horne, Tony, St. Louis	11	0	Johnson, Eric, Oakland	16	0
Harris, Raymont, Den.-N.E.	4	0	Houser, Kevin, New Orleans	16	0	Johnson, Garrett, New England	8	2
Harris, Sean, Chicago	15	13	Hovan, Chris, Minnesota	16	13	Johnson, J.J., Miami	13	1
Harris, Walt, Chicago	12	12	Howard, Chris, Jacksonville	2	1	Johnson, Joe, New Orleans	16	15
Harrison, Lloyd, Washington	2	0	Howard, Darren, New Orleans	16	16	Johnson, Kevin, Cleveland	16	16
Harrison, Marvin, Indianapolis	16	16	Howard, Desmond, Detroit	15	0	Johnson, Keyshawn, T.B.	16	16
Harrison, Nolan, Washington	16	2	Howard, Reggie, N.O.-Car.	2	0	Johnson, Lee, New England	16	0
Harrison, Rodney, San Diego	16	16	Howard, Ty, Tennessee	1	0	Johnson, Leon, N.Y. Jets	3	0
Hartings, Jeff, Detroit	16	16	Hoying, Bobby, Oakland	4	0	Johnson, Malcolm, Pit.-NYJ	5	0
Hartsell, Mark, Chicago	1	0	Huard, Brock, Seattle	5	4	Johnson, Olrick, New England	12	0
Harvey, Richard, San Diego	8	0	Huard, Damon, Miami	16	1	Johnson, Patrick, Baltimore	12	9
Hasselbach, Harald, Denver	16	1	Hudson, John, Baltimore	8	0	Johnson, Rob, Buffalo	12	11
Hasselbeck, Matt, Green Bay	16	0	Humphrey, Deon, Car.-S.D.	10	0	Johnson, Ted, New England	13	11
Hastings, Andre, Tampa Bay	3	0	Hunt, Cletidus, Green Bay	16	11	Johnson, Tre', Washington	4	4
Hasty, James, Kansas City	16	16	Huntley, Richard, Pittsburgh	13	0	Johnstone, Lance, Oakland	14	9
Hatcher, Armon, San Diego	4	0	Husak, Todd, Washington	1	0	Jones, Cedric, N.Y. Giants	16	16
Hatchette, Matthew, Minnesota	14	4	Husted, Michael, Washington	4	0	Jones, Clarence, Carolina	11	11
Hauck, Tim, Philadelphia	16	3	Hutson, Tony, Washington	3	0	Jones, Damon, Jacksonville	1	0
Hawkins, Artrell, Cincinnati	16	6	Hyder, Gaylon, St. Louis	5	1	Jones, Donta, New Orleans	12	0
Hawkins, Courtney, Pittsburgh	13	5	Irvin, Ken, Buffalo	16	16	Jones, Fred, Buffalo	15	0
Hawthorne, Duane, Dallas	14	0	Irvin, Sedrick, Detroit	6	0	Jones, Freddie, San Diego	16	16
Hawthorne, Michael, N.O.	11	1	Irwin, Heath, Miami	13	0	Jones, Greg, Washington	16	4
Hayes, Chris, N.Y. Jets	16	8	Isaia, Sale, New England	16	14	Jones, Henry, Buffalo	16	16
Hayes, Donald, Carolina	15	15	Ismail, Qadry, Baltimore	15	13	Jones, Isaac, Indianapolis	1	0
Hayes, Windrell, N.Y. Jets	8	1	Ismail, Raghib, Dallas	9	9	Jones, James, Detroit	16	16
Heard, Ronnie, San Francisco	13	3	Issa, Jabari, Arizona	10	0	Jones, John, Baltimore	8	0
Heath, Rodney, Cincinnati	13	9	Izzo, Larry, Miami	16	0	Jones, K.C., Denver	16	0
Heck, Andy, Washington	16	2	Jackson, Al, Dallas	3	0	Jones, Lenoy, Cleveland	8	1
Heffner-Liddiard, Brody, Miami	5	0	Jackson, Brad, Baltimore	10	0	Jones, Marcus, Tampa Bay	16	16
Hegamin, George, Tampa Bay	16	1	Jackson, Chris, Tennessee	1	0	Jones, Marvin, N.Y. Jets	16	16
Heiden, Steve, San Diego	15	3	Jackson, Curtis, New England	5	2	Jones, Mike A., St. Louis	16	16
Hellestrae, Dale, Dallas	16	0	Jackson, Darrell, Seattle	16	9	Jones, Reggie, San Diego	11	2
Henderson, William, Green Bay	16	6	Jackson, Dexter, Tampa Bay	13	0	Jones, Robert, Miami	16	16
Hendricks, Tommy, Miami	8	0	Jackson, Grady, Oakland	16	15	Jones, Rod, Cincinnati	16	11
Hennings, Chad, Dallas	8	8	Jackson, Greg, San Diego	2	1	Jones, Tebucky, New England	15	9
Henry, Kevin, Pittsburgh	15	15	Jackson, Jarious, Denver	2	0	Jones, Thomas, Arizona	14	4
Hentrich, Craig, Tennessee	16	0	Jackson, John, Cincinnati	8	5	Jones, Tony, Denver	16	16
Heppner, Kris, Sea.-Was.	8	0	Jackson, Lenzie, Cleveland	5	0	Jones, Walter, Seattle	16	16
Herndon, Jimmy, Chicago	10	2	Jackson, Raymond, Cleveland	9	1	Jordan, Andrew, Minnesota	16	4
Herring, Kim, Baltimore	16	16	Jackson, Sheldon, Buffalo	16	8	Jordan, Antony, Atlanta	8	0
Hetherington, Chris, Carolina	16	5	Jackson, Terry, San Francisco	15	1	Jordan, Randy, Oakland	16	0
Hicks, Eric, Kansas City	13	11	Jackson, Tyoka, Tampa Bay	16	1	Joseph, Kerry, Seattle	16	10
Hicks, Robert, Buffalo	14	7	Jackson, Waverly, Indianapolis	16	0	Joyce, Matt, Arizona	13	13
Hicks, Skip, Washington	10	1	Jackson, Willie, New Orleans	15	7	Junkin, Trey, Arizona	16	0
Hill, James, Seattle	10	0	Jacox, Kendyl, San Diego	16	3	Jurevicius, Joe, N.Y. Giants	14	3
Hill, Raion, Buffalo	16	0	Jacquet, Nate, S.D.-Min.	12	0	Kacyvenski, Isaiah, Seattle	16	0
Hill, Ray, Mia.-Buf.	8	0	James, Edgerrin, Indianapolis	16	16	Kalu, Ndukwe, Washington	15	0
Hilliard, Ike, N.Y. Giants	14	14	James, Jeno, Carolina	16	4	Kanell, Danny, Atlanta	5	1
Hilliard, John, Seattle	5	0	James, Tory, Oakland	16	1	Katzenmoyer, Andy, N.E.	8	3
Hitchcock, Jimmy, Carolina	16	2	Janikowski, Sebastian, Oakland	14	0	Kaufman, Napoleon, Oakland	14	2
Hobgood-Chittick, N., St.L.-S.F.	10	0	Jansen, Jon, Washington	16	16	Kearse, Jevon, Tennessee	16	16
Hodge, Damon, Dallas	8	0	Jasper, Edward, Atlanta	15	15	Keaton, Curtis, Cincinnati	6	0
Hodgins, James, St. Louis	15	2	Jefferson, Shawn, Atlanta	16	14	Keith, John, San Francisco	6	3
Holcombe, Robert, St. Louis	14	9	Jeffries, Greg, Miami	11	0	Kelly, Ben, Miami	2	0
Holdman, Warrick, Chicago	10	10	Jenkins, Billy, Denver	16	16	Kelly, Brian, Tampa Bay	16	3
Holecek, John, Buffalo	16	16	Jenkins, DeRon, San Diego	15	14	Kelly, Jeff, Atlanta	12	6
Holland, Darius, Cleveland	16	1	Jenkins, James, Washington	13	6	Kelly, Maurice, Seattle	16	0
Holliday, Vonnie, Green Bay	12	9	Jenkins, Kerry, N.Y. Jets	16	16	Kelly, Reggie, Atlanta	16	16
Hollier, Dwight, Indianapolis	16	15	Jenkins, MarTay, Arizona	16	2	Kelly, Rob, New Orleans	12	0
Hollis, Mike, Jacksonville	12	0	Jenkins, Ronney, San Diego	16	0	Kendall, Pete, Seattle	16	16
Holmberg, Rob, New England	16	5	Jennings, Brandon, Oakland	2	0	Kennedy, Cortez, Seattle	16	16
Holmes, Earl, Pittsburgh	16	16	Jennings, Brian, San Francisco	16	0	Kennedy, Kenoy, Denver	13	0
Holmes, Jaret, N.Y. Giants	4	0	Jervey, Travis, San Francisco	8	0	Kennedy, Lincoln, Oakland	16	16
Holmes, Kenny, Tennessee	14	13	Jett, James, Oakland	16	13	Kennison, Eddie, Chicago	16	10
Holmes, Lester, Arizona	12	12	Jett, John, Detroit	16	0	Kight, Danny, Indianapolis	16	0
Holmes, Priest, Baltimore	16	2	Johnson, Anthony, Jacksonville	12	3	Killens, Terry, Tennessee	16	0
Holsey, Bernard, Indianapolis	16	13	Johnson, Brad, Washington	12	11	Killings, Cedric, San Francisco	14	1
Holt, Torry, St. Louis	16	15	Johnson, Bryan, Washington	1	0	Kinchen, Brian, Carolina	16	0
Hoover, Brad, Carolina	16	4	Johnson, Charles, Philadelphia	16	16	King, Lamar, Seattle	14	14
Hopkins, Brad, Tennessee	15	15	Johnson, Doug, Atlanta	4	2	King, Shaun, Tampa Bay	16	16

Player, Team	GP	GS
Kinney, Erron, Tennessee	16	9
Kirby, Charles, Tampa Bay	6	2
Kirby, Terry, Oakland	2	0
Kirkland, Levon, Pittsburgh	16	16
Kirschke, Travis, Detroit	13	0
Kitna, Jon, Seattle	15	12
Kleinsasser, Jimmy, Minnesota	14	8
Klemm, Adrian, New England	5	4
Knight, Sammy, New Orleans	16	16
Knight, Tom, Arizona	16	15
Knorr, Micah, Dallas	14	0
Koch, Aaron, Jacksonville	8	0
Konrad, Rob, Miami	15	14
Koonce, George, Seattle	16	16
Kowalkowski, Scott, Detroit	16	2
Kozlowski, Brian, Atlanta	16	3
Kreider, Dan, Pittsburgh	10	7
Kreutz, Olin, Chicago	7	7
Kriewaldt, Clint, Detroit	13	1
Kuehl, Ryan, Cleveland	16	0
Kyle, Jason, San Francisco	2	0
LaBounty, Matt, Seattle	12	2
Lacina, Corbin, Minnesota	15	15
LaFleur, David, Dallas	15	10
LaMontagne, Noel, Cleveland	2	0
Landeta, Sean, Philadelphia	16	0
Lane, Max, New England	6	5
Lang, Kenard, Washington	16	0
Langford, Jevon, Cincinnati	11	3
Langham, Antonio, N.E.	15	7
Larrimore, Kareem, Dallas	15	4
Larsen, Leif, Buffalo	6	0
Lassiter, Kwamie, Arizona	16	16
Law, Ty, New England	15	15
Leach, Mike, Tennessee	15	0
Leaf, Ryan, San Diego	11	9
Lechler, Shane, Oakland	16	0
Ledford, Dwayne, San Francisco	1	0
Ledyard, Courtney, N.Y. Jets	4	0
Lee, Amp, Philadelphia	3	0
Lee, Charles, Green Bay	15	1
Leeuwenburg, Jay, Washington	16	12
Lepsis, Matt, Denver	16	16
Leroy, Emarlos, Jacksonville	9	1
Lett, Leon, Dallas	9	7
Levens, Dorsey, Green Bay	5	5
Levingston, Bashir, N.Y. Giants	3	0
Lewis, Chad, Philadelphia	16	16
Lewis, Darryll, San Diego	15	7
Lewis, Jamal, Baltimore	16	13
Lewis, Jeff, Carolina	5	0
Lewis, Jermaine, Baltimore	15	1
Lewis, Jonas, San Francisco	10	0
Lewis, Kevin, N.Y. Giants	7	0
Lewis, Mo, N.Y. Jets	16	16
Lewis, Ray, Baltimore	16	16
Lincoln, Jeremy, Detroit	3	0
Lindell, Rian, Seattle	12	0
Lindsay, Everett, Cleveland	16	16
Lindsey, Steve, Jac.-Den.	16	0
Linton, Jonathan, Buffalo	14	2
Little, Earl, Cleveland	16	0
Little, Leonard, St. Louis	14	0
Liwienski, Chris, Minnesota	14	1
Lockett, Kevin, Kansas City	16	2
Lodish, Mike, Denver	16	0
Logan, Ernie, N.Y. Jets	16	4
Logan, James, Seattle	16	0
Logan, Mike, Jacksonville	15	11
Long, Kevin, Tennessee	16	16
Longwell, Ryan, Green Bay	16	0
Love, Clarence, Baltimore	1	0
Loverne, David, N.Y. Jets	16	0
Lucas, Al, Carolina	13	0
Lucas, Justin, Arizona	16	0
Lucas, Ray, N.Y. Jets	7	0
Lyght, Todd, St. Louis	14	12
Lyle, Keith, St. Louis	16	16
Lyle, Rick, N.Y. Jets	14	14
Lyman, Dustin, Chicago	14	7
Lynch, Ben, San Francisco	9	0
Lynch, John, Tampa Bay	16	16
Lyon, Billy, Green Bay	11	1
Lytle, Matt, Seattle	2	0
Machado, J.P., N.Y. Jets	16	0
Mack, Stacey, Jacksonville	16	2
Mack, Tremain, Cincinnati	16	0
Macklin, David, Indianapolis	16	2
Maddox, Mark, Arizona	14	0
Madison, Sam, Miami	16	16
Makovicka, Joel, Arizona	14	10
Malbrough, Anthony, Cleveland	9	1
Mamula, Mike, Philadelphia	15	6
Mangum, Kris, Carolina	15	7
Mannelly, Patrick, Chicago	16	0
Manning, Peyton, Indianapolis	16	16
Mare, Olindo, Miami	16	0
Marion, Brock, Miami	16	16
Martin, Cecil, Philadelphia	16	9
Martin, Curtis, N.Y. Jets	16	16
Martin, Jamie, Jacksonville	5	0
Martin, Steve, Kansas City	16	0
Martin, Tony, Miami	10	5
Marts, Lonnie, Jacksonville	7	3
Maryland, Russell, Green Bay	16	16
Maslowski, Mike, Kansas City	16	5
Mason, Derrick, Tennessee	16	10
Mason, Eddie, Washington	16	2
Mathews, Jason, Tennessee	16	1
Mathis, Kevin, New Orleans	16	16
Mathis, Terance, Atlanta	16	16
Matthews, Bruce, Tennessee	16	16
Matthews, Shane, Chicago	6	5
Mawae, Kevin, N.Y. Jets	16	16
Mayberry, Jermane, Philadelphia	16	16
Mayes, Alonzo, Chicago	5	3
Mayes, Derrick, Seattle	13	8
Maynard, Brad, N.Y. Giants	16	0
McAfee, Fred, New Orleans	12	0
McAlister, Chris, Baltimore	16	16
McBride, Tod, Green Bay	15	6
McBurrows, Gerald, Atlanta	16	4
McCaffrey, Ed, Denver	16	16
McCardell, Keenan, Jacksonville	16	16
McCaslin, Eugene, Green Bay	1	0
McCleary, Norris, Kansas City	3	0
McCleon, Dexter, St. Louis	16	16
McClure, Todd, Atlanta	10	7
McCollum, Andy, St. Louis	16	16
McCoy, Tony, Arizona	6	6
McCrary, Fred, San Diego	15	12
McCrary, Michael, Baltimore	16	16
McCullough, George, Ten.	11	0
McCutcheon, Daylon, Cleveland	15	15
McDaniel, Ed, Minnesota	16	15
McDaniel, Emmanuel, NYG	16	3
McDaniel, Jeremy, Buffalo	16	5
McDaniel, Randall, Tampa Bay	16	16
McDonald, Ramos, N.Y. Giants	3	0
McDougal, Kevin, Indianapolis	6	0
McDougle, Stockar, Detroit	8	8
McDuffie, O.J., Miami	9	1
McElroy, Ray, Chicago	13	0
McFarland, Anthony, Tampa Bay	16	16
McGarity, Wane, Dallas	14	0
McGarrahan, Scott, Green Bay	16	0
McGee, Tony, Cincinnati	14	14
McGinest, Willie, New England	14	14
McGlockton, Chester, K.C.	15	15
McGrew, Reggie, San Francisco	10	0
McGriff, Travis, Denver	15	0
McIntosh, Chris, Seattle	14	10
McIntosh, Damion, San Diego	3	0
McKenzie, Keith, Cleveland	16	16
McKenzie, Mike, Green Bay	10	8
McKenzie, Raleigh, Green Bay	3	0
McKinley, Alvin, Carolina	7	0
McKinley, Dennis, Arizona	16	0
McKinney, Steve, Indianapolis	16	16
McKinnon, Ronald, Arizona	16	16
McKnight, James, Dallas	16	15
McLaughlin, John, Tampa Bay	6	0
McMillon, Todd, Chicago	3	0
McNabb, Donovan, Philadelphia	16	16
McNair, Steve, Tennessee	16	15
McNeil, Ryan, Dallas	16	16
McNown, Cade, Chicago	10	9
McQuarters, R.W., Chicago	15	2
McWilliams, Johnny, Minnesota	15	7
Meadows, Adam, Indianapolis	16	16
Means, Natrone, Carolina	1	0
Meester, Brad, Jacksonville	16	16
Megna, Marc, Cin.-N.E.	6	0
Meier, Rob, Jacksonville	16	0
Mickell, Darren, San Diego	16	16
Mickens, Ray, N.Y. Jets	16	0
Middleton, Frank, Tampa Bay	16	16
Milburn, Glyn, Chicago	16	0
Milem, John, San Francisco	16	0
Mili, Itula, Seattle	16	6
Miller, Arnold, Cleveland	12	0
Miller, Billy, Denver	12	0
Miller, Bubba, Philadelphia	16	16
Miller, Craig, Jacksonville	4	2
Miller, Fred, Tennessee	16	16
Miller, Jamir, Cleveland	16	16
Miller, Jim, Chicago	3	2
Miller, Josh, Pittsburgh	16	0
Miller, Keith, St. Louis	16	0
Milloy, Lawyer, New England	16	16
Milne, Brian, New Orleans	16	2
Minor, Kory, Carolina	15	0
Minter, Barry, Chicago	15	2
Minter, Mike, Carolina	16	16
Miranda, Paul, Seattle	3	0
Mirer, Rick, San Francisco	1	0
Mitchell, Anthony, Baltimore	16	0
Mitchell, Basil, Green Bay	1	0
Mitchell, Brandon, New England	11	9
Mitchell, Brian, Philadelphia	16	1
Mitchell, Jeff, Baltimore	14	14
Mitchell, Keith, New Orleans	16	14
Mitchell, Kevin, Washington	16	0
Mitchell, Pete, N.Y. Giants	14	5
Mitchell, Scott, Cincinnati	8	5
Mitchell, Tywan, Arizona	10	1
Mixon, Kenny, Miami	16	16
Mobley, John, Denver	15	14
Mohr, Chris, Buffalo	16	0
Mohring, Mike, San Diego	7	0
Molden, Alex, New Orleans	15	6
Montgomery, Joe, N.Y. Giants	3	0
Montgomery, Monty, S.F.	15	9
Montgomery, Scottie, Denver	4	0
Monty, Pete, N.Y. Giants	16	1
Moon, Warren, Kansas City	2	1

Player, Team	GP	GS
Moore, Corey, Buffalo	9	4
Moore, Damon, Philadelphia	16	16
Moore, Dave, Tampa Bay	16	16
Moore, Herman, Detroit	15	11
Moore, Jason, G.B.-S.F.	8	0
Moore, Jerald, New Orleans	11	1
Moore, Larry, Indianapolis	16	16
Moore, Marty, Cleveland	16	9
Moore, Mookie, Washington	5	1
Morabito, Tim, Carolina	16	13
Moran, Sean, St. Louis	15	3
Moreau, Frank, Kansas City	11	0
Moreland, Earthwind, N.Y. Jets	1	0
Moreland, Jake, N.Y. Jets	7	1
Moreno, Moses, San Diego	6	2
Morgan, Don, Minnesota	2	0
Morris, Aric, Tennessee	15	0
Morris, Rob, Indianapolis	7	0
Morris, Sammy, Buffalo	12	9
Morris, Sylvester, Kansas City	15	14
Morrow, Harold, Minnesota	16	0
Morton, Chad, New Orleans	16	3
Morton, Johnnie, Detroit	16	16
Morton, Mike, Green Bay	16	0
Moss, Randy, Minnesota	16	16
Moulds, Eric, Buffalo	16	16
Muhammad, Muhsin, Carolina	16	16
Muhammad, Mustafah, Ind.	13	3
Mulitalo, Edwin, Baltimore	16	16
Murphy, Frank, Tampa Bay	1	0
Murray, Eddie, Washington	6	0
Murrell, Adrian, Washington	15	0
Myers, Bobby, Tennessee	16	1
Myers, Greg, Dallas	6	4
Myers, Michael, Dallas	13	7
Myslinski, Tom, Pittsburgh	6	0
Naeole, Chris, New Orleans	16	16
Nails, Jamie, Buffalo	16	16
Nalen, Tom, Denver	16	16
Navies, Hannibal, Carolina	13	1
Neal, Lorenzo, Tennessee	16	6
Nedney, Joe, Den.-Car.	15	0
Neil, Dallas, Atlanta	6	0
Neil, Dan, Denver	16	16
Nelson, Jim, Minnesota	16	0
Nelson, Reggie, Jacksonville	1	0
Nesbit, Jamar, Carolina	16	16
Neufeld, Ryan, Jacksonville	3	0
Neujahr, Quentin, Jacksonville	16	2
Newberry, Jeremy, S.F.	16	16
Newkirk, Robert, Chicago	5	0
Newman, Keith, Buffalo	16	16
Nguyen, Dat, Dallas	10	5
Nickerson, Hardy, Jacksonville	6	6
Noble, Brandon, Dallas	16	9
Northcutt, Dennis, Cleveland	15	8
Northern, Gabe, Minnesota	9	2
Norton, Ken, San Francisco	16	16
Nugent, David, New England	6	0
Nutten, Tom, St. Louis	16	16
Nwokorie, Chukie, Indianapolis	2	0
Oben, Roman, Cleveland	16	16
O'Donnell, Neil, Tennessee	7	1
O'Dwyer, Matt, Cincinnati	10	10
Ogden, Jeff, Miami	16	0
Ogden, Jonathan, Baltimore	15	15
O'Hara, Shaun, Cleveland	8	4
Okeafor, Chike, San Francisco	15	0
Oldham, Chris, New Orleans	13	1
Oliver, Winslow, Atlanta	12	0
Olivo, Brock, Detroit	13	0
Olson, Benji, Tennessee	16	16
Olson, Erik, Jacksonville	14	0
O'Neal, Andre, Kansas City	10	0
O'Neal, Deltha, Denver	16	0
O'Neill, Kevin, Detroit	11	0
Ostroski, Jerry, Buffalo	16	16
Ostrowski, Phil, San Francisco	13	0
Ottis, Brad, Arizona	15	11
Owens, Rich, Miami	12	3
Owens, Terrell, San Francisco	14	13
Pace, Orlando, St. Louis	16	16
Page, Craig, Dallas	2	0
Page, Solomon, Dallas	16	16
Palmer, David, Minnesota	6	0
Palmer, Mitch, Minnesota	16	0
Panos, Joe, Buffalo	13	0
Parker, Anthony, San Francisco	16	0
Parker, De'Mond, Green Bay	8	0
Parker, Glenn, N.Y. Giants	13	13
Parker, Jeremiah, N.Y. Giants	4	0
Parker, Larry, Kansas City	16	0
Parker, Riddick, Seattle	16	16
Parker, Sirr, Cincinnati	2	0
Parker, Vaughn, San Diego	16	16
Parmalee, Bernie, N.Y. Jets	14	0
Parrella, John, San Diego	16	16
Parrish, Tony, Chicago	16	16
Parten, Ty, Kansas City	2	0
Pass, Patrick, New England	5	2
Pathon, Jerome, Indianapolis	16	10
Patten, David, Cleveland	14	11
Patton, Marvcus, Kansas City	16	15
Paulk, Jeff, New England	1	0
Paup, Bryce, Minnesota	10	0
Paxton, Lonie, New England	16	0
Payne, Seth, Jacksonville	16	14
Pederson, Doug, Cleveland	11	8
Pelshak, Troy, St.L.-Jac.	4	0
Pennington, Chad, N.Y. Jets	1	0
Perry, Darren, New Orleans	16	16
Perry, Ed, Miami	9	0
Perry, Jason, San Diego	1	0
Perry, Todd, Chicago	16	16
Peter, Christian, N.Y. Giants	16	15
Peter, Jason, Carolina	9	0
Peterson, Julian, San Francisco	13	7
Peterson, Mike, Indianapolis	16	16
Peterson, Todd, Kansas City	11	0
Petitgout, Luke, N.Y. Giants	16	16
Phenix, Perry, Tennessee	16	0
Phifer, Roman, N.Y. Jets	16	10
Phillips, Ryan, N.Y. Giants	16	15
Philyaw, Mareno, Atlanta	1	0
Pickens, Carl, Tennessee	9	6
Pierson, Pete, Tampa Bay	15	15
Pilgrim, Evan, Atlanta	7	1
Piller, Zach, Tennessee	16	0
Pinkston, Todd, Philadelphia	16	1
Pittman, Kavika, Denver	15	15
Pittman, Michael, Arizona	16	12
Player, Scott, Arizona	16	0
Pleasant, Anthony, S.F.	16	16
Plummer, Ahmed, S.F.	16	14
Plummer, Chad, Indianapolis	3	0
Plummer, Jake, Arizona	14	14
Poindexter, Anthony, Baltimore	10	0
Polk, DaShon, Buffalo	5	0
Pollard, Marcus, Indianapolis	16	14
Poole, Keith, New Orleans	15	4
Poole, Tyrone, Indianapolis	15	12
Pope, Daniel, Cincinnati	16	0
Pope, Marquez, Oakland	15	14
Porcher, Robert, Detroit	16	16
Porter, Daryl, Buffalo	16	0
Porter, Jerry, Oakland	12	0
Porter, Joey, Pittsburgh	16	16
Posey, Jeff, San Francisco	16	9
Poteat, Hank, Pittsburgh	15	0
Pounds, Darryl, Denver	9	0
Pourdanesh, Shar, Pittsburgh	5	2
Powell, Carl, Baltimore	2	0
Prentice, Travis, Cleveland	16	11
Price, Marcus, New Orleans	7	0
Price, Peerless, Buffalo	16	16
Price, Shawn, Buffalo	13	6
Pringley, Mike, San Diego	2	0
Prioleau, Pierson, S.F.	14	6
Pritchett, Kelvin, Detroit	15	0
Pritchett, Stanley, Philadelphia	16	2
Proehl, Ricky, St. Louis	12	4
Pryce, Trevor, Denver	16	16
Pupunu, Alfred, Detroit	9	0
Pyne, Jim, Cleveland	2	2
Quarles, Shelton, Tampa Bay	14	13
Quinn, Jonathan, Jacksonville	1	0
Rackers, Neil, Cincinnati	16	0
Rackley, Derek, Atlanta	16	0
Rainer, Wali, Cleveland	16	16
Randle, John, Minnesota	16	16
Ransom, Derrick, Kansas City	10	0
Rasby, Walter, Detroit	16	8
Rattay, Tim, San Francisco	1	0
Reagor, Montae, Denver	13	0
Redman, Chris, Baltimore	2	0
Redmon, Anthony, Atlanta	4	4
Redmond, J.R., New England	12	5
Reed, Andre, Washington	13	0
Reed, Jake, New Orleans	7	6
Reese, Ike, Philadelphia	16	0
Reese, Izell, Dallas	16	7
Reeves, John, San Diego	9	0
Rehberg, Scott, Cincinnati	10	6
Rhett, Errict, Cleveland	5	4
Rice, Jerry, San Francisco	16	16
Rice, Ron, Detroit	14	14
Rice, Simeon, Arizona	15	11
Richardson, Damien, Carolina	16	1
Richardson, Kyle, Baltimore	16	0
Richardson, Tony, Kansas City	16	16
Richey, Wade, San Francisco	16	0
Richie, David, Jacksonville	1	0
Ricks, Mikhael, S.D.-K.C.	4	1
Riemersma, Jay, Buffalo	12	12
Riley, Earl, Dallas	1	0
Riley, Victor, Kansas City	16	16
Rison, Andre, Oakland	16	0
Ritchie, Jon, Oakland	13	12
Rivera, Marco, Green Bay	16	16
Rivers, Ron, Atlanta	6	0
Roaf, Willie, New Orleans	16	16
Roan, Michael, Tennessee	1	1
Robbins, Austin, Oak.-G.B.	5	0
Robbins, Barret, Oakland	16	16
Robbins, Fred, Minnesota	8	0
Roberts, Ray, Detroit	10	10
Robertson, Marcus, Tennessee	15	15
Robinson, Bryan, Chicago	16	16
Robinson, Damien, Tampa Bay	16	16
Robinson, Eddie, Tennessee	16	16
Robinson, Eugene, Carolina	16	16
Robinson, Jeff, St. Louis	16	2
Robinson, Marcus, Chicago	11	11
Robinson-Randall, Greg, N.E.	12	4
Rodgers, Derrick, Miami	16	14
Rogers, Charlie, Seattle	15	0

Player, Team	GP	GS	Player, Team	GP	GS	Player, Team	GP	GS
Rogers, Sam, Buffalo	11	11	Shelton, L.J., Arizona	14	14	Spicer, Paul, Jacksonville	3	0
Rogers, Tyrone, Cleveland	16	0	Shepherd, Jacoby, St. Louis	15	1	Spikes, Cameron, St. Louis	9	0
Rolle, Samari, Tennessee	15	15	Shepherd, Leslie, Miami	13	11	Spikes, Takeo, Cincinnati	16	16
Roman, Mark, Cincinnati	8	2	Shields, Paul, Indianapolis	7	0	Spires, Greg, New England	16	2
Romanowski, Bill, Denver	16	16	Shields, Scott, Pittsburgh	10	1	Spriggs, Marcus, Cleveland	8	0
Rosenthal, Mike, N.Y. Giants	8	2	Shields, Will, Kansas City	16	16	Spriggs, T. Marcus, Buffalo	16	11
Ross, Adrian, Cincinnati	13	4	Shittle, Jason, N.Y. Giants	16	2	Springs, Shawn, Seattle	16	16
Rossum, Allen, Green Bay	16	0	Shivers, Wes, Atlanta	3	0	St. Louis, Brad, Cincinnati	16	0
Rouen, Tom, Denver	16	0	Short, Brandon, N.Y. Giants	11	0	Staat, Jeremy, Pittsburgh	7	0
Roundtree, Raleigh, San Diego	16	15	Sidney, Dainon, Tennessee	11	2	Stablein, Brian, Detroit	14	4
Royals, Mark, Tampa Bay	16	0	Simmons, Anthony, Seattle	16	16	Stachelski, Dave, New Orleans	4	0
Roye, Orpheus, Cleveland	16	16	Simmons, Brian, Cincinnati	1	1	Stai, Brenden, Jacksonville	16	16
Rucker, Mike, Carolina	16	1	Simmons, Clyde, Chicago	16	2	Staley, Duce, Philadelphia	5	5
Rudd, Dwayne, Minnesota	14	13	Simmons, Jason, Pittsburgh	15	0	Stanley, Chad, San Francisco	16	0
Ruddy, Tim, Miami	16	16	Simmons, Tony, New England	12	2	Starkey, Jason, Arizona	2	0
Ruegamer, Grey, New England	6	0	Simon, Corey, Philadelphia	16	16	Starks, Duane, Baltimore	15	15
Ruff, Orlando, San Diego	16	14	Simoneau, Mark, Atlanta	14	4	Stecker, Aaron, Tampa Bay	10	0
Runyan, Jon, Philadelphia	16	16	Simpson, Antoine, San Diego	7	0	Steele, Glen, Cincinnati	16	1
Rusk, Reggie, San Diego	7	0	Sims, Barry, Oakland	16	8	Stephens, Jamain, Cincinnati	5	0
Russ, Steve, Denver	2	0	Sims, Keith, Washington	13	13	Stephens, Reggie, N.Y. Giants	15	1
Russell, Darrell, Oakland	16	16	Sinceno, Kaseem, Chicago	11	11	Stepnoski, Mark, Dallas	11	11
Russell, Twan, Miami	16	2	Sinclair, Michael, Seattle	16	16	Steussie, Todd, Minnesota	16	16
Rutledge, Johnny, Arizona	11	3	Singleton, Alshermond, T.B.	13	1	Stevens, Matt, Was.-N.E.	16	4
Rutledge, Rod, New England	16	11	Siragusa, Tony, Baltimore	15	15	Stewart, James, Detroit	16	16
Salaam, Ephraim, Atlanta	14	10	Sirmon, Peter, Tennessee	5	0	Stewart, Kordell, Pittsburgh	16	11
Salave'a, Joe, Tennessee	15	1	Slade, Chris, New England	16	15	Stewart, Rayna, Jacksonville	12	10
Saleh, Tarek, Cleveland	16	0	Slaughter, T.J., Jacksonville	16	7	Stewart, Ryan, Detroit	1	0
Samuel, Khari, Chicago	16	0	Sloan, David, Detroit	15	10	Stills, Gary, Kansas City	12	0
Samuels, Chris, Washington	16	16	Small, Torrance, Philadelphia	14	14	Stinchcomb, Matt, Oakland	13	9
Sanders, Chris, Tennessee	16	14	Smeenge, Joel, Jacksonville	12	1	Stith, Shyrone, Jacksonville	14	0
Sanders, Deion, Washington	16	15	Smith, Aaron, Pittsburgh	16	15	Stoerner, Clint, Dallas	1	0
Sanders, Frank, Arizona	16	16	Smith, Akili, Cincinnati	12	11	Stokes, Barry, Green Bay	8	0
Sanders, Lewis, Cleveland	11	1	Smith, Antowain, Buffalo	11	3	Stokes, J.J., San Francisco	16	3
Sanderson, Scott, Tennessee	9	0	Smith, Brady, Atlanta	15	14	Stokley, Brandon, Baltimore	7	1
Santiago, O.J., Dallas	11	0	Smith, Brent, Miami	16	2	Stoltenberg, Bryan, Carolina	8	1
Sanyika, Sekou, Arizona	16	0	Smith, Bruce, Washington	16	16	Stone, Dwight, N.Y. Jets	12	0
Sapp, Warren, Tampa Bay	16	15	Smith, Chuck, Carolina	2	2	Stone, Ron, N.Y. Giants	15	15
Saturday, Jeff, Indianapolis	16	16	Smith, Darrin, New Orleans	16	11	Storz, Erik, Jacksonville	10	2
Sauer, Craig, Minnesota	9	0	Smith, Derek M., Washington	16	14	Stoutmire, Omar, N.Y. Giants	16	0
Sauerbrun, Todd, Kansas City	16	0	Smith, Detron, Denver	16	0	Stover, Matt, Baltimore	16	0
Sawyer, Talance, Minnesota	16	16	Smith, Emanuel, Jacksonville	1	0	Stoyanovich, Pete, K.C.-St.L.	8	0
Scarlett, Noel, Dallas	1	0	Smith, Emmitt, Dallas	16	16	Strahan, Michael, N.Y. Giants	16	16
Schau, Ryan, Philadelphia	10	0	Smith, Fernando, St.L.-Min.	3	0	Streets, Tai, San Francisco	15	1
Schlereth, Mark, Denver	8	8	Smith, Frankie, Chicago	14	0	Stringer, Korey, Minnesota	16	16
Schlesinger, Cory, Detroit	16	8	Smith, Hunter, Indianapolis	16	0	Strong, Mack, Seattle	16	13
Schneck, Mike, Pittsburgh	16	0	Smith, Jeff, Jacksonville	14	12	Stryzinski, Dan, Atlanta	16	0
Schroeder, Bill, Green Bay	16	16	Smith, Jimmy, Jacksonville	15	14	Stubblefield, Dana, Washington	15	14
Schulters, Lance, San Francisco	12	12	Smith, Lamar, Miami	15	15	Styles, Lorenzo, St. Louis	16	5
Schulz, Kurt, Detroit	11	11	Smith, Larry, Jacksonville	14	4	Sullivan, Chris, Pittsburgh	15	2
Scioli, Brad, Indianapolis	16	2	Smith, Mark, Arizona	14	7	Supernaw, Kywin, Detroit	13	3
Scott, Chad, Pittsburgh	16	16	Smith, Marquis, Cleveland	16	16	Surtain, Patrick, Miami	16	16
Scott, Tony, N.Y. Jets	16	0	Smith, Marvel, Pittsburgh	12	9	Suttle, Jason, Denver	5	0
Scott, Yusuf, Arizona	9	0	Smith, Maurice, Atlanta	10	0	Swann, Eric, Carolina	16	3
Scroggins, Tracy, Detroit	16	15	Smith, Neil, San Diego	10	0	Swanson, Pete, St. Louis	3	0
Sears, Corey, Arizona	8	2	Smith, Otis, New England	16	14	Swayda, Shawn, Atlanta	16	0
Seau, Junior, San Diego	16	16	Smith, Paul, San Francisco	10	0	Swayne, Harry, Baltimore	13	13
Seder, Tim, Dallas	15	0	Smith, Robaire, Tennessee	7	0	Swift, Justin, San Francisco	16	1
Sehorn, Jason, N.Y. Giants	14	14	Smith, Robert, Minnesota	16	16	Swift, Michael, Jacksonville	1	0
Sellers, Mike, Washington	15	7	Smith, Rod, Denver	16	16	Sword, Sam, Indianapolis	3	0
Semple, Tony, Detroit	11	8	Smith, Terrelle, New Orleans	14	9	Symonette, Josh, Washington	3	0
Serwanga, Kato, New England	15	0	Smith, Thomas, Chicago	16	16	Szott, David, Kansas City	1	1
Serwanga, Wasswa, Minnesota	7	2	Smith, Travian, Oakland	16	0	Tait, John, Kansas City	15	15
Shade, Sam, Washington	16	14	Snider, Matt, Green Bay	16	0	Tanner, Barron, Arizona	4	0
Sharpe, Shannon, Baltimore	16	15	Snow, Justin, Indianapolis	16	0	Tant, Jay, Arizona	5	0
Sharper, Darren, Green Bay	16	16	Soward, R. Jay, Jacksonville	13	2	Tanuvasa, Maa, Denver	16	16
Sharper, Jamie, Baltimore	16	16	Sowell, Jerald, N.Y. Jets	16	0	Tarle, Jim, Jacksonville	6	0
Shaw, Bobby, Pittsburgh	16	0	Sparks, Phillippi, Dallas	16	12	Tate, Robert, Minnesota	16	16
Shaw, Harold, New England	16	0	Spearman, Armegis, Cincinnati	15	11	Tauscher, Mark, Green Bay	16	14
Shaw, Terrance, Miami	11	3	Spears, Marcus, Kansas City	13	0	Taves, Josh, Oakland	16	0
Shea, Aaron, Cleveland	15	8	Spellman, Alonzo, Dallas	16	15	Taylor, Bobby, Philadelphia	16	15
Shedd, Kenny, Washington	1	0	Spence, Blake, Tampa Bay	3	0	Taylor, Fred, Jacksonville	13	13
Shelton, Daimon, Jacksonville	16	9	Spencer, Jimmy, Denver	16	6	Taylor, Henry, Atlanta	5	0

Player, Team	GP	GS	Player, Team	GP	GS	Player, Team	GP	GS
Taylor, Jason, Miami	16	16	Ulbrich, Jeff, San Francisco	4	0	Wetnight, Ryan, Green Bay	10	0
Taylor, Ryan, Cleveland	4	0	Ulmer, Artie, San Francisco	12	2	Whalen, James, Dallas	3	0
Taylor, Shannon, San Diego	11	0	Underwood, Dimitrius, Dallas	15	0	Wheatley, Austin, New Orleans	4	0
Taylor, Travis, Baltimore	9	8	Unutoa, Morris, Tampa Bay	16	0	Wheatley, Tyrone, Oakland	14	13
Teague, George, Dallas	9	9	Upshaw, Regan, Oakland	16	7	Whigham, Larry, New England	14	4
Teague, Trey, Denver	2	0	Urlacher, Brian, Chicago	16	14	White, Chris, Atlanta	5	0
Terrell, Daryl, New Orleans	16	0	Uwaezuoke, Iheanyi, Carolina	11	2	White, Dez, Chicago	15	0
Terrell, David, Washington	16	0	Van Dyke, Alex, Philadelphia	4	0	White, Jamel, Cleveland	13	0
Terry, Chris, Carolina	16	16	Van Pelt, Alex, Buffalo	1	0	White, Reggie, Carolina	16	16
Terry, Corey, New Orleans	7	0	Vance, Eric, Tampa Bay	14	0	White, Steve, Tampa Bay	15	0
Terry, Tim, Seattle	6	0	Vanderjagt, Mike, Indianapolis	16	0	Whitehead, Willie, New Orleans	16	2
Testaverde, Vinny, N.Y. Jets	16	16	Vaughn, Darrick, Atlanta	16	0	Whitfield, Bob, Atlanta	15	15
Tharpe, Larry, Pittsburgh	12	5	Verba, Ross, Green Bay	16	16	Whiting, Brandon, Philadelphia	16	11
Thibodeaux, Keith, Minnesota	16	0	Vickers, Kipp, Baltimore	12	2	Whitted, Alvis, Jacksonville	16	3
Thierry, John, Green Bay	16	16	Villarrial, Chris, Chicago	16	15	Whittington, Bernard, Ind.	15	12
Thigpen, Yancey, Tennessee	12	0	Vinatieri, Adam, New England	16	0	Wiegert, Zach, Jacksonville	8	8
Thomas, Adalius, Baltimore	3	0	Vincent, Troy, Philadelphia	16	16	Wiegmann, Casey, Chicago	16	10
Thomas, Chris, St. Louis	16	0	von Oelhoffen, Kimo, Pittsburgh	16	16	Wiggins, Jermaine, NYJ-N.E.	15	2
Thomas, Dave, N.Y. Giants	16	16	Vrabel, Mike, Pittsburgh	15	0	Wiley, Chuck, Atlanta	16	0
Thomas, Edward, S.F.-Jac.	8	0	Wade, John, Jacksonville	2	2	Wiley, Marcellus, Buffalo	16	15
Thomas, Fred, New Orleans	11	0	Wade, Todd, Miami	16	16	Wiley, Michael, Dallas	10	0
Thomas, Henry, New England	16	5	Wadsworth, Andre, Arizona	9	8	Wilkins, Jeff, St. Louis	11	0
Thomas, Hollis, Philadelphia	16	16	Wahle, Mike, Green Bay	16	6	Wilkins, Terrence, Indianapolis	14	7
Thomas, Kiwaukee, Jacksonville	16	3	Wainright, Frank, Baltimore	8	0	Wilkinson, Dan, Washington	16	16
Thomas, Mark, Indianapolis	14	1	Walendy, Craig, N.Y. Giants	12	0	Williams, Aeneas, Arizona	16	16
Thomas, Orlando, Minnesota	9	9	Walker, Bracey, Kansas City	16	0	Williams, Brian, Green Bay	4	3
Thomas, Randy, N.Y. Jets	16	16	Walker, Brian, Miami	16	16	Williams, Charlie, Dallas	11	0
Thomas, Ratcliff, Indianapolis	12	0	Walker, Darnell, Detroit	10	2	Williams, Clarence, Arizona	2	0
Thomas, Robert, Dallas	16	15	Walker, Darwin, Arizona	1	0	Williams, Dan, Kansas City	12	10
Thomas, Rodney, Tennessee	16	0	Walker, Denard, Tennessee	15	14	Williams, Darryl, Cincinnati	16	16
Thomas, Thurman, Miami	9	0	Walker, Gary, Jacksonville	15	14	Williams, Elijah, Atlanta	15	3
Thomas, Tra, Philadelphia	16	16	Walker, Marquis, Detroit	12	2	Williams, Erik, Dallas	16	16
Thomas, William, Oakland	16	16	Walls, Wesley, Carolina	8	8	Williams, George, N.Y. Giants	13	0
Thomas, Zach, Miami	11	11	Walsh, Chris, Minnesota	16	0	Williams, Grant, New England	15	8
Thomason, Jeff, Philadelphia	16	5	Walter, Ken, Carolina	16	0	Williams, Jamal, San Diego	16	16
Thompson, Derrius, Washington	4	0	Walters, Troy, Minnesota	12	0	Williams, James, Seattle	10	0
Thompson, Donnel, Pittsburgh	8	0	Walz, Zack, Arizona	6	5	Williams, James O., Chicago	16	16
Thompson, Kevin, Cleveland	1	0	Ward, Dedric, N.Y. Jets	16	16	Williams, Jay, Carolina	16	14
Thompson, Michael, Atlanta	2	2	Ward, Hines, Pittsburgh	16	15	Williams, Jermaine, Jacksonville	7	0
Thompson, Mike, Cleveland	12	0	Ward, Phillip, New Orleans	2	0	Williams, Josh, Indianapolis	14	7
Thompson, Raynoch, Arizona	11	9	Warfield, Eric, Kansas City	13	3	Williams, K.D., Green Bay	16	3
Thornton, John, Tennessee	16	16	Warner, Kurt, St. Louis	11	11	Williams, Karl, Tampa Bay	13	0
Thrash, James, Washington	16	9	Warren, Chris, Dal.-Phi.	14	1	Williams, Kevin L., NYJ-Mia.	11	7
Tillman, Pat, Arizona	16	16	Warren, Steve, Green Bay	13	0	Williams, Kevin R., S.F.	16	0
Tillman, Travares, Buffalo	15	4	Warrick, Peter, Cincinnati	16	16	Williams, Moe, Minnesota	16	0
Timmerman, Adam, St. Louis	16	15	Washington, Damon, NYG	3	0	Williams, Nick, Cincinnati	14	4
Tobeck, Robbie, Seattle	4	0	Washington, Dewayne, Pit.	16	16	Williams, Pat, Buffalo	16	3
Tomich, Jared, New Orleans	15	0	Washington, Keith, Baltimore	16	0	Williams, Payton, Indianapolis	7	0
Tongue, Reggie, Seattle	16	6	Washington, Marcus, Ind.	16	0	Williams, Ricky, New Orleans	10	10
Toomer, Amani, N.Y. Giants	16	14	Washington, Ted, Buffalo	16	16	Williams, Roland, St. Louis	16	11
Tosi, Mao, Arizona	15	10	Washington, Todd, Tampa Bay	10	0	Williams, Sammy, Baltimore	1	0
Tovar, Steve, San Diego	16	0	Waters, Brian, Kansas City	6	0	Williams, Shaun, N.Y. Giants	16	16
Towns, Lester, Carolina	16	14	Watson, Chris, Buffalo	16	4	Williams, Tony, Minnesota	14	12
Townsend, Deshea, Pittsburgh	16	0	Watson, Justin, St. Louis	14	2	Williams, Tyrone M., Phi.-K.C.	13	0
Trapp, James, Baltimore	16	1	Watters, Ricky, Seattle	16	16	Williams, U. Tyrone, Green Bay	16	16
Traylor, Keith, Denver	16	16	Wayne, Nate, Green Bay	16	13	Williams, Wally, New Orleans	16	16
Treu, Adam, Oakland	16	0	Weary, Fred, New Orleans	12	12	Williams, Willie, Seattle	16	15
Trotter, Jeremiah, Philadelphia	16	16	Weathers, Andre, N.Y. Giants	1	0	Willig, Matt, San Francisco	16	3
Tubbs, Winfred, San Francisco	14	14	Weaver, Jed, Miami	16	0	Willis, Donald, Kansas City	16	2
Tucker, Jason, Dallas	16	7	Webb, Richmond, Miami	14	14	Wilson, Al, Denver	15	14
Tucker, Rex, Chicago	6	0	Webster, Jason, San Francisco	16	10	Wilson, Antonio, Minnesota	1	0
Tucker, Ryan, St. Louis	16	16	Webster, Larry, Baltimore	5	0	Wilson, Jerry, Miami	16	1
Tuggle, Jessie, Atlanta	8	7	Webster, Nate, Tampa Bay	16	0	Wilson, Reinard, Cincinnati	14	0
Tuinei, Van, Chicago	14	2	Wedderburn, Floyd, Seattle	16	0	Wilson, Robert, New Orleans	16	0
Tuitele, Ula, New England	1	0	Weiner, Todd, Seattle	16	6	Wilson, Troy, Chicago	6	0
Tuman, Jerame, Pittsburgh	16	1	Welbourn, John, Philadelphia	16	16	Wiltz, Jason, N.Y. Jets	15	1
Tupa, Tom, N.Y. Jets	16	0	Wells, Dean, Carolina	16	14	Winfield, Antoine, Buffalo	11	11
Turk, Matt, Miami	16	0	Wells, Mike, Chicago	16	14	Winters, Frank, Green Bay	14	14
Turley, Kyle, New Orleans	16	16	Wesley, Greg, Kansas City	16	16	Wisniewski, Steve, Oakland	16	16
Turner, Scott, San Diego	16	2	West, Lyle, N.Y. Giants	16	1	Wistrom, Grant, St. Louis	16	16
Tuten, Melvin, Carolina	3	0	Westbrook, Bryant, Detroit	13	13	Withrow, Cory, Minnesota	12	0
Tylski, Rich, Pittsburgh	16	16	Westbrook, Michael, Was.	2	2	Witman, Jon, Pittsburgh	6	5

2000 REVIEW *Player participation*

Player, Team	GP	GS
Wohlabaugh, Dave, Cleveland ...	12	12
Wong, Kailee, Minnesota	16	16
Woodall, Lee, Carolina	16	16
Wooden, Shawn, Chicago	11	0
Woods, Jerome, Kansas City	16	16
Woodson, Charles, Oakland	16	16
Woodson, Darren, Dallas	11	11
Woodson, Rod, Baltimore	16	16
Woody, Damien, New England ..	16	16
Wortham, Barron, Dallas	16	11
Wright, Anthony, Dallas	4	2
Wright, Kenny, Minnesota	16	7
Wright, Kenyatta, Buffalo	16	0
Wuerffel, Danny, Green Bay	1	0
Wunsch, Jerry, Tampa Bay	16	16
Wycheck, Frank, Tennessee	16	16
Wynn, Renaldo, Jacksonville	14	14
Wynn, Spergon, Cleveland	7	1
Wyrick, Jimmy, Detroit	6	0
Yamini, Bashir, Tennessee	6	0
Yeast, Craig, Cincinnati	15	7
Yoder, Todd, Tampa Bay	9	0
Young, Brian, St. Louis	11	0
Young, Bryant, San Francisco ...	15	15
Young, Floyd, Tampa Bay	7	0
Young, Ryan, N.Y. Jets	16	16
Zahursky, Steve, Cleveland	16	16
Zeier, Eric, Tampa Bay	3	0
Zeigler, Dusty, N.Y. Giants	16	16
Zelenka, Joe, Washington	16	0
Zellner, Peppi, Dallas	12	0
Zereoue, Amos, Pittsburgh	12	0
Zgonina, Jeff, St. Louis	16	11
Ziemann, Chris, N.Y. Giants	8	0

PLAYERS WITH TWO OR MORE CLUBS

Player, Team	GP	GS
Akins, Chris, Dallas	8	0
Akins, Chris, Green Bay	2	0
Barnes, Lionel, St. Louis	1	0
Barnes, Lionel, Indianapolis	1	0
Bentley, Scott, Denver	1	0
Bentley, Scott, Washington	6	0
Canty, Chris, Seattle	12	1
Canty, Chris, New Orleans	3	0
Conway, Brett, Washington	2	0
Conway, Brett, Oakland	1	0
Conway, Brett, N.Y. Jets	1	0
Dukes, Chad, Washington	1	0
Dukes, Chad, Jacksonville	1	0
Dunn, Damon, N.Y. Jets	1	0
Dunn, Damon, Cleveland	3	0
Fletcher, Derrick, New England..	2	2
Fletcher, Derrick, Washington ...	1	0
Floyd, Chris, New England	11	0
Floyd, Chris, Cleveland	2	0
Franz, Todd, New Orleans	5	0
Franz, Todd, Cleveland	2	0
Hamilton, Michael, Miami	3	0
Hamilton, Michael, Cleveland	1	0
Harris, Raymont, Denver	3	0
Harris, Raymont, New England .	1	0
Heppner, Kris, Seattle	4	0
Heppner, Kris, Washington	4	0
Hill, Ray, Miami	3	0
Hill, Ray, Buffalo	5	0
Hobgood-Chittick, Nate, St.L.	5	0
Hobgood-Chittick, Nate, S.F.	5	0
Howard, Reggie, New Orleans...	1	0
Howard, Reggie, Carolina	1	0
Humphrey, Deon, Carolina	3	0
Humphrey, Deon, San Diego	7	0
Jacquet, Nate, San Diego	11	0
Jacquet, Nate, Minnesota	1	0
Johnson, Malcolm, Pittsburgh ..	4	0
Johnson, Malcolm, N.Y. Jets	1	0
Lindsey, Steve, Jacksonville	10	0
Lindsey, Steve, Denver	6	0
Megna, Marc, Cincinnati	2	0
Megna, Marc, New England	4	0
Moore, Jason, Green Bay	3	0
Moore, Jason, San Francisco	5	0
Nedney, Joe, Denver	3	0
Nedney, Joe, Carolina	12	0
Pelshak, Troy, St. Louis	3	0
Pelshak, Troy, Jacksonville	1	0
Ricks, Mikhael, San Diego	3	1
Ricks, Mikhael, Kansas City	1	0
Robbins, Austin, Oakland	3	0
Robbins, Austin, Green Bay	2	0
Smith, Fernando, St. Louis	2	0
Smith, Fernando, Minnesota	1	0
Stevens, Matt, Washington	15	4
Stevens, Matt, New England	1	0
Stoyanovich, Pete, Kansas City .	5	0
Stoyanovich, Pete, St. Louis	3	0
Thomas, Edward, San Francisco.	4	0
Thomas, Edward, Jacksonville ..	4	0
Warren, Chris, Dallas	13	0
Warren, Chris, Philadelphia	1	1
Wiggins, Jermaine, N.Y. Jets.....	11	0
Wiggins, Jermaine, N.E.	4	2
Williams, Kevin L., N.Y. Jets.....	9	7
Williams, Kevin L., Miami	2	0
Williams, Tyrone M., Phi.	3	0
Williams, Tyrone M., K.C.	10	0

2000 REVIEW Player participation

ATTENDANCE

REGULAR SEASON

Team	Home Attendance	Average	NFL Rank	Road Attendance	Average	NFL Rank
Arizona	387,475	48,434	31	506,451	63,306	27
Atlanta	422,814	52,852	30	541,765	67,721	11
Baltimore	551,695	68,962	11	510,678	63,835	25
Buffalo	555,695	69,462	10	537,892	67,237	12
Carolina	583,489	72,936	8	511,703	63,963	23
Chicago	535,552	66,944	14	545,132	68,142	9
Cincinnati	469,992	58,749	25	497,442	62,180	28
Cleveland	581,544	72,693	9	475,595	59,449	31
Dallas	504,360	63,045	20	571,110	71,389	1
Denver	604,042	75,505	6	535,988	66,999	14
Detroit	607,076	75,885	5	533,850	66,731	15
Green Bay	478,747	59,843	24	565,855	70,732	2
Indianapolis	454,319	56,790	27	553,694	69,212	4
Jacksonville	482,510	60,314	22	509,447	63,681	26
Kansas City	631,365	78,921	2	483,907	60,488	29
Miami	589,909	73,739	7	528,974	66,122	16
Minnesota	513,322	64,165	18	515,940	64,493	22
N.Y. Giants	624,085	78,011	3	511,370	63,921	24
N.Y. Jets	623,711	77,964	4	521,435	65,179	18
New England	482,336	60,292	23	548,258	68,532	7
New Orleans	504,315	63,039	21	476,488	59,561	30
Oakland	462,515	57,814	26	536,140	67,018	13
Philadelphia	523,531	65,441	17	516,325	64,541	20
Pittsburgh	440,426	55,053	28	546,611	68,326	8
San Diego	433,459	54,182	29	548,404	68,551	6
San Francisco	541,964	67,746	13	515,990	64,499	21
Seattle	508,367	63,546	19	520,718	65,090	19
St. Louis	528,402	66,050	15	552,966	69,121	5
Tampa Bay	524,775	65,597	16	555,954	69,494	3
Tennessee	547,524	68,441	12	543,750	67,969	10
Washington	647,424	80,928	1	526,908	65,864	17
NFL total	16,346,740	65,914		16,346,740	65,914	

Note: Attendance figures are unofficial and are based on box scores of games.

HISTORICAL

TOP REGULAR-SEASON HOME CROWDS

Team	Attendance	Date	Site	Opponent
Arizona	73,400	October 30, 1994	Sun Devil Stadium	Pittsburgh
Atlanta	71,253	November 21, 1993	Georgia Dome	Dallas
Baltimore	69,416	November 19, 2000	PSINet Stadium	Dallas
Buffalo	80,368	October 4, 1992	Rich Stadium	Miami
Carolina	76,136	December 10, 1995	Clemson Memorial Stadium	San Francisco
Chicago	66,944	Occurred many times. Last time: December 10, 2000	Soldier Field	New England
Cincinnati	64,006	September 10, 2000	Paul Brown Stadium	Cleveland
Cleveland	85,703	September 21, 1970	Cleveland Stadium	N.Y. Jets
Dallas	80,259	November 24, 1966	Cotton Bowl	Cleveland
Denver	76,098	December 23, 2000	Mile High Stadium	San Francisco
Detroit	80,444	December 20, 1981	Pontiac Silverdome	Tampa Bay
Green Bay	60,766	September 1, 1997	Lambeau Field	Chicago
Indianapolis	61,282	December 14, 1997	RCA Dome	Miami
Jacksonville	74,143	December 28, 1998	ALLTEL Stadium	Pittsburgh
Kansas City	82,893	October 2, 2000	Arrowhead Stadium	Seattle
Miami	78,914	November 19, 1972	Orange Bowl	N.Y. Jets
Minnesota	64,471	November 22, 1998	Metrodome	Green Bay
New England	61,457	December 5, 1971	Schaefer Stadium*	Miami
New Orleans	83,437	November 12, 1967 November 26, 1967	Tulane Stadium Tulane Stadium	Dallas Atlanta
New York Giants	78,216	September 24, 2000	Giants Stadium	Washington
New York Jets	79,469	September 20, 1998	Giants Stadium	Indianapolis
Oakland	74,121	September 23, 1973	Memorial Stadium; Berkeley, Cal.	Miami

Team	Attendance	Date	Site	Opponent
Philadelphia	72,111	November 1, 1981	Veterans Stadium	Dallas
Pittsburgh	60,808	December 18, 1994	Three Rivers Stadium	Cleveland
St. Louis	66,273	December 10, 2000	Trans World Dome	Minnesota
San Diego	68,274	October 24, 1999	Qualcomm Stadium	Green Bay
San Francisco	69,014	November 14, 1994	Candlestick Park	Dallas
Seattle	68,681	December 16, 2000	Husky Stadium	Oakland
Tampa Bay	73,523	December 12, 1997	Houlihan's Stadium	Green Bay
Tennessee	68,498	Occurred five times in 2000 season. Last time: December 25, 2000	Adelphia Coliseum	Dallas
Washington	84,431	September 18, 2000	FedEx Field	Dallas

*Now known as Foxboro Stadium.

YEAR BY YEAR

NATIONAL FOOTBALL LEAGUE

Year	Regular season*		Average	Postseason†	
1934	492,684	(60)	8,211	35,059	(1)
1935	638,178	(53)	12,041	15,000	(1)
1936	816,007	(54)	15,111	29,545	(1)
1937	963,039	(55)	17,510	15,878	(1)
1938	937,197	(55)	17,040	48,120	(1)
1939	1,071,200	(55)	19,476	32,279	(1)
1940	1,063,025	(55)	19,328	36,034	(1)
1941	1,108,615	(55)	20,157	55,870	(2)
1942	887,920	(55)	16,144	36,006	(1)
1943	969,128	(50)	19,383	71,315	(2)
1944	1,019,649	(50)	20,393	46,016	(1)
1945	1,270,401	(50)	25,408	32,178	(1)
1946	1,732,135	(55)	31,493	58,346	(1)
1947	1,837,437	(60)	30,624	66,268	(2)
1948	1,525,243	(60)	25,421	36,309	(1)
1949	1,391,735	(60)	23,196	27,980	(1)
1950	1,977,753	(78)	25,356	136,647	(3)
1951	1,913,019	(72)	26,570	57,522	(1)
1952	2,052,126	(72)	28,502	97,507	(2)
1953	2,164,585	(72)	30,064	54,577	(1)
1954	2,190,571	(72)	30,425	43,827	(1)
1955	2,521,836	(72)	35,026	85,693	(1)
1956	2,551,263	(72)	35,434	56,836	(1)
1957	2,836,318	(72)	39,393	119,579	(2)
1958	3,006,124	(72)	41,752	123,659	(2)
1959	3,140,000	(72)	43,617	57,545	(1)
1960	3,128,296	(78)	40,106	67,325	(1)
1961	3,986,159	(98)	40,675	39,029	(1)
1962	4,003,421	(98)	40,851	64,892	(1)
1963	4,163,643	(98)	42,486	45,801	(1)
1964	4,563,049	(98)	46,562	79,544	(1)
1965	4,634,021	(98)	47,296	100,304	(2)
1966	5,337,044	(105)	50,829	135,098	(2)
1967	5,938,924	(112)	53,026	241,754	(4)
1968	5,882,313	(112)	52,521	291,279	(4)
1969	6,096,127	(112)	54,430	242,841	(4)
1970	9,533,333	(182)	52,381	410,371	(7)
1971	10,076,035	(182)	55,363	430,244	(7)
1972	10,445,827	(182)	57,395	435,466	(7)
1973	10,730,933	(182)	58,961	458,515	(7)
1974	10,236,322	(182)	56,224	412,180	(7)
1975	10,213,193	(182)	56,116	443,811	(7)
1976	11,070,543	(196)	56,482	428,733	(7)
1977	11,018,632	(196)	56,218	483,588	(7)
1978	12,771,800	(224)	57,017	578,107	(9)
1979	13,182,039	(224)	58,848	582,266	(9)
1980	13,392,230	(224)	59,787	577,186	(9)
1981	13,606,990	(224)	60,745	587,361	(9)
1982§	7,367,438	(126)	58,472	985,952	(15)
1983	13,277,222	(224)	59,273	625,068	(9)
1984	13,398,112	(224)	59,813	614,809	(9)
1985	13,345,047	(224)	59,567	660,667	(9)
1986	13,588,551	(224)	60,663	683,901	(9)
1987∞	10,032,493	(168)	59,717	606,864	(9)
1988	13,539,848	(224)	60,446	608,204	(9)
1989	13,625,662	(224)	60,829	635,326	(9)
1990	14,266,240	(224)	63,689	797,198	(11)
1991	13,187,478	(224)	58,873	758,186	(11)
1992	13,159,387	(224)	58,747	756,005	(11)
1993	13,328,760	(224)	59,503	755,625	(11)
1994	13,479,680	(224)	60,177	719,143	(11)
1995	14,196,205	(240)	59,151	733,729	(11)
1996	13,695,748	(240)	57,066	711,601	(11)
1997	14,691,416	(240)	61,214	751,884	(11)
1998	14,977,358	(240)	62,406	776,225	(11)
1999	16,105,716	(248)	64,942	758,045	(11)
2000	16,346,740	(248)	65,914	760,710	(11)

*Number of tickets sold, including no-shows; number of regular-season games in parentheses.

†Includes conference, league championship and Super Bowl games, but not Pro Bowl; number of postseason games in parentheses.

‡A 57-day players strike reduced 224-game schedule to 126 games.

§A 24-day players strike reduced 224-game schedule to 168 non-strike games.

AMERICAN FOOTBALL LEAGUE

Champ. Year	Regular season*	Average	AFL Game
1960	926,156 (56)	16,538	32,183
1961	1,002,657 (56)	17,904	29,556
1962	1,147,302 (56)	20,487	37,981
1963	1,241,741 (56)	22,174	30,127
1964	1,447,875 (56)	25,855	40,242
1965	1,782,384 (56)	31,828	30,361
1966	2,160,369 (63)	34,291	42,080
1967	2,295,697 (63)	36,439	53,330
1968	2,635,004 (70)	37,643	62,627
1969	2,843,373 (70)	40,620	53,564

*Number of regular-season games in parentheses.

2000 REVIEW Attendance

TRADES

(Covering June 2000 through May 2001)

JUNE 5

San Francisco traded CB R.W. McQuarters to Chicago for a 2001 sixth-round conditional draft choice. San Francisco selected WR Cedrick Wilson (Tennessee).

JULY 11

New Orleans traded FB Marvin Powell to Green Bay for TE Lawrence Hart.

JULY 31

Green Bay traded QB Aaron Brooks and TE Lamont Hall to New Orleans for LB K.D. Williams and a 2001 third-round draft choice. Green Bay later traded the pick.

AUGUST 7

St. Louis traded WR Dane Looker to New England for an undisclosed draft choice.

AUGUST 9

Green Bay traded WR Robert Scott to Denver for a 2001 undisclosed draft choice.

AUGUST 10

New Orleans traded TE Lawrence Hart to Dallas for a conditional draft choice.

AUGUST 15

Denver traded LB Nate Wayne to Green Bay for a conditional draft choice.

AUGUST 16

Kansas City traded G Brenden Stai to Jacksonville for an undisclosed draft choice.

AUGUST 22

Dallas traded WR Jeff Ogden to Miami for a future seventh-round draft choice.

Indianapolis traded P John Baker to St. Louis for an undisclosed draft choice.

Miami traded WR-PR Nate Jacquet to San Diego for an undisclosed draft choice.

AUGUST 25

Philadelphia traded PR Allen Rossum to Green Bay for a 2001 fifth-round draft choice. Philadelphia selected TE Tony Stewart (Penn State).

AUGUST 27

Denver traded DB-KR Chris Watson to Buffalo for a 2001 fourth-round draft choice. Denver later traded the pick back to Buffalo.

Chicago traded T Chad Overhauser to Seattle for an undisclosed draft choice.

Atlanta traded TE O.J. Santiago to Dallas for a 2001 fourth-round choice and a 2002 seventh-round choice. Atlanta selected LB Matt Stewart (Vanderbilt).

Oakland traded DT Chuck Osborne to Green Bay for an undisclosed draft choice.

Oakland traded OL Gennaro DiNapoli to Tennessee for an undisclosed draft choice.

OCTOBER 2

Chicago traded TE Alonzo Mayes to Miami for an undisclosed draft choice.

MARCH 2

Green Bay traded QB Matt Hasselbeck to Seattle for 2001 undisclosed draft choices.

MARCH 6

Tampa Bay traded QB Eric Zeier to Atlanta for a 2001 seventh-round draft choice. Tampa Bay selected TE Dauntae' Finger (North Carolina).

MARCH 28

St. Louis traded DE Kevin Carter to Tennessee for a 2001 first-round draft choice. St. Louis selected DT Ryan Pickett (Ohio State).

APRIL 20

Green Bay traded 2001 second-, sixth-, seventh- and two third-round draft choices to San Francisco for 2001 second-, third- and fourth-round draft choices. Green Bay selected WR Robert Ferguson (Texas A&M), DB Bhawoh Jue (Penn State) and G Bill Ferrario (Wisconsin). San Francisco selected LB Jamie Winborn (Vanderbilt), DB Rashad Holman (Louisville) and RB Kevan Barlow (Pittsburgh). San Francisco later traded the seventh- and the other third-round picks to Seattle.

St. Louis traded TE Roland Williams to Oakland for a 2001 fourth-round draft choice. St. Louis later traded the fourth-round pick to Arizona.

St. Louis traded QB Trent Green and a 2001 fifth-round draft choice to Kansas City for a 2001 first-round draft choice. St. Louis selected DT Damione Lewis (Miami, Fla.). Kansas City selected RB Derrick Blaylock (Stephen F. Austin State).

Atlanta traded WR Tim Dwight, 2001 first- and third-round draft choices and a 2002 second-round draft choice to San Diego for a 2001 first-round draft choice. Atlanta selected QB Michael Vick (Virginia Tech). San Diego selected RB LaDainian Tomlinson (Texas Christian) and DB Tay Cody (Florida State).

APRIL 21

Arizona traded CB Aeneas Williams to St. Louis for 2001 second- and fourth-round draft choices. Arizona selected DB Michael Stone (Memphis) and DT Marcus Bell (Memphis).

Seattle traded 2001 first- and sixth-round draft choices to San Francisco for 2001 first-, third- and seventh-round draft choices. Seattle selected WR Koren Robinson (North Carolina State), RB Heath Evans (Auburn) and T Dennis Norman (Princeton). San Francisco selected DE Andre Carter (California) and DE Menson Holloway (Texas-El Paso).

Buffalo traded a 2001 first-round draft choice to Tampa Bay for 2001 first- and second-round draft choices. Buffalo selected DB Nate Clements (Ohio State) and later traded the second-round pick to Denver. Tampa Bay selected T Kenyatta Walker (Florida).

Pittsburgh traded a 2001 first-round draft choice to N.Y. Jets for 2001 first-, fourth- and sixth-round draft choices. Pittsburgh selected DT Casey Hampton (Texas), T Mathias Nkwenti (Temple) and DE Rodney Bailey (Ohio State). The Jets selected WR Santana Moss (Miami, Fla.).

Indianapolis traded a 2001 first-round draft choice to N.Y. Giants for 2001 first-, third- and sixth-round draft choices. Indianapolis selected WR Reggie Wayne (Miami, Fla.), DB Cory Bird (Virginia Tech) and DB Jason Doering (Wisconsin). The Giants selected DB Will Allen (Syracuse).

2000 REVIEW *Trades*

Dallas traded a 2001 second-round draft choice to Indianapolis for 2001 second- and third-round draft choices. Dallas later traded the second-round pick to Miami and the third-round pick to New Orleans. Indianapolis selected DB Idrees Bashir (Memphis).

New England traded a 2001 second-round draft choice to Pittsburgh for 2001 second- and fourth-round draft choices. New England later traded the second-round pick to Detroit and the fourth-round pick to San Diego. Pittsburgh selected LB Kendrell Bell (Georgia).

Detroit traded a 2001 second-round draft choice to New England for 2001 second- and sixth-round draft choices. Detroit selected C Dominic Raiola (Nebraska) and LB Jason Glenn (Texas A&M). New England selected G Matt Light (Purdue).

Buffalo traded a 2001 second-round draft choice to Denver for 2001 second- and fourth-round draft choices. Buffalo selected RB Travis Henry (Tennessee) and LB Brandon Spoon (North Carolina). Denver selected DE Paul Toviessi (Marshall).

Dallas traded a 2001 second-round draft choice to Miami for 2001 second- and fourth-round draft choices. Dallas selected DB Tony Dixon (Alabama). Miami selected WR Chris Chambers (Wisconsin).

New Orleans traded a 2001 second-round draft choice to Dallas for two 2001 third-round draft choices. New Orleans selected LB Sedrick Hodge (North Carolina) and DT Kenny Smith (Alabama). Dallas selected QB Quincy Carter (Georgia).

N.Y. Giants traded a 2001 second-round draft choice to Detroit for 2001 third- and fourth-round draft choices. The Giants selected DB William Peterson (Western Illinois) and DE Cedric Scott (Southern Mississippi). Detroit selected DT Shaun Rogers (Texas).

New England traded a 2001 third-round draft choice to Minnesota for 2001 third- and fourth-round draft choices. New England selected DB Brock Williams (Notre Dame) and TE Jabari Holloway (Notre Dame). Minnesota selected DB Eric Kelly (Kentucky).

Philadelphia traded 2001 third- and sixth-round draft choices to Miami for a 2002 second-round draft choice. Miami selected LB Morlon Greenwood (Syracuse) and DE Otis Leverette (Alabama-Birmingham).

APRIL 22

San Diego traded a 2001 fourth-round draft choice to New England for 2001 fourth- and fifth-round draft choices. San Diego selected LB Carlos Polk (Nebraska) and LB Zeke Moreno (Southern California). New England selected G Kenyatta Jones (South Florida).

Washington traded a 2001 fifth-round draft choice to St. Louis for 2001 fifth- and sixth-round draft choices. Washington selected WR Darnerien McCants (Delaware State) and DT Mario Monds (Cincinnati). St. Louis selected DB Jeremetrius Butler (Kansas State).

New England traded a 2001 fifth-round draft choice to Detroit for 2001 sixth- and seventh-round draft choices. New England selected TE Arther Love (South Carolina State) and K Owen Pochman (Brigham Young). Detroit selected QB Mike McMahon (Rutgers).

New England traded a 2001 sixth-round draft choice to Jacksonville for a 2002 fifth-round draft choice. Jacksonville selected G Chad Ward (Washington).

Denver traded three 2001 seventh-round draft choices to Atlanta for a 2002 fourth-round draft choice. Atlanta selected DB Corey Hall (Appalachian State), G Kynan Forney (Hawaii) and DE Ronald Flemons (Texas A&M).

2000 STATISTICS

Rushing
Passing
Receiving
Scoring
Interceptions
Sacks
Fumbles
Field goals
Punting
Punt returns
Kickoff returns
Miscellaneous

RUSHING

AFC

Team	Att.	Yds.	Avg.	Long	TD
Oakland	520	2470	4.8	t80	23
Cincinnati	495	2314	4.7	t80	13
Denver	516	2311	4.5	t80	21
Pittsburgh	527	2248	4.3	t45	19
Baltimore	511	2199	4.3	45	9
Tennessee	547	2084	3.8	t35	14
Jacksonville	481	2032	4.2	71	18
Buffalo	475	1922	4.0	59	11
Miami	496	1894	3.8	t68	16
Indianapolis	435	1859	4.3	30	14
Seattle	403	1720	4.3	55	10
N.Y. Jets	418	1471	3.5	55	11
Kansas City	383	1465	3.8	69	12
New England	424	1390	3.3	35	9
Cleveland	336	1085	3.2	42	7
San Diego	351	1062	3.0	26	7
AFC total	7318	29526	4.0	t80	214
AFC average	457.4	1845.4	4.0	...	13.4

t—touchdown.

NFC

Team	Att.	Yds.	Avg.	Long	TD
Minnesota	428	2129	5.0	t72	14
New Orleans	505	2068	4.1	40	14
Tampa Bay	490	2066	4.2	t70	18
N.Y. Giants	507	2009	4.0	t78	16
Dallas	463	1953	4.2	52	15
Philadelphia	397	1882	4.7	t85	13
St. Louis	383	1843	4.8	49	26
San Francisco	416	1801	4.3	42	15
Washington	445	1748	3.9	t50	15
Detroit	448	1747	3.9	34	15
Chicago	417	1736	4.2	52	6
Green Bay	404	1643	4.1	t39	13
Arizona	343	1278	3.7	29	6
Atlanta	350	1214	3.5	42	6
Carolina	363	1186	3.3	43	7
NFC total	6359	26303	4.1	t85	198
NFC average	423.9	1753.5	4.1	...	13.2
NFL total	13677	55829	...	t85	412
NFL average	441.2	1800.9	4.1	...	13.3

BESTS OF THE SEASON

Yards, season

AFC: 1709—Edgerrin James, Indianapolis.
NFC: 1521—Robert Smith, Minnesota.

Yards, game

AFC: 278—Corey Dillon, Cincinnati vs. Denver, Oct. 22 (22 attempts, 2 TDs).
NFC: 220—Marshall Faulk, St. Louis at New Orleans, Dec. 24 (32 attempts, 2 TDs).

Longest gain

NFC: 85—Brian Mitchell, Philadelphia vs. Atlanta, Oct. 1 (TD).
AFC: 80—Corey Dillon, Cincinnati vs. Tennessee, Oct. 8 (TD), Tyrone Wheatley, Oakland vs. Seattle, Oct. 22 (TD), Mike Anderson, Denver at Seattle, Nov. 26 (TD).

Attempts, season

AFC: 403—Eddie George, Tennessee.
NFC: 339—James Stewart, Detroit.

Attempts, game

AFC: 38—Edgerrin James, Indianapolis at Seattle, Oct. 15 (219 yards, 3 TDs).
NFC: 38—Ricky Williams, New Orleans vs. Carolina, Oct. 15 (144 yards, 2 TDs).

Yards per attempt, season

NFC: 5.4—Marshall Faulk, St. Louis.
AFC: 5.0—Mike Anderson, Denver.

Touchdowns, season

NFC: 18—Marshall Faulk, St. Louis.
AFC: 15—Mike Anderson, Denver.

Team leaders, yards

AFC:

Team	Yds	Player
Baltimore	1364	Jamal Lewis
Buffalo	591	Shawn Bryson
Cincinnati	1435	Corey Dillon
Cleveland	512	Travis Prentice
Denver	1487	Mike Anderson
Indianapolis	1709	Edgerrin James

Team	Yds	Player
Jacksonville	1399	Fred Taylor
Kansas City	697	Tony Richardson
Miami	1139	Lamar Smith
New England	570	Kevin Faulk
N.Y. Jets	1204	Curtis Martin
Oakland	1046	Tyrone Wheatley
Pittsburgh	1341	Jerome Bettis
San Diego	384	Terrell Fletcher
Seattle	1242	Ricky Watters
Tennessee	1509	Eddie George

NFC:

Team	Yds	Player
Arizona	719	Michael Pittman
Atlanta	1024	Jamal Anderson
Carolina	627	Tim Biakabutuka
Chicago	1120	James Allen
Dallas	1203	Emmitt Smith
Detroit	1184	James Stewart
Green Bay	1175	Ahman Green
Minnesota	1521	Robert Smith
New Orleans	1000	Ricky Williams
N.Y. Giants	1006	Tiki Barber
Philadelphia	629	Donovan McNabb
St. Louis	1359	Marshall Faulk
San Francisco	1142	Charlie Garner
Tampa Bay	1133	Warrick Dunn
Washington	1318	Stephen Davis

NFL LEADERS

Player, Team	Att.	Yds.	Avg.	Long	TD
James, Edgerrin, Indianapolis*	387	1709	4.4	30	13
Smith, Robert, Minnesota	295	1521	5.2	t72	7
George, Eddie, Tennessee*	403	1509	3.7	t35	14
Anderson, Mike, Denver*	297	1487	5.0	t80	15
Dillon, Corey, Cincinnati*	315	1435	4.6	t80	7
Taylor, Fred, Jacksonville*	292	1399	4.8	71	12
Lewis, Jamal, Baltimore*	309	1364	4.4	45	6
Faulk, Marshall, St. Louis	253	1359	5.4	36	18
Bettis, Jerome, Pittsburgh*	355	1341	3.8	30	8
Davis, Stephen, Washington	332	1318	4.0	t50	11
Watters, Ricky, Seattle*	278	1242	4.5	55	7

Player, Team	Att.	Yds.	Avg.	Long	TD
Martin, Curtis, N.Y. Jets*	316	1204	3.8	55	9
Smith, Emmitt, Dallas	294	1203	4.1	52	9
Stewart, James, Detroit	339	1184	3.5	34	10
Green, Ahman, Green Bay	263	1175	4.5	t39	10
Garner, Charlie, San Francisco	258	1142	4.4	42	7
Smith, Lamar, Miami*	309	1139	3.7	t68	14
Dunn, Warrick, Tampa Bay	248	1133	4.6	t70	5
Allen, James, Chicago	290	1120	3.9	29	2
Wheatley, Tyrone, Oakland*	232	1046	4.5	t80	9
Anderson, Jamal, Atlanta	282	1024	3.6	42	6
Barber, Tiki, N.Y. Giants	213	1006	4.7	t78	8
Williams, Ricky, New Orleans	248	1000	4.0	t26	8
Dayne, Ron, N.Y. Giants	228	770	3.4	50	5
Pittman, Michael, Arizona	184	719	3.9	29	4
Richardson, Tony, Kansas City*	147	697	4.7	33	3
McNabb, Donovan, Philadelphia	86	629	7.3	54	6
Biakabutuka, Tim, Carolina	173	627	3.6	43	2
Bryson, Shawn, Buffalo*	161	591	3.7	24	0
Holmes, Priest, Baltimore*	137	588	4.3	21	2

*AFC.

t—touchdown.

Leader based on yards gained.

AFC

Player, Team	Att.	Yds.	Avg.	Long	TD
Alexander, Derrick, Kansas City	3	45	15.0	26	0
Alexander, Shaun, Seattle	64	313	4.9	50	2
al-Jabbar, Abdul-Karim, Ind.	1	-2	-2.0	-2	0
Anders, Kimble, Kansas City	76	331	4.4	69	2
Anderson, Mike, Denver	297	1487	5.0	t80	15
Anderson, Richie, N.Y. Jets	27	63	2.3	9	0
Ayanbadejo, Obafemi, Baltimore	15	37	2.5	8	1
Banks, Tony, Baltimore	19	57	3.0	10	0
Bennett, Brandon, Cincinnati	90	324	3.6	t37	3
Bennett, Donnell, Kansas City	27	24	0.9	6	1
Bettis, Jerome, Pittsburgh	355	1341	3.8	30	8
Bishop, Michael, New England	7	-1	-.1	2	0
Bledsoe, Drew, New England	47	158	3.4	16	2
Brown, Reggie, Seattle	3	6	2.0	3	0
Brown, Tim, Oakland	3	12	4.0	7	0
Brown, Troy, New England	6	46	7.7	35	0
Brunell, Mark, Jacksonville	48	236	4.9	16	2
Bryson, Shawn, Buffalo	161	591	3.7	24	0
Bynum, Kenny, San Diego	7	26	3.7	9	0
Carter, Tony, New England	37	90	2.4	9	2
Chancey, Robert, San Diego	42	141	3.4	14	2
Chrebet, Wayne, N.Y. Jets	3	-3	-1.0	8	0
Cloud, Mike, Kansas City	30	84	2.8	t15	1
Coleman, KaRon, Denver	54	183	3.4	t24	1
Coles, Laveranues, N.Y. Jets	2	15	7.5	8	0
Conway, Curtis, San Diego	3	31	10.3	13	0
Couch, Tim, Cleveland	12	45	3.8	31	0
Crockett, Zack, Oakland	43	130	3.0	11	7
Davis, Terrell, Denver	78	282	3.6	24	2
Denson, Autry, Miami	31	108	3.5	12	0
Dilfer, Trent, Baltimore	20	75	3.8	19	0
Dillon, Corey, Cincinnati	315	1435	4.6	t80	7
Dudley, Rickey, Oakland	1	-7	-7.0	-7	0
Dukes, Chad, Jacksonville	2	2	1.0	2	0
Edwards, Marc, Cleveland	2	9	4.5	6	0
Edwards, Troy, Pittsburgh	3	4	1.3	15	0
Emanuel, Bert, Miami	3	-2	-.7	0	0
Faulk, Kevin, New England	164	570	3.5	18	4
Fazande, Jermaine, San Diego	119	368	3.1	26	2
Fiedler, Jay, Miami	54	267	4.9	30	1
Finn, Jim, Indianapolis	1	1	1.0	1	0
Fletcher, Terrell, San Diego	116	384	3.3	21	3
Floyd, Chris, New England	2	-1	-.5	0	0
Flutie, Doug, Buffalo	36	161	4.5	32	1
Frerotte, Gus, Denver	22	64	2.9	t13	1
Fuamatu-Ma'afala, Chris, Pit.	21	149	7.1	23	1
Gannon, Rich, Oakland	89	529	5.9	23	4
Gary, Olandis, Denver	13	80	6.2	25	0
Gash, Sam, Baltimore	2	2	1.0	1	0
George, Eddie, Tennessee	403	1509	3.7	t35	14
Glenn, Terry, New England	4	39	9.8	35	0
Gordon, Lennox, Indianapolis	4	13	3.3	6	0
Graham, Kent, Pittsburgh	8	7	0.9	7	0
Grbac, Elvis, Kansas City	30	110	3.7	22	1
Griese, Brian, Denver	29	102	3.5	18	1
Griffith, Howard, Denver	5	4	0.8	3	0
Groce, Clif, Cincinnati	3	4	1.3	5	0
Harbaugh, Jim, San Diego	16	24	1.5	7	0
Harris, Raymont, Den.-N.E.	13	36	2.8	7	0
Hayes, Windrell, N.Y. Jets	1	2	2.0	2	0
Holmes, Priest, Baltimore	137	588	4.3	21	2
Howard, Chris, Jacksonville	21	52	2.5	t9	1
Hoying, Bobby, Oakland	2	-3	-1.5	-1	0
Huard, Brock, Seattle	5	29	5.8	10	0
Huntley, Richard, Pittsburgh	46	215	4.7	t30	3
Izzo, Larry, Miami	1	39	39.0	39	0
Jackson, Darrell, Seattle	1	-1	-1.0	-1	0
Jackson, Jarious, Denver	1	-1	-1.0	-1	0
James, Edgerrin, Indianapolis	387	1709	4.4	30	13
Jenkins, Ronney, San Diego	8	6	0.8	4	0
Johnson, Anthony, Jacksonville	28	112	4.0	19	1
Johnson, J.J., Miami	50	168	3.4	16	1
Johnson, Lee, New England	2	-1	-.5	0	0
Johnson, Pat, Baltimore	2	21	10.5	19	0
Johnson, Rob, Buffalo	42	307	7.3	23	1
Jordan, Randy, Oakland	46	213	4.6	t43	3
Kaufman, Napoleon, Oakland	93	499	5.4	60	0
Keaton, Curtis, Cincinnati	6	24	4.0	8	0
Kirby, Terry, Oakland	11	51	4.6	28	0
Kitna, Jon, Seattle	48	127	2.6	13	1
Konrad, Rob, Miami	15	39	2.6	5	0
Kreider, Dan, Pittsburgh	2	24	12.0	22	0
Leaf, Ryan, San Diego	28	54	1.9	14	0
Lewis, Jamal, Baltimore	309	1364	4.4	45	6
Lewis, Jermaine, Baltimore	3	38	12.7	23	0
Lewis, Mo, N.Y. Jets	1	3	3.0	3	0
Linton, Jonathan, Buffalo	38	112	2.9	12	0
Lucas, Ray, N.Y. Jets	6	42	7.0	17	0
Mack, Stacey, Jacksonville	54	145	2.7	14	1
Manning, Peyton, Indianapolis	37	116	3.1	14	1
Martin, Curtis, N.Y. Jets	316	1204	3.8	55	9
Martin, Jamie, Jacksonville	7	-6	-.9	2	0
Mason, Derrick, Tennessee	1	1	1.0	1	0
McCrary, Fred, San Diego	7	8	1.1	4	0
McDuffie, O.J., Miami	1	-3	-3.0	-3	0
McNair, Steve, Tennessee	72	403	5.6	25	0
Miller, Josh, Pittsburgh	1	0	0.0	0	0
Mitchell, Scott, Cincinnati	10	61	6.1	t12	1
Moon, Warren, Kansas City	2	2	1.0	2	0
Moreau, Frank, Kansas City	67	179	2.7	22	4
Moreno, Moses, San Diego	5	20	4.0	13	0
Morris, Sammy, Buffalo	93	341	3.7	t32	5
Moulds, Eric, Buffalo	2	24	12.0	20	0
Neal, Lorenzo, Tennessee	1	-2	-2.0	-2	0
Northcutt, Dennis, Cleveland	9	33	3.7	13	0
O'Donnell, Neil, Tennessee	9	-2	-.2	4	0
Parker, Larry, Kansas City	1	-7	-7.0	-7	0
Parmalee, Bernie, N.Y. Jets	27	87	3.2	t18	2
Pass, Patrick, New England	18	58	3.2	11	0
Pathon, Jerome, Indianapolis	1	3	3.0	3	0
Pederson, Doug, Cleveland	18	68	3.8	15	0
Pennington, Chad, N.Y. Jets	1	0	0.0	0	0
Pope, Daniel, Cincinnati	2	22	11.0	22	0
Prentice, Travis, Cleveland	173	512	3.0	17	7
Price, Peerless, Buffalo	2	32	16.0	27	0
Quinn, Jonathan, Jacksonville	2	-2	-1.0	-1	0
Rackers, Neil, Cincinnati	1	-5	-5.0	-5	0
Redman, Chris, Baltimore	1	0	0.0	0	0

2000 STATISTICS Rushing

Player, Team	Att.	Yds.	Avg.	Long	TD
Redmond, J.R., New England	125	406	3.2	20	1
Rhett, Errict, Cleveland	71	258	3.6	42	0
Richardson, Tony, Kansas City	147	697	4.7	33	3
Rouen, Tom, Denver	1	-11	-11.0	-11	0
Shaw, Harold, New England	9	12	1.3	5	0
Shelton, Daimon, Jacksonville	2	3	1.5	2	0
Shepherd, Leslie, Miami	4	3	0.8	14	0
Smith, Akili, Cincinnati	41	232	5.7	21	0
Smith, Antowain, Buffalo	101	354	3.5	59	4
Smith, Hunter, Indianapolis	1	11	11.0	11	0
Smith, Lamar, Miami	309	1139	3.7	t68	14
Smith, Rod, Denver	6	99	16.5	t50	1
Soward, R. Jay, Jacksonville	3	28	9.3	20	0
Sowell, Jerald, N.Y. Jets	2	0	0.0	1	0
Stewart, Kordell, Pittsburgh	78	436	5.6	t45	7
Stith, Shyrone, Jacksonville	20	55	2.8	12	1
Stokley, Brandon, Baltimore	1	6	6.0	6	0
Stone, Dwight, N.Y. Jets	3	3	1.0	9	0
Strong, Mack, Seattle	3	9	3.0	4	0
Taylor, Fred, Jacksonville	292	1399	4.8	71	12
Taylor, Travis, Baltimore	2	11	5.5	12	0
Testaverde, Vinny, N.Y. Jets	25	32	1.3	15	0
Thomas, Rodney, Tennessee	61	175	2.9	20	0
Thomas, Thurman, Miami	28	136	4.9	25	0
Thompson, Kevin, Cleveland	1	0	0.0	0	0
Ward, Dedric, N.Y. Jets	4	23	5.8	12	0
Ward, Hines, Pittsburgh	4	53	13.3	23	0
Warrick, Peter, Cincinnati	16	148	9.3	t77	2
Watters, Ricky, Seattle	278	1242	4.5	55	7
Wheatley, Tyrone, Oakland	232	1046	4.5	t80	9
White, Jamel, Cleveland	47	145	3.1	14	0
Wilkins, Terrence, Indianapolis	3	8	2.7	6	0
Williams, James, Seattle	1	-5	-5.0	-5	0
Williams, Jermaine, Jacksonville	2	8	4.0	4	0
Williams, Nick, Cincinnati	10	54	5.4	13	0
Witman, Jon, Pittsburgh	3	5	1.7	2	0
Wynn, Spergon, Cleveland	3	15	5.0	11	0
Yeast, Craig, Cincinnati	1	15	15.0	15	0
Zereoue, Amos, Pittsburgh	6	14	2.3	11	0

t—touchdown.

NFC

Player, Team	Att.	Yds.	Avg.	Long	TD
Abdullah, Rabih, Tampa Bay	16	70	4.4	19	0
Aikman, Troy, Dallas	10	13	1.3	5	0
Akers, David, Philadelphia	1	15	15.0	15	0
Allen, James, Chicago	290	1120	3.9	29	2
Allen, Terry, New Orleans	46	179	3.9	18	2
Alstott, Mike, Tampa Bay	131	465	3.5	t20	5
Anderson, Jamal, Atlanta	282	1024	3.6	42	6
Autry, Darnell, Philadelphia	112	334	3.0	15	3
Bailey, Champ, Washington	1	7	7.0	t7	1
Barber, Tiki, N.Y. Giants	213	1006	4.7	t78	8
Barnes, Marlon, Chicago	15	81	5.4	20	0
Barnhardt, Tommy, Washington	1	11	11.0	11	0
Batch, Charlie, Detroit	44	199	4.5	19	2
Bates, D'Wayne, Chicago	1	-2	-2.0	-2	0
Bates, Mario, Detroit	31	127	4.1	23	2
Bates, Michael, Carolina	5	13	2.6	8	0
Beasley, Fred, San Francisco	50	147	2.9	9	3
Beuerlein, Steve, Carolina	44	106	2.4	15	1
Biakabutuka, Tim, Carolina	173	627	3.6	43	2
Blake, Jeff, New Orleans	57	243	4.3	20	1
Booker, Marty, Chicago	2	-1	-.5	5	0
Boston, David, Arizona	3	9	3.0	24	0
Brister, Bubby, Minnesota	5	20	4.0	12	0
Brooks, Aaron, New Orleans	41	170	4.1	29	2
Brown, Dave, Arizona	1	0	0.0	0	0
Bruce, Isaac, St. Louis	1	11	11.0	11	0
Canidate, Trung, St. Louis	3	6	2.0	3	0
Case, Stoney, Detroit	16	117	7.3	27	1

Player, Team	Att.	Yds.	Avg.	Long	TD
Centers, Larry, Washington	19	103	5.4	14	0
Chandler, Chris, Atlanta	21	60	2.9	16	0
Christian, Bob, Atlanta	9	19	2.1	7	0
Coakley, Dexter, Dallas	1	26	26.0	26	0
Collins, Kerry, N.Y. Giants	41	65	1.6	15	1
Comella, Greg, N.Y. Giants	10	45	4.5	16	0
Conwell, Ernie, St. Louis	2	23	11.5	17	0
Craig, Dameyune, Carolina	2	4	2.0	5	0
Crowell, Germane, Detroit	1	12	12.0	12	0
Culpepper, Daunte, Minnesota	89	470	5.3	t27	7
Cunningham, Randall, Dallas	23	89	3.9	19	1
Davis, Stephen, Washington	332	1318	4.0	t50	11
Dayne, Ron, N.Y. Giants	228	770	3.4	50	5
Detmer, Koy, Philadelphia	1	8	8.0	8	0
Dixon, Ron, N.Y. Giants	2	13	6.5	12	0
Driver, Donald, Green Bay	1	4	4.0	4	0
Dunn, Warrick, Tampa Bay	248	1133	4.6	t70	8
Dwight, Tim, Atlanta	5	8	1.6	5	0
Engram, Bobby, Chicago	1	1	1.0	1	0
Enis, Curtis, Chicago	36	84	2.3	t11	1
Faulk, Marshall, St. Louis	253	1359	5.4	36	18
Favre, Brett, Green Bay	27	108	4.0	18	0
Floyd, William, Carolina	16	33	2.1	8	1
Foster, Larry, Detroit	2	31	15.5	16	0
Freeman, Antonio, Green Bay	2	5	2.5	3	0
Fryar, Irving, Washington	2	16	8.0	15	0
Garcia, Jeff, San Francisco	72	414	5.8	33	4
Garner, Charlie, San Francisco	258	1142	4.4	42	7
Garrett, Jason, N.Y. Giants	4	-4	-1.0	-1	0
George, Jeff, Washington	7	24	3.4	14	0
Goodman, Herbert, Green Bay	3	-2	-.7	3	0
Gowin, Toby, New Orleans	1	5	5.0	5	0
Green, Ahman, Green Bay	263	1175	4.5	t39	10
Green, Jacquez, Tampa Bay	5	13	2.6	6	0
Green, Trent, St. Louis	20	69	3.5	t18	1
Greisen, Chris, Arizona	1	1	1.0	1	0
Hakim, Az-Zahir, St. Louis	5	19	3.8	5	0
Hambrick, Troy, Dallas	6	28	4.7	13	0
Hamilton, Joe, Tampa Bay	1	-2	-2.0	-2	0
Hasselbeck, Matt, Green Bay	4	-5	-1.3	-1	0
Henderson, William, Green Bay	2	16	8.0	12	0
Hetherington, Chris, Carolina	23	65	2.8	14	2
Hicks, Skip, Washington	29	78	2.7	12	1
Hilliard, Ike, N.Y. Giants	3	19	6.3	17	0
Hodgins, James, St. Louis	1	3	3.0	3	0
Holcombe, Robert, St. Louis	21	70	3.3	11	3
Holt, Torry, St. Louis	2	7	3.5	7	0
Hoover, Brad, Carolina	89	290	3.3	35	1
Horn, Joe, New Orleans	6	10	1.7	16	0
Horne, Tony, St. Louis	2	6	3.0	9	0
Husak, Todd, Washington	1	-1	-1.0	-1	0
Irvin, Sedrick, Detroit	9	49	5.4	32	0
Ismail, Raghib, Dallas	8	73	9.1	37	0
Jackson, Terry, San Francisco	5	6	1.2	3	1
Jefferson, Shawn, Atlanta	1	1	1.0	1	0
Jenkins, MarTay, Arizona	1	-4	-4.0	-4	0
Jervey, Travis, San Francisco	1	0	0.0	0	0
Jett, John, Detroit	1	0	0.0	0	0
Johnson, Brad, Washington	22	58	2.6	21	1
Johnson, Charles, Philadelphia	5	18	3.6	15	0
Johnson, Doug, Atlanta	3	11	3.7	8	0
Johnson, Keyshawn, Tampa Bay	2	5	2.5	3	0
Jones, Thomas, Arizona	112	373	3.3	29	2
Kanell, Danny, Atlanta	1	0	0.0	0	0
Kennison, Eddie, Chicago	3	72	24.0	52	0
King, Shaun, Tampa Bay	73	353	4.8	19	5
Kleinsasser, Jim, Minnesota	12	43	3.6	7	0
Lee, Amp, Philadelphia	1	2	2.0	2	0
Levens, Dorsey, Green Bay	77	224	2.9	17	3
Lewis, Jeff, Carolina	8	36	4.5	19	0
Lewis, Jonas, San Francisco	1	6	6.0	6	0
Lyle, Keith, St. Louis	1	4	4.0	4	0

Player, Team	Att.	Yds.	Avg.	Long	TD
Makovicka, Joel, Arizona	3	8	2.7	7	0
Martin, Cecil, Philadelphia	13	77	5.9	23	0
Mathis, Terance, Atlanta	1	-5	-5.0	-5	0
Matthews, Shane, Chicago	10	35	3.5	14	0
McAfee, Fred, New Orleans	2	37	18.5	40	0
McGarity, Wane, Dallas	6	49	8.2	t22	1
McNabb, Donovan, Philadelphia	86	629	7.3	54	6
McNown, Cade, Chicago	50	326	6.5	30	3
Milburn, Glyn, Chicago	1	6	6.0	6	0
Miller, Jim, Chicago	7	5	0.7	3	0
Milne, Brian, New Orleans	2	1	0.5	1	0
Mirer, Rick, San Francisco	3	0	0.0	3	0
Mitchell, Basil, Green Bay	2	8	4.0	4	0
Mitchell, Brian, Philadelphia	25	187	7.5	t85	2
Montgomery, Joe, N.Y. Giants	1	4	4.0	t4	1
Moore, Jerald, New Orleans	37	156	4.2	40	1
Morton, Chad, New Orleans	36	136	3.8	16	0
Morton, Johnnie, Detroit	4	25	6.3	27	0
Moss, Randy, Minnesota	3	5	1.7	9	0
Muhammad, Muhsin, Carolina	2	12	6.0	8	0
Murrell, Adrian, Washington	20	50	2.5	13	0
Owens, Terrell, San Francisco	3	11	3.7	5	0
Parker, De'Mond, Green Bay	18	85	4.7	24	0
Pittman, Michael, Arizona	184	719	3.9	29	4
Player, Scott, Arizona	1	-11	-11.0	-11	0
Plummer, Jake, Arizona	37	183	4.9	24	0
Pritchett, Stanley, Philadelphia	58	225	3.9	16	1
Rattay, Tim, San Francisco	2	-1	-.5	0	0
Rice, Jerry, San Francisco	1	-2	-2.0	-2	0
Rivers, Ron, Atlanta	8	27	3.4	10	0
Robinson, Marcus, Chicago	1	9	9.0	9	0
Rossum, Allen, Green Bay	1	16	16.0	16	0
Schlesinger, Cory, Detroit	1	3	3.0	3	0
Schroeder, Bill, Green Bay	2	11	5.5	12	0
Seder, Tim, Dallas	1	1	1.0	t1	1
Sellers, Mike, Washington	1	2	2.0	2	0
Small, Torrance, Philadelphia	1	1	1.0	1	0
Smith, Emmitt, Dallas	294	1203	4.1	52	9
Smith, Maurice, Atlanta	19	69	3.6	16	0
Smith, Paul, San Francisco	18	72	4.0	14	0
Smith, Robert, Minnesota	295	1521	5.2	t72	7
Smith, Terrelle, New Orleans	29	131	4.5	16	0
Staley, Duce, Philadelphia	79	344	4.4	60	1
Stecker, Aaron, Tampa Bay	12	31	2.6	14	0
Stewart, James, Detroit	339	1184	3.5	34	10
Stokes, J.J., San Francisco	1	6	6.0	6	0
Streets, Tai, San Francisco	1	0	0.0	0	0
Thomas, Robert, Dallas	15	51	3.4	9	0
Thrash, James, Washington	10	82	8.2	34	0
Toomer, Amani, N.Y. Giants	5	91	18.2	28	1
Tucker, Jason, Dallas	4	42	10.5	t17	1
Walter, Ken, Carolina	1	0	0.0	0	0
Walters, Troy, Minnesota	1	3	3.0	3	0
Warner, Kurt, St. Louis	18	17	0.9	11	0
Warren, Chris, Dal.-Phi.	74	296	4.0	t32	2
Watson, Justin, St. Louis	54	249	4.6	49	4
Wiley, Michael, Dallas	24	88	3.7	11	0
Williams, Moe, Minnesota	23	67	2.9	10	0
Williams, Ricky, New Orleans	248	1000	4.0	t26	8
Wright, Anthony, Dallas	12	36	3.0	19	0
Wuerffel, Danny, Green Bay	2	-2	-1.0	-1	0
Zeier, Eric, Tampa Bay	2	-2	-1.0	-1	0

t—touchdown.

PLAYERS WITH TWO CLUBS

Player, Team	Att.	Yds.	Avg.	Long	TD
Harris, Raymont, Denver	10	22	2.2	6	0
Harris, Raymont, New England	3	14	4.7	7	0
Warren, Chris, Dallas	59	254	4.3	t32	2
Warren, Chris, Philadelphia	15	42	2.8	11	0

PASSING

TEAM
AFC

Team	Att.	Comp.	Pct. Comp.	Gross Yds.	Sack	Yds. Lost	Net Yds.	Yds./ Att.	Yds./ Comp.	TD	Pct. TD	Long	Had Int.	Pct. Int.
Denver	569	354	62.2	4464	30	221	4243	7.85	12.61	28	4.92	61	12	2.1
Indianapolis	571	357	62.5	4413	20	131	4282	7.73	12.36	33	5.78	t78	15	2.6
Kansas City	582	342	58.8	4408	34	259	4149	7.57	12.89	29	4.98	t81	15	2.6
N.Y. Jets	637	352	55.3	4023	20	99	3924	6.32	11.43	23	3.61	63	29	4.6
Jacksonville	545	333	61.1	3947	54	289	3658	7.24	11.85	22	4.04	t67	15	2.8
Buffalo	546	312	57.1	3936	59	360	3576	7.21	12.62	20	3.66	t74	10	1.8
San Diego	578	311	53.8	3540	53	302	3238	6.12	11.38	19	3.29	t83	30	5.2
New England	565	328	58.1	3461	48	280	3181	6.13	10.55	18	3.19	59	15	2.7
Tennessee	462	286	61.9	3430	27	164	3266	7.42	11.99	18	3.90	67	16	3.5
Oakland	475	284	59.8	3430	28	124	3306	7.22	12.08	28	5.89	t84	11	2.3
Seattle	507	308	60.7	3198	46	238	2960	6.31	10.38	21	4.14	71	21	4.1
Baltimore	504	287	56.9	3102	43	287	2815	6.15	10.81	20	3.97	t59	19	3.8
Pittsburgh	439	217	49.4	2738	43	220	2518	6.24	12.62	12	2.73	t77	10	2.3
Cleveland	483	278	57.6	2728	40	283	2445	5.65	9.81	9	1.86	79	19	3.9
Miami	421	243	57.7	2720	28	153	2567	6.46	11.19	15	3.56	61	17	4.0
Cincinnati	454	207	45.6	2219	52	273	1946	4.89	10.72	6	1.32	46	14	3.1
AFC total	8338	4799	...	55757	625	3683	52074	...	...	321	...	t84	268	3.2
AFC average	521.1	299.9	57.6	3484.8	39.1	230.2	3254.6	6.69	11.62	20.1	3.8	...	16.8	3.2

t—touchdown.

NFC

Team	Att.	Comp.	Pct. Comp.	Gross Yds.	Sack	Yds. Lost	Net Yds.	Yds./ Att.	Yds./ Comp.	TD	Pct. TD	Long	Had Int.	Pct. Int.
St. Louis	587	380	64.7	5492	44	260	5232	9.36	14.45	37	6.30	t85	23	3.9
San Francisco	583	366	62.8	4400	25	161	4239	7.55	12.02	32	5.49	t69	10	1.7
Minnesota	495	307	62.0	4019	35	187	3832	8.12	13.09	33	6.67	t78	18	3.6
Green Bay	600	348	58.0	3916	34	238	3678	6.53	11.25	21	3.50	t67	16	2.7
Washington	561	343	61.1	3892	32	244	3648	6.94	11.35	18	3.21	t77	21	3.7
Carolina	566	340	60.1	3850	69	382	3468	6.80	11.32	19	3.36	54	19	3.4
N.Y. Giants	529	311	58.8	3610	28	243	3367	6.82	11.61	22	4.16	59	13	2.5
New Orleans	497	298	60.0	3573	39	244	3329	7.19	11.99	22	4.43	t53	15	3.0
Arizona	554	316	57.0	3478	35	228	3250	6.28	11.01	16	2.89	t70	24	4.3
Philadelphia	575	331	57.6	3386	45	262	3124	5.89	10.23	21	3.65	t70	15	2.6
Atlanta	514	285	55.4	3166	61	386	2780	6.16	11.11	14	2.72	55	20	3.9
Chicago	542	304	56.1	3005	34	200	2805	5.54	9.88	12	2.21	t68	16	3.0
Detroit	503	277	55.1	2992	53	317	2675	5.95	10.80	14	2.78	59	19	3.8
Tampa Bay	433	237	54.7	2824	38	241	2583	6.52	11.92	18	4.16	75	13	3.0
Dallas	445	255	57.3	2771	35	249	2522	6.23	10.87	14	3.15	t76	21	4.7
NFC total	7984	4698	...	54374	607	3842	50532	...	...	313	...	t85	263	3.3
NFC average	532.3	313.2	58.8	3624.9	40.5	256.1	3368.8	6.81	11.57	20.9	3.9	...	17.5	3.3
NFL total	16322	9497	...	110131	1232	7525	102606	...	...	634	...	t85	531	...
NFL average	526.5	306.4	58.2	3552.6	39.7	242.7	3309.9	6.75	11.60	20.5	3.9	...	17.1	3.3

INDIVIDUAL

BESTS OF THE SEASON

Highest rating, season
AFC: 102.9—Brian Griese, Denver.
NFC: 101.8—Trent Green, St. Louis.

Completion percentage, season
NFC: 67.7—Kurt Warner, St. Louis.
AFC: 64.3—Brian Griese, Denver.

Attempts, season
AFC: 590—Vinny Testaverde, N.Y. Jets.
NFC: 580—Brett Favre, Green Bay.

Completions, season
AFC: 357—Peyton Manning, Indianapolis.
NFC: 355—Jeff Garcia, San Francisco.

Yards, season
AFC: 4413—Peyton Manning, Indianapolis.
NFC: 4278—Jeff Garcia, San Francisco.

Yards, game
AFC: 504—Elvis Grbac, Kansas City at Oakland, Nov. 5 (39-53, 2 TDs).
NFC: 441—Kurt Warner, St. Louis vs. Denver, Sept. 4 (25-35, 3 TDs); Aaron Brooks, New Orleans vs. Denver, Dec. 3 (30-48, 2 TDs).

Longest gain
NFC: 85—Kurt Warner (to Torry Holt), St. Louis at Atlanta, Sept. 24 (TD).
AFC: 84—Rich Gannon (to James Jett), Oakland vs. Atlanta, Nov. 26 (TD).

Yards per attempt, season
NFC: 9.88—Kurt Warner, St. Louis.
AFC: 8.00—Brian Griese, Denver.

Touchdown passes, season
AFC: 33—Peyton Manning, Indianapolis.
NFC: 33—Daunte Culpepper, Minnesota.

Touchdown passes, game

AFC: 5—Tony Banks, Baltimore vs. Jacksonville, Sept. 10 (23-40, 262 yards); Elvis Grbac, Kansas City vs. San Diego, Sept. 17 (20-33, 235 yards); Vinny Testaverde, N.Y. Jets vs. Miami, Oct. 23 (36-59, 378 yards); Gus Frerotte, Denver vs. San Diego, Nov. 19 (36-58, 462 yards); Rich Gannon, Oakland vs. Carolina, Dec. 24 (26-32, 230 yards).

NFC: 4—Jeff Garcia, San Francisco at Dallas, Sept. 24 (16-26, 178 yards); Kurt Warner, St. Louis vs. San Diego, Oct. 1 (24-30, 390 yards); Kurt Warner, St. Louis at Atlanta, Sept. 24 (12-19, 336 yards); Jeff Garcia, San Francisco vs. Oakland, Oct. 8 (28-41, 336 yards); Jeff Garcia, San Francisco at Green Bay, Oct. 15 (27-42, 336 yards); Shaun King, Tampa Bay vs. Minnesota, Oct. 29 (16-23, 267 yards); Donovan McNabb, Philadelphia at Cleveland, Dec. 10 (23-36, 390 yards); Trent Green, St. Louis at N.Y. Giants, Nov. 12 (27-45, 272 yards).

Lowest interception percentage, season

AFC: 1.2—Brian Griese, Denver.
NFC: 1.8—Jeff Garcia, San Francisco.

NFL LEADERS

Player, Team	Att.	Comp.	Pct. Comp.	Yds.	Avg. Gain	TD	Pct. TD	Long	Int.	Pct. Int.	Sack	Yds. Lost	Rat. Pts.
Griese, Brian, Denver*	336	216	64.3	2688	8.00	19	5.7	61	4	1.2	17	139	102.9
Green, Trent, St. Louis	240	145	60.4	2063	8.60	16	6.7	64	5	2.1	24	145	101.8
Warner, Kurt, St. Louis	347	235	67.7	3429	9.88	21	6.1	t85	18	5.2	20	115	98.3
Culpepper, Daunte, Minnesota	474	297	62.7	3937	8.31	33	7.0	t78	16	3.4	34	181	98.0
Garcia, Jeff, San Francisco	561	355	63.3	4278	7.63	31	5.5	t69	10	1.8	24	155	97.6
Manning, Peyton, Indianapolis*	571	357	62.5	4413	7.73	33	5.8	t78	15	2.6	20	131	94.7
Gannon, Rich, Oakland*	473	284	60.0	3430	7.25	28	5.9	t84	11	2.3	28	124	92.4
Grbac, Elvis, Kansas City*	547	326	59.6	4169	7.62	28	5.1	t81	14	2.6	29	213	89.9
Flutie, Doug, Buffalo*	231	132	57.1	1700	7.36	8	3.5	52	3	1.3	10	68	86.5
Brunell, Mark, Jacksonville*	512	311	60.7	3640	7.11	20	3.9	t67	14	2.7	54	289	84.0
McNair, Steve, Tennessee*	396	248	62.6	2847	7.19	15	3.8	t56	13	3.3	24	141	83.2
Collins, Kerry, N.Y. Giants	529	311	58.8	3610	6.82	22	4.2	59	13	2.5	28	243	83.1
Blake, Jeff, New Orleans	302	184	60.9	2025	6.71	13	4.3	t49	9	3.0	24	150	82.7
Johnson, Rob, Buffalo*	306	175	57.2	2125	6.94	12	3.9	t74	7	2.3	49	292	82.2
Frerotte, Gus, Denver*	232	138	59.5	1776	7.66	9	3.9	44	8	3.4	12	77	82.1
Beuerlein, Steve, Carolina	533	324	60.8	3730	7.00	19	3.6	54	18	3.4	62	331	79.7
Favre, Brett, Green Bay	580	338	58.3	3812	6.57	20	3.4	t67	16	2.8	33	236	78.0
McNabb, Donovan, Philadelphia	569	330	58.0	3365	5.91	21	3.7	t70	13	2.3	45	262	77.8
Bledsoe, Drew, New England*	531	312	58.8	3291	6.20	17	3.2	59	13	2.4	45	264	77.3
Dilfer, Trent, Baltimore*	226	134	59.3	1502	6.65	12	5.3	t59	11	4.9	23	135	76.6
King, Shaun, Tampa Bay	428	233	54.4	2769	6.47	18	4.2	75	13	3.0	37	240	75.8
Johnson, Brad, Washington	365	228	62.5	2505	6.86	11	3.0	t77	15	4.1	20	150	75.7
Kitna, Jon, Seattle*	418	259	62.0	2658	6.36	18	4.3	71	19	4.5	33	166	75.6
Fiedler, Jay, Miami*	357	204	57.1	2402	6.73	14	3.9	61	14	3.9	23	129	74.5
Stewart, Kordell, Pittsburgh*	289	151	52.2	1860	6.44	11	3.8	t45	8	2.8	30	150	73.6
Chandler, Chris, Atlanta	331	192	58.0	2236	6.76	10	3.0	55	12	3.6	40	251	73.5
Banks, Tony, Baltimore*	274	150	54.7	1578	5.76	8	2.9	t53	8	2.9	20	152	69.3
Testaverde, Vinny, N.Y. Jets*	590	328	55.6	3732	6.33	21	3.6	63	25	4.2	13	71	69.0
McNown, Cade, Chicago	280	154	55.0	1646	5.88	8	2.9	t68	9	3.2	27	169	68.5
Batch, Charlie, Detroit	412	221	53.6	2489	6.04	13	3.2	59	15	3.6	41	242	67.3

*AFC.
t—touchdown.
Leader based on rating points, minimum 224 attempts.

AFC

Player, Team	Att.	Comp.	Pct. Comp.	Yds.	Avg. Gain	TD	Pct. TD	Long	Int.	Pct. Int.	Sack	Yds. Lost	Rat. Pts.
Banks, Tony, Baltimore	274	150	54.7	1578	5.76	8	2.9	t53	8	2.9	20	152	69.3
Bettis, Jerome, Pittsburgh	2	0	0.0	0	0.00	0	0.0	0	1	50.0	0	0	0.0
Bishop, Michael, New England	9	3	33.3	80	8.89	1	11.1	t44	1	11.1	0	0	64.4
Bledsoe, Drew, New England	531	312	58.8	3291	6.20	17	3.2	59	13	2.4	45	264	77.3
Brady, Tom, New England	3	1	33.3	6	2.00	0	0.0	6	0	0.0	0	0	42.4
Brown, Travis, Seattle	1	0	0.0	0	0.00	0	0.0	0	0	0.0	0	0	39.6
Brunell, Mark, Jacksonville	512	311	60.7	3640	7.11	20	3.9	t67	14	2.7	54	289	84.0
Chancey, Robert, San Diego	1	0	0.0	0	0.00	0	0.0	0	0	0.0	0	0	39.6
Couch, Tim, Cleveland	215	137	63.7	1483	6.90	7	3.3	79	9	4.2	10	78	77.3
Dilfer, Trent, Baltimore	226	134	59.3	1502	6.65	12	5.3	t59	11	4.9	23	135	76.6
Feagles, Jeff, Seattle	1	0	0.0	0	0.00	0	0.0	0	0	0.0	0	0	39.6
Fiedler, Jay, Miami	357	204	57.1	2402	6.73	14	3.9	61	14	3.9	23	129	74.5
Flutie, Doug, Buffalo	231	132	57.1	1700	7.36	8	3.5	52	3	1.3	10	68	86.5
Frerotte, Gus, Denver	232	138	59.5	1776	7.66	9	3.9	44	8	3.4	12	77	82.1
Friesz, John, New England	21	11	52.4	66	3.14	0	0.0	17	1	4.8	3	16	39.0
Gannon, Rich, Oakland	473	284	60.0	3430	7.25	28	5.9	t84	11	2.3	28	124	92.4
Graham, Kent, Pittsburgh	148	66	44.6	878	5.93	1	0.7	t77	1	0.7	13	70	63.4
Grbac, Elvis, Kansas City	547	326	59.6	4169	7.62	28	5.1	t81	14	2.6	29	213	89.9
Griese, Brian, Denver	336	216	64.3	2688	8.00	19	5.7	61	4	1.2	17	139	102.9

2000 STATISTICS Passing

Player, Team	Att.	Comp.	Pct. Comp.	Yds.	Avg. Gain	TD	Pct. TD	Long	Int.	Pct. Int.	Sack	Yds. Lost	Rat. Pts.
Harbaugh, Jim, San Diego	202	123	60.9	1416	7.01	8	4.0	t62	10	5.0	14	96	74.6
Hoying, Bobby, Oakland	2	0	0.0	0	0.00	0	0.0	0	0	0.0	0	0	39.6
Huard, Brock, Seattle	87	49	56.3	540	6.21	3	3.4	45	2	2.3	13	72	76.8
Huard, Damon, Miami	63	39	61.9	318	5.05	1	1.6	29	3	4.8	4	22	60.2
Jackson, Jarious, Denver	1	0	0.0	0	0.00	0	0.0	0	0	0.0	1	5	39.6
Johnson, Kevin, Cleveland	3	1	33.3	23	7.67	0	0.0	23	1	33.3	0	0	22.2
Johnson, Lee, New England	1	1	100.0	18	18.00	0	0.0	18	0	0.0	0	0	118.8
Johnson, Rob, Buffalo	306	175	57.2	2125	6.94	12	3.9	t74	7	2.3	49	292	82.2
Kitna, Jon, Seattle	418	259	62.0	2658	6.36	18	4.3	71	19	4.5	33	166	75.6
Leaf, Ryan, San Diego	322	161	50.0	1883	5.85	11	3.4	t83	18	5.6	31	155	56.2
Lewis, Jermaine, Baltimore	1	1	100.0	3	3.00	0	0.0	3	0	0.0	0	0	79.2
Lucas, Ray, N.Y. Jets	41	21	51.2	206	5.02	0	0.0	30	4	9.8	6	24	26.1
Manning, Peyton, Indianapolis	571	357	62.5	4413	7.73	33	5.8	t78	15	2.6	20	131	94.7
Martin, Curtis, N.Y. Jets	1	1	100.0	18	18.00	1	100.0	t18	0	0.0	0	0	158.3
Martin, Jamie, Jacksonville	33	22	66.7	307	9.30	2	6.1	t65	1	3.0	0	0	104.0
McNair, Steve, Tennessee	396	248	62.6	2847	7.19	15	3.8	t56	13	3.3	24	141	83.2
Mitchell, Scott, Cincinnati	187	89	47.6	966	5.17	3	1.6	38	8	4.3	16	82	50.8
Mohr, Chris, Buffalo	1	1	100.0	44	44.00	0	0.0	44	0	0.0	0	0	118.8
Moon, Warren, Kansas City	34	15	44.1	208	6.12	1	2.9	41	1	2.9	5	46	61.9
Moreno, Moses, San Diego	53	27	50.9	241	4.55	0	0.0	26	2	3.8	8	51	47.8
Morris, Sylvester, Kansas City	1	1	100.0	31	31.00	0	0.0	31	0	0.0	0	0	118.8
O'Donnell, Neil, Tennessee	64	36	56.3	530	8.28	2	3.1	67	3	4.7	3	23	74.3
Pederson, Doug, Cleveland	210	117	55.7	1047	4.99	2	1.0	67	8	3.8	17	116	56.6
Pennington, Chad, N.Y. Jets	5	2	40.0	67	13.40	1	20.0	62	0	0.0	1	4	127.1
Redman, Chris, Baltimore	3	2	66.7	19	6.33	0	0.0	12	0	0.0	0	0	84.0
Smith, Akili, Cincinnati	267	118	44.2	1253	4.69	3	1.1	46	6	2.2	36	191	52.8
Smith, Lamar, Miami	1	0	0.0	0	0.00	0	0.0	0	0	0.0	0	0	39.6
Stewart, Kordell, Pittsburgh	289	151	52.2	1860	6.44	11	3.8	t45	8	2.8	30	150	73.6
Testaverde, Vinny, N.Y. Jets	590	328	55.6	3732	6.33	21	3.6	63	25	4.2	13	71	69.0
Thomas, Thurman, Miami	0	0	...	0	0.00	0	...	0	0	...	1	2	...
Thompson, Kevin, Cleveland	1	1	100.0	8	8.00	0	0.0	8	0	0.0	0	0	100.0
Van Pelt, Alex, Buffalo	8	4	50.0	67	8.38	0	0.0	36	0	0.0	0	0	78.6
Wycheck, Frank, Tennessee	2	2	100.0	53	26.50	1	50.0	t30	0	0.0	0	0	158.3
Wynn, Spergon, Cleveland	54	22	40.7	167	3.09	0	0.0	32	1	1.9	13	89	41.2

t—touchdown.

NFC

Player, Team	Att.	Comp.	Pct. Comp.	Yds.	Avg. Gain	TD	Pct. TD	Long	Int.	Pct. Int.	Sack	Yds. Lost	Rat. Pts.
Aguiar, Louie, Chicago	1	1	100.0	13	13.00	0	0.0	13	0	0.0	0	0	118.8
Aikman, Troy, Dallas	262	156	59.5	1632	6.23	7	2.7	48	14	5.3	13	91	64.3
Alstott, Mike, Tampa Bay	1	0	0.0	0	0.00	0	0.0	0	0	0.0	0	0	39.6
Batch, Charlie, Detroit	412	221	53.6	2489	6.04	13	3.2	59	15	3.6	41	242	67.3
Berger, Mitch, Minnesota	1	0	0.0	0	0.00	0	0.0	0	1	100.0	0	0	0.0
Beuerlein, Steve, Carolina	533	324	60.8	3730	7.00	19	3.6	54	18	3.4	62	331	79.7
Blake, Jeff, New Orleans	302	184	60.9	2025	6.71	13	4.3	t49	9	3.0	24	150	82.7
Brister, Bubby, Minnesota	20	10	50.0	82	4.10	0	0.0	20	1	5.0	1	6	40.0
Brooks, Aaron, New Orleans	194	113	58.2	1514	7.80	9	4.6	t53	6	3.1	15	94	85.7
Brown, Dave, Arizona	69	40	58.0	467	6.77	2	2.9	t44	3	4.3	10	53	70.1
Case, Stoney, Detroit	91	56	61.5	503	5.53	1	1.1	t40	4	4.4	12	75	61.7
Chandler, Chris, Atlanta	331	192	58.0	2236	6.76	10	3.0	55	12	3.6	40	251	73.5
Collins, Kerry, N.Y. Giants	529	311	58.8	3610	6.82	22	4.2	59	13	2.5	28	243	83.1
Culpepper, Daunte, Minnesota	474	297	62.7	3937	8.31	33	7.0	t78	16	3.4	34	181	98.0
Cunningham, Randall, Dallas	125	74	59.2	849	6.79	6	4.8	t76	4	3.2	8	45	82.4
Detmer, Koy, Philadelphia	1	0	0.0	0	0.00	0	0.0	0	1	100.0	0	0	0.0
Favre, Brett, Green Bay	580	338	58.3	3812	6.57	20	3.4	t67	16	2.8	33	236	78.0
Garcia, Jeff, San Francisco	561	355	63.3	4278	7.63	31	5.5	t69	10	1.8	24	155	97.6
George, Jeff, Washington	194	113	58.2	1389	7.16	7	3.6	50	6	3.1	12	94	79.6
Green, Ahman, Green Bay	1	0	0.0	0	0.00	0	0.0	0	0	0.0	0	0	39.6
Green, Trent, St. Louis	240	145	60.4	2063	8.60	16	6.7	64	5	2.1	24	145	101.8
Greisen, Chris, Arizona	10	6	60.0	65	6.50	1	10.0	t26	0	0.0	3	24	112.5
Hamilton, Joe, Tampa Bay	0	0	...	0	...	0	...	0	0	...	1	1	...
Hartsell, Mark, Chicago	1	0	0.0	0	0.00	0	0.0	0	0	0.0	0	0	39.6
Hasselbeck, Matt, Green Bay	19	10	52.6	104	5.47	1	5.3	t27	0	0.0	1	2	86.3
Husak, Todd, Washington	2	2	100.0	-2	-1.00	0	0.0	6	0	0.0	0	0	79.2
Johnson, Brad, Washington	365	228	62.5	2505	6.86	11	3.0	t77	15	4.1	20	150	75.7
Johnson, Doug, Atlanta	67	36	53.7	406	6.06	2	3.0	26	3	4.5	13	75	63.4
Kanell, Danny, Atlanta	116	57	49.1	524	4.52	2	1.7	35	5	4.3	8	60	49.6
King, Shaun, Tampa Bay	428	233	54.4	2769	6.47	18	4.2	75	13	3.0	37	240	75.8
Lewis, Jeff, Carolina	32	16	50.0	120	3.75	0	0.0	16	1	3.1	7	51	46.4

Player, Team	Att.	Comp.	Pct. Comp.	Yds.	Avg. Gain	TD	Pct. TD	Long	Int.	Pct. Int.	Sack	Yds. Lost	Rat. Pts.
Matthews, Shane, Chicago	178	102	57.3	964	5.42	3	1.7	41	6	3.4	5	24	64.0
McNabb, Donovan, Philadelphia	569	330	58.0	3365	5.91	21	3.7	t70	13	2.3	45	262	77.8
McNown, Cade, Chicago	280	154	55.0	1646	5.88	8	2.9	t68	9	3.2	27	169	68.5
Miller, Jim, Chicago	82	47	57.3	382	4.66	1	1.2	t34	1	1.2	2	7	68.2
Mirer, Rick, San Francisco	20	10	50.0	126	6.30	1	5.0	26	0	0.0	1	6	86.7
Mitchell, Brian, Philadelphia	4	1	25.0	21	5.25	0	0.0	21	0	0.0	0	0	49.0
Plummer, Jake, Arizona	475	270	56.8	2946	6.20	13	2.7	t70	21	4.4	22	151	66.0
Rattay, Tim, San Francisco	1	1	100.0	-4	-4.00	0	0.0	-4	0	0.0	0	0	79.2
Rice, Jerry, San Francisco	1	0	0.0	0	0.00	0	0.0	0	0	0.0	0	0	39.6
Royals, Mark, Tampa Bay	1	1	100.0	36	36.00	0	0.0	36	0	0.0	0	0	118.8
Small, Torrance, Philadelphia	1	0	0.0	0	0.00	0	0.0	0	1	100.0	0	0	0.0
Stoerner, Clint, Dallas	5	3	60.0	53	10.60	1	20.0	29	0	0.0	2	21	135.8
Walter, Ken, Carolina	1	0	0.0	0	0.00	0	0.0	0	0	0.0	0	0	39.6
Warner, Kurt, St. Louis	347	235	67.7	3429	9.88	21	6.1	t85	18	5.2	20	115	98.3
Williams, Ricky, New Orleans	1	1	100.0	34	34.00	0	0.0	34	0	0.0	0	0	118.8
Wright, Anthony, Dallas	53	22	41.5	237	4.47	0	0.0	46	3	5.7	12	92	31.7
Zeier, Eric, Tampa Bay	3	3	100.0	19	6.33	0	0.0	14	0	0.0	0	0	93.1

RECEIVING

BESTS OF THE SEASON

Receptions, season
AFC: 102—Marvin Harrison, Indianapolis.
NFC: 102—Muhsin Muhammad, Carolina.

Receptions, game
NFC: 20—Terrell Owens, San Francisco vs. Chicago, Dec. 17 (283 yards; 1 TD).
AFC: 15—Jimmy Smith, Jacksonville at Baltimore, Sept. 10 (291 yards; 3 TDs).

Yards, season
NFC: 1635—Torry Holt, St. Louis.
AFC: 1602—Rod Smith, Denver.

Yards, game
AFC: 291—Jimmy Smith, Jacksonville at Baltimore, Sept. 10 (15 receptions, 3 TDs).
NFC: 283—Terrell Owens, San Francisco vs. Chicago, Dec. 17 (20 receptions, 1 TD).

Longest gain
NFC: 85—Torry Holt (from Kurt Warner), St. Louis at Atlanta, Sept. 24 (TD).
AFC: 84—James Jett (from Rich Gannon), Oakland vs. Atlanta, Nov. 26 (TD).

Yards per reception, season
NFC: 19.9—Torry Holt, St. Louis.
AFC: 17.8—Derrick Alexander, Kansas City.

Touchdowns, season
NFC: 15—Randy Moss, Minnesota.
AFC: 14—Marvin Harrison, Indianapolis.

Team leaders, receptions

AFC:

Team	No.	Player
Baltimore	67	Shannon Sharpe
Buffalo	94	Eric Moulds
Cincinnati	51	Peter Warrick
Cleveland	57	Kevin Johnson
Denver	101	Ed McCaffrey
Indianapolis	102	Marvin Harrison
Jacksonville	94	Keenan McCardell
Kansas City	93	Tony Gonzalez
Miami	56	Oronde Gadsden
New England	83	Troy Brown
N.Y. Jets	88	Richie Anderson
Oakland	76	Tim Brown
Pittsburgh	48	Hines Ward
San Diego	71	Freddie Jones
Seattle	63	Ricky Watters
		Sean Dawkins
Tennessee	70	Frank Wycheck

NFC:

Team	No.	Player
Arizona	73	Michael Pittman
Atlanta	60	Shawn Jefferson
Carolina	102	M. Muhammad
Chicago	55	Eddie Kennison
		Marcus Robinson
Dallas	52	James McKnight
Detroit	61	Johnnie Morton
Green Bay	73	Ahman Green
Minnesota	96	Cris Carter
New Orleans	94	Joe Horn
N.Y. Giants	78	Amani Toomer
Philadelphia	69	Chad Lewis
St. Louis	87	Isaac Bruce
San Francisco	97	Terrell Owens
Tampa Bay	71	Keyshawn Johnson
Washington	81	Larry Centers

NFL LEADERS

Player, Team	No.	Yds.	Avg.	Long	TD
Harrison, Marvin, Indianapolis*	102	1413	13.9	t78	14
Muhammad, Muhsin, Carolina	102	1183	11.6	36	6
McCaffrey, Ed, Denver*	101	1317	13.0	61	9
Smith, Rod, Denver*	100	1602	16.0	49	8
Owens, Terrell, San Francisco	97	1451	15.0	t69	13
Carter, Cris, Minnesota	96	1274	13.3	53	9
Horn, Joe, New Orleans	94	1340	14.3	52	8
Moulds, Eric, Buffalo*	94	1326	14.1	52	5
McCardell, Keenan, Jacksonville*	94	1207	12.8	t67	5
Gonzalez, Tony, Kansas City*	93	1203	12.9	39	9
Smith, Jimmy, Jacksonville*	91	1213	13.3	t65	8
Anderson, Richie, N.Y. Jets*	88	853	9.7	41	2
Bruce, Isaac, St. Louis	87	1471	16.9	t78	9
Brown, Troy, New England*	83	944	11.4	t44	4
Holt, Torry, St. Louis	82	1635	19.9	t85	6
Faulk, Marshall, St. Louis	81	830	10.2	t72	8
Centers, Larry, Washington	81	600	7.4	26	3
Glenn, Terry, New England*	79	963	12.2	t39	6
Alexander, Derrick, Kansas City*	78	1391	17.8	t81	10
Toomer, Amani, N.Y. Giants	78	1094	14.0	t54	7
Moss, Randy, Minnesota	77	1437	18.7	t78	15
Brown, Tim, Oakland*	76	1128	14.8	45	11
Rice, Jerry, San Francisco	75	805	10.7	t68	7
Pittman, Michael, Arizona	73	579	7.9	36	2
Green, Ahman, Green Bay	73	559	7.7	31	3
Boston, David, Arizona	71	1156	16.3	t70	7
Johnson, Keyshawn, Tampa Bay	71	874	12.3	38	8
Jones, Freddie, San Diego*	71	766	10.8	44	5
Barber, Tiki, N.Y. Giants	70	719	10.3	36	1
Wycheck, Frank, Tennessee*	70	636	9.1	26	4

*AFC.
t—touchdown.
Leader based on most passes caught.

AFC

Player, Team	No.	Yds.	Avg.	Long	TD
Alexander, Derrick, Kansas City	78	1391	17.8	t81	10
Alexander, Shaun, Seattle	5	41	8.2	18	0
Anders, Kimble, Kansas City	15	76	5.1	12	0
Anderson, Mike, Denver	23	169	7.3	18	0
Anderson, Richie, N.Y. Jets	88	853	9.7	41	2
Ayanbadejo, Obafemi, Baltimore	23	168	7.3	26	1
Bailey, Karsten, Seattle	6	62	10.3	22	1
Barlow, Reggie, Jacksonville	1	28	28.0	28	0
Battaglia, Marco, Cincinnati	13	105	8.1	15	0
Baxter, Fred, N.Y. Jets	4	22	5.5	t12	2
Becht, Anthony, N.Y. Jets	16	144	9.0	30	2
Bennett, Brandon, Cincinnati	19	168	8.8	25	0
Bennett, Donnell, Kansas City	2	17	8.5	13	0
Bettis, Jerome, Pittsburgh	13	97	7.5	25	0
Bjornson, Eric, New England	20	152	7.6	19	2
Blackwell, Will, Pittsburgh	2	23	11.5	14	0
Brady, Kyle, Jacksonville	64	729	11.4	36	3
Brigham, Jeremy, Oakland	13	107	8.2	19	2
Brisby, Vincent, N.Y. Jets	4	60	15.0	19	0
Brooks, Robert, Denver	3	51	17.0	25	0
Brown, Bobby, Cleveland	2	14	7.0	8	0
Brown, Reggie, Seattle	2	9	4.5	6	0
Brown, Tim, Oakland	76	1128	14.8	45	11
Brown, Troy, New England	83	944	11.4	t44	4
Bruener, Mark, Pittsburgh	17	192	11.3	t30	3
Bryson, Shawn, Buffalo	32	271	8.5	32	2
Burress, Plaxico, Pittsburgh	22	273	12.4	39	0

Player, Team	No.	Yds.	Avg.	Long	TD
Bush, Steve, Cincinnati	3	39	13.0	18	0
Bynum, Kenny, San Diego	2	13	6.5	7	0
Calloway, Chris, New England	5	95	19.0	28	0
Campbell, Mark, Cleveland	12	80	6.7	17	1
Carswell, Dwayne, Denver	49	495	10.1	t43	3
Carter, Tony, New England	9	73	8.1	21	0
Cavil, Kwame, Buffalo	4	66	16.5	39	0
Chamberlain, Byron, Denver	22	283	12.9	38	1
Chancey, Robert, San Diego	1	6	6.0	6	0
Chiaverini, Darrin, Cleveland	8	68	8.5	18	1
Chrebet, Wayne, N.Y. Jets	69	937	13.6	50	8
Clark, Desmond, Denver	27	339	12.6	44	3
Cloud, Mike, Kansas City	2	16	8.0	13	0
Coates, Ben, Baltimore	9	84	9.3	28	0
Coleman, KaRon, Denver	1	5	5.0	5	0
Coleman, Marcus, N.Y. Jets	1	45	45.0	t45	1
Coles, Laveranues, N.Y. Jets	22	370	16.8	63	1
Collins, Bobby, Buffalo	6	72	12.0	23	0
Conway, Curtis, San Diego	53	712	13.4	t68	5
Crockett, Zack, Oakland	10	62	6.2	15	0
Cushing, Matt, Pittsburgh	4	17	4.3	5	0
Davis, Billy, Baltimore	3	62	20.7	28	0
Davis, Reginald, San Diego	1	8	8.0	8	0
Davis, Shockmain, New England	2	12	6.0	9	0
Davis, Terrell, Denver	2	4	2.0	5	0
Dawkins, Sean, Seattle	63	731	11.6	40	5
Dawson, JaJuan, Cleveland	9	97	10.8	26	1
Denson, Autry, Miami	14	105	7.5	28	0
Dilfer, Trent, Baltimore	1	-1	-1.0	-1	0
Dilger, Ken, Indianapolis	47	538	11.4	32	3
Dillon, Corey, Cincinnati	18	158	8.8	31	0
Drayton, Troy, Kansas City	8	70	8.8	21	2
Dudley, Rickey, Oakland	29	350	12.1	30	4
Dugans, Ron, Cincinnati	14	125	8.9	17	1
Dunn, Damon, Cleveland	1	6	6.0	6	0
Dunn, David, Oakland	4	33	8.3	14	0
Dunn, Jason, Kansas City	2	26	13.0	20	0
Dyer, Deon, Miami	2	14	7.0	13	0
Dyson, Kevin, Tennessee	6	104	17.3	t30	1
Edwards, Marc, Cleveland	16	128	8.0	t21	2
Edwards, Troy, Pittsburgh	18	215	11.9	27	0
Elliott, Jumbo, N.Y. Jets	1	3	3.0	t3	1
Emanuel, Bert, Miami	7	132	18.9	t53	1
Farmer, Danny, Cincinnati	19	268	14.1	38	0
Faulk, Kevin, New England	51	465	9.1	t52	1
Fauria, Christian, Seattle	28	237	8.5	16	2
Fazande, Jermaine, San Diego	16	104	6.5	17	0
Finn, Jim, Indianapolis	4	13	3.3	6	1
Fletcher, Terrell, San Diego	48	355	7.4	26	1
Floyd, Chris, New England	1	21	21.0	21	0
Fuamatu-Ma'afala, Chris, Pit.	11	107	9.7	25	0
Gadsden, Oronde, Miami	56	786	14.0	61	6
Gary, Olandis, Denver	3	10	3.3	7	0
Gash, Sam, Baltimore	6	30	5.0	9	1
Gaylor, Trevor, San Diego	13	182	14.0	t62	1
Geason, Corey, Pittsburgh	3	66	22.0	36	0
George, Eddie, Tennessee	50	453	9.1	24	2
Glenn, Terry, New England	79	963	12.2	t39	6
Gonzalez, Tony, Kansas City	93	1203	12.9	39	9
Goodwin, Hunter, Miami	6	36	6.0	t9	1
Graham, Jeff, San Diego	55	907	16.5	t83	4
Green, E.G., Indianapolis	18	201	11.2	t34	1
Griffin, Damon, Cincinnati	2	25	12.5	16	0
Griffith, Howard, Denver	16	101	6.3	16	2
Groce, Clif, Cincinnati	11	45	4.1	14	0
Harris, Raymont, Den.-N.E.	4	20	5.0	16	0
Harrison, Marvin, Indianapolis	102	1413	13.9	t78	14
Hawkins, Courtney, Pittsburgh	19	238	12.5	33	1
Hayes, Windrell, N.Y. Jets	6	126	21.0	32	0
Heiden, Steve, San Diego	6	32	5.3	10	1
Holmes, Priest, Baltimore	32	221	6.9	27	0
Howard, Chris, Jacksonville	3	26	8.7	13	0
Huntley, Richard, Pittsburgh	10	91	9.1	19	0
Ismail, Qadry, Baltimore	49	655	13.4	t53	5
Jackson, Curtis, New England	5	44	8.8	13	0
Jackson, Darrell, Seattle	53	713	13.5	71	6
Jackson, Lenzie, Cleveland	1	5	5.0	5	0
Jackson, Sheldon, Buffalo	5	36	7.2	12	1
Jacquet, Nate, San Diego	1	25	25.0	25	0
James, Edgerrin, Indianapolis	63	594	9.4	60	5
Jenkins, Ronney, San Diego	1	1	1.0	1	0
Jett, James, Oakland	20	356	17.8	t84	2
Johnson, Anthony, Jacksonville	12	153	12.8	48	0
Johnson, J.J., Miami	10	61	6.1	11	0
Johnson, Kevin, Cleveland	57	669	11.7	79	0
Johnson, Pat, Baltimore	12	156	13.0	t46	2
Johnson, Rob, Buffalo	1	-6	-6.0	-6	0
Jones, Damon, Jacksonville	1	12	12.0	12	0
Jones, Freddie, San Diego	71	766	10.8	44	5
Jones, Reggie, San Diego	22	253	11.5	34	0
Jordan, Randy, Oakland	27	299	11.1	55	1
Kaufman, Napoleon, Oakland	13	127	9.8	25	1
Kinney, Erron, Tennessee	19	197	10.4	19	1
Kirby, Terry, Oakland	3	19	6.3	9	0
Konrad, Rob, Miami	14	83	5.9	18	0
Kreider, Dan, Pittsburgh	5	42	8.4	14	0
Lewis, Jamal, Baltimore	27	296	11.0	45	0
Lewis, Jermaine, Baltimore	19	161	8.5	26	1
Linton, Jonathan, Buffalo	3	8	2.7	t4	1
Lockett, Kevin, Kansas City	33	422	12.8	t34	2
Martin, Curtis, N.Y. Jets	70	508	7.3	31	2
Martin, Tony, Miami	26	393	15.1	44	0
Mason, Derrick, Tennessee	63	895	14.2	34	5
Mayes, Derrick, Seattle	29	264	9.1	40	1
McCaffrey, Ed, Denver	101	1317	13.0	61	9
McCardell, Keenan, Jacksonville	94	1207	12.8	t67	5
McCrary, Fred, San Diego	18	141	7.8	19	2
McDaniel, Jeremy, Buffalo	43	697	16.2	t74	2
McDuffie, O.J., Miami	14	143	10.2	24	0
McGee, Tony, Cincinnati	26	309	11.9	39	1
McGriff, Travis, Denver	2	51	25.5	t43	1
Mili, Itula, Seattle	28	288	10.3	34	3
Miller, Billy, Denver	1	7	7.0	7	0
Montgomery, Scottie, Denver	1	10	10.0	10	0
Morris, Sammy, Buffalo	37	268	7.2	24	1
Morris, Sylvester, Kansas City	48	678	14.1	47	3
Moulds, Eric, Buffalo	94	1326	14.1	52	5
Neal, Lorenzo, Tennessee	9	31	3.4	8	2
Northcutt, Dennis, Cleveland	39	422	10.8	37	0
Ogden, Jeff, Miami	2	24	12.0	12	0
Parker, Larry, Kansas City	3	41	13.7	27	0
Parmalee, Bernie, N.Y. Jets	9	66	7.3	18	0
Pass, Patrick, New England	4	17	4.3	15	0
Pathon, Jerome, Indianapolis	50	646	12.9	38	3
Patten, David, Cleveland	38	546	14.4	65	1
Pickens, Carl, Tennessee	10	242	24.2	67	0
Pollard, Marcus, Indianapolis	30	439	14.6	t50	3
Porter, Daryl, Buffalo	1	44	44.0	44	0
Porter, Jerry, Oakland	1	6	6.0	6	0
Prentice, Travis, Cleveland	37	191	5.2	13	1
Price, Peerless, Buffalo	52	762	14.7	42	3
Redmond, J.R., New England	20	126	6.3	20	2
Rhett, Errict, Cleveland	14	78	5.6	16	0
Richardson, Tony, Kansas City	58	468	8.1	24	3
Ricks, Mikhael, San Diego	3	35	11.7	23	0
Riemersma, Jay, Buffalo	31	372	12.0	35	5
Rison, Andre, Oakland	41	606	14.8	49	6
Ritchie, Jon, Oakland	26	173	6.7	17	0
Roan, Michael, Tennessee	3	12	4.0	6	0
Rutledge, Rod, New England	15	103	6.9	16	1
Saleh, Tarek, Cleveland	1	22	22.0	22	0
Sanders, Chris, Tennessee	33	536	16.2	54	0
Sharpe, Shannon, Baltimore	67	810	12.1	t59	5
Shaw, Bobby, Pittsburgh	40	672	16.8	t45	4

Player, Team	No.	Yds.	Avg.	Long	TD
Shaw, Harold, New England	2	11	5.5	8	0
Shea, Aaron, Cleveland	30	302	10.1	37	2
Shelton, Daimon, Jacksonville	4	48	12.0	16	0
Shepherd, Leslie, Miami	35	446	12.7	t46	4
Simmons, Tony, New England	14	231	16.5	46	1
Smith, Antowain, Buffalo	3	20	6.7	9	0
Smith, Detron, Denver	1	1	1.0	t1	1
Smith, Jimmy, Jacksonville	91	1213	13.3	t65	8
Smith, Lamar, Miami	31	201	6.5	28	2
Smith, Rod, Denver	100	1602	16.0	49	8
Soward, R. Jay, Jacksonville	14	154	11.0	45	1
Sowell, Jerald, N.Y. Jets	6	84	14.0	62	0
Stokley, Brandon, Baltimore	11	184	16.7	32	2
Strong, Mack, Seattle	23	141	6.1	24	1
Taylor, Fred, Jacksonville	36	240	6.7	19	2
Taylor, Travis, Baltimore	28	276	9.9	40	3
Thigpen, Yancey, Tennessee	15	289	19.3	t56	2
Thomas, Rodney, Tennessee	8	35	4.4	t9	1
Thomas, Thurman, Miami	16	117	7.3	15	1
Ward, Dedric, N.Y. Jets	54	801	14.8	61	3
Ward, Hines, Pittsburgh	48	672	14.0	t77	4
Warrick, Peter, Cincinnati	51	592	11.6	46	4
Watters, Ricky, Seattle	63	613	9.7	59	2
Weaver, Jed, Miami	10	179	17.9	41	0
Wheatley, Tyrone, Oakland	20	156	7.8	17	1
White, Jamel, Cleveland	13	100	7.7	25	0
Whitted, Alvis, Jacksonville	13	137	10.5	t37	3
Wiggins, Jermaine, NYJ-N.E.	18	207	11.5	59	2
Wilkins, Terrence, Indianapolis	43	569	13.2	t43	3
Williams, James, Seattle	8	99	12.4	18	0
Williams, Nick, Cincinnati	7	84	12.0	20	0
Witman, Jon, Pittsburgh	5	33	6.6	11	0
Woodson, Charles, Oakland	1	8	8.0	8	0
Wycheck, Frank, Tennessee	70	636	9.1	26	4
Yeast, Craig, Cincinnati	24	301	12.5	27	0
t—touchdown.					

NFC

Player, Team	No.	Yds.	Avg.	Long	TD
Abdullah, Rabih, Tampa Bay	2	14	7.0	11	0
Alexander, Stephen, Washington	47	510	10.9	30	2
Allen, James, Chicago	39	291	7.5	26	1
Allen, Terry, New Orleans	1	7	7.0	7	0
Allred, John, Chicago	9	109	12.1	25	1
Alstott, Mike, Tampa Bay	13	93	7.2	21	0
Anderson, Jamal, Atlanta	42	382	9.1	55	0
Anthony, Reidel, Tampa Bay	15	232	15.5	t46	4
Autry, Darnell, Philadelphia	24	275	11.5	37	1
Bailey, Champ, Washington	3	78	26.0	42	0
Barber, Tiki, N.Y. Giants	70	719	10.3	36	1
Barnes, Marlon, Chicago	1	7	7.0	7	0
Bates, D'Wayne, Chicago	4	42	10.5	18	0
Bates, Mario, Detroit	15	109	7.3	17	0
Bates, Michael, Carolina	5	38	7.6	23	0
Beasley, Fred, San Francisco	31	233	7.5	34	3
Biakabutuka, Tim, Carolina	34	341	10.0	25	2
Booker, Marty, Chicago	47	490	10.4	41	2
Boston, David, Arizona	71	1156	16.3	t70	7
Brazzell, Chris, Dallas	2	12	6.0	10	0
Brooks, Macey, Chicago	26	216	8.3	27	0
Broughton, Luther, Philadelphia	12	104	8.7	21	0
Brown, Na, Philadelphia	9	80	8.9	18	1
Bruce, Isaac, St. Louis	87	1471	16.9	t78	9
Byrd, Isaac, Carolina	22	241	11.0	t34	2
Campbell, Daniel, N.Y. Giants	8	46	5.8	13	3
Canidate, Trung, St. Louis	1	4	4.0	4	0
Carter, Cris, Minnesota	96	1274	13.3	53	9
Centers, Larry, Washington	81	600	7.4	26	3
Chandler, Chris, Atlanta	1	-4	-4.0	-4	0
Christian, Bob, Atlanta	44	315	7.2	19	0
Clark, Greg, San Francisco	38	342	9.0	34	2

Player, Team	No.	Yds.	Avg.	Long	TD
Cody, Mac, Arizona	17	212	12.5	24	0
Comella, Greg, N.Y. Giants	36	274	7.6	25	0
Connell, Albert, Washington	39	762	19.5	t77	3
Conwell, Ernie, St. Louis	5	40	8.0	17	0
Craig, Dameyune, Carolina	2	4	2.0	4	0
Crawford, Casey, Carolina	4	47	11.8	t16	1
Cross, Howard, N.Y. Giants	4	30	7.5	18	0
Crowell, Germane, Detroit	34	430	12.6	t50	3
Davis, John, Minnesota	17	202	11.9	37	1
Davis, Stephen, Washington	33	313	9.5	39	0
Davis, Thabiti, N.Y. Giants	2	40	20.0	27	0
Davis, Tyrone, Green Bay	19	197	9.3	41	2
Dayne, Ron, N.Y. Giants	3	11	3.7	12	0
Dixon, Ron, N.Y. Giants	6	92	15.3	t34	1
Douglas, Dameane, Philadelphia	1	9	9.0	9	0
Dragos, Scott, Chicago	4	28	7.0	10	0
Driver, Donald, Green Bay	21	322	15.3	49	1
Dunn, Warrick, Tampa Bay	44	422	9.6	45	1
Dwight, Tim, Atlanta	26	406	15.6	t52	1
Engram, Bobby, Chicago	16	109	6.8	25	0
Enis, Curtis, Chicago	8	68	8.5	18	0
Faulk, Marshall, St. Louis	81	830	10.2	t72	8
Finneran, Brian, Atlanta	7	60	8.6	14	0
Flemister, Zeron, Washington	1	8	8.0	8	0
Floyd, William, Carolina	17	114	6.7	15	1
Foster, Larry, Detroit	17	175	10.3	t40	1
Franks, Bubba, Green Bay	34	363	10.7	t27	1
Freeman, Antonio, Green Bay	62	912	14.7	t67	9
Fryar, Irving, Washington	41	548	13.4	t34	5
Galloway, Joey, Dallas	4	62	15.5	22	1
Garner, Charlie, San Francisco	68	647	9.5	62	3
Gedney, Chris, Arizona	10	75	7.5	24	0
German, Jammi, Atlanta	1	10	10.0	10	0
Glover, Andrew, New Orleans	21	281	13.4	39	4
Goodman, Herbert, Green Bay	1	0	0.0	0	0
Green, Ahman, Green Bay	73	559	7.7	31	3
Green, Jacquez, Tampa Bay	51	773	15.2	75	1
Hakim, Az-Zahir, St. Louis	53	734	13.8	t80	4
Hall, Lamont, New Orleans	5	33	6.6	13	1
Hankton, Karl, Carolina	4	38	9.5	14	0
Hape, Patrick, Tampa Bay	6	39	6.5	13	0
Hardy, Terry, Arizona	27	160	5.9	13	1
Harris, Jackie, Dallas	39	306	7.8	21	5
Hatchette, Matthew, Minnesota	16	190	11.9	t39	2
Hayes, Donald, Carolina	66	926	14.0	t43	3
Henderson, William, Green Bay	35	234	6.7	25	1
Hetherington, Chris, Carolina	14	116	8.3	19	1
Hicks, Skip, Washington	5	43	8.6	25	0
Hilliard, Ike, N.Y. Giants	55	787	14.3	59	8
Hodge, Damon, Dallas	4	60	15.0	20	0
Hodgins, James, St. Louis	2	5	2.5	3	0
Holcombe, Robert, St. Louis	8	90	11.3	19	1
Holt, Torry, St. Louis	82	1635	19.9	t85	6
Hoover, Brad, Carolina	15	112	7.5	16	0
Horn, Joe, New Orleans	94	1340	14.3	52	8
Horne, Tony, St. Louis	4	32	8.0	t18	2
Howard, Desmond, Detroit	2	14	7.0	10	0
Irvin, Sedrick, Detroit	8	90	11.3	18	0
Ismail, Raghib, Dallas	25	350	14.0	44	1
Jackson, Terry, San Francisco	5	48	9.6	16	1
Jackson, Willie, New Orleans	37	523	14.1	t53	6
Jefferson, Shawn, Atlanta	60	822	13.7	49	2
Jenkins, MarTay, Arizona	17	219	12.9	34	0
Johnson, Charles, Philadelphia	56	642	11.5	59	7
Johnson, Keyshawn, Tampa Bay	71	874	12.3	38	8
Jones, Thomas, Arizona	32	208	6.5	20	0
Jordan, Andrew, Minnesota	8	63	7.9	12	0
Jurevicius, Joe, N.Y. Giants	24	272	11.3	43	1
Kelly, Reggie, Atlanta	31	340	11.0	t37	2
Kennison, Eddie, Chicago	55	549	10.0	26	2
Kinchen, Brian, Carolina	1	7	7.0	7	0
Kleinsasser, Jim, Minnesota	10	98	9.8	21	0

2000 STATISTICS *Receiving*

Player, Team	No.	Yds.	Avg.	Long	TD
Kozlowski, Brian, Atlanta	15	151	10.1	30	2
LaFleur, David, Dallas	12	109	9.1	19	1
Lee, Amp, Philadelphia	1	20	20.0	20	0
Lee, Charles, Green Bay	10	134	13.4	38	0
Levens, Dorsey, Green Bay	16	146	9.1	37	0
Lewis, Chad, Philadelphia	69	735	10.7	52	3
Lyman, Dustin, Chicago	1	4	4.0	4	0
Makovicka, Joel, Arizona	6	18	3.0	5	0
Mangum, Kris, Carolina	19	215	11.3	31	1
Martin, Cecil, Philadelphia	31	219	7.1	26	0
Mathis, Terance, Atlanta	57	679	11.9	t44	5
Mayes, Alonzo, Chicago	4	40	10.0	19	0
McDaniel, Randall, Tampa Bay	1	2	2.0	t2	1
McGarity, Wane, Dallas	25	250	10.0	25	0
McKinley, Dennis, Arizona	2	13	6.5	9	0
McKnight, James, Dallas	52	926	17.8	48	2
McNabb, Donovan, Philadelphia	2	5	2.5	3	0
McWilliams, Johnny, Minnesota	22	180	8.2	26	3
Milburn, Glyn, Chicago	1	8	8.0	8	0
Miller, Bubba, Philadelphia	1	9	9.0	9	0
Milne, Brian, New Orleans	5	33	6.6	15	1
Mitchell, Brian, Philadelphia	13	89	6.8	21	1
Mitchell, Pete, N.Y. Giants	25	245	9.8	22	1
Mitchell, Tywan, Arizona	5	80	16.0	42	0
Moore, Dave, Tampa Bay	29	288	9.9	28	3
Moore, Herman, Detroit	40	434	10.9	t30	3
Morrow, Harold, Minnesota	1	2	2.0	2	0
Morton, Chad, New Orleans	30	213	7.1	35	0
Morton, Johnnie, Detroit	61	788	12.9	t42	3
Moss, Randy, Minnesota	77	1437	18.7	t78	15
Muhammad, Muhsin, Carolina	102	1183	11.6	36	6
Murrell, Adrian, Washington	16	93	5.8	12	0
Olivo, Brock, Detroit	3	50	16.7	19	0
Owens, Terrell, San Francisco	97	1451	15.0	t69	13
Palmer, David, Minnesota	1	-2	-2.0	-2	0
Parker, De'Mond, Green Bay	9	50	5.6	10	0
Pinkston, Todd, Philadelphia	10	181	18.1	45	0
Pittman, Michael, Arizona	73	579	7.9	t36	2
Poole, Keith, New Orleans	21	293	14.0	t49	1
Pritchett, Stanley, Philadelphia	25	193	7.7	17	0
Proehl, Ricky, St. Louis	31	441	14.2	29	4
Pupunu, Alfred, Detroit	3	32	10.7	17	0
Rasby, Walter, Detroit	10	78	7.8	17	1
Reed, Andre, Washington	10	103	10.3	t21	1
Reed, Jake, New Orleans	16	206	12.9	22	0
Rice, Jerry, San Francisco	75	805	10.7	t68	7
Robinson, Damien, Tampa Bay	1	36	36.0	36	0
Robinson, Jeff, St. Louis	5	52	10.4	27	0
Robinson, Marcus, Chicago	55	738	13.4	t68	5
Sanders, Frank, Arizona	54	749	13.9	t53	6
Schlesinger, Cory, Detroit	12	73	6.1	13	0
Schroeder, Bill, Green Bay	65	999	15.4	t55	4
Sellers, Mike, Washington	8	78	9.8	24	2
Sinceno, Kaseem, Chicago	23	206	9.0	28	0
Sloan, David, Detroit	32	379	11.8	59	2
Small, Torrance, Philadelphia	40	569	14.2	t70	3
Smith, Emmitt, Dallas	11	79	7.2	19	0
Smith, Maurice, Atlanta	1	5	5.0	5	0
Smith, Paul, San Francisco	2	55	27.5	47	0
Smith, Robert, Minnesota	36	348	9.7	t53	3
Smith, Terrelle, New Orleans	12	65	5.4	10	0
Stablein, Brian, Detroit	8	53	6.6	11	0
Staley, Duce, Philadelphia	25	201	8.0	26	0
Stecker, Aaron, Tampa Bay	1	15	15.0	15	0
Stewart, James, Detroit	32	287	9.0	32	1
Stokes, J.J., San Francisco	30	524	17.5	53	3
Streets, Tai, San Francisco	19	287	15.1	39	0
Swift, Justin, San Francisco	1	8	8.0	8	0
Tant, Jay, Arizona	1	4	4.0	4	0
Thomas, Robert, Minnesota	23	117	5.1	14	2
Thomason, Jeff, Philadelphia	10	46	4.6	11	5
Thrash, James, Washington	50	653	13.1	50	2
Toomer, Amani, N.Y. Giants	78	1094	14.0	t54	7
Tucker, Jason, Dallas	13	126	9.7	18	0
Turley, Kyle, New Orleans	1	16	16.0	16	0
Uwaezuoke, Iheanyi, Carolina	4	46	11.5	21	0
Van Dyke, Alex, Philadelphia	1	8	8.0	8	0
Walls, Wesley, Carolina	31	422	13.6	54	2
Walsh, Chris, Minnesota	18	191	10.6	21	0
Walters, Troy, Minnesota	1	5	5.0	5	0
Warren, Chris, Dal.-Phi.	32	303	9.5	t76	1
Watson, Justin, St. Louis	10	56	5.6	15	0
Wells, Mike, Chicago	1	13	13.0	13	0
Westbrook, Michael, Washington	9	103	11.4	21	0
Wetnight, Ryan, Green Bay	3	20	6.7	9	0
White, Dez, Chicago	10	87	8.7	t25	1
Wiley, Michael, Dallas	14	72	5.1	t15	1
Williams, Clarence, Arizona	1	5	5.0	5	0
Williams, Karl, Tampa Bay	2	35	17.5	27	0
Williams, Moe, Minnesota	4	31	7.8	12	0
Williams, Ricky, New Orleans	44	409	9.3	24	1
Williams, Roland, St. Louis	11	102	9.3	t31	3
Wilson, Robert, New Orleans	11	154	14.0	30	0
Yoder, Todd, Tampa Bay	1	1	1.0	1	0

t—touchdown.

PLAYERS WITH TWO CLUBS

Player, Team	No.	Yds.	Avg.	Long	TD
Harris, Raymont, Denver	2	19	9.5	16	0
Harris, Raymont, New England	2	1	0.5	2	0
Warren, Chris, Dallas	31	302	9.7	t76	1
Warren, Chris, Philadelphia	1	1	1.0	1	0
Wiggins, Jermaine, N.Y. Jets	2	4	2.0	3	1
Wiggins, Jermaine, New England	16	203	12.7	59	1

SCORING

TEAM

AFC

Team	Total TD	TD Rush	TD Pass	TD Misc.	XP	2Pt.	XPA	FG	FGA	Safeties	Total Pts.
Denver	58	21	28	9	53	2	53	26	34	1	485
Oakland	58	23	28	7	56	1	56	23	34	2	479
Indianapolis	50	14	33	3	46	2	46	25	27	2	429
Jacksonville	40	18	22	0	38	1	38	29	33	0	367
Kansas City	44	12	29	3	40	0	40	17	24	0	355
Tennessee	38	14	18	6	37	0	38	27	34	0	346
Baltimore	32	9	20	3	30	2	30	35	39	1	333
Miami	34	16	15	3	33	0	34	28	31	1	323
N.Y. Jets	36	11	23	2	32	2	32	23	34	0	321
Pittsburgh	35	19	12	4	32	1	33	25	30	1	321
Seattle	37	10	21	6	33	0	33	21	26	1	320
Buffalo	34	11	20	3	31	1	31	26	35	0	315
New England	28	9	18	1	25	1	25	27	33	0	276
San Diego	31	7	19	5	27	0	27	18	25	1	269
Cincinnati	21	13	6	2	21	0	21	12	21	1	185
Cleveland	17	7	9	1	17	0	17	14	17	0	161
AFC total	593	214	321	58	551	13	554	376	477	11	5285
AFC average	37.1	13.4	20.1	3.6	34.4	0.8	34.6	23.5	29.8	0.7	330.3

NFC

Team	Total TD	TD Rush	TD Pass	TD Misc.	XP	2Pt.	XPA	FG	FGA	Safeties	Total Pts.
St. Louis	67	26	37	4	58	4	58	24	27	0	540
Minnesota	47	14	33	0	45	2	45	22	23	0	397
San Francisco	49	15	32	2	43	3	45	15	22	0	388
Tampa Bay	43	18	18	7	42	1	42	28	34	1	388
New Orleans	41	14	22	5	37	1	37	23	29	0	354
Green Bay	36	13	21	2	32	2	32	33	38	1	353
Philadelphia	38	13	21	4	34	1	36	29	33	0	351
N.Y. Giants	39	16	22	1	37	0	37	19	25	0	328
Carolina	31	7	19	5	29	1	29	31	35	0	310
Detroit	33	15	14	4	29	4	29	24	30	0	307
Dallas	31	15	14	2	27	2	27	25	33	1	294
Washington	32	14	18	0	27	0	29	20	30	1	281
Atlanta	25	6	14	5	23	1	23	25	31	1	252
Chicago	22	6	12	4	21	0	21	21	27	0	216
Arizona	24	6	16	2	18	0	19	16	23	0	210
NFC total	558	198	313	47	502	22	509	355	440	5	4969
NFC average	37.2	13.2	20.9	3.1	33.5	1.5	33.9	23.7	29.3	0.3	331.3
NFL total	1151	412	634	105	1053	35	1063	731	917	16	10254
NFL average	37.1	13.3	20.5	3.4	34.0	1.1	34.3	23.6	29.6	0.5	330.8

INDIVIDUAL

BESTS OF THE SEASON

Points, season
NFC: 160—Marshall Faulk, St. Louis.
AFC: 135—Matt Stover, Baltimore.

Touchdowns, season
NFC: 26—Marshall Faulk, St. Louis.
AFC: 18—Edgerrin James, Indianapolis.

Extra points, season
AFC: 49—Jason Elam, Denver.
NFC: 45—Gary Anderson, Minnesota.

Field goals, season
AFC: 35—Matt Stover, Baltimore.
NFC: 34—Joe Nedney, Denver-Carolina.

Field goal attempts, season
AFC: 39—Matt Stover, Baltimore.
NFC: 38—Ryan Longwell, Green Bay; Joe Nedney, Denver-Carolina.

Longest field goal
NFC: 55—Martin Gramatica, Tampa Bay vs. Detroit, Oct. 19.
AFC: 54—John Carney, San Diego at Kansas City, Sept. 17; Sebastian Janikowski, Oakland at San Diego, Oct. 29.

Most points, game
AFC: 24—Fred Taylor, Jacksonville at Pittsburgh, Nov. 19 (4 TDs); Mike Anderson, Denver at New Orleans, Dec. 3 (4 TDs).
NFC: 24—Marshall Faulk, St. Louis at San Francisco, Oct. 29 (4 TDs); Marshall Faulk, St. Louis vs. Minnesota, Dec. 10 (4 TDs); Marshall Faulk, St. Louis at Tampa Bay, Dec. 18 (4 TDs).

Team leaders, points
AFC:

Baltimore	135	Matt Stover
Buffalo	109	Steve Christie
Cincinnati	57	Neil Rackers
Cleveland	59	Phil Dawson
Denver	103	Jason Elam

AFC:

Indianapolis	121	Mike Vanderjagt
Jacksonville	105	Mike Hollis
Kansas City	70	Todd Peterson
Miami	117	Olindo Mare
New England	106	Adam Vinatieri
N.Y. Jets	93	John Hall
Oakland	112	S. Janikowski
Pittsburgh	107	Kris Brown
San Diego	81	John Carney
Seattle	70	Rian Lindell
Tennessee	118	Al Del Greco

NFC:

Arizona	66	Cary Blanchard
Atlanta	98	Morten Andersen
Carolina	126	Joe Nedney
Chicago	84	Paul Edinger
Dallas	108	Tim Seder
Detroit	101	Jason Hanson
Green Bay	131	Ryan Longwell
Minnesota	111	Gary Anderson
New Orleans	106	Doug Brien
N.Y. Giants	85	Brad Daluiso
Philadelphia	121	David Akers
St. Louis	160	Marshall Faulk
San Francisco	88	Wade Richey
Tampa Bay	126	Martin Gramatica
Washington	66	Stephen Davis

NFL LEADERS

KICKERS

Player, Team	XPM	XPA	FGM	FGA	Tot. Pts.
Stover, Matt, Baltimore*	30	30	35	39	135
Longwell, Ryan, Green Bay	32	32	33	38	131
Nedney, Joe, Carolina	24	24	34	38	126
Gramatica, Martin, Tampa Bay	42	42	28	34	126
Vanderjagt, Mike, Indianapolis*	46	46	25	27	121
Akers, David, Philadelphia	34	36	29	33	121
Del Greco, Al, Tennessee*	37	38	27	33	118
Mare, Olindo, Miami*	33	34	28	31	117
Janikowski, Sebastian, Oakland*	46	46	22	32	112
Anderson, Gary, Minnesota	45	45	22	23	111
Christie, Steve, Buffalo*	31	31	26	35	109
Brown, Kris, Pittsburgh*	32	33	25	30	107
Brien, Doug, New Orleans	37	37	23	29	106
Vinatieri, Adam, New England*	25	25	27	33	106
Hollis, Mike, Jacksonville*	33	33	24	26	105
Elam, Jason, Denver*	49	49	18	24	103
Seder, Tim, Dallas	27	27	25	33	102
Hanson, Jason, Detroit	29	29	24	30	101
Andersen, Morten, Atlanta	23	23	25	31	98
Hall, John, N.Y. Jets*	30	30	21	32	93

*AFC.

NON-KICKERS

Player, Team	TD	RTD	PTD	MTD	2Pt.	Tot. Pts.
Faulk, Marshall, St. Louis	26	18	8	0	2	160
James, Edgerrin, Ind.*	18	13	5	0	1	110
Smith, Lamar, Miami*	16	14	2	0	0	96
George, Eddie, Tennessee*	16	14	2	0	0	96
Moss, Randy, Minnesota	15	0	15	0	1	92
Anderson, Mike, Denver*	15	15	0	0	1	92
Harrison, Marvin, Ind.*	14	0	14	0	0	84
Taylor, Fred, Jacksonville*	14	12	2	0	0	84
Owens, Terrell, San Francisco	13	0	13	0	1	80
Green, Ahman, Green Bay	13	10	3	0	0	78
Stewart, James, Detroit	11	10	1	0	3	72
Brown, Tim, Oakland*	11	0	11	0	0	66
Martin, Curtis, N.Y. Jets*	11	9	2	0	0	66

Player, Team	Tot. TD	RTD	PTD	MTD	2Pt.	Tot. Pts.
Davis, Stephen, Washington	11	11	0	0	0	66
Smith, Robert, Minnesota	10	7	3	0	0	60
Alexander, Derrick, K.C.*	10	0	10	0	0	60
Garner, Charlie, San Francisco	10	7	3	0	0	60
Wheatley, Tyrone, Oakland*	10	9	1	0	0	60
McCaffrey, Ed, Denver*	9	0	9	0	1	56
Carter, Cris, Minnesota	9	0	9	0	0	54
Smith, Emmitt, Dallas	9	9	0	0	0	54
Watters, Ricky, Seattle*	9	7	2	0	0	54
Bruce, Isaac, St. Louis	9	0	9	0	0	54
Smith, Rod, Denver*	9	1	8	0	0	54
Freeman, Antonio, Green Bay	9	0	9	0	0	54
Dunn, Warrick, Tampa Bay	9	8	1	0	0	54
Barber, Tiki, N.Y. Giants	9	8	1	0	0	54
Gonzalez, Tony, Kansas City*	9	0	9	0	0	54
Williams, Ricky, New Orleans	9	8	1	0	0	54
Smith, Jimmy, Jacksonville*	8	0	8	0	0	48

*AFC.

AFC

KICKERS

Player, Team	XPM	XPA	FGM	FGA	Tot. Pts.
Brown, Kris, Pittsburgh	32	33	25	30	107
Carney, John, San Diego	27	27	18	25	81
Christie, Steve, Buffalo	31	31	26	35	109
Conway, Brett, Was.-Oak.-NYJ*	8	8	6	6	26
Dawson, Phil, Cleveland	17	17	14	17	59
Del Greco, Al, Tennessee	37	38	27	33	118
Elam, Jason, Denver	49	49	18	24	103
Hall, John, N.Y. Jets	30	30	21	32	93
Hollis, Mike, Jacksonville	33	33	24	26	105
Janikowski, Sebastian, Oakland	46	46	22	32	112
Lechler, Shane, Oakland	7	7	0	1	7
Lindell, Rian, Seattle	25	25	15	17	70
Lindsey, Steve, Jacksonville	5	5	5	7	20
Mare, Olindo, Miami	33	34	28	31	117
Peterson, Todd, Kansas City	25	25	15	20	70
Rackers, Neil, Cincinnati	21	21	12	21	57
Stover, Matt, Baltimore	30	30	35	39	135
Vanderjagt, Mike, Indianapolis	46	46	25	27	121
Vinatieri, Adam, New England	25	25	27	33	106

*Includes both NFC and AFC statistics.

NON-KICKERS

Player, Team	Tot. TD	RTD	PTD	MTD	2Pt.	Tot. Pts.
Alexander, Derrick, K.C.	10	0	10	0	0	60
Alexander, Shaun, Seattle	2	2	0	0	0	12
Allen, Eric, Oakland	3	0	0	3	0	18
Anders, Kimble, Kansas City	2	2	0	0	0	12
Anderson, Mike, Denver	15	15	0	0	1	92
Anderson, Richie, N.Y. Jets	2	0	2	0	0	12
Ayanbadejo, Obafemi, Bal.	2	1	1	0	0	12
Bailey, Karsten, Seattle	1	0	1	0	0	6
Baxter, Fred, N.Y. Jets	2	0	2	0	0	12
Becht, Anthony, N.Y. Jets	2	0	2	0	0	12
Bellamy, Jay, Seattle	1	0	0	1	0	6
Bennett, Brandon, Cincinnati	3	3	0	0	0	18
Bennett, Donnell, Kansas City	1	1	0	0	0	6
Bettis, Jerome, Pittsburgh	8	8	0	0	0	48
Bjornson, Eric, New England	2	0	2	0	0	12
Blackwell, Will, Pittsburgh	1	0	0	1	0	6
Bledsoe, Drew, New England	2	2	0	0	0	12
Brady, Kyle, Jacksonville	3	0	3	0	1	20
Bratzke, Chad, Indianapolis	0	0	0	0	0	†2
Brigham, Jeremy, Oakland	2	0	2	0	0	12
Brown, Chad, Seattle	1	0	0	1	0	6
Brown, Tim, Oakland	11	0	11	0	0	66

Player, Team	Tot. TD	RTD	PTD	MTD	2Pt.	Tot. Pts.
Brown, Troy, New England	5	0	4	1	0	30
Bruener, Mark, Pittsburgh	3	0	3	0	0	18
Brunell, Mark, Jacksonville	2	2	0	0	0	12
Bryson, Shawn, Buffalo	2	0	2	0	1	14
Buckley, Terrell, Denver	1	0	0	1	0	6
Bulluck, Keith, Tennessee	1	0	0	1	0	6
Burris, Jeff, Indianapolis	1	0	0	1	0	6
Campbell, Mark, Cleveland	1	0	1	0	0	6
Carswell, Dwayne, Denver	3	0	3	0	0	18
Carter, Tony, New England	2	2	0	0	0	12
Chamberlain, Byron, Denver	1	0	1	0	0	6
Chancey, Robert, San Diego	2	2	0	0	0	12
Chiaverini, Darrin, Cleveland	1	0	1	0	0	6
Chrebet, Wayne, N.Y. Jets	8	0	8	0	0	48
Clark, Desmond, Denver	3	0	3	0	0	18
Cloud, Mike, Kansas City	2	1	0	1	0	12
Coates, Ben, Baltimore	0	0	0	0	1	2
Coleman, KaRon, Denver	1	1	0	0	0	6
Coleman, Marcus, N.Y. Jets	1	0	1	0	1	8
Coles, Laveranues, N.Y. Jets	1	0	1	0	1	8
Conway, Curtis, San Diego	5	0	5	0	0	30
Crockett, Ray, Denver	1	0	0	1	0	6
Crockett, Zack, Oakland	7	7	0	0	0	42
Davis, Terrell, Denver	2	2	0	0	0	12
Dawkins, Sean, Seattle	5	0	5	0	0	30
Dawson, JaJuan, Cleveland	1	0	1	0	0	6
Dilger, Ken, Indianapolis	3	0	3	0	0	18
Dillon, Corey, Cincinnati	7	7	0	0	0	42
Dixon, Gerald, San Diego	1	0	0	1	0	6
Drayton, Troy, Kansas City	2	0	2	0	0	12
Dudley, Rickey, Oakland	4	0	4	0	0	24
Dugans, Ron, Cincinnati	1	0	1	0	0	6
Dumas, Mike, San Diego	1	0	0	1	0	6
Dunn, David, Oakland	1	0	0	1	0	6
Dyson, Kevin, Tennessee	1	0	1	0	0	6
Edwards, Donnie, Kansas City	1	0	0	1	0	6
Edwards, Marc, Cleveland	2	0	2	0	0	12
Elliott, Jumbo, N.Y. Jets	1	0	1	0	0	6
Ellsworth, Percy, Cleveland	1	0	0	1	0	6
Emanuel, Bert, Miami	1	0	1	0	0	6
Faulk, Kevin, New England	5	4	1	0	1	32
Fauria, Christian, Seattle	2	0	2	0	0	12
Fazande, Jermaine, San Diego	2	2	0	0	0	12
Fiedler, Jay, Miami	1	1	0	0	0	6
Finn, Jim, Indianapolis	1	0	1	0	0	6
Fletcher, Terrell, San Diego	4	3	1	0	0	24
Flutie, Doug, Buffalo	1	1	0	0	0	6
Fontenot, Al, San Diego	0	0	0	0	0	†2
Ford, Henry, Tennessee	1	0	0	1	0	6
Frerotte, Gus, Denver	1	1	0	0	0	6
Fuamatu-Ma'afala, Chris, Pit.	1	1	0	0	0	6
Gadsden, Oronde, Miami	6	0	6	0	0	36
Gannon, Rich, Oakland	4	4	0	0	1	26
Gash, Sam, Baltimore	1	0	1	0	0	6
Gaylor, Trevor, San Diego	1	0	1	0	0	6
George, Eddie, Tennessee	16	14	2	0	0	96
Gildon, Jason, Pittsburgh	1	0	0	1	0	6
Glenn, Terry, New England	6	0	6	0	0	36
Godfrey, Randall, Tennessee	1	0	0	1	0	6
Gold, Ian, Denver	1	0	0	1	0	6
Gonzalez, Tony, Kansas City	9	0	9	0	0	54
Goodwin, Hunter, Miami	1	0	1	0	0	6
Gordon, Darrien, Oakland	1	0	0	1	0	6
Graham, Jeff, San Diego	4	0	4	0	0	24
Grbac, Elvis, Kansas City	1	1	0	0	0	6
Green, E.G., Indianapolis	1	0	1	0	0	6
Green, Victor, N.Y. Jets	1	0	1	0	0	6
Griese, Brian, Denver	1	1	0	0	0	6
Griffith, Howard, Denver	2	0	2	0	0	12
Haley, Jermaine, Miami	0	0	0	0	0	†2
Harrison, Marvin, Indianapolis	14	0	14	0	0	84
Harrison, Rodney, San Diego	1	0	0	1	0	6
Hawkins, Courtney, Pittsburgh	1	0	1	0	0	6
Heiden, Steve, San Diego	1	0	1	0	0	6
Holmes, Priest, Baltimore	2	2	0	0	0	12
Holsey, Bernard, Indianapolis	1	0	0	1	0	6
Howard, Chris, Jacksonville	1	1	0	0	0	6
Huntley, Richard, Pittsburgh	3	3	0	0	1	20
Ismail, Qadry, Baltimore	5	0	5	0	0	30
Jackson, Darrell, Seattle	6	0	6	0	0	36
Jackson, Sheldon, Buffalo	1	0	1	0	0	6
James, Edgerrin, Indianapolis	18	13	5	0	1	110
Jenkins, Billy, Denver	1	0	0	1	0	6
Jenkins, Ronney, San Diego	1	0	1	0	0	6
Jett, James, Oakland	2	0	2	0	0	12
Johnson, Anthony, Jac.	1	1	0	0	0	6
Johnson, J.J., Miami	1	1	0	0	0	6
Johnson, Pat, Baltimore	2	0	2	0	0	12
Johnson, Rob, Buffalo	1	1	0	0	0	6
Jones, Freddie, San Diego	5	0	5	0	0	30
Jones, Henry, Buffalo	1	0	0	1	0	6
Jordan, Randy, Oakland	5	3	1	1	0	30
Kaufman, Napoleon, Oakland	1	0	1	0	0	6
Kinney, Erron, Tennessee	1	0	1	0	0	6
Kitna, Jon, Seattle	1	1	0	0	0	6
Koonce, George, Seattle	1	0	0	1	0	6
Lewis, Jamal, Baltimore	6	6	0	0	1	38
Lewis, Jermaine, Baltimore	3	0	1	2	0	18
Linton, Jonathan, Buffalo	1	0	1	0	0	6
Lockett, Kevin, Kansas City	2	0	2	0	0	12
Mack, Stacey, Jacksonville	1	1	0	0	0	6
Madison, Sam, Miami	1	0	0	1	0	6
Manning, Peyton, Ind.	1	1	0	0	0	6
Martin, Curtis, N.Y. Jets	11	9	2	0	0	66
Mason, Derrick, Tennessee	6	0	5	1	0	36
Mayes, Derrick, Seattle	1	0	1	0	0	6
McAlister, Chris, Baltimore	1	0	0	1	0	6
McCaffrey, Ed, Denver	9	0	9	0	1	56
McCardell, Keenan, Jac.	5	0	5	0	0	30
McCrary, Fred, San Diego	2	0	2	0	0	12
McCrary, Michael, Baltimore	0	0	0	0	0	†2
McDaniel, Jeremy, Buffalo	2	0	2	0	0	12
McGee, Tony, Cincinnati	1	0	1	0	0	6
McGriff, Travis, Denver	1	0	1	0	0	6
Mili, Itula, Seattle	3	0	3	0	0	18
Mitchell, Scott, Cincinnati	1	1	0	0	0	6
Moreau, Frank, Kansas City	4	4	0	0	0	24
Morris, Sammy, Buffalo	6	5	1	0	0	36
Morris, Sylvester, Kansas City	3	0	3	0	0	18
Moulds, Eric, Buffalo	5	0	5	0	0	30
Muhammad, Mustafah, Ind.	1	0	0	1	0	6
Neal, Lorenzo, Tennessee	2	0	2	0	0	12
Ogden, Jeff, Miami	1	0	0	1	0	6
O'Neal, Deltha, Denver	1	0	0	1	0	6
Ostroski, Jerry, Buffalo	1	0	0	1	0	6
Parmalee, Bernie, N.Y. Jets	2	2	0	0	0	12
Pathon, Jerome, Indianapolis	3	0	3	0	0	18
Patten, David, Cleveland	1	0	1	0	0	6
Patton, Marvcus, Kansas City	1	0	0	1	0	6
Phenix, Perry, Tennessee	1	0	0	1	0	6
Pollard, Marcus, Indianapolis	3	0	3	0	1	20
Porter, Daryl, Buffalo	1	0	0	1	0	6
Porter, Joey, Pittsburgh	1	0	0	1	0	*8
Poteat, Hank, Pittsburgh	1	0	0	1	0	6
Prentice, Travis, Cleveland	8	7	1	0	0	48
Price, Peerless, Buffalo	3	0	3	0	0	18
Pryce, Trevor, Denver	1	0	0	1	0	6
Redmond, J.R., New England	3	1	2	0	0	18
Richardson, Tony, K.C.	6	3	3	0	0	36
Riemersma, Jay, Buffalo	5	0	5	0	0	30
Rison, Andre, Oakland	6	0	6	0	0	36
Rogers, Charlie, Seattle	1	0	0	1	0	6

Player, Team	Tot. TD	RTD	PTD	MTD	2Pt	Tot. Pts.
Rolle, Samari, Tennessee........	1	0	0	1	0	6
Russell, Darrell, Oakland.........	0	0	0	0	0	†2
Rutledge, Rod, New England..	1	0	1	0	0	6
Sharpe, Shannon, Baltimore...	5	0	5	0	0	30
Shaw, Bobby, Pittsburgh	4	0	4	0	0	24
Shea, Aaron, Cleveland..........	2	0	2	0	0	12
Shepherd, Leslie, Miami	4	0	4	0	0	24
Simmons, Tony, New England	1	0	1	0	0	6
Sinclair, Michael, Seattle........	1	0	0	1	0	6
Smith, Antowain, Buffalo........	4	4	0	0	0	24
Smith, Detron, Denver...........	1	0	1	0	0	6
Smith, Jimmy, Jacksonville....	8	0	8	0	0	48
Smith, Lamar, Miami	16	14	2	0	0	96
Smith, Rod, Denver	9	1	8	0	0	54
Soward, R. Jay, Jacksonville ..	1	0	1	0	0	6
Spencer, Jimmy, Denver	2	0	0	2	0	12
Stewart, Kordell, Pittsburgh....	7	7	0	0	0	42
Stith, Shyrone, Jacksonville....	1	1	0	0	0	6
Stokley, Brandon, Baltimore ...	2	0	2	0	0	12
Strong, Mack, Seattle	1	0	1	0	0	6
Suttle, Jason, Denver.............	1	0	0	1	0	6
Taylor, Fred, Jacksonville	14	12	2	0	0	84
Taylor, Jason, Miami	1	0	0	1	0	6
Taylor, Travis, Baltimore.........	3	0	3	0	0	18
Thigpen, Yancey, Tennessee ...	2	0	2	0	0	12
Thomas, Rodney, Tennessee ..	1	0	1	0	0	6
Thomas, Thurman, Miami	1	0	1	0	0	6
Thomas, William, Oakland	1	0	0	1	0	6
Turner, Scott, San Diego	1	0	0	1	0	6
Ward, Dedric, N.Y. Jets	3	0	3	0	0	18
Ward, Hines, Pittsburgh	4	0	4	0	0	24
Warrick, Peter, Cincinnati.......	7	2	4	1	0	42
Watters, Ricky, Seattle	9	7	2	0	0	54
Wheatley, Tyrone, Oakland......	10	9	1	0	0	60
Whitted, Alvis, Jacksonville	3	0	3	0	0	18
Wiggins, Jer., N.Y. J.-N.E.^.....	2	0	2	0	0	12
Wilkins, Terrence, Indianapolis	3	0	3	0	0	18
Williams, Darryl, Cincinnati	1	0	0	1	0	6
Williams, James, Seattle.........	0	0	0	0	0	†2
Williams, Josh, Indianapolis...	0	0	0	0	0	†2
Williams, Kevin, N.Y. Jets	1	0	0	1	0	6
Williams, Willie, Seattle..........	1	0	0	1	0	6
Wycheck, Frank, Tennessee....	4	0	4	0	0	24

†Includes safety.

NOTE: One team safety apiece credited to Cincinnati, Denver and Oakland.

NFC

KICKERS

Player, Team	XPM	XPA	FGM	FGA	Tot. Pts.
Akers, David, Philadelphia............	34	36	29	33	121
Andersen, Morten, Atlanta............	23	23	25	31	98
Anderson, Gary, Minnesota.........	45	45	22	23	111
Bentley, Scott, Washington	0	0	1	1	3
Blanchard, Cary, Arizona	18	19	16	23	66
Brien, Doug, New Orleans	37	37	23	29	106
Cunningham, Richie, Carolina.....	9	9	5	7	24
Daluiso, Brad, N.Y. Giants	34	34	17	23	85
Edinger, Paul, Chicago	21	21	21	27	84
Gramatica, Martin, Tampa Bay	42	42	28	34	126
Hall, Jeff, St. Louis	9	9	4	5	21
Hanson, Jason, Detroit................	29	29	24	30	101
Heppner, Kris, Sea.-Was.*	17	17	10	15	47
Holmes, Jaret, N.Y. Giants...........	3	3	2	2	9
Husted, Michael, Washington.......	8	9	4	8	20
Longwell, Ryan, Green Bay	32	32	33	38	131
Murray, Eddie, Washington	7	8	8	12	31
Nedney, Joe, Den.-Car.*	24	24	34	38	126

Player, Team	XPM	XPA	FGM	FGA	Tot. Pts.
Richey, Wade, San Francisco	43	45	15	22	88
Seder, Tim, Dallas	27	27	25	33	102
Stoyanovich, Pete, K.C.-St.L.*	26	26	5	9	41
Wilkins, Jeff, St. Louis	38	38	17	17	89

NON-KICKERS

Player, Team	Tot. TD	RTD	PTD	MTD	2Pt	Tot. Pts.
Abraham, Donnie, Tampa Bay.	1	0	0	1	0	6
Alexander, Stephen, Was.	2	0	2	0	0	12
Allen, James, Chicago	3	2	1	0	0	18
Allen, Terry, New Orleans.......	2	2	0	0	1	14
Allred, John, Chicago..............	1	0	1	0	0	6
Alstott, Mike, Tampa Bay	5	5	0	0	0	30
Ambrose, Ashley, Atlanta........	1	0	0	1	0	6
Anderson, Jamal, Atlanta........	6	6	0	0	1	38
Anthony, Reidel, Tampa Bay ...	4	0	4	0	0	24
Autry, Darnell, Philadelphia.....	4	3	1	0	0	24
Bailey, Champ, Washington	1	1	0	0	0	6
Barber, Ronde, Tampa Bay......	2	0	0	2	0	12
Barber, Tiki, N.Y. Giants	9	8	1	0	0	54
Batch, Charlie, Detroit.............	2	2	0	0	0	12
Bates, Mario, Detroit...............	2	2	0	0	0	12
Bates, Michael, Carolina	1	0	0	1	0	6
Beasley, Fred, San Francisco ..	6	3	3	0	0	36
Beuerlein, Steve, Carolina......	1	1	0	0	1	8
Biakabutuka, Tim, Carolina	4	2	2	0	0	24
Blake, Jeff, New Orleans.........	1	1	0	0	0	6
Booker, Marty, Chicago	2	0	2	0	0	12
Boston, David, Arizona	7	0	7	0	0	42
Brooks, Aaron, New Orleans...	2	2	0	0	0	12
Brooks, Derrick, Tampa Bay ...	1	0	0	1	0	6
Brown, Mike, Chicago.............	1	0	0	1	0	6
Brown, Na, Philadelphia.........	1	0	1	0	0	6
Bruce, Isaac, St. Louis	9	0	9	0	0	54
Bush, Devin, St. Louis	1	0	0	1	0	6
Byrd, Isaac, Carolina..............	2	0	2	0	0	12
Caldwell, Mike, Philadelphia ...	1	0	0	1	0	6
Campbell, Daniel, N.Y. Giants .	3	0	3	0	0	18
Campbell, Lamar, Detroit........	1	0	0	1	0	6
Carter, Cris, Minnesota	9	0	9	0	0	54
Case, Stoney, Detroit	1	1	0	0	0	6
Centers, Larry, Washington	3	0	3	0	0	18
Clark, Greg, San Francisco	2	0	2	0	0	12
Collins, Kerry, N.Y. Giants.......	1	1	0	0	0	6
Connell, Albert, Washington ...	3	0	3	0	0	18
Crawford, Casey, Carolina......	1	0	1	0	0	6
Crowell, Germane, Detroit.......	3	0	3	0	0	18
Culpepper, Daunte, Minnesota	7	7	0	0	0	42
Cunningham, Randall, Dallas..	1	1	0	0	0	6
Davis, John, Minnesota	1	0	1	0	0	6
Davis, Stephen, Washington...	11	11	0	0	0	66
Davis, Tyrone, Green Bay........	2	0	2	0	1	14
Dayne, Ron, N.Y. Giants	5	5	0	0	0	30
Dixon, Ron, N.Y. Giants	1	0	1	0	0	6
Driver, Donald, Green Bay.......	1	0	1	0	1	8
Duncan, Jamie, Tampa Bay.....	1	0	0	1	0	6
Dunn, Warrick, Tampa Bay......	9	8	1	0	0	54
Dwight, Tim, Atlanta	4	0	3	1	0	24
Enis, Curtis, Chicago	1	1	0	0	0	6
Evans, Doug, Carolina	1	0	0	1	0	6
Faulk, Marshall, St. Louis	26	18	8	0	2	160
Fletcher, London, St. Louis.....	0	0	0	0	1	2
Floyd, William, Carolina..........	2	1	1	0	0	12
Foster, Larry, Detroit...............	1	0	1	0	0	6
Franks, Bubba, Green Bay.......	1	0	1	0	0	6
Freeman, Antonio, Green Bay .	9	0	9	0	0	54
Fryar, Irving, Washington	5	0	5	0	0	30
Galloway, Joey, Dallas............	1	0	1	0	0	6
Garcia, Jeff, San Francisco	4	4	0	0	0	24
Garner, Charlie, San Francisco .	10	7	3	0	0	60

Player, Team	Tot. TD	RTD	PTD	MTD	2Pt.	Tot. Pts.
Glover, Andrew, New Orleans .	4	0	4	0	0	24
Green, Ahman, Green Bay	13	10	3	0	0	78
Green, Jacquez, Tampa Bay	1	0	1	0	0	6
Green, Trent, St. Louis	1	1	0	0	0	6
Hakim, Az-Zahir, St. Louis	5	0	4	1	0	30
Hall, Lamont, New Orleans	1	0	1	0	0	6
Hardy, Terry, Arizona	1	0	1	0	0	6
Harris, Jackie, Dallas	5	0	5	0	1	32
Harris, Walt, Chicago	1	0	0	1	0	6
Hartings, Jeff, Detroit	1	0	0	1	0	6
Hatchette, Matthew, Min.	2	0	2	0	0	12
Hayes, Donald, Carolina	3	0	3	0	0	18
Henderson, William, G.B.	1	0	1	0	0	6
Hetherington, Chris, Carolina..	3	2	1	0	0	18
Hicks, Skip, Washington	1	1	0	0	0	6
Hilliard, Ike, N.Y. Giants	8	0	8	0	0	48
Hitchcock, Jimmy, Carolina	1	0	0	1	0	6
Holcombe, Robert, St. Louis ..	4	3	1	0	0	24
Holt, Torry, St. Louis	6	0	6	0	0	36
Hoover, Brad, Carolina	1	1	0	0	0	6
Horn, Joe, New Orleans	8	0	8	0	0	48
Horne, Tony, St. Louis	3	0	2	1	0	18
Howard, Desmond, Detroit	1	0	0	1	0	6
Ismail, Raghib, Dallas	1	0	1	0	1	8
Jackson, Terry, San Francisco..	2	1	1	0	1	14
Jackson, Willie, New Orleans..	6	0	6	0	0	36
Jefferson, Shawn, Atlanta	2	0	2	0	0	12
Jenkins, MarTay, Arizona	1	0	0	1	0	6
Johnson, Brad, Washington	1	1	0	0	0	6
Johnson, Charles, Phi.	7	0	7	0	0	42
Johnson, Keyshawn, T.B.	8	0	8	0	0	48
Jones, Thomas, Arizona	2	2	0	0	0	12
Jurevicius, Joe, N.Y. Giants	1	0	1	0	0	6
Kelly, Brian, Tampa Bay	1	0	0	1	0	6
Kelly, Reggie, Atlanta	2	0	2	0	0	12
Kennison, Eddie, Chicago	2	0	2	0	0	12
King, Shaun, Tampa Bay	5	5	0	0	1	32
Knight, Sammy, New Orleans .	2	0	0	2	0	12
Kozlowski, Brian, Atlanta	2	0	2	0	0	12
LaFleur, David, Dallas	1	0	1	0	0	6
Levens, Dorsey, Green Bay	3	3	0	0	0	18
Lewis, Chad, Philadelphia	3	0	3	0	0	18
Lyle, Keith, St. Louis	1	0	0	1	0	6
Mangum, Kris, Carolina	1	0	1	0	0	6
Maryland, Russell, Green Bay.	0	0	0	0	0	†2
Mathis, Terance, Atlanta	5	0	5	0	0	30
McDaniel, Randall, T.B.	1	0	1	0	0	6
McGarity, Wane, Dallas	3	1	0	2	0	18
McKnight, James, Dallas	2	0	2	0	0	12
McNabb, Donovan, Phi.	6	6	0	0	0	36
McNown, Cade, Chicago	3	3	0	0	0	18
McQuarters, R.W., Chicago	1	0	0	1	0	6
McWilliams, Johnny, Min.	3	0	3	0	0	18
Milne, Brian, New Orleans	1	0	1	0	0	6
Minter, Mike, Carolina	1	0	0	1	0	6
Mitchell, Brian, Philadelphia	5	2	1	2	0	30
Mitchell, Keith, New Orleans...	2	0	0	2	0	12
Mitchell, Pete, N.Y. Giants	1	0	1	0	0	6
Montgomery, Delmonico, S.F. .	1	0	0	1	0	6
Montgomery, Joe, N.Y. Giants..	1	1	0	0	0	6
Moore, Dave, Tampa Bay	3	0	3	0	0	18
Moore, Herman, Detroit	3	0	3	0	0	18
Moore, Jerald, New Orleans ...	1	1	0	0	0	6
Morton, Johnnie, Detroit	3	0	3	0	1	20
Moss, Randy, Minnesota	15	0	15	0	1	92
Muhammad, Muhsin, Carolina .	6	0	6	0	0	36
Owens, Terrell, San Francisco.	13	0	13	0	1	80
Parrish, Tony, Chicago	1	0	0	1	0	6
Pittman, Michael, Arizona	6	4	2	0	0	36
Poole, Keith, New Orleans	1	0	1	0	0	6
Pritchett, Stanley, Phi.	1	1	0	0	0	6
Proehl, Ricky, St. Louis	4	0	4	0	0	24
Rasby, Walter, Detroit	1	0	1	0	0	6
Reed, Andre, Washington	1	0	1	0	0	6
Reese, Izell, Dallas	0	0	0	0	0	†2
Rice, Jerry, San Francisco	7	0	7	0	0	42
Robinson, Marcus, Chicago....	5	0	5	0	0	30
Rossum, Allen, Green Bay	1	0	0	1	0	6
Sanders, Frank, Arizona	6	0	6	0	0	36
Schroeder, Bill, Green Bay	4	0	4	0	0	24
Seder, Tim, Dallas	1	1	0	0	0	6
Sehorn, Jason, N.Y. Giants	1	0	0	1	0	6
Sellers, Mike, Washington	2	0	2	0	0	12
Sloan, David, Detroit	2	0	2	0	0	12
Small, Torrance, Philadelphia .	3	0	3	0	1	20
Smith, Bruce, Washington	0	0	0	0	0	†2
Smith, Darrin, New Orleans	1	0	0	1	0	6
Smith, Emmitt, Dallas	9	9	0	0	0	54
Smith, Robert, Minnesota	10	7	3	0	0	60
Staley, Duce, Philadelphia	1	1	0	0	0	6
Stewart, James, Detroit	11	10	1	0	3	72
Stokes, J.J., San Francisco	3	0	3	0	1	20
Thomas, Robert, Dallas	2	0	2	0	0	12
Thomason, Jeff, Philadelphia..	5	0	5	0	0	30
Thrash, James, Washington ...	2	0	2	0	0	12
Toomer, Amani, N.Y. Giants ...	8	1	7	0	0	48
Trotter, Jeremiah, Philadelphia.	1	0	0	1	0	6
Tucker, Jason, Dallas	1	1	0	0	0	6
Uwaezuoke, Iheanyi, Carolina .	1	0	0	1	0	6
Vaughn, Darrick, Atlanta	3	0	0	3	0	18
Walls, Wesley, Carolina	2	0	2	0	0	12
Warren, Chris, Dallas	3	2	1	0	0	18
Watson, Justin, St. Louis	4	4	0	0	0	24
Webster, Jason, S.F.	1	0	0	1	0	6
Westbrook, Bryant, Detroit	1	0	0	1	0	6
White, Dez, Chicago	1	0	1	0	0	6
Wiley, Michael, Dallas	1	0	1	0	0	6
Williams, Aeneas, Arizona	1	0	0	1	0	6
Williams, Karl, Tampa Bay	1	0	0	1	0	6
Williams, Moe, Minnesota	0	0	0	0	1	2
Williams, Ricky, New Orleans .	9	8	1	0	0	54
Williams, Roland, St. Louis	3	0	3	0	1	20
Williams, Tyrone, Green Bay...	1	0	0	1	0	6

†Includes safety.
NOTE: One team safety apiece credited to Atlanta and Tampa Bay.

INTERCEPTIONS

TEAM

AFC

Team	No.	Yds.	Avg.	Long	TD
Miami	28	311	11.1	43	0
Denver	27	343	12.7	t79	5
Baltimore	23	477	20.7	t98	1
Oakland	21	323	15.4	t50	4
N.Y. Jets	21	229	10.9	43	1
Seattle	17	300	17.6	t84	3
Tennessee	17	285	16.8	t87	4
Pittsburgh	17	154	9.1	33	0
San Diego	16	313	19.6	t75	4
Buffalo	16	131	8.2	t45	1
Kansas City	15	198	13.2	t42	2
Indianapolis	14	125	8.9	t40	2
Jacksonville	12	145	12.1	39	0
Cleveland	12	68	5.7	t33	1
New England	10	161	16.1	56	0
Cincinnati	9	107	11.9	t36	1
AFC total	275	3670	13.3	t98	29
AFC average	17.2	229.4	13.3	...	1.8

t—touchdown.

NFC

Team	No.	Yds.	Avg.	Long	TD
Detroit	25	340	13.6	t101	2
Tampa Bay	25	275	11.0	t37	4
Green Bay	21	315	15.0	47	1
New Orleans	20	264	13.2	46	4
N.Y. Giants	20	149	7.5	40	0
Philadelphia	19	255	13.4	38	2
St. Louis	19	135	7.1	23	0
Washington	17	219	12.9	48	0
Carolina	17	199	11.7	t88	2
Dallas	16	167	10.4	46	0
Atlanta	15	287	19.1	60	1
San Francisco	13	278	21.4	t70	2
Chicago	11	254	23.1	t61	4
Arizona	10	151	15.1	48	0
Minnesota	8	65	8.1	25	0
NFC total	256	3353	13.1	t101	22
NFC average	17.1	223.5	13.1	...	1.5
NFL total	531	7023	...	t101	51
NFL average	17.1	226.5	13.2	...	1.6

INDIVIDUAL

BESTS OF THE SEASON

Interceptions, season
NFC: 9—Darren Sharper, Green Bay.
AFC: 7—Samari Rolle, Tennessee; Brian Walker, Miami.

Interceptions, game
NFC: 3—Kurt Schulz, Detroit at Chicago, Sept. 24.
AFC: 3—Marcus Coleman, N.Y. Jets vs. Miami, Oct. 23.

Yards, season
AFC: 165—Chris McAlister, Baltimore.
NFC: 139—Ashley Ambrose, Atlanta.

Longest
NFC: 101—Bryant Westbrook, Detroit vs. New England, Nov. 23 (TD).
AFC: 98—Chris McAlister, Baltimore vs. N.Y. Jets, Dec. 24 (TD).

Touchdowns, season
AFC: 3—Eric Allen, Oakland.
NFC: 2—Sammy Knight, New Orleans.

Team leaders, interceptions
AFC:

Baltimore	6	Duane Starks
Buffalo	5	Keion Carpenter
Cincinnati	2	Tom Carter
		Takeo Spikes
Cleveland	3	Corey Fuller
Denver	6	Terrell Buckley
Indianapolis	4	Jeff Burris
Jacksonville	2	Rayna Stewart
		Donovin Darius
		Mike Logan
Kansas City	4	James Hasty
Miami	7	Brian Walker
New England	2	Ty Law
		Tebucky Jones
		Lawyer Milloy
N.Y. Jets	6	Victor Green
Oakland	6	Eric Allen
		William Thomas
Pittsburgh	5	Dewayne Washington
		Chad Scott
San Diego	6	Rodney Harrison
Seattle	4	Jay Bellamy
		Willie Williams
Tennessee	7	Samari Rolle

NFC:

Arizona	5	Aeneas Williams
Atlanta	6	Ray Buchanan
Carolina	5	Eric Davis
Chicago	3	Tony Parrish
Dallas	5	Phillippi Sparks
Detroit	7	Kurt Schulz
Green Bay	9	Darren Sharper
Minnesota	2	Kailee Wong
		Robert Tate
N.Y. Giants	6	Emmanuel McDaniel
New Orleans	5	Sammy Knight
Philadelphia	5	Troy Vincent
San Francisco	3	Zack Bronson
		Delmonico Montgomery
St. Louis	8	Dexter McCleon
Tampa Bay	7	Donnie Abraham
Washington	5	Champ Bailey

NFL LEADERS

Player, Team	No.	Yds.	Avg.	Long	TD
Sharper, Darren, Green Bay	9	109	12.1	47	0
McCleon, Dexter, St. Louis	8	28	3.5	23	0
Rolle, Samari, Tennessee*	7	140	20.0	t81	1
Abraham, Donnie, Tampa Bay	7	82	11.7	23	0
Walker, Brian, Miami*	7	80	11.4	31	0
Schulz, Kurt, Detroit	7	53	7.6	19	0
Allen, Eric, Oakland*	6	145	24.2	t50	3
Green, Victor, N.Y. Jets*	6	144	24.0	43	0
Westbrook, Bryant, Detroit	6	126	21.0	t101	1
Starks, Duane, Baltimore*	6	125	20.8	64	0
Buchanan, Ray, Atlanta	6	114	19.0	60	0
Buckley, Terrell, Denver*	6	110	18.3	33	1

Player, Team	No.	Yds.	Avg.	Long	TD
Harrison, Rodney, San Diego*	6	97	16.2	t63	1
Thomas, William, Oakland*	6	68	11.3	t46	1
McDaniel, Emmanuel, N.Y. Giants	6	30	5.0	17	0
Robinson, Damien, Tampa Bay	6	1	0.2	1	0

*AFC.
t—touchdown.
Leader based on most interceptions.

AFC

Player, Team	No.	Yds.	Avg.	Long	TD
Alexander, Brent, Pittsburgh	3	31	10.3	15	0
Allen, Eric, Oakland	6	145	24.2	t50	3
Bean, Robert, Cincinnati	1	0	0.0	0	0
Beasley, Aaron, Jacksonville	1	39	39.0	39	0
Beckett, Rogers, San Diego	1	7	7.0	7	0
Bell, Marcus, Seattle	1	30	30.0	30	0
Bellamy, Jay, Seattle	4	132	33.0	t84	1
Booker, Michael, Tennessee	1	2	2.0	2	0
Bowens, Tim, Miami	1	0	0.0	0	0
Boyer, Brant, Jacksonville	1	12	12.0	12	0
Brackens, Tony, Jacksonville	1	7	7.0	7	0
Brown, Chad, Seattle	1	0	0.0	0	0
Brown, Eric, Denver	3	9	3.0	9	0
Brown, Fakhir, San Diego	1	0	0.0	0	0
Browning, John, Kansas City	1	0	0.0	0	0
Bryant, Fernando, Jacksonville	1	0	0.0	0	0
Buckley, Terrell, Denver	6	110	18.3	33	1
Bulluck, Keith, Tennessee	1	8	8.0	t8	1
Burnett, Rob, Baltimore	1	3	3.0	3	0
Burris, Jeff, Indianapolis	4	38	9.5	t27	1
Bush, Lewis, Kansas City	1	33	33.0	33	0
Carpenter, Keion, Buffalo	5	63	12.6	22	0
Carter, Chris, Cincinnati	1	6	6.0	6	0
Carter, Tom, Cincinnati	2	40	20.0	30	0
Chapman, Lamar, Cleveland	1	0	0.0	0	0
Codie, Nikia, Pittsburgh	1	14	14.0	14	0
Coleman, Marcus, N.Y. Jets	4	6	1.5	7	0
Cota, Chad, Indianapolis	2	3	1.5	3	0
Cowart, Sam, Buffalo	2	4	2.0	2	0
Crockett, Ray, Denver	4	31	7.8	t26	1
Darius, Donovin, Jacksonville	2	26	13.0	21	0
Dennis, Pat, Kansas City	1	0	0.0	0	0
Dixon, Gerald, San Diego	1	36	36.0	t36	1
Dumas, Mike, San Diego	1	56	56.0	t56	1
Edwards, Donnie, Kansas City	2	45	22.5	t42	1
Ellis, Shaun, N.Y. Jets	1	1	1.0	1	0
Ellsworth, Percy, Cleveland	1	33	33.0	t33	1
Farrior, James, N.Y. Jets	1	0	0.0	0	0
Ferguson, Nick, N.Y. Jets	1	20	20.0	20	0
Flowers, Erik, Buffalo	1	0	0.0	0	0
Flowers, Lethon, Pittsburgh	1	0	0.0	0	0
Foley, Steve, Cincinnati	1	1	1.0	1	0
Frost, Scott, N.Y. Jets	1	1	1.0	1	0
Fuller, Corey, Cleveland	3	0	0.0	0	0
Glenn, Aaron, N.Y. Jets	4	34	8.5	34	0
Godfrey, Randall, Tennessee	2	25	12.5	t24	1
Green, Victor, N.Y. Jets	6	144	24.0	43	1
Hall, Cory, Cincinnati	1	12	12.0	12	0
Hardy, Kevin, Jacksonville	1	0	0.0	0	0
Harris, Antwan, New England	1	11	11.0	11	0
Harris, Corey, Baltimore	2	44	22.0	42	0
Harrison, Rodney, San Diego	6	97	16.2	t63	1
Hasty, James, Kansas City	4	53	13.3	38	0
Hayes, Chris, N.Y. Jets	1	0	0.0	0	0
Herring, Kim, Baltimore	3	74	24.7	30	0
Holecek, John, Buffalo	1	0	0.0	0	0
Holland, Darius, Cleveland	1	0	0.0	0	0
Irvin, Ken, Buffalo	2	1	0.5	1	0
James, Tory, Oakland	2	25	12.5	25	0
Jeffries, Greg, Miami	1	3	3.0	3	0
Jenkins, Billy, Denver	4	61	15.3	t36	1
Jenkins, DeRon, San Diego	1	16	16.0	16	0

Player, Team	No.	Yds.	Avg.	Long	TD
Johnson, Ellis, Indianapolis	1	-1	-1.0	0	0
Jones, Henry, Buffalo	2	45	22.5	t45	1
Jones, Tebucky, New England	2	20	10.0	20	0
Kacyvenski, Isaiah, Seattle	1	0	0.0	0	0
Kennedy, Cortez, Seattle	1	14	14.0	14	0
Kennedy, Kenoy, Denver	1	0	0.0	0	0
Kirkland, Levon, Pittsburgh	1	1	1.0	1	0
Koonce, George, Seattle	1	27	27.0	t27	1
Langham, Antonio, New England	1	24	24.0	24	0
Law, Ty, New England	2	32	16.0	32	0
Lewis, Darryll, San Diego	1	6	6.0	3	0
Lewis, Mo, N.Y. Jets	1	23	23.0	23	0
Lewis, Ray, Baltimore	2	1	0.5	1	0
Little, Earl, Cleveland	1	7	7.0	7	0
Logan, Mike, Jacksonville	2	14	7.0	14	0
Macklin, David, Indianapolis	2	35	17.5	35	0
Madison, Sam, Miami	5	80	16.0	34	0
Marion, Brock, Miami	5	72	14.4	24	0
McAlister, Chris, Baltimore	4	165	41.3	t98	1
McCutcheon, Daylon, Cleveland	1	20	20.0	20	0
Miller, Jamir, Cleveland	1	0	0.0	0	0
Milloy, Lawyer, New England	2	2	1.0	2	0
Mobley, John, Denver	1	9	9.0	9	0
Moore, Marty, Cleveland	1	3	3.0	3	0
Muhammad, Mustafah, Ind.	1	40	40.0	t40	1
Nickerson, Hardy, Jacksonville	1	10	10.0	10	0
Patton, Marvcus, Kansas City	2	39	19.5	t24	1
Peterson, Mike, Indianapolis	2	8	4.0	5	0
Phenix, Perry, Tennessee	1	87	87.0	t87	1
Poole, Tyrone, Indianapolis	1	1	1.0	1	0
Pope, Marquez, Oakland	2	25	12.5	25	0
Porter, Daryl, Buffalo	1	0	0.0	0	0
Porter, Joey, Pittsburgh	1	0	0.0	0	0
Rainer, Wali, Cleveland	1	5	5.0	5	0
Rogers, Sam, Buffalo	1	10	10.0	10	0
Rolle, Samari, Tennessee	7	140	20.0	t81	1
Romanowski, Bill, Denver	2	0	0.0	3	0
Ruff, Orlando, San Diego	1	18	18.0	18	0
Sanders, Lewis, Cleveland	1	0	0.0	0	0
Scott, Chad, Pittsburgh	5	49	9.8	33	0
Scott, Tony, N.Y. Jets	1	0	0.0	0	0
Seau, Junior, San Diego	2	2	1.0	2	0
Sharper, Jamie, Baltimore	1	45	45.0	45	0
Shaw, Terrance, Miami	1	0	0.0	0	0
Sidney, Dainon, Tennessee	3	19	6.3	19	0
Simmons, Anthony, Seattle	2	15	7.5	8	0
Smith, Otis, New England	1	56	56.0	56	0
Spencer, Jimmy, Denver	3	102	34.0	t79	2
Spikes, Takeo, Cincinnati	2	12	6.0	7	0
Springs, Shawn, Seattle	2	8	4.0	8	0
Starks, Duane, Baltimore	6	125	20.8	64	0
Stewart, Rayna, Jacksonville	2	37	18.5	24	0
Surtain, Patrick, Miami	5	55	11.0	43	0
Taves, Josh, Oakland	1	24	24.0	24	0
Taylor, Jason, Miami	1	2	2.0	2	0
Thomas, Henry, New England	1	16	16.0	16	0
Thomas, William, Oakland	6	68	11.3	t46	1
Thomas, Zach, Miami	1	0	0.0	0	0
Turner, Scott, San Diego	1	75	75.0	t75	1
Walker, Brian, Miami	7	80	11.4	31	0
Walker, Denard, Tennessee	2	4	2.0	4	0
Washington, Dewayne, Pittsburgh	5	59	11.8	31	0
Washington, Marcus, Indianapolis	1	1	1.0	1	0
Wesley, Greg, Kansas City	2	28	14.0	28	0
Williams, Darryll, Cincinnati	1	36	36.0	t36	1
Williams, Willie, Seattle	4	74	18.5	t69	1
Wilson, Al, Denver	3	21	7.0	20	0
Wilson, Jerry, Miami	1	19	19.0	19	0
Winfield, Antoine, Buffalo	1	8	8.0	8	0
Woods, Jerome, Kansas City	2	0	0.0	0	0
Woodson, Charles, Oakland	4	36	9.0	23	0
Woodson, Rod, Baltimore	4	20	5.0	18	0

t—touchdown.

NFC

Player, Team	No.	Yds.	Avg.	Long	TD
Abraham, Donnie, Tampa Bay	7	82	11.7	23	0
Aldridge, Allen, Detroit	1	4	4.0	4	0
Ambrose, Ashley, Atlanta	4	139	34.8	42	1
Armstead, Jessie, N.Y. Giants	1	-2	-2.0	0	0
Azumah, Jerry, Chicago	1	2	2.0	2	0
Bailey, Champ, Washington	5	48	9.6	48	0
Barber, Ronde, Tampa Bay	2	46	23.0	t37	1
Barrow, Micheal, N.Y. Giants	1	7	7.0	7	0
Bly, Dre', St. Louis	3	44	14.7	22	0
Boyd, Stephen, Detroit	1	0	0.0	0	0
Bradford, Ronnie, Atlanta	3	25	8.3	13	0
Bronson, Zack, San Francisco	3	75	25.0	43	0
Brooks, Derrick, Tampa Bay	1	34	34.0	t34	1
Brown, Corwin, Detroit	2	12	6.0	12	0
Brown, Mike, Chicago	1	35	35.0	t35	1
Buchanan, Ray, Atlanta	6	114	19.0	60	0
Butler, LeRoy, Green Bay	2	25	12.5	22	0
Caldwell, Mike, Philadelphia	1	26	26.0	t26	1
Campbell, Lamar, Detroit	1	42	42.0	t42	1
Carrier, Mark, Washington	1	30	30.0	30	0
Chavous, Corey, Arizona	1	0	0.0	0	0
Claiborne, Chris, Detroit	1	1	1.0	1	0
Davis, Eric, Carolina	5	14	2.8	8	0
Dawkins, Brian, Philadelphia	4	62	15.5	32	0
Dishman, Cris, Minnesota	1	0	0.0	0	0
Douglas, Hugh, Philadelphia	1	9	9.0	9	0
Duncan, Jamie, Tampa Bay	4	55	13.8	t31	1
Edwards, Antuan, Green Bay	2	4	2.0	4	0
Emmons, Carlos, Philadelphia	2	8	4.0	8	0
Evans, Doug, Carolina	2	17	8.5	17	0
Fair, Terry, Detroit	2	0	0.0	0	0
Fletcher, London, St. Louis	4	33	8.3	12	0
Fredrickson, Rob, Arizona	1	8	8.0	8	0
Garnes, Sam, N.Y. Giants	1	4	4.0	4	0
Gilbert, Sean, Carolina	1	0	0.0	0	0
Green, Darrell, Washington	3	35	11.7	33	0
Griffith, Robert, Minnesota	1	25	25.0	25	0
Harris, Al, Philadelphia	0	1	...	1	0
Harris, Walt, Chicago	2	35	17.5	t35	1
Hitchcock, Jimmy, Carolina	3	116	38.7	t88	1
Holliday, Vonnie, Green Bay	1	3	3.0	3	0
Howard, Darren, New Orleans	1	46	46.0	46	0
Keith, John, San Francisco	1	0	0.0	0	0
Kelly, Brian, Tampa Bay	1	9	9.0	t9	1
Kerney, Patrick, Atlanta	1	8	8.0	8	0
Knight, Sammy, New Orleans	5	68	13.6	t37	2
Lassiter, Kwamie, Arizona	1	11	11.0	11	0
Lyght, Todd, St. Louis	2	21	10.5	21	0
Lyle, Keith, St. Louis	1	9	9.0	9	0
Lynch, John, Tampa Bay	3	43	14.3	36	0
Mathis, Kevin, New Orleans	1	0	0.0	0	0
McBride, Tod, Green Bay	2	43	21.5	43	0
McCleon, Dexter, St. Louis	8	28	3.5	23	0
McDaniel, Emmanuel, N.Y. Giants	6	30	5.0	17	0
McKenzie, Mike, Green Bay	1	26	26.0	26	0
McNeil, Ryan, Dallas	2	4	2.0	4	0
McQuarters, R.W., Chicago	1	61	61.0	t61	1
Minter, Mike, Carolina	2	38	19.0	t30	1
Mitchell, Keith, New Orleans	1	40	40.0	t40	1
Mitchell, Kevin, Washington	1	0	0.0	0	0
Molden, Alex, New Orleans	3	24	8.0	24	0
Montgomery, Delmonico, S.F.	3	68	22.7	t46	1
Moore, Damon, Philadelphia	2	24	12.0	20	0
Navies, Hannibal, Carolina	1	0	0.0	0	0
Nguyen, Dat, Dallas	2	31	15.5	24	0
Oldham, Chris, New Orleans	2	0	0.0	0	0
Parrish, Tony, Chicago	3	81	27.0	t38	1
Perry, Darren, New Orleans	3	3	1.0	3	0
Peterson, Julian, San Francisco	2	33	16.5	31	0
Phillips, Ryan, N.Y. Giants	2	22	11.0	12	0
Prioleau, Pierson, San Francisco	1	13	13.0	13	0
Pritchett, Kelvin, Detroit	1	78	78.0	78	0
Quarles, Shelton, Tampa Bay	1	5	5.0	5	0
Reese, Izell, Dallas	2	60	30.0	46	0
Rice, Ron, Detroit	1	7	7.0	7	0
Robinson, Damien, Tampa Bay	6	1	0.2	1	0
Robinson, Eugene, Carolina	1	0	0.0	0	0
Sanders, Deion, Washington	4	91	22.8	32	0
Schulz, Kurt, Detroit	7	53	7.6	19	0
Sehorn, Jason, N.Y. Giants	2	32	16.0	32	0
Shade, Sam, Washington	2	15	7.5	15	0
Sharper, Darren, Green Bay	9	109	12.1	47	0
Shepherd, Jacoby, St. Louis	1	0	0.0	0	0
Smith, Darrin, New Orleans	2	56	28.0	t41	1
Sparks, Phillippi, Dallas	5	59	11.8	43	0
Stephens, Reggie, N.Y. Giants	3	4	1.3	4	0
Stevens, Matt, Washington	1	0	0.0	0	0
Tate, Robert, Minnesota	2	12	6.0	12	0
Taylor, Bobby, Philadelphia	3	64	21.3	38	0
Thibodeaux, Keith, Minnesota	1	0	0.0	0	0
Thomas, Dave, N.Y. Giants	1	0	0.0	0	0
Thomas, Orlando, Minnesota	1	0	0.0	0	0
Tillman, Pat, Arizona	1	30	30.0	27	0
Trotter, Jeremiah, Philadelphia	1	27	27.0	t27	1
Tubbs, Winfred, San Francisco	1	11	11.0	11	0
Urlacher, Brian, Chicago	2	19	9.5	19	0
Vincent, Troy, Philadelphia	5	34	6.8	17	0
Walker, Darnell, Detroit	1	5	5.0	5	0
Walker, Marquis, Detroit	1	12	12.0	12	0
Walz, Zack, Arizona	1	0	0.0	0	0
Weary, Fred, New Orleans	2	27	13.5	27	0
Webster, Jason, San Francisco	2	78	39.0	t70	1
Wells, Dean, Carolina	1	14	14.0	14	0
Wells, Mike, Chicago	1	21	21.0	21	0
Westbrook, Bryant, Detroit	6	126	21.0	t101	1
Williams, Aeneas, Arizona	5	102	20.4	48	0
Williams, Charlie, Dallas	1	0	0.0	0	0
Williams, Elijah, Atlanta	1	1	1.0	1	0
Williams, Shaun, N.Y. Giants	3	52	17.3	40	0
Williams, Tyrone, Green Bay	4	105	26.3	46	1
Wong, Kailee, Minnesota	2	28	14.0	14	0
Woodall, Lee, Carolina	1	0	0.0	0	0
Woodson, Darren, Dallas	2	12	6.0	12	0
Wortham, Barron, Dallas	2	1	0.5	1	0

t—touchdown.

SACKS

AFC

Team	Sacks	Yards
Tennessee	55	338
Kansas City	51	266
Miami	48	270
Denver	44	251
Oakland	43	278
Buffalo	42	308
Cleveland	42	270
Indianapolis	42	252
Jacksonville	40	247
N.Y. Jets	40	234
San Diego	39	249
Pittsburgh	39	229
Baltimore	35	178
New England	29	172
Seattle	27	152
Cincinnati	26	168
AFC total	642	3862
AFC average	40.1	241.4

NFC

Team	Sacks	Yards
New Orleans	66	378
Tampa Bay	55	332
St. Louis	51	288
Philadelphia	50	291
Washington	45	283
N.Y. Giants	44	279
San Francisco	38	270
Green Bay	38	244
Chicago	36	230
Minnesota	31	214
Atlanta	31	142
Detroit	28	162
Carolina	27	226
Dallas	25	189
Arizona	25	135
NFC total	590	3663
NFC average	39.3	244.2
NFL total	1232	7525
NFL average	39.7	242.7

INDIVIDUAL

BESTS OF THE SEASON

Sacks, season
NFC: 17.0—La'Roi Glover, New Orleans.
AFC: 16.5—Trace Armstrong, Miami.

Sacks, game
NFC: 4.0—Marcus Jones, Tampa Bay vs. Detroit, Oct. 19.
AFC: 3.5—Trace Armstrong, Miami vs. Buffalo, Oct. 8.

NFL LEADERS

Player, Team	No.
Glover, La'Roi, New Orleans	17.0
Sapp, Warren, Tampa Bay	16.5
Armstrong, Trace, Miami*	16.5
Douglas, Hugh, Philadelphia	15.0
Taylor, Jason, Miami*	14.5
Hicks, Eric, Kansas City*	14.0
Gildon, Jason, Pittsburgh*	13.5
Jones, Marcus, Tampa Bay	13.0
Coleman, Marco, Washington	12.0
Pryce, Trevor, Denver*	12.0
Johnson, Joe, New Orleans	12.0
Kearse, Jevon, Tennessee*	11.5
Wistrom, Grant, St. Louis	11.0
Howard, Darren, New Orleans	11.0
Wiley, Marcellus, Buffalo*	10.5
Porter, Joey, Pittsburgh*	10.5
Burnett, Rob, Baltimore*	10.5
Carter, Kevin, St. Louis	10.5
*AFC.	

AFC

Player, Team	No.
Abdullah, Rahim, Cleveland	2.0
Abraham, John, N.Y. Jets	4.5
Adams, Sam, Baltimore	2.0
Alexander, Brent, Pittsburgh	1.5
Alexander, Elijah, Oakland	2.0
Allen, Eric, Oakland	1.0

Player, Team	No.
Armstrong, Trace, Miami	16.5
Bartee, William, Kansas City	1.0
Battles, Ainsley, Pittsburgh	1.0
Beasley, Aaron, Jacksonville	5.0
Beckett, Rogers, San Diego	1.0
Bellamy, Jay, Seattle	2.0
Belser, Jason, Indianapolis	5.0
Bennett, Cornelius, Indianapolis	3.0
Biekert, Greg, Oakland	2.0
Bishop, Blaine, Tennessee	2.5
Boulware, Peter, Baltimore	7.0
Bowens, Tim, Miami	2.5
Boyer, Brant, Jacksonville	3.5
Brackens, Tony, Jacksonville	7.5
Bratzke, Chad, Indianapolis	7.5
Bromell, Lorenzo, Miami	2.0
Brown, Chad, Seattle	6.0
Brown, Cornell, Baltimore	3.0
Brown, Courtney, Cleveland	4.5
Brown, Eric, Denver	1.0
Browning, John, Kansas City	6.0
Bruschi, Tedy, New England	1.0
Bryant, Tony, Oakland	5.5
Burnett, Rob, Baltimore	10.5
Burris, Jeff, Indianapolis	3.0
Burton, Shane, N.Y. Jets	1.0
Bush, Lewis, Kansas City	1.0
Carter, Chris, Cincinnati	1.0
Chester, Larry, Indianapolis	2.5
Clemons, Duane, Kansas City	7.5
Cochran, Antonio, Seattle	0.5
Coleman, Roderick, Oakland	6.0
Colinet, Stalin, Cleveland	3.5
Copeland, John, Cincinnati	1.0
Cowart, Sam, Buffalo	5.5
Cox, Bryan, N.Y. Jets	6.0
Crockett, Ray, Denver	1.0
Curtis, Canute, Cincinnati	2.0
Darius, Donovin, Jacksonville	1.0
Dingle, Adrian, San Diego	2.5

Player, Team	No.	Player, Team	No.
Dixon, Gerald, San Diego	5.0	Newman, Keith, Buffalo	8.0
Dorsett, Anthony, Oakland	1.0	Nickerson, Hardy, Jacksonville	1.0
Dumas, Mike, San Diego	1.0	Owens, Rich, Miami	0.5
Eaton, Chad, New England	2.5	Parrella, John, San Diego	7.0
Edwards, Donnie, Kansas City	1.0	Patton, Marvcus, Kansas City	1.0
Ellis, Shaun, N.Y. Jets	8.5	Payne, Seth, Jacksonville	2.0
Embray, Keith, Tennessee	3.5	Phifer, Roman, N.Y. Jets	4.0
Farrior, James, N.Y. Jets	1.0	Pittman, Kavika, Denver	7.0
Favors, Gregory, Tennessee	5.5	Pope, Marquez, Oakland	1.0
Ferguson, Jason, N.Y. Jets	1.0	Porter, Joey, Pittsburgh	10.5
Fisk, Jason, Tennessee	2.0	Price, Shawn, Buffalo	1.0
Flowers, Erik, Buffalo	2.0	Pryce, Trevor, Denver	12.0
Flowers, Lethon, Pittsburgh	1.0	Rainer, Wali, Cleveland	1.0
Foley, Steve, Cincinnati	4.0	Reagor, Montae, Denver	2.0
Fontenot, Al, San Diego	4.0	Robinson, Eddie, Tennessee	4.0
Ford, Henry, Tennessee	2.0	Rodgers, Derrick, Miami	0.5
Frost, Scott, N.Y. Jets	1.0	Rogers, Sam, Buffalo	5.0
Gardener, Daryl, Miami	2.5	Rogers, Tyrone, Cleveland	2.0
Gibson, Oliver, Cincinnati	4.0	Rolle, Samari, Tennessee	1.5
Gildon, Jason, Pittsburgh	13.5	Romanowski, Bill, Denver	3.5
Godfrey, Randall, Tennessee	3.0	Ross, Adrian, Cincinnati	1.0
Gold, Ian, Denver	2.0	Roye, Orpheus, Cleveland	2.0
Haley, Jermaine, Miami	1.5	Rusk, Reggie, San Diego	1.0
Hall, Cory, Cincinnati	4.0	Russell, Darrell, Oakland	3.0
Hamilton, Bobby, New England	1.5	Salave'a, Joe, Tennessee	4.0
Hansen, Phil, Buffalo	2.0	Scioli, Brad, Indianapolis	2.0
Hardy, Kevin, Jacksonville	3.0	Seau, Junior, San Diego	3.5
Harris, Antwan, New England	1.0	Serwanga, Kato, New England	2.0
Harrison, Rodney, San Diego	6.0	Simmons, Anthony, Seattle	4.0
Hasselbach, Harald, Denver	2.5	Simmons, Brian, Cincinnati	1.0
Hasty, James, Kansas City	1.0	Sinclair, Michael, Seattle	3.5
Herring, Kim, Baltimore	1.0	Slade, Chris, New England	4.0
Hicks, Eric, Kansas City	14.0	Smeenge, Joel, Jacksonville	6.0
Holland, Darius, Cleveland	1.0	Smith, Aaron, Pittsburgh	4.0
Hollier, Dwight, Indianapolis	1.0	Smith, Marquis, Cleveland	1.0
Holmes, Earl, Pittsburgh	1.0	Smith, Robaire, Tennessee	2.5
Holmes, Kenny, Tennessee	8.0	Spearman, Armegis, Cincinnati	1.0
Holsey, Bernard, Indianapolis	2.0	Spencer, Jimmy, Denver	1.0
Jackson, Grady, Oakland	8.0	Spicer, Paul, Jacksonville	1.0
Johnson, Ellis, Indianapolis	5.0	Spikes, Takeo, Cincinnati	2.0
Johnson, Ted, New England	0.5	Spires, Greg, New England	6.0
Johnstone, Lance, Oakland	3.5	Spriggs, Marcus, Cleveland	2.0
Jones, Fred, Buffalo	1.0	Steele, Glen, Cincinnati	2.0
Jones, Lenoy, Cleveland	2.5	Surtain, Patrick, Miami	1.0
Jones, Marvin, N.Y. Jets	1.0	Tanuvasa, Maa, Denver	4.0
Kearse, Jevon, Tennessee	11.5	Taves, Josh, Oakland	3.0
Kennedy, Cortez, Seattle	1.0	Taylor, Jason, Miami	14.5
Killens, Terry, Tennessee	1.0	Thomas, Henry, New England	4.5
King, Lamar, Seattle	6.0	Thomas, Mark, Indianapolis	5.0
Koonce, George, Seattle	1.5	Thomas, William, Oakland	1.0
LaBounty, Matt, Seattle	0.5	Thomas, Zach, Miami	1.5
Larsen, Leif, Buffalo	1.0	Thompson, Mike, Cincinnati	1.0
Lewis, Darryll, San Diego	1.0	Thornton, John, Tennessee	4.0
Lewis, Mo, N.Y. Jets	10.0	Townsend, Deshea, Pittsburgh	3.5
Lewis, Ray, Baltimore	3.0	Trapp, James, Baltimore	2.0
Logan, Mike, Jacksonville	1.0	Traylor, Keith, Denver	1.0
Lyle, Rick, N.Y. Jets	1.0	Upshaw, Regan, Oakland	6.0
Maslowski, Mike, Kansas City	2.0	von Oelhoffen, Kimo, Pittsburgh	1.0
McCrary, Michael, Baltimore	6.5	Vrabel, Mike, Pittsburgh	1.0
McCutcheon, Daylon, Cleveland	4.0	Walker, Brian, Miami	2.0
McGinest, Willie, New England	6.0	Walker, Gary, Jacksonville	5.0
McGlockton, Chester, Kansas City	4.0	Washington, Marcus, Indianapolis	2.0
McKenzie, Keith, Cleveland	8.0	Washington, Ted, Buffalo	2.5
Meier, Rob, Jacksonville	0.5	Wesley, Greg, Kansas City	1.0
Mickell, Darren, San Diego	6.0	Whittington, Bernard, Indianapolis	1.0
Miller, Arnold, Cleveland	1.5	Wiley, Marcellus, Buffalo	10.5
Miller, Jamir, Cleveland	5.0	Williams, Dan, Kansas City	7.5
Mixon, Kenny, Miami	2.5	Williams, Jamal, San Diego	1.0
Mobley, John, Denver	2.0	Williams, Josh, Indianapolis	3.0
Moore, Corey, Buffalo	1.0	Williams, Pat, Buffalo	2.5
Moore, Marty, Cleveland	1.0	Williams, Tyrone, Kansas City	2.0

Player, Team / No.

Player, Team	No.
Williams, Willie, Seattle	1.0
Wilson, Al, Denver	5.0
Wilson, Jerry, Miami	0.5
Wilson, Reinard, Cincinnati	3.0
Wiltz, Jason, N.Y. Jets	1.0
Woods, Jerome, Kansas City	2.0
Wynn, Renaldo, Jacksonville	3.5

NFC

Player, Team	No.
Agnew, Ray, St. Louis	4.0
Ahanotu, Chidi, Tampa Bay	3.5
Aldridge, Allen, Detroit	2.0
Armstead, Jessie, N.Y. Giants	5.0
Arrington, LaVar, Washington	4.0
Barber, Ronde, Tampa Bay	5.5
Barber, Shawn, Washington	2.0
Barrow, Micheal, N.Y. Giants	3.5
Bly, Dre', St. Louis	1.0
Bowens, David, Green Bay	3.5
Boyd, Stephen, Detroit	0.5
Brooking, Keith, Atlanta	1.0
Brooks, Derrick, Tampa Bay	1.0
Brown, Corwin, Detroit	0.5
Buckner, Brentson, San Francisco	7.0
Burrough, John, Minnesota	2.0
Bush, Devin, St. Louis	1.0
Butler, LeRoy, Green Bay	2.0
Cannida, James, Tampa Bay	2.0
Carter, Kevin, St. Louis	10.5
Carter, Marty, Atlanta	2.0
Claiborne, Chris, Detroit	0.5
Clarke, Phil, New Orleans	1.0
Coleman, Marco, Washington	12.0
Collins, Todd, St. Louis	1.0
Colvin, Rosevelt, Chicago	3.0
Crockett, Henri, Atlanta	2.0
Culpepper, Brad, Chicago	1.0
Daniels, Phillip, Chicago	6.0
Darling, James, Philadelphia	0.5
Davis, Russell, Arizona	0.5
Dawkins, Brian, Philadelphia	2.0
Dotson, Santana, Green Bay	6.0
Douglas, Hugh, Philadelphia	15.0
Draft, Chris, Atlanta	1.0
Dronett, Shane, Atlanta	1.0
Ekuban, Ebenezer, Dallas	6.5
Ellis, Greg, Dallas	3.0
Elliss, Luther, Detroit	3.0
Emmons, Carlos, Philadelphia	0.5
Engelberger, John, San Francisco	3.0
Farr, D'Marco, St. Louis	1.0
Fields, Mark, New Orleans	2.0
Flanigan, Jim, Chicago	4.0
Fletcher, London, St. Louis	5.5
Folston, James, Arizona	2.0
Fredrickson, Rob, Arizona	1.0
Gardner, Barry, Philadelphia	1.0
Garnes, Sam, N.Y. Giants	1.0
Gbaja-Biamila, Kabeer, Green Bay	1.5
Gilbert, Sean, Carolina	4.0
Glover, La'Roi, New Orleans	17.0
Grasmanis, Paul, Philadelphia	3.5
Griffin, Cornelius, N.Y. Giants	5.0
Griffith, Robert, Minnesota	1.0
Hall, James, Detroit	1.0
Hall, Travis, Atlanta	4.5
Hambrick, Darren, Dallas	1.0
Hamilton, Keith, N.Y. Giants	10.0
Hand, Norman, New Orleans	3.0
Harris, Bernardo, Green Bay	2.0

Player, Team / No.

Player, Team	No.
Harris, Sean, Chicago	1.0
Harrison, Nolan, Washington	1.0
Heard, Ronnie, San Francisco	2.0
Hobgood-Chittick, Nate, St. Louis	1.0
Holliday, Vonnie, Green Bay	5.0
Hovan, Chris, Minnesota	2.0
Howard, Darren, New Orleans	11.0
Hunt, Cletidus, Green Bay	5.0
Issa, Jabari, Arizona	1.0
Jackson, Tyoka, Tampa Bay	2.0
Jasper, Edward, Atlanta	3.5
Johnson, Joe, New Orleans	12.0
Jones, Cedric, N.Y. Giants	3.5
Jones, Greg, Washington	1.0
Jones, James, Detroit	3.0
Jones, Marcus, Tampa Bay	13.0
Jones, Mike, St. Louis	2.0
Kalu, Ndukwe, Washington	1.0
Keith, John, San Francisco	1.0
Kerney, Patrick, Atlanta	2.5
Killings, Cedric, San Francisco	3.0
Kirschke, Travis, Detroit	0.5
Knight, Sammy, New Orleans	2.0
Knight, Tom, Arizona	1.0
Lang, Kenard, Washington	3.0
Lett, Leon, Dallas	2.5
Little, Leonard, St. Louis	5.0
Lyght, Todd, St. Louis	1.0
Lynch, John, Tampa Bay	1.0
Lyon, Billy, Green Bay	1.0
Maddox, Mark, Arizona	1.5
Mamula, Mike, Philadelphia	5.5
Mason, Eddie, Washington	2.0
McBurrows, Gerald, Atlanta	2.0
McCleon, Dexter, St. Louis	2.0
McDaniel, Ed, Minnesota	2.0
McDaniel, Emmanuel, N.Y. Giants	1.0
McFarland, Anthony, Tampa Bay	6.5
McGarrahan, Scott, Green Bay	0.5
McKinnon, Ronald, Arizona	4.0
McQuarters, R.W., Chicago	1.0
Minter, Mike, Carolina	2.0
Mitchell, Keith, New Orleans	6.5
Mitchell, Kevin, Washington	1.0
Montgomery, Delmonico, San Francisco	0.5
Monty, Pete, N.Y. Giants	2.0
Morabito, Tim, Carolina	2.0
Moran, Sean, St. Louis	2.0
Navies, Hannibal, Carolina	2.0
Noble, Brandon, Dallas	1.0
Okeafor, Chike, San Francisco	2.0
Oldham, Chris, New Orleans	2.0
Ottis, Brad, Arizona	1.0
Parrish, Tony, Chicago	2.0
Paup, Bryce, Minnesota	2.0
Peter, Christian, N.Y. Giants	1.0
Peter, Jason, Carolina	2.0
Peterson, Julian, San Francisco	4.0
Phillips, Ryan, N.Y. Giants	1.5
Pleasant, Anthony, San Francisco	2.0
Porcher, Robert, Detroit	8.0
Posey, Jeff, San Francisco	0.5
Pritchett, Kelvin, Detroit	2.5
Quarles, Shelton, Tampa Bay	2.0
Randle, John, Minnesota	8.0
Rice, Simeon, Arizona	7.5
Robbins, Fred, Minnesota	1.0
Robinson, Bryan, Chicago	4.5
Rucker, Mike, Carolina	2.5
Sapp, Warren, Tampa Bay	16.5
Sawyer, Talance, Minnesota	6.0

Player, Team	No.	Player, Team	No.
Schulters, Lance, San Francisco	0.5	Tuinei, Van, Chicago	1.0
Scroggins, Tracy, Detroit	6.5	Ulmer, Artie, San Francisco	1.0
Shade, Sam, Washington	1.0	Underwood, Dimitrius, Dallas	4.0
Sharper, Darren, Green Bay	1.0	Urlacher, Brian, Chicago	8.0
Simmons, Clyde, Chicago	0.5	Vincent, Troy, Philadelphia	1.0
Simon, Corey, Philadelphia	9.5	Wadsworth, Andre, Arizona	1.0
Simoneau, Mark, Atlanta	0.5	Wayne, Nate, Green Bay	2.0
Smith, Brady, Atlanta	4.5	Weary, Fred, New Orleans	2.0
Smith, Bruce, Washington	10.0	Wells, Mike, Chicago	1.0
Smith, Darrin, New Orleans	2.0	White, Reggie, Carolina	5.5
Smith, Derek, Washington	1.0	White, Steve, Tampa Bay	2.0
Smith, Frankie, Chicago	2.0	Whitehead, William, New Orleans	5.5
Smith, Mark, Arizona	3.0	Whiting, Brandon, Philadelphia	3.5
Spellman, Alonzo, Dallas	5.0	Wiley, Chuck, Atlanta	4.0
Strahan, Michael, N.Y. Giants	9.5	Wilkinson, Dan, Washington	3.5
Stubblefield, Dana, Washington	2.5	Williams, Brian, Green Bay	0.5
Styles, Lorenzo, St. Louis	1.0	Williams, Jay, Carolina	6.0
Swann, Eric, Carolina	1.0	Williams, K.D., Green Bay	0.5
Swayda, Shawn, Atlanta	1.5	Williams, Tony, Minnesota	4.0
Thierry, John, Green Bay	6.5	Wilson, Troy, Chicago	1.0
Thomas, Hollis, Philadelphia	4.0	Wistrom, Grant, St. Louis	11.0
Thomas, Orlando, Minnesota	1.0	Wong, Kailee, Minnesota	2.0
Tillman, Pat, Arizona	1.5	Young, Bryant, San Francisco	9.5
Trotter, Jeremiah, Philadelphia	3.0	Zellner, Peppi, Dallas	2.0
Tubbs, Winfred, San Francisco	2.0	Zgonina, Jeff, St. Louis	2.0

2000 STATISTICS *Sacks*

FUMBLES

AFC

Team	Fum.	Own Fum. Rec.	Own Fum. *O.B.	Own Fum. Lost	TD	Opp Fum. Rec.	TD	†Yards	Total Rec.
Baltimore	26	16	3	7	0	26	0	4	42
Miami	12	2	2	8	0	13	2	41	15
Cleveland	21	12	0	9	0	13	0	38	25
Oakland	18	8	1	9	0	16	1	88	24
New England	23	13	0	10	0	13	0	6	26
Kansas City	23	10	2	11	0	14	0	9	24
N.Y. Jets	18	7	0	11	0	14	0	1	21
Pittsburgh	24	13	0	11	0	17	2	30	30
Buffalo	28	15	1	12	2	13	0	128	28
Denver	26	11	2	13	0	17	2	70	28
Indianapolis	20	5	2	13	0	8	1	53	13
Tennessee	24	10	0	14	0	13	1	-1	23
Jacksonville	27	12	1	14	0	18	0	80	30
Seattle	35	17	1	17	0	10	2	84	27
San Diego	38	17	1	20	0	6	0	34	23
Cincinnati	37	13	3	21	0	12	0	-36	25
AFC total	400	181	19	200	2	223	11	629	404
AFC average	25.0	11.3	1.2	12.5	0.1	13.9	0.7	39.3	25.3

*Fumbled out of bounds.

†Includes all fumble yardage (aborted plays and recoveries of own and opponents' fumbles).

NFC

Team	Fum.	Own Fum. Rec.	Own Fum. *O.B.	Own Fum. Lost	TD	Opp Fum. Rec.	TD	†Yards	Total Rec.
San Francisco	22	12	2	8	0	8	0	11	20
Minnesota	26	15	1	10	0	10	0	-11	25
New Orleans	26	14	1	11	0	15	1	80	28
N.Y. Giants	25	12	2	11	0	11	0	-5	23
Tampa Bay	16	5	0	11	0	16	1	42	21
Washington	22	10	1	11	0	16	0	-29	26
Detroit	21	7	2	12	1	16	0	-2	23
St. Louis	24	12	0	12	1	6	1	118	18
Chicago	27	13	1	13	0	9	0	-2	22
Atlanta	27	11	2	14	0	10	0	-4	21
Philadelphia	22	8	0	14	0	12	0	2	20
Carolina	25	7	2	16	0	20	0	7	27
Green Bay	30	12	1	17	0	7	0	49	19
Dallas	31	12	1	18	0	9	0	3	21
Arizona	32	11	1	20	0	10	1	98	21
NFC total	376	161	17	198	2	175	4	357	336
NFC average	25.1	10.7	1.1	13.2	0.1	11.7	0.3	23.8	22.4
NFL total	776	342	36	398	4	398	15	986	740
NFL average	25.0	11.0	1.2	12.8	0.1	12.8	0.5	31.8	23.9

INDIVIDUAL

BESTS OF THE SEASON

Fumbles, season

AFC: 17—Jon Kitna, Seattle.
NFC: 11—Daunte Culpepper, Minnesota.

Fumbles, game

AFC: 4—Jon Kitna, Seattle vs. Buffalo, Dec. 23.
NFC: 4—Cade McNown, Chicago vs. Detroit, Sept. 24.

Own fumbles recovered, season

AFC: 9—Jon Kitna, Seattle.
NFC: 5—Tiki Barber, N.Y. Giants; Daunte Culpepper, Minnesota.

Own fumbles recovered, game

AFC: 3—Jon Kitna, Seattle at Jacksonville, Nov. 12; Doug Pederson, Cleveland vs. Philadelphia, Dec. 10.
NFC: 3—Tiki Barber, N.Y. Giants vs. Philadelphia, Oct. 29; Kyle Turley, New Orleans vs. St. Louis, Dec. 24.

Opponents' fumbles recovered, season

AFC: 5—Rob Burnett, Baltimore; Marquez Pope, Oakland.
NFC: 5—Doug Evans, Carolina.

Opponents' fumbles recovered, game

AFC: 2—Sam Cowart, Buffalo vs. N.Y. Jets, Oct. 29; Michael Sinclair, Seattle at Atlanta, Dec. 3; Lethon Flowers, Pittsburgh vs. Oakland, Dec. 3; Takeo Spikes, Cincinnati at Philadelphia, Dec. 24.

NFC: 2—Doug Evans, Carolina at St. Louis, Nov. 5; Keith Mitchell, New Orleans at Carolina, Nov. 12; Michael Strahan, N.Y. Giants at Arizona, Nov. 26; Shawn Barber, Washington vs. N.Y. Giants, Dec. 3.

Yards returning fumbles, season
NFC: 103—Aeneas Williams, Arizona.
AFC: 74—Darrien Gordon, Oakland.

Longest fumble return
NFC: 104—Aeneas Williams, Arizona vs. Washington, Nov. 5 (TD).
AFC: 74—Darrien Gordon, Oakland vs. Carolina, Dec. 24 (TD).

AFC

Player, Team	Fum.	Own Rec.	Opp. Rec.	Yds.	Tot. Rec.	TD
Adams, Sam, Baltimore	0	0	1	0	1	0
Albright, Ethan, Buffalo	0	0	1	19	1	0
Alexander, Brent, Pittsburgh	0	0	1	0	1	0
Alexander, Shaun, Seattle	2	0	0	0	0	0
Anders, Kimble, Kansas City	1	0	0	0	0	0
Anderson, Mike, Denver	4	0	0	0	0	0
Anderson, Richie, N.Y. Jets	2	0	0	0	0	0
Anderson, Willie, Cincinnati	0	1	0	0	1	0
Andruzzi, Joe, New England	0	1	0	2	1	0
Atkins, Larry, Kansas City	0	0	1	0	1	0
Bailey, Robert, Baltimore	0	0	1	27	1	0
Banks, Tony, Baltimore	5	2	0	-2	2	0
Barndt, Tom, Cincinnati	0	0	1	0	1	0
Battles, Ainsley, Pittsburgh	1	2	0	-1	2	0
Baxter, Fred, N.Y. Jets	0	1	0	0	1	0
Beasley, Aaron, Jacksonville	0	0	1	0	1	0
Becht, Anthony, N.Y. Jets	1	0	0	0	0	0
Belser, Jason, Indianapolis	0	0	1	0	1	0
Bennett, Brandon, Cincinnati	2	1	0	0	1	0
Bennett, Cornelius, Ind.	0	0	1	0	1	0
Bettis, Jerome, Pittsburgh	1	1	0	1	1	0
Biekert, Greg, Oakland	0	0	2	0	2	0
Bjornson, Eric, New England	0	1	0	0	1	0
Bledsoe, Drew, New England	9	3	0	-20	3	0
Blevins, Tony, Indianapolis	0	0	1	0	1	0
Brackens, Tony, Jacksonville	0	0	2	15	2	0
Braham, Rich, Cincinnati	1	0	0	-16	0	0
Branch, Calvin, Oakland	0	1	0	6	1	0
Bratzke, Chad, Indianapolis	0	0	1	0	1	0
Brigance, O.J., Baltimore	0	0	1	0	1	0
Brown, Chad, Seattle	0	0	3	16	3	1
Brown, Cornell, Baltimore	1	0	0	0	0	0
Brown, Courtney, Cleveland	0	0	1	0	1	0
Brown, Eric, Denver	0	0	3	8	3	0
Brown, Troy, New England	2	0	0	0	0	0
Browning, John, Kansas City	0	0	1	0	1	0
Brunell, Mark, Jacksonville	7	3	0	-2	3	0
Bryant, Fernando, Jacksonville	0	0	1	5	1	0
Bryant, Tony, Oakland	0	0	1	3	1	0
Bryson, Shawn, Buffalo	1	0	0	0	0	0
Bundren, Jim, Cleveland	0	1	0	0	1	0
Burnett, Rob, Baltimore	0	0	5	0	5	0
Burns, Keith, Denver	0	0	1	0	1	0
Burress, Plaxico, Pittsburgh	1	0	0	0	0	0
Burton, Shane, N.Y. Jets	0	0	1	4	1	0
Bush, Lewis, Kansas City	0	1	0	0	1	0
Carter, Chris, Cincinnati	0	0	1	0	1	0
Chanoine, Roger, Cleveland	0	1	0	0	1	0
Chapman, Lamar, Cleveland	1	0	0	0	0	0
Chester, Larry, Indianapolis	0	0	1	0	1	0
Chiaverini, Darrin, Cleveland	1	0	0	0	0	0
Chrebet, Wayne, N.Y. Jets	0	1	0	0	1	0
Clark, Danny, Jacksonville	0	0	2	44	2	0
Clemons, Duane, Kansas City	0	0	1	0	1	0
Coleman, KaRon, Denver	2	1	0	0	1	0
Coleman, Marcus, N.Y. Jets	1	0	0	0	0	0
Coleman, Roderick, Oakland	0	0	1	0	1	0

Player, Team	Fum.	Own Rec.	Opp. Rec.	Yds.	Tot. Rec.	TD
Colinet, Stalin, Cleveland	0	0	1	0	1	0
Copeland, John, Cincinnati	0	0	1	4	1	0
Couch, Tim, Cleveland	2	0	0	-8	0	0
Cowart, Sam, Buffalo	0	0	2	3	2	0
Cox, Bryan, N.Y. Jets	0	0	2	0	2	0
Craft, Jason, Jacksonville	0	1	0	4	1	0
Crockett, Zack, Oakland	0	0	1	0	1	0
Curtis, Canute, Cincinnati	0	0	1	0	1	0
Dalton, Antico, New England	0	1	0	0	1	0
Davis, Reginald, San Diego	0	1	0	0	1	0
Davis, Terrell, Denver	1	0	0	0	0	0
Dennis, Pat, Kansas City	0	0	2	-5	2	0
Denson, Autry, Miami	1	0	0	0	0	0
Dilfer, Trent, Baltimore	8	1	0	-7	1	0
Dilger, Ken, Indianapolis	1	0	0	0	0	0
Dillon, Corey, Cincinnati	4	0	0	0	0	0
Dixon, Gerald, San Diego	0	0	1	0	1	0
Dudley, Rickey, Oakland	1	1	0	0	1	0
Duffy, Roger, Pittsburgh	1	0	0	-10	0	0
Dunn, Damon, N.Y. Jets	1	0	0	0	0	0
Edwards, Donnie, Kansas City	0	0	1	11	1	0
Edwards, Marc, Cleveland	2	1	0	0	1	0
Edwards, Troy, Pittsburgh	1	0	0	0	0	0
Ellis, Shaun, N.Y. Jets	0	0	2	2	2	0
Ellsworth, Percy, Cleveland	0	0	1	16	1	0
Emanuel, Bert, Miami	1	0	0	0	0	0
Faneca, Alan, Pittsburgh	0	1	0	0	1	0
Farmer, Danny, Cincinnati	1	0	0	0	0	0
Farrior, James, N.Y. Jets	0	1	0	0	1	0
Faulk, Kevin, New England	6	1	0	0	1	0
Fauria, Christian, Seattle	1	1	0	0	1	0
Fazande, Jermaine, San Diego	1	1	0	0	1	0
Fiedler, Jay, Miami	2	0	0	-8	0	0
Fina, John, Buffalo	0	1	0	0	1	0
Finn, Jim, Indianapolis	1	0	0	0	0	0
Fletcher, Terrell, San Diego	2	0	0	0	0	0
Flowers, Lethon, Pittsburgh	0	0	3	0	3	0
Flutie, Doug, Buffalo	5	2	0	-9	2	0
Flynn, Mike, Baltimore	1	2	0	-18	2	0
Foley, Steve, Cincinnati	0	0	1	0	1	0
Ford, Henry, Tennessee	0	0	1	30	1	1
Fordham, Todd, Jacksonville	1	0	0	0	0	0
Fortin, Roman, San Diego	3	0	0	-1	0	0
Frerotte, Gus, Denver	5	0	0	0	0	0
Friedman, Lennie, Denver	0	2	0	0	2	0
Fuller, Corey, Cleveland	0	0	1	0	1	0
Gadsden, Oronde, Miami	0	1	1	0	2	0
Gamble, Trent, Miami	0	0	1	0	1	0
Gandy, Wayne, Pittsburgh	0	1	0	0	1	0
Gannon, Rich, Oakland	9	2	0	-1	2	0
Gaylor, Trevor, San Diego	0	1	0	13	1	0
George, Eddie, Tennessee	6	2	0	0	2	0
George, Tony, New England	0	1	1	24	2	0
Gildon, Jason, Pittsburgh	0	0	4	22	4	1
Godfrey, Randall, Tennessee	0	0	1	0	1	0
Goff, Mike, Cincinnati	0	2	0	0	2	0
Gold, Ian, Denver	0	1	1	0	2	0
Gonzalez, Tony, Kansas City	0	1	0	0	1	0
Gordon, Darrien, Oakland	2	0	1	74	1	1
Graham, Jeff, San Diego	1	0	0	0	0	0
Graham, Kent, Pittsburgh	1	0	0	0	0	0
Granville, Billy, Cincinnati	0	0	1	0	1	0
Gray, Chris, Seattle	0	1	0	0	1	0
Grbac, Elvis, Kansas City	7	2	0	-6	2	0
Green, Victor, N.Y. Jets	0	0	4	0	4	0
Greer, Donovan, Buffalo	0	0	1	0	1	0
Griese, Brian, Denver	5	2	0	-8	2	0
Griffith, Howard, Denver	0	1	0	0	1	0
Grunhard, Tim, Kansas City	0	1	0	0	1	0
Hall, Dante, Kansas City	1	0	0	0	0	0

Player, Team	Fum.	Own Rec.	Opp. Rec.	Yds.	Tot. Rec.	TD
Hamilton, Bobby, New England .	0	0	1	0	1	0
Hansen, Phil, Buffalo	0	0	1	29	1	0
Harbaugh, Jim, San Diego	5	1	0	-5	1	0
Hardy, Kevin, Jacksonville	0	0	2	2	2	0
Harris, Antwan, New England .	0	1	0	0	1	0
Harris, Corey, Baltimore.........	1	0	0	0	0	0
Harrison, Marvin, Indianapolis .	2	0	0	0	0	0
Hasty, James, Kansas City......	0	0	2	0	2	0
Hawkins, Artrell, Cincinnati.....	0	0	1	12	1	0
Hayes, Chris, N.Y. Jets...........	0	0	1	0	1	0
Heath, Rodney, Cincinnati......	0	0	1	0	1	0
Heiden, Steve, San Diego	0	0	1	0	1	0
Henry, Kevin, Pittsburgh.........	0	0	1	0	1	0
Hicks, Eric, Kansas City.........	0	0	1	0	1	0
Holmes, Earl, Pittsburgh.........	0	0	1	4	1	0
Holmes, Priest, Baltimore	2	1	0	0	1	0
Holsey, Bernard, Indianapolis .	0	0	1	48	1	1
Howard, Chris, Jacksonville....	2	0	0	0	0	0
Huard, Brock, Seattle..............	2	1	0	0	1	0
Humphrey, Deon, San Diego...	0	1	0	0	1	0
Huntley, Richard, Pittsburgh....	1	0	0	0	0	0
Isaia, Sale, New England........	0	1	0	0	1	0
Izzo, Larry, Miami	1	0	0	0	0	0
Jackson, Brad, Baltimore........	0	0	2	0	2	0
Jackson, Curtis, New England	1	0	0	0	0	0
Jackson, Darrell, Seattle	2	1	0	18	1	0
Jackson, Grady, Oakland........	0	0	1	0	1	0
Jackson, Sheldon, Buffalo	0	1	0	0	1	0
Jacquet, Nate, San Diego.......	3	2	0	0	2	0
James, Edgerrin, Indianapolis.	5	0	0	0	0	0
Jenkins, Billy, Denver..............	1	1	0	0	1	0
Jenkins, DeRon, San Diego	1	0	0	0	0	0
Jenkins, Ronney, San Diego ...	3	2	0	0	2	0
Johnson, Garrett, N.E.	0	0	1	0	1	0
Johnson, Lee, New England ...	2	1	0	-12	1	0
Johnson, Rob, Buffalo	4	2	0	0	2	0
Johnson, Ted, New England ...	0	0	3	0	3	0
Jones, Freddie, San Diego	3	1	0	0	1	0
Jones, Henry, Buffalo	0	0	1	14	1	0
Jones, Lenoy, Cleveland	0	0	1	0	1	0
Jones, Marvin, N.Y. Jets	0	0	1	0	1	0
Jones, Reggie, San Diego.......	1	1	0	0	1	0
Jones, Robert, Miami	0	1	0	0	1	0
Jordan, Randy, Oakland..........	1	0	0	0	0	0
Kacyvenski, Isaiah, Seattle......	0	0	1	0	1	0
Kaufman, Napoleon, Oakland..	1	0	0	0	0	0
Kendall, Pete, Seattle	0	1	0	0	1	0
Kennedy, Lincoln, Oakland	0	2	0	0	2	0
Kinney, Erron, Tennessee........	1	1	0	0	1	0
Kirkland, Levon, Pittsburgh	0	0	1	0	1	0
Kitna, Jon, Seattle...................	17	9	0	-19	9	0
Koonce, George, Seattle	0	0	1	0	1	0
Leaf, Ryan, San Diego	12	4	0	-18	4	0
Lepsis, Matt, Denver..............	0	1	0	0	1	0
Lewis, Darryll, San Diego	0	0	1	29	1	0
Lewis, Jamal, Baltimore...........	6	3	0	0	3	0
Lewis, Mo, N.Y. Jets	0	0	2	0	2	0
Lewis, Ray, Baltimore	0	0	3	0	3	0
Lindsay, Everett, Cleveland	0	1	0	0	1	0
Linton, Jonathan, Buffalo........	3	1	0	0	1	0
Little, Earl, Cleveland	1	0	1	0	1	0
Lockett, Kevin, Kansas City.....	3	1	0	0	1	0
Logan, Mike, Jacksonville.......	0	0	1	3	1	0
Long, Kevin, Tennessee	0	1	0	0	1	0
Loverne, David, N.Y. Jets........	0	1	0	0	1	0
Lucas, Ray, N.Y. Jets	2	1	0	0	1	0
Mack, Stacey, Jacksonville	3	1	0	0	1	0
Mack, Tremain, Cincinnati.......	3	1	0	0	1	0
Madison, Sam, Miami.............	1	0	2	20	2	1
Manning, Peyton, Indianapolis.	5	1	0	-3	1	0

Player, Team	Fum.	Own Rec.	Opp. Rec.	Yds.	Tot. Rec.	TD
Marion, Brock, Miami	0	0	1	0	1	0
Martin, Curtis, N.Y. Jets..........	2	0	0	0	0	0
Marts, Lonnie, Jacksonville	0	0	1	3	1	0
Maslowski, Mike, Kansas City.	0	0	1	0	1	0
Mason, Derrick, Tennessee.....	1	1	0	0	1	0
McAlister, Chris, Baltimore......	0	0	1	0	1	0
McCardell, Keenan, Jac.	3	1	0	4	1	0
McCrary, Fred, San Diego.......	1	0	0	0	0	0
McCrary, Michael, Baltimore....	0	0	3	0	3	0
McGinest, Willie, New England	0	0	2	0	2	0
McGlockton, Chester, K.C.	0	1	0	0	1	0
McKenzie, Keith, Cleveland.....	0	0	1	29	1	0
McKinney, Steve, Indianapolis .	0	0	1	0	1	0
McNair, Steve, Tennessee......	11	3	0	-31	3	0
Meester, Brad, Jacksonville	0	1	0	0	1	0
Mili, Itula, Seattle...................	1	0	0	0	0	0
Miller, Fred, Tennessee	0	2	0	0	2	0
Miller, Josh, Pittsburgh...........	1	1	0	-18	1	0
Mitchell, Anthony, Baltimore....	0	1	0	0	1	0
Mitchell, Scott, Cincinnati.......	4	0	0	-6	0	0
Mixon, Kenny, Miami	0	0	1	0	1	0
Moon, Warren, Kansas City	1	1	0	0	1	0
Moore, Corey, Buffalo	0	0	1	0	1	0
Moore, Larry, Indianapolis......	0	1	0	0	1	0
Moreau, Frank, Kansas City	2	0	0	0	0	0
Moreno, Moses, San Diego	3	1	0	-1	1	0
Morris, Aric, Tennessee..........	0	0	1	0	1	0
Morris, Sammy, Buffalo	2	1	0	0	1	0
Morris, Sylvester, Kansas City..	3	0	0	0	0	0
Moulds, Eric, Buffalo	1	1	0	0	1	0
Muhammad, Mustafah, Ind. ..	1	0	0	0	0	0
Mulitalo, Edwin, Baltimore......	0	2	0	0	2	0
Myslinski, Tom, Pittsburgh.....	0	1	0	0	1	0
Nails, Jamie, Buffalo...............	0	1	0	5	1	0
Nalen, Tom, Denver	1	0	0	-2	0	0
Newman, Keith, Buffalo	1	0	1	25	1	0
Northcutt, Dennis, Cleveland ..	1	0	0	0	0	0
Ogden, Jeff, Miami	1	0	0	0	0	0
Ogden, Jonathan, Baltimore ...	0	2	0	0	2	0
O'Hara, Shaun, Cleveland	1	0	0	-7	0	0
O'Neal, Deltha, Denver............	6	2	1	6	3	0
Ostroski, Jerry, Buffalo	1	1	0	-12	1	1
Parker, Larry, Kansas City.......	1	0	0	0	0	0
Parmalee, Bernie, N.Y. Jets.....	0	0	1	0	1	0
Pass, Patrick, New England	0	1	0	0	1	0
Patten, David, Cleveland	2	0	0	0	0	0
Patton, Marvcus, Kansas City.	0	0	1	0	1	0
Pederson, Doug, Cleveland.....	4	3	0	0	3	0
Phenix, Perry, Tennessee........	0	0	1	0	1	0
Pittman, Kavika, Denver..........	0	0	1	0	1	0
Poole, Tyrone, Indianapolis	0	1	0	8	1	0
Pope, Daniel, Cincinnati..........	1	1	0	-19	1	0
Pope, Marquez, Oakland.........	0	0	5	-2	5	0
Porter, Daryl, Buffalo	0	1	1	54	2	1
Porter, Joey, Pittsburgh...........	0	0	1	32	1	1
Poteat, Hank, Pittsburgh.........	3	0	0	0	0	0
Prentice, Travis, Cleveland	4	1	0	0	1	0
Price, Peerless, Buffalo	4	1	0	0	1	0
Pryce, Trevor, Denver	0	0	1	28	1	1
Rainer, Wali, Cleveland	0	0	1	0	1	0
Redmond, J.R., New England .	2	0	0	0	0	0
Richardson, Tony, Kansas City.	3	0	0	0	0	0
Riemersma, Jay, Buffalo..........	1	0	0	0	0	0
Robertson, Marcus, Ten.	0	0	1	0	1	0
Robinson, Eddie, Tennessee...	0	0	3	0	3	0
Rogers, Charlie, Seattle	5	1	0	0	1	0
Rogers, Sam, Buffalo..............	0	0	1	0	1	0
Rogers, Tyrone, Cleveland	0	0	3	0	3	0
Rolle, Samari, Tennessee........	0	0	1	0	1	0
Roman, Mark, Cincinnati	0	2	0	0	2	0

Player, Team	Fum.	Own Rec.	Opp. Rec.	Yds.	Tot. Rec.	TD
Romanowski, Bill, Denver	0	0	2	0	2	0
Roundtree, Raleigh, San Diego	0	1	0	0	1	0
Roye, Orpheus, Cleveland	0	0	1	8	1	0
Ruff, Orlando, San Diego	0	0	1	0	1	0
Rusk, Reggie, San Diego	0	0	1	17	1	0
Russell, Darrell, Oakland	0	0	1	0	1	0
Russell, Twan, Miami	0	0	1	0	1	0
Rutledge, Rod, New England	0	1	0	0	1	0
Saleh, Tarek, Cleveland	0	1	0	0	1	0
Sanders, Chris, Tennessee	1	0	0	0	0	0
Saturday, Jeff, Indianapolis	1	1	0	0	1	0
Scott, Chad, Pittsburgh	0	1	1	6	2	0
Scott, Tony, N.Y. Jets	0	1	0	0	1	0
Serwanga, Kato, New England	0	0	2	0	2	0
Sharper, Jamie, Baltimore	0	0	2	0	2	0
Shaw, Bobby, Pittsburgh	2	0	0	0	0	0
Shea, Aaron, Cleveland	1	0	0	0	0	0
Shelton, Daimon, Jacksonville	0	1	1	0	2	0
Shields, Scott, Pittsburgh	1	1	1	-5	2	0
Shields, Will, Kansas City	0	1	0	0	1	0
Sidney, Dainon, Tennessee	0	0	2	0	2	0
Simpson, Antoine, San Diego	0	0	1	0	1	0
Sims, Barry, Oakland	0	1	0	0	1	0
Sinclair, Michael, Seattle	0	0	4	69	4	1
Siragusa, Tony, Baltimore	0	0	1	0	1	0
Smith, Akili, Cincinnati	14	2	0	-14	2	0
Smith, Antowan, Buffalo	1	0	0	0	0	0
Smith, Jeff, Jacksonville	1	0	0	0	0	0
Smith, Jimmy, Jacksonville	1	0	0	0	0	0
Smith, Lamar, Miami	3	0	0	0	0	0
Smith, Larry, Jacksonville	0	0	3	1	3	0
Smith, Otis, New England	0	0	1	12	1	0
Smith, Rod, Denver	1	0	0	0	0	0
Soward, R. Jay, Jacksonville	3	1	0	0	1	0
Spencer, Jimmy, Denver	0	0	1	0	1	0
Spikes, Takeo, Cincinnati	0	0	3	0	3	0
Spires, Greg, New England	0	0	1	0	1	0
Spriggs, Marcus, Cleveland	0	0	1	0	1	0
Starks, Duane, Baltimore	1	1	1	0	2	0
Stewart, Kordell, Pittsburgh	8	3	0	-1	3	0
Stewart, Rayna, Jacksonville	0	0	2	2	2	0
Stills, Gary, Kansas City	0	0	1	0	1	0
Stith, Shyrone, Jacksonville	1	0	0	0	0	0
Stone, Dwight, N.Y. Jets	1	1	0	0	1	0
Storz, Erik, Jacksonville	0	0	1	0	1	0
Sullivan, Chris, Pittsburgh	0	0	2	0	2	0
Surtain, Patrick, Miami	0	0	1	0	1	0
Suttle, Jason, Denver	0	0	1	0	1	1
Swayne, Harry, Baltimore	0	1	0	0	1	0
Tait, John, Kansas City	0	1	0	0	1	0
Tanuvasa, Maa, Denver	0	0	4	38	4	0
Taylor, Fred, Jacksonville	4	2	0	-1	2	0
Taylor, Jason, Miami	0	0	4	29	4	1
Taylor, Travis, Baltimore	1	0	0	0	0	0
Testaverde, Vinny, N.Y. Jets	7	0	0	-5	0	0
Thomas, Henry, New England	0	0	1	0	1	0
Thomas, Kiwaukee, Jac.	0	0	1	0	1	0
Thomas, Rodney, Tennessee	1	0	1	0	1	0
Thomas, Thurman, Miami	1	0	0	0	0	0
Thomas, Zach, Miami	0	0	1	0	1	0
Thompson, Kevin, Cleveland	1	1	0	0	1	0
Thornton, John, Tennessee	0	0	1	0	1	0
Traylor, Keith, Denver	0	0	1	0	1	0
Upshaw, Regan, Oakland	0	0	2	8	2	0
Vrabel, Mike, Pittsburgh	0	0	1	0	1	0
Walker, Denard, Tennessee	1	0	0	0	0	0
Ward, Dedric, N.Y. Jets	1	0	0	0	0	0
Ward, Hines, Pittsburgh	2	1	0	0	1	0
Warrick, Peter, Cincinnati	2	1	0	0	1	0
Washington, Keith, Baltimore	0	0	1	0	1	0
Watson, Chris, Buffalo	4	2	0	0	2	0
Watters, Ricky, Seattle	5	2	0	0	2	0
Weaver, Jed, Miami	1	0	0	0	0	0
Webster, Larry, Baltimore	0	0	1	0	1	0
Wesley, Greg, Kansas City	0	0	1	0	1	0
Wheatley, Tyrone, Oakland	4	1	0	0	1	0
Whitted, Alvis, Jacksonville	1	0	0	0	0	0
Wiegert, Zach, Jacksonville	0	1	0	0	1	0
Wiggins, Jermaine, N.E.	1	0	0	0	0	0
Wiley, Marcellus, Buffalo	0	0	1	0	1	0
Wilkins, Terrence, Indianapolis	4	1	0	0	1	0
Williams, Dan, Kansas City	1	0	1	9	1	0
Williams, Josh, Indianapolis	0	0	1	0	1	0
Williams, Nick, Cincinnati	2	1	0	0	1	0
Williams, Pat, Buffalo	0	0	2	0	2	0
Williams, Willie, Seattle	0	0	1	0	1	0
Wilson, Reinard, Cincinnati	0	0	1	3	1	0
Woodson, Charles, Oakland	0	0	1	0	1	0
Woodson, Rod, Baltimore	0	0	3	4	3	0
Wycheck, Frank, Tennessee	2	0	0	0	0	0
Wynn, Spergon, Cleveland	2	0	0	0	0	0
Yeast, Craig, Cincinnati	3	1	0	0	1	0
Zahursky, Steve, Cleveland	0	3	0	0	3	0

NFC

Player, Team	Fum.	Own Rec.	Opp. Rec.	Yds.	Tot. Rec.	TD
Ahanotu, Chidi, Tampa Bay	0	0	1	0	1	0
Aikman, Troy, Dallas	2	0	0	0	0	0
Aldridge, Allen, Detroit	0	0	1	0	1	0
Alexander, Stephen, Was.	2	0	0	0	0	0
Allen, James, Chicago	5	0	0	0	0	0
Allen, Larry, Dallas	0	2	0	0	2	0
Alstott, Mike, Tampa Bay	3	1	0	0	1	0
Anderson, Jamal, Atlanta	6	1	0	0	1	0
Armstead, Jessie, N.Y. Giants	0	0	1	0	1	0
Autry, Darnell, Philadelphia	2	1	0	0	1	0
Badger, Brad, Minnesota	0	1	0	0	1	0
Bailey, Champ, Washington	0	0	1	0	1	0
Barber, Ronde, Tampa Bay	0	0	1	24	1	1
Barber, Shawn, Washington	0	0	3	0	3	0
Barber, Tiki, N.Y. Giants	9	5	0	0	5	0
Barnes, Marlon, Chicago	1	0	0	0	0	0
Barrett, David, Arizona	0	0	1	0	1	0
Barrow, Micheal, N.Y. Giants	0	0	1	0	1	0
Bartrum, Mike, Philadelphia	0	0	1	0	1	0
Batch, Charlie, Detroit	6	1	0	-5	1	0
Bates, Michael, Carolina	4	1	0	0	1	0
Beuerlein, Steve, Carolina	9	0	0	-5	0	0
Biakabutuka, Tim, Carolina	4	0	0	0	0	0
Bidwell, Josh, Green Bay	1	1	0	0	1	0
Birk, Matt, Minnesota	1	0	0	0	0	0
Blake, Jeff, New Orleans	7	3	0	-2	3	0
Bly, Dre', St. Louis	1	1	0	0	1	0
Booker, Marty, Chicago	2	1	0	0	1	0
Bostic, Jason, Philadelphia	1	0	0	0	0	0
Boston, David, Arizona	2	1	0	0	1	0
Bowens, David, Green Bay	0	0	1	0	1	0
Boyd, Stephen, Detroit	0	0	1	0	1	0
Brister, Bubby, Minnesota	1	1	0	0	1	0
Brooks, Aaron, New Orleans	4	0	0	-4	0	0
Broughton, Luther, Phi.	1	0	0	0	0	0
Brown, Dave, Arizona	2	0	0	-3	0	0
Brown, Lomas, N.Y. Giants	0	1	0	0	1	0
Brown, Mike, Chicago	0	0	1	12	1	0
Brown, Ray, San Francisco	0	1	0	0	1	0
Bruce, Isaac, St. Louis	1	0	0	0	0	0
Buchanan, Ray, Atlanta	0	0	2	1	2	0
Bush, Devin, St. Louis	0	1	0	15	1	1

Player, Team	Fum.	Own Rec.	Opp. Rec.	Yds.	Tot. Rec.	TD
Butler, LeRoy, Green Bay	0	0	1	0	1	0
Byrd, Isaac, Carolina	0	1	0	0	1	0
Campbell, Daniel, N.Y. Giants	1	0	0	0	0	0
Carter, Cris, Minnesota	3	2	0	0	2	0
Carter, Kevin, St. Louis	1	0	1	0	1	0
Carter, Marty, Atlanta	0	0	2	0	2	0
Case, Stoney, Detroit	1	0	0	0	0	0
Centers, Larry, Washington	1	1	0	0	1	0
Chandler, Chris, Atlanta	7	4	0	-13	4	0
Cherry, Je'Rod, Philadelphia	0	0	1	0	1	0
Christian, Bob, Atlanta	0	0	1	10	1	0
Clark, Greg, San Francisco	1	1	0	0	1	0
Clarke, Phil, New Orleans	0	0	1	0	1	0
Clement, Anthony, Arizona	0	1	0	0	1	0
Coakley, Dexter, Dallas	0	0	1	8	1	0
Cody, Mac, Arizona	4	1	0	0	1	0
Collins, Kerry, N.Y. Giants	7	1	0	-13	1	0
Colvin, Rosevelt, Chicago	0	0	1	0	1	0
Comella, Greg, N.Y. Giants	2	0	0	0	0	0
Culpepper, Daunte, Minnesota	11	5	0	-23	5	0
Cunningham, Randall, Dallas	4	3	0	-2	3	0
Daniels, Phillip, Chicago	0	0	1	0	1	0
Davis, Eric, Carolina	1	1	0	0	1	0
Davis, Robert, Green Bay	0	0	1	0	1	0
Davis, Stephen, Washington	4	1	0	0	1	0
Davis, Tyrone, Green Bay	2	0	0	0	0	0
Dawkins, Brian, Philadelphia	0	1	1	0	2	0
Dayne, Ron, N.Y. Giants	1	0	0	0	0	0
DeVries, Jared, Detroit	0	0	1	0	1	0
Dexter, James, Carolina	0	1	0	0	1	0
Diggs, Na'il, Green Bay	0	0	1	52	1	0
Dishman, Chris, Arizona	1	1	0	0	1	0
Dixon, David, Minnesota	0	1	0	0	1	0
Dotson, Earl, Green Bay	0	1	0	0	1	0
Downs, Gary, Atlanta	0	0	1	0	1	0
Driver, Donald, Green Bay	0	1	0	0	1	0
Duncan, Jamie, Tampa Bay	0	0	1	0	1	0
Dunn, Warrick, Tampa Bay	1	0	0	0	0	0
Dwight, Tim, Atlanta	3	1	0	0	1	0
Ekuban, Ebenezer, Dallas	0	0	1	0	1	0
Ellis, Greg, Dallas	0	0	2	0	2	0
Elliss, Luther, Detroit	0	0	2	3	2	0
Emmons, Carlos, Philadelphia	0	0	1	2	1	0
Engram, Bobby, Chicago	1	1	0	0	1	0
Evans, Doug, Carolina	0	0	5	-3	5	0
Fair, Terry, Detroit	1	0	1	2	1	0
Faulk, Marshall, St. Louis	0	2	0	0	2	0
Favre, Brett, Green Bay	9	2	0	-12	2	0
Fischer, Mark, Washington	1	0	0	-18	0	0
Flanigan, Jim, Chicago	0	0	1	0	1	0
Fontenot, Jerry, New Orleans	0	1	0	0	1	0
Foster, Larry, Detroit	2	0	1	0	1	0
Franks, Bubba, Green Bay	1	0	0	0	0	0
Freeman, Antonio, Green Bay	1	0	0	0	0	0
Fricke, Ben, Dallas	2	0	0	0	0	0
Garcia, Frank, Carolina	0	1	0	0	1	0
Garcia, Jeff, San Francisco	7	4	0	-6	4	0
Garner, Charlie, San Francisco	4	0	0	0	0	0
George, Jeff, Washington	3	1	0	-3	1	0
Gilbert, Sean, Carolina	0	0	1	0	1	0
Glover, La'Roi, New Orleans	0	0	1	0	1	0
Golden, Jack, N.Y. Giants	0	0	1	0	1	0
Goodman, Herbert, G.B.	2	0	0	0	0	0
Gragg, Scott, San Francisco	0	1	0	0	1	0
Grant, Orantes, Dallas	0	0	2	0	2	0
Green, Ahman, Green Bay	6	1	0	0	1	0
Green, Barrett, Detroit	0	0	1	0	1	0
Green, Trent, St. Louis	3	0	0	0	0	0
Greisen, Chris, Arizona	1	0	0	0	0	0
Griffith, Robert, Minnesota	0	0	2	0	2	0
Hakim, Az-Zahir, St. Louis	7	1	0	0	1	0
Hall, Lemanski, Minnesota	0	0	1	1	1	0
Hall, Travis, Atlanta	0	0	1	0	1	0
Hamilton, Joe, Tampa Bay	1	0	0	0	0	0
Hankton, Karl, Carolina	0	0	1	0	1	0
Hardy, Terry, Arizona	2	0	0	0	0	0
Hartings, Jeff, Detroit	0	1	0	0	1	1
Hastings, Andre, Tampa Bay	1	0	0	0	0	0
Hauck, Tim, Philadelphia	0	0	1	0	1	0
Hawthorne, Michael, N.O.	0	0	1	0	1	0
Hayes, Donald, Carolina	1	0	0	0	0	0
Heck, Andy, Washington	0	1	0	0	1	0
Henderson, William, G.B.	1	1	0	0	1	0
Hennings, Chad, Dallas	0	0	1	0	1	0
Hetherington, Chris, Carolina	0	0	1	0	1	0
Hicks, Skip, Washington	1	0	0	0	0	0
Hitchcock, Jimmy, Carolina	1	0	0	0	0	0
Hobgood-Chittick, Nate, S.F.	0	0	1	0	1	0
Hodgins, James, St. Louis	0	1	0	0	1	0
Holt, Torry, St. Louis	2	1	0	0	1	0
Hoover, Brad, Carolina	1	0	1	0	1	0
Horn, Joe, New Orleans	1	1	0	0	1	0
Horne, Tony, St. Louis	3	0	1	0	1	0
Howard, Darren, New Orleans	1	0	2	0	2	0
Howard, Desmond, Detroit	2	1	0	0	1	0
Irvin, Sedrick, Detroit	1	0	0	0	0	0
Ismail, Raghib, Dallas	1	0	0	0	0	0
Jackson, Dexter, Tampa Bay	0	0	1	0	1	0
Jackson, Terry, S.F.	0	1	0	0	1	0
Jackson, Willie, New Orleans	2	0	0	0	0	0
Jefferson, Shawn, Atlanta	1	0	0	0	0	0
Jenkins, MarTay, Arizona	3	0	0	0	0	0
Jett, John, Detroit	1	1	0	-10	1	0
Johnson, Brad, Washington	5	2	0	-14	2	0
Johnson, Doug, Atlanta	4	0	0	0	0	0
Johnson, Joe, New Orleans	0	0	2	0	2	0
Johnson, Keyshawn, T.B.	2	0	0	0	0	0
Jones, Greg, Washington	0	0	1	0	1	0
Jones, James, Detroit	0	0	1	0	1	0
Jones, Marcus, Tampa Bay	0	0	1	0	1	0
Jones, Thomas, Arizona	4	1	0	0	1	0
Jurevicius, Joe, N.Y. Giants	1	0	0	0	0	0
Kalu, Ndukwe, Washington	0	0	1	4	1	0
Kanell, Danny, Atlanta	2	2	0	-2	2	0
Kelly, Brian, Tampa Bay	0	0	2	0	2	0
Kelly, Reggie, Atlanta	0	0	0	0	0	0
Kennison, Eddie, Chicago	1	1	0	0	1	0
King, Shaun, Tampa Bay	4	3	0	0	3	0
Kirschke, Travis, Detroit	0	0	1	0	1	0
Kowalkowski, Scott, Detroit	0	0	1	2	1	0
Kozlowski, Brian, Atlanta	0	2	0	0	2	0
Kriewaldt, Clint, Detroit	0	0	1	0	1	0
Lang, Kenard, Washington	0	0	1	0	1	0
Lassiter, Kwamie, Arizona	0	0	1	0	1	0
Levingston, Bashir, NYG	2	0	0	0	0	0
Lewis, Jeff, Carolina	1	0	0	0	0	0
Lewis, Jonas, San Francisco	0	0	1	0	1	0
Lincoln, Jeremy, Detroit	0	0	1	0	1	0
Lucas, Albert, Carolina	0	0	1	0	1	0
Lyle, Keith, St. Louis	0	0	1	94	1	1
Lynch, John, Tampa Bay	0	0	2	8	2	0
Maddox, Mark, Arizona	0	1	0	-2	1	0
Martin, Cecil, Philadelphia	1	0	0	0	0	0
Mathis, Kevin, New Orleans	1	0	0	0	0	0
Mathis, Terance, Atlanta	1	0	0	0	0	0
Matthews, Shane, Chicago	2	1	0	0	1	0
McAfee, Fred, New Orleans	0	0	1	0	1	0
McBurrows, Gerald, Atlanta	0	0	2	0	2	0
McCleon, Dexter, St. Louis	1	0	1	21	1	0
McCollum, Andy, St. Louis	1	0	0	-4	0	0

Player, Team	Fum.	Own Rec.	Opp. Rec.	Yds.	Tot. Rec.	TD
McDaniel, Emmanuel, NYG	0	1	0	0	1	0
McElroy, Ray, Chicago	0	0	1	0	1	0
McFarland, Anthony, T.B.	0	0	1	0	1	0
McGarity, Wane, Dallas	2	2	0	0	2	0
McKenzie, Mike, Green Bay	1	0	0	0	0	0
McKenzie, Raleigh, Green Bay	0	1	0	0	1	0
McKinnon, Ronald, Arizona	0	0	1	0	1	0
McKnight, James, Dallas	1	0	0	0	0	0
McNabb, Donovan, Phi.	7	2	0	-5	2	0
McNown, Cade, Chicago	8	4	0	-17	4	0
Milburn, Glyn, Chicago	4	3	0	0	3	0
Miller, Jim, Chicago	1	0	0	0	0	0
Miller, Keith, St. Louis	0	1	0	0	1	0
Minter, Mike, Carolina	0	0	1	0	1	0
Mitchell, Basil, Green Bay	1	1	0	0	1	0
Mitchell, Brian, Philadelphia	3	1	0	0	1	0
Mitchell, Keith, New Orleans	0	0	4	90	4	1
Mitchell, Pete, N.Y. Giants	1	1	0	0	1	0
Monty, Pete, N.Y. Giants	0	1	0	0	1	0
Moore, Damon, Philadelphia	1	0	0	0	0	0
Morabito, Tim, Carolina	0	0	1	0	1	0
Morrow, Harold, Minnesota	0	0	1	0	1	0
Morton, Chad, New Orleans	2	1	0	0	1	0
Morton, Johnnie, Detroit	1	0	0	0	0	0
Moss, Randy, Minnesota	2	0	0	0	0	0
Muhammad, Muhsin, Car.	1	0	1	0	1	0
Murrell, Adrian, Washington	1	0	0	0	0	0
Myers, Michael, Dallas	0	0	1	0	1	0
Nguyen, Dat, Dallas	0	1	0	0	1	0
Norton, Ken, San Francisco	0	0	1	0	1	0
Nutten, Tom, St. Louis	0	1	0	0	1	0
Oldham, Chris, New Orleans	0	0	2	2	2	0
Oliver, Winslow, Atlanta	1	0	0	0	0	0
Owens, Terrell, San Francisco	3	0	0	0	0	0
Palmer, David, Minnesota	1	0	0	0	0	0
Petitgout, Luke, N.Y. Giants	0	1	0	0	1	0
Pittman, Michael, Arizona	5	0	0	0	0	0
Plummer, Jake, Arizona	8	4	0	-1	4	0
Poole, Keith, New Orleans	1	1	0	0	1	0
Porcher, Robert, Detroit	0	0	1	0	1	0
Posey, Jeff, San Francisco	0	0	1	0	1	0
Pritchett, Stanley, Phi.	1	0	0	0	0	0
Quarles, Shelton, Tampa Bay	0	0	2	5	2	0
Rasby, Walter, Detroit	0	1	0	0	1	0
Redmon, Anthony, Atlanta	0	1	0	0	1	0
Rice, Jerry, San Francisco	3	1	0	0	1	0
Rice, Ron, Detroit	0	0	1	6	1	0
Rice, Simeon, Arizona	0	0	1	0	1	0
Robinson, Damien, Tampa Bay	0	0	3	5	3	0
Robinson, Eugene, Carolina	0	0	3	26	3	0
Robinson, Jeff, St. Louis	0	1	0	0	1	0
Robinson, Marcus, Chicago	1	0	0	0	0	0
Rossum, Allen, Green Bay	4	3	0	0	3	0
Runyan, Jon, Philadelphia	0	1	0	0	1	0
Rutledge, Johnny, Arizona	0	0	1	0	1	0
Sanders, Deion, Washington	3	2	0	0	2	0
Sapp, Warren, Tampa Bay	0	0	1	0	1	0
Sawyer, Talance, Minnesota	0	0	2	0	2	0
Schroeder, Bill, Green Bay	1	0	0	0	0	0
Schulters, Lance, S.F.	0	0	1	16	1	0
Sears, Corey, Arizona	0	0	1	0	1	0
Sehorn, Jason, N.Y. Giants	0	0	1	8	1	0
Shade, Sam, Washington	0	0	4	1	4	0
Shelton, L.J., Arizona	0	1	0	0	1	0
Simmons, Clyde, Chicago	0	0	1	0	1	0
Simon, Corey, Philadelphia	0	0	1	5	1	0
Sims, Keith, Washington	0	1	0	0	1	0
Smith, Derek, Washington	0	0	1	0	1	0
Smith, Emmitt, Dallas	6	1	0	0	1	0
Smith, Paul, San Francisco	2	2	0	0	2	0
Smith, Robert, Minnesota	4	3	0	0	3	0
Smith, Terrelle, New Orleans	1	0	0	0	0	0
Smith, Thomas, Chicago	0	0	1	0	1	0
Stablein, Brian, Detroit	1	0	0	0	0	0
Stachelski, Dave, New Orleans	0	0	1	0	1	0
Staley, Duce, Philadelphia	3	1	0	0	1	0
Stecker, Aaron, Tampa Bay	1	0	0	0	0	0
Stepnoski, Mark, Dallas	1	0	0	0	0	0
Stevens, Matt, Washington	0	0	1	1	1	0
Stewart, James, Detroit	4	1	0	0	1	0
Strahan, Michael, N.Y. Giants	0	0	4	0	4	0
Streets, Tai, San Francisco	1	0	0	0	0	0
Stubblefield, Dana, Was.	0	0	1	0	1	0
Tate, Robert, Minnesota	0	0	1	0	1	0
Taylor, Bobby, Philadelphia	0	0	1	0	1	0
Terrell, David, Washington	0	1	1	0	2	0
Thomas, Chris, St. Louis	0	0	1	0	1	0
Thomas, Hollis, Philadelphia	0	0	1	0	1	0
Thomas, Orlando, Minnesota	0	0	2	0	2	0
Thomas, Robert, Dallas	2	1	0	0	1	0
Thrash, James, Washington	1	0	1	0	1	0
Tillman, Pat, Arizona	0	0	2	0	2	0
Toomer, Amani, N.Y. Giants	1	1	0	0	1	0
Towns, Lester, Carolina	0	0	2	0	2	0
Tubbs, Winfred, San Francisco	0	0	1	0	1	0
Tucker, Jason, Dallas	3	0	0	0	0	0
Turley, Kyle, New Orleans	0	4	0	-6	4	0
Urlacher, Brian, Chicago	0	0	1	0	1	0
Vaughn, Darrick, Atlanta	1	0	1	0	1	0
Vincent, Troy, Philadelphia	0	0	2	0	2	0
Walker, Marquis, Detroit	1	1	1	0	2	0
Walter, Ken, Carolina	2	2	0	-11	2	0
Walters, Troy, Minnesota	2	1	0	0	1	0
Warner, Kurt, St. Louis	4	0	0	-8	0	0
Warren, Chris, Dal.-Phi.	3	0	0	0	0	0
Wayne, Nate, Green Bay	0	0	1	9	1	0
Webster, Jason, S.F.	0	0	1	1	1	0
Welbourn, John, Philadelphia	0	1	0	0	1	0
West, Lyle, N.Y. Giants	0	0	1	0	1	0
White, Dez, Chicago	1	0	0	0	0	0
White, Reggie, Carolina	0	0	1	0	1	0
Whiting, Brandon, Philadelphia	0	0	2	0	2	0
Wiegmann, Casey, Chicago	0	1	0	0	1	0
Wiley, Michael, Dallas	3	1	0	0	1	0
Williams, Aeneas, Arizona	0	0	2	104	2	1
Williams, Brian, Green Bay	0	0	1	0	1	0
Williams, George, N.Y. Giants	0	0	1	0	1	0
Williams, James, Chicago	0	1	0	0	1	0
Williams, K.D., Green Bay	0	0	1	0	1	0
Williams, Karl, Tampa Bay	2	1	0	0	1	0
Williams, Kevin, S.F.	1	1	0	0	1	0
Williams, Moe, Minnesota	0	0	1	0	1	0
Williams, Ricky, New Orleans	6	2	0	0	2	0
Williams, Shaun, N.Y. Giants	0	0	1	0	1	0
Williams, Wally, New Orleans	1	0	0	0	0	0
Wong, Kailee, Minnesota	1	0	0	0	0	0
Woodall, Lee, Carolina	0	0	1	0	1	0
Wooden, Shawn, Chicago	0	0	1	3	1	0
Wortham, Barron, Dallas	0	0	1	0	1	0
Wright, Anthony, Dallas	3	1	0	-3	1	0
Wright, Kenny, Minnesota	0	1	0	11	1	0
Yoder, Todd, Tampa Bay	1	0	0	0	0	0
Young, Bryant, San Francisco	0	0	1	0	1	0
Zgonina, Jeff, St. Louis	0	2	1	0	3	0

PLAYERS WITH TWO CLUBS

Player, Team	Fum.	Own Rec.	Opp. Rec.	Yds.	Tot. Rec.	TD
Warren, Chris, Dallas	1	0	0	0	0	0
Warren, Chris, Philadelphia	2	0	0	0	0	0

FIELD GOALS

TEAM

AFC

Team	Made	Att.	Pct.	Long
Indianapolis	25	27	.926	48
Miami	28	31	.903	49
Baltimore	35	39	.897	51
Jacksonville	29	33	.879	51
Pittsburgh	25	30	.833	52
Cleveland	14	17	.824	45
New England	27	33	.818	53
Seattle	21	26	.808	52
Tennessee	27	34	.794	50
Denver	26	34	.765	51
Buffalo	26	35	.743	48
San Diego	18	25	.720	54
Kansas City	17	24	.708	42
Oakland	23	34	.676	54
N.Y. Jets	23	34	.676	52
Cincinnati	12	21	.571	45
AFC total	376	477	...	54
AFC average	23.5	29.8	.788	...

NFC

Team	Made	Att.	Pct.	Long
Minnesota	22	23	.957	49
St. Louis	24	27	.889	51
Carolina	31	35	.886	52
Philadelphia	29	33	.879	51
Green Bay	33	38	.868	52
Tampa Bay	28	34	.824	55
Atlanta	25	31	.806	51
Detroit	24	30	.800	54
New Orleans	23	29	.793	48
Chicago	21	27	.778	54
N.Y. Giants	19	25	.760	46
Dallas	25	33	.758	48
Arizona	16	23	.696	54
San Francisco	15	22	.682	47
Washington	20	30	.667	50
NFC total	355	440	...	55
NFC average	23.7	29.3	.807	...
NFL total	731	917	...	55
NFL average	23.6	29.6	.797	...

INDIVIDUAL

BESTS OF THE SEASON

Field goal percentage, season
NFC: 1.000—Jeff Wilkins, St. Louis.
AFC: .926—Mike Vanderjagt, Indianapolis.

Field goals, season
AFC: 35—Matt Stover, Baltimore.
NFC: 34—Joe Nedney, Denver-Carolina.

Field goal attempts, season
AFC: 39—Matt Stover, Baltimore.
NFC: 38—Ryan Longwell, Green Bay; Joe Nedney, Denver-
    Carolina.

Longest field goal
NFC: 55—Martin Gramatica, Tampa Bay vs. Detroit, Oct. 19.
AFC: 54—John Carney, San Diego at Kansas City, Sept. 17;
    Sebastian Janikowski, Oakland at San Diego, Oct. 29.

Average yards made, season
AFC: 40.1—Rian Lindell, Seattle.
NFC: 37.8—Ryan Longwell, Green Bay.

NFL LEADERS

Team	Made	Att.	Pct.	Long
Wilkins, Jeff, St. Louis	17	17	1.000	51
Anderson, Gary, Minnesota	22	23	.957	49
Vanderjagt, Mike, Indianapolis*	25	27	.926	48
Hollis, Mike, Jacksonville*	24	26	.923	51
Mare, Olindo, Miami*	28	31	.903	49
Stover, Matt, Baltimore*	35	39	.897	51
Nedney, Joe, Carolina	34	38	.895	52
Lindell, Rian, Seattle*	15	17	.882	52
Akers, David, Philadelphia	29	33	.879	51
Longwell, Ryan, Green Bay	33	38	.868	52

*AFC.
Leader based on percentage, minimum 16 attempts.

AFC

Player, Team	1-19	20-29	30-39	40-49	Over	Totals	Avg. Yds. Att.	Avg. Yds. Made	Avg. Yds. Miss	Long
Brown, Kris	1-1	8-8	9-10	6-9	1-2	25-30	34.9	33.2	43.4	52
Pittsburgh	1.000	1.000	.900	.667	.500	.833				
Carney, John	1-1	3-3	5-7	7-10	2-4	18-25	39.5	37.9	43.6	54
San Diego	1.000	1.000	.714	.700	.500	.720				
Christie, Steve	2-2	11-13	4-6	9-13	0-1	26-35	34.2	32.8	38.3	48
Buffalo	1.000	.846	.667	.692	.000	.743				
Conway, Brett	2-2	3-3	0-0	1-1	0-0	6-6	24.8	24.8	...	40
Was.-Oak.-NYJ*	1.000	1.000	...	1.000	...	1.000				
Dawson, Phil	3-3	4-4	5-5	2-5	0-0	14-17	32.7	30.7	42.0	45
Cleveland	1.000	1.000	1.000	.400	...	.824				
Del Greco, Al	0-0	13-15	7-8	6-9	1-1	27-33	32.5	31.7	36.3	50
Tennessee	...	.867	.875	.667	1.000	.818				
Elam, Jason	0-0	7-7	6-7	4-9	1-1	18-24	35.8	33.3	43.5	51
Denver	...	1.000	.857	.444	1.000	.750				
Hall, John	0-0	8-9	6-8	6-12	1-3	21-32	37.6	34.3	43.9	51
N.Y. Jets	...	.889	.750	.500	.333	.656				

Player, Team	1-19	20-29	30-39	40-49	Over	Totals	Avg. Yds. Att.	Avg. Yds. Made	Avg. Yds. Miss	Long
Hentrich, Craig	0-0	0-0	0-0	0-0	0-1	0-1	60.0	...	60.0	0
Tennessee	...	...	...	...	.000	.000				
Hollis, Mike	0-0	6-7	8-8	7-8	3-3	24-26	36.9	36.8	38.5	51
Jacksonville	...	.857	1.000	.875	1.000	.923				
Janikowski, Sebastian	1-1	6-6	6-7	8-14	1-4	22-32	38.3	34.9	45.8	54
Oakland	1.000	1.000	.857	.571	.250	.688				
Lechler, Shane	0-0	0-0	0-1	0-0	0-0	0-1	33.0	...	33.0	0
Oakland	...	...	.000	...	...	.000				
Lindell, Rian	0-0	4-5	1-1	7-8	3-3	15-17	39.1	40.1	32.0	52
Seattle	...	.800	1.000	.875	1.000	.882				
Lindsey, Steve	2-2	0-0	1-3	2-2	0-0	5-7	32.7	33.0	32.0	49
Jacksonville	1.000	...	.333	1.000	...	.714				
Mare, Olindo	0-0	7-8	9-10	12-13	0-0	28-31	35.6	35.5	37.0	49
Miami	...	.875	.900	.923	...	.903				
Peterson, Todd	1-1	5-5	7-9	2-5	0-0	15-20	33.4	31.3	39.6	42
Kansas City	1.000	1.000	.778	.400	...	.750				
Rackers, Neil	0-0	5-5	5-9	2-7	0-0	12-21	35.7	32.8	39.6	45
Cincinnati	...	1.000	.556	.286	...	.571				
Stover, Matt	2-2	9-9	12-13	10-12	2-3	35-39	35.5	34.6	43.3	51
Baltimore	1.000	1.000	.923	.833	.667	.897				
Vanderjagt, Mike	1-1	6-6	13-13	5-6	0-1	25-27	34.8	33.3	53.0	48
Indianapolis	1.000	1.000	1.000	.833	.000	.926				
Vinatieri, Adam	0-0	11-13	8-9	7-8	1-3	27-33	34.6	33.2	40.8	53
New England	...	.846	.889	.875	.333	.818				

*Includes both NFC and AFC statistics.

NFC

Player, Team	1-19	20-29	30-39	40-49	Over	Totals	Avg. Yds. Att.	Avg. Yds. Made	Avg. Yds. Miss	Long
Akers, David	1-1	6-6	14-15	7-10	1-1	29-33	35.8	34.9	41.8	51
Philadelphia	1.000	1.000	.933	.700	1.000	.879				
Andersen, Morten	0-0	6-6	6-7	11-15	2-3	25-31	38.9	37.8	43.8	51
Atlanta	...	1.000	.857	.733	.667	.806				
Anderson, Gary	1-1	5-5	9-9	7-7	0-1	22-23	35.3	34.6	51.0	49
Minnesota	1.000	1.000	1.000	1.000	.000	.957				
Bentley, Scott	0-0	0-0	0-0	0-0	1-1	1-1	50.0	50.0	...	50
Washington	...	...	...	...	1.000	1.000				
Blanchard, Cary	1-1	2-2	9-11	2-5	2-4	16-23	37.8	35.4	43.3	54
Arizona	1.000	1.000	.818	.400	.500	.696				
Brien, Doug	1-1	6-6	4-5	12-15	0-2	23-29	36.8	34.7	44.7	48
New Orleans	1.000	1.000	.800	.800	.000	.793				
Cunningham, Richie	0-0	3-5	2-2	0-0	0-0	5-7	28.6	29.6	26.0	39
Carolina	...	.600	1.000	...	...	.714				
Daluiso, Brad	0-0	8-8	5-8	4-7	0-0	17-23	33.4	31.6	38.3	46
N.Y. Giants	...	1.000	.625	.571	...	.739				
Edinger, Paul	1-1	5-5	7-9	6-10	2-2	21-27	37.6	36.6	41.3	54
Chicago	1.000	1.000	.778	.600	1.000	.778				
Gramatica, Martin	0-0	8-8	8-10	7-9	5-7	28-34	38.3	37.4	42.5	55
Tampa Bay	...	1.000	.800	.778	.714	.824				
Hall, Jeff	0-0	1-1	1-1	1-2	1-1	4-5	39.6	37.8	47.0	50
St. Louis	...	1.000	1.000	.500	1.000	.800				
Hanson, Jason	2-2	6-7	10-12	4-7	2-2	24-30	34.1	33.4	37.0	54
Detroit	1.000	.857	.833	.571	1.000	.800				
Heppner, Kris	1-1	4-4	3-6	2-2	0-2	10-15	35.0	31.8	41.4	45
Sea.-Was.*	1.000	1.000	.500	1.000	.000	.667				
Holmes, Jaret	0-0	1-1	1-1	0-0	0-0	2-2	30.5	30.5	...	34
N.Y. Giants	...	1.000	1.000	...	...	1.000				
Husted, Michael	0-0	4-4	0-3	0-1	0-0	4-8	29.6	24.3	35.0	28
Washington	...	1.000	.000	.000	...	.500				
Longwell, Ryan	0-0	7-8	10-10	13-15	3-5	33-38	38.6	37.8	43.8	52
Green Bay	...	.875	1.000	.867	.600	.868				
Murray, Eddie	0-0	2-2	3-4	3-6	0-0	8-12	38.2	35.4	43.8	47
Washington	...	1.000	.750	.500	...	.667				
Nedney, Joe	1-1	16-16	7-8	8-10	2-3	34-38	33.5	32.3	43.8	52
Den.-Car.*	1.000	1.000	.875	.800	.667	.895				
Richey, Wade	0-0	6-7	6-8	3-6	0-1	15-22	35.8	33.2	41.3	47
San Francisco	...	.857	.750	.500	.000	.682				

Player, Team	1-19	20-29	30-39	40-49	Over	Totals	Avg. Yds. Att.	Avg. Yds. Made	Avg. Yds. Miss	Long
Seder, Tim	2-2	5-6	9-11	9-13	0-1	25-33	36.3	34.7	41.5	48
Dallas	1.000	.833	.818	.692	.000	.758				
Stoyanovich, Pete	0-0	2-2	0-3	3-3	0-1	5-9	39.0	38.2	40.0	48
K.C.-St.L.*	...	1.000	.000	1.000	.000	.556				
Wilkins, Jeff	2-2	5-5	6-6	3-3	1-1	17-17	32.5	32.5	...	51
St. Louis	1.000	1.000	1.000	1.000	1.000	1.000				

*Includes both NFC and AFC statistics.

PLAYERS WITH TWO OR MORE CLUBS

Player, Team	1-19	20-29	30-39	40-49	Over	Totals	Avg. Yds. Att.	Avg. Yds. Made	Avg. Yds. Miss	Long
Conway, Brett	0-0	3-3	0-0	0-0	0-0	3-3	23.7	23.7	-	26
Washington	...	1.000	...	...	...	1.000				
Conway, Brett	1-1	0-0	0-0	0-0	0-0	1-1	19.0	19.0	-	19
Oakland	1.000	...	...	...	...	1.000				
Conway, Brett	1-1	0-0	0-0	1-1	0-0	2-2	29.5	29.5	-	40
N.Y. Jets	1.000	...	...	1.000	...	1.000				
Heppner, Kris	1-1	2-2	1-3	2-2	0-1	6-9	34.7	31.5	41.0	45
Seattle	1.000	1.000	.333	1.000	.000	.667				
Heppner, Kris	0-0	2-2	2-3	0-0	0-1	4-6	35.5	32.3	42.0	37
Washington	...	1.000	.667	...	.000	.667				
Nedney, Joe	0-0	6-6	1-1	1-2	0-1	8-10	29.7	25.5	46.5	43
Denver	...	1.000	1.000	.500	.000	.800				
Nedney, Joe	1-1	10-10	6-7	7-8	2-2	26-28	34.8	34.3	41.0	52
Carolina	1.000	1.000	.857	.875	1.000	.929				
Stoyanovich, Pete	0-0	1-1	0-2	1-1	0-0	2-4	35.5	34.5	36.5	42
Kansas City	...	1.000	.000	1.000	...	.500				
Stoyanovich, Pete	0-0	1-1	0-1	2-2	0-1	3-5	41.8	40.7	43.5	48
St. Louis	...	1.000	.000	1.000	.000	.600				

2000 STATISTICS Field goals

PUNTING

TEAM

AFC

Team	Total Punts	Yards	Long	Avg.	TB	Blocked	Opp. Ret.	Ret. Yards	Inside 20	Net Avg.
San Diego	92	4248	66	46.2	10	0	51	722	23	36.2
Cleveland	108	4919	67	45.5	5	0	69	793	25	37.3
Oakland	66	2984	69	45.2	10	1	30	279	24	38.0
N.Y. Jets	83	3714	70	44.7	15	0	42	660	18	33.2
Indianapolis	65	2906	65	44.7	9	0	28	357	20	36.4
Kansas City	82	3656	68	44.6	8	0	43	559	28	35.8
Pittsburgh	91	3944	67	43.3	8	1	44	371	34	37.5
New England	90	3798	62	42.2	5	1	43	384	31	36.8
Miami	92	3870	70	42.1	14	0	36	258	25	36.2
Jacksonville	79	3311	65	41.9	6	0	38	478	29	34.3
Tennessee	76	3101	67	40.8	9	0	28	160	33	36.3
Baltimore	86	3457	55	40.2	8	0	41	382	35	33.9
Cincinnati	94	3775	57	40.2	14	0	40	387	18	33.1
Denver	62	2455	62	39.6	9	1	23	270	18	32.3
Seattle	75	2960	57	39.5	2	1	32	151	24	36.9
Buffalo	96	3661	57	38.1	5	1	51	544	19	31.4
AFC total	1337	56759	70	...	137	6	639	6755	404	...
AFC average	83.6	3547.4	...	42.5	8.6	0.4	39.9	422.2	25.3	35.4

Leader based on average.

NFC

Team	Total Punts	Yards	Long	Avg.	TB	Blocked	Opp. Ret.	Ret. Yards	Inside 20	Net Avg.
Minnesota	62	2773	60	44.7	11	0	32	310	16	36.2
Arizona	65	2871	55	44.2	5	0	37	347	17	37.3
Detroit	95	4044	59	42.6	12	2	53	498	33	34.8
Philadelphia	86	3635	60	42.3	8	0	47	375	23	36.0
Dallas	68	2848	60	41.9	8	0	29	282	15	35.4
Tampa Bay	85	3551	63	41.8	8	0	41	408	17	35.1
New Orleans	74	3043	58	41.1	8	0	37	494	22	32.3
Atlanta	85	3447	60	40.6	5	1	29	126	27	37.9
N.Y. Giants	80	3210	64	40.1	8	1	28	353	26	33.7
Washington	79	3160	53	40.0	5	0	33	342	23	34.4
St. Louis	44	1736	59	39.5	5	1	17	132	13	34.2
San Francisco	70	2727	56	39.0	7	1	32	332	15	32.2
Green Bay	79	3033	53	38.4	6	0	27	205	22	34.3
Chicago	96	3624	56	37.8	7	0	36	251	20	33.7
Carolina	66	2459	66	37.3	2	2	25	187	19	33.8
NFC total	1134	46161	66	...	105	8	503	4642	308	...
NFC average	75.6	3077.4	...	40.7	7.0	0.5	33.5	309.5	20.5	34.8
NFL total	2471	102920	70	...	242	14	1142	11397	712	...
NFL average	79.7	3320.0	...	41.7	7.8	0.5	36.8	367.6	23.0	35.1

INDIVIDUAL

BESTS OF THE SEASON

Average yards per punt, season
AFC: 46.2—Darren Bennett, San Diego.
NFC: 44.7—Mitch Berger, Minnesota.

Net average yards per punt, season
AFC: 38.0—Shane Lechler, Oakland.
NFC: 37.9—Dan Stryzinski, Atlanta.

Longest
AFC: 70—Tom Tupa, N.Y. Jets vs. Buffalo, Sept. 17; Matt Turk, Miami at Cincinnati, Oct. 1; Matt Turk, Miami at Indianapolis, Nov. 26.
NFC: 66—Ken Walter, Carolina vs. San Diego, Dec. 17.

Punts, season
AFC: 108—Chris Gardocki, Cleveland.
NFC: 93—John Jett, Detroit.

Punts, game
AFC: 12—Josh Miller, Pittsburgh vs. Cincinnati, Oct. 15; Chris Gardocki, Cleveland at Jacksonville, Dec. 3.
NFC: 11—Mark Royals, Tampa Bay at Green Bay, Dec. 24 (OT).
10—Held by many players.

2000 STATISTICS Punting

Player, Team	Net Punts	Yards	Long	Avg.	Total Punts	TB	Blk.	Opp. Ret.	Ret. Yds.	In 20	Net Avg.
Bennett, Darren, San Diego	92	4248	66	46.2	92	10	0	51	722	23	36.2
Lechler, Shane, Oakland	65	2984	69	45.9	66	10	1	30	279	24	38.0
Gardocki, Chris, Cleveland	108	4919	67	45.5	108	5	0	69	793	25	37.3
Berger, Mitch, Minnesota	62	2773	60	44.7	62	11	0	32	310	16	36.2
Smith, Hunter, Indianapolis	65	2906	65	44.7	65	9	0	28	357	20	36.4
Tupa, Tom, N.Y. Jets	83	3714	70	44.7	83	15	0	42	660	18	33.2
Sauerbrun, Todd, Kansas City	82	3656	68	44.6	82	8	0	43	559	28	35.8
Player, Scott, Arizona	65	2871	55	44.2	65	5	0	37	347	17	37.3
Miller, Josh, Pittsburgh	90	3944	67	43.8	91	8	1	44	371	34	37.5
Jett, John, Detroit	93	4044	59	43.5	95	12	2	53	498	33	34.8
Knorr, Micah, Dallas	58	2481	60	42.8	58	8	0	25	248	12	35.7
Johnson, Lee, New England	89	3798	62	42.7	90	5	1	43	384	31	36.8
Landeta, Sean, Philadelphia	86	3635	60	42.3	86	8	0	47	375	23	36.0
Turk, Matt, Miami	92	3870	70	42.1	92	14	0	36	258	25	36.2
Barker, Bryan, Jacksonville	76	3194	65	42.0	76	5	0	38	478	29	34.4
Royals, Mark, Tampa Bay	85	3551	63	41.8	85	8	0	41	408	17	35.1
Gowin, Toby, New Orleans	74	3043	58	41.1	74	8	0	37	494	22	32.3
Stryzinski, Dan, Atlanta	84	3447	60	41.0	85	5	1	29	126	27	37.9
Hentrich, Craig, Tennessee	76	3101	67	40.8	76	9	0	28	160	33	36.3
Maynard, Brad, N.Y. Giants	79	3210	64	40.6	80	8	1	28	353	26	33.7
Baker, John, St. Louis	43	1736	59	40.4	44	5	1	17	132	13	34.2
Pope, Daniel, Cincinnati	94	3775	57	40.2	94	14	0	40	387	18	33.1
Richardson, Kyle, Baltimore	86	3457	55	40.2	86	8	0	41	382	35	33.9
Rouen, Tom, Denver	61	2455	62	40.2	62	9	1	23	270	18	32.3
Barnhardt, Tommy, Washington	79	3160	53	40.0	79	5	0	33	342	23	34.4
Feagles, Jeff, Seattle	74	2960	57	40.0	75	2	1	32	151	24	36.9
Stanley, Chad, San Francisco	69	2727	56	39.5	70	7	1	32	332	15	32.2
Aguiar, Louie, Chicago	52	2017	56	38.8	52	4	0	21	121	8	34.9
Bidwell, Josh, Green Bay	78	3003	53	38.5	78	5	0	27	205	22	34.6
Mohr, Chris, Buffalo	95	3661	57	38.5	96	5	1	51	544	19	31.4
Walter, Ken, Carolina	64	2459	66	38.4	66	2	2	25	187	19	33.8
Bartholomew, Brent, Chicago	44	1607	52	36.5	44	3	0	15	130	12	32.2

*AFC.
Leader based on average, minimum 40 punts.

AFC

Player, Team	Net Punts	Yards	Long	Avg.	Total Punts	TB	Blk.	Opp. Ret.	Ret. Yds.	In 20	Net Avg.
Barker, Bryan, Jacksonville	76	3194	65	42.0	76	5	0	38	478	29	34.4
Bennett, Darren, San Diego	92	4248	66	46.2	92	10	0	51	722	23	36.2
Feagles, Jeff, Seattle	74	2960	57	40.0	75	2	1	32	151	24	36.9
Gardocki, Chris, Cleveland	108	4919	67	45.5	108	5	0	69	793	25	37.3
Hentrich, Craig, Tennessee	76	3101	67	40.8	76	9	0	28	160	33	36.3
Johnson, Lee, New England	89	3798	62	42.7	90	5	1	43	384	31	36.8
Lechler, Shane, Oakland	65	2984	69	45.9	66	10	1	30	279	24	38.0
Lindsey, Steve, Jacksonville	3	117	46	39.0	3	1	0	0	0	0	32.3
Miller, Josh, Pittsburgh	90	3944	67	43.8	91	8	1	44	371	34	37.5
Mohr, Chris, Buffalo	95	3661	57	38.5	96	5	1	51	544	19	31.4
Pope, Daniel, Cincinnati	94	3775	57	40.2	94	14	0	40	387	18	33.1
Richardson, Kyle, Baltimore	86	3457	55	40.2	86	8	0	41	382	35	33.9
Rouen, Tom, Denver	61	2455	62	40.2	62	9	1	23	270	18	32.3
Sauerbrun, Todd, Kansas City	82	3656	68	44.6	82	8	0	43	559	28	35.8
Smith, Hunter, Indianapolis	65	2906	65	44.7	65	9	0	28	357	20	36.4
Tupa, Tom, N.Y. Jets	83	3714	70	44.7	83	15	0	42	660	18	33.2
Turk, Matt, Miami	92	3870	70	42.1	92	14	0	36	258	25	36.2

NFC

Player, Team	Net Punts	Yards	Long	Avg.	Total Punts	TB	Blk.	Opp. Ret.	Ret. Yds.	In 20	Net Avg.
Aguiar, Louie, Chicago	52	2017	56	38.8	52	4	0	21	121	8	34.9
Baker, John, St. Louis	43	1736	59	40.4	44	5	1	17	132	13	34.2
Barnhardt, Tommy, Washington	79	3160	53	40.0	79	5	0	33	342	23	34.4
Bartholomew, Brent, Chicago	44	1607	52	36.5	44	3	0	15	130	12	32.2
Berger, Mitch, Minnesota	62	2773	60	44.7	62	11	0	32	310	16	36.2
Bidwell, Josh, Green Bay	78	3003	53	38.5	78	5	0	27	205	22	34.6
Cantrell, Barry, Dallas	10	367	40	36.7	10	0	0	4	34	3	33.3

2000 STATISTICS Punting

Player, Team	Net Punts	Yards	Long	Avg.	Total Punts	TB	Blk.	Opp. Ret.	Ret. Yds.	In 20	Net Avg.
Gowin, Toby, New Orleans	74	3043	58	41.1	74	8	0	37	494	22	32.3
Jett, John, Detroit	93	4044	59	43.5	95	12	2	53	498	33	34.8
Knorr, Micah, Dallas	58	2481	60	42.8	58	8	0	25	248	12	35.7
Landeta, Sean, Philadelphia	86	3635	60	42.3	86	8	0	47	375	23	36.0
Longwell, Ryan, Green Bay	1	30	30	30.0	1	1	0	0	0	0	10.0
Maynard, Brad, N.Y. Giants	79	3210	64	40.6	80	8	1	28	353	26	33.7
Player, Scott, Arizona	65	2871	55	44.2	65	5	0	37	347	17	37.3
Royals, Mark, Tampa Bay	85	3551	63	41.8	85	8	0	41	408	17	35.1
Stanley, Chad, San Francisco	69	2727	56	39.5	70	7	1	32	332	15	32.2
Stryzinski, Dan, Atlanta	84	3447	60	41.0	85	5	1	29	126	27	37.9
Walter, Ken, Carolina	64	2459	66	38.4	66	2	2	25	187	19	33.8

PUNT RETURNS

TEAM

AFC

Team	No.	FC	Yds.	Avg.	Long	TD
Baltimore	45	10	713	15.8	t89	2
Miami	39	19	518	13.3	t81	1
Seattle	30	14	384	12.8	43	0
Tennessee	53	18	671	12.7	t69	1
New England	45	22	562	12.5	t66	1
Pittsburgh	42	20	499	11.9	54	1
Cleveland	29	14	294	10.1	30	0
Denver	36	12	364	10.1	64	0
Oakland	37	13	357	9.6	36	0
Indianapolis	38	14	352	9.3	40	0
Cincinnati	42	15	357	8.5	t82	1
Kansas City	37	12	295	8.0	26	0
N.Y. Jets	38	19	276	7.3	19	0
Jacksonville	46	19	333	7.2	22	0
San Diego	44	17	272	6.2	35	0
Buffalo	38	23	190	5.0	20	0
AFC total	639	261	6437	10.1	t89	7
AFC average	39.9	16.3	402.3	10.1	...	0.4

t—touchdown.

NFC

Team	No.	FC	Yds.	Avg.	Long	TD
St. Louis	34	18	521	15.3	t86	1
Detroit	33	24	472	14.3	t95	1
Carolina	21	12	238	11.3	t64	1
Dallas	35	14	364	10.4	t64	2
Philadelphia	33	33	335	10.2	t72	1
Minnesota	26	28	261	10.0	63	0
Washington	36	13	356	9.9	57	0
Atlanta	37	20	348	9.4	t70	1
Chicago	36	27	314	8.7	25	0
Tampa Bay	39	19	337	8.6	t73	1
Green Bay	35	26	300	8.6	43	0
New Orleans	40	17	339	8.5	51	0
San Francisco	26	13	220	8.5	25	0
N.Y. Giants	40	20	332	8.3	31	0
Arizona	32	11	223	7.0	25	0
NFC total	503	295	4960	9.9	t95	8
NFC average	33.5	19.7	330.7	9.9	...	0.5
NFL total	1142	556	11397	...	t95	15
NFL average	36.8	17.9	367.6	10.0	...	0.5

INDIVIDUAL

BESTS OF THE SEASON

Yards per attempt, season
AFC: 16.1—Jermaine Lewis, Baltimore.
NFC: 15.3—Az-Zahir Hakim, St. Louis.

Yards, season
AFC: 662—Derrick Mason, Tennessee.
NFC: 489—Az-Zahir Hakim, St. Louis.

Yards, game
AFC: 173—Jermaine Lewis, Baltimore vs. N.Y. Jets, Dec. 24 (4 returns, 2 TDs).
NFC: 119—Desmond Howard, Detroit at New Orleans, Sept. 3 (4 returns, 1 TD).

Longest
NFC: 95—Desmond Howard, Detroit at New Orleans, Sept. 3 (TD).
AFC: 89—Jermaine Lewis, Baltimore vs. N.Y. Jets, Dec. 24 (TD).

Returns, season
AFC: 51—Derrick Mason, Tennessee.
NFC: 39—Tiki Barber, N.Y. Giants.

Returns, game
NFC: 8—Tim Dwight, Atlanta at Detroit, Nov. 12 (34 yards).
AFC: 7—Craig Yeast, Cincinnati vs. Cleveland, Sept. 10 (35 yards).

Fair catches, season
NFC: 33—Brian Mitchell, Philadelphia.
AFC: 19—Troy Brown, New England; Dedric Ward, N.Y. Jets.

Touchdowns, season
AFC: 2—Jermaine Lewis, Baltimore.
NFC: 2—Wane McGarity, Dallas.

NFL LEADERS

Player, Team	No.	FC	Yds.	Avg.	Long	TD
Lewis, Jermaine, Baltimore*	36	9	578	16.1	t89	2
Hakim, Az-Zahir, St. Louis	32	17	489	15.3	t86	1
Howard, Desmond, Detroit	31	24	457	14.7	t95	1
Rogers, Charlie, Seattle*	26	12	363	14.0	43	0
Mason, Derrick, Tennessee*	51	17	662	13.0	t69	1
Poteat, Hank, Pittsburgh*	36	7	467	13.0	54	1
Brown, Troy, New England*	39	19	504	12.9	t66	1
McGarity, Wane, Dallas	30	9	353	11.8	t64	2
Northcutt, Dennis, Cleveland*..	27	12	289	10.7	30	0
Mitchell, Brian, Philadelphia	32	33	335	10.5	t72	1
O'Neal, Deltha, Denver*	34	11	354	10.4	64	0
Dwight, Tim, Atlanta	33	17	309	9.4	t70	1
Morton, Chad, New Orleans	30	14	278	9.3	51	0
Williams, Karl, Tampa Bay	31	18	286	9.2	t73	1
Gordon, Darrien, Oakland*	29	10	258	8.9	36	0

*AFC.

t—touchdown.

Leader based on average return, minimum 20.

AFC

Player, Team	No.	FC	Yds.	Avg.	Long	TD
Barlow, Reggie, Jacksonville	29	14	200	6.9	21	0
Barnes, Rashidi, Cleveland	1	0	0	0.0	0	0
Brown, Troy, New England	39	19	504	12.9	t66	1
Buckley, Terrell, Denver	2	1	10	5.0	11	0
Chapman, Lamar, Cleveland	1	2	5	5.0	5	0
Dumas, Mike, San Diego	1	0	1	1.0	1	0
Dunn, Damon, N.Y. Jets	1	0	0	0.0	0	0
Dunn, David, Oakland	8	3	99	12.4	25	0
Edwards, Troy, Pittsburgh	0	1	0	...	...	0
Faulk, Kevin, New England	6	3	58	9.7	35	0
Gordon, Darrien, Oakland	29	10	258	8.9	36	0
Graham, Jeff, San Diego	3	6	7	2.3	7	0
Griffin, Damon, Cincinnati	1	0	9	9.0	9	0
Hall, Dante, Kansas City	6	5	37	6.2	22	0
Hawkins, Courtney, Pittsburgh.	4	11	15	3.8	9	0
Jacquet, Nate, San Diego	30	8	211	7.0	35	0
Jenkins, DeRon, San Diego	1	0	0	0.0	0	0
Johnson, Leon, N.Y. Jets	10	0	62	6.2	16	0
Jones, Reggie, San Diego	9	3	53	5.9	17	0
Joseph, Kerry, Seattle	0	1	0	...	...	0
Kelly, Ben, Miami	5	0	31	6.2	10	0
Lewis, Jermaine, Baltimore	36	9	578	16.1	t89	2
Lockett, Kevin, Kansas City	26	6	208	8.0	26	0
Mason, Derrick, Tennessee	51	17	662	13.0	t69	1

Player, Team	No.	FC	Yds.	Avg.	Long	TD
McCardell, Keenan, Jac.	3	0	25	8.3	22	0
McDuffie, O.J., Miami	0	1	0	...	...	0
Muhammad, Mustafah, Ind.	2	0	4	2.0	4	0
Northcutt, Dennis, Cleveland....	27	12	289	10.7	30	0
Ogden, Jeff, Miami..................	19	11	323	17.0	t81	1
O'Neal, Deltha, Denver............	34	11	354	10.4	64	0
Parker, Larry, Kansas City	5	1	50	10.0	17	0
Poteat, Hank, Pittsburgh	36	7	467	13.0	54	1
Price, Peerless, Buffalo	5	5	27	5.4	12	0
Rogers, Charlie, Seattle...........	26	12	363	14.0	43	0
Shaw, Bobby, Pittsburgh.........	2	1	17	8.5	10	0
Shepherd, Leslie, Miami	15	7	164	10.9	32	0
Soward, R. Jay, Jacksonville....	14	5	108	7.7	18	0
Starks, Duane, Baltimore	9	1	135	15.0	47	0
Thigpen, Yancey, Tennessee.....	1	1	9	9.0	9	0
Walker, Denard, Tennessee	1	0	0	0.0	0	0
Ward, Dedric, N.Y. Jets	27	19	214	7.9	19	0
Warrick, Peter, Cincinnati	7	1	123	17.6	t82	1
Watson, Chris, Buffalo	33	18	163	4.9	20	0
Wilkins, Terrence, Indianapolis..	29	13	240	8.3	36	0
Williams, Payton, Indianapolis.	7	1	108	15.4	40	0
Yeast, Craig, Cincinnati	34	14	225	6.6	27	0

t—touchdown.

NFC

Player, Team	No.	FC	Yds.	Avg.	Long	TD
Bailey, Champ, Washington	1	1	65	65.0	54	0
Barber, Tiki, N.Y. Giants...........	39	20	332	8.5	31	0
Bates, Michael, Carolina..........	7	3	31	4.4	12	0
Bly, Dre', St. Louis	0	1	0	...	...	0
Bostic, Jason, Philadelphia	1	0	0	0.0	0	0
Byrd, Isaac, Carolina...............	1	1	10	10.0	10	0
Canty, Chris, Sea.-N.O.*..........	13	3	66	5.1	13	0
Cody, Mac, Arizona.................	31	11	222	7.2	25	0
Comella, Greg, N.Y. Giants.......	1	0	0	0.0	0	0
Davis, Eric, Carolina................	2	2	24	12.0	20	0
Dwight, Tim, Atlanta................	33	17	309	9.4	t70	1
Fair, Terry, Detroit...................	2	0	15	7.5	11	0

Player, Team	No.	FC	Yds.	Avg.	Long	TD
Galloway, Joey, Dallas..............	1	0	2	2.0	2	0
Green, Jacquez, Tampa Bay	2	0	1	0.5	1	0
Hakim, Az-Zahir, St. Louis........	32	17	489	15.3	t86	1
Harris, Walt, Chicago	1	1	14	14.0	14	0
Hastings, Andre, Tampa Bay	5	1	50	10.0	16	0
Hitchcock, Jimmy, Carolina......	1	0	0	0.0	0	0
Horne, Tony, St. Louis..............	1	0	16	16.0	16	0
Howard, Desmond, Detroit	31	24	457	14.7	t95	1
Jenkins, MarTay, Arizona	1	0	1	1.0	1	0
Lee, Charles, Green Bay	5	2	52	10.4	16	0
Lyght, Todd, St. Louis..............	0	0	16	...	16	0
Mathis, Kevin, New Orleans	1	1	5	5.0	5	0
McCleon, Dexter, St. Louis.......	1	0	0	0.0	0	0
McGarity, Wane, Dallas	30	9	353	11.8	t64	2
McKenzie, Mike, Green Bay......	1	0	0	0.0	0	0
Milburn, Glyn, Chicago	35	26	300	8.6	25	0
Mitchell, Brian, Philadelphia.....	32	33	335	10.5	t72	1
Morton, Chad, New Orleans	30	14	278	9.3	51	0
Oliver, Winslow, Atlanta	4	3	39	9.8	40	0
Palmer, David, Minnesota	10	12	33	3.3	16	0
Rossum, Allen, Green Bay	29	24	248	8.6	43	0
Sanders, Deion, Washington....	25	6	185	7.4	57	0
Thrash, James, Washington.....	10	6	106	10.6	25	0
Tucker, Jason, Dallas...............	4	5	9	2.3	8	0
Uwaezuoke, Iheanyi, Carolina ..	10	6	173	17.3	t64	1
Walsh, Chris, Minnesota	1	0	11	11.0	11	0
Walters, Troy, Minnesota	15	16	217	14.5	63	0
Williams, Karl, Tampa Bay	31	18	286	9.2	t73	1
Williams, Kevin, San Francisco	26	13	220	8.5	25	0
Wilson, Robert, New Orleans ...	0	0	11	...	11	0
Yoder, Todd, Tampa Bay..........	1	0	0	0.0	0	0

t—touchdown.
*Includes both AFC and NFC statistics.

PLAYERS WITH TWO CLUBS

Player, Team	No.	FC	Yds.	Avg.	Long	TD
Canty, Chris, Seattle................	4	1	21	5.3	8	0
Canty, Chris, New Orleans.......	9	2	45	5.0	13	0

2000 STATISTICS Punt returns

KICKOFF RETURNS

TEAM

AFC

Team	No.	Yds.	Avg.	Long	TD
Tennessee	47	1227	26.1	66	0
Seattle	80	1932	24.2	t81	1
Oakland	56	1336	23.9	t88	1
Denver	66	1477	22.4	t87	1
Baltimore	45	1005	22.3	41	0
Miami	51	1133	22.2	56	0
San Diego	83	1792	21.6	t93	1
Jacksonville	62	1323	21.3	47	0
Pittsburgh	58	1221	21.1	t98	1
N.Y. Jets	74	1552	21.0	t97	1
Kansas City	70	1466	20.9	38	0
New England	64	1335	20.9	47	0
Cleveland	85	1710	20.1	62	0
Indianapolis	58	1155	19.9	48	0
Cincinnati	77	1423	18.5	50	0
Buffalo	69	1262	18.3	37	0
AFC total	1045	22349	21.4	t98	6
AFC average	65.3	1396.8	21.4	...	0.4

t—touchdown.

NFC

Team	No.	Yds.	Avg.	Long	TD
Arizona	86	2296	26.7	t98	1
Green Bay	64	1570	24.5	t92	1
New Orleans	62	1473	23.8	68	0
Philadelphia	53	1237	23.3	t89	1
Detroit	69	1600	23.2	70	0
Tampa Bay	55	1255	22.8	48	0
Atlanta	83	1890	22.8	t100	3
Chicago	68	1512	22.2	38	0
St. Louis	80	1771	22.1	t103	1
Minnesota	67	1456	21.7	38	0
Dallas	69	1456	21.1	90	0
Carolina	55	1160	21.1	t92	1
N.Y. Giants	53	1102	20.8	47	1
Washington	63	1301	20.7	49	0
San Francisco	68	1299	19.1	68	0
NFC total	995	22378	22.5	t103	9
NFC average	66.3	1491.9	22.5	...	0.6
NFL total	2040	44727	...	t103	15
NFL average	65.8	1442.8	21.9	...	0.5

INDIVIDUAL

BESTS OF THE SEASON

Yards per attempt, season
NFC: 27.7—Darrick Vaughn, Atlanta.
AFC: 27.0—Derrick Mason, Tennessee.

Yards, season
NFC: 2186—MarTay Jenkins, Arizona.
AFC: 1629—Charlie Rogers, Seattle.

Yards, game
NFC: 267—Tony Horne, St. Louis at Kansas City, Oct. 22 (8 returns).
AFC: 221—Ronney Jenkins, San Diego vs. New Orleans, Sept. 10 (6 returns, 1 TD).

Longest
NFC: 103—Tony Horne, St. Louis vs. Atlanta, Oct. 15 (TD).
AFC: 98—Will Blackwell, Pittsburgh at San Diego, Dec. 24 (TD).

Returns, season
NFC: 82—MarTay Jenkins, Arizona.
AFC: 67—Ronney Jenkins, San Diego.

Returns, game
AFC: 8—Ronney Jenkins, San Diego at St. Louis, Oct. 1 (187 yards); Ronney Jenkins, San Diego vs. San Francisco, Dec. 3 (164 yards).
NFC: 8—Tony Horne, St. Louis vs. Denver, Sept. 4 (145 yards); Tony Horne, St. Louis at Kansas City, Oct. 22 (267 yards); MarTay Jenkins, Arizona at Jacksonville, Dec. 10 (193 yards); Troy Walters, Minnesota vs. Green Bay, Dec. 17 (177 yards).

Touchdowns, season
NFC: 3—Darrick Vaughn, Atlanta.
AFC: 1—Held by six players.

NFL LEADERS

Player, Team	No.	Yds.	Avg.	Long	TD
Vaughn, Darrick, Atlanta	39	1082	27.7	t100	3
Mason, Derrick, Tennessee*	42	1132	27.0	66	0
Jenkins, MarTay, Arizona	82	2186	26.7	t98	1
Rossum, Allen, Green Bay	50	1288	25.8	t92	1

Player, Team	No.	Yds.	Avg.	Long	TD
Williams, Kevin, Miami*	24	615	25.6	t97	1
Denson, Autry, Miami*	20	495	24.8	56	0
Rogers, Charlie, Seattle*	66	1629	24.7	t81	1
Howard, Desmond, Detroit	57	1401	24.6	70	0
Dunn, David, Oakland*	44	1073	24.4	t88	0
Horne, Tony, St. Louis	57	1379	24.2	t103	1
O'Neal, Deltha, Denver*	46	1102	24.0	t87	1
Mitchell, Brian, Philadelphia	47	1124	23.9	t89	1
Stith, Shyrone, Jacksonville*	33	785	23.8	47	0
Morton, Chad, New Orleans	44	1029	23.4	68	0
Marion, Brock, Miami*	22	513	23.3	47	0

*AFC.
t—touchdown.
Leader based on average return, minimum 20.

AFC

Player, Team	No.	Yds.	Avg.	Long	TD
Anders, Kimble, Kansas City	1	14	14.0	14	0
Barlow, Reggie, Jacksonville	11	224	20.4	27	0
Battaglia, Marco, Cincinnati	f0	0	...	...	0
Baxter, Fred, N.Y. Jets	1	15	15.0	15	0
Becht, Anthony, N.Y. Jets	2	0	0.0	0	0
Black, Avion, Buffalo	9	165	18.3	26	0
Blackwell, Will, Pittsburgh	10	281	28.1	t98	1
Bownes, Fabien, Seattle	3	83	27.7	38	0
Branch, Calvin, Oakland	2	48	24.0	24	0
Brown, Cornell, Baltimore	1	0	0.0	0	0
Brown, Reggie, Seattle	2	19	9.5	19	0
Brown, Troy, New England	2	15	7.5	9	0
Bruschi, Tedy, New England	2	13	6.5	7	0
Bryson, Shawn, Buffalo	8	122	15.3	26	0
Burnett, Chester, Cleveland	1	18	18.0	18	0
Bush, Steve, Cincinnati	3	18	6.0	8	0
Bynum, Kenny, San Diego	13	242	18.6	39	0
Campbell, Mark, Cleveland	3	30	10.0	13	0
Carswell, Dwayne, Denver	1	0	0.0	0	0
Carter, Tony, New England	1	16	16.0	16	0
Cavil, Kwame, Buffalo	1	1	1.0	1	0
Chamberlain, Byron, Denver	2	25	12.5	13	0
Cloud, Mike, Kansas City	36	779	21.6	38	0

Player, Team	No.	Yds.	Avg.	Long	TD
Cole, Chris, Denver	11	264	24.0	37	0
Coleman, Chris, Tennessee	2	54	27.0	27	0
Coles, Laveranues, N.Y. Jets	11	207	18.8	24	0
Davis, Shockmain, New England	2	45	22.5	32	0
Denson, Autry, Miami	20	495	24.8	56	0
Dilger, Ken, Indianapolis	1	0	0.0	0	0
Dunn, Damon, N.Y. Jets	2	35	17.5	21	0
Dunn, David, Oakland	44	1073	24.4	t88	1
Edwards, Marc, Cleveland	1	24	24.0	24	0
Edwards, Troy, Pittsburgh	15	298	19.9	37	0
Faulk, Kevin, New England	38	816	21.5	40	0
Fauria, Christian, Seattle	1	9	9.0	9	0
Fordham, Todd, Jacksonville	1	0	0.0	0	0
Foreman, Jay, Buffalo	1	19	19.0	19	0
Glenn, Aaron, N.Y. Jets	3	51	17.0	22	0
Goodwin, Hunter, Miami	2	6	3.0	6	0
Gordon, Darrien, Oakland	1	17	17.0	17	0
Graham, DeMingo, San Diego	1	0	0.0	0	0
Griffin, Damon, Cincinnati	8	129	16.1	29	0
Hall, Dante, Kansas City	17	358	21.1	36	0
Hamilton, Bobby, New England	1	0	0.0	0	0
Harris, Corey, Baltimore	39	907	23.3	41	0
Heath, Rodney, Cincinnati	1	22	22.0	22	0
Holmes, Priest, Baltimore	1	7	7.0	7	0
Holsey, Bernard, Indianapolis	1	10	10.0	10	0
Ismail, Qadry, Baltimore	2	51	25.5	38	0
Jackson, Curtis, New England	13	323	24.8	47	0
Jackson, Lenzie, Cleveland	9	168	18.7	30	0
Jacox, Kendyl, San Diego	1	8	8.0	8	0
Jenkins, Ronney, San Diego	67	1531	22.9	t93	1
Johnson, J.J., Miami	2	26	13.0	26	0
Johnson, Leon, N.Y. Jets	6	117	19.5	27	0
Jones, Henry, Buffalo	1	4	4.0	4	0
Jones, Reggie, San Diego	1	11	11.0	11	0
Joseph, Kerry, Seattle	3	71	23.7	34	0
Kaufman, Napoleon, Oakland	9	198	22.0	31	0
Keaton, Curtis, Cincinnati	6	100	16.7	25	0
Kreider, Dan, Pittsburgh	1	0	0.0	0	0
Leach, Mike, Tennessee	1	10	10.0	10	0
Leroy, Emarlos, Jacksonville	1	0	0.0	0	0
Lewis, Jermaine, Baltimore	1	23	23.0	23	0
Linton, Jonathan, Buffalo	3	40	13.3	17	0
Little, Earl, Cleveland	2	20	10.0	12	0
Lockett, Kevin, Kansas City	1	25	25.0	25	0
Mack, Stacey, Jacksonville	6	104	17.3	35	0
Mack, Tremain, Cincinnati	50	1036	20.7	50	0
Macklin, David, Indianapolis	1	0	0.0	0	0
Marion, Brock, Miami	22	513	23.3	47	0
Mason, Derrick, Tennessee	42	1132	27.0	66	0
Mili, Itula, Seattle	1	19	19.0	19	0
Miller, Billy, Denver	1	13	13.0	13	0
Morris, Sammy, Buffalo	1	17	17.0	17	0
Muhammad, Mustafah, Ind.	2	45	22.5	26	0
Neal, Lorenzo, Tennessee	1	15	15.0	15	0
O'Neal, Deltha, Denver	46	1102	24.0	t87	1
Parker, Larry, Kansas City	14	279	19.9	27	0
Pathon, Jerome, Indianapolis	26	583	22.4	48	0
Patten, David, Cleveland	22	469	21.3	62	0
Poteat, Hank, Pittsburgh	24	465	19.4	31	0
Redmond, J.R., New England	1	25	25.0	25	0
Rogers, Charlie, Seattle	66	1629	24.7	t81	1
Saleh, Tarek, Cleveland	4	46	11.5	15	0
Scott, Tony, N.Y. Jets	1	0	0.0	0	0
Shaw, Bobby, Pittsburgh	0	-8	...	-8	0
Shepherd, Leslie, Miami	1	14	14.0	14	0
Simmons, Tony, New England	4	82	20.5	39	0
Smith, Antowain, Buffalo	1	0	0.0	0	0
Smith, Detron, Denver	5	73	14.6	17	0
Soward, R. Jay, Jacksonville	4	93	23.3	28	0
Sowell, Jerald, N.Y. Jets	1	9	9.0	9	0
Spears, Marcus, Kansas City	1	11	11.0	11	0
Stith, Shyrone, Jacksonville	33	785	23.8	47	0

Player, Team	No.	Yds.	Avg.	Long	TD
Stone, Dwight, N.Y. Jets	25	555	22.2	43	0
Strong, Mack, Seattle	1	26	26.0	26	0
Thornton, John, Tennessee	1	16	16.0	16	0
Tuman, Jerame, Pittsburgh	1	-1	-1.0	-1	0
Ward, Hines, Pittsburgh	7	186	26.6	57	0
Washington, Keith, Baltimore	1	17	17.0	17	0
Watson, Chris, Buffalo	44	894	20.3	37	0
Weaver, Jed, Miami	1	15	15.0	15	0
White, Jamel, Cleveland	43	935	21.7	40	0
Whitted, Alvis, Jacksonville	4	67	16.8	20	0
Wiggins, Jermaine, N.Y. Jets	1	12	12.0	12	0
Wilkins, Terrence, Indianapolis	15	279	18.6	30	0
Williams, James, Seattle	3	76	25.3	40	0
Williams, Jermaine, Jacksonville	2	50	25.0	30	0
Williams, Kevin, NYJ-Mia.	24	615	25.6	t97	1
Williams, Nick, Cincinnati	2	12	6.0	12	0
Williams, Payton, Indianapolis	12	238	19.8	29	0
Yeast, Craig, Cincinnati	7	106	15.1	29	0

t—touchdown.
f—includes at least one fair catch.

NFC

Player, Team	No.	Yds.	Avg.	Long	TD
Abdullah, Rabih, Tampa Bay	1	16	16.0	16	0
Allen, Terry, New Orleans	0	6	...	6	0
Anthony, Reidel, Tampa Bay	3	88	29.3	45	0
Arrington, LaVar, Washington	1	39	39.0	23	0
Barber, Tiki, N.Y. Giants	1	28	28.0	28	0
Barrett, David, Arizona	0	46	...	41	0
Bates, Michael, Carolina	42	941	22.4	t92	1
Bennett, Tommy, Arizona	1	17	17.0	17	0
Berry, Gary, Green Bay	1	22	22.0	22	0
Beverly, Eric, Detroit	1	0	0.0	0	0
Blevins, Darrius, St. Louis	9	173	19.2	26	0
Bly, Dre', St. Louis	9	163	18.1	36	0
Bowens, David, Green Bay	1	12	12.0	12	0
Broughton, Luther, Philadelphia	1	20	20.0	20	0
Burks, Diaello, Carolina	1	25	25.0	25	0
Byrd, Isaac, Carolina	9	172	19.1	30	0
Carter, Tyrone, Minnesota	17	389	22.9	38	0
Cody, Mac, Arizona	1	18	18.0	18	0
Comella, Greg, N.Y. Giants	2	20	10.0	11	0
Dixon, Ron, N.Y. Giants	31	658	21.2	44	0
Douglas, Dameane, Philadelphia	2	50	25.0	41	0
Dwight, Tim, Atlanta	32	680	21.3	48	0
Enis, Curtis, Chicago	2	30	15.0	19	0
Fair, Terry, Detroit	6	149	24.8	31	0
Faulk, Marshall, St. Louis	1	18	18.0	18	0
Finneran, Brian, Atlanta	1	2	2.0	2	0
Fletcher, London, St. Louis	1	17	17.0	17	0
Goodman, Herbert, Green Bay	4	129	32.3	54	0
Goodrich, Dwayne, Dallas	1	12	12.0	12	0
Green, Jacquez, Tampa Bay	1	11	11.0	11	0
Green, Ray, Carolina	1	1	1.0	1	0
Hakim, Az-Zahir, St. Louis	1	2	2.0	2	0
Henderson, William, Green Bay	5	80	16.0	22	0
Hetherington, Chris, Carolina	2	21	10.5	11	0
Hicks, Skip, Washington	1	17	17.0	17	0
Horne, Tony, St. Louis	57	1379	24.2	t103	1
Howard, Desmond, Detroit	57	1401	24.6	70	0
Jackson, Terry, San Francisco	1	9	9.0	9	0
Jenkins, MarTay, Arizona	82	2186	26.7	t98	1
Jervey, Travis, San Francisco	8	209	26.1	68	0
Jurevicius, Joe, N.Y. Giants	1	3	3.0	3	0
Kozlowski, Brian, Atlanta	1	77	11.0	21	0
LaFleur, David, Dallas	2	21	10.5	13	0
Levingston, Bashir, N.Y. Giants	7	153	21.9	43	0
Lewis, Jonas, San Francisco	9	168	18.7	26	0
Mathis, Kevin, New Orleans	8	187	23.4	40	0
McAfee, Fred, New Orleans	10	251	25.1	52	0
McKinley, Dennis, Arizona	1	20	20.0	20	0

Player, Team	No.	Yds.	Avg.	Long	TD
McKinnon, Ronald, Arizona............	1	9	9.0	9	0
Milburn, Glyn, Chicago................	63	1468	23.3	38	0
Milem, John, San Francisco.........	1	13	13.0	13	0
Mitchell, Basil, Green Bay.............	1	26	26.0	26	0
Mitchell, Brian, Philadelphia........	47	1124	23.9	t89	1
Moran, Sean, St. Louis................	1	17	17.0	17	0
Morrow, Harold, Minnesota..........	1	17	17.0	17	0
Morton, Chad, New Orleans.........	44	1029	23.4	68	0
Morton, Mike, Green Bay.............	1	13	13.0	13	0
Murphy, Frank, Tampa Bay...........	2	24	12.0	19	0
Murrell, Adrian, Washington........	12	214	17.8	30	0
Noble, Brandon, Dallas..............	1	8	8.0	8	0
Okeafor, Chike, San Francisco......	1	17	17.0	17	0
Oliver, Winslow, Atlanta...............	2	15	7.5	11	0
Olivo, Brock, Detroit...................	3	25	8.3	13	0
Palmer, David, Minnesota.............	6	120	20.0	24	0
Plummer, Ahmed, San Francisco ..	1	0	0.0	0	0
Pritchett, Stanley, Philadelphia......	1	15	15.0	15	0
Proehl, Ricky, St. Louis................	1	2	2.0	2	0
Rossum, Allen, Green Bay............	50	1288	25.8	t92	1
Sanders, Deion, Washington.........	1	-1	-1.0	-1	0
Santiago, O.J., Dallas..................	1	13	13.0	13	0
Schlesinger, Cory, Detroit.............	2	25	12.5	14	0
Sehorn, Jason, N.Y. Giants...........	2	31	15.5	t38	1
Sellers, Mike, Washington.............	3	32	10.7	21	0
Sinceno, Kaseem, Chicago............	1	12	12.0	12	0
Smith, Paul, San Francisco..........	9	167	18.6	28	0
Stecker, Aaron, Tampa Bay............	29	663	22.9	48	0

Player, Team	No.	Yds.	Avg.	Long	TD
Stephens, Reggie, N.Y. Giants.......	3	69	23.0	40	0
Stoutmire, Omar, N.Y. Giants........	6	140	23.3	47	0
Streets, Tai, San Francisco...........	8	180	22.5	37	0
Thomas, Orlando, Minnesota........	1	15	15.0	15	0
Thomason, Jeff, Philadelphia........	1	10	10.0	10	0
Thrash, James, Washington..........	45	1000	22.2	49	0
Tucker, Jason, Dallas....................	51	1099	21.5	90	0
Tucker, Rex, Chicago	1	0	0.0	0	0
Tuinei, Van, Chicago	1	2	2.0	2	0
Vaughn, Darrick, Atlanta...............	39	1082	27.7	t100	3
Walsh, Chris, Minnesota...............	2	9	4.5	6	0
Walters, Troy, Minnesota..............	30	692	23.1	38	0
Wetnight, Ryan, Green Bay............	1	0	0.0	0	0
Whiting, Brandon, Philadelphia	1	18	18.0	18	0
Wiley, Michael, Dallas...................	13	303	23.3	38	0
Williams, Elijah, Atlanta	2	34	17.0	19	0
Williams, Karl, Tampa Bay.............	19	453	23.8	41	0
Williams, Kevin, San Francisco	30	536	17.9	33	0
Williams, Moe, Minnesota.............	10	214	21.4	34	0

t—touchdown.
f—includes at least one fair catch.

PLAYERS WITH TWO CLUBS

Player, Team	No.	Yds.	Avg.	Long	TD
Williams, Kevin, N.Y. Jets..............	21	551	26.2	t97	1
Williams, Kevin, Miami..................	3	64	21.3	24	0

2000 STATISTICS *Kickoff returns*

MISCELLANEOUS

CLUB RANKINGS BY YARDS

Team	OFFENSE Total	Rush	Pass	DEFENSE Total	Rush	Pass
Arizona	24	27	17	30	30	11
Atlanta	30	28	24	25	27	24
Baltimore	16	5	22	2	*1	8
Buffalo	9	13	11	3	6	4
Carolina	20	29	12	27	26	26
Chicago	23	21	23	16	19	17
Cincinnati	29	2	31	22	24	23
Cleveland	31	30	30	26	29	12
Dallas	25	12	28	19	31	3
Denver	2	3	3	24	7	31
Detroit	27	20	25	14	18	15
Green Bay	15	23	8	15	8	19
Indianapolis	3	16	2	21	25	18
Jacksonville	7	10	9	12	11	14
Kansas City	8	25	5	18	17	20
Miami	26	14	27	6	14	5
Minnesota	5	6	7	28	15	28
New England	22	26	19	20	21	21
New Orleans	10	8	14	8	10	10
N.Y. Giants	13	11	13	5	2	16
N.Y. Jets	12	24	6	T10	23	6
Oakland	6	*1	15	17	5	25
Philadelphia	17	15	20	T10	20	7
Pittsburgh	18	4	29	7	12	9
St. Louis	*1	17	*1	23	13	27
San Diego	28	31	18	13	4	22
San Francisco	4	18	4	29	16	29
Seattle	19	22	21	31	28	30
Tampa Bay	21	9	26	9	9	13
Tennessee	14	7	16	*1	3	*1
Washington	11	19	10	4	22	2

*NFL leader.

TAKEAWAYS/GIVEAWAYS

AFC

	TAKEAWAYS Int.	Fum.	Tot.	GIVEAWAYS Int.	Fum.	Tot.	Net Diff.
Baltimore	23	26	49	19	7	26	23
Denver	27	17	44	12	13	25	19
Oakland	21	16	37	11	9	20	17
Miami	28	13	41	17	9	26	15
Pittsburgh	17	18	35	10	11	21	14
Buffalo	16	13	29	10	13	23	6
Kansas City	15	14	29	15	11	26	3
Jacksonville	12	18	30	15	14	29	1
Tennessee	17	13	30	16	14	30	0
New England	10	13	23	15	10	25	-2
Cleveland	12	13	25	19	9	28	-3
N.Y. Jets	21	14	35	29	11	40	-5
Indianapolis	14	8	22	15	14	29	-7
Seattle	17	12	29	21	17	38	-9
Cincinnati	9	12	21	14	21	35	-14
San Diego	16	6	22	30	20	50	-28

NFC

	TAKEAWAYS Int.	Fum.	Tot.	GIVEAWAYS Int.	Fum.	Tot.	Net Diff.
Tampa Bay	25	16	41	13	11	24	17
Detroit	25	17	42	19	12	31	11
New Orleans	20	15	35	15	11	26	9
N.Y. Giants	20	11	31	13	11	24	7
Carolina	17	21	38	19	16	35	3
Philadelphia	19	12	31	15	14	29	2
San Francisco	13	8	21	10	9	19	2
Washington	17	16	33	21	12	33	0
Green Bay	21	7	28	16	17	33	-5
Atlanta	15	10	25	20	14	34	-9
Chicago	11	9	20	16	13	29	-9
Minnesota	8	10	18	18	10	28	-10
St. Louis	19	6	25	23	12	35	-10
Dallas	16	9	25	21	18	39	-14
Arizona	10	10	20	24	20	44	-24

CLUB LEADERS

	Offense	Defense
First downs	Den. 383	Ten. 215
Rushing	Oak. 128	Bal. 59
Passing	St.L. 247	Ten., Was. 134
Penalty	Car. 40	Car. 13
Rushes	Ten. 547	Den. 344
Net yards gained	Oak. 2470	Bal. 970
Average gain	Min. 5.0	Bal. 2.7
Passes attempted	NYJ 637	Dal., Jac. 458
Completed	St.L. 380	Ten. 242
Percent completed	St.L. 64.7	NYJ 51.3
Total yards gained	St.L. 5492	Ten. 2761
Times sacked	Ind., NYJ 20	N.O. 66
Yards lost	NYJ 99	N.O. 378
Net yards gained	St.L. 5232	Ten. 2423
Net yards per pass play	St.L. 8.29	Ten. 4.65
Yards gained per completion	St.L. 14.45	T.B. 10.28
Combined net yards gained	St.L. 7075	Ten. 3813
Percent total yards rushing	Cin. 54.3	Bal. 24.5
Percent total yards passing	S.D. 75.3	Dal. 50.5
Ball-control plays	Den. 1115	Ten. 908
Average yards per play	St.L. 6.98	Ten. 4.20
Avg. time of possession	Ten. 33:48	—
Third-down efficiency	St.L. 47.5	Ten. 30.8
Interceptions	—	Mia. 28
Yards returned	—	Bal. 477
Returned for TD	—	Den. 5
Punts	Cle. 108	—
Yards punted	Cle. 4919	—
Average yards per punt	S.D. 46.2	—
Punt returns	Ten. 53	St.L. 17
Yards returned	Bal. 713	Atl. 126
Average yds. per return	Bal. 15.8	Atl. 4.3
Returned for TD	Bal., Dal. 2	—
Kickoff returns	Ari. 86	Cin., Cle. 42
Yards returned	Ari. 2296	Ari. 827
Average yards per return	Ari. 26.7	Car. 17.5
Returned for TD	Atl. 3	—
Total points scored	St.L. 540	Bal. 165
Total TDs	St.L. 67	Bal. 18
TDs rushing	St.L. 26	Bal. 5
TDs passing	St.L. 37	Ten. 10
TDs on ret. and recov.	Den. 9	NYG 0
Extra point kicks	St.L. 58	—
2-Pt. conversions	Det., St.L. 4	12 tied with 0
Safeties	Ind., Oak. 2	—
Field goals made	Bal. 35	NYG 13
Field goals attempted	Bal. 39	Bal. 19
Percent successful	Min. 95.7	NYG 54.2
Extra points	St.L. 62	Bal. 15

OFFENSE

	Bal.	Buf.	Cin.	Cle.	Den.	Ind.	Jac.	K.C.	Mia.	N.E.	NYJ	Oak.	Pit.	S.D.	Sea.	Ten.
First downs	288	309	254	176	383	357	321	318	251	283	308	337	283	251	281	299
Rushing	116	111	119	53	124	111	109	84	104	80	84	128	124	63	98	107
Passing	156	174	109	110	223	213	193	207	122	172	192	177	128	156	168	167
Penalty	16	24	26	13	36	33	16	30	25	31	32	32	31	32	15	25
Rushes	511	475	495	336	516	435	481	383	496	424	418	520	527	351	403	547
Net yards gained	2199	1922	2314	1085	2311	1859	2032	1465	1894	1390	1471	2470	2248	1062	1720	2084
Average gain	4.3	4.0	4.7	3.2	4.5	4.3	4.2	3.8	3.8	3.3	3.5	4.8	4.3	3.0	4.3	3.8
Average yards per game	137.4	120.1	144.6	67.8	144.4	116.2	127.0	91.6	118.4	86.9	91.9	154.4	140.5	66.4	107.5	130.3
Passes attempted	504	546	454	483	569	571	545	582	421	565	637	475	439	578	507	462
Completed	287	312	207	278	354	357	333	342	243	328	352	284	217	311	308	286
Percent completed	56.9	57.1	45.6	57.6	62.2	62.5	61.1	58.8	57.7	58.1	55.3	59.8	49.4	53.8	60.7	61.9
Total yards gained	3102	3936	2219	2728	4464	4413	3947	4408	2720	3461	4023	3430	2738	3540	3198	3430
Times sacked	43	59	52	40	30	20	54	34	28	48	20	28	43	53	46	27
Yards lost	287	360	273	283	221	131	289	259	153	280	99	124	220	302	238	164
Net yards gained	2815	3576	1946	2445	4243	4282	3658	4149	2567	3181	3924	3306	2518	3238	2960	3266
Average yards per game	175.9	223.5	121.6	152.8	265.2	267.6	228.6	259.3	160.4	198.8	245.3	206.6	157.4	202.4	185.0	204.1
Net yards per pass play	5.15	5.91	3.85	4.67	7.08	7.25	6.11	6.74	5.72	5.19	5.97	6.57	5.22	5.13	5.35	6.68
Yards gained per completion	10.81	12.62	10.72	9.81	12.61	12.36	11.85	12.89	11.19	10.55	11.43	12.08	12.62	11.38	10.38	11.99
Combined net yards gained	5014	5498	4260	3530	6554	6141	5690	5614	4461	4571	5395	5776	4766	4300	4680	5350
Percent total yards rushing	43.9	35.0	54.3	30.7	35.3	30.3	35.7	26.1	42.5	30.4	27.3	42.8	47.2	24.7	36.8	39.0
Percent total yards passing	56.1	65.0	45.7	69.3	64.7	69.7	64.3	73.9	57.5	69.6	72.7	57.2	52.8	75.3	63.2	61.0
Average yards per game	313.4	343.6	266.3	220.6	409.6	383.8	355.6	350.9	278.8	285.7	337.2	361.0	297.9	268.8	292.5	334.4
Ball-control plays	1058	1080	1001	859	1115	1026	1080	999	945	1037	1075	1023	1009	982	956	1036
Average yards per play	4.7	5.1	4.3	4.1	5.9	6.0	5.3	5.6	4.7	4.4	5.0	5.6	4.7	4.4	4.9	5.2
Average time of possession	33:19	31:25	27:13	25:59	33:15	29:33	31:32	27:36	30:43	28:56	30:20	31:53	31:27	28:08	27:31	33:48
Third-down efficiency	40.3	37.2	33.9	27.6	44.5	46.8	42.6	36.8	35.0	35.0	38.2	43.2	37.6	32.9	40.5	42.5
Had intercepted	19	10	14	19	12	15	15	15	17	15	29	11	10	30	21	16
Yards opponents returned	234	112	138	228	144	212	168	295	102	208	545	93	150	515	191	236
Returned by opponents for TD	2	1	0	2	1	1	0	3	1	2	4	0	2	3	2	3
Punts	86	96	94	108	62	65	79	82	92	90	83	66	91	92	75	76
Yards punted	3457	3661	3775	4919	2455	2906	3311	3656	3870	3798	3714	2984	3944	4248	2960	3101
Average yards per punt	40.2	38.1	40.2	45.5	39.6	44.7	41.9	44.6	42.1	42.2	44.7	45.2	43.3	46.2	39.5	40.8
Punt returns	45	38	42	29	36	38	46	37	39	45	38	37	42	44	30	53
Yards returned	713	190	357	294	364	352	333	295	518	562	276	357	499	272	384	671
Average yards per return	15.8	5.0	8.5	10.1	10.1	9.3	7.2	8.0	13.3	12.5	7.3	9.6	11.9	6.2	12.8	12.7
Returned for TD	2	0	0	1	0	0	0	0	1	1	0	0	1	0	0	1
Kickoff returns	45	69	77	85	66	58	62	70	51	64	74	56	58	83	80	47
Yards returned	1005	1262	1423	1710	1477	1155	1323	1466	1133	1335	1552	1336	1221	1792	1932	1227
Average yards per return	22.3	18.3	18.5	20.1	22.4	19.9	21.3	20.9	22.2	20.9	21.0	23.9	21.1	21.6	24.2	26.1
Returned for TD	0	0	0	0	1	0	0	0	0	0	1	1	1	1	1	0
Fumbles	26	28	37	21	26	20	27	23	12	23	18	18	24	38	35	24
Lost	7	13	21	9	13	14	14	11	9	10	11	9	11	20	17	14
Out of bounds	3	1	3	0	2	2	1	2	2	0	0	1	0	1	1	0
Recovered for TD	0	2	0	0	0	0	0	0	0	0	0	0	0	0	0	0
Penalties	95	101	99	103	89	94	95	118	115	99	76	118	81	121	89	107
Yards penalized	730	913	878	925	792	866	703	848	920	815	626	940	667	1036	728	870
Total points scored	333	315	185	161	485	429	367	355	323	276	321	479	321	269	320	346
Total TDs	32	34	21	17	58	50	40	44	34	28	36	58	35	31	37	38
TDs rushing	9	11	13	7	21	14	18	12	16	9	11	23	19	7	10	14
TDs passing	20	20	6	9	28	33	22	29	15	18	23	28	12	19	21	18
TDs on returns and recoveries	3	3	2	1	9	3	0	3	3	1	2	7	4	5	6	6
Extra point kicks	30	31	21	17	53	46	38	40	33	25	32	56	32	27	33	37
Extra point kicks attempted	30	31	21	17	53	46	38	40	34	25	32	56	33	27	33	38
2-Pt. conversions	2	1	0	0	2	2	1	0	0	1	2	1	1	0	0	0
2-Pt. conversions attempted	2	3	0	0	5	4	1	4	0	3	4	2	2	4	4	0
Safeties	1	0	1	0	1	2	0	0	1	0	0	2	1	1	1	0
Field goals made	35	26	12	14	26	25	29	17	28	27	23	23	25	18	21	27
Field goals attempted	39	35	21	17	34	27	33	24	31	33	34	34	30	25	26	34
Percent successful	89.7	74.3	57.1	82.4	76.5	92.6	87.9	70.8	90.3	81.8	67.6	67.6	83.3	72.0	80.8	79.4
Extra points	32	32	21	17	55	48	39	40	33	26	34	57	33	27	33	37
Field goals blocked	1	4	2	0	0	1	1	1	0	0	0	1	0	0	2	0

DEFENSE

	Bal.	Buf.	Cin.	Cle.	Den.	Ind.	Jac.	K.C.	Mia.	N.E.	NYJ	Oak.	Pit.	S.D.	Sea.	Ten.
First downs	216	252	307	343	294	310	252	330	289	326	267	320	252	312	331	215
Rushing	59	76	101	147	80	109	85	103	92	108	98	85	82	76	126	62
Passing	135	153	182	169	189	177	144	201	156	184	152	202	153	195	185	134
Penalty	22	23	24	27	25	24	23	26	41	34	17	33	17	41	20	19
Rushes	361	444	504	594	344	446	436	441	417	495	476	383	425	470	503	387
Net yards gained	970	1559	1925	2505	1598	1935	1685	1809	1736	1831	1888	1551	1693	1422	2454	1390
Average gain	2.7	3.5	3.8	4.2	4.6	4.3	3.9	4.1	4.2	3.7	4.0	4.0	4.0	3.0	4.9	3.6
Average yards per game	60.6	97.4	120.3	156.6	99.9	120.9	105.3	113.1	108.5	114.4	118.0	96.9	105.8	88.9	153.4	86.9
Passes attempted	528	480	538	486	574	530	458	549	530	544	517	588	521	552	489	466
Completed	295	283	318	262	310	317	258	358	282	321	265	359	280	326	309	242
Percent completed	55.9	59.0	59.1	53.9	54.0	59.8	56.3	65.2	53.2	59.0	51.3	61.1	53.7	59.1	63.2	51.9
Total yards gained	3175	3175	3730	3408	4197	3674	3407	3737	3170	3694	3166	3976	3249	3786	4089	2761
Times sacked	35	42	26	42	44	42	40	51	48	29	40	43	39	39	27	55
Yards lost	178	308	168	270	251	252	247	266	270	172	234	278	229	249	152	338
Net yards gained	2997	2867	3562	3138	3946	3422	3160	3471	2900	3522	2932	3698	3020	3537	3937	2423
Average yards per game	187.3	179.2	222.6	196.1	246.6	213.9	197.5	216.9	181.3	220.1	183.3	231.1	188.8	221.1	246.1	151.4
Net yards per pass play	5.32	5.49	6.32	5.94	6.39	5.98	6.35	5.79	5.02	6.15	5.26	5.86	5.39	5.98	7.63	4.65
Yards gained per completion	10.76	11.22	11.73	13.01	13.54	11.59	13.21	10.44	11.24	11.51	11.06	11.08	11.60	11.61	13.23	11.41
Combined net yards gained	3967	4426	5487	5643	5544	5357	4845	5280	4636	5353	4820	5249	4713	4959	6391	3813
Percent total yards rushing	24.5	35.2	35.1	44.4	28.8	36.1	34.8	34.3	37.4	34.2	39.2	29.5	35.9	28.7	38.4	36.5
Percent total yards passing	75.5	64.8	64.9	55.6	71.2	63.9	65.2	65.7	62.6	65.8	60.8	70.5	64.1	71.3	61.6	63.5
Average yards per game	247.9	276.6	342.9	352.7	346.5	334.8	302.8	330.0	289.8	334.6	301.3	328.1	294.6	309.9	399.4	238.3
Ball-control plays	924	966	1068	1122	962	1018	934	1041	995	1068	1033	1014	985	1061	1019	908
Average yards per play	4.3	4.6	5.1	5.0	5.8	5.3	5.2	5.1	4.7	5.0	4.7	5.2	4.8	4.7	6.3	4.2
Average time of possession	26:41	28:35	32:47	34:01	26:45	30:27	28:28	32:24	29:17	31:04	29:40	28:07	28:33	31:52	32:29	26:12
Third-down efficiency	34.1	37.0	42.7	43.2	34.6	38.7	36.5	40.6	33.2	43.5	39.1	39.5	35.1	37.6	44.3	30.8
Intercepted by	23	16	9	12	27	14	12	15	28	10	21	21	17	16	17	17
Yards returned by	477	131	107	68	343	125	145	198	311	161	229	323	154	313	300	285
Returned for TD	1	1	1	1	5	2	1	2	0	0	1	4	0	4	3	4
Punts	87	92	80	68	73	82	90	78	87	87	88	79	84	91	62	105
Yards punted	3872	3865	3338	2868	3196	3503	3822	3363	3532	3513	3523	3289	3641	3780	2571	4480
Average yards per punt	44.5	42.0	41.7	42.2	43.8	42.7	42.5	43.1	40.6	40.4	40.0	41.6	43.3	41.5	41.5	42.7
Punt returns	41	51	40	69	23	28	38	43	36	43	42	30	44	51	32	28
Yards returned	382	544	387	793	270	357	478	559	258	384	660	279	371	722	151	160
Average yards per return	9.3	10.7	9.7	11.5	11.7	12.8	12.6	13.0	7.2	8.9	15.7	9.3	8.4	14.2	4.7	5.7
Returned for TD	0	1	0	0	1	0	1	0	0	0	2	0	0	1	0	0
Kickoff returns	73	70	42	42	90	73	73	70	68	62	62	80	69	61	64	76
Yards returned	1558	1524	898	1012	1934	1736	1523	1679	1260	1350	1424	1689	1496	1471	1236	1587
Average yards per return	21.3	21.8	21.4	24.1	21.5	23.8	20.9	24.0	18.5	21.8	23.0	21.1	21.7	24.1	19.3	20.9
Returned for TD	0	2	0	0	1	1	1	0	0	1	0	0	0	1	0	0
Fumbles	45	30	22	27	31	16	26	19	30	27	21	29	25	17	28	39
Recovered by	26	13	12	13	17	8	18	14	13	13	14	16	18	6	12	13
Out of bounds	0	1	1	0	2	0	1	1	0	0	1	1	1	0	3	2
Recovered for TD	0	0	0	0	0	0	0	0	0	0	1	0	0	1	1	0
Penalties	84	103	115	71	109	103	96	108	86	95	100	117	105	106	96	97
Yards penalized	535	905	924	626	898	820	814	1020	793	897	832	912	876	851	694	778
Total points scored	165	350	359	419	369	326	327	354	226	338	321	299	255	440	405	191
Total TDs	18	37	40	46	45	37	39	42	23	38	33	35	24	50	46	20
TDs rushing	5	13	12	26	13	13	14	13	9	12	9	8	9	10	20	7
TDs passing	11	18	26	18	26	22	23	25	13	23	17	25	13	33	23	10
TDs on returns and recoveries.	2	6	2	2	6	2	2	4	1	3	7	2	2	7	3	3
Extra point kicks	15	33	39	44	42	33	36	39	20	34	32	30	24	46	45	20
Extra point kicks attempted	18	33	40	44	43	33	36	39	20	34	32	30	24	46	45	20
2-Pt. conversions	0	3	0	1	0	3	2	0	1	1	1	0	0	1	0	0
2-Pt. conversions attempted	0	4	0	2	2	4	3	3	3	4	1	5	0	4	1	0
Safeties	0	1	1	2	0	1	1	0	0	1	1	1	0	1	0	0
Field goals made	14	29	26	31	19	21	17	21	22	24	29	19	29	30	28	17
Field goals attempted	19	33	36	34	23	28	24	30	30	32	34	25	34	34	33	22
Percent successful	73.7	87.9	72.2	91.2	82.6	75.0	70.8	70.0	73.3	75.0	85.3	76.0	85.3	88.2	84.8	77.3
Extra points	15	36	39	45	42	36	38	39	21	35	33	30	24	47	45	20
Field goals blocked	0	1	0	1	0	1	0	0	2	2	2	2	1	0	0	1

OFFENSE

	Ari.	Atl.	Car.	Chi.	Dal.	Det.	G.B.	Min.	N.O.	NYG	Phi.	S.F.	St.L.	T.B.	Was.
First downs	253	256	304	239	276	264	315	319	312	310	295	334	380	275	308
Rushing	71	65	63	89	116	101	88	107	117	100	88	98	112	111	98
Passing	156	156	201	143	128	143	197	193	169	195	182	211	247	144	185
Penalty	26	35	40	7	32	20	30	19	26	15	25	25	21	20	25
Rushes	343	350	363	417	463	448	404	428	505	507	397	416	383	490	445
Net yards gained	1278	1214	1186	1736	1953	1747	1643	2129	2068	2009	1882	1801	1843	2066	1748
Average gain	3.7	3.5	3.3	4.2	4.2	3.9	4.1	5.0	4.1	4.0	4.7	4.3	4.8	4.2	3.9
Average yards per game	79.9	75.9	74.1	108.5	122.1	109.2	102.7	133.1	129.3	125.6	117.6	112.6	115.2	129.1	109.3
Passes attempted	554	514	566	542	445	503	600	495	497	529	575	583	587	433	561
Completed	316	285	340	304	255	277	348	307	298	311	331	366	380	237	343
Percent completed	57.0	55.4	60.1	56.1	57.3	55.1	58.0	62.0	60.0	58.8	57.6	62.8	64.7	54.7	61.1
Total yards gained	3478	3166	3850	3005	2771	2992	3916	4019	3573	3610	3386	4400	5492	2824	3892
Times sacked	35	61	69	34	35	53	34	35	39	28	45	25	44	38	32
Yards lost	228	386	382	200	249	317	238	187	244	243	262	161	260	241	244
Net yards gained	3250	2780	3468	2805	2522	2675	3678	3832	3329	3367	3124	4239	5232	2583	3648
Average yards per game	203.1	173.8	216.8	175.3	157.6	167.2	229.9	239.5	208.1	210.4	195.3	264.9	327.0	161.4	228.0
Net yards per pass play	5.52	4.83	5.46	4.87	5.25	4.81	5.80	7.23	6.21	6.04	5.04	6.97	8.29	5.48	6.15
Yards gained per completion	11.01	11.11	11.32	9.88	10.87	10.80	11.25	13.09	11.99	11.61	10.23	12.02	14.45	11.92	11.35
Combined net yards gained	4528	3994	4654	4541	4475	4422	5321	5961	5397	5376	5006	6040	7075	4649	5396
Percent total yards rushing	28.2	30.4	25.5	38.2	43.6	39.5	30.9	35.7	38.3	37.4	37.6	29.8	26.0	44.4	32.4
Percent total yards passing	71.8	69.6	74.5	61.8	56.4	60.5	69.1	64.3	61.7	62.6	62.4	70.2	74.0	55.6	67.6
Average yards per game	283.0	249.6	290.9	283.8	279.7	276.4	332.6	372.6	337.3	336.0	312.9	377.5	442.2	290.6	337.3
Ball-control plays	932	925	998	993	943	1004	1038	958	1041	1064	1017	1024	1014	961	1038
Average yards per play	4.9	4.3	4.7	4.6	4.7	4.4	5.1	6.2	5.2	5.1	4.9	5.9	7.0	4.8	5.2
Average time of possession	26:32	29:35	29:54	28:30	28:40	30:10	30:45	29:28	31:27	31:39	29:01	29:38	30:54	29:38	31:29
Third-down efficiency	37.7	28.9	39.4	30.2	35.9	32.1	39.0	45.7	42.7	40.2	40.2	41.6	47.5	33.3	39.4
Had intercepted	24	20	19	16	21	19	16	18	15	13	15	10	23	13	21
Yards opponents returned	383	271	365	150	179	270	201	181	125	172	146	94	386	155	374
Returned by opponents for TD	2	3	2	1	3	2	1	1	1	0	0	2	4	1	1
Punts	65	85	66	96	68	95	79	62	74	80	86	70	44	85	79
Yards punted	2871	3447	2459	3624	2848	4044	3033	2773	3043	3210	3635	2727	1736	3551	3160
Average yards per punt	44.2	40.6	37.3	37.8	41.9	42.6	38.4	44.7	41.1	40.1	42.3	39.0	39.5	41.8	40.0
Punt returns	32	37	21	36	35	33	35	26	40	40	33	26	34	39	36
Yards returned	223	348	238	314	364	472	300	261	339	332	335	220	521	337	356
Average yards per return	7.0	9.4	11.3	8.7	10.4	14.3	8.6	10.0	8.5	8.3	10.2	8.5	15.3	8.6	9.9
Returned for TD	0	1	1	0	2	1	0	0	0	0	1	0	1	1	0
Kickoff returns	86	83	55	68	69	69	64	67	62	53	53	68	80	55	63
Yards returned	2296	1890	1160	1512	1456	1600	1570	1456	1473	1102	1237	1299	1771	1255	1301
Average yards per return	26.7	22.8	21.1	22.2	21.1	23.2	24.5	21.7	23.8	20.8	23.3	19.1	22.1	22.8	20.7
Returned for TD	1	3	1	0	0	0	1	0	0	1	1	0	1	0	0
Fumbles	32	27	25	27	31	21	30	26	26	25	22	22	24	16	22
Lost	20	14	16	13	18	12	17	10	11	11	14	9	12	11	12
Out of bounds	1	2	2	1	1	2	1	1	1	2	0	2	0	0	1
Recovered for TD	0	0	0	0	0	1	0	0	0	0	0	0	1	0	0
Penalties	96	97	84	90	108	106	88	106	124	91	113	134	111	82	115
Yards penalized	785	720	683	696	963	805	685	908	1024	839	980	1135	942	702	1009
Total points scored	210	252	310	216	294	307	353	397	354	328	351	388	540	388	281
Total TDs	24	25	31	22	31	33	36	47	41	39	38	49	67	43	32
TDs rushing	6	6	7	6	15	15	13	14	14	16	13	15	26	18	14
TDs passing	16	14	19	12	14	14	21	33	22	22	21	32	37	18	18
TDs on returns and recoveries.	2	5	5	4	2	4	2	0	5	1	4	2	4	7	0
Extra point kicks	18	23	29	21	27	29	32	45	37	37	34	43	58	42	27
Extra point kicks attempted	19	23	29	21	27	29	32	45	37	37	36	45	58	42	29
2-Pt. conversions	0	1	1	0	2	4	2	2	1	0	1	3	4	1	0
2-Pt. conversions attempted	5	2	2	1	4	4	3	2	4	2	2	4	9	1	3
Safeties	0	1	0	0	1	0	1	0	0	0	0	0	0	1	1
Field goals made	16	25	31	21	25	24	33	22	23	19	29	15	24	28	20
Field goals attempted	23	31	35	27	33	30	38	23	29	25	33	22	27	34	30
Percent successful	69.6	80.6	88.6	77.8	75.8	80.0	86.8	95.7	79.3	76.0	87.9	68.2	88.9	82.4	66.7
2-Pt. conversions	0	1	1	0	2	4	2	2	1	0	1	3	4	1	0
Extra points	18	24	30	21	29	33	34	47	38	37	35	46	62	43	27
Field goals blocked	0	0	1	0	1	2	1	1	2	3	0	1	0	1	1

DEFENSE

	Ari.	Atl.	Car.	Chi.	Dal.	Det.	G.B.	Min.	N.O.	NYG	Phi.	S.F.	St.L.	T.B.	Was.
First downs	345	308	304	297	309	279	284	344	279	274	295	347	321	283	254
Rushing	149	113	107	106	137	96	84	110	95	62	105	110	95	84	97
Passing	175	175	184	172	145	159	186	208	159	181	159	194	195	180	134
Penalty	21	20	13	19	27	24	14	26	25	31	31	43	31	19	23
Rushes	578	453	426	469	538	421	417	396	395	359	453	435	383	398	430
Net yards gained	2609	1983	1944	1827	2636	1823	1618	1788	1672	1156	1830	1794	1697	1648	1853
Average gain	4.5	4.4	4.6	3.9	4.9	4.3	3.9	4.5	4.2	3.2	4.0	4.1	4.4	4.1	4.3
Average yards per game	163.1	123.9	121.5	114.2	164.8	113.9	101.1	111.8	104.5	72.3	114.4	112.1	106.1	103.0	115.8
Passes attempted	459	515	552	530	458	544	557	584	488	585	552	558	534	594	462
Completed	296	306	352	332	277	311	307	369	285	327	314	320	323	339	254
Percent completed	64.5	59.4	63.8	62.6	60.5	57.2	55.1	63.2	58.4	55.9	56.9	57.3	60.5	57.1	55.0
Total yards gained	3263	3766	3938	3637	2882	3372	3695	4127	3449	3669	3281	4185	4085	3484	2904
Times sacked	25	31	27	36	25	28	38	31	66	44	50	38	51	55	45
Yards lost	135	142	226	230	189	162	244	214	378	279	291	270	288	332	283
Net yards gained	3128	3624	3712	3407	2693	3210	3451	3913	3071	3390	2990	3915	3797	3152	2621
Average yards per game	195.5	226.5	232.0	212.9	168.3	200.6	215.7	244.6	191.9	211.9	186.9	244.7	237.3	197.0	163.8
Net yards per pass play	6.46	6.64	6.41	6.02	5.58	5.61	5.80	6.36	5.54	5.39	4.97	6.57	6.49	4.86	5.17
Yards gained per completion	11.02	12.31	11.19	10.95	10.40	10.84	12.04	11.18	12.10	11.22	10.45	13.08	12.65	10.28	11.43
Combined net yards gained	5737	5607	5656	5234	5329	5033	5069	5701	4743	4546	4820	5709	5494	4800	4474
Percent total yards rushing	45.5	35.4	34.4	34.9	49.5	36.2	31.9	31.4	35.3	25.4	38.0	31.4	30.9	34.3	41.4
Percent total yards passing	54.5	64.6	65.6	65.1	50.5	63.8	68.1	68.6	64.7	74.6	62.0	68.6	69.1	65.7	58.6
Average yards per game	358.6	350.4	353.5	327.1	333.1	314.6	316.8	356.3	296.4	284.1	301.3	356.8	343.4	300.0	279.6
Ball-control plays	1062	999	1005	1035	1021	993	1012	1011	949	988	1055	1031	968	1047	937
Average yards per play	5.4	5.6	5.6	5.1	5.2	5.1	5.0	5.6	5.0	4.6	4.6	5.5	5.7	4.6	4.8
Average time of possession	33:28	30:25	30:06	31:30	31:20	29:50	29:15	30:32	28:33	28:21	30:59	30:22	29:06	30:22	28:33
Third-down efficiency	47.3	35.9	43.3	36.8	40.4	37.2	36.6	45.5	39.2	35.6	32.6	39.2	38.5	32.9	35.1
Intercepted by	10	15	17	11	16	25	21	8	20	20	19	13	19	25	17
Yards returned by	151	287	199	254	167	340	315	65	264	149	255	278	135	275	219
Returned for TD	0	1	2	4	0	2	1	0	4	0	2	2	0	4	0
Punts	59	70	58	91	70	84	94	65	74	86	87	65	67	89	79
Yards punted	2422	2932	2311	3629	2838	3501	3888	2593	3024	3570	3516	2773	2825	3556	3386
Average yards per punt	41.1	41.9	39.8	39.9	40.5	41.7	41.4	39.9	40.9	41.5	40.4	42.7	42.2	40.0	42.9
Punt returns	37	29	25	36	29	53	27	32	37	28	47	32	17	41	33
Yards returned	347	126	187	251	282	498	205	310	494	353	375	332	132	408	342
Average yards per return	9.4	4.3	7.5	7.0	9.7	9.4	7.6	9.7	13.4	12.6	8.0	10.4	7.8	10.0	10.4
Returned for TD	2	0	0	0	0	0	1	0	2	0	1	0	0	1	2
Kickoff returns	46	50	64	51	56	59	76	69	71	67	72	63	87	74	60
Yards returned	827	1230	1120	1105	1205	1327	1639	1519	1743	1509	1519	1358	2032	1688	1529
Average yards per return	18.0	24.6	17.5	21.7	21.5	22.5	21.6	22.0	24.5	22.5	21.1	21.6	23.4	22.8	25.5
Returned for TD	0	3	0	0	0	0	0	1	2	0	0	0	1	0	1
Fumbles	17	18	37	20	23	36	16	17	24	17	27	19	19	26	28
Recovered	10	10	21	9	9	17	7	10	15	11	12	8	6	16	16
Out of bounds	2	2	2	1	2	3	0	1	1	1	3	2	2	0	0
Recovered for TD	0	0	0	1	0	0	0	0	0	0	0	0	0	0	0
Penalties	96	122	128	78	108	112	101	104	105	80	111	102	101	95	106
Yards penalized	914	1010	1073	727	999	913	992	747	837	728	936	857	747	688	790
Total points scored	443	413	310	355	361	307	323	371	305	246	245	422	471	269	269
Total TDs	52	46	35	43	41	32	37	43	36	30	23	49	56	29	26
TDs rushing	29	16	12	15	17	14	7	17	14	7	10	22	18	12	9
TDs passing	19	23	19	25	20	16	28	23	17	23	11	25	32	15	12
TDs on returns and recoveries	4	7	4	3	4	2	2	3	5	0	2	2	6	2	5
Extra point kicks	50	38	30	41	37	31	36	38	31	25	21	46	49	25	23
Extra point kicks attempted	51	38	31	41	37	31	36	38	31	27	21	46	50	25	23
2-Pt. conversions	0	6	2	1	0	1	1	0	2	1	1	2	3	2	0
2-Pt. conversions attempted	1	8	4	2	3	1	1	4	5	3	2	6	6	4	3
Safeties	0	0	3	0	2	0	2	0	0	0	0	0	1	0	0
Field goals made	27	29	20	18	26	26	21	25	18	13	28	26	26	22	30
Field goals attempted	34	31	30	26	31	31	25	29	24	24	33	31	31	32	34
Percent successful	79.4	93.5	66.7	69.2	83.9	83.9	84.0	86.2	75.0	54.2	84.8	83.9	83.9	68.8	88.2
Extra points	50	44	32	42	37	32	37	38	33	26	22	48	52	27	23
Field goals blocked	0	1	2	3	2	1	0	0	0	0	0	0	0	4	1

2000 STATISTICS *Miscellaneous*

	AFC Offense Total	AFC Offense Average	AFC Defense Total	AFC Defense Average	NFC Offense Total	NFC Offense Average	NFC Defense Total	NFC Defense Average	NFL Total	NFL Average
First downs	4699	293.7	4616	288.5	4440	296.0	4523	301.5	9139	294.8
Rushing	1615	100.9	1489	93.1	1424	94.9	1550	103.3	3039	98.0
Passing	2667	166.7	2711	169.4	2650	176.7	2606	173.7	5317	171.5
Penalty	417	26.1	416	26.0	366	24.4	367	24.5	783	25.3
Rushes	7318	457.4	7126	445.4	6359	423.9	6551	436.7	13677	441.2
Net yards gained	29526	1845.4	27951	1746.9	26303	1753.5	27878	1858.5	55829	1800.9
Average gain	....	4.0	....	3.9	....	4.1	....	4.3	....	4.1
Average yards per game	....	115.3	....	109.2	....	109.6	....	116.2	....	112.6
Passes attempted	8338	521.1	8350	521.9	7984	532.3	7972	531.5	16322	526.5
Completed	4799	299.9	4785	299.1	4698	313.2	4712	314.1	9497	306.4
Percent completed	....	57.6	....	57.3	....	58.8	....	59.1	....	58.2
Total yards gained	55757	3484.8	56394	3524.6	54374	3624.9	53737	3582.5	110131	3552.6
Times sacked	625	39.1	642	40.1	607	40.5	590	39.3	1232	39.7
Yards lost	3683	230.2	3862	241.4	3842	256.1	3663	244.2	7525	242.7
Net yards gained	52074	3254.6	52532	3283.3	50532	3368.8	50074	3338.3	102606	3309.9
Average yards per game	....	203.4	....	205.2	....	210.6	....	208.6	....	206.9
Net yards per pass play	....	5.81	....	5.84	....	5.88	....	5.85	....	5.85
Yards gained per completion	....	11.62	....	11.79	....	11.57	....	11.40	....	11.60
Combined net yards gained	81600	5100.0	80483	5030.2	76835	5122.3	77952	5196.8	158435	5110.8
Percent total yards rushing	....	36.2	....	34.7	....	34.2	....	35.8	....	35.2
Percent total yards passing	....	63.8	....	65.3	....	65.8	....	64.2	....	64.8
Average yards per game	....	318.8	....	314.4	....	320.1	....	324.8	....	319.4
Ball-control plays	16281	1017.6	16118	1007.4	14950	996.7	15113	1007.5	31231	1007.5
Average yards per play	....	5.0	....	5.0	....	5.1	....	5.2	....	5.1
Third-down efficiency	....	38.4	....	38.2	....	38.2	....	38.4	....	38.3
Interceptions	268	16.8	275	17.2	263	17.5	256	17.1	531	17.1
Yards returned	3571	223.2	3670	229.4	3452	230.1	3353	223.5	7023	226.2
Returned for TD	27	1.7	29	1.8	24	1.6	22	1.5	51	1.6
Punts	1337	83.6	1333	83.3	1134	75.6	1138	75.9	2471	79.7
Yards punted	56759	3547.4	56160	3510.0	46165	3077.7	46764	3117.6	102924	3320.1
Average yards per punt	....	42.5	....	42.1	....	40.7	....	41.1	....	41.7
Punt returns	639	39.9	639	39.9	503	33.5	503	33.5	1142	36.8
Yards returned	6437	402.3	6755	422.2	4960	330.7	4642	309.5	11397	367.6
Average yards per return	....	10.1	....	10.6	....	9.9	....	9.2	....	10.0
Returned for TD	7	0.4	6	0.4	8	0.5	9	0.6	15	0.5
Kickoff returns	1045	65.3	1075	67.2	995	66.3	965	64.3	2040	65.8
Yards returned	22349	1396.8	23377	1461.1	22378	1491.9	21350	1423.3	44727	1442.8
Average yards per return	....	21.4	....	21.7	....	22.5	....	22.1	....	21.9
Returned for TD	6	0.4	7	0.4	9	0.6	8	0.5	15	0.5
Fumbles	400	25.0	432	27.0	376	25.1	344	22.9	776	25.0
Lost	203	12.7	226	14.1	200	13.3	177	11.8	403	13.0
Out of bounds	19	1.2	14	0.9	17	1.1	22	1.5	36	1.2
Own recovered for TD	2	0.1	3	0.2	2	0.1	1	0.1	4	0.1
Opponents recovered by	223	13.9	200	12.5	175	11.7	198	13.2	398	12.8
Opponents recovered for TD	11	0.7	8	0.5	4	0.3	7	0.5	15	0.5
Penalties	1595	99.7	1591	99.4	1545	103.0	1549	103.3	3140	101.3
Yards penalized	13257	828.6	13175	823.4	12876	858.4	12958	863.9	26133	843.0
Total points scored	5285	330.3	5144	321.5	4969	331.3	5110	340.7	10254	330.8
Total TDs	593	37.1	573	35.8	558	37.2	578	38.5	1151	37.1
TDs rushing	214	13.4	193	12.1	198	13.2	219	14.6	412	13.3
TDs passing	321	20.1	326	20.4	313	20.9	308	20.5	634	20.5
TDs on returns and recoveries	58	3.6	54	3.4	47	3.1	51	3.4	105	3.4
Extra point kicks	551	34.4	532	33.3	502	33.5	521	34.7	1053	34.0
Extra point kicks attempted	554	34.6	537	33.6	509	33.9	526	35.1	1063	34.3
2-Pt. conversions	13	0.8	13	0.8	22	1.5	22	1.5	35	1.1
2-Pt. conversions attempted	37	2.3	36	2.3	48	3.2	49	3.3	85	2.7
Safeties	11	0.7	10	0.6	5	0.3	6	0.4	16	0.5
Field goals made	376	23.5	376	23.5	355	23.7	355	23.7	731	23.6
Field goals attempted	477	29.8	471	29.4	440	29.3	446	29.7	917	29.6
Percent successful	....	78.8	....	79.8	....	80.7	....	79.6	....	79.7
Extra points	564	35.3	545	66.5	524	34.9	543	36.2	1088	35.1
Field goals blocked	13	0.8	13	0.8	14	0.9	14	0.9	27	0.9

2000 STATISTICS *Miscellaneous*

RUSHING

Player, Team	Opponent	Date	Att.	Yds.	TD
Corey Dillon, Cincinnati	vs. Denver	October 22	22	278	2
Mike Anderson, Denver	at New Orleans	December 3	37	251	4
Fred Taylor, Jacksonville	at Pittsburgh	November 19	30	234	3
Marshall Faulk, St. Louis	at New Orleans	December 24	32	220	2
Edgerrin James, Indianapolis	at Seattle	October 15	38	219	3
Corey Dillon, Cincinnati	vs. Arizona	December 3	35	216	1
Warrick Dunn, Tampa Bay	vs. Dallas	December 3	22	210	2
Marshall Faulk, St. Louis	vs. Atlanta	October 15	25	208	1
Curtis Martin, N.Y. Jets	vs. Indianapolis	December 3	30	203	1
Duce Staley, Philadelphia	at Dallas	September 3	26	201	1
Charlie Garner, San Francisco	at Dallas	September 24	36	201	1
Mike Anderson, Denver	at Seattle	November 26	30	195	2
Mike Anderson, Denver	at Oakland	September 17	32	187	0
Jamal Lewis, Baltimore	vs. Dallas	November 19	28	187	0
Eddie George, Tennessee	at Cincinnati	October 8	36	181	1
Fred Taylor, Jacksonville	vs. Cleveland	December 3	30	181	3
Eddie George, Tennessee	at Cleveland	December 17	34	176	3
Robert Smith, Minnesota	at Chicago	October 15	23	170	1
Jamal Lewis, Baltimore	vs. Cleveland	November 26	30	170	2
Ricky Watters, Seattle	vs. Oakland	December 16	26	168	0
Eddie George, Tennessee	vs. Jacksonville	October 16	29	167	1
James Stewart, Detroit	at N.Y. Jets	December 17	37	164	0
Ahman Green, Green Bay	at Minnesota	December 17	25	161	0
Ricky Williams, New Orleans	at Atlanta	October 22	29	156	3
Tyrone Wheatley, Oakland	vs. Seattle	October 22	15	156	1
Tony Richardson, Kansas City	vs. Denver	December 17	23	156	1
Lamar Smith, Miami	at N.Y. Jets	October 23*	23	155	2
Ahman Green, Green Bay	vs. Indianapolis	November 19	24	153	0
Emmitt Smith, Dallas	vs. Washington	December 10	23	150	1
Robert Smith, Minnesota	at Dallas	November 23	21	148	1
Antowain Smith, Buffalo	at Seattle	December 23	17	147	3
Tyrone Wheatley, Oakland	at Seattle	December 16	26	146	0
Lamar Smith, Miami	vs. Seattle	September 3	27	145	1
Warrick Dunn, Tampa Bay	vs. St. Louis	December 18	22	145	3
Tiki Barber, N.Y. Giants	vs. Arizona	September 3	13	144	2
Ricky Williams, New Orleans	vs. Carolina	October 15	38	144	2
Curtis Martin, N.Y. Jets	at New England	October 15	34	143	3
Stephen Davis, Washington	vs. Tampa Bay	October 1*	28	141	1
Edgerrin James, Indianapolis	vs. Detroit	October 29	31	139	1
Corey Dillon, Cincinnati	at Cleveland	October 29	27	137	1
Fred Taylor, Jacksonville	vs. Arizona	December 10	23	137	2
Marshall Faulk, St. Louis	vs. Minnesota	December 10	25	135	4
Marshall Faulk, St. Louis	vs. San Francisco	September 17	25	134	3
Robert Smith, Minnesota	at Detroit	October 1	16	134	1
Emmitt Smith, Dallas	at Philadelphia	November 5*	26	134	1
Jerome Bettis, Pittsburgh	vs. Philadelphia	November 12*	30	134	1
Eddie George, Tennessee	vs. Cleveland	November 19	36	134	3
Stephen Davis, Washington	vs. Carolina	September 3	23	133	1
Jerome Bettis, Pittsburgh	at Cleveland	September 17	24	133	1
Emmitt Smith, Dallas	at Carolina	October 1*	24	132	1
Mike Anderson, Denver	vs. Atlanta	September 10	31	131	2
Edgerrin James, Indianapolis	vs. N.Y. Jets	November 12	31	131	1
Mike Anderson, Denver	vs. Seattle	December 10	29	131	2
Ricky Williams, New Orleans	at Chicago	October 8	30	128	1
Corey Dillon, Cincinnati	vs. Pittsburgh	November 26	23	128	2
Jerome Bettis, Pittsburgh	vs. Oakland	December 3	24	128	0
Edgerrin James, Indianapolis	vs. Minnesota	December 24	26	128	0
Jamal Lewis, Baltimore	at Arizona	December 17	29	126	1
Eddie George, Tennessee	vs. N.Y. Giants	October 1	35	125	1
Lamar Smith, Miami	at Detroit	November 5	24	125	2
Donovan McNabb, Philadelphia	at Washington	November 26	11	125	1
Edgerrin James, Indianapolis	at Kansas City	September 3	28	124	1
Edgerrin James, Indianapolis	vs. New England	October 22	20	124	1
Fred Taylor, Jacksonville	vs. Washington	October 22	22	124	0
Stephen Davis, Washington	at Arizona	November 5	30	124	1
James Stewart, Detroit	vs. Minnesota	October 1	20	123	0
Robert Smith, Minnesota	at Green Bay	November 6*	24	122	0
James Allen, Chicago	at N.Y. Jets	November 26	25	122	0
Stephen Davis, Washington	vs. Arizona	December 24	27	120	0
Priest Holmes, Baltimore	at Pittsburgh	September 3	27	119	0
Jamal Anderson, Atlanta	at Detroit	November 12	25	119	1
Edgerrin James, Indianapolis	vs. Miami	November 26	26	118	0

Player, Team	Opponent	Date	Att.	Yds.	TD
Ahman Green, Green Bay	vs. Detroit	December 10	27	118	1
Robert Smith, Minnesota	vs. Arizona	November 12	20	117	0
Brad Hoover, Carolina	vs. Green Bay	November 27	24	117	1
Jamal Lewis, Baltimore	vs. Cincinnati	September 24	25	116	1
James Stewart, Detroit	at Tampa Bay	October 19	29	116	3
Terrell Davis, Denver	at N.Y. Jets	November 5	33	115	1
Robert Smith, Minnesota	vs. Detroit	November 30	17	115	2
Stephen Davis, Washington	at Jacksonville	October 22	24	114	2
Fred Taylor, Jacksonville	at Tennessee	October 16	20	112	0
Emmitt Smith, Dallas	vs. Arizona	October 22	24	112	1
Tyrone Wheatley, Oakland	vs. Kansas City	November 5	20	112	1
Edgerrin James, Indianapolis	at Miami	December 17	32	112	0
Edgerrin James, Indianapolis	vs. Buffalo	December 11	27	111	3
Curtis Martin, N.Y. Jets	at Green Bay	September 3	30	110	1
Corey Dillon, Cincinnati	vs. Miami	October 1	22	110	0
Fred Taylor, Jacksonville	at Cincinnati	December 17	32	110	1
Robert Smith, Minnesota	vs. Chicago	September 3	14	109	0
Charlie Garner, San Francisco	vs. Oakland	October 8*	24	109	0
Jamal Lewis, Baltimore	at Cincinnati	November 5	22	109	0
Ron Dayne, N.Y. Giants	vs. Dallas	October 15	21	108	1
Aaron Brooks, New Orleans	at San Francisco	December 10	11	108	0
Ricky Williams, New Orleans	at Seattle	September 17	23	107	0
Michael Pittman, Arizona	vs. Cleveland	October 8	16	107	0
Jerome Bettis, Pittsburgh	at N.Y. Jets	October 8	25	107	1
Fred Taylor, Jacksonville	at Dallas	October 29*	31	107	0
Jamal Anderson, Atlanta	vs. Kansas City	December 24	28	107	0
Warrick Dunn, Tampa Bay	vs. Buffalo	November 26	20	106	2
Ricky Watters, Seattle	vs. New Orleans	September 17	22	105	1
Brian Mitchell, Philadelphia	vs. Atlanta	October 1	2	105	1
Jerome Bettis, Pittsburgh	vs. Cleveland	October 22	33	105	1
Fred Taylor, Jacksonville	vs. Tennessee	November 26	24	104	0
Jerome Bettis, Pittsburgh	vs. Washington	December 16	25	104	0
Ricky Williams, New Orleans	vs. Philadelphia	September 24	20	103	0
Tim Biakabutuka, Carolina	vs. Seattle	October 8	23	103	0
Mike Anderson, Denver	vs. Cleveland	October 15	20	103	1
Fred Taylor, Jacksonville	vs. Seattle	November 12	21	103	1
Robert Smith, Minnesota	vs. Carolina	November 19	23	103	1
Justin Watson, St. Louis	vs. San Diego	October 1	14	102	1
Kimble Anders, Kansas City	vs. St. Louis	October 22	13	102	2
Emmitt Smith, Dallas	vs. Jacksonville	October 29*	24	102	0
Charlie Garner, San Francisco	vs. Kansas City	November 12	25	102	1
Jerome Bettis, Pittsburgh	vs. Cincinnati	October 15	29	101	0
Eddie George, Tennessee	at Philadelphia	December 3	32	101	0
Emmitt Smith, Dallas	vs. Minnesota	November 23	12	100	0
Lamar Smith, Miami	at Buffalo	December 3	28	100	0

*Overtime game.

PASSING

Player, Team	Opponent	Date	Att.	Comp.	Yds.	TD	Int.
Elvis Grbac, Kansas City	at Oakland	November 5	53	39	504	2	2
Vinny Testaverde, N.Y. Jets	at Baltimore	December 24	69	36	481	2	3
Gus Frerotte, Denver	vs. San Diego	November 19	58	36	462	5	4
Kurt Warner, St. Louis	vs. Denver	September 4	35	25	441	3	3
Aaron Brooks, New Orleans	vs. Denver	December 3	48	30	441	2	2
Peyton Manning, Indianapolis	vs. Jacksonville	September 25	36	23	440	4	0
Trent Green, St. Louis	vs. Carolina	November 5	42	29	431	2	0
Jeff Garcia, San Francisco	vs. Chicago	December 17	44	36	402	2	0
Kurt Warner, St. Louis	vs. San Francisco	September 17	34	23	394	2	2
Kurt Warner, St. Louis	vs. San Diego	October 1	30	24	390	4	0
Donovan McNabb, Philadelphia	at Cleveland	December 10	36	23	390	4	0
Mark Brunell, Jacksonville	at Baltimore	September 10	50	28	386	3	2
Kurt Warner, St. Louis	at Seattle	September 10	47	35	386	1	1
Rich Gannon, Oakland	at Denver	November 13	53	30	382	1	2
Vinny Testaverde, N.Y. Jets	vs. Miami	October 23*	59	36	378	5	3
Peyton Manning, Indianapolis	vs. Oakland	September 10	48	33	367	3	2
Trent Green, St. Louis	vs. Washington	November 20	38	23	366	2	1
Doug Flutie, Buffalo	at Seattle	December 23	25	20	366	3	0
Brian Griese, Denver	at Cincinnati	October 22	45	30	365	2	1
Steve Beuerlein, Carolina	at San Francisco	September 10	32	24	364	3	1
Brian Griese, Denver	vs. New England	October 1	50	31	361	1	1
Daunte Culpepper, Minnesota	vs. Carolina	November 19	29	22	357	3	0
Daunte Culpepper, Minnesota	vs. Miami	September 10	37	23	355	1	1
Kerry Collins, N.Y. Giants	vs. Detroit	November 19	51	29	350	2	1
Elvis Grbac, Kansas City	at New England	December 4	46	25	350	3	1
Jim Harbaugh, San Diego	at St. Louis	October 1	40	27	348	2	1
Kurt Warner, St. Louis	vs. Minnesota	December 10	32	27	346	0	0

Player, Team	Opponent	Date	Att.	Comp.	Yds.	TD	Int.
Elvis Grbac, Kansas City	at Seattle	October 29	35	22	342	3	3
Elvis Grbac, Kansas City	vs. Buffalo	November 19	48	28	341	2	1
Mark Brunell, Jacksonville	vs. Seattle	November 12	33	24	340	1	0
Peyton Manning, Indianapolis	at N.Y. Jets	December 3	51	27	339	2	2
Kurt Warner, St. Louis	at Atlanta	September 24	19	12	336	4	1
Jeff Garcia, San Francisco	vs. Oakland	October 8*	41	28	336	4	0
Jeff Garcia, San Francisco	at Green Bay	October 15	42	27	336	4	0
Brian Griese, Denver	vs. Cleveland	October 15	34	19	336	3	0
Daunte Culpepper, Minnesota	vs. Green Bay	December 17	38	23	335	3	1
Peyton Manning, Indianapolis	at New England	October 8	54	31	334	1	3
Brett Favre, Green Bay	vs. Chicago	October 1	48	31	333	3	1
Kerry Collins, N.Y. Giants	vs. Pittsburgh	December 10	35	24	333	2	0
Steve Beuerlein, Carolina	vs. Seattle	October 8	39	27	332	2	1
Brian Griese, Denver	at N.Y. Jets	November 5	35	22	327	2	1
Jeff Garcia, San Francisco	at San Diego	December 3	32	18	323	2	0
Rob Johnson, Buffalo	vs. San Diego	October 15*	47	29	321	1	1
Kerry Collins, N.Y. Giants	vs. Jacksonville	December 23	39	22	321	2	1
Jake Plummer, Arizona	at N.Y. Giants	September 3	49	28	318	2	3
Tim Couch, Cleveland	vs. Pittsburgh	September 17	31	23	316	2	0
Kurt Warner, St. Louis	at Tampa Bay	December 18	32	20	316	2	3
Elvis Grbac, Kansas City	vs. Carolina	December 10	44	31	315	1	2
Kurt Warner, St. Louis	vs. Atlanta	October 15	40	24	313	3	1
Daunte Culpepper, Minnesota	at Tampa Bay	October 29	53	29	313	1	2
Drew Bledsoe, New England	vs. Miami	December 24	34	18	312	2	2
Donovan McNabb, Philadelphia	vs. Atlanta	October 1	44	30	311	2	1
Ryan Leaf, San Diego	at Denver	November 19	27	13	311	3	1
Rich Gannon, Oakland	at San Francisco	October 8*	43	21	310	2	1
Trent Green, St. Louis	at San Francisco	October 29	39	22	310	2	1
Steve Beuerlein, Carolina	vs. San Francisco	October 22	44	28	309	3	0
Doug Pederson, Cleveland	vs. Philadelphia	December 10	40	29	309	1	2
Troy Aikman, Dallas	vs. Cincinnati	November 12	37	24	308	1	0
Brian Griese, Denver	at St. Louis	September 4	29	19	307	2	0
Jeff Garcia, San Francisco	at Carolina	October 22	39	25	307	2	1
Jeff Garcia, San Francisco	vs. New Orleans	December 10	38	25	305	2	2
Peyton Manning, Indianapolis	at Chicago	November 5	39	26	302	2	1
Daunte Culpepper, Minnesota	vs. Arizona	November 12	32	25	302	3	1
Mark Brunell, Jacksonville	at Cleveland	September 3	34	24	301	1	0
Brett Favre, Green Bay	vs. Indianapolis	November 19	36	23	301	2	1

*Overtime game.

RECEIVING

Player, Team	Opponent	Date	Rec.	Yds.	TD
Jimmy Smith, Jacksonville	at Baltimore	September 10	15	291	3
Terrell Owens, San Francisco	vs. Chicago	December 17	20	283	1
Albert Connell, Washington	at Jacksonville	October 22	7	211	3
Amani Toomer, N.Y. Giants	vs. Jacksonville	December 23	8	193	1
Torry Holt, St. Louis	at Atlanta	September 24	3	189	2
Isaac Bruce, St. Louis	vs. San Francisco	September 17	8	188	1
Rod Smith, Denver	vs. San Diego	November 19	11	187	1
David Boston, Arizona	at Cincinnati	December 3	9	184	2
Joe Horn, New Orleans	vs. San Francisco	November 5	10	180	1
Terrell Owens, San Francisco	vs. Oakland	October 8*	12	176	2
Tim Brown, Oakland	at San Francisco	October 8*	7	172	2
Torry Holt, St. Louis	vs. Minnesota	December 10	9	172	0
Eric Moulds, Buffalo	vs. San Diego	October 15*	11	170	0
Joe Horn, New Orleans	vs. Denver	December 3	10	170	0
Cris Carter, Minnesota	vs. Miami	September 10	9	168	0
Randy Moss, Minnesota	at Detroit	October 1	7	168	3
Isaac Bruce, St. Louis	vs. San Diego	October 1	9	167	1
Torry Holt, St. Louis	at Tampa Bay	December 18	9	165	1
James McKnight, Dallas	vs. Cincinnati	November 12	8	164	1
Rod Smith, Denver	vs. New England	October 1	13	160	1
Marvin Harrison, Indianapolis	at New England	October 8	13	159	1
Marvin Harrison, Indianapolis	vs. New England	October 22	5	156	2
Keenan McCardell, Jacksonville	vs. Seattle	November 12	6	156	1
Bill Schroeder, Green Bay	vs. Indianapolis	November 19	8	155	0
Derrick Alexander, Kansas City	vs. Seattle	October 2	5	153	1
Shawn Jefferson, Atlanta	vs. San Francisco	September 3	7	148	1
Terrence Wilkins, Indianapolis	vs. Jacksonville	September 25	9	148	1
Ed McCaffrey, Denver	vs. San Diego	November 19	10	148	2
Az-Zahir Hakim, St. Louis	vs. Carolina	November 5	8	147	1
Tony Gonzalez, Kansas City	at New England	December 4	11	147	1
Jimmy Smith, Jacksonville	vs. Arizona	December 10	8	147	1
Dedric Ward, N.Y. Jets	at Baltimore	December 24	8	147	1
Derrick Alexander, Kansas City	vs. Buffalo	November 19	7	146	0
Jeff Graham, San Diego	at Denver	November 19	4	144	2

Player, Team	Opponent	Date	Rec.	Yds.	TD
Randy Moss, Minnesota	at Dallas	November 23	7	144	2
Curtis Conway, San Diego	at Buffalo	October 15*	7	143	1
Marvin Harrison, Indianapolis	vs. Oakland	September 10	10	141	1
Wayne Chrebet, N.Y. Jets	at Indianapolis	November 12	8	140	0
Derrick Alexander, Kansas City	at Oakland	November 5	9	139	2
Richie Anderson, N.Y. Jets	at Baltimore	December 24	11	139	1
Kyle Brady, Jacksonville	at Dallas	October 29*	10	138	1
Cris Carter, Minnesota	vs. Carolina	November 19	8	138	1
Keenan McCardell, Jacksonville	vs. Pittsburgh	October 1	11	137	1
Eric Moulds, Buffalo	vs. N.Y. Jets	October 29	6	137	0
Derrick Alexander, Kansas City	at Seattle	October 29	4	137	2
Ed McCaffrey, Denver	at Cincinnati	October 22	10	136	0
Amani Toomer, N.Y. Giants	vs. Pittsburgh	December 10	9	136	1
Randy Moss, Minnesota	vs. Green Bay	December 17	4	136	1
Eric Moulds, Buffalo	at Minnesota	October 22	12	135	1
Rod Smith, Denver	vs. Kansas City	September 24	8	134	0
Marvin Harrison, Indianapolis	at Seattle	October 15	7	134	0
Rod Smith, Denver	at N.Y. Jets	November 5	5	134	0
Tony Gonzalez, Kansas City	at Oakland	November 5	9	134	0
Jimmy Smith, Jacksonville	at Indianapolis	September 25	9	132	2
Peerless Price, Buffalo	at Seattle	December 23	8	132	1
Jacquez Green, Tampa Bay	at Minnesota	October 9	11	131	0
Laveranues Coles, N.Y. Jets	at Buffalo	October 29	5	131	0
Muhsin Muhammad, Carolina	vs. Green Bay	November 27	11	131	2
Keenan McCardell, Jacksonville	at N.Y. Giants	December 23	11	131	0
Torry Holt, St. Louis	vs. Carolina	November 5	4	130	0
Randy Moss, Minnesota	at Green Bay	November 6*	6	130	0
James McKnight, Dallas	vs. San Francisco	September 24	6	129	0
Ed McCaffrey, Denver	vs. Cleveland	October 15	5	129	0
Isaac Bruce, St. Louis	at Kansas City	October 22	8	129	2
Isaac Bruce, St. Louis	at San Francisco	October 29	8	129	0
Terry Glenn, New England	vs. Cincinnati	November 19	11	129	0
Terrell Owens, San Francisco	vs. New Orleans	December 10	6	129	1
David Boston, Arizona	at N.Y. Giants	September 3	9	128	2
Tony Gonzalez, Kansas City	at Denver	September 24	10	127	1
Muhsin Muhammad, Carolina	vs. San Francisco	October 22	9	127	0
Marcus Robinson, Chicago	at Green Bay	October 1	2	126	2
Ricky Watters, Seattle	vs. Denver	November 26	9	126	0
Torry Holt, St. Louis	vs. Washington	November 20	4	125	0
David Boston, Arizona	vs. Philadelphia	October 15	6	123	1
Albert Connell, Washington	at N.Y. Giants	September 24	4	122	0
Torrance Small, Philadelphia	vs. Atlanta	October 1	4	122	1
Tim Brown, Oakland	at Denver	November 13	10	122	1
Robert Wilson, New Orleans	vs. Denver	December 3	8	122	0
Keyshawn Johnson, Tampa Bay	vs. Minnesota	October 29	6	121	1
James Thrash, Washington	vs. Philadelphia	November 26	5	121	0
Torry Holt, St. Louis	at New Orleans	December 24	5	121	0
Tony Martin, Miami	at Minnesota	September 10	6	120	0
Oronde Gadsden, Miami	at N.Y. Jets	October 23*	7	119	0
Cris Carter, Minnesota	vs. Arizona	November 12	11	119	1
Bill Schroeder, Green Bay	at Chicago	December 3	6	119	0
Troy Brown, New England	vs. Kansas City	December 4	12	119	1
Randy Moss, Minnesota	vs. Tampa Bay	October 9	5	118	1
Sean Dawkins, Seattle	vs. Indianapolis	October 15	6	118	0
Antonio Freeman, Green Bay	vs. Minnesota	November 6*	5	118	1
Curtis Conway, San Diego	at Denver	November 19	4	118	1
Rod Smith, Denver	vs. Atlanta	September 10	7	117	2
Derrick Alexander, Kansas City	vs. St. Louis	October 22	5	117	1
Tony Gonzalez, Kansas City	vs. St. Louis	October 22	5	117	1
Jimmy Smith, Jacksonville	vs. Seattle	November 12	10	117	0
Andre Rison, Oakland	at Denver	November 13	6	117	0
Az-Zahir Hakim, St. Louis	vs. Denver	September 4	5	116	1
Joe Horn, New Orleans	at San Diego	September 10	12	116	2
Marshall Faulk, St. Louis	vs. San Diego	October 1	6	116	2
Antonio Freeman, Green Bay	vs. San Francisco	October 15	6	116	1
Derrick Alexander, Kansas City	at New England	December 4	5	116	1
Joe Horn, New Orleans	vs. Atlanta	December 17	7	116	0
Keyshawn Johnson, Tampa Bay	vs. St. Louis	December 18	7	116	0
Marvin Harrison, Indianapolis	at Kansas City	September 3	9	115	0
Keenan McCardell, Jacksonville	at Cleveland	September 3	9	115	0
Ed McCaffrey, Denver	at St. Louis	September 4	7	115	0
Donald Hayes, Carolina	at San Francisco	September 10	6	115	1
Cris Carter, Minnesota	at Tampa Bay	October 29	7	115	0
Terrell Owens, San Francisco	vs. St. Louis	October 29	8	115	2
Muhsin Muhammad, Carolina	at Oakland	December 24	10	114	0
David Patten, Cleveland	vs. Baltimore	October 1	7	113	0

Player, Team	Opponent	Date	Rec.	Yds.	TD
Jeff Graham, San Diego	at Buffalo	October 15*	9	113	1
James McKnight, Dallas	vs. Jacksonville	October 29*	6	113	0
Jeff Graham, San Diego	vs. Pittsburgh	December 24	5	113	1
Sylvester Morris, Kansas City	vs. San Diego	September 17	6	112	3
Eric Moulds, Buffalo	vs. Indianapolis	October 1	9	112	1
Charlie Garner, San Francisco	at Carolina	October 22	7	112	0
Ed McCaffrey, Denver	vs. Seattle	December 10	8	112	1
Rod Smith, Denver	vs. Cleveland	October 15	5	111	3
Cris Carter, Minnesota	at Chicago	October 15	7	111	0
Kyle Brady, Jacksonville	vs. Washington	October 22	8	111	0
Freddie Jones, San Diego	vs. Oakland	October 29	10	111	2
Rod Smith, Denver	at Cincinnati	October 22	7	110	1
Randy Moss, Minnesota	vs. Buffalo	October 22	5	110	1
Ike Hilliard, N.Y. Giants	vs. St. Louis	November 12	5	110	2
Troy Brown, New England	vs. Cincinnati	November 19	8	110	0
Richie Anderson, N.Y. Jets	vs. Miami	October 23*	12	109	0
Marvin Harrison, Indianapolis	vs. Detroit	October 29	9	109	1
Shawn Jefferson, Atlanta	at Oakland	November 26	7	109	0
Eddie George, Tennessee	at Jacksonville	November 26	7	109	0
Terrence Wilkins, Indianapolis	at N.Y. Jets	December 3	7	109	1
Marvin Harrison, Indianapolis	vs. Minnesota	December 24	12	109	3
Muhsin Muhammad, Carolina	at San Francisco	September 10	8	108	1
Keenan McCardell, Jacksonville	vs. Cincinnati	September 17	10	108	1
Terrell Owens, San Francisco	at St. Louis	September 17	6	108	1
Bill Schroeder, Green Bay	vs. Chicago	October 1	8	108	2
Troy Brown, New England	at Denver	October 1	5	108	2
Amani Toomer, N.Y. Giants	vs. Philadelphia	October 29	9	108	1
Amani Toomer, N.Y. Giants	vs. Detroit	November 19	8	108	0
Jeff Graham, San Diego	at St. Louis	October 1	7	107	0
Cris Carter, Minnesota	vs. Buffalo	October 22	7	107	2
Randy Moss, Minnesota	vs. Carolina	November 19	5	106	1
Larry Foster, Detroit	at Minnesota	November 30	8	106	1
Carl Pickens, Tennessee	at Pittsburgh	September 24	2	105	0
Joe Horn, New Orleans	at San Francisco	December 10	5	105	0
Dedric Ward, N.Y. Jets	at Green Bay	September 3	5	104	0
Jacquez Green, Tampa Bay	vs. Chicago	September 10	5	104	1
Kevin Dyson, Tennessee	vs. Kansas City	September 10*	6	104	1
Az-Zahir Hakim, St. Louis	vs. San Diego	October 1	5	104	0
Shannon Sharpe, Baltimore	vs. Tennessee	October 22	8	104	0
Wayne Chrebet, N.Y. Jets	vs. Miami	October 23*	6	104	2
Randy Moss, Minnesota	vs. Arizona	November 12	7	104	1
Jimmy Smith, Jacksonville	vs. Cleveland	December 3	6	104	0
Torry Holt, St. Louis	vs. Denver	September 4	6	103	0
Eric Moulds, Buffalo	vs. Green Bay	September 10	7	103	0
Marvin Harrison, Indianapolis	vs. Jacksonville	September 25	2	103	1
Derrick Mason, Tennessee	vs. N.Y. Giants	October 1	6	103	1
Richie Anderson, N.Y. Jets	at Oakland	December 10	8	103	0
David Patten, Cleveland	vs. Philadelphia	December 10	7	103	1
Qadry Ismail, Baltimore	at Pittsburgh	September 3	7	102	1
David Boston, Arizona	vs. Dallas	September 10	6	102	0
Wesley Walls, Carolina	vs. Seattle	October 8	7	102	0
Kevin Johnson, Cleveland	vs. Cincinnati	October 29	6	102	0
Sylvester Morris, Kansas City	at Oakland	November 5	6	102	0
James Thrash, Washington	at Arizona	November 5	8	102	1
Eric Moulds, Buffalo	at Tampa Bay	November 26	8	102	0
Muhsin Muhammad, Carolina	at Kansas City	December 10	5	102	0
Danny Farmer, Cincinnati	vs. Jacksonville	December 17	8	102	0
Troy Brown, New England	vs. Miami	December 24	6	101	0
Torry Holt, St. Louis	at Seattle	September 10	7	101	0
Reggie Jones, San Diego	vs. Denver	October 8	8	101	0
Tony Gonzalez, Kansas City	at Seattle	October 29	5	101	1
Shannon Sharpe, Baltimore	vs. Dallas	November 19	6	101	0
Rod Smith, Denver	at Kansas City	December 17	4	101	1
Eric Moulds, Buffalo	at Seattle	December 23	4	100	1
Marshall Faulk, St. Louis	vs. Denver	September 4	4	100	0
Dedric Ward, N.Y. Jets	vs. New England	September 11	7	100	1
Tony Gonzalez, Kansas City	vs. Oakland	October 15	6	100	2
Amani Toomer, N.Y. Giants	at Cleveland	November 5	8	100	1
Eddie Kennison, Chicago	vs. New England	December 10	5	100	0
Chad Lewis, Philadelphia	at Cleveland	December 10			

*Overtime game.

OFFENSE

TOTAL SCORES

Team	Series	TD Rush	TD Pass	Total TDs	TD Efficiency Pct.	FGM	Total Scores	Scoring Efficiency Pct.
St. Louis	78	26	23	49	62.82	17	66	84.62
Oakland	65	21	17	38	58.46	17	55	84.62
Denver	59	16	17	33	55.93	20	53	89.83
Indianapolis	53	12	20	32	60.38	17	49	92.45
Green Bay	55	11	16	27	49.09	21	48	87.27
San Francisco	62	15	22	37	59.68	11	48	77.42
Buffalo	56	11	16	27	48.21	18	45	80.36
Tennessee	55	12	14	26	47.27	19	45	81.82
Philadelphia	50	11	14	25	50.00	20	45	90.00
Jacksonville	57	15	12	27	47.37	18	45	78.95
Carolina	57	7	15	22	38.60	22	44	77.19
Detroit	54	16	8	24	44.44	19	43	79.63
Kansas City	55	11	18	29	52.73	13	42	76.36
New England	53	9	14	23	43.40	19	42	79.25
Pittsburgh	49	17	6	23	46.94	19	42	85.71
Tampa Bay	47	14	13	27	57.45	15	42	89.36
Miami	46	14	11	25	54.35	16	41	89.13
N.Y. Giants	46	13	12	25	54.35	15	40	86.96
N.Y. Jets	53	11	17	28	52.83	12	40	75.47
Minnesota	46	10	15	25	54.35	14	39	84.78
New Orleans	48	13	11	24	50.00	15	39	81.25
Seattle	46	10	18	28	60.87	11	39	84.78
Washington	48	12	11	23	47.92	16	39	81.25
Baltimore	50	8	12	20	40.00	19	39	78.00
Dallas	47	13	10	23	48.94	15	38	80.85
Arizona	44	6	8	14	31.82	13	27	61.36
Atlanta	37	5	8	13	35.14	13	26	70.27
San Diego	38	7	8	15	39.47	11	26	68.42
Cleveland	32	7	8	15	46.88	10	25	78.13
Chicago	26	6	5	11	42.31	12	23	88.46
Cincinnati	33	7	6	13	39.39	10	23	69.70
Totals	1545	366	405	771	49.90	487	1258	81.42
Average	49.8	11.8	13.1	24.9	49.90	15.7	40.6	81.42

SCORING EFFICIENCY

Team	Series	TD Rush	TD Pass	Total TDs	TD Efficiency Pct.	FGM	Total Scores	Scoring Efficiency Pct.
Indianapolis	53	12	20	32	60.38	17	49	92.45
Philadelphia	50	11	14	25	50.00	20	45	90.00
Denver	59	16	17	33	55.93	20	53	89.83
Tampa Bay	47	14	13	27	57.45	15	42	89.36
Miami	46	14	11	25	54.35	16	41	89.13
Chicago	26	6	5	11	42.31	12	23	88.46
Green Bay	55	11	16	27	49.09	21	48	87.27
N.Y. Giants	46	13	12	25	54.35	15	40	86.96
Pittsburgh	49	17	6	23	46.94	19	42	85.71
Minnesota	46	10	15	25	54.35	14	39	84.78
Seattle	46	10	18	28	60.87	11	39	84.78
St. Louis	78	26	23	49	62.82	17	66	84.62
Oakland	65	21	17	38	58.46	17	55	84.62
Tennessee	55	12	14	26	47.27	19	45	81.82
New Orleans	48	13	11	24	50.00	15	39	81.25
Washington	48	12	11	23	47.92	16	39	81.25
Dallas	47	13	10	23	48.94	15	38	80.85
Buffalo	56	11	16	27	48.21	18	45	80.36
Detroit	54	16	8	24	44.44	19	43	79.63
New England	53	9	14	23	43.40	19	42	79.25
Jacksonville	57	15	12	27	47.37	18	45	78.95
Cleveland	32	7	8	15	46.88	10	25	78.13
Baltimore	50	8	12	20	40.00	19	39	78.00
San Francisco	62	15	22	37	59.68	11	48	77.42
Carolina	57	7	15	22	38.60	22	44	77.19
Kansas City	55	11	18	29	52.73	13	42	76.36
N.Y. Jets	53	11	17	28	52.83	12	40	75.47
Atlanta	37	5	8	13	35.14	13	26	70.27
Cincinnati	33	7	6	13	39.39	10	23	69.70
San Diego	38	7	8	15	39.47	11	26	68.42
Arizona	44	6	8	14	31.82	13	27	61.36
Totals	1545	366	405	771	49.90	487	1258	81.42
Average	49.8	11.8	13.1	24.9	49.90	15.7	40.6	81.42

TOTAL SCORES

Team	Series	TD Rush	TD Pass	Total TDs	TD Efficiency Pct.	FGM	Total Scores	Scoring Efficiency Pct.
Baltimore	27	4	4	8	29.63	6	14	51.85
Tennessee	30	6	8	14	46.67	9	23	76.67
Miami	38	9	8	17	44.74	11	28	73.68
Detroit	36	9	11	20	55.56	11	31	86.11
N.Y. Giants	45	6	16	22	48.89	9	31	68.89
Pittsburgh	42	4	9	13	30.95	18	31	73.81
Philadelphia	40	9	5	14	35.00	19	33	82.50
New Orleans	49	14	8	22	44.90	12	34	69.39
Washington	44	6	7	13	29.55	21	34	77.27
Denver	50	9	14	23	46.00	12	35	70.00
Tampa Bay	45	10	8	18	40.00	17	35	77.78
Green Bay	45	7	17	24	53.33	13	37	82.22
Carolina	61	10	11	21	34.43	17	38	62.30
Jacksonville	40	13	13	26	65.00	12	38	95.00
Chicago	46	13	16	29	63.04	10	39	84.78
Kansas City	50	12	19	31	62.00	10	41	82.00
Oakland	47	8	22	30	63.83	12	42	89.36
Indianapolis	51	13	15	28	54.90	15	43	84.31
N.Y. Jets	50	9	12	21	42.00	22	43	86.00
New England	54	12	16	28	51.85	17	45	83.33
Atlanta	55	13	13	26	47.27	20	46	83.64
Buffalo	54	12	14	26	48.15	21	47	87.04
Dallas	53	16	12	28	52.83	19	47	78.69
Cincinnati	61	12	16	28	45.90	20	48	87.50
San Francisco	56	21	14	35	62.50	14	49	83.61
Seattle	61	16	15	31	50.82	20	51	83.87
Minnesota	62	17	15	32	51.61	20	52	88.33
Cleveland	60	23	11	34	56.67	19	53	93.10
St. Louis	58	17	17	34	58.62	20	54	84.85
Arizona	66	26	13	39	59.09	17	56	86.96
San Diego	69	10	26	36	52.17	24	60	81.42
Totals	1545	366	405	771	49.90	487	1258	81.42
Average	49.8	11.8	13.1	24.9	49.90	15.7	40.6	81.42

SCORING EFFICIENCY

Team	Series	TD Rush	TD Pass	Total TDs	TD Efficiency Pct.	FGM	Total Scores	Scoring Efficiency Pct.
Baltimore	27	4	4	8	29.63	6	14	51.85
Carolina	61	10	11	21	34.43	17	38	62.30
N.Y. Giants	45	6	16	22	48.89	9	31	68.89
New Orleans	49	14	8	22	44.90	12	34	69.39
Denver	50	9	14	23	46.00	12	35	70.00
Miami	38	9	8	17	44.74	11	28	73.68
Pittsburgh	42	4	9	13	30.95	18	31	73.81
Tennessee	30	6	8	14	46.67	9	23	76.67
Washington	44	6	7	13	29.55	21	34	77.27
Tampa Bay	45	10	8	18	40.00	17	35	77.78
Cincinnati	61	12	16	28	45.90	20	48	78.69
Kansas City	50	12	19	31	62.00	10	41	82.00
Green Bay	45	7	17	24	53.33	13	37	82.22
Philadelphia	40	9	5	14	35.00	19	33	82.50
New England	54	12	16	28	51.85	17	45	83.33
Seattle	61	16	15	31	50.82	20	51	83.61
Atlanta	55	13	13	26	47.27	20	46	83.64
Minnesota	62	17	15	32	51.61	20	52	83.87
Indianapolis	51	13	15	28	54.90	15	43	84.31
Chicago	46	13	16	29	63.04	10	39	84.78
Arizona	66	26	13	39	59.09	17	56	84.85
N.Y. Jets	50	9	12	21	42.00	22	43	86.00
Detroit	36	9	11	20	55.56	11	31	86.11
San Diego	69	10	26	36	52.17	24	60	86.96
Buffalo	54	12	14	26	48.15	21	47	87.04
San Francisco	56	21	14	35	62.50	14	49	87.50
Cleveland	60	23	11	34	56.67	19	53	88.33
Dallas	53	16	12	28	52.83	19	47	88.68
Oakland	47	8	22	30	63.83	12	42	89.36
St. Louis	58	17	17	34	58.62	20	54	93.10
Jacksonville	40	13	13	26	65.00	12	38	95.00
Totals	1545	366	405	771	49.90	487	1258	81.42
Average	49.8	11.8	13.1	24.9	49.90	15.7	40.6	81.42

2000 STATISTICS *Miscellaneous*

HISTORY

Championship games
Year-by-year standings
Super Bowls
Pro Bowls
Records
Statistical leaders
Coaching records
Hall of Fame
The Sporting News awards
First-round draft choices
Team by team

CHAMPIONSHIP GAMES

NFL (1933-1969); NFC (1970-2000)
RESULTS

Sea.	Date	Winner (Share)	Loser (Share)	Score	Site	Attendance
1933	Dec. 17	Chicago Bears ($210.34)	N.Y. Giants ($140.22)	23-21	Chicago	26,000
1934	Dec. 9	N.Y. Giants ($621)	Chicago Bears ($414.02)	30-13	N.Y. Giants	35,059
1935	Dec. 15	Detroit ($313.35)	N.Y. Giants ($200.20)	26-7	Detroit	15,000
1936	Dec. 13	Green Bay ($250)	Boston Redskins ($180)	21-6	N.Y. Giants	29,545
1937	Dec. 12	Washington ($225.90)	Chicago Bears ($127.78)	28-21	Chicago	15,870
1938	Dec. 11	N.Y. Giants ($504.45)	Green Bay ($368.81)	23-17	N.Y. Giants	48,120
1939	Dec. 10	Green Bay ($703.97)	N.Y. Giants ($455.57)	27-0	Milwaukee	32,279
1940	Dec. 8	Chicago Bears ($873)	Washington ($606)	73-0	Washington	36,034
1941	Dec. 21	Chicago Bears ($430)	N.Y. Giants ($288)	37-9	Chicago	13,341
1942	Dec. 13	Washington ($965)	Chicago Bears ($637)	14-6	Washington	36,006
1943	Dec. 26	Chicago Bears ($1,146)	Washington ($765)	41-21	Chicago	34,320
1944	Dec. 17	Green Bay ($1,449)	N.Y. Giants ($814)	14-7	N.Y. Giants	46,016
1945	Dec. 16	Cleveland Rams ($1,469)	Washington ($902)	15-14	Cleveland	32,178
1946	Dec. 15	Chicago Bears ($1,975)	N.Y. Giants ($1,295)	24-14	N.Y. Giants	58,346
1947	Dec. 28	Chicago Cardinals ($1,132)	Philadelphia ($754)	28-21	Chicago	30,759
1948	Dec. 19	Philadelphia ($1,540)	Chicago Cardinals ($874)	7-0	Philadelphia	36,309
1949	Dec. 18	Philadelphia ($1,094)	L.A. Rams ($739)	14-0	L.A. Rams	27,980
1950	Dec. 24	Cleveland Browns ($1,113)	L.A. Rams ($686)	30-28	Cleveland	29,751
1951	Dec. 23	L.A. Rams ($2,108)	Cleve. Browns ($1,483)	24-17	L.A. Rams	57,522
1952	Dec. 28	Detroit ($2,274)	Cleveland Browns ($1,712)	17-7	Cleveland	50,934
1953	Dec. 27	Detroit ($2,424)	Cleveland Browns ($1,654)	17-16	Detroit	54,577
1954	Dec. 26	Cleveland Browns ($2,478)	Detroit ($1,585)	56-10	Cleveland	43,827
1955	Dec. 26	Cleveland Browns ($3,508)	L.A. Rams ($2,316)	38-14	L.A. Rams	85,693
1956	Dec. 30	N.Y. Giants ($3,779)	Chicago Bears ($2,485)	47-7	N.Y. Giants	56,836
1957	Dec. 29	Detroit ($4,295)	Cleveland Browns ($2,750)	59-14	Detroit	55,263
1958	Dec. 28	Baltimore ($4,718)	N.Y. Giants ($3,111)	23-17*	N.Y. Giants	64,185
1959	Dec. 27	Baltimore ($4,674)	N.Y. Giants ($3,083)	31-16	Baltimore	57,545
1960	Dec. 26	Philadelphia ($5,116)	Green Bay ($3,105)	17-13	Philadelphia	67,325
1961	Dec. 31	Green Bay ($5,195)	N.Y. Giants ($3,339)	37-0	Green Bay	39,029
1962	Dec. 30	Green Bay ($5,888)	N.Y. Giants ($4,166)	16-7	N.Y. Giants	64,892
1963	Dec. 29	Chicago Bears ($5,899)	N.Y. Giants ($4,218)	14-10	Chicago	45,801
1964	Dec. 27	Cleveland Browns ($8,052)	Baltimore ($5,571)	27-0	Cleveland	79,544
1965	Jan. 2	Green Bay ($7,819)	Cleveland Browns ($5,288)	23-12	Green Bay	50,777
1966	Jan. 1	Green Bay ($9,813)	Dallas ($6,527)	34-27	Dallas	74,152
1967	Dec. 31	Green Bay ($7,950)	Dallas ($5,299)	21-17	Green Bay	50,861
1968	Dec. 29	Baltimore ($9,306)	Cleveland Browns ($5,963)	34-0	Cleveland	78,410
1969	Jan. 4	Minnesota ($7,930)	Cleveland Browns ($5,118)	27-7	Minnesota	46,503
1970	Jan. 3	Dallas ($8,500)	San Francisco ($5,500)	17-10	San Francisco	59,364
1971	Jan. 2	Dallas ($8,500)	San Francisco ($5,500)	14-3	Dallas	63,409
1972	Dec. 31	Washington ($8,500)	Dallas ($5,500)	26-3	Washington	53,129
1973	Dec. 30	Minnesota ($8,500)	Dallas ($5,500)	27-10	Dallas	64,422
1974	Dec. 29	Minnesota ($8,500)	L.A. Rams ($5,500)	14-10	Minnesota	48,444
1975	Jan. 4	Dallas ($8,500)	L.A. Rams ($5,500)	37-7	L.A. Rams	88,919
1976	Dec. 26	Minnesota ($8,500)	L.A. Rams ($5,500)	24-13	Minnesota	48,379
1977	Jan. 1	Dallas ($9,000)	Minnesota ($9,000)	23-6	Dallas	64,293
1978	Jan. 7	Dallas ($9,000)	L.A. Rams ($9,000)	28-0	L.A. Rams	71,086
1979	Jan. 6	L.A. Rams ($9,000)	Tampa Bay ($9,000)	9-0	Tampa Bay	72,033
1980	Jan. 11	Philadelphia ($9,000)	Dallas ($9,000)	20-7	Philadelphia	70,696
1981	Jan. 10	San Francisco ($9,000)	Dallas ($9,000)	28-27	San Francisco	60,525
1982	Jan. 22	Washington ($18,000)	Dallas ($18,000)	31-17	Washington	55,045
1983	Jan. 8	Washington ($18,000)	San Francisco ($18,000)	24-21	Washington	55,363
1984	Jan. 6	San Francisco ($18,000)	Chicago Bears ($18,000)	23-0	San Francisco	61,040
1985	Jan. 12	Chicago Bears ($18,000)	L.A. Rams ($18,000)	24-0	Chicago	63,522
1986	Jan. 11	N.Y. Giants ($18,000)	Washington ($18,000)	17-0	N.Y. Giants	76,633
1987	Jan. 17	Washington ($18,000)	Minnesota ($18,000)	17-10	Washington	55,212
1988	Jan. 8	San Francisco ($18,000)	Chicago Bears ($18,000)	28-3	Chicago	64,830
1989	Jan. 14	San Francisco ($18,000)	L.A. Rams ($18,000)	30-3	San Francisco	64,769
1990	Jan. 20	N.Y. Giants ($18,000)	San Francisco ($18,000)	15-13	San Francisco	65,750
1991	Jan. 12	Washington ($18,000)	Detroit ($18,000)	41-10	Washington	55,585
1992	Jan. 17	Dallas ($18,000)	San Francisco ($18,000)	30-20	San Francisco	64,920
1993	Jan. 23	Dallas ($23,500)	San Francisco ($23,500)	38-21	Dallas	64,902
1994	Jan. 15	San Francisco ($26,000)	Dallas ($26,000)	38-28	San Francisco	69,125
1995	Jan. 14	Dallas ($27,000)	Green Bay ($27,000)	38-27	Dallas	65,135
1996	Jan. 12	Green Bay ($29,000)	Carolina ($29,000)	30-13	Green Bay	60,216
1997	Jan. 11	Green Bay ($30,000)	San Francisco ($30,000)	23-10	San Francisco	68,987
1998	Jan. 17	Atlanta ($32,500)	Minnesota ($32,500)	30-27*	Minnesota	64,060
1999	Jan. 23	St. Louis ($33,000)	Tampa Bay ($33,000)	11-6	St. Louis	66,496
2000	Jan. 14	N.Y. Giants ($34,500)	Minnesota ($34,500)	41-0	New York	79,310

*Overtime.

COMPOSITE STANDINGS

	W	L	Pct.	PF	PA		W	L	Pct.	PF	PA
Atlanta Falcons	1	0	1.000	30	27	Minnesota Vikings	4	4	.500	135	151
Philadelphia Eagles	4	1	.800	79	48	Phoenix Cardinals*	1	1	.500	28	28
Green Bay Packers	10	3	.769	303	177	San Francisco 49ers	5	7	.417	245	222
Baltimore Colts	3	1	.750	88	60	Cleveland Browns	4	7	.364	224	253
Detroit Lions	4	2	.667	139	141	New York Giants	6	11	.353	281	322
Washington Redskins†	7	5	.583	222	255	St. Louis Rams‡	4	9	.308	134	276
Chicago Bears	7	6	.538	286	245	Carolina Panthers	0	1	.000	13	30
Dallas Cowboys	8	8	.500	361	319	Tampa Bay Buccaneers	0	2	.000	6	20

*Both games played when franchise was in Chicago; won 28-21, lost 7-0.
†One game played when franchise was in Boston; lost 21-6.
‡One game played when franchise was in Cleveland; won 15-14. 11 games played when franchise was in Los Angeles, record of 2-9.

AFL (1960-1969); AFC (1970-2000)
RESULTS

Sea.	Date	Winner (Share)	Loser (Share)	Score	Site	Attendance
1960	Jan. 1	Houston ($1,025)	L.A. Chargers ($718)	24-16	Houston	32,183
1961	Dec. 24	Houston ($1,792)	San Diego ($1,111)	10-3	San Diego	29,556
1962	Dec. 23	Dallas Texans ($2,206)	Houston ($1,471)	20-17*	Houston	37,981
1963	Jan. 5	San Diego ($2,498)	Boston Patriots ($1,596)	51-10	San Diego	30,127
1964	Dec. 26	Buffalo ($2,668)	San Diego ($1,738)	20-7	Buffalo	40,242
1965	Dec. 26	Buffalo ($5,189)	San Diego ($3,447)	23-0	San Diego	30,361
1966	Jan. 1	Kansas City ($5,309)	Buffalo ($3,799)	31-7	Buffalo	42,080
1967	Dec. 31	Oakland ($6,321)	Houston ($4,996)	40-7	Oakland	53,330
1968	Dec. 29	N.Y. Jets ($7,007)	Oakland ($5,349)	27-23	New York	62,627
1969	Jan. 4	Kansas City ($7,755)	Oakland ($6,252)	17-7	Oakland	53,564
1970	Jan. 3	Baltimore ($8,500)	Oakland ($5,500)	27-17	Baltimore	54,799
1971	Jan. 2	Miami ($8,500)	Baltimore ($5,500)	21-0	Miami	76,622
1972	Dec. 31	Miami ($8,500)	Pittsburgh ($5,500)	21-17	Pittsburgh	50,845
1973	Dec. 30	Miami ($8,500)	Oakland ($5,500)	27-10	Miami	79,325
1974	Dec. 29	Pittsburgh ($8,500)	Oakland ($5,500)	24-13	Oakland	53,800
1975	Jan. 4	Pittsburgh ($8,500)	Oakland ($5,500)	16-10	Pittsburgh	50,609
1976	Dec. 28	Oakland ($8,500)	Pittsburgh ($5,500)	24-7	Oakland	53,821
1977	Jan. 1	Denver ($9,000)	Oakland ($9,000)	20-17	Denver	75,044
1978	Jan. 7	Pittsburgh ($9,000)	Houston ($9,000)	34-5	Pittsburgh	50,725
1979	Jan. 6	Pittsburgh ($9,000)	Houston ($9,000)	27-13	Pittsburgh	50,475
1980	Jan. 11	Oakland ($9,000)	San Diego ($9,000)	34-27	San Diego	52,428
1981	Jan. 10	Cincinnati ($9,000)	San Diego ($9,000)	27-7	Cincinnati	46,302
1982	Jan. 23	Miami ($18,000)	N.Y. Jets ($18,000)	14-0	Miami	67,396
1983	Jan. 8	L.A. Raiders ($18,000)	Seattle ($18,000)	30-14	Los Angeles	88,734
1984	Jan. 6	Miami ($18,000)	Pittsburgh ($18,000)	45-28	Miami	76,029
1985	Jan. 12	New England ($18,000)	Miami ($18,000)	31-14	Miami	74,978
1986	Jan. 11	Denver ($18,000)	Cleveland ($18,000)	23-20*	Cleveland	79,915
1987	Jan. 17	Denver ($18,000)	Cleveland ($18,000)	38-33	Denver	75,993
1988	Jan. 8	Cincinnati ($18,000)	Buffalo ($18,000)	21-10	Cincinnati	59,747
1989	Jan. 14	Denver ($18,000)	Cleveland ($18,000)	37-21	Denver	76,046
1990	Jan. 20	Buffalo ($18,000)	L.A. Raiders ($18,000)	51-3	Buffalo	80,234
1991	Jan. 12	Buffalo ($18,000)	Denver ($18,000)	10-7	Buffalo	80,272
1992	Jan. 17	Buffalo ($18,000)	Miami ($18,000)	29-10	Miami	72,703
1993	Jan. 23	Buffalo ($23,500)	Kansas City ($23,500)	30-13	Buffalo	76,642
1994	Jan. 15	San Diego ($26,000)	Pittsburgh ($26,000)	17-13	Pittsburgh	61,545
1995	Jan. 14	Pittsburgh ($27,000)	Indianapolis ($27,000)	20-16	Pittsburgh	61,062
1996	Jan. 12	New England ($29,000)	Jacksonville ($29,000)	20-6	New England	60,190
1997	Jan. 11	Denver ($30,000)	Pittsburgh ($30,000)	24-21	Pittsburgh	61,382
1998	Jan. 17	Denver ($32,500)	N.Y. Jets ($32,500)	23-10	Denver	75,482
1999	Jan. 23	Tennessee ($33,000)	Jacksonville ($33,000)	33-14	Jacksonville	75,206
2000	Jan. 14	Baltimore ($34,500)	Oakland ($34,500)	16-3	Oakland	62,784

*Overtime.

COMPOSITE STANDINGS

	W	L	Pct.	PF	PA		W	L	Pct.	PF	PA
Cincinnati Bengals	2	0	1.000	48	17	Tennessee Titans▲	3	4	.429	109	154
Baltimore Ravens	1	0	1.000	16	3	New York Jets	1	2	.333	37	60
Denver Broncos	6	1	.857	172	132	Indianapolis Colts∞	1	2	.333	43	58
Buffalo Bills	6	2	.750	180	92	Oakland Raiders§	4	9	.308	231	280
Kansas City Chiefs†	3	1	.750	81	61	San Diego Chargers*	2	6	.250	128	161
Miami Dolphins	5	2	.714	152	115	Seattle Seahawks	0	1	.000	14	30
New England Patriots‡	2	1	.667	61	71	Jacksonville Jaguars	0	2	.000	20	53
Pittsburgh Steelers	5	5	.500	207	188	Cleveland Browns	0	3	.000	74	98

*One game played when franchise was in Los Angeles; lost 24-16.
†One game played when franchise was in Dallas (Texans); won 20-17.
‡One game played when franchise was in Boston; lost 51-10.
§Two games played when franchise was in Los Angeles; record of 1-1.
∞Two games played when franchise was in Baltimore; record of 1-1.
▲Six games played when franchise was in Houston (Oilers); record of 2-4.

POSTSEASON GAME COMPOSITE STANDINGS

	W	L	Pct.	PF	PA		W	L	Pct.	PF	PA
Baltimore Ravens	4	0	1.000	95	23	New York Giants	16	20	.444	619	660
Green Bay Packers	22	10	.688	772	558	Tennessee Titans▼	12	15	.444	471	626
San Francisco 49ers	24	15	.615	984	759	St. Louis Rams†	16	21	.432	612	787
Dallas Cowboys	32	21	.604	1271	979	Minnesota Vikings	17	23	.425	779	913
Washington Redskins‡	22	15	.595	778	652	Kansas City Chiefs*	8	11	.421	301	384
Pittsburgh Steelers	21	15	.583	801	707	Cincinnati Bengals	5	7	.417	246	257
Oakland Raiders◆	22	16	.579	885	675	Detroit Lions	7	10	.412	365	404
Denver Broncos	16	12	.571	616	657	New England Patriots§	7	10	.412	320	357
Miami Dolphins	19	18	.526	777	828	Atlanta Falcons	4	6	.400	208	260
Chicago Bears	14	14	.500	579	552	San Diego Chargers▲	7	11	.389	332	428
Jacksonville Jaguars	4	4	.500	208	200	Seattle Seahawks	3	5	.375	145	159
Carolina Panthers	1	1	.500	39	47	Cleveland Browns	11	19	.367	596	702
Buffalo Bills	14	15	.483	681	658	Tampa Bay Buccaneers	3	6	.333	91	170
New York Jets	6	7	.462	260	247	Arizona Cardinals∞	2	5	.286	122	182
Indianapolis Colts■	10	12	.455	393	431	New Orleans Saints	1	5	.167	103	185
Philadelphia Eagles	10	12	.455	387	392						

*One game played when franchise was in Dallas (Texans); won 20-17.
†One game played when franchise was in Cleveland; won 15-14. 32 games played when franchise was in Los Angeles; record of 12-20.
‡One game played when franchise was in Boston; lost 21-6.
§Two games played when franchise was in Boston; won 26-8, lost 51-10.
∞Two games played when franchise was in Chicago; won 28-21, lost 7-0. Three games played when franchise was in St. Louis; lost 35-23, lost 30-14, lost 41-16.
▲One game played when franchise was in Los Angeles; lost 24-16.
◆12 games played when franchise was in Los Angeles; record of 6-6.
■15 games played when franchise was in Baltimore; record of 8-7.
▼22 games played when franchise was in Houston; record of 9-13.

CHAMPIONS OF DEFUNCT PRO FOOTBALL LEAGUES

ALL-AMERICAN FOOTBALL CONFERENCE

Year	Winner	Coach	Loser	Coach	Score, Site
1946	Cleveland Browns	Paul Brown	N.Y. Yankees	Ray Flaherty	14-9, Cleveland
1947	Cleveland Browns	Paul Brown	N.Y. Yankees	Ray Flaherty	14-3, New York
1948	Cleveland Browns	Paul Brown	Buffalo Bills	Red Dawson	49-7, Cleveland
1949	Cleveland Browns	Paul Brown	S.F. 49ers	Buck Shaw	21-7, Cleveland

NOTE: Cleveland Browns and San Francisco 49ers joined the NFL after the AAFC folded in 1949.

WORLD FOOTBALL LEAGUE

Year	Winner	Coach	Loser	Coach	Score, Site
1974	Birmingham Americans	Jack Gotta	Florida Blazers	Jack Pardee	22-21, Birmingham
1975	League folded October 22				

UNITED STATES FOOTBALL LEAGUE

Year	Winner	Coach	Loser	Coach	Score, Site
1983	Michigan Panthers	Jim Stanley	Philadelphia Stars	Jim Mora	24-22, Denver
1984	Philadelphia Stars	Jim Mora	Arizona Wranglers	George Allen	23-3, Tampa
1985	Baltimore Stars	Jim Mora	Oakland Invaders	Charlie Sumner	28-24, E. Rutherford, N.J.

YEAR-BY-YEAR STANDINGS

1920

Team	W	L	T	Pct.
Akron Pros*	8	0	3	1.000
Decatur Staleys	10	1	2	.909
Buffalo All-Americans	9	1	1	.900
Chicago Cardinals	6	2	2	.750
Rock Island Independents	6	2	2	.750
Dayton Triangles	5	2	2	.714
Rochester Jeffersons	6	3	2	.667
Canton Bulldogs	7	4	2	.636
Detroit Heralds	2	3	3	.400
Cleveland Tigers	2	4	2	.333
Chicago Tigers	2	5	1	.286
Hammond Pros	2	5	0	.286
Columbus Panhandles	2	6	2	.250
Muncie Flyers	0	1	0	.000

*No official standings were maintained for the 1920 season, and the championship was awarded to the Akron Pros in a League meeting on April 30, 1921. Clubs played schedules which included games against non-league opponents. Records of clubs against all opponents are listed above.

1921

Team	W	L	T	Pct.
Chicago Staleys	9	1	1	.900
Buffalo All-Americans	9	1	2	.900
Akron Pros	8	3	1	.727
Canton Bulldogs	5	2	3	.714
Rock Island Independents	4	2	1	.667
Evansville Crimson Giants	3	2	0	.600
Green Bay Packers	3	2	1	.600
Dayton Triangles	4	4	1	.500
Chicago Cardinals	3	3	2	.500
Rochester Jeffersons	2	3	0	.400
Cleveland Indians	3	5	0	.375
Washington Senators	1	2	0	.333
Cincinnati Celts	1	3	0	.250
Hammond Pros	1	3	1	.250
Minneapolis Marines	1	3	1	.250
Detroit Heralds	1	5	1	.167
Columbus Panhandles	1	8	0	.111
Tonawanda Kardex	0	1	0	.000
Muncie Flyers	0	2	0	.000
Louisville Brecks	0	2	0	.000
New York Giants	0	2	0	.000

1922

Team	W	L	T	Pct.
Canton Bulldogs	10	0	2	1.000
Chicago Bears	9	3	0	.750
Chicago Cardinals	8	3	0	.727
Toledo Maroons	5	2	2	.714
Rock Island Independents	4	2	1	.667
Racine Legion	6	4	1	.600
Dayton Triangles	4	3	1	.571
Green Bay Packers	4	3	3	.571
Buffalo All-Americans	5	4	1	.556
Akron Pros	3	5	2	.375
Milwaukee Badgers	2	4	3	.333
Oorang Indians	2	6	0	.250
Minneapolis Marines	1	3	0	.250
Louisville Brecks	1	3	0	.250
Evansville Crimson Giants	0	3	0	.000
Rochester Jeffersons	0	4	1	.000
Hammond Pros	0	5	1	.000
Columbus Panhandles	0	7	0	.000

1923

Team	W	L	T	Pct.
Canton Bulldogs	11	0	1	1.000
Chicago Bears	9	2	1	.818
Green Bay Packers	7	2	1	.778
Milwaukee Badgers	7	2	3	.778
Cleveland Indians	3	1	3	.750
Chicago Cardinals	8	4	0	.667
Duluth Kelleys	4	3	0	.571
Columbus Tigers	5	4	1	.556
Buffalo All-Americans	4	4	3	.500
Racine Legion	4	4	2	.500
Toledo Maroons	2	3	2	.400
Rock Island Independents	2	3	3	.400
Minneapolis Marines	2	5	2	.286
St. Louis All-Stars	1	4	2	.200
Hammond Pros	1	5	1	.167
Dayton Triangles	1	6	1	.143
Akron Indians	1	6	0	.143
Oorang Indians	1	10	0	.091
Rochester Jeffersons	0	2	0	.000
Louisville Brecks	0	3	0	.000

1924

Team	W	L	T	Pct.
Cleveland Bulldogs	7	1	1	.875
Chicago Bears	6	1	4	.857
Frankford Yellow Jackets	11	2	1	.846
Duluth Kelleys	5	1	0	.833
Rock Island Independents	6	2	2	.750
Green Bay Packers	7	4	0	.636
Racine Legion	4	3	3	.571
Chicago Cardinals	5	4	1	.556
Buffalo Bisons	6	5	0	.545
Columbus Tigers	4	4	0	.500
Hammond Pros	2	2	1	.500
Milwaukee Badgers	5	8	0	.385
Akron Indians	2	6	0	.250
Dayton Triangles	2	6	0	.250
Kansas City Blues	2	7	0	.222
Kenosha Maroons	0	5	1	.000
Minneapolis Marines	0	6	0	.000
Rochester Jeffersons	0	7	0	.000

1925

Team	W	L	T	Pct.
Chicago Cardinals	11	2	1	.846
Pottsville Maroons	10	2	0	.833
Detroit Panthers	8	2	2	.800
New York Giants	8	4	0	.667
Akron Indians	4	2	2	.667
Frankford Yellow Jackets	13	7	0	.650
Chicago Bears	9	5	3	.643
Rock Island Independents	5	3	3	.625
Green Bay Packers	8	5	0	.615
Providence Steam Roller	6	5	1	.545
Canton Bulldogs	4	4	0	.500
Cleveland Bulldogs	5	8	0	.385
Kansas City Cowboys	2	5	1	.286
Hammond Pros	1	4	0	.200
Buffalo Bisons	1	6	2	.143
Duluth Kelleys	0	3	0	.000
Rochester Jeffersons	0	6	1	.000
Milwaukee Badgers	0	6	0	.000
Dayton Triangles	0	7	1	.000
Columbus Tigers	0	9	0	.000

1926

Team	W	L	T	Pct.
Frankford Yellow Jackets	14	1	1	.933
Chicago Bears	12	1	3	.923
Pottsville Maroons	10	2	1	.833
Kansas City Cowboys	8	3	0	.727
Green Bay Packers	7	3	3	.700
Los Angeles Buccaneers	6	3	1	.667
New York Giants	8	4	1	.667
Duluth Eskimos	6	5	3	.545
Buffalo Rangers	4	4	2	.500
Chicago Cardinals	5	6	1	.455
Providence Steam Roller	5	7	1	.417
Detroit Panthers	4	6	2	.400
Hartford Blues	3	7	0	.300
Brooklyn Lions	3	8	0	.273
Milwaukee Badgers	2	7	0	.222
Akron Pros	1	4	3	.200
Dayton Triangles	1	4	1	.200
Racine Tornadoes	1	4	0	.200
Columbus Tigers	1	6	0	.143
Canton Bulldogs	1	9	3	.100
Hammond Pros	0	4	0	.000
Louisville Colonels	0	4	0	.000

1927

Team	W	L	T	Pct.
New York Giants	11	1	1	.917
Green Bay Packers	7	2	1	.778
Chicago Bears	9	3	2	.750
Cleveland Bulldogs	8	4	1	.667
Providence Steam Roller	8	5	1	.615
New York Yankees	7	8	1	.467
Frankford Yellow Jackets	6	9	3	.400
Pottsville Maroons	5	8	0	.385
Chicago Cardinals	3	7	1	.300
Dayton Triangles	1	6	1	.143
Duluth Eskimos	1	8	0	.111
Buffalo Bisons	0	5	0	.000

1928

Team	W	L	T	Pct.
Providence Steam Roller	8	1	2	.889
Frankford Yellow Jackets	11	3	2	.786
Detroit Wolverines	7	2	1	.778
Green Bay Packers	6	4	3	.600
Chicago Bears	7	5	1	.583
New York Giants	4	7	2	.364
New York Yankees	4	8	1	.333
Pottsville Maroons	2	8	0	.200
Chicago Cardinals	1	5	0	.167
Dayton Triangles	0	7	0	.000

1929

Team	W	L	T	Pct.
Green Bay Packers	12	0	1	1.000
New York Giants	13	1	1	.929
Frankford Yellow Jackets	9	4	5	.692
Chicago Cardinals	6	6	1	.500
Boston Bulldogs	4	4	0	.500
Orange Tornadoes	3	4	4	.429
Staten Island Stapletons	3	4	3	.429
Providence Steam Roller	4	6	2	.400
Chicago Bears	4	9	2	.308
Buffalo Bisons	1	7	1	.125
Minneapolis Red Jackets	1	9	0	.100
Dayton Triangles	0	6	0	.000

1930

Team	W	L	T	Pct.
Green Bay Packers	10	3	1	.769
New York Giants	13	4	0	.765
Chicago Bears	9	4	1	.692
Brooklyn Dodgers	7	4	1	.636
Providence Steam Roller	6	4	1	.600
Staten Island Stapletons	5	5	2	.500
Chicago Cardinals	5	6	2	.455
Portsmouth Spartans	5	6	3	.455
Frankford Yellow Jackets	4	13	1	.222
Minneapolis Red Jackets	1	7	1	.125
Newark Tornadoes	1	10	1	.091

1931

Team	W	L	T	Pct.
Green Bay Packers	12	2	0	.857
Portsmouth Spartans	11	3	0	.786
Chicago Bears	8	5	0	.615
Chicago Cardinals	5	4	0	.556
New York Giants	7	6	1	.538
Providence Steam Roller	4	4	3	.500
Staten Island Stapletons	4	6	1	.400
Cleveland Indians	2	8	0	.200
Brooklyn Dodgers	2	12	0	.143
Frankford Yellow Jackets	1	6	1	.143

1932

Team	W	L	T	Pct.
Chicago Bears	7	1	6	.875
Green Bay Packers	10	3	1	.769
Portsmouth Spartans	6	2	4	.750
Boston Braves	4	4	2	.500
New York Giants	4	6	2	.400
Brooklyn Dodgers	3	9	0	.250
Chicago Cardinals	2	6	2	.250
Staten Island Stapletons	2	7	3	.222

NOTE: Chicago Bears and Portsmouth finished regularly scheduled games tied for first place. Bears won playoff game, which counted in standings, 9-0.

1933

EASTERN DIVISION

Team	W	L	T	Pct.	PF	PA
N.Y. Giants	11	3	0	.786	244	101
Brooklyn	5	4	1	.556	93	54
Boston	5	5	2	.500	103	97
Philadelphia	3	5	1	.375	77	158
Pittsburgh	3	6	2	.333	67	208

WESTERN DIVISION

Team	W	L	T	Pct.	PF	PA
Chicago Bears	10	2	1	.833	133	82
Portsmouth	6	5	0	.545	128	87
Green Bay	5	7	1	.417	170	107
Cincinnati	3	6	1	.333	38	110
Chi. Cardinals	1	9	1	.100	52	101

PLAYOFFS

NFL championship
Chicago Bears 23 vs. N.Y. Giants 21

1934

EASTERN DIVISION

Team	W	L	T	Pct.	PF	PA
N.Y. Giants	8	5	0	.615	147	107
Boston	6	6	0	.500	107	94
Brooklyn	4	7	0	.364	61	153
Philadelphia	4	7	0	.364	127	85
Pittsburgh	2	10	0	.167	51	206

WESTERN DIVISION

Team	W	L	T	Pct.	PF	PA
Chicago Bears	13	0	0	1.000	286	86
Detroit	10	3	0	.769	238	59
Green Bay	7	6	0	.538	156	112
Chi. Cardinals	5	6	0	.455	80	84
St. Louis	1	2	0	.333	27	61
Cincinnati	0	8	0	.000	10	243

PLAYOFFS

NFL championship
N.Y. Giants 30 vs. Chicago Bears 13

1935

EASTERN DIVISION

Team	W	L	T	Pct.	PF	PA
N.Y. Giants	9	3	0	.750	180	96
Brooklyn	5	6	1	.455	90	141
Pittsburgh	4	8	0	.333	100	209
Boston	2	8	1	.200	65	123
Philadelphia	2	9	0	.182	60	179

NOTE: One game between Boston and Philadelphia was cancelled.

WESTERN DIVISION

Team	W	L	T	Pct.	PF	PA
Detroit	7	3	2	.700	191	111
Green Bay	8	4	0	.667	181	96
Chicago Bears	6	4	2	.600	192	106
Chi. Cardinals	6	4	2	.600	99	97

PLAYOFFS

NFL championship
Detroit 26 vs. N.Y. Giants 7

1936

EASTERN DIVISION

Team	W	L	T	Pct.	PF	PA
Boston	7	5	0	.583	149	110
Pittsburgh	6	6	0	.500	98	187
N.Y. Giants	5	6	1	.455	115	163
Brooklyn	3	8	1	.273	92	161
Philadelphia	1	11	0	.083	51	206

WESTERN DIVISION

Team	W	L	T	Pct.	PF	PA
Green Bay	10	1	1	.909	248	118
Chicago Bears	9	3	0	.750	222	94
Detroit	8	4	0	.667	235	102
Chi. Cardinals	3	8	1	.273	74	143

PLAYOFFS

NFL championship
Green Bay 21, Boston 6, at New York.

1937

EASTERN DIVISION

Team	W	L	T	Pct.	PF	PA
Washington	8	3	0	.727	195	120
N.Y. Giants	6	3	2	.667	128	109
Pittsburgh	4	7	0	.364	122	145
Brooklyn	3	7	1	.300	82	174
Philadelphia	2	8	1	.200	86	177

WESTERN DIVISION

Team	W	L	T	Pct.	PF	PA
Chicago Bears	9	1	1	.900	201	100
Green Bay	7	4	0	.636	220	122
Detroit	7	4	0	.636	180	105
Chi. Cardinals	5	5	1	.500	135	165
Cleveland	1	10	0	.091	75	207

PLAYOFFS

NFL championship
Washington 28 at Chicago Bears 21

1938

EASTERN DIVISION

Team	W	L	T	Pct.	PF	PA
N.Y. Giants	8	2	1	.800	194	79
Washington	6	3	2	.667	148	154
Brooklyn	4	4	3	.500	131	161
Philadelphia	5	6	0	.455	154	164
Pittsburgh	2	9	0	.182	79	169

WESTERN DIVISION

Team	W	L	T	Pct.	PF	PA
Green Bay	8	3	0	.727	223	118
Detroit	7	4	0	.636	119	108
Chicago Bears	6	5	0	.545	194	148
Cleveland	4	7	0	.364	131	215
Chi. Cardinals	2	9	0	.182	111	168

PLAYOFFS

NFL championship
N.Y. Giants 23 vs. Green Bay 17

1939

EASTERN DIVISION

Team	W	L	T	Pct.	PF	PA
N.Y. Giants	9	1	1	.900	168	85
Washington	8	2	1	.800	242	94
Brooklyn	4	6	1	.400	108	219
Philadelphia	1	9	1	.100	105	200
Pittsburgh	1	9	1	.100	114	216

WESTERN DIVISION

Team	W	L	T	Pct.	PF	PA
Green Bay	9	2	0	.818	233	153
Chicago Bears	8	3	0	.727	298	157
Detroit	6	5	0	.545	145	150
Cleveland	5	5	1	.500	195	164
Chi. Cardinals	1	10	0	.091	84	254

PLAYOFFS

NFL championship
Green Bay 27 vs. N.Y. Giants 0

1940

EASTERN DIVISION

Team	W	L	T	Pct.	PF	PA
Washington	9	2	0	.818	245	142
Brooklyn	8	3	0	.727	186	120
N.Y. Giants	6	4	1	.600	131	133
Pittsburgh	2	7	2	.222	60	178
Philadelphia	1	10	0	.091	111	211

WESTERN DIVISION

Team	W	L	T	Pct.	PF	PA
Chicago Bears	8	3	0	.727	238	152
Green Bay	6	4	1	.600	238	155
Detroit	5	5	1	.500	138	153
Cleveland	4	6	1	.400	171	191
Chi. Cardinals	2	7	2	.222	139	222

PLAYOFFS

NFL championship
Chicago Bears 73 at Washington 0

– 307 –

1941

EASTERN DIVISION

Team	W	L	T	Pct.	PF	PA
N.Y. Giants	8	3	0	.727	238	114
Brooklyn	7	4	0	.636	158	127
Washington	6	5	0	.545	176	174
Philadelphia	2	8	1	.200	119	218
Pittsburgh	1	9	1	.100	103	276

WESTERN DIVISION

Team	W	L	T	Pct.	PF	PA
Chicago Bears	10	1	0	.909	396	147
Green Bay	10	1	0	.909	258	120
Detroit	4	6	1	.400	121	195
Chi. Cardinals	3	7	1	.300	127	197
Cleveland	2	9	0	.182	116	244

PLAYOFFS

Western Division playoff
Chicago Bears 33 vs. Green Bay 14

NFL championship
Chicago Bears 37 vs. N.Y. Giants 9

1942

EASTERN DIVISION

Team	W	L	T	Pct.	PF	PA
Washington	10	1	0	.909	227	102
Pittsburgh	7	4	0	.636	167	119
N.Y. Giants	5	5	1	.500	155	139
Brooklyn	3	8	0	.273	100	168
Philadelphia	2	9	0	.182	134	239

WESTERN DIVISION

Team	W	L	T	Pct.	PF	PA
Chicago Bears	11	0	0	1.000	376	84
Green Bay	8	2	1	.800	300	215
Cleveland	5	6	0	.455	150	207
Chi. Cardinals	3	8	0	.273	98	209
Detroit	0	11	0	.000	38	263

PLAYOFFS

NFL championship
Washington 14 vs. Chicago Bears 6

1943

EASTERN DIVISION

Team	W	L	T	Pct.	PF	PA
Washington	6	3	1	.667	229	137
N.Y. Giants	6	3	1	.667	197	170
Phil.-Pitt.	5	4	1	.556	225	230
Brooklyn	2	8	0	.200	65	234

NOTE: Cleveland Rams did not play in 1943.

WESTERN DIVISION

Team	W	L	T	Pct.	PF	PA
Chicago Bears	8	1	1	.889	303	157
Green Bay	7	2	1	.778	264	172
Detroit	3	6	1	.333	178	218
Chi. Cardinals	0	10	0	.000	95	238

PLAYOFFS

Eastern Division playoff
Washington 28 at N.Y. Giants 0

NFL championship
Chicago Bears 41 vs. Washington 21

1944

EASTERN DIVISION

Team	W	L	T	Pct.	PF	PA
N.Y. Giants	8	1	1	.889	206	75
Philadelphia	7	1	2	.875	267	131
Washington	6	3	1	.667	169	180
Boston	2	8	0	.200	82	233
Brooklyn	0	10	0	.000	69	166

WESTERN DIVISION

Team	W	L	T	Pct.	PF	PA
Green Bay	8	2	0	.800	238	141
Chicago Bears	6	3	1	.667	258	172
Detroit	6	3	1	.667	216	151
Cleveland	4	6	0	.400	188	224
Card-Pitt	0	10	0	.000	108	328

PLAYOFFS

NFL championship
Green Bay 14 at N.Y. Giants 7

1945

EASTERN DIVISION

Team	W	L	T	Pct.	PF	PA
Washington	8	2	0	.800	209	121
Philadelphia	7	3	0	.700	272	133
N.Y. Giants	3	6	1	.333	179	198
Boston	3	6	1	.333	123	211
Pittsburgh	2	8	0	.200	79	220

WESTERN DIVISION

Team	W	L	T	Pct.	PF	PA
Cleveland	9	1	0	.900	244	136
Detroit	7	3	0	.700	195	194
Green Bay	6	4	0	.600	258	173
Chicago Bears	3	7	0	.300	192	235
Chi. Cardinals	1	9	0	.100	98	228

PLAYOFFS

NFL championship
Cleveland 15 vs. Washington 14

1946

AAFC

EASTERN DIVISION

Team	W	L	T	Pct.	PF	PA
New York	10	3	1	.769	270	192
Brooklyn	3	10	1	.231	226	339
Buffalo	3	10	1	.231	249	370
Miami	3	11	0	.154	167	378

WESTERN DIVISION

Team	W	L	T	Pct.	PF	PA
Cleveland	12	2	0	.857	423	137
San Francisco	9	5	0	.643	307	189
Los Angeles	7	5	2	.583	305	290
Chicago	5	6	3	.455	263	315

PLAYOFFS

AAFC championship
Cleveland 14 vs. New York 9

NFL

EASTERN DIVISION

Team	W	L	T	Pct.	PF	PA
N.Y. Giants	7	3	1	.700	236	162
Philadelphia	6	5	0	.545	231	220
Washington	5	5	1	.500	171	191
Pittsburgh	5	5	1	.500	136	117
Boston	2	8	1	.200	189	273

WESTERN DIVISION

Team	W	L	T	Pct.	PF	PA
Chicago Bears	8	2	1	.800	289	193
Los Angeles	6	4	1	.600	277	257
Green Bay	6	5	0	.545	148	158
Chi. Cardinals	6	5	0	.545	260	198
Detroit	1	10	0	.091	142	310

PLAYOFFS

NFL championship
Chicago Bears 24 at N.Y. Giants 14

1947

AAFC

EASTERN DIVISION

Team	W	L	T	Pct.	PF	PA
New York	11	2	1	.846	378	239
Buffalo	8	4	2	.667	320	288
Brooklyn	3	10	1	.231	181	340
Baltimore	2	11	1	.154	167	377

WESTERN DIVISION

Team	W	L	T	Pct.	PF	PA
Cleveland	12	1	1	.923	410	185
San Francisco	8	4	2	.667	327	264
Los Angeles	7	7	0	.500	328	256
Chicago	1	13	0	.071	263	425

PLAYOFFS

AAFC championship
Cleveland 14 at New York 3

NFL

EASTERN DIVISION

Team	W	L	T	Pct.	PF	PA
Philadelphia	8	4	0	.667	308	242
Pittsburgh	8	4	0	.667	240	259
Boston	4	7	1	.364	168	256
Washington	4	8	0	.333	295	367
N.Y. Giants	2	8	2	.200	190	309

WESTERN DIVISION

Team	W	L	T	Pct.	PF	PA
Chi. Cardinals	9	3	0	.750	306	231
Chicago Bears	8	4	0	.667	363	241
Green Bay	6	5	1	.545	274	210
Los Angeles	6	6	0	.500	259	214
Detroit	3	9	0	.250	231	305

PLAYOFFS

Eastern Division playoff
Philadelphia 21 at Pittsburgh 0
NFL championship
Chicago Cardinals 28 vs. Philadelphia 21

1948

AAFC

EASTERN DIVISION

Team	W	L	T	Pct.	PF	PA
Buffalo	7	7	0	.500	360	358
Baltimore	7	7	0	.500	333	327
New York	6	8	0	.429	265	301
Brooklyn	2	12	0	.143	253	387

WESTERN DIVISION

Team	W	L	T	Pct.	PF	PA
Cleveland	14	0	0	1.000	389	190
San Francisco	12	2	0	.857	495	248
Los Angeles	7	7	0	.500	258	305
Chicago	1	13	0	.071	202	439

PLAYOFFS

Eastern Division playoff
Buffalo 28 vs. Baltimore 17
AAFC championship
Cleveland 49 vs. Buffalo 7

NFL

EASTERN DIVISION

Team	W	L	T	Pct.	PF	PA
Philadelphia	9	2	1	.818	376	156
Washington	7	5	0	.583	291	287
N.Y. Giants	4	8	0	.333	297	388
Pittsburgh	4	8	0	.333	200	243
Boston	3	9	0	.250	174	372

WESTERN DIVISION

Team	W	L	T	Pct.	PF	PA
Chi. Cardinals	11	1	0	.917	395	226
Chicago Bears	10	2	0	.833	375	151
Los Angeles	6	5	1	.545	327	269
Green Bay	3	9	0	.250	154	290
Detroit	2	10	0	.167	200	407

PLAYOFFS

NFL championship
Philadelphia 7 vs. Chicago Cardinals 0

1949

AAFC

Team	W	L	T	Pct.	PF	PA
Cleveland	9	1	2	.900	339	171
San Francisco	9	3	0	.750	416	227
Brooklyn-N.Y.	8	4	0	.667	196	206
Buffalo	5	5	2	.500	236	256
Chicago	4	8	0	.333	179	268
Los Angeles	4	8	0	.333	253	322
Baltimore	1	11	0	.083	172	341

PLAYOFFS

AAFC Semifinals
Cleveland 31 vs. Buffalo 21
San Francisco 17 vs. Brooklyn-N.Y. 7
AAFC championship
Cleveland 21 vs. San Francisco 7

NFL

EASTERN DIVISION

Team	W	L	T	Pct.	PF	PA
Philadelphia	11	1	0	.917	364	134
Pittsburgh	6	5	1	.545	224	214
N.Y. Giants	6	6	0	.500	287	298
Washington	4	7	1	.364	268	339
N.Y. Bulldogs	1	10	1	.091	153	365

WESTERN DIVISION

Team	W	L	T	Pct.	PF	PA
Los Angeles	8	2	2	.800	360	239
Chicago Bears	9	3	0	.750	332	218
Chi. Cardinals	6	5	1	.545	360	301
Detroit	4	8	0	.333	237	259
Green Bay	2	10	0	.167	114	329

PLAYOFFS

NFL championship
Philadelphia 14 at Los Angeles 0

1950

AMERICAN CONFERENCE

Team	W	L	T	Pct.	PF	PA
Cleveland	10	2	0	.833	310	144
N.Y. Giants	10	2	0	.833	268	150
Philadelphia	6	6	0	.500	254	141
Pittsburgh	6	6	0	.500	180	195
Chi. Cardinals	5	7	0	.417	233	287
Washington	3	9	0	.250	232	326

NATIONAL CONFERENCE

Team	W	L	T	Pct.	PF	PA
Los Angeles	9	3	0	.750	466	309
Chicago Bears	9	3	0	.750	279	207
N.Y. Yanks	7	5	0	.583	366	367
Detroit	6	6	0	.500	321	285
Green Bay	3	9	0	.250	244	406
San Francisco	3	9	0	.250	213	300
Baltimore	1	11	0	.083	213	462

PLAYOFFS

American Conference playoff
Cleveland 8 vs. N.Y. Giants 3
National Conference playoff
Los Angeles 24 vs. Chicago Bears 14
NFL championship
Cleveland 30 vs. Los Angeles 28

1951

AMERICAN CONFERENCE

Team	W	L	T	Pct.	PF	PA
Cleveland	11	1	0	.917	331	152
N.Y. Giants	9	2	1	.818	254	161
Washington	5	7	0	.417	183	296
Pittsburgh	4	7	1	.364	183	235
Philadelphia	4	8	0	.333	234	264
Chi. Cardinals	3	9	0	.250	210	287

NATIONAL CONFERENCE

Team	W	L	T	Pct.	PF	PA
Los Angeles	8	4	0	.667	392	261
Detroit	7	4	1	.636	336	259
San Francisco	7	4	1	.636	255	205
Chicago Bears	7	5	0	.583	286	282
Green Bay	3	9	0	.250	254	375
N.Y. Yanks	1	9	2	.100	241	382

PLAYOFFS

NFL championship
Los Angeles 24 vs. Cleveland 17

1952

AMERICAN CONFERENCE

Team	W	L	T	Pct.	PF	PA
Cleveland	8	4	0	.667	310	213
N.Y. Giants	7	5	0	.583	234	231
Philadelphia	7	5	0	.583	252	271
Pittsburgh	5	7	0	.417	300	273
Chi. Cardinals	4	8	0	.333	172	221
Washington	4	8	0	.333	240	287

NATIONAL CONFERENCE

Team	W	L	T	Pct.	PF	PA
Detroit	9	3	0	.750	344	192
Los Angeles	9	3	0	.750	349	234
San Francisco	7	5	0	.583	285	221
Green Bay	6	6	0	.500	295	312
Chicago Bears	5	7	0	.417	245	326
Dallas Texans	1	11	0	.083	182	427

PLAYOFFS

National Conference playoff
Detroit 31 vs. Los Angeles 21

NFL championship
Detroit 17 at Cleveland 7

1953

EASTERN CONFERENCE

Team	W	L	T	Pct.	PF	PA
Cleveland	11	1	0	.917	348	162
Philadelphia	7	4	1	.636	352	215
Washington	6	5	1	.545	208	215
Pittsburgh	6	6	0	.500	211	263
N.Y. Giants	3	9	0	.250	179	277
Chi. Cardinals	1	10	1	.091	190	337

WESTERN CONFERENCE

Team	W	L	T	Pct.	PF	PA
Detroit	10	2	0	.833	271	205
San Francisco	9	3	0	.750	372	237
Los Angeles	8	3	1	.727	366	236
Chicago Bears	3	8	1	.273	218	262
Baltimore	3	9	0	.250	182	350
Green Bay	2	9	1	.182	200	338

PLAYOFFS

NFL championship
Detroit 17 vs. Cleveland 16

1954

EASTERN CONFERENCE

Team	W	L	T	Pct.	PF	PA
Cleveland	9	3	0	.750	336	162
Philadelphia	7	4	1	.636	284	230
N.Y. Giants	7	5	0	.583	293	184
Pittsburgh	5	7	0	.417	219	263
Washington	3	9	0	.250	207	432
Chi. Cardinals	2	10	0	.167	183	347

WESTERN CONFERENCE

Team	W	L	T	Pct.	PF	PA
Detroit	9	2	1	.818	337	189
Chicago Bears	8	4	0	.667	301	279
San Francisco	7	4	1	.636	313	251
Los Angeles	6	5	1	.545	314	285
Green Bay	4	8	0	.333	234	251
Baltimore	3	9	0	.250	131	279

PLAYOFFS

NFL championship
Cleveland 56 vs. Detroit 10

1955

EASTERN CONFERENCE

Team	W	L	T	Pct.	PF	PA
Cleveland	9	2	1	.818	349	218
Washington	8	4	0	.667	246	222
N.Y. Giants	6	5	1	.545	267	223
Chi. Cardinals	4	7	1	.364	224	252
Philadelphia	4	7	1	.364	248	231
Pittsburgh	4	8	0	.333	195	285

WESTERN CONFERENCE

Team	W	L	T	Pct.	PF	PA
Los Angeles	8	3	1	.727	260	231
Chicago Bears	8	4	0	.667	294	251
Green Bay	6	6	0	.500	258	276
Baltimore	5	6	1	.455	214	239
San Francisco	4	8	0	.333	216	298
Detroit	3	9	0	.250	230	275

PLAYOFFS

NFL championship
Cleveland 38 at Los Angeles 14

1956

EASTERN CONFERENCE

Team	W	L	T	Pct.	PF	PA
N.Y. Giants	8	3	1	.727	264	197
Chi. Cardinals	7	5	0	.583	240	182
Washington	6	6	0	.500	183	225
Cleveland	5	7	0	.417	167	177
Pittsburgh	5	7	0	.417	217	250
Philadelphia	3	8	1	.273	143	215

WESTERN CONFERENCE

Team	W	L	T	Pct.	PF	PA
Chicago Bears	9	2	1	.818	363	246
Detroit	9	3	0	.750	300	188
San Francisco	5	6	1	.455	233	284
Baltimore	5	7	0	.417	270	322
Green Bay	4	8	0	.333	264	342
Los Angeles	4	8	0	.333	291	307

PLAYOFFS

NFL championship
N.Y. Giants 47 vs. Chicago Bears 7

1957

EASTERN CONFERENCE

Team	W	L	T	Pct.	PF	PA
Cleveland	9	2	1	.818	269	172
N.Y. Giants	7	5	0	.583	254	211
Pittsburgh	6	6	0	.500	161	178
Washington	5	6	1	.455	251	230
Philadelphia	4	8	0	.333	173	230
Chi. Cardinals	3	9	0	.250	200	299

WESTERN CONFERENCE

Team	W	L	T	Pct.	PF	PA
Detroit	8	4	0	.667	251	231
San Francisco	8	4	0	.667	260	264
Baltimore	7	5	0	.583	303	235
Los Angeles	6	6	0	.500	307	278
Chicago Bears	5	7	0	.417	203	211
Green Bay	3	9	0	.250	218	311

PLAYOFFS

Western Conference playoff
Detroit 31 at San Francisco 27

NFL championship
Detroit 59 vs. Cleveland 14

1958

EASTERN CONFERENCE

Team	W	L	T	Pct.	PF	PA
N.Y. Giants	9	3	0	.750	246	183
Cleveland	9	3	0	.750	302	217
Pittsburgh	7	4	1	.636	261	230
Washington	4	7	1	.364	214	268
Chi. Cardinals	2	9	1	.182	261	356
Philadelphia	2	9	1	.182	235	306

WESTERN CONFERENCE

Team	W	L	T	Pct.	PF	PA
Baltimore	9	3	0	.750	381	203
Chicago Bears	8	4	0	.667	298	230
Los Angeles	8	4	0	.667	344	278
San Francisco	6	6	0	.500	257	324
Detroit	4	7	1	.364	261	276
Green Bay	1	10	1	.091	193	382

PLAYOFFS

Eastern Conference playoff
N.Y. Giants 10 vs. Cleveland 0

NFL championship
Baltimore 23 at N.Y. Giants 17 (OT)

1959

EASTERN CONFERENCE

Team	W	L	T	Pct.	PF	PA
N.Y. Giants	10	2	0	.833	284	170
Cleveland	7	5	0	.583	270	214
Philadelphia	7	5	0	.583	268	278
Pittsburgh	6	5	1	.545	257	216
Washington	3	9	0	.250	185	350
Chi. Cardinals	2	10	0	.167	234	324

WESTERN CONFERENCE

Team	W	L	T	Pct.	PF	PA
Baltimore	9	3	0	.750	374	251
Chicago Bears	8	4	0	.667	252	196
Green Bay	7	5	0	.583	248	246
San Francisco	7	5	0	.583	255	237
Detroit	3	8	1	.273	203	275
Los Angeles	2	10	0	.167	242	315

PLAYOFFS

NFL championship
Baltimore 31 vs. N.Y. Giants 16

1960

AFL

EASTERN DIVISION

Team	W	L	T	Pct.	PF	PA
Houston	10	4	0	.714	379	285
N.Y. Titans	7	7	0	.500	382	399
Buffalo	5	8	1	.385	296	303
Boston Patriots	5	9	0	.357	286	349

WESTERN DIVISION

Team	W	L	T	Pct.	PF	PA
L.A. Chargers	10	4	0	.714	373	336
Dallas Texans	8	6	0	.571	362	253
Oakland	6	8	0	.429	319	388
Denver	4	9	1	.308	309	393

PLAYOFFS

AFL championship
Houston 24 vs. L.A. Chargers 16

NFL

EASTERN CONFERENCE

Team	W	L	T	Pct.	PF	PA
Philadelphia	10	2	0	.833	321	246
Cleveland	8	3	1	.727	362	217
N.Y. Giants	6	4	2	.600	271	261
St. Louis	6	5	1	.545	288	230
Pittsburgh	5	6	1	.455	240	275
Washington	1	9	2	.100	178	309

WESTERN CONFERENCE

Team	W	L	T	Pct.	PF	PA
Green Bay	8	4	0	.667	332	209
Detroit	7	5	0	.583	239	212
San Francisco	7	5	0	.583	208	205
Baltimore	6	6	0	.500	288	234
Chicago	5	6	1	.455	194	299
L.A. Rams	4	7	1	.364	265	297
Dallas Cowboys	0	11	1	.000	177	369

PLAYOFFS

NFL championship
Philadelphia 17 vs. Green Bay 13

1961

AFL

EASTERN DIVISION

Team	W	L	T	Pct.	PF	PA
Houston	10	3	1	.769	513	242
Boston Patriots	9	4	1	.692	413	313
N.Y. Titans	7	7	0	.500	301	390
Buffalo	6	8	0	.429	294	342

WESTERN DIVISION

Team	W	L	T	Pct.	PF	PA
San Diego	12	2	0	.857	396	219
Dallas Texans	6	8	0	.429	334	343
Denver	3	11	0	.214	251	432
Oakland	2	12	0	.143	237	458

PLAYOFFS

AFL championship
Houston 10 at San Diego 3

NFL

EASTERN CONFERENCE

Team	W	L	T	Pct.	PF	PA
N.Y. Giants	10	3	1	.769	368	220
Philadelphia	10	4	0	.714	361	297
Cleveland	8	5	1	.615	319	270
St. Louis	7	7	0	.500	279	267
Pittsburgh	6	8	0	.429	295	287
Dallas Cowboys	4	9	1	.308	236	380
Washington	1	12	1	.077	174	392

WESTERN CONFERENCE

Team	W	L	T	Pct.	PF	PA
Green Bay	11	3	0	.786	391	223
Detroit	8	5	1	.615	270	258
Baltimore	8	6	0	.571	302	307
Chicago	8	6	0	.571	326	302
San Francisco	7	6	1	.538	346	272
Los Angeles	4	10	0	.286	263	333
Minnesota	3	11	0	.214	285	407

PLAYOFFS

NFL championship
Green Bay 37 vs. N.Y. Giants 0

1962

AFL

EASTERN DIVISION

Team	W	L	T	Pct.	PF	PA
Houston	11	3	0	.786	387	270
Boston Patriots	9	4	1	.692	346	295
Buffalo	7	6	1	.538	309	272
N.Y. Titans	5	9	0	.357	278	423

WESTERN DIVISION

Team	W	L	T	Pct.	PF	PA
Dallas Texans	11	3	0	.786	389	233
Denver	7	7	0	.500	353	334
San Diego	4	10	0	.286	314	392
Oakland	1	13	0	.071	213	370

PLAYOFFS

AFL championship
Dallas Texans 20 at Houston 17 (OT)

NFL

EASTERN CONFERENCE

Team	W	L	T	Pct.	PF	PA
N.Y. Giants	12	2	0	.857	398	283
Pittsburgh	9	5	0	.643	312	363
Cleveland	7	6	1	.538	291	257
Washington	5	7	2	.417	305	376
Dallas Cowboys	5	8	1	.385	398	402
St. Louis	4	9	1	.308	287	361
Philadelphia	3	10	1	.231	282	356

WESTERN CONFERENCE

Team	W	L	T	Pct.	PF	PA
Green Bay	13	1	0	.929	415	148
Detroit	11	3	0	.786	315	177
Chicago	9	5	0	.643	321	287
Baltimore	7	7	0	.500	293	288
San Francisco	6	8	0	.429	282	331
Minnesota	2	11	1	.154	254	410
Los Angeles	1	12	1	.077	220	334

PLAYOFFS

NFL championship
Green Bay 16 at N.Y. Giants 7

1963

AFL

EASTERN DIVISION

Team	W	L	T	Pct.	PF	PA
Boston Patriots	7	6	1	.538	327	257
Buffalo	7	6	1	.538	304	291
Houston	6	8	0	.429	302	372
N.Y. Jets	5	8	1	.385	249	399

WESTERN DIVISION

Team	W	L	T	Pct.	PF	PA
San Diego	11	3	0	.786	399	256
Oakland	10	4	0	.714	363	288
Kansas City	5	7	2	.417	347	263
Denver	2	11	1	.154	301	473

PLAYOFFS

Eastern Division playoff
Boston 26 at Buffalo 8
AFL championship
San Diego 51 vs. Boston 10

NFL

EASTERN CONFERENCE

Team	W	L	T	Pct.	PF	PA
N.Y. Giants	11	3	0	.786	448	280
Cleveland	10	4	0	.714	343	262
St. Louis	9	5	0	.643	341	283
Pittsburgh	7	4	3	.636	321	295
Dallas	4	10	0	.286	305	378
Washington	3	11	0	.214	279	398
Philadelphia	2	10	2	.167	242	381

WESTERN CONFERENCE

Team	W	L	T	Pct.	PF	PA
Chicago	11	1	2	.917	301	144
Green Bay	11	2	1	.846	369	206
Baltimore	8	6	0	.571	316	285
Detroit	5	8	1	.385	326	265
Minnesota	5	8	1	.385	309	390
Los Angeles	5	9	0	.357	210	350
San Francisco	2	12	0	.143	198	391

PLAYOFFS

NFL championship
Chicago 14 vs. N.Y. Giants 10

1964

AFL

EASTERN DIVISION

Team	W	L	T	Pct.	PF	PA
Buffalo	12	2	0	.857	400	242
Boston Patriots	10	3	1	.769	365	297
N.Y. Jets	5	8	1	.385	278	315
Houston	4	10	0	.286	310	355

WESTERN DIVISION

Team	W	L	T	Pct.	PF	PA
San Diego	8	5	1	.615	341	300
Kansas City	7	7	0	.500	366	306
Oakland	5	7	2	.417	303	350
Denver	2	11	1	.154	240	438

PLAYOFFS

AFL championship
Buffalo 20 vs. San Diego 7

NFL

EASTERN CONFERENCE

Team	W	L	T	Pct.	PF	PA
Cleveland	10	3	1	.769	415	293
St. Louis	9	3	2	.750	357	331
Philadelphia	6	8	0	.429	312	313
Washington	6	8	0	.429	307	305
Dallas	5	8	1	.385	250	289
Pittsburgh	5	9	0	.357	253	315
N.Y. Giants	2	10	2	.167	241	399

WESTERN CONFERENCE

Team	W	L	T	Pct.	PF	PA
Baltimore	12	2	0	.857	428	225
Green Bay	8	5	1	.615	342	245
Minnesota	8	5	1	.615	355	296
Detroit	7	5	2	.583	280	260
Los Angeles	5	7	2	.417	283	339
Chicago	5	9	0	.357	260	379
San Francisco	4	10	0	.286	236	330

PLAYOFFS

NFL championship
Cleveland 27 vs. Baltimore 0

1965

AFL

EASTERN DIVISION

Team	W	L	T	Pct.	PF	PA
Buffalo	10	3	1	.769	313	226
N.Y. Jets	5	8	1	.385	285	303
Boston Patriots	4	8	2	.333	244	302
Houston	4	10	0	.286	298	429

WESTERN DIVISION

Team	W	L	T	Pct.	PF	PA
San Diego	9	2	3	.818	340	227
Oakland	8	5	1	.615	298	239
Kansas City	7	5	2	.583	322	285
Denver	4	10	0	.286	303	392

PLAYOFFS

AFL championship
Buffalo 23 at San Diego 0

NFL

EASTERN CONFERENCE

Team	W	L	T	Pct.	PF	PA
Cleveland	11	3	0	.786	363	325
Dallas	7	7	0	.500	325	280
N.Y. Giants	7	7	0	.500	270	338
Washington	6	8	0	.429	257	301
Philadelphia	5	9	0	.357	363	359
St. Louis	5	9	0	.357	296	309
Pittsburgh	2	12	0	.143	202	397

WESTERN CONFERENCE

Team	W	L	T	Pct.	PF	PA
Green Bay	10	3	1	.769	316	224
Baltimore	10	3	1	.769	389	284
Chicago	9	5	0	.643	409	275
San Francisco	7	6	1	.538	421	402
Minnesota	7	7	0	.500	383	403
Detroit	6	7	1	.462	257	295
Los Angeles	4	10	0	.286	269	328

PLAYOFFS

Western Conference playoff
Green Bay 13 vs. Baltimore 10 (OT)

NFL championship
Green Bay 23 vs. Cleveland 12

1966

AFL

EASTERN DIVISION

Team	W	L	T	Pct.	PF	PA
Buffalo	9	4	1	.692	358	255
Boston Patriots	8	4	2	.667	315	283
N.Y. Jets	6	6	2	.500	322	312
Houston	3	11	0	.214	335	396
Miami	3	11	0	.214	213	362

WESTERN DIVISION

Team	W	L	T	Pct.	PF	PA
Kansas City	11	2	1	.846	448	276
Oakland	8	5	1	.615	315	288
San Diego	7	6	1	.538	335	284
Denver	4	10	0	.286	196	381

PLAYOFFS

AFL championship
Kansas City 31 at Buffalo 7

NFL

EASTERN CONFERENCE

Team	W	L	T	Pct.	PF	PA
Dallas	10	3	1	.769	445	239
Cleveland	9	5	0	.643	403	259
Philadelphia	9	5	0	.643	326	340
St. Louis	8	5	1	.615	264	265
Washington	7	7	0	.500	351	355
Pittsburgh	5	8	1	.385	316	347
Atlanta	3	11	0	.214	204	437
N.Y. Giants	1	12	1	.077	263	501

WESTERN CONFERENCE

Team	W	L	T	Pct.	PF	PA
Green Bay	12	2	0	.857	335	163
Baltimore	9	5	0	.643	314	226
Los Angeles	8	6	0	.571	289	212
San Francisco	6	6	2	.500	320	325
Chicago	5	7	2	.417	234	272
Detroit	4	9	1	.308	206	317
Minnesota	4	9	1	.308	292	304

PLAYOFFS

NFL championship
Green Bay 34 at Dallas 27

Super Bowl 1
Green Bay 35, Kansas City 10, at Los Angeles.

1967

AFL

EASTERN DIVISION

Team	W	L	T	Pct.	PF	PA
Houston	9	4	1	.692	258	199
N.Y. Jets	8	5	1	.615	371	329
Buffalo	4	10	0	.286	237	285
Miami	4	10	0	.286	219	407
Boston Patriots	3	10	1	.231	280	389

WESTERN DIVISION

Team	W	L	T	Pct.	PF	PA
Oakland	13	1	0	.929	468	233
Kansas City	9	5	0	.643	408	254
San Diego	8	5	1	.615	360	352
Denver	3	11	0	.214	256	409

PLAYOFFS

AFL championship
Oakland 40 vs. Houston 7

NFL

EASTERN CONFERENCE

CAPITOL DIVISION

Team	W	L	T	Pct.	PF	PA
Dallas	9	5	0	.643	342	268
Philadelphia	6	7	1	.462	351	409
Washington	5	6	3	.455	347	353
New Orleans	3	11	0	.214	233	379

CENTURY DIVISION

Team	W	L	T	Pct.	PF	PA
Cleveland	9	5	0	.643	334	297
N.Y. Giants	7	7	0	.500	369	379
St. Louis	6	7	1	.462	333	356
Pittsburgh	4	9	1	.308	281	320

WESTERN CONFERENCE

COASTAL DIVISION

Team	W	L	T	Pct.	PF	PA
Los Angeles	11	1	2	.917	398	196
Baltimore	11	1	2	.917	394	198
San Francisco	7	7	0	.500	273	337
Atlanta	1	12	1	.077	175	422

CENTRAL DIVISION

Team	W	L	T	Pct.	PF	PA
Green Bay	9	4	1	.692	332	209
Chicago	7	6	1	.538	239	218
Detroit	5	7	2	.417	260	259
Minnesota	3	8	3	.273	233	294

PLAYOFFS

Conference championships
Dallas 52 vs. Cleveland 14
Green Bay 28 vs. Los Angeles 7

NFL championship
Green Bay 21 vs. Dallas 17

Super Bowl 2
Green Bay 33, Oakland 14, at Miami.

1968

AFL

EASTERN DIVISION

Team	W	L	T	Pct.	PF	PA
N.Y. Jets	11	3	0	.786	419	280
Houston	7	7	0	.500	303	248
Miami	5	8	1	.385	276	355
Boston Patriots	4	10	0	.286	229	406
Buffalo	1	12	1	.077	199	367

WESTERN DIVISION

Team	W	L	T	Pct.	PF	PA
Oakland	12	2	0	.857	453	233
Kansas City	12	2	0	.857	371	170
San Diego	9	5	0	.643	382	310
Denver	5	9	0	.357	255	404
Cincinnati	3	11	0	.214	215	329

PLAYOFFS

Western Division playoff
Oakland 41 vs. Kansas City 6

AFL championship
N.Y. Jets 27 vs. Oakland 23

NFL

EASTERN CONFERENCE

CAPITOL DIVISION

Team	W	L	T	Pct.	PF	PA
Dallas	12	2	0	.857	431	186
N.Y. Giants	7	7	0	.500	294	325
Washington	5	9	0	.357	249	358
Philadelphia	2	12	0	.143	202	351

CENTURY DIVISION

Team	W	L	T	Pct.	PF	PA
Cleveland	10	4	0	.714	394	273
St. Louis	9	4	1	.692	325	289
New Orleans	4	9	1	.308	246	327
Pittsburgh	2	11	1	.154	244	397

WESTERN CONFERENCE

COASTAL DIVISION

Team	W	L	T	Pct.	PF	PA
Baltimore	13	1	0	.929	402	144
Los Angeles	10	3	1	.769	312	200
San Francisco	7	6	1	.538	303	310
Atlanta	2	12	0	.143	170	389

CENTRAL DIVISION

Team	W	L	T	Pct.	PF	PA
Minnesota	8	6	0	.571	282	242
Chicago	7	7	0	.500	250	333
Green Bay	6	7	1	.462	281	227
Detroit	4	8	2	.333	207	241

PLAYOFFS

Conference championships
Cleveland 31 vs. Dallas 20
Baltimore 24 vs. Minnesota 14

NFL championship
Baltimore 34 at Cleveland 0

Super Bowl 3
N.Y. Jets 16, Baltimore 7, at Miami.

1969

AFL

EASTERN DIVISION

Team	W	L	T	Pct.	PF	PA
N.Y. Jets	10	4	0	.714	353	269
Houston	6	6	2	.500	278	279
Boston Patriots	4	10	0	.286	266	316
Buffalo	4	10	0	.286	230	359
Miami	3	10	1	.231	233	332

WESTERN DIVISION

Team	W	L	T	Pct.	PF	PA
Oakland	12	1	1	.923	377	242
Kansas City	11	3	0	.786	359	177
San Diego	8	6	0	.571	288	276
Denver	5	8	1	.385	297	344
Cincinnati	4	9	1	.308	280	367

PLAYOFFS

Divisional games
Kansas City 13 at N.Y. Jets 6
Oakland 56 vs. Houston 7

AFL championship
Kansas City 17 at Oakland 7

NFL

EASTERN CONFERENCE

CAPITOL DIVISION

Team	W	L	T	Pct.	PF	PA
Dallas	11	2	1	.846	369	223
Washington	7	5	2	.583	307	319
New Orleans	5	9	0	.357	311	393
Philadelphia	4	9	1	.308	279	377

CENTURY DIVISION

Team	W	L	T	Pct.	PF	PA
Cleveland	10	3	1	.769	351	300
N.Y. Giants	6	8	0	.429	264	298
St. Louis	4	9	1	.308	314	389
Pittsburgh	1	13	0	.071	218	404

WESTERN CONFERENCE

COASTAL DIVISION

Team	W	L	T	Pct.	PF	PA
Los Angeles	11	3	0	.786	320	243
Baltimore	8	5	1	.615	279	268
Atlanta	6	8	0	.429	276	268
San Francisco	4	8	2	.333	277	319

CENTRAL DIVISION

Team	W	L	T	Pct.	PF	PA
Minnesota	12	2	0	.857	379	133
Detroit	9	4	1	.692	259	188
Green Bay	8	6	0	.571	269	221
Chicago	1	13	0	.071	210	339

PLAYOFFS

Conference championships
Cleveland 38 at Dallas 14
Minnesota 23 vs. Los Angeles 20

NFL championship
Minnesota 27 vs. Cleveland 7

Super Bowl 4
Kansas City 23, Minnesota 7, at New Orleans.

1970

AMERICAN CONFERENCE

EASTERN DIVISION

Team	W	L	T	Pct.	PF	PA
Baltimore*	11	2	1	.846	321	234
Miami†	10	4	0	.714	297	228
N.Y. Jets	4	10	0	.286	255	286
Buffalo	3	10	1	.231	204	337
Boston Patriots	2	12	0	.143	149	361

CENTRAL DIVISION

Team	W	L	T	Pct.	PF	PA
Cincinnati*	8	6	0	.571	312	255
Cleveland	7	7	0	.500	286	265
Pittsburgh	5	9	0	.357	210	272
Houston	3	10	1	.231	217	352

WESTERN DIVISION

Team	W	L	T	Pct.	PF	PA
Oakland*	8	4	2	.667	300	293
Kansas City	7	5	2	.583	272	244
San Diego	5	6	3	.455	282	278
Denver	5	8	1	.385	253	264

*Division champion.
†Wild-card team.

NATIONAL CONFERENCE

EASTERN DIVISION

Team	W	L	T	Pct.	PF	PA
Dallas*	10	4	0	.714	299	221
N.Y. Giants	9	5	0	.643	301	270
St. Louis	8	5	1	.615	325	228
Washington	6	8	0	.429	297	314
Philadelphia	3	10	1	.231	241	332

CENTRAL DIVISION

Team	W	L	T	Pct.	PF	PA
Minnesota*	12	2	0	.857	335	143
Detroit†	10	4	0	.714	347	202
Chicago	6	8	0	.429	256	261
Green Bay	6	8	0	.429	196	293

WESTERN DIVISION

Team	W	L	T	Pct.	PF	PA
San Francisco*	10	3	1	.769	352	267
Los Angeles	9	4	1	.692	325	202
Atlanta	4	8	2	.333	206	261
New Orleans	2	11	1	.154	172	347

PLAYOFFS

AFC divisional games
Baltimore 17 vs. Cincinnati 0
Oakland 21 vs. Miami 14

AFC championship
Baltimore 27 vs. Oakland 17

NFC divisional games
Dallas 5 vs. Detroit 0
San Francisco 17 at Minnesota 14

NFC championship
Dallas 17 at San Francisco 10

Super Bowl 5
Baltimore 16, Dallas 13, at Miami.

1971

AMERICAN CONFERENCE

EASTERN DIVISION

Team	W	L	T	Pct.	PF	PA
Miami*	10	3	1	.769	315	174
Baltimore†	10	4	0	.714	313	140
New England	6	8	0	.429	238	325
N.Y. Jets	6	8	0	.429	212	299
Buffalo	1	13	0	.071	184	394

CENTRAL DIVISION

Team	W	L	T	Pct.	PF	PA
Cleveland*	9	5	0	.643	285	273
Pittsburgh	6	8	0	.429	246	292
Houston	4	9	1	.308	251	330
Cincinnati	4	10	0	.286	284	265

WESTERN DIVISION

Team	W	L	T	Pct.	PF	PA
Kansas City*	10	3	1	.769	302	208
Oakland	8	4	2	.667	344	278
San Diego	6	8	0	.429	311	341
Denver	4	9	1	.308	203	275

*Division champion.
†Wild-card team.

NATIONAL CONFERENCE

EASTERN DIVISION

Team	W	L	T	Pct.	PF	PA
Dallas*	11	3	0	.786	406	222
Washington†	9	4	1	.692	276	190
Philadelphia	6	7	1	.462	221	302
St. Louis	4	9	1	.308	231	279
N.Y. Giants	4	10	0	.286	228	362

CENTRAL DIVISION

Team	W	L	T	Pct.	PF	PA
Minnesota*	11	3	0	.786	245	139
Detroit	7	6	1	.538	341	286
Chicago	6	8	0	.429	185	276
Green Bay	4	8	2	.333	274	298

WESTERN DIVISION

Team	W	L	T	Pct.	PF	PA
San Francisco*	9	5	0	.643	300	216
Los Angeles	8	5	1	.615	313	260
Atlanta	7	6	1	.538	274	277
New Orleans	4	8	2	.333	266	347

PLAYOFFS

AFC divisional games
Miami 27 at Kansas City 24 (OT)
Baltimore 20 at Cleveland 3

AFC championship
Miami 21 vs. Baltimore 0

NFC divisional games
Dallas 20 at Minnesota 12
San Francisco 24 vs. Washington 20

NFC championship
Dallas 14 vs. San Francisco 3

Super Bowl 6
Dallas 24, Miami 3, at New Orleans.

FOOTBALL COMES TO MONDAY NIGHT

Although few people at the time could have guessed at the kind of popularity the show would come to enjoy, ABC's Monday Night Football debuted on September 21, 1970 with the telecast of a Jets-Browns game from Cleveland Stadium. With 85,703 fans looking on, coach Blanton Collier's Browns beat Weeb Ewbank's Jets, 31-21. Though the game had little of the excitement of future Monday night encounters, it did have a few noteworthy accomplishments. Jets quarterback Joe Namath completed 19 of 32 passes for 299 yards and one touchdown, but he also was intercepted three times, turnovers that proved crucial to the Browns' victory. Homer Jones returned a kickoff 94 yards for a Cleveland touchdown.

1972

AMERICAN CONFERENCE

EASTERN DIVISION

Team	W	L	T	Pct.	PF	PA
Miami*	14	0	0	1.000	385	171
N.Y. Jets	7	7	0	.500	367	324
Baltimore	5	9	0	.357	235	252
Buffalo	4	9	1	.321	257	377
New England	3	11	0	.214	192	446

CENTRAL DIVISION

Team	W	L	T	Pct.	PF	PA
Pittsburgh*	11	3	0	.786	343	175
Cleveland†	10	4	0	.714	268	249
Cincinnati	8	6	0	.571	299	229
Houston	1	13	0	.071	164	380

WESTERN DIVISION

Team	W	L	T	Pct.	PF	PA
Oakland*	10	3	1	.750	365	248
Kansas City	8	6	0	.571	287	254
Denver	5	9	0	.357	325	350
San Diego	4	9	1	.321	264	344

*Division champion.
†Wild-card team.

NATIONAL CONFERENCE

EASTERN DIVISION

Team	W	L	T	Pct.	PF	PA
Washington*	11	3	0	.786	336	218
Dallas†	10	4	0	.714	319	240
N.Y. Giants	8	6	0	.571	331	247
St. Louis	4	9	1	.321	193	303
Philadelphia	2	11	1	.179	145	352

CENTRAL DIVISION

Team	W	L	T	Pct.	PF	PA
Green Bay*	10	4	0	.714	304	226
Detroit	8	5	1	.607	339	290
Minnesota	7	7	0	.500	301	252
Chicago	4	9	1	.321	225	275

WESTERN DIVISION

Team	W	L	T	Pct.	PF	PA
San Francisco*	8	5	1	.607	353	249
Atlanta	7	7	0	.500	269	274
Los Angeles	6	7	1	.464	291	286
New Orleans	2	11	1	.179	215	361

PLAYOFFS

AFC divisional games
Pittsburgh 13 vs. Oakland 7
Miami 20 vs. Cleveland 14

AFC championship
Miami 21 at Pittsburgh 17

NFC divisional games
Dallas 30 at San Francisco 28
Washington 16 vs. Green Bay 3

NFC championship
Washington 26 vs. Dallas 3

Super Bowl 7
Miami 14, Washington 7, at Los Angeles.

1973

AMERICAN CONFERENCE

EASTERN DIVISION

Team	W	L	T	Pct.	PF	PA
Miami*	12	2	0	.857	343	150
Buffalo	9	5	0	.643	259	230
New England	5	9	0	.357	258	300
Baltimore	4	10	0	.286	226	341
N.Y. Jets	4	10	0	.286	240	306

CENTRAL DIVISION

Team	W	L	T	Pct.	PF	PA
Cincinnati*	10	4	0	.714	286	231
Pittsburgh†	10	4	0	.714	347	210
Cleveland	7	5	2	.571	234	255
Houston	1	13	0	.071	199	447

WESTERN DIVISION

Team	W	L	T	Pct.	PF	PA
Oakland*	9	4	1	.679	292	175
Denver	7	5	2	.571	354	296
Kansas City	7	5	2	.571	231	192
San Diego	2	11	1	.179	188	386

*Division champion.
†Wild-card team.

NATIONAL CONFERENCE

EASTERN DIVISION

Team	W	L	T	Pct.	PF	PA
Dallas*	10	4	0	.714	382	203
Washington†	10	4	0	.714	325	198
Philadelphia	5	8	1	.393	310	393
St. Louis	4	9	1	.321	286	365
N.Y. Giants	2	11	1	.179	226	362

CENTRAL DIVISION

Team	W	L	T	Pct.	PF	PA
Minnesota*	12	2	0	.857	296	168
Detroit	6	7	1	.464	271	247
Green Bay	5	7	2	.429	202	259
Chicago	3	11	0	.214	195	334

WESTERN DIVISION

Team	W	L	T	Pct.	PF	PA
Los Angeles*	12	2	0	.857	388	178
Atlanta	9	5	0	.643	318	224
New Orleans	5	9	0	.357	163	312
San Francisco	5	9	0	.357	262	319

PLAYOFFS

AFC divisional games
Oakland 33 vs. Pittsburgh 14
Miami 34 vs. Cincinnati 16

AFC championship
Miami 27 vs. Oakland 10

NFC divisional games
Minnesota 27 vs. Washington 20
Dallas 27 vs. Los Angeles 16

NFC championship
Minnesota 27 at Dallas 10

Super Bowl 8
Miami 24, Minnesota 7, at Houston.

1974

AMERICAN CONFERENCE

EASTERN DIVISION

Team	W	L	T	Pct.	PF	PA
Miami*	11	3	0	.786	327	216
Buffalo†	9	5	0	.643	264	244
New England	7	7	0	.500	348	289
N.Y. Jets	7	7	0	.500	279	300
Baltimore	2	12	0	.143	190	329

CENTRAL DIVISION

Team	W	L	T	Pct.	PF	PA
Pittsburgh*	10	3	1	.750	305	189
Cincinnati	7	7	0	.500	283	259
Houston	7	7	0	.500	236	282
Cleveland	4	10	0	.286	251	344

WESTERN DIVISION

Team	W	L	T	Pct.	PF	PA
Oakland*	12	2	0	.857	355	228
Denver	7	6	1	.536	302	294
Kansas City	5	9	0	.357	233	293
San Diego	5	9	0	.357	212	285

*Division champion.
†Wild-card team.

NATIONAL CONFERENCE

EASTERN DIVISION

Team	W	L	T	Pct.	PF	PA
St. Louis*	10	4	0	.714	285	218
Washington†	10	4	0	.714	320	196
Dallas	8	6	0	.571	297	235
Philadelphia	7	7	0	.500	242	217
N.Y. Giants	2	12	0	.143	195	299

CENTRAL DIVISION

Team	W	L	T	Pct.	PF	PA
Minnesota*	10	4	0	.714	310	195
Detroit	7	7	0	.500	256	270
Green Bay	6	8	0	.429	210	206
Chicago	4	10	0	.286	152	279

WESTERN DIVISION

Team	W	L	T	Pct.	PF	PA
Los Angeles*	10	4	0	.714	263	181
San Francisco	6	8	0	.429	226	236
New Orleans	5	9	0	.357	166	263
Atlanta	3	11	0	.214	111	271

PLAYOFFS

AFC divisional games
Oakland 28 vs. Miami 26
Pittsburgh 32 vs. Buffalo 14

AFC championship
Pittsburgh 24 at Oakland 13

NFC divisional games
Minnesota 30 vs. St. Louis 14
Los Angeles 19 vs. Washington 10

NFC championship
Minnesota 14 vs. Los Angeles 10

Super Bowl 9
Pittsburgh 16, Minnesota 6, at New Orleans.

AMERICAN CONFERENCE

EASTERN DIVISION

Team	W	L	T	Pct.	PF	PA
Baltimore*	10	4	0	.714	395	269
Miami	10	4	0	.714	357	222
Buffalo	8	6	0	.571	420	355
New England	3	11	0	.214	258	358
N.Y. Jets	3	11	0	.214	258	433

CENTRAL DIVISION

Team	W	L	T	Pct.	PF	PA
Pittsburgh*	12	2	0	.857	373	162
Cincinnati†	11	3	0	.786	340	246
Houston	10	4	0	.714	293	226
Cleveland	3	11	0	.214	218	372

WESTERN DIVISION

Team	W	L	T	Pct.	PF	PA
Oakland*	11	3	0	.786	375	255
Denver	6	8	0	.429	254	307
Kansas City	5	9	0	.357	282	341
San Diego	2	12	0	.143	189	345

*Division champion.
†Wild-card team.

NATIONAL CONFERENCE

EASTERN DIVISION

Team	W	L	T	Pct.	PF	PA
St. Louis*	11	3	0	.786	356	276
Dallas†	10	4	0	.714	350	268
Washington	8	6	0	.571	325	276
N.Y. Giants	5	9	0	.357	216	306
Philadelphia	4	10	0	.286	225	302

CENTRAL DIVISION

Team	W	L	T	Pct.	PF	PA
Minnesota*	12	2	0	.857	377	180
Detroit	7	7	0	.500	245	262
Chicago	4	10	0	.286	191	379
Green Bay	4	10	0	.286	226	285

WESTERN DIVISION

Team	W	L	T	Pct.	PF	PA
Los Angeles*	12	2	0	.857	312	135
San Francisco	5	9	0	.357	255	286
Atlanta	4	10	0	.286	240	289
New Orleans	2	12	0	.143	165	360

PLAYOFFS

AFC divisional games
Pittsburgh 28 vs. Baltimore 10
Oakland 31 vs. Cincinnati 28

AFC championship
Pittsburgh 16 vs. Oakland 10

NFC divisional games
Los Angeles 35 vs. St. Louis 23
Dallas 17 at Minnesota 14

NFC championship
Dallas 37 at Los Angeles 7

Super Bowl 10
Pittsburgh 21, Dallas 17, at Miami.

AMERICAN CONFERENCE

EASTERN DIVISION

Team	W	L	T	Pct.	PF	PA
Baltimore*	11	3	0	.786	417	246
New England†	11	3	0	.786	376	236
Miami	6	8	0	.429	263	264
N.Y. Jets	3	11	0	.214	169	383
Buffalo	2	12	0	.143	245	363

CENTRAL DIVISION

Team	W	L	T	Pct.	PF	PA
Pittsburgh*	10	4	0	.714	342	138
Cincinnati	10	4	0	.714	335	210
Cleveland	9	5	0	.643	267	287
Houston	5	9	0	.357	222	273

WESTERN DIVISION

Team	W	L	T	Pct.	PF	PA
Oakland*	13	1	0	.929	350	237
Denver	9	5	0	.643	315	206
San Diego	6	8	0	.429	248	285
Kansas City	5	9	0	.357	290	376
Tampa Bay	0	14	0	.000	125	412

*Division champion.
†Wild-card team.

NATIONAL CONFERENCE

EASTERN DIVISION

Team	W	L	T	Pct.	PF	PA
Dallas*	11	3	0	.786	296	194
Washington†	10	4	0	.714	291	217
St. Louis	10	4	0	.714	309	267
Philadelphia	4	10	0	.286	165	286
N.Y. Giants	3	11	0	.214	170	250

CENTRAL DIVISION

Team	W	L	T	Pct.	PF	PA
Minnesota*	11	2	1	.821	305	176
Chicago	7	7	0	.500	253	216
Detroit	6	8	0	.429	262	220
Green Bay	5	9	0	.357	218	299

WESTERN DIVISION

Team	W	L	T	Pct.	PF	PA
Los Angeles*	10	3	1	.750	351	190
San Francisco	8	6	0	.571	270	190
Atlanta	4	10	0	.286	172	312
New Orleans	4	10	0	.286	253	346
Seattle	2	12	0	.143	229	429

PLAYOFFS

AFC divisional games
Oakland 24 vs. New England 21
Pittsburgh 40 at Baltimore 14

AFC championship
Oakland 24 vs. Pittsburgh 7

NFC divisional games
Minnesota 35 vs. Washington 20
Los Angeles 14 at Dallas 12

NFC championship
Minnesota 24 vs. Los Angeles 13

Super Bowl 11
Oakland 32, Minnesota 14, at Pasadena, Calif.

THE '76 BUCS: THE WRONG KIND OF FAME

Four seasons after the Miami Dolphins went through an entire season without losing a game, another Florida team also made NFL history, but not the kind it would have preferred. In their inaugural season the Tampa Bay Buccaneers failed to win a game, going 0-16 as a member of the AFC's Western Division. Coach John McKay's Bucs scored a league-low 125 points and allowed 412, a total surpassed only by the league's other 1976 expansion team, the Seattle Seahawks. Tampa Bay failed to score more than 20 points in any game and did not come within three points of winning a game. One of those three-point defeats came in Week 6, when the Seahawks beat the Bucs, 13-10, a victory preserved when veteran linebacker Mike Curtis blocked a 35-yard field goal attempt by Bucs kicker Dave Green with 42 seconds left.

1977

AMERICAN CONFERENCE

EASTERN DIVISION

Team	W	L	T	Pct.	PF	PA
Baltimore*	10	4	0	.714	295	221
Miami	10	4	0	.714	313	197
New England	9	5	0	.643	278	217
N.Y. Jets	3	11	0	.214	191	300
Buffalo	3	11	0	.214	160	313

CENTRAL DIVISION

Team	W	L	T	Pct.	PF	PA
Pittsburgh*	9	5	0	.643	283	243
Houston	8	6	0	.571	299	230
Cincinnati	8	6	0	.571	238	235
Cleveland	6	8	0	.429	269	267

WESTERN DIVISION

Team	W	L	T	Pct.	PF	PA
Denver*	12	2	0	.857	274	148
Oakland†	11	3	0	.786	351	230
San Diego	7	7	0	.500	222	205
Seattle	5	9	0	.357	282	373
Kansas City	2	12	0	.143	225	349

*Division champion.
†Wild-card team.

NATIONAL CONFERENCE

EASTERN DIVISION

Team	W	L	T	Pct.	PF	PA
Dallas*	12	2	0	.857	345	212
Washington	9	5	0	.643	196	189
St. Louis	7	7	0	.500	272	287
Philadelphia	5	9	0	.357	220	207
N.Y. Giants	5	9	0	.357	181	265

CENTRAL DIVISION

Team	W	L	T	Pct.	PF	PA
Minnesota*	9	5	0	.643	231	227
Chicago†	9	5	0	.643	255	253
Detroit	6	8	0	.429	183	252
Green Bay	4	10	0	.286	134	219
Tampa Bay	2	12	0	.143	103	223

WESTERN DIVISION

Team	W	L	T	Pct.	PF	PA
Los Angeles*	10	4	0	.714	302	146
Atlanta	7	7	0	.500	179	129
San Francisco	5	9	0	.357	220	260
New Orleans	3	11	0	.214	232	336

PLAYOFFS

AFC divisional games
Denver 34 vs. Pittsburgh 21
Oakland 37 at Baltimore 31 (OT)

AFC championship
Denver 20 vs. Oakland 17

NFC divisional games
Dallas 37 vs. Chicago 7
Minnesota 14 at Los Angeles 7

NFC championship
Dallas 23 vs. Minnesota 6

Super Bowl 12
Dallas 27, Denver 10, at New Orleans.

1978

AMERICAN CONFERENCE

EASTERN DIVISION

Team	W	L	T	Pct.	PF	PA
New England*	11	5	0	.688	358	286
Miami†	11	5	0	.688	372	254
N.Y. Jets	8	8	0	.500	359	364
Buffalo	5	11	0	.313	302	354
Baltimore	5	11	0	.313	239	421

CENTRAL DIVISION

Team	W	L	T	Pct.	PF	PA
Pittsburgh*	14	2	0	.875	356	195
Houston†	10	6	0	.625	283	298
Cleveland	8	8	0	.500	334	356
Cincinnati	4	12	0	.250	252	284

WESTERN DIVISION

Team	W	L	T	Pct.	PF	PA
Denver*	10	6	0	.625	282	198
Oakland	9	7	0	.563	311	283
Seattle	9	7	0	.563	345	358
San Diego	9	7	0	.563	355	309
Kansas City	4	12	0	.250	243	327

*Division champion.
†Wild-card team.

NATIONAL CONFERENCE

EASTERN DIVISION

Team	W	L	T	Pct.	PF	PA
Dallas*	12	4	0	.750	384	208
Philadelphia†	9	7	0	.563	270	250
Washington	8	8	0	.500	273	283
St. Louis	6	10	0	.375	248	296
N.Y. Giants	6	10	0	.375	264	298

CENTRAL DIVISION

Team	W	L	T	Pct.	PF	PA
Minnesota*	8	7	1	.531	294	306
Green Bay	8	7	1	.531	249	269
Detroit	7	9	0	.438	290	300
Chicago	7	9	0	.438	253	274
Tampa Bay	5	11	0	.313	241	259

WESTERN DIVISION

Team	W	L	T	Pct.	PF	PA
Los Angeles*	12	4	0	.750	316	245
Atlanta†	9	7	0	.563	240	290
New Orleans	7	9	0	.438	281	298
San Francisco	2	14	0	.125	219	350

PLAYOFFS

AFC wild-card game
Houston 17 at Miami 9

AFC divisional games
Houston 31 at New England 14
Pittsburgh 33 vs. Denver 10

AFC championship
Pittsburgh 34 vs. Houston 5

NFC wild-card game
Atlanta 14 vs. Philadelphia 13

NFC divisional games
Dallas 27 vs. Atlanta 20
Los Angeles 34 vs. Minnesota 10

NFC championship
Dallas 28 at Los Angeles 0

Super Bowl 13
Pittsburgh 35, Dallas 31, at Miami.

SMASHING DEBUT FOR BIG EARL

Houston running back Earl Campbell, winner of the Heisman Trophy at Texas the year before and the league's top draft pick, gave NFL fans a preview of things to come by rushing for a league-high 1,450 yards and scoring 13 touchdowns in one of the most electrifying rookie seasons in NFL history. Campbell dethroned defending league rushing champ Walter Payton by 55 yards despite carrying the ball 31 fewer times. More important, he took a team that had not been to the playoffs in eight years to the AFC championship game. Campbell's best game of 1978 came under the brightest of lights: a 199-yard, four-touchdown performance in a 35-30 victory over Miami on Monday, November 20. He capped his big evening by scoring the Oilers' final touchdown on an 81-yard run in the fourth quarter.

AMERICAN CONFERENCE

EASTERN DIVISION

Team	W	L	T	Pct.	PF	PA
Miami*	10	6	0	.625	341	257
New England	9	7	0	.563	411	326
N.Y. Jets	8	8	0	.500	337	383
Buffalo	7	9	0	.438	268	279
Baltimore	5	11	0	.313	271	351

CENTRAL DIVISION

Team	W	L	T	Pct.	PF	PA
Pittsburgh*	12	4	0	.750	416	262
Houston†	11	5	0	.688	362	331
Cleveland	9	7	0	.563	359	352
Cincinnati	4	12	0	.250	337	421

WESTERN DIVISION

Team	W	L	T	Pct.	PF	PA
San Diego*	12	4	0	.750	411	246
Denver†	10	6	0	.625	289	262
Seattle	9	7	0	.563	378	372
Oakland	9	7	0	.563	365	337
Kansas City	7	9	0	.438	238	262

*Division champion.
†Wild-card team.

NATIONAL CONFERENCE

EASTERN DIVISION

Team	W	L	T	Pct.	PF	PA
Dallas*	11	5	0	.688	371	313
Philadelphia†	11	5	0	.688	339	282
Washington	10	6	0	.625	348	295
N.Y. Giants	6	10	0	.375	237	323
St. Louis	5	11	0	.313	307	358

CENTRAL DIVISION

Team	W	L	T	Pct.	PF	PA
Tampa Bay*	10	6	0	.625	273	237
Chicago†	10	6	0	.625	306	249
Minnesota	7	9	0	.438	259	337
Green Bay	5	11	0	.313	246	316
Detroit	2	14	0	.125	219	365

WESTERN DIVISION

Team	W	L	T	Pct.	PF	PA
Los Angeles*	9	7	0	.563	323	309
New Orleans	8	8	0	.500	370	360
Atlanta	6	10	0	.375	300	388
San Francisco	2	14	0	.125	308	416

PLAYOFFS

AFC wild-card game
Houston 13 vs. Denver 7

AFC divisional games
Houston 17 at San Diego 14
Pittsburgh 34 vs. Miami 14

AFC championship
Pittsburgh 27 vs. Houston 13

NFC wild-card game
Philadelphia 27 vs. Chicago 17

NFC divisional games
Tampa Bay 24 vs. Philadelphia 17
Los Angeles 21 at Dallas 19

NFC championship
Los Angeles 9 at Tampa Bay 0

Super Bowl 14
Pittsburgh 31, Los Angeles 19, at Pasadena, Calif.

AMERICAN CONFERENCE

EASTERN DIVISION

Team	W	L	T	Pct.	PF	PA
Buffalo*	11	5	0	.688	320	260
New England	10	6	0	.625	441	325
Miami	8	8	0	.500	266	305
Baltimore	7	9	0	.438	355	387
N.Y. Jets	4	12	0	.250	302	395

CENTRAL DIVISION

Team	W	L	T	Pct.	PF	PA
Cleveland*	11	5	0	.688	357	310
Houston†	11	5	0	.688	295	251
Pittsburgh	9	7	0	.563	352	313
Cincinnati	6	10	0	.375	244	312

WESTERN DIVISION

Team	W	L	T	Pct.	PF	PA
San Diego*	11	5	0	.688	418	327
Oakland†	11	5	0	.688	364	306
Kansas City	8	8	0	.500	319	336
Denver	8	8	0	.500	310	323
Seattle	4	12	0	.250	291	408

*Division champion.
†Wild-card team.

NATIONAL CONFERENCE

EASTERN DIVISION

Team	W	L	T	Pct.	PF	PA
Philadelphia*	12	4	0	.750	384	222
Dallas†	12	4	0	.750	454	311
Washington	6	10	0	.375	261	293
St. Louis	5	11	0	.313	299	350
N.Y. Giants	4	12	0	.250	249	425

CENTRAL DIVISION

Team	W	L	T	Pct.	PF	PA
Minnesota*	9	7	0	.563	317	308
Detroit	9	7	0	.563	334	272
Chicago	7	9	0	.438	304	264
Tampa Bay	5	10	1	.344	271	341
Green Bay	5	10	1	.344	231	371

WESTERN DIVISION

Team	W	L	T	Pct.	PF	PA
Atlanta*	12	4	0	.750	405	272
Los Angeles†	11	5	0	.688	424	289
San Francisco	6	10	0	.375	320	415
New Orleans	1	15	0	.063	291	487

PLAYOFFS

AFC wild-card game
Oakland 27 vs. Houston 7

AFC divisional games
San Diego 20 vs. Buffalo 14
Oakland 14 at Cleveland 12

AFC championship
Oakland 34 at San Diego 27

NFC wild-card game
Dallas 34 vs. Los Angeles 13

NFC divisional games
Philadelphia 31 vs. Minnesota 16
Dallas 30 at Atlanta 27

NFC championship
Philadelphia 20 vs. Dallas 7

Super Bowl 15
Oakland 27, Philadelphia 10, at New Orleans.

AIR CORYELL TAKES TO THE SKIES

Although their season would end in disappointment—a loss to Oakland in the AFC championship game—few teams were more exciting to watch in 1980 than coach Don Coryell's San Diego Chargers. Only eight receivers caught passes for 1,000 or more yards that year, but San Diego had three of them: John Jefferson (who led the league with 1,340 yards), Kellen Winslow (1,290) and Charlie Joiner (1,132). It marked the first time in history that three receivers on the same team each topped 1,000 yards in the same season. In addition, Winslow caught 89 passes to set a record for receptions by a tight end and Jefferson became the first player to begin his NFL career with three consecutive 1,000-yard seasons. Not surprisingly, the Chargers won the AFC West title for the second year in a row, the only team to repeat from the 1979 season.

1981

AMERICAN CONFERENCE

EASTERN DIVISION

Team	W	L	T	Pct.	PF	PA
Miami*	11	4	1	.719	345	275
N.Y. Jets†	10	5	1	.656	355	287
Buffalo†	10	6	0	.625	311	276
Baltimore	2	14	0	.125	259	533
New England	2	14	0	.125	322	370

CENTRAL DIVISION

Team	W	L	T	Pct.	PF	PA
Cincinnati*	12	4	0	.750	421	304
Pittsburgh	8	8	0	.500	356	297
Houston	7	9	0	.438	281	355
Cleveland	5	11	0	.313	276	375

WESTERN DIVISION

Team	W	L	T	Pct.	PF	PA
San Diego*	10	6	0	.625	478	390
Denver	10	6	0	.625	321	289
Kansas City	9	7	0	.563	343	290
Oakland	7	9	0	.438	273	343
Seattle	6	10	0	.375	322	388

*Division champion.
†Wild-card team.

NATIONAL CONFERENCE

EASTERN DIVISION

Team	W	L	T	Pct.	PF	PA
Dallas*	12	4	0	.750	367	277
Philadelphia†	10	6	0	.625	368	221
N.Y. Giants†	9	7	0	.563	295	257
Washington	8	8	0	.500	347	349
St. Louis	7	9	0	.438	315	408

CENTRAL DIVISION

Team	W	L	T	Pct.	PF	PA
Tampa Bay*	9	7	0	.563	315	268
Detroit	8	8	0	.500	397	322
Green Bay	8	8	0	.500	324	361
Minnesota	7	9	0	.438	325	369
Chicago	6	10	0	.375	253	324

WESTERN DIVISION

Team	W	L	T	Pct.	PF	PA
San Francisco*	13	3	0	.813	357	250
Atlanta	7	9	0	.438	426	355
Los Angeles	6	10	0	.375	303	351
New Orleans	4	12	0	.250	207	378

PLAYOFFS

AFC wild-card game
Buffalo 31 at New York Jets 27

AFC divisional games
San Diego 41 at Miami 38 (OT)
Cincinnati 28 vs. Buffalo 21

AFC championship
Cincinnati 27 vs. San Diego 7

NFC wild-card game
N.Y. Giants 27 at Philadelphia 21

NFC divisional games
Dallas 38 vs. Tampa Bay 0
San Francisco 38 vs. N.Y. Giants 24

NFC championship
San Francisco 28 vs. Dallas 27

Super Bowl 16
San Francisco 26, Cincinnati 21, at Pontiac, Mich.

1982

AMERICAN CONFERENCE

Team	W	L	T	Pct.	PF	PA
L.A. Raiders	8	1	0	.889	260	200
Miami	7	2	0	.778	198	131
Cincinnati	7	2	0	.778	232	177
Pittsburgh	6	3	0	.667	204	146
San Diego	6	3	0	.667	288	221
N.Y. Jets	6	3	0	.667	245	166
New England	5	4	0	.556	143	157
Cleveland	4	5	0	.444	140	182
Buffalo	4	5	0	.444	150	154
Seattle	4	5	0	.444	127	147
Kansas City	3	6	0	.333	176	184
Denver	2	7	0	.222	148	226
Houston	1	8	0	.111	136	245
Baltimore	0	8	1	.056	113	236

NATIONAL CONFERENCE

Team	W	L	T	Pct.	PF	PA
Washington	8	1	0	.889	190	128
Dallas	6	3	0	.667	226	145
Green Bay	5	3	1	.611	226	169
Minnesota	5	4	0	.556	187	198
Atlanta	5	4	0	.556	183	199
St. Louis	5	4	0	.556	135	170
Tampa Bay	5	4	0	.556	158	178
Detroit	4	5	0	.444	181	176
New Orleans	4	5	0	.444	129	160
N.Y. Giants	4	5	0	.444	164	160
San Francisco	3	6	0	.333	209	206
Chicago	3	6	0	.333	141	174
Philadelphia	3	6	0	.333	191	195
L.A. Rams	2	7	0	.222	200	250

As a result of a 57-day players' strike, the 1982 NFL regular season schedule was reduced from 16 weeks to 9. At the conclusion of the regular season, a 16-team Super Bowl Tournament was held. Eight teams from each conference were seeded 1 through 8 based on their records during regular season play.

Miami finished ahead of Cincinnati based on a better conference record. Pittsburgh won common games tiebreaker with San Diego after New York Jets were eliminated from three-way tie based on conference record. Cleveland finished ahead of Buffalo and Seattle based on better conference record. Minnesota, Atlanta, St. Louis and Tampa Bay seeds were determined by best won-lost record in conference games. Detroit finished ahead of New Orleans and the New York Giants based on a better conference record.

PLAYOFFS

AFC first round
Miami 28 vs. New England 13
L.A. Raiders 27 vs. Cleveland 10
New York Jets 44 at Cincinnati 17
San Diego 31 at Pittsburgh 28

AFC second round
N.Y. Jets 17 at L.A. Raiders 14
Miami 34 vs. San Diego 13

AFC championship
Miami 14 vs. New York Jets 0

NFC first round
Washington 31 vs. Detroit 7
Green Bay 41 vs. St. Louis 16
Minnesota 30 vs. Atlanta 24
Dallas 30 vs. Tampa Bay 17

NFC second round
Washington 21 vs. Minnesota 7
Dallas 37 vs. Green Bay 26

NFC championship
Washington 31 vs. Dallas 17

Super Bowl 17
Washington 27, Miami 17, at Pasadena, Calif.

LT: A ROOKIE TO REMEMBER

The 1981 season was a big one for rookies (six made the Pro Bowl), but none had more impact than Giants linebacker Lawrence Taylor, who had no problem adjusting to the pro game after an All-American career at North Carolina. The second player drafted in 1981, Taylor was simply marvelous, helping to make a good New York defense with veterans like linebacker Harry Carson and cornerback Mark Haynes great. In 16 games (all starts) Taylor had 133 tackles, 10.5 sacks, recovered a fumble and intercepted a pass. He followed that up with 14 tackles and two sacks in two playoff games, the Giants' first postseason action since 1963. For his efforts Taylor was a unanimous All-NFL first-team selection, a Pro Bowl starter and the Associated Press Defensive Player of the Year.

AMERICAN CONFERENCE

EASTERN DIVISION

Team	W	L	T	Pct.	PF	PA
Miami*	12	4	0	.750	389	250
New England	8	8	0	.500	274	289
Buffalo	8	8	0	.500	283	351
Baltimore	7	9	0	.438	264	354
N.Y. Jets	7	9	0	.438	313	331

CENTRAL DIVISION

Team	W	L	T	Pct.	PF	PA
Pittsburgh*	10	6	0	.625	355	303
Cleveland	9	7	0	.563	356	342
Cincinnati	7	9	0	.438	346	302
Houston	2	14	0	.125	288	460

WESTERN DIVISION

Team	W	L	T	Pct.	PF	PA
L.A. Raiders*	12	4	0	.750	442	338
Seattle†	9	7	0	.563	403	397
Denver†	9	7	0	.563	302	327
San Diego	6	10	0	.375	358	462
Kansas City	6	10	0	.375	386	367

*Division champion.
†Wild-card team.

NATIONAL CONFERENCE

EASTERN DIVISION

Team	W	L	T	Pct.	PF	PA
Washington*	14	2	0	.875	541	332
Dallas†	12	4	0	.750	479	360
St. Louis	8	7	1	.531	374	428
Philadelphia	5	11	0	.313	233	322
N.Y. Giants	3	12	1	.219	267	347

CENTRAL DIVISION

Team	W	L	T	Pct.	PF	PA
Detroit*	9	7	0	.563	347	286
Green Bay	8	8	0	.500	429	439
Chicago	8	8	0	.500	311	301
Minnesota	8	8	0	.500	316	348
Tampa Bay	2	14	0	.125	241	380

WESTERN DIVISION

Team	W	L	T	Pct.	PF	PA
San Francisco*	10	6	0	.625	432	293
L.A. Rams†	9	7	0	.563	361	344
New Orleans	8	8	0	.500	319	337
Atlanta	7	9	0	.438	370	389

PLAYOFFS

AFC wild-card game
Seattle 31 vs. Denver 7

AFC divisional games
Seattle 27 at Miami 20
L.A. Raiders 38 vs. Pittsburgh 10

AFC championship game
L.A. Raiders 30 vs. Seattle 14

NFC wild-card game
Los Angeles Rams 24 at Dallas 17

NFC divisional games
San Francisco 24 vs. Detroit 23
Washington 51 vs. L.A. Rams 7

NFC championship game
Washington 24 vs. San Francisco 21

Super Bowl 18
L.A. Raiders 38, Washington 9, at Tampa, Fla.

AMERICAN CONFERENCE

EASTERN DIVISION

Team	W	L	T	Pct.	PF	PA
Miami*	14	2	0	.875	513	298
New England	9	7	0	.563	362	352
N.Y. Jets	7	9	0	.438	332	364
Indianapolis	4	12	0	.250	239	414
Buffalo	2	14	0	.125	250	454

CENTRAL DIVISION

Team	W	L	T	Pct.	PF	PA
Pittsburgh*	9	7	0	.563	387	310
Cincinnati	8	8	0	.500	339	339
Cleveland	5	11	0	.313	250	297
Houston	3	13	0	.188	240	437

WESTERN DIVISION

Team	W	L	T	Pct.	PF	PA
Denver*	13	3	0	.813	353	241
Seattle†	12	4	0	.750	418	282
L.A. Raiders†	11	5	0	.688	368	278
Kansas City	8	8	0	.500	314	324
San Diego	7	9	0	.438	394	413

*Division champion.
†Wild-card team.

NATIONAL CONFERENCE

EASTERN DIVISION

Team	W	L	T	Pct.	PF	PA
Washington*	11	5	0	.688	426	310
N.Y. Giants†	9	7	0	.563	299	301
St. Louis	9	7	0	.563	423	345
Dallas	9	7	0	.563	308	308
Philadelphia	6	9	1	.406	278	320

CENTRAL DIVISION

Team	W	L	T	Pct.	PF	PA
Chicago*	10	6	0	.625	325	248
Green Bay	8	8	0	.500	390	309
Tampa Bay	6	10	0	.375	335	380
Detroit	4	11	1	.281	283	408
Minnesota	3	13	0	.188	276	484

WESTERN DIVISION

Team	W	L	T	Pct.	PF	PA
San Francisco*	15	1	0	.938	475	227
L.A. Rams†	10	6	0	.625	346	316
New Orleans	7	9	0	.438	298	361
Atlanta	4	12	0	.250	281	382

PLAYOFFS

AFC wild-card game
Seattle 13 vs. Los Angeles Raiders 7

AFC divisional games
Miami 31 vs. Seattle 10
Pittsburgh 24 at Denver 17

AFC championship
Miami 45 vs. Pittsburgh 28

NFC wild-card game
N.Y. Giants 16 at L.A. Rams 13

NFC divisional games
San Francisco 21 vs. N.Y. Giants 10
Chicago 23 at Washington 19

NFC championship
San Francisco 23 vs. Chicago 0

Super Bowl 19
San Francisco 38, Miami 16, at Palo Alto, Calif.

CAPITAL GAINS FOR THE REDSKINS

Although they failed to successfully defend their Super Bowl championship, the Washington Redskins did just about everything else right in 1983, especially on offense. Washington scored 541 points, the most in NFL history and 62 more than the next highest scoring team that year. Running back John Riggins scored a record 24 touchdowns, rushed for a club-record 1,347 yards and set a league mark by rushing for a TD in 13 consecutive games. Mark Moseley's 161 points set a new league standard for kickers. But as good as Riggins and Moseley were, the league's Most Valuable Player, in voting conducted by the Associated Press, was quarterback Joe Theismann, who threw 29 TD passes, compiled a 97.0 passer rating and had streaks of 161 and 104 consecutive passes without an interception.

1985

AMERICAN CONFERENCE

EASTERN DIVISION

Team	W	L	T	Pct.	PF	PA
Miami*	12	4	0	.750	428	320
N.Y. Jets†	11	5	0	.688	393	264
New England†	11	5	0	.688	362	290
Indianapolis	5	11	0	.313	320	386
Buffalo	2	14	0	.125	200	381

CENTRAL DIVISION

Team	W	L	T	Pct.	PF	PA
Cleveland*	8	8	0	.500	287	294
Cincinnati	7	9	0	.438	441	437
Pittsburgh	7	9	0	.438	379	355
Houston	5	11	0	.313	284	412

WESTERN DIVISION

Team	W	L	T	Pct.	PF	PA
L.A. Raiders*	12	4	0	.750	354	308
Denver	11	5	0	.688	380	329
Seattle	8	8	0	.500	349	303
San Diego	8	8	0	.500	467	435
Kansas City	6	10	0	.375	317	360

*Division champion.
†Wild-card team.

NATIONAL CONFERENCE

EASTERN DIVISION

Team	W	L	T	Pct.	PF	PA
Dallas*	10	6	0	.625	357	333
N.Y. Giants†	10	6	0	.625	399	283
Washington	10	6	0	.625	297	312
Philadelphia	7	9	0	.438	286	310
St. Louis	5	11	0	.313	278	414

CENTRAL DIVISION

Team	W	L	T	Pct.	PF	PA
Chicago*	15	1	0	.938	456	198
Green Bay	8	8	0	.500	337	355
Minnesota	7	9	0	.438	346	359
Detroit	7	9	0	.438	307	366
Tampa Bay	2	14	0	.125	294	448

WESTERN DIVISION

Team	W	L	T	Pct.	PF	PA
L.A. Rams*	11	5	0	.688	340	277
San Francisco†	10	6	0	.625	411	263
New Orleans	5	11	0	.313	294	401
Atlanta	4	12	0	.250	282	452

PLAYOFFS

AFC wild-card game
New England 26 at N.Y. Jets 14

AFC divisional games
Miami 24 vs. Cleveland 21
New England 27 at L.A. Raiders 20

AFC championship
New England 31 at Miami 14

NFC wild-card game
N.Y. Giants 17 vs. San Francisco 3

NFC divisional games
Los Angeles Rams 20 vs. Dallas 0
Chicago 21 vs. New York Giants 0

NFC championship
Chicago 24 vs. Los Angeles Rams 0

Super Bowl 20
Chicago 46, New England 10, at New Orleans.

1986

AMERICAN CONFERENCE

EASTERN DIVISION

Team	W	L	T	Pct.	PF	PA
New England*	11	5	0	.688	412	307
N.Y. Jets†	10	6	0	.625	364	386
Miami	8	8	0	.500	430	405
Buffalo	4	12	0	.250	287	348
Indianapolis	3	13	0	.188	229	400

CENTRAL DIVISION

Team	W	L	T	Pct.	PF	PA
Cleveland*	12	4	0	.750	391	310
Cincinnati	10	6	0	.625	409	394
Pittsburgh	6	10	0	.375	307	336
Houston	5	11	0	.313	274	329

WESTERN DIVISION

Team	W	L	T	Pct.	PF	PA
Denver*	11	5	0	.688	378	327
Kansas City†	10	6	0	.625	358	326
Seattle	10	6	0	.625	366	293
L.A. Raiders	8	8	0	.500	323	346
San Diego	4	12	0	.250	335	396

*Division champion.
†Wild-card team.

NATIONAL CONFERENCE

EASTERN DIVISION

Team	W	L	T	Pct.	PF	PA
N.Y. Giants*	14	2	0	.875	371	236
Washington†	12	4	0	.750	368	296
Dallas	7	9	0	.438	346	337
Philadelphia	5	10	1	.344	256	312
St. Louis	4	11	1	.281	218	351

CENTRAL DIVISION

Team	W	L	T	Pct.	PF	PA
Chicago*	14	2	0	.875	352	187
Minnesota	9	7	0	.563	398	273
Detroit	5	11	0	.313	277	326
Green Bay	4	12	0	.250	254	418
Tampa Bay	2	14	0	.125	239	473

WESTERN DIVISION

Team	W	L	T	Pct.	PF	PA
San Francisco*	10	5	1	.656	374	247
L.A. Rams†	10	6	0	.625	309	267
Atlanta	7	8	1	.469	280	280
New Orleans	7	9	0	.438	288	287

PLAYOFFS

AFC wild-card game
N.Y. Jets 35 vs. Kansas City 15

AFC divisional games
Cleveland 23 vs. N.Y. Jets 20 (OT)
Denver 22 vs. New England 17

AFC championship
Denver 23 at Cleveland 20 (OT)

NFC wild-card game
Washington 19 vs. L.A. Rams 7

NFC divisional games
Washington 27 at Chicago 13
N.Y. Giants 49 vs. San Francisco 3

NFC championship
N.Y. Giants 17 vs. Washington 0

Super Bowl 21
New York Giants 39, Denver 20, at Pasadena, Calif.

DA BEARS

The 1985 Chicago Bears may not have been the best team ever, but they were certainly among the most colorful. Running back Walter Payton suggested his teammates could have stepped right from the pages of "One Flew Over the Cuckoo's Nest." Rookie defensive tackle William Perry, whose girth earned him the nickname "The Refrigerator," said "I was big when I was little" when queried about his weight. The players cut a popular music video "The Super Bowl Shuffle"—while the regular season was still in progress. But there were good reasons for the cockiness: the Bears were good. They scored 456 points and allowed 198, one of the lowest totals ever for a 16-game season. Their final record, including the playoffs, was 18-1, and they outscored their three postseason opponents by a combined 91-10. Chicago's 46-10 rout of New England in the Super Bowl was the most lopsided in the game's first 20 years.

AMERICAN CONFERENCE

EASTERN DIVISION

Team	W	L	T	Pct.	PF	PA
Indianapolis*	9	6	0	.600	300	238
New England	8	7	0	.533	320	293
Miami	8	7	0	.533	362	335
Buffalo	7	8	0	.467	270	305
N.Y. Jets	6	9	0	.400	334	360

CENTRAL DIVISION

Team	W	L	T	Pct.	PF	PA
Cleveland*	10	5	0	.667	390	239
Houston†	9	6	0	.600	345	349
Pittsburgh	8	7	0	.533	285	299
Cincinnati	4	11	0	.267	285	370

WESTERN DIVISION

Team	W	L	T	Pct.	PF	PA
Denver*	10	4	1	.700	379	288
Seattle†	9	6	0	.600	371	314
San Diego	8	7	0	.533	253	317
L.A. Raiders	5	10	0	.333	301	289
Kansas City	4	11	0	.267	273	388

*Division champion.
†Wild-card team.

NOTE: The 1987 NFL regular season was reduced from 224 games to 210 (16 to 15 for each team) due to players' strike.

NATIONAL CONFERENCE

EASTERN DIVISION

Team	W	L	T	Pct.	PF	PA
Washington*	11	4	0	.733	379	285
Dallas	7	8	0	.467	340	348
St. Louis	7	8	0	.467	362	368
Philadelphia	7	8	0	.467	337	380
N.Y. Giants	6	9	0	.400	280	312

CENTRAL DIVISION

Team	W	L	T	Pct.	PF	PA
Chicago*	11	4	0	.733	356	282
Minnesota†	8	7	0	.533	336	335
Green Bay	5	9	1	.367	255	300
Tampa Bay	4	11	0	.267	286	360
Detroit	4	11	0	.267	269	384

WESTERN DIVISION

Team	W	L	T	Pct.	PF	PA
San Francisco*	13	2	0	.867	459	253
New Orleans†	12	3	0	.800	422	283
L.A. Rams	6	9	0	.400	317	361
Atlanta	3	12	0	.200	205	436

PLAYOFFS

AFC wild-card game
Houston 23 vs. Seattle 20 (OT)
AFC divisional games
Cleveland 38 vs. Indianapolis 21
Denver 34 vs. Houston 10
AFC championship
Denver 38 vs. Cleveland 33
NFC wild-card game
Minnesota 44 at New Orleans 10
NFC divisional games
Minnesota 36 at San Francisco 24
Washington 21 at Chicago 17
NFC championship
Washington 17 vs. Minnesota 10
Super Bowl 22
Washington 42, Denver 10, at San Diego.

AMERICAN CONFERENCE

EASTERN DIVISION

Team	W	L	T	Pct.	PF	PA
Buffalo*	12	4	0	.750	329	237
Indianapolis	9	7	0	.563	354	315
New England	9	7	0	.563	250	284
N.Y. Jets	8	7	1	.531	372	354
Miami	6	10	0	.375	319	380

CENTRAL DIVISION

Team	W	L	T	Pct.	PF	PA
Cincinnati*	12	4	0	.750	448	329
Cleveland†	10	6	0	.625	304	288
Houston†	10	6	0	.625	424	365
Pittsburgh	5	11	0	.313	336	421

WESTERN DIVISION

Team	W	L	T	Pct.	PF	PA
Seattle*	9	7	0	.563	339	329
Denver	8	8	0	.500	327	352
L.A. Raiders	7	9	0	.438	325	369
San Diego	6	10	0	.375	231	332
Kansas City	4	11	1	.281	254	320

*Division champion.
†Wild-card team.

NATIONAL CONFERENCE

EASTERN DIVISION

Team	W	L	T	Pct.	PF	PA
Philadelphia*	10	6	0	.625	379	319
N.Y. Giants	10	6	0	.625	359	304
Washington	7	9	0	.438	345	387
Phoenix	7	9	0	.438	344	398
Dallas	3	13	0	.188	265	381

CENTRAL DIVISION

Team	W	L	T	Pct.	PF	PA
Chicago*	12	4	0	.750	312	215
Minnesota†	11	5	0	.688	406	233
Tampa Bay	5	11	0	.313	261	350
Detroit	4	12	0	.250	220	313
Green Bay	4	12	0	.250	240	315

WESTERN DIVISION

Team	W	L	T	Pct.	PF	PA
San Francisco*	10	6	0	.625	369	294
L.A. Rams†	10	6	0	.625	407	293
New Orleans	10	6	0	.625	312	283
Atlanta	5	11	0	.313	244	315

PLAYOFFS

AFC wild-card game
Houston 24 at Cleveland 23
AFC divisional games
Cincinnati 21 vs. Seattle 13
Buffalo 17 vs. Houston 10
AFC championship
Cincinnati 21 vs. Buffalo 10
NFC wild-card game
Minnesota 28 vs. L.A. Rams 17
NFC divisional games
Chicago 20 vs. Philadelphia 12
San Francisco 34 vs. Minnesota 9
NFC championship
San Francisco 28 at Chicago 3
Super Bowl 23
San Francisco 20, Cincinnati 16, at Miami.

REPLACEMENT BALL

Frustrated in their attempts to gain a fairer form of unrestricted free agency, NFL players went on strike for the second time in league history on September 22, 1987. The work stoppage forced the cancellation of all Week 3 games and brought about three subsequent weeks of what came to be called "replacement football." With their regular players on strike, team owners quickly assembled new squads consisting of former NFL and United States Football League players, castoffs and amateur dreamers willing to cross a picket line. The result? There was a wide discrepancy in the quality of the teams, depending largely on how much effort management invested in assembling new rosters. The defending Super Bowl champion Giants, for example, lost all three of their replacement games (which counted in the standings) and never recovered once their regular players returned, finishing the season 6-9 and out of the playoffs. The Redskins, meanwhile, went 3-0 in replacement ball, helping to propel them to an 11-4 regular-season finish en route to the club's second Super Bowl title in six years.

1989

AMERICAN CONFERENCE

EASTERN DIVISION

Team	W	L	T	Pct.	PF	PA
Buffalo*	9	7	0	.563	409	317
Indianapolis	8	8	0	.500	298	301
Miami	8	8	0	.500	331	379
New England	5	11	0	.313	297	391
N.Y. Jets	4	12	0	.250	253	411

CENTRAL DIVISION

Team	W	L	T	Pct.	PF	PA
Cleveland*	9	6	1	.594	334	254
Houston†	9	7	0	.563	365	412
Pittsburgh†	9	7	0	.563	265	326
Cincinnati	8	8	0	.500	404	285

WESTERN DIVISION

Team	W	L	T	Pct.	PF	PA
Denver*	11	5	0	.688	362	226
Kansas City	8	7	1	.531	318	286
L.A. Raiders	8	8	0	.500	315	297
Seattle	7	9	0	.438	241	327
San Diego	6	10	0	.375	266	290

*Division champion.
†Wild-card team.

NATIONAL CONFERENCE

EASTERN DIVISION

Team	W	L	T	Pct.	PF	PA
N.Y. Giants*	12	4	0	.750	348	252
Philadelphia†	11	5	0	.688	342	274
Washington	10	6	0	.625	386	308
Phoenix	5	11	0	.313	258	377
Dallas	1	15	0	.063	204	393

CENTRAL DIVISION

Team	W	L	T	Pct.	PF	PA
Minnesota*	10	6	0	.625	351	275
Green Bay	10	6	0	.625	362	356
Detroit	7	9	0	.438	312	364
Chicago	6	10	0	.375	358	377
Tampa Bay	5	11	0	.313	320	419

WESTERN DIVISION

Team	W	L	T	Pct.	PF	PA
San Francisco*	14	2	0	.875	442	253
L.A. Rams†	11	5	0	.688	426	344
New Orleans	9	7	0	.563	386	301
Atlanta	3	13	0	.188	279	437

PLAYOFFS

AFC wild-card game
Pittsburgh 26 at Houston 23 (OT)

AFC divisional games
Cleveland 34 vs. Buffalo 30
Denver 24 vs. Pittsburgh 23

AFC championship
Denver 37 vs. Cleveland 21

NFC wild-card game
L.A. Rams 21 at Philadelphia 7

NFC divisional games
L.A. Rams 19 at N.Y. Giants 13 (OT)
San Francisco 41 vs. Minnesota 13

NFC championship
San Francisco 30 vs. L.A. Rams 3

Super Bowl 24
San Francisco 55, Denver 10, at New Orleans.

1990

AMERICAN CONFERENCE

EASTERN DIVISION

Team	W	L	T	Pct.	PF	PA
Buffalo*	13	3	0	.813	428	263
Miami†	12	4	0	.750	336	242
Indianapolis	7	9	0	.438	281	353
N.Y. Jets	6	10	0	.375	295	345
New England	1	15	0	.063	181	446

CENTRAL DIVISION

Team	W	L	T	Pct.	PF	PA
Cincinnati*	9	7	0	.563	360	352
Houston†	9	7	0	.563	405	307
Pittsburgh	9	7	0	.563	292	240
Cleveland	3	13	0	.188	228	462

WESTERN DIVISION

Team	W	L	T	Pct.	PF	PA
L.A. Raiders*	12	4	0	.750	337	268
Kansas City†	11	5	0	.688	369	257
Seattle	9	7	0	.563	306	286
San Diego	6	10	0	.375	315	281
Denver	5	11	0	.313	331	374

*Division champion.
†Wild-card team.

NATIONAL CONFERENCE

EASTERN DIVISION

Team	W	L	T	Pct.	PF	PA
N.Y. Giants*	13	3	0	.813	335	211
Philadelphia†	10	6	0	.625	396	299
Washington†	10	6	0	.625	381	301
Dallas	7	9	0	.438	244	308
Phoenix	5	11	0	.313	268	396

CENTRAL DIVISION

Team	W	L	T	Pct.	PF	PA
Chicago*	11	5	0	.688	348	280
Tampa Bay	6	10	0	.375	264	367
Detroit	6	10	0	.375	373	413
Green Bay	6	10	0	.375	271	347
Minnesota	6	10	0	.375	351	326

WESTERN DIVISION

Team	W	L	T	Pct.	PF	PA
San Francisco*	14	2	0	.875	353	239
New Orleans†	8	8	0	.500	274	275
L.A. Rams	5	11	0	.313	345	412
Atlanta	5	11	0	.313	348	365

PLAYOFFS

AFC wild-card playoffs
Miami 17 vs. Kansas City 16
Cincinnati 41 vs. Houston 14

AFC divisional playoffs
Buffalo 44 vs. Miami 34
L.A. Raiders 20 vs. Cincinnati 10

AFC championship
Buffalo 51 vs. L.A. Raiders 3

NFC wild-card playoffs
Washington 20 at Philadelphia 6
Chicago 16 vs. New Orleans 6

NFC divisional playoffs
San Francisco 28 vs. Washington 10
N.Y. Giants 31 vs. Chicago 3

NFC championship
N.Y. Giants 15 at San Francisco 13

Super Bowl 25
N.Y. Giants 20 vs. Buffalo 19, at Tampa, Fla.

GIANTS AND BILLS GO DOWN TO THE WIRE

One year after the most lopsided Super Bowl ever, the Giants and Bills staged the closest, with New York edging Buffalo, 20-19, at Tampa Stadium in Super Bowl 25 when Bills kicker Scott Norwood missed a 47-yard field goal attempt with eight seconds left. Although Norwood wore the goat horns afterward, his teammates did little early in the contest to prevent the game from coming down to a last-minute kick. A Buffalo offense that had scored a league-high 428 points during the regular season and 95 in the first two playoff games did little in its biggest test of the season. Only running back Thurman Thomas (135 yards rushing) had what could be considered a superior game. The Giants' offense, meanwhile, put together scoring drives of 87, 75 and 74 yards. A 14-play, 75-yard drive that took 9 minutes, 29 seconds off the clock went into the books as the most time-consuming drive in Super Bowl history.

1991

AMERICAN CONFERENCE

EASTERN DIVISION

Team	W	L	T	Pct.	PF	PA
Buffalo*	13	3	0	.813	458	318
N.Y. Jets†	8	8	0	.500	314	293
Miami	8	8	0	.500	343	349
New England	6	10	0	.375	211	305
Indianapolis	1	15	0	.063	143	381

CENTRAL DIVISION

Team	W	L	T	Pct.	PF	PA
Houston*	11	5	0	.688	386	251
Pittsburgh	7	9	0	.438	292	344
Cleveland	6	10	0	.375	293	298
Cincinnati	3	13	0	.188	263	435

WESTERN DIVISION

Team	W	L	T	Pct.	PF	PA
Denver*	12	4	0	.750	304	235
Kansas City†	10	6	0	.625	322	252
L.A. Raiders†	9	7	0	.563	298	297
Seattle	7	9	0	.438	276	261
San Diego	4	12	0	.250	274	342

*Division champion.
†Wild-card team.

NATIONAL CONFERENCE

EASTERN DIVISION

Team	W	L	T	Pct.	PF	PA
Washington*	14	2	0	.875	485	224
Dallas†	11	5	0	.688	342	310
Philadelphia	10	6	0	.625	285	244
N.Y. Giants	8	8	0	.500	281	297
Phoenix	4	12	0	.250	196	344

CENTRAL DIVISION

Team	W	L	T	Pct.	PF	PA
Detroit*	12	4	0	.750	339	295
Chicago†	11	5	0	.688	299	269
Minnesota	8	8	0	.500	301	306
Green Bay	4	12	0	.250	273	313
Tampa Bay	3	13	0	.188	199	365

WESTERN DIVISION

Team	W	L	T	Pct.	PF	PA
New Orleans*	11	5	0	.688	341	211
Atlanta†	10	6	0	.625	361	338
San Francisco	10	6	0	.625	393	239
L.A. Rams	3	13	0	.188	234	390

PLAYOFFS

AFC wild-card playoffs
Kansas City 10 vs. L.A. Raiders 6
Houston 17 vs. N.Y. Jets 10

AFC divisional playoffs
Denver 26 vs. Houston 24
Buffalo 37 vs. Kansas City 14

AFC championship
Buffalo 10 vs. Denver 7

NFC wild-card playoffs
Atlanta 27 at New Orleans 20
Dallas 17 at Chicago 13

NFC divisional playoffs
Washington 24 vs. Atlanta 7
Detroit 38 vs. Dallas 6

NFC championship
Washington 41 vs. Detroit 10

Super Bowl 26
Washington 37 vs. Buffalo 24, at Minneapolis.

1992

AMERICAN CONFERENCE

EASTERN DIVISION

Team	W	L	T	Pct.	PF	PA
Miami*	11	5	0	.688	340	281
Buffalo†	11	5	0	.688	381	283
Indianapolis	9	7	0	.563	216	302
N.Y. Jets	4	12	0	.250	220	315
New England	2	14	0	.125	205	363

CENTRAL DIVISION

Team	W	L	T	Pct.	PF	PA
Pittsburgh*	11	5	0	.688	299	225
Houston†	10	6	0	.625	352	258
Cleveland	7	9	0	.438	272	275
Cincinnati	5	11	0	.313	274	364

WESTERN DIVISION

Team	W	L	T	Pct.	PF	PA
San Diego*	11	5	0	.688	335	241
Kansas City†	10	6	0	.625	348	282
Denver	8	8	0	.500	262	329
L.A. Raiders	7	9	0	.438	249	281
Seattle	2	14	0	.125	140	312

*Division champion.
†Wild-card team.

NATIONAL CONFERENCE

EASTERN DIVISION

Team	W	L	T	Pct.	PF	PA
Dallas*	13	3	0	.813	409	243
Philadelphia†	11	5	0	.688	354	245
Washington†	9	7	0	.563	300	255
N.Y. Giants	6	10	0	.375	306	367
Phoenix	4	12	0	.250	243	332

CENTRAL DIVISION

Team	W	L	T	Pct.	PF	PA
Minnesota*	11	5	0	.688	374	249
Green Bay	9	7	0	.563	276	296
Tampa Bay	5	11	0	.313	267	365
Chicago	5	11	0	.313	295	361
Detroit	5	11	0	.313	273	332

WESTERN DIVISION

Team	W	L	T	Pct.	PF	PA
San Francisco*	14	2	0	.875	431	236
New Orleans†	12	4	0	.750	330	202
Atlanta	6	10	0	.375	327	414
L.A. Rams	6	10	0	.375	313	383

PLAYOFFS

AFC wild-card playoffs
San Diego 17 vs. Kansas City 0
Buffalo 41 vs. Houston 38 (OT)

AFC divisional playoffs
Buffalo 24 at Pittsburgh 3
Miami 31 vs. San Diego 0

AFC championship
Buffalo 29 at Miami 10

NFC wild-card playoffs
Washington 24 at Minnesota 7
Philadelphia 36 at New Orleans 20

NFC divisional playoffs
San Francisco 20 vs. Washington 13
Dallas 34 vs. Philadelphia 10

NFC championship
Dallas 30 at San Francisco 20

Super Bowl 27
Dallas 52 vs. Buffalo 17, at Pasadena, Calif.

COWBOYS HIT THE HEIGHTS AGAIN

Three years after hitting the lowest point in franchise history, the Dallas Cowboys were back on top of the football world following a 52-17 romp over Buffalo in Super Bowl 27. In their fourth year under Jimmy Johnson, who replaced legendary coach Tom Landry following an ownership change in February 1989, the Cowboys won a franchise-record 13 regular season games and rolled through the playoffs, beating the Eagles, 49ers and Bills by a combined score of 116-47. Troy Aikman, the first player Johnson drafted after taking over, was superb in the playoffs, compiling an NFL-record 116.7 quarterback rating in the three games. With the win Johnson joined Paul Brown as the only men to coach championship teams in both college and the NFL.

1993

AMERICAN CONFERENCE

EASTERN DIVISION

Team	W	L	T	Pct.	PF	PA
Buffalo*	12	4	0	.750	329	242
Miami	9	7	0	.563	349	351
N.Y. Jets	8	8	0	.500	270	247
New England	5	11	0	.313	238	286
Indianapolis	4	12	0	.250	189	378

CENTRAL DIVISION

Team	W	L	T	Pct.	PF	PA
Houston*	12	4	0	.750	368	238
Pittsburgh†	9	7	0	.563	308	281
Cleveland	7	9	0	.438	304	307
Cincinnati	3	13	0	.188	187	319

WESTERN DIVISION

Team	W	L	T	Pct.	PF	PA
Kansas City*	11	5	0	.688	328	291
L.A. Raiders†	10	6	0	.625	306	326
Denver†	9	7	0	.563	373	284
San Diego	8	8	0	.500	322	290
Seattle	6	10	0	.375	280	314

*Division champion.
†Wild-card team.

NATIONAL CONFERENCE

EASTERN DIVISION

Team	W	L	T	Pct.	PF	PA
Dallas*	12	4	0	.750	376	229
N.Y. Giants†	11	5	0	.688	288	205
Philadelphia	8	8	0	.500	293	315
Phoenix	7	9	0	.438	326	269
Washington	4	12	0	.250	230	345

CENTRAL DIVISION

Team	W	L	T	Pct.	PF	PA
Detroit*	10	6	0	.625	298	292
Minnesota†	9	7	0	.563	277	290
Green Bay†	9	7	0	.563	340	282
Chicago	7	9	0	.438	234	230
Tampa Bay	5	11	0	.313	237	376

WESTERN DIVISION

Team	W	L	T	Pct.	PF	PA
San Francisco*	10	6	0	.625	473	295
New Orleans	8	8	0	.500	317	343
Atlanta	6	10	0	.375	316	385
L.A. Rams	5	11	0	.313	221	367

PLAYOFFS

AFC wild-card playoffs
Kansas City 27 vs. Pittsburgh 24 (OT)
L.A. Raiders 42 vs. Denver 24

AFC divisional playoffs
Buffalo 29 vs. L.A. Raiders 23
Kansas City 28 at Houston 20

AFC championship
Buffalo 30 vs. Kansas City 13

NFC wild-card playoffs
Green Bay 28 at Detroit 24
N.Y. Giants 17 vs. Minnesota 10

NFC divisional playoffs
San Francisco 44 vs. N.Y. Giants 3
Dallas 27 vs. Green Bay 17

NFC championship
Dallas 38 vs. San Francisco 21

Super Bowl 28
Dallas 30 vs. Buffalo 13, at Atlanta.

1994

AMERICAN CONFERENCE

EASTERN DIVISION

Team	W	L	T	Pct.	PF	PA
Miami*	10	6	0	.625	389	327
New England†	10	6	0	.625	351	312
Indianapolis	8	8	0	.500	307	320
Buffalo	7	9	0	.438	340	356
N.Y. Jets	6	10	0	.375	264	320

CENTRAL DIVISION

Team	W	L	T	Pct.	PF	PA
Pittsburgh*	12	4	0	.750	316	234
Cleveland†	11	5	0	.688	340	204
Cincinnati	3	13	0	.188	276	406
Houston	2	14	0	.125	226	352

WESTERN DIVISION

Team	W	L	T	Pct.	PF	PA
San Diego*	11	5	0	.688	381	306
Kansas City†	9	7	0	.563	319	298
L.A. Raiders	9	7	0	.563	303	327
Denver	7	9	0	.438	347	396
Seattle	6	10	0	.375	287	323

*Division champion.
†Wild-card team.

NATIONAL CONFERENCE

EASTERN DIVISION

Team	W	L	T	Pct.	PF	PA
Dallas*	12	4	0	.750	414	248
N.Y. Giants	9	7	0	.563	279	305
Arizona	8	8	0	.500	235	267
Philadelphia	7	9	0	.438	308	308
Washington	3	13	0	.188	320	412

CENTRAL DIVISION

Team	W	L	T	Pct.	PF	PA
Minnesota*	10	6	0	.625	356	314
Detroit†	9	7	0	.563	357	342
Green Bay†	9	7	0	.563	382	287
Chicago†	9	7	0	.563	271	307
Tampa Bay	6	10	0	.375	251	351

WESTERN DIVISION

Team	W	L	T	Pct.	PF	PA
San Francisco*	13	3	0	.813	505	296
New Orleans	7	9	0	.438	348	407
Atlanta	7	9	0	.438	313	389
L.A. Rams	4	12	0	.250	286	365

PLAYOFFS

AFC wild-card playoffs
Miami 27 vs. Kansas City 17
Cleveland 20 vs. New England 13

AFC divisional playoffs
Pittsburgh 29 vs. Cleveland 9
San Diego 22 vs. Miami 21

AFC championship
San Diego 17 at Pittsburgh 13

NFC wild-card playoffs
Green Bay 16 vs. Detroit 12
Chicago 35 at Minnesota 18

NFC divisional playoffs
San Francisco 44 vs. Chicago 15
Dallas 35 vs. Green Bay 9

NFC championship
San Francisco 38 vs. Dallas 28

Super Bowl 29
San Francisco 49 vs. San Diego 26 at Miami.

MONTANA IN THE MIDWEST

Although he was unable to take the Chiefs to the same heights he did the San Francisco 49ers a decade earlier, Joe Montana closed out his illustrious career with two relatively productive, if injury plagued, seasons in Kansas City. Montana, who never completely recovered from injuries suffered in the 1990 NFC title game against the Giants (broken right hand, bruised sternum) that forced him to miss the entire 1991 season and all but one game in '92, played only 38 of 64 quarters for the Chiefs in 1993. Nevertheless, he was the AFC's No. 2-rated quarterback and guided Kansas City to within one game of the Super Bowl. Using the old Montana magic, he spearheaded come-from-behind playoff victories over the Steelers and Oilers before the Chiefs finally succumbed, 30-13, at Buffalo in the AFC championship game.

AMERICAN CONFERENCE

EASTERN DIVISION

	W	L	T	Pct.	Pts.	Opp.
Buffalo*	10	6	0	.625	350	335
Indianapolis†	9	7	0	.563	331	316
Miami†	9	7	0	.563	398	332
New England	6	10	0	.375	294	377
N.Y. Jets	3	13	0	.188	233	384

CENTRAL DIVISION

	W	L	T	Pct.	Pts.	Opp.
Pittsburgh*	11	5	0	.689	407	327
Cincinnati	7	9	0	.438	349	374
Houston	7	9	0	.438	348	324
Cleveland	5	11	0	.313	289	356
Jacksonville	4	12	0	.250	275	404

WESTERN DIVISION

	W	L	T	Pct.	Pts.	Opp.
Kansas City*	13	3	0	.813	358	241
San Diego†	9	7	0	.563	321	323
Seattle	8	8	0	.500	363	366
Denver	8	8	0	.500	388	345
Oakland	8	8	0	.500	348	332

*Division champion.
†Wild-card team.

NATIONAL CONFERENCE

EASTERN DIVISION

	W	L	T	Pct.	Pts.	Opp.
Dallas*	12	4	0	.750	435	291
Philadelphia†	10	6	0	.625	318	338
Washington	6	10	0	.375	326	359
N.Y. Giants	5	11	0	.313	290	340
Arizona	4	12	0	.250	275	422

CENTRAL DIVISION

	W	L	T	Pct.	Pts.	Opp.
Green Bay*	11	5	0	.689	404	314
Detroit†	10	6	0	.625	436	336
Chicago	9	7	0	.563	392	360
Minnesota	8	8	0	.500	412	385
Tampa Bay	7	9	0	.438	238	335

WESTERN DIVISION

	W	L	T	Pct.	Pts.	Opp.
San Francisco*	11	5	0	.688	457	258
Atlanta†	9	7	0	.563	362	349
St. Louis	7	9	0	.438	309	418
Carolina	7	9	0	.438	289	325
New Orleans	7	9	0	.438	319	348

PLAYOFFS

AFC wild-card playoffs
Buffalo 37 vs. Miami 22
Indianapolis 35 at San Diego 20

AFC divisional playoffs
Pittsburgh 40 vs. Buffalo 21
Indianapolis 10 at Kansas City 7

AFC championship
Pittsburgh 20 vs. Indianapolis 16

NFC wild-card playoffs
Philadelphia 58 vs. Detroit 37
Green Bay 37 vs. Atlanta 20

NFC divisional playoffs
Green Bay 27 at San Francisco 17
Dallas 30 vs. Philadelphia 11

NFC championship
Dallas 38 vs. Green Bay 27

Super Bowl 30
Dallas 27 vs Pittsburgh 17, at Tempe, Ariz.

HISTORY *Year-by-year standings*

AMERICAN CONFERENCE

EASTERN DIVISION

	W	L	T	Pct.	Pts.	Opp.
New England*	11	5	0	.687	418	313
Buffalo†	10	6	0	.625	319	266
Indianapolis†	9	7	0	.563	317	334
Miami	8	8	0	.500	339	325
N.Y. Jets	1	15	0	.063	279	454

CENTRAL DIVISION

	W	L	T	Pct.	Pts.	Opp.
Pittsburgh*	10	6	0	.625	344	257
Jacksonville†	9	7	0	.563	325	335
Cincinnati	8	8	0	.500	372	369
Houston	8	8	0	.500	345	319
Baltimore	4	12	0	.250	371	441

WESTERN DIVISION

	W	L	T	Pct.	Pts.	Opp.
Denver*	13	3	0	.813	391	275
Kansas City	9	7	0	.563	297	300
San Diego	8	8	0	.500	310	376
Oakland	7	9	0	.438	340	293
Seattle	7	9	0	.438	317	376

*Division champion.
†Wild-card team.

NATIONAL CONFERENCE

EASTERN DIVISION

	W	L	T	Pct.	Pts.	Opp.
Dallas*	10	6	0	.625	286	250
Philadelphia†	10	6	0	.625	363	341
Washington	9	7	0	.563	364	312
Arizona	7	9	0	.438	300	397
N.Y. Giants	6	10	0	.375	242	297

CENTRAL DIVISION

	W	L	T	Pct.	Pts.	Opp.
Green Bay*	13	3	0	.813	456	210
Minnesota†	9	7	0	.563	298	315
Chicago	7	9	0	.438	283	305
Tampa Bay	6	10	0	.375	221	293
Detroit	5	11	0	.313	302	368

WESTERN DIVISION

	W	L	T	Pct.	Pts.	Opp.
Carolina*	12	4	0	.750	367	218
San Francisco†	12	4	0	.750	398	257
St. Louis	6	10	0	.375	303	409
Atlanta	3	13	0	.188	309	465
New Orleans	3	13	0	.188	229	339

PLAYOFFS

AFC wild-card playoffs
Jacksonville 30, Buffalo 27
Pittsburgh 42, Indianapolis 14

AFC divisional playoffs
Jacksonville 30, Denver 27
New England 28, Pittsburgh 3

AFC championship
New England 20, Jacksonville 16

NFC wild-card playoffs
Dallas 40, Minnesota 15
San Francisco 14, Philadelphia 0

NFC divisional playoffs
Green Bay 35, San Francisco 14
Carolina 26, Dallas 17

NFC championship
Green Bay 30, Carolina 13

Super Bowl 31
Green Bay 35, New England 21, at New Orleans.

LOMBARDI WOULD BE PROUD

Six coaches and 29 years after last winning the Super Bowl, the Green Bay Packers were NFL champions again following a 35-21 victory over New England in Super Bowl 31. The title was not unexpected, despite the many years that had passed since the franchise's last title in Vince Lombardi's final season as coach. The Packers scored the most points of any team and allowed the fewest en route to finishing the 1996 regular season at 13-3. They had the league's best player in quarterback Brett Favre and arguably its best coach (Mike Holmgren) and best general manager (Ron Wolf). Just as important, the '96 Packers were a playoff-hardened team, having lost to Dallas in the NFC title game the previous year and been ousted in the second round in each of the two seasons before that.

1997

AMERICAN CONFERENCE

EASTERN DIVISION

	W	L	T	Pct.	Pts.	Opp.
New England*	10	6	0	.625	369	289
Miami†	9	7	0	.563	339	327
N.Y. Jets	9	7	0	.563	348	287
Buffalo	6	10	0	.375	255	367
Indianapolis	3	13	0	.188	313	401

CENTRAL DIVISION

	W	L	T	Pct.	Pts.	Opp.
Pittsburgh*	11	5	0	.688	372	307
Jacksonville†	11	5	0	.688	394	318
Tennessee	8	8	0	.500	333	310
Cincinnati	7	9	0	.438	355	405
Baltimore	6	9	1	.406	326	345

WESTERN DIVISION

	W	L	T	Pct.	Pts.	Opp.
Kansas City*	13	3	0	.813	375	232
Denver†	12	4	0	.750	472	287
Seattle	8	8	0	.500	365	362
Oakland	4	12	0	.250	324	419
San Diego	4	12	0	.250	266	425

*Division champion.
†Wild-card team.

NATIONAL CONFERENCE

EASTERN DIVISION

	W	L	T	Pct.	Pts.	Opp.
N.Y. Giants*	10	5	1	.656	307	265
Washington	8	7	1	.531	327	289
Philadelphia	6	9	1	.406	317	372
Dallas	6	10	0	.375	304	314
Arizona	4	12	0	.250	283	379

CENTRAL DIVISION

	W	L	T	Pct.	Pts.	Opp.
Green Bay*	13	3	0	.813	422	282
Tampa Bay†	10	6	0	.625	299	263
Detroit†	9	7	0	.563	379	306
Minnesota†	9	7	0	.563	354	359
Chicago	4	12	0	.250	263	421

WESTERN DIVISION

	W	L	T	Pct.	Pts.	Opp.
San Francisco*	13	3	0	.813	375	265
Carolina	7	9	0	.438	265	314
Atlanta	7	9	0	.438	320	361
New Orleans	6	10	0	.375	237	327
St. Louis	5	11	0	.313	299	359

PLAYOFFS

AFC wild-card playoffs
Denver 42, Jacksonville 17
New England 17, Miami 3
AFC divisional playoffs
Pittsburgh 7, New England 6
Denver 14, Kansas City 10
AFC championship
Denver 24, Pittsburgh 21
NFC wild-card playoffs
Minnesota 23, N.Y. Giants 22
Tampa Bay 20, Detroit 10
NFC divisional playoffs
San Francisco 38, Minnesota 22
Green Bay 21, Tampa Bay 7
NFC championship
Green Bay 23, San Francisco 10
Super Bowl 32
Denver 31, Green Bay 24, at San Diego.

1998

AMERICAN CONFERENCE

EASTERN DIVISION

	W	L	T	Pct.	Pts.	Opp.
N.Y. Jets*	12	4	0	.750	416	266
Buffalo†	10	6	0	.625	400	333
Miami†	10	6	0	.625	321	265
New England†	9	7	0	.563	337	329
Indianapolis	3	13	0	.188	310	444

CENTRAL DIVISION

	W	L	T	Pct.	Pts.	Opp.
Jacksonville*	11	5	0	.688	392	338
Tennessee	8	8	0	.500	330	320
Pittsburgh	7	9	0	.438	263	303
Baltimore	6	10	0	.375	269	335
Cincinnati	3	13	0	.188	268	452

WESTERN DIVISION

	W	L	T	Pct.	Pts.	Opp.
Denver*	14	2	0	.875	501	309
Oakland	8	8	0	.500	288	356
Seattle	8	8	0	.500	372	310
Kansas City	7	9	0	.438	327	363
San Diego	5	11	0	.313	241	342

*Division champion.
†Wild-card team.

NATIONAL CONFERENCE

EASTERN DIVISION

	W	L	T	Pct.	Pts.	Opp.
Dallas*	10	6	0	.625	381	275
Arizona†	9	7	0	.563	325	378
N.Y. Giants	8	8	0	.500	287	309
Washington	6	10	0	.375	319	421
Philadelphia	3	13	0	.188	161	344

CENTRAL DIVISION

	W	L	T	Pct.	Pts.	Opp.
Minnesota*	15	1	0	.938	556	296
Green Bay†	11	5	0	.688	408	319
Tampa Bay	8	8	0	.500	314	295
Detroit	5	11	0	.313	306	378
Chicago	4	12	0	.250	276	368

WESTERN DIVISION

	W	L	T	Pct.	Pts.	Opp.
Atlanta*	14	2	0	.875	442	289
San Francisco†	12	4	0	.750	479	328
New Orleans	6	10	0	.375	305	359
Carolina	4	12	0	.250	336	413
St. Louis	4	12	0	.250	285	378

PLAYOFFS

AFC wild-card playoffs
Miami 24, Buffalo 17
Jacksonville 25, New England 10
AFC divisional playoffs
Denver 38, Miami 3
New York Jets 34, Jacksonville 24
AFC championship
Denver 23, New York Jets 10
NFC wild-card playoffs
Arizona 20, Dallas 7
San Francisco 30, Green Bay 27
NFC divisional playoffs
Atlanta 20, San Francisco 18
Minnesota 41, Arizona 21
NFC championship
Atlanta 30, Minnesota 27 (OT)
Super Bowl 33
Denver 34, Atlanta 19, at Miami.

ELWAY, BRONCOS REACH THE TOP

One year after a humbling first-round playoff loss at home to Jacksonville, the Denver Broncos made sure history did not repeat, whipping the Jaguars, 42-17, in a first-round rematch at Mile High Stadium. That was impressive, but what happened next was more impressive: three straight road playoff victories and the franchise's first-ever Super Bowl title. Prior to the three-game winning streak, the Broncos had won just one other road playoff game in their 37-year history. Although running back Terrell Davis was the Broncos' star and won Super Bowl 32 MVP honors, their leader was veteran quarterback John Elway, who finally scaled the NFL mountaintop after three crushing Super Bowl defeats earlier in his career. Denver thus became the first AFC team in 14 years and only the second wild-card team to win the Super Bowl.

AMERICAN CONFERENCE

EASTERN DIVISION

	W	L	T	Pct.	Pts.	Opp.
Indianapolis*	13	3	0	.813	423	333
Buffalo†	11	5	0	.688	320	229
Miami†	9	7	0	.563	326	336
N.Y. Jets	8	8	0	.500	308	309
New England	8	8	0	.500	299	284

CENTRAL DIVISION

	W	L	T	Pct.	Pts.	Opp.
Jacksonville*	14	2	0	.875	396	217
Tennessee†	13	3	0	.813	392	324
Baltimore	8	8	0	.500	324	277
Pittsburgh	6	10	0	.375	317	320
Cincinnati	4	12	0	.250	283	460
Cleveland	2	14	0	.125	217	437

WESTERN DIVISION

	W	L	T	Pct.	Pts.	Opp.
Seattle*	9	7	0	.563	338	298
Kansas City	9	7	0	.563	390	322
San Diego	8	8	0	.500	269	316
Oakland	8	8	0	.500	390	329
Denver	6	10	0	.375	314	318

*Division champion.
†Wild-card team.

NATIONAL CONFERENCE

EASTERN DIVISION

	W	L	T	Pct.	Pts.	Opp.
Washington*	10	6	0	.625	443	377
Dallas†	8	8	0	.500	352	276
N.Y. Giants	7	9	0	.438	299	358
Arizona	6	10	0	.375	245	382
Philadelphia	5	11	0	.313	272	357

CENTRAL DIVISION

	W	L	T	Pct.	Pts.	Opp.
Tampa Bay*	11	5	0	.688	270	235
Minnesota†	10	6	0	.625	399	335
Detroit†	8	8	0	.500	322	323
Green Bay	8	8	0	.500	357	341
Chicago	6	10	0	.375	272	341

WESTERN DIVISION

	W	L	T	Pct.	Pts.	Opp.
St. Louis*	13	3	0	.813	526	242
Carolina	8	8	0	.500	421	381
Atlanta	5	11	0	.313	285	380
San Francisco	4	12	0	.250	295	453
New Orleans	3	13	0	.188	260	434

PLAYOFFS

AFC wild-card playoffs
Miami 20, Seattle 17
Tennessee 22, Buffalo 16
AFC divisional playoffs
Tennessee 19, Indianapolis 16
Jacksonville 62, Miami 7
AFC championship
Tennessee 33, Jacksonville 14
NFC wild-card playoffs
Minnesota 27, Dallas 10
Washington 27, Detroit 13
NFC divisional playoffs
St. Louis 49, Minnesota 37
Tampa Bay 14, Washington 13
NFC championship
St. Louis 11, Tampa Bay 6
Super Bowl 34
St. Louis 23, Tennessee 16

In perhaps the most dramatic final play in Super Bowl history, Rams linebacker Mike Jones preserves St. Louis' 23-16 victory in Super Bowl 34 by tackling Tennessee receiver Kevin Dyson a yard short of the end zone. (Photo by Dilip Vishwanat/The Sporting News.)

SUPER BOWLS

SUMMARIES

SUPER BOWL 1
JANUARY 15, 1967, AT LOS ANGELES

Kansas City (AFL)	0	10	0	0 — 10
Green Bay (NFL)	7	7	14	7 — 35

Winning coach—Vince Lombardi.
Most Valuable Player—Bart Starr.
Attendance—61,946.

SUPER BOWL 2
JANUARY 14, 1968, AT MIAMI

Green Bay (NFL)	3	13	10	7 — 33
Oakland (AFL)	0	7	0	7 — 14

Winning coach—Vince Lombardi.
Most Valuable Player—Bart Starr.
Attendance—75,546.

SUPER BOWL 3
JANUARY 12, 1969, AT MIAMI

New York (AFL)	0	7	6	3 — 16
Baltimore (NFL)	0	0	0	7 — 7

Winning coach—Weeb Ewbank.
Most Valuable Player—Joe Namath.
Attendance—75,389.

SUPER BOWL 4
JANUARY 11, 1970, AT NEW ORLEANS

Minnesota (NFL)	0	0	7	0 — 7
Kansas City (AFL)	3	13	7	0 — 23

Winning coach—Hank Stram.
Most Valuable Player—Len Dawson.
Attendance—80,562.

SUPER BOWL 5
JANUARY 17, 1971, AT MIAMI

Baltimore (AFC)	0	6	0	10 — 16
Dallas (NFC)	3	10	0	0 — 13

Winning coach—Don McCafferty.
Most Valuable Player—Chuck Howley.
Attendance—79,204.

SUPER BOWL 6
JANUARY 16, 1972, AT NEW ORLEANS

Dallas (NFC)	3	7	7	7 — 24
Miami (AFC)	0	3	0	0 — 3

Winning coach—Tom Landry.
Most Valuable Player—Roger Staubach.
Attendance—81,023.

SUPER BOWL 7
JANUARY 14, 1973, AT LOS ANGELES

Miami (AFC)	7	7	0	0 — 14
Washington (NFC)	0	0	0	7 — 7

Winning coach—Don Shula.
Most Valuable Player—Jake Scott.
Attendance—90,182.

SUPER BOWL 8
JANUARY 13, 1974, AT HOUSTON

Minnesota (NFC)	0	0	0	7 — 7
Miami (AFC)	14	3	7	0 — 24

Winning coach—Don Shula.
Most Valuable Player—Larry Csonka.
Attendance—71,882.

SUPER BOWL 9
JANUARY 12, 1975, AT NEW ORLEANS

Pittsburgh (AFC)	0	2	7	7 — 16
Minnesota (NFC)	0	0	0	6 — 6

Winning coach—Chuck Noll.
Most Valuable Player—Franco Harris.
Attendance—80,997.

SUPER BOWL 10
JANUARY 18, 1976, AT MIAMI

Dallas (NFC)	7	3	0	7 — 17
Pittsburgh (AFC)	7	0	0	14 — 21

Winning coach—Chuck Noll.
Most Valuable Player—Lynn Swann.
Attendance—80,187.

SUPER BOWL 11
JANUARY 9, 1977, AT PASADENA, CALIF.

Oakland (AFC)	0	16	3	13 — 32
Minnesota (NFC)	0	0	7	7 — 14

Winning coach—John Madden.
Most Valuable Player—Fred Biletnikoff.
Attendance—103,428.

SUPER BOWL 12
JANUARY 15, 1978, AT NEW ORLEANS

Dallas (NFC)	10	3	7	7 — 27
Denver (AFC)	0	0	10	0 — 10

Winning coach—Tom Landry.
Most Valuable Players—Harvey Martin and Randy White.
Attendance—75,804.

SUPER BOWL 13
JANUARY 21, 1979, AT MIAMI

Pittsburgh (AFC)	7	14	0	14 — 35
Dallas (NFC)	7	7	3	14 — 31

Winning coach—Chuck Noll.
Most Valuable Player—Terry Bradshaw.
Attendance—78,656.

SUPER BOWL 14
JANUARY 20, 1980, PASADENA, CALIF.

Los Angeles (NFC)	7	6	6	0 — 19
Pittsburgh (AFC)	3	7	7	14 — 31

Winning coach—Chuck Noll.
Most Valuable Player—Terry Bradshaw.
Attendance—103,985.

SUPER BOWL 15
JANUARY 25, 1981, AT NEW ORLEANS

Oakland (AFC)	14	0	10	3 — 27
Philadelphia (NFC)	0	3	0	7 — 10

Winning coach—Tom Flores.
Most Valuable Player—Jim Plunkett.
Attendance—75,500.

SUPER BOWL 16
JANUARY 24, 1982, AT PONTIAC, MICH.

San Francisco (NFC)	7	13	0	6 — 26
Cincinnati (AFC)	0	0	7	14 — 21

Winning coach—Bill Walsh.
Most Valuable Player—Joe Montana.
Attendance—81,270.

SUPER BOWL 17
JANUARY 30, 1983, AT PASADENA, CALIF.

Miami (AFC)	7	10	0	0 — 17
Washington (NFC)	0	10	3	14 — 27

Winning coach—Joe Gibbs.
Most Valuable Player—John Riggins.
Attendance—103,667.

SUPER BOWL 18
JANUARY 22, 1984, AT TAMPA

Washington (NFC)	0	3	6	0 — 9
Los Angeles (AFC)	7	14	14	3 — 38

Winning coach—Tom Flores.
Most Valuable Player—Marcus Allen.
Attendance—72,920.

SUPER BOWL 19
JANUARY 20, 1985, AT PALO ALTO, CALIF.
Miami (AFC)	10	6	0	0 — 16
San Francisco (NFC)	7	21	10	0 — 38

Winning coach—Bill Walsh.
Most Valuable Player—Joe Montana.
Attendance—84,059.

SUPER BOWL 20
JANUARY 26, 1986, AT NEW ORLEANS
Chicago (NFC)	13	10	21	2 — 46
New England (AFC)	3	0	0	7 — 10

Winning coach—MIke Ditka.
Most Valuable—Richard Dent.
Attendance—73,818.

SUPER BOWL 21
JANUARY 25, 1987, AT PASADENA, CALIF.
Denver (AFC)	10	0	0	10 — 20
N.Y. Giants (NFC)	7	2	17	13 — 39

Winning coach—Bill Parcells.
Most Valuable Player—Phil Simms.
Attendance—101,063.

SUPER BOWL 22
JANUARY 31, 1988, AT SAN DIEGO
Washington (NFC)	0	35	0	7 — 42
Denver (AFC)	10	0	0	0 — 10

Winning coach—Joe Gibbs.
Most Valuable Player—Doug Williams.
Attendance—73,302.

SUPER BOWL 23
JANUARY 22, 1989, AT MIAMI
Cincinnati (AFC)	0	3	10	3 — 16
San Francisco (NFC)	3	0	3	14 — 20

Winning coach—Bill Walsh.
Most Valuable Player—Jerry Rice.
Attendance—75,179.

SUPER BOWL 24
JANUARY 28, 1990, AT NEW ORLEANS
San Francisco (NFC)	13	14	14	14 — 55
Denver (AFC)	3	0	7	0 — 10

Winning coach—George Seifert.
Most Valuable Player—Joe Montana.
Attendance—72,919.

SUPER BOWL 25
JANUARY 27, 1991, AT TAMPA
Buffalo (AFC)	3	9	0	7 — 19
New York (NFC)	3	7	7	3 — 20

Winning coach—Bill Parcells.
Most Valuable Player—Ottis Anderson.
Attendance—73,813.

SUPER BOWL 26
JANUARY 26, 1992, AT MINNEAPOLIS
Washington (NFC)	0	17	14	6 — 37
Buffalo (AFC)	0	0	10	14 — 24

Winning coach—Joe Gibbs.
Most Valuable Player—Mark Rypien.
Attendance—63,130.

SUPER BOWL 27
JANUARY 31, 1993, AT PASADENA, CALIF.
Buffalo (AFC)	7	3	7	0 — 17
Dallas (NFC)	14	14	3	21 — 52

Winning coach—Jimmy Johnson.
Most Valuable Player—Troy Aikman.
Attendance—98,374.

SUPER BOWL 28
JANUARY 30, 1994, AT ATLANTA, GA.
Dallas (NFC)	6	0	14	10 — 30
Buffalo (AFC)	3	10	0	0 — 13

Winning coach—Jimmy Johnson.
Most Valuable Player—Emmitt Smith.
Attendance—72,817.

SUPER BOWL 29
JANUARY 29, 1995, AT MIAMI, FLA.
San Diego (AFC)	7	3	8	8 — 26
San Francisco (NFC)	14	14	14	7 — 49

Winning coach—George Seifert.
Most Valuable Player—Steve Young.
Attendance—74,107.

SUPER BOWL 30
JANUARY 28, 1996, AT TEMPE, ARIZ.
Dallas (NFC)	10	3	7	7 — 27
Pittsburgh (AFC)	0	7	0	10 — 17

Winning coach—Barry Switzer.
Most Valuable Player—Larry Brown.
Attendance—76,347.

SUPER BOWL 31
JANUARY 26, 1997, AT NEW ORLEANS
New England (AFC)	14	0	7	0 — 21
Green Bay (NFC)	10	17	8	0 — 35

Winning coach—Mike Holmgren.
Most Valuable Player—Desmond Howard.
Attendance—72,301.

SUPER BOWL 32
JANUARY 25, 1998, AT SAN DIEGO
Green Bay (NFC)	7	7	3	7 — 24
Denver (AFC)	7	10	7	7 — 31

Winning coach—Mike Shanahan.
Most Valuable Player—Terrell Davis.
Attendance—68,912.

SUPER BOWL 33
JANUARY 31, 1999, AT MIAMI
Denver (AFC)	7	10	0	17 — 34
Atlanta (NFC)	3	3	0	13 — 19

Winning coach—Mike Shanahan.
Most Valuable Player—John Elway.
Attendance—74,803.

SUPER BOWL 34
JANUARY 30, 2000, AT ATLANTA
St. Louis (NFC)	3	6	7	7 — 23
Tennessee (AFC)	0	0	6	10 — 16

Winning coach—Dick Vermeil.
Most Valuable Player—Kurt Warner.
Attendance—72,625.

SUPER BOWL 35
JANUARY 28, 2001, AT TAMPA
Baltimore (AFC)	7	3	14	10 — 34
N.Y. Giants (NFC)	0	0	7	0 — 7

Winning coach—Brian Billick.
Most Valuable Player—Ray Lewis.
Attendance—71,921.

PRO BOWLS

RESULTS

Date	Site	Winning team, score	Losing team, score	Att.
1-15-39	Wrigley Field, Los Angeles	New York Giants, 13	Pro All-Stars, 10	†20,000
1-14-40	Gilmore Stadium, Los Angeles	Green Bay Packers, 16	NFL All-Stars, 7	†18,000
12-29-40	Gilmore Stadium, Los Angeles	Chicago Bears, 28	NFL All-Stars, 14	21,624
1-4-42	Polo Grounds, New York	Chicago Bears, 35	NFL All-Stars, 24	17,725
12-27-42	Shibe Park, Philadelphia	NFL All-Stars, 17	Washington Redskins, 14	18,671
1943-50	No game was played.			
1-14-51	Los Angeles Memorial Coliseum	American Conference, 28	National Conference, 27	53,676
1-12-52	Los Angeles Memorial Coliseum	National Conference, 30	American Conference, 13	19,400
1-10-53	Los Angeles Memorial Coliseum	National Conference, 27	American Conference, 7	34,208
1-17-54	Los Angeles Memorial Coliseum	East, 20	West, 9	44,214
1-16-55	Los Angeles Memorial Coliseum	West, 26	East, 19	43,972
1-15-56	Los Angeles Memorial Coliseum	East, 31	West, 30	37,867
1-13-57	Los Angeles Memorial Coliseum	West, 19	East, 10	44,177
1-12-58	Los Angeles Memorial Coliseum	West, 26	East, 7	66,634
1-11-59	Los Angeles Memorial Coliseum	East, 28	West, 21	72,250
1-17-60	Los Angeles Memorial Coliseum	West, 38	East, 21	56,876
1-15-61	Los Angeles Memorial Coliseum	West, 35	East, 31	62,971
1-7-62*	Balboa Stadium, San Diego	West, 47	East, 27	20,973
1-14-62	Los Angeles Memorial Coliseum	West, 31	East, 30	57,409
1-13-63*	Balboa Stadium, San Diego	West, 21	East, 14	27,641
1-13-63	Los Angeles Memorial Coliseum	East, 30	West, 20	61,374
1-12-64	Los Angeles Memorial Coliseum	West, 31	East, 17	67,242
1-19-64*	Balboa Stadium, San Diego	West, 27	East, 24	20,016
1-10-65	Los Angeles Memorial Coliseum	West, 34	East, 14	60,598
1-16-65*	Jeppesen Stadium, Houston	West, 38	East, 14	15,446
1-15-66*	Rice Stadium, Houston	AFL All-Stars, 30	Buffalo Bills, 19	35,572
1-15-66	Los Angeles Memorial Coliseum	East, 36	West, 7	60,124
1-21-67*	Oakland-Alameda County Coliseum	East, 30	West, 23	18,876
1-22-67	Los Angeles Memorial Coliseum	East, 20	West, 10	15,062
1-21-68*	Gator Bowl, Jacksonville, Fla.	East, 25	West, 24	40,103
1-21-68	Los Angeles Memorial Coliseum	West, 38	East, 20	53,289
1-19-69*	Gator Bowl, Jacksonville, Fla.	West, 38	East, 25	41,058
1-19-69	Los Angeles Memorial Coliseum	West, 10	East, 7	32,050
1-17-70*	Astrodome, Houston	West, 26	East, 3	30,170
1-18-70	Los Angeles Memorial Coliseum	West, 16	East, 13	57,786
1-24-71	Los Angeles Memorial Coliseum	NFC, 27	AFC, 6	48,222
1-23-72	Los Angeles Memorial Coliseum	AFC, 26	NFC, 13	53,647
1-21-73	Texas Stadium, Irving	AFC, 33	NFC, 28	37,091
1-20-74	Arrowhead Stadium, Kansas City	AFC, 15	NFC, 13	66,918
1-20-75	Orange Bowl, Miami	NFC, 17	AFC, 10	26,484
1-26-76	Louisiana Superdome, New Orleans	NFC, 23	AFC, 20	30,546
1-17-77	Kingdome, Seattle	AFC, 24	NFC, 14	64,752
1-23-78	Tampa Stadium	NFC, 14	AFC, 13	51,337
1-29-79	Los Angeles Memorial Coliseum	NFC, 13	AFC, 7	46,281
1-27-80	Aloha Stadium, Honolulu	NFC, 37	AFC, 27	49,800
2-1-81	Aloha Stadium, Honolulu	NFC, 21	AFC, 7	50,360
1-31-82	Aloha Stadium, Honolulu	AFC, 16	NFC, 13	50,402
2-6-83	Aloha Stadium, Honolulu	NFC, 20	AFC, 19	49,883
1-29-84	Aloha Stadium, Honolulu	NFC, 45	AFC, 3	50,445
1-27-85	Aloha Stadium, Honolulu	AFC, 22	NFC, 14	50,385
2-2-86	Aloha Stadium, Honolulu	NFC, 28	AFC, 24	50,101
2-1-87	Aloha Stadium, Honolulu	AFC, 10	NFC, 6	50,101
2-7-88	Aloha Stadium, Honolulu	AFC, 15	NFC, 6	50,113
1-29-89	Aloha Stadium, Honolulu	NFC, 34	AFC, 3	50,113
2-4-90	Aloha Stadium, Honolulu	NFC, 27	AFC, 21	50,445
2-3-91	Aloha Stadium, Honolulu	AFC, 23	NFC, 21	50,345
2-2-92	Aloha Stadium, Honolulu	NFC, 21	AFC, 15	50,209
2-7-93	Aloha Stadium, Honolulu	AFC, 23 (OT)	NFC, 20	50,007
2-6-94	Aloha Stadium, Honolulu	NFC, 17	AFC, 3	50,026
2-5-95	Aloha Stadium, Honolulu	AFC, 41	NFC, 13	49,121
2-4-96	Aloha Stadium, Honolulu	NFC, 20	AFC, 13	50,034
2-2-97	Aloha Stadium, Honolulu	AFC, 26 (OT)	NFC, 23	50,031
2-1-98	Aloha Stadium, Honolulu	AFC, 29	NFC, 24	49,995
2-7-99	Aloha Stadium, Honolulu	AFC, 23	NFC, 10	50,075
2-6-00	Aloha Stadium, Honolulu	NFC, 51	AFC, 31	50,112
2-4-01	Aloha Stadium, Honolulu	AFC, 38	NFC, 17	50,128

*AFL game.
†Estimated figure.

Year—Name, team

1951— Otto Graham, Cleveland Browns
1952— Dan Towler, Los Angeles Rams
1953— Dan Doll, Detroit Lions
1954— Chuck Bednarik, Philadelphia Eagles
1955— Billy Wilson, San Francisco 49ers
1956— Ollie Matson, Chicago Cardinals
1957— Bert Rechichar, Baltimore Colts (back)
　　　 Ernie Stautner, Pittsburgh Steelers (lineman)
1958— Hugh McElhenny, San Francisco 49ers (back)
　　　 Gene Brito, Washington Redskins (lineman)
1959— Frank Gifford, New York Giants (back)
　　　 Doug Atkins, Chicago Bears (lineman)
1960— Johnny Unitas, Baltimore Colts (back)
　　　 Gene Lipscomb, Baltimore Colts (lineman)
1961— Johnny Unitas, Baltimore Colts (back)
　　　 Sam Huff, New York Giants (lineman)
1962— Cotton Davidson, Dallas Texans*
　　　 Jim Brown, Cleveland Browns (back)
　　　 Henry Jordan, Green Bay Packers (lineman)
1963— Curtis McClinton, Dallas Texans* (offense)
　　　 Earl Faison, San Diego Chargers* (defense)
　　　 Jim Brown, Cleveland Browns (back)
　　　 Gene Lipscomb, Pittsburgh Steelers (lineman)
1964— Keith Lincoln, San Diego Chargers* (offense)
　　　 Archie Matsos, Oakland Raiders* (defense)
　　　 Johnny Unitas, Baltimore Colts (back)
　　　 Gino Marchetti, Baltimore Colts (lineman)
1965— Keith Lincoln, San Diego Chargers* (offense)
　　　 Willie Brown, Denver Broncos* (defense)
　　　 Fran Tarkenton, Minnesota Vikings (back)
　　　 Terry Barr, Detroit Lions (lineman)
1966— Joe Namath, New York Jets* (offense)
　　　 Frank Buncom, San Diego Chargers* (defense)
　　　 Jim Brown, Cleveland Browns (back)
　　　 Dale Meinert, St. Louis Cardinals (lineman)
1967— Babe Parilli, Boston Patriots* (offense)
　　　 Verlon Biggs, New York Jets* (defense)
　　　 Gale Sayers, Chicago Bears (back)
　　　 Floyd Peters, Philadelphia Eagles (lineman)
1968— Joe Namath, New York Jets* (offense)
　　　 Don Maynard, New York Jets* (offense)
　　　 Speedy Duncan, San Diego Chargers (defense)
　　　 Gale Sayers, Chicago Bears (back)
　　　 Dave Robinson, Green Bay Packers (lineman)

Year—Name, team

1969— Len Dawson, Kansas City Chiefs* (offense)
　　　 George Webster, Houston* (defense)
　　　 Roman Gabriel, Los Angeles Rams (back)
　　　 Merlin Olsen, Los Angeles Rams (lineman)
1970— John Hadl, San Diego Chargers*
　　　 Gale Sayers, Chicago Bears (back)
　　　 George Andrie, Dallas Cowboys (lineman)
1971— Mel Renfro, Dallas Cowboys (back)
　　　 Fred Carr, Green Bay Packers (lineman)
1972— Jan Stenerud, Kansas City Chiefs (offense)
　　　 Willie Lanier, Kansas City Chiefs (defense)
1973— O.J. Simpson, Buffalo Bills
1974— Garo Yepremian, Miami Dolphins
1975— James Harris, Los Angeles Rams
1976— Billy Johnson, Houston Oilers
1977— Mel Blount, Pittsburgh Steelers
1978— Walter Payton, Chicago Bears
1979— Ahmad Rashad, Minnesota Vikings
1980— Chuck Muncie, New Orleans Saints
1981— Eddie Murray, Detroit Lions
1982— Kellen Winslow, San Diego Chargers
　　　 Lee Roy Selmon, Tampa Bay Buccaneers
1983— Dan Fouts, San Diego Chargers
　　　 John Jefferson, Green Bay Packers
1984— Joe Theismann, Washington Redskins
1985— Mark Gastineau, New York Jets
1986— Phil Simms, New York Giants
1987— Reggie White, Philadelphia Eagles
1988— Bruce Smith, Buffalo Bills
1989— Randall Cunningham, Philadelphia Eagles
1990— Jerry Gray, Los Angeles Rams
1991— Jim Kelly, Buffalo Bills
1992— Michael Irvin, Dallas Cowboys
1993— Steve Tasker, Buffalo Bills
1994— Andre Rison, Atlanta Falcons
1995— Marshall Faulk, Indianapolis Colts
1996— Jerry Rice, San Francisco 49ers
1997— Mark Brunell, Jacksonville Jaguars
1998— Warren Moon, Seattle Seahawks
1999— Ty Law, New England Patriots
　　　 Keyshawn Johnson, New York Jets
2000— Randy Moss, Minnesota Vikings
2001— Rich Gannon, Oakland Raiders
　　　 *AFL game.

RECORDS

INDIVIDUAL SERVICE

PLAYERS

Most years played
26—George Blanda, Chicago Bears, Baltimore, Houston, Oakland, 1949 through 1975, except 1959.

Most years with one club
20—Jackie Slater, L.A. Rams, St. Louis Rams, 1976 through 1995.

Most games played, career
340—George Blanda, Chicago Bears, Baltimore, Houston, Oakland, 1949 through 1975, except 1959.

Most consecutive games played, career
282—Jim Marshall, Cleveland, Minnesota, September 25, 1960 through December 16, 1979.

COACHES

Most years as head coach
40—George Halas, Chicago Bears, 1920 through 1929, 1933 through 1942, 1946 through 1955 and 1958 through 1967.

Most games won as head coach
328—Don Shula, Baltimore, 1963 through 1969; Miami, 1970 through 1995.

Most games lost as head coach
162—Tom Landry, Dallas, 1960 through 1988.

INDIVIDUAL OFFENSE

RUSHING

YARDS

Most yards, career
16,726—Walter Payton, Chicago, 1975 through 1987.

Most yards, season
2,105—Eric Dickerson, Los Angeles Rams, 1984.

Most years leading league in yards
8—Jim Brown, Cleveland, 1957 through 1965, except 1962.

Most consecutive years leading league in yards
5—Jim Brown, Cleveland, 1957 through 1961.

Most years with 1,000 or more yards
10—Walter Payton, Chicago, 1976 through 1986, except 1982.
Barry Sanders, Detroit, 1989 through 1998.
Emmitt Smith, Dallas, 1991 through 2000.

Most consecutive years with 1,000 or more yards
10—Barry Sanders, Detroit, 1989 through 1998.
Emmitt Smith, Dallas, 1991 through 2000.

Most yards, game
278—Corey Dillon, Cincinnati vs. Denver, October 22, 2000.

Most games with 200 or more yards, career
6—O.J. Simpson, Buffalo, San Francisco, 1969 through 1979.

Most games with 200 or more yards, season
4—Earl Campbell, Houston, 1980.

Most consecutive games with 200 or more yards, season
2—O.J. Simpson, Buffalo, December 9 through 16, 1973.
O.J. Simpson, Buffalo, November 25 through December 5, 1976.
Earl Campbell, Houston, October 19 through 26, 1980.

Most games with 100 or more yards, career
77—Walter Payton, Chicago, 1975 through 1987.

Most games with 100 or more yards, season
14—Barry Sanders, Detroit, 1997.

Most consecutive games with 100 or more yards, career
14—Barry Sanders, Detroit, September 14 through December 21, 1997.

Most consecutive games with 100 or more yards, season
14—Barry Sanders, Detroit, September 14 through December 21, 1997.

Longest run from scrimmage
99 yards—Tony Dorsett, Dallas at Minnesota, January 3, 1983 (touchdown).

ATTEMPTS

Most attempts, career
3,838—Walter Payton, Chicago, 1975 through 1987.

Most attempts, season
410—Jamal Anderson, Atlanta, 1998.

Most attempts, game
45—Jamie Morris, Washington at Cincinnati, December 17, 1988, overtime.
43—Butch Woolfolk, New York Giants at Philadelphia, November 20, 1983.
James Wilder, Tampa Bay vs. Green Bay, September 30, 1984, overtime.

Most years leading league in attempts
6—Jim Brown, Cleveland, 1958 through 1965, except 1960 and 1962.

Most consecutive years leading league in attempts
4—Steve Van Buren, Philadelphia, 1947 through 1950.
Walter Payton, Chicago, 1976 through 1979.

TOUCHDOWNS

Most touchdowns, career
145—Emmitt Smith, Dallas, 1990 through 2000.

Most touchdowns, season
25—Emmitt Smith, Dallas, 1995.

Most years leading league in touchdowns
5—Jim Brown, Cleveland, 1957 through 1959, 1963, 1965.

Most consecutive years leading league in touchdowns
3—Steve Van Buren, Philadelphia, 1947 through 1949.
Jim Brown, Cleveland, 1957 through 1959.
Abner Haynes, Dallas Texans, 1960 through 1962.
Cookie Gilchrist, Buffalo, 1962 through 1964.
Leroy Kelly, Cleveland, 1966 through 1968.

Most touchdowns, game
6—Ernie Nevers, Chicago Cardinals vs. Chicago Bears, November 28, 1929.

Most consecutive games with one or more touchdowns, career
13—John Riggins, Washington, December 26, 1982 through November 27, 1983.
George Rogers, Washington, November 24, 1985 through November 2, 1986.

Most consecutive games with one or more touchdowns, season
12—John Riggins, Washington, September 5 through November 27, 1983.

PASSING

PASSER RATING

Highest rating, career (1,500 or more attempts)
96.8—Steve Young, Tampa Bay, San Francisco, 1985 through 1999.

Highest rating, season (qualifiers)
112.8—Steve Young, San Francisco, 1994.

ATTEMPTS

Most attempts, career
8,358—Dan Marino, Miami, 1983 through 1999.

Most attempts, season
691—Drew Bledsoe, New England, 1994.

Most years leading league in attempts
5—Dan Marino, Miami, 1984, 1986, 1988, 1992, 1997.

Most consecutive years leading league in attempts
3—Johnny Unitas, Baltimore, 1959 through 1961.
    George Blanda, Houston, 1963 through 1965.

Most attempts, game
70—Drew Bledsoe, New England vs. Minnesota, November 13, 1994 (overtime).
68—George Blanda, Houston vs. Buffalo, November 1, 1964.

COMPLETIONS

Most completions, career
4,967—Dan Marino, Miami, 1983 through 1999.

Most completions, season
404—Warren Moon, Houston, 1991.

Most years leading league in completions
6—Dan Marino, Miami, 1984, 1985, 1986, 1988, 1992, 1997.

Most consecutive years leading league in completions
3—George Blanda, Houston, 1963 through 1965.
    Dan Marino, Miami, 1984 through 1986.

Most completions, game
45—Drew Bledsoe, New England vs. Minnesota, November 13, 1994 (overtime).
42—Richard Todd, New York Jets vs. San Francisco, September 21, 1980.

YARDS

Most yards, career
61,361—Dan Marino, Miami, 1983 through 1999.

Most yards, season
5,084—Dan Marino, Miami, 1984.

Most years leading league in yards
5—Sonny Jurgensen, Philadelphia, Washington, 1961, 1962, 1966, 1967, 1969.
    Dan Marino, Miami, 1984 through 1986, 1988, 1992.

Most consecutive years leading league in yards
4—Dan Fouts, San Diego, 1979 through 1982.

Most years with 3,000 or more yards
13—Dan Marino, Miami, 1984 through 1998, except 1993 and 1996.

Most yards, game
554—Norm Van Brocklin, Los Angeles at New York Yanks, September 28, 1951.

Most games with 400 or more yards, career
13—Dan Marino, Miami, 1983 through 1996.

Most games with 400 or more yards, season
4—Dan Marino, Miami, 1984.

Most consecutive games with 400 or more yards, season
2—Dan Fouts, San Diego, December 11 through 20, 1982.
    Dan Marino, Miami, December 2 through 9, 1984.
    Phil Simms, New York Giants, October 6 through 13, 1985.

Most games with 300 or more yards, career
63—Dan Marino, Miami, 1983 through 1999.

Most games with 300 or more yards, season
9—Dan Marino, Miami, 1984.
    Warren Moon, Houston, 1990.
    Kurt Warner, St. Louis, 1999.

Most consecutive games with 300 or more yards, season
6—Steve Young, San Francisco, September 6 through October 18, 1998.

Longest pass completion
99 yards—Frank Filchock, Washington vs. Pittsburgh, October 15, 1939 (touchdown).

George Izo, Washington at Cleveland, September 15, 1963 (touchdown).
Karl Sweetan, Detroit at Baltimore, October 16, 1966 (touchdown).
Sonny Jurgensen, Washington at Chicago, September 15, 1968 (touchdown).
Jim Plunkett, Los Angeles Raiders vs. Washington, October 2, 1983 (touchdown).
Ron Jaworski, Philadelphia vs. Atlanta, November 10, 1985 (touchdown).
Stan Humphries, San Diego at Seattle, September 18, 1994 (touchdown).
Brett Favre, Green Bay at Chicago, September 11, 1995 (touchdown).

YARDS PER ATTEMPT

Most yards per attempt, career (1,500 or more attempts)
8.63—Otto Graham, Cleveland, 1950 through 1955 (13,499 yards, 1,565 attempts).

Most yards per attempt, season (qualifiers)
11.17—Tommy O'Connell, Cleveland, 1957 (1,229 yards, 110 attempts).

Most years leading league in yards per attempt
7—Sid Luckman, Chicago Bears, 1939 through 1943, 1946, 1947.

Most consecutive years leading league in yards per attempt
5—Sid Luckman, Chicago Bears, 1939 through 1943.

Most yards per attempt, game (20 or more attempts)
18.58—Sammy Baugh, Washington vs. Boston, October 31, 1948 (446 yards, 24 attempts).

TOUCHDOWNS

Most touchdowns, career
420—Dan Marino, Miami, 1983 through 1999.

Most touchdowns, season
48—Dan Marino, Miami, 1984.

Most years leading league in touchdowns
4—Johnny Unitas, Baltimore, 1957 through 1960.
    Len Dawson, Dallas Texans, Kansas City, 1962 through 1966, except 1964.
    Steve Young, San Francisco, 1992 through 1994, 1998.

Most consecutive years leading league in touchdowns
4—Johnny Unitas, Baltimore, 1957 through 1960.

Most touchdowns, game
7—Sid Luckman, Chicago Bears at New York Giants, November 14, 1943.
    Adrian Burk, Philadelphia at Washington, October 17, 1954.
    George Blanda, Houston vs. New York Titans, November 19, 1961.
    Y.A. Tittle, New York Giants vs. Washington, October 28, 1962.
    Joe Kapp, Minnesota vs. Baltimore, September 28, 1969.

INTERCEPTIONS

Most interceptions, career
277—George Blanda, Chicago Bears, Baltimore, Houston, Oakland, 1949 through 1975, except 1959.

Most interceptions, season
42—George Blanda, Houston, 1962.

Most interceptions, game
8—Jim Hardy, Chicago Cardinals vs. Philadelphia, September 24, 1950.

Most attempts with no interceptions, game
70—Drew Bledsoe, New England vs. Minnesota, November 13, 1994 (overtime).
63—Rich Gannon, Minnesota at New England, October 20, 1991 (overtime).
60—Davey O'Brien, Philadelphia at Washington, December 1, 1940.

INTERCEPTION PERCENTAGE

Lowest interception percentage, career (1,500 or more attempts)
2.08—Neil O'Donnell, Pittsburgh, N.Y. Jets, Cincinnati, Tennessee, 1991 through 2000 (3,121 attempts, 65 interceptions).

Lowest interception percentage, season (qualifiers)
0.66—Joe Ferguson, Buffalo, 1976 (151 attempts, one interception).

Most years leading league in lowest interception percentage
5—Sammy Baugh, Washington, 1940, 1942, 1944, 1945, 1947.

SACKS (SINCE 1963)

Most times sacked, career
516—John Elway, Denver, 1983 through 1998.

Most times sacked, season
72—Randall Cunningham, Philadelphia, 1986.

Most times sacked, game
12—Bert Jones, Baltimore vs. St. Louis, October 26, 1980.
Warren Moon, Houston vs. Dallas, September 29, 1985.

RECEIVING

RECEPTIONS

Most receptions, career
1,281—Jerry Rice, San Francisco, 1985 through 2000.

Most receptions, season
123—Herman Moore, Detroit, 1995.

Most years leading league in receptions
8—Don Hutson, Green Bay, 1936 through 1945, except 1938 and 1940.

Most consecutive years leading league in receptions
5—Don Hutson, Green Bay, 1941 through 1945.

Most receptions, game
20—Terrell Owens, San Francisco vs. Chicago, December 17, 2000.

Most consecutive games with one or more receptions
225—Jerry Rice, San Francisco, December 9, 1985 through December 23, 2000 (current).

YARDS

Most yards, career
19,247—Jerry Rice, San Francisco, 1985 through 2000.

Most yards, season
1,848—Jerry Rice, San Francisco, 1995.

Most years leading league in yards
7—Don Hutson, Green Bay, 1936 through 1944, except 1937 and 1940.

Most consecutive years leading league in yards
4—Don Hutson, Green Bay, 1941 through 1944.

Most years with 1,000 or more yards
12—Jerry Rice, San Francisco, 1986 through 1998, except 1997.

Most yards, game
336—Willie Anderson, Los Angeles Rams at New Orleans, November 26, 1989 (overtime).
309—Stephone Paige, Kansas City vs. San Diego, December 22, 1985.

Most games with 200 or more yards, career
5—Lance Alworth, San Diego, Dallas, 1962 through 1972.

Most games with 200 or more yards, season
3—Charley Hennigan, Houston, 1961.

Most games with 100 or more yards, career
66—Jerry Rice, San Francisco, 1985 through 2000.

Most games with 100 or more yards, season
11—Michael Irvin, Dallas, 1995.

Most consecutive games with 100 or more yards, season
7—Charley Hennigan, Houston, 1961.
Bill Groman, Houston, 1961.
Michael Irvin, Dallas, 1995.

Longest reception
99 yards—Andy Farkas, Washington vs. Pittsburgh, October 15, 1939 (touchdown).
Bobby Mitchell, Washington at Cleveland, September 15, 1963 (touchdown).
Pat Studstill, Detroit at Baltimore, October 16, 1966 (touchdown).
Gerry Allen, Washington at Chicago, September 15, 1968 (touchdown).
Cliff Branch, Los Angeles Raiders vs. Washington, October 2, 1983 (touchdown).
Mike Quick, Philadelphia vs. Atlanta, November 10, 1985 (touchdown).
Tony Martin, San Diego at Seattle, September 18, 1994 (touchdown).
Robert Brooks, Green Bay at Chicago, September 11, 1995 (touchdown).

TOUCHDOWNS

Most touchdowns, career
176—Jerry Rice, San Francisco, 1985 through 2000.

Most touchdowns, season
22—Jerry Rice, San Francisco, 1987.

Most years leading league in touchdowns
9—Don Hutson, Green Bay, 1935 through 1944, except 1939.

Most consecutive years leading league in touchdowns
5—Don Hutson, Green Bay, 1940 through 1944.

Most touchdowns, game
5—Bob Shaw, Chicago Cardinals vs. Baltimore, October 2, 1950.
Kellen Winslow, San Diego at Oakland, November 22, 1981.
Jerry Rice, San Francisco at Atlanta, October 14, 1990.

Most consecutive games with one or more touchdowns
13—Jerry Rice, San Francisco, December 19, 1986 through December 27, 1987.

COMBINED NET YARDS

(Rushing, receiving, interception returns, punt returns, kickoff returns and fumble returns)

ATTEMPTS

Most attempts, career
4,368—Walter Payton, Chicago, 1975 through 1987.

Most attempts, season
496—James Wilder, Tampa Bay, 1984.

Most attempts, game
48—James Wilder, Tampa Bay at Pittsburgh, October 30, 1983.

YARDS

Most yards, career
21,803—Walter Payton, Chicago, 1975 through 1987.

Most yards, season
2,535—Lionel James, San Diego, 1985.

Most years leading league in yards
5—Jim Brown, Cleveland, 1958 through 1961, 1964.

Most consecutive years leading league in yards
4—Jim Brown, Cleveland, 1958 through 1961.

Most yards, game
404—Glyn Milburn, Denver vs. Seattle, December 10, 1995.

SCORING

POINTS

Most points, career
2,059—Gary Anderson, Pittsburgh, Philadelphia, San Francisco, Minnesota, 1982 through 2000.

Most points, season
176—Paul Hornung, Green Bay, 1960.

Most years leading league in points
5—Don Hutson, Green Bay, 1940 through 1944.
Gino Cappelletti, Boston, 1961 through 1966, except 1962.

Most consecutive years leading league in points
5—Don Hutson, Green Bay, 1940 through 1944.

Most years with 100 or more points
12—Morten Andersen, New Orleans, Atlanta, 1985 through 1998, except 1990 and 1996.

Most points, game
40—Ernie Nevers, Chicago Cardinals vs. Chicago Bears, November 28, 1929.

Most consecutive games with one or more points
270—Morten Andersen, New Orleans, Atlanta, December 11, 1983 through December 24, 2000 (current).

TOUCHDOWNS

Most touchdowns, career
187—Jerry Rice, San Francisco, 1985 through 2000.

Most touchdowns, season
26—Marshall Faulk, St. Louis, 2000.

Most years leading league in touchdowns
8—Don Hutson, Green Bay, 1935 through 1938 and 1941 through 1944.

Most consecutive years leading league in touchdowns
4—Don Hutson, Green Bay, 1935 through 1938 and 1941 through 1944.

Most touchdowns, game
6—Ernie Nevers, Chicago Cardinals vs. Chicago Bears, November 28, 1929.
Dub Jones, Cleveland vs. Chicago Bears, November 25, 1951.
Gale Sayers, Chicago vs. San Francisco, December 12, 1965.

Most consecutive games with one or more touchdowns
18—Lenny Moore, Baltimore, October 27, 1963 through September 19, 1965.

EXTRA POINTS

Most extra points attempted, career
959—George Blanda, Chicago Bears, Baltimore, Houston, Oakland, 1949 through 1975, except 1959.

Most extra points made, career
943—George Blanda, Chicago Bears, Baltimore, Houston, Oakland, 1949 through 1975, except 1959.

Most extra points attempted, season
70—Uwe von Schamann, Miami, 1984.

Most extra points made, season
66—Uwe von Schamann, Miami, 1984.

Most extra points attempted, game
10—Charlie Gogolak, Washington vs. New York Giants, November 27, 1966.

Most extra points made, game
9—Pat Harder, Chicago Cardinals at New York Giants, October 17, 1948.
Bob Waterfield, Los Angeles vs. Baltimore, October 22, 1950.
Charlie Gogolak, Washington vs. New York Giants, November 27, 1966.

FIELD GOALS AND FIELD-GOAL PERCENTAGE

Most field goals attempted, career
637—George Blanda, Chicago Bears, Baltimore, Houston, Oakland, 1949 through 1975, except 1959.

Most field goals made, career
461—Gary Anderson, Pittsburgh, Philadelphia, San Francisco, Minnesota, 1982 through 2000.

Most field goals attempted, season
49—Bruce Gossett, Los Angeles, 1966.
Curt Knight, Washington, 1971.

Most field goals made, season
39—Olindo Mare, Miami, 1999.

Most field goals attempted, game
9—Jim Bakken, St. Louis at Pittsburgh, September 24, 1967.

Most field goals made, game
7—Jim Bakken, St. Louis at Pittsburgh, September 24, 1967.
Rich Karlis, Minnesota vs. Los Angeles Rams, November 5, 1989 (overtime).
Chris Boniol, Dallas vs. Green Bay, November 18, 1996.

Most field goals made, one quarter
4—Garo Yepremian, Detroit vs. Minnesota, November 13, 1966, second quarter.
Curt Knight, Washington at New York Giants, November 15, 1970, second quarter.
Roger Ruzek, Dallas vs. New York Giants, November 2, 1987, fourth quarter.

Most consecutive games with one or more field goals made, career
31—Fred Cox, Minnesota, November 17, 1968 through December 5, 1970.

Most consecutive field goals made, career
40—Gary Anderson, San Francisco, Minnesota, December 15, 1997 through December 26, 1998.

Most field goals of 50 or more yards, career
37—Morten Andersen, New Orleans, Atlanta, 1982 through 2000.

Most field goals of 50 or more yards, season
8—Morten Andersen, Atlanta, 1995.

Most field goals of 50 or more yards, game
3—Morten Andersen, Atlanta vs. New Orleans, December 10, 1995.

Longest field goal made
63 yards—Tom Dempsey, New Orleans vs. Detroit, November 8, 1970.
Jason Elam, Denver vs. Jacksonville, October 25, 1998.

Highest field-goal percentage, career (100 or more made)
84.73—Ryan Longwell, Green Bay, 1997 through 2000 (131 attempted, 111 made).

Highest field-goal percentage, season (qualifiers)
100.00—Tony Zendejas, Los Angeles Rams, 1991 (17 made).
Gary Anderson, Minnesota, 1998 (35 made).
Jeff Wilkins, St. Louis, 2000 (17 made).

SAFETIES

Most safeties, career
4—Ted Hendricks, Baltimore, Green Bay, Oakland, Los Angeles Raiders, 1969 through 1983.
Doug English, Detroit, 1975 through 1985, except 1980.

Most safeties, season
2—Held by many players.

Most safeties, game
2—Fred Dryer, Los Angeles vs. Green Bay, October 21, 1973.

PUNTING

Most punts, career
1,154—Dave Jennings, New York Giants, New York Jets, 1974 through 1987.

Most punts, season
114—Bob Parsons, Chicago, 1981.

Most seasons leading league in punting
4—Sammy Baugh, Washington, 1940 through 1943.
 Jerrel Wilson, Kansas City, 1965, 1968, 1972, 1973.

Most consecutive seasons leading league in punting
4—Sammy Baugh, Washington, 1940 through 1943.

Most punts, game
16— Leo Araguz, Oakland vs. San Diego, October 11, 1998.

Longest punt
98 yards—Steve O'Neal, New York Jets at Denver, September
 21, 1969.

FUMBLES

Most fumbles, career
161—Warren Moon, Houston, Minnesota, Seattle, Kansas City,
 1984 through 2000.

Most fumbles, season
21—Tony Banks, St. Louis, 1996.

Most fumbles, game
7—Len Dawson, Kansas City vs. San Diego, November 15, 1964.

PUNT RETURNS

Most punt returns, career
349—Dave Meggett, N.Y. Giants, New England, N.Y. Jets, 1989
 through 1998.
 Brian Mitchell, Washington, Philadelphia, 1990 through
 2000.

Most punt returns, season
70—Danny Reece, Tampa Bay, 1979.

Most years leading league in punt returns
3—Les "Speedy" Duncan, San Diego, Washington, 1965, 1966,
 1971.
 Rick Upchurch, Denver, 1976, 1978, 1982.

Most punt returns, game
11—Eddie Brown, Washington at Tampa Bay, October 9, 1977.

YARDS

Most yards, career
3,811—Brian Mitchell, Washington, Philadelphia, 1990 through
 2000.

Most yards, season
875—Desmond Howard, Green Bay, 1996.

Most yards, game
207—LeRoy Irvin, Los Angeles at Atlanta, October 11, 1981.

Longest punt return
103 yards—Robert Bailey, Los Angeles Rams at New Orleans,
 October 23, 1994 (touchdown).

FAIR CATCHES

Most fair catches, career
184—Brian Mitchell, Washington, Philadelphia, 1990 through
 2000.

Most fair catches, season
33—Brian Mitchell, Philadelphia, 2000.

Most fair catches, game
7—Lem Barney, Detroit vs. Chicago, November 21, 1976.
 Bobby Morse, Philadelphia vs. Buffalo, December 27, 1987.

TOUCHDOWNS

Most touchdowns, career
9—Eric Metcalf, Cleveland, Atlanta, San Diego, Arizona, Carolina,
 1989 through 1999.

Most touchdowns, season
4—Jack Christiansen, Detroit, 1951.
 Rick Upchurch, Denver, 1976.

Most touchdowns, game
2—Jack Christiansen, Detroit vs. Los Angeles, October 14, 1951.
 Jack Christiansen, Detroit vs. Green Bay, November 22, 1951.
 Dick Christy, New York Titans vs. Denver, September 24, 1961.
 Rick Upchurch, Denver vs. Cleveland, September 26, 1976.
 LeRoy Irvin, Los Angeles at Atlanta, October 11, 1981.
 Vai Sikahema, St. Louis vs. Tampa Bay, December 21, 1986.
 Todd Kinchen, Los Angeles Rams vs. Atlanta, December 27,
 1992.
 Eric Metcalf, San Diego at Cincinnati, November 2, 1997.
 Darrien Gordon, Denver vs. Carolina, November 9, 1997.
 Jermaine Lewis, Baltimore vs. Seattle, December 7, 1997.
 Jermaine Lewis, Baltimore vs. N.Y. Jets, December 24, 2000.

KICKOFF RETURNS

Most kickoff returns, career
468—Brian Mitchell, Washington, Philadelphia, 1990 through 2000.

Most kickoff returns, season
82—MarTay Jenkins, Arizona, 2000.

Most years leading league in kickoff returns
3—Abe Woodson, San Francisco, 1959, 1962, 1963.
 Tyrone Hughes, New Orleans, 1994 through 1996.

Most kickoff returns, game
10—Desmond Howard, Oakland at Seattle, October 26, 1997.

YARDS

Most yards, career
10,710—Brian Mitchell, Washington, Philadelphia, 1990 through
 2000.

Most yards, season
2,186—MarTay Jenkins, Arizona, 2000.

Most years leading league in yards
3—Bruce Harper, New York Jets, 1977 through 1979.
 Tyrone Hughes, New Orleans, 1994 through 1996.

Most yards, game
304—Tyrone Hughes, New Orleans vs. Los Angeles Rams, October
 23, 1994.

Longest kickoff return
106 yards—Al Carmichael, Green Bay vs. Chicago Bears,
 October 7, 1956 (touchdown).
 Noland Smith, Kansas City at Denver, December 17, 1967.
 Roy Green, St. Louis at Dallas, October 21, 1979.

TOUCHDOWNS

Most touchdowns, career
6—Ollie Matson, Chicago Cardinals, Los Angeles Rams, Detroit,
 Philadelphia, 1952 through 1964, except 1953.
 Gale Sayers, Chicago, 1965 through 1971.
 Travis Williams, Green Bay, Los Angeles, 1967 through 1971.
 Mel Gray, New Orleans, Detroit, Houston, Tennessee, Phila-
 delphia, 1986 through 1997.

Most touchdowns, season
4—Travis Williams, Green Bay, 1967.
 Cecil Turner, Chicago, 1970.

Most touchdowns, game
2—Timmy Brown, Philadelphia vs. Dallas, November 6, 1966.
 Travis Williams, Green Bay vs. Cleveland, November 12, 1967.
 Ron Brown, Los Angeles Rams vs. Green Bay, November
 24, 1985.
 Tyrone Hughes, New Orleans vs. Los Angeles Rams,
 October 23, 1994.

COMBINED KICK RETURNS

(KICKOFFS AND PUNTS)

Most kick returns, career
818—Brian Mitchell, Washington, Philadelphia, 1990 through 2000.

Most kick returns, season
102—Glyn Milburn, Detroit, 1997.

Most kick returns, game
13—Stump Mitchell, St. Louis at Atlanta, October 18, 1981.
Ron Harris, New England at Pittsburgh, December 5, 1993.

YARDS

Most yards, career
14,521—Brian Mitchell, Washington, Philadelphia, 1990 through 2000.

Most yards, season
2,187—MarTay Jenkins, Arizona, 2000.

Most yards, game
347—Tyrone Hughes, New Orleans vs. Los Angeles Rams, October 23, 1994.

TOUCHDOWNS

Most touchdowns, career
11—Eric Metcalf, Cleveland, Atlanta, San Diego, Arizona, Carolina, 1989 through 1999.
Brian Mitchell, Washington, Philadelphia, 1990 through 2000.

Most touchdowns, season
4—Jack Christiansen, Detroit, 1951.
Emlen Tunnell, New York Giants, 1951.
Gale Sayers, Chicago, 1967.
Travis Williams, Green Bay, 1967.
Cecil Turner, Chicago, 1970.
Billy "White Shoes" Johnson, Houston, 1975.
Rick Upchurch, Denver, 1976.

Most touchdowns, game
2—Held by many players.

INDIVIDUAL DEFENSE

INTERCEPTIONS

Most interceptions, career
81—Paul Krause, Washington, Minnesota, 1964 through 1979.

Most interceptions, season
14—Dick "Night Train" Lane, Los Angeles, 1952.

Most interceptions, game
4—Held by many players.

Most consecutive games with one or more interceptions
8—Tom Morrow, Oakland, 1962 through 1963.

Most yards on interceptions, career
1,282—Emlen Tunnell, New York Giants, Green Bay, 1948 through 1961.

Most yards on interceptions, season
349—Charlie McNeil, San Diego, 1961.

Most yards on interceptions, game
177—Charlie McNeil, San Diego vs. Houston, September 24, 1961.

Longest interception return
103—Vencie Glenn, San Diego vs. Denver, November 29, 1987.
Louis Oliver, Miami vs. Buffalo, October 4, 1992.
(Note: James Willis, 14 yards, and Troy Vincent, 90 yards, combined for a 104-yard interception return for Philadelphia vs. Dallas, November 3, 1996.)

TOUCHDOWNS

Most touchdowns, career
9—Ken Houston, Houston, Washington, 1967 through 1980.
Rod Woodson, Pittsburgh, San Francisco, Baltimore, 1987 through 2000.

Most touchdowns, season
4—Ken Houston, Houston, 1971.
Jim Kearney, Kansas City, 1972.
Eric Allen, Philadelphia, 1993.

Most touchdowns, game
2—Held by many players.

FUMBLES RECOVERED

Most fumbles recovered (own and opponents'), career
56—Warren Moon, Houston, Minnesota, Seattle, Kansas City, 1984 through 2000.

Most fumbles recovered (own), career
56—Warren Moon, Houston, Minnesota, Seattle, Kansas City, 1984 through 2000.

Most opponents' fumbles recovered, career
29—Jim Marshall, Cleveland, Minnesota, 1960 through 1979.

Most fumbles recovered (own and opponents'), season
9—Don Hultz, Minnesota, 1963.
Dave Krieg, Seattle, 1989.
Brian Griese, Denver, 1999.
Jon Kitna, Seattle, 2000.

Most fumbles recovered (own), season
9—Dave Krieg, Seattle, 1989.
Brian Griese, Denver, 1999.
Jon Kitna, Seattle, 2000.

Most opponents' fumbles recovered, season
9—Don Hultz, Minnesota, 1963.

Most fumbles recovered (own and opponents'), game
4—Otto Graham, Cleveland at New York Giants, October 25, 1953.
Sam Etcheverry, St. Louis at New York Giants, September 17, 1961.
Roman Gabriel, Los Angeles at San Francisco, October 12, 1969.
Joe Ferguson, Buffalo vs. Miami, September 18, 1977.
Randall Cunningham, Philadelphia at Los Angeles Raiders, November 30, 1986 (overtime).

Most fumbles recovered (own), game
4—Otto Graham, Cleveland at New York Giants, October 25, 1953.
Sam Etcheverry, St. Louis at New York Giants, September 17, 1961.
Roman Gabriel, Los Angeles at San Francisco, October 12, 1969.
Joe Ferguson, Buffalo vs. Miami, September 18, 1977.
Randall Cunningham, Philadelphia at Los Angeles Raiders, November 30, 1986 (overtime).

Most opponents' fumbles recovered, game
3—Held by many players.

Longest fumble return
104 yards—Jack Tatum, Oakland at Green Bay, September 24, 1972 (touchdown).
Aeneas Williams, Arizona vs. Washington, November 5, 2000 (touchdown).

TOUCHDOWNS

Most touchdowns (own and opponents' recovered), career
5—Jessie Tuggle, Atlanta, 1987 through 2000.

Most touchdowns (own recovered), career
2—Held by many players.

Most touchdowns (opponents' recovered), career
4—Jessie Tuggle, Atlanta, 1987 through 2000.

Most touchdowns, season
2—Held by many players.

Most touchdowns, game
2—Fred "Dippy" Evans, Chicago Bears vs. Washington, November 28, 1948.

SACKS (SINCE 1982)

Most sacks, career
198—Reggie White, Philadelphia, Green Bay, Carolina, 1985 through 2000, except 1999.

Most sacks, season
22—Mark Gastineau, New York Jets, 1984.

Most sacks, game
7—Derrick Thomas, Kansas City vs. Seattle, November 11, 1990.

TEAM MISCELLANEOUS
CHAMPIONSHIPS

Most league championships won
12—Green Bay, 1929, 1930, 1931, 1936, 1939, 1944, 1961, 1962, 1965, 1966, 1967, 1996.

Most consecutive league championships won
3—Green Bay, 1929 through 1931.
Green Bay, 1965 through 1967.

Most first-place finishes during regular season (since 1933)
18—Cleveland Browns, 1950 through 1955, 1957, 1964, 1965, 1967, 1968, 1969, 1971, 1980, 1985, 1986, 1987, 1989.

Most consecutive first-place finishes during regular season (since 1933)
7—Los Angeles, 1973 through 1979.

GAMES WON

Most games won, season
15—San Francisco, 1984.
Chicago, 1985.
Minnesota, 1998.

Most consecutive games won, season
14—Miami, September 17 through December 16, 1972.

Most consecutive games won from start of season
14—Miami, September 17 through December 16, 1972 (entire season).

Most consecutive games won at end of season
14—Miami, September 17 through December 16, 1972 (entire season).

Most consecutive undefeated games, season
14—Miami, September 17 through December 16, 1972 (entire season).

Most consecutive games won
17—Chicago Bears, November 26, 1933 through December 2, 1934.

Most consecutive undefeated games
25—Canton, 1921 through 1923 (won 22, tied three).

Most consecutive home games won
27—Miami, October 17, 1971 through December 15, 1974.

Most consecutive undefeated home games
30—Green Bay, 1928 through 1933 (won 27, tied three).

Most consecutive road games won
18—San Francisco, November 27, 1988 through December 30, 1990.

Most consecutive undefeated road games
18—San Francisco, November 27, 1988 through December 30, 1990 (won 18).

GAMES LOST

Most games lost, season
15—New Orleans, 1980.
Dallas, 1989.
New England, 1990.
Indianapolis, 1991.
New York Jets, 1996.
San Diego, 2000.

Most consecutive games lost
26—Tampa Bay, September 12, 1976 through December 4, 1977.

Most consecutive winless games
26—Tampa Bay, September 12, 1976 through December 4, 1977 (lost 26).

Most consecutive games lost, season
14—Tampa Bay, September 12 through December 12, 1976.
New Orleans, September 7 through December 7, 1980.
Baltimore, September 13 through December 13, 1981.
New England, September 23 through December 30, 1990.

Most consecutive games lost from start of season
14—Tampa Bay, September 12 through December 12, 1976 (entire season).
New Orleans, September 7 through December 7, 1980.

Most consecutive games lost at end of season
14—Tampa Bay, September 12 through December 12, 1976 (entire season).
New England, September 23 through December 30, 1990.

Most consecutive winless games, season
14—Tampa Bay, September 12 through December 12, 1976 (lost 14; entire season).
New Orleans, September 7 through December 7, 1980 (lost 14).
Baltimore, September 13 through December 13, 1981 (lost 14).
New England, September 23 through December 30, 1990 (lost 14).

Most consecutive home games lost
14—Dallas, October 9, 1988 through December 24, 1989.

Most consecutive winless home games
14—Dallas, October 9, 1988 through December 24, 1989 (lost 14).

Most consecutive road games lost
23—Houston, September 27, 1981 through November 4, 1984.

Most consecutive winless road games
23—Houston, September 27, 1981 through November 4, 1984 (lost 23).

TIE GAMES

Most tie games, season
6—Chicago Bears, 1932.

Most consecutive tie games
3—Chicago Bears, September 25 through October 9, 1932.

TEAM OFFENSE
RUSHING

Most years leading league in rushing
16—Chicago Bears, 1932, 1934, 1935, 1939, 1940, 1941, 1942, 1951, 1955, 1956, 1968, 1977, 1983, 1984, 1985, 1986.

Most consecutive years leading league in rushing
4—Chicago Bears, 1939 through 1942.
Chicago Bears, 1983 through 1986.

ATTEMPTS

Most attempts, season
681—Oakland, 1977.

Most attempts, game
72—Chicago Bears vs. Brooklyn, October 20, 1935.

Most attempts by both teams, game
108—Chicago Cardinals 70, Green Bay 38, December 5, 1948.

Fewest attempts, game
6—Chicago Cardinals at Boston, October 29, 1933.

Fewest attempts by both teams, game
35—New Orleans 20, Seattle 15, September 1, 1991.

YARDS

Most yards, season
3,165—New England, 1978.

Fewest yards, season
298—Philadelphia, 1940.

Most yards, game
426—Detroit vs. Pittsburgh, November 4, 1934.

Most yards by both teams, game
595—Los Angeles 371, New York Yanks 224, November 18, 1951.

Fewest yards, game
-53—Detroit at Chicago Cardinals, October 17, 1943.

Fewest yards by both teams, game
-15—Detroit -53, Chicago Cardinals 38, October 17, 1943.

TOUCHDOWNS

Most touchdowns, season
36—Green Bay, 1962.

Fewest touchdowns, season
1—Brooklyn, 1934.

Most touchdowns, game
7—Los Angeles vs. Atlanta, December 4, 1976.

Most touchdowns by both teams, game
8—Los Angeles 6, New York Yanks 2, November 18, 1951.
Chicago Bears 5, Green Bay 3, November 6, 1955.
Cleveland 6, Los Angeles 2, November 24, 1957.

PASSING

ATTEMPTS

Most attempts, season
709—Minnesota, 1981.

Fewest attempts, season
102—Cincinnati, 1933.

Most attempts, game
70—New England vs. Minnesota, November 13, 1994 (overtime).
68—Houston at Buffalo, November 1, 1964.

Most attempts by both teams, game
112—New England 70, Minnesota 42, November 13, 1994 (overtime).
104—Miami 55, New York Jets 49, October 18, 1987 (overtime).
102—San Francisco 57, Atlanta 45, October 6, 1985.

Fewest attempts, game
0—Green Bay vs. Portsmouth, October 8, 1933.
Detroit at Cleveland, September 10, 1937.
Pittsburgh vs. Brooklyn, November 16, 1941.
Pittsburgh vs. Los Angeles, November 13, 1949.
Cleveland vs. Philadelphia, December 3, 1950.

Fewest attempts by both teams, game
4—Detroit 3, Chicago Cardinals 1, November 3, 1935.
Cleveland 4, Detroit 0, September 10, 1937.

COMPLETIONS

Most completions, season
432—San Francisco, 1995.

Fewest completions, season
25—Cincinnati, 1933.

Most completions, game
45—New England vs. Minnesota, November 13, 1994 (overtime).
42—New York Jets vs. San Francisco, September 21, 1980.

Most completions by both teams, game
71—New England 45, Minnesota 26, November 13, 1994 (overtime).
68—San Francisco 37, Atlanta 31, October 6, 1985.

Fewest completions, game
0—Held by many teams. Last team: Buffalo vs. New York Jets, September 29, 1974.

Fewest completions by both teams, game
1—Philadelphia 1, Chicago Cardinals 0, November 8, 1936.
Cleveland 1, Detroit 0, September 10, 1937.
Detroit 1, Chicago Cardinals 0, September 15, 1940.
Pittsburgh 1, Brooklyn 0, November 29, 1942.

YARDS

Most yards, season
5,232—St. Louis, 2000.

Most years leading league in yards
10—San Diego, 1965, 1968, 1971, 1978 through 1983, 1985.

Most consecutive years leading league in yards
6—San Diego, 1978 through 1983.

Fewest yards, season
302—Chicago Cardinals, 1934.

Most yards, game
554—Los Angeles at New York Yanks, September 28, 1951.

Most yards by both teams, game
884—New York Jets 449, Miami 435, September 21, 1986 (overtime).
883—San Diego 486, Cincinnati 397, December 20, 1982.

Fewest yards, game
-53—Denver at Oakland, September 10, 1967.

Fewest yards by both teams, game
-11—Green Bay -10, Dallas -1, October 24, 1965.

TOUCHDOWNS

Most touchdowns, season
49—Miami, 1984.

Fewest touchdowns, season
0—Cincinnati, 1933.
Pittsburgh, 1945.

Most touchdowns, game
7—Chicago Bears at New York Giants, November 14, 1943.
Philadelphia at Washington, October 17, 1954.
Houston vs. New York Titans, November 19, 1961.
Houston vs. New York Titans, October 14, 1962.
New York Giants vs. Washington, October 28, 1962.
Minnesota vs. Baltimore, September 28, 1969.
San Diego at Oakland, November 22, 1981.

Most touchdowns by both teams, game
12—New Orleans 6, St. Louis 6, November 2, 1969.

INTERCEPTIONS

Most interceptions, season
48—Houston, 1962.

Fewest interceptions, season
5—Cleveland, 1960.
Green Bay, 1966.
Kansas City, 1990.
New York Giants, 1990.

Most interceptions, game
9—Detroit vs. Green Bay, October 24, 1943.
Pittsburgh vs. Philadelphia, December 12, 1965.

Most interceptions by both teams, game
13—Denver 8, Houston 5, December 2, 1962.

SACKS

Most sacks allowed, season
104—Philadelphia, 1986.

Most years leading league in fewest sacks allowed
10—Miami, 1973 and 1982 through 1990.

Most consecutive years leading league in fewest sacks allowed
9—Miami, 1982 through 1990.

Fewest sacks allowed, season
7—Miami, 1988.

Most sacks allowed, game
12—Pittsburgh at Dallas, November 20, 1966.
Baltimore vs. St. Louis, October 26, 1980.
Detroit vs. Chicago, December 16, 1984.
Houston vs. Dallas, September 29, 1985.

Most sacks allowed by both teams, game
18—Green Bay 10, San Diego 8, September 24, 1978.

SCORING

POINTS

Most points, season
556—Minnesota, 1998.

Most points, game
72—Washington vs. New York Giants, November 27, 1966.

Most points by both teams, game
113—Washington 72, New York Giants 41, November 27, 1966.

Fewest points by both teams, game
0—Occurred many times. Last time: New York Giants 0, Detroit 0, November 7, 1943.

Most points in a shutout victory
64—Philadelphia vs. Cincinnati, November 6, 1934.

Fewest points in a shutout victory
2—Green Bay at Chicago Bears, October 16, 1932.
Chicago Bears at Green Bay, September 18, 1938.

Most points in first half of game
49—Green Bay vs. Tampa Bay, October 2, 1983.

Most points in first half of game by both teams
70—Houston 35, Oakland 35, December 22, 1963.

Most points in second half of game
49—Chicago Bears at Philadelphia, November 30, 1941.

Most points in second half of game by both teams
65—Washington 38, New York Giants 27, November 27, 1966.

Most points in one quarter
41—Green Bay vs. Detroit, October 7, 1945, second quarter.
Los Angeles vs. Detroit, October 29, 1950, third quarter.

Most points in one quarter by both teams
49—Oakland 28, Houston 21, December 22, 1963, second quarter.

Most points in first quarter
35—Green Bay vs. Cleveland, November 12, 1967.

Most points in first quarter by both teams
42—Green Bay 35, Cleveland 7, November 12, 1967.

Most points in second quarter
41—Green Bay vs. Detroit, October 7, 1945.

Most points in second quarter by both teams
49—Oakland 28, Houston 21, December 22, 1963.

Most points in third quarter
41—Los Angeles vs. Detroit, October 29, 1950.

Most points in third quarter by both teams
48—Los Angeles 41, Detroit 7, October 29, 1950.

Most points in fourth quarter
31—Oakland vs. Denver, December 17, 1960.
Oakland vs. San Diego, December 8, 1963.
Atlanta at Green Bay, September 13, 1981.

Most points in fourth quarter by both teams
42—Chicago Cardinals 28, Philadelphia 14, December 7, 1947.
Green Bay 28, Chicago Bears 14, November 6, 1955.
New York Jets 28, Boston 14, October 27, 1968.
Pittsburgh 21, Cleveland 21, October 18, 1969.

Most consecutive games without being shut out
370—San Francisco, October 16, 1977 through December 23, 2000 (current).

TIMES SHUT OUT

Most times shut out, season
8—Frankford, 1927 (lost six, tied two).
Brooklyn, 1931 (lost eight).

Most consecutive times shut out
8—Rochester, 1922 through 1924 (lost eight).

TOUCHDOWNS

Most touchdowns, season
70—Miami, 1984.

Most years leading league in touchdowns
13—Chicago Bears, 1932, 1934, 1935, 1939, 1941, 1942, 1943, 1944, 1946, 1947, 1948, 1956, 1965.

Most consecutive years leading league in touchdowns
4—Chicago Bears, 1941 through 1944.
Los Angeles, 1949 through 1952.

Most touchdowns, game
10—Philadelphia vs. Cincinnati, November 6, 1934.
Los Angeles vs. Baltimore, October 22, 1950.
Washington vs. New York Giants, November 27, 1966.

Most touchdowns by both teams, game
16—Washington 10, New York Giants 6, November 27, 1966.

Most consecutive games with one or more touchdowns
166—Cleveland, 1957 through 1969.

EXTRA POINTS

Most extra points, season
66—Miami, 1984.

Fewest extra points, season
2—Chicago Cardinals, 1933.

Most extra points, game
10—Los Angeles vs. Baltimore, October 22, 1950.

Most extra points by both teams, game
14—Chicago Cardinals 9, New York Giants 5, October 17, 1948.
Houston 7, Oakland 7, December 22, 1963.
Washington 9, New York Giants 5, November 27, 1966.

FIELD GOALS

Most field goals attempted, season
49—Los Angeles, 1966.
Washington, 1971.

Most field goals made, season
39—Miami, 1999.

Most field goals attempted, game
9—St. Louis at Pittsburgh, September 24, 1967.

Most field goals made, game
7—St. Louis at Pittsburgh, September 24, 1967.
Minnesota vs. Los Angeles Rams, November 5, 1989 (overtime).

Most field goals attempted by both teams, game
11—St. Louis 6, Pittsburgh 5, November 13, 1966.
Washington 6, Chicago 5, November 14, 1971.
Green Bay 6, Detroit 5, September 29, 1974.
Washington 6, New York Giants 5, November 14, 1976.

Most field goals made by both teams, game
8—Cleveland 4, St. Louis 4, September 20, 1964.
Chicago 5, Philadelphia 3, October 20, 1968.
Washington 5, Chicago 3, November 14, 1971.
Kansas City 5, Buffalo 3, December 19, 1971.
Detroit 4, Green Bay 4, September 29, 1974.
Cleveland 5, Denver 3, October 19, 1975.
New England 4, San Diego 4, November 9, 1975.
San Francisco 6, New Orleans 2, October 16, 1983.
Seattle 5, Los Angeles Raiders 3, December 18, 1988.

Most consecutive games with one or more field goals made
31—Minnesota, November 17, 1968 through December 5, 1970.

SAFETIES

Most safeties, season
4—Cleveland, 1927.
Detroit, 1962.
Seattle, 1993.

Most safeties, game
3—Los Angeles Rams vs. New York Giants, September 30, 1984.

Most safeties by both teams, game
3—Los Angeles Rams 3, New York Giants 0, September 30, 1984.

FIRST DOWNS

Most first downs, season
387—Miami, 1984.

Most first downs, game
39—New York Jets vs. Miami, November 27, 1988.
Washington at Detroit, November 4, 1990 (overtime).

Most first downs by both teams, game
62—San Diego 32, Seattle 30, September 15, 1985.

PUNTING

Most punts, season
114—Chicago, 1981.

Fewest punts, season
23—San Diego, 1982.

Most punts, game
17—Chicago Bears vs. Green Bay, October 22, 1933.
Cincinnati vs. Pittsburgh, October 22, 1933.

Most punts by both teams, game
31—Chicago Bears 17, Green Bay 14, October 22, 1933.
Cincinnati 17, Pittsburgh 14, October 22, 1933.

Fewest punts, game
0—Held by many teams.

Fewest punts by both teams, game
0—Buffalo 0, San Francisco 0, September 13, 1992.

FUMBLES

Most fumbles, season
56—Chicago Bears, 1938.
San Francisco, 1978.

Fewest fumbles, season
8—Cleveland, 1959.

Most fumbles, game
10—Philadelphia/Pittsburgh vs. New York, October 9, 1943.
Detroit at Minnesota, November 12, 1967.
Kansas City vs. Houston, October 12, 1969.
San Francisco at Detroit, December 17, 1978.

Most fumbles by both teams, game
14—Washington 8, Pittsburgh 6, November 14, 1937.
Chicago Bears 7, Cleveland 7, November 24, 1940.
St. Louis 8, New York Giants 6, September 17, 1961.
Kansas City 10, Houston 4, October 12, 1969.

LOST

Most fumbles lost, season
36—Chicago Cardinals, 1959.

Fewest fumbles lost, season
3—Philadelphia, 1938.
Minnesota, 1980.

Most fumbles lost, game
8—St. Louis at Washington, October 25, 1976.
Cleveland at Pittsburgh, December 23, 1990.

RECOVERED

Most fumbles recovered (own and opponents'), season
58—Minnesota, 1963.

Fewest fumbles recovered (own and opponents'), season
9—San Francisco, 1982.

Most fumbles recovered (own and opponents'), game
10—Denver vs. Buffalo, December 13, 1964.
Pittsburgh vs. Houston, December 9, 1973.
Washington vs. St. Louis, October 25, 1976.

Most fumbles recovered (own), season
37—Chicago Bears, 1938.

Fewest fumbles recovered (own), season
2—Washington, 1958.

TOUCHDOWNS

Most touchdowns on fumbles recovered (own and opponents'), season
5—Chicago Bears, 1942.
Los Angeles, 1952.
San Francisco, 1965.
Oakland, 1978.

Most touchdowns on own fumbles recovered, season
2—Held by many teams. Last team: Miami, 1996.

Most touchdowns on fumbles recovered (own and opponents'), game
2—Held by many teams.

Most touchdowns on fumbles recovered (own and opponents'), game
3—Detroit 2, Minnesota 1, December 9, 1962.
Green Bay 2, Dallas 1, November 29, 1964.
Oakland 2, Buffalo 1, December 24, 1967.

Most touchdowns on own fumbles recovered, game
1—Held by many teams.

Most touchdowns on opponents' fumbles recovered by both teams, game
3—Green Bay 2, Dallas 1, November 29, 1964.
Oakland 2, Buffalo 1, December 24, 1967.

TURNOVERS

Most turnovers, season
63—San Francisco, 1978.

Fewest turnovers, season
12—Kansas City, 1982.

Most turnovers, game
12—Detroit vs. Chicago Bears, November 22, 1942.
Chicago Cardinals vs. Philadelphia, September 24, 1950.
Pittsburgh vs. Philadelphia, December 12, 1965.

Most turnovers by both teams, game
17—Detroit 12, Chicago Bears 5, November 22, 1942.
Boston 9, Philadelphia 8, December 8, 1946.

PUNT RETURNS

Most punt returns, season
71—Pittsburgh, 1976.
Tampa Bay, 1979.
Los Angeles Raiders, 1985.

Fewest punt returns, season
12—Baltimore, 1981.
San Diego, 1982.

Most punt returns, game
12—Philadelphia at Cleveland, December 3, 1950.

Most punt returns by both teams, game
17—Philadelphia 12, Cleveland 5, December 3, 1950.

YARDS

Most yards, season
785—Los Angeles Raiders, 1985.

Fewest yards, season
27—St. Louis, 1965.

Most yards, game
231—Detroit vs. San Francisco, October 6, 1963.

Most yards by both teams, game
282—Los Angeles 219, Atlanta 63, October 11, 1981.

TOUCHDOWNS

Most touchdowns, season
5—Chicago Cardinals, 1959.

Most touchdowns, game
2—Held by many teams. Last team: Baltimore vs. N.Y. Jets, December 24, 2000.

Most touchdowns by both teams, game
2—Occurred many times. Last time: Baltimore 2, N.Y. Jets 0, December 24, 2000.

KICKOFF RETURNS

Most kickoff returns, season
89—Cleveland, 1999.

Fewest kickoff returns, season
17—New York Giants, 1944.

Most kickoff returns, game
12—New York Giants at Washington, November 27, 1966.

Most kickoff returns by both teams, game
19—New York Giants 12, Washington 7, November 27, 1966.

YARDS

Most yards, season
2,296—Arizona, 2000.

Fewest yards, season
282—New York Giants, 1940.

Most yards, game
362—Detroit at Los Angeles, October 29, 1950.

Most yards by both teams, game
560—Detroit 362, Los Angeles 198, October 29, 1950.

TOUCHDOWNS

Most touchdowns, season
4—Green Bay, 1967.
Chicago, 1970.
Detroit, 1994.

Most touchdowns, game
2—Chicago Bears at Green Bay, September 22, 1940.
Chicago Bears vs. Green Bay, November 9, 1952.
Philadelphia vs. Dallas, November 6, 1966.
Green Bay vs. Cleveland, November 12, 1967.
Los Angeles Rams vs. Green Bay, November 24, 1985.
New Orleans vs. Los Angeles Rams, October 23, 1994.

Most touchdowns by both teams, game (each team scoring)
2—Occurred many times. Last time: Atlanta 1, St. Louis 1, October 15, 2000.

PENALTIES

Most penalties, season
158—Kansas City, 1998.

Fewest penalties, season
19—Detroit, 1937.

Most penalties, game
22—Brooklyn at Green Bay, September 17, 1944.
Chicago Bears at Philadelphia, November 26, 1944.
San Francisco at Buffalo, October 4, 1998.

Most penalties by both teams, game
37—Cleveland 21, Chicago Bears 16, November 25, 1951.

Fewest penalties, game
0—Held by many teams. Last team: San Francisco vs. Philadelphia, November 29, 1992.

Fewest penalties by both teams, game
0—Brooklyn 0, Pittsburgh 0, October 28, 1934.
Brooklyn 0, Boston 0, September 28, 1936.
Cleveland 0, Chicago Bears 0, October 9, 1938.
Pittsburgh 0, Philadelphia 0, November 10, 1940.

YARDS PENALIZED

Most yards penalized, season
1,304—Kansas City, 1998.

Fewest yards penalized, season
139—Detroit, 1937.

Most yards penalized, game
209—Cleveland vs. Chicago Bears, November 25, 1951.

Most yards penalized by both teams, game
374—Cleveland 209, Chicago Bears 165, November 25, 1951.

Fewest yards penalized, game
0—Held by many teams. Last team: San Francisco vs. Philadelphia, November 29, 1992.

Fewest yards penalized by both teams, game
0—Brooklyn 0, Pittsburgh 0, October 28, 1934.
Brooklyn 0, Boston 0, September 28, 1936.
Cleveland 0, Chicago Bears 0, October 9, 1938.
Pittsburgh 0, Philadelphia 0, November 10, 1940.

TEAM DEFENSE
RUSHING

YARDS ALLOWED

Most yards allowed, season
3,228—Buffalo, 1978.

Fewest yards allowed, season
519—Chicago Bears, 1942.

TOUCHDOWNS ALLOWED

Most touchdowns allowed, season
36—Oakland, 1961.

Fewest touchdowns allowed, season
2—Detroit, 1934.
Dallas, 1968.
Minnesota, 1971.

PASSING

YARDS ALLOWED

Most yards allowed, season
4,751—Atlanta, 1995.

Fewest yards allowed, season
545—Philadelphia, 1934.

TOUCHDOWNS ALLOWED

Most touchdowns allowed, season
40—Denver, 1963.

Fewest touchdowns allowed, season
1—Portsmouth, 1932.
   Philadelphia, 1934.

YARDS ALLOWED

(RUSHING AND PASSING)

Most yards allowed rushing and passing, season
6,793—Baltimore, 1981.

Fewest yards allowed rushing and passing, season
1,539—Chicago Cardinals, 1934.

SCORING

POINTS ALLOWED

Most points allowed, season
533—Baltimore, 1981.

Fewest points allowed, season (since 1932)
44—Chicago Bears, 1932.

SHUTOUTS

Most shutouts, season
10—Pottsville, 1926 (won nine, tied one).
   New York Giants, 1927 (won nine, tied one).

Most consecutive shutouts
13—Akron, 1920 through 1921 (won 10, tied three).

TOUCHDOWNS ALLOWED

Most touchdowns allowed, season
68—Baltimore, 1981.

Fewest touchdowns allowed, season (since 1932)
6—Chicago Bears, 1932.
   Brooklyn, 1933.

FIRST DOWNS ALLOWED

Most first downs allowed, season
406—Baltimore, 1981.

Fewest first downs allowed, season
77—Detroit, 1935.

Most first downs allowed by rushing, season
179—Detroit, 1985.

Fewest first downs allowed by rushing, season
35—Chicago Bears, 1942.

Most first downs allowed by passing, season
230—Atlanta, 1995.

Fewest first downs allowed by passing, season
33—Chicago Bears, 1943.

Most first downs allowed by penalties, season
56—Kansas City, 1998.

Fewest first downs allowed by penalties, season
1—Boston, 1944.

INTERCEPTIONS

Most interceptions, season
49—San Diego, 1961.

Fewest interceptions, season
3—Houston, 1982.

Most interceptions, game
9—Green Bay at Detroit, October 24, 1943.
   Philadelphia at Pittsburgh, December 12, 1965.

Most yards returning interceptions, season
929—San Diego, 1961.

Fewest yards returning interceptions, season
5—Los Angeles, 1959.

Most yards returning interceptions, game
325—Seattle vs. Kansas City, November 4, 1984.

Most touchdowns returning interceptions, season
9—San Diego, 1961.

Most touchdowns returning interceptions, game
4—Seattle vs. Kansas City, November 4, 1984.

Most touchdowns returning interceptions by both teams, game
4—Philadelphia 3, Pittsburgh 1, December 12, 1965.
   Seattle 4, Kansas City 0, November 4, 1984.

FUMBLES

Most opponents' fumbles forced, season
50—Minnesota, 1963.
   San Francisco, 1978.

Fewest opponents' fumbles forced, season
11—Cleveland, 1956.
   Baltimore, 1982.
   Tennessee, 1998.

RECOVERED

Most opponents' fumbles recovered, season
31—Minnesota, 1963.

Fewest opponents' fumbles recovered, season
3—Los Angeles, 1974.

Most opponents' fumbles recovered, game
8—Washington vs. St. Louis, October 25, 1976.
   Pittsburgh vs. Cleveland, December 23, 1990.

TOUCHDOWNS

Most touchdowns on opponents' fumbles recovered, season
4—Held by many teams. Last team: Cincinnati, 1998.

Most touchdowns on opponents' fumbles recovered, game
2—Held by many teams. Last team: Cincinnati at Pittsburgh,
   December 20, 1998.

TURNOVERS

Most opponents' turnovers, season
66—San Diego, 1961.

Fewest opponents' turnovers, season
11—Baltimore, 1982.

Most opponents' turnovers, game
12—Chicago Bears at Detroit, November 22, 1942.
   Philadelphia at Chicago Cardinals, September 24, 1950.
   Philadelphia at Pittsburgh, December 12, 1965.

SACKS

Most sacks, season
72—Chicago, 1984.

Fewest sacks, season
11—Baltimore, 1982.

Most sacks, game
12—Dallas at Pittsburgh, November 20, 1966.
   St. Louis at Baltimore, October 26, 1980.
   Chicago at Detroit, December 16, 1984.
   Dallas at Houston, September 29, 1985.

PUNTS RETURNED

Most punts returned by opponents, season
71—Tampa Bay, 1976.
   Tampa Bay, 1977.

Fewest punts returned by opponents, season
7—Washington, 1962.
   San Diego, 1982.

Most yards allowed on punts returned by opponents, season
932—Green Bay, 1949.

Fewest yards allowed on punts returned by opponents, season
22—Green Bay, 1967.

Most touchdowns allowed on punts returned by opponents, season
4—New York, 1959.
   Atlanta, 1992.

KICKOFFS RETURNED

Most kickoffs returned by opponents, season
91—Washington, 1983.

Fewest kickoffs returned by opponents, season
10—Brooklyn, 1943.

Most yards allowed on kickoffs returned by opponents, season
2,045—Kansas City, 1966.

Fewest yards allowed on kickoffs returned by opponents, season
225—Brooklyn, 1943.

Most touchdowns allowed on kickoffs returned by opponents, season
4—Minnesota, 1998.

STATISTICAL LEADERS

CAREER MILESTONES
TOP 20 RUSHERS

Player	League	Years	Att.	Yds.	Avg.	Long	TD
Walter Payton	NFL	13	3838	16726	4.4	76	110
Barry Sanders	NFL	10	3062	15269	5.0	85	99
Emmitt Smith*	NFL	11	3537	15166	4.3	75	145
Eric Dickerson	NFL	11	2996	13259	4.4	85	90
Tony Dorsett	NFL	12	2936	12739	4.3	99	77
Jim Brown	NFL	9	2359	12312	5.2	80	106
Marcus Allen	NFL	16	3022	12243	4.1	61	123
Franco Harris	NFL	13	2949	12120	4.1	75	91
Thurman Thomas*	NFL	13	2877	12074	4.2	80	65
John Riggins	NFL	14	2916	11352	3.9	66	104
O.J. Simpson	AFL-NFL	11	2404	11236	4.7	94	61
Ricky Watters*	NFL	9	2550	10325	4.0	57	77
Ottis Anderson	NFL	14	2562	10273	4.0	76	81
Jerome Bettis*	NFL	8	2461	9804	4.0	71	49
Joe Perry	AAFC-NFL	16	1929	9723	5.0	78	71
Earl Campbell	NFL	8	2187	9407	4.3	81	74
Jim Taylor	NFL	10	1941	8597	4.4	84	83
Earnest Byner	NFL	14	2095	8261	3.9	54	56
Herschel Walker	NFL	12	1954	8225	4.2	91	61
Roger Craig	NFL	11	1991	8189	4.1	71	56

*Active through 2000 season.

TOP 20 PASSERS

Player	League	Years	Att.	Comp.	Yds.	TD	Int.	Rating Pts.
Steve Young	NFL	15	4149	2667	33124	232	107	96.8
Joe Montana	NFL	15	5391	3409	40551	273	139	92.3
Otto Graham	AAFC-NFL	10	2626	1464	23584	174	135	86.6
Dan Marino	NFL	17	8358	4967	61361	420	252	86.4
Brett Favre*	NFL	10	4932	2997	34706	255	157	86.0
Peyton Manning*	NFL	3	1679	1014	12287	85	58	85.4
Mark Brunell*	NFL	8	2972	1608	19212	106	66	85.1
Brad Johnson*	NFL	9	1821	1126	12973	79	57	84.7
Jim Kelly	NFL	11	4779	2874	35467	237	175	84.4
Roger Staubach	NFL	11	2958	1685	22700	153	109	83.4
Neil Lomax	NFL	8	3153	1817	22771	136	90	82.7
Sonny Jurgensen	NFL	18	4262	2433	32224	255	189	82.63
Len Dawson	NFL-AFL	19	3741	2136	28711	239	183	82.56
Neil O'Donnell*	NFL	10	3121	1802	20938	116	65	81.863
Ken Anderson	NFL	16	4475	2654	32838	197	160	81.858
Bernie Kosar	NFL	12	3365	1994	23301	124	87	81.8
Danny White	NFL	13	2950	1761	21959	155	132	81.72
Elvis Grbac*	NFL	7	1978	1181	13741	84	63	81.67
Troy Aikman*	NFL	12	4715	2898	32942	165	141	81.6
Dave Krieg	NFL	19	5311	3105	38147	261	199	81.5

*Active through 2000 season.

TOP 20 RECEIVERS

Player	League	Years	No.	Yds.	Avg.	Long	TD
Jerry Rice*	NFL	16	1281	19247	15.0	96	176
Cris Carter*	NFL	14	1020	12962	12.7	80	123
Andre Reed*	NFL	16	951	13198	13.9	83	87
Art Monk	NFL	16	940	12721	13.5	79	68
Irving Fryar*	NFL	17	851	12785	15.0	80	84
Tim Brown*	NFL	13	846	12072	14.3	80	86
Steve Largent	NFL	14	819	13089	16.0	74	100
Henry Ellard	NFL	16	814	13777	16.9	81	65
James Lofton	NFL	16	764	14004	18.3	80	75
Charlie Joiner	AFL-NFL	18	750	12146	16.2	87	65
Michael Irvin	NFL	12	750	11904	15.9	87	65
Andre Rison*	NFL	12	743	10205	13.7	80	84
Gary Clark	NFL	11	699	10856	15.5	84	65
Larry Centers*	NFL	11	685	5683	8.3	87	25
Herman Moore*	NFL	10	666	9098	13.7	93	62

Player	League	Years	No.	Yds.	Avg.	Long	TD
Ozzie Newsome	NFL	13	662	7980	12.1	74	47
Charley Taylor	NFL	13	649	9110	14.0	88	79
Drew Hill	NFL	15	634	9831	15.5	81	60
Don Maynard	NFL-AFL	15	633	11834	18.7	87	88
Raymond Berry	NFL	13	631	9275	14.7	70	68

*Active through 2000 season.

TOP 20 SCORERS

Player	League	Years	TD	XP Made	FG Made	Total
Gary Anderson*	NFL	19	0	676	461	2059
George Blanda	NFL-AFL	26	9	943	335	2002
Morten Andersen*	NFL	19	0	615	441	1938
Norm Johnson	NFL	18	0	638	366	1736
Nick Lowery	NFL	18	0	562	383	1711
Jan Stenerud	AFL-NFL	19	0	580	373	1699
Lou Groza	AAFC-NFL	21	1	810	264	1608
Eddie Murray*	NFL	19	0	538	352	1594
Al Del Greco*	NFL	17	0	543	347	1584
Pat Leahy	NFL	18	0	558	304	1470
Jim Turner	AFL-NFL	16	1	521	304	1439
Matt Bahr	NFL	17	0	522	300	1422
Mark Moseley	NFL	16	0	482	300	1382
Jim Bakken	NFL	17	0	534	282	1380
Fred Cox	NFL	15	0	519	282	1365
Jim Breech	NFL	14	0	517	243	1246
Pete Stoyanovich*	NFL	12	0	420	272	1236
Chris Bahr	NFL	14	0	490	241	1213
Kevin Butler	NFL	13	0	413	265	1208
Steve Christie*	NFL	11	0	358	272	1174

*Active through 2000 season.
†Includes four two-point conversions.

YEAR BY YEAR

AFC

RUSHING

(Based on most net yards)

	Net Yds.	Att.	TD
1960—Abner Haynes, Dallas	875	156	9
1961—Billy Cannon, Houston	948	200	6
1962—Cookie Gilchrist, Buffalo	1096	214	13
1963—Clem Daniels, Oakland	1099	215	3
1964—Cookie Gilchrist, Buffalo	981	230	6
1965—Paul Lowe, San Diego	1121	222	7
1966—Jim Nance, Boston	1458	299	11
1967—Jim Nance, Boston	1216	269	7
1968—Paul Robinson, Cincinnati	1023	238	8
1969—Dick Post, San Diego	873	182	6
1970—Floyd Little, Denver	901	209	3
1971—Floyd Little, Denver	1133	284	6
1972—O.J. Simpson, Buffalo	1251	292	6
1973—O.J. Simpson, Buffalo	2003	332	12
1974—Otis Armstrong, Denver	1407	263	9
1975—O.J. Simpson, Buffalo	1817	329	16
1976—O.J. Simpson, Buffalo	1503	290	8
1977—Mark van Eeghen, Oakland	1273	324	7
1978—Earl Campbell, Houston	1450	302	13
1979—Earl Campbell, Houston	1697	368	19
1980—Earl Campbell, Houston	1934	373	13
1981—Earl Campbell, Houston	1376	361	10
1982—Freeman McNeil, N.Y. Jets	786	151	6
1983—Curt Warner, Seattle	1449	335	13
1984—Earnest Jackson, San Diego	1179	296	8
1985—Marcus Allen, L.A. Raiders	1759	380	11
1986—Curt Warner, Seattle	1481	319	13
1987—Eric Dickerson, Indianapolis	1288	283	6
1988—Eric Dickerson, Indianapolis	1659	388	14
1989—Christian Okoye, Kansas City	1480	370	12

	Net Yds.	Att.	TD
1990—Thurman Thomas, Buffalo	1297	271	11
1991—Thurman Thomas, Buffalo	1407	288	7
1992—Barry Foster, Pittsburgh	1690	390	11
1993—Thurman Thomas, Buffalo	1315	355	6
1994—Chris Warren, Seattle	1545	333	9
1995—Curtis Martin, New England	1487	368	14
1996—Terrell Davis, Denver	1538	345	13
1997—Terrell Davis, Denver	1750	369	15
1998—Terrell Davis, Denver	2008	392	21
1999—Edgerrin James, Indianapolis	1553	369	13
2000—Edgerrin James, Indianapolis	1709	387	13

PASSING

(Based on highest passer rating among qualifiers*)

	Att.	Com.	Yds.	TD	Int.	Rat.
1960—Jack Kemp, Chargers	406	211	3018	20	25	67.1
1961—George Blanda, Hou.	362	187	3330	36	22	91.3
1962—Len Dawson, Dal.	310	189	2759	29	17	98.3
1963—Tobin Rote, S.D.	286	170	2510	20	17	86.7
1964—Len Dawson, K.C.	354	199	2879	30	18	89.9
1965—John Hadl, S.D.	348	174	2798	20	21	71.3
1966—Len Dawson, K.C.	284	159	2527	26	10	101.7
1967—Daryle Lamonica, Oak.	425	220	3228	30	20	80.8
1968—Len Dawson, K.C.	224	131	2109	17	9	98.6
1969—Greg Cook, Cin.	197	106	1854	15	11	88.3
1970—Daryle Lamonica, Oak.	356	179	2516	22	15	76.5
1971—Bob Griese, Mia.	263	145	2089	19	9	90.9
1972—Earl Morrall, Mia.	150	83	1360	11	7	91.0
1973—Ken Stabler, Oak.	260	163	1997	14	10	88.5
1974—Ken Anderson, Cin.	328	213	2667	18	10	95.9
1975—Ken Anderson, Cin.	377	228	3169	21	11	94.1
1976—Ken Stabler, Oak.	291	194	2737	27	17	103.7
1977—Bob Griese, Mia.	307	180	2252	22	13	88.0
1978—Terry Bradshaw, Pit.	368	207	2915	28	20	84.8
1979—Dan Fouts, S.D.	530	332	4082	24	24	82.6

	Att.	Com.	Yds.	TD	Int.	Rat.
1980— Brian Sipe, Cle.	554	337	4132	30	14	91.4
1981— Ken Anderson, Cin.	479	300	3754	29	10	98.5
1982— Ken Anderson, Cin.	309	218	2495	12	9	95.5
1983— Dan Marino, Mia.	296	173	2210	20	6	96.0
1984— Dan Marino, Mia.	564	362	5084	48	17	108.9
1985— Ken O'Brien, NYJ	488	297	3888	25	8	96.2
1986— Dan Marino, Mia.	623	378	4746	44	23	92.5
1987— Bernie Kosar, Cle.	389	241	3033	22	9	95.4
1988— Boomer Esiason, Cin.	388	223	3572	28	14	97.4
1989— Boomer Esiason, Cin.	455	258	3525	28	11	92.1
1990— Jim Kelly, Buf.	346	219	2829	24	9	101.2
1991— Jim Kelly, Buf.	474	304	3844	33	17	97.6
1992— Warren Moon, Hou.	346	224	2521	18	12	89.3
1993— John Elway, Den.	551	348	4030	25	10	92.8
1994— Dan Marino, Mia.	615	385	4453	30	17	89.2
1995— Jim Harbaugh, Ind.	314	200	2575	17	5	100.7
1996— John Elway, Den.	466	287	3328	26	14	89.2
1997— Mark Brunell, Jac.	435	264	3281	18	7	†91.17
1998— Vinny Testaverde, NYJ	421	259	3256	29	7	101.6
1999— Peyton Manning, Ind.	533	331	4135	26	15	90.7
2000— Brian Griese, Den.	336	216	2688	19	4	102.9

*This chart includes passer rating points for all leaders, although the same rating system was not used for determining leading quarterbacks prior to 1973. The old system was less equitable, yet similar to the new in that the rating was based on percentage of completions, touchdown passes, percentage of interceptions and average gain in yards.

†Brunell and Jeff George of Oakland (521, 290, 3917, 29, 9), tied with 91.2 rating points, but rounded to another decimal place, Brunell's rating is higher, 91.17 to 91.15.

RECEIVING

(Based on most receptions)

	No.	Yds.	TD
1960— Lionel Taylor, Denver	92	1235	12
1961— Lionel Taylor, Denver	100	1176	4
1962— Lionel Taylor, Denver	77	908	4
1963— Lionel Taylor, Denver	78	1101	10
1964— Charley Hennigan, Houston	101	1546	8
1965— Lionel Taylor, Denver	85	1131	6
1966— Lance Alworth, San Diego	73	1383	13
1967— George Sauer, N.Y. Jets	75	1189	6
1968— Lance Alworth, San Diego	68	1312	10
1969— Lance Alworth, San Diego	64	1003	4
1970— Marlin Briscoe, Buffalo	57	1036	8
1971— Fred Biletnikoff, Oakland	61	929	9
1972— Fred Biletnikoff, Oakland	58	802	7
1973— Fred Willis, Houston	57	371	1
1974— Lydell Mitchell, Baltimore	72	544	2
1975— Reggie Rucker, Cleveland	60	770	3
Lydell Mitchell, Baltimore	60	544	4
1976— MacArthur Lane, Kansas City	66	686	1
1977— Lydell Mitchell, Baltimore	71	620	4
1978— Steve Largent, Seattle	71	1168	8
1979— Joe Washington, Baltimore	82	750	3
1980— Kellen Winslow, San Diego	89	1290	9
1981— Kellen Winslow, San Diego	88	1075	10
1982— Kellen Winslow, San Diego	54	721	6
1983— Todd Christensen, L.A. Raiders	92	1247	12
1984— Ozzie Newsome, Cleveland	89	1001	5
1985— Lionel James, San Diego	86	1027	6
1986— Todd Christensen, L.A. Raiders	95	1153	8
1987— Al Toon, N.Y. Jets	68	976	5
1988— Al Toon, N.Y. Jets	93	1067	5
1989— Andre Reed, Buffalo	88	1312	9
1990— Haywood Jeffires, Houston	74	1048	8
Drew Hill, Houston	74	1019	5
1991— Haywood Jeffires, Houston	100	1181	7
1992— Haywood Jeffires, Houston	90	913	9
1993— Reggie Langhorne, Indianapolis	85	1038	3
1994— Ben Coates, New England	96	1174	7
1995— Carl Pickens, Cincinnati	99	1234	17
1996— Carl Pickens, Cincinnati	100	1180	12
1997— Tim Brown, Oakland	104	1408	5
1998— O.J. McDuffie, Miami	90	1050	7
1999— Jimmy Smith, Jacksonville	116	1636	6
2000— Marvin Harrison, Indianapolis	102	1413	14

SCORING

(Based on most total points)

	TD	PAT	FG	Tot.
1960— Gene Mingo, Denver	6	33	18	123
1961— Gino Cappelletti, Boston	8	48	17	147
1962— Gene Mingo, Denver	4	32	27	137
1963— Gino Cappelletti, Boston	2	35	22	113
1964— Gino Cappelletti, Boston	7	36	25	155
1965— Gino Cappelletti, Boston	9	27	17	132
1966— Gino Cappelletti, Boston	6	35	16	119
1967— George Blanda, Oakland	0	56	20	116
1968— Jim Turner, N.Y. Jets	0	43	34	145
1969— Jim Turner, N.Y. Jets	0	33	32	129
1970— Jan Stenerud, Kansas City	0	26	30	116
1971— Garo Yepremian, Miami	0	33	28	117
1972— Bobby Howfield, N.Y. Jets	0	40	27	121
1973— Roy Gerela, Pittsburgh	0	36	29	123
1974— Roy Gerela, Pittsburgh	0	33	20	93
1975— O.J. Simpson, Buffalo	23	0	0	138
1976— Toni Linhart, Baltimore	0	49	20	109
1977— Errol Mann, Oakland	0	39	20	99
1978— Pat Leahy, N.Y. Jets	0	41	22	107
1979— John Smith, New England	0	46	23	115
1980— John Smith, New England	0	51	26	129
1981— Jim Breech, Cincinnati	0	49	22	115
Nick Lowery, Kansas City	0	37	26	115
1982— Marcus Allen, L.A. Raiders	14	0	0	84
1983— Gary Anderson, Pittsburgh	0	38	27	119
1984— Gary Anderson, Pittsburgh	0	45	24	117
1985— Gary Anderson, Pittsburgh	0	40	33	139
1986— Tony Franklin, New England	0	44	32	140
1987— Jim Breech, Cincinnati	0	25	24	97
1988— Scott Norwood, Buffalo	0	33	32	129
1989— David Treadwell, Denver	0	39	27	120
1990— Nick Lowery, Kansas City	0	37	34	139
1991— Pete Stoyanovich, Miami	0	28	31	121
1992— Pete Stoyanovich, Miami	0	34	30	124
1993— Jeff Jaeger, L.A. Raiders	0	27	35	132
1994— John Carney, San Diego	0	33	34	135
1995— Norm Johnson, Pittsburgh	0	39	34	141
1996— Cary Blanchard, Indianapolis	0	27	36	135
1997— Mike Hollis, Jacksonville	0	41	31	134
1998— Steve Christie, Buffalo	0	41	33	140
1999— Mike Vanderjagt, Indianapolis	0	43	34	145
2000— Matt Stover, Baltimore	0	30	35	135

FIELD GOALS

	No.
1960— Gene Mingo, Denver	18
1961— Gino Cappelletti, Boston	17
1962— Gene Mingo, Denver	27
1963— Gino Cappelletti, Boston	22
1964— Gino Cappelletti, Boston	25
1965— Pete Gogolak, Buffalo	28
1966— Mike Mercer, Oakland-Kansas City	21
1967— Jan Stenerud, Kansas City	21
1968— Jim Turner, N.Y. Jets	34
1969— Jim Turner, N.Y. Jets	32
1970— Jan Stenerud, Kansas City	30
1971— Garo Yepremian, Miami	28
1972— Roy Gerela, Pittsburgh	28
1973— Roy Gerela, Pittsburgh	29
1974— Roy Gerela, Pittsburgh	20
1975— Jan Stenerud, Kansas City	22
1976— Jan Stenerud, Kansas City	21
1977— Errol Mann, Oakland	20
1978— Pat Leahy, N.Y. Jets	22

		No.
1979—	John Smith, New England	23
1980—	John Smith, New England	26
	Fred Steinfort, Denver	26
1981—	Nick Lowery, Kansas City	26
1982—	Nick Lowery, Kansas City	19
1983—	Raul Allegre, Baltimore	30
1984—	Gary Anderson, Pittsburgh	24
	Matt Bahr, Cleveland	24
1985—	Gary Anderson, Pittsburgh	33
1986—	Tony Franklin, New England	32
1987—	Dean Biasucci, Indianapolis	24
	Jim Breech, Cincinnati	24
1988—	Scott Norwood, Buffalo	32
1989—	David Treadwell, Denver	27
1990—	Nick Lowery, Kansas City	34
1991—	Pete Stoyanovich, Miami	31
1992—	Pete Stoyanovich, Miami	30
1993—	Jeff Jaeger, L.A. Raiders	35
1994—	John Carney, San Diego	34
1995—	Norm Johnson, Pittsburgh	34
1996—	Cary Blanchard, Indianapolis	36
1997—	Cary Blanchard, Indianapolis	32
1998—	Al Del Greco, Tennessee	36
1999—	Olinda Mare, Miami	39
2000—	Matt Stover, Baltimore	35

INTERCEPTIONS

		No.	Yds.
1960—	Austin Gonsoulin, Denver	11	98
1961—	Bill Atkins, Buffalo	10	158
1962—	Lee Riley, N.Y. Jets	11	122
1963—	Fred Glick, Houston	12	180
1964—	Dainard Paulson, N.Y. Jets	12	157
1965—	W.K. Hicks, Houston	9	156
1966—	Johnny Robinson, Kansas City	10	136
	Bobby Hunt, Kansas City	10	113
1967—	Miller Farr, Houston	10	264
	Tom Janik, Buffalo	10	222
	Dick Westmoreland, Miami	10	127
1968—	Dave Grayson, Oakland	10	195
1969—	Emmitt Thomas, Kansas City	9	146
1970—	Johnny Robinson, Kansas City	10	155
1971—	Ken Houston, Houston	9	220
1972—	Mike Sensibaugh, Kansas City	8	65
1973—	Dick Anderson, Miami	8	136
	Mike Wagner, Pittsburgh	8	134
1974—	Emmitt Thomas, Kansas City	12	214
1975—	Mel Blount, Pittsburgh	11	121
1976—	Ken Riley, Cincinnati	9	141
1977—	Lyle Blackwood, Baltimore	10	163
1978—	Thom Darden, Cleveland	10	200
1979—	Mike Reinfeldt, Houston	12	205
1980—	Lester Hayes, Oakland	13	273
1981—	John Harris, Seattle	10	155
1982—	Ken Riley, Cincinnati	5	88
	Bobby Jackson, N.Y. Jets	5	84
	Dwayne Woodruff, Pittsburgh	5	53
	Donnie Shell, Pittsburgh	5	27
1983—	Ken Riley, Cincinnati	8	89
	Vann McElroy, Los Angeles	8	68
1984—	Kenny Easley, Seattle	10	126
1985—	Eugene Daniel, Indianapolis	8	53
	Albert Lewis, Kansas City	8	59
1986—	Deron Cherry, Kansas City	9	150
1987—	Mike Prior, Indianapolis	6	57
	Mark Kelso, Buffalo	6	25
	Keith Bostic, Houston	6	-14
1988—	Erik McMillan, N.Y. Jets	8	168
1989—	Felix Wright, Cleveland	9	91
1990—	Richard Johnson, Houston	8	100
1991—	Ronnie Lott, L.A. Raiders	8	52
1992—	Henry Jones, Buffalo	8	263

		No.	Yds.
1993—	Nate Odomes, Buffalo	9	65
	Eugene Robinson, Seattle	9	80
1994—	Eric Turner, Cleveland	9	199
1995—	Willie Williams, Pittsburgh	7	122
1996—	Tyrone Braxton, Denver	9	128
1997—	Mark McMillian, Kansas City	8	274
	Darryl Williams, Seattle	8	172
1998—	Ty Law, New England	9	133
1999—	Rod Woodson, Baltimore	7	195
	Sam Madison, Miami	7	164
	James Hasty, Kansas City	7	98
2000—	Samari Rolle, Tennessee	7	140
	Brian Walker, Miami	7	80

PUNTING

(Based on highest average yardage per punt by qualifiers)

		No.	Avg.
1960—	Paul Maguire, L.A. Chargers	43	40.5
1961—	Bill Atkins, Buffalo	85	44.5
1962—	Jim Fraser, Denver	55	43.6
1963—	Jim Fraser, Denver	81	44.4
1964—	Jim Fraser, Denver	73	44.2
1965—	Jerrel Wilson, Kansas City	69	45.4
1966—	Bob Scarpitto, Denver	76	45.8
1967—	Bob Scarpitto, Denver	105	44.9
1968—	Jerrel Wilson, Kansas City	63	45.1
1969—	Dennis Partee, San Diego	71	44.6
1970—	Dave Lewis, Cincinnati	79	46.2
1971—	Dave Lewis, Cincinnati	72	44.8
1972—	Jerrel Wilson, Kansas City	66	44.8
1973—	Jerrel Wilson, Kansas City	80	45.5
1974—	Ray Guy, Oakland	74	42.2
1975—	Ray Guy, Oakland	68	43.8
1976—	Marv Bateman, Buffalo	86	42.8
1977—	Ray Guy, Oakland	59	43.4
1978—	Pat McInally, Cincinnati	91	43.1
1979—	Bob Grupp, Kansas City	89	43.6
1980—	Luke Prestridge, Denver	70	43.9
1981—	Pat McInally, Cincinnati	72	45.4
1982—	Luke Prestridge, Denver	45	45.0
1983—	Rohn Stark, Baltimore	91	45.3
1984—	Jim Arnold, Kansas City	98	44.9
1985—	Rohn Stark, Indianapolis	78	45.9
1986—	Rohn Stark, Indianapolis	76	45.2
1987—	Ralf Mojsiejenko, San Diego	67	42.9
1988—	Harry Newsome, Pittsburgh	65	45.4
1989—	Greg Montgomery, Houston	56	43.3
1990—	Mike Horan, Denver	58	44.4
1991—	Reggie Roby, Miami	54	45.7
1992—	Greg Montgomery, Houston	53	46.9
1993—	Greg Montgomery, Houston	54	45.6
1994—	Jeff Gossett, L.A. Raiders	77	43.9
1995—	Rick Tuten, Seattle	83	45.0
1996—	John Kidd, Miami	78	46.3
1997—	Tom Tupa, New England	71	45.7
1998—	Craig Hentrich, Tennessee	69	47.2
1999—	Tom Rouen, Denver	84	46.5
2000—	Darren Bennett, San Diego	92	46.2

PUNT RETURNS

(Based on most total yards)

		No.	Yds.	Avg.
1960—	Abner Haynes, Dallas	14	215	15.4
1961—	Dick Christy, N.Y. Jets	18	383	21.3
1962—	Dick Christy, N.Y. Jets	15	250	16.7
1963—	Claude Gibson, Oakland	26	307	11.8
1964—	Bobby Jancik, Houston	12	220	18.3
1965—	Leslie Duncan, San Diego	30	464	15.5
1966—	Leslie Duncan, San Diego	18	238	13.2
1967—	Floyd Little, Denver	16	270	16.9
1968—	Noland Smith, Kansas City	18	270	15.0
1969—	Bill Thompson, Denver	25	288	11.5

	No.	Yds.	Avg.
1970—Ed Podolak, Kansas City	23	311	13.5
1971—Leroy Kelly, Cleveland	30	292	9.7
1972—Chris Farasopolous, N.Y. Jets	17	179	10.5
1973—Ron Smith, San Diego	27	352	15.0
1974—Lemar Parrish, Cincinnati	18	338	18.8
1975—Billy Johnson, Houston	40	612	18.8
1976—Rick Upchurch, Denver	39	536	13.7
1977—Billy Johnson, Houston	30	539	15.4
1978—Rick Upchurch, Denver	36	493	13.7
1979—Tony Nathan, Miami	28	306	10.9
1980—J.T. Smith, Kansas City	40	581	14.5
1981—James Brooks, San Diego	22	290	13.2
1982—Rick Upchurch, Denver	15	242	16.1
1983—Kirk Springs, N.Y. Jets	23	287	12.5
1984—Mike Martin, Cincinnati	24	376	15.7
1985—Irving Fryar, New England	37	520	14.1
1986—Bobby Joe Edmonds, Seattle	34	419	12.3
1987—Bobby Joe Edmonds, Seattle	20	251	12.6
1988—Jojo Townsell, N.Y. Jets	35	409	11.7
1989—Clarence Verdin, Indianapolis	23	296	12.9
1990—Clarence Verdin, Indianapolis	31	396	12.8
1991—Rod Woodson, Pittsburgh	28	320	11.4
1992—Rod Woodson, Pittsburgh	32	364	11.4
1993—Tim Brown, L.A. Raiders	40	465	11.6
1994—Tim Brown, L.A. Raiders	40	487	12.2
1995—Tamarick Vanover, Kansas City	51	540	10.6
1996—David Meggett, New England	52	588	11.3
1997—Leon Johnson, N.Y. Jets	51	619	12.1
1998—Reggie Barlow, Jacksonville	43	555	12.9
1999—Charlie Rogers, Seattle	22	318	14.5
2000—Derrick Mason, Tennessee	51	662	13.0

KICKOFF RETURNS

(Based on most total yards)

	No.	Yds.	Avg.
1960—Ken Hall, Houston	19	594	31.3
1961—Dave Grayson, Dallas	16	453	28.3
1962—Bobby Jancik, Houston	24	726	30.3
1963—Bobby Jancik, Houston	45	1317	29.3
1964—Bo Roberson, Oakland	36	975	27.1
1965—Abner Haynes, Denver	34	901	26.5
1966—Goldie Sellers, Denver	19	541	28.5
1967—Zeke Moore, Houston	14	405	28.9
1968—George Atkinson, Oakland	32	802	25.1
1969—Bill Thompson, Denver	19	594	31.3
1970—Jim Duncan, Baltimore	20	707	35.4
1971—Mercury Morris, Miami	15	423	28.2
1972—Bruce Laird, Baltimore	29	843	29.1
1973—Wallace Francis, Buffalo	23	687	29.9
1974—Greg Pruitt, Cleveland	22	606	27.5
1975—Harold Hart, Oakland	17	518	30.5
1976—Duriel Harris, Miami	17	559	32.9
1977—Raymond Clayborn, New England	20	869	31.0
1978—Keith Wright, Cleveland	30	789	26.3
1979—Larry Brunson, Oakland	17	441	25.9
1980—Horace Ivory, New England	36	992	27.6
1981—Carl Roaches, Houston	28	769	27.5
1982—Mike Mosley, Buffalo	18	487	27.1
1983—Fulton Walker, Miami	36	962	26.7
1984—Bobby Humphrey, N.Y. Jets	22	675	30.7
1985—Glen Young, Cleveland	35	898	25.7
1986—Lupe Sanchez, Pittsburgh	25	591	23.6
1987—Paul Palmer, Kansas City	38	923	24.3
1988—Tim Brown, L.A. Raiders	41	1098	26.8
1989—Rod Woodson, Pittsburgh	36	982	27.3
1990—Kevin Clark, Denver	20	505	25.3
1991—Nate Lewis, San Diego	23	578	25.1
1992—Jon Vaughn, New England	20	564	28.2
1993—Clarence Verdin, Indianapolis	50	1050	21.0
1994—Andre Coleman, San Diego	49	1293	26.4
1995—Andre Coleman, San Diego	62	1411	22.8
1996—Mel Gray, Houston	50	1224	24.5

	No.	Yds.	Avg.
1997—Kevin Williams, Arizona	59	1459	24.7
1998—Vaughn Hebron, Denver	46	1216	26.4
1999—Tremain Mack, Cincinnati	51	1382	27.1
2000—Charlie Rogers, Seattle	66	1629	24.7

SACKS

	No.
1982— Jesse Baker, Houston	7.5
1983— Mark Gastineau, N.Y. Jets	19.0
1984— Mark Gastineau, N.Y. Jets	22.0
1985— Andre Tippett, New England	16.5
1986— Sean Jones, L.A. Raiders	15.5
1987— Andre Tippett, New England	12.5
1988— Greg Townsend, L.A. Raiders	11.5
1989— Lee Williams, San Diego	14.0
1990— Derrick Thomas, Kansas City	20.0
1991— William Fuller, Houston	15.0
1992— Leslie O'Neal, San Diego	17.0
1993— Neil Smith, Kansas City	15.0
1994— Kevin Greene, Pittsburgh	14.0
1995— Bryce Paup, Buffalo	17.5
1996— Michael McCrary, Seattle	13.5
Bruce Smith, Buffalo	13.5
1997— Bruce Smith, Buffalo	15.0
1998— Michael Sinclair, Seattle	16.5
1999— Jevon Kearse, Tennessee	14.5
2000— Trace Armstrong, Miami	16.5

NFC

RUSHING

(Based on most net yards)

	Net Yds.	Att.	TD
1960—Jim Brown, Cleveland	1257	215	9
1961—Jim Brown, Cleveland	1408	305	8
1962—Jim Taylor, Green Bay	1474	272	19
1963—Jim Brown, Cleveland	1863	291	12
1964—Jim Brown, Cleveland	1446	280	7
1965—Jim Brown, Cleveland	1544	289	17
1966—Gale Sayers, Chicago	1231	229	8
1967—Leroy Kelly, Cleveland	1205	235	11
1968—Leroy Kelly, Cleveland	1239	248	16
1969—Gale Sayers, Chicago	1032	236	8
1970—Larry Brown, Washington	1125	237	5
1971—John Brockington, Green Bay	1105	216	4
1972—Larry Brown, Washington	1216	285	8
1973—John Brockington, Green Bay	1144	265	3
1974—Lawrence McCutcheon, L.A. Rams..	1109	236	3
1975—Jim Otis, St. Louis	1076	269	5
1976—Walter Payton, Chicago	1390	311	13
1977—Walter Payton, Chicago	1852	339	14
1978—Walter Payton, Chicago	1395	333	11
1979—Walter Payton, Chicago	1610	369	14
1980—Walter Payton, Chicago	1460	317	6
1981—George Rogers, New Orleans	1674	378	13
1982—Tony Dorsett, Dallas	745	177	5
1983—Eric Dickerson, L.A. Rams	1808	390	18
1984—Eric Dickerson, L.A. Rams	2105	379	14
1985—Gerald Riggs, Atlanta	1719	397	10
1986—Eric Dickerson, L.A. Rams	1821	404	11
1987—Charles White, L.A. Rams	1374	324	11
1988—Herschel Walker, Dallas	1514	361	5
1989—Barry Sanders, Detroit	1470	280	14
1990—Barry Sanders, Detroit	1304	255	13
1991—Emmitt Smith, Dallas	1563	365	12
1992—Emmitt Smith, Dallas	1713	373	18
1993—Emmitt Smith, Dallas	1486	283	9
1994—Barry Sanders, Detroit	1883	331	7
1995—Emmitt Smith, Dallas	1773	377	25
1996—Barry Sanders, Detroit	1553	307	11
1997—Barry Sanders, Detroit	2053	335	11

	Net Yds.	Att.	TD
1998—Jamal Anderson, Atlanta	1846	410	14
1999—Stephen Davis, Washington	1405	290	17
2000—Robert Smith, Minnesota	1521	295	7

PASSING

(Based on highest passer rating among qualifiers*)

	Att.	Com.	Yds.	TD	Int.	Rat.
1960— Milt Plum, Cle.	250	151	2297	21	5	110.4
1961— Milt Plum, Cle.	302	177	2416	18	10	90.3
1962— Bart Starr, G.B.	285	178	2438	12	9	90.7
1963— Y.A. Tittle, NYG	367	221	3145	36	14	104.8
1964— Bart Starr, G.B.	272	163	2144	15	4	97.1
1965— Rudy Bukich, Chi.	312	176	2641	20	9	93.7
1966— Bart Starr, G.B.	251	156	2257	14	3	105.0
1967— Sonny Jurgensen, Was.	508	288	3747	31	16	87.3
1968— Earl Morrall, Bal.	317	182	2909	26	17	93.2
1969— Sonny Jurgensen, Was.	442	274	3102	22	15	85.4
1970— John Brodie, S.F.	378	223	2941	24	10	93.8
1971— Roger Staubach, Dal.	211	126	1882	15	4	104.8
1972— Norm Snead, NYG	325	196	2307	17	12	84.0
1973— Roger Staubach, Dal.	286	179	2428	23	15	94.6
1974— Sonny Jurgensen, Was.	167	107	1185	11	5	94.6
1975— Fran Tarkenton, Min.	425	273	2994	25	13	91.7
1976— James Harris, L.A.	158	91	1460	8	6	89.8
1977— Roger Staubach, Dal.	361	210	2620	18	9	87.1
1978— Roger Staubach, Dal.	413	231	3190	25	16	84.9
1979— Roger Staubach, Dal.	461	267	3586	27	11	92.4
1980— Ron Jaworski, Phi.	451	257	3529	27	12	90.0
1981— Joe Montana, S.F.	488	311	3565	19	12	88.4
1982— Joe Theismann, Was.	252	161	2033	13	9	91.3
1983— Steve Bartkowski, Atl.	432	274	3167	22	5	97.6
1984— Joe Montana, S.F.	432	279	3630	28	10	102.9
1985— Joe Montana, S.F.	494	303	3653	27	13	91.3
1986— Tommy Kramer, Min.	372	208	3000	24	10	92.6
1987— Joe Montana, S.F.	398	266	3054	31	13	102.1
1988— Wade Wilson, Min.	332	204	2746	15	9	91.5
1989— Joe Montana, S.F.	386	271	3521	26	8	112.4
1990— Phil Simms, NYG	311	184	2284	15	4	92.7
1991— Steve Young, S.F.	279	180	2517	17	8	101.8
1992— Steve Young, S.F.	402	268	3465	25	7	107.0
1993— Steve Young, S.F.	462	314	4023	29	16	101.5
1994— Steve Young, S.F.	461	324	3969	35	10	112.8
1995— Brett Favre, G.B.	570	359	4413	38	13	99.5
1996— Steve Young, S.F.	316	214	2410	14	6	97.2
1997— Steve Young, S.F.	356	241	3029	19	6	104.7
1998— Ran. Cunningham, Min.	425	259	3704	34	10	106.0
1999— Kurt Warner, St.L.	499	325	4353	41	13	109.2
2000— Trent Green, St.L.	240	145	2063	16	5	101.8

*This chart includes passer rating points for all leaders, although the same rating system was not used for determining leading quarterbacks prior to 1973. The old system was less equitable, yet similar to the new in that the rating was based on percentage of completions, touchdown passes, percentage of interceptions and average gain in yards.

RECEIVING

(Based on most receptions)

	No.	Yds.	TD
1960—Raymond Berry, Baltimore	74	1298	10
1961—Jim Phillips, L.A. Rams	78	1092	5
1962—Bobby Mitchell, Washington	72	1384	11
1963—Bobby Joe Conrad, St. Louis	73	967	10
1964—Johnny Morris, Chicago	93	1200	10
1965—Dave Parks, San Francisco	80	1344	12
1966—Charley Taylor, Washington	72	1119	12
1967—Charley Taylor, Washington	70	990	9
1968—Clifton McNeil, San Francisco	71	994	7
1969—Dan Abramowicz, New Orleans	73	1015	7
1970—Dick Gordon, Chicago	71	1026	13
1971—Bob Tucker, N.Y. Giants	59	791	4
1972—Harold Jackson, Philadelphia	62	1048	4
1973—Harold Carmichael, Philadelphia	67	1116	9
1974—Charles Young, Philadelphia	63	696	3
1975—Chuck Foreman, Minnesota	73	691	9
1976—Drew Pearson, Dallas	58	806	6
1977—Ahmad Rashad, Minnesota	51	681	2
1978—Rickey Young, Minnesota	88	704	5
1979—Ahmad Rashad, Minnesota	80	1156	9
1980—Earl Cooper, San Francisco	83	567	4
1981—Dwight Clark, San Francisco	85	1105	4
1982—Dwight Clark, San Francisco	60	913	5
1983—Roy Green, St. Louis	78	1227	14
Charlie Brown, Washington	78	1225	8
Earnest Gray, N.Y. Giants	78	1139	5
1984—Art Monk, Washington	106	1372	7
1985—Roger Craig, San Francisco	92	1016	6
1986—Jerry Rice, San Francisco	86	1570	15
1987—J.T. Smith, St. Louis	91	1117	8
1988—Henry Ellard, L.A. Rams	86	1414	10
1989—Sterling Sharpe, Green Bay	90	1423	12
1990—Jerry Rice, San Francisco	100	1502	13
1991—Michael Irvin, Dallas	93	1523	8
1992—Sterling Sharpe, Green Bay	108	1461	13
1993—Sterling Sharpe, Green Bay	112	1274	11
1994—Cris Carter, Minnesota	122	1256	7
1995—Herman Moore, Detroit	123	1686	14
1996—Jerry Rice, San Francisco	108	1254	8
1997—Herman Moore, Detroit	104	1293	8
1998—Frank Sanders, Arizona	89	1145	3
1999—Muhsin Muhammad, Carolina	96	1253	8
2000—Muhsin Muhammad, Carolina	102	1183	6

SCORING

(Based on most total points)

	TD	PAT	FG	Tot.
1960— Paul Hornung, Green Bay	15	41	15	176
1961— Paul Hornung, Green Bay	10	41	15	146
1962— Jim Taylor, Green Bay	19	0	0	114
1963— Don Chandler, N.Y. Giants	0	52	18	106
1964— Lenny Moore, Baltimore	20	0	0	120
1965— Gale Sayers, Chicago	22	0	0	132
1966— Bruce Gossett, L.A. Rams	0	29	28	113
1967— Jim Bakken, St. Louis	0	36	27	117
1968— Leroy Kelly, Cleveland	20	0	0	120
1969— Fred Cox, Minnesota	0	43	26	121
1970— Fred Cox, Minnesota	0	35	30	125
1971— Curt Knight, Washington	0	27	29	114
1972— Chester Marcol, Green Bay	0	29	33	128
1973— David Ray, L.A. Rams	0	40	30	130
1974— Chester Marcol, Green Bay	0	19	25	94
1975— Chuck Foreman, Minnesota	22	0	0	132
1976— Mark Moseley, Washington	0	31	22	97
1977— Walter Payton, Chicago	16	0	0	96
1978— Frank Corral, L.A. Rams	0	31	29	118
1979— Mark Moseley, Washington	0	39	25	114
1980— Ed Murray, Detroit	0	35	27	116
1981— Ed Murray, Detroit	0	46	25	121
Rafael Septien, Dallas	0	40	27	121
1982— Wendell Tyler, L.A. Rams	13	0	0	78
1983— Mark Moseley, Washington	0	62	33	161
1984— Ray Wersching, S.F.	0	56	25	131
1985— Kevin Butler, Chicago	0	51	31	144
1986— Kevin Butler, Chicago	0	36	28	120
1987— Jerry Rice, San Francisco	23	0	0	138
1988— Mike Cofer, San Francisco	0	40	27	121
1989— Mike Cofer, San Francisco	0	49	29	136
1990— Chip Lohmiller, Washington	0	41	30	131
1991— Chip Lohmiller, Washington	0	56	31	149
1992— Morten Andersen, New Orleans	0	33	29	120
Chip Lohmiller, Washington	0	30	30	120
1993— Jason Hanson, Detroit	0	28	34	130
1994— Fuad Reveiz, Minnesota	0	30	34	132
1995— Emmitt Smith, Dallas	25	0	0	150

	TD	PAT	FG	Tot.
1996—John Kasay, Carolina	0	34	37	145
1997—Richie Cunningham, Dallas	0	24	34	126
1998—Gary Anderson, Minnesota	0	59	35	164
1999—Jeff Wilkins, St. Louis	0	64	20	124
2000—Marshall Faulk, St. Louis	26	0	0	*160

*Includes two 2-Pt. conversions.

FIELD GOALS

	No.
1960— Tommy Davis, San Francisco	19
1961— Steve Myhra, Baltimore	21
1962— Lou Michaels, Pittsburgh	26
1963— Jim Martin, Baltimore	24
1964— Jim Bakken, St. Louis	25
1965— Fred Cox, Minnesota	23
1966— Bruce Gossett, L.A. Rams	28
1967— Jim Bakken, St. Louis	27
1968— Mac Percival, Chicago	25
1969— Fred Cox, Minnesota	26
1970— Fred Cox, Minnesota	30
1971— Curt Knight, Washington	29
1972— Chester Marcol, Green Bay	33
1973— David Ray, L.A. Rams	30
1974— Chester Marcol, Green Bay	25
1975— Toni Fritsch, Dallas	22
1976— Mark Moseley, Washington	22
1977— Mark Moseley, Washington	21
1978— Frank Corral, L.A. Rams	29
1979— Mark Moseley, Washington	25
1980— Eddie Murray, Detroit	27
1981— Rafael Septien, Dallas	27
1982— Mark Moseley, Washington	20
1983— Ali Haji-Sheikh, N.Y. Giants	35
1984— Paul McFadden, Philadelphia	30
1985— Morten Andersen, New Orleans	31
Kevin Butler, Chicago	31
1986— Kevin Butler, Chicago	28
1987— Morten Andersen, New Orleans	28
1988— Mike Cofer, San Francisco	27
1989— Rich Karlis, Minnesota	31
1990— Chip Lohmiller, Washington	30
1991— Chip Lohmiller, Washington	31
1992— Chip Lohmiller, Washington	30
1993— Jason Hanson, Detroit	34
1994— Fuad Reveiz, Minnesota	34
1995— Morten Andersen, Atlanta	31
1996— John Kasay, Carolina	37
1997— Richie Cunningham, Dallas	34
1998— Gary Anderson, Minnesota	35
1999— Martin Gramatica, Tampa Bay	27
2000— Ryan Longwell, Green Bay	33

INTERCEPTIONS

	No.	Yds.
1960— Dave Baker, San Francisco	10	96
Jerry Norton, St. Louis	10	96
1961— Dick Lynch, N.Y. Giants	9	60
1962— Willie Wood, Green Bay	9	132
1963— Dick Lynch, N.Y. Giants	9	251
Rosie Taylor, Chicago	9	172
1964— Paul Krause, Washington	12	140
1965— Bobby Boyd, Baltimore	9	78
1966— Larry Wilson, St. Louis	10	180
1967— Lem Barney, Detroit	10	232
Dave Whitsell, New Orleans	10	178
1968— Willie Williams, N.Y. Giants	10	103
1969— Mel Renfro, Dallas	10	118
1970— Dick Le Beau, Detroit	9	96
1971— Bill Bradley, Philadelphia	11	248
1972— Bill Bradley, Philadelphia	9	73
1973— Bob Bryant, Minnesota	7	105
1974— Ray Brown, Atlanta	8	164

	No.	Yds.
1975— Paul Krause, Minnesota	10	201
1976— Monte Jackson, L.A. Rams	10	173
1977— Rolland Lawrence, Atlanta	7	138
1978— Ken Stone, St. Louis	9	139
Willie Buchanon, Green Bay	9	93
1979— Lemar Parrish, Washington	9	65
1980— Nolan Cromwell, L.A. Rams	8	140
1981— Everson Walls, Dallas	11	133
1982— Everson Walls, Dallas	7	61
1983— Mark Murphy, Washington	9	127
1984— Tom Flynn, Green Bay	9	106
1985— Everson Walls, Dallas	9	31
1986— Ronnie Lott, San Francisco	10	134
1987— Barry Wilburn, Washington	9	135
1988— Scott Case, Atlanta	10	47
1989— Eric Allen, Philadelphia	8	38
1990— Mark Carrier, Chicago	10	39
1991— Ray Crockett, Detroit	6	141
Tim McKyer, Atlanta	6	24
Deion Sanders, Atlanta	6	119
Aeneas Williams, Phoenix	6	60
1992— Aubray McMillian, Minnesota	8	157
1993— Deion Sanders, Atlanta	7	91
1994— Aeneas Williams, Arizona	9	89
1995— Orlando Thomas, Minnesota	9	108
1996— Keith Lyle, St. Louis	9	152
1997— Ryan McNeil, St. Louis	9	127
1998— Kwamie Lassiter, Arizona	8	80
1999— Donnie Abraham, Tampa Bay	7	115
Troy Vincent, Philadelphia	7	91
2000— Darren Sharper, Green Bay	9	109

PUNTING

(Based on highest average yardage per punt by qualifiers)

	No.	Avg.
1960— Jerry Norton, St. Louis	39	45.6
1961— Yale Lary, Detroit	52	48.4
1962— Tommy Davis, San Francisco	48	45.8
1963— Yale Lary, Detroit	35	48.9
1964— Bobby Walden, Minnesota	72	46.4
1965— Gary Collins, Cleveland	65	46.7
1966— David Lee, Baltimore	49	45.6
1967— Billy Lothridge, Atlanta	87	43.7
1968— Billy Lothridge, Atlanta	75	44.3
1969— David Lee, Baltimore	50	45.3
1970— Julian Fagan, New Orleans	77	42.5
1971— Tom McNeill, Philadelphia	73	42.0
1972— Dave Chapple, L.A. Rams	53	44.2
1973— Tom Wittum, San Francisco	79	43.7
1974— Tom Blanchard, New Orleans	88	42.1
1975— Herman Weaver, Detroit	80	42.0
1976— John James, Atlanta	101	42.1
1977— Tom Blanchard, New Orleans	82	42.4
1978— Tom Skladany, Detroit	86	42.5
1979— Dave Jennings, N.Y. Giants	104	42.7
1980— Dave Jennings, N.Y. Giants	94	44.8
1981— Tom Skladany, Detroit	64	43.5
1982— Carl Birdsong, St. Louis	54	43.8
1983— Frank Garcia, Tampa Bay	95	42.2
1984— Brian Hansen, New Orleans	69	43.8
1985— Rick Donnelly, Atlanta	59	43.6
1986— Sean Landeta, N.Y. Giants	79	44.8
1987— Rick Donnelly, Atlanta	61	44.0
1988— Jim Arnold, Detroit	97	42.4
1989— Rich Camarillo, Phoenix	76	43.4
1990— Sean Landeta, N.Y. Giants	75	44.1
1991— Harry Newsome, Minnesota	68	45.5
1992— Harry Newsome, Minnesota	72	45.0
1993— Jim Arnold, Detroit	72	44.5
1994— Sean Landeta, L.A. Rams	78	44.8
1995— Sean Landeta, St. Louis	83	44.3
1996— Matt Turk, Washington	75	45.1

	No.	Avg.
1997— Mark Royals, New Orleans	88	45.9
1998— Mark Royals, New Orleans	88	45.6
1999— Mitch Berger, Minnesota	61	45.4
2000— Mitch Berger, Minnesota	62	44.7

PUNT RETURNS

(Based on most total yards)

	No.	Yds.	Avg.
1960— Abe Woodson, San Francisco	13	174	13.4
1961— Willie Wood, Green Bay	14	225	16.1
1962— Pat Studstill, Detroit	29	457	15.8
1963— Dick James, Washington	16	214	13.4
1964— Tommy Watkins, Detroit	16	238	14.9
1965— Leroy Kelly, Cleveland	17	265	15.6
1966— Johnny Roland, St. Louis	20	221	11.1
1967— Ben Davis, Cleveland	18	229	12.7
1968— Bob Hayes, Dallas	15	312	20.8
1969— Alvin Haymond, L.A. Rams	33	435	13.2
1970— Bruce Taylor, San Francisco	43	516	12.0
1971— Les Duncan, Washington	22	233	10.6
1972— Ken Ellis, Green Bay	14	215	15.4
1973— Bruce Taylor, San Francisco	15	207	13.8
1974— Dick Jauron, Detroit	17	286	16.8
1975— Terry Metcalf, St. Louis	23	285	12.4
1976— Eddie Brown, Washington	48	646	13.5
1977— Larry Marshall, Philadelphia	46	489	10.6
1978— Jackie Wallace, L.A. Rams	52	618	11.9
1979— John Sciarra, Philadelphia	16	182	11.4
1980— Kenny Johnson, Atlanta	23	281	12.2
1981— LeRoy Irvin, L.A. Rams	46	615	13.4
1982— Billy Johnson, Atlanta	24	273	11.4
1983— Henry Ellard, L.A. Rams	16	217	13.6
1984— Henry Ellard, L.A. Rams	30	403	13.4
1985— Henry Ellard, L.A. Rams	37	501	13.5
1986— Vai Sikahema, St. Louis	43	522	12.1
1987— Mel Gray, New Orleans	24	352	14.7
1988— John Taylor, San Francisco	44	556	12.6
1989— Walter Stanley, Detroit	36	496	13.8
1990— Johnny Bailey, Chicago	36	399	11.1
1991— Mel Gray, Detroit	25	385	15.4
1992— Johnny Bailey, Phoenix	20	263	13.2
1993— Tyrone Hughes, New Orleans	37	503	13.6
1994— Brian Mitchell, Washington	32	452	14.1
1995— Eric Guliford, Carolina	43	475	11.0
1996— Desmond Howard, Green Bay	58	875	15.1
1997— Karl Williams, Tampa Bay	46	597	13.0
1998— Brian Mitchell, Washington	44	506	11.5
1999— Glyn Milburn, Chicago	29	346	11.9
2000— Az-Zahir Hakim, St. Louis	32	489	15.3

KICKOFF RETURNS

(Based on most total yards)

	No.	Yds.	Avg.
1960— Tom Moore, Green Bay	12	397	33.1
1961— Dick Bass, L.A. Rams	23	698	30.3
1962— Abe Woodson, San Francisco	37	1157	31.3
1963— Abe Woodson, San Francisco	29	935	32.3
1964— Clarence Childs, N.Y. Giants	34	987	29.0
1965— Tommy Watkins, Detroit	17	584	34.4
1966— Gale Sayers, Chicago	23	718	31.2

	No.	Yds.	Avg.
1967— Travis Williams, Green Bay	18	739	41.1
1968— Preston Pearson, Baltimore	15	527	35.1
1969— Bobby Williams, Detroit	17	563	33.1
1970— Cecil Turner, Chicago	23	752	32.7
1971— Travis Williams, L.A. Rams	25	743	29.7
1972— Ron Smith, Chicago	30	924	30.8
1973— Carl Garrett, Chicago	16	486	30.4
1974— Terry Metcalf, St. Louis	20	623	31.2
1975— Walter Payton, Chicago	14	444	31.7
1976— Cullen Bryant, L.A. Rams	16	459	28.7
1977— Wilbert Montgomery, Phila.	23	619	26.9
1978— Steve Odom, Green Bay	25	677	27.1
1979— Jimmy Edwards, Minnesota	44	1103	25.1
1980— Rich Mauti, New Orleans	31	798	27.6
1981— Mike Nelms, Washington	37	1099	29.7
1982— Alvin Hall, Detroit	16	426	26.6
1983— Darrin Nelson, Minnesota	18	445	24.7
1984— Barry Redden, L.A. Rams	23	530	23.0
1985— Ron Brown, L.A. Rams	28	918	32.8
1986— Dennis Gentry, Chicago	20	576	28.8
1987— Sylvester Stamps, Atlanta	24	660	27.5
1988— Donnie Elder, Tampa Bay	34	772	22.7
1989— Mel Gray, Detroit	24	640	26.7
1990— Dave Meggett, N.Y. Giants	21	492	23.4
1991— Mel Gray, Detroit	36	929	25.8
1992— Deion Sanders, Atlanta	40	1067	26.7
1993— Tony Smith, Atlanta	38	948	24.9
1994— Tyrone Hughes, New Orleans	63	1556	24.7
1995— Tyrone Hughes, New Orleans	66	1617	24.5
1996— Tyrone Hughes, New Orleans	70	1791	25.6
1997— Glyn Milburn, Detroit	55	1315	23.9
1998— Glyn Milburn, Chicago	62	1550	25.0
1999— Tony Horne, St. Louis	30	892	29.7
2000— MarTay Jenkins, Arizona	82	2186	26.7

SACKS

	No.
1982— Doug Martin, Minnesota	11.5
1983— Fred Dean, San Francisco	17.5
1984— Richard Dent, Chicago	17.5
1985— Richard Dent, Chicago	17.0
1986— Lawrence Taylor, N.Y. Giants	20.5
1987— Reggie White, Philadelphia	21.0
1988— Reggie White, Philadelphia	18.0
1989— Chris Doleman, Minnesota	21.0
1990— Charles Haley, San Francisco	16.0
1991— Pat Swilling, New Orleans	17.0
1992— Clyde Simmons, Philadelphia	19.0
1993— Renaldo Turnbull, New Orleans	13.0
Reggie White, Green Bay	13.0
1994— Ken Harvey, Washington	13.5
John Randle, Minnesota	13.5
1995— William Fuller, Philadelphia	13.0
Wayne Martin, New Orleans	13.0
1996— Kevin Greene, Carolina	14.5
1997— John Randle, Minnesota	15.5
1998— Reggie White, Green Bay	16.0
1999— Kevin Carter, St. Louis	17.0
2000— La'Roi Glover, New Orleans	17.0

COACHING RECORDS

COACHES WITH 100 OR MORE CAREER VICTORIES

(Ranked according to career wins)

	Yrs.	REGULAR SEASON				POSTSEASON			CAREER			
		Won	Lost	Tied	Pct.	Won	Lost	Pct.	Won	Lost	Tied	Pct.
Don Shula	33	328	156	6	.676	19	17	.528	347	173	6	.665
George Halas	40	318	148	31	.671	6	3	.667	324	151	31	.671
Tom Landry	29	250	162	6	.605	20	16	.556	270	178	6	.601
Curly Lambeau	33	226	132	22	.624	3	2	.600	229	134	22	.623
Chuck Noll	23	193	148	1	.566	16	8	.667	209	156	1	.572
Chuck Knox	22	186	147	1	.558	7	11	.389	193	158	1	.550
*Dan Reeves	20	171	140	1	.550	10	8	.556	181	148	1	.550
Paul Brown	21	166	100	6	.621	4	9	.308	170	109	6	.607
Bud Grant	18	158	96	5	.620	10	12	.455	168	108	5	.607
Steve Owen	23	153	100	17	.598	2	8	.200	155	108	17	.584
Marv Levy	17	143	112	0	.561	11	8	.579	154	120	0	.562
Marty Schottenheimer	15	145	85	1	.630	5	11	.313	150	96	1	.609
Bill Parcells	15	138	100	1	.579	11	6	.647	149	106	1	.584
Joe Gibbs	12	124	60	0	.674	16	5	.762	140	65	0	.683
Hank Stram	17	131	97	10	.571	5	3	.625	136	100	10	.573
Weeb Ewbank	20	130	129	7	.502	4	1	.800	134	130	7	.507
Mike Ditka	14	121	95	0	.560	6	6	.500	127	101	0	.557
Sid Gillman	18	122	99	7	.550	1	5	.167	123	104	7	.541
*George Seifert	10	113	47	0	.706	10	5	.667	123	52	0	.703
George Allen	12	116	47	5	.705	4	7	.364	120	54	5	.684
*Jim Mora	14	119	96	0	.553	0	6	.000	119	102	0	.538
Don Coryell	14	111	83	1	.572	3	6	.333	114	89	1	.561
John Madden	10	103	32	7	.750	9	7	.563	112	39	7	.731
Buddy Parker	15	104	75	9	.577	3	2	.600	107	77	9	.578
Vince Lombardi	10	96	34	6	.728	9	1	.900	105	35	6	.740
Bill Walsh	10	92	59	1	.609	10	4	.714	102	63	1	.617

*Active NFL coaches in 2000.

ACTIVE COACHES CAREER RECORDS

(Ranked according to career NFL percentages)

	Yrs.	REGULAR SEASON				POSTSEASON			CAREER			
		Won	Lost	Tied	Pct.	Won	Lost	Pct.	Won	Lost	Tied	Pct.
George Seifert	10	113	47	0	.706	10	5	.667	123	52	0	.703
Brian Billick	2	20	12	0	.625	4	0	1.000	24	12	0	.667
Mike Shanahan	8	72	44	0	.621	7	2	.778	79	46	0	.632
Mike Holmgren	9	90	54	0	.625	9	6	.600	99	60	0	.623
Dennis Green	9	92	52	0	.639	4	8	.333	96	60	0	.615
Jim Haslett	1	10	6	0	.625	1	1	.500	11	7	0	.611
Marty Schottenheimer	15	145	85	1	.630	5	11	.313	150	96	1	.609
Mike Martz	1	10	6	0	.625	0	1	.000	10	7	0	.588
Bill Cowher	9	86	58	0	.597	5	6	.455	91	64	0	.587
Jim Fassel	4	37	26	1	.586	2	2	.500	39	28	1	.581
Jon Gruden	3	28	20	0	.583	1	1	.500	29	21	0	.580
Tom Coughlin	6	56	40	0	.583	4	4	.500	60	44	0	.577
Jeff Fisher	7	58	44	0	.569	3	2	.600	61	46	0	.570
Mike Sherman	1	9	7	0	.563	0	0	.000	9	7	0	.563
Tony Dungy	5	45	35	0	.563	2	3	.400	47	38	0	.553
Dan Reeves	20	171	140	1	.550	10	8	.556	181	148	1	.550
Steve Mariucci	4	35	29	0	.547	2	2	.500	37	31	0	.544
Jim Mora	14	119	96	0	.553	0	6	.000	119	102	0	.538
USFL Totals	3	41	12	1	.769	7	1	.875	48	13	1	.782
Dick Vermeil	10	76	73	0	.510	6	4	.600	82	77	0	.516
Andy Reid	2	16	16	0	.500	1	1	.500	17	17	0	.500
Dave Wannstedt	7	51	61	0	.455	2	2	.500	53	63	0	.457
Bill Belichick	6	41	55	0	.427	1	1	.500	42	56	0	.429
Dick Jauron	2	11	21	0	.344	0	0	.000	11	21	0	.344
Dave Campo	1	5	11	0	.313	0	0	.000	5	11	0	.313
Dick LeBeau	1	4	9	0	.308	0	0	.000	4	9	0	.308
Mike Riley	2	9	23	0	.281	0	0	.000	9	23	0	.281
Dave McGinnis	1	1	8	0	.111	0	0	.000	1	8	0	.111
Butch Davis	0	0	0	0	.000	0	0	.000	0	0	0	.000
Herman Edwards	0	0	0	0	.000	0	0	.000	0	0	0	.000
Marty Mornhinweg	0	0	0	0	.000	0	0	.000	0	0	0	.000
Gregg Williams	0	0	0	0	.000	0	0	.000	0	0	0	.000

HALL OF FAME

ROSTER OF MEMBERS

SEVEN NEW INDUCTEES IN 2001

Nick Buoniconti, Marv Levy, Mike Munchak, Jackie Slater, Lynn Swann, Ron Yary and Jack Youngblood were inducted into Pro Football's Hall of Fame in 2001, expanding the list of former stars honored at Canton, Ohio, to 211.

Name	Elec. year	College	Pos.	NFL teams
Adderley, Herb	1980	Michigan State	CB	Green Bay Packers, 1961-69; Dallas Cowboys, 1970-72
Alworth, Lance†	1978	Arkansas	WR	San Diego Chargers, 1962-70; Dallas Cowboys, 1971-72.
Atkins, Doug	1982	Tennessee	DE	Cleveland Browns, 1953-54; Chicago Bears, 1955-66; New Orleans Saints, 1967-69
Badgro, Morris (Red)	1981	Southern California	E	New York Yankees, 1926; New York Giants, 1930-35
Barney, Lem	1992	Jackson State	CB	Detroit Lions, 1967-77
Battles, Cliff	1968	W. Virginia Wesleyan	HB/QB	Boston Braves, Boston Redskins, Washington Redskins, 1932-37; coach, Brooklyn Dodgers, 1946-47
Baugh, Sammy	1963	Texas Christian	QB	Washington Redskins, 1937-52; coach, New York Titans, 1960-61; Houston Oilers, 1964
Bednarik, Chuck	1967	Pennsylvania	C/LB	Philadelphia Eagles, 1949-62
Bell, Bert	1963	Pennsylvania	*	NFL Commissioner, 1946-59
Bell, Bobby	1983	Minnesota	LB	Kansas City Chiefs, 1963-74
Berry, Raymond†	1973	Southern Methodist	E	Baltimore Colts, 1955-67; coach, New England Patriots, 1984-89
Bidwill, Charles W.	1967	Loyola	*	Owner, Chicago Cardinals, 1933-47
Biletnikoff, Fred	1988	Florida State	WR	Oakland Raiders, 1965-78
Blanda, George†	1981	Kentucky	QB/PK	Chicago Bears, 1949-58; Baltimore Colts, 1950; Houston Oilers, 1960-66; Oakland Raiders, 1967-73
Blount, Mel†	1989	Southern	CB	Pittsburgh Steelers, 1970-83
Bradshaw, Terry†	1989	Louisiana Tech	QB	Pittsburgh Steelers, 1970-83
Brown, Jim†	1971	Syracuse	FB	Cleveland Browns, 1957-65
Brown, Paul	1967	Miami of Ohio	*	Coach, Cleveland Browns, 1946-62; Cincinnati Bengals, 1968-75
Brown, Roosevelt	1975	Morgan State	T	New York Giants, 1953-66
Brown, Willie†	1984	Grambling	DB	Denver Broncos, 1963-66; Oakland Raiders, 1967-78
Buchanan, Buck	1990	Grambling	DT	Kansas City Chiefs, 1963-75
Buoniconti, Nick	2001	Notre Dame	LB	Boston Patriots, 1962-68; Miami Dolphins, 1969-76
Butkus, Dick†	1979	Illinois	LB	Chicago Bears, 1965-73
Campbell, Earl†	1991	Texas	RB	Houston Oilers, 1978-84; New Orleans Saints, 1984-85
Canadeo, Tony	1974	Gonzaga	HB	Green Bay Packers, 1941-44, 46-52
Carr, Joe	1963			NFL President, 1921-39
Chamberlin, Guy	1965	Nebraska	E/WB*	Player/coach, Canton Bulldogs, Cleveland, Frankford Yellowjackets, Chicago Bears, Chicago Cardinals, 1919-28
Christiansen, Jack	1970	Colorado A&M	DB	Detroit Lions, 1951-58; coach, San Francisco 49ers, 1963-67
Clark, Dutch	1963	Colorado College	QB	Portsmouth Spartans, Detroit Lions, 1931-38
Connor, George	1975	Notre Dame	T/LB	Chicago Bears, 1948-55
Conzelman, Jimmy	1964	Washington (Mo.)	HB*	Coach/executive, Decatur, Rock Island, Milwaukee, Detroit, Providence, Chicago Cardinals, 1920-48
Creekmur, Lou	1996	William & Mary	T/G	Detroit Lions, 1950-59
Csonka, Larry	1987	Syracuse	RB	Miami Dolphins, 1968-74, 79; New York Giants, 1976-78
Davis, Al	1992	Syracuse	*	Coach/general manager/president, Oakland-Los Angeles Raiders, 1963-present
Davis, Willie	1981	Grambling	DE	Cleveland Browns, 1958-59; Green Bay Packers, 1960-69
Dawson, Len	1987	Purdue	QB	Pittsburgh Steelers, 1957-58; Cleveland Browns, 1960-61; Dallas Texans, 1962; Kansas City Chiefs, 1963-75
Dickerson, Eric†	1999	Southern Methodist	RB	Los Angeles Rams, 1983-87; Indianapolis Colts, 1987-91; Los Angeles Raiders, 1992; Atlanta Falcons, 1993
Dierdorf, Dan	1996	Michigan	T/C	St. Louis Cardinals, 1971-83
Ditka, Mike	1988	Pittsburgh	TE	Chicago Bears, 1961-66; Philadelphia Eagles, 1967-68; Dallas Cowboys, 1969-72; coach, Chicago Bears, 1982-92; New Orleans Saints, 1997-99
Donovan, Art	1968	Boston College	DT	Baltimore Colts, New York Yanks, Dallas Texans, 1950-61
Dorsett, Tony	1994	Pittsburgh	RB	Dallas Cowboys, 1977-87; Denver Broncos, 1988
Driscoll, Paddy	1965	Northwestern	TB/HB/QB	Player/coach, Chicago Cardinals, Chicago Bears, 1919-31, 41-68
Dudley, Bill	1966	Virginia	HB	Pittsburgh Steelers, Detroit Lions, Washington Redskins, 1942-53
Edwards, Turk	1969	Washington State	T	Boston Braves, Boston Redskins, Washington Redskins, 1932-40
Ewbank, Weeb	1978	Miami of Ohio	*	Coach, Baltimore Colts, 1954-62; New York Jets, 1963-73
Fears, Tom	1970	Santa Clara	E	Los Angeles Rams, 1948-56; coach, New Orleans Saints, 1967-70
Finks, Jim	1995	Tulsa	QB*	Pittsburgh Steelers, 1949-55; administrator, Minnesota Vikings, 1964-73; Chicago Bears, 1974-86; New Orleans Saints, 1987-93

Name	Elec. year	College	Pos.	NFL teams
Flaherty, Ray	1976	Gonzaga	E*	Player/coach, Los Angeles Wildcats, New York Yankees, AFL; New York Giants, Boston Redskins, Washington Redskins, New York Yankees, AAFC; Chicago Hornets, 1926-49
Ford, Len	1976	Michigan	E	Los Angeles Dons, Cleveland Browns, 1948-58
Fortmann, Danny	1965	Colgate	G	Chicago Bears, 1936-43
Fouts, Dan†	1993	Oregon	QB	San Diego Chargers, 1973-87
Gatski, Frank	1985	Marshall	C	Cleveland Browns, 1946-56; Detroit Lions, 1957
George, Bill	1974	Wake Forest	LB	Chicago Bears, Los Angeles Rams, 1952-66
Gibbs, Joe	1996	San Diego State	*	Washington Redskins, 1981-92
Gifford, Frank	1977	Southern California	HB/E	New York Giants, 1952-60, 62-64
Gillman, Sid	1983	Ohio State	E*	Coach, Los Angeles Rams, 1955-59; Los Angeles Chargers, 1960; San Diego Chargers, 1961-69, 71; Houston Oilers, 1973-74
Graham, Otto	1965	Northwestern	QB	Cleveland Browns, 1946-55; coach, Washington Redskins, 1966-68
Grange, Red	1963	Illinois	HB	Chicago Bears, 1925, 29-34; New York Yankees, 1926-27
Grant, Bud	1994	Minnesota	WR*	Philadelphia Eagles, 1951-52; coach, Minnesota Vikings, 1967-83, 1985
Greene, Joe†	1987	North Texas State	DT	Pittsburgh Steelers, 1969-81
Gregg, Forrest†	1977	Southern Methodist	T	Green Bay Packers, Dallas Cowboys, 1956, 58-71; coach, Cleveland Browns, 1975-77; Cincinnati Bengals, 1980-83; Green Bay Packers, 1984-87
Griese, Bob	1990	Purdue	QB	Miami Dolphins, 1967-80
Groza, Lou	1974	Ohio State	T/PK	Cleveland Browns, 1946-59, 61-67
Guyon, Joe	1966	Carlisle, Georgia Tech	HB	Canton Bulldogs, Cleveland Indians, Oorang Indians, Rock Island Independents, Kansas City Cowboys, New York Giants, 1918-27
Halas, George	1963	Illinois	E*	Player/coach/ founder, Chicago Bears, 1920-83
Ham, Jack†	1988	Penn State	LB	Pittsburgh Steelers, 1971-82
Hannah, John†	1991	Alabama	G	New England Patriots, 1973-85
Harris, Franco†	1990	Penn State	RB	Pittsburgh Steelers, 1972-83; Seattle Seahawks, 1984
Haynes, Mike	1997	Arizona State	CB	New England Patriots, 1976-82; Los Angeles Raiders, 1983-89
Healey, Ed	1964	Dartmouth	T	Rock Island, Chicago Bears, 1920-27
Hein, Mel	1963	Washington State	C	New York Giants, 1931-45
Hendricks, Ted	1990	Miami, Fla.	LB	Baltimore Colts, 1969-73; Green Bay Packers, 1974; Oakland/Los Angeles Raiders, 1975-83
Henry, Wilbur	1963	Wash'ton & Jefferson	T	Canton Bulldogs, Akron Indians, New York Giants, Pottsville Maroons, Pittsburgh Steelers, 1920-30
Herber, Arnie	1966	Regis	HB	Green Bay Packers, New York Giants, 1930-45
Hewitt, Bill	1971	Michigan	E	Chicago Bears, 1932-36; Philadelphia Eagles, 1937-39; Philadelphia/Pittsburgh, 1943
Hinkle, Clarke	1964	Bucknell	FB	Green Bay Packers, 1932-41
Hirsch, Elroy (Crazylegs)	1968	Wisconsin	E/HB	Chicago Rockets, Los Angeles Rams, 1946-57
Hornung, Paul	1986	Notre Dame	RB	Green Bay Packers, 1957-62, 64-66
Houston, Ken†	1986	Prairie View	DB	Houston Oilers, 1967-72; Washington Redskins, 1973-80
Hubbard, Cal	1963	Centenary, Geneva	T/E	New York Giants, Green Bay Packers, Pittsburgh Steelers, 1927-36
Huff, Sam	1982	West Virginia	LB	New York Giants, 1956-63; Washington Redskins, 1964-67, 69
Hunt, Lamar	1972	Southern Methodist	*	Founder, American Football League, 1959; president, Dallas Texans, 1960-62; Kansas City Chiefs, 1963-present
Hutson, Don	1963	Alabama	E	Green Bay Packers, 1935-45
Johnson, Jimmy	1994	UCLA	DB	San Francisco 49ers, 1961-76
Johnson, John Henry	1987	Arizona State	FB	San Francisco 49ers, 1954-56; Detroit Lions, 1957-59; Pittsburgh Steelers, 1960-65; Houston Oilers, 1966
Joiner, Charlie	1996	Grambling	WR	Houston Oilers, 1969-72; Cincinnati Bengals, 1972-75; San Diego Chargers, 1976-86
Jones, Deacon†	1980	South Carolina State	DE	Los Angeles Rams, 1961-71; San Diego Chargers, 1972-73; Washington Redskins, 1974
Jones, Stan	1991	Maryland	G/DT	Chicago Bears, 1954-65; Washington Redskins, 1966
Jordan, Henry	1995	Virginia	DT	Cleveland Browns, 1957-58; Green Bay Packers, 1959-69
Jurgensen, Sonny	1983	Duke	QB	Philadelphia Eagles, 1957-63; Washington Redskins, 1964-74
Kelly, Leroy	1994	Morgan State	RB	Cleveland Browns, 1964-73
Kiesling, Walter	1966	St. Thomas	G/T*	Player/coach, Duluth Eskimos, Pottsville Maroons, Boston Braves, Chicago Cardinals, Chicago Bears, Green Bay Packers, Pittsburgh Steelers, 1926-56
Kinard, Frank (Bruiser)	1971	Mississippi	T	Brooklyn Dodgers, 1938-45; New York Yankees, 1946-47
Krause, Paul	1998	Iowa	S	Washington Redskins, 1964-67; Minnesota Vikings, 1968-79
Lambeau, Curly	1963	Notre Dame	TB/FB/E*	Founder/player/coach, Green Bay Packers, 1919-49
Lambert, Jack†	1990	Kent State	LB	Pittsburgh Steelers, 1974-84
Landry, Tom†	1990	Texas	*	Coach, Dallas Cowboys, 1960-88
Lane, Dick (Night Train)	1974	Scottsbluff J.C.	DB	Los Angeles Rams, Chicago Cardinals, Detroit Lions, 1952-65
Langer, Jim†	1987	South Dakota State	C	Miami Dolphins, 1970-79; Minnesota Vikings, 1980-81
Lanier, Willie	1986	Morgan State	LB	Kansas City Chiefs, 1967-77
Largent, Steve†	1995	Tulsa	WR	Seattle Seahawks, 1976-89

Name	Elec. year	College	Pos.	NFL teams
Lary, Yale	1979	Texas A&M	DB	Detroit Lions, 1952-53, 56-64
Lavelli, Dante	1975	Ohio State	E	Cleveland Browns, 1946-56
Layne, Bobby	1967	Texas	QB	Chicago Bears, New York Bulldogs, Detroit Lions, Pittsburgh Steelers, 1948-62
Leemans, Tuffy	1978	George Washington	FB	New York Giants, 1936-43
Levy, Marv†	2001	Coe College	*	Kansas City Chiefs, 1978-82; Buffalo Bills, 1986-96
Lilly, Bob†	1980	Texas Christian	DT	Dallas Cowboys, 1961-74
Little, Larry	1993	Bethune Cookman	G	San Diego Chargers, 1967-68; Miami Dolphins, 1969-80
Lombardi, Vince	1971	Fordham	*	Coach, Green Bay Packers, 1959-67; Washington Redskins, 1969
Long, Howie	2000	Villanova	DE	Oakland/Los Angeles Raiders, 1981-93
Lott, Ronnie†	2000	Southern California	DB	San Francisco 49ers, 1981-90; Los Angeles Raiders, 1991-92; New York Jets, 1993-94
Luckman, Sid	1965	Columbia	QB	Chicago Bears, 1939-50
Lyman, Roy (Link)	1964		T	Canton Bulldogs, Cleveland, Chicago Bears, 1922-34
Mack, Tom	1999	Michigan	G	Los Angeles Rams, 1966-78
Mackey, John	1992	Syracuse	TE	Baltimore Colts, 1963-71; San Diego Chargers, 1972
Mara, Tim	1963		*	Founder, New York Giants, 1925-65
Mara, Wellington	1997	Fordham	*	President, New York Giants, 1965-present
Marchetti, Gino†	1972	San Francisco	DE	Dallas Texans, 1952; Baltimore Colts, 1953-66
Marshall, George Preston	1963		*	Founder, Washington Redskins, 1932-65
Matson, Ollie†	1972	San Francisco	HB	Chicago Cardinals, 1952, 54-58; Los Angeles Rams, 1959-62; Detroit Lions, 1963; Philadelphia Eagles, 1964-66
Maynard, Don	1987	Texas Western College	WR	New York Giants, 1958; New York Jets, 1960-72; St. Louis Cardinals, 1973
McAfee, George	1966	Duke	HB	Chicago Bears, 1940-41, 45-50
McCormack, Mike	1984	Kansas	T	New York Yanks, 1951; Cleveland Browns, 1954-62
McDonald, Tommy	1998	Oklahoma	WR	Philadelphia Eagles,1957-63; Dallas Cowboys, 1964; Los Angeles Rams, 1965-66; Atlanta Falcons, 1967; Cleveland Browns,1968
McElhenny, Hugh†	1970	Washington	HB	San Francisco 49ers, Minnesota Vikings, New York Giants, Detroit Lions, 1952-64
McNally, Johnny Blood	1963	St. John's	HB	Milwaukee Badgers, Duluth Eskimos, Pottsville Maroons, Green Bay Packers, Pittsburgh Steelers, 1925-39
Michalske, August (Mike)	1964	Penn State	G	New York Yankees, Green Bay Packers, 1927-37
Millner, Wayne	1968	Notre Dame	E	Boston Redskins, Washington Redskins, 1936-41, 45
Mitchell, Bobby	1983	Illinois	RB/FL/WR	Cleveland Browns, 1958-61; Washington Redskins, 1962-68
Mix, Ron	1979	Southern California	T	Los Angeles Chargers, 1960; San Diego Chargers, 1961-69; Oakland Raiders, 1971
Montana, Joe†	2000	Notre Dame	QB	San Francisco 49ers, 1979-92; Kansas City Chiefs, 1993-94
Moore, Lenny	1975	Penn State	HB	Baltimore Colts, 1956-67
Motley, Marion	1968	Nevada	FB/LB	Cleveland Browns, Pittsburgh Steelers, 1946-55
Munchak, Mike	2001	Penn State	G	Houston Oilers, 1982-93
Munoz, Anthony†	1998	Southern California	OT	Cincinnati Bengals, 1980-92
Musso, George	1982	Milliken	G/DT	Chicago Bears, 1933-44
Nagurski, Bronko	1963	Minnesota	FB/T	Chicago Bears, 1930-37, 43
Namath, Joe	1985	Alabama	QB	New York Jets, 1965-76; Los Angeles Rams, 1977
Neale, Earle (Greasy)	1969	W. Virginia Wesleyan	*	Coach, Philadelphia Eagles, 1941-50
Nevers, Ernie	1963	Stanford	FB	Duluth Eskimos, Chicago Cardinals, 1926-37
Newsome, Ozzie	1999	Alabama	TE	Cleveland Browns, 1978-90
Nitschke, Ray†	1978	Illinois	LB	Green Bay Packers, 1958-72
Noll, Chuck†	1993	Dayton	*	Coach, Pittsburgh Steelers, 1969-91
Nomellini, Leo†	1969	Minnesota	DT	San Francisco 49ers, 1953-63
Olsen, Merlin†	1982	Utah State	DT	Los Angeles Rams, 1962-76
Otto, Jim†	1980	Miami, Fla.	C	Oakland Raiders, 1960-74
Owen, Steve	1966	Phillips	T/G	Player/coach, Kansas City Cowboys, New York Giants, 1924-53
Page, Alan	1988	Notre Dame	DT	Minnesota Vikings, 1967-78; Chicago Bears, 1978-81
Parker, Clarence (Ace)	1972	Duke	HB	Brooklyn Dodgers, 1937-41; Boston Yanks, 1945; New York Yankees, 1946
Parker, Jim†	1973	Ohio State	G	Baltimore Colts, 1957-67
Payton, Walter†	1993	Jackson State	RB	Chicago Bears, 1975-87
Perry, Joe†	1969	Compton J.C.	FB	San Francisco 49ers, Baltimore Colts, 1948-63
Pihos, Pete	1970	Indiana	E	Philadelphia Eagles, 1947-55
Ray, Hugh (Shorty)	1966	Illinois	*	NFL technical adviser and supervisor of officials, 1938-56
Reeves, Daniel F.	1967	Georgetown	*	Founder, Los Angeles Rams, 1941-71
Renfro, Mel	1996	Oregon	DB	Dallas Cowboys, 1964-77
Riggins, John	1992	Kansas	FB	New York Jets, 1971-75; Washington Redskins, 1976-85
Ringo, Jim	1981	Syracuse	C	Green Bay Packers, 1953-63; Philadelphia Eagles, 1964-67
Robustelli, Andy	1971	Arnold	DE	Los Angeles Rams, 1951-55; New York Giants, 1956-64
Rooney, Arthur J.	1964	Georgetown	*	Founder, Pittsburgh Steelers, 1933-82
Rooney, Dan	2000	Duquesne	*	Pittsburgh Steelers, 1955-present
Rozelle, Pete	1985	San Francisco	*	NFL Commissioner, 1960-89

Name	Elec. year	College	Pos.	NFL teams
St. Clair, Bob	1990	Tulsa	T	San Francisco 49ers, 1953-63
Sayers, Gale†	1977	Kansas	RB	Chicago Bears, 1965-71
Schmidt, Joe	1973	Pittsburgh	LB	Detroit Lions, 1953-65; coach, Detroit Lions, 1967-72
Schramm, Tex	1991	Texas	*	President/general manager, Dallas Cowboys, 1960-88
Selmon, Lee Roy	1995	Oklahoma	DE	Tampa Bay Buccaneers, 1976-84
Shaw, Billy	1999	Georgia Tech	G	Buffalo Bills, 1961-69
Shell, Art	1989	Md.-Eastern Shore	T	Oakland-Los Angeles Raiders, 1968-82; coach, Los Angeles Raiders, 1989-94
Shula, Don†	1997	John Carroll	DB	Cleveland Browns, 1951-52; Baltimore Colts, 1953-56; Washington Redskins, 1957; coach, Baltimore Colts, 1963-69, Miami Dolphins, 1970-95
Simpson, O.J.†	1985	Southern California	RB	Buffalo Bills, 1969-77; San Francisco 49ers, 1978
Singletary, Mike†	1998	Baylor	LB	Chicago Bears, 1981-92
Slater, Jackie†	2001	Jackson State	T	Los Angeles Rams, 1976-94; St. Louis Rams, 1995
Smith, Jackie	1994	N'western Louisiana	TE	St. Louis Cardinals, 1963-77; Dallas Cowboys, 1978
Starr, Bart†	1977	Alabama	QB	Green Bay Packers, 1956-71; coach, Green Bay Packers, 1975-83
Staubach, Roger†	1985	Navy	QB	Dallas Cowboys, 1969-79
Stautner, Ernie†	1969	West Virginia	DT	Pittsburgh Steelers, 1950-63
Stenerud, Jan†	1991	Montana State	PK	Kansas City Chiefs, 1967-79; Green Bay Packers, 1980-83; Minnesota Vikings, 1984-85
Stephenson, Dwight	1998	Alabama	C	Miami Dolphins, 1980-87
Strong, Ken	1967	New York U.	HB/PK	Staten Island Stapletons, New York Yankees, New York Giants, 1929-39, 44-47
Stydahar, Joe	1967	West Virginia	T	Chicago Bears, 1936-42, 45-46
Swann, Lynn	2001	Southern California	WR	Pittsburgh Steelers, 1974-82
Tarkenton, Fran	1986	Georgia	QB	Minnesota Vikings, 1961-66, 72-78; New York Giants, 1967-71
Taylor, Charley	1984	Arizona State	WR	Washington Redskins, 1964-75, 77
Taylor, Lawrence†	1999	North Carolina	LB	New York Giants, 1981-93
Taylor, Jim	1976	Louisiana State	FB	Green Bay Packers, 1958-66; New Orleans Saints, 1967
Thorpe, Jim	1963	Carlisle	HB	Canton Bulldogs, Oorang Indians, Cleveland Indians, Toledo Maroons, Rock Island Independents, New York Giants, 1915-26, 29
Tittle, Y.A.	1971	Louisiana State	QB	Baltimore Colts, 1948-50; San Francisco 49ers, 1951-60; New York Giants, 1961-64
Trafton, George	1964	Notre Dame	C	Chicago Bears, 1920-32
Trippi, Charley	1968	Georgia	HB	Chicago Cardinals, 1947-55
Tunnell, Emlen	1967	Iowa	DB	New York Giants, Green Bay Packers, 1948-61
Turner, Clyde (Bulldog)	1966	Hardin-Simmons	C/LB	Chicago Bears, 1940-52; coach, New York Titans, 1962
Unitas, John†	1979	Louisville	QB	Baltimore Colts, 1956-72; San Diego Chargers, 1973
Upshaw, Gene†	1987	Texas A&I	G	Oakland Raiders, 1967-81
Van Brocklin, Norm	1971	Oregon	QB	Los Angeles Rams, 1949-57; Philadelphia Eagles, 1958-60; coach, Minnesota Vikings, 1961-66; Atlanta Falcons, 1968-74
Van Buren, Steve	1965	Louisiana State	HB	Philadelphia Eagles, 1944-51
Walker, Doak	1986	Southern Methodist	RB	Detroit Lions, 1950-55
Walsh, Bill	1993	San Jose State	*	Coach, San Francisco 49ers, 1979-88
Warfield, Paul†	1983	Ohio State	WR	Cleveland Browns, 1964-69, 76-77; Miami Dolphins, 1970-74
Waterfield, Bob	1965	UCLA	QB	Cleveland Rams, Los Angeles Rams, 1945-52; coach, Los Angeles Rams, 1960-62
Webster, Mike	1997	Wisconsin	C-G	Pittsburgh Steelers, 1974-88; Kansas City Chiefs, 1989-90
Weinmeister, Arnie	1984	Washington	T	New York Yankees, 1948-49; New York Giants, 1950-53
White, Randy	1994	Maryland	DT	Dallas Cowboys, 1975-88
Wilcox, Dave	2000	Oregon	LB	San Francisco 49ers, 1964-74
Willis, Bill	1977	Ohio State	G	Cleveland Browns, 1946-53
Wilson, Larry†	1978	Utah	DB	St. Louis Cardinals, 1960-72
Winslow, Kellen	1995	Missouri	TE	San Diego Chargers, 1979-87
Wojciechowicz, Alex	1968	Fordham	C/LB	Detroit Lions, Philadelphia Eagles, 1938-50
Wood, Willie	1989	Southern California	S	Green Bay Packers, 1960-71
Yary, Ron	2001	Southern California	OT	Minnesota Vikings, 1968-81; Los Angeles Rams, 1982
Youngblood, Jack	2001	Florida	DE	Los Angeles Rams, 1971-84

*Hall of Fame member was selected for contributions other than as a player.
†Elected in his first year of eligibility.
Abbreviations of positions: C—Center, CB—Cornerback, DB—Defensive back, DE—Defensive end, DT—Defensive tackle, E—End, FB—Fullback, FL—Flanker, G—Guard, HB—Halfback, LB—Linebacker, PK—Placekicker, QB—Quarterback, RB—Running back, S—Safety, T—Tackle, TB—Tailback, TE—Tight end.

THE SPORTING NEWS AWARDS

PLAYER OF THE YEAR

1954—Lou Groza, OT/K, Cleveland
1955—Otto Graham, QB, Cleveland
1956—Frank Gifford, HB, N.Y. Giants
1957—Jim Brown, RB, Cleveland
1958—Jim Brown, RB, Cleveland
1959—Johnny Unitas, QB, Baltimore
1960—Norm Van Brocklin, QB, Philadelphia
1961—Paul Hornung, HB, Green Bay
1962—Y.A. Tittle, QB, N.Y. Giants
1963—Y.A. Tittle, QB, N.Y. Giants
1964—Johnny Unitas, QB, Baltimore
1965—Jim Brown, RB, Cleveland
1966—Bart Starr, QB, Green Bay
1967—Johnny Unitas, QB, Baltimore
1968—Earl Morrall, QB, Baltimore
1969—Roman Gabriel, QB, L.A. Rams
1970—NFC: John Brodie, QB, San Francisco
    AFC: George Blanda, QB/PK, Oakland
1971—NFC: Roger Staubach, QB, Dallas
    AFC: Bob Griese, QB, Miami
1972—NFC: Larry Brown, RB, Washington
    AFC: Earl Morrall, QB, Miami
1973—NFC: John Hadl, QB, L.A. Rams
    AFC: O.J. Simpson, RB, Buffalo
1974—NFC: Chuck Foreman, RB, Minnesota
    AFC: Ken Stabler, QB, Oakland
1975—NFC: Fran Tarkenton, QB, Minnesota
    AFC: O.J. Simpson, RB, Buffalo
1976—NFC: Walter Payton, RB, Chicago
    AFC: Ken Stabler, QB, Oakland
1977—NFC: Walter Payton, RB, Chicago
    AFC: Craig Morton, QB, Denver

1978—NFC: Archie Manning, QB, New Orleans
    AFC: Earl Campbell, RB, Houston
1979—NFC: Ottis Anderson, RB, St. Louis
    AFC: Dan Fouts, QB, San Diego
1980—Brian Sipe, QB, Cleveland
1981—Ken Anderson, QB, Cincinnati
1982—Mark Moseley, PK, Washington
1983—Eric Dickerson, RB, L.A. Rams
1984—Dan Marino, QB, Miami
1985—Marcus Allen, RB, L.A. Raiders
1986—Lawrence Taylor, LB, N.Y. Giants
1987—Jerry Rice, WR, San Francisco
1988—Boomer Esiason, QB, Cincinnati
1989—Joe Montana, QB, San Francisco
1990—Jerry Rice, WR, San Francisco
1991—Thurman Thomas, RB, Buffalo
1992—Steve Young, QB, San Francisco
1993—Emmitt Smith, RB, Dallas
1994—Steve Young, QB, San Francisco
1995—Brett Favre, QB, Green Bay
1996—Brett Favre, QB, Green Bay
1997—Barry Sanders, RB, Detroit
1998—Terrell Davis, RB, Denver
1999—Kurt Warner, QB, St. Louis
2000—Marshall Faulk, RB, St. Louis
    NOTE: From 1970-79, a player was selected as Player of the Year for both the NFC and AFC. In 1980 The Sporting News reinstated the selection of one player as Player of the Year for the entire NFL.

ROOKIE OF THE YEAR

1955—Alan Ameche, FB, Baltimore
1956—J.C. Caroline, HB, Chicago
1957—Jim Brown, FB, Cleveland
1958—Bobby Mitchell, HB, Cleveland
1959—Nick Pietrosante, FB, Detroit
1960—Gail Cogdill, E, Detroit
1961—Mike Ditka, E, Chicago
1962—Ronnie Bull, HB, Chicago
1963—Paul Flatley, WR, Minnesota
1964—Charley Taylor, HB, Washington
1965—Gale Sayers, RB, Chicago
1966—Tommy Nobis, LB, Atlanta
1967—Mel Farr, RB, Detroit
1968—Earl McCullouch, WR, Detroit
1969—Calvin Hill, RB, Dallas
1970—NFC: Bruce Taylor, CB, San Francisco
    AFC: Dennis Shaw, QB, Buffalo
1971—NFC: John Brockington, RB, Green Bay
    AFC: Jim Plunkett, QB, New England
1972—NFC: Chester Marcol, PK, Green Bay
    AFC: Franco Harris, RB, Pittsburgh
1973—NFC: Chuck Foreman, RB, Minnesota
    AFC: Boobie Clark, RB, Cincinnati
1974—NFC: Wilbur Jackson, RB, San Francisco
    AFC: Don Woods, RB, San Diego
1975—NFC: Steve Bartkowski, QB, Atlanta
    AFC: Robert Brazile, LB, Houston
1976—NFC: Sammy White, WR, Minnesota
    AFC: Mike Haynes, CB, New England

1977—NFC: Tony Dorsett, RB, Dallas
    AFC: A.J. Duhe, DT, Miami
1978—NFC: Al Baker, DE, Detroit
    AFC: Earl Campbell, RB, Houston
1979—NFC: Ottis Anderson, RB, St. Louis
    AFC: Jerry Butler, WR, Buffalo
1980—Billy Sims, RB, Detroit
1981—George Rogers, RB, New Orleans
1982—Marcus Allen, RB, L.A. Raiders
1983—Dan Marino, QB, Miami
1984—Louis Lipps, WR, Pittsburgh
1985—Eddie Brown, WR, Cincinnati
1986—Rueben Mayes, RB, New Orleans
1987—Robert Awalt, TE, St. Louis
1988—Keith Jackson, TE, Philadelphia
1989—Barry Sanders, RB, Detroit
1990—Richmond Webb, T, Miami
1991—Mike Croel, LB, Denver
1992—Santana Dotson, DL, Tampa Bay
1993—Jerome Bettis, RB, L.A. Rams
1994—Marshall Faulk, RB, Indianapolis
1995—Curtis Martin, RB, New England
1996—Eddie George, RB, Houston
1997—Warrick Dunn, RB, Tampa Bay
1998—Randy Moss, WR, Minnesota
1999—Edgerrin James, RB, Indianapolis
2000—Brian Urlacher, LB, Chicago
    NOTE: In 1980, The Sporting News began selecting one rookie as Rookie of the Year for the entire NFL.

1947—Jimmy Conzelman, Chi. Cardinals
1948—Earle (Greasy) Neale, Philadelphia
1949—Paul Brown, Cleveland (AAFC)
1950—Steve Owen, N.Y. Giants
1951—Paul Brown, Cleveland
1952—J. Hampton Pool, L.A. Rams
1953—Paul Brown, Cleveland
1954—None
1955—Joe Kuharich, Washington
1956—Jim Lee Howell, N.Y. Giants
1957—None
1958—None
1959—None
1960—None
1961—Vince Lombardi, Green Bay
1962—None
1963—George Halas, Chicago
1964—Don Shula, Baltimore
1965—George Halas, Chicago
1966—Tom Landry, Dallas
1967—George Allen, L.A. Rams
1968—Don Shula, Baltimore
1969—Bud Grant, Minnesota
1970—Don Shula, Miami
1971—George Allen, Washington
1972—Don Shula, Miami
1973—Chuck Knox, L.A. Rams

1974—Don Coryell, St. Louis
1975—Ted Marchibroda, Baltimore
1976—Chuck Fairbanks, New England
1977—Red Miller, Denver
1978—Jack Patera, Seattle
1979—Dick Vermeil, Philadelphia
1980—Chuck Knox, Buffalo
1981—Bill Walsh, San Francisco
1982—Joe Gibbs, Washington
1983—Joe Gibbs, Washington
1984—Chuck Knox, Seattle
1985—Mike Ditka, Chicago
1986—Bill Parcells, N.Y. Giants
1987—Jim Mora, New Orleans
1988—Marv Levy, Buffalo
1989—Lindy Infante, Green Bay
1990—George Seifert, San Francisco
1991—Joe Gibbs, Washington
1992—Bill Cowher, Pittsburgh
1993—Dan Reeves, N.Y. Giants
1994—George Seifert, San Francisco
1995—Ray Rhodes, Philadelphia
1996—Dom Capers, Carolina
1997—Jim Fassel, N.Y. Giants
1998—Dan Reeves, Atlanta
1999—Dick Vermeil, St. Louis
2000—Andy Reid, Philadelphia

NFL EXECUTIVE OF THE YEAR

1955—Dan Reeves, L.A. Rams
1956—George Halas, Chicago
1972—Dan Rooney, Pittsburgh
1973—Jim Finks, Minnesota
1974—Art Rooney, Pittsburgh
1975—Joe Thomas, Baltimore
1976—Al Davis, Oakland
1977—Tex Schramm, Dallas
1978—John Thompson, Seattle
1979—John Sanders, San Diego
1980—Eddie LeBaron, Atlanta
1981—Paul Brown, Cincinnati
1982—Bobby Beathard, Washington
1983—Bobby Beathard, Washington
1984—George Young, N.Y. Giants
1985—Mike McCaskey, Chicago
1986—George Young, N.Y. Giants

1987—Jim Finks, New Orleans
1988—Bill Polian, Buffalo
1989—John McVay, San Francisco
1990—George Young, N.Y. Giants
1991—Bill Polian, Buffalo
1992—Ron Wolf, Green Bay
1993—George Young, N.Y. Giants
1994—Carmen Policy, San Francisco
1995—Bill Polian, Carolina
1996—Bill Polian, Carolina
1997—George Young, N.Y. Giants
1998—Jeff Diamond, Minnesota
1999—Bill Polian, Indianapolis
2000—Randy Mueller, New Orleans
  NOTE: The Executive of the Year Award was not given from 1957-71.

2000 NFL ALL-PRO TEAM

OFFENSE

WR—Randy Moss, Minnesota
   Marvin Harrison, Indianapolis
TE—Tony Gonzalez, Kansas City
T—Jonathan Ogden, Baltimore
   Orlando Pace, St. Louis
C—Tom Nalen, Denver
G—Larry Allen, Dallas
   Bruce Matthews, Tennessee
QB—Rich Gannon, Oakland
RB—Marshall Faulk, St. Louis
   Edgerrin James, Indianapolis

DEFENSE

DE—Hugh Douglas, Philadelphia
   Jason Taylor, Miami
DT—Warren Sapp, Tampa Bay
   La'Roi Glover, New Orleans
LB—Ray Lewis, Baltimore
   Derrick Brooks, Tampa Bay
   Junior Seau, San Diego
CB—Sam Madison, Miami
   Samari Rolle, Tennessee
S—John Lynch, Tampa Bay
   Darren Sharper, Green Bay

SPECIALISTS

PR—Az-Zahir Hakim, St. Louis
KR—Derrick Mason, Tennessee
K—Matt Stover, Baltimore
P—Shane Lechler, Oakland

FIRST-ROUND DRAFT CHOICES

(Note: Players in boldface are in Pro Football's Hall of Fame and those in italics are former Heisman Trophy winners. In years in which draft order was not announced, players are arranged alphabetically by team.)

1936

FIRST ROUND—NFL

No.	Team	Player selected	Pos.	College
1.	Philadelphia	*Jay Berwanger*	B	Chicago
2.	Boston	Riley Smith	B	Alabama
3.	Pittsburgh	Bill Shakespeare	B	Notre Dame
4.	Brooklyn	Dick Crayne	B	Iowa
5.	Chi. Cardinals	Jim Lawrence	B	Texas Christian
6.	Chi. Bears	**Joe Stydahar**	T	West Virginia
7.	Green Bay	Russ Letlow	G	San Francisco
8.	Detroit	Sid Wagner	G	Michigan State
9.	New York	Art Lewis	T	Ohio

Total number of picks in draft: 81.

OTHER NOTEWORTHY PICKS

Round/Overall—Team, Player selected, Pos., College
2/18—New York, **Tuffy Leemans**, B, George Washington; 3/23—Chi. Cardinals, Eddie Erdelatz, E, St. Mary's (Calif.); 4/31—Brooklyn, Bear Bryant, E, Alabama; 8/65—Boston, **Wayne Millner**, E, Notre Dame; 9/78—Chi. Bears, **Dan Fortmann**, G, Colgate.

1937

FIRST ROUND—NFL

No.	Team	Player selected	Pos.	College
1.	Philadelphia	Sam Francis	B	Nebraska
2.	Brooklyn	Ed Goddard	B	Washington State
3.	Chi. Cardinals	Buzz Buivid	B	Marquette
4.	New York	Ed Widseth	T	Minnesota
5.	Pittsburgh	Mike Basrak	C	Duquesne
6.	Boston	**Sammy Baugh**	QB	Texas Christian
7.	Detroit	Lloyd Cardwell	B	Nebraska
8.	Chi. Bears	Les McDonald	E	Nebraska
9.	Green Bay	Eddie Jankowski	B	Wisconsin
10.	League*	Johnny Drake	B	Purdue

*The league selected for an extra franchise under the likelihood that one would be awarded. The Cleveland Rams received Drake when they were admitted to the league prior to the 1937 season.
Total number of picks in draft: 100.

OTHER NOTEWORTHY PICKS

Round/Overall—Team, Player selected, Pos., College
2/13—Brooklyn, **Ace Parker**, B, Duke; 3/29—Green Bay, Bud Wilkinson, T, Minnesota; 9/87—Detroit, *Larry Kelley*, E, Yale.

1938

FIRST ROUND—NFL

No.	Team	Player selected	Pos.	College
1.	Cleveland	Corbett Davis	B	Indiana
2.	Philadelphia	Jim McDonald	B	Ohio State
3.	Brooklyn	Boyd Brumbaugh	B	Duquesne
4.	Pittsburgh	Whizzer White	B	Colorado
5.	Chi. Cardinals	Jack Robbins	B	Arkansas
6.	Detroit	**Alex Wojciechowicz**	C	Fordham
7.	Green Bay	Cecil Isbell	B	Purdue
8.	New York	George Karamatic	B	Gonzaga
9.	Washington	Andy Farkas	B	Detroit
10.	Chi. Bears	Joe Gray	B	Oregon State

Total number of picks in draft: 110.

OTHER NOTEWORTHY PICKS

Round/Overall—Team, Player selected, Pos., College
3/18—Brooklyn, **Frank (Bruiser) Kinard**, T, Mississippi; 12/106—Detroit, *Clint Frank*, B, Yale.

1939

FIRST ROUND—NFL

No.	Team	Player selected	Pos.	College
1.	Chi. Cardinals	Ki Aldrich	C	Texas Christian
2.	Chi. Bears	**Sid Luckman**	QB	Columbia
3.	Cleveland	Parker Hall	B	Mississippi
4.	Philadelphia	*Davey O'Brien*	B	Texas Christian
5.	Brooklyn	Bob MacLeod	B	Dartmouth
6.	Chi. Bears	Bill Osmanski	B	Holy Cross
7.	Detroit	John Pingel	B	Michigan State
8.	Washington	I.B. Hale	T	Texas Christian
9.	Green Bay	Larry Buhler	B	Minnesota
10.	New York	Walt Neilson	B	Arizona

Team not selecting in first round: Pittsburgh.
Total number of picks in draft: 200.

OTHER NOTEWORTHY PICKS

Round/Overall—Team, Player selected, Pos., College
11/91—Chi. Cardinals, Bowden Wyatt, E, Tennessee.

1940

FIRST ROUND—NFL

No.	Team	Player selected	Pos.	College
1.	Chi. Cardinals	George Cafego	B	Tennessee
2.	Philadelphia	**George McAfee**	B	Duke
3.	Pittsburgh	Kay Eakin	B	Arkansas
4.	Brooklyn	Banks McFadden	B	Clemson
5.	Cleveland	Olie Cordill	B	Rice
6.	Detroit	Doyle Nave	B	USC
7.	Chi. Bears	**Bulldog Turner**	C	Hardin-Simmons
8.	Washington	Ed Boell	B	New York U.
9.	Green Bay	Hal Van Every	B	Minnesota
10.	New York	Grenny Lansdell	B	USC

Total number of picks in draft: 200.

OTHER NOTEWORTHY PICKS

Round/Overall—Team, Player selected, Pos., College
2/11—Chi. Cardinals, George (Snuffy) Stirnweiss, B, North Carolina; 2/14—Brooklyn, *Nile Kinnick*, B, Iowa; 4/27—Pittsburgh, Frank (Pop) Ivy, E, Oklahoma; 9/77—Chi. Bears, Hampton Pool, E, Stanford.

1941

FIRST ROUND—NFL

No.	Team	Player selected	Pos.	College
1.	Chi. Bears	*Tom Harmon*	B	Michigan
2.	Chi. Cardinals	John Kimbrough	B	Texas A&M
3.	Chi. Bears	Norm Standlee	B	Stanford
4.	Cleveland	Rudy Mucha	C	Washington
5.	Detroit	Jim Thomason	B	Texas A&M
6.	New York	George Franck	B	Minnesota
7.	Green Bay	George Paskvan	B	Wisconsin
8.	Brooklyn	Dean McAdams	B	Washington
9.	Chi. Bears	Don Scott	B	Ohio State
10.	Washington	Forest Evashevski	B	Michigan

Teams not selecting in first round: Philadelphia, Pittsburgh.
Total number of picks in draft: 200.

OTHER NOTEWORTHY PICKS

Round/Overall—Team, Player selected, Pos., College
2/13—Chi. Cardinals, Paul Christman, QB, Missouri; 9/77—Green Bay, **Tony Canadeo**, B, Gonzaga.

1942
FIRST ROUND—NFL

No.	Team	Player selected	Pos.	College
1.	Pittsburgh	**Bill Dudley**	B	Virginia
2.	Cleveland	Jack Wilson	B	Baylor
3.	Philadelphia	Pete Kmetovic	B	Stanford
4.	Chi. Cardinals	Steve Lach	B	Duke
5.	Detroit	Bob Westfall	B	Michigan
6.	Washington	Spec Sanders	B	Texas
7.	Brooklyn	Bob Robertson	B	USC
8.	New York	Merle Hapes	B	Mississippi
9.	Green Bay	Urban Odson	T	Minnesota
10.	Chi. Bears	Frankie Albert	B	Stanford

Total number of picks in draft: 200.

OTHER NOTEWORTHY PICKS

Round/Overall—Team, Player selected, Pos., College
7/58—New York, Tommy Prothro, B, Duke; 13/119—Green Bay, *Bruce Smith*, B, Minnesota; 15/134—Chi. Cardinals, Marv Harshman, B, Pacific Lutheran; 15/135—Detroit, Mac Speedie, E, Utah; 18/167—Brooklyn, Ralph Miller, B, Kansas.

1943
FIRST ROUND—NFL

No.	Team	Player selected	Pos.	College
1.	Detroit	*Frank Sinkwich*	B	Georgia
2.	Philadelphia	Joe Muha	B	Virginia Military
3.	Chi. Cardinals	Glenn Dobbs	B	Tulsa
4.	Brooklyn	Paul Governali	B	Columbia
5.	Cleveland	Mike Holovak	B	Boston College
6.	New York	Steve Filipowicz	B	Fordham
7.	Pittsburgh	Bill Daley	B	Minnesota
8.	Green Bay	Dick Wildung	T	Minnesota
9.	Chi. Bears	Bob Steuber	B	Missouri
10.	Washington	Jack Jenkins	B	Vanderbilt

Note: Philadelphia and Pittsburgh franchises merged for 1943 season (but after draft); Cleveland franchise suspended operations for one year (but after draft).
Total number of picks in draft: 300.

OTHER NOTEWORTHY PICKS

Round/Overall—Team, Player selected, Pos., College
6/45—Cleveland, *Les Horvath*, B, Ohio State, 13/116—New York, Don McCafferty, T, Ohio State; 17/157—Nick Skorich, G, Cincinnati.

1944
FIRST ROUND—NFL

No.	Team	Player selected	Pos.	College
1.	Boston	*Angelo Bertelli*	QB	Notre Dame
2.	Chi. Cardinals	Pat Harder	B	Wisconsin
3.	Brooklyn	Creighton Miller	B	Notre Dame
4.	Detroit	**Otto Graham**	QB	Northwestern
5.	Philadelphia	**Steve Van Buren**	B	Louisiana State
6.	New York	Billy Hillenbrand	B	Indiana
7.	Green Bay	Merv Pregulman	G	Michigan
8.	Washington	Mike Micka	B	Colgate
9.	Chi. Bears	Ray Evans	B	Kansas
10.	Pittsburgh	Johnny Podesto	B	St. Mary's (Cal.)
11.	Cleveland	Tony Butkovich	B	Illinois

Note: Chi. Cardinals and Pittsburgh franchises merged for 1944 season (but after draft).
Total number of picks in draft: 330.

OTHER NOTEWORTHY PICKS

Round/Overall—Team, Player selected, Pos., College
5/42—Cleveland, **Bob Waterfield**, B, UCLA; 8/71—Green Bay, Alex Agase, G, Illinois; 10/88—Chi. Cardinals, Lou Saban, B, Indiana; 12/112—Detroit, Jack Lescoulie, G, UCLA.

1945
FIRST ROUND—NFL

No.	Team	Player selected	Pos.	College
1.	Chi. Cardinals	**Charley Trippi**	B	Georgia
2.	Pittsburgh	Paul Duhart	B	Florida
3.	Brooklyn	Joe Renfroe	B	Tulane
4.	Boston	Eddie Prokop	B	Georgia Tech
5.	Cleveland	**Crazylegs Hirsch**	B	Wisconsin
6.	Detroit	Frank Szymanski	C	Notre Dame
7.	Chi. Bears	Don Lund	B	Michigan
8.	Washington	Jim Hardy	QB	USC
9.	Philadelphia	John Yonaker	E	Notre Dame
10.	New York	Elmer Barbour	B	Wake Forest
11.	Green Bay	Walt Schlinkman	B	Texas Tech

Note: Boston and Brooklyn franchises merged for 1945 season (but after draft).
Total number of picks in draft: 330.

OTHER NOTEWORTHY PICKS

Round/Overall—Team, Player selected, Pos., College
3/25—Philadelphia, Alvin Dark, B, Louisiana State; 5/41—Philadelphia, **Pete Pihos**, E, Indiana; 11/103—Cleveland, **Tom Fears**, E, UCLA; 13/127—Washington, Charlie Conerly, QB, Mississippi; 15/145—Pittsburgh, **George Connor**, T, Notre Dame; 17/166—Brooklyn, **Arnie Weinmeister**, E, Washington.

1946
FIRST ROUND—NFL

No.	Team	Player selected	Pos.	College
1.	Boston	Frank Dancewicz	QB	Notre Dame
2.	Chi. Cardinals	Dub Jones	B	Tulane
3.	Pittsburgh	*Doc Blanchard*	B	Army
4.	Chi. Bears	*Johnny Lujack*	QB	Notre Dame
5.	New York	**George Connor**	T	Notre Dame
6.	Green Bay	Johnny Strzykalski	B	Marquette
7.	Philadelphia	Leo Riggs	B	USC
8.	Detroit	Bill Dellastatious	B	Missouri
9.	Washington	Cal Rossi	B	UCLA
10.	Los Angeles	Emil Sitko	B	Notre Dame

Total number of picks in draft: 300.

OTHER NOTEWORTHY PICKS

Round/Overall—Team, Player selected, Pos., College
3/19—Chi. Bears, Frank Broyles, QB, Georgia Tech; 9/74—Chi. Bears, Walt Dropo, E, Connecticut.

1947
SPECIAL SELECTIONS—AAFC

These special selections were made prior to the regular AAFC draft and the draft order was not announced.

Team	Player selected	Pos.	College
Brooklyn	*Doc Blanchard*	B	Army
Brooklyn	Choo-Choo Roberts	B	UT-Chattanooga
Buffalo	Bob Fenimore	B	Oklahoma State
Buffalo	Frank Aschenbrenner	B	Northwestern
Buffalo	Cal Richardson	E	Tulsa
Buffalo	Red Cochran	B	Wake Forest
Chicago	*Johnny Lujack*	QB	Notre Dame
Chicago	Bernie Gallagher	T	Penn State
Cleveland	Dick Hoerner	B	Iowa
Cleveland	Robert Lawrence Rice	C	Tulane
Los Angeles	Herman Wedemeyer	B	St. Mary's (Cal.)
Miami	Arnold Tucker	QB	Army
Miami	Ernie Case	B	UCLA
New York	Buddy Young	B	Illinois
New York	**Charley Trippi**	B	Georgia
San Francisco	*Glenn Davis*	B	Army

Note: Miami dropped out of league after draft, but Miami's selections went to new Baltimore franchise formed after draft.
Total number of special selection picks: 16.

FIRST ROUND—AAFC

No. Team	Player selected	Pos.	College
1. Miami	Elmer Madar	E	Michigan
2. Buffalo	Alton Baldwin	E	Arkansas
3. Brooklyn	Neill Armstrong	E	Oklahoma State
4. Chicago	George Sullivan	T	Notre Dame
5. Los Angeles	Burr Baldwin	E	UCLA
6. San Francisco	Clyde LeForce	B	Tulsa
7. New York	Ben Raimondi	B	Indiana
8. Cleveland	Bob Chappuis	B	Michigan

Note: Miami dropped out of league after draft, but Miami's selections went to new Baltimore franchise formed after draft.
Total number of picks in regular rounds of draft (excluding special selections): 170.

OTHER NOTEWORTHY PICKS

Round/Overall—Team, Player selected, Pos., College
2/11—Charlie Conerly, QB, Mississippi; 6/47—New York, Walt Dropo, E, Connecticut; 10/78—San Francisco, Frank Broyles, QB, Georgia Tech.

FIRST ROUND—NFL

No. Team	Player selected	Pos.	College
1. Chi. Bears	Bob Fenimore	B	Oklahoma State
2. Detroit	*Glenn Davis*	B	Army
3. Boston	Fritz Barzilauskas	G	Yale
4. Washington	Cal Rossi	B	UCLA
5. Pittsburgh	Hub Bechtol	E	Texas
6. Green Bay	Ernie Case	B	UCLA
7. Chi. Cardinals	Tex Coulter	T	Army
8. Philadelphia	Neill Armstrong	E	Oklahoma State
9. Los Angeles	Herman Wedemeyer	B	St. Mary's (Cal.)
10. New York	Vic Schwall	B	Northwestern
11. Chi. Bears	Don Kindt	B	Wisconsin

Note: From 1947-58 one team was granted a "bonus selection," which became the first overall pick in the draft. Each team was allowed only one bonus selection during this period.
Total number of picks in draft: 300.

OTHER NOTEWORTHY PICKS

Round/Overall—Team, Player selected, Pos., College
12/103—Los Angeles, **Dante Lavelli**, E, Ohio State; 13/109—Pittsburgh, Ara Parseghian, B, Miami of Ohio; 20/184—New York, **Tom Landry**, B, Texas; 22/204—New York, **Art Donovan**, T, Boston College; 31/293—Ed Ehlers, B, Purdue.

1948

FIRST ROUND—AAFC

No. Team	Player selected	Pos.	College
1. Chicago	Tony (Skippy) Minisi	B	Pennsylvania
2. Baltimore	**Bobby Layne**	QB	Texas
3. Brooklyn	Harry Gilmer	QB	Alabama
4. Los Angeles	Vaughn Mancha	C	Alabama
5. San Francisco	Joe Scott	B	San Francisco
6. Buffalo	Clyde Scott	B	Arkansas
7. New York	Lowell Tew	B	Alabama
8. Cleveland	Jeff Durkota	B	Penn State

Total number of picks in draft: 217.

OTHER NOTEWORTHY PICKS

Round/Overall—Team, Player selected, Pos., College
3/14—Los Angeles, **Len Ford**, E, Michigan; 19/128—New York, **Tom Landry**, B, Texas; 25/177—Cleveland, Ara Parseghian, B, Miami of Ohio; 28/198—Los Angeles, **Lou Creekmur**, T, William & Mary.

FIRST ROUND—NFL

No. Team	Player selected	Pos.	College
1. Washington	Harry Gilmer	QB	Alabama
2. New York	Tony (Skippy) Minisi	B	Pennsylvania
3. Chi. Bears	**Bobby Layne**	QB	Texas
4. Washington	Lowell Tew	B	Alabama
5. Boston	Vaughn Mancha	C	Alabama
6. Detroit	Y.A. Tittle	QB	Louisiana State
7. Green Bay	Earl (Jug) Girard	B	Wisconsin
8. Philadelphia	Clyde Scott	B	Arkansas
9. Pittsburgh	Dan Edwards	E	Georgia
10. Chi. Bears	Max Baumgardner	E	Texas
11. Chi. Cardinals	Jim Spavital	B	Oklahoma State

Note: From 1947-58 one team was granted a "bonus selection," which became the first overall pick in the draft. Each team was allowed only one bonus selection during this period; team not selecting in first round: Los Angeles.
Total number of picks in draft: 300.

OTHER NOTEWORTHY PICKS

Round/Overall—Team, Player selected, Pos., College
26/243—Philadelphia, **Lou Creekmur**, T, William & Mary; 29/274—Pittsburgh, Abe Gibron, G, Purdue.

1949

SECRET DRAFT—AAFC

These players were selected in the first round of a secret two-round draft in July, 1948, in order for the AAFC to have a chance of luring star college players before the NFL could negotiate with them.

Team	Player selected	Pos.	College
Baltimore	Dick Harris	C	Texas
Brooklyn	**Chuck Bednarik**	C	Pennsylvania
Buffalo	Abe Gibron	G	Purdue
Chicago	Terry Brennan	B	Notre Dame
Chicago	Pete Elliott	B	Michigan
Cleveland	Gene Derricotte	B	Michigan
Los Angeles	Dan Dworsky	C	Michigan
San Francisco	**Ernie Stautner**	T	Boston College

Team not selecting in first round: New York.
Total number of picks in secret draft: 16.

FIRST ROUND—AAFC

No. Team	Player selected	Pos.	College
1. Chicago	Stan Heath	QB	Nevada
2. Brooklyn	Joe Sullivan	B	Dartmouth
3. New York	Bobby Thomason	QB	Virginia Military
4. Baltimore	George Sims	B	Baylor
5. Los Angeles	George Taliaferro	B	Indiana
6. Buffalo	Bill Kay	T	Iowa
7. San Francisco	Chester Fritz	T	Missouri
8. Cleveland	Jack Mitchell	QB	Oklahoma

Note: Brooklyn and New York franchises merged for 1949 season (but after draft).
Total number of picks in regular rounds of draft (excluding secret draft selections): 192.

OTHER NOTEWORTHY PICKS

Round/Overall—Team, Player selected, Pos., College
2/9—Chicago, **George Blanda**, QB, Kentucky; 4/22—Chicago, **Jim Finks**, QB, Tulsa; 9/69—Cleveland, **Doak Walker**, B, SMU; 11/78—Chicago, **Norm Van Brocklin**, QB, Oregon.

FIRST ROUND—NFL

No. Team	Player selected	Pos.	College
1. Philadelphia	**Chuck Bednarik**	C	Pennsylvania
2. Detroit	Johnny Rauch	QB	Georgia
3. Boston	*Doak Walker*	B	SMU

No.	Team	Player selected	Pos.	College
4.	New York	Paul Page	B	SMU
5.	Green Bay	Stan Heath	QB	Nevada
6.	Pittsburgh	Bobby Gage	B	Clemson
7.	Los Angeles	Bobby Thomason	QB	Virginia Military
8.	Washington	Rob Goode	B	Texas A&M
9.	Philadelphia	Frank Tripucka	QB	Notre Dame
10.	Chi. Cardinals	Bill Fischer	G	Notre Dame
11.	Chi. Bears	Dick Harris	C	Texas

Note: From 1947-58 one team was granted a "bonus selection," which became the first overall pick in the draft. Each team was allowed only one bonus selection during this period.

Total number of picks in draft: 251.

OTHER NOTEWORTHY PICKS

Round/Overall—Team, Player selected, Pos., College
2/14—New York, Al DeRogatis, T, Duke; 4/37—Los Angeles, **Norm Van Brocklin**, QB, Oregon; 6/55—New York, Abe Gibron, G, Purdue; 12/116—Pittsburgh, **Jim Finks**, B, Tulsa; 12/119—Chi. Bears, **George Blanda**, QB, Kentucky; 25/247—Los Angeles, Clay Matthews Sr., T, Georgia Tech.

1950
FIRST ROUND—NFL

No.	Team	Player selected	Pos.	College
1.	Detroit	*Leon Hart*	E	Notre Dame
2.	Baltimore	Adrian Burk	QB	Baylor
3.	Chi. Bears	Chuck Hunsinger	B	Florida
4.	Green Bay	Clayton Tonnemaker	C	Minnesota
5.	Detroit	Joe Watson	C	Rice
6.	Washington	George Thomas	B	Oklahoma
7.	N.Y. Giants	Travis Tidwell	B	Auburn
8.	Pittsburgh	Lynn Chandnois	B	Michigan State
9.	Los Angeles	Ralph Pasquariello	B	Villanova
10.	Chi. Bears	Fred (Curly) Morrison	B	Ohio State
11.	San Francisco	**Leo Nomellini**	T	Minnesota
12.	Los Angeles	Stan West	G	Oklahoma
13.	Cleveland	Ken Carpenter	B	Oregon State
14.	Philadelphia	**Bud Grant**	E	Minnesota

Note: From 1947-58 one team was granted a "bonus selection," which became the first overall pick in the draft. Each team was allowed only one bonus selection during this period; teams not selecting in first round: Chi. Cardinals, N.Y. Bulldogs.

Total number of picks in draft: 391.

OTHER NOTEWORTHY PICKS

Round/Overall—Team, Player selected, Pos., College
2/22—Pittsburgh, **Ernie Stautner**, T, Boston College; 10/123—Eddie LeBaron, QB, Pacific; 16/201—Washington, Charlie (Choo-Choo) Justice, B, North Carolina; 20/250—N.Y. Bulldogs, Darrell Royal, B, Oklahoma.

1951
FIRST ROUND—NFL

No.	Team	Player selected	Pos.	College
1.	N.Y. Giants	Kyle Rote	B	SMU
2.	Chi. Bears	Bob Williams	QB	Notre Dame*
3.	San Francisco	**Y.A. Tittle**	QB	Louisiana State*
4.	Washington	Leon Heath	B	Oklahoma
5.	Green Bay	Bob Gain	T	Kentucky
6.	Chi. Cardinals	Jerry Groom	C	Notre Dame
7.	Philadelphia	Ebert Van Buren	B	Louisiana State
8.	Philadelphia	Chet Mutryn	B	Xavier*
9.	Pittsburgh	Butch Avinger	B	Alabama
10.	Chi. Bears	Billy Stone	B	Bradley*
11.	Los Angeles	Bud McFadin	G	Texas
12.	Chi. Bears	Gene Schroeder	E	Virginia
13.	N.Y. Giants	Jim Spavital	B	Oklahoma State*
14.	Cleveland	Kenny Konz	B	Louisiana State

*Players drafted from Baltimore franchise, which disbanded following 1950 season.

Note: From 1947-58 one team was granted a "bonus selection," which became the first overall pick in the draft. Each team was allowed only one bonus selection during this period; teams not selecting in first round: Detroit, N.Y. Yanks.

Total number of picks in draft: 362.

OTHER NOTEWORTHY PICKS

Round/Overall—Team, Player selected, Pos., College
2/23—Chi. Bears, **Bill George**, T, Wake Forest; 3/34—N.Y. Yanks, **Mike McCormack**, T, Kansas; 4/50—Cleveland, **Art Donovan**, T, Boston College; 6/69—Detroit, **Jack Christiansen**, B, Colorado State; 9/110—Cleveland, **Don Shula**, B, John Carroll; 19/228—Los Angeles, **Andy Robustelli**, E, Arnold.

1952
FIRST ROUND—NFL

No.	Team	Player selected	Pos.	College
1.	Los Angeles	Bill Wade	QB	Vanderbilt
2.	N.Y. Yanks	Les Richter	G	California
3.	Chi. Cardinals	**Ollie Matson**	B	San Francisco
4.	Green Bay	Babe Parilli	QB	Kentucky
5.	Philadelphia	Johnny Bright	B	Drake
6.	Pittsburgh	Ed Modzelewski	B	Maryland
7.	Washington	Larry Isbell	B	Baylor
8.	Chi. Bears	Jim Dooley	B	Miami, Fla.
9.	San Francisco	**Hugh McElhenny**	B	Washington
10.	Cleveland	Bert Rechichar	B	Tennessee
11.	N.Y. Giants	**Frank Gifford**	B	USC
12.	Cleveland	Harry Agganis	QB	Boston University
13.	Los Angeles	Bob Carey	E	Michigan State

Note: Shortly after draft, N.Y. Yanks franchise was sold back to league and the club played in 1952 as Dallas Texans; from 1947-58 one team was granted a "bonus selection," which became the first overall pick in the draft. Each team was allowed only one bonus selection during this period; team not selecting in first round: Detroit.

Total number of picks in draft: 360.

OTHER NOTEWORTHY PICKS

Round/Overall—Team, Player selected, Pos., College
2/14—N.Y. Yanks, **Gino Marchetti**, T, San Francisco; 3/26—Cleveland, Don Klosterman, QB, Loyola, Calif.; 3/34—Detroit, **Yale Lary**, B, Texas A&M; 4/45—Detroit, Pat Summerall, E, Arkansas; 7/79—Washington, *Vic Janowicz*, B, Ohio State; 15/176—Chi. Bears, *Dick Kazmaier*, B, Princeton.

1953
FIRST ROUND—NFL

No.	Team	Player selected	Pos.	College
1.	San Francisco	Harry Babcock	E	Georgia
2.	Baltimore	*Billy Vessels*	B	Oklahoma
3.	Washington	Jack Scarbath	B	Maryland
4.	Chi. Cardinals	Johnny Olszewski	B	California
5.	Pittsburgh	Ted Marchibroda	QB	Detroit
6.	Chi. Bears	Billy Anderson	B	Compton J.C.
7.	Green Bay	Al Carmichael	B	USC
8.	New York	Bobby Marlow	B	Alabama
9.	Los Angeles	Donn Moomaw	C	UCLA
10.	San Francisco	Tom Stolhanske	E	Texas
11.	Cleveland	**Doug Atkins**	T	Tennessee
12.	Los Angeles	Ed Barker	E	Washington State
13.	Detroit	Harley Sewell	G	Texas

Note: From 1947-58 one team was granted a "bonus selection," which became the first overall pick in the draft. Each team was allowed only one bonus selection during this period; team not selecting in first round: Philadelphia.

Total number of picks in draft: 360.

OTHER NOTEWORTHY PICKS

Round/Overall—Team, Player selected, Pos., College
2/17—Chi. Bears, Zeke Bratkowski, QB, Georgia; 2/18—Pittsburgh, **John Henry Johnson**, B, Arizona State; 3/32—San Francisco, **Bob St. Clair**, T, Tulsa; 5/54—Chi. Bears, **Stan Jones**, T, Maryland; 7/79—Green Bay, **Jim Ringo**, C, Syracuse; 7/81—Philadelphia, Ray Malavasi, G, Mississippi State; 7/85—Detroit, **Joe Schmidt**, C, Pittsburgh; 10/117—Philadelphia, Tom Brookshier, B, Colorado; 20/239—Cleveland, **Chuck Noll**, T, Dayton; 25/292—Chi. Cardinals, Haywood Sullivan, B, Florida; 27/321—New York, **Roosevelt Brown**, T, Morgan State; 30/352—Washington, Bob Mathias, B, Stanford.

1954
FIRST ROUND—NFL

No. Team	Player selected	Pos.	College
1. Cleveland	Bobby Garrett	QB	Stanford
2. Chi. Cardinals	Lamar McHan	QB	Arkansas
3. Green Bay	Art Hunter	T	Notre Dame
4. Green Bay	Veryl Switzer	B	Kansas State
5. Baltimore	Cotton Davidson	QB	Baylor
6. Chi. Bears	Stan Wallace	B	Illinois
7. Pittsburgh	*Johnny Lattner*	B	Notre Dame
8. Washington	Steve Meilinger	E	Kentucky
9. Philadelphia	Neil Worden	B	Notre Dame
10. Los Angeles	Ed Beatty	C	Mississippi
11. San Francisco	Bernie Faloney	B	Maryland
12. Cleveland	John Bauer	G	Illinois
13. Detroit	Dick Chapman	T	Rice

Note: From 1947-58 one team was granted a "bonus selection," which became the first overall pick in the draft. Each team was allowed only one bonus selection during this period; team not selecting in first round: New York.
Total number of picks in draft: 360.

OTHER NOTEWORTHY PICKS

Round/Overall—Team, Player selected, Pos., College
4/41—New York, Dick Nolan, B, Maryland; 5/51—Green Bay, Max McGee, B, Tulane; 15/174—Chi. Bears, Harlon Hill, E, North Alabama; 20/232—Baltimore, **Raymond Berry**, E, Southern Methodist; 25/293—Baltimore, Pepper Rodgers, B, Georgia Tech.

1955
FIRST ROUND—NFL

No. Team	Player selected	Pos.	College
1. Baltimore	George Shaw	B	Oregon
2. Chi. Cardinals	Max Boydston	E	Oklahoma
3. Baltimore	*Alan Ameche*	B	Wisconsin
4. Washington	Ralph Guglielmi	QB	Notre Dame
5. Green Bay	Tom Bettis	G	Purdue
6. Pittsburgh	Frank Varrichione	T	Notre Dame
7. Los Angeles	Larry Morris	C	Georgia Tech
8. New York	Joe Heap	B	Notre Dame
9. Philadelphia	Dick Bielski	B	Maryland
10. San Francisco	Dickie Moegle	B	Rice
11. Chi. Bears	Ron Drzewiecki	B	Marquette
12. Detroit	Dave Middleton	B	Auburn
13. Cleveland	Kurt Burris	C	Oklahoma

Total number of picks in draft: 360.

OTHER NOTEWORTHY PICKS

Round/Overall—Team, Player selected, Pos., College
3/31—New York, Rosey Grier, T, Penn State; 3/34—San Francisco, Carroll Hardy, B, Colorado; 9/102—Pittsburgh, **Johnny Unitas**, QB, Louisville; 12/139—Los Angeles, Jim Hanifan, E, California; 13/155—Chi. Bears, Norm Cash, B, Sul Ross; 30/354—Los Angeles, K.C. Jones, E, San Francisco.

1956
FIRST ROUND—NFL

No. Team	Player selected	Pos.	College
1. Pittsburgh	Gary Glick	QB	Colorado State
2. San Francisco	Earl Morrall	QB	Michigan State
3. Detroit	*Hopalong Cassady*	B	Ohio State
4. Philadelphia	Bob Pellegrini	C	Maryland
5. Pittsburgh	Art Davis	B	Mississippi State
6. Los Angeles	Joe Marconi	B	West Virginia
7. Chi. Cardinals	Joe Childress	B	Auburn
8. Green Bay	Jack Losch	B	Miami, Fla.
9. Baltimore	**Lenny Moore**	B	Penn State
10. Chi. Bears	Menan (Tex) Schriewer	E	Texas
11. Los Angeles	Charlie Horton	B	Vanderbilt
12. Washington	Ed Vereb	B	Maryland
13. Cleveland	Preston Carpenter	B	Arkansas

Note: From 1947-58 one team was granted a "bonus selection," which became the first overall pick in the draft. Each team was allowed only one bonus selection during this period; team not selecting in first round: New York.
Total number of picks in draft: 360.

OTHER NOTEWORTHY PICKS

Round/Overall—Team, Player selected, Pos., College
2/20—Green Bay, **Forrest Gregg**, T, SMU; 3/30—New York, **Sam Huff**, T, West Virginia; 5/54—Philadelphia, Fuzzy Thurston, G, Valparaiso; 15/181—Cleveland, **Willie Davis**, E, Grambling; 16/186—Chi. Cardinals, George Welsh, QB, Navy; 17/200—Green Bay, **Bart Starr**, QB, Alabama; 21/251—Washington, Howard Schnellenberger, E, Kentucky.

1957
FIRST ROUND—NFL

No. Team	Player selected	Pos.	College
1. Green Bay	*Paul Hornung*	QB	Notre Dame
2. Los Angeles	Jon Arnett	B	USC
3. San Francisco	John Brodie	QB	Stanford
4. Green Bay	Ron Kramer	E	Michigan
5. Pittsburgh	**Len Dawson**	QB	Purdue
6. Cleveland	**Jim Brown**	B	Syracuse
7. Philadelphia	Clarence Peaks	B	Michigan State
8. Baltimore	**Jim Parker**	G	Ohio State
9. Washington	Don Bosseler	B	Miami, Fla.
10. Chi. Cardinals	Jerry Tubbs	C	Oklahoma
11. Los Angeles	Del Shofner	B	Baylor
12. Detroit	Bill Glass	G	Baylor
13. Chi. Bears	Earl Leggett	T	Louisiana State

Note: From 1947-58 one team was granted a "bonus selection," which became the first overall pick in the draft. Each team was allowed only one bonus selection during this period; team not selecting in first round: New York.
Total number of picks in draft: 360.

OTHER NOTEWORTHY PICKS

Round/Overall—Team, Player selected, Pos., College
2/14—Los Angeles, Jack Pardee, B, Texas A&M; 3/31—Philadelphia, **Tommy McDonald**, B, Oklahoma; 4/43—Philadelphia, **Sonny Jurgensen**, QB, Duke; 5/52—Cleveland, **Henry Jordan**, T, Virginia; 5/53—Cleveland, Milt Campbell, B, Indiana; 9/109—New York, **Don Maynard**, B, Texas Western College; 17/203—Detroit, Jack Kemp, QB, Occidental; 29/346—Chi. Cardinals, Lee Corso, B, Florida State.

1958
FIRST ROUND—NFL

No. Team	Player selected	Pos.	College
1. Chi. Cardinals	King Hill	QB	Rice
2. Chi. Cardinals	*John David Crow*	B	Texas A&M
3. Green Bay	Dan Currie	C	Michigan State

No.	Team	Player selected	Pos.	College
4.	Los Angeles	Lou Michaels	T	Kentucky
5.	Los Angeles	Jim Phillips	E	Auburn
6.	Philadelphia	Walt Kowalczyk	B	Michigan State
7.	Chi. Bears	Chuck Howley	G	West Virginia
8.	San Francisco	Jim Pace	B	Michigan
9.	San Francisco	Charlie Krueger	T	Texas A&M
10.	Detroit	Alex Karras	T	Iowa
11.	Baltimore	Lenny Lyles	B	Louisville
12.	New York	Phil King	B	Vanderbilt
13.	Cleveland	Jim Shofner	B	Texas Christian

Note: From 1947-58 one team was granted a "bonus selection," which became the first overall pick in the draft. Each team was allowed only one bonus selection during this period; teams not selecting in first round: Pittsburgh, Washington.

Total number of picks in draft: 360.

OTHER NOTEWORTHY PICKS

Round/Overall—Team, Player selected, Pos., College
2/15—Green Bay, **Jim Taylor**, B, Louisiana State; 3/36—Green Bay, **Ray Nitschke**, B, Illinois; 4/39—Green Bay, Jerry Kramer, G, Idaho; 7/84—Cleveland, **Bobby Mitchell**, B, Illinois; 13/154—Baltimore, Jerry Richardson, E, Wofford; 19/223—Pittsburgh, Gene Keady, B, Kansas State; 21/244—Philadelphia, John Madden, T, Cal Poly-SLO.

1959

FIRST ROUND—NFL

No.	Team	Player selected	Pos.	College
1.	Green Bay	Randy Duncan	QB	Iowa
2.	Los Angeles	Dick Bass	B	Pacific
3.	Chi. Cardinals	Billy Stacy	B	Mississippi State
4.	Washington	Don Allard	QB	Boston College
5.	San Francisco	Dave Baker	QB	Oklahoma
6.	Detroit	Nick Pietrosante	B	Notre Dame
7.	Chi. Bears	Don Clark	B	Ohio State
8.	San Francisco	Dan James	C	Ohio State
9.	Los Angeles	Paul Dickson	T	Baylor
10.	New York	Lee Grosscup	QB	Utah
11.	Cleveland	Rich Kreitling	E	Illinois
12.	Baltimore	Jackie Burkett	C	Auburn

Teams not selecting in first round: Philadelphia, Pittsburgh.
Total number of picks in draft: 360.

OTHER NOTEWORTHY PICKS

Round/Overall—Team, Player selected, Pos., College
5/58—Cleveland, Dick LeBeau, B, Ohio State; 18/209—Washington, Joe Kapp, QB, California; 19/222—San Francisco, Tom Osborne, B, Hastings.

1960

AFL

Eight players were selected as territorial picks by the AFL prior to its first draft. The actual draft was held in two stages consisting of a total of 53 rounds. The draft order was not announced. Shortly after the draft, Minneapolis withdrew from the league when it was offered an NFL franchise (to begin play in 1961). Oakland was then allowed to join as the eighth AFL team, and it received the Minneapolis draft list. Before Oakland was admitted to the league, however, other AFL teams had signed a number of players drafted by Minneapolis. The AFL then held an allocation draft for Oakland. Each AFL team protected 11 players and Oakland was allowed to choose 24 unprotected players. Below is the list of AFL territorial picks.

Team	Player selected	Pos.	College
Boston	Gerhard Schwedes	HB	Syracuse
Buffalo	Richie Lucas	QB	Penn State
Dallas	Don Meredith	QB	SMU
Denver	Roger LeClerc	C	Trinity (Ct.)
Houston	*Billy Cannon*	B	Louisiana State

Team	Player selected	Pos.	College
Los Angeles	Monty Stickles	E	Notre Dame
Minneapolis	Dale Hackbart	QB	Wisconsin
New York	George Izo	QB	Notre Dame

Total number of territorial picks: 8.
Total number of regular draft picks (including territorial): 424.
Total number of allocation picks for Oakland franchise: 24

OTHER NOTEWORTHY PICKS

Team, Player selected, Pos., College
Boston, Foge Fazio, C, Pittsburgh; Boston, **Ron Mix**, T, USC; Buffalo, **Larry Wilson**, DB, Utah; Houston, Jim Marshall, T/G, Ohio State; Los Angeles, Paul Maguire, E, The Citadel; Minneapolis, **Jim Otto**, C, Miami, Fla.

FIRST ROUND—NFL

No.	Team	Player selected	Pos.	College
1.	Los Angeles	*Billy Cannon*	B	Louisiana State
2.	Chi. Cardinals	George Izo	QB	Notre Dame
3.	Detroit	Johnny Robinson	HB	Louisiana State
4.	Washington	Richie Lucas	QB	Penn State
5.	Green Bay	Tom Moore	B	Vanderbilt
6.	Pittsburgh	Jack Spikes	FB	Texas Christian
7.	Chi. Bears	Roger Davis	G	Syracuse
8.	Cleveland	Jim Houston	E	Ohio State
9.	Philadelphia	Ron Burton	HB	Northwestern
10.	Baltimore	**Ron Mix**	T	USC
11.	San Francisco	Monty Stickles	E	Notre Dame
12.	New York	Lou Cordileone	T	Clemson

Note: Chi. Cardinals moved to St. Louis prior to 1960 season (but after draft); expansion Dallas team joined league after draft.
Total number of picks in draft: 240.

OTHER NOTEWORTHY PICKS

Round/Overall—Team, Player selected, Pos., College
3/32—Chi. Bears, Don Meredith, QB, SMU; 4/44—Cleveland, Jim Marshall, T, Ohio State; 7/74—Chi. Cardinals, **Larry Wilson**, DB, Utah.

1961

FIRST ROUND—AFL

Team	Player selected	Pos.	College
Boston	Tommy Mason	HB	Tulane
Buffalo	Ken Rice	T	Auburn
Dallas	E.J. Holub	C	Texas Tech
Denver	Bob Gaiters	HB	New Mexico St.
Houston	**Mike Ditka**	E	Pittsburgh
Los Angeles	Earl Faison	E	Indiana
New York	Tom Brown	G	Minnesota
Oakland	Joe Rutgens	T	Illinois

Note: Los Angeles team moved to San Diego prior to 1960 season (but after draft).
Total number of picks in draft: 240.

OTHER NOTEWORTHY PICKS

Round—Team, Player selected, Pos., College
2—Buffalo, **Billy Shaw**, T, Georgia Tech; 2—Dallas, **Bob Lilly**, T, Texas Christian; 2—New York, **Herb Adderley**, HB, Michigan State; 4—Los Angeles, **Jimmy Johnson**, HB, UCLA; 5—Boston, **Fran Tarkenton**, QB, Georgia; 5—Buffalo, Norm Snead, QB, Wake Forest; 5—Los Angeles, Billy Kilmer, QB, UCLA; 6—Houston, Jake Gibbs, QB, Mississippi; 19—Boston, *Joe Bellino*, B, Navy.

FIRST ROUND—NFL

No.	Team	Player selected	Pos.	College
1.	Minnesota	Tommy Mason	HB	Tulane
2.	Washington	Norm Snead	QB	Wake Forest
3.	Washington	Joe Rutgens	T	Illinois

No.	Team	Player selected	Pos.	College
4.	Los Angeles	Marlin McKeever	LB	USC
5.	Chicago	**Mike Ditka**	E	Pittsburgh
6.	San Francisco	**Jimmy Johnson**	B	UCLA
7.	Baltimore	Tom Matte	HB	Ohio State
8.	St. Louis	Ken Rice	T	Auburn
9.	San Francisco	Bernie Casey	B	Bowling Green
10.	Cleveland	Bobby Crespino	E	Mississippi
11.	San Francisco	Billy Kilmer	QB	UCLA
12.	Green Bay	**Herb Adderley**	B	Michigan State
13.	Dallas	**Bob Lilly**	T	Texas Christian
14.	Philadelphia	Art Baker	FB	Syracuse

Teams not selecting in first round: Dallas, Detroit, New York, Pittsburgh.
Total number of picks in draft: 280.

OTHER NOTEWORTHY PICKS

Round/Overall—Team, Player selected, Pos., College
3/29—Minnesota, **Fran Tarkenton**, QB, Georgia; 9/125—Cleveland, Jake Gibbs, QB, Mississippi; 14/184—Dallas, **Billy Shaw**, T, Georgia Tech; 14/186—Los Angeles, **Deacon Jones**, T, South Carolina State; 17/227—Washington, *Joe Bellino*, B, Navy.

1962

FIRST ROUND—AFL

No.	Team	Player selected	Pos.	College
1.	Oakland	Roman Gabriel	QB	N. Carolina State
2.	Denver	**Merlin Olsen**	T	Utah State
3.	Dallas	Ronnie Bull	B	Baylor
4.	Buffalo	*Ernie Davis*	B	Syracuse
5.	New York	Sandy Stephens	QB	Minnesota
6.	Boston	Gary Collins	E	Maryland
7.	Houston	Ray Jacobs	T	Howard Payne
8.	San Diego	Bob Ferguson	B	Ohio State

Total number of picks in draft: 272.

OTHER NOTEWORTHY PICKS

Round—Team, Player selected, Pos., College
2/9—Oakland, **Lance Alworth**, HB, Arkansas; 3/24—San Diego, John Hadl, QB, Kansas; 13/102—Boston, **Nick Buoniconti**, G, Notre Dame.

FIRST ROUND—NFL

No.	Team	Player selected	Pos.	College
1.	Washington	*Ernie Davis*	B	Syracuse
2.	Los Angeles	Roman Gabriel	QB	N. Carolina State
3.	Los Angeles	**Merlin Olsen**	T	Utah State
4.	Cleveland	Gary Collins	E	Maryland
5.	Pittsburgh	Bob Ferguson	B	Ohio State
6.	St. Louis	Fate Echols	T	Northwestern
7.	Chicago	Ronnie Bull	B	Baylor
8.	San Francisco	**Lance Alworth**	B	Arkansas
9.	Baltimore	Wendell Harris	B	Louisiana State
10.	Detroit	John Hadl	QB	Kansas
11.	Cleveland	Leroy Jackson	B	Western Illinois
12.	St. Louis	Irv Goode	C	Kentucky
13.	New York	Jerry Hillebrand	E	Colorado
14.	Green Bay	Earl Gros	B	Louisiana State

Teams not selecting in first round: Dallas, Minnesota, Philadelphia.
Total number of picks in draft: 280.

OTHER NOTEWORTHY PICKS

Round/Overall—Team, Player selected, Pos., College
7/95—Cleveland, John Havlicek, E, Ohio State; 17/238—Green Bay, **Buck Buchanan**, T, Grambling.

1963

FIRST ROUND—AFL

No.	Team	Player selected	Pos.	College
1.	Dallas	**Buck Buchanan**	T	Grambling
2.	San Diego	Walt Sweeney	E	Syracuse
3.	New York	Jerry Stovall	B	Louisiana State
4.	Buffalo	Dave Behrman	C	Michigan State
5.	Denver	Kermit Alexander	B	UCLA
6.	Houston	Danny Brabham	FB	Arkansas
7.	Boston	Art Graham	E	Boston College
8.	Dallas	Ed Budde	T	Michigan State

Team not selecting in first round: Oakland.
Total number of picks in draft: 232.

OTHER NOTEWORTHY PICKS

Round/Overall—Team, Player selected, Pos., College
5/35—New York, **John Mackey**, E, Syracuse; 7/56—Dallas, **Bobby Bell**, T, Minnesota; 12/90—San Diego, *Terry Baker*, QB, Oregon State; 24/188—Buffalo, Daryle Lamonica, QB, Notre Dame.

FIRST ROUND—NFL

No.	Team	Player selected	Pos.	College
1.	Los Angeles	*Terry Baker*	B	Oregon State
2.	St. Louis	Jerry Stovall	B	Louisiana State
3.	Minnesota	Jim Dunaway	T	Mississippi
4.	Philadelphia	Ed Budde	T	Michigan State
5.	Baltimore	Bob Vogel	T	Ohio State
6.	Dallas	Lee Roy Jordan	LB	Alabama
7.	Washington	Pat Richter	E	Wisconsin
8.	San Francisco	Kermit Alexander	B	UCLA
9.	Cleveland	Tom Hutchinson	E	Kentucky
10.	Los Angeles	Rufus Guthrie	G	Georgia Tech
11.	Chicago	Dave Behrman	C	Michigan State
12.	Detroit	Daryl Sanders	T	Ohio State
13.	St. Louis	Don Brumm	DE	Purdue
14.	Green Bay	Dave Robinson	E	Penn State

Teams not selecting in first round: New York, Pittsburgh.
Total number of picks in draft: 280.

OTHER NOTEWORTHY PICKS

Round/Overall—Team, Player selected, Pos., College
2/16—Minnesota, **Bobby Bell**, T, Minnesota; 2/19—Baltimore, **John Mackey**, E, Syracuse; 10/129—St. Louis, **Jackie Smith**, E, Northwestern (La.) State; 12/168—Green Bay, Daryle Lamonica, QB, Notre Dame; 19/265—New York, **Buck Buchanan**, T, Grambling.

1964

FIRST ROUND—AFL

No.	Team	Player selected	Pos.	College
1.	Boston	Jack Concannon	QB	Boston College
2.	Kansas City	Pete Beathard	QB	USC
3.	New York	Matt Snell	FB	Ohio State
4.	Denver	Bob Brown	T	Nebraska
5.	Buffalo	Carl Eller	T	Minnesota
6.	Houston	Scott Appleton	T	Texas
7.	Oakland	Tony Lorick	HB	Arizona State
8.	San Diego	Ted Davis	E	Georgia Tech

Total number of picks in draft: 208.

OTHER NOTEWORTHY PICKS

Round/Overall—Team, Player selected, Pos., College
2/9—Houston, **Charley Taylor**, HB, Arizona State; 4/28—Buffalo, **Paul Warfield**, HB, Ohio State; 6/46—Houston, **Dave Wilcox**, DE, Oregon; 9/67—New York, Sherman Lewis, HB, Michigan State; 10/79—Oakland, **Mel Renfro**, HB, Oregon; 12/89—Denver, **Paul Krause**, DB, Iowa; 14/105—Denver, Bob Hayes, HB, Florida A&M; 16/122—Kansas City, *Roger Staubach*, QB, Navy; 18/140—Boston, Joe Tiller, T, Montana State; 23/183—Oakland, Bill Curry, C, Georgia Tech.

FIRST ROUND—NFL

No.	Team	Player selected	Pos.	College
1.	San Francisco	Dave Parks	E	Texas Tech
2.	Philadelphia	Bob Brown	T	Nebraska
3.	Washington	**Charley Taylor**	HB	Arizona State
4.	Dallas	Scott Appleton	T	Texas
5.	Detroit	Pete Beathard	QB	USC
6.	Minnesota	Carl Eller	T	Minnesota
7.	Los Angeles	Bill Munson	QB	Utah State
8.	Baltimore	Marv Woodson	HB	Indiana
9.	St. Louis	Ken Kortas	T	Louisville
10.	Pittsburgh	Paul Martha	HB	Pittsburgh
11.	Cleveland	**Paul Warfield**	HB	Ohio State
12.	New York	Joe Don Looney	B	Oklahoma
13.	Green Bay	Lloyd Voss	T	Nebraska
14.	Chicago	Dick Evey	T	Tennessee

Total number of picks in draft: 280.

OTHER NOTEWORTHY PICKS

Round/Overall—Team, Player selected, Pos., College
2/17—Dallas, **Mel Renfro**, B, Oregon; 2/18—Washington, **Paul Krause**, B, Iowa; 3/29—San Francisco, **Dave Wilcox**, DE, Oregon; 7/88—Dallas, Bob Hayes, HB, Florida A&M; 7/89—Detroit, Bill Parcells, T, Wichita State; 8/110—Cleveland, **Leroy Kelly**, HB, Morgan State; 10/129—Dallas, *Roger Staubach*, QB, Navy; 18/250—Cleveland, Sherman Lewis, HB, Michigan State.

1965

FIRST ROUND—AFL

Team	Player selected	Pos.	College
Boston	Jerry Rush	T	Michigan State
Buffalo	Jim Davidson	T	Ohio State
Houston	Lawrence Elkins	E	Baylor
Kansas City	**Gale Sayers**	HB	Kansas
New York	**Joe Namath**	QB	Alabama
New York	Tom Nowatzke	FB	Indiana
Oakland	Harry Schuh	T	Memphis State
San Diego	Steve DeLong	DE	Tennessee

Team not selecting in first round: Denver.
Total number of picks in draft: 160.

OTHER NOTEWORTHY PICKS

Round—Team, Player selected, Pos., College
2—Denver, **Dick Butkus**, LB, Illinois; 2—New York, *John Huarte*, QB, Notre Dame; 2—Oakland, **Fred Biletnikoff**, E, Florida State; 7—Buffalo, Marty Schottenheimer, LB, Pittsburgh; 7—San Diego, Jack Snow, E, Notre Dame; 10—Oakland, Craig Morton, QB, California.

REDSHIRT—AFL

The AFL held a separate draft for future picks in 1965 and 1966.

Team	Player selected	Pos.	College
Boston	Dave McCormick	T	Louisiana State
Buffalo	Ken Ambrusko	HB	Maryland
Denver	Miller Farr	HB	Wichita State
Houston	Donny Anderson	HB	Texas Tech
Kansas City	Alphonse Dotson	T	Grambling
New York	Johnny Roland	HB	Missouri
Oakland	Larry Todd	HB	Arizona State
San Diego	Gary Garrison	E	San Diego State

Total number of picks in draft: 96.

OTHER NOTEWORTHY PICKS

Round—Team, Player selected, Pos., College
9—New York, Rich Kotite, E, Wagner.

FIRST ROUND—NFL

No.	Team	Player selected	Pos.	College
1.	New York	Tucker Frederickson	B	Auburn
2.	San Francisco	Ken Willard	FB	North Carolina
3.	Chicago	**Dick Butkus**	LB	Illinois
4.	Chicago	**Gale Sayers**	HB	Kansas
5.	Dallas	Craig Morton	QB	California
6.	Chicago	Steve DeLong	DE	Tennessee
7.	Green Bay	Donny Anderson	HB	Texas Tech
8.	Minnesota	Jack Snow	E	Notre Dame
9.	Los Angeles	Clancy Williams	HB	Washington State
10.	Green Bay	Lawrence Elkins	E	Baylor
11.	Detroit	Tom Nowatzke	FB	Indiana
12.	St. Louis	**Joe Namath**	QB	Alabama
13.	San Francisco	George Donnelly	B	Illinois
14.	Baltimore	Mike Curtis	LB	Duke

Teams not selecting in first round: Cleveland, Philadelphia, Pittsburgh, Washington.
Total number of picks in draft: 280.

OTHER NOTEWORTHY PICKS

Round/Overall—Team, Player selected, Pos., College
3/39—Detroit, **Fred Biletnikoff**, E, Florida State; 4/49—Baltimore, Marty Schottenheimer, LB, Pittsburgh; 6/76—Philadelphia, *John Huarte*, QB, Notre Dame; 17/238—Baltimore, Rick Reichardt, HB, Wisconsin; 19/257—Dallas, Merv Rettenmund, HB, Ball State.

1966

FIRST ROUND—AFL

Team	Player selected	Pos.	College
Boston	Karl Singer	T	Purdue
Buffalo	Mike Dennis	HB	Mississippi
Denver	Jerry Shay	T	Purdue
Houston	Tommy Nobis	LB	Texas
Kansas City	Aaron Brown	E	Minnesota
Miami	Jim Grabowski	FB	Illinois
Miami	Rick Norton	QB	Kentucky
New York	Bill Yearby	T	Michigan
Oakland	Rodger Bird	HB	Kentucky
San Diego	Don Davis	T	Cal State-L.A.

Total number of picks in draft: 181.

OTHER NOTEWORTHY PICKS

Round—Team, Player selected, Pos., College
15—Oakland, Steve Renko, FB, Kansas; 17—Kansas City, Walt Garrison, FB, Oklahoma State; 20—Kansas City, *Mike Garrett*, HB, USC.

REDSHIRT—AFL

The AFL held a separate draft for future picks in 1965 and 1966.

Team	Player selected	Pos.	College
Boston	Willie Townes	T	Tulsa
Buffalo	Jack Gregory	E	UT-Chattanooga
Denver	Nick Eddy	HB	Notre Dame
Houston	Tom Fisher	LB	Tennessee
Kansas City	George Youngblood	E/DB	Cal State-L.A.
Miami	John Roderick	E	SMU
New York	Don Parker	E	Virginia
Oakland	Rod Sherman	HB	USC
San Diego	Bob Windsor	E	Kentucky

Total number of picks in draft: 99.

OTHER NOTEWORTHY PICKS

Round—Team, Player selected, Pos., College
3—Kansas City, **Jan Stenerud**, K, Montana State; Boston, Ray Perkins, E, Alabama.

FIRST ROUND—NFL

No. Team	Player selected	Pos.	College
1. Atlanta	Tommy Nobis	LB	Texas
2. Los Angeles	**Tom Mack**	T	Michigan
3. Pittsburgh	Dick Leftridge	FB	West Virginia
4. Philadelphia	Randy Beisler	DE	Indiana
5. Dallas	John Niland	G	Iowa
6. Washington	Charlie Gogolak	K	Princeton
7. Minnesota	Jerry Shay	T	Purdue
8. St. Louis	Carl McAdams	LB	Oklahoma
9. Green Bay	Jim Grabowski	FB	Illinois
10. New York	Francis Peay	T	Missouri
11. San Francisco	Stan Hindman	T	Mississippi
12. Chicago	George Rice	T	Louisiana State
13. Green Bay	Gale Gillingham	T	Minnesota
14. Cleveland	Milt Morin	E	Massachusetts
15. Baltimore	Sam Ball	T	Kentucky
16. Atlanta	Randy Johnson	QB	Texas A&I

Team not selecting in first round: Detroit.
Total number of picks in draft: 305.

OTHER NOTEWORTHY PICKS

Round/Overall—Team, Player selected, Pos., College
2/18—Los Angeles, *Mike Garrett*, HB, USC; 5/79—Dallas, Walt Garrison, HB, Oklahoma State; 7/110—Baltimore, Ray Perkins, E, Alabama; 20/296—Dallas, Lou Hudson, FL, Minnesota.

1967

FIRST ROUND—AFL-NFL

From 1967 through 1969 the AFL and NFL held a combined draft. The league is noted in parentheses after each team's name.

No. Team	Player selected	Pos.	College
1. Baltimore (N)	Bubba Smith	DT	Michigan State
2. Minnesota (N)	Clint Jones	HB	Michigan State
3. San Fran. (N)	*Steve Spurrier*	QB	Florida
4. Miami (A)	**Bob Griese**	QB	Purdue
5. Houston (A)	George Webster	LB	Michigan State
6. Denver (A)	Floyd Little	HB	Syracuse
7. Detroit (N)	Mel Farr	HB	UCLA
8. Minnesota (N)	Gene Washington	FL	Michigan State
9. Green Bay (N)	Bob Hyland	G	Boston College
10. Chicago (N)	Loyd Phillips	DE	Arkansas
11. San Fran. (N)	Cas Banaszek	TE/LB	Northwestern
12. N.Y. Jets (A)	Paul Seiler	G	Notre Dame
13. Wash. (N)	Ray McDonald	FB	Idaho
14. San Diego (A)	Ron Billingsley	DT	Wyoming
15. Minnesota (N)	**Alan Page**	DE	Notre Dame
16. St. Louis (N)	Dave Williams	FL	Washington
17. Oakland (A)	**Gene Upshaw**	G/T	Texas A&I
18. Cleveland (N)	Bob Matheson	LB	Duke
19. Phil. (N)	Harry Jones	HB	Arkansas
20. Baltimore (N)	Jim Detwiler	HB	Michigan
21. Boston (A)	John Charles	DB	Purdue
22. Buffalo (A)	John Pitts	FL/DB	Arizona State
23. Houston (A)	Tom Regner	G	Notre Dame
24. Kan. City (A)	Gene Trosch	DT	Miami, Fla.
25. Green Bay (N)	Don Horn	QB	San Diego State
26. New Orl. (N)	Les Kelley	HB	Alabama

Teams not selecting in first round: Atlanta (N), Dallas (N), Los Angeles (N), N.Y. Giants (N), Pittsburgh (N).
Total number of picks in draft: 445.

OTHER NOTEWORTHY PICKS

Round/Overall—Team, Player selected, Pos., College
2/34—Detroit (N), **Lem Barney**, DB, Jackson State; 2/50—Kansas City (A), **Willie Lanier**, LB, Morgan State; 9/214—Houston (A), **Ken Houston**, DB, Prairie View A&M; 9/226—Los Angeles, Tommie Smith, HB, San Jose State; 11/285—Dallas (N), Pat Riley, FL, Kentucky; 17/443—Kansas City, Dave Lattin, FL, Texas-El Paso; 17/445—New Orleans, Jimmy Walker, E, Providence.

1968

FIRST ROUND—AFL-NFL

From 1967 through 1969 the AFL and NFL held a combined draft. The league is noted in parentheses after each team's name.

No. Team	Player selected	Pos.	College
1. Minnesota (N)	**Ron Yary**	T	USC
2. Cincinnati (A)	Bob Johnson	C	Tennessee
3. Atlanta (N)	Claude Humphrey	DE	Tennessee State
4. San Diego (A)	Russ Washington	T	Missouri
5. Green Bay (N)	Fred Carr	LB	Texas-El Paso
6. Boston (A)	Dennis Byrd	DT	N. Carolina State
7. New Orl. (N)	Kevin Hardy	DE	Notre Dame
8. Miami (A)	**Larry Csonka**	RB	Syracuse
9. Buffalo (A)	Haven Moses	E	San Diego State
10. Pittsburgh (N)	Mike Taylor	T	USC
11. Detroit (N)	Greg Landry	QB	Massachusetts
12. Wash. (N)	Jim Smith	DB	Oregon
13. St. Louis (N)	MacArthur Lane	RB	Utah State
14. Phil. (N)	Tim Rossovich	DE	USC
15. San Fran. (N)	Forrest Blue	C	Auburn
16. Chicago (N)	Mike Hull	RB	USC
17. N.Y. Jets (N)	Lee White	RB	Weber State
18. San Diego (A)	Jim Hill	DB	Texas A&I
19. Kan. City (A)	Mo Moorman	G	Texas A&M
20. Dallas (N)	Dennis Homan	E	Alabama
21. Cleveland (N)	Marvin Upshaw	DE	Trinity (Tex.)
22. Kan. City (A)	George Daney	G	Texas-El Paso
23. Baltimore (N)	John Williams	G	Minnesota
24. Detroit (N)	Earl McCullouch	E	USC
25. Oakland (A)	Eldridge Dickey	QB	Tennessee State
26. Green Bay (N)	Bill Lueck	G	Arizona
27. Miami (A)	Doug Crusan	T	Indiana

Teams not selecting in first round: Denver (A), Houston (A), Los Angeles (N), N.Y. Giants (N).
Total number of picks in draft: 461.

OTHER NOTEWORTHY PICKS

Round/Overall—Team, Player selected, Pos., College
2/30—Los Angeles (N), *Gary Beban*, QB, UCLA; 2/52—Oakland (A), Ken Stabler, QB, Alabama; 3/80—Oakland (A), **Art Shell**, T, Maryland-Eastern Shore; 9/240—Miami (A), Tom Paciorek, DB, Houston; 16/417—Pittsburgh (N), Rocky Bleier, RB, Notre Dame.

1969

FIRST ROUND—AFL-NFL

From 1967 through 1969 the AFL and NFL held a combined draft. The league is noted in parentheses after each team's name.

No. Team	Player selected	Pos.	College
1. Buffalo (A)	*O.J. Simpson*	RB	USC
2. Atlanta (N)	George Kunz	T	Notre Dame
3. Phil. (N)	Leroy Keyes	RB	Purdue
4. Pittsburgh (N)	**Joe Greene**	DT	North Texas State
5. Cincinnati (A)	Greg Cook	QB	Cincinnati
6. Boston (A)	Ron Sellers	SE	Florida State
7. San Fran. (N)	Ted Kwalick	TE	Penn State
8. Los Ang. (N)	Larry Smith	RB	Florida
9. San Diego (A)	Marty Domres	QB	Columbia
10. Los Ang. (N)	Jim Seymour	SE	Notre Dame
11. Miami (A)	Bill Stanfill	DE	Georgia
12. Green Bay (N)	Rich Moore	DT	Villanova
13. N.Y. Giants (N)	Fred Dryer	DE	San Diego State
14. Chicago (N)	Rufus Mayes	T	Ohio State
15. Houston (A)	Ron Pritchard	LB	Arizona State
16. San Fran. (N)	Gene Washington	FL	Stanford
17. New Orl. (N)	John Shinners	G	Xavier
18. San Diego (A)	Bob Babich	LB	Miami of Ohio
19. St. Louis (N)	Roger Wehrli	DB	Missouri
20. Cleveland (N)	Ron Johnson	RB	Michigan

No. Team	Player selected	Pos.	College
21. Los Ang. (N)	Bob Klein	TE	USC
22. Oakland (A)	Art Thoms	DT	Syracuse
23. Kan. City (A)	Jim Marsalis	DB	Tennessee State
24. Dallas (N)	Calvin Hill	RB	Yale
25. Baltimore (N)	Eddie Hinton	FL	Oklahoma
26. N.Y. Jets (A)	Dave Foley	T	Ohio State

Teams not selecting in first round: Denver (A), Detroit (N), Minnesota (N), Washington (N).

Total number of picks in draft: 442.

OTHER NOTEWORTHY PICKS

Round/Overall—Team, Player selected, Pos., College
2/33—Baltimore (N), **Ted Hendricks**, LB, Miami, Fla.; 3/63—Miami (A), Mercury Morris, RB, West Texas State; 4/93—Houston (A), **Charlie Joiner**, DB, Grambling; 8/192—Buffalo (A), James Harris, QB, Grambling; 17/429—N.Y. Giants (N), Ken Riley, LB, Texas-Arlington.

1970

FIRST ROUND—NFL

No. Team	Player selected	Pos.	College
1. Pittsburgh	**Terry Bradshaw**	QB	Louisiana Tech
2. Green Bay	Mike McCoy	DT	Notre Dame
3. Cleveland	Mike Phipps	QB	Purdue
4. Boston	Phil Olsen	DT	Utah State
5. Buffalo	Al Cowlings	DE	USC
6. Philadelphia	Steve Zabel	TE	Oklahoma
7. Cincinnati	Mike Reid	DT	Penn State
8. St. Louis	Larry Stegent	RB	Texas A&M
9. San Francisco	Cedrick Hardman	DE	North Texas State
10. New Orleans	Ken Burrough	WR	Texas Southern
11. Denver	Bobby Anderson	RB	Colorado
12. Atlanta	John Small	LB	The Citadel
13. N.Y. Giants	Jim Files	LB	Oklahoma
14. Houston	Doug Wilkerson	G	N.C. Central
15. San Diego	Walker Gillette	WR	Richmond
16. Green Bay	Rich McGeorge	TE	Elon
17. San Francisco	Bruce Taylor	DB	Boston University
18. Baltimore	Norm Bulaich	RB	Texas Christian
19. Detroit	*Steve Owens*	RB	Oklahoma
20. N.Y. Jets	Steve Tannen	DB	Florida
21. Cleveland	Bob McKay	T	Texas
22. Los Angeles	Jack Reynolds	LB	Tennessee
23. Dallas	Duane Thomas	RB	West Texas State
24. Oakland	Raymond Chester	TE	Morgan State
25. Minnesota	John Ward	T	Oklahoma State
26. Kansas City	Sid Smith	T	USC

Teams not selecting in first round: Chicago, Miami, Washington.
Total number of picks in draft: 442.

OTHER NOTEWORTHY PICKS

Round/Overall—Team, Player selected, Pos., College
3/53—Pittsburgh, **Mel Blount**, DB, Southern (La.); 7/159—Miami, Jake Scott, DB, Georgia; 8/201—St. Louis, Mike Holmgren, QB, USC; 14/346—Philadelphia, Mark Moseley, K, Stephen F. Austin.

1971

FIRST ROUND—NFL

No. Team	Player selected	Pos.	College
1. Boston	*Jim Plunkett*	QB	Stanford
2. New Orleans	Archie Manning	QB	Mississippi
3. Houston	Dan Pastorini	QB	Santa Clara
4. Buffalo	J.D. Hill	WR	Arizona State
5. Philadelphia	Richard Harris	DE	Grambling
6. N.Y. Jets	**John Riggins**	RB	Kansas
7. Atlanta	Joe Profit	RB	N.E. Louisiana

No. Team	Player selected	Pos.	College
8. Pittsburgh	Frank Lewis	WR	Grambling
9. Green Bay	John Brockington	RB	Ohio State
10. Los Angeles	Isiah Robertson	LB	Southern (La.)
11. Chicago	Joe Moore	RB	Missouri
12. Denver	Marv Montgomery	T	USC
13. San Diego	Leon Burns	RB	Long Beach State
14. Cleveland	Clarence Scott	DB	Kansas State
15. Cincinnati	Vernon Holland	T	Tennessee State
16. Kansas City	Elmo Wright	WR	Houston
17. St. Louis	Norm Thompson	DB	Utah
18. N.Y. Giants	Rocky Thompson	WR	West Texas State
19. Oakland	Jack Tatum	DB	Ohio State
20. Los Angeles	**Jack Youngblood**	DE	Florida
21. Detroit	Bob Bell	DT	Cincinnati
22. Baltimore	Don McCauley	RB	North Carolina
23. San Francisco	Tim Anderson	DB	Ohio State
24. Minnesota	Leo Hayden	RB	Ohio State
25. Dallas	Tody Smith	DE	USC
26. Baltimore	Leonard Dunlap	DB	North Texas State

Note: Boston franchise changed its name to New England (but after draft); teams not selecting in first round: Miami, Washington.
Total number of picks in draft: 442.

OTHER NOTEWORTHY PICKS

Round/Overall—Team, Player selected, Pos., College
2/34—Pittsburgh, **Jack Ham**, LB, Penn State; 2/43—St. Louis, **Dan Dierdorf**, T, Michigan; 3/67—Cincinnati, Ken Anderson, QB, Augustana (Ill.); 4/99—Miami, Joe Theismann, QB, Notre Dame; 7/161—Philadelphia, Harold Carmichael, WR, Southern (La).

1972

FIRST ROUND—NFL

No. Team	Player selected	Pos.	College
1. Buffalo	Walt Patulski	DE	Notre Dame
2. Cincinnati	Sherman White	DE	California
3. Chicago	Lionel Antoine	T	Southern Illinois
4. St. Louis	Bobby Moore	WR	Oregon
5. Denver	Riley Odoms	TE	Houston
6. Houston	Gregory Sampson	DE	Stanford
7. Green Bay	Willie Buchanon	DB	San Diego State
8. New Orleans	Royce Smith	G	Georgia
9. N.Y. Jets	Jerome Barkum	WR	Jackson State
10. Minnesota	Jeff Siemon	LB	Stanford
11. Green Bay	Jerry Tagge	QB	Nebraska
12. Chicago	Craig Clemons	DB	Iowa
13. Pittsburgh	**Franco Harris**	RB	Penn State
14. Philadelphia	John Reaves	QB	Florida
15. Atlanta	Clarence Ellis	DB	Notre Dame
16. Detroit	Herb Orvis	DE	Colorado
17. N.Y. Giants	Eldridge Small	DB	Texas A&I
18. Cleveland	Thom Darden	DB	Michigan
19. San Francisco	Terry Beasley	WR	Auburn
20. N.Y. Jets	Mike Taylor	LB	Michigan
21. Oakland	Mike Siani	WR	Villanova
22. Baltimore	Tom Drougas	T	Oregon
23. Kansas City	Jeff Kinney	RB	Nebraska
24. N.Y. Giants	Larry Jacobson	DE	Nebraska
25. Miami	Mike Kadish	DT	Notre Dame
26. Dallas	Bill Thomas	RB	Boston College

Teams not selecting in first round: Los Angeles, New England, San Diego, Washington.
Total number of picks in draft: 442.

OTHER NOTEWORTHY PICKS

Round/Overall—Team, Player selected, Pos., College
2/40—Atlanta, *Pat Sullivan*, QB, Auburn; 2/50—Minnesota, Ed Marinaro, RB, Cornell; 7/167—Chicago, Jim Fassel, QB, Long Beach State; 13/330—Cleveland, Brian Sipe, QB, San Diego State.

1973
FIRST ROUND—NFL

No. Team	Player selected	Pos.	College
1. Houston	John Matuszak	DE	Tampa
2. Baltimore	Bert Jones	QB	Louisiana State
3. Philadelphia	Jerry Sisemore	T	Texas
4. New England	**John Hannah**	G	Alabama
5. St. Louis	Dave Butz	DT	Purdue
6. Philadelphia	Charle Young	TE	USC
7. Buffalo	Paul Seymour	T	Michigan
8. Chicago	Wally Chambers	DE	Eastern Kentucky
9. Denver	Otis Armstrong	RB	Purdue
10. Baltimore	Joe Ehrmann	DT	Syracuse
11. New England	Sam Cunningham	RB	USC
12. Minnesota	Chuck Foreman	RB	Miami, Fla.
13. N.Y. Jets	Burgess Owens	DB	Miami, Fla.
14. Houston	George Amundson	RB	Iowa State
15. Cincinnati	Isaac Curtis	WR	San Diego State
16. Cleveland	Steve Holden	WR	Arizona State
17. Detroit	Ernest Price	DE	Texas A&I
18. San Francisco	Mike Holmes	DB	Texas Southern
19. New England	Darryl Stingley	WR	Purdue
20. Dallas	Billy Joe Dupree	TE	Michigan State
21. Green Bay	Barry Smith	WR	Florida State
22. Cleveland	Pete Adams	T	USC
23. Oakland	Ray Guy	P	Southern Miss
24. Pittsburgh	James Thomas	DB	Florida State
25. San Diego	*Johnny Rodgers*	WR	Nebraska
26. Buffalo	Joe DeLamielleure	G	Michigan State

Teams not selecting in first round: Atlanta, Kansas City, Los Angeles, Miami, New Orleans, N.Y. Giants, Washington.
Total number of picks in draft: 442.

OTHER NOTEWORTHY PICKS

Round/Overall—Team, Player selected, Pos., College
2/37—Los Angeles, Ron Jaworski, QB, Youngstown State; 3/84—San Diego, **Dan Fouts**, QB, Oregon; 4/91—Detroit, Dick Jauron, RB, Yale; 17/423—Buffalo, John Stearns, DB, Colorado; 17/429—Minnesota, Dave Winfield, TE, Minnesota.

1974
FIRST ROUND—NFL

No. Team	Player selected	Pos.	College
1. Dallas	Ed Jones	DE	Tennessee State
2. San Diego	Bo Matthews	RB	Colorado
3. N.Y. Giants	John Hicks	G	Ohio State
4. Chicago	Waymond Bryant	LB	Tennessee State
5. Baltimore	John Dutton	DE	Nebraska
6. N.Y. Jets	Carl Barzilauskas	DT	Indiana
7. St. Louis	J.V. Cain	TE	Colorado
8. Detroit	Ed O'Neil	LB	Penn State
9. San Francisco	Wilbur Jackson	RB	Alabama
10. San Francisco	Bill Sandifer	DT	UCLA
11. Los Angeles	*John Cappelletti*	RB	Penn State
12. Green Bay	Barty Smith	RB	Richmond
13. New Orleans	Rick Middleton	LB	Ohio State
14. Denver	Randy Gradishar	LB	Ohio State
15. San Diego	Don Goode	LB	Kansas
16. Kansas City	Woody Green	RB	Arizona State
17. Minnesota	Fred McNeill	LB	UCLA
18. Buffalo	Reuben Gant	TE	Oklahoma State
19. Oakland	Henry Lawrence	T	Florida A&M
20. Chicago	Dave Gallagher	DL	Michigan
21. Pittsburgh	**Lynn Swann**	WR	USC
22. Dallas	Charley Young	RB	N. Carolina State
23. Cincinnati	Bill Kollar	DT	Montana State
24. Baltimore	Roger Carr	WR	Louisiana Tech
25. Minnesota	Steve Riley	T	USC
26. Miami	Donald Reese	DE	Jackson State

Teams not selecting in first round: Atlanta, Cleveland, Houston, New England, Philadelphia, Washington.
Total number of picks in draft: 442.

OTHER NOTEWORTHY PICKS

Round/Overall—Team, Player selected, Pos., College
2/45—Oakland, Dave Casper, TE, Notre Dame; 2/46—Pittsburgh, **Jack Lambert**, LB, Kent State; 4/82—Pittsburgh, John Stallworth, WR, Alabama A&M; 5/125—Pittsburgh, **Mike Webster**, C, Wisconsin; 10/236—N.Y. Giants, Ray Rhodes, WR, Tulsa; 15/365—Houston, Billy (White Shoes) Johnson, WR, Widener; 15/376—Green Bay, Dave Wannstedt, T, Pittsburgh.

1975
FIRST ROUND—NFL

No. Team	Player selected	Pos.	College
1. Atlanta	Steve Bartkowski	QB	California
2. Dallas	**Randy White**	DE/LB	Maryland
3. Baltimore	Ken Huff	G	North Carolina
4. Chicago	**Walter Payton**	RB	Jackson State
5. Cleveland	Mack Mitchell	DE	Houston
6. Houston	Robert Brazile	LB	Jackson State
7. New Orleans	Larry Burton	WR	Purdue
8. San Diego	Gary Johnson	DT	Grambling
9. Los Angeles	Mike Fanning	DT	Notre Dame
10. San Francisco	Jimmy Webb	DT	Mississippi State
11. Los Angeles	Dennis Harrah	T	Miami, Fla.
12. New Orleans	Kurt Schumacher	T	Ohio State
13. Detroit	Lynn Boden	G	South Dakota St.
14. Cincinnati	Glenn Cameron	LB	Florida
15. Houston	Don Hardeman	RB	Texas A&I
16. New England	Russ Francis	TE	Oregon
17. Denver	Louis Wright	DB	San Jose State
18. Dallas	Thomas Henderson	LB	Langston
19. Buffalo	Tom Ruud	LB	Nebraska
20. Los Angeles	Doug France	T	Ohio State
21. St. Louis	Tim Gray	DB	Texas A&M
22. San Diego	Mike Williams	DB	Louisiana State
23. Miami	Darryl Carlton	T	Tampa
24. Oakland	Neal Colzie	DB	Ohio State
25. Minnesota	Mark Mullaney	DE	Colorado State
26. Pittsburgh	Dave Brown	DB	Michigan

Teams not selecting in first round: Green Bay, Kansas City, N.Y. Giants, N.Y. Jets, Philadelphia, Washington.
Total number of picks in draft: 442.

OTHER NOTEWORTHY PICKS

Round/Overall—Team, Player selected, Pos., College
4/95—Denver, Rick Upchurch, WR, Minnesota; 5/116—New England, Steve Grogan, QB, Kansas State; 7/176—Los Angeles, Pat Haden, QB, USC.

1976
FIRST ROUND—NFL

No. Team	Player selected	Pos.	College
1. Tampa Bay	**Lee Roy Selmon**	DE	Oklahoma
2. Seattle	Steve Niehaus	DT	Notre Dame
3. New Orleans	Chuck Muncie	RB	California
4. San Diego	Joe Washington	RB	Oklahoma
5. New England	**Mike Haynes**	DB	Arizona State
6. N.Y. Jets	Richard Todd	QB	Alabama
7. Cleveland	Mike Pruitt	RB	Purdue
8. Chicago	Dennis Lick	T	Wisconsin
9. Atlanta	Bubba Bean	RB	Texas A&M
10. Detroit	James Hunter	DB	Grambling
11. Cincinnati	Billy Brooks	WR	Oklahoma
12. New England	Pete Brock	C	Colorado

No.	Team	Player selected	Pos.	College
13.	N.Y. Giants	Troy Archer	DE	Colorado
14.	Kansas City	Rod Walters	G	Iowa
15.	Denver	Tom Glassic	G	Virginia
16.	Detroit	Lawrence Gaines	RB	Wyoming
17.	Miami	Larry Gordon	LB	Arizona State
18.	Buffalo	Mario Clark	DB	Oregon
19.	Miami	Kim Bokamper	LB	San Jose State
20.	Baltimore	Ken Novak	DT	Purdue
21.	New England	Tim Fox	DB	Ohio State
22.	St. Louis	Mike Dawson	DT	Arizona
23.	Green Bay	Mark Koncar	T	Colorado
24.	Cincinnati	*Archie Griffin*	RB	Ohio State
25.	Minnesota	James White	DT	Oklahoma State
26.	Los Angeles	Kevin McLain	LB	Colorado State
27.	Dallas	Aaron Kyle	DB	Wyoming
28.	Pittsburgh	Bennie Cunningham	TE	Clemson

Teams not selecting in first round: Houston, Oakland, Philadelphia, San Francisco, Washington.

Total number of picks in draft: 487.

OTHER NOTEWORTHY PICKS

Round/Overall—Team, Player selected, Pos., College
3/86—Los Angeles, **Jackie Slater**, G, Jackson State; 4/117—Houston, **Steve Largent**, WR, Tulsa; 14/393—Washington, Quinn Buckner, DB, Indiana.

1977

FIRST ROUND—NFL

No.	Team	Player selected	Pos.	College
1.	Tampa Bay	Ricky Bell	RB	USC
2.	Dallas	*Tony Dorsett*	RB	Pittsburgh
3.	Cincinnati	Eddie Edwards	DT	Miami, Fla.
4.	N.Y. Jets	Marvin Powell	T	USC
5.	N.Y. Giants	Gary Jeter	DT	USC
6.	Atlanta	Warren Bryant	T	Kentucky
7.	New Orleans	Joe Campbell	DE	Maryland
8.	Cincinnati	Wilson Whitley	DT	Houston
9.	Green Bay	Mike Butler	DE	Kansas
10.	Kansas City	Gary Green	DB	Baylor
11.	Houston	Morris Towns	T	Missouri
12.	Buffalo	Phil Dokes	DT	Oklahoma State
13.	Miami	A.J. Duhe	DT	Louisiana State
14.	Seattle	Steve August	G	Tulsa
15.	Chicago	Ted Albrecht	T	California
16.	New England	Raymond Clayborn	DB	Texas
17.	Cleveland	Robert Jackson	LB	Texas A&M
18.	Denver	Steve Schindler	G	Boston College
19.	St. Louis	Steve Pisarkiewicz	QB	Missouri
20.	Atlanta	Wilson Faumina	DT	San Jose State
21.	Pittsburgh	Robin Cole	LB	New Mexico
22.	Cincinnati	Mike Cobb	TE	Michigan State
23.	Los Angeles	Bob Brudzinski	LB	Ohio State
24.	San Diego	Bob Rush	C	Memphis State
25.	New England	Stanley Morgan	WR	Tennessee
26.	Baltimore	Randy Burke	WR	Kentucky
27.	Minnesota	Tommy Kramer	QB	Rice
28.	Green Bay	Ezra Johnson	DE	Morris Brown

Teams not selecting in first round: Detroit, Oakland, Philadelphia, San Francisco, Washington.

Total number of picks in draft: 335.

OTHER NOTEWORTHY PICKS

Round/Overall—Team, Player selected, Pos., College
2/31—Los Angeles, Nolan Cromwell, DB, Kansas; 4/91—Los Angeles, Vince Ferragamo, QB, Nebraska; 6/140—Chicago, Vince Evans, QB, USC; 10/275—Dallas, Steve DeBerg, QB, San Jose State; 11/295—San Francisco, Brian Billick, TE, Brigham Young.

1978

FIRST ROUND—NFL

No.	Team	Player selected	Pos.	College
1.	Houston	*Earl Campbell*	RB	Texas
2.	Kansas City	Art Still	DE	Kentucky
3.	New Orleans	Wes Chandler	WR	Florida
4.	N.Y. Jets	Chris Ward	T	Ohio State
5.	Buffalo	Terry Miller	RB	Oklahoma State
6.	Green Bay	James Lofton	WR	Stanford
7.	San Francisco	Ken MacAfee	TE	Notre Dame
8.	Cincinnati	Ross Browner	DE	Notre Dame
9.	Seattle	Keith Simpson	DB	Memphis State
10.	N.Y. Giants	Gordon King	T	Stanford
11.	Detroit	Luther Bradley	DB	Notre Dame
12.	Cleveland	Clay Matthews	LB	USC
13.	Atlanta	Mike Kenn	T	Michigan
14.	San Diego	John Jefferson	WR	Arizona State
15.	St. Louis	Steve Little	K	Arkansas
16.	Cincinnati	Blair Bush	C	Washington
17.	Tampa Bay	Doug Williams	QB	Grambling
18.	New England	Bob Cryder	G	Alabama
19.	St. Louis	Ken Greene	DB	Washington State
20.	Los Angeles	Elvis Peacock	RB	Oklahoma
21.	Minnesota	Randy Holloway	DE	Pittsburgh
22.	Pittsburgh	Ron Johnson	DB	Eastern Michigan
23.	Cleveland	*Ozzie Newsome*	WR	Alabama
24.	San Francisco	Dan Bunz	LB	Long Beach State
25.	Baltimore	Reese McCall	TE	Auburn
26.	Green Bay	John Anderson	LB	Michigan
27.	Denver	Don Latimer	DT	Miami, Fla.
28.	Dallas	Larry Bethea	DE	Michigan State

Teams not selecting in first round: Chicago, Miami, Oakland, Philadelphia, Washington.

Total number of picks in draft: 334.

OTHER NOTEWORTHY PICKS

Round/Overall—Team, Player selected, Pos., College
2/56—Dallas, Todd Christensen, RB, Brigham Young; 8/206—Cincinnati, Jim Breech, K, California; 8/215—New England, Mosi Tatupu, RB, USC.

1979

FIRST ROUND—NFL

No.	Team	Player selected	Pos.	College
1.	Buffalo	Tom Cousineau	LB	Ohio State
2.	Kansas City	Mike Bell	DE	Colorado State
3.	Cincinnati	Jack Thompson	QB	Washington State
4.	Chicago	Dan Hampton	DT	Arkansas
5.	Buffalo	Jerry Butler	WR	Clemson
6.	Baltimore	Barry Krauss	LB	Alabama
7.	N.Y. Giants	Phil Simms	QB	Morehead State
8.	St. Louis	Ottis Anderson	RB	Miami, Fla.
9.	Chicago	Al Harris	DE	Arizona State
10.	Detroit	Keith Dorney	T	Penn State
11.	New Orleans	Russell Erxleben	K/P	Texas
12.	Cincinnati	Charles Alexander	RB	Louisiana State
13.	San Diego	**Kellen Winslow**	TE	Missouri
14.	N.Y. Jets	Marty Lyons	DE	Alabama
15.	Green Bay	Eddie Lee Ivery	RB	Georgia Tech
16.	Minnesota	Ted Brown	RB	N. Carolina State
17.	Atlanta	Don Smith	DE	Miami, Fla.
18.	Seattle	Manu Tuiasosopo	DT	UCLA
19.	Los Angeles	George Andrews	LB	Nebraska
20.	Cleveland	Willis Adams	WR	Houston
21.	Philadelphia	Jerry Robinson	LB	UCLA
22.	Denver	Kelvin Clark	T	Nebraska
23.	Kansas City	Steve Fuller	QB	Clemson
24.	Miami	Jon Giesler	T	Michigan

No. Team	Player selected	Pos.	College
25. New England	Rick Sanford	DB	South Carolina
26. Los Angeles	Kent Hill	T	Georgia Tech
27. Dallas	Robert Shaw	C	Tennessee
28. Pittsburgh	Greg Hawthorne	RB	Baylor

Teams not selecting in first round: Houston, Oakland, San Francisco, Tampa Bay, Washington.
Total number of picks in draft: 330.

OTHER NOTEWORTHY PICKS

Round/Overall—Team, Player selected, Pos., College
2/41—N.Y. Jets, Mark Gastineau, DE, East Central Oklahoma; 2/51—Buffalo, Jim Haslett, LB, Indiana, Pa.; 3/82—San Francisco, **Joe Montana**, QB, Notre Dame; 7/173—St. Louis, Kirk Gibson, WR, Michigan State; 10/249—San Francisco, Dwight Clark, WR, Clemson.

1980
FIRST ROUND—NFL

No. Team	Player selected	Pos.	College
1. Detroit	*Billy Sims*	RB	Oklahoma
2. N.Y. Jets	Johnny (Lam) Jones	WR	Texas
3. Cincinnati	**Anthony Munoz**	T	USC
4. Green Bay	Bruce Clark	DE	Penn State
5. Baltimore	Curtis Dickey	RB	Texas A&M
6. St. Louis	Curtis Greer	DE	Michigan
7. Atlanta	Junior Miller	TE	Nebraska
8. N.Y. Giants	Mark Haynes	DB	Colorado
9. Minnesota	Doug Martin	DT	Washington
10. Seattle	Jacob Green	DE	Texas A&M
11. Kansas City	Brad Budde	G	USC
12. New Orleans	Stan Brock	T	Colorado
13. San Francisco	Earl Cooper	RB	Rice
14. New England	Roland James	DB	Tennessee
15. Oakland	Marc Wilson	QB	Brigham Young
16. Buffalo	Jim Ritcher	C	N. Carolina State
17. Los Angeles	Johnnie Johnson	DB	Texas
18. Washington	Art Monk	WR	Syracuse
19. Chicago	Otis Wilson	LB	Louisville
20. San Francisco	Jim Stuckey	DT	Clemson
21. Miami	Don McNeal	DB	Alabama
22. Tampa Bay	Ray Snell	G	Wisconsin
23. Philadelphia	Roynell Young	DB	Alcorn State
24. Baltimore	Derrick Hatchett	DB	Texas
25. New England	Vagas Ferguson	RB	Notre Dame
26. Green Bay	George Cumby	LB	Oklahoma
27. Cleveland	*Charles White*	RB	USC
28. Pittsburgh	Mark Malone	QB	Arizona State

Teams not selecting in first round: Dallas, Denver, Houston, San Diego.
Total number of picks in draft: 333.

OTHER NOTEWORTHY PICKS

Round/Overall—Team, Player selected, Pos., College
2/29—Buffalo, Joe Cribbs, RB, Auburn; 2/43—Oakland, Matt Millen, LB, Penn State; 2/48—Miami, **Dwight Stephenson**, C, Alabama; 7/166—Detroit, Eddie Murray, K, Tulane.

1981
FIRST ROUND—NFL

No. Team	Player selected	Pos.	College
1. New Orleans	*George Rogers*	RB	South Carolina
2. N.Y. Giants	**Lawrence Taylor**	LB	North Carolina
3. N.Y. Jets	Freeman McNeil	RB	UCLA
4. Seattle	Kenny Easley	DB	UCLA
5. St. Louis	E.J. Junior	LB	Alabama
6. Green Bay	Rich Campbell	QB	California
7. Tampa Bay	Hugh Green	LB	Pittsburgh
8. San Francisco	**Ronnie Lott**	DB	USC

No. Team	Player selected	Pos.	College
9. Los Angeles	Mel Owens	LB	Michigan
10. Cincinnati	David Verser	WR	Kansas
11. Chicago	Keith Van Horne	T	USC
12. Baltimore	Randy McMillan	RB	Pittsburgh
13. Miami	David Overstreet	RB	Oklahoma
14. Kansas City	Willie Scott	TE	South Carolina
15. Denver	Dennis Smith	DB	USC
16. Detroit	Mark Nichols	WR	San Jose State
17. Pittsburgh	Keith Gary	DE	Oklahoma
18. Baltimore	Donnell Thompson	DT	North Carolina
19. New England	Brian Holloway	T	Stanford
20. Washington	Mark May	T	Pittsburgh
21. Oakland	Ted Watts	DB	Texas Tech
22. Cleveland	Hanford Dixon	DB	Southern Miss
23. Oakland	Curt Marsh	T	Washington
24. San Diego	James Brooks	RB	Auburn
25. Atlanta	Bobby Butler	DB	Florida State
26. Dallas	Howard Richards	T	Missouri
27. Philadelphia	Leonard Mitchell	DE	Houston
28. Buffalo	Booker Moore	RB	Penn State

Teams not selecting in first round: Houston, Minnesota.
Total number of picks in draft: 332.

OTHER NOTEWORTHY PICKS

Round/Overall—Team, Player selected, Pos., College
2/37—Cincinnati, Cris Collinsworth, WR, Florida; 2/38—Chicago, **Mike Singletary**, LB, Baylor; 2/48—Oakland, **Howie Long**, DT, Villanova; 7/177—Chicago, Jeff Fisher, DB, USC; 8/213—N.Y. Jets, J.C. Watts, DB, Oklahoma; Supplemental—New Orleans, Dave Wilson, QB, Illinois.

1982
FIRST ROUND—NFL

No. Team	Player selected	Pos.	College
1. New England	Ken Sims	DT	Texas
2. Baltimore	Johnie Cooks	LB	Mississippi State
3. Cleveland	Chip Banks	LB	USC
4. Baltimore	Art Schlichter	QB	Ohio State
5. Chicago	Jim McMahon	QB	Brigham Young
6. Seattle	Jeff Bryant	DE	Clemson
7. Minnesota	Darrin Nelson	RB	Stanford
8. Houston	**Mike Munchak**	G	Penn State
9. Atlanta	Gerald Riggs	RB	Arizona State
10. Oakland	*Marcus Allen*	RB	USC
11. Kansas City	Anthony Hancock	WR	Tennessee
12. Pittsburgh	Walter Abercrombie	RB	Baylor
13. New Orleans	Lindsay Scott	WR	Georgia
14. Los Angeles	Barry Redden	RB	Richmond
15. Detroit	Jimmy Williams	LB	Nebraska
16. St. Louis	Luis Sharpe	T	UCLA
17. Tampa Bay	Sean Farrell	G	Penn State
18. N.Y. Giants	Butch Woolfolk	RB	Michigan
19. Buffalo	Perry Tuttle	WR	Clemson
20. Philadelphia	Mike Quick	WR	N. Carolina State
21. Denver	Gerald Willhite	RB	San Jose State
22. Green Bay	Ron Hallstrom	G	Iowa
23. N.Y. Jets	Bob Crable	LB	Notre Dame
24. Miami	Roy Foster	G	USC
25. Dallas	Rod Hill	DB	Kentucky State
26. Cincinnati	Glen Collins	DE	Mississippi State
27. New England	Lester Williams	DT	Miami, Fla.

Note: Oakland franchise moved to Los Angeles (but after draft); teams not selecting in first round: San Diego, San Francisco, Washington.
Total number of picks in draft: 334.

OTHER NOTEWORTHY PICKS

Round/Overall—Team, Player selected, Pos., College
2/45—N.Y. Giants, Joe Morris, RB, Syracuse; 2/52—Miami, Mark Duper, WR, Northwestern (La.) State; 5/131—Denver, Sammy Winder, RB, Southern Mississippi.

1983

FIRST ROUND—NFL

No.	Team	Player selected	Pos.	College
1.	Baltimore	John Elway	QB	Stanford
2.	L.A. Rams	Eric Dickerson	RB	SMU
3.	Seattle	Curt Warner	RB	Penn State
4.	Denver	Chris Hinton	G	Northwestern
5.	San Diego	Billy Ray Smith	LB	Arkansas
6.	Chicago	Jimbo Covert	T	Pittsburgh
7.	Kansas City	Todd Blackledge	QB	Penn State
8.	Philadelphia	Michael Haddix	RB	Mississippi State
9.	Houston	Bruce Matthews	G	USC
10.	N.Y. Giants	Terry Kinard	DB	Clemson
11.	Green Bay	Tim Lewis	DB	Pittsburgh
12.	Buffalo	Tony Hunter	TE	Notre Dame
13.	Detroit	James Jones	RB	Florida
14.	Buffalo	Jim Kelly	QB	Miami, Fla.
15.	New England	Tony Eason	QB	Illinois
16.	Atlanta	Mike Pitts	DE	Alabama
17.	St. Louis	Leonard Smith	DB	McNeese State
18.	Chicago	Willie Gault	WR	Tennessee
19.	Minnesota	Joey Browner	DB	USC
20.	San Diego	Gary Anderson	WR	Arkansas
21.	Pittsburgh	Gabriel Rivera	DT	Texas Tech
22.	San Diego	Gill Byrd	DB	San Jose State
23.	Dallas	Jim Jeffcoat	DE	Arizona State
24.	N.Y. Jets	Ken O'Brien	QB	UC Davis
25.	Cincinnati	Dave Rimington	C	Nebraska
26.	L.A. Raiders	Don Mosebar	T	USC
27.	Miami	Dan Marino	QB	Pittsburgh
28.	Washington	Darrell Green	DB	Texas A&I

Teams not selecting in first round: Cleveland, New Orleans, San Francisco, Tampa Bay.
Total number of picks in draft: 335.

OTHER NOTEWORTHY PICKS

Round/Overall—Team, Player selected, Pos., College
2/49—San Francisco, Roger Craig, RB, Nebraska; 3/84—Washington, Charles Mann, DE, Nevada; 8/203—Chicago, Richard Dent, DE, Tennessee State; 12/334—Miami, Anthony Carter, WR, Michigan.

1984

FIRST ROUND—NFL

No.	Team	Player selected	Pos.	College
1.	New England	Irving Fryar	WR	Nebraska
2.	Houston	Dean Steinkuhler	T	Nebraska
3.	N.Y. Giants	Carl Banks	LB	Michigan State
4.	Philadelphia	Kenny Jackson	WR	Penn State
5.	Kansas City	Bill Maas	DT	Pittsburgh
6.	San Diego	Mossy Cade	DB	Texas
7.	Cincinnati	Ricky Hunley	LB	Arizona
8.	Indianapolis	Leonard Coleman	DB	Vanderbilt
9.	Atlanta	Rick Bryan	DT	Oklahoma
10.	N.Y. Jets	Russell Carter	DB	SMU
11.	Chicago	Wilber Marshall	LB	Florida
12.	Green Bay	Alphonso Carreker	DE	Florida State
13.	Minnesota	Keith Millard	DE	Washington State
14.	Miami	Jackie Shipp	LB	Oklahoma
15.	N.Y. Jets	Ron Faurot	DE	Arkansas
16.	Cincinnati	Pete Koch	DE	Maryland
17.	St. Louis	Clyde Duncan	WR	Tennessee
18.	Cleveland	Don Rogers	DB	UCLA
19.	Indianapolis	Ron Solt	G	Maryland
20.	Detroit	David Lewis	TE	California
21.	Kansas City	John Alt	T	Iowa
22.	Seattle	Terry Taylor	DB	Southern Illinois
23.	Pittsburgh	Louis Lipps	WR	Southern Miss
24.	San Francisco	Todd Shell	LB	Brigham Young
25.	Dallas	Billy Cannon Jr.	LB	Texas A&M
26.	Buffalo	Greg Bell	RB	Notre Dame

No.	Team	Player selected	Pos.	College
27.	N.Y. Giants	Bill Roberts	T	Ohio State
28.	Cincinnati	Brian Blados	T	North Carolina

Teams not selecting in first round: Denver, L.A. Raiders, L.A. Rams, New Orleans, Tampa Bay, Washington.
Total number of picks in draft: 336.

OTHER NOTEWORTHY PICKS

Round/Overall—Team, Player selected, Pos., College
2/38—Cincinnati, Boomer Esiason, QB, Maryland; 3/59—N.Y. Giants, Jeff Hostetler, QB, West Virginia; 10/280—Cleveland, Earnest Byner, RB, East Carolina.

FIRST ROUND—NFL SUPPLEMENTAL

In 1984, the NFL held a three-round supplemental draft for the contract rights to USFL and CFL players.

No.	Team	Player selected	Pos.	College
1.	Tampa Bay	Steve Young	QB	Brigham Young
2.	Houston	*Mike Rozier*	RB	Nebraska
3.	N.Y. Giants	Gary Zimmerman	G	Oregon
4.	Philadelphia	Reggie White	DE	Tennessee
5.	Kansas City	Mark Adickes	T	Baylor
6.	San Diego	Lee Williams	DE	Bethune-Cookman
7.	Cincinnati	Wayne Peace	QB	Florida
8.	Indianapolis	Paul Bergmann	TE	UCLA
9.	Atlanta	Joey Jones	WR	Alabama
10.	N.Y. Jets	Ken Hobart	QB	Idaho
11.	Cleveland	Kevin Mack	RB	Clemson
12.	Green Bay	Buford Jordan	RB	McNeese State
13.	Minnesota	Allanda Smith	DB	Texas Christian
14.	Buffalo	Dwight Drane	DB	Oklahoma
15.	New Orleans	Vaughan Johnson	LB	N. Carolina State
16.	New England	Ricky Sanders	WR/PR	SW Texas State
17.	St. Louis	Mike Ruether	C	Texas
18.	Cleveland	Mike Johnson	LB	Virginia Tech
19.	Denver	Freddie Gilbert	DE	Georgia
20.	Detroit	Alphonso Williams	WR	Nevada
21.	L.A. Rams	William Fuller	DE	North Carolina
22.	Seattle	Gordon Hudson	TE	Brigham Young
23.	Pittsburgh	Duane Gunn	WR	Indiana
24.	San Francisco	Derrick Crawford	WR	Memphis State
25.	Dallas	Todd Fowler	TE	Stephen F. Austin
26.	Miami	Danny Knight	WR	Mississippi State
27.	Washington	Tony Zendejas	K	Nevada
28.	L.A. Raiders	Chris Woods	WR	Auburn

Team not selecting in first round: Chicago.
Total number of picks in supplemental draft: 84.

1985

FIRST ROUND—NFL

No.	Team	Player selected	Pos.	College
1.	Buffalo	Bruce Smith	DE	Virginia Tech
2.	Atlanta	Bill Fralic	T	Pittsburgh
3.	Houston	Ray Childress	DE	Texas A&M
4.	Minnesota	Chris Doleman	LB	Pittsburgh
5.	Indianapolis	Duane Bickett	LB	USC
6.	Detroit	Lomas Brown	T	Florida
7.	Green Bay	Ken Ruettgers	T	USC
8.	Tampa Bay	Ron Holmes	DE	Washington
9.	Philadelphia	Kevin Allen	T	Indiana
10.	N.Y. Jets	Al Toon	WR	Wisconsin
11.	Houston	Richard Johnson	DB	Wisconsin
12.	San Diego	Jim Lachey	G	Ohio State
13.	Cincinnati	Eddie Brown	WR	Miami, Fla.
14.	Buffalo	Derrick Burroughs	DB	Memphis State
15.	Kansas City	Ethan Horton	RB	North Carolina
16.	San Francisco	Jerry Rice	WR	Miss Valley
17.	Dallas	Kevin Brooks	DE	Michigan
18.	St. Louis	Freddie Joe Nunn	LB	Mississippi
19.	N.Y. Giants	George Adams	RB	Kentucky

– 375 –

No.	Team	Player selected	Pos.	College
20.	Pittsburgh	Darryl Sims	DE	Wisconsin
21.	L.A. Rams	Jerry Gray	DB	Texas
22.	Chicago	William Perry	DT	Clemson
23.	L.A. Raiders	Jessie Hester	WR	Florida State
24.	New Orleans	Alvin Toles	LB	Tennessee
25.	Cincinnati	Emanuel King	LB	Alabama
26.	Denver	Steve Sewell	RB	Oklahoma
27.	Miami	Lorenzo Hampton	RB	Florida
28.	New England	Trevor Matich	C	Brigham Young

Teams not selecting in first round: Cleveland, Seattle, Washington.

Total number of picks in draft: 336.

OTHER NOTEWORTHY PICKS

Round/Overall—Team, Player selected, Pos., College
2/37—Philadelphia, Randall Cunningham, QB/P, UNLV; 4/86—Buffalo, Andre Reed, WR, Kutztown; 5/114—Dallas, *Herschel Walker*, RB, Georgia; 11/285—L.A. Rams, *Doug Flutie*, QB, Boston College; Supplemental—Cleveland, Bernie Kosar, QB, Miami, Fla.

1986

FIRST ROUND—NFL

No.	Team	Player selected	Pos.	College
1.	Tampa Bay	*Bo Jackson*	RB	Auburn
2.	Atlanta	Tony Casillas	NT	Oklahoma
3.	Houston	Jim Everett	QB	Purdue
4.	Indianapolis	Jon Hand	DE	Alabama
5.	St. Louis	Anthony Bell	LB	Michigan State
6.	New Orleans	Jim Dombrowski	T	Virginia
7.	Kansas City	Brian Jozwiak	T	West Virginia
8.	San Diego	Leslie O'Neal	DE	Oklahoma State
9.	Pittsburgh	John Rienstra	G	Temple
10.	Philadelphia	Keith Byars	RB	Ohio State
11.	Cincinnati	Joe Kelly	LB	Washington
12.	Detroit	Chuck Long	QB	Iowa
13.	San Diego	James Fitzpatrick	T	USC
14.	Minnesota	Gerald Robinson	DE	Auburn
15.	Seattle	John L. Williams	RB	Florida
16.	Buffalo	Ronnie Harmon	RB	Iowa
17.	Atlanta	Tim Green	LB	Syracuse
18.	Dallas	Mike Sherrard	WR	UCLA
19.	N.Y. Giants	Eric Dorsey	DE	Notre Dame
20.	Buffalo	Will Wolford	T	Vanderbilt
21.	Cincinnati	Tim McGee	WR	Tennessee
22.	N.Y. Jets	Mike Haight	T	Iowa
23.	L.A. Rams	Mike Schad	T	Queens (Canada)
24.	L.A. Raiders	Bob Buczkowski	DE	Pittsburgh
25.	Tampa Bay	Roderick Jones	DB	SMU
26.	New England	Reggie Dupard	RB	SMU
27.	Chicago	Neal Anderson	RB	Florida

Teams not selecting in first round: Cleveland, Denver, Green Bay, Miami, San Francisco, Washington.

Total number of picks in draft: 333.

OTHER NOTEWORTHY PICKS

Round/Overall—Team, Player selected, Pos., College
3/76—San Francisco, John Taylor, WR, Delaware State; 4/96—San Francisco, Charles Haley, LB, James Madison; 6/146—Washington, Mark Rypien, QB, Washington State; 9/233—Philadelphia, Clyde Simmons, DE, Western Carolina; 12/327—L.A. Rams, Marcus Dupree, RB, Oklahoma.

1987

FIRST ROUND—NFL

No.	Team	Player selected	Pos.	College
1.	Tampa Bay	*Vinny Testaverde*	QB	Miami, Fla.
2.	Indianapolis	Cornelius Bennett	LB	Alabama
3.	Houston	Alonzo Highsmith	RB	Miami, Fla.

No.	Team	Player selected	Pos.	College
4.	Green Bay	Brent Fullwood	RB	Auburn
5.	Cleveland	Mike Junkin	LB	Duke
6.	St. Louis	Kelly Stouffer	QB	Colorado State
7.	Detroit	Reggie Rogers	DE	Washington
8.	Buffalo	Shane Conlan	LB	Penn State
9.	Philadelphia	Jerome Brown	DT	Miami, Fla.
10.	Pittsburgh	Rod Woodson	DB	Purdue
11.	New Orleans	Shawn Knight	DT	Brigham Young
12.	Dallas	Danny Noonan	DT	Nebraska
13.	Atlanta	Chris Miller	QB	Oregon
14.	Minnesota	D.J. Dozier	RB	Penn State
15.	L.A. Raiders	John Clay	T	Missouri
16.	Miami	John Bosa	DE	Boston College
17.	Cincinnati	Jason Buck	DE	Brigham Young
18.	Seattle	Tony Woods	LB	Pittsburgh
19.	Kansas City	Paul Palmer	RB	Temple
20.	Houston	Haywood Jeffires	WR	N. Carolina State
21.	N.Y. Jets	Roger Vick	RB	Texas A&M
22.	San Francisco	Harris Barton	T	North Carolina
23.	New England	Bruce Armstrong	T	Louisville
24.	San Diego	Rod Bernstine	TE	Texas A&M
25.	San Francisco	Terrence Flagler	RB	Clemson
26.	Chicago	Jim Harbaugh	QB	Michigan
27.	Denver	Ricky Nattiel	WR	Florida
28.	N.Y. Giants	Mark Ingram	WR	Michigan State

Teams not selecting in first round: L.A. Rams, Washington.

Total number of picks in draft: 335.

OTHER NOTEWORTHY PICKS

Round/Overall—Team, Player selected, Pos., College
2/53—San Diego, Louis Brock, DB, USC; 5/117—Washington, Timmy Smith, RB, Texas Tech; 7/183—L.A. Raiders, *Bo Jackson*, RB, Auburn; 10/261—Pittsburgh, Merril Hoge, RB, Idaho State; 12/313—Tampa Bay, Mike Shula, QB, Alabama; Supplemental—Seattle, Brian Bosworth, LB, Oklahoma; Supplemental—Philadelphia, Cris Carter, WR, Ohio State.

1988

FIRST ROUND—NFL

No.	Team	Player selected	Pos.	College
1.	Atlanta	Aundray Bruce	LB	Auburn
2.	Kansas City	Neil Smith	DE	Nebraska
3.	Detroit	Bennie Blades	DB	Miami, Fla.
4.	Tampa Bay	Paul Gruber	T	Wisconsin
5.	Cincinnati	Rickey Dixon	DB	Oklahoma
6.	L.A. Raiders	*Tim Brown*	WR	Notre Dame
7.	Green Bay	Sterling Sharpe	WR	South Carolina
8.	N.Y. Jets	Dave Cadigan	T	USC
9.	L.A. Raiders	Terry McDaniel	DB	Tennessee
10.	N.Y. Giants	Eric Moore	T	Indiana
11.	Dallas	Michael Irvin	WR	Miami, Fla.
12.	Phoenix	Ken Harvey	LB	California
13.	Philadelphia	Keith Jackson	TE	Oklahoma
14.	L.A. Rams	Gaston Green	RB	UCLA
15.	San Diego	Anthony Miller	WR	Tennessee
16.	Miami	Eric Kumerow	DE	Ohio State
17.	New England	John Stephens	RB	NW (La.) State
18.	Pittsburgh	Aaron Jones	DE	Eastern Kentucky
19.	Minnesota	Randall McDaniel	G	Arizona State
20.	L.A. Rams	Aaron Cox	WR	Arizona State
21.	Cleveland	Clifford Charlton	LB	Florida
22.	Houston	Lorenzo White	RB	Michigan State
23.	Chicago	Brad Muster	RB	Stanford
24.	New Orleans	Craig Heyward	RB	Pittsburgh
25.	L.A. Raiders	Scott Davis	DE	Illinois
26.	Denver	Ted Gregory	NT	Syracuse
27.	Chicago	Wendell Davis	WR	Louisiana State

Teams not selecting in first round: Buffalo, Indianapolis, San Francisco, Seattle, Washington.

Total number of picks in draft: 333.

OTHER NOTEWORTHY PICKS

Round/Overall—Team, Player selected, Pos., College
2/40—Buffalo, Thurman Thomas, RB, Oklahoma State; 2/41—Dallas, Ken Norton Jr., LB, UCLA; 2/44—Pittsburgh, Dermontti Dawson, G, Kentucky; 2/46—Willie (Flipper) Anderson, WR, UCLA; 3/80—San Francisco, Bill Romanowski, LB, Boston College.

1989

FIRST ROUND—NFL

No. Team	Player selected	Pos.	College
1. Dallas	Troy Aikman	QB	UCLA
2. Green Bay	Tony Mandarich	T	Michigan State
3. Detroit	*Barry Sanders*	RB	Oklahoma State
4. Kansas City	Derrick Thomas	LB	Alabama
5. Atlanta	Deion Sanders	CB	Florida State
6. Tampa Bay	Broderick Thomas	LB	Nebraska
7. Pittsburgh	Tim Worley	RB	Georgia
8. San Diego	Burt Grossman	DE	Pittsburgh
9. Miami	Sammie Smith	RB	Florida State
10. Phoenix	Eric Hill	LB	Louisiana State
11. Chicago	Donnell Woolford	CB	Clemson
12. Chicago	Trace Armstrong	DE	Florida
13. Cleveland	Eric Metcalf	RB	Texas
14. N.Y. Jets	Jeff Lageman	LB	Virginia
15. Seattle	Andy Heck	T	Notre Dame
16. New England	Hart Lee Dykes	WR	Oklahoma State
17. Phoenix	Joe Wolf	G	Boston College
18. N.Y. Giants	Brian Williams	G	Minnesota
19. New Orleans	Wayne Martin	DE	Arkansas
20. Denver	Steve Atwater	S	Arkansas
21. L.A. Rams	Bill Hawkins	DE	Miami, Fla.
22. Indianapolis	Andre Rison	WR	Michigan State
23. Houston	David Williams	T	Florida
24. Pittsburgh	Tom Ricketts	T	Pittsburgh
25. Miami	Louis Oliver	S	Florida
26. L.A. Rams	Cleveland Gary	RB	Miami, Fla.
27. Atlanta	Shawn Collins	WR	Northern Arizona
28. San Francisco	Keith DeLong	LB	Tennessee

Teams not selecting in first round: Buffalo, Cincinnati, L.A. Raiders, Minnesota, Philadelphia, Washington.
Total number of picks in draft: 335.

OTHER NOTEWORTHY PICKS

Round/Overall—Team, Player selected, Pos., College
2/34—Pittsburgh, Carnell Lake, DB, UCLA; 7/173—Buffalo, Brian Jordan, DB, Richmond; Supplemental—Dallas, Steve Walsh, QB, Miami, Fla.; Supplemental—Denver, Bobby Humphrey, RB, Alabama; Supplemental—Phoenix, Timm Rosenbach, QB, Washington State.

1990

FIRST ROUND—NFL

No. Team	Player selected	Pos.	College
1. Indianapolis	Jeff George	QB	Illinois
2. N.Y. Jets	Blair Thomas	RB	Penn State
3. Seattle	Cortez Kennedy	DT	Miami, Fla.
4. Tampa Bay	Keith McCants	LB	Alabama
5. San Diego	Junior Seau	LB	USC
6. Chicago	Mark Carrier	DB	USC
7. Detroit	*Andre Ware*	QB	Houston
8. New England	Chris Singleton	LB	Arizona
9. Miami	Richmond Webb	T	Texas A&M
10. New England	Ray Agnew	DE	N. Carolina State
11. L.A. Raiders	Anthony Smith	DE	Arizona
12. Cincinnati	James Francis	LB	Baylor
13. Kansas City	Percy Snow	LB	Michigan State
14. New Orleans	Renaldo Turnbull	DE	West Virginia
15. Houston	Lamar Lathon	LB	Houston

No. Team	Player selected	Pos.	College
16. Buffalo	James Williams	DB	Fresno State
17. Dallas	Emmitt Smith	RB	Florida
18. Green Bay	Tony Bennett	LB	Mississippi
19. Green Bay	Darrell Thompson	RB	Minnesota
20. Atlanta	Steve Broussard	RB	Washington State
21. Pittsburgh	Eric Green	TE	Liberty, Va.
22. Philadelphia	Ben Smith	DB	Georgia
23. L.A. Rams	Bern Brostek	C	Washington
24. N.Y. Giants	Rodney Hampton	RB	Georgia
25. San Francisco	Dexter Carter	RB	Florida State

Teams not selecting in first round: Cleveland, Denver, Minnesota, Phoenix, Washington.
Total number of picks in draft: 331.

OTHER NOTEWORTHY PICKS

Round/Overall—Team, Player selected, Pos., College
3/70—Pittsburgh, Neil O'Donnell, QB, Maryland; 5/130—Washington, Brian Mitchell, RB, Southwestern Louisiana; 7/192—Denver, Shannon Sharpe, WR, Savannah State; 9/241—Minnesota, Terry Allen, RB, Clemson; 10/265—Buffalo, Mike Lodish, DT, UCLA.

1991

FIRST ROUND—NFL

No. Team	Player selected	Pos.	College
1. Dallas	Russell Maryland	DL	Miami, Fla.
2. Cleveland	Eric Turner	S	UCLA
3. Atlanta	Bruce Pickens	CB	Nebraska
4. Denver	Mike Croel	LB	Nebraska
5. L.A. Rams	Todd Lyght	CB	Notre Dame
6. Phoenix	Eric Swann	DL	No college
7. Tampa Bay	Charles McRae	T	Tennessee
8. Philadelphia	Antone Davis	T	Tennessee
9. San Diego	Stanley Richard	CB	Texas
10. Detroit	Herman Moore	WR	Virginia
11. New England	Pat Harlow	T	USC
12. Dallas	Alvin Harper	WR	Tennessee
13. Atlanta	Mike Pritchard	WR	Colorado
14. New England	Leonard Russell	RB	Arizona State
15. Pittsburgh	Huey Richardson	LB	Florida
16. Seattle	Dan McGwire	QB	San Diego State
17. Washington	Bobby Wilson	DT	Michigan State
18. Cincinnati	Alfred Williams	LB	Colorado
19. Green Bay	Vincent Clark	DB	Ohio State
20. Dallas	Kelvin Pritchett	DT	Mississippi
21. Kansas City	Harvey Williams	RB	Louisiana State
22. Chicago	Stan Thomas	T	Texas
23. Miami	Randal Hill	WR	Miami, Fla.
24. L.A. Raiders	Todd Marinovich	QB	USC
25. San Francisco	Ted Washington	DL	Louisville
26. Buffalo	Henry Jones	S	Illinois
27. N.Y. Giants	Jarrod Bunch	FB	Michigan

Teams not selecting in first round: Houston, Indianapolis, Minnesota, New Orleans, N.Y. Jets.
Total number of picks in draft: 334.

OTHER NOTEWORTHY PICKS

Round/Overall—Team, Player selected, Pos., College
2/33—Atlanta, Brett Favre, QB, Southern Mississippi; 2/45—San Francisco, Ricky Watters, RB, Notre Dame; 4/100—L.A. Raiders, Rocket Ismail, WR, Notre Dame; 5/113—Miami, Bryan Cox, LB, Western Illinois; 7/173—Dallas, Leon Lett, DT, Emporia State; 12/326—Washington, Keenan McCardell, WR, UNLV.

1992

FIRST ROUND—NFL

No. Team	Player selected	Pos.	College
1. Indianapolis	Steve Emtman	DL	Washington
2. Indianapolis	Quentin Coryatt	LB	Texas A&M

No.	Team	Player selected	Pos.	College
3.	L.A. Rams	Sean Gilbert	DL	Pittsburgh
4.	Washington	*Desmond Howard*	WR	Michigan
5.	Green Bay	Terrell Buckley	DB	Florida State
6.	Cincinnati	David Klingler	QB	Houston
7.	Miami	Troy Vincent	DB	Wisconsin
8.	Atlanta	Bob Whitfield	OL	Stanford
9.	Cleveland	Tommy Vardell	FB	Stanford
10.	Seattle	Ray Roberts	OL	Virginia
11.	Pittsburgh	Leon Searcy	T	Miami, Fla.
12.	Miami	Marco Coleman	LB	Georgia Tech
13.	New England	Eugene Chung	OL	Virginia Tech
14.	N.Y. Giants	Derek Brown	TE	Notre Dame
15.	N.Y. Jets	Johnny Mitchell	TE	Nebraska
16.	L.A. Raiders	Chester McGlockton	DT	Clemson
17.	Dallas	Kevin Smith	DB	Texas A&M
18.	San Francisco	Dana Hall	DB	Washington
19.	Atlanta	Tony Smith	RB	Southern Miss
20.	Kansas City	Dale Carter	DB	Tennessee
21.	New Orleans	Vaughn Dunbar	RB	Indiana
22.	Chicago	Alonzo Spellman	DL	Ohio State
23.	San Diego	Chris Mims	DL	Tennessee
24.	Dallas	Robert Jones	LB	East Carolina
25.	Denver	Tommy Maddox	QB	UCLA
26.	Detroit	Robert Porcher	DL	S. Carolina State
27.	Buffalo	John Fina	OL	Arizona
28.	Cincinnati	Darryl Williams	DB	Miami, Fla.

Teams not selecting in first round: Houston, Minnesota, Philadelphia, Phoenix, Tampa Bay.
Total number of picks in draft: 336.

OTHER NOTEWORTHY PICKS

Round/Overall—Team, Player selected, Pos., College
2/36—Dallas, Jimmy Smith, WR, Jackson State; 2/56—Detroit, Jason Hanson, K, Washington; 9/227—Minnesota, Brad Johnson, QB, Florida State; 9/230—Green Bay, *Ty Detmer*, QB, Brigham Young; Supplemental—N.Y. Giants, Dave Brown, QB, Duke.

1993
FIRST ROUND—NFL

No.	Team	Player selected	Pos.	College
1.	New England	Drew Bledsoe	QB	Washington State
2.	Seattle	Rick Mirer	QB	Notre Dame
3.	Phoenix	Garrison Hearst	RB	Georgia
4.	N.Y. Jets	Marvin Jones	LB	Florida State
5.	Cincinnati	John Copeland	DT	Alabama
6.	Tampa Bay	Eric Curry	DE	Alabama
7.	Chicago	Curtis Conway	WR	USC
8.	New Orleans	Willie Roaf	T	Louisiana Tech
9.	Atlanta	Lincoln Kennedy	T	Washington
10.	L.A. Rams	Jerome Bettis	RB	Notre Dame
11.	Denver	Dan Williams	DE	Toledo
12.	L.A. Raiders	Patrick Bates	DB	Texas A&M
13.	Houston	Brad Hopkins	G	Illinois
14.	Cleveland	Steve Everitt	C	Michigan
15.	Green Bay	Wayne Simmons	LB	Clemson
16.	Indianapolis	Sean Dawkins	WR	California
17.	Washington	Tom Carter	DB	Notre Dame
18.	Phoenix	Ernest Dye	T	South Carolina
19.	Philadelphia	Lester Holmes	T	Jackson State
20.	New Orleans	Irv Smith	TE	Notre Dame
21.	Minnesota	Robert Smith	RB	Ohio State
22.	San Diego	Darrien Gordon	DB	Stanford
23.	Pittsburgh	Deon Figures	DB	Colorado
24.	Philadelphia	Leonard Renfro	DE	Colorado
25.	Miami	O.J. McDuffie	WR	Penn State
26.	San Francisco	Dana Stubblefield	DT	Kansas
27.	San Francisco	Todd Kelly	DE	Tennessee

No.	Team	Player selected	Pos.	College
28.	Buffalo	Thomas Smith	DB	North Carolina
29.	Green Bay	George Teague	DB	Alabama

Teams not selecting in first round: Dallas, Detroit, Kansas City, N.Y. Giants.
Total number of picks in draft: 224.

OTHER NOTEWORTHY PICKS

Round/Overall—Team, Player selected, Pos., College
3/82—Tampa Bay, John Lynch, DB, Stanford; 5/118—Green Bay, Mark Brunell, QB, Washington; 6/160—Washington, Frank Wycheck, TE, Maryland; 7/192—Minnesota, *Gino Torretta*, QB, Miami, Fla.; 8/219—San Francisco, Elvis Grbac, QB, Michigan; 8/222—San Diego, Trent Green, QB, Indiana.

1994
FIRST ROUND—NFL

No.	Team	Player selected	Pos.	College
1.	Cincinnati	Dan Wilkinson	DT	Ohio State
2.	Indianapolis	Marshall Faulk	RB	San Diego State
3.	Washington	Heath Shuler	QB	Tennessee
4.	New England	Willie McGinest	DE	USC
5.	Indianapolis	Trev Alberts	LB	Nebraska
6.	Tampa Bay	Trent Dilfer	QB	Fresno State
7.	San Francisco	Bryant Young	DT	Notre Dame
8.	Seattle	Sam Adams	DE	Texas A&M
9.	Cleveland	Antonio Langham	DB	Alabama
10.	Arizona	Jamir Miller	LB	UCLA
11.	Chicago	John Thierry	LB	Alcorn State
12.	N.Y. Jets	Aaron Glenn	DB	Texas A&M
13.	New Orleans	Joe Johnson	DE	Louisville
14.	Philadelphia	Bernard Williams	T	Georgia
15.	L.A. Rams	Wayne Gandy	T	Auburn
16.	Green Bay	Aaron Taylor	T	Notre Dame
17.	Pittsburgh	Charles Johnson	WR	Colorado
18.	Minnesota	Dewayne Washington	CB	N. Carolina State
19.	Minnesota	Todd Steussie	T	California
20.	Miami	Tim Bowens	DT	Mississippi
21.	Detroit	Johnnie Morton	WR	USC
22.	L.A. Raiders	Rob Fredrickson	LB	Michigan State
23.	Dallas	Shante Carver	DE	Arizona State
24.	N.Y. Giants	Thomas Lewis	WR	Indiana
25.	Kansas City	Greg Hill	RB	Texas A&M
26.	Houston	Henry Ford	DE	Arkansas
27.	Buffalo	Jeff Burris	DB	Notre Dame
28.	San Francisco	William Floyd	RB	Florida State
29.	Cleveland	Derrick Alexander	WR	Michigan

Teams not selecting in first round: Atlanta, Denver, San Diego.
Total number of picks in draft: 222.

OTHER NOTEWORTHY PICKS

Round/Overall—Team, Player selected, Pos., College
2/33—L.A. Rams, Isaac Bruce, WR, Memphis State; 2/46—Dallas, Larry Allen, G, Sonoma State; 2/59—N.Y. Giants, Jason Sehorn, DB, USC; 7/201—Atlanta, Jamal Anderson, RB, Utah; 7/218—Denver, Tom Nalen, C, Boston College.

1995
FIRST ROUND—NFL

No.	Team	Player selected	Pos.	College
1.	Cincinnati	Ki-Jana Carter	RB	Penn State
2.	Jacksonville	Tony Boselli	T	USC
3.	Houston	Steve McNair	QB	Alcorn State
4.	Washington	Michael Westbrook	WR	Colorado
5.	Carolina	Kerry Collins	QB	Penn State
6.	St. Louis	Kevin Carter	DE	Florida
7.	Philadelphia	Mike Mamula	DE	Boston College
8.	Seattle	Joey Galloway	WR	Ohio State

No.	Team	Player selected	Pos.	College
9.	N.Y. Jets	Kyle Brady	TE	Penn State
10.	San Francisco	J.J. Stokes	WR	UCLA
11.	Minnesota	Derrick Alexander	DE	Florida State
12.	Tampa Bay	Warren Sapp	DT	Miami, Fla.
13.	New Orleans	Mark Fields	LB	Washington State
14.	Buffalo	Ruben Brown	G	Pittsburgh
15.	Indianapolis	Ellis Johnson	DT	Florida
16.	N.Y. Jets	Hugh Douglas	DE	Central State, O.
17.	N.Y. Giants	Tyrone Wheatley	RB	Michigan
18.	Los Angeles	Napoleon Kaufman	RB	Washington
19.	Jacksonville	James Stewart	RB	Tennessee
20.	Detroit	Luther Elliss	DT	Utah
21.	Chicago	*Rashaan Salaam*	RB	Colorado
22.	Carolina	Tyrone Poole	DB	Ft. Valley (Ga.) St.
23.	New England	Ty Law	DB	Michigan
24.	Minnesota	Korey Stringer	T	Ohio State
25.	Miami	Billy Milner	T	Houston
26.	Atlanta	Devin Bush	DB	Florida State
27.	Pittsburgh	Mark Bruener	TE	Washington
28.	Tampa Bay	Derrick Brooks	LB	Florida State
29.	Carolina	Blake Brockermeyer	T	Texas
30.	Cleveland	Craig Powell	LB	Ohio State
31.	Kansas City	Trezelle Jenkins	T	Michigan
32.	Green Bay	Craig Newsome	DB	Arizona State

Note: Los Angeles franchise moved to Oakland (but after draft); teams not selecting in first round: Arizona, Dallas, Denver, San Diego.
Total number of picks in draft: 249.

OTHER NOTEWORTHY PICKS

Round/Overall—Team, Player selected, Pos., College
3/90—Green Bay, Antonio Freeman, WR, Virginia Tech; 4/99—Jacksonville, Rob Johnson, QB, USC; 6/196—Denver, Terrell Davis, RB, Georgia.

1996
FIRST ROUND—NFL

No.	Team	Player selected	Pos.	College
1.	N.Y. Jets	Keyshawn Johnson	WR	USC
2.	Jacksonville	Kevin Hardy	LB	Illinois
3.	Arizona	Simeon Rice	DE	Illinois
4.	Baltimore	Jonathan Ogden	T	UCLA
5.	N.Y. Giants	Cedric Jones	DE	Oklahoma
6.	St. Louis	Lawrence Phillips	RB	Nebraska
7.	New England	Terry Glenn	WR	Ohio State
8.	Carolina	Tim Biakabutuka	RB	Michigan
9.	Oakland	Rickey Dudley	TE	Ohio State
10.	Cincinnati	Willie Anderson	T	Auburn
11.	New Orleans	Alex Molden	DB	Oregon
12.	Tampa Bay	Regan Upshaw	DE	California
13.	Chicago	Walt Harris	DB	Miss. State
14.	Houston	*Eddie George*	RB	Ohio State
15.	Denver	John Mobley	LB	Kutztown, Pa.
16.	Minnesota	Duane Clemons	DE	California
17.	Detroit	Reggie Brown	LB	Texas A&M
18.	St. Louis	Eddie Kennison	WR	Louisiana State
19.	Indianapolis	Marvin Harrison	WR	Syracuse
20.	Miami	Daryl Gardener	DT	Baylor
21.	Seattle	Pete Kendall	T	Boston College
22.	Tampa Bay	Marcus Jones	DT	North Carolina
23.	Detroit	Jeff Hartings	G	Penn State
24.	Buffalo	Eric Moulds	WR	Miss. State
25.	Philadelphia	Jermane Mayberry	T	Tex. A&M-K'ville
26.	Baltimore	Ray Lewis	LB	Miami, Fla.
27.	Green Bay	John Michels	T	USC
28.	Kansas City	Jerome Woods	DB	Memphis
29.	Pittsburgh	Jamain Stephens	T	N. Carolina A&T
30.	Washington	Andre Johnson	T	Penn State

Teams not selecting in first round: Atlanta, Dallas, San Diego, San Francisco.
Total number of picks in draft: 254.

OTHER NOTEWORTHY PICKS

Round/Overall—Team, Player selected, Pos., College
2/33—Jacksonville, Tony Brackens, DE, Texas; 3/89—San Francisco, Terrell Owens, WR, UT-Chattanooga; 4/102—Washington, Stephen Davis, RB, Auburn.

1997
FIRST ROUND—NFL

No.	Team	Player selected	Pos.	College
1.	St. Louis	Orlando Pace	T	Ohio State
2.	Oakland	Darrell Russell	DT	USC
3.	Seattle	Shawn Springs	CB	Ohio State
4.	Baltimore	Peter Boulware	DE	Florida State
5.	Detroit	Bryant Westbrook	DB	Texas
6.	Seattle	Walter Jones	T	Florida State
7.	N.Y. Giants	Ike Hilliard	WR	Florida
8.	N.Y. Jets	James Farrior	LB	Virginia
9.	Arizona	Tom Knight	DB	Iowa
10.	New Orleans	Chris Naeole	G	Colorado
11.	Atlanta	Michael Booker	DB	Nebraska
12.	Tampa Bay	Warrick Dunn	RB	Florida State
13.	Kansas City	Tony Gonzalez	TE	California
14.	Cincinnati	Reinard Wilson	LB	Florida State
15.	Miami	Yatil Green	WR	Miami, Fla.
16.	Tampa Bay	Reidel Anthony	WR	Florida
17.	Washington	Kenard Lang	DE	Miami, Fla.
18.	Houston	Kenny Holmes	DE	Miami, Fla.
19.	Indianapolis	Tarik Glenn	T	California
20.	Minnesota	Dwayne Rudd	LB	Alabama
21.	Jacksonville	Renaldo Wynn	DT	Notre Dame
22.	Dallas	David LaFleur	TE	Louisiana State
23.	Buffalo	Antowain Smith	RB	Houston
24.	Pittsburgh	Chad Scott	DB	Maryland
25.	Philadelphia	Jon Harris	DE	Virginia
26.	San Francisco	Jim Druckenmiller	QB	Virginia Tech
27.	Carolina	Rae Carruth	WR	Colorado
28.	Denver	Trevor Pryce	DT	Clemson
29.	New England	Chris Canty	DB	Kansas State
30.	Green Bay	Ross Verba	T	Iowa

Teams not selecting in first round: Chicago, San Diego.
Total number of picks in draft: 240.

OTHER NOTEWORTHY PICKS

Round/Overall—Team, Player selected, Pos., College
2/43—Cincinnati, Corey Dillon, RB, Washington; 2/60—Green Bay, Darren Sharper, DB, William & Mary; 3/73—Miami, Jason Taylor, DE, Akron; 4/99—New Orleans, *Danny Wuerffel*, QB, Florida.

1998
FIRST ROUND—NFL

No.	Team	Player selected	Pos.	College
1.	Indianapolis	Peyton Manning	QB	Tennessee
2.	San Diego	Ryan Leaf	QB	Washington State
3.	Arizona	Andre Wadsworth	DE	Florida State
4.	Oakland	*Charles Woodson*	DB	Michigan
5.	Chicago	Curtis Enis	RB	Penn State
6.	St. Louis	Grant Wistrom	DE	Nebraska
7.	New Orleans	Kyle Turley	T	San Diego State
8.	Dallas	Greg Ellis	DE	North Carolina
9.	Jacksonville	Fred Taylor	RB	Florida
10.	Baltimore	Duane Starks	DB	Miami, Fla.
11.	Philadelphia	Tra Thomas	T	Florida State
12.	Atlanta	Keith Brooking	LB	Georgia Tech
13.	Cincinnati	Takeo Spikes	LB	Auburn
14.	Carolina	Jason Peter	DT	Nebraska
15.	Seattle	Anthony Simmons	LB	Clemson

No. Team	Player selected	Pos.	College
16. Tennessee	Kevin Dyson	WR	Utah
17. Cincinnati	Brian Simmons	LB	North Carolina
18. New England	Robert Edwards	RB	Georgia
19. Green Bay	Vonnie Holliday	DT	North Carolina
20. Detroit	Terry Fair	DB	Tennessee
21. Minnesota	Randy Moss	WR	Marshall
22. New England	Tebucky Jones	DB	Syracuse
23. Oakland	Mo Collins	T	Florida
24. N.Y. Giants	Shaun Williams	DB	UCLA
25. Jacksonville	Donovin Darius	DB	Syracuse
26. Pittsburgh	Alan Faneca	G	Louisiana State
27. Kansas City	Victor Riley	T	Auburn
28. San Francisco	R.W. McQuarters	DB	Oklahoma State
29. Miami	John Avery	RB	Mississippi
30. Denver	Marcus Nash	WR	Tennessee

Teams not selecting in first round: Buffalo, N.Y. Jets, Tampa Bay, Washington.

Total number of picks in draft: 241.

OTHER NOTEWORTHY PICKS

Round/Overall—Team, Player selected, Pos., College
2/60—Detroit, Charlie Batch, QB, Eastern Michigan; 3/76—Seattle, Ahman Green, RB, Nebraska; 3/91—Denver, Brian Griese, QB, Michigan; 6/187—Green Bay, Matt Hasselbeck, QB, Boston College.

1999

FIRST ROUND—NFL

No. Team	Player selected	Pos.	College
1. Cleveland	Tim Couch	QB	Kentucky
2. Philadelphia	Donovan McNabb	QB	Syracuse
3. Cincinnati	Akili Smith	QB	Oregon
4. Indianapolis	Edgerrin James	RB	Miami, Fla.
5. New Orleans	*Ricky Williams*	RB	Texas
6. St. Louis	Torry Holt	WR	N. Carolina State
7. Washington	Champ Bailey	DB	Georgia
8. Arizona	David Boston	WR	Ohio State
9. Detroit	Chris Claiborne	LB	USC
10. Baltimore	Chris McAlister	DB	Arizona
11. Minnesota	Daunte Culpepper	QB	Central Florida
12. Chicago	Cade McNown	QB	UCLA
13. Pittsburgh	Troy Edwards	WR	Louisiana Tech
14. Kansas City	John Tait	T	Brigham Young
15. Tampa Bay	Anthony McFarland	DT	Louisiana State
16. Tennessee	Jevon Kearse	DE	Florida
17. New England	Damien Woody	C	Boston College
18. Oakland	Matt Stinchcomb	T	Georgia
19. N.Y. Giants	Luke Petitgout	T	Notre Dame
20. Dallas	Ebenezer Ekuban	DE	North Carolina
21. Arizona	L.J. Shelton	T	Eastern Michigan
22. Seattle	Lamar King	DE	Saginaw Valley St.
23. Buffalo	Antoine Winfield	DB	Ohio State
24. San Francisco	Reggie McGrew	DT	Florida
25. Green Bay	Antuan Edwards	DB	Clemson
26. Jacksonville	Fernando Bryant	DB	Alabama
27. Detroit	Aaron Gibson	T	Wisconsin
28. New England	Andy Katzenmoyer	LB	Ohio State
29. Minnesota	Dimitrius Underwood	DE	Michigan State
30. Atlanta	Patrick Kerney	DE	Virginia
31. Denver	Al Wilson	LB	Tennessee

Teams not selecting in first round: Carolina, Miami, N.Y. Jets, San Diego.

Total number of picks in draft: 253.

OTHER NOTEWORTHY PICKS

Round/Overall—Team, Player selected, Pos., College
3/80—Tampa Bay, Martin Gramatica, K, Kansas State; 4/127—Denver, Olandis Gary, RB, Georgia; 4/131—Green Bay, Aaron Brooks, QB, Virginia.

2000

FIRST ROUND—NFL

No. Team	Player selected	Pos.	College
1. Cleveland	Courtney Brown	DE	Penn State
2. Washington	LaVar Arrington	LB	Penn State
3. Washington	Chris Samuels	T	Alabama
4. Cincinnati	Peter Warrick	WR	Florida State
5. Baltimore	Jamal Lewis	RB	Tennessee
6. Philadelphia	Corey Simon	DT	Florida State
7. Arizona	Thomas Jones	RB	Virginia
8. Pittsburgh	Plaxico Burress	WR	Michigan State
9. Chicago	Brian Urlacher	LB	New Mexico
10. Baltimore	Travis Taylor	WR	Florida
11. N.Y. Giants	*Ron Dayne*	RB	Wisconsin
12. N.Y. Jets	Shaun Ellis	DE	Tennessee
13. N.Y. Jets	John Abraham	LB	South Carolina
14. Green Bay	Bubba Franks	TE	Miami, Fla.
15. Denver	Deltha O'Neal	DB	California
16. San Francisco	Julian Peterson	LB	Michigan State
17. Oakland	Sebastian Janikowski	K	Florida State
18. N.Y. Jets	Chad Pennington	QB	Marshall
19. Seattle	Shaun Alexander	RB	Alabama
20. Detroit	Stockar McDougle	T	Oklahoma
21. Kansas City	Sylvester Morris	WR	Jackson State
22. Seattle	Chris McIntosh	T	Wisconsin
23. Carolina	Rashard Anderson	DB	Jackson State
24. San Francisco	Ahmed Plummer	DB	Ohio State
25. Minnesota	Chris Hovan	DT	Boston College
26. Buffalo	Erik Flowers	DE	Arizona State
27. N.Y. Jets	Anthony Becht	TE	West Virginia
28. Indianapolis	Rob Morris	LB	Brigham Young
29. Jacksonville	R. Jay Soward	WR	USC
30. Tennessee	Keith Bulluck	LB	Syracuse
31. St. Louis	Trung Canidate	RB	Arizona

Teams not selecting in first round: Atlanta, Dallas, Miami, New England, New Orleans, San Diego, Tampa Bay.

Total number of picks in draft: 254.

OTHER NOTEWORTHY PICKS

Round/Overall—Team, Player selected, Pos., College
2/33—New Orleans, Darren Howard, DE, Kansas State; 3/80—Seattle, Darrell Jackson, WR, Florida; 5/142—Oakland, Shane Lechler, P, Texas A&M.

TEAM BY TEAM

ARIZONA CARDINALS

YEAR-BY-YEAR RECORDS

			REGULAR SEASON					PLAYOFFS		
Year	W	L	T	Pct.	PF	PA	Finish	W	L	Highest round	Coach
1920*	6	2	2	.750	...	...	T4th				Paddy Driscoll
1921*	3	3	2	.500	...	...	T8th				Paddy Driscoll
1922*	8	3	0	.727	...	...	3rd				Paddy Driscoll
1923*	8	4	0	.667	...	...	6th				Arnold Horween
1924*	5	4	1	.556	...	...	8th				Arnold Horween
1925*	11	2	1	.846	...	...	1st				Norman Barry
1926*	5	6	1	.455	...	...	10th				Norman Barry
1927*	3	7	1	.300	...	...	9th				Guy Chamberlin
1928*	1	5	0	.167	...	...	9th				Fred Gillies
1929*	6	6	1	.500	...	...	T4th				Dewey Scanlon
1930*	5	6	2	.455	...	...	T7th				Ernie Nevers
1931*	5	4	0	.556	...	...	4th				LeRoy Andrews, E. Nevers
1932*	2	6	2	.250	...	...	7th				Jack Chevigny
1933*	1	9	1	.100	52	101	5th/Western Div.	—	—		Paul Schissler
1934*	5	6	0	.455	80	84	4th/Western Div.	—	—		Paul Schissler
1935*	6	4	2	.600	99	97	T3rd/Western Div.	—	—		Milan Creighton
1936*	3	8	1	.273	74	143	4th/Western Div.	—	—		Milan Creighton
1937*	5	5	1	.500	135	165	4th/Western Div.	—	—		Milan Creighton
1938*	2	9	0	.182	111	168	5th/Western Div.	—	—		Milan Creighton
1939*	1	10	0	.091	84	254	5th/Western Div.	—	—		Ernie Nevers
1940*	2	7	2	.222	139	222	5th/Western Div.	—	—		Jimmy Conzelman
1941*	3	7	1	.300	127	197	4th/Western Div.	—	—		Jimmy Conzelman
1942*	3	8	0	.273	98	209	4th/Western Div.	—	—		Jimmy Conzelman
1943*	0	10	0	.000	95	238	4th/Western Div.	—	—		Phil Handler
1944†	0	10	0	.000	108	328	5th/Western Div.	—	—		P. Handler-Walt Kiesling
1945*	1	9	0	.100	98	228	5th/Western Div.	—	—		Phil Handler
1946*	6	5	0	.545	260	198	T3rd/Western Div.	—	—		Jimmy Conzelman
1947*	9	3	0	.750	306	231	1st/Western Div.	1	0	NFL champ	Jimmy Conzelman
1948*	11	1	0	.917	395	226	1st/Western Div.	0	1	NFL championship game	Jimmy Conzelman
1949*	6	5	1	.545	360	301	3rd/Western Div.	—	—		P. Handler-Buddy Parker
1950*	5	7	0	.417	233	287	5th/American Conf.	—	—		Curly Lambeau
1951*	3	9	0	.250	210	287	6th/American Conf.	—	—		Curly Lambeau, P. Handler-Cecil Isbell
1952*	4	8	0	.333	172	221	T5th/American Conf.	—	—		Joe Kuharich
1953*	1	10	1	.091	190	337	6th/Eastern Conf.	—	—		Joe Stydahar
1954*	2	10	0	.167	183	347	6th/Eastern Conf.	—	—		Joe Stydahar
1955*	4	7	1	.364	224	252	T4th/Eastern Conf.	—	—		Ray Richards
1956*	7	5	0	.583	240	182	2nd/Eastern Conf.	—	—		Ray Richards
1957*	3	9	0	.250	200	299	6th/Eastern Conf.	—	—		Ray Richards
1958*	2	9	1	.182	261	356	T5th/Eastern Conf.	—	—		Pop Ivy
1959*	2	10	0	.167	234	324	6th/Eastern Conf.	—	—		Pop Ivy
1960‡	6	5	1	.545	288	230	4th/Eastern Conf.	—	—		Pop Ivy
1961‡	7	7	0	.500	279	267	4th/Eastern Conf.	—	—		Pop Ivy
1962‡	4	9	1	.308	287	361	6th/Eastern Conf.	—	—		Wally Lemm
1963‡	9	5	0	.643	341	283	3rd/Eastern Conf.	—	—		Wally Lemm
1964‡	9	3	2	.750	357	331	4th/Eastern Conf.	—	—		Wally Lemm
1965‡	5	9	0	.357	296	309	T5th/Eastern Conf.	—	—		Wally Lemm
1966‡	8	5	1	.615	264	265	4th/Eastern Conf.	—	—		Charley Winner
1967‡	6	7	1	.462	333	356	3rd/Century Div.	—	—		Charley Winner
1968‡	9	4	1	.692	325	289	2nd/Century Div.	—	—		Charley Winner
1969‡	4	9	1	.308	314	389	3rd/Century Div.	—	—		Charley Winner
1970‡	8	5	1	.615	325	228	3rd/NFC Eastern Div.	—	—		Charley Winner
1971‡	4	9	1	.308	231	279	4th/NFC Eastern Div.	—	—		Bob Hollway
1972‡	4	9	1	.308	193	303	4th/NFC Eastern Div.	—	—		Bob Hollway
1973‡	4	9	1	.308	286	365	4th/NFC Eastern Div.	—	—		Don Coryell
1974‡	10	4	0	.714	285	218	1st/NFC Eastern Div.	0	1	NFC div. playoff game	Don Coryell
1975‡	11	3	0	.786	356	276	1st/NFC Eastern Div.	0	1	NFC div. playoff game	Don Coryell
1976‡	10	4	0	.714	309	267	3rd/NFC Eastern Div.	—	—		Don Coryell
1977‡	7	7	0	.500	272	287	3rd/NFC Eastern Div.	—	—		Don Coryell
1978‡	6	10	0	.375	248	296	T4th/NFC Eastern Div.	—	—		Bud Wilkinson
1979‡	5	11	0	.313	307	358	5th/NFC Eastern Div.	—	—		B. Wilkinson, Larry Wilson
1980‡	5	11	0	.313	299	350	4th/NFC Eastern Div.	—	—		Jim Hanifan
1981‡	7	9	0	.438	315	408	5th/NFC Eastern Div.	—	—		Jim Hanifan
1982‡	5	4	0	.556	135	170	T4th/NFC	0	1	NFC first-round pl. game	Jim Hanifan

				REGULAR SEASON					PLAYOFFS		
Year	W	L	T	Pct.	PF	PA	Finish	W	L	Highest round	Coach
1983‡	8	7	1	.531	374	428	3rd/NFC Eastern Div.	—	—		Jim Hanifan
1984‡	9	7	0	.563	423	345	T3rd/NFC Eastern Div.	—	—		Jim Hanifan
1985‡	5	11	0	.313	278	414	5th/NFC Eastern Div.	—	—		Jim Hanifan
1986‡	4	11	1	.281	218	351	5th/NFC Eastern Div.	—	—		Gene Stallings
1987‡	7	8	0	.467	362	368	T2nd/NFC Eastern Div.	—	—		Gene Stallings
1988§	7	9	0	.438	344	398	T3rd/NFC Eastern Div.	—	—		Gene Stallings
1989§	5	11	0	.313	258	377	4th/NFC Eastern Div.	—	—		G. Stallings, Hank Kuhlmann
1990§	5	11	0	.313	268	396	5th/NFC Eastern Div.	—	—		Joe Bugel
1991§	4	12	0	.250	196	344	5th/NFC Eastern Div.	—	—		Joe Bugel
1992§	4	12	0	.250	243	332	5th/NFC Eastern Div.	—	—		Joe Bugel
1993§	7	9	0	.438	326	269	4th/NFC Eastern Div.	—	—		Joe Bugel
1994	8	8	0	.500	235	267	3rd/NFC Eastern Div.	—	—		Buddy Ryan
1995	4	12	0	.250	275	422	5th/NFC Eastern Div.	—	—		Buddy Ryan
1996	7	9	0	.438	300	397	4th/NFC Eastern Div.	—	—		Vince Tobin
1997	4	12	0	.250	283	379	5th/NFC Eastern Div.	—	—		Vince Tobin
1998	9	7	0	.563	325	378	2nd/NFC Eastern Div.	1	1	NFC div. playoff game	Vince Tobin
1999	6	10	0	.375	245	382	4th/NFC Eastern Div.	—	—		Vince Tobin
2000	3	13	0	.188	210	443	5th/NFC Eastern Div.	—	—		V. Tobin, Dave McGinnis

*Chicago Cardinals.
†Card-Pitt, a combined squad of Chicago Cardinals and Pittsburgh Steelers.
‡St. Louis Cardinals.
§Phoenix Cardinals.

FIRST-ROUND DRAFT PICKS

1936—Jim Lawrence, B, Texas Christian
1937—Ray Buivid, B, Marquette
1938—Jack Robbins, B, Arkansas
1939—Charles Aldrich, C, Texas Christian*
1940—George Cafego, B, Tennessee*
1941—John Kimbrough, B, Texas A&M
1942—Steve Lach, B, Duke
1943—Glenn Dobbs, B, Tulsa
1944—Pat Harder, B, Wisconsin*
1945—Charley Trippi, B, Georgia*
1946—Dub Jones, B, Louisiana State
1947—DeWitt (Tex) Coulter, T, Army
1948—Jim Spavital, B, Oklahoma A&M
1949—Bill Fischer, G, Notre Dame
1950—None
1951—Jerry Groom, C, Notre Dame
1952—Ollie Matson, B, San Francisco
1953—Johnny Olszewski, QB, California
1954—Lamar McHan, B, Arkansas
1955—Max Boydston, E, Oklahoma
1956—Joe Childress, B, Auburn
1957—Jerry Tubbs, C, Oklahoma
1958—King Hill, B, Rice*
1959—Billy Stacy, B, Mississippi State
1960—George Izo, QB, Notre Dame
1961—Ken Rice, T, Auburn
1962—Fate Echols, DT, Northwestern
        Irv Goode, C, Kentucky
1963—Jerry Stovall, DB, Louisiana State
        Don Brumm, E, Purdue
1964—Ken Kortas, DT, Louisville
1965—Joe Namath, QB, Alabama
1966—Carl McAdams, LB, Oklahoma
1967—Dave Williams, WR, Washington
1968—MacArthur Lane, RB, Utah State
1969—Roger Wehrli, DB, Missouri
1970—Larry Stegent, RB, Texas A&M

1971—Norm Thompson, DB, Utah
1972—Bobby Moore, RB, Oregon
1973—Dave Butz, DT, Purdue
1974—J.V. Cain, TE, Colorado
1975—Tim Gray, DB, Texas A&M
1976—Mike Dawson, DT, Arizona
1977—Steve Pisarkiewicz, QB, Missouri
1978—Steve Little, K, Arkansas
        Ken Greene, DB, Washington St.
1979—Ottis Anderson, RB, Miami, Fla.
1980—Curtis Greer, DE, Michigan
1981—E.J. Junior, LB, Alabama
1982—Luis Sharpe, T, UCLA
1983—Leonard Smith, DB, McNeese State
1984—Clyde Duncan, WR, Tennessee
1985—Freddie Joe Nunn, LB, Mississippi
1986—Anthony Bell, LB, Michigan St.
1987—Kelly Stouffer, QB, Colorado St.
1988—Ken Harvey, LB, California
1989—Eric Hill, LB, Louisiana State
        Joe Wolf, G, Boston College
1990—None
1991—Eric Swann, DL, None
1992—None
1993—Garrison Hearst, RB, Georgia
        Ernest Dye, T, South Carolina
1994—Jamir Miller, LB, UCLA
1995—None
1996—Simeon Rice, DE, Illinois
1997—Tom Knight, DB, Iowa
1998—Andre Wadsworth, DE, Florida State
1999—David Boston, WR, Ohio State
        L.J. Shelton, T, Eastern Michigan
2000—Thomas Jones, RB, Virginia
2001—Leonard Davis, T, Texas
        *First player chosen in draft.

FRANCHISE RECORDS

Most rushing yards, career
7,999—Ottis Anderson
Most rushing yards, season
1,605—Ottis Anderson, 1979

Most rushing yards, game
214—LeShon Johnson at N.O., Sept. 22,
        1996

Most rushing touchdowns, season
14—John David Crow, 1962
Most passing attempts, season
560—Neil Lomax, 1984

Most passing attempts, game
61—Neil Lomax at S.D., Sept. 20, 1987

Most passes completed, season
345—Neil Lomax, 1984

Most passes completed, game
37—Neil Lomax at Was., Dec. 16, 1984
  Kent Graham vs. St.L., Sept. 29,
  1996 (OT)

Most passing yards, career
34,639—Jim Hart

Most passing yards, season
4,614—Neil Lomax, 1984

Most passing yards, game
522—Boomer Esiason at Was., Nov. 10,
  1996 (OT)
468—Neil Lomax at Was., Dec. 16, 1984

Most touchdown passes, season
28—Charley Johnson, 1963
  Neil Lomax, 1984

Most pass receptions, career
535—Larry Centers

Most pass receptions, season
101—Larry Centers, 1995

Most pass receptions, game
16—Sonny Randle at NYG, Nov. 4, 1962

Most receiving yards, career
8,497—Roy Green

Most receiving yards, season
1,555—Roy Green, 1984

Most receiving yards, game
256—Sonny Randle vs. NYG, Nov. 4, 1962

Most receiving touchdowns, season
16—Sonny Randle, 1960

Most touchdowns, career
69—Roy Green

Most field goals, season
30—Greg Davis, 1995

Longest field goal
55 yards—Greg Davis at Sea., Dec. 19,
  1993
  Greg Davis at Det., Sept. 17, 1995

Most interceptions, career
52—Larry Wilson

Most interceptions, season
12—Bob Nussbaumer, 1949

SERIES RECORDS

Arizona vs.: Atlanta 13-7; Baltimore 1-1; Buffalo 3-4; Carolina 0-1; Chicago 26-54-6; Cincinnati 2-5; Cleveland 11-32-3; Dallas 25-51-1; Denver 0-4-1; Detroit 17-28-3; Green Bay 21-43-4; Indianapolis 6-6; Jacksonville 0-1; Kansas City 1-5-1; Miami 0-8; Minnesota 8-8; New England 6-4; New Orleans 12-11; N.Y. Giants 39-76-2; N.Y. Jets 2-3; Oakland 1-3; Philadelphia 51-51-5; Pittsburgh 21-30-3; St. Louis 14-16-2; San Diego 2-6; San Francisco 9-12; Seattle 5-1; Tampa Bay 7-7; Tennessee 4-3; Washington 42-64-1.
NOTE: Includes records for entire franchise, from 1920 to present.

COACHING RECORDS

LeRoy Andrews, 0-1-0; Norman Barry, 16-8-2; Joe Bugel, 20-44-0; Guy Chamberlain, 3-7-1; Jack Chevigny, 2-6-2; Jimmy Conzelman, 34-31-3 (1-1); Don Coryell, 42-27-1 (0-2); Milan Creighton, 16-26-4; Paddy Driscoll, 17-8-4; Chuck Drulis-Ray Prochaska-Ray Willsey*, 2-0-0; Fred Gillies, 1-5-0; Phil Handler, 1-29-0; Phil Handler-Cecil Isbell*, 1-1-0; Phil Handler-Buddy Parker*, 2-4-0; Jim Hanifan, 39-49-1 (0-1); Bob Hollway, 8-18-2; Arnold Horween, 13-8-1; Frank Ivy, 17-29-2; Joe Kuharich, 4-8-0; Hank Kuhlmann, 0-5-0; Curly Lambeau, 7-15-0; Wally Lemm, 27-26-3; Dave McGinnis, 1-8-0; Ernie Nevers, 11-19-2; Buddy Parker, 4-1-1; Ray Richards, 14-21-1; Buddy Ryan, 12-20-0; Dewey Scanlon, 6-6-1; Paul Schissler, 6-15-1; Gene Stallings, 23-34-1; Joe Stydahar, 3-20-1; Vince Tobin, 28-43-0 (1-1); Bud Wilkinson, 9-20-0; Larry Wilson, 2-1-0; Charley Winner, 35-30-5.
NOTE: Playoff games in parentheses.
*Co-coaches.

RETIRED UNIFORM NUMBERS

No.	Player
8	Larry Wilson
77	Stan Mauldin
88	J.V. Cain
99	Marshall Goldberg

ATLANTA FALCONS
YEAR-BY-YEAR RECORDS

	REGULAR SEASON							PLAYOFFS			
Year	W	L	T	Pct.	PF	PA	Finish	W	L	Highest round	Coach
1966	3	11	0	.214	204	437	7th/Eastern Conf.	—	—		Norb Hecker
1967	1	12	1	.077	175	422	4th/Coastal Div.	—	—		Norb Hecker
1968	2	12	0	.143	170	389	4th/Coastal Div.	—	—		N. Hecker, N. Van Brocklin
1969	6	8	0	.429	276	268	3rd/Coastal Div.	—	—		Norm Van Brocklin
1970	4	8	2	.333	206	261	3rd/NFC Western Div.	—	—		Norm Van Brocklin
1971	7	6	1	.538	274	277	3rd/NFC Western Div.	—	—		Norm Van Brocklin
1972	7	7	0	.500	269	274	2nd/NFC Western Div.	—	—		Norm Van Brocklin
1973	9	5	0	.643	318	224	2nd/NFC Western Div.	—	—		Norm Van Brocklin
1974	3	11	0	.214	111	271	4th/NFC Western Div.	—	—		N. Van Brocklin, M. Campbell
1975	4	10	0	.286	240	289	3rd/NFC Western Div.	—	—		Marion Campbell
1976	4	10	0	.286	172	312	T3rd/NFC Western Div.	—	—		M. Campbell, Pat Peppler
1977	7	7	0	.500	179	129	2nd/NFC Western Div.	—	—		Leeman Bennett
1978	9	7	0	.563	240	290	2nd/NFC Western Div.	1	1	NFC div. playoff game	Leeman Bennett
1979	6	10	0	.375	300	388	3rd/NFC Western Div.	—	—		Leeman Bennett
1980	12	4	0	.750	405	272	1st/NFC Western Div.	0	1	NFC div. playoff game	Leeman Bennett
1981	7	9	0	.438	426	355	2nd/NFC Western Div.	—	—		Leeman Bennett
1982	5	4	0	.556	183	199	T4th/NFC	0	1	NFC first-round pl. game	Leeman Bennett
1983	7	9	0	.438	370	389	4th/NFC Western Div.	—	—		Dan Henning
1984	4	12	0	.250	281	382	4th/NFC Western Div.	—	—		Dan Henning
1985	4	12	0	.250	282	452	4th/NFC Western Div.	—	—		Dan Henning
1986	7	8	1	.469	280	280	3rd/NFC Western Div.	—	—		Dan Henning
1987	3	12	0	.200	205	436	4th/NFC Western Div.	—	—		Marion Campbell
1988	5	11	0	.313	244	315	4th/NFC Western Div.	—	—		Marion Campbell

			REGULAR SEASON						PLAYOFFS		
Year	W	L	T	Pct.	PF	PA	Finish	W	L	Highest round	Coach
1989	3	13	0	.188	279	437	4th/NFC Western Div.	—	—		M. Campbell, Jim Hanifan
1990	5	11	0	.313	348	365	T3rd/NFC Western Div.	—	—		Jerry Glanville
1991	10	6	0	.625	361	338	2nd/NFC Western Div.	1	1	NFC div. playoff game	Jerry Glanville
1992	6	10	0	.375	327	414	T3rd/NFC Western Div.	—	—		Jerry Glanville
1993	6	10	0	.375	316	385	3rd/NFC Western Div.	—	—		Jerry Glanville
1994	7	9	0	.438	313	389	T2nd/NFC Western Div.	—	—		June Jones
1995	9	7	0	.563	362	349	2nd/NFC Western Div.	0	1	NFC wild-card game	June Jones
1996	3	13	0	.188	309	465	T4th/NFC Western Div.	—	—		June Jones
1997	7	9	0	.438	320	361	T2nd/NFC Western Div.	—	—		Dan Reeves
1998	14	2	0	.875	442	289	1st/NFC Western Div.	2	1	Super Bowl	Dan Reeves
1999	5	11	0	.313	285	380	3rd/NFC Western Div.	—	—		Dan Reeves
2000	4	12	0	.250	252	413	5th/NFC Western Div.	—	—		Dan Reeves

FIRST-ROUND DRAFT PICKS

1966—Tommy Nobis, LB, Texas*
　　　Randy Johnson, QB, Texas A&I
1967—None
1968—Claude Humphrey, DE, Tennessee State
1969—George Kunz, T, Notre Dame
1970—John Small, LB, Citadel
1971—Joe Profit, RB, Northeast Louisiana State
1972—Clarence Ellis, DB, Notre Dame
1973—None
1974—None
1975—Steve Bartkowski, QB, California*
1976—Bubba Bean, RB, Texas A&M
1977—Warren Bryant, T, Kentucky
　　　Wilson Faumuina, DT, San Jose State
1978—Mike Kenn, T, Michigan
1979—Don Smith, DE, Miami, Fla.
1980—Junior Miller, TE, Nebraska
1981—Bobby Butler, DB, Florida State
1982—Gerald Riggs, RB, Arizona State
1983—Mike Pitts, DE, Alabama
1984—Rick Bryan, DT, Oklahoma
1985—Bill Fralic, T, Pittsburgh

1986—Tony Casillas, DT, Oklahoma
　　　Tim Green, LB, Syracuse
1987—Chris Miller, QB, Oregon
1988—Aundray Bruce, LB, Auburn*
1989—Deion Sanders, DB, Florida State
　　　Shawn Collins, WR, Northern Arizona
1990—Steve Broussard, RB, Washington State
1991—Bruce Pickens, CB, Nebraska
　　　Mike Pritchard, WR, Colorado
1992—Bob Whitfield, T, Stanford
　　　Tony Smith, RB, Southern Mississippi
1993—Lincoln Kennedy, T, Washington
1994—None
1995—Devin Bush, DB, Florida State
1996—None
1997—Michael Booker, DB, Nebraska
1998—Keith Brooking, LB, Georgia Tech
1999—Patrick Kerney, DE, Virginia
2000—None
2001—Michael Vick, QB, Virginia Tech*
　　　*First player chosen in draft.

FRANCHISE RECORDS

Most rushing yards, career
6,631—Gerald Riggs
Most rushing yards, season
1,846—Jamal Anderson, 1998
Most rushing yards, game
202—Gerald Riggs at N.O., Sept. 2, 1984
Most rushing touchdowns, season
14—Jamal Anderson, 1998
Most passing attempts, season
557—Jeff George, 1995
Most passing attempts, game
66—Chris Miller vs. Det., Dec. 24, 1989
Most passes completed, season
336—Jeff George, 1995
Most passes completed, game
37—Chris Miller vs. Det., Dec. 24, 1989
Most passing yards, career
23,468—Steve Bartkowski
Most passing yards, season
4,143—Jeff George, 1995

Most passing yards, game
416—Steve Bartkowski vs. Pit., Nov. 15, 1981
Most touchdown passes, season
31—Steve Bartkowski, 1980
Most pass receptions, career
522—Terance Mathis
Most pass receptions, season
111—Terance Mathis, 1994
Most pass receptions, game
15—William Andrews vs. Pit., Nov. 15, 1981
Most receiving yards, career
6,785—Terance Mathis
Most receiving yards, season
1,358—Alfred Jenkins, 1981
Most receiving yards, game
198—Terance Mathis at N.O., Dec. 13, 1998

Most receiving touchdowns, season
15—Andre Rison, 1993
Most touchdowns, career
56—Andre Rison
Most field goals, season
31—Morten Andersen, 1995
Longest field goal
59 yards—Morten Andersen vs. S.F., Dec. 24, 1995
Most interceptions, career
39—Rolland Lawrence
Most interceptions, season
10—Scott Case, 1988
Most sacks, career
62.5—Claude Humphrey
Most sacks, season
16—Joel Williams, 1980

SERIES RECORDS

Atlanta vs.: Arizona 7-13; Baltimore 0-1; Buffalo 3-4; Carolina 7-5; Chicago 10-9; Cincinnati 2-7; Cleveland 2-8; Dallas 6-12; Denver 3-7; Detroit 7-21; Green Bay 9-10; Indianapolis 1-10; Jacksonville 0-2; Kansas City 1-4; Miami 2-6; Minnesota 6-14; New England 6-3; New Orleans 37-26; N.Y. Giants 7-7; N.Y. Jets 4-4; Oakland 3-7; Philadelphia 9-10-1; Pittsburgh 1-11; St. Louis 23-43-2; San Diego 5-1; San Francisco 25-42-1; Seattle 2-6; Tampa Bay 8-9; Tennessee 5-5; Washington 4-13-1.

COACHING RECORDS

Leeman Bennett, 46-41-0 (1-3); Marion Campbell, 17-51-0; Jerry Glanville, 27-37-0 (1-1); Jim Hanifan, 0-4-0; Norb Hecker, 4-26-1; Dan Henning, 22-41-1; June Jones, 19-29-0 (0-1); Pat Peppler, 3-6-0; Dan Reeves, 30-34-0 (2-1); Norm Van Brocklin, 37-49-3. NOTE: Playoff games in parentheses.

BALTIMORE RAVENS
YEAR-BY-YEAR RECORDS

	REGULAR SEASON						PLAYOFFS			
Year	W	L	T	Pct.	PF	PA	Finish	W	L	Highest round	Coach
1996	4	12	0	.250	371	441	5th/AFC Central Div.	—	—		Ted Marchibroda
1997	6	9	1	.406	326	345	5th/AFC Central Div.	—	—		Ted Marchibroda
1998	6	10	0	.375	269	335	4th/AFC Central Div.	—	—		Ted Marchibroda
1999	8	8	0	.500	324	277	3rd/AFC Central Div.	—	—		Brian Billick
2000	12	4	0	.750	333	165	2nd/AFC Central Div.	4	0	Super Bowl champ	Brian Billick

FIRST-ROUND DRAFT PICKS

1996—Jonathan Ogden, T, UCLA
Ray Lewis, LB, Miami, Fla.
1997—Peter Boulware, DE, Florida State

1998—Duane Starks, DB, Miami, Fla.
1999—Chris McAlister, DB, Arizona

2000—Jamal Lewis, RB, Tennessee
Travis Taylor, WR, Florida
2001—Todd Heap, TE, Arizona State

FRANCHISE RECORDS

Most rushing yards, career
2,102—Priest Holmes
Most rushing yards, season
1,364—Jamal Lewis, 2000
Most rushing yards, game
227—Priest Holmes at Cin., Nov. 22, 1998
Most rushing touchdowns, season
7—Priest Holmes, 1998
Most passing attempts, season
549—Vinny Testaverde, 1996
Most passing attempts, game
51—Vinny Testaverde vs. St.L., Oct. 27, 1996 (OT)
50—Vinny Testaverde vs. Jac., Nov. 24, 1996 (OT)
47—Vinny Testaverde vs. Pit., Oct. 5, 1997
Vinny Testaverde at Mia., Oct. 19, 1997
Most passes completed, season
325—Vinny Testaverde, 1996
Most passes completed, game
32—Vinny Testaverde vs. Mia., Oct. 19, 1997

Most passing yards, career
7,148—Vinny Testaverde
Most passing yards, season
4,177—Vinny Testaverde, 1996
Most passing yards, game
429—Vinny Testaverde vs. St.L., Oct. 27, 1996 (OT)
366—Vinny Testaverde vs. Jac., Nov. 24, 1996 (OT)
353—Vinny Testaverde vs. N.E., Oct. 6, 1996
Most touchdown passes, season
33—Vinny Testaverde, 1996
Most pass receptions, career
183—Michael Jackson
Most pass receptions, season
76—Michael Jackson, 1996
Most pass receptions, game
13—Priest Holmes vs. Ten., Oct. 11, 1998
Most receiving yards, career
2,596—Michael Jackson
Most receiving yards, season
1,201—Michael Jackson, 1996

Most receiving yards, game
258—Qadry Ismail at Pit., Dec. 12, 1999
Most receiving touchdowns, season
14—Michael Jackson, 1996
Most touchdowns, career
25—Jermaine Lewis
Most field goals, season
35—Matt Stover, 2000
Longest field goal
51 yards—Matt Stover at Was., Oct. 15, 2000
Matt Stover vs. Ten., Oct. 29, 2000
Most interceptions, career
17—Rod Woodson
Most interceptions, season
7—Rod Woodson, 1999
Most sacks, career
41.5—Michael McCrary
Most sacks, season
14.5—Michael McCrary, 1998

SERIES RECORDS

Baltimore vs.: Arizona 1-1; Atlanta, 1-0; Buffalo 0-1; Carolina 0-1; Chicago 0-1; Cincinnati 7-3; Cleveland 4-0; Dallas 1-0; Denver 0-1; Detroit 1-0; Green Bay 0-1; Indianapolis 1-1; Jacksonville 2-8; Kansas City 0-1; Miami 0-2; Minnesota 0-1; New England 0-2; New Orleans 2-0; N.Y. Giants 1-0; N.Y. Jets 2-1; Oakland 2-0; Philadelphia, 0-0-1; Pittsburgh 3-7; St. Louis 1-1; San Diego 1-2; San Francisco 0-1; Seattle, 1-0; Tennessee 4-6; Washington 1-1.

COACHING RECORDS

Brian Billick, 20-12-0 (4-0); Ted Marchibroda, 16-31-1.
NOTE: Playoff games in parentheses.

BUFFALO BILLS
YEAR-BY-YEAR RECORDS

	REGULAR SEASON							PLAYOFFS			
Year	W	L	T	Pct.	PF	PA	Finish	W	L	Highest round	Coach
1960*	5	8	1	.385	296	303	3rd/Eastern Div.	—	—		Buster Ramsey
1961*	6	8	0	.429	294	342	4th/Eastern Div.	—	—		Buster Ramsey
1962*	7	6	1	.538	309	272	3rd/Eastern Div.	—	—		Lou Saban
1963*	7	6	1	.538	304	291	2nd/Eastern Div.	0	1	E. Div. championship game	Lou Saban
1964*	12	2	0	.857	400	242	1st/Eastern Div.	1	0	AFL champ	Lou Saban
1965*	10	3	1	.769	313	226	1st/Eastern Div.	1	0	AFL champ	Lou Saban
1966*	9	4	1	.692	358	255	1st/Eastern Div.	0	1	AFL championship game	Joe Collier
1967*	4	10	0	.286	237	285	T3rd/Eastern Div.	—	—		Joe Collier
1968*	1	12	1	.077	199	367	5th/Eastern Div.	—	—		J. Collier, H. Johnson
1969*	4	10	0	.286	230	359	T3rd/Eastern Div.	—	—		John Rauch
1970	3	10	1	.231	204	337	4th/AFC Eastern Div.	—	—		John Rauch
1971	1	13	0	.071	184	394	5th/AFC Eastern Div.	—	—		Harvey Johnson
1972	4	9	1	.321	257	377	4th/AFC Eastern Div.	—	—		Lou Saban
1973	9	5	0	.643	259	230	2nd/AFC Eastern Div.	—	—		Lou Saban
1974	9	5	0	.643	264	244	2nd/AFC Eastern Div.	0	1	AFC div. playoff game	Lou Saban
1975	8	6	0	.571	420	355	3rd/AFC Eastern Div.	—	—		Lou Saban
1976	2	12	0	.143	245	363	5th/AFC Eastern Div.	—	—		Lou Saban, Jim Ringo
1977	3	11	0	.214	160	313	T4th/AFC Eastern Div.	—	—		Jim Ringo
1978	5	11	0	.313	302	354	T4th/AFC Eastern Div.	—	—		Chuck Knox
1979	7	9	0	.438	268	279	4th/AFC Eastern Div.	—	—		Chuck Knox
1980	11	5	0	.688	320	260	1st/AFC Eastern Div.	0	1	AFC div. playoff game	Chuck Knox
1981	10	6	0	.625	311	276	3rd/AFC Eastern Div.	1	1	AFC div. playoff game	Chuck Knox
1982	4	5	0	.444	150	154	T8th/AFC	—	—		Chuck Knox
1983	8	8	0	.500	283	351	T2nd/AFC Eastern Div.	—	—		Kay Stephenson
1984	2	14	0	.125	250	454	5th/AFC Eastern Div.	—	—		Kay Stephenson
1985	2	14	0	.125	200	381	5th/AFC Eastern Div.	—	—		Hank Bullough
1986	4	12	0	.250	287	348	4th/AFC Eastern Div.	—	—		H. Bullough, M. Levy
1987	7	8	0	.467	270	305	4th/AFC Eastern Div.	—	—		Marv Levy
1988	12	4	0	.750	329	237	1st/AFC Eastern Div.	1	1	AFC championship game	Marv Levy
1989	9	7	0	.563	409	317	1st/AFC Eastern Div.	0	1	AFC div. playoff game	Marv Levy
1990	13	3	0	.813	428	263	1st/AFC Eastern Div.	2	1	Super Bowl	Marv Levy
1991	13	3	0	.813	458	318	1st/AFC Eastern Div.	2	1	Super Bowl	Marv Levy
1992	11	5	0	.688	381	283	2nd/AFC Eastern Div.	3	1	Super Bowl	Marv Levy
1993	12	4	0	.750	329	242	1st/AFC Eastern Div.	2	1	Super Bowl	Marv Levy
1994	7	9	0	.438	340	356	4th/AFC Eastern Div.	—	—		Marv Levy
1995	10	6	0	.625	350	335	1st/AFC Eastern Div.	1	1	AFC div. playoff game	Marv Levy
1996	10	6	0	.625	319	266	2nd/AFC Eastern Div.	0	1	AFC wild-card game	Marv Levy
1997	6	10	0	.375	255	367	4th/AFC Eastern Div.	—	—		Marv Levy
1998	10	6	0	.625	400	333	T2nd/AFC Eastern Div.	0	1	AFC wild-card game	Wade Phillips
1999	11	5	0	.688	320	229	2nd/AFC Eastern Div.	0	1	AFC wild-card game	Wade Phillips
2000	8	8	0	.500	315	350	4th/AFC Eastern Div.	—	—		Wade Phillips

*American Football League.

FIRST-ROUND DRAFT PICKS

1960—Richie Lucas, QB, Penn State
1961—Ken Rice, T, Auburn* (AFL)
1962—Ernie Davis, RB, Syracuse
1963—Dave Behrman, C, Michigan State
1964—Carl Eller, DE, Minnesota
1965—Jim Davidson, T, Ohio State
1966—Mike Dennis, RB, Mississippi
1967—John Pitts, DB, Arizona State
1968—Haven Moses, WR, San Diego St.
1969—O.J. Simpson, RB, Southern California*
1970—Al Cowlings, DE, Southern California
1971—J.D. Hill, WR, Arizona State
1972—Walt Patulski, DE, Notre Dame*
1973—Paul Seymour, T, Michigan
    Joe DeLamielleure, G, Michigan State
1974—Reuben Gant, TE, Oklahoma State
1975—Tom Ruud, LB, Nebraska
1976—Mario Clark, DB, Oregon
1977—Phil Dokes, DT, Oklahoma State
1978—Terry Miller, RB, Oklahoma State
1979—Tom Cousineau, LB, Ohio State*

    Jerry Butler, WR, Clemson
1980—Jim Ritcher, C, North Carolina State
1981—Booker Moore, RB, Penn State
1982—Perry Tuttle, WR, Clemson
1983—Tony Hunter, TE, Notre Dame
    Jim Kelly, QB, Miami, Fla.
1984—Greg Bell, RB, Notre Dame
1985—Bruce Smith, DT, Virginia Tech*
    Derrick Burroughs, DB, Memphis State
1986—Ronnie Harmon, RB, Iowa
    Will Wolford, T, Vanderbilt
1987—Shane Conlan, LB, Penn State
1988—None
1989—None
1990—James Williams, DB, Fresno State
1991—Henry Jones, S, Illinois
1992—John Fina, T, Arizona
1993—Thomas Smith, DB, North Carolina
1994—Jeff Burris, DB, Notre Dame
1995—Ruben Brown, G, Pittsburgh
1996—Eric Moulds, WR, Mississippi State

1997—Antowain Smith, RB, Houston
1998—None

1999—Antoine Winfield, DB, Ohio State
2000—Erik Flowers, DE, Arizona State

2001—Nate Clements, DB, Ohio State
*First player chosen in draft.

FRANCHISE RECORDS

Most rushing yards, career
11,938—Thurman Thomas
Most rushing yards, season
2,003—O.J. Simpson, 1973
Most rushing yards, game
273—O.J. Simpson at Det., Nov. 25, 1976
Most rushing touchdowns, season
16—O.J. Simpson, 1975
Most passing attempts, season
508—Joe Ferguson, 1983
Most passing attempts, game
55—Joe Ferguson at Mia., Oct. 9, 1983
Most passes completed, season
304—Jim Kelly, 1991
Most passes completed, game
38—Joe Ferguson at Mia., Oct. 9, 1983
Most passing yards, career
35,467—Jim Kelly

Most passing yards, season
3,844—Jim Kelly, 1991
Most passing yards, game
419—Joe Ferguson at Mia., Oct. 9, 1983
Most touchdown passes, season
33—Jim Kelly, 1991
Most pass receptions, career
941—Andre Reed
Most pass receptions, season
94—Eric Moulds, 2000
Most pass receptions, game
15—Andre Reed vs. G.B., Nov. 20, 1994
Most receiving yards, career
13,095—Andre Reed
Most receiving yards, season
1,368—Eric Moulds, 1998
Most receiving yards, game
255—Jerry Butler vs. NYJ, Sept. 23, 1979

Most receiving touchdowns, season
11—Bill Brooks, 1995
Most touchdowns, career
87—Andre Reed
    Thurman Thomas
Most field goals, season
33—Steve Christie, 1998
Longest field goal
59 yards—Steve Christie vs. Mia., Sept. 26, 1993
Most interceptions, career
40—George Byrd
Most interceptions, season
10—Billy Atkins, 1961
    Tom Janik, 1967
Most sacks, career
171—Bruce Smith
Most sacks, season
19—Bruce Smith, 1990

SERIES RECORDS

Buffalo vs.: Arizona 4-3; Atlanta 4-3; Baltimore 1-0; Carolina 2-0; Chicago 3-5; Cincinnati 9-10; Cleveland 4-7; Dallas 3-3; Denver 17-12-1; Detroit 2-3-1; Green Bay 6-2; Indianapolis 34-26-1; Jacksonville 1-1; Kansas City 18-14-1; Miami 25-44-1; Minnesota 2-7; New England 39-42-1; New Orleans 4-2; N.Y. Giants 5-3; N.Y. Jets 46-35; Oakland 15-16; Philadelphia 5-4; Pittsburgh 8-8; St. Louis 4-4; San Diego 8-17-2; San Francisco 4-3; Seattle 3-5; Tampa Bay 2-5; Tennessee 14-22; Washington 5-4.

COACHING RECORDS

Hank Bullough, 4-17-0; Joe Collier, 13-16-1 (0-1); Harvey Johnson, 2-23-1; Chuck Knox, 37-36-0 (1-2); Marv Levy, 112-70-0 (11-8); Wade Phillips, 29-19-0 (0-2); Buster Ramsey, 11-16-1; John Rauch, 7-20-1; Jim Ringo, 3-20-0; Lou Saban, 68-45-4 (2-2); Kay Stephenson, 10-26-0.
NOTE: Playoff games in parentheses.

RETIRED UNIFORM NUMBERS

No.	Player
	None

CAROLINA PANTHERS
YEAR-BY-YEAR RECORDS

	REGULAR SEASON						PLAYOFFS			
Year	W	L	T	Pct.	PF	PA	Finish	W	L	Highest round	Coach
1995	7	9	0	.438	289	325	T3rd/NFC Western Div.	—	—		Dom Capers
1996	12| 4	0	.750	367	218	1st/NFC Western Div.	1	1	NFC championship game	Dom Capers
1997	7	9	0	.438	265	314	T2nd/NFC Western Div.	—	—		Dom Capers
1998	4	12	0	.250	336	413	T4th/NFC Western Div.	—	—		Dom Capers
1999	8	8	0	.500	421	381	2nd/NFC Western Div.	—	—		George Seifert
2000	7	9	0	.438	310	310	3rd/NFC Western Div.	—	—		George Seifert

FIRST-ROUND DRAFT PICKS

1995—Kerry Collins, QB, Penn State
    Tyrone Poole, DB, Fort Valley (Ga.) St.
    Blake Brockermeyer, T, Texas
1996—Tim Biakabutuka, RB, Michigan
1997—Rae Carruth, WR, Colorado

1998—Jason Peter, DT, Nebraska
1999—None
2000—Rashard Anderson, DB, Jackson State
2001—Dan Morgan, LB, Miami, Fla.

FRANCHISE RECORDS

Most rushing yards, career
2,300—Tim Biakabutuka
Most rushing yards, season
1,120—Anthony Johnson, 1996

Most rushing yards, game
147—Fred Lane vs. Oak., Nov. 2, 1997
Most rushing touchdowns, season
7—Fred Lane, 1997

Most passing attempts, season
571—Steve Beuerlein, 1999
Most passing attempts, game
53—Kerry Collins vs. G.B., Sept. 27, 1998

Most passes completed, season
343—Steve Beuerlein, 1999
Most passes completed, game
29—Steve Beuerlein at Green Bay, Dec.
12, 1999
Most passing yards, career
12,690—Steve Beuerlein
Most passing yards, season
4,436—Steve Beuerlein, 1999
Most passing yards, game
373—Steve Beuerlein at Green Bay,
Dec. 12, 1999
Most touchdown passes, season
36—Steve Beuerlein, 1999
Most pass receptions, career
318—Muhsin Muhammad

Most pass receptions, season
102—Muhsin Muhammad, 2000
Most pass receptions, game
11—Muhsin Muhammad vs. S.F., Dec.
18, 1999
Muhsin Muhammad vs. G.B., Nov.
27, 2000
Most receiving yards, career
4,101—Muhsin Muhammad
Most receiving yards, season
1,253—Muhsin Muhammad, 1999
Most receiving yards, game
192—Muhsin Muhammad at N.O., Sept.
13, 1998
Most receiving touchdowns, season
12—Patrick Jeffers, 1999

Most touchdowns, career
35—Wesley Walls
Most field goals, season
37—John Kasay, 1996
Longest field goal
56 yards—John Kasay vs. G.B., Sept. 27,
1998
Most interceptions, career
25—Eric Davis
Most interceptions, season
6—Brett Maxie, 1995
Most sacks, career
41.5—Kevin Greene
Most sacks, season
15—Kevin Greene, 1998

SERIES RECORDS

Carolina vs.: Arizona 1-0; Atlanta 5-7; Buffalo 0-2; Baltimore 1-0; Chicago 0-1; Cincinnati 1-0; Cleveland 1-0; Dallas 1-2; Denver 0-1; Detroit 0-1; Green Bay 2-2; Indianapolis 2-0; Jacksonville 0-2; Kansas City 0-2; Miami 0-1; Minnesota 0-3; New England 1-0; New Orleans 6-6; N.Y. Giants 1-0; N.Y. Jets 1-1; Oakland 1-1; Philadelphia 1-1; Pittsburgh 1-1; St. Louis 7-5; San Diego 2-0; San Francisco 7-5; Seattle 1-0; Tampa Bay 1-2; Tennessee 1-0; Washington 0-5.

COACHING RECORDS

Dom Capers, 30-34-0 (1-1); George Seifert, 15-17-0.
NOTE: Playoff games in parentheses.

RETIRED UNIFORM NUMBERS

No.	Player
None	

CHICAGO BEARS
YEAR-BY-YEAR RECORDS

			REGULAR SEASON						PLAYOFFS		
Year	W	L	T	Pct.	PF	PA	Finish	W	L	Highest round	Coach
1920*	10	1	2	.909	...	...	2nd				George Halas
1921†	9	1	1	.900	...	...	1st				George Halas
1922	9	3	0	.750	...	...	2nd				George Halas
1923	9	2	1	.818	...	...	2nd				George Halas
1924	6	1	4	.857	...	...	2nd				George Halas
1925	9	5	3	.643	...	...	7th				George Halas
1926	12	1	3	.923	...	...	2nd				George Halas
1927	9	3	2	.750	...	...	3rd				George Halas
1928	7	5	1	.583	...	...	5th				George Halas
1929	4	9	2	.308	...	...	9th				George Halas
1930	9	4	1	.692	...	...	3rd				Ralph Jones
1931	8	5	0	.615	...	...	3rd				Ralph Jones
1932	7	1	6	.875	...	...	1st				Ralph Jones
1933	10	2	1	.833	133	82	1st/Western Div.	1	0	NFL champ	George Halas
1934	13	0	0	1.000	286	86	1st/Western Div.	0	1	NFL championship game	George Halas
1935	6	4	2	.600	192	106	T3rd/Western Div.	—	—		George Halas
1936	9	3	0	.750	222	94	2nd/Western Div.	—	—		George Halas
1937	9	1	1	.900	201	100	1st/Western Div.	0	1	NFL championship game	George Halas
1938	6	5	0	.545	194	148	3rd/Western Div.	—	—		George Halas
1939	8	3	0	.727	298	157	2nd/Western Div.	—	—		George Halas
1940	8	3	0	.727	238	152	1st/Western Div.	1	0	NFL champ	George Halas
1941	10	1	0	.909	396	147	1st/Western Div.	2	0	NFL champ	George Halas
1942	11	0	0	1.000	376	84	1st/Western Div.	0	1	NFL championship game	George Halas, Hunk Anderson-Luke Johnsos
1943	8	1	1	.889	303	157	1st/Western Div.	1	0	NFL champ	H. Anderson-L. Johnsos
1944	6	3	1	.667	258	172	T2nd/Western Div.	—	—		H. Anderson-L. Johnsos
1945	3	7	0	.300	192	235	4th/Western Div.	—	—		H. Anderson-L. Johnsos
1946	8	2	1	.800	289	193	1st/Western Div.	1	0	NFL champ	George Halas
1947	8	4	0	.667	363	241	2nd/Western Div.	—	—		George Halas
1948	10	2	0	.833	375	151	2nd/Western Div.	—	—		George Halas
1949	9	3	0	.750	332	218	2nd/Western Div.	—	—		George Halas
1950	9	3	0	.750	279	207	2nd/National Conf.	0	1	Nat. Conf. champ. game	George Halas
1951	7	5	0	.583	286	282	4th/National Conf.	—	—		George Halas
1952	5	7	0	.417	245	326	5th/National Conf.	—	—		George Halas
1953	3	8	1	.273	218	262	T4th/Western Conf.	—	—		George Halas

Year	W	L	T	Pct.	PF	PA	Finish	W	L	Highest round	Coach
							REGULAR SEASON			PLAYOFFS	
1954	8	4	0	.667	301	279	2nd/Western Conf.	—	—		George Halas
1955	8	4	0	.667	294	251	2nd/Western Conf.	—	—		George Halas
1956	9	2	1	.818	363	246	1st/Western Conf.	0	1	NFL championship game	Paddy Driscoll
1957	5	7	0	.417	203	211	5th/Western Conf.	—	—		Paddy Driscoll
1958	8	4	0	.667	298	230	T2nd/Western Conf.	—	—		George Halas
1959	8	4	0	.667	252	196	2nd/Western Conf.	—	—		George Halas
1960	5	6	1	.455	194	299	5th/Western Conf.	—	—		George Halas
1961	8	6	0	.571	326	302	T3rd/Western Conf.	—	—		George Halas
1962	9	5	0	.643	321	287	3rd/Western Conf.	—	—		George Halas
1963	11	1	2	.917	301	144	1st/Western Conf.	1	0	NFL champ	George Halas
1964	5	9	0	.357	260	379	6th/Western Conf.	—	—		George Halas
1965	9	5	0	.643	409	275	3rd/Western Conf.	—	—		George Halas
1966	5	7	2	.417	234	272	5th/Western Conf.	—	—		George Halas
1967	7	6	1	.538	239	218	2nd/Central Div.	—	—		George Halas
1968	7	7	0	.500	250	333	2nd/Central Div.	—	—		Jim Dooley
1969	1	13	0	.071	210	339	4th/Central Div.	—	—		Jim Dooley
1970	6	8	0	.429	256	261	T3rd/NFC Central Div.	—	—		Jim Dooley
1971	6	8	0	.429	185	276	3rd/NFC Central Div.	—	—		Jim Dooley
1972	4	9	1	.321	225	275	4th/NFC Central Div.	—	—		Abe Gibron
1973	3	11	0	.214	195	334	4th/NFC Central Div.	—	—		Abe Gibron
1974	4	10	0	.286	152	279	4th/NFC Central Div.	—	—		Abe Gibron
1975	4	10	0	.286	191	379	T3rd/NFC Central Div.	—	—		Jack Pardee
1976	7	7	0	.500	253	216	2nd/NFC Central Div.	—	—		Jack Pardee
1977	9	5	0	.643	255	253	2nd/NFC Central Div.	0	1	NFC div. playoff game	Jack Pardee
1978	7	9	0	.438	253	274	T3rd/NFC Central Div.	—	—		Neill Armstrong
1979	10	6	0	.625	306	249	2nd/NFC Central Div.	0	1	NFC wild-card game	Neill Armstrong
1980	7	9	0	.438	304	264	3rd/NFC Central Div.	—	—		Neill Armstrong
1981	6	10	0	.375	253	324	5th/NFC Central Div.	—	—		Neill Armstrong
1982	3	6	0	.333	141	174	T11th/NFC	—	—		Mike Ditka
1983	8	8	0	.500	311	301	T2nd/NFC Central Div.	—	—		Mike Ditka
1984	10	6	0	.625	325	248	1st/NFC Central Div.	1	1	NFC championship game	Mike Ditka
1985	15	1	0	.938	456	198	1st/NFC Central Div.	3	0	Super Bowl champ	Mike Ditka
1986	14	2	0	.875	352	187	1st/NFC Central Div.	0	1	NFC div. playoff game	Mike Ditka
1987	11	4	0	.733	356	282	1st/NFC Central Div.	0	1	NFC div. playoff game	Mike Ditka
1988	12	4	0	.750	312	215	1st/NFC Central Div.	1	1	NFC championship game	Mike Ditka
1989	6	10	0	.375	358	377	4th/NFC Central Div.	—	—		Mike Ditka
1990	11	5	0	.688	348	280	1st/NFC Central Div.	1	1	NFC div. playoff game	Mike Ditka
1991	11	5	0	.688	299	269	2nd/NFC Central Div.	0	1	NFC wild-card game	Mike Ditka
1992	5	11	0	.313	295	361	T3rd/NFC Central Div.	—	—		Mike Ditka
1993	7	9	0	.438	234	230	4th/NFC Central Div.	—	—		Dave Wannstedt
1994	9	7	0	.563	271	307	T2nd/NFC Central Div.	1	1	NFC div. playoff game	Dave Wannstedt
1995	9	7	0	.563	392	360	3rd/NFC Central Div.	—	—		Dave Wannstedt
1996	7	9	0	.438	283	305	3rd/NFC Central Div.	—	—		Dave Wannstedt
1997	4	12	0	.250	263	421	5th/NFC Central Div.	—	—		Dave Wannstedt
1998	4	12	0	.250	276	368	5th/NFC Central Div.	—	—		Dave Wannstedt
1999	6	10	0	.375	272	341	5th NFC Central Div.	—	—		Dick Jauron
2000	5	11	0	.313	216	355	5th/NFC Central Div.	—	—		Dick Jauron

*Decatur Staleys.
†Chicago Staleys.

FIRST-ROUND DRAFT PICKS

1936—Joe Stydahar, T, West Virginia
1937—Les McDonald, E, Nebraska
1938—Joe Gray, B, Oregon State
1939—Sid Luckman, B, Columbia
Bill Osmanski, B, Holy Cross
1940—C. Turner, C, Hardin-Simmons
1941—Tom Harmon, B, Michigan*
Norm Standlee, B, Stanford
Don Scott, B, Ohio State
1942—Frankie Albert, B, Stanford
1943—Bob Steuber, B, Missouri
1944—Ray Evans, B, Kansas
1945—Don Lund, B, Michigan
1946—Johnny Lujack, QB, Notre Dame
1947—Bob Fenimore, B, Oklahoma A&M*
1948—Bobby Layne, QB, Texas
Max Baumgardner, E, Texas
1949—Dick Harris, C, Texas

1950—Chuck Hunsinger, B, Florida
1951—Bob Williams, B, Notre Dame
Billy Stone, B, Bradley
Gene Schroeder, E, Virginia
1952—Jim Dooley, B, Miami
1953—Billy Anderson, B, Compton (Ca.) J.C.
1954—Stan Wallace, B, Illinois
1955—Ron Drzewiecki, B, Marquette
1956—Menan (Tex) Schriewer, E, Texas
1957—Earl Leggett, DT, Louisiana State
1958—Chuck Howley, LB, West Virginia
1959—Don Clark, B, Ohio State
1960—Roger Davis, G, Syracuse
1961—Mike Ditka, E, Pittsburgh
1962—Ron Bull, RB, Baylor
1963—Dave Behrman, C, Michigan State
1964—Dick Evey, DT, Tennessee
1965—Dick Butkus, LB, Illinois

Gale Sayers, RB, Kansas
Steve DeLong, DE, Tennessee
1966—George Rice, DT, Louisiana State
1967—Loyd Phillips, DE, Arkansas
1968—Mike Hull, RB, Southern California
1969—Rufus Mayes, T, Ohio State
1970—None
1971—Joe Moore, RB, Missouri
1972—Lionel Antoine, T, Southern Illinois
Craig Clemons, DB, Iowa
1973—Wally Chambers, DE, Eastern Kentucky
1974—Waymond Bryant, LB, Tennessee State
Dave Gallagher, DE, Michigan
1975—Walter Payton, RB, Jackson State
1976—Dennis Lick, T, Wisconsin
1977—Ted Albrecht, T, California
1978—None
1979—Dan Hampton, DT, Arkansas
Al Harris, DE, Arizona State
1980—Otis Wilson, LB, Louisville
1981—Keith Van Horne, T, Southern California
1982—Jim McMahon, QB, Brigham Young
1983—Jimbo Covert, T, Pittsburgh

Willie Gault, WR, Tennessee
1984—Wilber Marshall, LB, Florida
1985—William Perry, DT, Clemson
1986—Neal Anderson, RB, Florida
1987—Jim Harbaugh, QB, Michigan
1988—Brad Muster, RB, Stanford
Wendell Davis, WR, Louisiana State
1989—Donnell Woolford, DB, Clemson
Trace Armstrong, DE, Florida
1990—Mark Carrier, DB, Southern California
1991—Stan Thomas, T, Texas
1992—Alonzo Spellman, DE, Ohio State
1993—Curtis Conway, WR, Southern California
1994—John Thierry, LB, Alcorn State
1995—Rashaan Salaam, RB, Colorado
1996—Walt Harris, DB, Mississippi State
1997—None
1998—Curtis Enis, RB, Penn State
1999—Cade McNown, QB, UCLA
2000—Brian Urlacher, LB, New Mexico
2001—David Terrell, WR, Michigan
*First player chosen in draft.

FRANCHISE RECORDS

Most rushing yards, career
16,726—Walter Payton
Most rushing yards, season
1,852—Walter Payton, 1977
Most rushing yards, game
275—Walter Payton vs. Min., Nov. 20, 1977
Most rushing touchdowns, season
14—Gale Sayers, 1965
Walter Payton, 1977
Walter Payton, 1979
Most passing attempts, season
522—Erik Kramer, 1995
Most passing attempts, game
60—Erik Kramer vs. NYJ, Nov. 16, 1997
Most passes completed, season
315—Erik Kramer, 1995
Most passes completed, game
34—Jim Miller vs. Min., Nov. 14, 1999 (OT)
33—Bill Wade at Was., Oct. 25, 1964

Most passing yards, career
14,686—Sid Luckman
Most passing yards, season
3,838—Erik Kramer, 1995
Most passing yards, game
468—Johnny Lujack vs. Chi. Cards, Dec. 11, 1949
Most touchdown passes, season
29—Erik Kramer, 1995
Most pass receptions, career
492—Walter Payton
Most pass receptions, season
93—Johnny Morris, 1964
Most pass receptions, game
14—Jim Keane at NYG, Oct. 23, 1949
Most receiving yards, career
5,059—Johnny Morris
Most receiving yards, season
1,400—Marcus Robinson, 1999
Most receiving yards, game
214—Harlon Hill at S.F., Oct. 31, 1954

Most receiving touchdowns, season
13—Ken Kavanaugh, 1947
Dick Gordon, 1970
Most touchdowns, career
125—Walter Payton
Most field goals, season
31—Kevin Butler, 1985
Longest field goal
55 yards—Bob Thomas at L.A. Rams, Nov. 23, 1975
Kevin Butler vs. Min., Oct. 25, 1993
Kevin Butler at T.B., Dec. 12, 1993
Most interceptions, career
38—Gary Fencik
Most interceptions, season
10—Mark Carrier, 1990
Most sacks, career
124.5—Richard Dent
Most sacks, season
17.5—Richard Dent, 1984

SERIES RECORDS

Chicago vs.: Arizona 54-26-6; Atlanta 9-10; Baltimore 1-0; Buffalo 5-3; Carolina 1-0; Cincinnati 2-4; Cleveland 3-8; Dallas 8-9; Denver 5-6; Detroit 74-56-3; Green Bay 84-71-6; Indianapolis 17-21; Jacksonville 1-1; Kansas City 5-3; Miami 3-5; Minnesota 33-44-2; New England 3-5; New Orleans 11-8; N.Y. Giants 25-17-2; N.Y. Jets 4-3; Oakland 4-6; Philadelphia 25-6-1; Pittsburgh 19-6-1; St. Louis 36-27-3; San Diego 4-4; San Francisco 25-26-1; Seattle 2-5; Tampa Bay 31-15; Tennessee 4-4; Washington 14-14.
NOTE: Includes records as Decatur Staleys in 1920 and Chicago Staleys in 1921.

COACHING RECORDS

Hunk Anderson-Luke Johnsos*, 23-11-2 (1-1); Neill Armstrong, 30-34-0 (0-1); Mike Ditka, 106-62-0 (6-6); Jim Dooley, 20-36-0; Paddy Driscoll, 14-9-1 (0-1); Abe Gibron, 11-30-1; George Halas, 318-148-31 (6-3); Dick Jauron, 11-21-0; Ralph Jones, 24-10-7; Jack Pardee, 20-22-0 (0-1); Dave Wannstedt, 40-56-0 (1-1).
NOTE: Playoff games in parentheses.
*Co-coaches.

RETIRED UNIFORM NUMBERS

No.	Player	No.	Player
3	Bronko Nagurski	42	Sid Luckman
5	George McAfee	51	Dick Butkus
7	George Halas	56	Bill Hewitt
28	Willie Galimore	61	Bill George
34	Walter Payton	66	Bulldog Turner
40	Gale Sayers	77	Red Grange
41	Brian Piccolo		

CINCINNATI BENGALS
YEAR-BY-YEAR RECORDS

		REGULAR SEASON						PLAYOFFS			
Year	W	L	T	Pct.	PF	PA	Finish	W	L	Highest round	Coach
1968*	3	11	0	.214	215	329	5th/Western Div.	—	—		Paul Brown
1969*	4	9	1	.308	280	367	5th/Western Div.	—	—		Paul Brown
1970	8	6	0	.571	312	255	1st/AFC Central Div.	0	1	AFC div. playoff game	Paul Brown
1971	4	10	0	.286	284	265	4th/AFC Central Div.	—	—		Paul Brown
1972	8	6	0	.571	299	229	3rd/AFC Central Div.	—	—		Paul Brown
1973	10	4	0	.714	286	231	1st/AFC Central Div.	0	1	AFC div. playoff game	Paul Brown
1974	7	7	0	.500	283	259	T2nd/AFC Central Div.	—	—		Paul Brown
1975	11	3	0	.786	340	246	2nd/AFC Central Div.	0	1	AFC div. playoff game	Paul Brown
1976	10	4	0	.714	335	210	2nd/AFC Central Div.	—	—		Bill Johnson
1977	8	6	0	.571	238	235	T2nd/AFC Central Div.	—	—		Bill Johnson
1978	4	12	0	.250	252	284	4th/AFC Central Div.	—	—		B. Johnson, H. Rice
1979	4	12	0	.250	337	421	4th/AFC Central Div.	—	—		Homer Rice
1980	6	10	0	.375	244	312	4th/AFC Central Div.	—	—		Forrest Gregg
1981	12	4	0	.750	421	304	1st/AFC Central Div.	2	1	Super Bowl	Forrest Gregg
1982	7	2	0	.778	232	177	T2nd/AFC	0	1	AFC first-round pl. game	Forrest Gregg
1983	7	9	0	.438	346	302	3rd/AFC Central Div.	—	—		Forrest Gregg
1984	8	8	0	.500	339	339	2nd/AFC Central Div.	—	—		Sam Wyche
1985	7	9	0	.438	441	437	T2nd/AFC Central Div.	—	—		Sam Wyche
1986	10	6	0	.625	409	394	2nd/AFC Central Div.	—	—		Sam Wyche
1987	4	11	0	.267	285	370	4th/AFC Central Div.	—	—		Sam Wyche
1988	12	4	0	.750	448	329	1st/AFC Central Div.	2	1	Super Bowl	Sam Wyche
1989	8	8	0	.500	404	285	4th/AFC Central Div.	—	—		Sam Wyche
1990	9	7	0	.563	360	352	1st/AFC Central Div.	1	1	AFC div. playoff game	Sam Wyche
1991	3	13	0	.188	263	435	4th/AFC Central Div.	—	—		Sam Wyche
1992	5	11	0	.313	274	364	4th/AFC Central Div.	—	—		David Shula
1993	3	13	0	.188	187	319	4th/AFC Central Div.	—	—		David Shula
1994	3	13	0	.188	276	406	3rd/AFC Central Div.	—	—		David Shula
1995	7	9	0	.438	349	374	T2nd/AFC Central Div.	—	—		David Shula
1996	8	8	0	.500	372	369	T3rd/AFC Central Div.	—	—		D. Shula, B. Coslet
1997	7	9	0	.438	355	405	4th/AFC Central Div.	—	—		Bruce Coslet
1998	3	13	0	.188	268	452	5th/AFC Central Div.	—	—		Bruce Coslet
1999	4	12	0	.250	283	460	5th/AFC Central Div.	—	—		Bruce Coslet
2000	4	12	0	.333	185	359	5th/AFC Central Div.	—	—		B. Coslet, Dick LeBeau

*American Football League.

FIRST-ROUND DRAFT PICKS

1968—Bob Johnson, C, Tennessee
1969—Greg Cook, QB, Cincinnati
1970—Mike Reid, DT, Penn State
1971—Vernon Holland, T, Tennessee State
1972—Sherman White, DE, California
1973—Issac Curtis, WR, San Diego State
1974—Bill Kollar, DT, Montana State
1975—Glenn Cameron, LB, Florida
1976—Billy Brooks, WR, Oklahoma
　　　Archie Griffin, RB, Ohio State
1977—Eddie Edwards, DT, Miami, Fla.
　　　Wilson Whitley, DT, Houston
　　　Mike Cobb, TE, Michigan State
1978—Ross Browner, DE, Notre Dame
　　　Blair Bush, C, Washington
1979—Jack Thompson, QB, Washington State
　　　Charles Alexander, RB, Louisiana State
1980—Anthony Munoz, T, Southern California
1981—David Verser, WR, Kansas
1982—Glen Collins, DE, Mississippi State
1983—Dave Rimington, C, Nebraska
1984—Ricky Hunley, LB, Arizona
　　　Pete Koch, DE, Maryland

　　　Brian Blados, T, North Carolina
1985—Eddie Brown, WR, Miami, Fla.
　　　Emanuel King, LB, Alabama
1986—Joe Kelly, LB, Washington
　　　Tim McGee, WR, Tennessee
1987—Jason Buck, DT, Brigham Young
1988—Rickey Dixon, S, Oklahoma
1989—None
1990—James Francis, LB, Baylor
1991—Alfred Williams, LB, Colorado
1992—David Klingler, QB, Houston
　　　Darryl Williams, DB, Miami, Fla.
1993—John Copeland, DE, Alabama
1994—Dan Wilkinson, DT, Ohio State*
1995—Ki-Jana Carter, RB, Penn State*
1996—Willie Anderson, T, Auburn
1997—Reinard Wilson, LB, Florida State
1998—Takeo Spikes, LB, Auburn
　　　Brian Simmons, LB, North Carolina
1999—Akili Smith, QB, Oregon
2000—Peter Warrick, WR, Florida State
2001—Justin Smith, DE, Missouri
　　　*First player chosen in draft.

FRANCHISE RECORDS

Most rushing yards, career
6,447—James Brooks
Most rushing yards, season
1,435—Corey Dillon, 2000

Most rushing yards, game
278—Corey Dillon vs. Den., Oct. 22, 2000
Most rushing touchdowns, season
15—Ickey Woods, 1988

Most passing attempts, season
567—Jeff Blake, 1995
Most passing attempts, game
56—Ken Anderson at S.D., Dec. 20, 1982

Most passes completed, season 326—Jeff Blake, 1995	**Most pass receptions, season** 100—Carl Pickens, 1996	**Most field goals, season** 29—Doug Pelfrey, 1995
Most passes completed, game 40—Ken Anderson at S.D., Dec. 20, 1982	**Most pass receptions, game** 13—Carl Pickens vs. Pit., Oct. 11, 1998	**Longest field goal** 55 yards—Chris Bahr vs. Hou., Sept. 23, 1979
Most passing yards, career 32,838—Ken Anderson	**Most receiving yards, career** 7,101—Isaac Curtis	**Most interceptions, career** 65—Ken Riley
Most passing yards, season 3,959—Boomer Esiason, 1986	**Most receiving yards, season** 1,273—Eddie Brown, 1988	**Most interceptions, season** 9—Ken Riley, 1976
Most passing yards, game 490—Boomer Esiason at L.A. Rams, Oct. 7, 1990	**Most receiving yards, game** 216—Eddie Brown vs. Pit., Nov. 16, 1988	**Most sacks, career** 83.5—Eddie Edwards
Most touchdown passes, season 29—Ken Anderson, 1981	**Most receiving touchdowns, season** 17—Carl Pickens, 1995	**Most sacks, season** 21.5—Coy Bacon, 1976
Most pass receptions, career 473—Carl Pickens	**Most touchdowns, career** 70—Pete Johnson	

SERIES RECORDS

Cincinnati vs.: Arizona 5-2; Atlanta 7-2; Baltimore 3-7; Buffalo 10-9; Carolina 0-1; Chicago 4-2; Cleveland 27-28; Dallas 3-5; Denver 7-14; Detroit 4-3; Green Bay 4-5; Indianapolis 8-12; Jacksonville 5-7; Kansas City 9-11; Miami 3-13; Minnesota 4-5; New England 7-10; New Orleans 4-5; N.Y. Giants 4-2; N.Y. Jets 6-10; Oakland 7-16; Philadelphia 6-3; Pittsburgh 26-35; St. Louis 5-4; San Diego 9-15; San Francisco 2-7; Seattle 7-8; Tampa Bay 3-3; Tennessee 28-35-1; Washington 2-4.

COACHING RECORDS

Paul Brown, 55-56-1 (0-3); Bruce Coslet, 21-39-0; Forrest Gregg, 32-25-0 (2-2); Bill Johnson, 18-15-0; Dick LeBeau, 4-9-0; Homer Rice, 8-19-0; Dave Shula, 19-52-0; Sam Wyche, 61-66-0 (3-2).
NOTE: Playoff games in parentheses.

RETIRED UNIFORM NUMBERS

No.	Player
54	Bob Johnson

CLEVELAND BROWNS
YEAR-BY-YEAR RECORDS

	REGULAR SEASON							PLAYOFFS			
Year	W	L	T	Pct.	PF	PA	Finish	W	L	Highest round	Coach
1946*	12	2	0	.857	423	137	1st/Western Div.	—	—		Paul Brown
1947*	12	1	1	.923	410	185	1st/Western Div.	—	—		Paul Brown
1948*	14	0	0	1.000	389	190	1st/Western Div.	—	—		Paul Brown
1949*	9	1	2	.900	339	171	1st	—	—		Paul Brown
1950	10	2	0	.833	310	144	1st/American Conf.	2	0	NFL champ	Paul Brown
1951	11	1	0	.917	331	152	1st/American Conf.	0	1	NFL championship game	Paul Brown
1952	8	4	0	.667	310	213	1st/American Conf.	0	1	NFL championship game	Paul Brown
1953	11	1	0	.917	348	162	1st/Eastern Conf.	0	1	NFL championship game	Paul Brown
1954	9	3	0	.750	336	162	1st/Eastern Conf.	1	0	NFL champ	Paul Brown
1955	9	2	1	.818	349	218	1st/Eastern Conf.	1	0	NFL champ	Paul Brown
1956	5	7	0	.417	167	177	4th/Eastern Conf.	—	—		Paul Brown
1957	9	2	1	.818	269	172	1st/Eastern Conf.	0	1	NFL championship game	Paul Brown
1958	9	3	0	.750	302	217	1st/Eastern Conf.	0	1	E. Conf. championship game	Paul Brown
1959	7	5	0	.583	270	214	T2nd/Eastern Conf.	—	—		Paul Brown
1960	8	3	1	.727	362	217	2nd/Eastern Conf.	—	—		Paul Brown
1961	8	5	1	.615	319	270	3rd/Eastern Conf.	—	—		Paul Brown
1962	7	6	1	.538	291	257	3rd/Eastern Conf.	—	—		Paul Brown
1963	10	4	0	.714	343	262	2nd/Eastern Conf.	—	—		Blanton Collier
1964	10	3	1	.769	415	293	1st/Eastern Conf.	1	0	NFL champ	Blanton Collier
1965	11	3	0	.786	363	325	1st/Eastern Conf.	0	1	NFL championship game	Blanton Collier
1966	9	5	0	.643	403	259	T2nd/Eastern Conf.	—	—		Blanton Collier
1967	9	5	0	.643	334	297	1st/Century Div.	0	1	E. Conf. championship game	Blanton Collier
1968	10	4	0	.714	394	273	1st/Century Div.	1	1	NFL championship game	Blanton Collier
1969	10	3	1	.769	351	300	1st/Century Div.	1	1	NFL championship game	Blanton Collier
1970	7	7	0	.500	286	265	2nd/AFC Central Div.	—	—		Blanton Collier
1971	9	5	0	.643	285	273	1st/AFC Central Div.	0	1	AFC div. playoff game	Nick Skorich
1972	10	4	0	.714	268	249	2nd/AFC Central Div.	0	1	AFC div. playoff game	Nick Skorich
1973	7	5	2	.571	234	255	3rd/AFC Central Div.	—	—		Nick Skorich
1974	4	10	0	.286	251	344	4th/AFC Central Div.	—	—		Nick Skorich
1975	3	11	0	.214	218	372	4th/AFC Central Div.	—	—		Forrest Gregg
1976	9	5	0	.643	267	287	3rd/AFC Central Div.	—	—		Forrest Gregg
1977	6	8	0	.429	269	267	4th/AFC Central Div.	—	—		F. Gregg, Dick Modzelewski
1978	8	8	0	.500	334	356	3rd/AFC Central Div.	—	—		Sam Rutigliano
1979	9	7	0	.563	359	352	3rd/AFC Central Div.	—	—		Sam Rutigliano
1980	11	5	0	.688	357	310	1st/AFC Central Div.	0	1	AFC div. playoff game	Sam Rutigliano

						REGULAR SEASON			PLAYOFFS		
Year	W	L	T	Pct.	PF	PA	Finish	W	L	Highest round	Coach
1981	5	11	0	.313	276	375	4th/AFC Central Div.	—	—		Sam Rutigliano
1982	4	5	0	.444	140	182	T8th/AFC	0	1	AFC first-round pl. game	Sam Rutigliano
1983	9	7	0	.563	356	342	2nd/AFC Central Div.	—	—		Sam Rutigliano
1984	5	11	0	.313	250	297	3rd/AFC Central Div.	—	—		Rutigliano, Schottenheimer
1985	8	8	0	.500	287	294	1st/AFC Central Div.	0	1	AFC div. playoff game	Marty Schottenheimer
1986	12	4	0	.750	391	310	1st/AFC Central Div.	1	1	AFC championship game	Marty Schottenheimer
1987	10	5	0	.667	390	239	1st/AFC Central Div.	1	1	AFC championship game	Marty Schottenheimer
1988	10	6	0	.625	304	288	T2nd/AFC Central Div.	0	1	AFC wild-card game	Marty Schottenheimer
1989	9	6	1	.594	334	254	1st/AFC Central Div.	1	1	AFC championship game	Bud Carson
1990	3	13	0	.188	228	462	4th/AFC Central Div.	—	—		Bud Carson, Jim Shofner
1991	6	10	0	.375	293	298	3rd/AFC Central Div.	—	—		Bill Belichick
1992	7	9	0	.438	272	275	3rd/AFC Central Div.	—	—		Bill Belichick
1993	7	9	0	.438	304	307	3rd/AFC Central Div.	—	—		Bill Belichick
1994	11	5	0	.688	340	204	2nd/AFC Central Div.	1	1	AFC div. playoff game	Bill Belichick
1995	5	11	0	.313	289	356	4th/AFC Central Div.	—	—		Bill Belichick
1999	2	14	0	.125	217	437	6th/AFC Central Div.	—	—		Chris Palmer
2000	3	13	0	.188	161	419	6th/AFC Central Div.	—	—		Chris Palmer

*All-America Football Conference.

FIRST-ROUND DRAFT PICKS

1950—Ken Carpenter, B, Oregon State
1951—Ken Konz, B, Louisiana State
1952—Bert Rechichar, DB, Tennessee
　　　Harry Agganis, QB, Boston University
1953—Doug Atkins, DT, Tennessee
1954—Bobby Garrett, QB, Stanford*
　　　John Bauer, G, Illinois
1955—Kent Burris, C, Oklahoma
1956—Preston Carpenter, B, Arkansas
1957—Jim Brown, B, Syracuse
1958—Jim Shofner, DB, Texas Christian
1959—Rich Kreitling, DE, Illinois
1960—Jim Houston, DE, Ohio State
1961—None
1962—Gary Collins, WR, Maryland
　　　Leroy Jackson, B, Western Illinois
1963—Tom Hutchinson, TE, Kentucky
1964—Paul Warfield, WR, Ohio State
1965—None
1966—Milt Morin, TE, Massachusetts
1967—Bob Matheson, LB, Duke
1968—M. Upshaw, DE, Trinity (Tex.)
1969—Ron Johnson, RB, Michigan
1970—Mike Phipps, QB, Purdue
　　　Bob McKay, T, Texas
1971—Clarence Scott, DB, Kansas State
1972—Thom Darden, DB, Michigan
1973—Steve Holden, WR, Arizona State
　　　Pete Adams, G, Southern California

1974—None
1975—Mack Mitchell, DE, Houston
1976—Mike Pruitt, RB, Purdue
1977—Robert Jackson, LB, Texas A&M
1978—Clay Matthews, LB, Southern California
　　　Ozzie Newsome, WR, Alabama
1979—Willis Adams, WR, Houston
1980—Charles White, RB, Southern California
1981—Hanford Dixon, CB, Southern Mississippi
1982—Chip Banks, LB, Southern California
1983—None
1984—Don Rogers, DB, UCLA
1985—None
1986—None
1987—Mike Junkin, LB, Duke
1988—Clifford Charlton, LB, Florida
1989—Eric Metcalf, RB, Texas
1990—None
1991—Eric Turner, S, UCLA
1992—Tommy Vardell, FB, Stanford
1993—Steve Everitt, C, Michigan
1994—Antonio Langham, DB, Alabama
　　　Derrick Alexander, WR, Michigan
1995—Craig Powell, LB, Ohio State
1999—Tim Couch, QB, Kentucky*
2000—Courtney Brown, DE, Penn State*
2001—Gerard Warren, DT, Florida
　　　*First player chosen in draft.

FRANCHISE RECORDS

Most rushing yards, career
12,312—Jim Brown
Most rushing yards, season
1,863—Jim Brown, 1963
Most rushing yards, game
237—Jim Brown vs. L.A., Nov. 24, 1957
　　　Jim Brown vs. Phi., Nov. 19, 1961
Most rushing touchdowns, season
17— Jim Brown, 1958
　　　Jim Brown, 1965
Most passing attempts, season
567—Brian Sipe, 1981
Most passing attempts, game
57—Brian Sipe vs. S.D., Sept. 7, 1981
Most passes completed, season
337—Brian Sipe, 1980

Most passes completed, game
33—Brian Sipe vs. S.D., Dec. 5, 1982
Most passing yards, career
23,713—Brian Sipe
Most passing yards, season
4,132—Brian Sipe, 1980
Most passing yards, game
444—Brian Sipe vs. Bal., Oct. 25, 1981
Most touchdown passes, season
30—Brian Sipe, 1980
Most pass receptions, career
662—Ozzie Newsome
Most pass receptions, season
89—Ozzie Newsome, 1983
　　　Ozzie Newsome, 1984

Most pass receptions, game
14—Ozzie Newsome vs. NYJ, Oct. 14, 1984
Most receiving yards, career
7,980—Ozzie Newsome
Most receiving yards, season
1,236—Webster Slaughter, 1989
Most receiving yards, game
191—Ozzie Newsome vs. NYJ, Oct. 14, 1984
Most receiving touchdowns, season
13—Gary Collins, 1963
Most touchdowns, career
126—Jim Brown
Most field goals, season
29—Matt Stover, 1995

Longest field goal
60 yards—Steve Cox at Cin., Oct. 21, 1984
Most interceptions, career
45—Thom Darden

Most interceptions, season
10—Thom Darden, 1978
Most sacks, career
63.5—Clay Matthews

Most sacks, season
14.5—Bill Glass, 1965

SERIES RECORDS

Cleveland vs.: Arizona 32-11-3; Atlanta 8-2; Baltimore 0-4; Buffalo 7-4; Carolina 0-1; Chicago 8-3; Cincinnati 28-27; Dallas 15-9; Denver 5-14; Detroit 3-12; Green Bay 6-8; Indianapolis 13-8; Jacksonville 0-6; Kansas City 8-7-2; Miami 4-6; Minnesota 3-8; New England 11-5; New Orleans 10-3; N.Y. Giants 25-18-2; N.Y. Jets 9-6; Oakland 3-10; Philadelphia 31-13-1; Pittsburgh 54-42; St. Louis 8-8; San Diego 6-10-1; San Francisco 9-6; Seattle 4-9; Tampa Bay 5-0; Tennessee 30-25; Washington 32-9-1.

COACHING RECORDS

Bill Belichick, 36-44 (1-1); Paul Brown, 158-48-8 (4-5); Bud Carson, 11-12-1 (1-1); Blanton Collier, 76-34-2 (3-4); Forrest Gregg (18-23); Dick Modzelewski, 0-1; Chris Palmer, 5-27-0; Sam Rutigliano, 47-50 (0-2); Marty Schottenheimer, 44-27 (2-4); Jim Shofner, 1-7; Nick Skorich, 30-24-2 (0-2).
NOTE: Playoff games in parentheses.

RETIRED UNIFORM NUMBERS

No.	Player
14	Otto Graham
32	Jim Brown
45	Ernie Davis
46	Don Fleming
76	Lou Groza

DALLAS COWBOYS
YEAR-BY-YEAR RECORDS

		REGULAR SEASON						PLAYOFFS			
Year	W	L	T	Pct.	PF	PA	Finish	W	L	Highest round	Coach
1960	0	11	1	.000	177	369	7th/Western Conf.	—	—		Tom Landry
1961	4	9	1	.308	236	380	6th/Eastern Conf.	—	—		Tom Landry
1962	5	8	1	.385	398	402	5th/Eastern Conf.	—	—		Tom Landry
1963	4	10	0	.286	305	378	5th/Eastern Conf.	—	—		Tom Landry
1964	5	8	1	.385	250	289	5th/Eastern Conf.	—	—		Tom Landry
1965	7	7	0	.500	325	280	T2nd/Eastern Conf.	—	—		Tom Landry
1966	10	3	1	.769	445	239	1st/Eastern Conf.	0	1	NFL championship game	Tom Landry
1967	9	5	0	.643	342	268	1st/Capitol Div.	1	1	NFL championship game	Tom Landry
1968	12	2	0	.857	431	186	1st/Capitol Div.	0	1	E. Conf. championship game	Tom Landry
1969	11	2	1	.846	369	223	1st/Capitol Div.	0	1	E. Conf. championship game	Tom Landry
1970	10	4	0	.714	299	221	1st/NFC Eastern Div.	2	1	Super Bowl	Tom Landry
1971	11	3	0	.786	406	222	1st/NFC Eastern Div.	3	0	Super Bowl champ	Tom Landry
1972	10	4	0	.714	319	240	2nd/NFC Eastern Div.	1	1	NFC championship game	Tom Landry
1973	10	4	0	.714	382	203	1st/NFC Eastern Div.	1	1	NFC championship game	Tom Landry
1974	8	6	0	.571	297	235	3rd/NFC Eastern Div.	—	—		Tom Landry
1975	10	4	0	.714	350	268	2nd/NFC Eastern Div.	2	1	Super Bowl	Tom Landry
1976	11	3	0	.786	296	194	1st/NFC Eastern Div.	0	1	NFC div. playoff game	Tom Landry
1977	12	2	0	.857	345	212	1st/NFC Eastern Div.	3	0	Super Bowl champ	Tom Landry
1978	12	4	0	.750	384	208	1st/NFC Eastern Div.	2	1	Super Bowl	Tom Landry
1979	11	5	0	.688	371	313	1st/NFC Eastern Div.	0	1	NFC div. playoff game	Tom Landry
1980	12	4	0	.750	454	311	2nd/NFC Eastern Div.	2	1	NFC championship game	Tom Landry
1981	12	4	0	.750	367	277	1st/NFC Eastern Div.	1	1	NFC championship game	Tom Landry
1982	6	3	0	.667	226	145	2nd/NFC	2	1	NFC championship game	Tom Landry
1983	12	4	0	.750	479	360	2nd/NFC Eastern Div.	0	1	NFC wild-card game	Tom Landry
1984	9	7	0	.563	308	308	T3rd/NFC Eastern Div.	—	—		Tom Landry
1985	10	6	0	.625	357	333	1st/NFC Eastern Div.	0	1	NFC div. playoff game	Tom Landry
1986	7	9	0	.438	346	337	3rd/NFC Eastern Div.	—	—		Tom Landry
1987	7	8	0	.467	340	348	T2nd/NFC Eastern Div.	—	—		Tom Landry
1988	3	13	0	.188	265	381	5th/NFC Eastern Div.	—	—		Tom Landry
1989	1	15	0	.063	204	393	5th/NFC Eastern Div.	—	—		Jimmy Johnson
1990	7	9	0	.438	244	308	4th/NFC Eastern Div.	—	—		Jimmy Johnson
1991	11	5	0	.688	342	310	2nd/NFC Eastern Div.	1	1	NFC div. playoff game	Jimmy Johnson
1992	13	3	0	.813	409	243	1st/NFC Eastern Div.	3	0	Super Bowl champ	Jimmy Johnson
1993	12	4	0	.750	376	229	1st/NFC Eastern Div.	3	0	Super Bowl champ	Jimmy Johnson
1994	12	4	0	.750	414	248	1st/NFC Eastern Div.	1	1	NFC championship game	Barry Switzer
1995	12	4	0	.750	435	291	1st/NFC Eastern Div.	3	0	Super Bowl champ	Barry Switzer
1996	10	6	0	.625	286	250	1st/NFC Eastern Div.	1	1	NFC div. playoff game	Barry Switzer
1997	6	10	0	.375	304	314	4th/NFC Eastern Div.	—	—		Barry Switzer
1998	10	6	0	.625	381	275	1st/NFC Eastern Div.	0	1	NFC wild-card game	Chan Gailey
1999	8	8	0	.500	352	276	2nd/NFC Eastern Div.	0	1	NFC wild-card game	Chan Gailey
2000	5	11	0	.313	294	361	4th/NFC Eastern Div.	—	—		Dave Campo

FIRST-ROUND DRAFT PICKS

1961—Bob Lilly, DT, Texas Christian
1962—None
1963—Lee Roy Jordan, LB, Alabama
1964—Scott Appleton, DT, Texas
1965—Craig Morton, QB, California
1966—John Niland, G, Iowa
1967—None
1968—Dennis Homan, WR, Alabama
1969—Calvin Hill, RB, Yale
1970—Duane Thomas, RB, West Texas State
1971—Tody Smith, DE, Southern California
1972—Bill Thomas, RB, Boston College
1973—Billy Joe DuPree, TE, Michigan State
1974—Ed Jones, DE, Tennessee State*
    Charles Young, RB, North Carolina State
1975—Randy White, LB, Maryland
    Thomas Henderson, LB, Langston
1976—Aaron Kyle, DB, Wyoming
1977—Tony Dorsett, RB, Pittsburgh
1978—Larry Bethea, DE, Michigan State
1979—Robert Shaw, C, Tennessee
1980—None
1981—Howard Richards, T, Missouri
1982—Rod Hill, DB, Kentucky State

1983—Jim Jeffcoat, DE, Arizona State
1984—Billy Cannon Jr., LB, Texas A&M
1985—Kevin Brooks, DE, Michigan
1986—Mike Sherrard, WR, UCLA
1987—Danny Noonan, DT, Nebraska
1988—Michael Irvin, WR, Miami, Fla.
1989—Troy Aikman, QB, UCLA*
1990—Emmitt Smith, RB, Florida
1991—Russell Maryland, DL, Miami, Fla.*
    Alvin Harper, WR, Tennessee
    Kelvin Pritchett, DT, Mississippi
1992—Kevin Smith, DB, Texas A&M
    Robert Jones, LB, East Carolina
1993—None
1994—Shante Carver, DE, Arizona State
1995—None
1996—None
1997—David LaFleur, TE, Louisiana State
1998—Greg Ellis, DE, North Carolina
1999—Ebenezer Ekuban, DE, North Carolina
2000—None
2001—None
    *First player chosen in draft.

FRANCHISE RECORDS

Most rushing yards, career
15,166—Emmitt Smith

Most rushing yards, season
1,773—Emmitt Smith, 1995

Most rushing yards, game
237—Emmitt Smith at Phi., Oct. 31, 1993

Most rushing touchdowns, season
25—Emmitt Smith, 1995

Most passing attempts, season
533—Danny White, 1983

Most passing attempts, game
57—Troy Aikman vs. Min., Nov. 26, 1998

Most passes completed, season
334—Danny White, 1983

Most passes completed, game
34—Troy Aikman at NYG, Oct. 5, 1997
    Troy Aikman vs. Min., Nov. 26, 1998

Most passing yards, career
32,942—Troy Aikman

Most passing yards, season
3,980—Danny White, 1983

Most passing yards, game
460—Don Meredith at S.F., Nov. 10, 1963

Most touchdown passes, season
29—Danny White, 1983

Most pass receptions, career
750—Michael Irvin

Most pass receptions, season
111—Michael Irvin, 1995

Most pass receptions, game
13—Lance Rentzel vs. Was., Nov. 19, 1967

Most receiving yards, career
11,904—Michael Irvin

Most receiving yards, season
1,603—Michael Irvin, 1995

Most receiving yards, game
246—Bob Hayes at Was., Nov. 13, 1966

Most receiving touchdowns, season
14—Frank Clarke, 1962

Most touchdowns, career
156—Emmitt Smith

Most field goals, season
34—Richie Cunningham, 1997

Longest field goal
54 yards—Toni Fritsch at NYG,
    Sept. 24, 1972
    Ken Willis at Cle., Sept. 1, 1991
    Richie Cunningham at Den., Sept.
    13, 1998

Most interceptions, career
52—Mel Renfro

Most interceptions, season
11—Everson Walls, 1981

Most sacks, career
114—Harvey Martin

Most sacks, season
20—Harvey Martin, 1977

SERIES RECORDS

Dallas vs.: Arizona 51-25-1; Atlanta 12-6; Baltimore 0-1; Buffalo 3-3; Carolina 2-1; Chicago 9-8; Cincinnati 5-3; Cleveland 9-15; Denver 4-3; Detroit 7-6; Green Bay 9-10; Indianapolis 7-4; Jacksonville 1-1; Kansas City 4-3; Miami 3-6; Minnesota 9-9; New England 7-1; New Orleans 14-5; N.Y. Giants 47-28-2; N.Y. Jets 5-2; Oakland 3-4; Philadelphia 48-32; Pittsburgh 14-11; St. Louis 8-9; San Diego 5-1; San Francisco 7-13-1; Seattle 5-1; Tampa Bay 6-1; Tennessee 5-5; Washington 47-31-2.

COACHING RECORDS

Dave Campo, 5-11-0; Chan Gailey, 18-14-0 (0-2); Jimmy Johnson, 44-36-0 (7-1); Tom Landry, 250-162-6 (20-16); Barry Switzer, 40-24-0 (5-2).
NOTE: Playoff games in parentheses.

RETIRED UNIFORM NUMBERS

No.	Player
	None

DENVER BRONCOS
YEAR-BY-YEAR RECORDS

	REGULAR SEASON						PLAYOFFS			
Year	W	L	T	Pct.	PF	PA	Finish	W	L	Highest round	Coach
1960*	4	9	1	.308	309	393	4th/Western Div.	—	—		Frank Filchock
1961*	3	11	0	.214	251	432	3rd/Western Div.	—	—		Frank Filchock
1962*	7	7	0	.500	353	334	2nd/Western Div.	—	—		Jack Faulkner
1963*	2	11	1	.154	301	473	4th/Western Div.	—	—		Jack Faulkner
1964*	2	11	1	.154	240	438	4th/Western Div.	—	—		J. Faulkner, M. Speedie
1965*	4	10	0	.286	303	392	4th/Western Div.	—	—		Mac Speedie
1966*	4	10	0	.286	196	381	4th/Western Div.	—	—		M. Speedie, Ray Malavasi
1967*	3	11	0	.214	256	409	4th/Western Div.	—	—		Lou Saban
1968*	5	9	0	.357	255	404	4th/Western Div.	—	—		Lou Saban
1969*	5	8	1	.385	297	344	4th/Western Div.	—	—		Lou Saban
1970	5	8	1	.385	253	264	4th/AFC Western Div.	—	—		Lou Saban
1971	4	9	1	.308	203	275	4th/AFC Western Div.	—	—		Lou Saban, Jerry Smith
1972	5	9	0	.357	325	350	3rd/AFC Western Div.	—	—		John Ralston
1973	7	5	2	.571	354	296	T2nd/AFC Western Div.	—	—		John Ralston
1974	7	6	1	.536	302	294	2nd/AFC Western Div.	—	—		John Ralston
1975	6	8	0	.429	254	307	2nd/AFC Western Div.	—	—		John Ralston
1976	9	5	0	.643	315	206	2nd/AFC Western Div.	—	—		John Ralston
1977	12	2	0	.857	274	148	1st/AFC Western Div.	2	1	Super Bowl	Red Miller
1978	10	6	0	.625	282	198	1st/AFC Western Div.	0	1	AFC div. playoff game	Red Miller
1979	10	6	0	.625	289	262	2nd/AFC Western Div.	0	1	AFC wild-card game	Red Miller
1980	8	8	0	.500	310	323	T3rd/AFC Western Div.	—	—		Red Miller
1981	10	6	0	.625	321	289	2nd/AFC Western Div.	—	—		Dan Reeves
1982	2	7	0	.222	148	226	12th/AFC	—	—		Dan Reeves
1983	9	7	0	.563	302	327	T2nd/AFC Western Div.	0	1	AFC wild-card game	Dan Reeves
1984	13	3	0	.813	353	241	1st/AFC Western Div.	0	1	AFC div. playoff game	Dan Reeves
1985	11	5	0	.688	380	329	2nd/AFC Western Div.	—	—		Dan Reeves
1986	11	5	0	.688	378	327	1st/AFC Western Div.	2	1	Super Bowl	Dan Reeves
1987	10	4	1	.700	379	288	1st/AFC Western Div.	2	1	Super Bowl	Dan Reeves
1988	8	8	0	.500	327	352	2nd/AFC Western Div.	—	—		Dan Reeves
1989	11	5	0	.688	362	226	1st/AFC Western Div.	2	1	Super Bowl	Dan Reeves
1990	5	11	0	.313	331	374	5th/AFC Western Div.	—	—		Dan Reeves
1991	12	4	0	.750	304	235	1st/AFC Western Div.	1	1	AFC championship game	Dan Reeves
1992	8	8	0	.500	262	329	3rd/AFC Western Div.	—	—		Dan Reeves
1993	9	7	0	.563	373	284	3rd/AFC Western Div.	0	1	AFC wild-card game	Wade Phillips
1994	7	9	0	.438	347	396	4th/AFC Western Div.	—	—		Wade Phillips
1995	8	8	0	.500	388	345	T3rd/AFC Western Div.	—	—		Mike Shanahan
1996	13	3	0	.813	391	275	1st/AFC Western Div.	0	1	AFC div. playoff game	Mike Shanahan
1997	12	4	0	.750	472	287	2nd/AFC Western Div.	4	0	Super Bowl champ	Mike Shanahan
1998	14	2	0	.875	501	309	1st/AFC Western Div.	3	0	Super Bowl champ	Mike Shanahan
1999	6	10	0	.375	314	318	5th/AFC Western Div.	—	—		Mike Shanahan
2000	11	5	0	.688	485	369	2nd/AFC Western Div.	0	1	AFC wild-card game	Mike Shanahan

*American Football League.

FIRST-ROUND DRAFT PICKS

1960—Roger Leclerc, C, Trinity (Conn.)
1961—Bob Gaiters, RB, New Mexico State
1962—Merlin Olsen, DT, Utah State
1963—Kermit Alexander, DB, UCLA
1964—Bob Brown, T, Nebraska
1965—None
1966—Jerry Shay, DT, Purdue
1967—Floyd Little, RB, Syracuse
1968—None
1969—None
1970—Bob Anderson, RB, Colorado
1971—Marv Montgomery, T, Southern California
1972—Riley Odoms, TE, Houston
1973—Otis Armstrong, RB, Purdue
1974—Randy Gradishar, LB, Ohio State
1975—Louis Wright, DB, San Jose State
1976—Tom Glassic, G, Virginia
1977—Steve Schindler, G, Boston College
1978—Don Latimer, DT, Miami, Fla.
1979—Kevin Clark, T, Nebraska
1980—None

1981—Dennis Smith, DB, Southern California
1982—Gerald Willhite, RB, San Jose State
1983—Chris Hinton, G, Northwestern
1984—None
1985—Steve Sewell, RB, Oklahoma
1986—None
1987—Ricky Nattiel, WR, Florida
1988—Ted Gregory, DT, Syracuse
1989—Steve Atwater, DB, Arkansas
1990—None
1991—Mike Croel, LB, Nebraska
1992—Tommy Maddox, QB, UCLA
1993—Dan Williams, DE, Toledo
1994—None
1995—None
1996—John Mobley, LB, Kutztown (Pa.)
1997—Trevor Pryce, DT, Clemson
1998—Marcus Nash, WR, Tennessee
1999—Al Wilson, LB, Tennessee
2000—Deltha O'Neal, DB, California
2001—Willie Middlebrooks, DB, Minnesota

FRANCHISE RECORDS

Most rushing yards, career
6,906—Terrell Davis
Most rushing yards, season
2,008—Terrell Davis, 1998
Most rushing yards, game
251—Mike Anderson at N.O., Dec. 3, 2000
Most rushing touchdowns, season
21—Terrell Davis, 1998
Most passing attempts, season
605—John Elway, 1985
Most passing attempts, game
59—John Elway at G.B., Oct. 10, 1993
Most passes completed, season
348—John Elway, 1993
Most passes completed, game
36—John Elway vs. S.D., Sept. 4, 1994
Gus Frerotte vs. S.D., Nov. 19, 2000
Most passing yards, career
51,475—John Elway
Most passing yards, season
4,030—John Elway, 1993

Most passing yards, game
462—Gus Frerotte vs. S.D., Nov. 19, 2000
Most touchdown passes, season
27—John Elway, 1997
Most pass receptions, career
552—Shannon Sharpe
Most pass receptions, season
101—Ed McCaffrey, 2000
Most pass receptions, game
13—Lionel Taylor vs. Oak., Nov. 29, 1964
Robert Anderson vs. Chi., Sept. 30, 1973
Shannon Sharpe vs. S.D., Oct. 6, 1996
Rod Smith vs. N.E., Oct. 1, 2000
Most receiving yards, career
6,983—Shannon Sharpe
Most receiving yards, season
1,602—Rod Smith, 2000
Most receiving yards, game
199—Lionel Taylor vs. Buf., Nov. 27, 1960

Most receiving touchdowns, season
13—Steve Watson, 1981
Most touchdowns, career
63—Terrell Davis
Most field goals, season
31—Jason Elam, 1995
Longest field goal
63 yards—Jason Elam vs. Jac., Oct. 25, 1998
Most interceptions, career
44—Steve Foley
Most interceptions, season
11—Goose Gonsoulin, 1960
Most sacks, career
97.5—Simon Fletcher
Most sacks, season
16—Simon Fletcher, 1992

SERIES RECORDS

Denver vs.: Arizona 4-0-1; Atlanta 7-3; Baltimore 1-0; Buffalo 12-17-1; Carolina 1-0; Chicago 6-5; Cincinnati 14-7; Cleveland 14-5; Dallas 3-4; Detroit 5-3; Green Bay 5-3-1; Indianapolis 9-2; Jacksonville 2-1; Kansas City 34-47; Miami 2-7-1; Minnesota 4-6; New England 20-14; New Orleans 5-2; N.Y. Giants 3-4; N.Y. Jets 14-13-1; Oakland 30-49-2; Philadelphia 3-6; Pittsburgh 10-6-1; San Diego 45-36-1; St. Louis 4-5; San Francisco 5-4; Seattle 31-16; Tampa Bay 3-2; Tennessee 11-20-1; Washington 5-3.

COACHING RECORDS

Jack Faulkner, 9-22-1; Frank Filchock, 7-20-1; Ray Malavasi, 4-8-0; Red Miller, 40-22 (2-3); Wade Phillips, 16-16-0 (0-1); John Ralston, 34-33-3; Dan Reeves, 110-73-1 (7-6); Lou Saban, 20-42-3; Mike Shanahan, 64-32-0 (7-2); Jerry Smith, 2-3; Mac Speedie, 6-19-1.
NOTE: Playoff games in parentheses.

RETIRED UNIFORM NUMBERS

No.	Player
7	John Elway
18	Frank Tripucka
44	Floyd Little

DETROIT LIONS

YEAR-BY-YEAR RECORDS

Year	W	L	T	Pct.	PF	PA	Finish	W	L	Highest round	Coach
				REGULAR SEASON					PLAYOFFS		
1930*	5	6	3	.455	...	...	T7th				Tubby Griffen
1931*	11	3	0	.786	...	...	2nd				Potsy Clark
1932*	6	2	4	.750	...	...	3rd				Potsy Clark
1933*	6	5	0	.545	128	87	2nd/Western Div.	—	—		Potsy Clark
1934	10	3	0	.769	238	59	2nd/Western Div.	—	—		Potsy Clark
1935	7	3	2	.700	191	111	1st/Western Div.	1	0	NFL champ	Potsy Clark
1936	8	4	0	.667	235	102	3rd/Western Div.	—	—		Potsy Clark
1937	7	4	0	.636	180	105	T2nd/Western Div.	—	—		Dutch Clark
1938	7	4	0	.636	119	108	2nd/Western Div.	—	—		Dutch Clark
1939	6	5	0	.545	145	150	3rd/Western Div.	—	—		Gus Henderson
1940	5	5	1	.500	138	153	3rd/Western Div.	—	—		Potsy Clark
1941	4	6	1	.400	121	195	3rd/Western Div.	—	—		Bill Edwards
1942	0	11	0	.000	38	263	5th/Western Div.	—	—		B. Edwards, John Karcis
1943	3	6	1	.333	178	218	3rd/Western Div.	—	—		Gus Dorais
1944	6	3	1	.667	216	151	T2nd/Western Div.	—	—		Gus Dorais
1945	7	3	0	.700	195	194	2nd/Western Div.	—	—		Gus Dorais
1946	1	10	0	.091	142	310	2nd/Western Div.	—	—		Gus Dorais
1947	3	9	0	.250	231	305	5th/Western Div.	—	—		Gus Dorais
1948	2	10	0	.167	200	407	5th/Western Div.	—	—		Bo McMillin
1949	4	8	0	.333	237	259	4th/Western Div.	—	—		Bo McMillin
1950	6	6	0	.500	321	285	4th/National Conf.	—	—		Bo McMillin
1951	7	4	1	.636	336	259	T2nd/National Conf.	—	—		Buddy Parker
1952	9	3	0	.750	344	192	1st/National Conf.	2	0	NFL champ	Buddy Parker
1953	10	2	0	.833	271	205	1st/Western Conf.	1	0	NFL champ	Buddy Parker
1954	9	2	1	.818	337	189	1st/Western Conf.	0	1	NFL championship game	Buddy Parker

	REGULAR SEASON							PLAYOFFS			
Year	W	L	T	Pct.	PF	PA	Finish	W	L	Highest round	Coach
1955	3	9	0	.250	230	275	6th/Western Conf.	—	—		Buddy Parker
1956	9	3	0	.750	300	188	2nd/Western Conf.	—	—		Buddy Parker
1957	8	4	0	.667	251	231	1st/Western Conf.	2	0	NFL champ	George Wilson
1958	4	7	1	.364	261	276	5th/Western Conf.	—	—		George Wilson
1959	3	8	1	.273	203	275	5th/Western Conf.	—	—		George Wilson
1960	7	5	0	.583	239	212	T2nd/Western Conf.	—	—		George Wilson
1961	8	5	1	.615	270	258	2nd/Western Conf.	—	—		George Wilson
1962	11	3	0	.786	315	177	2nd/Western Conf.	—	—		George Wilson
1963	5	8	1	.385	326	265	T4th/Western Conf.	—	—		George Wilson
1964	7	5	2	.583	280	260	4th/Western Conf.	—	—		George Wilson
1965	6	7	1	.462	257	295	6th/Western Conf.	—	—		Harry Gilmer
1966	4	9	1	.308	206	317	T6th/Western Conf.	—	—		Harry Gilmer
1967	5	7	2	.417	260	259	3rd/Central Div.	—	—		Joe Schmidt
1968	4	8	2	.333	207	241	4th/Central Div.	—	—		Joe Schmidt
1969	9	4	1	.692	259	188	2nd/Central Div.	—	—		Joe Schmidt
1970	10	4	0	.714	347	202	2nd/NFC Central Div.	0	1	NFC div. playoff game	Joe Schmidt
1971	7	6	1	.538	341	286	2nd/NFC Central Div.	—	—		Joe Schmidt
1972	8	5	1	.607	339	290	2nd/NFC Central Div.	—	—		Joe Schmidt
1973	6	7	1	.464	271	247	2nd/NFC Central Div.	—	—		Don McCafferty
1974	7	7	0	.500	256	270	2nd/NFC Central Div.	—	—		Rick Forzano
1975	7	7	0	.500	245	262	2nd/NFC Central Div.	—	—		Rick Forzano
1976	6	8	0	.429	262	220	3rd/NFC Central Div.	—	—		R. Forzano, T. Hudspeth
1977	6	8	0	.429	183	252	3rd/NFC Central Div.	—	—		Tommy Hudspeth
1978	7	9	0	.438	290	300	T3rd/NFC Central Div.	—	—		Monte Clark
1979	2	14	0	.125	219	365	5th/NFC Central Div.	—	—		Monte Clark
1980	9	7	0	.563	334	272	2nd/NFC Central Div.	—	—		Monte Clark
1981	8	8	0	.500	397	322	2nd/NFC Central Div.	—	—		Monte Clark
1982	4	5	0	.444	181	176	T8th/NFC	0	1	NFC first-round pl. game	Monte Clark
1983	9	7	0	.563	347	286	1st/NFC Central Div.	0	1	NFC div. playoff game	Monte Clark
1984	4	11	1	.281	283	408	4th/NFC Central Div.	—	—		Monte Clark
1985	7	9	0	.438	307	366	T3rd/NFC Central Div.	—	—		Darryl Rogers
1986	5	11	0	.313	277	326	3rd/NFC Central Div.	—	—		Darryl Rogers
1987	4	11	0	.267	269	384	T4th/NFC Central Div.	—	—		Darryl Rogers
1988	4	12	0	.250	220	313	T4th/NFC Central Div.	—	—		Darryl Rogers
1989	7	9	0	.438	312	364	3rd/NFC Central Div.	—	—		Wayne Fontes
1990	6	10	0	.375	373	413	T2nd/NFC Central Div.	—	—		Wayne Fontes
1991	12	4	0	.750	339	295	1st/NFC Central Div.	1	1	NFC championship game	Wayne Fontes
1992	5	11	0	.313	273	332	T3rd/NFC Central Div.	—	—		Wayne Fontes
1993	10	6	0	.625	298	292	1st/NFC Central Div.	0	1	NFC wild-card game	Wayne Fontes
1994	9	7	0	.563	357	342	T2nd/NFC Central Div.	0	1	NFC wild-card game	Wayne Fontes
1995	10	6	0	.625	436	336	2nd/NFC Central Div.	0	1	NFC wild-card game	Wayne Fontes
1996	5	11	0	.313	302	368	5th/NFC Central Div.	—	—		Wayne Fontes
1997	9	7	0	.563	379	306	T3rd/NFC Central Div.	0	1	NFC wild-card game	Bobby Ross
1998	5	11	0	.313	306	378	4th/NFC Central Div.	—	—		Bobby Ross
1999	8	8	0	.500	322	323	3rd/NFC Central Div.	0	1	NFC wild-card game	Bobby Ross
2000	9	7	0	.563	307	307	4th/NFC Central Div.	—	—		B. Ross, Gary Moeller

*Portsmouth Spartans.

FIRST-ROUND DRAFT PICKS

1936—Sid Wagner, G, Michigan State
1937—Lloyd Cardwell, B, Nebraska
1938—Alex Wojciechowicz, C, Fordham
1939—John Pingel, B, Michigan State
1940—Doyle Nave, B, Southern California
1941—Jim Thomason, B, Texas A&M
1942—Bob Westfall, B, Michigan
1943—Frank Sinkwich, B, Georgia*
1944—Otto Graham, B, Northwestern
1945—Frank Szymanski, B, Notre Dame
1946—Bill Dellastatious, B, Missouri
1947—Glenn Davis, B, Army
1948—Y.A. Tittle, B, Louisiana State
1949—John Rauch, B, Georgia
1950—Leon Hart, E, Notre Dame*
    Joe Watson, C, Rice
1951—None
1952—None
1953—Harley Sewell, G, Texas
1954—Dick Chapman, T, Rice

1955—Dave Middleton, B, Auburn
1956—Howard Cassidy, B, Ohio State
1957—Bill Glass, G, Baylor
1958—Alex Karras, DT, Iowa
1959—Nick Pietrosante, B, Notre Dame
1960—John Robinson, DB, Louisiana State
1961—None
1962—John Hadl, QB, Kansas
1963—Daryl Sanders, T, Ohio State
1964—Pete Beathard, QB, Southern California
1965—Tom Nowatzke, RB, Indiana
1966—None
1967—Mel Farr, RB, UCLA
1968—Greg Landry, QB, Massachusetts
    Earl McCullouch, E, Southern California
1969—None
1970—Steve Owens, RB, Oklahoma
1971—Bob Bell, DT, Cincinnati
1972—Herb Orvis, DE, Colorado
1973—Ernie Price, DE, Texas A&I

1974—Ed O'Neil, LB, Penn State
1975—Lynn Boden, G, South Dakota State
1976—James Hunter, DB, Grambling State
      Lawrence Gaines, FB, Wyoming
1977—None
1978—Luther Bradley, DB, Notre Dame
1979—Keith Dorney, T, Penn State
1980—Billy Sims, RB, Oklahoma*
1981—Mark Nichols, WR, San Jose State
1982—Jimmy Williams, LB, Nebraska
1983—James Jones, RB, Florida
1984—David Lewis, TE, California
1985—Lomas Brown, T, Florida
1986—Chuck Long, QB, Iowa
1987—Reggie Rogers, DE, Washington
1988—Bennie Blades, S, Miami, Fla.

1989—Barry Sanders, RB, Oklahoma State
1990—Andre Ware, QB, Houston
1991—Herman Moore, WR, Virginia
1992—Robert Porcher, DE, South Carolina State
1993—None
1994—Johnnie Morton, WR, Southern California
1995—Luther Elliss, DT, Utah
1996—Reggie Brown, LB, Texas A&M
      Jeff Hartings, G, Penn State
1997—Bryant Westbrook, DB, Texas
1998—Terry Fair, DB, Tennessee
1999—Chris Claiborne, LB, Southern California
      Aaron Gibson, T, Wisconsin
2000—Stockar McDougle, T, Oklahoma
2001—Jeff Backus, T, Michigan
    *First player chosen in draft.

FRANCHISE RECORDS

Most rushing yards, career
15,269—Barry Sanders
Most rushing yards, season
2,053—Barry Sanders, 1997
Most rushing yards, game
237—Barry Sanders vs. T.B., Nov. 13, 1994
Most rushing touchdowns, season
16—Barry Sanders, 1991
Most passing attempts, season
583—Scott Mitchell, 1995
Most passing attempts, game
50—Eric Hipple at L.A. Rams, Oct. 19, 1986
    Scott Mitchell at Was., Oct. 22, 1995
    Scott Mitchell at Atl., Nov. 5, 1995
    Scott Mitchell at Oak., Oct. 13, 1996
    Scott Mitchell vs. T.B., Sept. 7, 1997
Most passes completed, season
346—Scott Mitchell, 1995
Most passes completed, game
33—Eric Hipple at Cle., Sept. 28, 1986
    Chuck Long vs. G.B., Oct. 25, 1987

Most passing yards, career
15,710—Bobby Layne
Most passing yards, season
4,338—Scott Mitchell, 1995
Most passing yards, game
410—Scott Mitchell vs. Min., Nov. 23, 1995
Most touchdown passes, season
32—Scott Mitchell, 1995
Most pass receptions, career
666—Herman Moore
Most pass receptions, season
123—Herman Moore, 1995
Most pass receptions, game
14—Herman Moore vs. Chi., Dec. 4, 1995
Most receiving yards, career
9,098—Herman Moore
Most receiving yards, season
1,686—Herman Moore, 1995
Most receiving yards, game
302—Cloyce Box vs. Bal., Dec. 3, 1950

Most receiving touchdowns, season
15—Cloyce Box, 1952
Most touchdowns, career
109—Barry Sanders
Most field goals, season
34—Jason Hanson, 1993
Longest field goal
56 yards—Jason Hanson vs. Cle., Oct. 8, 1995
Most interceptions, career
62—Dick LeBeau
Most interceptions, season
12—Don Doll, 1950
    Jack Christiansen, 1953
Most sacks, career
75.5—Al Baker
Most sacks, season
23—Al Baker, 1978

SERIES RECORDS

Detroit vs.: Arizona 28-17-3; Atlanta 21-7; Baltimore 0-1; Buffalo 3-2-1; Carolina 1-0; Chicago 56-74-3; Cincinnati 3-4; Cleveland 12-3; Dallas 6-7; Denver 3-5; Green Bay 60-69-6; Indianapolis 19-18-2; Jacksonville 1-1; Kansas City 3-6; Miami 2-5; Minnesota 28-49-2; New England 4-3; New Orleans 7-8-1; N.Y. Giants 15-14-1; N.Y. Jets 6-3; Oakland 2-6; Philadelphia 11-11-2; Pittsburgh 14-12-1; St. Louis 28-32-1; San Diego 3-4; San Francisco 26-29-1; Seattle 4-4; Tampa Bay 26-20; Tennessee 3-4; Washington 5-24.
NOTE: Includes records only from 1934 to present.

COACHING RECORDS

Dutch Clark, 14-8-0; Monte Clark, 43-61-1 (0-2); Potsy Clark, 53-25-7 (1-0); Gus Dorais, 20-31-2; Bill Edwards, 4-9-1; Wayne Fontes, 66-67-0 (1-4); Rick Forzano, 15-17-0; Harry Gilmer, 10-16-2; Hal Griffen, 5-6-3; Elmer Henderson, 6-5-0; Tommy Hudspeth, 11-13-0; John Karcis, 0-8-0; Don McCafferty, 6-7-1; Alvin McMillin, 12-24-0; Gary Moeller, 4-3-0; Buddy Parker, 47-23-2 (3-1); Darryl Rogers, 18-40-0; Bobby Ross, 27-30-0 (0-2); Joe Schmidt, 43-34-7 (0-1); George Wilson, 53-45-6 (2-0).
NOTE: Playoff games in parentheses.

RETIRED UNIFORM NUMBERS

No.	Player
7	Dutch Clark
22	Bobby Layne
37	Doak Walker
56	Joe Schmidt
85	Chuck Hughes
88	Charlie Sanders

GREEN BAY PACKERS
YEAR-BY-YEAR RECORDS

	REGULAR SEASON							PLAYOFFS			
Year	W	L	T	Pct.	PF	PA	Finish	W	L	Highest round	Coach
1921	3	2	1	.600	...	...	T6th				Curly Lambeau
1922	4	3	3	.571	...	...	T7th				Curly Lambeau
1923	7	2	1	.778	...	...	3rd				Curly Lambeau
1924	7	4	0	.636	...	...	6th				Curly Lambeau

Year	W	L	T	Pct.	PF	PA	Finish	W	L	Highest round	Coach
							REGULAR SEASON			**PLAYOFFS**	
1925	8	5	0	.615	...	...	9th				Curly Lambeau
1926	7	3	3	.700	...	...	5th				Curly Lambeau
1927	7	2	1	.778	...	...	2nd				Curly Lambeau
1928	6	4	3	.600	...	...	4th				Curly Lambeau
1929	12	0	1	1.000	...	...	1st				Curly Lambeau
1930	10	3	1	.769	...	...	1st				Curly Lambeau
1931	12	2	0	.857	...	...	1st				Curly Lambeau
1932	10	3	1	.769	...	...	2nd				Curly Lambeau
1933	5	7	1	.417	170	107	3rd/Western Div.	—	—		Curly Lambeau
1934	7	6	0	.538	156	112	3rd/Western Div.	—	—		Curly Lambeau
1935	8	4	0	.667	181	96	2nd/Western Div.	—	—		Curly Lambeau
1936	10	1	1	.909	248	118	1st/Western Div.	1	0	NFL champ	Curly Lambeau
1937	7	4	0	.636	220	122	T2nd/Western Div.	—	—		Curly Lambeau
1938	8	3	0	.727	223	118	1st/Western Div.	0	1	NFL championship game	Curly Lambeau
1939	9	2	0	.818	233	153	1st/Western Div.	1	0	NFL champ	Curly Lambeau
1940	6	4	1	.600	238	155	2nd/Western Div.	—	—		Curly Lambeau
1941	10	1	0	.909	258	120	2nd/Western Div.	0	1	W. Div. championship game	Curly Lambeau
1942	8	2	1	.800	300	215	2nd/Western Div.	—	—		Curly Lambeau
1943	7	2	1	.778	264	172	2nd/Western Div.	—	—		Curly Lambeau
1944	8	2	0	.800	238	141	1st/Western Div.	1	0	NFL champ	Curly Lambeau
1945	6	4	0	.600	258	173	3rd/Western Div.	—	—		Curly Lambeau
1946	6	5	0	.545	148	158	T3rd/Western Div.	—	—		Curly Lambeau
1947	6	5	1	.545	274	210	3rd/Western Div.	—	—		Curly Lambeau
1948	3	9	0	.250	154	290	4th/Western Div.	—	—		Curly Lambeau
1949	2	10	0	.167	114	329	5th/Western Div.	—	—		Curly Lambeau
1950	3	9	0	.250	244	406	T5th/National Conf.	—	—		Gene Ronzani
1951	3	9	0	.250	254	375	5th/National Conf.	—	—		Gene Ronzani
1952	6	6	0	.500	295	312	4th/National Conf.	—	—		Gene Ronzani
1953	2	9	1	.182	200	338	6th/Western Conf.	—	—		Gene Ronzani, Hugh Devore-S. McLean
1954	4	8	0	.333	234	251	5th/Western Conf.	—	—		Lisle Blackbourn
1955	6	6	0	.500	258	276	3rd/Western Conf.	—	—		Lisle Blackbourn
1956	4	8	0	.333	264	342	5th/Western Conf.	—	—		Lisle Blackbourn
1957	3	9	0	.250	218	311	6th/Western Conf.	—	—		Lisle Blackbourn
1958	1	10	1	.091	193	382	6th/Western Conf.	—	—		Scooter McLean
1959	7	5	0	.583	248	246	T3rd/Western Conf.	—	—		Vince Lombardi
1960	8	4	0	.667	332	209	1st/Western Conf.	0	1	NFL championship game	Vince Lombardi
1961	11	3	0	.786	391	223	1st/Western Conf.	1	0	NFL champ	Vince Lombardi
1962	13	1	0	.929	415	148	1st/Western Conf.	1	0	NFL champ	Vince Lombardi
1963	11	2	1	.846	369	206	2nd/Western Conf.	—	—		Vince Lombardi
1964	8	5	1	.615	342	245	T2nd/Western Conf.	—	—		Vince Lombardi
1965	10	3	1	.769	316	224	1st/Western Conf.	2	0	NFL champ	Vince Lombardi
1966	12	2	0	.857	335	163	1st/Western Conf.	2	0	Super Bowl champ	Vince Lombardi
1967	9	4	1	.692	332	209	1st/Central Div.	3	0	Super Bowl champ	Vince Lombardi
1968	6	7	1	.462	281	227	3rd/Central Div.	—	—		Phil Bengtson
1969	8	6	0	.571	269	221	3rd/Central Div.	—	—		Phil Bengtson
1970	6	8	0	.429	196	293	T3rd/NFC Central Div.	—	—		Phil Bengtson
1971	4	8	2	.333	274	298	4th/NFC Central Div.	—	—		Dan Devine
1972	10	4	0	.714	304	226	1st/NFC Central Div.	0	1	NFC div. playoff game	Dan Devine
1973	5	7	2	.429	202	259	3rd/NFC Central Div.	—	—		Dan Devine
1974	6	8	0	.429	210	206	3rd/NFC Central Div.	—	—		Dan Devine
1975	4	10	0	.286	226	285	T3rd/NFC Central Div.	—	—		Bart Starr
1976	5	9	0	.357	218	299	4th/NFC Central Div.	—	—		Bart Starr
1977	4	10	0	.286	134	219	4th/NFC Central Div.	—	—		Bart Starr
1978	8	7	1	.531	249	269	2nd/NFC Central Div.	—	—		Bart Starr
1979	5	11	0	.313	246	316	4th/NFC Central Div.	—	—		Bart Starr
1980	5	10	1	.344	231	371	T4th/NFC Central Div.	—	—		Bart Starr
1981	8	8	0	.500	324	361	3rd/NFC Central Div.	—	—		Bart Starr
1982	5	3	1	.611	226	169	3rd/NFC	1	1	NFC second-round pl. game	Bart Starr
1983	8	8	0	.500	429	439	T2nd/NFC Central Div.	—	—		Bart Starr
1984	8	8	0	.500	390	309	2nd/NFC Central Div.	—	—		Forrest Gregg
1985	8	8	0	.500	337	355	2nd/NFC Central Div.	—	—		Forrest Gregg
1986	4	12	0	.250	254	418	4th/NFC Central Div.	—	—		Forrest Gregg
1987	5	9	1	.367	255	300	3rd/NFC Central Div.	—	—		Forrest Gregg
1988	4	12	0	.250	240	315	T4th/NFC Central Div.	—	—		Lindy Infante
1989	10	6	0	.625	362	356	2nd/NFC Central Div.	—	—		Lindy Infante
1990	6	10	0	.375	271	347	T2nd/NFC Central Div.	—	—		Lindy Infante
1991	4	12	0	.250	273	313	4th/NFC Central Div.	—	—		Lindy Infante
1992	9	7	0	.563	276	296	2nd/NFC Central Div.	—	—		Mike Holmgren
1993	9	7	0	.563	340	282	T2nd/NFC Central Div.	1	1	NFC div. playoff game	Mike Holmgren
1994	9	7	0	.563	382	287	T2nd/NFC Central Div.	1	1	NFC div. playoff game	Mike Holmgren

				REGULAR SEASON					PLAYOFFS		
Year	W	L	T	Pct.	PF	PA	Finish	W	L	Highest round	Coach
1995	11	5	0	.689	404	314	1st/NFC Central Div.	2	1	NFC championship game	Mike Holmgren
1996	13	3	0	.813	456	210	1st/NFC Central Div.	3	0	Super Bowl champ	Mike Holmgren
1997	13	3	0	.813	422	282	1st/NFC Central Div.	2	1	Super Bowl	Mike Holmgren
1998	11	5	0	.688	408	319	2nd/NFC Central Div.	0	1	NFC wild-card game	Mike Holmgren
1999	8	8	0	.500	357	341	4th/NFC Central Div.	—	—		Ray Rhodes
2000	9	7	0	.563	353	323	3rd/NFC Central Div.	—	—		Mike Sherman

FIRST-ROUND DRAFT PICKS

1936—Russ Letlow, G, San Francisco
1937—Ed Jankowski, B, Wisconsin
1938—Cecil Isbell, B, Purdue
1939—Larry Buhler, B, Minnesota
1940—Hal Van Every, B, Marquette
1941—George Paskvan, B, Wisconsin
1942—Urban Odson, T, Minnesota
1943—Dick Wildung, T, Minnesota
1944—Merv Pregulman, G, Michigan
1945—Walt Schlinkman, G, Texas Tech
1946—Johnny Strzykalski, B, Marquette
1947—Ernie Case, B, UCLA
1948—Earl Girard, B, Wisconsin
1949—Stan Heath, B, Nevada
1950—Clayton Tonnemaker, G, Minnesota
1951—Bob Gain, T, Kentucky
1952—Babe Parilli, QB, Kentucky
1953—Al Carmichael, B, Southern California
1954—Art Hunter, T, Notre Dame
    Veryl Switzer, B, Kansas State
1955—Tom Bettis, G, Purdue
1956—Jack Losch, B, Miami
1957—Paul Hornung, B, Notre Dame*
    Ron Kramer, E, Michigan
1958—Dan Currie, C, Michigan State
1959—Randy Duncan, B, Iowa*
1960—Tom Moore, RB, Vanderbilt
1961—Herb Adderley, DB, Michigan State
1962—Earl Gros, RB, Louisiana State
1963—Dave Robinson, LB, Penn State
1964—Lloyd Voss, DT, Nebraska
1965—Donny Anderson, RB, Texas Tech
    Larry Elkins, E, Baylor
1966—Jim Grabowski, RB, Illinois
    Gale Gillingham, G, Minnesota
1967—Bob Hyland, C, Boston College
    Don Horn, QB, San Diego State
1968—Fred Carr, LB, Texas-El Paso
    Bill Lueck, G, Arizona
1969—Rich Moore, DT, Villanova

1970—Mike McCoy, DT, Notre Dame
    Rich McGeorge, TE, Elon
1971—John Brockington, RB, Ohio State
1972—Willie Buchanon, DB, San Diego State
    Jerry Tagge, QB, Nebraska
1973—Barry Smith, WR, Florida State
1974—Barty Smith, RB, Richmond
1975—None
1976—Mark Koncar, T, Colorado
1977—Mike Butler, DE, Kansas
    Ezra Johnson, DE, Morris Brown
1978—James Lofton, WR, Stanford
    John Anderson, LB, Michigan
1979—Eddie Lee Ivery, RB, Georgia Tech
1980—Bruce Clark, DT, Penn State
    George Cumby, LB, Oklahoma
1981—Rich Campbell, QB, California
1982—Ron Hallstrom, G, Iowa
1983—Tim Lewis, DB, Pittsburgh
1984—Alphonso Carreker, DT, Florida State
1985—Ken Ruettgers, T, Southern California
1986—None
1987—Brent Fullwood, RB, Auburn
1988—Sterling Sharpe, WR, South Carolina
1989—Tony Mandarich, T, Michigan State
1990—Tony Bennett, LB, Mississippi
    Darrell Thompson, RB, Minnesota
1991—Vincent Clark, DB, Ohio State
1992—Terrell Buckley, DB, Florida State
1993—Wayne Simmons, LB, Clemson
    George Teague, DB, Alabama
1994—Aaron Taylor, T, Notre Dame
1995—Craig Newsome, DB, Arizona State
1996—John Michaels, T, Southern California
1997—Ross Verba, T, Iowa
1998—Vonnie Holliday, DT, North Carolina
1999—Antuan Edwards, DB, Clemson
2000—Bubba Franks, TE, Miami, Fla.
2001—Jamal Reynolds, DE, Florida State
    *First player chosen in draft.

FRANCHISE RECORDS

Most rushing yards, career
8,207—Jim Taylor
Most rushing yards, season
1,474—Jim Taylor, 1962
Most rushing yards, game
190—Dorsey Levens vs. Dal., Nov. 23, 1997
Most rushing touchdowns, season
19—Jim Taylor, 1962
Most passing attempts, season
599—Don Majkowski, 1989
Most passing attempts, game
61—Brett Favre vs. S.F., Oct. 14, 1996 (OT)
59—Don Majkowski at Det., Nov. 12, 1989
Most passes completed, season
363—Brett Favre, 1994

Most passes completed, game
36—Brett Favre at Chi., Dec. 5, 1993
Most passing yards, career
34,706—Brett Favre
Most passing yards, season
4,458—Lynn Dickey, 1983
Most passing yards, game
418—Lynn Dickey at T.B., Oct. 12, 1980
Most touchdown passes, season
39—Brett Favre, 1996
Most pass receptions, career
595—Sterling Sharpe
Most pass receptions, season
112—Sterling Sharpe, 1993

Most pass receptions, game
14—Don Hutson at NYG, Nov. 22, 1942
Most receiving yards, career
9,656—James Lofton
Most receiving yards, season
1,497—Robert Brooks, 1995
Most receiving yards, game
257—Bill Howton vs. L.A. Rams, Oct. 21, 1956
Most receiving touchdowns, season
18—Sterling Sharpe, 1994
Most touchdowns, career
105—Don Hutson

Most field goals, season
33—Chester Marcol, 1972
    Ryan Longwell, 2000
Longest field goal
54 yards—Chris Jacke at Det., Jan. 2, 1994

Most interceptions, career
52—Bobby Dillon
Most interceptions, season
10—Irv Comp, 1943

Most sacks, career
84—Ezra Johnson
Most sacks, season
20.5—Ezra Johnson, 1978

SERIES RECORDS

Green Bay vs.: Arizona 43-21-4; Atlanta 10-9; Baltimore 1-0; Buffalo 2-6; Carolina 2-2; Chicago 71-84-6; Cincinnati 5-4; Cleveland 8-6; Dallas 10-9; Denver 3-5-1; Detroit 69-60-6; Indianapolis 19-19-1; Jacksonville 1-0; Kansas City 1-5-1; Miami 1-9; Minnesota 39-39-1; New England 3-3; New Orleans 13-4; N.Y. Giants 23-20-2; N.Y. Jets 2-6; Oakland 3-5; Philadelphia 22-9; Pittsburgh 21-12; St. Louis 27-40-1; San Diego 6-1; San Francisco 25-25-1; Seattle 4-4; Tampa Bay 27-16-1; Tennessee 4-3; Washington 9-11.

COACHING RECORDS

Phil Bengtson, 20-21-1; Lisle Blackbourn, 17-31-0; Dan Devine, 25-27-4 (0-1); Hugh Devore-Ray (Scooter) McLean, 0-2-0; Forrest Gregg, 25-37-1; Mike Holmgren, 75-37-0 (9-5); Lindy Infante, 24-40-0; Curly Lambeau, 209-104-21 (3-2); Vince Lombardi, 89-29-4 (9-1); Ray (Scooter) McLean, 1-10-1; Ray Rhodes, 8-8-0; Gene Ronzani, 14-31-1; Mike Sherman, 9-7-0; Bart Starr, 52-76-3 (1-1).
NOTE: Playoff games in parentheses.

RETIRED UNIFORM NUMBERS

No.	Player
3	Tony Canadeo
14	Don Hutson
15	Bart Starr
66	Ray Nitschke

INDIANAPOLIS COLTS
YEAR-BY-YEAR RECORDS

Year	W	L	T	Pct.	PF	PA	Finish	W	L	Highest round	Coach
				REGULAR SEASON						PLAYOFFS	
1953*	3	9	0	.250	182	350	5th/Western Conf.	—	—		Keith Molesworth
1954*	3	9	0	.250	131	279	6th/Western Conf.	—	—		Weeb Ewbank
1955*	5	6	1	.455	214	239	4th/Western Conf.	—	—		Weeb Ewbank
1956*	5	7	0	.417	270	322	4th/Western Conf.	—	—		Weeb Ewbank
1957*	7	5	0	.583	303	235	3rd/Western Conf.	—	—		Weeb Ewbank
1958*	9	3	0	.750	381	203	1st/Western Conf.	1	0	NFL champ	Weeb Ewbank
1959*	9	3	0	.750	374	251	1st/Western Conf.	1	0	NFL champ	Weeb Ewbank
1960*	6	6	0	.500	288	234	4th/Western Conf.	—	—		Weeb Ewbank
1961*	8	6	0	.571	302	307	T3rd/Western Conf.	—	—		Weeb Ewbank
1962*	7	7	0	.500	293	288	4th/Western Conf.	—	—		Weeb Ewbank
1963*	8	6	0	.571	316	285	3rd/Western Conf.	—	—		Don Shula
1964*	12	2	0	.857	428	225	1st/Western Conf.	0	1	NFL championship game	Don Shula
1965*	10	3	1	.769	389	284	2nd/Western Conf.	0	1	W. Conf. champ. game	Don Shula
1966*	9	5	0	.643	314	226	2nd/Western Conf.	—	—		Don Shula
1967*	11	1	2	.917	394	198	2nd/Coastal Div.	—	—		Don Shula
1968*	13	1	0	.929	402	144	1st/Coastal Div.	2	1	Super Bowl	Don Shula
1969*	8	5	1	.615	279	268	2nd/Coastal Div.	—	—		Don Shula
1970*	11	2	1	.846	321	234	1st/AFC Eastern Div.	3	0	Super Bowl champ	Don McCafferty
1971*	10	4	0	.714	313	140	2nd/AFC Eastern Div.	1	1	AFC championship game	Don McCafferty
1972*	5	9	0	.357	235	252	3rd/AFC Eastern Div.	—	—		McCafferty, John Sandusky
1973*	4	10	0	.286	226	341	T4th/AFC Eastern Div.	—	—		Howard Schnellenberger
1974*	2	12	0	.143	190	329	5th/AFC Eastern Div.	—	—		H. Schnellenberger, Joe Thomas
1975*	10	4	0	.714	395	269	1st/AFC Eastern Div.	0	1	AFC div. playoff game	Ted Marchibroda
1976*	11	3	0	.786	417	246	1st/AFC Eastern Div.	0	1	AFC div. playoff game	Ted Marchibroda
1977*	10	4	0	.714	295	221	1st/AFC Eastern Div.	0	1	AFC div. playoff game	Ted Marchibroda
1978*	5	11	0	.313	239	421	T4th/AFC Eastern Div.	—	—		Ted Marchibroda
1979*	5	11	0	.313	271	351	5th/AFC Eastern Div.	—	—		Ted Marchibroda
1980*	7	9	0	.438	355	387	4th/AFC Eastern Div.	—	—		Mike McCormack
1981*	2	14	0	.125	259	533	T4th/AFC Eastern Div.	—	—		Mike McCormack
1982*	0	8	1	.056	113	236	14th/AFC	—	—		Frank Kush
1983*	7	9	0	.438	264	354	T4th/AFC Eastern Div.	—	—		Frank Kush
1984	4	12	0	.250	239	414	4th/AFC Eastern Div.	—	—		Frank Kush, Hal Hunter
1985	5	11	0	.313	320	386	4th/AFC Eastern Div.	—	—		Rod Dowhower
1986	3	13	0	.188	229	400	5th/AFC Eastern Div.	—	—		Rod Dowhower, Ron Meyer
1987	9	6	0	.600	300	238	1st/AFC Eastern Div.	0	1	AFC div. playoff game	Ron Meyer
1988	9	7	0	.563	354	315	T2nd/AFC Eastern Div.	—	—		Ron Meyer
1989	8	8	0	.500	298	301	T2nd/AFC Eastern Div.	—	—		Ron Meyer
1990	7	9	0	.438	281	353	3rd/AFC Eastern Div.	—	—		Ron Meyer
1991	1	15	0	.063	143	381	5th/AFC Eastern Div.	—	—		Ron Meyer, Rick Venturi
1992	9	7	0	.563	216	302	3rd/AFC Eastern Div.	—	—		Ted Marchibroda
1993	4	12	0	.250	189	378	5th/AFC Eastern Div.	—	—		Ted Marchibroda
1994	8	8	0	.500	307	320	3rd/AFC Eastern Div.	—	—		Ted Marchibroda
1995	9	7	0	.563	331	316	T2nd/AFC Eastern Div.	2	1	AFC championship game	Ted Marchibroda

	REGULAR SEASON						PLAYOFFS			
Year	W	L	T	Pct.	PF	PA	Finish	W	L	Highest round	Coach
1996	9	7	0	.563	317	334	3rd/AFC Eastern Div.	0	1	AFC wild-card game	Lindy Infante
1997	3	13	0	.188	313	401	5th/AFC Eastern Div.	—	—		Lindy Infante
1998	3	13	0	.188	310	444	5th/AFC Eastern Div.	—	—		Jim Mora
1999	13	3	0	.813	423	333	1st/AFC Eastern Div.	0	1	AFC div. playoff game	Jim Mora
2000	10	6	0	.625	429	326	2nd/AFC Eastern Div.	0	1	AFC wild-card game	Jim Mora

*Baltimore Colts.

FIRST-ROUND DRAFT PICKS

1953—Billy Vessels, B, Oklahoma
1954—Cotton Davidson, B, Baylor
1955—George Shaw, B, Oregon*
     Alan Ameche, B, Wisconsin
1956—Lenny Moore, B, Penn State
1957—Jim Parker, T, Ohio State
1958—Lenny Lyles, B, Louisville
1959—Jackie Burkett, C, Auburn
1960—Ron Mix, T, Southern California
1961—Tom Matte, RB, Ohio State
1962—Wendell Harris, DB, Louisiana State
1963—Bob Vogel, T, Ohio State
1964—Marv Woodson, DB, Indiana
1965—Mike Curtis, LB, Duke
1966—Sam Ball, T, Kentucky
1967—Bubba Smith, DT, Michigan State*
     Jim Detwiler, RB, Michigan
1968—John Williams, G, Minnesota
1969—Eddie Hinton, WR, Oklahoma
1970—Norm Bulaich, RB, Texas Christian
1971—Don McCauley, RB, North Carolina
     Leonard Dunlap, DB, North Texas State
1972—Tom Drougas, T, Oregon
1973—Bert Jones, QB, Louisiana State
     Joe Ehrmann, DT, Syracuse
1974—John Dutton, DE, Nebraska
     Roger Carr, WR, Louisiana Tech
1975—Ken Huff, G, North Carolina
1976—Ken Novak, DT, Purdue
1977—Randy Burke, WR, Kentucky
1978—Reese McCall, TE, Auburn

1979—Barry Krauss, LB, Alabama
1980—Curtis Dickey, RB, Texas A&M
     Derrick Hatchett, DB, Texas
1981—Randy McMillan, RB, Pittsburgh
     Donnell Thompson, DT, North Carolina
1982—Johnie Cooks, LB, Mississippi State
     Art Schlichter, QB, Ohio State
1983—John Elway, QB, Stanford*
1984—L. Coleman, DB, Vanderbilt
     Ron Solt, G, Maryland
1985—Duane Bickett, LB, Southern California
1986—Jon Hand, DT, Alabama
1987—Cornelius Bennett, LB, Alabama
1988—None
1989—Andre Rison, WR, Michigan State
1990—Jeff George, QB, Illinois*
1991—None
1992—Steve Emtman, DE, Washington*
     Quentin Coryatt, LB, Texas A&M
1993—Sean Dawkins, WR, California
1994—Marshall Faulk, RB, San Diego State
     Trev Alberts, LB, Nebraska
1995—Ellis Johnson, DT, Florida
1996—Marvin Harrison, WR, Syracuse
1997—Tarik Glenn, T, California
1998—Peyton Manning, QB, Tennessee*
1999—Edgerrin James, RB, Miami, Fla.
2000—Rob Morris, LB, Brigham Young
2001—Reggie Wayne, WR, Miami, Fla.
     *First player chosen in draft.

FRANCHISE RECORDS

Most rushing yards, career
5,487—Lydell Mitchell
Most rushing yards, season
1,709—Edgerrin James, 2000
Most rushing yards, game
219—Edgerrin James at Sea., Oct. 15, 2000
Most rushing touchdowns, season
16—Lenny Moore, 1964
Most passing attempts, season
575—Peyton Manning, 1998
Most passing attempts, game
59—Jeff George at Was., Nov. 7, 1993
Most passes completed, season
357—Peyton Manning, 2000
Most passes completed, game
37—Jeff George at Was., Nov. 7, 1993
Most passing yards, career
39,768—Johnny Unitas
Most passing yards, season
4,413—Peyton Manning, 2000

Most passing yards, game
440—Peyton Manning vs. Jac., Sept. 25, 2000
Most touchdown passes, season
33—Peyton Manning, 2000
Most pass receptions, career
631—Raymond Berry
Most pass receptions, season
115—Marvin Harrison, 1999
Most pass receptions, game
14—Marvin Harrison at Cle., Dec. 26, 1999
Most receiving yards, career
9,275—Raymond Berry
Most receiving yards, season
1,663—Marvin Harrison, 1999
Most receiving yards, game
224—Raymond Berry at Was., Nov. 10, 1957
Most receiving touchdowns, season
14—Raymond Berry, 1959
     Marvin Harrison, 2000

Most touchdowns, career
113—Lenny Moore
Most field goals, season
36—Cary Blanchard, 1996
Longest field goal
58 yards—Dan Miller at S.D., Dec. 26, 1982
Most interceptions, career
57—Bob Boyd
Most interceptions, season
11—Tom Keane, 1953
Most sacks, career
56.5—Fred Cook
Most sacks, season
17—John Dutton, 1975

SERIES RECORDS

Indianapolis vs.: Arizona 6-6; Atlanta 10-1; Baltimore 0-1; Buffalo 26-34-1; Carolina 0-2; Chicago 21-17; Cincinnati 12-8; Cleveland 8-13; Dallas 4-7; Denver 2-9; Detroit 18-19-2; Green Bay 19-19-1; Jacksonville 2-0; Kansas City 7-6; Miami 21-41; Minnesota 12-7-1; New England 24-37; New Orleans 3-4; N.Y. Giants 6-5; N.Y. Jets 37-24; Oakland 2-6; Philadelphia 8-6; Pittsburgh 4-13; St. Louis 21-17-2; San Diego 8-11; San Francisco 22-17; Seattle 5-3; Tampa Bay 5-4; Tennessee 7-7; Washington 17-9.
NOTE: Includes records as Baltimore Colts from 1953 through 1983.

COACHING RECORDS

Rod Dowhower, 5-24-0; Weeb Ewbank, 59-52-1 (2-0); Hal Hunter, 0-1-0; Lindy Infante, 12-19-0 (0-1); Frank Kush, 11-28-1; Ted Marchibroda, 71-67-0 (2-4); Don McCafferty, 22-10-1 (4-1); Mike McCormack, 9-23-0; Ron Meyer, 36-35-0 (0-1); Keith Molesworth, 3-9-0; Jim Mora, 26-22-0 (0-2); John Sandusky, 4-5-0; Howard Schnellenberger, 4-13-0; Don Shula, 71-23-4 (2-3); Joe Thomas, 2-9-0; Rick Venturi, 1-10.
NOTE: Playoff games in parentheses.

RETIRED UNIFORM NUMBERS

No.	Player
19	Johnny Unitas
22	Buddy Young
24	Lenny Moore
70	Art Donovan
77	Jim Parker
82	Raymond Berry
89	Gino Marchetti

JACKSONVILLE JAGUARS
YEAR-BY-YEAR RECORDS

Year	REGULAR SEASON W	L	T	Pct.	PF	PA	Finish	PLAYOFFS W	L	Highest round	Coach
1995	4	12	0	.250	275	404	5th/AFC Central Div.	—	—		Tom Coughlin
1996	9	7	0	.563	325	335	2nd/AFC Central Div.	2	1	AFC championship game	Tom Coughlin
1997	11	5	0	.688	394	318	2nd/AFC Central Div.	0	1	AFC wild-card game	Tom Coughlin
1998	11	5	0	.688	392	338	1st/AFC Central Div.	1	1	AFC div. playoff game	Tom Coughlin
1999	14	2	0	.875	396	217	1st/AFC Central Div.	1	1	AFC championship game	Tom Coughlin
2000	7	9	0	.438	367	327	4th/AFC Central Div.	—	—		Tom Coughlin

FIRST-ROUND DRAFT PICKS

1995—Tony Boselli, T, Southern California
    James Stewart, RB, Tennessee
1996—Kevin Hardy, LB, Illinois
1997—Renaldo Wynn, DT, Notre Dame
1998—Fred Taylor, RB, Florida
    Donovin Darius, DB, Syracuse
1999—Fernando Bryant, DB, Alabama
2000—R. Jay Soward, WR, Southern California
2001—Marcus Stroud, DT, Georgia

FRANCHISE RECORDS

Most rushing yards, career
3,354—Fred Taylor
Most rushing yards, season
1,399—Fred Taylor, 2000
Most rushing yards, game
234—Fred Taylor at Pit., Nov. 19, 2000
Most rushing touchdowns, season
14—Fred Taylor, 1998
Most passing attempts, season
557—Mark Brunell, 1996
Most passing attempts, game
52—Mark Brunell at St.L., Oct. 20, 1996
Most passes completed, season
353—Mark Brunell, 1996
Most passes completed, game
37—Mark Brunell at St.L., Oct. 20, 1996
Most passing yards, career
19,117—Mark Brunell

Most passing yards, season
4,367—Mark Brunell, 1996
Most passing yards, game
432—Mark Brunell at N.E., Sept. 22, 1996
Most touchdown passes, season
20—Mark Brunell, 1998, 2000
Most pass receptions, career
472—Jimmy Smith
Most pass receptions, season
116—Jimmy Smith, 1999
Most pass receptions, game
16—Keenan McCardell at St.L., Oct. 20, 1996
Most receiving yards, career
6,887—Jimmy Smith
Most receiving yards, season
1,636—Jimmy Smith, 1999
Most receiving yards, game
291—Jimmy Smith at Bal., Sept. 10, 2000

Most receiving touchdowns, season
8—Jimmy Smith, 1998, 2000
Most touchdowns, career
38—James Stewart
    Jimmy Smith
Most field goals, season
31—Mike Hollis, 1997, 1999
Longest field goal
53 yards—Mike Hollis vs. Pit., Oct. 8, 1995
    Mike Hollis vs. Car., Sept. 29, 1996
Most interceptions, career
11—Aaron Beasley
Most interceptions, season
6—Aaron Beasley
Most sacks, career
37—Tony Brackens
Most sacks, season
12—Tony Brackens, 1999

SERIES RECORDS

Jacksonville vs.: Arizona 1-0; Atlanta 2-0; Baltimore 8-2; Buffalo 1-1; Carolina 2-0; Chicago 1-1; Cincinnati 7-5; Cleveland 6-0; Dallas 1-1; Denver 1-2; Detroit 1-1; Green Bay 0-1; Indianapolis 0-2; Kansas City 2-0; Miami 1-0; Minnesota 0-1; New England 0-2; New Orleans 1-1; N.Y. Giants 1-1; N.Y. Jets 2-1; Oakland 1-1; Philadelphia 1-0; Pittsburgh 7-5; St. Louis 0-1; San Diego 0-0; San Francisco 1-0; Seattle 1-2; Tampa Bay 1-1; Tennessee 5-7; Washington 0-2.

COACHING RECORDS

Tom Coughlin, 56-40-0 (4-4).
NOTE: Playoff games in parentheses.

KANSAS CITY CHIEFS
YEAR-BY-YEAR RECORDS

	REGULAR SEASON						PLAYOFFS			
Year	W	L	T	Pct.	PF	PA	Finish	W	L	Highest round	Coach

Year	W	L	T	Pct.	PF	PA	Finish	W	L	Highest round	Coach
1960*†	8	6	0	.571	362	253	2nd/Western Div.	—	—		Hank Stram
1961*†	6	8	0	.429	334	343	2nd/Western Div.	—	—		Hank Stram
1962*†	11	3	0	.786	389	233	1st/Western Div.	1	0	AFL champ	Hank Stram
1963*	5	7	2	.417	347	263	3rd/Western Div.	—	—		Hank Stram
1964*	7	7	0	.500	366	306	2nd/Western Div.	—	—		Hank Stram
1965*	7	5	2	.583	322	285	3rd/Western Div.	—	—		Hank Stram
1966*	11	2	1	.846	448	276	1st/Western Div.	1	1	Super Bowl	Hank Stram
1967*	9	5	0	.643	408	254	2nd/Western Div.	—	—		Hank Stram
1968*	12	2	0	.857	371	170	2nd/Western Div.	0	1	W. Div. champ. game	Hank Stram
1969*	11	3	0	.786	359	177	2nd/Western Div.	3	0	Super Bowl champ	Hank Stram
1970	7	5	2	.583	272	244	2nd/AFC Western Div.	—	—		Hank Stram
1971	10	3	1	.769	302	208	1st/AFC Western Div.	0	1	AFC div. playoff game	Hank Stram
1972	8	6	0	.571	287	254	2nd/AFC Western Div.	—	—		Hank Stram
1973	7	5	2	.571	231	192	T2nd/AFC Western Div.	—	—		Hank Stram
1974	5	9	0	.357	233	293	T3rd/AFC Western Div.	—	—		Hank Stram
1975	5	9	0	.357	282	341	3rd/AFC Western Div.	—	—		Paul Wiggin
1976	5	9	0	.357	290	376	4th/AFC Western Div.	—	—		Paul Wiggin
1977	2	12	0	.143	225	349	5th/AFC Western Div.	—	—		Paul Wiggin, Tom Bettis
1978	4	12	0	.250	243	327	5th/AFC Western Div.	—	—		Marv Levy
1979	7	9	0	.438	238	262	5th/AFC Western Div.	—	—		Marv Levy
1980	8	8	0	.500	319	336	T3rd/AFC Western Div.	—	—		Marv Levy
1981	9	7	0	.563	343	290	3rd/AFC Western Div.	—	—		Marv Levy
1982	3	6	0	.333	176	184	11th/AFC	—	—		Marv Levy
1983	6	10	0	.375	386	367	T4th/AFC Western Div.	—	—		John Mackovic
1984	8	8	0	.500	314	324	4th/AFC Western Div.	—	—		John Mackovic
1985	6	10	0	.375	317	360	5th/AFC Western Div.	—	—		John Mackovic
1986	10	6	0	.625	358	326	2nd/AFC Western Div.	0	1	AFC wild-card game	John Mackovic
1987	4	11	0	.267	273	388	5th/AFC Western Div.	—	—		Frank Gansz
1988	4	11	1	.281	254	320	5th/AFC Western Div.	—	—		Frank Gansz
1989	8	7	1	.531	318	286	2nd/AFC Western Div.	—	—		Marty Schottenheimer
1990	11	5	0	.688	369	257	2nd/AFC Western Div.	0	1	AFC wild-card game	Marty Schottenheimer
1991	10	6	0	.625	322	252	2nd/AFC Western Div.	1	1	AFC div. playoff game	Marty Schottenheimer
1992	10	6	0	.625	348	282	2nd/AFC Western Div.	0	1	AFC wild-card game	Marty Schottenheimer
1993	11	5	0	.688	328	291	1st/AFC Western Div.	2	1	AFC championship game	Marty Schottenheimer
1994	9	7	0	.563	319	298	2nd/AFC Western Div.	0	1	AFC wild-card game	Marty Schottenheimer
1995	13	3	0	.813	358	241	1st/AFC Western Div.	0	1	AFC div. playoff game	Marty Schottenheimer
1996	9	7	0	.563	297	300	2nd/AFC Western Div.	—	—		Marty Schottenheimer
1997	13	3	0	.813	375	232	1st/AFC Western Div.	0	1	AFC div. playoff game	Marty Schottenheimer
1998	7	9	0	.438	327	363	4th/AFC Western Div.	—	—		Marty Schottenheimer
1999	9	7	0	.563	390	322	2nd/AFC Western Div.	—	—		Gunther Cunningham
2000	7	9	0	.438	355	354	3rd/AFC Western Div.	—	—		Gunther Cunningham

*American Football League.
†Dallas Texans.

FIRST-ROUND DRAFT PICKS

1960—Don Meredith, QB, Southern Methodist
1961—E.J. Holub, C, Texas Tech
1962—Ronnie Bull, RB, Baylor
1963—Buck Buchanan, DT, Grambling* (AFL)
      Ed Budde, G, Michigan State
1964—Pete Beathard, QB, Southern California
1965—Gale Sayers, RB, Kansas
1966—Aaron Brown, DE, Minnesota
1967—Gene Trosch, DE, Miami
1968—Mo Moorman, G, Texas A&M
      George Daney, G, Texas-El Paso
1969—Jim Marsalis, DB, Tennessee State
1970—Sid Smith, T, Southern California
1971—Elmo Wright, WR, Houston
1972—Jeff Kinney, RB, Nebraska
1973—None

1974—Woody Green, RB, Arizona State
1975—None
1976—Rod Walters, G, Iowa
1977—Gary Green, DB, Baylor
1978—Art Still, DE, Kentucky
1979—Mike Bell, DE, Colorado State
      Steve Fuller, QB, Clemson
1980—Brad Budde, G, Southern California
1981—Willie Scott, TE, South Carolina
1982—Anthony Hancock, WR, Tennessee
1983—Todd Blackledge, QB, Penn State
1984—Bill Maas, DT, Pittsburgh
      John Alt, T, Iowa
1985—Ethan Horton, RB, North Carolina
1986—Brian Jozwiak, T, West Virginia
1987—Paul Palmer, RB, Temple

1988—Neil Smith, DE, Nebraska
1989—Derrick Thomas, LB, Alabama
1990—Percy Snow, LB, Michigan State
1991—Harvey Williams, RB, Louisiana State
1992—Dale Carter, DB, Tennessee
1993—None
1994—Greg Hill, RB, Texas A&M
1995—Trezelle Jenkins, T, Michigan

1996—Jerome Woods, DB, Memphis
1997—Tony Gonzalez, TE, California
1998—Victor Riley, T, Auburn
1999—John Tait, T, Brigham Young
2000—Sylvester Morris, WR, Jackson State
2001—None
*First player chosen in draft.

FRANCHISE RECORDS

Most rushing yards, career
4,897—Christian Okoye
Most rushing yards, season
1,480—Christian Okoye, 1989
Most rushing yards, game
200—Barry Word vs. Det., Oct. 14, 1990
Most rushing touchdowns, season
13—Abner Haynes, 1962
Most passing attempts, season
603—Bill Kenney, 1983
Most passing attempts, game
55—Joe Montana at S.D., Oct. 9, 1994
 Steve Bono at Mia., Dec. 12, 1994
Most passes completed, season
346—Bill Kenney, 1983
Most passes completed, game
39—Elvis Grbac at Oak., Nov. 5, 2000
Most passing yards, career
28,507—Len Dawson

Most passing yards, season
4,348—Bill Kenney, 1983
Most passing yards, game
504—Elvis Grbac at Oak., Nov. 5, 2000
Most touchdown passes, season
30—Len Dawson, 1964
Most pass receptions, career
416—Henry Marshall
Most pass receptions, season
93—Tony Gonzalez, 2000
Most pass receptions, game
12—Ed Podolak vs. Den., Oct. 7, 1973
Most receiving yards, career
7,306—Otis Taylor
Most receiving yards, season
1,391—Derrick Alexander, 2000
Most receiving yards, game
309—Stephone Paige vs. S.D., Dec. 22, 1985

Most receiving touchdowns, season
12—Chris Burford, 1962
Most touchdowns, career
60—Otis Taylor
Most field goals, season
34—Nick Lowery, 1990
Longest field goals
58 yards—Nick Lowery at Was., Sept. 18, 1983
 Nick Lowery vs. L.A. Raiders, Sept. 12, 1985
Most interceptions, career
58—Emmitt Thomas
Most interceptions, season
12—Emmitt Thomas, 1974
Most sacks, career
126.5—Derrick Thomas
Most sacks, season
20—Derrick Thomas, 1990

SERIES RECORDS

Kansas City vs.: Arizona 5-1-1; Atlanta 4-1; Baltimore 1-0; Buffalo 14-18-1; Carolina 2-0; Chicago 3-5; Cincinnati 11-9; Cleveland 7-8-2; Dallas 3-4; Denver 47-34; Detroit 6-3; Green Bay 5-1-1; Indianapolis 6-7; Jacksonville 0-2; Miami 10-10; Minnesota 4-3; New England 15-9-3; New Orleans 4-3; N.Y. Giants 3-7; N.Y. Jets 14-13-1; Oakland 40-39-2; Philadelphia 2-1; Pittsburgh 7-15; St. Louis 3-4; San Diego 42-38-1; San Francisco 3-5; Seattle 29-15; Tampa Bay 5-3; Tennessee 24-18; Washington 4-1.
NOTE: Includes records as Dallas Texans from 1960 through 1962.

COACHING RECORDS

Tom Bettis, 1-6-0; Gunther Cunningham, 16-16-0; Frank Gansz, 8-22-1; Marv Levy, 31-42-0; John Mackovic, 30-34-0 (0-1); Marty Schottenheimer, 101-58-1 (3-7); Hank Stram, 124-76-10 (5-3); Paul Wiggin, 11-24-0.
NOTE: Playoff games in parentheses.

RETIRED UNIFORM NUMBERS

No.	Player
3	Jan Stenerud
16	Len Dawson
28	Abner Haynes
33	Stone Johnson
36	Mack Lee Hill
63	Willie Lanier
78	Bobby Bell
86	Buck Buchanan

MIAMI DOLPHINS
YEAR-BY-YEAR RECORDS

	REGULAR SEASON							PLAYOFFS			
Year	W	L	T	Pct.	PF	PA	Finish	W	L	Highest round	Coach
1966*	3	11	0	.214	213	362	T4th/Eastern Div.	—	—		George Wilson
1967*	4	10	0	.286	219	407	T3rd/Eastern Div.	—	—		George Wilson
1968*	5	8	1	.385	276	355	3rd/Eastern Div.	—	—		George Wilson
1969*	3	10	1	.231	233	332	5th/Eastern Div.	—	—		George Wilson
1970	10	4	0	.714	297	228	2nd/AFC Eastern Div.	0	1	AFC div. playoff game	Don Shula
1971	10	3	1	.769	315	174	1st/AFC Eastern Div.	2	1	Super Bowl	Don Shula
1972	14	0	0	1.000	385	171	1st/AFC Eastern Div.	3	0	Super Bowl champ	Don Shula
1973	12	2	0	.857	343	150	1st/AFC Eastern Div.	3	0	Super Bowl champ	Don Shula
1974	11	3	0	.786	327	216	1st/AFC Eastern Div.	0	1	AFC div. playoff game	Don Shula
1975	10	4	0	.714	357	222	2nd/AFC Eastern Div.	—	—		Don Shula
1976	6	8	0	.429	263	264	3rd/AFC Eastern Div.	—	—		Don Shula
1977	10	4	0	.714	313	197	2nd/AFC Eastern Div.	—	—		Don Shula

			REGULAR SEASON						PLAYOFFS		
Year	W	L	T	Pct.	PF	PA	Finish	W	L	Highest round	Coach
1978	11	5	0	.688	372	254	2nd/AFC Eastern Div.	0	1	AFC wild-card game	Don Shula
1979	10	6	0	.625	341	257	1st/AFC Eastern Div.	0	1	AFC div. playoff game	Don Shula
1980	8	8	0	.500	266	305	3rd/AFC Eastern Div.	—	—		Don Shula
1981	11	4	1	.719	345	275	1st/AFC Eastern Div.	0	1	AFC div. playoff game	Don Shula
1982	7	2	0	.778	198	131	T2nd/AFC	3	1	Super Bowl	Don Shula
1983	12	4	0	.750	389	250	1st/AFC Eastern Div.	0	1	AFC div. playoff game	Don Shula
1984	14	2	0	.875	513	298	1st/AFC Eastern Div.	2	1	Super Bowl	Don Shula
1985	12	4	0	.750	428	320	1st/AFC Eastern Div.	1	1	AFC championship game	Don Shula
1986	8	8	0	.500	430	405	3rd/AFC Eastern Div.	—	—		Don Shula
1987	8	7	0	.533	362	335	T2nd/AFC Eastern Div.	—	—		Don Shula
1988	6	10	0	.375	319	380	5th/AFC Eastern Div.	—	—		Don Shula
1989	8	8	0	.500	331	379	T2nd/AFC Eastern Div.	—	—		Don Shula
1990	12	4	0	.750	336	242	2nd/AFC Eastern Div.	1	1	AFC div. playoff game	Don Shula
1991	8	8	0	.500	343	349	3rd/AFC Eastern Div.	—	—		Don Shula
1992	11	5	0	.688	340	281	1st/AFC Eastern Div.	1	1	AFC championship game	Don Shula
1993	9	7	0	.563	349	351	2nd/AFC Eastern Div.	—	—		Don Shula
1994	10	6	0	.625	389	327	1st/AFC Eastern Div.	1	1	AFC div. playoff game	Don Shula
1995	9	7	0	.563	398	332	T2nd/AFC Eastern Div.	0	1	AFC wild-card game	Don Shula
1996	8	8	0	.500	279	454	4th/AFC Eastern Div.	—	—		Jimmy Johnson
1997	9	7	0	.563	339	327	T2nd/AFC Eastern Div.	0	1	AFC wild-card game	Jimmy Johnson
1998	10	6	0	.625	321	265	T2nd/AFC Eastern Div.	1	1	AFC div. playoff game	Jimmy Johnson
1999	9	7	0	.563	326	336	3rd/AFC Eastern Div.	1	1	AFC div. playoff game	Jimmy Johnson
2000	11	5	0	.688	323	226	1st/AFC Eastern Div.	1	1	AFC div. playoff game	Dave Wannstedt

*American Football League.

FIRST-ROUND DRAFT PICKS

1966—Jim Grabowski, RB, Illinois*
    Rick Norton, QB, Kentucky
1967—Bob Griese, QB, Purdue
1968—Larry Csonka, RB, Syracuse
    Doug Crusan, T, Indiana
1969—Bill Stanfill, DE, Georgia
1970—None
1971—None
1972—Mike Kadish, DT, Notre Dame
1973—None
1974—Don Reese, DE, Jackson State
1975—Darryl Carlton, T, Tampa
1976—Larry Gordon, LB, Arizona State
    Kim Bokamper, LB, San Jose State
1977—A.J. Duhe, DE, Louisiana State
1978—None
1979—Jon Giesler, T, Michigan
1980—Don McNeal, DB, Alabama
1981—David Overstreet, RB, Oklahoma
1982—Roy Foster, G, Southern California
1983—Dan Marino, QB, Pittsburgh

1984—Jackie Shipp, LB, Oklahoma
1985—Lorenzo Hampton, RB, Florida
1986—None
1987—John Bosa, DE, Boston College
1988—Eric Kumerow, DE, Ohio State
1989—Sammie Smith, RB, Florida State
    Louis Oliver, DB, Florida
1990—Richmond Webb, T, Texas A&M
1991—Randal Hill, WR, Miami, Fla.
1992—Troy Vincent, DB, Wisconsin
    Marco Coleman, LB, Georgia Tech
1993—O.J. McDuffie, WR, Penn State
1994—Tim Bowens, DT, Mississippi
1995—Billy Milner, T, Houston
1996—Daryl Gardener, DT, Baylor
1997—Yatil Green, WR, Miami, Fla.
1998—John Avery, RB, Mississippi
1999—None
2000—None
2001—Jamar Fletcher, DB, Wisconsin
    *First player chosen in draft.

FRANCHISE RECORDS

Most rushing yards, career
6,737—Larry Csonka
Most rushing yards, season
1,258—Delvin Williams, 1978
Most rushing yards, game
197—Mercury Morris vs. N.E., Sept. 30, 1973
Most rushing touchdowns, season
15—Karim Abdul-Jabbar, 1997
Most passing attempts, season
623—Dan Marino, 1986
Most passing attempts, game
60—Dan Marino vs. NYJ, Oct. 23, 1988
    Dan Marino at N.E., Nov. 23, 1997
Most passes completed, season
385—Dan Marino, 1994

Most passes completed, game
39—Dan Marino at Buf., Nov. 16, 1986
Most passing yards, career
58,913—Dan Marino
Most passing yards, season
5,084—Dan Marino, 1984
Most passing yards, game
521—Dan Marino vs. NYJ, Oct. 23, 1988
Most touchdown passes, season
48—Dan Marino, 1984
Most pass receptions, career
550—Mark Clayton
Most pass receptions, season
90—O.J. McDuffie, 1998
Most pass receptions, game
12—Jim Jensen at N.E., Nov. 6, 1988

Most receiving yards, career
8,869—Mark Duper
Most receiving yards, season
1,389—Mark Clayton, 1984
Most receiving yards, game
217—Mark Duper vs. NYJ, Nov. 10, 1985
Most receiving touchdowns, season
18—Mark Clayton, 1984
Most touchdowns, career
82—Mark Clayton
Most field goals, season
39—Olindo Mare, 1999
Longest field goal
59 yards—Pete Stoyanovich at NYJ, Nov. 12, 1989
Most interceptions, career
35—Jake Scott

Most interceptions, season	Most sacks, career	Most sacks, season
10—Dick Westmoreland, 1967	67.5—Bill Stanfill	18.5—Bill Stanfill, 1973

SERIES RECORDS

Miami vs.: Arizona 8-0; Atlanta 6-2; Baltimore 2-0; Buffalo 44-25-1; Carolina 1-0; Chicago 5-3; Cincinnati 13-3; Cleveland 6-4; Dallas 6-3; Denver 7-2-1; Detroit 5-2; Green Bay 9-1; Indianapolis 41-21; Jacksonville 0-1; Kansas City 10-10; Minnesota 4-3; New England 42-27; New Orleans 6-4; N.Y. Giants 1-3; N.Y. Jets 33-34-1; Oakland 8-15-1; Philadelphia 7-3; Pittsburgh 9-7; St. Louis 7-1; San Diego 8-10; San Francisco 4-3; Seattle 5-2; Tampa Bay 4-3; Tennessee 14-11; Washington 5-3.

COACHING RECORDS

Jimmy Johnson, 36-28-0 (2-3); Don Shula, 257-133-2 (17-14); Dave Wannstedt, 11-5-0 (1-1); George Wilson, 15-39-2.
NOTE: Playoff games in parentheses.

RETIRED UNIFORM NUMBERS

No.	Player
12	Bob Griese
13	Dan Marino

MINNESOTA VIKINGS
YEAR-BY-YEAR RECORDS

		REGULAR SEASON						PLAYOFFS		
Year	W	L	T	Pct.	PF	PA	Finish	W	L	Highest round	Coach
1961	3	11	0	.214	285	407	7th/Western Conf.	—	—		Norm Van Brocklin
1962	2	11	1	.154	254	410	6th/Western Conf.	—	—		Norm Van Brocklin
1963	5	8	1	.385	309	390	T4th/Western Conf.	—	—		Norm Van Brocklin
1964	8	5	1	.615	355	296	T2nd/Western Conf.	—	—		Norm Van Brocklin
1965	7	7	0	.500	383	403	5th/Western Conf.	—	—		Norm Van Brocklin
1966	4	9	1	.308	292	304	T6th/Western Conf.	—	—		Norm Van Brocklin
1967	3	8	3	.273	233	294	4th/Central Div.	—	—		Bud Grant
1968	8	6	0	.571	282	242	1st/Central Div.	0	1	W. Conf. champ. game	Bud Grant
1969	12	2	0	.857	379	133	1st/Central Div.	2	1	Super Bowl	Bud Grant
1970	12	2	0	.857	335	143	1st/NFC Central Div.	0	1	NFC div. playoff game	Bud Grant
1971	11	3	0	.786	245	139	1st/NFC Central Div.	0	1	NFC div. playoff game	Bud Grant
1972	7	7	0	.500	301	252	3rd/NFC Central Div.	—	—		Bud Grant
1973	12	2	0	.857	296	168	1st/NFC Central Div.	2	1	Super Bowl	Bud Grant
1974	10	4	0	.714	310	195	1st/NFC Central Div.	2	1	Super Bowl	Bud Grant
1975	12	2	0	.857	377	180	1st/NFC Central Div.	0	1	NFC div. playoff game	Bud Grant
1976	11	2	1	.821	305	176	1st/NFC Central Div.	2	1	Super Bowl	Bud Grant
1977	9	5	0	.643	231	227	1st/NFC Central Div.	1	1	NFC championship game	Bud Grant
1978	8	7	1	.531	294	306	1st/NFC Central Div.	0	1	NFC div. playoff game	Bud Grant
1979	7	9	0	.438	259	337	3rd/NFC Central Div.	—	—		Bud Grant
1980	9	7	0	.563	317	308	1st/NFC Central Div.	0	1	NFC div. playoff game	Bud Grant
1981	7	9	0	.438	325	369	4th/NFC Central Div.	—	—		Bud Grant
1982	5	4	0	.556	187	198	T4th/NFC	1	1	NFC second-round pl. game	Bud Grant
1983	8	8	0	.500	316	348	T2nd/NFC Central Div.	—	—		Bud Grant
1984	3	13	0	.188	276	484	5th/NFC Central Div.	—	—		Les Steckel
1985	7	9	0	.438	346	359	T3rd/NFC Central Div.	—	—		Bud Grant
1986	9	7	0	.563	398	273	2nd/NFC Central Div.	—	—		Jerry Burns
1987	8	7	0	.533	336	335	2nd/NFC Central Div.	2	1	NFC championship game	Jerry Burns
1988	11	5	0	.688	406	233	2nd/NFC Central Div.	1	1	NFC div. playoff game	Jerry Burns
1989	10	6	0	.625	351	275	1st/NFC Central Div.	0	1	NFC div. playoff game	Jerry Burns
1990	6	10	0	.375	351	326	T2nd/NFC Central Div.	—	—		Jerry Burns
1991	8	8	0	.500	301	306	3rd/NFC Central Div.	—	—		Jerry Burns
1992	11	5	0	.688	374	249	1st/NFC Central Div.	0	1	NFC wild-card game	Dennis Green
1993	9	7	0	.563	277	290	T2nd/NFC Central Div.	0	1	NFC wild-card game	Dennis Green
1994	10	6	0	.625	356	314	1st/NFC Central Div.	0	1	NFC wild-card game	Dennis Green
1995	8	8	0	.500	412	385	4th/NFC Central Div.	—	—		Dennis Green
1996	9	7	0	.563	298	315	2nd/NFC Central Div.	0	1	NFC wild-card game	Dennis Green
1997	9	7	0	.563	354	359	T3rd/NFC Central Div.	1	1	NFC div. playoff game	Dennis Green
1998	15	1	0	.938	556	296	1st/NFC Central Div.	1	1	NFC championship game	Dennis Green
1999	10	6	0	.625	399	335	2nd/NFC Central Div.	1	1	NFC div. playoff game	Dennis Green
2000	11	5	0	.688	397	371	1st/NFC Central Div.	1	1	NFC championship game	Dennis Green

FIRST-ROUND DRAFT PICKS

1961—Tommy Mason, RB, Tulane*
1962—None
1963—Jim Dunaway, T, Mississippi
1964—Carl Eller, DE, Minnesota
1965—Jack Snow, WR, Notre Dame
1966—Jerry Shay, DT, Purdue

1967—Clint Jones, RB, Michigan State
      Gene Washington, WR, Michigan State
      Alan Page, DT, Notre Dame
1968—Ron Yary, T, Southern California*
1969—None
1970—John Ward, DT, Oklahoma State

1971—Leo Hayden, RB, Ohio State
1972—Jeff Siemon, LB, Stanford
1973—Chuck Foreman, RB, Miami, Fla.
1974—Fred McNeill, LB, UCLA
    Steve Riley, T, Southern California
1975—Mark Mullaney, DE, Colorado State
1976—James White, DT, Oklahoma State
1977—Tommy Kramer, QB, Rice
1978—Randy Holloway, DE, Pittsburgh
1979—Ted Brown, RB, North Carolina State
1980—Doug Martin, DT, Washington
1981—None
1982—Darrin Nelson, RB, Stanford
1983—Joey Browner, DB, Southern California
1984—Keith Millard, DE, Washington State
1985—Chris Doleman, LB, Pittsburgh
1986—Gerald Robinson, DE, Auburn
1987—D.J. Dozier, RB, Penn State

1988—Randall McDaniel, G, Arizona State
1989—None
1990—None
1991—None
1992—None
1993—Robert Smith, RB, Ohio State
1994—DeWayne Washington, CB, North Carolina State
    Todd Steussie, T, California
1995—Derrick Alexander, DE, Florida State
    Korey Stringer, T, Ohio State
1996—Duane Clemons, DE, California
1997—Dwayne Rudd, LB, Alabama
1998—Randy Moss, WR, Marshall
1999—Daunte Culpepper, QB, Central Florida
    Dimitrius Underwood, DE, Michigan State
2000—Chris Hovan, DT, Boston College
2001—Michael Bennett, RB, Wisconsin
    *First player chosen in draft.

FRANCHISE RECORDS

Most rushing yards, career
6,818—Robert Smith
Most rushing yards, season
1,521—Robert Smith, 2000
Most rushing yards, game
200—Chuck Foreman at Phi., Oct. 24, 1976
Most rushing touchdowns, season
13—Chuck Foreman, 1975
    Chuck Foreman, 1976
    Terry Allen, 1992
Most passing attempts, season
606—Warren Moon, 1995
Most passing attempts, game
63—Rich Gannon at N.E., Oct. 20, 1991
Most passes completed, season
377—Warren Moon, 1995
Most passes completed, game
38—Tommy Kramer vs. Cle., Dec. 14, 1980
    Tommy Kramer vs. G.B., Nov. 29, 1981

Most passing yards, career
33,098—Fran Tarkenton
Most passing yards, season
4,264—Warren Moon, 1994
Most passing yards, game
490—Tommy Kramer at Was., Nov. 2, 1986
Most touchdown passes, season
34—Randall Cunningham, 1998
Most pass receptions, career
931—Cris Carter
Most pass receptions, season
122—Cris Carter, 1994, 1995
Most pass receptions, game
15—Rickey Young at N.E., Dec. 16, 1979
Most receiving yards, career
11,512—Cris Carter
Most receiving yards, season
1,437—Randy Moss, 2000
Most receiving yards, game
210—Sammy White vs. Det., Nov. 7, 1976

Most receiving touchdowns, season
17—Cris Carter, 1995
    Randy Moss, 1998
Most touchdowns, career
104—Cris Carter
Most field goals, season
46—Fred Cox, 1970
Longest field goal
54 yards—Jan Stenerud vs. Atl., Sept. 16, 1984
Most interceptions, career
53—Paul Krause
Most interceptions, season
10—Paul Krause, 1975
Most sacks, career
130—Carl Eller
Most sacks, season
21—Chris Doleman, 1989

SERIES RECORDS

Minnesota vs.: Arizona 8-8; Atlanta 14-6; Baltimore 1-0; Buffalo 7-2; Carolina 3-0; Chicago 44-33-2; Cincinnati 5-4; Cleveland 8-3; Dallas 9-9; Denver 6-4; Detroit 49-28-2; Green Bay 39-39-1; Indianapolis 7-12-1; Jacksonville 1-0; Kansas City 3-4; Miami 3-4; New England 4-4; New Orleans 14-6; N.Y. Giants 8-5; N.Y. Jets 1-5; Oakland 3-7; Philadelphia 11-6; Pittsburgh 8-4; St. Louis 16-12-2; San Diego 4-4; San Francisco 17-17-1; Seattle 2-4; Tampa Bay 30-16; Tennessee 5-3; Washington 5-6.

COACHING RECORDS

Jerry Burns, 52-43-0 (3-3); Bud Grant, 158-96-5 (10-12); Dennis Green, 92-52-0 (4-8); Les Steckel, 3-13-0; Norm Van Brocklin, 29-51-4.
NOTE: Playoff games in parentheses.

RETIRED UNIFORM NUMBERS

No.	Player
10	Fran Tarkenton
22	Paul Krause
88	Alan Page

NEW ENGLAND PATRIOTS
YEAR-BY-YEAR RECORDS

		REGULAR SEASON							PLAYOFFS		
Year	W	L	T	Pct.	PF	PA	Finish	W	L	Highest round	Coach
1960*†	5	9	0	.357	286	349	4th/Eastern Div.	—	—		Lou Saban
1961*†	9	4	1	.692	413	313	2nd/Eastern Div.	—	—		Lou Saban, Mike Holovak
1962*†	9	4	1	.692	346	295	2nd/Eastern Div.	—	—		Mike Holovak
1963*†	7	6	1	.538	327	257	1st/Eastern Div.	1	1	AFL championship game	Mike Holovak
1964*†	10	3	1	.769	365	297	2nd/Eastern Div.	—	—		Mike Holovak
1965*†	4	8	2	.333	244	302	3rd/Eastern Div.	—	—		Mike Holovak
1966*†	8	4	2	.667	315	283	2nd/Eastern Div.	—	—		Mike Holovak

Year	W	L	T	Pct.	PF	PA	Finish	W	L	Highest round	Coach
1967*†	3	10	1	.231	280	389	5th/Eastern Div.	—	—		Mike Holovak
1968*†	4	10	0	.286	229	406	4th/Eastern Div.	—	—		Mike Holovak
1969*†	4	10	0	.286	266	316	T3rd/Eastern Div.	—	—		Clive Rush
1970†	2	12	0	.143	149	361	5th/AFC Eastern Div.	—	—		Clive Rush, John Mazur
1971	6	8	0	.429	238	325	T3rd/AFC Eastern Div.	—	—		John Mazur
1972	3	11	0	.214	192	446	5th/AFC Eastern Div.	—	—		J. Mazur, Phil Bengtson
1973	5	9	0	.357	258	300	3rd/AFC Eastern Div.	—	—		Chuck Fairbanks
1974	7	7	0	.500	348	289	T3rd/AFC Eastern Div.	—	—		Chuck Fairbanks
1975	3	11	0	.214	258	358	T4th/AFC Eastern Div.	—	—		Chuck Fairbanks
1976	11	3	0	.786	376	236	2nd/Eastern Div.	0	1	AFC div. playoff game	Chuck Fairbanks
1977	9	5	0	.643	278	217	3rd/AFC Eastern Div.	—	—		Chuck Fairbanks
1978	11	5	0	.688	358	286	1st/AFC Eastern Div.	0	1	AFC div. playoff game	Chuck Fairbanks, Hank Bullough-R. Erhardt
1979	9	7	0	.563	411	326	2nd/AFC Eastern Div.	—	—		Ron Erhardt
1980	10	6	0	.625	441	325	2nd/AFC Eastern Div.	—	—		Ron Erhardt
1981	2	14	0	.125	322	370	T4th/AFC Eastern Div.	—	—		Ron Erhardt
1982	5	4	0	.556	143	157	7th/AFC	0	1	AFC first-round pl. game	Ron Meyer
1983	8	8	0	.500	274	289	T2nd/AFC Eastern Div.	—	—		Ron Meyer
1984	9	7	0	.563	362	352	2nd/AFC Eastern Div.	—	—		R. Meyer, R. Berry
1985	11	5	0	.688	362	290	T2nd/AFC Eastern Div.	3	1	Super Bowl	Raymond Berry
1986	11	5	0	.688	412	307	1st/AFC Eastern Div.	0	1	AFC div. playoff game	Raymond Berry
1987	8	7	0	.533	320	293	T2nd/AFC Eastern Div.	—	—		Raymond Berry
1988	9	7	0	.563	250	284	T2nd/AFC Eastern Div.	—	—		Raymond Berry
1989	5	11	0	.313	297	391	4th/AFC Eastern Div.	—	—		Raymond Berry
1990	1	15	0	.063	181	446	5th/AFC Eastern Div.	—	—		Rod Rust
1991	6	10	0	.375	211	305	4th/AFC Eastern Div.	—	—		Dick MacPherson
1992	2	14	0	.125	205	363	5th/AFC Eastern Div.	—	—		Dick MacPherson
1993	5	11	0	.313	238	286	4th/AFC Eastern Div.	—	—		Bill Parcells
1994	10	6	0	.625	351	312	2nd/AFC Eastern Div.	0	1	AFC wild-card game	Bill Parcells
1995	6	10	0	.375	294	377	4th/AFC Eastern Div.	—	—		Bill Parcells
1996	11	5	0	.687	418	313	1st/AFC Eastern Div.	2	1	Super Bowl	Bill Parcells
1997	10	6	0	.625	369	289	1st/AFC Eastern Div.	1	1	AFC div. playoff game	Pete Carroll
1998	9	7	0	.563	337	329	4th/AFC Eastern Div.	0	1	AFC wild-card game	Pete Carroll
1999	8	8	0	.500	299	284	5th/AFC Eastern Div.	—	—		Pete Carroll
2000	5	11	0	.313	276	338	5th/AFC Eastern Div.	—	—		Bill Belichick

*American Football League.
†Boston Patriots.

FIRST-ROUND DRAFT PICKS

1960—Ron Burton, RB, Northwestern
1961—Tommy Mason, RB, Tulane
1962—Gary Collins, WR, Maryland
1963—Art Graham, E, Boston College
1964—Jack Concannon, QB, Boston College* (AFL)
1965—Jerry Rush, DE, Michigan State
     Dave McCormick, T, Louisiana State
1966—Karl Singer, T, Purdue
     Willie Townes, T, Tulsa
1967—John Charles, DB, Purdue
1968—Dennis Byrd, DE, North Carolina State
1969—Ron Sellers, WR, Florida State
1970—Phil Olsen, DT, Utah State
1971—Jim Plunkett, QB, Stanford*
1972—None
1973—John Hannah, G, Alabama
     Sam Cunningham, RB, Southern California
     Darryl Stingley, WR, Purdue
1974—None
1975—Russ Francis, TE, Oregon
1976—Mike Haynes, DB, Arizona State
     Pete Brock, C, Colorado
     Tim Fox, DB, Ohio State
1977—Raymond Clayborn, DB, Texas
     Stanley Morgan, WR, Tennessee
1978—Bob Cryder, G, Alabama
1979—Rick Sanford, DB, South Carolina
1980—Roland James, DB, Tennessee
     Vagas Ferguson, RB, Notre Dame

1981—Brian Holloway, T, Stanford
1982—Kenneth Sims, DT, Texas*
     Lester Williams, DT, Nebraska
1983—Tony Eason, QB, Illinois
1984—Irving Fryar, WR, Nebraska*
1985—Trevor Matich, C, Brigham Young
1986—Reggie Dupard, RB, Southern Methodist
1987—Bruce Armstrong, G, Louisville
1988—J. Stephens, RB, Northwestern Louisiana State
1989—Hart Lee Dykes, WR, Oklahoma State
1990—Chris Singleton, LB, Arizona
     Ray Agnew, DL, North Carolina State
1991—Pat Harlow, T, Southern California
     Leonard Russell, RB, Arizona State
1992—Eugene Chung, T, Virginia Tech
1993—Drew Bledsoe, QB, Washington State*
1994—Willie McGinest, DE, Southern California
1995—Ty Law, DB, Michigan
1996—Terry Glenn, WR, Ohio State
1997—Chris Canty, DB, Kansas State
1998—Robert Edwards, RB, Georgia
     Tebucky Jones, DB, Syracuse
1999—Damien Woody, C, Boston College
     Andy Katzenmoyer, LB, Ohio State
2000—None
2001—Richard Seymour, DT, Georgia
     *First player chosen in draft.

FRANCHISE RECORDS

Most rushing yards, career
5,453—Sam Cunningham
Most rushing yards, season
1,487—Curtis Martin, 1995
Most rushing yards, game
212—Tony Collins vs. NYJ, Sept. 18, 1983
Most rushing touchdowns, season
14—Curtis Martin, 1995, 1996
Most passing attempts, season
691—Drew Bledsoe, 1994
Most passing attempts, game
70—Drew Bledsoe vs. Min., Nov. 13, 1994 (OT)
60—Drew Bledsoe at Pit., Dec. 16, 1995
Most passes completed, season
400—Drew Bledsoe, 1994
Most passes completed, game
45—Drew Bledsoe vs. Min., Nov. 13, 1994 (OT)
39—Drew Bledsoe at Pit., Dec. 16, 1995
Most passing yards, career
26,886—Steve Grogan

Most passing yards, season
4,555—Drew Bledsoe, 1994
Most passing yards, game
426—Drew Bledsoe vs. Min., Nov. 13, 1994 (OT)
423—Drew Bledsoe vs. Mia., Nov. 23, 1998
Most touchdown passes, season
31—Babe Parilli, 1964
Most pass receptions, career
534—Stanley Morgan
Most pass receptions, season
96—Ben Coates, 1994
Most pass receptions, game
13—Terry Glenn at Cle., Oct. 3, 1999
Most receiving yards, career
10,352—Stanley Morgan
Most receiving yards, season
1,491—Stanley Morgan, 1986
Most receiving yards, game
214—Terry Glenn at Cle., Oct. 3, 1999

Most receiving touchdowns, season
12—Stanley Morgan, 1979
Most touchdowns, career
68—Stanley Morgan
Most field goals, season
32—Tony Franklin, 1986
Longest field goal
55 yards—Matt Bahr at Mia., Nov. 12, 1995
Adam Vinatieri at St.L., Dec. 13, 1998
Most interceptions, career
36—Raymond Clayborn
Most interceptions, season
11—Ron Hall, 1964
Most sacks, career
100—Andre Tippett
Most sacks, season
18.5—Andre Tippett, 1984

SERIES RECORDS

New England vs.: Arizona 4-6; Atlanta 3-6; Baltimore 2-0; Buffalo 42-39-1; Carolina 0-1; Chicago 5-3; Cincinnati 10-7; Cleveland 5-11; Dallas 1-7; Denver 14-20; Detroit 3-4; Green Bay 3-3; Indianapolis 37-24; Jacksonville 2-0; Kansas City 9-15-3; Miami 27-42; Minnesota 4-4; New Orleans 6-3; N.Y. Giants 3-3; N.Y. Jets 35-45-1; Oakland 12-13-1; Philadelphia 2-6; Pittsburgh 4-11; St. Louis 3-4; San Diego 16-11-2; San Francisco 2-7; Seattle 6-7; Tampa Bay 3-2; Tennessee 18-14-1; Washington 1-5.
NOTE: Includes records as Boston Patriots from 1960 through 1970.

COACHING RECORDS

Bill Belichick, 5-11-0; Phil Bengtson, 1-4-0; Raymond Berry, 48-39-0 (3-2); Hank Bullough, 0-1-0; Pete Carroll, 27-21-0 (1-2); Ron Erhardt, 21-27-0; Chuck Fairbanks, 46-39-0 (0-2); Mike Holovak, 52-46-9 (1-1); Dick MacPherson, 8-24-0; John Mazur, 9-21-0; Ron Meyer, 18-15-0 (0-1); Bill Parcells, 32-32-0 (2-2); Clive Rush, 5-16-0; Rod Rust, 1-15-0; Lou Saban, 7-12-0.
NOTE: Playoff games in parentheses.

RETIRED UNIFORM NUMBERS

No.	Player
20	Gino Cappelletti
40	Mike Haynes
57	Steve Nelson
73	John Hannah
79	Jim Hunt
89	Bob Dee

NEW ORLEANS SAINTS
YEAR-BY-YEAR RECORDS

Year	W	L	T	Pct.	PF	PA	Finish	W	L	Highest round	Coach
1967	3	11	0	.214	233	379	4th/Capitol Div.	—	—		Tom Fears
1968	4	9	1	.308	246	327	3rd/Century Div.	—	—		Tom Fears
1969	5	9	0	.357	311	393	3rd/Capitol Div.	—	—		Tom Fears
1970	2	11	1	.154	172	347	4th/NFC Western Div.	—	—		Tom Fears, J.D. Roberts
1971	4	8	2	.333	266	347	4th/NFC Western Div.	—	—		J.D. Roberts
1972	2	11	1	.179	215	361	4th/NFC Western Div.	—	—		J.D. Roberts
1973	5	9	0	.357	163	312	T3rd/NFC Western Div.	—	—		John North
1974	5	9	0	.357	166	263	3rd/NFC Western Div.	—	—		John North
1975	2	12	0	.143	165	360	4th/NFC Western Div.	—	—		J. North, Ernie Hefferle
1976	4	10	0	.286	253	346	T3rd/NFC Western Div.	—	—		Hank Stram
1977	3	11	0	.214	232	336	4th/NFC Western Div.	—	—		Hank Stram
1978	7	9	0	.438	281	298	3rd/NFC Western Div.	—	—		Dick Nolan
1979	8	8	0	.500	370	360	2nd/NFC Western Div.	—	—		Dick Nolan
1980	1	15	0	.063	291	487	4th/NFC Western Div.	—	—		Dick Nolan, Dick Stanfel
1981	4	12	0	.250	207	378	4th/NFC Western Div.	—	—		Bum Phillips
1982	4	5	0	.444	129	160	T8th/NFC	—	—		Bum Phillips
1983	8	8	0	.500	319	337	3rd/NFC Western Div.	—	—		Bum Phillips
1984	7	9	0	.438	298	361	3rd/NFC Western Div.	—	—		Bum Phillips
1985	5	11	0	.313	294	401	3rd/NFC Western Div.	—	—		B. Phillips, Wade Phillips

			REGULAR SEASON						PLAYOFFS		
Year	W	L	T	Pct.	PF	PA	Finish	W	L	Highest round	Coach
1986	7	9	0	.438	288	287	4th/NFC Western Div.	—	—		Jim Mora
1987	12	3	0	.800	422	283	2nd/NFC Western Div.	0	1	NFC wild-card game	Jim Mora
1988	10	6	0	.625	312	283	3rd/NFC Western Div.	—	—		Jim Mora
1989	9	7	0	.563	386	301	3rd/NFC Western Div.	—	—		Jim Mora
1990	8	8	0	.500	274	275	2nd/NFC Western Div.	0	1	NFC wild-card game	Jim Mora
1991	11	5	0	.688	341	211	1st/NFC Western Div.	0	1	NFC wild-card game	Jim Mora
1992	12	4	0	.750	330	202	2nd/NFC Western Div.	0	1	NFC wild-card game	Jim Mora
1993	8	8	0	.500	317	343	2nd/NFC Western Div.	—	—		Jim Mora
1994	7	9	0	.438	348	407	T2nd/NFC Western Div.	—	—		Jim Mora
1995	7	9	0	.438	319	348	T3rd/NFC Western Div.	—	—		Jim Mora
1996	3	13	0	.188	229	339	T4th/NFC Western Div.	—	—		Jim Mora, Rick Venturi
1997	6	10	0	.375	237	327	4th/NFC Western Div.	—	—		Mike Ditka
1998	6	10	0	.375	305	359	3rd/NFC Western Div.	—	—		Mike Ditka
1999	3	13	0	.188	260	434	5th/NFC Western Div.	—	—		Mike Ditka
2000	10	6	0	.625	354	305	1st/NFC Western Div.	1	1	NFC div. playoff game	Jim Haslett

FIRST-ROUND DRAFT PICKS

1967—Les Kelley, RB, Alabama
1968—Kevin Hardy, DE, Notre Dame
1969—John Shinners, G, Xavier (Ohio)
1970—Ken Burrough, WR, Texas Southern
1971—Archie Manning, QB, Mississippi
1972—Royce Smith, G, Georgia
1973—None
1974—Rick Middleton, LB, Ohio State
1975—Larry Burton, WR, Purdue
       Kurt Schumacher, G, Ohio State
1976—Chuck Muncie, RB, California
1977—Joe Campbell, DE, Maryland
1978—Wes Chandler, WR, Florida
1979—Russell Erxleben, P, Texas
1980—Stan Brock, T, Colorado
1981—George Rogers, RB, South Carolina*
1982—Lindsay Scott, WR, Georgia
1983—None
1984—None

1985—Alvin Toles, LB, Tennessee
1986—Jim Dombrowski, T, Virginia
1987—Shawn Knight, DE, Brigham Young
1988—Craig Heyward, RB, Pittsburgh
1989—Wayne Martin, DE, Arkansas
1990—Renaldo Turnbull, DE, West Virginia
1991—None
1992—Vaughn Dunbar, RB, Indiana
1993—Willie Roaf, T, Louisiana Tech
       Irv Smith, TE, Notre Dame
1994—Joe Johnson, DE, Louisville
1995—Mark Fields, LB, Washington State
1996—Alex Molden, DB, Oregon
1997—Chris Naeole, G, Colorado
1998—Kyle Turley, T, San Diego State
1999—Ricky Williams, RB, Texas
2000—None
2001—Deuce McAllister, RB, Mississippi
    *First player chosen in draft.

FRANCHISE RECORDS

Most rushing yards, career
4,267—George Rogers
Most rushing yards, season
1,674—George Rogers, 1981
Most rushing yards, game
206—George Rogers vs. St.L., Sept. 4, 1983
Most rushing touchdowns, season
13—George Rogers, 1981
    Dalton Hilliard, 1989
Most passing attempts, season
567—Jim Everett, 1995
Most passing attempts, game
55—Jim Everett at S.F., Sept. 25, 1994
Most passes completed, season
346—Jim Everett, 1994
Most passes completed, game
33—Archie Manning at G.B., Sept. 10, 1978
    Jeff Blake at S.D., Sept. 10, 2000
Most passing yards, career
21,734—Archie Manning

Most passing yards, season
3,970—Jim Everett, 1995
Most passing yards, game
441—Aaron Brooks vs. Den., Dec. 3, 2000
Most touchdown passes, season
26—Jim Everett, 1995
Most pass receptions, career
532—Eric Martin
Most pass receptions, season
94—Joe Horn, 2000
Most pass receptions, game
14—Tony Galbreath at G.B., Sept. 10, 1978
Most receiving yards, career
7,854—Eric Martin
Most receiving yards, season
1,340—Joe Horn, 2000
Most receiving yards, game
205—Wes Chandler vs. Atl., Sept. 2, 1979
Most receiving touchdowns, season
9—Henry Childs, 1977

Most touchdowns, career
53—Dalton Hilliard
Most field goals, season
31—Morten Andersen, 1985
Longest field goal
63 yards—Tom Dempsey vs. Det., Nov. 8, 1970
Most interceptions, career
37—Dave Waymer
Most interceptions, season
10—Dave Whitsell, 1967
Most sacks, career
123—Rickey Jackson
Most sacks, season
17—Pat Swilling, 1991
    La'Roi Glover, 2000

SERIES RECORDS

New Orleans vs.: Arizona 11-12; Atlanta 26-37; Baltimore 0-2; Buffalo 2-4; Carolina 6-6; Chicago 8-11; Cincinnati 5-4; Cleveland 3-10; Dallas 5-14; Denver 2-5; Detroit 8-7-1; Green Bay 4-13; Indianapolis 4-3; Jacksonville 1-1; Kansas City 3-4; Miami 4-6; Minnesota 6-14; New England 3-6; N.Y. Giants 8-12; N.Y. Jets 4-4; Philadelphia 8-13; Oakland 3-5-1; Pittsburgh 5-6; St. Louis 26-34; San Diego 2-6; San Francisco 18-43-2; Seattle 4-3; Tampa Bay 13-6; Tennessee 4-5-1; Washington 5-12.

COACHING RECORDS

Mike Ditka, 15-33-0; Tom Fears, 13-34-2; Jim Haslett, 10-6-0 (1-1); Ernie Hefferle, 1-7-0; Jim Mora, 93-74-0 (0-4); Dick Nolan, 15-29-0; John North, 11-23-0; Bum Phillips, 27-42-0; Wade Phillips, 1-3-0; J.D. Roberts, 7-25-3; Dick Stanfel, 1-3-0; Hank Stram, 7-21-0; Rick Venturi, 1-7-0.
NOTE: Playoff games in parentheses.

NEW YORK GIANTS
YEAR-BY-YEAR RECORDS

	REGULAR SEASON							PLAYOFFS			
Year	W	L	T	Pct.	PF	PA	Finish	W	L	Highest round	Coach
1925	8	4	0	.667	122	67	T4th				Bob Folwell
1926	8	4	1	.667	147	51	T6th				Joe Alexander
1927	11	1	1	.917	197	20	1st				Earl Potteiger
1928	4	7	2	.364	79	136	6th				Earl Potteiger
1929	13	1	1	.929	312	86	2nd				LeRoy Andrews
1930	13	4	0	.765	308	98	2nd				L. Andrews, Benny Friedman-Steve Owen
1931	7	6	1	.538	154	100	5th				Steve Owen
1932	4	6	2	.400	93	113	5th				Steve Owen
1933	11	3	0	.786	244	101	1st/Eastern Div.	0	1	NFL championship game	Steve Owen
1934	8	5	0	.615	147	107	1st/Eastern Div.	1	0	NFL champ	Steve Owen
1935	9	3	0	.750	180	96	1st/Eastern Div.	0	1	NFL championship game	Steve Owen
1936	5	6	1	.455	115	163	3rd/Eastern Div.	—	—		Steve Owen
1937	6	3	2	.667	128	109	2nd/Eastern Div.	—	—		Steve Owen
1938	8	2	1	.800	194	79	1st/Eastern Div.	1	0	NFL champ	Steve Owen
1939	9	1	1	.900	168	85	1st/Eastern Div.	0	1	NFL championship game	Steve Owen
1940	6	4	1	.600	131	133	3rd/Eastern Div.	—	—		Steve Owen
1941	8	3	0	.727	238	114	1st/Eastern Div.	0	1	NFL championship game	Steve Owen
1942	5	5	1	.500	155	139	3rd/Eastern Div.	—	—		Steve Owen
1943	6	3	1	.667	197	170	2nd/Eastern Div.	0	1	E. Div. champ. game	Steve Owen
1944	8	1	1	.889	206	75	1st/Eastern Div.	0	1	NFL championship game	Steve Owen
1945	3	6	1	.333	179	198	T3rd/Eastern Div.	—	—		Steve Owen
1946	7	3	1	.700	236	162	1st/Eastern Div.	0	1	NFL championship game	Steve Owen
1947	2	8	2	.200	190	309	5th/Eastern Div.	—	—		Steve Owen
1948	4	8	0	.333	297	388	T3rd/Eastern Div.	—	—		Steve Owen
1949	6	6	0	.500	287	298	3rd/Eastern Div.	—	—		Steve Owen
1950	10	2	0	.833	268	150	2nd/American Conf.	0	1	Am. Conf. champ. game	Steve Owen
1951	9	2	1	.818	254	161	2nd/American Conf.	—	—		Steve Owen
1952	7	5	0	.583	234	231	T2nd/American Conf.	—	—		Steve Owen
1953	3	9	0	.250	179	277	5th/Eastern Conf.	—	—		Steve Owen
1954	7	5	0	.583	293	184	3rd/Eastern Conf.	—	—		Jim Lee Howell
1955	6	5	1	.545	267	223	3rd/Eastern Conf.	—	—		Jim Lee Howell
1956	8	3	1	.727	264	197	1st/Eastern Conf.	1	0	NFL champ	Jim Lee Howell
1957	7	5	0	.583	254	211	2nd/Eastern Conf.	—	—		Jim Lee Howell
1958	9	3	0	.750	246	183	1st/Eastern Conf.	1	1	NFL championship game	Jim Lee Howell
1959	10	2	0	.833	284	170	1st/Eastern Conf.	0	1	NFL championship game	Jim Lee Howell
1960	6	4	2	.600	271	261	3rd/Eastern Conf.	—	—		Jim Lee Howell
1961	10	3	1	.769	368	220	1st/Eastern Conf.	0	1	NFL championship game	Allie Sherman
1962	12	2	0	.857	398	283	1st/Eastern Conf.	0	1	NFL championship game	Allie Sherman
1963	11	3	0	.786	448	280	1st/Eastern Conf.	0	1	NFL championship game	Allie Sherman
1964	2	10	2	.167	241	399	7th/Eastern Conf.	—	—		Allie Sherman
1965	7	7	0	.500	270	338	T2nd/Eastern Conf.	—	—		Allie Sherman
1966	1	12	1	.077	263	501	8th/Eastern Conf.	—	—		Allie Sherman
1967	7	7	0	.500	369	379	2nd/Century Div.	—	—		Allie Sherman
1968	7	7	0	.500	294	325	2nd/Capitol Div.	—	—		Allie Sherman
1969	6	8	0	.429	264	298	2nd/Century Div.	—	—		Alex Webster
1970	9	5	0	.643	301	270	2nd/NFC Eastern Div.	—	—		Alex Webster
1971	4	10	0	.286	228	362	5th/NFC Eastern Div.	—	—		Alex Webster
1972	8	6	0	.571	331	247	3rd/NFC Eastern Div.	—	—		Alex Webster
1973	2	11	1	.179	226	362	5th/NFC Eastern Div.	—	—		Alex Webster
1974	2	12	0	.143	195	299	5th/NFC Eastern Div.	—	—		Bill Arnsparger
1975	5	9	0	.357	216	306	4th/NFC Eastern Div.	—	—		Bill Arnsparger
1976	3	11	0	.214	170	250	5th/NFC Eastern Div.	—	—		B. Arnsparger, J. McVay
1977	5	9	0	.357	181	265	T4th/NFC Eastern Div.	—	—		John McVay
1978	6	10	0	.375	264	298	T4th/NFC Eastern Div.	—	—		John McVay
1979	6	10	0	.375	237	323	4th/NFC Eastern Div.	—	—		Ray Perkins
1980	4	12	0	.250	249	425	5th/NFC Eastern Div.	—	—		Ray Perkins
1981	9	7	0	.563	295	257	3rd/NFC Eastern Div.	1	1	NFC div. playoff game	Ray Perkins

HISTORY Team by team

REGULAR SEASON							PLAYOFFS			
Year	W	L	T	Pct.	PF	PA	Finish	W	L	Highest round	Coach
---	---	---	---	---	---	---	---	---	---	---	---
1982	4	5	0	.444	164	160	T8th/NFC	—	—		Ray Perkins
1983	3	12	1	.219	267	347	5th/NFC Eastern Div.	—	—		Bill Parcells
1984	9	7	0	.563	299	301	2nd/NFC Eastern Div.	1	1	NFC div. playoff game	Bill Parcells
1985	10	6	0	.625	399	283	2nd/NFC Eastern Div.	1	1	NFC div. playoff game	Bill Parcells
1986	14	2	0	.875	371	236	1st/NFC Eastern Div.	3	0	Super Bowl champ	Bill Parcells
1987	6	9	0	.400	280	312	5th/NFC Eastern Div.	—	—		Bill Parcells
1988	10	6	0	.625	359	304	2nd/NFC Eastern Div.	—	—		Bill Parcells
1989	12	4	0	.750	348	252	1st/NFC Eastern Div.	0	1	NFC div. playoff game	Bill Parcells
1990	13	3	0	.813	335	211	1st/NFC Eastern Div.	3	0	Super Bowl champ	Bill Parcells
1991	8	8	0	.500	281	297	4th/NFC Eastern Div.	—	—		Ray Handley
1992	6	10	0	.375	306	367	4th/NFC Eastern Div.	—	—		Ray Handley
1993	11	5	0	.688	288	205	2nd/NFC Eastern Div.	1	1	NFC div. playoff game	Dan Reeves
1994	9	7	0	.563	279	305	2nd/NFC Eastern Div.	—	—		Dan Reeves
1995	5	11	0	.313	290	340	4th/NFC Eastern Div.	—	—		Dan Reeves
1996	6	10	0	.375	242	297	5th/NFC Eastern Div.	—	—		Dan Reeves
1997	10	5	1	.656	307	265	1st/NFC Eastern Div.	0	1	NFC wild-card game	Jim Fassel
1998	8	8	0	.500	287	309	3rd/NFC Eastern Div.	—	—		Jim Fassel
1999	7	9	0	.438	299	358	3rd/NFC Eastern Div.	—	—		Jim Fassel
2000	12	4	0	.750	328	246	1st/NFC Eastern Div.	2	1	Super Bowl	Jim Fassel

FIRST-ROUND DRAFT PICKS

1936—Art Lewis, T, Ohio
1937—Ed Widseth, T, Minnesota
1938—George Karamatic, B, Gonzaga
1939—Walt Nielson, B, Arizona
1940—Grenville Lansdell, B, Southern California
1941—George Franck, B, Minnesota
1942—Merle Hapes, B, Mississippi
1943—Steve Filipowicz, B, Fordham
1944—Billy Hillenbrand, B, Indiana
1945—Elmer Barbour, B, Wake Forest
1946—George Connor, T, Notre Dame
1947—Vic Schwall, B, Northwestern
1948—Tony Minisi, B, Pennsylvania
1949—Paul Page, B, Southern Methodist
1950—Travis Tidwell, B, Auburn
1951—Kyle Rote, B, Southern Methodist*
       Kim Spavital, B, Oklahoma A&M
1952—Frank Gifford, B, Southern California
1953—Bobby Marlow, B, Alabama
1954—None
1955—Joe Heap, B, Notre Dame
1956—Henry Moore, B, Arkansas
1957—None
1958—Phil King, B, Vanderbilt
1959—Lee Grosscup, B, Utah
1960—Lou Cordileone, G, Clemson
1961—None
1962—Jerry Hillebrand, LB, Colorado
1963—None
1964—Joe Don Looney, RB, Oklahoma
1965—T. Frederickson, RB, Auburn*
1966—Francis Peay, T, Missouri
1967—None
1968—None
1969—Fred Dryer, DE, San Diego State

1970—Jim Files, LB, Oklahoma
1971—Rocky Thompson, RB, West Texas State
1972—Eldridge Small, DB, Texas A&I
       Larry Jacobson, DT, Nebraska
1973—None
1974—John Hicks, G, Ohio State
1975—None
1976—Troy Archer, DE, Colorado
1977—Gary Jeter, DT, Southern Cal
1978—Gordon King, T, Stanford
1979—Phil Simms, QB, Morehead State
1980—Mark Haynes, DB, Colorado
1981—Lawrence Taylor, LB, North Carolina
1982—Butch Woolfolk, RB, Michigan
1983—Terry Kinard, DB, Clemson
1984—Carl Banks, LB, Michigan State
       Bill Roberts, T, Ohio State
1985—George Adams, RB, Kentucky
1986—Eric Dorsey, DT, Notre Dame
1987—Mark Ingram, WR, Michigan State
1988—Eric Moore, T, Indiana
1989—Brian Williams, G, Minnesota
1990—Rodney Hampton, RB, Georgia
1991—Jarrod Bunch, FB, Michigan
1992—Derek Brown, TE, Notre Dame
1993—None
1994—Thomas Lewis, WR, Indiana
1995—Tyrone Wheatley, RB, Michigan
1996—Cedric Jones, DE, Oklahoma
1997—Ike Hilliard, WR, Florida
1998—Shaun Williams, DB, UCLA
1999—Luke Petitgout, T, Notre Dame
2000—Ron Dayne, RB, Wisconsin
2001—Will Allen, DB, Syracuse
*First player chosen in draft.

FRANCHISE RECORDS

Most rushing yards, career
6,897—Rodney Hampton
Most rushing yards, season
1,516—Joe Morris, 1986
Most rushing yards, game
218—Gene Roberts vs. Chi. Cardinals,
       Nov. 12, 1950
Most rushing touchdowns, season
21—Joe Morris, 1985

Most passing attempts, season
533—Phil Simms, 1984
Most passing attempts, game
62—Phil Simms at Cin., Oct. 13, 1985
Most passes completed, season
311—Kerry Collins, 2000
Most passes completed, game
40—Phil Simms at Cin., Oct. 13, 1985

Most passing yards, career
33,462—Phil Simms
Most passing yards, season
4,044—Phil Simms, 1984
Most passing yards, game
513—Phil Simms at Cin., Oct. 13, 1985
Most touchdown passes, season
36—Y.A. Tittle, 1963

Most pass receptions, career
395—Joe Morrison

Most pass receptions, season
79—Amani Toomer, 1999

Most pass receptions, game
12—Mark Bavaro at Cin., Oct. 13, 1985

Most receiving yards, career
5,434—Frank Gifford

Most receiving yards, season
1,209—Homer Jones

Most receiving yards, game
269—Del Shofner vs. Was., Oct. 28, 1962

Most receiving touchdowns, season
13—Homer Jones, 1967

Most touchdowns, career
78—Frank Gifford

Most field goals, season
35—Ali Haji-Sheikh, 1983

Longest field goal
56 yards—Ali Haji-Sheikh at Det.,
Nov. 7, 1983

Most interceptions, career
74—Emlen Tunnell

Most interceptions, season
11—Otto Schellbacher, 1951
Jimmy Patton, 1958

Most sacks, career
132.5—Lawrence Taylor

Most sacks, season
20.5—Lawrence Taylor, 1986

SERIES RECORDS

N.Y. Giants vs.: Arizona 76-39-2; Atlanta 7-7; Baltimore, 0-1; Buffalo 3-5; Carolina 0-1; Chicago 17-25-2; Cincinnati 2-4; Cleveland 18-25-2; Dallas 28-47-2; Denver 4-3; Detroit 14-15-1; Green Bay 20-23-2; Indianapolis 5-6; Jacksonville 1-1; Kansas City 7-3; Miami 3-1; Minnesota 5-8; New England 3-3; New Orleans 12-8; N.Y. Jets 5-4; Oakland 2-6; Philadelphia 71-59-2; Pittsburgh 45-28-3; St. Louis 7-22; San Diego 5-3; San Francisco 11-12; Seattle 5-3; Tampa Bay 9-5; Tennessee 5-2; Washington 69-54-3.

COACHING RECORDS

Joe Alexander, 8-4-1; LeRoy Andrews, 24-5-1; Bill Arnsparger, 7-28-0; Jim Fassel, 37-26-1 (2-2); Bob Folwell, 8-4-0; Benny Friedman, 2-0-0; Ray Handley, 14-18-0; Jim Lee Howell, 53-27-4 (2-2); John McVay, 14-23-0; Steve Owen, 153-100-17 (2-8); Bill Parcells, 77-49-1 (8-3); Ray Perkins, 23-34-0 (1-1); Earl Potteiger, 15-8-3; Dan Reeves, 31-33-0 (1-1); Allie Sherman, 57-51-4 (0-3); Alex Webster, 29-40-1.
NOTE: Playoff games in parentheses.

RETIRED UNIFORM NUMBERS

No.	Player
1	Ray Flaherty
4	Tuffy Leemans
7	Mel Hein
11	Phil Simms
14	Y.A. Tittle
32	Al Blozis
40	Joe Morrison
42	Charlie Conerly
50	Ken Strong
56	Lawrence Taylor

NEW YORK JETS
YEAR-BY-YEAR RECORDS

	REGULAR SEASON							PLAYOFFS			
Year	W	L	T	Pct.	PF	PA	Finish	W	L	Highest round	Coach
1960*†	7	7	0	.500	382	399	2nd/Eastern Div.	—	—		Sammy Baugh
1961*†	7	7	0	.500	301	390	3rd/Eastern Div.	—	—		Sammy Baugh
1962*†	5	9	0	.357	278	423	4th/Eastern Div.	—	—		Bulldog Turner
1963*	5	8	1	.385	249	399	4th/Eastern Div.	—	—		Weeb Ewbank
1964*	5	8	1	.385	278	315	3rd/Eastern Div.	—	—		Weeb Ewbank
1965*	5	8	1	.385	285	303	2nd/Eastern Div.	—	—		Weeb Ewbank
1966*	6	6	2	.500	322	312	3rd/Eastern Div.	—	—		Weeb Ewbank
1967*	8	5	1	.615	371	329	2nd/Eastern Div.	—	—		Weeb Ewbank
1968*	11	3	0	.786	419	280	1st/Eastern Div.	2	0	Super Bowl champ	Weeb Ewbank
1969*	10	4	0	.714	353	269	1st/Eastern Div.	0	1	Div. playoff game	Weeb Ewbank
1970	4	10	0	.286	255	286	3rd/AFC Eastern Div.	—	—		Weeb Ewbank
1971	6	8	0	.429	212	299	T3rd/AFC Eastern Div.	—	—		Weeb Ewbank
1972	7	7	0	.500	367	324	2nd/AFC Eastern Div.	—	—		Weeb Ewbank
1973	4	10	0	.286	240	306	T4th/AFC Eastern Div.	—	—		Weeb Ewbank
1974	7	7	0	.500	279	300	T3rd/AFC Eastern Div.	—	—		Charley Winner
1975	3	11	0	.214	258	433	T4th/AFC Eastern Div.	—	—		C. Winner, Ken Shipp
1976	3	11	0	.214	169	383	4th/AFC Eastern Div.	—	—		Lou Holtz, Mike Holovak
1977	3	11	0	.214	191	300	T4th/AFC Eastern Div.	—	—		Walt Michaels
1978	8	8	0	.500	359	364	3rd/AFC Eastern Div.	—	—		Walt Michaels
1979	8	8	0	.500	337	383	3rd/AFC Eastern Div.	—	—		Walt Michaels
1980	4	12	0	.250	302	395	5th/AFC Eastern Div.	—	—		Walt Michaels
1981	10	5	1	.656	355	287	2nd/AFC Eastern Div.	0	1	AFC wild-card game	Walt Michaels
1982	6	3	0	.667	245	166	T4th/AFC	2	1	AFC championship game	Walt Michaels
1983	7	9	0	.438	313	331	T4th/AFC Eastern Div.	—	—		Joe Walton
1984	7	9	0	.438	332	364	3rd/AFC Eastern Div.	—	—		Joe Walton
1985	11	5	0	.688	393	264	T2nd/AFC Eastern Div.	0	1	AFC wild-card game	Joe Walton
1986	10	6	0	.625	364	386	2nd/AFC Eastern Div.	1	1	AFC div. playoff game	Joe Walton
1987	6	9	0	.400	334	360	5th/AFC Eastern Div.	—	—		Joe Walton
1988	8	7	1	.531	372	354	4th/AFC Eastern Div.	—	—		Joe Walton
1989	4	12	0	.250	253	411	5th/AFC Eastern Div.	—	—		Joe Walton
1990	6	10	0	.375	295	345	4th/AFC Eastern Div.	—	—		Bruce Coslet
1991	8	8	0	.500	314	293	2nd/AFC Eastern Div.	0	1	AFC wild-card game	Bruce Coslet

				REGULAR SEASON						PLAYOFFS		
Year	W	L	T	Pct.	PF	PA	Finish	W	L	Highest round		Coach
1992	4	12	0	.250	220	315	4th/AFC Eastern Div.	—	—			Bruce Coslet
1993	8	8	0	.500	270	247	3rd/AFC Eastern Div.	—	—			Bruce Coslet
1994	6	10	0	.375	264	320	5th/AFC Eastern Div.	—	—			Pete Carroll
1995	3	13	0	.188	233	384	5th/AFC Eastern Div.	—	—			Rich Kotite
1996	1	15	0	.063	279	454	5th/AFC Eastern Div.	—	—			Rich Kotite
1997	9	7	0	.563	348	287	T2nd/AFC Eastern Div.	—	—			Bill Parcells
1998	12	4	0	.750	416	266	1st/AFC Eastern Div.	1	1	AFC championship game		Bill Parcells
1999	8	8	0	.500	308	309	4th/AFC Eastern Div.	—	—			Bill Parcells
2000	9	7	0	.563	321	321	3rd/AFC Eastern Div.	—	—			Al Groh

*American Football League.
†New York Titans.

FIRST-ROUND DRAFT PICKS

1960—George Izo, QB, Notre Dame
1961—Tom Brown, G, Minnesota
1962—Sandy Stephens, QB, Minnesota
1963—Jerry Stovall, RB, Louisiana State
1964—Matt Snell, RB, Ohio State
1965—Joe Namath, QB, Alabama
    Tom Nowatzke, RB, Indiana
1966—Bill Yearby, DT, Michigan
1967—Paul Seiler, G, Notre Dame
1968—Lee White, RB, Weber State
1969—Dave Foley, T, Ohio State
1970—Steve Tannen, DB, Florida
1971—John Riggins, RB, Kansas
1972—Jerome Barkum, WR, Jackson State
1972—Mike Taylor, LB, Michigan
1973—Burgess Owens, DB, Miami
1974—Carl Barzilauskas, DT, Indiana
1975—None
1976—Richard Todd, QB, Alabama
1977—Marvin Powell, T, Southern California
1978—Chris Ward, T, Ohio State
1979—Marty Lyons, DT, Alabama
1980—Lam Jones, WR, Texas
1981—Freeman McNeil, RB, UCLA
1982—Bob Crable, LB, Notre Dame

1983—Ken O'Brien, QB, California-Davis
1984—Russell Carter, DB, Southern Methodist
    Ron Faurot, DE, Arkansas
1985—Al Toon, WR, Wisconsin
1986—Mike Haight, T, Iowa
1987—Roger Vick, FB, Texas A&M
1988—Dave Cadigan, T, Southern California
1989—Jeff Lageman, LB, Virginia
1990—Blair Thomas, RB, Penn State
1991—None
1992—Johnny Mitchell, TE, Nebraska
1993—Marvin Jones, LB, Florida State
1994—Aaron Glenn, DB, Texas A&M
1995—Kyle Brady, TE, Penn State
    Hugh Douglas, DE, Central State (O.)
1996—Keyshawn Johnson, WR, Southern California*
1997—James Farrior, LB, Virginia
1998—None
1999—None
2000—Shaun Ellis, DE, Tennessee
    John Abraham, LB, South Carolina
    Chad Pennington, QB, Marshall
    Anthony Becht, TE, West Virginia
2001—Santana Moss, WR, Miami, Fla.
*First player chosen in draft.

FRANCHISE RECORDS

Most rushing yards, career
8,074—Freeman McNeil
Most rushing yards, season
1,464—Curtis Martin, 1999
Most rushing yards, game
203—Curtis Martin vs. Ind., Dec. 3, 2000
Most rushing touchdowns, season
11—Emerson Boozer, 1972
    Johnny Hector, 1987
    Brad Baxter, 1991
Most passing attempts, season
590—Vinny Testaverde, 2000
Most passing attempts, game
69—Vinny Testaverde at Bal., Dec. 24, 2000
Most passes completed, season
328—Vinny Testaverde, 2000
Most passes completed, game
42—Richard Todd vs. S.F., Sept. 21, 1980
    Vinny Testaverde vs. Sea., Dec. 6, 1998

Most passing yards, career
27,057—Joe Namath
Most passing yards, season
4,007—Joe Namath, 1967
Most passing yards, game
496—Joe Namath at Bal., Sept. 24, 1972
Most touchdown passes, season
29—Vinny Testaverde, 1998
Most pass receptions, career
627—Don Maynard
Most pass receptions, season
93—Al Toon, 1988
Most pass receptions, game
17—Clark Gaines vs. S.F., Sept. 21, 1980
Most receiving yards, career
11,732—Don Maynard
Most receiving yards, season
1,434—Don Maynard, 1967
Most receiving yards, game
228—Don Maynard at Oak., Nov. 17, 1968

Most receiving touchdowns, season
14—Art Powell, 1960
    Don Maynard, 1965
Most touchdowns, career
88—Don Maynard
Most field goals, season
34—Jim Turner, 1968
Longest field goal
55 yards—Pat Leahy vs. Chi., Dec. 14, 1985
    John Hall at Sea., Aug. 31, 1997
Most interceptions, career
34—Bill Baird
Most interceptions, season
12—Dainard Paulson, 1964
Most sacks, career
107.5—Mark Gastineau
Most sacks, season
22—Mark Gastineau, 1984

SERIES RECORDS

N.Y. Jets vs.: Arizona 3-2; Atlanta 4-4; Baltimore 1-2; Buffalo 35-46; Carolina 1-1; Chicago 3-4; Cincinnati 10-6; Cleveland 6-9; Dallas 2-5; Denver 13-14-1; Detroit 3-6; Green Bay 6-2; Indianapolis 24-37; Jacksonville 1-2; Kansas City 13-14-1; Miami 34-33-1; Minnesota 5-1; New England 45-35-1; New Orleans 4-4; N.Y. Giants 4-5; Oakland 10-18-2; Philadelphia 0-6; Pittsburgh 1-14; St. Louis 2-7; San Diego 9-17-1; San Francisco 1-7; Seattle 7-8; Tampa Bay 7-1; Tennessee 13-20-1; Washington 1-6.
NOTE: Includes records as New York Titans from 1960 through 1962.

COACHING RECORDS

Sammy Baugh, 14-14-0; Pete Carroll, 6-10-0; Bruce Coslet, 26-38-0 (0-1); Weeb Ewbank, 71-77-6 (2-1); Al Groh, 9-7-0; Mike Holovak, 0-1-0; Lou Holtz, 3-10-0; Rich Kotite, 4-28-0; Walt Michaels, 39-47-1 (2-2); Bill Parcells, 29-19-0 (1-1); Ken Shipp, 1-4-0; Clyde Turner, 5-9-0; Joe Walton, 53-57-1 (1-2); Charley Winner, 9-14-0.
NOTE: Playoff games in parentheses.

RETIRED UNIFORM NUMBERS

No.	Player
12	Joe Namath
13	Don Maynard

OAKLAND RAIDERS
YEAR-BY-YEAR RECORDS

Year	\multicolumn{5}{c}{REGULAR SEASON}					\multicolumn{2}{c}{PLAYOFFS}		Coach
	W	L	T	Pct.	PF	PA	Finish	W	L	Highest round	Coach
1960*	6	8	0	.429	319	388	3rd/Western Div.	—	—		Eddie Erdelatz
1961*	2	12	0	.143	237	458	4th/Western Div.	—	—		E. Erdelatz, Marty Feldman
1962*	1	13	0	.071	213	370	4th/Western Div.	—	—		M. Feldman, Red Conkright
1963*	10	4	0	.714	363	288	2nd/Western Div.	—	—		Al Davis
1964*	5	7	2	.417	303	350	3rd/Western Div.	—	—		Al Davis
1965*	8	5	1	.615	298	239	2nd/Western Div.	—	—		Al Davis
1966*	8	5	1	.615	315	288	2nd/Western Div.	—	—		John Rauch
1967*	13	1	0	.929	468	233	1st/Western Div.	1	1	Super Bowl	John Rauch
1968*	12	2	0	.857	453	233	1st/Western Div.	1	1	AFL championship game	John Rauch
1969*	12	1	1	.923	377	242	1st/Western Div.	1	1	AFL championship game	John Madden
1970	8	4	2	.667	300	293	1st/AFC Western Div.	1	1	AFC championship game	John Madden
1971	8	4	2	.667	344	278	2nd/AFC Western Div.	—	—		John Madden
1972	10	3	1	.750	365	248	1st/AFC Western Div.	0	1	AFC div. playoff game	John Madden
1973	9	4	1	.679	292	175	1st/AFC Western Div.	1	1	AFC championship game	John Madden
1974	12	2	0	.857	355	228	1st/AFC Western Div.	1	1	AFC championship game	John Madden
1975	11	3	0	.786	375	255	1st/AFC Western Div.	1	1	AFC championship game	John Madden
1976	13	1	0	.929	350	237	1st/AFC Western Div.	3	0	Super Bowl champ	John Madden
1977	11	3	0	.786	351	230	2nd/AFC Western Div.	1	1	AFC championship game	John Madden
1978	9	7	0	.563	311	283	T2nd/AFC Western Div.	—	—		Tom Flores
1979	9	7	0	.563	365	337	T3rd/AFC Western Div.	—	—		Tom Flores
1980	11	5	0	.688	364	306	2nd/AFC Western Div.	4	0	Super Bowl champ	Tom Flores
1981	7	9	0	.438	273	343	4th/AFC Western Div.	—	—		Tom Flores
1982†	8	1	0	.889	260	200	1st/AFC	1	1	AFC second-round pl. game	Tom Flores
1983†	12	4	0	.750	442	338	1st/AFC Western Div.	3	0	Super Bowl champ	Tom Flores
1984†	11	5	0	.688	368	278	3rd/AFC Western Div.	0	1	AFC wild-card game	Tom Flores
1985†	12	4	0	.750	354	308	1st/AFC Western Div.	0	1	AFC div. playoff game	Tom Flores
1986†	8	8	0	.500	323	346	4th/AFC Western Div.	—	—		Tom Flores
1987†	5	10	0	.333	301	289	4th/AFC Western Div.	—	—		Mike Shanahan
1988†	7	9	0	.438	325	369	3rd/AFC Western Div.	—	—		Mike Shanahan, Art Shell
1989†	8	8	0	.500	315	297	3rd/AFC Western Div.	—	—		Art Shell
1990†	12	4	0	.750	337	268	1st/AFC Western Div.	1	1	AFC championship game	Art Shell
1991†	9	7	0	.563	298	297	3rd/AFC Western Div.	0	1	AFC wild-card game	Art Shell
1992†	7	9	0	.438	249	281	4th/AFC Western Div.	—	—		Art Shell
1993†	10	6	0	.625	306	326	2nd/AFC Western Div.	1	1	AFC div. playoff game	Art Shell
1994†	9	7	0	.563	303	327	3rd/AFC Western Div.	—	—		Mike White
1995	8	8	0	.500	348	332	T3rd/AFC Western Div.	—	—		Mike White
1996	7	9	0	.438	340	293	T4th/AFC Western Div.	—	—		Joe Bugel
1997	4	12	0	.250	324	419	T4th/AFC Western Div.	—	—		Jon Gruden
1998	8	8	0	.500	288	356	2nd/AFC Western Div.	—	—		Jon Gruden
1999	8	8	0	.500	390	329	4th/AFC Western Div.	—	—		Jon Gruden
2000	12	4	0	.750	479	299	1st/AFC Western Div.	1	1	AFC championship game	Jon Gruden

*American Football League.
†Los Angeles Raiders.

FIRST-ROUND DRAFT PICKS

1960—Dale Hackbart, DB, Wisconsin
1961—Joe Rutgens, DT, Illinois
1962—Roman Gabriel, QB, North Carolina State* (AFL)

1963—None
1964—Tony Lorick, RB, Arizona State
1965—Harry Schuh, T, Memphis State

1966—Rodger Bird, DB, Kentucky
1967—Gene Upshaw, G, Texas A&I
1968—Eldridge Dickey, QB, Tenn. State
1969—Art Thoms, DT, Syracuse
1970—Raymond Chester, TE, Morgan State
1971—Jack Tatum, DB, Ohio State
1972—Mike Siani, WR, Villanova
1973—Ray Guy, P, So. Mississippi
1974—Henry Lawrence, T, Florida A&M
1975—Neal Colzie, DB, Ohio State
1976—None
1977—None
1978—None
1979—None
1980—Marc Wilson, QB, Brigham Young
1981—Ted Watts, DB, Texas Tech
Curt Marsh, G, Washington
1982—Marcus Allen, RB, Southern California
1983—Don Mosebar, T, Southern California
1984—None
1985—Jessie Hester, WR, Florida State

1986—Bob Buczkowski, DT, Pittsburgh
1987—John Clay, T, Missouri
1988—Tim Brown, WR, Notre Dame
Terry McDaniel, CB, Tennessee
Scott Davis, DE, Illinois
1989—None
1990—Anthony Smith, DE, Arizona
1991—Todd Marinovich, QB, Southern California
1992—Chester McGlockton, DT, Clemson
1993—Patrick Bates, DB, Texas A&M
1994—Rob Fredrickson, LB, Michigan State
1995—Napoleon Kaufman, RB, Washington
1996—Rickey Dudley, TE, Ohio State
1997—Darrell Russell, DT, Southern California
1998—Charles Woodson, DB, Michigan
Mo Collins, T, Florida
1999—Matt Stinchcomb, T, Georgia
2000—Sebastian Janikowski, PK, Florida State
2001—Derrick Gibson, DB, Florida State
*First player chosen in draft.

FRANCHISE RECORDS

Most rushing yards, career
8,545—Marcus Allen
Most rushing yards, season
1,759—Marcus Allen, 1985
Most rushing yards, game
227—Napoleon Kaufman vs. Den., Oct. 19, 1997
Most rushing touchdowns, season
16—Pete Banaszak, 1975
Most passing attempts, season
521—Jeff George, 1997
Most passing attempts, game
59—Todd Marinovich vs. Cle., Sept. 20, 1992
Most passes completed, season
304—Ken Stabler, 1979
Rich Gannon, 1999
Most passes completed, game
34—Jim Plunkett at K.C., Sept. 12, 1985
Most passing yards, career
19,078—Ken Stabler

Most passing yards, season
3,917—Jeff George, 1997
Most passing yards, game
424—Jeff Hostetler vs. S.D., Oct. 18, 1993
Most touchdown passes, season
34—Daryle Lamonica, 1969
Most pass receptions, career
846—Tim Brown
Most pass receptions, season
104—Tim Brown, 1997
Most pass receptions, game
14—Tim Brown vs. Jac., Dec. 21, 1997
Most receiving yards, career
12,072—Tim Brown
Most receiving yards, season
1,408—Tim Brown, 1997
Most receiving yards, game
247—Art Powell vs. Hou., Dec. 22, 1963
Most receiving touchdowns, season
16—Art Powell, 1964

Most touchdowns, career
98—Marcus Allen
Most field goals, season
35—Jeff Jaeger, 1993
Longest field goal
54 yards—George Fleming vs. Den., Oct. 2, 1961
Sebastian Janikowski at S.D., Oct. 29, 2000
Most interceptions, career
39—Willie Brown
Lester Hayes
Most interceptions, season
13—Lester Hayes, 1980
Most sacks, career
107.5—Greg Townsend
Most sacks, season
17.5—Tony Cline, 1970

SERIES RECORDS

Oakland vs.: Arizona 3-1; Atlanta 7-3; Baltimore 0-2; Buffalo 16-15; Carolina 1-1; Chicago 6-4; Cincinnati 16-7; Cleveland 10-3; Dallas 4-3; Denver 49-30-2; Detroit 6-2; Green Bay 5-3; Indianapolis 6-2; Jacksonville 1-1; Kansas City 39-40-2; Miami 15-8-1; Minnesota 7-3; New England 13-12-1; New Orleans 5-3-1; N.Y. Giants 6-2; N.Y. Jets 18-10-2; Philadelphia 3-4; Pittsburgh 7-6; St. Louis 7-2; San Diego 50-30-2; San Francisco 6-3; Seattle 25-21; Tampa Bay 4-1; Tennessee 20-15; Washington 6-3.
NOTE: Includes records as Los Angeles Raiders from 1982 through 1994.

COACHING RECORDS

Joe Bugel, 4-12-0; Red Conkright, 1-8-0; Al Davis, 23-16-3; Eddie Erdelatz, 6-10-0; Marty Feldman, 2-15-0; Tom Flores, 83-53-0 (8-3); Jon Gruden, 28-20-0 (1-1); John Madden, 103-32-7 (9-7); John Rauch, 33-8-1 (2-2); Mike Shanahan, 8-12-0; Art Shell, 54-38-0 (2-3); Mike White, 15-17-0.
NOTE: Playoff games in parentheses.

RETIRED UNIFORM NUMBERS

No.	Player
	None

PHILADELPHIA EAGLES
YEAR-BY-YEAR RECORDS

		REGULAR SEASON							PLAYOFFS		
Year	W	L	T	Pct.	PF	PA	Finish	W	L	Highest round	Coach
1933	3	5	1	.375	77	158	4th/Eastern Div.	—	—		Lud Wray
1934	4	7	0	.364	127	85	T3rd/Eastern Div.	—	—		Lud Wray

	REGULAR SEASON							PLAYOFFS			
Year	W	L	T	Pct.	PF	PA	Finish	W	L	Highest round	Coach
1935	2	9	0	.182	60	179	5th/Eastern Div.	—	—		Lud Wray
1936	1	11	0	.083	51	206	5th/Eastern Div.	—	—		Bert Bell
1937	2	8	1	.200	86	177	5th/Eastern Div.	—	—		Bert Bell
1938	5	6	0	.455	154	164	4th/Eastern Div.	—	—		Bert Bell
1939	1	9	1	.100	105	200	T4th/Eastern Div.	—	—		Bert Bell
1940	1	10	0	.091	111	211	5th/Eastern Div.	—	—		Bert Bell
1941	2	8	1	.200	119	218	4th/Eastern Div.	—	—		Greasy Neale
1942	2	9	0	.182	134	239	5th/Eastern Div.	—	—		Greasy Neale
1943*	5	4	1	.556	225	230	3rd/Eastern Div.	—	—		G. Neale-Walt Kiesling
1944	7	1	2	.875	267	131	2nd/Eastern Div.	—	—		Greasy Neale
1945	7	3	0	.700	272	133	2nd/Eastern Div.	—	—		Greasy Neale
1946	6	5	0	.545	231	220	2nd/Eastern Div.	—	—		Greasy Neale
1947	8	4	0	.667	308	242	1st/Eastern Div.	1	1	NFL championship game	Greasy Neale
1948	9	2	1	.818	376	156	1st/Eastern Div.	1	0	NFL champ	Greasy Neale
1949	11	1	0	.917	364	134	1st/Eastern Div.	1	0	NFL champ	Greasy Neale
1950	6	6	0	.500	254	141	T3rd/American Conf.	—	—		Greasy Neale
1951	4	8	0	.333	234	264	5th/American Conf.	—	—		Bo McMillin, Wayne Millner
1952	7	5	0	.583	252	271	T2nd/American Conf.	—	—		Jim Trimble
1953	7	4	1	.636	352	215	2nd/Eastern Conf.	—	—		Jim Trimble
1954	7	4	1	.636	284	230	2nd/Eastern Conf.	—	—		Jim Trimble
1955	4	7	1	.364	248	231	T4th/Eastern Conf.	—	—		Jim Trimble
1956	3	8	1	.273	143	215	6th/Eastern Conf.	—	—		Hugh Devore
1957	4	8	0	.333	173	230	5th/Eastern Conf.	—	—		Hugh Devore
1958	2	9	1	.182	235	306	T5th/Eastern Conf.	—	—		Buck Shaw
1959	7	5	0	.583	268	278	T2nd/Eastern Conf.	—	—		Buck Shaw
1960	10	2	0	.833	321	246	1st/Eastern Conf.	1	0	NFL champ	Buck Shaw
1961	10	4	0	.714	361	297	2nd/Eastern Conf.	—	—		Nick Skorich
1962	3	10	1	.231	282	356	7th/Eastern Conf.	—	—		Nick Skorich
1963	2	10	2	.167	242	381	7th/Western Conf.	—	—		Nick Skorich
1964	6	8	0	.429	312	313	T3rd/Eastern Conf.	—	—		Joe Kuharich
1965	5	9	0	.357	363	359	T5th/Eastern Conf.	—	—		Joe Kuharich
1966	9	5	0	.643	326	340	T2nd/Eastern Conf.	—	—		Joe Kuharich
1967	6	7	1	.462	351	409	2nd/Capitol Div.	—	—		Joe Kuharich
1968	2	12	0	.143	202	351	4th/Capitol Div.	—	—		Joe Kuharich
1969	4	9	1	.308	279	377	4th/Capitol Div.	—	—		Jerry Williams
1970	3	10	1	.231	241	332	5th/NFC Eastern Div.	—	—		Jerry Williams
1971	6	7	1	.462	221	302	3rd/NFC Eastern Div.	—	—		J. Williams, Ed Khayat
1972	2	11	1	.179	145	352	5th/NFC Eastern Div.	—	—		Ed Khayat
1973	5	8	1	.393	310	393	3rd/NFC Eastern Div.	—	—		Mike McCormack
1974	7	7	0	.500	242	217	4th/NFC Eastern Div.	—	—		Mike McCormack
1975	4	10	0	.286	225	302	5th/NFC Eastern Div.	—	—		Mike McCormack
1976	4	10	0	.286	165	286	4th/NFC Eastern Div.	—	—		Dick Vermeil
1977	5	9	0	.357	220	207	T4th/NFC Eastern Div.	—	—		Dick Vermeil
1978	9	7	0	.563	270	250	2nd/NFC Eastern Div.	0	1	NFC wild-card game	Dick Vermeil
1979	11	5	0	.688	339	282	2nd/NFC Eastern Div.	1	1	NFC div. playoff game	Dick Vermeil
1980	12	4	0	.750	384	222	1st/NFC Eastern Div.	2	1	Super Bowl	Dick Vermeil
1981	10	6	0	.625	368	221	2nd/NFC Eastern Div.	0	1	NFC wild-card game	Dick Vermeil
1982	3	6	0	.333	191	195	T11th/NFC	—	—		Dick Vermeil
1983	5	11	0	.313	233	322	4th/NFC Eastern Div.	—	—		Marion Campbell
1984	6	9	1	.406	278	320	5th/NFC Eastern Div.	—	—		Marion Campbell
1985	7	9	0	.438	286	310	4th/NFC Eastern Div.	—	—		M. Campbell, Fred Bruney
1986	5	10	1	.344	256	312	4th/NFC Eastern Div.	—	—		Buddy Ryan
1987	7	8	0	.467	337	380	T2nd/NFC Eastern Div.	—	—		Buddy Ryan
1988	10	6	0	.625	379	319	1st/NFC Eastern Div.	0	1	NFC div. playoff game	Buddy Ryan
1989	11	5	0	.688	342	274	2nd/NFC Eastern Div.	0	1	NFC wild-card game	Buddy Ryan
1990	10	6	0	.625	396	299	T2nd/NFC Eastern Div.	0	1	NFC wild-card game	Buddy Ryan
1991	10	6	0	.625	285	244	3rd/NFC Eastern Div.	—	—		Rich Kotite
1992	11	5	0	.688	354	245	2nd/NFC Eastern Div.	1	1	NFC div. playoff game	Rich Kotite
1993	8	8	0	.500	293	315	3rd/NFC Eastern Div.	—	—		Rich Kotite
1994	7	9	0	.438	308	308	4th/NFC Eastern Div.	—	—		Rich Kotite
1995	10	6	0	.625	318	338	2nd/NFC Eastern Div.	1	1	NFC div. playoff game	Ray Rhodes
1996	10	6	0	.625	363	341	2nd/NFC Eastern Div.	0	1	NFC wild-card game	Ray Rhodes
1997	6	9	1	.406	317	372	3rd/NFC Eastern Div.	—	—		Ray Rhodes
1998	3	13	0	.188	161	344	5th/NFC Eastern Div.	—	—		Ray Rhodes
1999	5	11	0	.313	272	357	5th/NFC Eastern Div.	—	—		Andy Reid
2000	11	5	0	.688	351	245	2nd/NFC Eastern Div.	1	1	NFC div. playoff game	Andy Reid

*Phil-Pitt "Steagles," a combined squad of Philadelphia Eagles and Pittsburgh Steelers.

FIRST-ROUND DRAFT PICKS

1936—Jay Berwanger, B, Chicago*
1937—Sam Francis, B, Nebraska*
1938—John McDonald, B, Nebraska
1939—Davey O'Brien, QB, Texas Christian
1940—Wes McAfee, B, Duke
1941—None
1942—Pete Kmetovic, B, Stanford
1943—Joe Muha, B, Virginia Military
1944—Steve Van Buren, B, Louisiana State
1945—John Yonaker, E, Notre Dame
1946—Leo Riggs, B, Southern California
1947—Neil Armstrong, E, Oklahoma A&M
1948—Clyde Scott, B, Arkansas
1949—Chuck Bednarik, C, Pennsylvania*
      Frank Tripucka, QB, Notre Dame
1950—Bud Grant, E, Minnesota
1951—Ebert Van Buren, B, Louisiana State
      Chet Mutryn, B, Xavier
1952—John Bright, B, Drake
1953—None
1954—Neil Worden, B, Notre Dame
1955—Dick Bielski, B, Maryland
1956—Bob Pellegrini, C, Maryland
1957—Clarence Peaks, B, Michigan State
1958—Walter Kowalczyk, B, Michigan State
1959—None
1960—Ron Burton, B, Northwestern
1961—Art Baker, B, Syracuse
1962—None
1963—Ed Budde, T, Michigan State
1964—Bob Brown, T, Nebraska
1965—None
1966—Randy Beisler, T, Indiana
1967—Harry Jones, RB, Arkansas
1968—Tim Rossovich, DE, Southern California
1969—Leroy Keyes, RB, Purdue

1970—Steve Zabel, E, Oklahoma
1971—Richard Harris, DE, Grambling State
1972—John Reaves, QB, Florida
1973—Jerry Sisemore, T, Texas
      Charle Young, TE, Southern California
1974—None
1975—None
1976—None
1977—None
1978—None
1979—Jerry Robinson, LB, UCLA
1980—Roynell Young, DB, Alcorn State
1981—Leonard Mitchell, DE, Houston
1982—Mike Quick, WR, North Carolina State
1983—Michael Haddix, RB, Mississippi State
1984—Kenny Jackson, WR, Penn State
1985—Kevin Allen, T, Indiana
1986—Keith Byars, RB, Ohio State
1987—Jerome Brown, DT, Miami, Fla.
1988—Keith Jackson, TE, Oklahoma
1989—None
1990—Ben Smith, DB, Georgia
1991—Antone Davis, T, Tennessee
1992—None
1993—Lester Holmes, T, Jackson State
      Leonard Renfro, DT, Colorado
1994—Bernard Williams, T, Georgia
1995—Mike Mamula, DE, Boston College
1996—Jermane Mayberry, T, Texas A&M-Kingsville
1997—Jon Harris, DE, Virginia
1998—Tra Thomas, T, Florida State
1999—Donovan McNabb, QB, Syracuse
2000—Corey Simon, DT, Florida State
2001—Freddie Mitchell, WR, UCLA
      *First player chosen in draft.

FRANCHISE RECORDS

Most rushing yards, career
6,538—Wilbert Montgomery
Most rushing yards, season
1,512—Wilbert Montgomery, 1979
Most rushing yards, game
205—Steve Van Buren vs. Pit., Nov. 27,
      1949
Most rushing touchdowns, season
15—Steve Van Buren, 1945
Most passing attempts, season
569—Donovan McNabb, 2000
Most passing attempts, game
62—Randall Cunningham at Chi., Oct. 2,
      1989
Most passes completed, season
330—Donovan McNabb, 2000
Most passes completed, game
34—Randall Cunningham at Was., Sept.
      17, 1989
Most passing yards, career
26,963—Ron Jaworski

Most passing yards, season
3,808—Randall Cunningham, 1988
Most passing yards, game
447—Randall Cunningham at Was., Sept.
      17, 1989
Most touchdown passes, season
32—Sonny Jurgensen, 1961
Most pass receptions, career
589—Harold Carmichael
Most pass receptions, season
88—Irving Fryar, 1996
Most pass receptions, game
14—Don Looney at Was., Dec. 1, 1940
Most receiving yards, career
8,978—Harold Carmichael
Most receiving yards, season
1,409—Mike Quick, 1983
Most receiving yards, game
237—Tommy McDonald vs. NYG, Dec.
      10, 1961

Most receiving touchdowns, season
13—Tommy McDonald, 1960
      Tommy McDonald, 1961
      Mike Quick, 1983
Most touchdowns, career
79—Harold Carmichael
Most field goals, season
30—Paul McFadden, 1984
Longest field goal
59 yards—Tony Franklin at Dal.,
      Nov. 12, 1979
Most interceptions, career
34—Eric Allen
      Bill Bradley
Most interceptions, season
11—Bill Bradley, 1971
Most sacks, career
124—Reggie White
Most sacks, season
21—Reggie White, 1987

SERIES RECORDS

Philadelphia vs.: Arizona 51-51-5; Atlanta 10-9-1; Baltimore, 0-0-1; Buffalo 4-5; Carolina 1-1; Chicago 6-25-1; Cincinnati 3-6; Cleveland 13-31-1; Dallas 32-48; Denver 6-3; Detroit 11-11-2; Green Bay 9-22; Indianapolis 6-8; Jacksonville 0-1; Kansas City 1-2; Miami 3-7; Minnesota 6-11; New England 6-2; New Orleans 13-8; N.Y. Giants 59-71-2; N.Y. Jets 6-0; Oakland 4-3; Pittsburgh 45-26-3; St. Louis 14-14-1; San Diego 2-5; San Francisco 6-14-1; Seattle 4-3; Tampa Bay 3-3; Tennessee 6-1; Washington 57-67-6. NOTE: Includes records when team combined with Pittsburgh squad and was known as Phil-Pitt in 1943.

COACHING RECORDS

Bert Bell, 10-44-2; Fred Bruney, 1-0-0; Marion Campbell, 17-29-1; Hugh Devore, 7-16-1; Ed Khayat, 8-15-2; Rich Kotite, 36-28-0 (1-1); Joe Kuharich, 28-41-1; Mike McCormack, 16-25-1; Alvin McMillin, 2-0-0; Wayne Millner, 2-8-0; Earle (Greasy) Neale, 63-43-5 (3-1); Andy Reid, 16-16-0 (1-1); Ray Rhodes, 29-34-1 (1-2); Buddy Ryan, 43-35-1 (0-3); Buck Shaw, 19-16-1 (1-0); Nick Skorich, 15-24-3; Jim Trimble, 25-20-3; Dick Vermeil, 54-47-0 (3-4); Jerry Williams, 7-22-2; Lud Wray, 9-21-1.
NOTE: Playoff games in parentheses.

RETIRED UNIFORM NUMBERS

No.	Player
15	Steve Van Buren
40	Tom Brookshier
44	Pete Retzlaff
60	Chuck Bednarik
70	Al Wistert
99	Jerome Brown

PITTSBURGH STEELERS
YEAR-BY-YEAR RECORDS

	REGULAR SEASON							PLAYOFFS			
Year	W	L	T	Pct.	PF	PA	Finish	W	L	Highest round	Coach
1933*	3	6	2	.333	67	208	5th/Eastern Div.	—	—		Jap Douds
1934*	2	10	0	.167	51	206	5th/Eastern Div.	—	—		Luby DiMello
1935*	4	8	0	.333	100	209	3rd/Eastern Div.	—	—		Joe Bach
1936*	6	6	0	.500	98	187	2nd/Eastern Div.	—	—		Joe Bach
1937*	4	7	0	.364	122	145	3rd/Eastern Div.	—	—		Johnny Blood
1938*	2	9	0	.182	79	169	5th/Eastern Div.	—	—		Johnny Blood
1939*	1	9	1	.100	114	216	T4th/Eastern Div.	—	—		J. Blood-W. Kiesling
1940*	2	7	2	.222	60	178	4th/Eastern Div.	—	—		Walt Kiesling
1941	1	9	1	.100	103	276	5th/Eastern Div.	—	—		Bert Bell-Buff Donelli-Walt Kiesling
1942	7	4	0	.636	167	119	2nd/Eastern Div.	—	—		Walt Kiesling
1943†	5	4	1	.556	225	230	3rd/Eastern Div.	—	—		W. Kiesling-Greasy Neale
1944‡	0	10	0	.000	108	328	5th/Western Div.	—	—		W. Kiesling-Phil Handler
1945	2	8	0	.200	79	220	5th/Eastern Div.	—	—		Jim Leonard
1946	5	5	1	.500	136	117	T3rd/Eastern Div.	—	—		Jock Sutherland
1947	8	4	0	.667	240	259	2nd/Eastern Div.	0	1	E. Div. champ. game	Jock Sutherland
1948	4	8	0	.333	200	243	T3rd/Eastern Div.	—	—		John Michelosen
1949	6	5	1	.545	224	214	2nd/Eastern Div.	—	—		John Michelosen
1950	6	6	0	.500	180	195	T3rd/American Conf.	—	—		John Michelosen
1951	4	7	1	.364	183	235	4th/American Conf.	—	—		John Michelosen
1952	5	7	0	.417	300	273	3rd/American Conf.	—	—		Joe Bach
1953	6	6	0	.500	211	263	4th/Eastern Conf.	—	—		Joe Bach
1954	5	7	0	.417	219	263	4th/Eastern Conf.	—	—		Walt Kiesling
1955	4	8	0	.333	195	285	6th/Eastern Conf.	—	—		Walt Kiesling
1956	5	7	0	.417	217	250	5th/Eastern Conf.	—	—		Walt Kiesling
1957	6	6	0	.500	161	178	3rd/Eastern Conf.	—	—		Buddy Parker
1958	7	4	1	.636	261	230	3rd/Eastern Conf.	—	—		Buddy Parker
1959	6	5	1	.545	257	216	4th/Eastern Conf.	—	—		Buddy Parker
1960	5	6	1	.455	240	275	5th/Eastern Conf.	—	—		Buddy Parker
1961	6	8	0	.429	295	287	5th/Eastern Conf.	—	—		Buddy Parker
1962	9	5	0	.643	312	363	2nd/Eastern Conf.	—	—		Buddy Parker
1963	7	4	3	.636	321	295	4th/Eastern Conf.	—	—		Buddy Parker
1964	5	9	0	.357	253	315	6th/Eastern Conf.	—	—		Buddy Parker
1965	2	12	0	.143	202	397	7th/Eastern Conf.	—	—		Mike Nixon
1966	5	8	1	.385	316	347	6th/Eastern Conf.	—	—		Bill Austin
1967	4	9	1	.308	281	320	4th/Century Div.	—	—		Bill Austin
1968	2	11	1	.154	244	397	4th/Century Div.	—	—		Bill Austin
1969	1	13	0	.071	218	404	4th/Century Div.	—	—		Chuck Noll
1970	5	9	0	.357	210	272	3rd/AFC Central Div.	—	—		Chuck Noll
1971	6	8	0	.429	246	292	2nd/AFC Central Div.	—	—		Chuck Noll
1972	11	3	0	.786	343	175	1st/AFC Central Div.	1	1	AFC championship game	Chuck Noll
1973	10	4	0	.714	347	210	2nd/AFC Central Div.	0	1	AFC div. playoff game	Chuck Noll
1974	10	3	1	.750	305	189	1st/AFC Central Div.	3	0	Super Bowl champ	Chuck Noll
1975	12	2	0	.857	373	162	1st/AFC Central Div.	3	0	Super Bowl champ	Chuck Noll
1976	10	4	0	.714	342	138	1st/AFC Central Div.	1	1	AFC championship game	Chuck Noll
1977	9	5	0	.643	283	243	1st/AFC Central Div.	0	1	AFC div. playoff game	Chuck Noll
1978	14	2	0	.875	356	195	1st/AFC Central Div.	3	0	Super Bowl champ	Chuck Noll
1979	12	4	0	.750	416	262	1st/AFC Central Div.	3	0	Super Bowl champ	Chuck Noll
1980	9	7	0	.563	352	313	3rd/AFC Central Div.	—	—		Chuck Noll
1981	8	8	0	.500	356	297	2nd/AFC Central Div.	—	—		Chuck Noll
1982	6	3	0	.667	204	146	T4th/AFC	0	1	AFC first-round pl. game	Chuck Noll
1983	10	6	0	.625	355	303	1st/AFC Central Div.	0	1	AFC div. playoff game	Chuck Noll
1984	9	7	0	.563	387	310	1st/AFC Central Div.	1	1	AFC championship game	Chuck Noll
1985	7	9	0	.438	379	355	T2nd/AFC Central Div.	—	—		Chuck Noll
1986	6	10	0	.375	307	336	3rd/AFC Central Div.	—	—		Chuck Noll
1987	8	7	0	.533	285	299	3rd/AFC Central Div.	—	—		Chuck Noll

Year	REGULAR SEASON							PLAYOFFS			
	W	L	T	Pct.	PF	PA	Finish	W	L	Highest round	Coach
1988	5	11	0	.313	336	421	4th/AFC Central Div.	—	—		Chuck Noll
1989	9	7	0	.563	265	326	T2nd/AFC Central Div.	1	1	AFC div. playoff game	Chuck Noll
1990	9	7	0	.563	292	240	3rd/AFC Central Div.	—	—		Chuck Noll
1991	7	9	0	.438	292	344	2nd/AFC Central Div.	—	—		Chuck Noll
1992	11	5	0	.688	299	225	1st/AFC Central Div.	0	1	AFC div. playoff game	Bill Cowher
1993	9	7	0	.563	308	281	2nd/AFC Central Div.	0	1	AFC wild-card game	Bill Cowher
1994	12	4	0	.750	316	234	1st/AFC Central Div.	1	1	AFC championship game	Bill Cowher
1995	11	5	0	.689	407	327	1st/AFC Central Div.	2	1	Super Bowl	Bill Cowher
1996	10	6	0	.625	344	257	1st/AFC Central Div.	1	1	AFC div. playoff game	Bill Cowher
1997	11	5	0	.688	372	307	1st/AFC Central Div.	1	1	AFC championship game	Bill Cowher
1998	7	9	0	.438	263	303	3rd/AFC Central Div.	—	—		Bill Cowher
1999	6	10	0	.375	317	320	4th/AFC Central Div.	—	—		Bill Cowher
2000	9	7	0	.563	321	255	3rd/AFC Central Div.	—	—		Bill Cowher

*Pittsburgh Pirates.
†Phil-Pitt "Steagles," a combined squad of Philadelphia Eagles and Pittsburgh Steelers.
‡Card-Pitt, a combined squad of Chicago Cardinals and Pittsburgh Steelers.

FIRST-ROUND DRAFT PICKS

1936—Bill Shakespeare, B, Notre Dame
1937—Mike Basrak, C, Duquesne
1938—Byron White, B, Colorado
    Frank Filchock, B, Indiana
1939—None
1940—Kay Eakin, B, Arkansas
1941—Chet Gladchuk, C, Boston College
1942—Bill Dudley, B, Virginia*
1943—Bill Daley, B, Minnesota
1944—Johnny Podesto, B, St. Mary's (Calif.)
1945—Paul Duhart, B, Florida
1946—Doc Blanchard, B, Army
1947—Hub Bechtol, E, Texas
1948—Dan Edwards, E, Georgia
1949—Bobby Gage, B, Clemson
1950—Lynn Chandnois, B, Michigan State
1951—Clarence Avinger, B, Alabama
1952—Ed Modzelewski, B, Maryland
1953—Ted Marchibroda, QB, St. Bonaventure
1954—John Lattner, B, Notre Dame
1955—Frank Varrichione, T, Notre Dame
1956—Gary Glick, B, Colorado State*
    Art Davis, B, Mississippi State
1957—Len Dawson, QB, Purdue
1958—None
1959—None
1960—Jack Spikes, B, Texas Christian
1961—None
1962—Bob Ferguson, RB, Ohio State
1963—None
1964—Paul Martha, RB, Pittsburgh
1965—None
1966—Dick Leftridge, RB, West Virginia
1967—None
1968—Mike Taylor, T, Southern California

1969—Joe Greene, DT, North Texas State
1970—Terry Bradshaw, QB, Louisiana Tech*
1971—Frank Lewis, WR, Grambling State
1972—Franco Harris, RB, Penn State
1973—James Thomas, DB, Florida State
1974—Lynn Swann, WR, Southern California
1975—Dave Brown, DB, Michigan
1976—Bennie Cunningham, TE, Clemson
1977—Robin Cole, LB, New Mexico
1978—Ron Johnson, DB, Eastern Michigan
1979—Greg Hawthorne, RB, Baylor
1980—Mark Malone, QB, Arizona State
1981—Keith Gary, DE, Oklahoma
1982—Walter Abercrombie, RB, Baylor
1983—Gabriel Rivera, DT, Texas Tech
1984—Louis Lipps, WR, Southern Mississippi
1985—Darryl Sims, DT, Wisconsin
1986—John Rienstra, G, Temple
1987—Rod Woodson, DB, Purdue
1988—Aaron Jones, DE, Eastern Kentucky
1989—Tim Worley, RB, Georgia
    Tom Ricketts, T, Pittsburgh
1990—Eric Green, TE, Liberty (Va.)
1991—Huey Richardson, LB, Florida
1992—Leon Searcy, T, Miami, Fla.
1993—Deon Figures, DB, Colorado
1994—Charles Johnson, WR, Colorado
1995—Mark Bruener, TE, Washington
1996—Jermain Stephens, T, North Carolina A&T
1997—Chad Scott, DB, Maryland
1998—Alan Faneca, G, Louisiana State
1999—Troy Edwards, WR, Louisiana Tech
2000—Plaxico Burress, WR, Michigan State
2001—Casey Hampton, DT, Texas
    *First player chosen in draft.

FRANCHISE RECORDS

Most rushing yards, career
11,950—Franco Harris
Most rushing yards, season
1,690—Barry Foster, 1992
Most rushing yards, game
218—John Fuqua at Phi., Dec. 20, 1970
Most rushing touchdowns, season
14—Franco Harris, 1976
Most passing attempts, season
486—Neil O'Donnell, 1993

Most passing attempts, game
55—Neil O'Donnell vs. G.B., Dec. 24, 1995
Most passes completed, season
270—Neil O'Donnell, 1993
Most passes completed, game
34—Neil O'Donnell at Chi., Nov. 5, 1995
    (OT)
31—Joe Gilliam at Den., Sept. 22, 1974
    (OT)
30—Terry Bradshaw vs. Cle., Nov. 25,
    1979 (OT)

29—Terry Bradshaw vs. Cin., Sept. 19,
    1982 (OT)
28—Kent Nix vs. Dal., Oct. 22, 1967
Most passing yards, career
27,989—Terry Bradshaw
Most passing yards, season
3,724—Terry Bradshaw, 1979
Most passing yards, game
409—Bobby Layne vs. Chi. Cardinals,
    Dec. 13, 1958

Most touchdown passes, season
28—Terry Bradshaw, 1978
Most pass receptions, career
537—John Stallworth
Most pass receptions, season
85—Yancey Thigpen, 1995
Most pass receptions, game
14—Courtney Hawkins vs. Ten., Nov. 1, 1998
Most receiving yards, career
8,723—John Stallworth

Most receiving yards, season
1,398—Yancey Thigpen, 1997
Most receiving yards, game
235—Buddy Dial vs. Cle., Oct. 22, 1961
Most receiving touchdowns, season
12—Buddy Dial, 1961
Louis Lipps, 1985
Most touchdowns, career
100—Franco Harris
Most field goals, season
34—Norm Johnson, 1995

Longest field goal
55 yards—Gary Anderson vs. S.D., Nov. 25, 1984
Most interceptions, career
57—Mel Blount
Most interceptions, season
11—Mel Blount, 1975
Most sacks, career
73.5—L.C. Greenwood
Most sacks, season
15—Mike Merriweather, 1984

SERIES RECORDS

Pittsburgh vs.: Arizona 30-21-3; Atlanta 11-1; Baltimore 7-3; Buffalo 8-8; Carolina 1-1; Chicago 6-19-1; Cincinnati 35-26; Cleveland 42-54; Dallas 11-14; Denver 6-10-1; Detroit 12-14-1; Green Bay 12-21; Indianapolis 13-4; Jacksonville 5-7; Kansas City 15-7; Miami 6-9; Minnesota 4-8; New England 11-4; New Orleans 6-5; N.Y. Giants 28-45-3; N.Y. Jets 14-1; Oakland 6-7; Philadelphia 26-45-3; St. Louis 6-17-2; San Diego 17-5; San Francisco 8-9; Seattle 6-7; Tampa Bay 4-1; Tennessee 35-26; Washington 26-39-4.
NOTE: Includes records as Pittsburgh Pirates from 1933 through 1940; also includes records when team combined with Philadelphia squad and was known as Phil-Pitt in 1943 and when team combined with Chicago Cardinals squad and was known as Card-Pitt in 1944.

COACHING RECORDS

Bill Austin, 11-28-3; Joe Bach, 21-27-0; Bert Bell, 0-2-0; Bill Cowher, 86-58-0 (5-6); Luby DiMelio, 2-10-0; Aldo Donelli, 0-5-0; Forrest Douds, 3-6-2; Walt Kiesling, 30-55-5; Jim Leonard, 2-8-0; Johnny (Blood) McNally, 6-19-0; Johnny Michelosen, 20-26-2; Mike Nixon, 2-12-0; Chuck Noll, 193-148-1 (16-8); Buddy Parker, 51-47-6 (0-1); Jock Sutherland, 13-9-1 (0-1).
NOTE: Playoff games in parentheses.

RETIRED UNIFORM NUMBERS

No.	Player
	None

ST. LOUIS RAMS

YEAR-BY-YEAR RECORDS

	REGULAR SEASON						PLAYOFFS			
Year	W	L	T	Pct.	PF	PA	Finish	W	L	Highest round	Coach
1937*	1	10	0	.091	75	207	5th/Western Div.	—	—		Hugo Bezdek
1938*	4	7	0	.364	131	215	4th/Western Div.	—	—		Hugo Bezdek, Art Lewis
1939*	5	5	1	.500	195	164	4th/Western Div.	—	—		Dutch Clark
1940*	4	6	1	.400	171	191	4th/Western Div.	—	—		Dutch Clark
1941*	2	9	0	.182	116	244	5th/Western Div.	—	—		Dutch Clark
1942*	5	6	0	.455	150	207	3rd/Western Div.	—	—		Dutch Clark
1943*	Rams did not play in 1943.										
1944*	4	6	0	.400	188	224	4th/Western Div.	—	—		Buff Donelli
1945*	9	1	0	.900	244	136	1st/Western Div.	1	0	NFL champ	Adam Walsh
1946†	6	4	1	.600	277	257	2nd/Western Div.	—	—		Adam Walsh
1947†	6	6	0	.500	259	214	4th/Western Div.	—	—		Bob Snyder
1948†	6	5	1	.545	327	269	3rd/Western Div.	—	—		Clark Shaughnessy
1949†	8	2	2	.800	360	239	1st/Western Div.	0	1	NFL championship game	Clark Shaughnessy
1950†	9	3	0	.750	466	309	1st/National Conf.	1	1	NFL championship game	Joe Stydahar
1951†	8	4	0	.667	392	261	1st/National Conf.	1	0	NFL champ	Joe Stydahar
1952†	9	3	0	.750	349	234	2nd/National Conf.	0	1	Nat. Conf. champ. game	J. Stydahar, Hamp Pool
1953†	8	3	1	.727	366	236	3rd/Western Conf.	—	—		Hamp Pool
1954†	6	5	1	.545	314	285	4th/Western Conf.	—	—		Hamp Pool
1955†	8	3	1	.727	260	231	1st/Western Conf.	0	1	NFL championship game	Sid Gillman
1956†	4	8	0	.333	291	307	6th/Western Conf.	—	—		Sid Gillman
1957†	6	6	0	.500	307	278	4th/Western Conf.	—	—		Sid Gillman
1958†	8	4	0	.667	344	278	T2nd/Western Conf.	—	—		Sid Gillman
1959†	2	10	0	.167	242	315	6th/Western Conf.	—	—		Sid Gillman
1960†	4	7	1	.364	265	297	6th/Western Conf.	—	—		Bob Waterfield
1961†	4	10	0	.286	263	333	6th/Western Conf.	—	—		Bob Waterfield
1962†	1	12	1	.077	220	334	7th/Western Conf.	—	—		B. Waterfield, H. Svare
1963†	5	9	0	.357	210	350	6th/Western Conf.	—	—		Harland Svare
1964†	5	7	2	.417	283	339	5th/Western Conf.	—	—		Harland Svare
1965†	4	10	0	.286	269	328	7th/Western Conf.	—	—		Harland Svare
1966†	8	6	0	.571	289	212	3rd/Western Conf.	—	—		George Allen
1967†	11	1	2	.917	398	196	1st/Coastal Div.	0	1	W. Conf. champ. game	George Allen
1968†	10	3	1	.769	312	200	2nd/Coastal Div.	—	—		George Allen
1969†	11	3	0	.786	320	243	1st/Coastal Div.	0	1	W. Conf. champ. game	George Allen
1970†	9	4	1	.692	325	202	2nd/NFC Western Div.	—	—		George Allen
1971†	8	5	1	.615	313	260	2nd/NFC Western Div.	—	—		Tommy Prothro

Year	W	L	T	Pct.	PF	PA	Finish	W	L	Highest round	Coach
1972†	6	7	1	.464	291	286	3rd/NFC Western Div.	—	—		Tommy Prothro
1973†	12	2	0	.857	388	178	1st/NFC Western Div.	0	1	NFC div. playoff game	Chuck Knox
1974†	10	4	0	.714	263	181	1st/NFC Western Div.	1	1	NFC championship game	Chuck Knox
1975†	12	2	0	.857	312	135	1st/NFC Western Div.	1	1	NFC championship game	Chuck Knox
1976†	10	3	1	.750	351	190	1st/NFC Western Div.	1	1	NFC championship game	Chuck Knox
1977†	10	4	0	.714	302	146	1st/NFC Western Div.	0	1	NFC div. playoff game	Chuck Knox
1978†	12	4	0	.750	316	245	1st/NFC Western Div.	1	1	NFC championship game	Ray Malavasi
1979†	9	7	0	.563	323	309	1st/NFC Western Div.	2	1	Super Bowl	Ray Malavasi
1980†	11	5	0	.688	424	289	2nd/NFC Western Div.	0	1	NFC wild-card game	Ray Malavasi
1981†	6	10	0	.375	303	351	3rd/NFC Western Div.	—	—		Ray Malavasi
1982†	2	7	0	.222	200	250	14th/NFC	—	—		Ray Malavasi
1983†	9	7	0	.563	361	344	2nd/NFC Western Div.	1	1	NFC div. playoff game	John Robinson
1984†	10	6	0	.625	346	316	2nd/NFC Western Div.	0	1	NFC wild-card game	John Robinson
1985†	11	5	0	.688	340	277	1st/NFC Western Div.	1	1	NFC championship game	John Robinson
1986†	10	6	0	.625	309	267	2nd/NFC Western Div.	0	1	NFC wild-card game	John Robinson
1987†	6	9	0	.400	317	361	3rd/NFC Western Div.	—	—		John Robinson
1988†	10	6	0	.625	407	293	2nd/NFC Western Div.	0	1	NFC wild-card game	John Robinson
1989†	11	5	0	.688	426	344	2nd/NFC Western Div.	2	1	NFC championship game	John Robinson
1990†	5	11	0	.313	345	412	T3rd/NFC Western Div.	—	—		John Robinson
1991†	3	13	0	.188	234	390	4th/NFC Western Div.	—	—		John Robinson
1992†	6	10	0	.375	313	383	T3rd/NFC Western Div.	—	—		Chuck Knox
1993†	5	11	0	.313	221	367	4th/NFC Western Div.	—	—		Chuck Knox
1994†	4	12	0	.250	286	365	4th/NFC Western Div.	—	—		Chuck Knox
1995	7	9	0	.438	309	418	T3rd/NFC Western Div.	—	—		Rich Brooks
1996	6	10	0	.375	303	409	3rd/NFC Western Div.	—	—		Rich Brooks
1997	5	11	0	.313	299	359	5th/NFC Western Div.	—	—		Dick Vermeil
1998	4	12	0	.250	285	378	5th/NFC Western Div.	—	—		Dick Vermeil
1999	13	3	0	.813	526	242	1st/NFC Western Div.	3	0	Super Bowl champ	Dick Vermeil
2000	10	6	0	.625	540	471	2nd/NFC Western Div.	0	1	NFC wild-card game	Mike Martz

*Cleveland Rams.
†Los Angeles Rams.

FIRST-ROUND DRAFT PICKS

1937—Johnny Drake, B, Purdue
1938—Corbett Davis, B, Indiana*
1939—Parker Hall, B, Mississippi
1940—Ollie Cordill, B, Rice
1941—Rudy Mucha, C, Washington
1942—Jack Wilson, B, Baylor
1943—Mike Holovak, B, Boston College
1944—Tony Butkovich, B, Illinois
1945—Elroy Hirsch, B, Wisconsin
1946—Emil Sitko, B, Notre Dame
1947—Herman Wedemeyer, B, St. Mary's (Cal.)
1948—None
1949—Bobby Thomason, B, Virginia Military
1950—Ralph Pasquariello, B, Villanova
    Stan West, G, Oklahoma
1951—Bud McFadin, G, Texas
1952—Bill Wade, B, Vanderbilt*
    Bob Carey, E, Michigan State
1953—Donn Moomaw, C, UCLA
    Ed Barker, E, Washington State
1954—Ed Beatty, C, Cincinnati
1955—Larry Morris, C, Georgia Tech
1956—Joe Marconi, B, West Virginia
    Charlie Horton, B, Vanderbilt
1957—Jon Arnett, B, Southern California
    Del Shofner, B, Baylor
1958—Lou Michaels, T, Kentucky
    Jim Phillips, E, Auburn
1959—Dick Bass, B, Pacific
    Paul Dickson, G, Baylor
1960—Billy Cannon, RB, Louisiana State*
1961—Marlin McKeever, LB, Southern California
1962—Roman Gabriel, QB, North Carolina State
    Merlin Olsen, DT, Utah State
1963—Terry Baker, QB, Oregon State*
    Rufus Guthrie, G, Georgia Tech
1964—Bill Munson, QB, Utah State

1965—Clancy Williams, DB, Washington State
1966—Tom Mack, G, Michigan
1967—None
1968—None
1969—Larry Smith, RB, Florida
    Jim Seymour, E, Notre Dame
    Bob Klein, TE, Southern California
1970—Jack Reynolds, LB, Tennessee
1971—Isiah Robertson, LB, Southern
    Jack Youngblood, DE, Florida
1972—None
1973—None
1974—John Cappelletti, RB, Penn State
1975—Mike Fanning, DT, Notre Dame
    Dennis Harrah, G, Miami, Fla.
    Doug France, T, Ohio State
1976—Kevin McLain, LB, Colorado State
1977—Bob Brudzinski, LB, Ohio State
1978—Elvis Peacock, RB, Oklahoma
1979—George Andrews, LB, Nebraska
    Kent Hill, G, Georgia Tech
1980—Johnnie Johnson, DB, Texas
1981—Mel Owens, LB, Michigan
1982—Barry Redden, RB, Richmond
1983—Eric Dickerson, RB, Southern Methodist
1984—None
1985—Jerry Gray, DB, Texas
1986—Mike Schad, T, Queens College (Ont.)
1987—None
1988—Gaston Green, RB, UCLA
    Aaron Cox, WR, Arizona State
1989—Bill Hawkins, DE, Miami, Fla.
    Cleveland Gary, RB, Miami, Fla.
1990—Bern Brostek, C, Washington
1991—Todd Lyght, CB, Notre Dame
1992—Sean Gilbert, DE, Pittsburgh
1993—Jerome Bettis, RB, Notre Dame

1994—Wayne Gandy, T, Auburn
1995—Kevin Carter, DE, Florida
1996—Lawrence Phillips, RB, Nebraska
　　Eddie Kennison, WR, Louisiana State
1997—Orlando Pace, T, Ohio State*
1998—Grant Wistrom, DE, Nebraska

1999—Torry Holt, WR, North Carolina State
2000—Trung Canidate, RB, Arizona
2001—Damione Lewis, DT, Miami, Fla.
　　Adam Archuleta, DB, Arizona State
　　Ryan Pickett, DT, Ohio State
　　*First player chosen in draft.

FRANCHISE RECORDS

Most rushing yards, career
7,245—Eric Dickerson
Most rushing yards, season
2,105—Eric Dickerson, 1984
Most rushing yards, game
247—Willie Ellison vs. N.O., Dec. 5, 1971
Most rushing touchdowns, season
18—Eric Dickerson, 1983
　　Marshall Faulk, 2000
Most passing attempts, season
554—Jim Everett, 1990
Most passing attempts, game
55—Mark Rypien vs. Buf., Dec. 10, 1995
Most passes completed, season
325—Kurt Warner, 1999
Most passes completed, game
35—Dieter Brock vs. S.F., Oct. 27, 1985
　　Kurt Warner at Sea., Sept. 10, 2000
Most passing yards, career
23,758—Jim Everett

Most passing yards, season
4,353—Kurt Warner, 1999
Most passing yards, game
554—Norm Van Brocklin at N.Y. Yanks,
　　Sept. 28, 1951
Most touchdown passes, season
41—Kurt Warner, 1999
Most pass receptions, career
593—Henry Ellard
Most pass receptions, season
119—Isaac Bruce, 1995
Most pass receptions, game
18—Tom Fears vs. G.B., Dec. 3, 1950
Most receiving yards, career
9,761—Henry Ellard
Most receiving yards, season
1,781—Isaac Bruce, 1995
Most receiving yards, game
336—Willie Anderson at N.O., Nov. 26,
　　1989

Most receiving touchdowns, season
17—Elroy Hirsch, 1951
Most touchdowns, career
58—Eric Dickerson
Most field goals, season
30—David Ray, 1973
Longest field goal
57 yards—Jeff Wilkins vs. Ari., Sept. 27,
　　1998
Most interceptions, career
46—Ed Meador
Most interceptions, season
14—Night Train Lane, 1952
Most sacks, career
151.5—Deacon Jones
Most sacks, season
22—Deacon Jones, 1964
　　Deacon Jones, 1968

SERIES RECORDS

St. Louis vs.: Arizona 16-14-2; Atlanta 43-23-2; Baltimore 1-1; Buffalo 4-4; Carolina 5-7; Chicago 27-36-3; Cincinnati 4-5; Cleveland 8-8; Dallas 9-8; Denver 5-4; Detroit 32-28-1; Green Bay 40-27-1; Indianapolis 17-21-2; Jacksonville 1-0; Kansas City 4-3; Miami 1-7; Minnesota 12-16-2; New England 4-3; New Orleans 34-26; N.Y. Giants 22-7; N.Y. Jets 7-2; Oakland 2-7; Philadelphia 14-14-1; Pittsburgh 17-6-2; San Diego 4-3; San Francisco 51-47-2; Seattle 5-2; Tampa Bay 8-4; Tennessee 5-3; Washington 7-17-1. NOTE: Includes records as Los Angeles Rams from 1946 through 1994.

COACHING RECORDS

George Allen, 47-17-4 (2-2); Hugo Bezdek, 1-13-0; Rich Brooks, 13-19-0; Dutch Clark, 16-26-2; Aldo Donelli, 4-6-0; Sid Gillman, 28-31-1 (0-1); Chuck Knox, 69-48-1 (3-5); Art Lewis, 4-4-0; Ray Malavasi, 40-33-0 (3-3); Mike Martz, 10-6-0 (0-1); Hamp Pool, 23-10-2 (0-1); Tommy Prothro, 14-12-2; John Robinson, 75-68-0 (4-6); Clark Shaughnessy, 14-7-3 (0-1); Bob Snyder, 6-6-0; Joe Stydahar, 17-8-0 (2-1); Harland Svare, 14-31-3; Dick Vermeil, 22-26-0 (3-0); Adam Walsh, 15-5-1 (1-0); Bob Waterfield, 9-24-1. NOTE: Playoff games in parentheses.

RETIRED UNIFORM NUMBERS

No.	Player
7	Bob Waterfield
74	Merlin Olsen
78	Jackie Slater

SAN DIEGO CHARGERS
YEAR-BY-YEAR RECORDS

			REGULAR SEASON					PLAYOFFS			
Year	W	L	T	Pct.	PF	PA	Finish	W	L	Highest round	Coach
1960*†	10	4	0	.714	373	336	1st/Western Div.	0	1	AFL championship game	Sid Gillman
1961*	12	2	0	.857	396	219	1st/Western Div.	0	1	AFL championship game	Sid Gillman
1962*	4	10	0	.286	314	392	3rd/Western Div.	—	—		Sid Gillman
1963*	11	3	0	.786	399	256	1st/Western Div.	1	0	AFL champ	Sid Gillman
1964*	8	5	1	.615	341	300	1st/Western Div.	0	1	AFL championship game	Sid Gillman
1965*	9	2	3	.818	340	227	1st/Western Div.	0	1	AFL championship game	Sid Gillman
1966*	7	6	1	.538	335	284	3rd/Western Div.	—	—		Sid Gillman
1967*	8	5	1	.615	360	352	3rd/Western Div.	—	—		Sid Gillman
1968*	9	5	0	.643	382	310	3rd/Western Div.	—	—		Sid Gillman
1969*	8	6	0	.571	288	276	3rd/Western Div.	—	—		S. Gillman, C. Waller
1970	5	6	3	.455	282	278	3rd/AFC Western Div.	—	—		Charlie Waller
1971	6	8	0	.429	311	341	3rd/AFC Western Div.	—	—		Harland Svare
1972	4	9	1	.308	264	344	4th/AFC Western Div.	—	—		Harland Svare
1973	2	11	1	.179	188	386	4th/AFC Western Div.	—	—		H. Svare, Ron Waller
1974	5	9	0	.357	212	285	T3rd/AFC Western Div.	—	—		Tommy Prothro

Year	W	L	T	Pct.	PF	PA	Finish	W	L	Highest round	Coach
1975	2	12	0	.143	189	345	4th/AFC Western Div.	—	—		Tommy Prothro
1976	6	8	0	.429	248	285	3rd/AFC Western Div.	—	—		Tommy Prothro
1977	7	7	0	.500	222	205	3rd/AFC Western Div.	—	—		Tommy Prothro
1978	9	7	0	.563	355	309	T2nd/AFC Western Div.	—	—		T. Prothro, Don Coryell
1979	12	4	0	.750	411	246	1st/AFC Western Div.	0	1	AFC div. playoff game	Don Coryell
1980	11	5	0	.688	418	327	1st/AFC Western Div.	1	1	AFC championship game	Don Coryell
1981	10	6	0	.625	478	390	1st/AFC Western Div.	1	1	AFC championship game	Don Coryell
1982	6	3	0	.667	288	221	T4th/AFC	1	1	AFC second-round pl. game	Don Coryell
1983	6	10	0	.375	358	462	T4th/AFC Western Div.	—	—		Don Coryell
1984	7	9	0	.438	394	413	5th/AFC Western Div.	—	—		Don Coryell
1985	8	8	0	.500	467	435	T3rd/AFC Western Div.	—	—		Don Coryell
1986	4	12	0	.250	335	396	5th/AFC Western Div.	—	—		D. Coryell, Al Saunders
1987	8	7	0	.533	253	317	3rd/AFC Western Div.	—	—		Al Saunders
1988	6	10	0	.375	231	332	4th/AFC Western Div.	—	—		Al Saunders
1989	6	10	0	.375	266	290	5th/AFC Western Div.	—	—		Dan Henning
1990	6	10	0	.375	315	281	4th/AFC Western Div.	—	—		Dan Henning
1991	4	12	0	.250	274	342	5th/AFC Western Div.	—	—		Dan Henning
1992	11	5	0	.688	335	241	1st/AFC Western Div.	1	1	AFC div. playoff game	Bobby Ross
1993	8	8	0	.500	322	290	4th/AFC Western Div.	—	—		Bobby Ross
1994	11	5	0	.688	381	306	1st/AFC Western Div.	2	1	Super Bowl	Bobby Ross
1995	9	7	0	.563	321	323	2nd/AFC Western Div.	0	1	AFC wild-card game	Bobby Ross
1996	8	8	0	.500	310	376	3rd/AFC Western Div.	—	—		Bobby Ross
1997	4	12	0	.250	266	425	T4th/AFC Western Div.	—	—		Kevin Gilbride
1998	5	11	0	.313	241	342	5th/AFC Western Div.	—	—		K. Gilbride, June Jones
1999	8	8	0	.500	269	316	3rd/AFC Western Div.	—	—		Mike Riley
2000	1	15	0	.063	269	440	5th/AFC Western Div.	—	—		Mike Riley

*American Football League.
†Los Angeles Chargers.

FIRST-ROUND DRAFT PICKS

1960—Monty Stickles, E, Notre Dame
1961—Earl Faison, E, Indiana
1962—Bob Ferguson, RB, Ohio State
1963—Walt Sweeney, E, Syracuse
1964—Ted Davis, E, Georgia Tech
1965—Steve DeLong, DE, Tennessee
1966—Don Davis, T, Los Angeles State
1967—Ron Billingsley, DT, Wyoming
1968—Russ Washington, T, Missouri
       Jim Hill, DB, Texas A&I
1969—Marty Domres, QB, Columbia
       Bob Babich, LB, Miami of Ohio
1970—Walker Gillette, WR, Richmond
1971—Leon Burns, RB, Long Beach State
1972—None
1973—Johnny Rodgers, WR, Nebraska
1974—Bo Matthews, RB, Colorado
       Don Goode, LB, Kansas
1975—Gary Johnson, DT, Grambling State
       Mike Williams, DB, Louisiana State
1976—Joe Washington, RB, Oklahoma
1977—Bob Rush, C, Memphis State
1978—John Jefferson, WR, Arizona State
1979—Kellen Winslow, TE, Missouri
1980—None

1981—James Brooks, RB, Auburn
1982—None
1983—Billy Ray Smith, LB, Arkansas
       Gary Anderson, WR, Arkansas
       Gill Byrd, DB, San Jose State
1984—Mossy Cade, DB, Texas
1985—Jim Lachey, G, Ohio State
1986—Leslie O'Neal, DE, Oklahoma State
       Jim FitzPatrick, T, Southern California
1987—Rod Bernstine, TE, Texas A&M
1988—Anthony Miller, WR, Tennessee
1989—Burt Grossman, DE, Pittsburgh
1990—Junior Seau, LB, Southern California
1991—Stanley Richard, CB, Texas
1992—Chris Mims, DT, Tennessee
1993—Darrien Gordon, DB, Stanford
1994—None
1995—None
1996—None
1997—None
1998—Ryan Leaf, QB, Washington State
1999—None
2000—None
2001—LaDainian Tomlinson, RB, Texas Christian

FRANCHISE RECORDS

Most rushing yards, career
4,963—Paul Lowe
Most rushing yards, season
1,350—Natrone Means, 1994
Most rushing yards, game
217—Gary Anderson vs. K.C., Dec. 18, 1988
Most rushing touchdowns, season
19—Chuck Muncie, 1981

Most passing attempts, season
609—Dan Fouts, 1981
Most passing attempts, game
58—Mark Herrmann at K.C., Dec. 22, 1985
Most passes completed, season
360—Dan Fouts, 1981
Most passes completed, game
37—Dan Fouts vs. Mia., Nov. 18, 1984 (OT)
       Mark Herrmann at K.C., Dec. 22, 1985

Most passing yards, career
43,040—Dan Fouts
Most passing yards, season
4,802—Dan Fouts, 1981
Most passing yards, game
444—Dan Fouts vs. NYG, Oct. 19, 1980
       Dan Fouts at S.F., Dec. 11, 1982
Most touchdown passes, season
33—Dan Fouts, 1981

Most pass receptions, career
586—Charlie Joiner
Most pass receptions, season
90—Tony Martin, 1995
Most pass receptions, game
15—Kellen Winslow at G.B., Oct. 7, 1984
Most receiving yards, career
9,585—Lance Alworth
Most receiving yards, season
1,602—Lance Alworth, 1965
Most receiving yards, game
260—Wes Chandler vs. Cin., Dec. 20, 1982

Most receiving touchdowns, season
14—Lance Alworth, 1965
    Tony Martin, 1996
Most touchdowns, career
83—Lance Alworth
Most field goals, season
34—John Carney, 1994
Longest field goal
54 yards—John Carney vs. Sea., Nov. 10,
    1991
    John Carney vs. Buf., Sept. 6,
    1998
    John Carney at K.C., Sept. 17,
    2000

Most interceptions, career
42—Gill Byrd
Most interceptions, season
9—Charlie McNeil, 1961
Most sacks, career
105.5—Leslie O'Neal
Most sacks, season
17.5—Gary Johnson, 1980

SERIES RECORDS

San Diego vs.: Arizona 6-2; Atlanta 1-5; Baltimore 2-1; Buffalo 17-8-2; Carolina 0-2; Chicago 4-4; Cincinnati 15-9; Cleveland 10-6-1; Dallas 1-5; Denver 36-45-1; Detroit 4-3; Green Bay 1-6; Indianapolis 11-8; Jacksonville 0-0; Kansas City 38-42-1; Miami 10-8; Minnesota 4-4; New England 11-16-2; New Orleans 6-2; N.Y. Giants 3-5; N.Y. Jets 17-9-1; Oakland 30-50-2; Philadelphia 5-2; Pittsburgh 5-17; St. Louis 3-4; San Francisco 3-6; Seattle 22-22; Tampa Bay 6-1; Tennessee 19-13-1; Washington 0-6.
NOTE: Includes records as Los Angeles Chargers in 1960.

COACHING RECORDS

Don Coryell, 69-56-0 (3-4); Kevin Gilbride, 6-16-0; Sid Gillman, 86-53-6 (1-4); Dan Henning, 16-32-0; June Jones, 3-7-0; Tommy Prothro, 21-39-0; Mike Riley, 9-23-0; Bobby Ross, 47-33-0 (3-3); Al Saunders, 17-22-0; Harland Svare, 7-17-2; Charlie Waller, 9-7-3; Ron Waller, 1-5-0.
NOTE: Playoff games in parentheses.

RETIRED UNIFORM NUMBERS

No.	Player
14	Dan Fouts

SAN FRANCISCO 49ERS
YEAR-BY-YEAR RECORDS

			REGULAR SEASON						PLAYOFFS	
Year	W	L	T	Pct.	PF	PA	Finish	W	L	Highest round	Coach
1946*	9	5	0	.643	307	189	2nd/Western Div.	— —			Buck Shaw
1947*	8	4	2	.667	327	264	2nd/Western Div.	— —			Buck Shaw
1948*	12	2	0	.857	495	248	2nd/Western Div.	— —			Buck Shaw
1949*	9	3	0	.750	416	227	2nd	— —			Buck Shaw
1950	3	9	0	.250	213	300	T5th/National Conf.	— —			Buck Shaw
1951	7	4	1	.636	255	205	T2nd/National Conf.	— —			Buck Shaw
1952	7	5	0	.583	285	221	3rd/National Conf.	— —			Buck Shaw
1953	9	3	0	.750	372	237	2nd/Western Conf.	— —			Buck Shaw
1954	7	4	1	.636	313	251	3rd/Western Conf.	— —			Buck Shaw
1955	4	8	0	.333	216	298	5th/Western Conf.	— —			Red Strader
1956	5	6	1	.455	233	284	3rd/Western Conf.	— —			Frankie Albert
1957	8	4	0	.667	260	264	2nd/Western Conf.	0	1	W. Conf. champ. game	Frankie Albert
1958	6	6	0	.500	257	324	4th/Western Conf.	— —			Frankie Albert
1959	7	5	0	.583	255	237	T3rd/Western Conf.	— —			Red Hickey
1960	7	5	0	.583	208	205	T2nd/Western Conf.	— —			Red Hickey
1961	7	6	1	.538	346	272	5th/Western Conf.	— —			Red Hickey
1962	6	8	0	.429	282	331	5th/Western Conf.	— —			Red Hickey
1963	2	12	0	.143	198	391	7th/Western Conf.	— —			R. Hickey, J. Christiansen
1964	4	10	0	.286	236	330	7th/Western Conf.	— —			Jack Christiansen
1965	7	6	1	.538	421	402	4th/Western Conf.	— —			Jack Christiansen
1966	6	6	2	.500	320	325	4th/Western Conf.	— —			Jack Christiansen
1967	7	7	0	.500	273	337	3rd/Coastal Div.	— —			Jack Christiansen
1968	7	6	1	.538	303	310	3rd/Coastal Div.	— —			Dick Nolan
1969	4	8	2	.333	277	319	4th/Coastal Div.	— —			Dick Nolan
1970	10	3	1	.769	352	267	1st/NFC Western Div.	1	1	NFC championship game	Dick Nolan
1971	9	5	0	.643	300	216	1st/NFC Western Div.	1	1	NFC championship game	Dick Nolan
1972	8	5	1	.607	353	249	1st/NFC Western Div.	0	1	NFC div. playoff game	Dick Nolan
1973	5	9	0	.357	262	319	T3rd/NFC Western Div.	— —			Dick Nolan
1974	6	8	0	.429	226	236	2nd/NFC Western Div.	— —			Dick Nolan
1975	5	9	0	.357	255	286	2nd/NFC Western Div.	— —			Dick Nolan
1976	8	6	0	.571	270	190	2nd/NFC Western Div.	— —			Monte Clark
1977	5	9	0	.357	220	260	3rd/NFC Western Div.	— —			Ken Meyer
1978	2	14	0	.125	219	350	4th/NFC Western Div.	— —			Pete McCulley, Fred O'Connor

	REGULAR SEASON							PLAYOFFS			
Year	W	L	T	Pct.	PF	PA	Finish	W	L	Highest round	Coach
1979	2	14	0	.125	308	416	4th/NFC Western Div.	—	—		Bill Walsh
1980	6	10	0	.375	320	415	3rd/NFC Western Div.	—	—		Bill Walsh
1981	13	3	0	.813	357	250	1st/NFC Western Div.	3	0	Super Bowl champ	Bill Walsh
1982	3	6	0	.333	209	206	T11th/NFC	—	—		Bill Walsh
1983	10	6	0	.625	432	293	1st/NFC Western Div.	1	1	NFC championship game	Bill Walsh
1984	15	1	0	.938	475	227	1st/NFC Western Div.	3	0	Super Bowl champ	Bill Walsh
1985	10	6	0	.625	411	263	2nd/NFC Western Div.	0	1	NFC wild-card game	Bill Walsh
1986	10	5	1	.656	374	247	1st/NFC Western Div.	0	1	NFC div. playoff game	Bill Walsh
1987	13	2	0	.867	459	253	1st/NFC Western Div.	0	1	NFC div. playoff game	Bill Walsh
1988	10	6	0	.625	369	294	1st/NFC Western Div.	3	0	Super Bowl champ	Bill Walsh
1989	14	2	0	.875	442	253	1st/NFC Western Div.	3	0	Super Bowl champ	George Seifert
1990	14	2	0	.875	353	239	1st/NFC Western Div.	1	1	NFC championship game	George Seifert
1991	10	6	0	.625	393	239	3rd/NFC Western Div.	—	—		George Seifert
1992	14	2	0	.875	431	236	1st/NFC Western Div.	1	1	NFC championship game	George Seifert
1993	10	6	0	.625	473	295	1st/NFC Western Div.	1	1	NFC championship game	George Seifert
1994	13	3	0	.813	505	296	1st/NFC Western Div.	3	0	Super Bowl champ	George Seifert
1995	11	5	0	.688	457	258	1st/NFC Western Div.	0	1	NFC div. playoff game	George Seifert
1996	12	4	0	.750	398	257	2nd/NFC Western Div.	1	1	NFC div. playoff game	George Seifert
1997	13	3	0	.813	375	265	1st/NFC Western Div.	1	1	NFC championship game	Steve Mariucci
1998	12	4	0	.750	479	328	2nd/NFC Western Div.	1	1	NFC div. playoff game	Steve Mariucci
1999	4	12	0	.250	295	453	4th/NFC Western Div.	—	—		Steve Mariucci
2000	6	10	0	.375	388	422	4th/NFC Western Div.	—	—		Steve Mariucci

*All-America Football Conference.

FIRST-ROUND DRAFT PICKS

1950—Leo Nomellini, T, Minnesota
1951—Y.A. Tittle, QB, Louisiana State
1952—Hugh McElhenny, RB, Washington
1953—Harry Babcock, E, Georgia*
    Tom Stolhandske, E, Texas
1954—Bernie Faloney, QB, Maryland
1955—Dick Moegel, HB, Rice
1956—Earl Morrall QB, Michigan State
1957—John Brodie, QB, Stanford
1958—Jim Pace, RB, Michigan
    Charles Krueger, T, Texas A&M
1959—Dave Baker, RB, Oklahoma
    Dan James, C, Ohio State
1960—Monty Stickles, E, Notre Dame
1961—Jim Johnson, RB, UCLA
    Bernie Casey, RB, Bowling Green State
    Billy Kilmer, QB, UCLA
1962—Lance Alworth, RB, Arkansas
1963—Kermit Alexander, RB, UCLA
1964—Dave Parks, E, Texas Tech*
1965—Ken Willard, RB, North Carolina
    George Donnelly, DB, Illinois
1966—Stan Hindman, DE, Mississippi
1967—Steve Spurrier, QB, Florida
    Cas Banaszek, LB, Northwestern
1968—Forrest Blue, C, Auburn
1969—Ted Kwalick, TE, Penn State
    Gene Washington, WR, Stanford
1970—Cedrick Hardman, DE, North Texas State
    Bruce Taylor, DB, Boston University
1971—Tim Anderson, DB, Ohio State
1972—Terry Beasley, WR, Auburn
1973—Mike Holmes, DB, Tex. Southern
1974—Wilbur Jackson, RB, Alabama
    Bill Sandifer, DT, UCLA

1975—Jimmy Webb, DT, Mississippi State
1976—None
1977—None
1978—Ken McAfee, TE, Notre Dame
    Dan Bunz, LB, Long Beach State
1979—None
1980—Earl Cooper, RB, Rice
    Jim Stuckey, DE, Clemson
1981—Ronnie Lott, DB, Southern California
1982—None
1983—None
1984—Todd Shell, LB, Brigham Young
1985—Jerry Rice, WR, Mississippi Valley State
1986—None
1987—Harris Barton, T, North Carolina
    Terrence Flager, RB, Clemson
1988—None
1989—Keith DeLong, LB, Tennessee
1990—Dexter Carter, RB, Florida State
1991—Ted Washington, DL, Louisville
1992—Dana Hall, DB, Washington
1993—Dana Stubblefield, DT, Kansas
    Todd Kelly, DE, Tennessee
1994—Bryant Young, DT, Notre Dame
    William Floyd, RB, Florida State
1995—J.J. Stokes, WR, UCLA
1996—None
1997—Jim Druckenmiller, QB, Virginia Tech
1998—R.W. McQuarters, DB, Oklahoma State
1999—Reggie McGrew, DT, Florida
2000—Julian Peterson, LB, Michigan State
    Ahmed Plummer, DB, Ohio State
2001—Andre Carter, DE, California
    *First player chosen in draft.

FRANCHISE RECORDS

Most rushing yards, career
7,344—Joe Perry
Most rushing yards, season
1,570—Garrison Hearst, 1998

Most rushing yards, game
201—Charlie Garner at Dal., Sept. 24,
    2000

Most rushing touchdowns, season
10—Joe Perry, 1953
    J.D. Smith, 1959
    Billy Kilmer, 1961
    Ricky Watters, 1993
    Derek Loville, 1995

Most passing attempts, season
578—Steve DeBerg, 1979
Most passing attempts, game
60—Joe Montana at Was., Nov. 17, 1986
Most passes completed, season
355—Jeff Garcia, 2000
Most passes completed, game
37—Joe Montana at Atl., Nov. 6, 1985
Most passing yards, career
35,142—Joe Montana
Most passing yards, season
4,278—Jeff Garcia, 2000
Most passing yards, game
476—Joe Montana at Atl., Oct. 14, 1990
Most touchdown passes, season
36—Steve Young, 1998

Most pass receptions, career
1,281—Jerry Rice
Most pass receptions, season
122—Jerry Rice, 1995
Most pass receptions, game
16—Jerry Rice at L.A. Rams, Nov. 20, 1994
Most receiving yards, career
19,247—Jerry Rice
Most receiving yards, season
1,848—Jerry Rice, 1995
Most receiving yards, game
289—Jerry Rice vs. Min., Dec. 18, 1995
Most receiving touchdowns, season
22—Jerry Rice, 1987

Most touchdowns, career
187—Jerry Rice
Most field goals, season
30—Jeff Wilkins, 1996
Longest field goal
56 yards—Mike Cofer at Atl., Oct. 14, 1990
Most interceptions, career
51—Ronnie Lott
Most interceptions, season
10—Dave Baker, 1960
Ronnie Lott, 1986
Most sacks, career
112.5—Cedrick Hardman
Most sacks, season
18—Cedrick Hardman

SERIES RECORDS

San Francisco vs.: Arizona 12-9; Atlanta 42-25-1; Baltimore 1-0; Buffalo 3-4; Carolina 5-7; Chicago 26-25-1; Cincinnati 7-2; Cleveland 6-9; Dallas 13-7-1; Denver 4-5; Detroit 29-26-1; Green Bay 25-25-1; Indianapolis 17-22; Jacksonville 0-1; Kansas City 5-3; Miami 3-4; Minnesota 17-17-1; New England 7-2; New Orleans 43-18-2; N.Y. Giants 12-11; N.Y. Jets 7-1; Oakland 3-6; Philadelphia 14-6-1; Pittsburgh 9-8; St. Louis 47-51-2; San Diego 6-3; Seattle 4-2; Tampa Bay 12-2; Tennessee 7-3; Washington 12-7-1.
NOTE: Includes records only from 1950 to present.

COACHING RECORDS

Frankie Albert, 19-16-1 (0-1); Jack Christiansen, 26-38-3; Monte Clark, 8-6-0; Red Hickey, 27-27-1; Steve Mariucci, 35-29-0 (2-2); Pete McCulley, 1-8-0; Ken Meyer, 5-9-0; Dick Nolan, 54-53-5 (2-3); Fred O'Connor, 1-6-0; George Seifert, 98-30-0 (10-5); Buck Shaw, 33-25-2; Red Strader, 4-8-0; Bill Walsh, 92-59-1 (10-4).
NOTE: Playoff games in parentheses.

RETIRED UNIFORM NUMBERS

No.	Player
12	John Brodie
16	Joe Montana
34	Joe Perry
37	Jimmy Johnson
39	Hugh McElhenny
70	Charlie Krueger
73	Leo Nomellini
87	Dwight Clark

SEATTLE SEAHAWKS
YEAR-BY-YEAR RECORDS

		REGULAR SEASON					PLAYOFFS			
Year	W	L	T	Pct.	PF	PA	Finish	W	L	Highest round	Coach
1976	2	12	0	.143	229	429	5th/NFC Western Div.	—	—		Jack Patera
1977	5	9	0	.357	282	373	4th/AFC Western Div.	—	—		Jack Patera
1978	9	7	0	.563	345	358	T2nd/AFC Western Div.	—	—		Jack Patera
1979	9	7	0	.563	378	372	T3rd	—	—		Jack Patera
1980	4	12	0	.250	291	408	5th/AFC Western Div.	—	—		Jack Patera
1981	6	10	0	.375	322	388	5th/AFC Western Div.	—	—		Jack Patera
1982	4	5	0	.444	127	147	T8th/AFC	—	—		J. Patera, Mike McCormack
1983	9	7	0	.562	403	397	T2nd/AFC Western Div.	2	1	AFC championship game	Chuck Knox
1984	12	4	0	.750	418	282	2nd/AFC Western Div.	1	1	AFC div. playoff game	Chuck Knox
1985	8	8	0	.500	349	303	T3rd/AFC Western Div.	—	—		Chuck Knox
1986	10	6	0	.625	366	293	T2nd/AFC Western Div.	—	—		Chuck Knox
1987	9	6	0	.600	371	314	2nd/AFC Western Div.	0	1	AFC wild-card game	Chuck Knox
1988	9	7	0	.563	339	329	1st/AFC Western Div.	0	1	AFC div. playoff game	Chuck Knox
1989	7	9	0	.438	241	327	4th/AFC Western Div.	—	—		Chuck Knox
1990	9	7	0	.563	306	286	3rd/AFC Western Div.	—	—		Chuck Knox
1991	7	9	0	.438	276	261	4th/AFC Western Div.	—	—		Chuck Knox
1992	2	14	0	.125	140	312	5th/AFC Western Div.	—	—		Tom Flores
1993	6	10	0	.375	280	314	5th/AFC Western Div.	—	—		Tom Flores
1994	6	10	0	.375	287	323	5th/AFC Western Div.	—	—		Tom Flores
1995	8	8	0	.500	363	366	T3rd/AFC Western Div.	—	—		Dennis Erickson
1996	7	9	0	.438	317	376	T4th/AFC Western Div.	—	—		Dennis Erickson
1997	8	8	0	.500	365	362	3rd/AFC Western Div.	—	—		Dennis Erickson
1998	8	8	0	.500	372	310	3rd/AFC Western Div.	—	—		Dennis Erickson
1999	9	7	0	.563	338	298	1st/AFC Western Div.	0	1	AFC wild-card game	Mike Holmgren
2000	6	10	0	.375	320	405	4th/AFC Western Div.	—	—		Mike Holmgren

FIRST-ROUND DRAFT PICKS

1976—Steve Niehaus, DT, Notre Dame
1977—Steve August, G, Tulsa
1978—Keith Simpson, DB, Memphis State
1979—Manu Tuiasosopo, DT, UCLA
1980—Jacob Green, DE, Texas A&M
1981—Kenny Easley, DB, UCLA
1982—Jeff Bryant, DE, Clemson
1983—Curt Warner, RB, Penn State
1984—Terry Taylor, DB, Southern Illinois
1985—None
1986—John L. Williams, RB, Florida
1987—Tony Woods, LB, Pittsburgh
1988—None
1989—Andy Heck, T, Notre Dame
1990—Cortez Kennedy, DT, Miami, Fla.

1991—Dan McGwire, QB, San Diego State
1992—Ray Roberts, T, Virginia
1993—Rick Mirer, QB, Notre Dame
1994—Sam Adams, DE, Texas A&M
1995—Joey Galloway, WR, Ohio State
1996—Pete Kendall, T, Boston College
1997—Shawn Springs, CB, Ohio State
    Walter Jones, T, Florida State
1998—Anthony Simmons, LB, Clemson
1999—Lamar King, DE, Saginaw Valley State
2000—Shaun Alexander, RB, Alabama
    Chris McIntosh, T, Wisconsin
2001—Koren Robinson, WR, North Carolina State
    Steve Hutchinson, G, Michigan

FRANCHISE RECORDS

Most rushing yards, career
6,706—Chris Warren

Most rushing yards, season
1,545—Chris Warren, 1994

Most rushing yards, game
207—Curt Warner vs. K.C., Nov. 27, 1983 (OT)
192—Curt Warner vs. Den., Dec. 20, 1986

Most rushing touchdowns, season
15—Chris Warren, 1995

Most passing attempts, season
532—Dave Krieg, 1985

Most passing attempts, game
51—Dave Krieg vs. Atl., Oct. 13, 1985

Most passes completed, season
313—Warren Moon, 1997

Most passes completed, game
33—Dave Krieg vs. Atl., Oct. 13, 1985

Most passing yards, career
26,132—Dave Krieg

Most passing yards, season
3,678—Warren Moon, 1997

Most passing yards, game
418—Dave Krieg vs. Den., Nov. 20, 1983

Most touchdown passes, season
32—Dave Krieg, 1984

Most pass receptions, career
819—Steve Largent

Most pass receptions, season
81—Brian Blades, 1994

Most pass receptions, game
15—Steve Largent vs. Det., Oct. 18, 1987

Most receiving yards, career
13,089—Steve Largent

Most receiving yards, season
1,287—Steve Largent, 1985

Most receiving yards, game
261—Steve Largent vs. Det., Oct. 18, 1987

Most receiving touchdowns, season
13—Daryl Turner, 1985

Most touchdowns, career
101—Steve Largent

Most field goals, season
34—Todd Peterson, 1999

Longest field goal
55 yards—John Kasay vs. K.C., Jan. 2, 1994

Most interceptions, career
50—Dave Brown

Most interceptions, season
10—John Harris, 1981
    Kenny Easley, 1984

Most sacks, career
116—Jacob Green

Most sacks, season
16.5—Michael Sinclair, 1998

SERIES RECORDS

Seattle vs.: Arizona 1-5; Atlanta 6-2; Baltimore 0-1; Buffalo 5-3; Carolina 0-1; Chicago 5-2; Cincinnati 8-7; Cleveland 9-4; Dallas 1-5; Denver 16-31; Detroit 4-4; Green Bay 4-4; Indianapolis 3-5; Jacksonville 2-1; Kansas City 15-29; Miami 2-5; Minnesota 4-2; New England 7-6; New Orleans 3-4; N.Y. Giants 3-5; N.Y. Jets 8-7; Oakland 21-25; Philadelphia 3-4; Pittsburgh 7-6; St. Louis 2-5; San Diego 22-22; San Francisco 2-4; Tampa Bay 4-1; Tennessee 7-4; Washington 4-5.

COACHING RECORDS

Dennis Erickson, 31-33-0; Tom Flores, 14-34-0; Mike Holmgren, 15-17-0 (0-1); Chuck Knox, 80-63-0 (3-4); Mike McCormack, 4-3-0; Jack Patera, 35-59-0.
NOTE: Playoff games in parentheses.

RETIRED UNIFORM NUMBERS

No.	Player
80	Steve Largent

TAMPA BAY BUCCANEERS
YEAR-BY-YEAR RECORDS

	REGULAR SEASON							PLAYOFFS			
Year	W	L	T	Pct.	PF	PA	Finish	W	L	Highest round	Coach
1976	0	14	0	.000	125	412	5th/AFC Western Div.	—	—		John McKay
1977	2	12	0	.143	103	223	5th/NFC Central Div.	—	—		John McKay
1978	5	11	0	.313	241	259	5th/NFC Central Div.	—	—		John McKay
1979	10	6	0	.625	273	237	1st/NFC Central Div.	1	1	NFC championship game	John McKay
1980	5	10	1	.344	271	341	T4th/NFC Central Div.	—	—		John McKay
1981	9	7	0	.563	315	268	1st/NFC Central Div.	0	1	NFC div. playoff game	John McKay
1982	5	4	0	.556	158	178	T4th/NFC	0	1	NFC first-round pl. game	John McKay
1983	2	14	0	.125	241	380	5th/NFC Central Div.	—	—		John McKay
1984	6	10	0	.375	335	380	3rd/NFC Central Div.	—	—		John McKay

			REGULAR SEASON						PLAYOFFS		
Year	W	L	T	Pct.	PF	PA	Finish	W	L	Highest round	Coach
1985	2	14	0	.125	294	448	5th/NFC Central Div.	—	—		Leeman Bennett
1986	2	14	0	.125	239	473	5th/NFC Central Div.	—	—		Leeman Bennett
1987	4	11	0	.267	286	360	T4th/NFC Central Div.	—	—		Ray Perkins
1988	5	11	0	.313	261	350	3rd/NFC Central Div.	—	—		Ray Perkins
1989	5	11	0	.313	320	419	5th/NFC Central Div.	—	—		Ray Perkins
1990	6	10	0	.375	264	367	T2nd/NFC Central Div.	—	—		R. Perkins, R. Williamson
1991	3	13	0	.188	199	365	5th/NFC Central Div.	—	—		Richard Williamson
1992	5	11	0	.313	267	365	T3rd/NFC Central Div.	—	—		Sam Wyche
1993	5	11	0	.313	237	376	5th/NFC Central Div.	—	—		Sam Wyche
1994	6	10	0	.375	251	351	5th/NFC Central Div.	—	—		Sam Wyche
1995	7	9	0	.438	238	335	5th/NFC Central Div.	—	—		Sam Wyche
1996	6	10	0	.375	221	293	4th/NFC Central Div.	—	—		Tony Dungy
1997	10	6	0	.625	299	263	3rd/AFC Western Div.	1	1	NFC div. playoff game	Tony Dungy
1998	8	8	0	.500	314	295	3rd/AFC Western Div.	—	—		Tony Dungy
1999	11	5	0	.688	270	235	1st/NFC Central Div.	1	1	NFC championship game	Tony Dungy
2000	10	6	0	.625	388	269	2nd/NFC Central Div.	0	1	NFC wild-card game	Tony Dungy

FIRST-ROUND DRAFT PICKS

1976—Lee Roy Selmon, DE, Oklahoma*
1977—Ricky Bell, RB, Southern California*
1978—Doug Williams, QB, Grambling State
1979—None
1980—Ray Snell, T, Wisconsin
1981—Hugh Green, LB, Pittsburgh
1982—Sean Farrell, G, Penn State
1983—None
1984—None
1985—Ron Holmes, DE, Washington
1986—Bo Jackson, RB, Auburn*
　　　Rod Jones, DB, Southern Methodist
1987—Vinny Testaverde, QB, Miami, Fla.*
1988—Paul Gruber, T, Wisconsin
1989—Broderick Thomas, LB, Nebraska
1990—Keith McCants, LB, Alabama

1991—Charles McRae, T, Tennessee
1992—None
1993—Eric Curry, DE, Alabama
1994—Trent Dilfer, QB, Fresno State
1995—Warren Sapp, DT, Miami, Fla.
　　　Derrick Brooks, LB, Florida State
1996—Regan Upshaw, DE, California
　　　Marcus Jones, DT, North Carolina
1997—Warrick Dunn, RB, Florida State
　　　Reidel Anthony, WR, Florida
1998—None
1999—Anthony McFarland, DT, Louisiana State
2000—None
2001—Kenyatta Walker, T, Florida
　　　*First player chosen in draft.

FRANCHISE RECORDS

Most rushing yards, career
5,957—James Wilder
Most rushing yards, season
1,544—James Wilder, 1984
Most rushing yards, game
219—James Wilder at Min., Nov. 6, 1983
Most rushing touchdowns, season
13—James Wilder, 1984
Most passing attempts, season
521—Doug Williams, 1980
Most passing attempts, game
56—Doug Williams vs. Cle., Sept. 28, 1980
Most passes completed, season
308—Steve DeBerg, 1984
Most passes completed, game
31—Vinny Testaverde at Hou., Dec. 10, 1989
Most passing yards, career
14,820—Vinny Testaverde

Most passing yards, season
3,563—Doug Williams, 1981
Most passing yards, game
486—Doug Williams at Min., Nov. 16, 1980
Most touchdown passes, season
21—Trent Dilfer, 1997, 1998
Most pass receptions, career
430—James Wilder
Most pass receptions, season
86—Mark Carrier, 1989
Most pass receptions, game
13—James Wilder vs. Min., Sept. 15, 1985
Most receiving yards, career
5,018—Mark Carrier
Most receiving yards, season
1,422—Mark Carrier, 1989
Most receiving yards, game
212—Mark Carrier at N.O., Dec. 6, 1987

Most receiving touchdowns, season
9—Kevin House, 1981
　　Bruce Hill, 1988
　　Mark Carrier, 1989
Most touchdowns, career
46—James Wilder
Most field goals, season
28—Martin Gramatica, 2000
Longest field goal
57 yards—Michael Husted at L.A. Raiders, Dec. 19, 1993
Most interceptions, career
29—Cedric Brown
Most interceptions, season
9—Cedric Brown, 1981
Most sacks, career
78.5—Lee Roy Selmon
Most sacks, season
16.5—Warren Sapp, 2000

SERIES RECORDS

Tampa Bay vs.: Arizona 7-7; Atlanta 9-8; Buffalo 5-2; Carolina 2-1; Chicago 15-31; Cincinnati 3-3; Cleveland 0-5; Dallas 1-6; Denver 2-3; Detroit 20-26; Green Bay 16-27-1; Indianapolis 4-5; Jacksonville 1-1; Kansas City 3-5; Miami 3-4; Minnesota 16-30; New England 2-3; New Orleans 6-13; N.Y. Giants 5-9; N.Y. Jets 1-7; Oakland 1-4; Philadelphia 3-3; Pittsburgh 1-4; St. Louis 4-8; San Diego 1-6; San Francisco 2-12; Seattle 1-4; Tennessee 1-5; Washington 4-6.

COACHING RECORDS

Leeman Bennett, 4-28-0; Tony Dungy, 45-35-0 (2-3); John McKay, 44-88-1 (1-3); Ray Perkins, 19-41-0; Richard Williamson, 4-15-0; Sam Wyche, 23-41-0.
NOTE: Playoff games in parentheses.

RETIRED UNIFORM NUMBERS

No.	Player
63	Lee Roy Selmon

TENNESSEE TITANS
YEAR-BY-YEAR RECORDS

	REGULAR SEASON							PLAYOFFS			
Year	W	L	T	Pct.	PF	PA	Finish	W	L	Highest round	Coach
1960*†	10	4	0	.714	379	285	1st/Eastern Div.	1	0	AFL champ	Lou Rymkus
1961*†	10	3	1	.769	513	242	1st/Eastern Div.	1	0	AFL champ	L. Rymkus, Wally Lemm
1962*†	11	3	0	.786	387	270	1st/Eastern Div.	0	1	AFL championship game	Pop Ivy
1963*†	6	8	0	.429	302	372	3rd/Eastern Div.	—	—		Pop Ivy
1964*†	4	10	0	.286	310	355	4th/Eastern Div.	—	—		Sammy Baugh
1965*†	4	10	0	.286	298	429	4th/Eastern Div.	—	—		Hugh Taylor
1966*†	3	11	0	.214	335	396	T4th/Eastern Div.	—	—		Wally Lemm
1967*†	9	4	1	.692	258	199	1st/Eastern Div.	0	1	AFL championship game	Wally Lemm
1968*†	7	7	0	.500	303	248	2nd/Eastern Div.	—	—		Wally Lemm
1969*†	6	6	2	.500	278	279	2nd/Eastern Div.	0	1	Div. playoff game	Wally Lemm
1970†	3	10	1	.231	217	352	4th/AFC Central Div.	—	—		Wally Lemm
1971†	4	9	1	.308	251	330	3rd/AFC Central Div.	—	—		Ed Hughes
1972†	1	13	0	.071	164	380	4th/AFC Central Div.	—	—		Bill Peterson
1973†	1	13	0	.071	199	447	4th/AFC Central Div.	—	—		B. Peterson, S. Gillman
1974†	7	7	0	.500	236	282	T2nd/AFC Central Div.	—	—		Sid Gillman
1975†	10	4	0	.714	293	226	3rd/AFC Central Div.	—	—		Bum Phillips
1976†	5	9	0	.357	222	273	4th/AFC Central Div.	—	—		Bum Phillips
1977†	8	6	0	.571	299	230	T2nd/AFC Central Div.	—	—		Bum Phillips
1978†	10	6	0	.625	283	298	2nd/AFC Central Div.	2	1	AFC championship game	Bum Phillips
1979†	11	5	0	.688	362	331	2nd/AFC Central Div.	2	1	AFC championship game	Bum Phillips
1980†	11	5	0	.688	295	251	2nd/AFC Central Div.	0	1	AFC wild-card game	Bum Phillips
1981†	7	9	0	.438	281	355	3rd/AFC Central Div.	—	—		Ed Biles
1982†	1	8	0	.111	136	245	13th/AFC	—	—		Ed Biles
1983†	2	14	0	.125	288	460	4th/AFC Central Div.	—	—		Ed Biles, Chuck Studley
1984†	3	13	0	.188	240	437	4th/AFC Central Div.	—	—		Hugh Campbell
1985†	5	11	0	.313	284	412	4th/AFC Central Div.	—	—		H. Campbell, J. Glanville
1986†	5	11	0	.313	274	329	4th/AFC Central Div.	—	—		Jerry Glanville
1987†	9	6	0	.600	345	349	2nd/AFC Central Div.	1	1	AFC div. playoff game	Jerry Glanville
1988†	10	6	0	.625	424	365	T2nd/AFC Central Div.	1	1	AFC div. playoff game	Jerry Glanville
1989†	9	7	0	.563	365	412	T2nd/AFC Central Div.	0	1	AFC wild-card game	Jerry Glanville
1990†	9	7	0	.563	405	307	2nd/AFC Central Div.	0	1	AFC wild-card game	Jack Pardee
1991†	11	5	0	.688	386	251	1st/AFC Central Div.	1	1	AFC div. playoff game	Jack Pardee
1992†	10	6	0	.625	352	258	2nd/AFC Central Div.	0	1	AFC wild-card game	Jack Pardee
1993†	12	4	0	.750	368	238	1st/AFC Central Div.	0	1	AFC div. playoff game	Jack Pardee
1994†	2	14	0	.125	226	352	4th/AFC Central Div.	—	—		Jack Pardee, Jeff Fisher
1995†	7	9	0	.438	348	324	T2nd/AFC Central Div.	—	—		Jeff Fisher
1996†	8	8	0	.500	345	319	T3rd/AFC Central Div.	—	—		Jeff Fisher
1997‡	8	8	0	.500	333	310	3rd/AFC Central Div.	—	—		Jeff Fisher
1998‡	8	8	0	.500	330	320	2nd/AFC Central Div.	—	—		Jeff Fisher
1999	13	3	0	.813	392	324	2nd/AFC Central Div.	3	1	Super Bowl	Jeff Fisher
2000	13	3	0	.813	346	191	1st/AFC Central Div.	0	1	AFC div. playoff game	Jeff Fisher

*American Football League.
†Houston Oilers.
‡Tennessee Oilers.

FIRST-ROUND DRAFT PICKS

1960—Billy Cannon, RB, Louisiana State
1961—Mike Ditka, E, Pittsburgh
1962—Ray Jacobs, DT, Howard Payne
1963—Danny Brabham, LB, Arkansas
1964—Scott Appleton, DT, Texas
1965—Lawrence Elkins, WR, Baylor* (AFL)
1966—Tommy Nobis, LB, Texas
1967—George Webster, LB, Michigan State
       Tom Regner, G, Notre Dame
1968—None
1969—Ron Pritchard, LB, Arizona State
1970—Doug Wilkerson, G, North Carolina Central
1971—Dan Pastorini, QB, Santa Clara

1972—Greg Sampson, DE, Stanford
1973—John Matuszak, DE, Tampa*
       George Amundson, RB, Iowa State
1974—None
1975—Robert Brazile, LB, Jackson State
       Don Hardeman, RB, Texas A&I
1976—None
1977—Morris Towns, T, Missouri
1978—Earl Campbell, RB, Texas*
1979—None
1980—None
1981—None
1982—Mike Munchak, G, Penn State

1983—Bruce Matthews, G, Southern California
1984—Dean Steinkuhler, G, Nebraska
1985—Ray Childress, DE, Texas A&M
    Richard Johnson, DB, Wisconsin
1986—Jim Everett, QB, Purdue
1987—Alonzo Highsmith, FB, Miami, Fla.
    Haywood Jeffires, WR, North Carolina State
1988—Lorenzo White, RB, Michigan State
1989—David Williams, T, Florida
1990—Lamar Lathon, LB, Houston
1991—None

1992—None
1993—Brad Hopkins, G, Illinois
1994—Henry Ford, DE, Arkansas
1995—Steve McNair, QB, Alcorn State
1996—Eddie George, RB, Ohio State
1997—Kenny Holmes, DE, Miami, Fla.
1998—Kevin Dyson, WR, Utah
1999—Jevon Kearse, LB, Florida
2000—Keith Bulluck, LB, Syracuse
2001—None
*First player chosen in draft.

FRANCHISE RECORDS

Most rushing yards, career
8,574—Earl Campbell
Most rushing yards, season
1,934—Earl Campbell, 1980
Most rushing yards, game
216—Billy Cannon at N.Y. Titans, Dec.
    10, 1961
    Eddie George vs. Oak., Aug. 31,
    1997 (OT)
Most rushing touchdowns, season
19—Earl Campbell, 1979
Most passing attempts, season
655—Warren Moon, 1991
Most passing attempts, game
68—George Blanda at Buf., Nov. 1, 1964
Most passes completed, season
404—Warren Moon, 1991
Most passes completed, game
41—Warren Moon vs. Dal., Nov. 10, 1991

Most passing yards, career
33,685—Warren Moon
Most passing yards, season
4,690—Warren Moon, 1991
Most passing yards, game
527—Warren Moon at K.C., Dec. 16, 1990
Most touchdown passes, season
36—George Blanda, 1961
Most pass receptions, career
542—Ernest Givins
Most pass receptions, season
101—Charlie Hennigan, 1964
Most pass receptions, game
13—Charlie Hennigan at Boston, Oct.
    13, 1961
    Haywood Jeffires at NYJ, Oct. 13,
    1991
Most receiving yards, career
7,935—Ernest Givins
Most receiving yards, season
1,746—Charlie Hennigan, 1961

Most receiving yards, game
272—Charlie Hennigan at Boston, Oct.
    13, 1961
Most receiving touchdowns, season
17—Bill Groman, 1961
Most touchdowns, career
73—Earl Campbell
Most field goals, season
36—Al Del Greco, 1998
Longest field goal
56 yards—Al Del Greco vs. S.F., Oct. 27,
    1996
Most interceptions, career
45—Jim Norton
Most interceptions, season
12—Freddy Glick, 1963
    Mike Reinfeldt, 1979
Most sacks, season
15.5—Jesse Baker, 1979

SERIES RECORDS

Tennessee vs.: Arizona 3-4; Atlanta 5-5; Baltimore 6-4; Buffalo 22-14; Carolina 0-1; Chicago 4-4; Cincinnati 35-28-1; Cleveland 25-30; Dallas 5-5; Denver 20-11-1; Detroit 4-3; Green Bay 3-4; Indianapolis 7-7; Jacksonville 7-5; Kansas City 18-24; Miami 11-14; Minnesota 3-5; New England 14-18-1; New Orleans 5-4-1; N.Y. Giants 2-5; N.Y. Jets 20-13-1; Oakland 15-20; Philadelphia 1-6; Pittsburgh 26-35; St. Louis 3-5; San Diego 13-19-1; San Francisco 3-7; Seattle 4-7; Tampa Bay 5-1; Washington 5-3.
NOTE: Includes records as Houston Oilers from 1960 through 1996.

COACHING RECORDS

Sammy Baugh, 4-10-0; Ed Biles, 8-23-0; Hugh Campbell, 8-22-0; Jeff Fisher, 58-44-0 (3-2); Sid Gillman, 8-15-0; Jerry Glanville, 33-32-0 (2-3); Ed Hughes, 4-9-1; Frank Ivy, 17-11-0 (0-1); Wally Lemm, 37-38-4 (1-2); Jack Pardee, 43-31-0 (1-4); Bill Peterson, 1-18-0; Bum Phillips, 55-35-0 (4-3); Lou Rymkus, 11-7-1 (1-0); Chuck Studley, 2-8-0; Hugh Taylor, 4-10-0.
NOTE: Playoff games in parentheses.

RETIRED UNIFORM NUMBERS

No.	Player
34	Earl Campbell
43	Jim Norton
63	Mike Munchak
65	Elvin Bethea

WASHINGTON REDSKINS
YEAR-BY-YEAR RECORDS

	REGULAR SEASON						PLAYOFFS			
Year	W	L	T	Pct.	PF	PA	Finish	W	L	Highest round	Coach
1932*	4	4	2	.500	55	79	4th	—	—		Lud Wray
1933†	5	5	2	.500	103	97	3rd/Eastern Div.	—	—		Lone Star Dietz
1934†	6	6	0	.500	107	94	2nd/Eastern Div.	—	—		Lone Star Dietz
1935†	2	8	1	.200	65	123	4th/Eastern Div.	—	—		Eddie Casey
1936†	7	5	0	.583	149	110	1st/Eastern Div.	0	1	NFL championship game	Ray Flaherty
1937	8	3	0	.727	195	120	1st/Eastern Div.	1	0	NFL champ	Ray Flaherty
1938	6	3	2	.667	148	154	2nd/Eastern Div.	—	—		Ray Flaherty
1939	8	2	1	.800	242	94	2nd/Eastern Div.	—	—		Ray Flaherty
1940	9	2	0	.818	245	142	1st/Eastern Div.	0	1	NFL championship game	Ray Flaherty
1941	6	5	0	.545	176	174	3rd/Eastern Div.	—	—		Ray Flaherty
1942	10	1	0	.909	227	102	1st/Eastern Div.	1	0	NFL champ	Ray Flaherty

Year	W	L	T	Pct.	PF	PA	Finish	W	L	Highest round	Coach
1943	6	3	1	.667	229	137	1st/Eastern Div.	1	1	NFL championship game	Dutch Bergman
1944	6	3	1	.667	169	180	3rd/Eastern Div.	—	—		Dudley DeGroot
1945	8	2	0	.800	209	121	1st/Eastern Div.	0	1	NFL championship game	Dudley DeGroot
1946	5	5	1	.500	171	191	T3rd/Eastern Div.	—	—		Turk Edwards
1947	4	8	0	.333	295	367	4th/Eastern Div.	—	—		Turk Edwards
1948	7	5	0	.583	291	287	2nd/Eastern Div.	—	—		Turk Edwards
1949	4	7	1	.364	268	339	4th/Eastern Div.	—	—		John Whelchel, H. Ball
1950	3	9	0	.250	232	326	6th/American Conf.	—	—		Herman Ball
1951	5	7	0	.417	183	296	3rd/American Conf.	—	—		Herman Ball, Dick Todd
1952	4	8	0	.333	240	287	T5th/American Conf.	—	—		Curly Lambeau
1953	6	5	1	.545	208	215	3rd/Eastern Conf.	—	—		Curly Lambeau
1954	3	9	0	.250	207	432	5th/Eastern Conf.	—	—		Joe Kuharich
1955	8	4	0	.667	246	222	2nd/Eastern Conf.	—	—		Joe Kuharich
1956	6	6	0	.500	183	225	3rd/Eastern Conf.	—	—		Joe Kuharich
1957	5	6	1	.455	251	230	4th/Eastern Conf.	—	—		Joe Kuharich
1958	4	7	1	.364	214	268	4th/Eastern Conf.	—	—		Joe Kuharich
1959	3	9	0	.250	185	350	5th/Eastern Conf.	—	—		Mike Nixon
1960	1	9	2	.100	178	309	6th/Eastern Conf.	—	—		Mike Nixon
1961	1	12	1	.077	174	392	7th/Eastern Conf.	—	—		Bill McPeak
1962	5	7	2	.417	305	376	4th/Eastern Conf.	—	—		Bill McPeak
1963	3	11	0	.214	279	398	6th/Eastern Conf.	—	—		Bill McPeak
1964	6	8	0	.429	307	305	T3rd/Eastern Conf.	—	—		Bill McPeak
1965	6	8	0	.429	257	301	4th/Eastern Conf.	—	—		Bill McPeak
1966	7	7	0	.500	351	355	5th/Eastern Conf.	—	—		Otto Graham
1967	5	6	3	.455	347	353	3rd/Capitol Div.	—	—		Otto Graham
1968	5	9	0	.357	249	358	3rd/Capitol Div.	—	—		Otto Graham
1969	7	5	2	.583	307	319	2nd/Capitol Div.	—	—		Vince Lombardi
1970	6	8	0	.429	297	314	4th/NFC Eastern Div.	—	—		Bill Austin
1971	9	4	1	.692	276	190	2nd/NFC Eastern Div.	0	1	NFC div. playoff game	George Allen
1972	11	3	0	.786	336	218	1st/NFC Eastern Div.	2	1	Super Bowl	George Allen
1973	10	4	0	.714	325	198	2nd/NFC Eastern Div.	0	1	NFC div. playoff game	George Allen
1974	10	4	0	.714	320	196	2nd/NFC Eastern Div.	0	1	NFC div. playoff game	George Allen
1975	8	6	0	.571	325	276	3rd/NFC Eastern Div.	—	—		George Allen
1976	10	4	0	.714	291	217	2nd/NFC Eastern Div.	0	1	NFC div. playoff game	George Allen
1977	9	5	0	.643	196	189	2nd/NFC Eastern Div.	—	—		George Allen
1978	8	8	0	.500	273	283	3rd/NFC Eastern Div.	—	—		Jack Pardee
1979	10	6	0	.625	348	295	3rd/NFC Eastern Div.	—	—		Jack Pardee
1980	6	10	0	.375	261	293	3rd/NFC Eastern Div.	—	—		Jack Pardee
1981	8	8	0	.500	347	349	4th/NFC Eastern Div.	—	—		Joe Gibbs
1982	8	1	0	.889	190	128	1st/NFC	4	0	Super Bowl champ	Joe Gibbs
1983	14	2	0	.875	541	332	1st/NFC Eastern Div.	2	1	Super Bowl	Joe Gibbs
1984	11	5	0	.688	426	310	1st/NFC Eastern Div.	0	1	NFC div. playoff game	Joe Gibbs
1985	10	6	0	.625	297	312	3rd/NFC Eastern Div.	—	—		Joe Gibbs
1986	12	4	0	.750	368	296	2nd/NFC Eastern Div.	2	1	NFC championship game	Joe Gibbs
1987	11	4	0	.733	379	285	1st/NFC Eastern Div.	3	0	Super Bowl champ	Joe Gibbs
1988	7	9	0	.438	345	387	T3rd/NFC Eastern Div.	—	—		Joe Gibbs
1989	10	6	0	.625	386	308	3rd/NFC Eastern Div.	—	—		Joe Gibbs
1990	10	6	0	.625	381	301	T2nd/NFC Eastern Div.	1	1	NFC div. playoff game	Joe Gibbs
1991	14	2	0	.875	485	224	1st/NFC Eastern Div.	3	0	Super Bowl champ	Joe Gibbs
1992	9	7	0	.563	300	255	3rd/NFC Eastern Div.	1	1	NFC div. playoff game	Joe Gibbs
1993	4	12	0	.250	230	345	5th/NFC Eastern Div.	—	—		Richie Petitbon
1994	3	13	0	.188	320	412	5th/NFC Eastern Div.	—	—		Norv Turner
1995	6	10	0	.375	326	359	3rd/NFC Eastern Div.	—	—		Norv Turner
1996	9	7	0	.563	364	312	3rd/NFC Eastern Div.	—	—		Norv Turner
1997	8	7	1	.533	327	289	2nd/NFC Eastern Div.	—	—		Norv Turner
1998	6	10	0	.375	319	421	4th/NFC Eastern Div.	—	—		Norv Turner
1999	10	6	0	.625	443	377	1st/NFC Eastern Div.	1	1	NFC div. playoff game	Norv Turner
2000	8	8	0	.500	281	269	3rd/NFC Eastern Div.	—	—		Norv Turner

*Boston Braves.
†Boston Redskins.

FIRST-ROUND DRAFT PICKS

1936—Riley Smith, QB, Alabama
1937—Sammy Baugh, QB, Texas Christian
1938—Andy Farkas, B, Detroit
1939—I.B. Hale, T, Texas Christian
1940—Ed Boell, B, New York University
1941—Forrest Evashevski, B, Michigan
1942—Orban Sanders, B, Texas
1943—Jack Jenkins, B, Missouri
1944—Mike Micka, B, Colgate

1945—Jim Hardy, B, Southern California
1946—Cal Rossi, B, UCLA
1947—Cal Rossi, B, UCLA
1948—Harry Gilmer, QB, Alabama*
1949—Rob Goode, RB, Texas A&M
1950—George Thomas, RB, Oklahoma
1951—Leon Heath, RB, Oklahoma
1952—Larry Isbell, QB, Baylor
1953—Jack Scarbath, QB, Maryland

1954—Steve Meilinger, TE, Kentucky
1955—Ralph Guglielmi, QB, Notre Dame
1956—Ed Vereb, RB, Maryland
1957—Don Bosseler, RB, Miami, Fla.
1958—None
1959—Don Allard, QB, Boston College
1960—Richie Lucas, QB, Penn State
1961—Joe Rutgens, T, Illinois
        Norm Snead, QB, Wake Forest
1962—Ernie Davis, RB, Syracuse*
        Leroy Jackson, RB, Illinois Central
1963—Pat Richter, TE, Wisconsin
1964—Charley Taylor, RB, Arizona State
1965—None
1966—Charlie Gogolak, K, Princeton
1967—Ray McDonald, RB, Idaho
1968—Jim Smith, DB, Oregon
1969—None
1970—None
1971—None
1972—None
1973—None
1974—None
1975—None
1976—None
1977—None

1978—None
1979—None
1980—Art Monk, WR, Syracuse
1981—Mark May, T, Pittsburgh
1982—None
1983—Darrell Green, DB, Texas A&I
1984—None
1985—None
1986—None
1987—None
1988—None
1989—None
1990—None
1991—Bobby Wilson, DT, Michigan State
1992—Desmond Howard, WR, Michigan
1993—Tom Carter, DB, Notre Dame
1994—Heath Shuler, QB, Tennessee
1995—Michael Westbrook, WR, Colorado
1996—Andre Johnson, T, Penn State
1997—Kenard Lang, DE, Miami, Fla.
1998—None
1999—Champ Bailey, DB, Georgia
2000—LaVar Arrington, LB, Penn State
        Chris Samuels, T, Alabama
2001—Rod Gardner, WR, Clemson
*First player chosen in draft.

FRANCHISE RECORDS

Most rushing yards, career
7,472—John Riggins
Most rushing yards, season
1,405—Stephen Davis, 1999
Most rushing yards, game
221—Gerald Riggs vs. Phi., Sept. 17, 1989
Most rushing touchdowns, season
24—John Riggins, 1983
Most passing attempts, season
541—Jay Schroeder, 1986
Most passing attempts, game
58—Jay Schroeder vs. S.F., Dec. 1, 1985
Most passes completed, season
316—Brad Johnson, 1999
Most passes completed, game
32—Sonny Jurgensen at Cle., Nov. 26, 1967
        John Friesz at NYG, Sept. 18, 1994
        Brad Johnson at S.F., Dec. 26, 1999 (OT)
Most passing yards, career
25,206—Joe Theismann

Most passing yards, season
4,109—Jay Schroeder, 1986
Most passing yards, game
471—Brad Johnson at S.F. Dec. 26, 1999 (OT)
446—Sammy Baugh vs. N.Y. Yanks, Oct. 31, 1948
Most touchdown passes, season
31—Sonny Jurgensen, 1967
Most pass receptions, career
888—Art Monk
Most pass receptions, season
106—Art Monk, 1984
Most pass receptions, game
13—Art Monk vs. Cin., Dec. 15, 1985
        Kelvin Bryant vs. NYG, Dec. 7, 1986
        Art Monk at Det., Nov. 4, 1990
Most receiving yards, career
12,026—Art Monk
Most receiving yards, season
1,436—Bobby Mitchell, 1963

Most receiving yards, game
255—Anthony Allen vs. St.L., Oct. 4, 1987
Most receiving touchdowns, season
12—Hugh Taylor, 1952
        Charley Taylor, 1966
        Jerry Smith, 1967
        Ricky Sanders, 1988
Most touchdowns, career
90—Charley Taylor
Most field goals, season
33—Mark Moseley, 1983
Longest field goal
57 yards—Steve Cox vs. Sea., Sept. 28, 1986
Most interceptions, career
53—Darrell Green
Most interceptions, season
13—Dan Sandifer, 1948
Most sacks, career
97.5—Dexter Manley
Most sacks, season
18.0—Dexter Manley, 1986

SERIES RECORDS

Washington vs.: Arizona 64-42-1; Atlanta 13-4-1; Baltimore 1-1; Buffalo 4-5; Carolina 5-0; Chicago 14-14; Cincinnati 4-2; Cleveland 9-32-1; Dallas 31-47-2; Denver 3-5; Detroit 24-5; Green Bay 11-9; Indianapolis 9-17; Jacksonville 2-0; Kansas City 1-4; Miami 3-5; Minnesota 6-5; New England 5-1; New Orleans 12-5; N.Y. Giants 54-69-3; N.Y. Jets 6-1; Oakland 3-6; Philadelphia 67-57-6; Pittsburgh 39-26-4; St. Louis 17-7-1; San Diego 6-0; San Francisco 7-12-1; Seattle 5-4; Tampa Bay 6-4; Tennessee 3-5.
NOTE: Includes records only from 1937 to present.

COACHING RECORDS

George Allen, 67-30-1 (2-5); Bill Austin, 6-8-0; Herman Bell, 4-16-0; Dutch Bergman, 6-3-1 (1-1); Eddie Casey, 2-8-1; Dudley DeGroot, 14-5-1 (0-1); William Dietz, 11-11-2; Turk Edwards, 16-18-1; Ray Flaherty, 54-21-3 (2-2); Joe Gibbs, 124-60-0 (16-5); Otto Graham, 17-22-3; Joe Kuharich, 26-32-2; Curly Lambeau, 10-13-1; Vince Lombardi, 7-5-2; Bill McPeak, 21-46-3; Mike Nixon, 4-18-2; Jack Pardee, 24-24-0; Richie Petitbon, 4-12-0; Dick Todd, 5-4-0; Norv Turner, 50-61-1 (1-1); John Whelchel, 3-3-1; Lud Wray, 4-4-2.
NOTE: Playoff games in parentheses.

RETIRED UNIFORM NUMBERS

No.	Player
33	Sammy Baugh

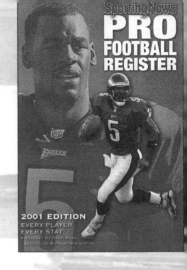

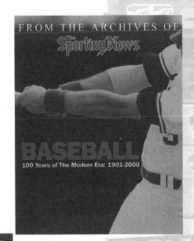

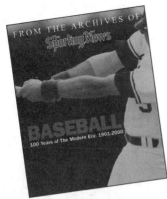

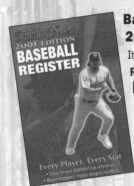
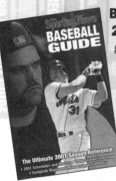
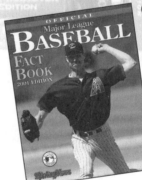